CHAMBERS

OFFICIAL

SCRABBLE®

W₄ O₁ R₁ D₂ S₁

INTERNATIONAL
EDITION

CHAMBERS

SCRABBLE® is a registered trademark owned in the USA by Hasbro Inc.,
in Canada by Hasbro Canada Corporation and throughout the rest of the
world by J W Spear & Sons, Maidenhead, SL6 4UB, England,
a Mattel Company, and is used under licence from Mattel Europa B.V.

CHAMBERS
An imprint of Chambers Harrap Publishers Ltd
7 Hopetoun Crescent
Edinburgh EH7 4AY, UK

www.chambers.co.uk

This edition published by Chambers 2002
Previously published in paperback by Chambers 2001

Copyright © Chambers Harrap Publishers Ltd 2001
Reprinted 2002

A CIP catalogue record for this book is available from the British Library.

We should like to make it clear that the presence of a word in this book in
no way affects its legal status as a trademark.

ISBN 0-550-10058-X

Managing Editor
Catherine Schwartz

Designed and typeset by Chambers Harrap Publishers Ltd
Printed and bound in Great Britain by Clays Ltd, St Ives plc

Preface

Official Scrabble® Words – International edition brings together in a single list the allowable words for Scrabble in the UK and the USA. *Official Scrabble® Words, 4th edition*, derived from *The Chambers Dictionary* (1998), is the authority for Scrabble in the UK; the *Official Tournament and Club Word List* is the authority for tournament play in the USA. Together, these word lists form an increasingly recognized authority for international tournament play worldwide.

Official Scrabble® Words – International edition will be a valuable adjudication and reference tool for all UK players who compete at an international level, be this by participating in international tournaments or by playing across the Internet, and also for any players who wish to play with this increased vocabulary.

Information on the compilation of these lists is given below, in the Introduction to *Official Scrabble® Words, 4th edition* and in the paragraph on the *Official Tournament and Club Word List*.

The Publisher

Introduction

Official Scrabble® Words – International edition

Official Scrabble® Words – International edition (OSWI) lists allowable words up to 9 letters in length and their inflections (plurals etc). For longer words, *The Chambers Dictionary* is the UK authority. A number of words in *The Chambers Dictionary*, and hence in OSWI, as well as a number of words in the *Official Tournament and Club Word List*, may be offensive to some people, or may not conform to notions of 'political correctness'. These words are however part of the English language, which dictionaries naturally reflect.

Words that are uniquely found in the *Official Tournament and Club Word List* are marked with an asterisk in this word list. Unmarked words are from *Official Scrabble® Words, 4th edition*, and meanings for all of these words can be found in *The Chambers Dictionary*. *Official Scrabble® Words, 4th edition* and the *Official Tournament and Club Word List* were compiled independently and at separate times; information on the compilation of these lists is included here.

Introduction to

Official Scrabble® Words, 4th edition

This fourth edition of *Official Scrabble® Words* is based on *The Chambers Dictionary* (1998), the latest in a long line of Chambers dictionaries. All words listed in that dictionary are permitted in Scrabble except:

 those only spelt with an initial capital letter;
 abbreviations and symbols;
 prefixes and suffixes;
 those requiring apostrophes and hyphens.

Official Scrabble® Words (OSW) lists, and is the official authority for, all allowable words of up to 9 letters long and their inflections (plurals etc). For longer words, *The Chambers Dictionary* is the authority. A number of words listed in *The Chambers Dictionary*, and hence in OSW, may be offensive to some people, or may not conform to 'political correctness'. These words are however part of the English language, which the Dictionary naturally reflects.

Every relevant entry in *The Chambers Dictionary* has been thoroughly examined and considered for inclusion in OSW. Derivative forms have been carefully considered too, and appropriate inflections – plurals, verb forms, and comparatives and superlatives – have been included. Many new words have been added to the Dictionary, and there have been other changes: some words have changed or augmented their labels (both part-of-speech and classification), some have changed their hyphenation or capitalization status, others have moved on from being abbreviations – all resulting in hundreds of new entries in this edition of OSW. Inevitably such changes, along with other Dictionary judgements, have resulted in a small number of deletions from the previous edition of OSW.

In the compilation of this edition of OSW, a small number of errors were found in *The Chambers Dictionary*. Those confirmed by the publisher have not been perpetuated in OSW.

Allowable words

This edition of *Official Scrabble® Words* is the final authority on allowed Scrabble words where the uninflected form of the word is up to 9 letters long. It is based on the 1998 edition of *The Chambers Dictionary*. All words listed in that dictionary are permitted in Scrabble except for those in the categories mentioned above.

It should be noted that the entries that are labelled 'symbol' (for example FF, LM) are now, as well as abbreviations, barred from Scrabble use.

One particular entry in OSW worthy of special mention is PH. Since in the Dictionary the capitalized letter is not the initial letter, and since PH is not deemed to be an abbreviation or a symbol, it has been included here, along with its plural PHS.

The approaches that have been taken to various groups of words in this edition of OSW are explained below.

Accents

Accents are not shown in this edition of *Official Scrabble® Words*. As there are no accented letters in the English-language Scrabble sets, it was felt unnecessary to retain accents in OSW. Where *The Chambers Dictionary* shows a word with an accent, the accent has been ignored in OSW.

Adverbs

Adverbs have been included in *Official Scrabble® Words* if they are included in *The Chambers Dictionary*. No attempt has been made to include adverbial forms which are not explicitly shown in the Dictionary.

Comparatives and Superlatives

This edition of *Official Scrabble® Words* sees the inclusion of more comparative and superlative forms than were in the previous edition. We have considered the possible comparative and superlative forms of all adjectives in OSW, and we have based our final selection on a range of criteria. These have included commonness or familiarity of the adjective, number of syllables, meaning, and whether the adjective is dialect, obsolete or foreign. We also took into account the euphony of the -ER and -EST forms, current usage, data from language corpora, including the British National Corpus®, and listings in other dictionaries. We cannot say that we have applied a mechanical formula in deciding which comparatives and superlatives to include. We have allowed the -IER and the -IEST forms of most one- and two-syllable adjectives ending in -Y, and some of three syllables, but not all. We have not excluded the comparative and superlative forms of all adjectives of three syllables or more – some have been included. We have not excluded the comparative and superlative forms of all adjectives ending in certain specific groups of letters, such as -ATE, -ENT, and -ID. Again, some have been included.

Definitions

To find the meaning of any word in OSW *The Chambers Dictionary* should be consulted.

Foreign Words

Foreign words appearing in *The Chambers Dictionary* have been included in *Official Scrabble® Words*. Where a specific plural form appears in the Dictionary, we have included only that form. Where no plural is shown in the Dictionary, we have used our judgement, and the appropriate plural form has been included. In some instances, this will be a foreign plural; in others, it will be an English plural (usually the addition of an -S). Occasionally, both types of plural will be included. Do be aware that not all plural forms in OSW are explicitly shown in *The Chambers Dictionary*. For example, as no plural form is shown in the Dictionary for STERNUM, we have included both of the plural forms STERNA and STERNUMS.

Interjections

Interjections are not treated as nouns, but as parts of speech which do not permit plurals. In *Official Scrabble® Words*, an interjection has no inflected forms, unless explicitly indicated in *The Chambers Dictionary*. A plural is only allowed if an interjection is also shown to be a noun; and verb forms are only allowed if an interjection is also shown to be a verb.

Some examples:

AW, QUOTHA and UM are interjections only, so no inflected forms are allowed;

EH is an interjection and a verb, so the inflected verb forms EHS, EHED and EHING are allowed;

OOH is an interjection, verb and noun, so the verb forms OOHS, OOHED and OOHING are allowed; OOHS is also the plural form of the noun.

If *The Chambers Dictionary* quite clearly lists a plural form of an interjection (for example, as at LO and OHO), then that is allowable.

Letters and letter sounds

Names of letters and letter sounds appearing in *The Chambers Dictionary* are included in *Official Scrabble® Words*, as there is nothing in the rules of Scrabble to bar the use of such words. Accordingly, OSW lists familiar letter names (for example, AITCH, MU, NU, and XI) as well as unfamiliar ones (for example, DIGAMMA, SAMPI, VAU and WYNN). Their plural forms are also included.

Obsolete Words

Obsolete words are included in *Official Scrabble® Words*, along with many of their relevant inflected forms (such as plurals and verb inflections). We have included plurals of obsolete nouns, and we have included verb inflections of obsolete verbs. We have not included comparative and superlative forms of obsolete adjectives, or derivatives of obsolete words, unless these are explicitly shown in *The Chambers Dictionary*. (For example, BROACH and BROACHER are both allowable words, and BROCH is in the Dictionary as an obsolete spelling of BROACH – so BROACH, BROACHER and BROCH are all allowable, but we have not included BROCHER.)

Words marked in *The Chambers Dictionary* as being from the works of Shakespeare, Spenser and Milton have been treated in the same way as obsolete words.

Order of Words

All the words in *Official Scrabble® Words* are listed in strict alphabetical sequence, regardless of length. It is important to bear this in mind, particularly when checking the validity of plurals.

For example:

the plural of FAD is not listed immediately after FAD but is shown at its correct alphabetical place between FADOS and FADY;
to determine whether FAB has a plural or not it is necessary to check between the entries FABRICS and FABULAR. It is not listed there, so FABS is not allowed.

Plurals

With few exceptions, we have included in *Official Scrabble® Words* the plurals of all nouns. Plural forms have been shown for all nouns ending in -ISM, -ITY and -NESS; while these plurals may be little used in regular English, all are available for use if needed in the English language. We have also included the plural forms of chemicals, chemical elements, minerals, man-made materials, natural minerals, fibres, drugs, gases, rocks, oils, vitamins, enzymes, diseases, illnesses and the like.

The plurals of many foreign words are included. For many words there are now two plural forms – an English plural and a foreign plural (for example, STERNUMS and STERNA). However, some words that previously only had an -S plural now only have a foreign plural. Where the compilers have found no evidence for these -S forms, only the foreign plurals are now included. For example, the plural of ANCILE is now only ANCILIA, although previously it was only ANCILES.

Word Lengths

Official Scrabble® Words users may well want to understand what criteria have been employed in considering word lengths. In compiling OSW we began by listing all the valid but uninflected words of length up to (and including) 9 letters. We then allowed the relevant inflections of these (namely plurals, verb forms, and comparatives and superlatives), resulting in words up to 13 letters long. (It is possible for a 9-letter verb to double a final consonant before adding -ING, giving 13 letters in all!)

Here are some examples:

the 9-letter noun CACODEMON gives rise to the 10-letter plural CACODEMONS;

the 9-letter noun CACOPHONY gives rise to the 11-letter plural CACOPHONIES;

the 9-letter noun CANTHARIS gives rise to the 11-letter plural CANTHARIDES;

the 9-letter verb CALCULATE gives rise to these verb inflections: CALCULATES, CALCULATED and CALCULATING, having 10 or 11 letters;

the 8-letter verb CARBURET gives rise to these verb inflections: CARBURETS, CARBURETTED and CARBURETTING, having 9, 11 or 12 letters.

If any inflected form of a 9-letter word is also a singular noun in its own right, then a plural form of that noun is also included.

For example:

the 9-letter verb CATERWAUL gives rise to these verb inflections: CATERWAULS, CATERWAULED and CATERWAULING; but since CATERWAULING is also shown in *The Chambers Dictionary* as a noun, the plural form of CATERWAULINGS has been included here;

the 8-letter verb CROSSCUT gives rise to these verb inflections: CROSSCUTS and CROSSCUTTING; but since CROSS-CUTTING is also shown in the Dictionary as a noun, the plural form CROSSCUTTINGS has been included here.

There are a few instances of 9-letter adjectives which add an -S to become 10-letter nouns. For example, CANONICAL thus becomes CANONICALS, which is included. For convenience in adjudication, other similar cases are treated likewise: for example, the adverbs EARTHWARD and EARTHWARDS are both included.

There are instances of singular nouns having more than 9 letters, but with plurals of 9 letters or less. The singulars have not been included here, but the plurals have. For example, the singular AUDITORIUM has 10 letters, so hasn't been included, but its plural AUDITORIA has 9 letters, so is included.

Official Tournament and Club Word List

This official tournament word list is derived from *The Official Scrabble®
Players Dictionary, Second Edition*, and *The Official Scrabble® Players
Dictionary, Third Edition*, supplemented with nine-letter words and their
inflected forms taken from *Merriam-Webster's Collegiate Dictionary,
Tenth Edition*. This list contains words only, no definitions or part-of-
speech labels, and includes all inflected forms spelled out in full. This list
contains all words eligible for play, including some that are considered
offensive; although qualified for play, such words may be inappropriate
for family use.

Keen-eyed users will notice that different approaches have been taken to
the inclusion and exclusion of words by the compilers of *Official
Scrabble® Words, 4th edition* and the *Official Tournament and Club
Word List*. For example, AUDITORIUM is too long for inclusion in
OSW, although a perfectly valid word for Scrabble in the UK; this word
is however included in the US word list and so duly included, and marked
with an asterisk, in this combined word list.

Official Scrabble® Words – International edition will not answer every
possible query regarding the validity of words. Remember that for words
longer than 9 letters, and their inflected forms, *The Chambers Dictionary*
is the UK authority. For example, PHOTOGRAPH is perfectly valid for
use in Scrabble; it's just that it isn't included here. There are plenty of other
10-15 letter words that could be played legitimately in Scrabble, and are in
The Chambers Dictionary.

A

AA
AAH*
AAHED*
AAHING*
AAHS*
AAL*
AALII*
AALIIS*
AALS*
AARDVARK
AARDVARKS
AARDWOLF
AARDWOLVES
AARGH*
AARRGH*
AARRGHH*
AAS
AASVOGEL
AASVOGELS
AB*
ABA
ABAC
ABACA
ABACAS
ABACI
ABACK
ABACS
ABACTINAL
ABACTOR
ABACTORS
ABACUS
ABACUSES
ABAFT
ABAKA*
ABAKAS*
ABALONE
ABALONES
ABAMP*
ABAMPERE
ABAMPERES
ABAMPS*
ABAND
ABANDED
ABANDING
ABANDON
ABANDONED
ABANDONEE
ABANDONEES
ABANDONER*
ABANDONERS*
ABANDONING
ABANDONS
ABANDS
ABAPICAL*
ABAS

ABASE
ABASED
ABASEDLY*
ABASEMENT
ABASEMENTS
ABASER*
ABASERS*
ABASES
ABASH
ABASHED
ABASHEDLY
ABASHES
ABASHING
ABASHLESS
ABASHMENT
ABASHMENTS
ABASIA*
ABASIAS*
ABASING
ABASK
ABATABLE
ABATE
ABATED
ABATEMENT
ABATEMENTS
ABATER*
ABATERS*
ABATES
ABATING
ABATIS
ABATISES*
ABATOR
ABATORS
ABATTIS
ABATTISES*
ABATTOIR
ABATTOIRS
ABATTU
ABATURE
ABATURES
ABAXIAL
ABAXILE*
ABAYA
ABAYAS
ABB
ABBA
ABBACIES
ABBACY
ABBAS
ABBATIAL
ABBE
ABBES
ABBESS
ABBESSES
ABBEY

ABBEYS
ABBOT
ABBOTCIES*
ABBOTCY*
ABBOTS
ABBOTSHIP
ABBOTSHIPS
ABBS
ABCEE
ABCEES
ABDABS
ABDICABLE
ABDICANT
ABDICATE
ABDICATED
ABDICATES
ABDICATING
ABDICATOR
ABDICATORS
ABDOMEN
ABDOMENS
ABDOMINA
ABDOMINAL
ABDUCE
ABDUCED
ABDUCENS*
ABDUCENT
ABDUCENTES*
ABDUCES
ABDUCING
ABDUCT
ABDUCTED
ABDUCTEE
ABDUCTEES
ABDUCTING
ABDUCTION
ABDUCTIONS
ABDUCTOR
ABDUCTORES*
ABDUCTORS
ABDUCTS
ABEAM
ABEAR
ABEARING
ABEARS
ABED
ABEIGH
ABELE
ABELES
ABELIA
ABELIAN*
ABELIAS
ABELMOSK*
ABELMOSKS*
ABERRANCE

ABERRANCES
ABERRANCIES
ABERRANCY
ABERRANT
ABERRANTS*
ABERRATE
ABERRATED
ABERRATES
ABERRATING
ABESSIVE
ABESSIVES
ABET
ABETMENT
ABETMENTS
ABETS
ABETTAL
ABETTALS
ABETTED
ABETTER
ABETTERS
ABETTING
ABETTOR
ABETTORS
ABEYANCE
ABEYANCES
ABEYANCIES
ABEYANCY
ABEYANT
ABFARAD*
ABFARADS*
ABHENRIES*
ABHENRY*
ABHENRYS*
ABHOR
ABHORRED
ABHORRENT
ABHORRER
ABHORRERS
ABHORRING
ABHORRINGS
ABHORS
ABID
ABIDANCE
ABIDANCES
ABIDDEN
ABIDE
ABIDED
ABIDER*
ABIDERS*
ABIDES
ABIDING
ABIDINGLY
ABIDINGS
ABIES
ABIGAIL

ABIGAILS
ABILITIES
ABILITY
ABIOGENIC*
ABIOSES
ABIOSIS
ABIOTIC
ABJECT
ABJECTED
ABJECTING
ABJECTION
ABJECTIONS
ABJECTLY
ABJECTS
ABJOINT
ABJOINTED
ABJOINTING
ABJOINTS
ABJURE
ABJURED
ABJURER
ABJURERS
ABJURES
ABJURING
ABLATE
ABLATED
ABLATES
ABLATING
ABLATION
ABLATIONS
ABLATIVAL
ABLATIVE
ABLATIVES
ABLATOR
ABLATORS
ABLAUT
ABLAUTS
ABLAZE
ABLE
ABLED
ABLEGATE*
ABLEGATES*
ABLEISM
ABLEISMS
ABLEIST
ABLER
ABLES
ABLEST
ABLET
ABLETS
ABLING
ABLINGS*
ABLINS
ABLOOM
ABLOW

ABLUENT*	ABORALLY*	ABRAYING	ABSCISSAS	ABSTERGE
ABLUENTS*	ABORD	ABRAYS	ABSCISSE	ABSTERGED
ABLUSH	ABORDED	ABRAZO	ABSCISSES	ABSTERGES
ABLUTED*	ABORDING	ABRAZOS	ABSCISSIN	ABSTERGING
ABLUTION	ABORDS	ABREACT	ABSCISSINS	ABSTINENT
ABLUTIONS	ABORE	ABREACTED	ABSCOND	ABSTRACT
ABLY	ABORIGEN	ABREACTING	ABSCONDED	ABSTRACTED
ABMHO*	ABORIGENS	ABREACTS	ABSCONDER	ABSTRACTER
ABMHOS*	ABORIGIN	ABREAST	ABSCONDERS	ABSTRACTERS
ABNEGATE	ABORIGINE	ABREGE	ABSCONDING	ABSTRACTEST
ABNEGATED	ABORIGINES	ABREGES	ABSCONDS	ABSTRACTING
ABNEGATES	ABORIGINS	ABRI*	ABSEIL	ABSTRACTS
ABNEGATING	ABORNE	ABRICOCK	ABSEILED	ABSTRICT
ABNEGATOR	ABORNING	ABRICOCKS	ABSEILING	ABSTRICTED
ABNEGATORS	ABORT	ABRIDGE	ABSEILINGS	ABSTRICTING
ABNORMAL	ABORTED	ABRIDGED	ABSEILS	ABSTRICTS
ABNORMALS	ABORTEE	ABRIDGER	ABSENCE	ABSTRUSE
ABNORMITIES	ABORTEES	ABRIDGERS	ABSENCES	ABSTRUSER
ABNORMITY	ABORTER*	ABRIDGES	ABSENT	ABSTRUSEST
ABNORMOUS	ABORTERS*	ABRIDGING	ABSENTED	ABSURD
ABO*	ABORTING	ABRIM	ABSENTEE	ABSURDER
ABOARD	ABORTION	ABRIN	ABSENTEES	ABSURDEST
ABODE	ABORTIONS	ABRINS	ABSENTER*	ABSURDISM
ABODED	ABORTIVE	ABRIS*	ABSENTERS*	ABSURDISMS
ABODEMENT	ABORTS	ABROACH	ABSENTING	ABSURDIST
ABODEMENTS	ABORTUARIES	ABROAD	ABSENTLY	ABSURDISTS
ABODES	ABORTUARY	ABROADS	ABSENTS	ABSURDITIES
ABODING	ABOS*	ABROGATE	ABSEY	ABSURDITY
ABOHM*	ABOUGHT	ABROGATED	ABSEYS	ABSURDLY
ABOHMS*	ABOULIA	ABROGATES	ABSINTH	ABSURDS*
ABOIDEAU	ABOULIAS	ABROGATING	ABSINTHE	ABTHANE
ABOIDEAUS	ABOULIC*	ABROGATOR	ABSINTHES	ABTHANES
ABOIDEAUX*	ABOUND	ABROGATORS	ABSINTHS	ABUBBLE*
ABOIL	ABOUNDED	ABROOKE	ABSIT	ABUILDING*
ABOITEAU	ABOUNDING	ABROOKED	ABSITS	ABULIA
ABOITEAUS	ABOUNDS	ABROOKES	ABSOLUTE	ABULIAS
ABOITEAUX*	ABOUT	ABROOKING	ABSOLUTER	ABULIC*
ABOLISH	ABOUTS	ABROSIA*	ABSOLUTES	ABUNA
ABOLISHED	ABOVE	ABROSIAS*	ABSOLUTEST	ABUNAS
ABOLISHER*	ABOVES*	ABRUPT	ABSOLVE	ABUNDANCE
ABOLISHERS*	ABRACHIA*	ABRUPTER	ABSOLVED	ABUNDANCES
ABOLISHES	ABRACHIAS*	ABRUPTEST	ABSOLVER	ABUNDANCIES
ABOLISHING	ABRADABLE*	ABRUPTION	ABSOLVERS	ABUNDANCY
ABOLITION	ABRADANT	ABRUPTIONS	ABSOLVES	ABUNDANT
ABOLITIONS	ABRADANTS	ABRUPTLY	ABSOLVING	ABUNE
ABOLLA	ABRADE	ABRUPTS	ABSONANT	ABURST
ABOLLAE	ABRADED	ABS*	ABSORB	ABUSABLE*
ABOLLAS	ABRADER*	ABSCESS	ABSORBANT*	ABUSAGE
ABOMA*	ABRADERS*	ABSCESSED	ABSORBANTS*	ABUSAGES
ABOMAS*	ABRADES	ABSCESSES	ABSORBATE	ABUSE
ABOMASA	ABRADING	ABSCESSING*	ABSORBATES	ABUSED
ABOMASAL	ABRAID	ABSCIND	ABSORBED	ABUSER
ABOMASI	ABRAIDED	ABSCINDED	ABSORBENT	ABUSERS
ABOMASUM	ABRAIDING	ABSCINDING	ABSORBENTS	ABUSES
ABOMASUS	ABRAIDS	ABSCINDS	ABSORBER	ABUSING
ABOMASUSES	ABRAM	ABSCISE	ABSORBERS	ABUSION
ABOMINATE	ABRASION	ABSCISED	ABSORBING	ABUSIONS
ABOMINATED	ABRASIONS	ABSCISES	ABSORBS	ABUSIVE
ABOMINATES	ABRASIVE	ABSCISIN	ABSTAIN	ABUSIVELY
ABOMINATING	ABRASIVES	ABSCISING	ABSTAINED	ABUT
ABONDANCE	ABRAXAS	ABSCISINS	ABSTAINER	ABUTILON
ABONDANCES	ABRAXASES	ABSCISS	ABSTAINERS	ABUTILONS
ABOON*	ABRAY	ABSCISSA	ABSTAINING	ABUTMENT
ABORAL	ABRAYED	ABSCISSAE	ABSTAINS	ABUTMENTS

ABUTS	ACARIASES	ACCESS	ACCORAGE	ACCRUING
ABUTTAL	ACARIASIS	ACCESSARIES	ACCORAGED	ACCUMBENT
ABUTTALS	ACARICIDE	ACCESSARY	ACCORAGES	ACCURACIES
ABUTTED	ACARICIDES	ACCESSED	ACCORAGING	ACCURACY
ABUTTER	ACARID	ACCESSES	ACCORD	ACCURATE
ABUTTERS	ACARIDAN	ACCESSING	ACCORDANT	ACCURSE
ABUTTING	ACARIDANS	ACCESSION	ACCORDED	ACCURSED
ABUZZ	ACARIDEAN	ACCESSIONED	ACCORDER	ACCURSES
ABVOLT	ACARIDEANS	ACCESSIONING	ACCORDERS	ACCURSING
ABVOLTS	ACARIDIAN	ACCESSIONS	ACCORDING	ACCURST
ABWATT*	ACARIDIANS	ACCESSORIES	ACCORDION	ACCUSABLE
ABWATTS*	ACARIDS	ACCESSORY	ACCORDIONS	ACCUSAL
ABY	ACARINE	ACCIDENCE	ACCORDS	ACCUSALS
ABYE	ACARINES*	ACCIDENCES	ACCOST	ACCUSANT*
ABYEING	ACAROID	ACCIDENT	ACCOSTED	ACCUSANTS*
ABYES	ACAROLOGIES	ACCIDENTS	ACCOSTING	ACCUSE
ABYING	ACAROLOGY	ACCIDIA*	ACCOSTS	ACCUSED
ABYS*	ACARPOUS	ACCIDIAS*	ACCOUNT	ACCUSER
ABYSM	ACARUS	ACCIDIE	ACCOUNTED	ACCUSERS
ABYSMAL	ACATER	ACCIDIES	ACCOUNTING	ACCUSES
ABYSMALLY	ACATERS	ACCINGE	ACCOUNTINGS	ACCUSING
ABYSMS	ACATES	ACCINGED	ACCOUNTS	ACCUSTOM
ABYSS	ACATOUR	ACCINGES	ACCOURAGE	ACCUSTOMED
ABYSSAL	ACATOURS	ACCINGING	ACCOURAGED	ACCUSTOMING
ABYSSES	ACAUDAL	ACCIPITER	ACCOURAGES	ACCUSTOMS
ACACIA	ACAUDATE	ACCIPITERS	ACCOURAGING	ACE
ACACIAS	ACAULINE	ACCITE	ACCOURT	ACED
ACADEME	ACAULOSE	ACCITED	ACCOURTED	ACEDIA
ACADEMES	ACAULOUS*	ACCITES	ACCOURTING	ACEDIAS
ACADEMIA	ACCABLE	ACCITING	ACCOURTS	ACELDAMA*
ACADEMIAS	ACCEDE	ACCLAIM	ACCOUTER	ACELDAMAS*
ACADEMIC	ACCEDED	ACCLAIMED	ACCOUTERED	ACELLULAR
ACADEMICS	ACCEDENCE	ACCLAIMER*	ACCOUTERING	ACENTRIC*
ACADEMIES	ACCEDENCES	ACCLAIMERS*	ACCOUTERS	ACEQUIA*
ACADEMISM	ACCEDER	ACCLAIMING	ACCOUTRE	ACEQUIAS*
ACADEMISMS	ACCEDERS	ACCLAIMS	ACCOUTRED	ACER
ACADEMIST	ACCEDES	ACCLIMATE	ACCOUTRES	ACERATE
ACADEMISTS	ACCEDING	ACCLIMATED	ACCOUTRING	ACERATED*
ACADEMY	ACCEND	ACCLIMATES	ACCOY	ACERB
ACAJOU	ACCENDED	ACCLIMATING	ACCOYED	ACERBATE
ACAJOUS	ACCENDING	ACCLIVITIES	ACCOYING	ACERBATED
ACALEPH	ACCENDS	ACCLIVITY	ACCOYLD	ACERBATES
ACALEPHAE*	ACCENSION	ACCLIVOUS	ACCOYS	ACERBATING
ACALEPHAN	ACCENSIONS	ACCLOY	ACCREDIT	ACERBER
ACALEPHANS	ACCENT	ACCLOYED	ACCREDITED	ACERBEST
ACALEPHE	ACCENTED	ACCLOYING	ACCREDITING	ACERBIC
ACALEPHES	ACCENTING	ACCLOYS	ACCREDITS	ACERBITIES
ACALEPHS	ACCENTOR	ACCOAST	ACCRETE	ACERBITY
ACANTH	ACCENTORS	ACCOASTED	ACCRETED	ACEROLA*
ACANTHA	ACCENTS	ACCOASTING	ACCRETES	ACEROLAS*
ACANTHAS	ACCENTUAL	ACCOASTS	ACCRETING	ACEROSE
ACANTHI*	ACCEPT	ACCOIED	ACCRETION	ACEROUS
ACANTHIN	ACCEPTANT	ACCOIL	ACCRETIONS	ACERS
ACANTHINE	ACCEPTANTS	ACCOILS	ACCRETIVE	ACERVATE
ACANTHINS	ACCEPTED	ACCOLADE	ACCREW	ACERVULI*
ACANTHOID	ACCEPTEE*	ACCOLADES	ACCREWED	ACERVULUS*
ACANTHOUS	ACCEPTEES*	ACCOMPANIED	ACCREWING	ACES
ACANTHS	ACCEPTER	ACCOMPANIES	ACCREWS	ACESCENCE
ACANTHUS	ACCEPTERS	ACCOMPANY	ACCRUABLE*	ACESCENCES
ACANTHUSES	ACCEPTING	ACCOMPANYING	ACCRUAL	ACESCENCIES
ACAPNIA	ACCEPTIVE	ACCOMPT	ACCRUALS	ACESCENCY
ACAPNIAS	ACCEPTOR	ACCOMPTED	ACCRUE	ACESCENT
ACARI	ACCEPTORS	ACCOMPTING	ACCRUED	ACESCENTS*
ACARIAN	ACCEPTS	ACCOMPTS	ACCRUES	ACETA*

The Chambers Dictionary is the authority for many longer words; see Introduction, page ix

ACETABULA	ACHIEVING	ACIDY	ACOUSTICS	ACROBATICS
ACETABULUM*	ACHILLEA	ACIERAGE	ACQUAINT	ACROBATS
ACETABULUMS*	ACHILLEAS	ACIERAGES	ACQUAINTED	ACRODONT*
ACETAL	ACHIMENES	ACIERATE	ACQUAINTING	ACRODONTS*
ACETALS	ACHINESS*	ACIERATED	ACQUAINTS	ACROGEN
ACETAMID*	ACHINESSES*	ACIERATES	ACQUEST	ACROGENIC
ACETAMIDE	ACHING	ACIERATING	ACQUESTS	ACROGENS
ACETAMIDES	ACHINGLY	ACIFORM	ACQUIESCE	ACROLECT*
ACETAMIDS*	ACHINGS	ACINAR*	ACQUIESCED	ACROLECTS*
ACETATE	ACHIOTE*	ACING	ACQUIESCES	ACROLEIN
ACETATED*	ACHIOTES*	ACINI	ACQUIESCING	ACROLEINS
ACETATES	ACHKAN	ACINIC*	ACQUIGHT	ACROLITH
ACETIC	ACHKANS	ACINIFORM	ACQUIGHTING	ACROLITHS
ACETIFIED	ACHOLIA*	ACINOSE	ACQUIGHTS	ACROMIA
ACETIFIES	ACHOLIAS*	ACINOUS	ACQUIRAL	ACROMIAL
ACETIFY	ACHOO*	ACINUS	ACQUIRALS	ACROMION
ACETIFYING	ACHROMAT	ACKEE	ACQUIRE	ACRONIC*
ACETIN*	ACHROMATS	ACKEES	ACQUIRED	ACRONICAL
ACETINS*	ACHROMIC*	ACKERS	ACQUIRER*	ACRONYCAL
ACETONE	ACHY	ACKNEW	ACQUIRERS*	ACRONYM
ACETONES	ACICULA*	ACKNOW	ACQUIRES	ACRONYMIC
ACETONIC*	ACICULAE*	ACKNOWING	ACQUIRING	ACRONYMS
ACETOSE	ACICULAR	ACKNOWN	ACQUIST	ACROPETAL
ACETOUS	ACICULAS*	ACKNOWNE	ACQUISTS	ACROPHOBE*
ACETOXYL*	ACICULATE	ACKNOWS	ACQUIT	ACROPHOBES*
ACETOXYLS*	ACICULUM*	ACLINIC	ACQUITE	ACROPHONIES
ACETUM*	ACICULUMS*	ACMATIC*	ACQUITES	ACROPHONY
ACETYL	ACID	ACME	ACQUITING	ACROPOLIS
ACETYLATE*	ACIDEMIA*	ACMES	ACQUITS	ACROPOLISES
ACETYLATED*	ACIDEMIAS*	ACMIC*	ACQUITTAL	ACROSOMAL*
ACETYLATES*	ACIDER	ACMITE	ACQUITTALS	ACROSOME
ACETYLATING*	ACIDEST	ACMITES	ACQUITTED	ACROSOMES
ACETYLENE	ACIDFREAK	ACNE	ACQUITTER*	ACROSPIRE
ACETYLENES	ACIDFREAKS	ACNED*	ACQUITTERS*	ACROSPIRES
ACETYLIC*	ACIDHEAD*	ACNES	ACQUITTING	ACROSS
ACETYLS	ACIDHEADS*	ACNODE*	ACRASIA	ACROSTIC
ACH	ACIDIC	ACNODES*	ACRASIAS	ACROSTICS
ACHAENIA	ACIDIER	ACOCK	ACRASIN*	ACROTER
ACHAENIUM	ACIDIEST	ACOEMETI	ACRASINS*	ACROTERIA
ACHAENIUMS	ACIDIFIED	ACOLD	ACRATIC	ACROTERS
ACHAGE	ACIDIFIER	ACOLUTHIC	ACRAWL	ACROTIC*
ACHAGES	ACIDIFIERS	ACOLYTE	ACRE	ACROTISM
ACHALASIA*	ACIDIFIES	ACOLYTES	ACREAGE	ACROTISMS
ACHALASIAS*	ACIDIFY	ACOLYTH	ACREAGES	ACRYLATE*
ACHARNE	ACIDIFYING	ACOLYTHS	ACRED	ACRYLATES*
ACHARYA	ACIDITIES	ACONITE	ACRES	ACRYLIC
ACHARYAS	ACIDITY	ACONITES	ACRID	ACRYLICS
ACHATES	ACIDLY	ACONITIC	ACRIDER	ACT
ACHE	ACIDNESS	ACONITINE	ACRIDEST	ACTA
ACHED	ACIDNESSES	ACONITINES	ACRIDIN	ACTABLE
ACHENE	ACIDOPHIL*	ACONITUM	ACRIDINE	ACTED
ACHENES	ACIDOPHILS*	ACONITUMS	ACRIDINES	ACTIN
ACHENIA	ACIDOSES	ACORN	ACRIDINS	ACTINAL
ACHENIAL	ACIDOSIS	ACORNED	ACRIDITIES	ACTINALLY
ACHENIUM	ACIDOTIC*	ACORNS	ACRIDITY	ACTING
ACHENIUMS	ACIDS	ACOSMISM	ACRIDLY*	ACTINGS
ACHES	ACIDULATE	ACOSMISMS	ACRIDNESS*	ACTINIA
ACHIER	ACIDULATED	ACOSMIST	ACRIDNESSES*	ACTINIAE
ACHIEST	ACIDULATES	ACOSMISTS	ACRIMONIES	ACTINIAN
ACHIEVE	ACIDULATING	ACOUCHI	ACRIMONY	ACTINIANS
ACHIEVED	ACIDULENT	ACOUCHIES	ACRITARCH*	ACTINIAS
ACHIEVER	ACIDULOUS	ACOUCHIS	ACRITARCHS*	ACTINIC
ACHIEVERS	ACIDURIA*	ACOUCHY	ACROBAT	ACTINIDE
ACHIEVES	ACIDURIAS*	ACOUSTIC	ACROBATIC	ACTINIDES

Words marked with an asterisk are from OTCWL

ACTINISM	ACTUATE	ADAMSITES*	ADDORSED	ADESPOTA
ACTINISMS	ACTUATED	ADAPT	ADDRESS	ADESSIVE
ACTINIUM	ACTUATES	ADAPTABLE	ADDRESSED	ADESSIVES
ACTINIUMS	ACTUATING	ADAPTED	ADDRESSEE	ADHARMA
ACTINOID	ACTUATION	ADAPTER	ADDRESSEES	ADHARMAS
ACTINOIDS	ACTUATIONS	ADAPTERS	ADDRESSER	ADHERE
ACTINON	ACTUATOR	ADAPTING	ADDRESSERS	ADHERED
ACTINONS	ACTUATORS	ADAPTION	ADDRESSES	ADHERENCE
ACTINS	ACTURE	ADAPTIONS	ADDRESSING	ADHERENCES
ACTION	ACTURES	ADAPTIVE	ADDRESSOR	ADHEREND*
ACTIONED	ACUATE*	ADAPTOR	ADDRESSORS	ADHERENDS*
ACTIONER	ACUITIES	ADAPTORS	ADDREST	ADHERENT
ACTIONERS	ACUITY	ADAPTS	ADDS	ADHERENTS
ACTIONING	ACULEATE	ADAW	ADDUCE	ADHERER
ACTIONIST	ACULEATED	ADAWED	ADDUCED	ADHERERS
ACTIONISTS	ACULEI	ADAWING	ADDUCENT	ADHERES
ACTIONS	ACULEUS	ADAWS	ADDUCER	ADHERING
ACTIVATE	ACUMEN	ADAXIAL	ADDUCERS	ADHESION
ACTIVATED	ACUMENS	ADAYS	ADDUCES	ADHESIONS
ACTIVATES	ACUMINATE	ADD	ADDUCIBLE	ADHESIVE
ACTIVATING	ACUMINATED	ADDABLE*	ADDUCING	ADHESIVES
ACTIVATOR	ACUMINATES	ADDAX	ADDUCT	ADHIBIT
ACTIVATORS	ACUMINATING	ADDAXES	ADDUCTED	ADHIBITED
ACTIVE	ACUMINOUS	ADDEBTED	ADDUCTING	ADHIBITING
ACTIVELY	ACUPOINT	ADDED	ADDUCTION	ADHIBITS
ACTIVES*	ACUPOINTS	ADDEDLY*	ADDUCTIONS	ADIABATIC
ACTIVISM	ACUSHLA	ADDEEM	ADDUCTIVE	ADIAPHORA
ACTIVISMS	ACUSHLAS	ADDEEMED	ADDUCTOR	ADIEU
ACTIVIST	ACUTANCE*	ADDEEMING	ADDUCTORS	ADIEUS
ACTIVISTS	ACUTANCES*	ADDEEMS	ADDUCTS	ADIEUX
ACTIVITIES	ACUTE	ADDEND	ADEEM	ADIOS
ACTIVITY	ACUTELY	ADDENDA	ADEEMED	ADIPIC*
ACTIVIZE*	ACUTENESS	ADDENDS	ADEEMING	ADIPOCERE
ACTIVIZED*	ACUTENESSES	ADDENDUM	ADEEMS	ADIPOCERES
ACTIVIZES*	ACUTER	ADDER	ADEMPTION	ADIPOCYTE*
ACTIVIZING*	ACUTES	ADDERS	ADEMPTIONS	ADIPOCYTES*
ACTON	ACUTEST	ADDERWORT	ADENINE	ADIPOSE
ACTONS	ACYCLIC	ADDERWORTS	ADENINES	ADIPOSES*
ACTOR	ACYCLOVIR	ADDIBLE*	ADENITIS	ADIPOSIS*
ACTORISH*	ACYCLOVIRS	ADDICT	ADENITISES	ADIPOSITIES
ACTORS	ACYL	ADDICTED	ADENOID	ADIPOSITY
ACTRESS	ACYLATE*	ADDICTING	ADENOIDAL	ADIPOUS*
ACTRESSES	ACYLATED*	ADDICTION	ADENOIDS	ADIT
ACTRESSY*	ACYLATES*	ADDICTIONS	ADENOMA	ADITS
ACTS	ACYLATING*	ADDICTIVE	ADENOMAS	ADJACENCIES
ACTUAL	ACYLATION*	ADDICTS	ADENOMATA	ADJACENCY
ACTUALISE	ACYLATIONS*	ADDING	ADENOSES*	ADJACENT
ACTUALISED	ACYLOIN*	ADDIO	ADENOSINE	ADJECTIVE
ACTUALISES	ACYLOINS*	ADDIOS	ADENOSINES	ADJECTIVES
ACTUALISING	ACYLS	ADDITION	ADENOSIS*	ADJOIN
ACTUALIST	AD	ADDITIONS	ADENYL*	ADJOINED
ACTUALISTS	ADAGE	ADDITIVE	ADENYLS*	ADJOINING
ACTUALITE	ADAGES	ADDITIVES	ADEPT	ADJOINS
ACTUALITES	ADAGIAL*	ADDITORY*	ADEPTER	ADJOINT
ACTUALITIES	ADAGIO	ADDLE	ADEPTEST	ADJOINTS
ACTUALITY	ADAGIOS	ADDLED	ADEPTLY	ADJOURN
ACTUALIZE	ADAMANCE*	ADDLEMENT	ADEPTNESS	ADJOURNED
ACTUALIZED	ADAMANCES*	ADDLEMENTS	ADEPTNESSES	ADJOURNING
ACTUALIZES	ADAMANCIES*	ADDLES	ADEPTS	ADJOURNS
ACTUALIZING	ADAMANCY*	ADDLING	ADEQUACIES	ADJUDGE
ACTUALLY	ADAMANT	ADDOOM	ADEQUACY	ADJUDGED
ACTUARIAL	ADAMANTLY	ADDOOMED	ADEQUATE	ADJUDGES
ACTUARIES	ADAMANTS	ADDOOMING	ADERMIN	ADJUDGING
ACTUARY	ADAMSITE*	ADDOOMS	ADERMINS	ADJUNCT

The Chambers Dictionary is the authority for many longer words; see Introduction, page ix

ADJUNCTLY	ADMITTERS*	ADORN	ADULTLY*	ADVERTISE
ADJUNCTS	ADMITTING	ADORNED	ADULTNESS*	ADVERTISED
ADJURE	ADMIX	ADORNER*	ADULTNESSES*	ADVERTISES
ADJURED	ADMIXED	ADORNERS*	ADULTS	ADVERTISING
ADJURER*	ADMIXES	ADORNING	ADUMBRAL*	ADVERTISINGS
ADJURERS*	ADMIXING	ADORNMENT	ADUMBRATE	ADVERTIZE
ADJURES	ADMIXT*	ADORNMENTS	ADUMBRATED	ADVERTIZED
ADJURING	ADMIXTURE	ADORNS	ADUMBRATES	ADVERTIZES
ADJUROR*	ADMIXTURES	ADOS	ADUMBRATING	ADVERTIZING
ADJURORS*	ADMONISH	ADOWN	ADUNC	ADVERTS
ADJUST	ADMONISHED	ADOZE*	ADUNCATE	ADVEW
ADJUSTED	ADMONISHES	ADPRESS	ADUNCATED	ADVEWED
ADJUSTER	ADMONISHING	ADPRESSED	ADUNCITIES	ADVEWING
ADJUSTERS	ADMONITOR	ADPRESSES	ADUNCITY	ADVEWS
ADJUSTING	ADMONITORS	ADPRESSING	ADUNCOUS	ADVICE
ADJUSTIVE*	ADNASCENT	ADRAD	ADUST	ADVICEFUL
ADJUSTOR	ADNATE	ADREAD	ADUSTED	ADVICES
ADJUSTORS	ADNATION	ADREADED	ADUSTING	ADVISABLE
ADJUSTS	ADNATIONS	ADREADING	ADUSTS	ADVISABLY
ADJUTAGE	ADNEXA*	ADREADS	ADVANCE	ADVISE
ADJUTAGES	ADNEXAL*	ADRED	ADVANCED	ADVISED
ADJUTANCIES	ADNOMINAL	ADRENAL	ADVANCER*	ADVISEDLY
ADJUTANCY	ADNOUN	ADRENALIN	ADVANCERS*	ADVISEE*
ADJUTANT	ADNOUNS	ADRENALINS	ADVANCES	ADVISEES*
ADJUTANTS	ADO	ADRENALS	ADVANCING	ADVISER
ADJUVANCIES	ADOBE	ADRIFT	ADVANTAGE	ADVISERS
ADJUVANCY	ADOBELIKE*	ADROIT	ADVANTAGED	ADVISES
ADJUVANT	ADOBES	ADROITER	ADVANTAGES	ADVISING
ADJUVANTS	ADOBO*	ADROITEST	ADVANTAGING	ADVISINGS
ADLAND	ADOBOS*	ADROITLY	ADVECT*	ADVISOR
ADLANDS	ADONIS*	ADRY	ADVECTED*	ADVISORIES*
ADMAN	ADONISE	ADS	ADVECTING*	ADVISORS
ADMASS	ADONISED	ADSCRIPT	ADVECTION	ADVISORY
ADMASSES	ADONISES	ADSCRIPTS	ADVECTIONS	ADVOCAAT
ADMEASURE	ADONISING	ADSORB	ADVECTIVE*	ADVOCAATS
ADMEASURED	ADONIZE	ADSORBATE	ADVECTS*	ADVOCACIES
ADMEASURES	ADONIZED	ADSORBATES	ADVENE	ADVOCACY
ADMEASURING	ADONIZES	ADSORBED	ADVENED	ADVOCATE
ADMEN	ADONIZING	ADSORBENT	ADVENES	ADVOCATED
ADMIN	ADOORS	ADSORBENTS	ADVENING	ADVOCATES
ADMINICLE	ADOPT	ADSORBER*	ADVENT	ADVOCATING
ADMINICLES	ADOPTABLE*	ADSORBERS*	ADVENTIVE	ADVOCATOR
ADMINS	ADOPTED	ADSORBING	ADVENTIVES	ADVOCATORS
ADMIRABLE	ADOPTEE	ADSORBS	ADVENTS	ADVOUTRER
ADMIRABLY	ADOPTEES	ADSUM	ADVENTURE	ADVOUTRERS
ADMIRAL	ADOPTER	ADULARIA	ADVENTURED	ADVOUTRIES
ADMIRALS	ADOPTERS	ADULARIAS	ADVENTURES	ADVOUTRY
ADMIRALTIES*	ADOPTING	ADULATE	ADVENTURING	ADVOWSON
ADMIRALTY*	ADOPTION	ADULATED	ADVERB	ADVOWSONS
ADMIRANCE	ADOPTIONS	ADULATES	ADVERBIAL	ADWARD
ADMIRANCES	ADOPTIOUS	ADULATING	ADVERBIALS*	ADWARDED
ADMIRE	ADOPTIVE	ADULATION	ADVERBS	ADWARDING
ADMIRED	ADOPTS	ADULATIONS	ADVERSARIES	ADWARDS
ADMIRER	ADORABLE	ADULATOR	ADVERSARY	ADYNAMIA
ADMIRERS	ADORABLY	ADULATORS	ADVERSE	ADYNAMIAS
ADMIRES	ADORATION	ADULATORY	ADVERSELY	ADYNAMIC
ADMIRING	ADORATIONS	ADULT	ADVERSER	ADYTA
ADMISSION	ADORE	ADULTERER	ADVERSEST	ADYTUM
ADMISSIONS	ADORED	ADULTERERS	ADVERSITIES	ADZ
ADMISSIVE	ADORER	ADULTERIES	ADVERSITY	ADZE
ADMIT	ADORERS	ADULTERY	ADVERT	ADZES
ADMITS	ADORES	ADULTHOOD	ADVERTED	ADZUKI*
ADMITTED	ADORING	ADULTHOODS	ADVERTENT	ADZUKIS*
ADMITTER*	ADORINGLY	ADULTLIKE*	ADVERTING	AE

Words marked with an asterisk are from OTCWL

AECIA	AERIFY*	AEROPHYTE	AFFAIRES	AFFIXIAL*
AECIAL*	AERIFYING*	AEROPHYTES	AFFAIRS	AFFIXING
AECIDIA	AERILY*	AEROPLANE	AFFEAR	AFFIXMENT*
AECIDIAL*	AERO	AEROPLANES	AFFEARD	AFFIXMENTS*
AECIDIUM	AEROBATIC*	AEROS	AFFEARE	AFFLATED
AECIUM	AEROBE	AEROSAT*	AFFEARED	AFFLATION
AEDES	AEROBES	AEROSATS*	AFFEARES	AFFLATIONS
AEDILE	AEROBIA*	AEROSHELL	AFFEARING	AFFLATUS
AEDILES	AEROBIC	AEROSHELLS	AFFEARS	AFFLATUSES
AEDINE*	AEROBICS	AEROSOL	AFFECT	AFFLICT
AEFALD	AEROBIONT	AEROSOLS	AFFECTED	AFFLICTED
AEFAULD	AEROBIONTS	AEROSPACE	AFFECTER	AFFLICTING
AEGIRINE	AEROBIUM*	AEROSPACES	AFFECTERS	AFFLICTINGS
AEGIRINES	AEROBOMB	AEROSTAT	AFFECTING	AFFLICTS
AEGIRITE	AEROBOMBS	AEROSTATS	AFFECTION	AFFLUENCE
AEGIRITES	AEROBRAKE*	AEROTAXES	AFFECTIONED	AFFLUENCES
AEGIS	AEROBRAKED*	AEROTAXIS	AFFECTIONING	AFFLUENCIES*
AEGISES	AEROBRAKES*	AEROTONE	AFFECTIONS	AFFLUENCY*
AEGLOGUE	AEROBRAKING*	AEROTONES	AFFECTIVE	AFFLUENT
AEGLOGUES	AEROBUS	AEROTRAIN	AFFECTS	AFFLUENTS
AEGROTAT	AEROBUSES	AEROTRAINS	AFFEER	AFFLUENZA
AEGROTATS	AEROBUSSES	AERUGO*	AFFEERED	AFFLUENZAS
AEMULE	AERODART	AERUGOS*	AFFEERING	AFFLUX
AEMULED	AERODARTS	AERY	AFFEERS	AFFLUXES
AEMULES	AERODROME	AESC	AFFERENT	AFFLUXION
AEMULING	AERODROMES	AESCES	AFFERENTS*	AFFLUXIONS
AENEOUS	AERODUCT*	AESCULIN	AFFIANCE	AFFOORD
AENEUS*	AERODUCTS*	AESCULINS	AFFIANCED	AFFOORDED
AEOLIAN	AERODYNE	AESIR	AFFIANCES	AFFOORDING
AEOLIPILE	AERODYNES	AESTHESES	AFFIANCING	AFFOORDS
AEOLIPILES	AEROFOIL	AESTHESIA	AFFIANT*	AFFORCE
AEOLIPYLE	AEROFOILS	AESTHESIAS	AFFIANTS*	AFFORCED
AEOLIPYLES	AEROGEL*	AESTHESIS	AFFICHE	AFFORCES
AEON	AEROGELS*	AESTHETE	AFFICHES	AFFORCING
AEONIAN	AEROGRAM	AESTHETES	AFFIDAVIT	AFFORD
AEONIC*	AEROGRAMS	AESTHETIC	AFFIDAVITS	AFFORDED
AEONS	AEROGRAPH	AESTHETICS	AFFIED	AFFORDING
AEPYORNIS*	AEROGRAPHS	AESTIVAL	AFFIES	AFFORDS
AEPYORNISES*	AEROLITE	AESTIVATE	AFFILIATE	AFFOREST
AEQUORIN*	AEROLITES	AESTIVATED	AFFILIATED	AFFORESTED
AEQUORINS*	AEROLITH	AESTIVATES	AFFILIATES	AFFORESTING
AERATE	AEROLITHS	AESTIVATING	AFFILIATING	AFFORESTS
AERATED	AEROLITIC	AETHER	AFFINAL*	AFFRAP
AERATES	AEROLOGIES	AETHERIC*	AFFINE	AFFRAPPED
AERATING	AEROLOGY	AETHERS	AFFINED	AFFRAPPING
AERATION	AEROMANCIES	AETIOLOGIES	AFFINELY*	AFFRAPS
AERATIONS	AEROMANCY	AETIOLOGY	AFFINES	AFFRAY
AERATOR	AEROMETER	AFALD	AFFINITIES	AFFRAYED
AERATORS	AEROMETERS	AFAR	AFFINITY	AFFRAYER*
AERIAL	AEROMETRIES	AFARA	AFFIRM	AFFRAYERS*
AERIALIST	AEROMETRY	AFARAS	AFFIRMANT	AFFRAYING
AERIALISTS	AEROMOTOR	AFARS*	AFFIRMANTS	AFFRAYS
AERIALITIES	AEROMOTORS	AFAWLD	AFFIRMED	AFFRENDED
AERIALITY	AERONAUT	AFEAR	AFFIRMER	AFFRET
AERIALLY	AERONAUTS	AFEARD	AFFIRMERS	AFFRETS
AERIALS	AERONOMER*	AFEARED	AFFIRMING	AFFRICATE
AERIE	AERONOMERS*	AFEARING	AFFIRMS	AFFRICATES
AERIED*	AERONOMIC*	AFEARS	AFFIX	AFFRIGHT
AERIER	AERONOMIES	AFEBRILE*	AFFIXABLE*	AFFRIGHTED
AERIES	AERONOMY	AFF*	AFFIXAL*	AFFRIGHTING
AERIEST	AEROPHOBE	AFFABLE	AFFIXED	AFFRIGHTS
AERIFIED*	AEROPHOBES	AFFABLY	AFFIXER*	AFFRONT
AERIFIES*	AEROPHONE	AFFAIR	AFFIXERS*	AFFRONTE
AERIFORM	AEROPHONES	AFFAIRE	AFFIXES	AFFRONTED

The Chambers Dictionary is the authority for many longer words; see Introduction, page ix

AFFRONTEE
AFFRONTING
AFFRONTINGS
AFFRONTS
AFFUSION
AFFUSIONS
AFFY
AFFYDE
AFFYING
AFGHAN
AFGHANI*
AFGHANIS*
AFGHANS
AFIELD
AFIRE
AFLAJ
AFLAME
AFLATOXIN
AFLATOXINS
AFLOAT
AFLUTTER
AFOOT
AFORE
AFOREHAND
AFORESAID
AFORETIME
AFOUL
AFRAID
AFREET
AFREETS
AFRESH
AFRIT
AFRITS
AFRO
AFRONT
AFROS
AFT
AFTER
AFTERCARE
AFTERCARES
AFTERCLAP*
AFTERCLAPS*
AFTERDECK
AFTERDECKS
AFTEREYE
AFTEREYED
AFTEREYEING
AFTEREYES
AFTEREYING
AFTERGAME
AFTERGAMES
AFTERGLOW
AFTERGLOWS
AFTERHEAT
AFTERHEATS
AFTERINGS
AFTERLIFE*
AFTERLIVES*
AFTERMATH
AFTERMATHS
AFTERMOST
AFTERNOON
AFTERNOONS
AFTERS

AFTERTAX*
AFTERTIME
AFTERTIMES
AFTERWARD
AFTERWARDS
AFTERWORD
AFTERWORDS
AFTMOST
AFTOSA*
AFTOSAS*
AG*
AGA
AGACANT
AGACANTE
AGACERIE
AGACERIES
AGAIN
AGAINST
AGALACTIA
AGALACTIAS
AGALLOCH
AGALLOCHS
AGALWOOD*
AGALWOODS*
AGAMA*
AGAMAS*
AGAMETE*
AGAMETES*
AGAMI
AGAMIC
AGAMID
AGAMIDS
AGAMIS
AGAMOID
AGAMOIDS
AGAMOUS
AGAPAE
AGAPAI*
AGAPE
AGAPEIC*
AGAR
AGARIC
AGARICS
AGAROSE*
AGAROSES*
AGARS
AGAS
AGAST
AGATE
AGATES
AGATEWARE
AGATEWARES
AGATIZE*
AGATIZED*
AGATIZES*
AGATIZING*
AGATOID*
AGAVE
AGAVES
AGAZE
AGAZED
AGE
AGED
AGEDLY*

AGEDNESS
AGEDNESSES
AGEE
AGEING
AGEINGS
AGEISM
AGEISMS
AGEIST
AGEISTS
AGELAST
AGELASTIC
AGELASTS
AGELESS
AGELESSLY*
AGELONG
AGEN
AGENCIES
AGENCY
AGENDA
AGENDAS
AGENDUM*
AGENDUMS*
AGENE
AGENES
AGENESES*
AGENESIA*
AGENESIAS*
AGENESIS*
AGENETIC*
AGENIZE*
AGENIZED*
AGENIZES*
AGENIZING*
AGENT
AGENTED
AGENTIAL
AGENTING
AGENTINGS*
AGENTIVE
AGENTIVES
AGENTRIES*
AGENTRY*
AGENTS
AGER*
AGERATUM
AGERATUMS
AGERS*
AGES
AGGADIC*
AGGER
AGGERS
AGGIE*
AGGIES*
AGGRACE
AGGRACED
AGGRACES
AGGRACING
AGGRADE
AGGRADED
AGGRADES
AGGRADING
AGGRATE
AGGRATED
AGGRATES

AGGRATING
AGGRAVATE
AGGRAVATED
AGGRAVATES
AGGRAVATING
AGGREGATE
AGGREGATED
AGGREGATES
AGGREGATING
AGGRESS
AGGRESSED
AGGRESSES
AGGRESSING
AGGRESSOR
AGGRESSORS
AGGRI
AGGRIEVE
AGGRIEVED
AGGRIEVES
AGGRIEVING
AGGRO
AGGROS
AGGRY
AGHA
AGHAS
AGHAST
AGILA
AGILAS
AGILE
AGILELY
AGILER
AGILEST
AGILITIES
AGILITY
AGIN
AGING
AGINGS
AGINNER
AGINNERS
AGIO
AGIOS
AGIOTAGE
AGIOTAGES
AGISM*
AGISMS*
AGIST
AGISTED
AGISTER
AGISTERS
AGISTING
AGISTMENT
AGISTMENTS
AGISTOR
AGISTORS
AGISTS
AGITABLE*
AGITATE
AGITATED
AGITATES
AGITATING
AGITATION
AGITATIONS
AGITATIVE
AGITATO

AGITATOR
AGITATORS
AGITPROP
AGITPROPS
AGLARE*
AGLEAM
AGLEE
AGLET
AGLETS
AGLEY
AGLIMMER
AGLITTER
AGLOW
AGLY*
AGLYCON*
AGLYCONE*
AGLYCONES*
AGLYCONS*
AGMA
AGMAS
AGMINATE*
AGNAIL
AGNAILS
AGNAME
AGNAMED
AGNAMES
AGNATE
AGNATES
AGNATIC
AGNATICAL
AGNATION
AGNATIONS
AGNISE
AGNISED
AGNISES
AGNISING
AGNIZE
AGNIZED
AGNIZES
AGNIZING
AGNOMEN
AGNOMENS
AGNOMINA
AGNOMINAL
AGNOSIA
AGNOSIAS
AGNOSTIC
AGNOSTICS
AGO
AGOG
AGOGE
AGOGES
AGOGIC
AGOGICS
AGOING
AGON
AGONAL*
AGONE
AGONES*
AGONIC
AGONIES
AGONISE
AGONISED
AGONISES

AGONISING	AGRIZE	AIBLINS	AIRBASE	AIRLIFT
AGONIST	AGRIZED	AID	AIRBASES	AIRLIFTED
AGONISTES	AGRIZES	AIDANCE	AIRBOAT*	AIRLIFTING
AGONISTIC	AGRIZING	AIDANCES	AIRBOATS*	AIRLIFTS
AGONISTICS	AGROLOGIES	AIDANT	AIRBORNE	AIRLIKE*
AGONISTS	AGROLOGY	AIDE	AIRBOUND*	AIRLINE
AGONIZE	AGRONOMIC	AIDED	AIRBRUSH*	AIRLINER
AGONIZED	AGRONOMICS	AIDER	AIRBRUSHED*	AIRLINERS
AGONIZES	AGRONOMIES	AIDERS	AIRBRUSHES*	AIRLINES
AGONIZING	AGRONOMY	AIDES	AIRBRUSHING*	AIRLOCK
AGONS	AGROUND	AIDFUL	AIRBURST	AIRLOCKS
AGONY	AGRYPNIA*	AIDING	AIRBURSTS	AIRMAIL
AGOOD	AGRYPNIAS*	AIDLESS	AIRBUS*	AIRMAILED
AGORA	AGRYZE	AIDMAN*	AIRBUSES*	AIRMAILING
AGORAE*	AGRYZED	AIDMEN*	AIRBUSSES	AIRMAILS
AGORAS	AGRYZES	AIDOI	AIRCHECK*	AIRMAN
AGOROT	AGRYZING	AIDOS	AIRCHECKS*	AIRMEN
AGOROTH*	AGUACATE	AIDS	AIRCOACH*	AIRMOBILE*
AGOUTA	AGUACATES	AIERIES	AIRCOACHES*	AIRN
AGOUTAS	AGUE	AIERY	AIRCRAFT	AIRNED
AGOUTI	AGUED	AIGLET	AIRCREW*	AIRNING
AGOUTIES	AGUELIKE*	AIGLETS	AIRCREWS*	AIRNS
AGOUTIS	AGUES	AIGRET*	AIRDATE*	AIRPARK*
AGOUTY	AGUEWEED*	AIGRETS*	AIRDATES*	AIRPARKS*
AGRAFE*	AGUEWEEDS*	AIGRETTE	AIRDRAWN	AIRPLANE
AGRAFES*	AGUISE	AIGRETTES	AIRDROME	AIRPLANES
AGRAFFE	AGUISED	AIGUILLE	AIRDROMES	AIRPLAY*
AGRAFFES	AGUISES	AIGUILLES	AIRDROP*	AIRPLAYS*
AGRAPHA	AGUISH	AIKIDO	AIRDROPPED*	AIRPORT
AGRAPHIA	AGUISHLY	AIKIDOS	AIRDROPPING*	AIRPORTS
AGRAPHIAS	AGUISING	AIKONA	AIRDROPS*	AIRPOST*
AGRAPHIC	AGUIZE	AIL	AIRED	AIRPOSTS*
AGRAPHON	AGUIZED	AILANTHUS	AIRER	AIRPOWER*
AGRARIAN	AGUIZES	AILANTHUSES	AIRERS	AIRPOWERS*
AGRARIANS*	AGUIZING	AILANTO	AIREST*	AIRPROOF*
AGRASTE	AGUTI	AILANTOS	AIRFARE*	AIRPROOFED*
AGRAVIC	AGUTIS	AILED	AIRFARES*	AIRPROOFING*
AGREE	AH	AILERON	AIRFIELD	AIRPROOFS*
AGREEABLE	AHA	AILERONS	AIRFIELDS	AIRS
AGREEABLY	AHCHOO*	AILETTE	AIRFLOW	AIRSCAPE*
AGREED	AHEAD	AILETTES	AIRFLOWS	AIRSCAPES*
AGREEING	AHEAP	AILING	AIRFOIL	AIRSCREW
AGREEMENT	AHED	AILMENT	AIRFOILS	AIRSCREWS
AGREEMENTS	AHEIGHT	AILMENTS	AIRFRAME	AIRSHAFT
AGREES	AHEM	AILS	AIRFRAMES	AIRSHAFTS
AGREGE	AHENT	AIM	AIRGAP	AIRSHED*
AGREGES	AHIGH	AIMED	AIRGAPS	AIRSHEDS*
AGREMENS	AHIMSA	AIMER*	AIRGLOW	AIRSHIP
AGREMENT	AHIMSAS	AIMERS*	AIRGLOWS	AIRSHIPS
AGREMENTS	AHIND	AIMFUL*	AIRGRAPH	AIRSICK
AGRESTAL	AHING	AIMFULLY*	AIRGRAPHS	AIRSIDE
AGRESTIAL	AHINT	AIMING	AIRHEAD	AIRSIDES
AGRESTIC	AHISTORIC*	AIMLESS	AIRHEADED*	AIRSPACE
AGRIA*	AHOLD	AIMLESSLY	AIRHEADS	AIRSPACES
AGRIAS*	AHOLDS*	AIMS	AIRHOLE	AIRSPEED
AGRIMONIES	AHORSE	AIN	AIRHOLES	AIRSPEEDS
AGRIMONY	AHOY	AINE	AIRIER	AIRSTOP
AGRIN	AHS	AINEE	AIRIEST	AIRSTOPS
AGRIOLOGIES	AHULL	AINS*	AIRILY	AIRSTREAM
AGRIOLOGY	AHUNGERED	AINSELL*	AIRINESS	AIRSTREAMS
AGRISE	AHUNGRY	AINSELLS*	AIRINESSES	AIRSTRIP
AGRISED	AI	AIOLI	AIRING	AIRSTRIPS
AGRISES	AIA	AIOLIS	AIRINGS	AIRT
AGRISING	AIAS	AIR	AIRLESS	AIRTED

The Chambers Dictionary is the authority for many longer words; see Introduction, page ix

AIRTH*	AKES	ALARMISM	ALBINOISM	ALCHEMY
AIRTHED*	AKIMBO	ALARMISMS	ALBINOISMS	ALCHERA
AIRTHING*	AKIN	ALARMIST	ALBINOS	ALCHERAS
AIRTHS*	AKINESES	ALARMISTS	ALBINOTIC	ALCHYMIES
AIRTIGHT	AKINESIA	ALARMS	ALBITE	ALCHYMY
AIRTIME	AKINESIAS	ALARUM	ALBITES	ALCID*
AIRTIMES	AKINESIS	ALARUMED	ALBITIC	ALCIDINE*
AIRTING	AKING	ALARUMING	ALBITISE	ALCIDS*
AIRTS	AKKAS	ALARUMS	ALBITISED	ALCOHOL
AIRWARD	AKOLUTHOS	ALARY	ALBITISES	ALCOHOLIC
AIRWARDS	AKOLUTHOSES	ALAS	ALBITISING	ALCOHOLICS
AIRWAVE	AKVAVIT	ALASKA*	ALBITIZE	ALCOHOLS
AIRWAVES	AKVAVITS	ALASKAS*	ALBITIZED	ALCOPOP
AIRWAY	AL*	ALASTOR*	ALBITIZES	ALCOPOPS
AIRWAYS	ALA	ALASTORS*	ALBITIZING	ALCORZA
AIRWISE*	ALAAP	ALASTRIM	ALBIZIA*	ALCORZAS
AIRWOMAN	ALAAPS	ALASTRIMS	ALBIZIAS*	ALCOVE
AIRWOMEN	ALABAMINE	ALATE	ALBIZZIA*	ALCOVED*
AIRWORTHY	ALABAMINES	ALATED	ALBIZZIAS*	ALCOVES
AIRY	ALABASTER	ALATES*	ALBRICIAS	ALDEA
AIS	ALABASTERS	ALATION*	ALBS	ALDEAS
AISLE	ALACK	ALATIONS*	ALBUGO	ALDEHYDE
AISLED	ALACRITIES	ALAY	ALBUGOS	ALDEHYDES
AISLES	ALACRITY	ALAYED	ALBUM	ALDEHYDIC*
AISLEWAY*	ALAE	ALAYING	ALBUMEN	ALDER
AISLEWAYS*	ALAIMENT	ALAYS	ALBUMENS	ALDERFLIES*
AISLING	ALAIMENTS	ALB	ALBUMIN	ALDERFLY*
AISLINGS	ALALAGMOI	ALBA*	ALBUMINS	ALDERMAN
AIT	ALALAGMOS	ALBACORE	ALBUMOSE*	ALDERMEN
AITCH	ALALIA	ALBACORES	ALBUMOSES*	ALDERN
AITCHBONE	ALALIAS	ALBARELLI	ALBUMS	ALDERS
AITCHBONES	ALAMEDA	ALBARELLO	ALBURNOUS	ALDOL*
AITCHES	ALAMEDAS	ALBARELLOS	ALBURNUM	ALDOLASE*
AITS	ALAMO*	ALBAS*	ALBURNUMS	ALDOLASES*
AITU	ALAMODE	ALBATA	ALCADE*	ALDOLS*
AITUS	ALAMODES	ALBATAS	ALCADES*	ALDOSE
AIVER*	ALAMORT	ALBATROSS	ALCAHEST	ALDOSES
AIVERS*	ALAMOS*	ALBATROSSES	ALCAHESTS	ALDRIN
AIZLE	ALAN*	ALBE	ALCAIC*	ALDRINS
AIZLES	ALAND	ALBEDO	ALCAICS*	ALE
AJAR	ALANDS*	ALBEDOES*	ALCAIDE	ALEATORIC
AJEE	ALANE*	ALBEDOS	ALCAIDES	ALEATORIES
AJIVA*	ALANG	ALBEE	ALCALDE	ALEATORY
AJIVAS*	ALANGS	ALBEIT	ALCALDES	ALEBENCH
AJOWAN	ALANIN*	ALBERGHI	ALCARRAZA	ALEBENCHES
AJOWANS	ALANINE	ALBERGO	ALCARRAZAS	ALEC*
AJUGA*	ALANINES	ALBERT	ALCATRAS	ALECOST
AJUGAS*	ALANINS*	ALBERTITE	ALCATRASES	ALECOSTS
AJUTAGE	ALANNAH	ALBERTITES	ALCAYDE	ALECS*
AJUTAGES	ALANNAHS	ALBERTS	ALCAYDES	ALECTRYON
AJWAN	ALANS*	ALBESCENT	ALCAZAR	ALECTRYONS
AJWANS	ALANT*	ALBESPINE	ALCAZARS	ALEE
AKARYOTE	ALANTS*	ALBESPINES	ALCHEMIC	ALEF*
AKARYOTES	ALANYL*	ALBESPYNE	ALCHEMIES	ALEFS*
AKE	ALANYLS*	ALBESPYNES	ALCHEMISE	ALEFT
AKED	ALAP	ALBICORE	ALCHEMISED	ALEGAR
AKEDAH	ALAPA	ALBICORES	ALCHEMISES	ALEGARS
AKEDAHS	ALAPAS	ALBINAL*	ALCHEMISING	ALEGGE
AKEE	ALAPS	ALBINESS	ALCHEMIST	ALEGGED
AKEES	ALAR	ALBINESSES	ALCHEMISTS	ALEGGES
AKELA*	ALARM	ALBINIC	ALCHEMIZE	ALEGGING
AKELAS*	ALARMED	ALBINISM	ALCHEMIZED	ALEHOUSE*
AKENE	ALARMEDLY	ALBINISMS	ALCHEMIZES	ALEHOUSES*
AKENES	ALARMING	ALBINO	ALCHEMIZING	ALEMBIC

ALEMBICS	ALFORJAS	ALIDAD	ALINING	ALKIES
ALEMBROTH	ALFRESCO	ALIDADE	ALIPED	ALKINE*
ALEMBROTHS	ALGA	ALIDADES	ALIPEDS	ALKINES*
ALENCON*	ALGAE	ALIDADS	ALIPHATIC	ALKOXIDE*
ALENCONS*	ALGAECIDE*	ALIEN	ALIQUANT	ALKOXIDES*
ALENGTH	ALGAECIDES*	ALIENABLE	ALIQUOT	ALKOXY*
ALEPH	ALGAL	ALIENAGE	ALIQUOTS*	ALKY
ALEPHS	ALGAROBA	ALIENAGES	ALISMA	ALKYD
ALEPINE	ALGAROBAS	ALIENATE	ALISMAS	ALKYDS
ALEPINES	ALGARROBA	ALIENATED	ALIST*	ALKYL
ALERCE	ALGARROBAS	ALIENATES	ALIT	ALKYLATE*
ALERCES	ALGARROBO	ALIENATING	ALITERACIES	ALKYLATED*
ALERION	ALGARROBOS	ALIENATOR	ALITERACY	ALKYLATES*
ALERIONS	ALGAS*	ALIENATORS	ALITERATE	ALKYLATING*
ALERT	ALGATE	ALIENED	ALITERATES*	ALKYLIC*
ALERTED	ALGATES	ALIENEE	ALIUNDE	ALKYLS
ALERTER	ALGEBRA	ALIENEES	ALIVE	ALKYNE
ALERTEST	ALGEBRAIC	ALIENER*	ALIVENESS	ALKYNES
ALERTING	ALGEBRAS	ALIENERS*	ALIVENESSES	ALL
ALERTLY	ALGERINE	ALIENING	ALIYA	ALLANITE*
ALERTNESS	ALGERINES	ALIENISM	ALIYAH	ALLANITES*
ALERTNESSES	ALGESES	ALIENISMS	ALIYAHS	ALLANTOIC
ALERTS	ALGESIA	ALIENIST	ALIYAS	ALLANTOID
ALES	ALGESIAS	ALIENISTS	ALIYOS*	ALLANTOIDES*
ALETHIC	ALGESIS	ALIENLY*	ALIYOT	ALLANTOIDS
ALEURON	ALGICIDAL*	ALIENNESS*	ALIYOTH	ALLANTOIN*
ALEURONE	ALGICIDE	ALIENNESSES*	ALIZARI	ALLANTOINS*
ALEURONES	ALGICIDES	ALIENOR	ALIZARIN	ALLANTOIS
ALEURONS	ALGID	ALIENORS	ALIZARINE	ALLANTOISES
ALEVIN	ALGIDITIES	ALIENS	ALIZARINS	ALLATIVE
ALEVINS	ALGIDITY	ALIF*	ALIZARIS	ALLATIVES
ALEW	ALGIN	ALIFORM	ALKAHEST	ALLAY
ALEWASHED	ALGINATE	ALIFS*	ALKAHESTS	ALLAYED
ALEWIFE	ALGINATES	ALIGARTA	ALKALI	ALLAYER
ALEWIVES	ALGINIC	ALIGARTAS	ALKALIC*	ALLAYERS
ALEWS	ALGINS	ALIGHT	ALKALIES	ALLAYING
ALEXANDER*	ALGOID	ALIGHTED	ALKALIFIED	ALLAYINGS
ALEXANDERS*	ALGOLOGIES	ALIGHTING	ALKALIFIES	ALLAYMENT
ALEXIA	ALGOLOGY	ALIGHTS	ALKALIFY	ALLAYMENTS
ALEXIAS	ALGOR*	ALIGN	ALKALIFYING	ALLAYS
ALEXIC	ALGORISM	ALIGNED	ALKALIN*	ALLCOMERS
ALEXIN	ALGORISMS	ALIGNER*	ALKALINE	ALLEDGE
ALEXINE*	ALGORITHM	ALIGNERS*	ALKALIS	ALLEDGED
ALEXINES*	ALGORITHMS	ALIGNING	ALKALISE	ALLEDGES
ALEXINS	ALGORS*	ALIGNMENT	ALKALISED	ALLEDGING
ALEYE	ALGUACIL	ALIGNMENTS	ALKALISES	ALLEE
ALEYED	ALGUACILS	ALIGNS	ALKALISING	ALLEES
ALEYES	ALGUAZIL	ALIKE	ALKALIZE	ALLEGE
ALEYING	ALGUAZILS	ALIKENESS*	ALKALIZED	ALLEGED
ALFA	ALGUM	ALIKENESSES*	ALKALIZES	ALLEGEDLY
ALFAKI*	ALGUMS	ALIMENT	ALKALIZING	ALLEGER
ALFAKIS*	ALIAS	ALIMENTAL	ALKALOID	ALLEGERS
ALFALFA	ALIASES	ALIMENTED	ALKALOIDS	ALLEGES
ALFALFAS	ALIASING	ALIMENTING	ALKALOSES	ALLEGGE
ALFAQUI	ALIASINGS	ALIMENTS	ALKALOSIS	ALLEGGED
ALFAQUIN*	ALIBI	ALIMONIES	ALKALOTIC*	ALLEGGES
ALFAQUINS*	ALIBIED*	ALIMONY	ALKANE	ALLEGGING
ALFAQUIS	ALIBIES*	ALINE	ALKANES	ALLEGIANT
ALFAS	ALIBIING*	ALINED	ALKANET	ALLEGING
ALFERECES	ALIBIS	ALINEMENT	ALKANETS	ALLEGORIC
ALFEREZ	ALIBLE*	ALINEMENTS	ALKENE	ALLEGORIES
ALFILARIA*	ALICANT	ALINER*	ALKENES	ALLEGORY
ALFILARIAS*	ALICANTS	ALINERS*	ALKIE	ALLEGRO
ALFORJA	ALICYCLIC	ALINES	ALKIE	ALLEGROS

ALLEL	ALLNESS	ALLOTTEES	ALMAH	ALOFT
ALLELE	ALLNESSES	ALLOTTER*	ALMAHS	ALOGIA
ALLELES	ALLNIGHT	ALLOTTERIES	ALMAIN	ALOGIAS
ALLELIC*	ALLOBAR*	ALLOTTERS*	ALMAINS	ALOGICAL
ALLELISM*	ALLOBARS*	ALLOTTERY	ALMANAC	ALOHA
ALLELISMS*	ALLOCABLE	ALLOTTING	ALMANACS	ALOHAS*
ALLELS	ALLOCARPIES	ALLOTYPE*	ALMANDINE	ALOIN*
ALLELUIA	ALLOCARPY	ALLOTYPES*	ALMANDINES	ALOINS*
ALLELUIAH	ALLOCATE	ALLOTYPIC*	ALMANDITE*	ALONE
ALLELUIAHS	ALLOCATED	ALLOTYPIES*	ALMANDITES*	ALONELY
ALLELUIAS	ALLOCATES	ALLOTYPY*	ALMAS	ALONENESS
ALLEMANDE	ALLOCATING	ALLOVER*	ALME	ALONENESSES
ALLEMANDES	ALLOCATOR*	ALLOVERS*	ALMEH	ALONG
ALLENARLY	ALLOCATORS*	ALLOW	ALMEHS	ALONGSIDE
ALLERGEN	ALLOD	ALLOWABLE	ALMEMAR*	ALONGST
ALLERGENS	ALLODIA*	ALLOWABLY	ALMEMARS*	ALOOF
ALLERGIC	ALLODIAL	ALLOWANCE	ALMERIES	ALOOFLY
ALLERGICS	ALLODIUM	ALLOWANCED	ALMERY	ALOOFNESS
ALLERGIES	ALLODIUMS	ALLOWANCES	ALMES	ALOOFNESSES
ALLERGIN*	ALLODS	ALLOWANCING	ALMIGHTY	ALOPECIA
ALLERGINS*	ALLOGAMIES	ALLOWED	ALMIRAH	ALOPECIAS
ALLERGIST	ALLOGAMY	ALLOWEDLY	ALMIRAHS	ALOPECIC*
ALLERGISTS	ALLOGENIC*	ALLOWING	ALMNER*	ALOPECOID
ALLERGY	ALLOGRAFT	ALLOWS	ALMNERS*	ALOUD
ALLERION	ALLOGRAFTED*	ALLOXAN*	ALMOND	ALOW
ALLERIONS	ALLOGRAFTING*	ALLOXANS*	ALMONDS	ALOWE
ALLETHRIN*	ALLOGRAFTS	ALLOY	ALMONER	ALP
ALLETHRINS*	ALLOGRAPH	ALLOYED	ALMONERS	ALPACA
ALLEVIATE	ALLOGRAPHS	ALLOYING	ALMONRIES	ALPACAS
ALLEVIATED	ALLOMETRIES	ALLOYS	ALMONRY	ALPARGATA
ALLEVIATES	ALLOMETRY	ALLS	ALMOST	ALPARGATAS
ALLEVIATING	ALLOMORPH	ALLSEED	ALMOUS	ALPEEN
ALLEY	ALLOMORPHS	ALLSEEDS	ALMS	ALPEENS
ALLEYCAT	ALLONGE	ALLSORTS	ALMSGIVER*	ALPENGLOW*
ALLEYCATS	ALLONGES	ALLSPICE	ALMSGIVERS*	ALPENGLOWS*
ALLEYED	ALLONS	ALLSPICES	ALMSHOUSE*	ALPENHORN
ALLEYS	ALLONYM	ALLUDE	ALMSHOUSES*	ALPENHORNS
ALLEYWAY	ALLONYMS	ALLUDED	ALMSMAN*	ALPHA
ALLEYWAYS	ALLOPATH	ALLUDES	ALMSMEN*	ALPHABET
ALLHEAL	ALLOPATHIES	ALLUDING	ALMUCE	ALPHABETED
ALLHEALS	ALLOPATHS	ALLURE	ALMUCES	ALPHABETING
ALLIABLE*	ALLOPATHY	ALLURED	ALMUD*	ALPHABETS
ALLIANCE	ALLOPATRIES*	ALLURER	ALMUDE*	ALPHAS
ALLIANCES	ALLOPATRY*	ALLURERS	ALMUDES*	ALPHASORT
ALLICE	ALLOPHANE*	ALLURES	ALMUDS*	ALPHASORTED
ALLICES	ALLOPHANES*	ALLURING	ALMUG	ALPHASORTING
ALLICHOLIES	ALLOPHONE	ALLUSION	ALMUGS	ALPHASORTS
ALLICHOLY	ALLOPHONES	ALLUSIONS	ALNAGE	ALPHORN
ALLICIN*	ALLOPLASM	ALLUSIVE	ALNAGER	ALPHORNS
ALLICINS*	ALLOPLASMS	ALLUVIA	ALNAGERS	ALPHOSIS*
ALLIED	ALLOSAUR	ALLUVIAL	ALNAGES	ALPHOSISES*
ALLIES	ALLOSAURS	ALLUVIALS*	ALNICO*	ALPHYL*
ALLIGARTA	ALLOSTERIES	ALLUVION	ALNICOES*	ALPHYLS*
ALLIGARTAS	ALLOSTERY	ALLUVIONS	ALOD	ALPINE
ALLIGATE	ALLOT	ALLUVIUM	ALODIA*	ALPINELY*
ALLIGATED	ALLOTMENT	ALLUVIUMS*	ALODIAL	ALPINES
ALLIGATES	ALLOTMENTS	ALLY	ALODIUM	ALPINISM
ALLIGATING	ALLOTROPE	ALLYING	ALODIUMS	ALPINISMS
ALLIGATOR	ALLOTROPES	ALLYL	ALODS	ALPINIST
ALLIGATORS	ALLOTROPIES	ALLYLIC*	ALOE	ALPINISTS
ALLIS	ALLOTROPY	ALLYLS	ALOED	ALPS
ALLISES	ALLOTS	ALMA	ALOES	ALREADY
ALLIUM	ALLOTTED	ALMAGEST*	ALOETIC	ALRIGHT
ALLIUMS	ALLOTTEE	ALMAGESTS*	ALOETICS	ALS

Words marked with an asterisk are from OTCWL

ALSIKE	ALTOS	ALYSSUMS	AMAZE	AMBIVERTS
ALSIKES	ALTRICES	AM	AMAZED	AMBLE
ALSO	ALTRICIAL	AMA*	AMAZEDLY	AMBLED
ALSOON	ALTRUISM	AMABILE	AMAZEMENT	AMBLER
ALSOONE	ALTRUISMS	AMADAVAT	AMAZEMENTS	AMBLERS
ALT	ALTRUIST	AMADAVATS	AMAZES	AMBLES
ALTAR	ALTRUISTS	AMADOU	AMAZING	AMBLING
ALTARAGE	ALTS	AMADOUS	AMAZINGLY	AMBLINGS
ALTARAGES	ALUDEL	AMAH	AMAZON	AMBLYOPIA
ALTARS	ALUDELS	AMAHS	AMAZONIAN	AMBLYOPIAS
ALTARWISE	ALULA	AMAIN	AMAZONITE	AMBLYOPIC*
ALTER	ALULAE	AMALGAM	AMAZONITES	AMBO
ALTERABLE	ALULAR*	AMALGAMS	AMAZONS	AMBOINA*
ALTERABLY*	ALUM	AMANDINE	AMBAGE	AMBOINAS*
ALTERANT	ALUMIN*	AMANDINES	AMBAGES	AMBONES
ALTERANTS	ALUMINA	AMANITA	AMBAGIOUS	AMBOS
ALTERCATE	ALUMINAS	AMANITAS	AMBAN	AMBOYNA*
ALTERCATED	ALUMINATE	AMANITIN*	AMBANS	AMBOYNAS*
ALTERCATES	ALUMINATES	AMANITINS*	AMBARI*	AMBRIES
ALTERCATING	ALUMINE*	AMARACUS	AMBARIES*	AMBROID
ALTERED	ALUMINES*	AMARACUSES	AMBARIS*	AMBROIDS
ALTERER*	ALUMINIC*	AMARANT	AMBARY*	AMBROSIA
ALTERERS*	ALUMINISE	AMARANTH	AMBASSAGE	AMBROSIAL
ALTERING	ALUMINISED	AMARANTHS	AMBASSAGES	AMBROSIAN
ALTERITIES	ALUMINISES	AMARANTIN	AMBASSIES	AMBROSIAS
ALTERITY	ALUMINISING	AMARANTS	AMBASSY	AMBROTYPE
ALTERN	ALUMINIUM	AMARELLE*	AMBATCH	AMBROTYPES
ALTERNANT	ALUMINIUMS	AMARELLES*	AMBATCHES	AMBRY
ALTERNANTS	ALUMINIZE	AMARETTI*	AMBEER*	AMBSACE*
ALTERNAT	ALUMINIZED	AMARETTO	AMBEERS*	AMBSACES*
ALTERNATE	ALUMINIZES	AMARETTOS	AMBER	AMBULACRA
ALTERNATED	ALUMINIZING	AMARNA*	AMBERED	AMBULACRUM*
ALTERNATES	ALUMINOUS	AMARYLLID	AMBERGRIS	AMBULANCE
ALTERNATING	ALUMINS*	AMARYLLIDS	AMBERGRISES	AMBULANCES
ALTERNATS	ALUMINUM	AMARYLLIS	AMBERIES*	AMBULANT
ALTERNE	ALUMINUMS	AMARYLLISES	AMBERINA*	AMBULANTS
ALTERNES	ALUMISH	AMAS*	AMBERINAS*	AMBULATE
ALTERS	ALUMIUM	AMASS	AMBERITE	AMBULATED
ALTESSE	ALUMIUMS	AMASSABLE	AMBERITES	AMBULATES
ALTESSES	ALUMNA	AMASSED	AMBERJACK	AMBULATING
ALTEZA	ALUMNAE	AMASSER*	AMBERJACKS	AMBULATOR
ALTEZAS	ALUMNI	AMASSERS*	AMBEROID	AMBULATORS
ALTEZZA	ALUMNUS	AMASSES	AMBEROIDS	AMBUSCADE
ALTEZZAS	ALUMROOT*	AMASSING	AMBEROUS	AMBUSCADED
ALTHAEA	ALUMROOTS*	AMASSMENT	AMBERS	AMBUSCADES
ALTHAEAS	ALUMS	AMASSMENTS	AMBERY	AMBUSCADING
ALTHEA	ALUNITE	AMATE	AMBIANCE	AMBUSCADO
ALTHEAS	ALUNITES	AMATED	AMBIANCES	AMBUSCADOES
ALTHO*	ALURE	AMATES	AMBIENCE	AMBUSCADOS
ALTHORN	ALURES	AMATEUR	AMBIENCES	AMBUSH
ALTHORNS	ALVEARIES	AMATEURS	AMBIENT	AMBUSHED
ALTHOUGH	ALVEARY	AMATING	AMBIENTS	AMBUSHER*
ALTIMETER	ALVEATED	AMATION	AMBIGUITIES	AMBUSHERS*
ALTIMETERS	ALVEOLAR	AMATIONS	AMBIGUITY	AMBUSHES
ALTIMETRIES	ALVEOLARS*	AMATIVE	AMBIGUOUS	AMBUSHING
ALTIMETRY	ALVEOLATE	AMATIVELY*	AMBIT	AMEARST
ALTIPLANO*	ALVEOLE	AMATOL	AMBITION	AMEBA
ALTIPLANOS*	ALVEOLES	AMATOLS	AMBITIONED*	AMEBAE
ALTISSIMO	ALVEOLI	AMATORIAL	AMBITIONING*	AMEBAN*
ALTITUDE	ALVEOLUS	AMATORIAN	AMBITIONS	AMEBAS
ALTITUDES	ALVINE	AMATORY	AMBITIOUS	AMEBEAN*
ALTO	ALWAY	AMAUROSES	AMBITS	AMEBIASES*
ALTOIST*	ALWAYS	AMAUROSIS	AMBITTY	AMEBIASIS*
ALTOISTS*	ALYSSUM	AMAUROTIC	AMBIVERT	AMEBIC

AMEBOCYTE*
AMEBOCYTES*
AMEBOID*
AMEER
AMEERATE*
AMEERATES*
AMEERS
AMEIOSES
AMEIOSIS
AMELCORN
AMELCORNS
AMELIA
AMELIAS
AMEN
AMENABLE
AMENABLY
AMENAGE
AMENAGED
AMENAGES
AMENAGING
AMENAUNCE
AMENAUNCES
AMEND
AMENDABLE
AMENDE
AMENDED
AMENDER
AMENDERS
AMENDES
AMENDING
AMENDMENT
AMENDMENTS
AMENDS
AMENE
AMENED
AMENING
AMENITIES
AMENITY
AMENS
AMENT
AMENTA
AMENTAL
AMENTIA
AMENTIAS
AMENTS
AMENTUM
AMERCE
AMERCED
AMERCER*
AMERCERS*
AMERCES
AMERCING
AMERICIUM
AMERICIUMS
AMESACE*
AMESACES*
AMETHYST
AMETHYSTS
AMETROPIA*
AMETROPIAS*
AMETROPIC*
AMI
AMIA*
AMIABLE

AMIABLY
AMIANTHUS
AMIANTHUSES
AMIANTUS
AMIANTUSES
AMIAS*
AMICABLE
AMICABLY
AMICE
AMICES
AMICI*
AMICUS*
AMID
AMIDASE*
AMIDASES*
AMIDE
AMIDES
AMIDIC*
AMIDIN*
AMIDINE*
AMIDINES*
AMIDINS*
AMIDMOST
AMIDO*
AMIDOGEN*
AMIDOGENS*
AMIDOL*
AMIDOLS*
AMIDONE*
AMIDONES*
AMIDS*
AMIDSHIP*
AMIDSHIPS
AMIDST
AMIE
AMIES
AMIGA*
AMIGAS*
AMIGO
AMIGOS
AMILDAR
AMILDARS
AMIN*
AMINE
AMINES
AMINIC*
AMINITIES*
AMINITY*
AMINO*
AMINS*
AMIR
AMIRATE*
AMIRATES*
AMIRS
AMIS
AMISES
AMISS
AMISSES
AMISSIBLE
AMISSING
AMITIES
AMITOSES
AMITOSIS
AMITOTIC

AMITROLE*
AMITROLES*
AMITY
AMLA
AMLAS
AMMAN
AMMANS
AMMETER
AMMETERS
AMMINE*
AMMINES*
AMMINO*
AMMIRAL
AMMIRALS
AMMO
AMMOCETE*
AMMOCETES*
AMMON
AMMONAL
AMMONALS
AMMONIA
AMMONIAC
AMMONIACS*
AMMONIAS
AMMONIATE*
AMMONIATED*
AMMONIATES*
AMMONIATING*
AMMONIC*
AMMONIFIED*
AMMONIFIES*
AMMONIFY*
AMMONIFYING*
AMMONITE
AMMONITES
AMMONITIC*
AMMONIUM
AMMONIUMS
AMMONO*
AMMONOID
AMMONOIDS
AMMONS
AMMOS
AMNESIA
AMNESIAC
AMNESIACS
AMNESIAS
AMNESIC
AMNESICS
AMNESTIC*
AMNESTIED
AMNESTIES
AMNESTY
AMNESTYING
AMNIA
AMNIC*
AMNIO
AMNION
AMNIONIC*
AMNIONS*
AMNIOS
AMNIOTE*
AMNIOTES*
AMNIOTIC

AMNIOTOMIES
AMNIOTOMY
AMOEBA
AMOEBAE
AMOEBAEAN
AMOEBAN*
AMOEBAS
AMOEBEAN*
AMOEBIC
AMOEBOID
AMOK
AMOKS*
AMOLE*
AMOLES*
AMOMUM
AMOMUMS
AMONG
AMONGST
AMOOVE
AMOOVED
AMOOVES
AMOOVING
AMORAL
AMORALISM
AMORALISMS
AMORALIST
AMORALISTS
AMORALITIES*
AMORALITY*
AMORALLY*
AMORANCE
AMORANCES
AMORANT
AMORCE
AMORCES
AMORET
AMORETS
AMORETTI
AMORETTO
AMORETTOS*
AMORINI
AMORINO
AMORISM
AMORISMS
AMORIST
AMORISTIC*
AMORISTS
AMORNINGS
AMOROSA
AMOROSAS
AMOROSITIES
AMOROSITY
AMOROSO
AMOROSOS
AMOROUS
AMOROUSLY
AMORPHISM
AMORPHISMS
AMORPHOUS
AMORT
AMORTISE
AMORTISED
AMORTISES
AMORTISING

AMORTIZE
AMORTIZED
AMORTIZES
AMORTIZING
AMOSITE
AMOSITES
AMOTION*
AMOTIONS*
AMOUNT
AMOUNTED
AMOUNTING
AMOUNTS
AMOUR
AMOURETTE
AMOURETTES
AMOURS
AMOVE
AMOVED
AMOVES
AMOVING
AMP
AMPASSIES
AMPASSY
AMPERAGE
AMPERAGES
AMPERE
AMPERES
AMPERSAND
AMPERSANDS
AMPERZAND
AMPERZANDS
AMPHIBIA*
AMPHIBIAN
AMPHIBIANS
AMPHIBOLE
AMPHIBOLES
AMPHIBOLIES
AMPHIBOLY
AMPHIGORIES
AMPHIGORY
AMPHIOXI*
AMPHIOXUS
AMPHIOXUSES
AMPHIPOD
AMPHIPODS
AMPHOLYTE
AMPHOLYTES
AMPHORA
AMPHORAE
AMPHORAL*
AMPHORAS*
AMPHORIC
AMPLE
AMPLENESS
AMPLENESSES
AMPLER
AMPLEST
AMPLEXUS
AMPLEXUSES*
AMPLIDYNE*
AMPLIDYNES*
AMPLIFIED
AMPLIFIER
AMPLIFIERS

AMPLIFIES	AMYGDALAE*	ANAEROBES	ANALYSES	ANASARCAS
AMPLIFY	AMYGDALAS	ANAEROBIC	ANALYSING	ANASTASES
AMPLIFYING	AMYGDALE	ANAGLYPH	ANALYSIS	ANASTASIS
AMPLITUDE	AMYGDALES	ANAGLYPHS	ANALYST	ANASTATIC
AMPLITUDES	AMYGDALIN	ANAGOGE	ANALYSTS	ANATASE
AMPLOSOME	AMYGDALINS	ANAGOGES	ANALYTIC	ANATASES
AMPLOSOMES	AMYGDALS	ANAGOGIC	ANALYTICS	ANATHEMA
AMPLY	AMYGDULE	ANAGOGIES	ANALYZE	ANATHEMAS
AMPOULE	AMYGDULES	ANAGOGY	ANALYZED	ANATHEMATA*
AMPOULES	AMYL	ANAGRAM	ANALYZER	ANATOMIC
AMPS	AMYLASE	ANAGRAMMED	ANALYZERS	ANATOMIES
AMPUL	AMYLASES	ANAGRAMMING	ANALYZES	ANATOMISE
AMPULE	AMYLENE	ANAGRAMS	ANALYZING	ANATOMISED
AMPULES	AMYLENES	ANAL	ANAMNESES	ANATOMISES
AMPULLA	AMYLIC*	ANALCIME	ANAMNESIS	ANATOMISING
AMPULLAE	AMYLOGEN*	ANALCIMES	ANAN	ANATOMIST
AMPULLAR*	AMYLOGENS*	ANALCITE	ANANA	ANATOMISTS
AMPULLARY*	AMYLOID	ANALCITES	ANANAS	ANATOMIZE
AMPULS	AMYLOIDAL	ANALECTA	ANANASES	ANATOMIZED
AMPUTATE	AMYLOIDS	ANALECTIC	ANANDROUS	ANATOMIZES
AMPUTATED	AMYLOPSIN	ANALECTS	ANANKE	ANATOMIZING
AMPUTATES	AMYLOPSINS	ANALEMMA	ANANKES	ANATOMY
AMPUTATING	AMYLOSE*	ANALEMMAS	ANANTHOUS	ANATOXIN*
AMPUTATOR	AMYLOSES*	ANALEMMATA	ANAPAEST	ANATOXINS*
AMPUTATORS	AMYLS	ANALEPTIC	ANAPAESTS	ANATROPIES
AMPUTEE	AMYLUM	ANALEPTICS	ANAPEST	ANATROPY
AMPUTEES	AMYLUMS	ANALGESIA	ANAPESTIC*	ANATTA
AMREETA*	AMYOTONIA*	ANALGESIAS	ANAPESTICS*	ANATTAS
AMREETAS*	AMYOTONIAS*	ANALGESIC	ANAPESTS	ANATTO
AMRIT	AMYTAL	ANALGESICS	ANAPHASE	ANATTOS
AMRITA	AMYTALS	ANALGETIC*	ANAPHASES	ANAXIAL
AMRITAS	AN	ANALGETICS*	ANAPHASIC*	ANBURIES
AMRITS	ANA	ANALGIA*	ANAPHOR*	ANBURY
AMTMAN	ANABAENA*	ANALGIAS*	ANAPHORA	ANCE
AMTMANS	ANABAENAS*	ANALITIES*	ANAPHORAS	ANCESTOR
AMTRAC*	ANABAS	ANALITY*	ANAPHORIC	ANCESTORED*
AMTRACK	ANABASES	ANALLY	ANAPHORS*	ANCESTORING*
AMTRACKS	ANABASIS	ANALOG	ANAPLASIA*	ANCESTORS
AMTRACS*	ANABATIC	ANALOGA	ANAPLASIAS*	ANCESTRAL
AMU*	ANABIOSES	ANALOGIC	ANAPLASTIES	ANCESTRIES
AMUCK	ANABIOSIS	ANALOGIES	ANAPLASTY	ANCESTRY
AMUCKS*	ANABIOTIC	ANALOGISE	ANAPTYXES	ANCHOR
AMULET	ANABLEPS	ANALOGISED	ANAPTYXIS	ANCHORAGE
AMULETIC	ANABLEPSES	ANALOGISES	ANARCH	ANCHORAGES
AMULETS	ANABOLIC	ANALOGISING	ANARCHAL	ANCHORED
AMUS*	ANABOLISM	ANALOGIST	ANARCHIAL	ANCHORESS
AMUSABLE	ANABOLISMS	ANALOGISTS	ANARCHIC	ANCHORESSES
AMUSE	ANABOLITE	ANALOGIZE	ANARCHIES	ANCHORET
AMUSED	ANABOLITES	ANALOGIZED	ANARCHISE	ANCHORETS
AMUSEDLY	ANABRANCH	ANALOGIZES	ANARCHISED	ANCHORING
AMUSEMENT	ANABRANCHES	ANALOGIZING	ANARCHISES	ANCHORITE
AMUSEMENTS	ANACHARIS	ANALOGON	ANARCHISING	ANCHORITES
AMUSER	ANACHARISES	ANALOGONS	ANARCHISM	ANCHORMAN*
AMUSERS	ANACLITIC*	ANALOGOUS	ANARCHISMS	ANCHORMEN*
AMUSES	ANACONDA	ANALOGS	ANARCHIST	ANCHORS
AMUSETTE	ANACONDAS	ANALOGUE	ANARCHISTS	ANCHOVETA
AMUSETTES	ANACRUSES	ANALOGUES	ANARCHIZE	ANCHOVETAS
AMUSIA*	ANACRUSIS	ANALOGY	ANARCHIZED	ANCHOVIES
AMUSIAS*	ANADEM	ANALYSAND	ANARCHIZES	ANCHOVY
AMUSING	ANADEMS	ANALYSANDS	ANARCHIZING	ANCHUSA*
AMUSINGLY	ANAEMIA	ANALYSE	ANARCHS	ANCHUSAS*
AMUSIVE	ANAEMIAS	ANALYSED	ANARCHY	ANCHUSIN*
AMYGDAL	ANAEMIC	ANALYSER	ANAS	ANCHUSINS*
AMYGDALA	ANAEROBE	ANALYSERS	ANASARCA	ANCHYLOSE

The Chambers Dictionary is the authority for many longer words; see Introduction, page ix

ANCHYLOSED	ANDVILE	ANGAKOKS*	ANGLICISTS	ANICONISTS
ANCHYLOSES	ANDVILES	ANGARIA*	ANGLICIZE	ANICUT
ANCHYLOSING	ANE	ANGARIAS*	ANGLICIZED	ANICUTS
ANCIENT	ANEAR	ANGARIES	ANGLICIZES	ANIGH
ANCIENTER*	ANEARED	ANGARY	ANGLICIZING	ANIGHT
ANCIENTEST*	ANEARING	ANGAS*	ANGLIFIED	ANIL
ANCIENTLY	ANEARS	ANGEKKOK	ANGLIFIES	ANILE
ANCIENTRIES	ANEATH	ANGEKKOKS	ANGLIFY	ANILIN*
ANCIENTRY	ANECDOTA*	ANGEKOK	ANGLIFYING	ANILINE
ANCIENTS	ANECDOTAL	ANGEKOKS	ANGLING	ANILINES
ANCILE	ANECDOTE	ANGEL	ANGLINGS	ANILINGUS*
ANCILIA	ANECDOTES	ANGELED*	ANGLIST	ANILINGUSES*
ANCILLA*	ANECDOTIC*	ANGELFISH*	ANGLISTS	ANILINS*
ANCILLAE*	ANECHOIC	ANGELFISHES*	ANGLOPHIL	ANILITIES
ANCILLARIES	ANELACE	ANGELHOOD	ANGLOPHILS	ANILITY
ANCILLARY	ANELACES	ANGELHOODS	ANGOLA	ANILS
ANCILLAS*	ANELASTIC*	ANGELIC	ANGOPHORA	ANIMA
ANCIPITAL	ANELE	ANGELICA	ANGOPHORAS	ANIMAL
ANCLE	ANELED	ANGELICAL	ANGORA	ANIMALIC
ANCLES	ANELES	ANGELICAS	ANGORAS	ANIMALIER*
ANCOME	ANELING	ANGELING*	ANGRIER	ANIMALIERS*
ANCOMES	ANEMIA	ANGELS	ANGRIES	ANIMALISE
ANCON	ANEMIAS	ANGELUS	ANGRIEST	ANIMALISED
ANCONAL*	ANEMIC	ANGELUSES	ANGRILY	ANIMALISES
ANCONE*	ANEMOGRAM	ANGER	ANGRINESS	ANIMALISING
ANCONEAL*	ANEMOGRAMS	ANGERED	ANGRINESSES	ANIMALISM
ANCONES	ANEMOLOGIES	ANGERING	ANGRY	ANIMALISMS
ANCONOID*	ANEMOLOGY	ANGERLESS	ANGST	ANIMALIST
ANCORA	ANEMONE	ANGERLY	ANGSTROM	ANIMALISTS
ANCRESS	ANEMONES	ANGERS	ANGSTROMS	ANIMALITIES
ANCRESSES	ANEMOSES*	ANGICO	ANGSTS	ANIMALITY
AND	ANEMOSIS*	ANGICOS	ANGUIFORM	ANIMALIZE
ANDANTE	ANENST*	ANGINA	ANGUINE	ANIMALIZED
ANDANTES	ANENT	ANGINAL	ANGUIPED	ANIMALIZES
ANDANTINO	ANERGIA*	ANGINAS	ANGUIPEDE	ANIMALIZING
ANDANTINOS	ANERGIAS*	ANGINOSE*	ANGUISH	ANIMALLY
ANDESINE	ANERGIC*	ANGINOUS*	ANGUISHED	ANIMALS
ANDESINES	ANERGIES*	ANGIOGRAM	ANGUISHES	ANIMAS
ANDESITE	ANERGY*	ANGIOGRAMS	ANGUISHING	ANIMATE
ANDESITES	ANERLY	ANGIOMA	ANGULAR	ANIMATED
ANDESITIC	ANEROID	ANGIOMAS	ANGULARLY*	ANIMATELY*
ANDESYTE*	ANEROIDS	ANGIOMATA	ANGULATE	ANIMATER
ANDESYTES*	ANES	ANGKLUNG	ANGULATED	ANIMATERS
ANDIRON	ANESTRA	ANGKLUNGS	ANGULATES*	ANIMATES
ANDIRONS	ANESTRI	ANGLE	ANGULATING*	ANIMATIC
ANDOUILLE*	ANESTROUS*	ANGLED	ANGULOSE*	ANIMATICS
ANDOUILLES*	ANESTRUM	ANGLEPOD*	ANGULOUS*	ANIMATING
ANDRADITE*	ANESTRUS	ANGLEPODS*	ANHEDONIA	ANIMATION
ANDRADITES*	ANETHOL*	ANGLER	ANHEDONIAS	ANIMATIONS
ANDROECIA	ANETHOLE*	ANGLERS	ANHEDONIC	ANIMATISM
ANDROECIUM*	ANETHOLES*	ANGLES	ANHEDRAL	ANIMATISMS
ANDROGEN	ANETHOLS*	ANGLESITE	ANHINGA*	ANIMATO*
ANDROGENS	ANETIC	ANGLESITES	ANHINGAS*	ANIMATOR
ANDROGYNE	ANEUPLOID	ANGLEWISE	ANHUNGRED	ANIMATORS
ANDROGYNES	ANEUPLOIDS	ANGLEWORM	ANHYDRIDE	ANIME
ANDROGYNIES	ANEURIN	ANGLEWORMS	ANHYDRIDES	ANIMES
ANDROGYNY	ANEURINS	ANGLICE	ANHYDRITE	ANIMI*
ANDROID	ANEURISM	ANGLICISE	ANHYDRITES	ANIMIS*
ANDROIDS	ANEURISMS	ANGLICISED	ANHYDROUS	ANIMISM
ANDROLOGIES	ANEURYSM	ANGLICISES	ANI	ANIMISMS
ANDROLOGY	ANEURYSMS	ANGLICISING	ANICONIC	ANIMIST
ANDROMEDA	ANEW	ANGLICISM	ANICONISM	ANIMISTIC
ANDROMEDAS	ANGA*	ANGLICISMS	ANICONISMS	ANIMISTS
ANDS	ANGAKOK*	ANGLICIST	ANICONIST	ANIMOSITIES

Words marked with an asterisk are from OTCWL

ANIMOSITY	ANNALIZES	ANNUALIZED	ANOMIC	ANSERINES*
ANIMUS	ANNALIZING	ANNUALIZES	ANOMIE	ANSEROUS*
ANIMUSES	ANNALS	ANNUALIZING	ANOMIES	ANSWER
ANION	ANNAS	ANNUALLY	ANOMY	ANSWERED
ANIONIC	ANNAT	ANNUALS	ANON	ANSWERER
ANIONS	ANNATES	ANNUITANT	ANONYM	ANSWERERS
ANIS	ANNATS	ANNUITANTS	ANONYMA	ANSWERING
ANISE	ANNATTA	ANNUITIES	ANONYMAS	ANSWERS
ANISEED	ANNATTAS	ANNUITY	ANONYMISE	ANT
ANISEEDS	ANNATTO	ANNUL	ANONYMISED	ANTA
ANISES	ANNATTOS	ANNULAR	ANONYMISES	ANTACID
ANISETTE	ANNEAL	ANNULARS	ANONYMISING	ANTACIDS
ANISETTES	ANNEALED	ANNULATE	ANONYMITIES	ANTAE
ANISIC*	ANNEALER	ANNULATED	ANONYMITY	ANTALGIC*
ANISOGAMIES*	ANNEALERS	ANNULATES	ANONYMIZE	ANTALGICS*
ANISOGAMY*	ANNEALING	ANNULET	ANONYMIZED	ANTAR
ANISOLE*	ANNEALINGS	ANNULETS	ANONYMIZES	ANTARA
ANISOLES*	ANNEALS	ANNULI	ANONYMIZING	ANTARAS
ANKER	ANNECTENT	ANNULLED	ANONYMOUS	ANTARCTIC*
ANKERITE	ANNELID	ANNULLING	ANONYMS	ANTARS
ANKERITES	ANNELIDAN*	ANNULMENT	ANOOPSIA*	ANTAS
ANKERS	ANNELIDANS*	ANNULMENTS	ANOOPSIAS*	ANTBEAR
ANKH	ANNELIDS	ANNULOSE	ANOPHELES	ANTBEARS
ANKHS	ANNEX	ANNULS	ANOPIA*	ANTBIRD
ANKLE	ANNEXE	ANNULUS	ANOPIAS*	ANTBIRDS
ANKLEBONE*	ANNEXED	ANNULUSES*	ANOPSIA*	ANTE
ANKLEBONES*	ANNEXES	ANOA	ANOPSIAS*	ANTEATER
ANKLED	ANNEXING	ANOAS	ANORAK	ANTEATERS
ANKLES	ANNEXION	ANODAL	ANORAKS	ANTECEDE
ANKLET	ANNEXIONS	ANODALLY*	ANORECTAL	ANTECEDED
ANKLETS	ANNEXMENT	ANODE	ANORECTIC	ANTECEDES
ANKLING*	ANNEXMENTS	ANODES	ANORECTICS	ANTECEDING
ANKLONG	ANNEXURE	ANODIC	ANORETIC	ANTECHOIR
ANKLONGS	ANNEXURES	ANODISE	ANORETICS	ANTECHOIRS
ANKLUNG	ANNICUT	ANODISED	ANOREXIA	ANTED
ANKLUNGS	ANNICUTS	ANODISES	ANOREXIAS	ANTEDATE
ANKUS	ANNO	ANODISING	ANOREXIC	ANTEDATED
ANKUSES	ANNOTATE	ANODIZE	ANOREXICS	ANTEDATES
ANKUSH*	ANNOTATED	ANODIZED	ANOREXIES	ANTEDATING
ANKUSHES*	ANNOTATES	ANODIZES	ANOREXY	ANTEED*
ANKYLOSE	ANNOTATING	ANODIZING	ANORTHIC	ANTEFIX
ANKYLOSED	ANNOTATOR	ANODYNE	ANORTHITE	ANTEFIXA
ANKYLOSES	ANNOTATORS	ANODYNES	ANORTHITES	ANTEFIXAE*
ANKYLOSING	ANNOUNCE	ANODYNIC*	ANOSMIA	ANTEFIXAL
ANKYLOSIS	ANNOUNCED	ANOESES	ANOSMIAS	ANTEFIXES
ANKYLOTIC*	ANNOUNCER	ANOESIS	ANOSMIC*	ANTEING
ANLACE	ANNOUNCERS	ANOESTRA	ANOTHER	ANTELOPE
ANLACES	ANNOUNCES	ANOESTRI	ANOUGH	ANTELOPES
ANLAGE	ANNOUNCING	ANOESTRUM	ANOUROUS	ANTELUCAN
ANLAGEN	ANNOY	ANOESTRUS	ANOVULANT	ANTENATAL
ANLAGES	ANNOYANCE	ANOETIC	ANOVULANTS	ANTENATI
ANLAS*	ANNOYANCES	ANOINT	ANOVULAR*	ANTENNA
ANLASES*	ANNOYED	ANOINTED	ANOW	ANTENNAE
ANN	ANNOYER	ANOINTER	ANOXEMIA*	ANTENNAL
ANNA	ANNOYERS	ANOINTERS	ANOXEMIAS*	ANTENNARY
ANNAL	ANNOYING	ANOINTING	ANOXEMIC*	ANTENNAS
ANNALISE	ANNOYS	ANOINTS	ANOXIA	ANTENNULE
ANNALISED	ANNS	ANOLE*	ANOXIAS	ANTENNULES
ANNALISES	ANNUAL	ANOLES*	ANOXIC	ANTEPAST
ANNALISING	ANNUALISE	ANOLYTE*	ANSA*	ANTEPASTS
ANNALIST	ANNUALISED	ANOLYTES*	ANSAE*	ANTERIOR
ANNALISTS	ANNUALISES	ANOMALIES	ANSATE	ANTEROOM
ANNALIZE	ANNUALISING	ANOMALOUS	ANSATED	ANTEROOMS
ANNALIZED	ANNUALIZE	ANOMALY	ANSERINE	ANTES

The Chambers Dictionary is the authority for many longer words; see Introduction, page ix

ANTETYPE*	ANTIC	ANTILEFT*	ANTIQUE	ANTIURBAN*
ANTETYPES*	ANTICALLY*	ANTILIFE*	ANTIQUED	ANTIVENIN
ANTEVERT	ANTICAR*	ANTILOCK*	ANTIQUELY	ANTIVENINS
ANTEVERTED	ANTICHLOR	ANTILOG	ANTIQUER*	ANTIVIRAL
ANTEVERTING	ANTICHLORS	ANTILOGIES	ANTIQUERS*	ANTIVIRUS
ANTEVERTS	ANTICITY*	ANTILOGS	ANTIQUES	ANTIWAR
ANTHELIA	ANTICIVIC	ANTILOGY	ANTIQUING	ANTIWEAR*
ANTHELICES	ANTICIZE	ANTIMACHO*	ANTIQUITIES	ANTIWEED*
ANTHELION	ANTICIZED	ANTIMALE*	ANTIQUITY	ANTIWHITE*
ANTHELIONS*	ANTICIZES	ANTIMAN*	ANTIRADAR*	ANTIWOMAN*
ANTHELIX	ANTICIZING	ANTIMASK	ANTIRAPE*	ANTLER
ANTHELIXES*	ANTICK	ANTIMASKS	ANTIRED*	ANTLERED
ANTHEM	ANTICKE	ANTIMERE*	ANTIRIOT	ANTLERS
ANTHEMED	ANTICKED	ANTIMERES*	ANTIROCK*	ANTLIA
ANTHEMIA	ANTICKING	ANTIMONIC	ANTIROLL*	ANTLIAE
ANTHEMIC	ANTICKS*	ANTIMONIES	ANTIRUST	ANTLIATE
ANTHEMING	ANTICLINE	ANTIMONY	ANTIRUSTS*	ANTLIKE*
ANTHEMION	ANTICLINES	ANTIMYCIN*	ANTIS	ANTLION
ANTHEMS	ANTICLING*	ANTIMYCINS*	ANTISAG*	ANTLIONS
ANTHER	ANTICLY*	ANTING	ANTISCIAN	ANTONYM
ANTHERAL*	ANTICODON*	ANTINGS	ANTISCIANS	ANTONYMIC
ANTHERID*	ANTICODONS*	ANTINODAL	ANTISENSE*	ANTONYMIES
ANTHERIDS*	ANTICOLD*	ANTINODE	ANTISERA	ANTONYMS
ANTHERS	ANTICOUS	ANTINODES	ANTISERUM	ANTONYMY
ANTHESES	ANTICRACK*	ANTINOISE	ANTISERUMS	ANTRA
ANTHESIS	ANTICRIME*	ANTINOMIC	ANTISEX*	ANTRAL*
ANTHILL*	ANTICS	ANTINOMIES	ANTISHARK*	ANTRE
ANTHILLS*	ANTICULT*	ANTINOMY	ANTISHIP	ANTRES
ANTHOCARP	ANTIDORA*	ANTINOVEL*	ANTISHOCK*	ANTRORSE
ANTHOCARPS	ANTIDOTAL	ANTINOVELS*	ANTISKID	ANTRUM
ANTHOCYAN	ANTIDOTE	ANTINUKE*	ANTISLEEP*	ANTRUMS*
ANTHOCYANS	ANTIDOTED*	ANTIPAPAL	ANTISLIP*	ANTS
ANTHODIA*	ANTIDOTES	ANTIPARTY*	ANTISMOG*	ANTSIER
ANTHODIUM*	ANTIDOTING*	ANTIPASTI*	ANTISMOKE*	ANTSIEST
ANTHOID	ANTIDRAFT*	ANTIPASTO	ANTISMUT*	ANTSY
ANTHOLOGIES	ANTIDRUG*	ANTIPASTOS	ANTISNOB*	ANUCLEATE
ANTHOLOGY	ANTIELITE*	ANTIPATHIES	ANTISOLAR*	ANURAL*
ANTHOZOAN*	ANTIENT	ANTIPATHY	ANTISPAST	ANURAN*
ANTHOZOANS*	ANTIENTS	ANTIPHON	ANTISPASTS	ANURANS*
ANTHRACES*	ANTIFAT*	ANTIPHONIES	ANTISTAT	ANURESES*
ANTHRACIC	ANTIFLU*	ANTIPHONS	ANTISTATE*	ANURESIS*
ANTHRAX	ANTIFOAM*	ANTIPHONY	ANTISTATS	ANURETIC*
ANTHRAXES	ANTIFRAUD*	ANTIPILL*	ANTISTICK*	ANURIA
ANTHROPIC	ANTIFUR*	ANTIPODAL	ANTISTORIES*	ANURIAS
ANTHURIUM	ANTIGAY	ANTIPODALS*	ANTISTORY*	ANURIC*
ANTHURIUMS	ANTIGEN	ANTIPODE	ANTITANK	ANUROUS
ANTI	ANTIGENE*	ANTIPODES	ANTITAX*	ANUS
ANTIAGING*	ANTIGENES*	ANTIPOLE	ANTITHEFT	ANUSES
ANTIAIR*	ANTIGENIC	ANTIPOLES	ANTITHET	ANVIL
ANTIALIEN*	ANTIGENS	ANTIPOPE	ANTITHETS	ANVILED*
ANTIAR	ANTIGLARE*	ANTIPOPES	ANTITOXIC	ANVILING*
ANTIARIN*	ANTIGUN*	ANTIPORN*	ANTITOXIN	ANVILLED*
ANTIARINS*	ANTIHELICES	ANTIPOT*	ANTITOXINS	ANVILLING*
ANTIARS	ANTIHELIX	ANTIPRESS*	ANTITRADE	ANVILS
ANTIATOM*	ANTIHERO*	ANTIPYIC*	ANTITRADES	ANVILTOP*
ANTIATOMS*	ANTIHEROES*	ANTIPYICS*	ANTITRAGI	ANVILTOPS*
ANTIAUXIN*	ANTIHUMAN*	ANTIQUARIES	ANTITRUST	ANXIETIES
ANTIAUXINS*	ANTIJAM*	ANTIQUARK	ANTITUMOR*	ANXIETY
ANTIBIAS*	ANTIKING*	ANTIQUARKS	ANTITYPAL	ANXIOUS
ANTIBLACK*	ANTIKINGS*	ANTIQUARY	ANTITYPE	ANXIOUSLY
ANTIBODIES	ANTIKNOCK	ANTIQUATE	ANTITYPES	ANY
ANTIBODY	ANTIKNOCKS	ANTIQUATED	ANTITYPIC	ANYBODIES
ANTIBOSS*	ANTILABOR*	ANTIQUATES	ANTIULCER*	ANYBODY
ANTIBUG*	ANTILEAK*	ANTIQUATING	ANTIUNION*	ANYHOW

ANYMORE*	APEDOM	APHICIDE	APISH	APOGEIC*
ANYONE	APEDOMS	APHICIDES	APISHLY	APOGRAPH
ANYONES	APEEK	APHID	APISHNESS	APOGRAPHS
ANYPLACE*	APEHOOD	APHIDES	APISHNESSES	APOLLO
ANYROAD	APEHOODS	APHIDIAN	APISM	APOLLOS
ANYTHING	APELIKE*	APHIDIANS	APISMS	APOLOG*
ANYTHINGS	APEMAN	APHIDIOUS	APIVOROUS	APOLOGAL*
ANYTIME	APEMEN	APHIDS	APLANAT	APOLOGIA
ANYWAY	APEPSIA	APHIS	APLANATIC	APOLOGIAE*
ANYWAYS	APEPSIAS	APHOLATE*	APLANATS	APOLOGIAS
ANYWHEN	APEPSIES	APHOLATES*	APLASIA	APOLOGIES
ANYWHERE	APEPSY	APHONIA	APLASIAS	APOLOGISE
ANYWHERES*	APER*	APHONIAS	APLASTIC	APOLOGISED
ANYWISE	APERCU	APHONIC	APLENTY	APOLOGISES
ANZIANI	APERCUS	APHONICS*	APLITE	APOLOGISING
AORIST	APERIENT	APHONIES	APLITES	APOLOGIST
AORISTIC	APERIENTS	APHONOUS	APLITIC*	APOLOGISTS
AORISTS	APERIES	APHONY	APLOMB	APOLOGIZE
AORTA	APERIODIC	APHORISE	APLOMBS	APOLOGIZED
AORTAE	APERITIF	APHORISED	APLUSTRE	APOLOGIZES
AORTAL	APERITIFS	APHORISER	APLUSTRES	APOLOGIZING
AORTAS	APERITIVE	APHORISERS	APNEA	APOLOGS*
AORTIC	APERITIVES	APHORISES	APNEAL*	APOLOGUE
AORTITIS	APERS*	APHORISING	APNEAS	APOLOGUES
AORTITISES	APERT	APHORISM	APNEIC*	APOLOGY
AOUDAD	APERTNESS	APHORISMS	APNOEA	APOLUNE*
AOUDADS	APERTNESSES	APHORIST	APNOEAL*	APOLUNES*
APACE	APERTURE	APHORISTS	APNOEAS	APOMICT*
APACHE	APERTURES	APHORIZE	APNOEIC*	APOMICTIC
APACHES	APERY	APHORIZED	APOAPSIDES*	APOMICTS*
APADANA	APES	APHORIZER	APOAPSIS*	APOMIXES
APADANAS	APETALIES	APHORIZERS	APOCARP*	APOMIXIS
APAGE	APETALOUS	APHORIZES	APOCARPIES*	APOOP
APAGOGE	APETALY	APHORIZING	APOCARPS*	APOPHASES
APAGOGES	APEX	APHOTIC	APOCARPY*	APOPHASIS
APAGOGIC	APEXES	APHTHA	APOCOPATE	APOPHATIC
APAID	APHAGIA	APHTHAE	APOCOPATED	APOPHONIES*
APANAGE	APHAGIAS	APHTHOUS	APOCOPATES	APOPHONY*
APANAGED	APHANITE	APHYLLIES	APOCOPATING	APOPHYGE
APANAGES	APHANITES	APHYLLOUS	APOCOPE	APOPHYGES
APAREJO*	APHANITIC*	APHYLLY	APOCOPES	APOPHYSES
APAREJOS*	APHASIA	APIAN	APOCOPIC*	APOPHYSIS
APART	APHASIAC	APIARIAN	APOCRINE	APOPLEX
APARTHEID	APHASIACS	APIARIANS*	APOCRYPHA	APOPLEXED
APARTHEIDS	APHASIAS	APIARIES	APOD	APOPLEXES
APARTMENT	APHASIC	APIARIST	APODAL	APOPLEXIES
APARTMENTS	APHASICS*	APIARISTS	APODE	APOPLEXING
APARTNESS	APHELIA	APIARY	APODES	APOPLEXY
APARTNESSES	APHELIAN	APICAL	APODICTIC	APOPTOSES
APATETIC	APHELION	APICALLY	APODOSES	APOPTOSIS
APATHATON	APHELIONS*	APICALS*	APODOSIS	APOPTOTIC
APATHATONS	APHERESES	APICES	APODOUS	APORIA
APATHETIC	APHERESIS	APICIAN	APODS	APORIAS
APATHIES	APHESES	APICULATE	APOENZYME	APORT
APATHY	APHESIS	APICULI*	APOENZYMES	APOSITIA
APATITE	APHETIC	APICULUS*	APOGAEIC	APOSITIAS
APATITES	APHETISE	APIECE	APOGAMIC	APOSITIC
APAY	APHETISED	APIMANIA*	APOGAMIES	APOSPORIES
APAYD	APHETISES	APIMANIAS*	APOGAMOUS	APOSPORY
APAYING	APHETISING	APING	APOGAMY	APOSTACIES*
APAYS	APHETIZE	APIOL	APOGEAL	APOSTACY*
APE	APHETIZED	APIOLOGIES*	APOGEAN	APOSTASIES
APEAK	APHETIZES	APIOLOGY*	APOGEE	APOSTASY
APED	APHETIZING	APIOLS	APOGEES	APOSTATE

The Chambers Dictionary is the authority for many longer words; see Introduction, page ix

APOSTATES
APOSTATIC
APOSTIL
APOSTILLE
APOSTILLES
APOSTILS
APOSTLE
APOSTLES
APOSTOLIC
APOTHECE*
APOTHECES*
APOTHECIA
APOTHECIUM*
APOTHEGM
APOTHEGMS
APOTHEM
APOTHEMS
APOZEM
APOZEMS
APPAID
APPAIR
APPAIRED
APPAIRING
APPAIRS
APPAL
APPALL*
APPALLED
APPALLING
APPALLS*
APPALS
APPALTI
APPALTO
APPANAGE
APPANAGED
APPANAGES
APPARAT
APPARATS
APPARATUS
APPARATUSES
APPAREL
APPARELED*
APPARELING*
APPARELLED
APPARELLING
APPARELS
APPARENCIES
APPARENCY
APPARENT
APPARENTS
APPARITOR
APPARITORS
APPAY
APPAYD
APPAYING
APPAYS
APPEACH
APPEACHED
APPEACHES
APPEACHING
APPEAL
APPEALED
APPEALER*
APPEALERS*
APPEALING

APPEALS
APPEAR
APPEARED
APPEARER
APPEARERS
APPEARING
APPEARS
APPEASE
APPEASED
APPEASER
APPEASERS
APPEASES
APPEASING
APPEL
APPELLANT
APPELLANTS
APPELLATE
APPELLEE*
APPELLEES*
APPELLOR*
APPELLORS*
APPELS
APPEND
APPENDAGE
APPENDAGES
APPENDANT
APPENDANTS
APPENDED
APPENDICES
APPENDING
APPENDIX
APPENDIXES
APPENDS
APPERIL
APPERILL
APPERILLS
APPERILS
APPERTAIN
APPERTAINED
APPERTAINING
APPERTAINS
APPESTAT
APPESTATS
APPETENCE
APPETENCES
APPETENCIES
APPETENCY
APPETENT
APPETIBLE
APPETISE
APPETISED
APPETISER
APPETISERS
APPETISES
APPETISING
APPETITE
APPETITES
APPETIZE
APPETIZED
APPETIZER
APPETIZERS
APPETIZES
APPETIZING
APPLAUD

APPLAUDED
APPLAUDER
APPLAUDERS
APPLAUDING
APPLAUDS
APPLAUSE
APPLAUSES
APPLE
APPLECART*
APPLECARTS*
APPLEJACK*
APPLEJACKS*
APPLES
APPLET
APPLETS
APPLIABLE
APPLIANCE
APPLIANCES
APPLICANT
APPLICANTS
APPLICATE
APPLIED
APPLIER
APPLIERS
APPLIES
APPLIQUE
APPLIQUED*
APPLIQUEING*
APPLIQUES
APPLY
APPLYING
APPOINT
APPOINTED
APPOINTEE
APPOINTEES
APPOINTING
APPOINTOR
APPOINTORS
APPOINTS
APPORT
APPORTION
APPORTIONED
APPORTIONING
APPORTIONS
APPORTS
APPOSE
APPOSED
APPOSER
APPOSERS
APPOSES
APPOSING
APPOSITE
APPRAISAL
APPRAISALS
APPRAISE
APPRAISED
APPRAISEE
APPRAISEES
APPRAISER
APPRAISERS
APPRAISES
APPRAISING
APPREHEND
APPREHENDED

APPREHENDING
APPREHENDS
APPRESS
APPRESSED
APPRESSES
APPRESSING
APPRISE
APPRISED
APPRISER
APPRISERS
APPRISES
APPRISING
APPRISINGS
APPRIZE
APPRIZED
APPRIZER
APPRIZERS
APPRIZES
APPRIZING
APPRIZINGS
APPROACH
APPROACHED
APPROACHES
APPROACHING
APPROBATE
APPROBATED
APPROBATES
APPROBATING
APPROOF
APPROOFS
APPROVAL
APPROVALS
APPROVE
APPROVED
APPROVER
APPROVERS
APPROVES
APPROVING
APPUI
APPUIED
APPUIS
APPULSE
APPULSES
APPUY
APPUYED
APPUYING
APPUYS
APRACTIC*
APRAXIA
APRAXIAS
APRAXIC*
APRES
APRICATE
APRICATED
APRICATES
APRICATING
APRICOCK
APRICOCKS
APRICOT
APRICOTS
APRIORISM
APRIORISMS
APRIORIST
APRIORISTS

APRIORITIES
APRIORITY
APRON
APRONED
APRONFUL
APRONFULS
APRONING
APRONS
APROPOS
APROTIC*
APSARAS
APSARASES
APSE
APSES
APSIDAL
APSIDES
APSIDIOLE
APSIDIOLES
APSIS
APT
APTED
APTER
APTERAL
APTERIA
APTERISM
APTERISMS
APTERIUM
APTEROUS
APTERYX
APTERYXES
APTEST
APTING
APTITUDE
APTITUDES
APTLY
APTNESS
APTNESSES
APTOTE
APTOTES
APTOTIC
APTS
APYRASE*
APYRASES*
APYRETIC
APYREXIA
APYREXIAS
AQUA
AQUABATIC
AQUABATICS
AQUABOARD
AQUABOARDS
AQUACADE
AQUACADES
AQUADROME
AQUADROMES
AQUAE
AQUAFER
AQUAFERS
AQUALUNG
AQUALUNGS
AQUANAUT
AQUANAUTS
AQUAPHOBE
AQUAPHOBES

Words marked with an asterisk are from OTCWL

AQUAPLANE	ARABISE	ARBITRAGING	ARCATURES*	ARCHITYPE
AQUAPLANED	ARABISED	ARBITRAL	ARCCOS	ARCHITYPES
AQUAPLANES	ARABISES	ARBITRARY	ARCCOSES	ARCHIVAL
AQUAPLANING	ARABISING	ARBITRATE	ARCCOSINE*	ARCHIVE
AQUAPLANINGS	ARABIZE	ARBITRATED	ARCCOSINES*	ARCHIVED
AQUARELLE	ARABIZED	ARBITRATES	ARCED	ARCHIVES
AQUARELLES	ARABIZES	ARBITRATING	ARCH	ARCHIVING
AQUARIA	ARABIZING	ARBITRESS	ARCHAEI	ARCHIVIST
AQUARIAL*	ARABLE	ARBITRESSES	ARCHAEUS	ARCHIVISTS
AQUARIAN	ARABLES*	ARBITRIUM	ARCHAIC	ARCHIVOLT
AQUARIANS	ARACEOUS	ARBITRIUMS	ARCHAISE	ARCHIVOLTS
AQUARIIST	ARACHIS	ARBLAST	ARCHAISED	ARCHLET
AQUARIISTS	ARACHISES	ARBLASTER	ARCHAISER	ARCHLETS
AQUARIST	ARACHNID	ARBLASTERS	ARCHAISERS	ARCHLUTE
AQUARISTS	ARACHNIDS	ARBLASTS	ARCHAISES	ARCHLUTES
AQUARIUM	ARACHNOID	ARBOR	ARCHAISING	ARCHLY
AQUARIUMS	ARACHNOIDS	ARBOREAL	ARCHAISM	ARCHNESS
AQUAROBIC	ARAGONITE	ARBORED*	ARCHAISMS	ARCHNESSES
AQUAROBICS	ARAGONITES	ARBOREOUS	ARCHAIST	ARCHOLOGIES
AQUAS	ARAISE	ARBORES	ARCHAISTS	ARCHOLOGY
AQUATIC	ARAISED	ARBORET	ARCHAIZE	ARCHON
AQUATICS	ARAISES	ARBORETA	ARCHAIZED	ARCHONS
AQUATINT	ARAISING	ARBORETS	ARCHAIZER	ARCHONTIC
AQUATINTA	ARAK	ARBORETUM	ARCHAIZERS	ARCHOSAUR*
AQUATINTAS	ARAKS	ARBORETUMS*	ARCHAIZES	ARCHOSAURS*
AQUATINTED	ARALIA	ARBORIST	ARCHAIZING	ARCHWAY
AQUATINTING	ARALIAS	ARBORISTS	ARCHANGEL	ARCHWAYS
AQUATINTS	ARAME	ARBORIZE*	ARCHANGELS	ARCHWISE
AQUATONE*	ARAMES	ARBORIZED*	ARCHDUCAL	ARCIFORM*
AQUATONES*	ARAMID*	ARBORIZES*	ARCHDUCHIES	ARCING
AQUAVIT	ARAMIDS*	ARBORIZING*	ARCHDUCHY	ARCINGS
AQUAVITS	ARANEID	ARBOROUS	ARCHDUKE	ARCKED
AQUEDUCT	ARANEIDS	ARBORS	ARCHDUKES	ARCKING
AQUEDUCTS	ARANEOUS	ARBOUR	ARCHED	ARCKINGS
AQUEOUS	ARAPAIMA	ARBOURED	ARCHEI	ARCO
AQUIFER	ARAPAIMAS	ARBOURS	ARCHENEMIES*	ARCOLOGIES
AQUIFERS	ARAPONGA	ARBOVIRUS	ARCHENEMY*	ARCOLOGY
AQUILEGIA	ARAPONGAS	ARBOVIRUSES	ARCHER	ARCS
AQUILEGIAS	ARAPUNGA	ARBS	ARCHERESS	ARCSECOND
AQUILINE	ARAPUNGAS	ARBUSCLE*	ARCHERESSES	ARCSECONDS
AQUILON	ARAR	ARBUSCLES*	ARCHERIES	ARCSIN
AQUILONS	ARAROBA	ARBUTE	ARCHERS	ARCSINE*
AQUIVER	ARAROBAS	ARBUTEAN*	ARCHERY	ARCSINES*
AR	ARARS	ARBUTES	ARCHES	ARCSINS
ARABA	ARAUCARIA	ARBUTUS	ARCHEST	ARCTAN
ARABAS	ARAUCARIAS	ARBUTUSES	ARCHETYPE	ARCTANS
ARABESK*	ARAYSE	ARC	ARCHETYPES	ARCTIC
ARABESKS*	ARAYSED	ARCADE	ARCHEUS	ARCTICS
ARABESQUE	ARAYSES	ARCADED	ARCHFIEND*	ARCTIID
ARABESQUES	ARAYSING	ARCADES	ARCHFIENDS*	ARCTIIDS
ARABIC*	ARB	ARCADIA*	ARCHIL	ARCTOID
ARABICA	ARBA	ARCADIAN*	ARCHILOWE	ARCTOPHIL
ARABICAS	ARBALEST	ARCADIANS*	ARCHILOWES	ARCTOPHILS
ARABICIZE*	ARBALESTS	ARCADIAS*	ARCHILS	ARCUATE
ARABICIZED*	ARBALIST	ARCADING	ARCHIMAGE	ARCUATED
ARABICIZES*	ARBALISTS	ARCADINGS	ARCHIMAGES	ARCUATELY*
ARABICIZING*	ARBAS	ARCANA	ARCHINE*	ARCUATION
ARABILITIES*	ARBELEST*	ARCANE	ARCHINES*	ARCUATIONS
ARABILITY*	ARBELESTS*	ARCANELY	ARCHING	ARCUS
ARABIN	ARBITER	ARCANIST	ARCHINGS*	ARCUSES
ARABINOSE	ARBITERS	ARCANISTS	ARCHITECT	ARD
ARABINOSES	ARBITRAGE	ARCANUM	ARCHITECTED	ARDEB
ARABINS	ARBITRAGED	ARCANUMS*	ARCHITECTING	ARDEBS
ARABIS	ARBITRAGES	ARCATURE*	ARCHITECTS	ARDENCIES

ARDENCY	AREOMETERS	ARGOTS	ARILLODES	ARMIGER
ARDENT	AREOSTYLE	ARGUABLE	ARILLOID	ARMIGERAL
ARDENTLY	AREOSTYLES	ARGUABLY	ARILLUS	ARMIGERO
ARDOR	ARERE	ARGUE	ARILS	ARMIGEROS
ARDORS	ARES	ARGUED	ARIOSE*	ARMIGERS
ARDOUR	ARET	ARGUER	ARIOSI	ARMIL
ARDOURS	ARETE	ARGUERS	ARIOSO	ARMILLA
ARDRI	ARETES	ARGUES	ARIOSOS	ARMILLAE
ARDRIGH	ARETHUSA*	ARGUFIED	ARIOT	ARMILLARY
ARDRIGHS	ARETHUSAS*	ARGUFIER	ARIPPLE	ARMILLAS
ARDRIS	ARETS	ARGUFIERS	ARIS	ARMILS
ARDS	ARETT	ARGUFIES	ARISE	ARMING
ARDUOUS	ARETTED	ARGUFY	ARISEN	ARMINGS*
ARDUOUSLY	ARETTING	ARGUFYING	ARISES	ARMISTICE
ARE	ARETTS	ARGUING	ARISH	ARMISTICES
AREA	AREW	ARGULI	ARISHES	ARMLESS
AREACH	ARF*	ARGULUS	ARISING	ARMLET
AREACHED	ARFS*	ARGUMENT	ARISTA	ARMLETS
AREACHES	ARGAL	ARGUMENTA	ARISTAE	ARMLIKE*
AREACHING	ARGALA	ARGUMENTS	ARISTAS	ARMLOAD*
AREAD	ARGALAS	ARGUMENTUM*	ARISTATE	ARMLOADS*
AREADING	ARGALI	ARGUS	ARISTO	ARMLOCK
AREADS	ARGALIS	ARGUSES	ARISTOS	ARMLOCKED
AREAE*	ARGALS*	ARGUTE	ARK	ARMLOCKING
AREAL	ARGAN	ARGUTELY	ARKED	ARMLOCKS
AREALLY*	ARGAND	ARGYLE	ARKING	ARMOIRE
AREAR	ARGANDS	ARGYLES	ARKITE	ARMOIRES
AREAS	ARGANS	ARGYLL*	ARKITES	ARMONICA*
AREAWAY	ARGEMONE	ARGYLLS*	ARKOSE	ARMONICAS*
AREAWAYS	ARGEMONES	ARGYRIA	ARKOSES	ARMOR
ARECA	ARGENT	ARGYRIAS	ARKOSIC*	ARMORED*
ARECAS	ARGENTAL*	ARGYRITE	ARKS	ARMORER*
ARECOLINE*	ARGENTIC*	ARGYRITES	ARLE	ARMORERS*
ARECOLINES*	ARGENTINE	ARHAT*	ARLED	ARMORIAL
ARED	ARGENTINES	ARHATS*	ARLES	ARMORIALS
AREDD	ARGENTITE	ARHATSHIP*	ARLING	ARMORIES
AREDE	ARGENTITES	ARHATSHIPS*	ARM	ARMORING*
AREDES	ARGENTS	ARHYTHMIA	ARMADA	ARMORIST
AREDING	ARGENTUM*	ARHYTHMIAS	ARMADAS	ARMORISTS
AREFIED	ARGENTUMS*	ARHYTHMIC	ARMADILLO	ARMORLESS*
AREFIES	ARGHAN	ARIA	ARMADILLOS	ARMORS
AREFY	ARGHANS	ARIAS	ARMAGNAC*	ARMORY
AREFYING	ARGIL	ARID	ARMAGNACS*	ARMOUR
AREG	ARGILLITE	ARIDER	ARMAMENT	ARMOURED
AREIC*	ARGILLITES	ARIDEST	ARMAMENTS	ARMOURER
ARENA	ARGILS	ARIDITIES	ARMATURE	ARMOURERS
ARENAS	ARGINASE*	ARIDITY	ARMATURED*	ARMOURIES
ARENATION	ARGINASES*	ARIDLY	ARMATURES	ARMOURING*
ARENATIONS	ARGININE	ARIDNESS	ARMATURING*	ARMOURS
ARENITE*	ARGININES	ARIDNESSES	ARMBAND	ARMOURY
ARENITES*	ARGLE*	ARIEL	ARMBANDS	ARMOZEEN
ARENOSE*	ARGLED*	ARIELS	ARMCHAIR	ARMOZEENS
ARENOUS*	ARGLES*	ARIETTA	ARMCHAIRS	ARMOZINE
AREOLA	ARGLING*	ARIETTAS	ARMED	ARMOZINES
AREOLAE	ARGOL	ARIETTE	ARMER*	ARMPIT
AREOLAR	ARGOLS	ARIETTES	ARMERS*	ARMPITS
AREOLAS*	ARGON	ARIGHT	ARMET	ARMREST*
AREOLATE	ARGONAUT	ARIL	ARMETS	ARMRESTS*
AREOLATED	ARGONAUTS	ARILED*	ARMFUL	ARMS
AREOLE	ARGONS	ARILLARY	ARMFULS	ARMSFUL*
AREOLES	ARGOSIES	ARILLATE	ARMGAUNT	ARMURE
AREOLOGIES*	ARGOSY	ARILLATED	ARMHOLE	ARMURES
AREOLOGY*	ARGOT	ARILLI	ARMHOLES	ARMY
AREOMETER	ARGOTIC*	ARILLODE	ARMIES	ARMYWORM*

ARMYWORMS*	ARRAIGNED	ARRISES	ARSES	ARTIFICES
ARNA	ARRAIGNER	ARRISH	ARSHEEN	ARTILLERIES
ARNAS	ARRAIGNERS	ARRISHES	ARSHEENS	ARTILLERY
ARNATTO*	ARRAIGNING	ARRIVAL	ARSHIN	ARTILY*
ARNATTOS*	ARRAIGNINGS	ARRIVALS	ARSHINE	ARTINESS
ARNICA	ARRAIGNS	ARRIVANCE	ARSHINES	ARTINESSES
ARNICAS	ARRANGE	ARRIVANCES	ARSHINS	ARTISAN
ARNOTTO	ARRANGED	ARRIVANCIES	ARSINE	ARTISANAL
ARNOTTOS	ARRANGER	ARRIVANCY	ARSINES	ARTISANS
ARNUT	ARRANGERS	ARRIVE	ARSINO*	ARTIST
ARNUTS	ARRANGES	ARRIVED	ARSIS	ARTISTE
AROBA	ARRANGING	ARRIVER*	ARSON	ARTISTES
AROBAS	ARRANT	ARRIVERS*	ARSONIST	ARTISTIC
AROID	ARRANTLY	ARRIVES	ARSONISTS	ARTISTRIES
AROIDS	ARRAS	ARRIVING	ARSONITE	ARTISTRY
AROINT	ARRASED	ARRIVISME	ARSONITES	ARTISTS
AROINTED	ARRASENE	ARRIVISMES	ARSONOUS*	ARTLESS
AROINTING	ARRASENES	ARRIVISTE	ARSONS	ARTLESSLY
AROINTS	ARRASES	ARRIVISTES	ART	ARTS
AROLLA	ARRAUGHT	ARROBA	ARTAL	ARTSIER
AROLLAS	ARRAY	ARROBAS	ARTEFACT	ARTSIES
AROMA	ARRAYAL	ARROGANCE	ARTEFACTS	ARTSIEST
AROMAS	ARRAYALS	ARROGANCES	ARTEL	ARTSMAN
AROMATIC	ARRAYED	ARROGANT	ARTELS	ARTSMEN
AROMATICS	ARRAYER	ARROGATE	ARTEMISIA	ARTSY
AROMATISE	ARRAYERS	ARROGATED	ARTEMISIAS	ARTWORK
AROMATISED	ARRAYING	ARROGATES	ARTERIAL	ARTWORKS
AROMATISES	ARRAYMENT	ARROGATING	ARTERIALS*	ARTY
AROMATISING	ARRAYMENTS	ARROW	ARTERIES	ARUGOLA*
AROMATIZE	ARRAYS	ARROWED	ARTERIOLE	ARUGOLAS*
AROMATIZED	ARREAR	ARROWHEAD*	ARTERIOLES	ARUGULA
AROMATIZES	ARREARAGE	ARROWHEADS*	ARTERITIDES*	ARUGULAS
AROMATIZING	ARREARAGES	ARROWING	ARTERITIS	ARUM
AROSE	ARREARS	ARROWROOT	ARTERITISES	ARUMS
AROUND	ARRECT	ARROWROOTS	ARTERY	ARUSPEX*
AROUSAL	ARREEDE	ARROWS	ARTESIAN	ARUSPICES*
AROUSALS	ARREEDES	ARROWWOOD	ARTFUL	ARVAL
AROUSE	ARREEDING	ARROWWOODS	ARTFULLY	ARVICOLE
AROUSED	ARREST	ARROWWORM*	ARTHRITIC	ARVICOLES
AROUSER	ARRESTANT*	ARROWWORMS*	ARTHRITICS	ARVO
AROUSERS	ARRESTANTS*	ARROWY	ARTHRITIDES*	ARVOS
AROUSES	ARRESTED	ARROYO	ARTHRITIS	ARY
AROUSING	ARRESTEE	ARROYOS	ARTHRITISES	ARYBALLOS
AROW	ARRESTEES	ARS	ARTHROPOD	ARYBALLOSES
AROYNT	ARRESTER	ARSE	ARTHROPODS	ARYL
AROYNTED	ARRESTERS	ARSEHOLE	ARTHROSES	ARYLS
AROYNTING	ARRESTING	ARSEHOLES	ARTHROSIS	ARYTENOID
AROYNTS	ARRESTIVE	ARSENAL	ARTIC	ARYTENOIDS
ARPEGGIO	ARRESTOR	ARSENALS	ARTICHOKE	ARYTHMIA*
ARPEGGIOS	ARRESTORS	ARSENATE	ARTICHOKES	ARYTHMIAS*
ARPEN*	ARRESTS	ARSENATES	ARTICLE	ARYTHMIC*
ARPENS*	ARRET	ARSENIATE	ARTICLED	AS
ARPENT	ARRETS	ARSENIATES	ARTICLES	ASAFETIDA
ARPENTS	ARRHIZAL*	ARSENIC	ARTICLING	ASAFETIDAS
ARPILLERA	ARRIAGE	ARSENICAL	ARTICS	ASANA
ARPILLERAS	ARRIAGES	ARSENICALS*	ARTICULAR	ASANAS
ARQUEBUS	ARRIDE	ARSENICS	ARTIER	ASAR
ARQUEBUSES	ARRIDED	ARSENIDE	ARTIES	ASARUM
ARRACACHA	ARRIDES	ARSENIDES	ARTIEST	ASARUMS
ARRACACHAS	ARRIDING	ARSENIOUS	ARTIFACT	ASBESTIC
ARRACK	ARRIERE	ARSENITE	ARTIFACTS	ASBESTINE
ARRACKS	ARRIERO	ARSENITES	ARTIFICE	ASBESTOS
ARRAH	ARRIEROS	ARSENO*	ARTIFICER	ASBESTOSES
ARRAIGN	ARRIS	ARSENOUS*	ARTIFICERS	ASBESTOUS

ASBESTUS*
ASBESTUSES*
ASCARID
ASCARIDES
ASCARIDS
ASCARIS
ASCAUNT
ASCEND
ASCENDANT
ASCENDANTS
ASCENDED
ASCENDENT
ASCENDENTS
ASCENDER
ASCENDERS
ASCENDING
ASCENDS
ASCENSION
ASCENSIONS
ASCENSIVE
ASCENT
ASCENTS
ASCERTAIN
ASCERTAINED
ASCERTAINING
ASCERTAINS
ASCESES
ASCESIS
ASCETIC
ASCETICAL
ASCETICS
ASCI
ASCIAN
ASCIANS
ASCIDIA
ASCIDIAN
ASCIDIANS
ASCIDIUM
ASCITES
ASCITIC
ASCITICAL
ASCLEPIAD
ASCLEPIADS
ASCLEPIAS
ASCLEPIASES
ASCOCARP*
ASCOCARPS*
ASCOGONIA*
ASCOGONIUM*
ASCONCE
ASCORBATE
ASCORBATES
ASCORBIC*
ASCOSPORE
ASCOSPORES
ASCOT
ASCOTS
ASCRIBE
ASCRIBED
ASCRIBES
ASCRIBING
ASCUS
ASDIC*
ASDICS*

ASEA*
ASEISMIC
ASEITIES
ASEITY
ASEPALOUS
ASEPSES
ASEPSIS
ASEPTATE
ASEPTIC
ASEPTICS
ASEXUAL
ASEXUALLY
ASH
ASHAKE
ASHAME
ASHAMED
ASHAMEDLY
ASHAMES
ASHAMING
ASHCAN*
ASHCANS*
ASHED*
ASHEN
ASHERIES
ASHERY
ASHES
ASHET
ASHETS
ASHFALL*
ASHFALLS*
ASHIER
ASHIEST
ASHINE
ASHINESS*
ASHINESSES*
ASHING*
ASHIVER
ASHLAR
ASHLARED
ASHLARING
ASHLARINGS
ASHLARS
ASHLER
ASHLERED
ASHLERING
ASHLERINGS
ASHLERS
ASHLESS*
ASHMAN*
ASHMEN*
ASHORE
ASHPLANT*
ASHPLANTS*
ASHRAM
ASHRAMA
ASHRAMAS
ASHRAMITE
ASHRAMITES
ASHRAMS
ASHTRAY*
ASHTRAYS*
ASHY
ASIDE
ASIDES

ASINICO
ASINICOS
ASININE
ASININELY*
ASININITIES
ASININITY
ASK
ASKANCE
ASKANCED
ASKANCES
ASKANCING
ASKANT
ASKANTED
ASKANTING
ASKANTS
ASKARI
ASKARIS
ASKED
ASKER
ASKERS
ASKESES
ASKESIS
ASKEW
ASKEWNESS*
ASKEWNESSES*
ASKING
ASKINGS*
ASKLENT
ASKOI*
ASKOS*
ASKS
ASLAKE
ASLAKED
ASLAKES
ASLAKING
ASLANT
ASLEEP
ASLOPE
ASMEAR
ASMOULDER
ASOCIAL
ASP
ASPARAGUS
ASPARAGUSES
ASPARKLE*
ASPARTAME
ASPARTAMES
ASPARTATE*
ASPARTATES*
ASPECT
ASPECTED
ASPECTING
ASPECTS
ASPECTUAL
ASPEN
ASPENS
ASPER
ASPERATE
ASPERATED
ASPERATES
ASPERATING
ASPERGE
ASPERGED
ASPERGER

ASPERGERS
ASPERGES
ASPERGILL
ASPERGILLS
ASPERGING
ASPERITIES
ASPERITY
ASPEROUS
ASPERS
ASPERSE
ASPERSED
ASPERSER*
ASPERSERS*
ASPERSES
ASPERSING
ASPERSION
ASPERSIONS
ASPERSIVE
ASPERSOIR
ASPERSOIRS
ASPERSOR*
ASPERSORIES
ASPERSORS*
ASPERSORY
ASPHALT
ASPHALTED
ASPHALTER
ASPHALTERS
ASPHALTIC
ASPHALTING
ASPHALTS
ASPHALTUM
ASPHALTUMS
ASPHERIC
ASPHODEL
ASPHODELS
ASPHYXIA
ASPHYXIAL
ASPHYXIAS
ASPHYXIES
ASPHYXY
ASPIC
ASPICK
ASPICKS
ASPICS
ASPIDIA
ASPIDIOID
ASPIDIUM
ASPINE
ASPINES
ASPIRANT
ASPIRANTS
ASPIRATA*
ASPIRATAE*
ASPIRATE
ASPIRATED
ASPIRATES
ASPIRATING
ASPIRATOR
ASPIRATORS
ASPIRE
ASPIRED
ASPIRER*
ASPIRERS*

ASPIRES
ASPIRIN
ASPIRING
ASPIRINS
ASPIS*
ASPISES*
ASPISH*
ASPLENIUM
ASPLENIUMS
ASPORT
ASPORTED
ASPORTING
ASPORTS
ASPOUT
ASPRAWL
ASPREAD
ASPROUT
ASPS
ASQUAT
ASQUINT
ASRAMA*
ASRAMAS*
ASS
ASSAGAI
ASSAGAIED
ASSAGAIING
ASSAGAIS
ASSAI
ASSAIL
ASSAILANT
ASSAILANTS
ASSAILED
ASSAILER
ASSAILERS
ASSAILING
ASSAILS
ASSAIS
ASSART
ASSARTED
ASSARTING
ASSARTS
ASSASSIN
ASSASSINS
ASSAULT
ASSAULTED
ASSAULTER
ASSAULTERS
ASSAULTING
ASSAULTS
ASSAY
ASSAYABLE
ASSAYED
ASSAYER
ASSAYERS
ASSAYING
ASSAYINGS
ASSAYS
ASSEGAAI
ASSEGAAIED
ASSEGAAIING
ASSEGAAIS
ASSEGAI
ASSEGAIED
ASSEGAIING

Words marked with an asterisk are from OTCWL

ASSEGAIS	ASSIGNORS	ASSUMERS*	ASTHENIC	ASTROID
ASSEMBLE	ASSIGNS	ASSUMES	ASTHENICS	ASTROIDS
ASSEMBLED	ASSIST	ASSUMING	ASTHENIES*	ASTROLABE
⌐SSEMBLER	ASSISTANT	ASSUMINGS	ASTHENY*	ASTROLABES
ASSEMBLERS	ASSISTANTS	ASSUMPSIT	ASTHMA	ASTROLOGIES
ASSEMBLES	ASSISTED	ASSUMPSITS	ASTHMAS	ASTROLOGY
ASSEMBLIES	ASSISTER*	ASSURABLE	ASTHMATIC	ASTRONAUT
ASSEMBLING	ASSISTERS*	ASSURANCE	ASTHMATICS*	ASTRONAUTS
ASSEMBLY	ASSISTING	ASSURANCES	ASTHORE	ASTRONOMIES
ASSENT	ASSISTOR*	ASSURE	ASTHORES	ASTRONOMY
ASSENTED	ASSISTORS*	ASSURED	ASTICHOUS	ASTROPHEL
ASSENTER	ASSISTS	ASSUREDLY	ASTIGMIA	ASTROPHELS
ASSENTERS	ASSIZE	ASSUREDS	ASTIGMIAS	ASTRUT
ASSENTING	ASSIZED	ASSURER	ASTILBE	ASTUCIOUS
ASSENTIVE	ASSIZER	ASSURERS	ASTILBES	ASTUCITIES
ASSENTOR	ASSIZERS	ASSURES	ASTIR	ASTUCITY
ASSENTORS	ASSIZES	ASSURGENT	ASTOMOUS	ASTUN
ASSENTS	ASSIZING	ASSURING	ASTONE	ASTUNNED
ASSERT	ASSLIKE*	ASSUROR*	ASTONED	ASTUNNING
ASSERTED	ASSOCIATE	ASSURORS*	ASTONES	ASTUNS
ASSERTER	ASSOCIATED	ASSWAGE	ASTONIED	ASTUTE
ASSERTERS	ASSOCIATES	ASSWAGED	ASTONIES	ASTUTELY
ASSERTING	ASSOCIATING	ASSWAGES	ASTONING	ASTUTER
ASSERTION	ASSOIL	ASSWAGING	ASTONISH	ASTUTEST
ASSERTIONS	ASSOILED	ASTABLE	ASTONISHED	ASTYLAR
ASSERTIVE	ASSOILING	ASTARE	ASTONISHES	ASUDDEN
ASSERTOR	ASSOILS	ASTART	ASTONISHING	ASUNDER
ASSERTORS	ASSOILZIE	ASTARTED	ASTONY	ASWARM
ASSERTORY	ASSOILZIED	ASTARTING	ASTONYING	ASWAY
ASSERTS	ASSOILZIEING	ASTARTS	ASTOOP	ASWIM
ASSES	ASSOILZIES	ASTASIA*	ASTOUND	ASWING
ASSESS	ASSONANCE	ASTASIAS*	ASTOUNDED	ASWIRL
ASSESSED	ASSONANCES	ASTATIC	ASTOUNDING	ASWOON
ASSESSES	ASSONANT	ASTATINE	ASTOUNDS	ASYLA*
ASSESSING	ASSONANTS*	ASTATINES	ASTRADDLE	ASYLUM
ASSESSOR	ASSONATE	ASTATKI	ASTRAGAL	ASYLUMS
ASSESSORS	ASSONATED	ASTATKIS	ASTRAGALI	ASYMMETRIES
ASSET	ASSONATES	ASTEISM	ASTRAGALS	ASYMMETRY
ASSETS	ASSONATING	ASTEISMS	ASTRAKHAN	ASYMPTOTE
ASSEVER	ASSORT	ASTELIC	ASTRAKHANS	ASYMPTOTES
ASSEVERED	ASSORTED	ASTELIES	ASTRAL	ASYNAPSES*
ASSEVERING	ASSORTER	ASTELY	ASTRALLY*	ASYNAPSIS*
ASSEVERS	ASSORTERS	ASTER	ASTRALS*	ASYNDETA*
ASSHOLE	ASSORTING	ASTERIA	ASTRAND	ASYNDETIC
ASSHOLES	ASSORTS	ASTERIAS	ASTRANTIA	ASYNDETON
ASSIDUITIES	ASSOT	ASTERID	ASTRANTIAS	ASYNDETONS
ASSIDUITY	ASSOTS	ASTERIDS	ASTRAY	ASYNERGIA
ASSIDUOUS	ASSOTT	ASTERISK	ASTRICT	ASYNERGIAS
ASSIEGE	ASSOTTED	ASTERISKED	ASTRICTED	ASYNERGIES
ASSIEGED	ASSOTTING	ASTERISKING	ASTRICTING	ASYNERGY
ASSIEGES	ASSUAGE	ASTERISKS	ASTRICTS	ASYSTOLE
ASSIEGING	ASSUAGED	ASTERISM	ASTRIDE	ASYSTOLES
ASSIENTO	ASSUAGES	ASTERISMS	ASTRINGE	AT
ASSIENTOS	ASSUAGING	ASTERN	ASTRINGED	ATABAL
ASSIGN	ASSUAGINGS	ASTERNAL*	ASTRINGER	ATABALS
ASSIGNAT	ASSUASIVE	ASTEROID	ASTRINGERS	ATABEG
ASSIGNATS	ASSUETUDE	ASTEROIDS	ASTRINGES	ATABEGS
ASSIGNED	ASSUETUDES	ASTERS	ASTRINGING	ATABEK
ASSIGNEE	ASSUMABLE	ASTERT	ASTROCYTE	ATABEKS
ASSIGNEES	ASSUMABLY	ASTERTED	ASTROCYTES	ATABRIN
ASSIGNER*	ASSUME	ASTERTING	ASTRODOME	ATABRINS
ASSIGNERS*	ASSUMED	ASTERTS	ASTRODOMES	ATACAMITE
ASSIGNING	ASSUMEDLY	ASTHENIA	ASTROFELL	ATACAMITES
ASSIGNOR	ASSUMER*	ASTHENIAS	ASTROFELLS	ATACTIC

The Chambers Dictionary is the authority for many longer words; see Introduction, page ix

ATAGHAN	ATHEMATIC	ATMOLYZE	ATONIES	ATTAINT
ATAGHANS	ATHENAEUM*	ATMOLYZED	ATONING	ATTAINTED
ATALAYA	ATHENAEUMS*	ATMOLYZES	ATONINGLY	ATTAINTING
ATALAYAS	ATHENEUM*	ATMOLYZING	ATONY	ATTAINTS
ATAMAN	ATHENEUMS*	ATMOMETER	ATOP	ATTAP
ATAMANS	ATHEOLOGIES	ATMOMETERS	ATOPIC	ATTAPS
ATAMASCO*	ATHEOLOGY	ATOC	ATOPIES	ATTAR
ATAMASCOS*	ATHEOUS	ATOCIA	ATOPY	ATTARS
ATAP	ATHERINE	ATOCIAS	ATRAMENT	ATTASK
ATAPS	ATHERINES	ATOCS	ATRAMENTS	ATTASKED
ATARACTIC	ATHEROMA	ATOK	ATRAZINE	ATTASKING
ATARACTICS	ATHEROMAS	ATOKAL	ATRAZINES	ATTASKS
ATARAXIA	ATHEROMATA	ATOKE	ATREMBLE	ATTASKT
ATARAXIAS	ATHETESES	ATOKES	ATRESIA	ATTEMPER
ATARAXIC	ATHETESIS	ATOKOUS	ATRESIAS	ATTEMPERED
ATARAXICS	ATHETISE	ATOKS	ATRIA	ATTEMPERING
ATARAXIES	ATHETISED	ATOLL	ATRIAL	ATTEMPERS
ATARAXY	ATHETISES	ATOLLS	ATRIP	ATTEMPT
ATAVIC*	ATHETISING	ATOM	ATRIUM	ATTEMPTED
ATAVISM	ATHETIZE	ATOMIC	ATRIUMS	ATTEMPTER
ATAVISMS	ATHETIZED	ATOMICAL	ATROCIOUS	ATTEMPTERS
ATAVIST*	ATHETIZES	ATOMICITIES	ATROCITIES	ATTEMPTING
ATAVISTIC	ATHETIZING	ATOMICITY	ATROCITY	ATTEMPTS
ATAVISTS*	ATHETOID	ATOMICS*	ATROPHIA*	ATTEND
ATAXIA	ATHETOSES	ATOMIES	ATROPHIAS*	ATTENDANT
ATAXIAS	ATHETOSIC	ATOMISE	ATROPHIC*	ATTENDANTS
ATAXIC	ATHETOSIS	ATOMISED	ATROPHIED	ATTENDED
ATAXICS*	ATHETOTIC	ATOMISER	ATROPHIES	ATTENDEE
ATAXIES	ATHIRST	ATOMISERS	ATROPHY	ATTENDEES
ATAXY	ATHLETA	ATOMISES	ATROPHYING	ATTENDER
ATCHIEVE	ATHLETAS	ATOMISING	ATROPIA	ATTENDERS
ATCHIEVED	ATHLETE	ATOMISM	ATROPIAS	ATTENDING
ATCHIEVES	ATHLETES	ATOMISMS	ATROPIN	ATTENDS
ATCHIEVING	ATHLETIC	ATOMIST	ATROPINE	ATTENT
ATE	ATHLETICS	ATOMISTIC	ATROPINES	ATTENTAT
ATEBRIN	ATHODYD*	ATOMISTS	ATROPINS	ATTENTATS
ATEBRINS	ATHODYDS*	ATOMIZE	ATROPISM	ATTENTION
ATECHNIC*	ATHRILL	ATOMIZED	ATROPISMS	ATTENTIONS
ATELIC*	ATHROB	ATOMIZER	ATROPOUS	ATTENTIVE
ATELIER	ATHROCYTE	ATOMIZERS	ATT*	ATTENTS
ATELIERS	ATHROCYTES	ATOMIZES	ATTABOY	ATTENUANT
ATEMOYA*	ATHWART	ATOMIZING	ATTACH	ATTENUANTS
ATEMOYAS*	ATILT	ATOMS	ATTACHE	ATTENUATE
ATEMPORAL*	ATIMIES	ATOMY	ATTACHED	ATTENUATED
ATES*	ATIMY	ATONABLE*	ATTACHER*	ATTENUATES
ATHANASIES	ATINGLE	ATONAL	ATTACHERS*	ATTENUATING
ATHANASY	ATISHOO	ATONALISM	ATTACHES	ATTERCOP
ATHANOR	ATISHOOS	ATONALISMS	ATTACHING	ATTERCOPS
ATHANORS	ATLANTES*	ATONALIST	ATTACK	ATTEST
ATHEISE	ATLAS	ATONALISTS	ATTACKED	ATTESTED
ATHEISED	ATLASES	ATONALITIES	ATTACKER	ATTESTER
ATHEISES	ATLATL	ATONALITY	ATTACKERS	ATTESTERS
ATHEISING	ATLATLS	ATONALLY*	ATTACKING	ATTESTING
ATHEISM	ATMA*	ATONE	ATTACKMAN*	ATTESTOR
ATHEISMS	ATMAN	ATONED	ATTACKMEN*	ATTESTORS
ATHEIST	ATMANS	ATONEMENT	ATTACKS	ATTESTS
ATHEISTIC	ATMAS*	ATONEMENTS	ATTAIN	ATTIC
ATHEISTS	ATMOLOGIES	ATONER	ATTAINDER	ATTICISM*
ATHEIZE	ATMOLOGY	ATONERS	ATTAINDERS	ATTICISMS*
ATHEIZED	ATMOLYSE	ATONES	ATTAINED	ATTICIST*
ATHEIZES	ATMOLYSED	ATONIC	ATTAINER*	ATTICISTS*
ATHEIZING	ATMOLYSES	ATONICITIES	ATTAINERS*	ATTICS
ATHELING	ATMOLYSING	ATONICITY	ATTAINING	ATTIRE
ATHELINGS	ATMOLYSIS	ATONICS*	ATTAINS	ATTIRED

Words marked with an asterisk are from OTCWL

ATTIRES	ATWEEN	AUDITIONED	AULDEST	AURICULAS
ATTIRING	ATWITTER	AUDITIONING	AULIC	AURIFIED
ATTIRINGS	ATWIXT	AUDITIONS	AULNAGE	AURIFIES
ATTITUDE	ATYPIC*	AUDITIVE	AULNAGER	AURIFORM
ATTITUDES	ATYPICAL	AUDITIVES*	AULNAGERS	AURIFY
ATTOLLENS	AUBADE	AUDITOR	AULNAGES	AURIFYING
ATTOLLENT	AUBADES	AUDITORIA	AULOI	AURIS*
ATTOLLENTS	AUBERGE	AUDITORIES	AULOS	AURISCOPE
ATTONCE	AUBERGES	AUDITORIUM*	AUMAIL	AURISCOPES
ATTONE	AUBERGINE	AUDITORIUMS*	AUMAILED	AURIST
ATTONES	AUBERGINES	AUDITORS	AUMAILING	AURISTS
ATTORN	AUBRETIA	AUDITORY	AUMAILS	AUROCHS
ATTORNED	AUBRETIAS	AUDITRESS	AUMBRIES	AUROCHSES
ATTORNEY	AUBRIETA	AUDITRESSES	AUMBRY	AURORA
ATTORNEYED	AUBRIETAS	AUDITS	AUMIL	AURORAE
ATTORNEYING	AUBRIETIA	AUF	AUMILS	AURORAL
ATTORNEYS	AUBRIETIAS	AUFGABE	AUNE	AURORALLY
ATTORNING	AUBURN	AUFGABES	AUNES	AURORAS
ATTORNS	AUBURNS*	AUFS	AUNT	AUROREAN
ATTRACT	AUCEPS	AUGEND*	AUNTER	AUROUS
ATTRACTED	AUCEPSES	AUGENDS*	AUNTERS	AURUM*
ATTRACTING	AUCTION	AUGER	AUNTHOOD*	AURUMS*
ATTRACTOR	AUCTIONED	AUGERS	AUNTHOODS*	AUSFORM*
ATTRACTORS	AUCTIONING	AUGHT	AUNTIE	AUSFORMED*
ATTRACTS	AUCTIONS	AUGHTS	AUNTIES	AUSFORMING*
ATTRAHENS	AUCTORIAL	AUGITE	AUNTLIER	AUSFORMS*
ATTRAHENT	AUCUBA	AUGITES	AUNTLIEST	AUSLANDER*
ATTRAHENTS	AUCUBAS	AUGITIC	AUNTLIKE*	AUSLANDERS*
ATTRAP	AUDACIOUS	AUGMENT	AUNTLY	AUSPEX*
ATTRAPPED	AUDACITIES	AUGMENTED	AUNTS	AUSPICATE
ATTRAPPING	AUDACITY	AUGMENTER	AUNTY	AUSPICATED
ATTRAPS	AUDAD*	AUGMENTERS	AURA	AUSPICATES
ATTRIBUTE	AUDADS*	AUGMENTING	AURAE	AUSPICATING
ATTRIBUTED	AUDIAL*	AUGMENTOR	AURAL	AUSPICE
ATTRIBUTES	AUDIBLE	AUGMENTORS	AURALLY	AUSPICES
ATTRIBUTING	AUDIBLES	AUGMENTS	AURAR*	AUSTENITE
ATTRIST	AUDIBLY	AUGUR	AURAS	AUSTENITES
ATTRISTED	AUDIENCE	AUGURAL	AURATE	AUSTERE
ATTRISTING	AUDIENCES	AUGURED	AURATED	AUSTERELY
ATTRISTS	AUDIENCIA	AUGURER	AURATES	AUSTERER
ATTRIT	AUDIENCIAS	AUGURERS	AUREATE	AUSTEREST
ATTRITE	AUDIENT	AUGURIES	AUREI	AUSTERITIES
ATTRITED	AUDIENTS	AUGURING	AUREITIES	AUSTERITY
ATTRITES	AUDILE	AUGURS	AUREITY	AUSTRAL
ATTRITING	AUDILES	AUGURSHIP	AURELIA	AUSTRALES
ATTRITION	AUDING*	AUGURSHIPS	AURELIAN	AUSTRALS*
ATTRITIONS	AUDINGS*	AUGURY	AURELIANS	AUSUBO*
ATTRITS	AUDIO	AUGUST	AURELIAS	AUSUBOS*
ATTRITTED	AUDIOGRAM	AUGUSTE	AUREOLA	AUTACOID
ATTRITTING	AUDIOGRAMS	AUGUSTER	AUREOLAE*	AUTACOIDS
ATTUENT	AUDIOLOGIES	AUGUSTES	AUREOLAS	AUTARCHIC
ATTUITE	AUDIOLOGY	AUGUSTEST	AUREOLE	AUTARCHIES
ATTUITED	AUDIOPHIL	AUGUSTLY	AUREOLED	AUTARCHY
ATTUITES	AUDIOPHILS	AUGUSTS	AUREOLES	AUTARKIC
ATTUITING	AUDIOS	AUK	AUREOLING*	AUTARKIES
ATTUITION	AUDIOTAPE	AUKLET	AURES*	AUTARKIST
ATTUITIONS	AUDIOTAPES	AUKLETS	AUREUS	AUTARKISTS
ATTUITIVE	AUDIPHONE	AUKS	AURIC	AUTARKY
ATTUNE	AUDIPHONES	AULA	AURICLE	AUTECISM*
ATTUNED	AUDIT	AULARIAN	AURICLED	AUTECISMS*
ATTUNES	AUDITABLE*	AULARIANS	AURICLES	AUTEUR
ATTUNING	AUDITED	AULAS	AURICULA	AUTEURIST*
ATWAIN	AUDITING	AULD	AURICULAE*	AUTEURISTS*
ATWEEL	AUDITION	AULDER	AURICULAR	AUTEURS

The Chambers Dictionary is the authority for many longer words; see Introduction, page ix

AUTHENTIC	AUTOFOCUS	AUTOPHOBY	AVADAVAT	AVERAGING
AUTHOR	AUTOFOCUSES	AUTOPHONIES	AVADAVATS	AVERMENT
AUTHORED	AUTOGAMIC	AUTOPHONY	AVAIL	AVERMENTS
AUTHORESS	AUTOGAMIES	AUTOPILOT	AVAILABLE	AVERRED
AUTHORESSES	AUTOGAMY	AUTOPILOTS	AVAILABLY	AVERRING
AUTHORIAL	AUTOGENIC	AUTOPISTA	AVAILE	AVERS
AUTHORING	AUTOGENICS	AUTOPISTAS	AVAILED	AVERSE
AUTHORINGS	AUTOGENIES	AUTOPOINT	AVAILES	AVERSELY
AUTHORISE	AUTOGENY	AUTOPOINTS	AVAILFUL	AVERSION
AUTHORISED	AUTOGIRO	AUTOPSIA	AVAILING	AVERSIONS
AUTHORISES	AUTOGIROS	AUTOPSIAS	AVAILS	AVERSIVE
AUTHORISH	AUTOGRAFT	AUTOPSIC*	AVAL	AVERT
AUTHORISING	AUTOGRAFTED	AUTOPSIED	AVALANCHE	AVERTABLE
AUTHORISM	AUTOGRAFTING	AUTOPSIES	AVALANCHED	AVERTED
AUTHORISMS	AUTOGRAFTS	AUTOPSY	AVALANCHES	AVERTEDLY
AUTHORITIES	AUTOGRAPH	AUTOPSYING	AVALANCHING	AVERTIBLE
AUTHORITY	AUTOGRAPHED	AUTOPTIC	AVALE	AVERTING
AUTHORIZE	AUTOGRAPHING	AUTOROUTE	AVALED	AVERTS
AUTHORIZED	AUTOGRAPHS	AUTOROUTES	AVALES	AVES
AUTHORIZES	AUTOGUIDE	AUTOS	AVALING	AVGAS
AUTHORIZING	AUTOGUIDES	AUTOSCOPIES	AVANT	AVGASES
AUTHORS	AUTOGYRO	AUTOSCOPY	AVANTI	AVGASSES*
AUTISM	AUTOGYROS	AUTOSOMAL	AVARICE	AVIAN
AUTISMS	AUTOHARP	AUTOSOME	AVARICES	AVIANIZE*
AUTISTIC	AUTOHARPS	AUTOSOMES	AVAS	AVIANIZED*
AUTISTICS	AUTOING*	AUTOTELIC	AVASCULAR	AVIANIZES*
AUTO	AUTOLATRIES	AUTOTIMER	AVAST	AVIANIZING*
AUTOBAHN	AUTOLATRY	AUTOTIMERS	AVATAR	AVIANS*
AUTOBAHNEN*	AUTOLOGIES	AUTOTOMIES	AVATARS	AVIARIES
AUTOBAHNS	AUTOLOGY	AUTOTOMY	AVAUNT	AVIARIST
AUTOBUS	AUTOLYSE	AUTOTOXIN	AVAUNTED	AVIARISTS
AUTOBUSES	AUTOLYSED	AUTOTOXINS	AVAUNTING	AVIARY
AUTOBUSSES	AUTOLYSES	AUTOTROPH	AVAUNTS	AVIATE
AUTOCADE	AUTOLYSING	AUTOTROPHS	AVE	AVIATED
AUTOCADES	AUTOLYSIS	AUTOTYPE	AVELLAN*	AVIATES
AUTOCAR	AUTOLYTIC	AUTOTYPED	AVELLANE*	AVIATING
AUTOCARP	AUTOLYZE	AUTOTYPES	AVENGE	AVIATION
AUTOCARPS	AUTOLYZED	AUTOTYPIES*	AVENGED	AVIATIONS
AUTOCARS	AUTOLYZES	AUTOTYPING	AVENGEFUL	AVIATOR
AUTOCLAVE	AUTOLYZING	AUTOTYPY*	AVENGER	AVIATORS
AUTOCLAVED	AUTOMAKER*	AUTOVAC	AVENGERS	AVIATRESS
AUTOCLAVES	AUTOMAKERS*	AUTOVACS	AVENGES	AVIATRESSES
AUTOCLAVING	AUTOMAN*	AUTUMN	AVENGING	AVIATRICES
AUTOCOID*	AUTOMAT	AUTUMNAL	AVENIR	AVIATRIX
AUTOCOIDS*	AUTOMATA	AUTUMNS	AVENIRS	AVIATRIXES
AUTOCRACIES	AUTOMATE	AUTUMNY	AVENS	AVICULAR*
AUTOCRACY	AUTOMATED	AUTUNITE	AVENSES	AVID
AUTOCRAT	AUTOMATES	AUTUNITES	AVENTAIL	AVIDER
AUTOCRATS	AUTOMATIC	AUXESES	AVENTAILE	AVIDEST
AUTOCRIME	AUTOMATICS	AUXESIS	AVENTAILES	AVIDIN
AUTOCRIMES	AUTOMATING	AUXETIC	AVENTAILS	AVIDINS
AUTOCROSS	AUTOMATON	AUXETICS	AVENTRE	AVIDITIES
AUTOCROSSES	AUTOMATONS	AUXILIAR	AVENTRED	AVIDITY
AUTOCUE	AUTOMATS	AUXILIARIES	AVENTRES	AVIDLY
AUTOCUES	AUTOMEN*	AUXILIARS	AVENTRING	AVIDNESS
AUTOCYCLE	AUTONOMIC	AUXILIARY	AVENTURE	AVIDNESSES
AUTOCYCLES	AUTONOMICS	AUXIN	AVENTURES	AVIETTE
AUTODYNE	AUTONOMIES	AUXINIC*	AVENUE	AVIETTES
AUTODYNES*	AUTONOMY	AUXINS	AVENUES	AVIFAUNA
AUTOECISM*	AUTONYM	AUXOMETER	AVER	AVIFAUNAE
AUTOECISMS*	AUTONYMS	AUXOMETERS	AVERAGE	AVIFAUNAL*
AUTOED*	AUTOPHAGIES	AUXOTROPH*	AVERAGED	AVIFAUNAS
AUTOFLARE	AUTOPHAGY	AUXOTROPHS*	AVERAGELY*	AVIFORM
AUTOFLARES	AUTOPHOBIES	AVA	AVERAGES	AVIGATOR*

AVIGATORS*	AVOW	AWARNS	AWNIER	AXMEN
AVINE	AVOWABLE	AWASH	AWNIEST	AXOID
AVION	AVOWABLY*	AWATCH	AWNING	AXOIDS
AVIONIC	AVOWAL	AWAVE	AWNINGED*	AXOLOTL
AVIONICS	AVOWALS	AWAY	AWNINGS	AXOLOTLS
AVIONS	AVOWED	AWAYES	AWNLESS	AXON
AVIRULENT*	AVOWEDLY	AWAYNESS*	AWNS	AXONAL*
AVISANDUM	AVOWER	AWAYNESSES*	AWNY	AXONE*
AVISANDUMS	AVOWERS	AWAYS	AWOKE	AXONEMAL*
AVISE	AVOWING	AWDL	AWOKEN	AXONEME*
AVISED	AVOWRIES	AWDLS	AWOL*	AXONEMES*
AVISEMENT	AVOWRY	AWE	AWOLS*	AXONES*
AVISEMENTS	AVOWS	AWEARIED	AWORK	AXONIC*
AVISES	AVOYER	AWEARY	AWRACK	AXONS
AVISING	AVOYERS	AWEATHER*	AWRONG	AXOPLASM
AVISO	AVULSE	AWED	AWRY	AXOPLASMS
AVISOS	AVULSED	AWEE*	AWSOME	AXSEED*
AVITAL	AVULSES	AWEEL	AX	AXSEEDS*
AVIZANDUM	AVULSING	AWEIGH	AXAL*	AY
AVIZANDUMS	AVULSION	AWEING*	AXE	AYAH
AVIZE	AVULSIONS	AWELESS	AXED	AYAHS
AVIZED	AVUNCULAR	AWES	AXEL	AYAHUASCA*
AVIZEFULL	AVYZE	AWESOME	AXELS	AYAHUASCAS*
AVIZES	AVYZED	AWESOMELY	AXEMAN	AYAHUASCO
AVIZING	AVYZES	AWESTRIKE	AXEMEN	AYAHUASCOS
AVO*	AVYZING	AWESTRIKES	AXENIC*	AYATOLLAH
AVOCADO	AW	AWESTRIKING	AXES	AYATOLLAHS
AVOCADOES*	AWA	AWESTRUCK	AXIAL	AYE
AVOCADOS	AWAIT	AWETO	AXIALITIES	AYELP
AVOCATION	AWAITED	AWETOS	AXIALITY	AYENBITE
AVOCATIONS	AWAITER*	AWFUL	AXIALLY	AYENBITES
AVOCET	AWAITERS*	AWFULLER	AXIL	AYES
AVOCETS	AWAITING	AWFULLEST	AXILE	AYGRE
AVODIRE*	AWAITS	AWFULLY	AXILLA	AYIN*
AVODIRES*	AWAKE	AWFULNESS	AXILLAE	AYINS*
AVOID	AWAKED	AWFULNESSES	AXILLAR	AYONT
AVOIDABLE	AWAKEN	AWHAPE	AXILLARIES*	AYRE
AVOIDABLY*	AWAKENED	AWHAPED	AXILLARS*	AYRES
AVOIDANCE	AWAKENER*	AWHAPES	AXILLARY	AYRIE
AVOIDANCES	AWAKENERS*	AWHAPING	AXILLAS*	AYRIES
AVOIDED	AWAKENING	AWHEEL	AXILS	AYS
AVOIDER*	AWAKENINGS	AWHEELS	AXING	AYU
AVOIDERS*	AWAKENS	AWHILE	AXINITE	AYURVEDA
AVOIDING	AWAKES	AWHIRL*	AXINITES	AYURVEDAS
AVOIDS	AWAKING	AWING	AXIOLOGIES	AYURVEDIC
AVOISION	AWAKINGS	AWKWARD	AXIOLOGY	AYUS
AVOISIONS	AWANTING	AWKWARDER	AXIOM	AYWORD
AVOS*	AWARD	AWKWARDEST	AXIOMATIC	AYWORDS
AVOSET	AWARDABLE*	AWKWARDLY	AXIOMATICS	AZALEA
AVOSETS	AWARDED	AWL	AXIOMS	AZALEAS
AVOUCH	AWARDEE*	AWLBIRD	AXION*	AZAN
AVOUCHED	AWARDEES*	AWLBIRDS	AXIONS*	AZANS
AVOUCHER*	AWARDER*	AWLESS*	AXIS	AZEOTROPE
AVOUCHERS*	AWARDERS*	AWLS	AXISED*	AZEOTROPES
AVOUCHES	AWARDING	AWLWORT*	AXISES	AZIDE
AVOUCHING	AWARDS	AWLWORTS*	AXITE*	AZIDES
AVOURE	AWARE	AWMOUS	AXITES*	AZIDO*
AVOURES	AWARENESS	AWMRIE	AXLE	AZIMUTH
AVOUTERER	AWARENESSES	AWMRIES	AXLED*	AZIMUTHAL
AVOUTERERS	AWARER	AWMRY	AXLES	AZIMUTHS
AVOUTRER	AWAREST	AWN	AXLETREE*	AZINE
AVOUTRERS	AWARN	AWNED	AXLETREES*	AZINES
AVOUTRIES	AWARNED	AWNER	AXLIKE*	AZIONE
AVOUTRY	AWARNING	AWNERS	AXMAN	AZIONES

The Chambers Dictionary is the authority for many longer words; see Introduction, page ix

AZLON*
AZLONS*
AZO*
AZOIC
AZOLE*
AZOLES*
AZOLLA
AZOLLAS
AZON*
AZONAL
AZONIC

AZONS*
AZOTE
AZOTED*
AZOTEMIA*
AZOTEMIAS*
AZOTEMIC*
AZOTES
AZOTH
AZOTHS
AZOTIC
AZOTISE

AZOTISED
AZOTISES
AZOTISING
AZOTIZE
AZOTIZED
AZOTIZES
AZOTIZING
AZOTOUS
AZOTURIA
AZOTURIAS
AZULEJO

AZULEJOS
AZURE
AZUREAN
AZURES
AZURINE
AZURINES
AZURITE
AZURITES
AZURN
AZURY
AZYGIES

AZYGOS
AZYGOSES
AZYGOUS
AZYGY
AZYM
AZYME
AZYMES
AZYMITE
AZYMITES
AZYMOUS
AZYMS

B

BA
BAA
BAAED
BAAING
BAAINGS
BAAL*
BAALIM*
BAALISM*
BAALISMS*
BAALS*
BAAS
BAASES
BAASKAAP*
BAASKAAPS*
BAASSKAP
BAASSKAPS
BABA
BABACO
BABACOOTE
BABACOOTES
BABACOS
BABAS
BABASSU
BABASSUS
BABBITT
BABBITTED
BABBITTING
BABBITTS
BABBLE
BABBLED
BABBLER
BABBLERS
BABBLES
BABBLIER
BABBLIEST
BABBLING
BABBLINGS
BABBLY
BABE
BABEL
BABELDOM
BABELDOMS
BABELISH
BABELISM
BABELISMS
BABELS
BABES
BABESIA*
BABESIAS*
BABICHE
BABICHES
BABIED
BABIER
BABIES
BABIEST

BABIRUSA
BABIRUSAS
BABIRUSSA
BABIRUSSAS
BABKA*
BABKAS*
BABLAH
BABLAHS
BABOO
BABOOL*
BABOOLS*
BABOON
BABOONERIES
BABOONERY
BABOONISH
BABOONS
BABOOS
BABOOSH
BABOOSHES
BABOUCHE
BABOUCHES
BABU
BABUCHE
BABUCHES
BABUDOM
BABUDOMS
BABUISM
BABUISMS
BABUL
BABULS
BABUS
BABUSHKA
BABUSHKAS
BABY
BABYFOOD
BABYFOODS
BABYHOOD
BABYHOODS
BABYING
BABYISH
BAC
BACALAO*
BACALAOS*
BACCA
BACCAE
BACCARA
BACCARAS
BACCARAT
BACCARATS
BACCARE
BACCAS
BACCATE
BACCATED*
BACCHANAL
BACCHANALS

BACCHANT
BACCHANTE
BACCHANTES
BACCHANTS
BACCHIAC
BACCHIAN
BACCHIC
BACCHII
BACCHIUS
BACCIES
BACCIFORM
BACCO
BACCOES
BACCOS
BACCY
BACH
BACHARACH
BACHARACHS
BACHED
BACHELOR
BACHELORS
BACHES
BACHING
BACHS
BACILLAR
BACILLARY
BACILLI
BACILLUS
BACK
BACKACHE
BACKACHES
BACKARE
BACKBAND
BACKBANDS
BACKBEAT
BACKBEATS
BACKBENCH*
BACKBENCHES*
BACKBEND*
BACKBENDS*
BACKBIT
BACKBITE
BACKBITER
BACKBITERS
BACKBITES
BACKBITING
BACKBITINGS
BACKBITTEN
BACKBLOCK*
BACKBLOCKS*
BACKBOARD*
BACKBOARDS*
BACKBOND
BACKBONDS
BACKBONE

BACKBONED
BACKBONES
BACKCAST*
BACKCASTS*
BACKCHAT
BACKCHATS
BACKCHATTED
BACKCHATTING
BACKCLOTH*
BACKCLOTHS*
BACKCOURT
BACKCOURTS
BACKCROSS*
BACKCROSSED*
BACKCROSSES*
BACKCROSSING*
BACKDATE*
BACKDATED*
BACKDATES*
BACKDATING*
BACKDOOR*
BACKDOWN
BACKDOWNS
BACKDROP
BACKDROPPED*
BACKDROPPING*
BACKDROPS
BACKDROPT*
BACKED
BACKER
BACKERS
BACKET
BACKETS
BACKFALL
BACKFALLS
BACKFIELD
BACKFIELDS*
BACKFILE
BACKFILES
BACKFILL
BACKFILLED
BACKFILLING
BACKFILLS
BACKFIRE
BACKFIRED
BACKFIRES
BACKFIRING
BACKFISCH
BACKFISCHES
BACKFIT*
BACKFITS*
BACKFITTED*
BACKFITTING*
BACKFLOW*
BACKFLOWS*

BACKHAND
BACKHANDED*
BACKHANDING*
BACKHANDS
BACKHAUL*
BACKHAULED*
BACKHAULING*
BACKHAULS*
BACKHOE
BACKHOES
BACKHOUSE*
BACKHOUSES*
BACKING
BACKINGS
BACKLAND
BACKLANDS
BACKLASH
BACKLASHED*
BACKLASHES
BACKLASHING*
BACKLESS*
BACKLIFT
BACKLIFTS
BACKLIGHT*
BACKLIGHTED*
BACKLIGHTING*
BACKLIGHTS*
BACKLIST
BACKLISTED*
BACKLISTING*
BACKLISTS
BACKLIT*
BACKLOG
BACKLOGGED*
BACKLOGGING*
BACKLOGS
BACKLOT
BACKLOTS
BACKMOST
BACKOUT*
BACKOUTS*
BACKPACK
BACKPACKED
BACKPACKING
BACKPACKINGS
BACKPACKS
BACKPAY
BACKPAYS
BACKPEDAL*
BACKPEDALED*
BACKPEDALING*
BACKPEDALLED*
BACKPEDALLING*
BACKPEDALS*
BACKPIECE

BACKPIECES	BACKSWEPT*	BADASS	BAGASSE	BAIGNOIRE
BACKRA	BACKSWING	BADASSED	BAGASSES	BAIGNOIRES
BACKRAS	BACKSWINGS	BADASSES	BAGATELLE	BAIL
BACKREST*	BACKSWORD	BADDER*	BAGATELLES	BAILABLE
BACKRESTS*	BACKSWORDS	BADDEST*	BAGEL	BAILBOND
BACKROOM	BACKTRACK	BADDIE	BAGELS	BAILBONDS
BACKRUSH*	BACKTRACKED	BADDIES	BAGFUL	BAILED
BACKRUSHES*	BACKTRACKING	BADDISH	BAGFULS	BAILEE
BACKS	BACKTRACKINGS	BADDY	BAGGAGE	BAILEES
BACKSAW	BACKTRACKS	BADE	BAGGAGES	BAILER
BACKSAWS	BACKUP*	BADGE	BAGGED	BAILERS
BACKSEAT*	BACKUPS*	BADGED	BAGGER*	BAILEY
BACKSEATS*	BACKVELD	BADGER	BAGGERS*	BAILEYS
BACKSET	BACKVELDS	BADGERED	BAGGIE*	BAILIE
BACKSETS	BACKWARD	BADGERING	BAGGIER	BAILIES
BACKSEY	BACKWARDS	BADGERLY	BAGGIES	BAILIFF
BACKSEYS	BACKWASH	BADGERS	BAGGIEST	BAILIFFS
BACKSHISH	BACKWASHED	BADGES	BAGGILY	BAILING
BACKSHISHED	BACKWASHES	BADGING	BAGGINESS	BAILIWICK
BACKSHISHES	BACKWASHING	BADINAGE	BAGGINESSES	BAILIWICKS
BACKSHISHING	BACKWATER	BADINAGED*	BAGGING	BAILLI
BACKSIDE	BACKWATERS	BADINAGES	BAGGINGS	BAILLIAGE
BACKSIDES	BACKWOOD*	BADINAGING*	BAGGIT	BAILLIAGES
BACKSIGHT	BACKWOODS	BADIOUS	BAGGITS	BAILLIE
BACKSIGHTS	BACKWORD	BADLAND*	BAGGY	BAILLIES
BACKSLAP*	BACKWORDS	BADLANDS	BAGHOUSE*	BAILLIS
BACKSLAPPED*	BACKWORK	BADLY	BAGHOUSES*	BAILMENT
BACKSLAPPING*	BACKWORKS	BADMAN	BAGMAN	BAILMENTS
BACKSLAPS*	BACKWRAP*	BADMASH	BAGMEN	BAILOR
BACKSLASH	BACKWRAPS*	BADMASHES	BAGNIO	BAILORS
BACKSLASHES	BACKYARD	BADMEN	BAGNIOS	BAILOUT*
BACKSLID	BACKYARDS	BADMINTON	BAGPIPE	BAILOUTS*
BACKSLIDDEN*	BACLAVA	BADMINTONS	BAGPIPER	BAILS
BACKSLIDE	BACLAVAS	BADMOUTH	BAGPIPERS	BAILSMAN
BACKSLIDES	BACON	BADMOUTHED	BAGPIPES	BAILSMEN
BACKSLIDING	BACONER	BADMOUTHING	BAGPIPING	BAININ
BACKSLIDINGS	BACONERS	BADMOUTHS	BAGPIPINGS	BAININS
BACKSPACE	BACONS	BADNESS	BAGS	BAINITE
BACKSPACED	BACS	BADNESSES	BAGSFUL*	BAINITES
BACKSPACES	BACTERIA	BADS	BAGUET*	BAIRN
BACKSPACING	BACTERIAL	BAEL	BAGUETS*	BAIRNISH*
BACKSPEER	BACTERIAN	BAELS	BAGUETTE	BAIRNLIER
BACKSPEERED	BACTERIAS*	BAETYL	BAGUETTES	BAIRNLIEST
BACKSPEERING	BACTERIC	BAETYLS	BAGUIO	BAIRNLIKE
BACKSPEERS	BACTERIN*	BAFF	BAGUIOS	BAIRNLY
BACKSPEIR	BACTERINS*	BAFFED	BAGWASH	BAIRNS
BACKSPEIRED	BACTERISE	BAFFIES	BAGWASHES	BAISEMAIN
BACKSPEIRING	BACTERISED	BAFFING	BAGWIG	BAISEMAINS
BACKSPEIRS	BACTERISES	BAFFLE	BAGWIGS	BAIT
BACKSPIN	BACTERISING	BAFFLED	BAGWORM*	BAITED
BACKSPINS	BACTERIUM	BAFFLEGAB	BAGWORMS*	BAITER
BACKSTAB*	BACTERIZE	BAFFLEGABS	BAH	BAITERS
BACKSTABBED*	BACTERIZED	BAFFLER	BAHADA	BAITFISH
BACKSTABBING*	BACTERIZES	BAFFLERS	BAHADAS	BAITFISHES
BACKSTABS*	BACTERIZING	BAFFLES	BAHADUR*	BAITH*
BACKSTAGE	BACTEROID	BAFFLING	BAHADURS*	BAITING
BACKSTALL	BACTEROIDS	BAFFS	BAHT	BAITINGS
BACKSTALLS	BACULA	BAFFY	BAHTS	BAITS
BACKSTAY*	BACULINE	BAFT	BAHUT	BAIZA*
BACKSTAYS*	BACULITE	BAFTS	BAHUTS	BAIZAS*
BACKSTOP	BACULITES	BAG	BAHUVRIHI	BAIZE
BACKSTOPPED*	BACULUM	BAGARRE	BAHUVRIHIS	BAIZED
BACKSTOPPING*	BACULUMS	BAGARRES	BAIDARKA*	BAIZES
BACKSTOPS	BAD	BAGASS*	BAIDARKAS*	BAIZING

Words marked with an asterisk are from OTCWL

BAJADA	BALANCERS	BALISTAE	BALLCLAYS	BALLUPS
BAJADAS	BALANCES	BALISTAS	BALLCOCK	BALLUTE*
BAJAN	BALANCING	BALK	BALLCOCKS	BALLUTES*
BAJANS	BALANITIS	BALKANISE	BALLED	BALLY
BAJRA	BALANITISES	BALKANISED	BALLER*	BALLYHOO
BAJRAS	BALAS	BALKANISES	BALLERINA	BALLYHOOED
BAJREE	BALASES	BALKANISING	BALLERINAS	BALLYHOOING
BAJREES	BALATA	BALKANIZE	BALLERINE	BALLYHOOS
BAJRI	BALATAS	BALKANIZED	BALLERS*	BALLYRAG
BAJRIS	BALBOA	BALKANIZES	BALLET	BALLYRAGGED
BAJU	BALBOAS	BALKANIZING	BALLETED	BALLYRAGGING
BAJUS	BALCONET	BALKED	BALLETIC	BALLYRAGS
BAKE	BALCONETS	BALKER	BALLETING	BALM
BAKEAPPLE	BALCONIED	BALKERS	BALLETS	BALMACAAN
BAKEAPPLES	BALCONIES	BALKIER	BALLGAME*	BALMACAANS
BAKEBOARD	BALCONY	BALKIEST	BALLGAMES*	BALMED
BAKEBOARDS	BALD	BALKILY*	BALLHAWK*	BALMIER
BAKED	BALDACHIN	BALKINESS	BALLHAWKS*	BALMIEST
BAKEHOUSE	BALDACHINS	BALKINESSES	BALLIES*	BALMILY
BAKEHOUSES	BALDAQUIN	BALKING	BALLING	BALMINESS
BAKEMEAT	BALDAQUINS	BALKINGLY	BALLINGS	BALMINESSES
BAKEMEATS	BALDED*	BALKINGS	BALLISTA	BALMING
BAKEN	BALDER	BALKLINE	BALLISTAE	BALMLIKE*
BAKER	BALDEST	BALKLINES	BALLISTAS	BALMORAL
BAKERIES	BALDHEAD*	BALKS	BALLISTIC	BALMORALS
BAKERS	BALDHEADS*	BALKY	BALLISTICS	BALMS
BAKERY	BALDICOOT	BALL	BALLIUM	BALMY
BAKES	BALDICOOTS	BALLABILE	BALLIUMS	BALNEAL
BAKESHOP*	BALDIER	BALLABILES	BALLOCKS	BALNEARIES
BAKESHOPS*	BALDIES	BALLABILI	BALLOCKSED	BALNEARY
BAKESTONE	BALDIEST	BALLAD	BALLOCKSES	BALONEY
BAKESTONES	BALDING	BALLADE	BALLOCKSING	BALONEYS
BAKEWARE	BALDISH	BALLADED	BALLON	BALOO
BAKEWARES	BALDLY	BALLADEER	BALLONET	BALOOS
BAKHSHISH	BALDMONEY	BALLADEERED	BALLONETS	BALS*
BAKHSHISHED	BALDMONEYS	BALLADEERING	BALLONNE*	BALSA
BAKHSHISHES	BALDNESS	BALLADEERS	BALLONNES*	BALSAM
BAKHSHISHING	BALDNESSES	BALLADES	BALLONS	BALSAMED
BAKING	BALDPATE	BALLADIC*	BALLOON	BALSAMIC
BAKINGS	BALDPATED	BALLADIN	BALLOONED	BALSAMING
BAKLAVA	BALDPATES	BALLADINE	BALLOONING	BALSAMS
BAKLAVAS	BALDRIC	BALLADINES	BALLOONINGS	BALSAMY
BAKLAWA*	BALDRICK	BALLADING	BALLOONS	BALSAS
BAKLAWAS*	BALDRICKS	BALLADINS	BALLOT	BALSAWOOD
BAKSHEESH	BALDRICS	BALLADIST	BALLOTED	BALSAWOODS
BAKSHEESHED	BALDS*	BALLADISTS	BALLOTEE	BALTHASAR
BAKSHEESHES	BALDY	BALLADRIES	BALLOTEES	BALTHASARS
BAKSHEESHING	BALE	BALLADRY	BALLOTER*	BALTHAZAR
BAKSHISH*	BALECTION	BALLADS	BALLOTERS*	BALTHAZARS
BAKSHISHED*	BALECTIONS	BALLAN	BALLOTING	BALU
BAKSHISHES*	BALED	BALLANS	BALLOTS	BALUS
BAKSHISHING*	BALEEN	BALLANT	BALLOW	BALUSTER
BAL*	BALEENS	BALLANTED	BALLOWS	BALUSTERS
BALACLAVA	BALEFIRE*	BALLANTING	BALLPARK	BALZARINE
BALACLAVAS	BALEFIRES*	BALLANTS	BALLPARKS*	BALZARINES
BALADIN	BALEFUL	BALLAST	BALLPOINT	BAM
BALADINE	BALEFULLY	BALLASTED	BALLPOINTS	BAMBINI
BALADINES	BALER	BALLASTING	BALLROOM	BAMBINO
BALADINS	BALERS	BALLASTS	BALLROOMS	BAMBINOS
BALALAIKA	BALES	BALLAT	BALLS	BAMBOO
BALALAIKAS	BALING	BALLATED	BALLSIER	BAMBOOS
BALANCE	BALISAUR*	BALLATING	BALLSIEST	BAMBOOZLE
BALANCED	BALISAURS*	BALLATS	BALLSY	BAMBOOZLED
BALANCER	BALISTA	BALLCLAY	BALLUP	BAMBOOZLES

The Chambers Dictionary is the authority for many longer words; see Introduction, page ix

BAMBOOZLING	BANDEROLS	BANE	BANKNOTE*	BANTERS
BAMMED	BANDERS*	BANEBERRIES	BANKNOTES*	BANTIES*
BAMMER	BANDICOOT	BANEBERRY	BANKROLL	BANTING
BAMMERS	BANDICOOTED	BANED	BANKROLLED	BANTINGS
BAMMING	BANDICOOTING	BANEFUL	BANKROLLING	BANTLING
BAMPOT	BANDICOOTS	BANEFULLY	BANKROLLS	BANTLINGS
BAMPOTS	BANDIED	BANES	BANKRUPT	BANTS
BAMS	BANDIER	BANG	BANKRUPTED	BANTU
BAN	BANDIES	BANGED	BANKRUPTING	BANTUS
BANAL	BANDIEST	BANGER	BANKRUPTS	BANTY*
BANALER	BANDING	BANGERS	BANKS	BANXRING
BANALEST	BANDINGS	BANGING	BANKSIA	BANXRINGS
BANALISE	BANDIT	BANGINGS	BANKSIAS	BANYAN
BANALISED	BANDITRIES	BANGKOK*	BANKSIDE*	BANYANS
BANALISES	BANDITRY	BANGKOKS*	BANKSIDES*	BANZAI
BANALISING	BANDITS	BANGLE	BANKSMAN	BANZAIS
BANALITIES	BANDITTI	BANGLED	BANKSMEN	BAOBAB
BANALITY	BANDITTIS	BANGLES	BANLIEUE	BAOBABS
BANALIZE	BANDOBAST	BANGS	BANLIEUES	BAP
BANALIZED	BANDOBASTS	BANGSRING	BANNED	BAPS
BANALIZES	BANDOG	BANGSRINGS	BANNER	BAPTISE
BANALIZING	BANDOGS	BANGSTER	BANNERALL	BAPTISED
BANALLY	BANDOLEER	BANGSTERS	BANNERALLS	BAPTISES
BANANA	BANDOLEERS	BANGTAIL*	BANNERED	BAPTISIA*
BANANAS	BANDOLEON	BANGTAILS*	BANNERET	BAPTISIAS*
BANAUSIAN	BANDOLEONS	BANI	BANNERETS	BAPTISING
BANAUSIC	BANDOLERO	BANIA	BANNERING*	BAPTISM
BANC	BANDOLEROS	BANIAN	BANNEROL	BAPTISMAL
BANCO	BANDOLIER	BANIANS	BANNEROLS	BAPTISMS
BANCOS	BANDOLIERS	BANIAS	BANNERS	BAPTIST
BANCS	BANDOLINE	BANING	BANNET*	BAPTISTRIES
BAND	BANDOLINED	BANISH	BANNETS*	BAPTISTRY
BANDA	BANDOLINES	BANISHED	BANNING	BAPTISTS
BANDAGE	BANDOLINING	BANISHER*	BANNISTER	BAPTIZE
BANDAGED	BANDONEON	BANISHERS*	BANNISTERS	BAPTIZED
BANDAGER*	BANDONEONS	BANISHES	BANNOCK	BAPTIZER*
BANDAGERS*	BANDONION	BANISHING	BANNOCKS	BAPTIZERS*
BANDAGES	BANDONIONS	BANISTER	BANNS	BAPTIZES
BANDAGING	BANDOOK	BANISTERS	BANQUET	BAPTIZING
BANDALORE	BANDOOKS	BANJAX	BANQUETED	BAPU
BANDALORES	BANDORA	BANJAXED	BANQUETER	BAPUS
BANDANA	BANDORAS	BANJAXES	BANQUETERS	BAR
BANDANAS	BANDORE	BANJAXING	BANQUETING	BARACAN
BANDANNA	BANDORES	BANJO	BANQUETINGS	BARACANS
BANDANNAS	BANDROL	BANJOES	BANQUETS	BARAGOUIN
BANDAR	BANDROLS	BANJOIST	BANQUETTE	BARAGOUINS
BANDARS	BANDS	BANJOISTS	BANQUETTES	BARASINGA
BANDAS	BANDSMAN	BANJOS	BANS	BARASINGAS
BANDBOX*	BANDSMEN	BANJULELE	BANSHEE	BARATHEA
BANDBOXES*	BANDSTAND	BANJULELES	BANSHEES	BARATHEAS
BANDBRAKE	BANDSTANDS	BANK	BANSHIE*	BARATHRUM
BANDBRAKES	BANDSTER	BANKABLE	BANSHIES*	BARATHRUMS
BANDEAU	BANDSTERS	BANKBOOK*	BANT	BARAZA
BANDEAUS*	BANDURA	BANKBOOKS*	BANTAM	BARAZAS
BANDEAUX	BANDURAS	BANKCARD*	BANTAMS	BARB
BANDED	BANDWAGON	BANKCARDS*	BANTED	BARBAL*
BANDELET	BANDWAGONS	BANKED	BANTENG	BARBARIAN
BANDELETS	BANDWIDTH	BANKER	BANTENGS	BARBARIANS
BANDELIER	BANDWIDTHS	BANKERLY	BANTER	BARBARIC
BANDELIERS	BANDY	BANKERS	BANTERED	BARBARISE
BANDER*	BANDYING	BANKET	BANTERER	BARBARISED
BANDEROL	BANDYINGS	BANKETS	BANTERERS	BARBARISES
BANDEROLE	BANDYMAN	BANKING	BANTERING	BARBARISING
BANDEROLES	BANDYMEN	BANKINGS	BANTERINGS	BARBARISM

Words marked with an asterisk are from OTCWL

BARBARISMS
BARBARITIES
BARBARITY
BARBARIZE
BARBARIZED
BARBARIZES
BARBARIZING
BARBAROUS
BARBASCO
BARBASCOES*
BARBASCOS
BARBASTEL
BARBASTELS
BARBATE
BARBATED
BARBE
BARBECUE
BARBECUED
BARBECUER*
BARBECUERS*
BARBECUES
BARBECUING
BARBED
BARBEL
BARBELL*
BARBELLS*
BARBELS
BARBEQUE
BARBEQUED
BARBEQUES
BARBEQUING
BARBER
BARBERED
BARBERING
BARBERRIES
BARBERRY
BARBERS
BARBES
BARBET
BARBETS
BARBETTE
BARBETTES
BARBICAN
BARBICANS
BARBICEL
BARBICELS
BARBIE
BARBIES
BARBING
BARBITAL
BARBITALS
BARBITONE
BARBITONES
BARBLESS*
BARBOLA
BARBOLAS
BARBOTINE
BARBOTINES
BARBS
BARBULE
BARBULES
BARBUT*
BARBUTS*
BARBWIRE*

BARBWIRES*
BARCA
BARCAROLE
BARCAROLES
BARCAS
BARCHAN
BARCHANE
BARCHANES
BARCHANS
BARD
BARDASH
BARDASHES
BARDE*
BARDED
BARDES*
BARDIC
BARDIER
BARDIEST
BARDING
BARDLING
BARDLINGS
BARDO
BARDOS
BARDS
BARDSHIP
BARDSHIPS
BARDY
BARE
BAREBACK
BAREBOAT
BAREBOATS*
BAREBONE
BAREBONES
BARED
BAREFACED
BAREFIT*
BAREFOOT
BAREGE
BAREGES
BAREGINE
BAREGINES
BAREHEAD*
BARELY
BARENESS
BARENESSES
BARER
BARES
BARESARK
BARESARKS
BAREST
BARF
BARFED
BARFING
BARFLIES
BARFLY
BARFS
BARFUL
BARGAIN
BARGAINED
BARGAINER
BARGAINERS
BARGAINING
BARGAINS
BARGANDER

BARGANDERS
BARGE
BARGED
BARGEE
BARGEES
BARGEESE
BARGELLO
BARGELLOS
BARGEMAN
BARGEMEN
BARGEPOLE
BARGEPOLES
BARGES
BARGEST
BARGESTS
BARGHAIST
BARGHAISTS
BARGHEST
BARGHESTS
BARGING
BARGOOSE
BARGUEST*
BARGUESTS*
BARHOP*
BARHOPPED*
BARHOPPING*
BARHOPS*
BARIC
BARILLA
BARILLAS
BARING
BARISH
BARITE
BARITES
BARITONAL*
BARITONE
BARITONES
BARIUM
BARIUMS
BARK
BARKAN
BARKANS
BARKED
BARKEEP*
BARKEEPER
BARKEEPERS
BARKEEPS*
BARKEN
BARKENED
BARKENING
BARKENS
BARKER
BARKERS
BARKHAN
BARKHANS
BARKIER
BARKIEST
BARKING
BARKLESS
BARKS
BARKY
BARLEDUC*
BARLEDUCS*
BARLESS*

BARLEY
BARLEYS
BARLOW*
BARLOWS*
BARM
BARMAID
BARMAIDS
BARMAN
BARMBRACK
BARMBRACKS
BARMEN
BARMIE*
BARMIER
BARMIEST
BARMINESS
BARMINESSES
BARMKIN
BARMKINS
BARMS
BARMY
BARN
BARNACLE
BARNACLED
BARNACLES
BARNED
BARNEY
BARNEYS
BARNIER*
BARNIEST*
BARNING
BARNLIKE*
BARNS
BARNSTORM
BARNSTORMED
BARNSTORMING
BARNSTORMINGS
BARNSTORMS
BARNY*
BARNYARD
BARNYARDS
BAROCCO
BAROCCOS
BAROCK
BAROCKS
BAROGRAM
BAROGRAMS
BAROGRAPH
BAROGRAPHS
BAROMETER
BAROMETERS
BAROMETRIES
BAROMETRY
BAROMETZ
BAROMETZES
BARON
BARONAGE
BARONAGES
BARONESS
BARONESSES
BARONET
BARONETCIES
BARONETCY
BARONETS
BARONG

BARONGS
BARONIAL
BARONIES
BARONNE
BARONNES
BARONS
BARONY
BAROQUE
BAROQUELY*
BAROQUES
BAROSCOPE
BAROSCOPES
BAROSTAT
BAROSTATS
BAROUCHE
BAROUCHES
BARP
BARPERSON
BARPERSONS
BARPS
BARQUE
BARQUES
BARQUETTE*
BARQUETTES*
BARRABLE*
BARRACAN
BARRACANS
BARRACE
BARRACES
BARRACK
BARRACKED
BARRACKER
BARRACKERS
BARRACKING
BARRACKINGS
BARRACKS
BARRACOON
BARRACOONS
BARRACUDA
BARRACUDAS
BARRAGE
BARRAGED*
BARRAGES
BARRAGING*
BARRANCA
BARRANCAS
BARRANCO
BARRANCOS
BARRAT
BARRATER*
BARRATERS*
BARRATOR
BARRATORS
BARRATRIES
BARRATRY
BARRATS
BARRE
BARRED
BARREFULL
BARREL
BARRELAGE
BARRELAGES
BARRELED*
BARRELFUL

The Chambers Dictionary is the authority for many longer words; see Introduction, page ix

BARRELFULS	BARTERS	BASER	BASIS	BASTARDIES
BARRELING*	BARTISAN	BASES	BASK	BASTARDLY
BARRELLED	BARTISANS	BASEST	BASKED	BASTARDS
BARRELLING	BARTIZAN	BASH	BASKET	BASTARDY
BARRELS	BARTIZANS	BASHAW	BASKETFUL	BASTE
BARRELSFUL*	BARTON	BASHAWISM	BASKETFULS	BASTED
BARREN	BARTONS	BASHAWISMS	BASKETRIES	BASTER
BARRENER	BARWARE*	BASHAWS	BASKETRY	BASTERS
BARRENEST	BARWARES*	BASHED	BASKETS	BASTES
BARRENLY*	BARWOOD	BASHER	BASKETSFUL*	BASTIDE
BARRENS*	BARWOODS	BASHERS	BASKING	BASTIDES
BARRES	BARYE	BASHES	BASKS	BASTILE*
BARRET	BARYES	BASHFUL	BASMATI*	BASTILES*
BARRETOR*	BARYON	BASHFULLY	BASMATIS*	BASTILLE
BARRETORS*	BARYONIC*	BASHING	BASNET	BASTILLES
BARRETRIES*	BARYONS	BASHINGS	BASNETS	BASTINADE
BARRETRY*	BARYTA	BASHLESS	BASOCHE	BASTINADED
BARRETS	BARYTAS	BASHLIK	BASOCHES	BASTINADES
BARRETTE	BARYTE*	BASHLIKS	BASON	BASTINADING
BARRETTER	BARYTES	BASHLYK*	BASONS	BASTINADO
BARRETTERS	BARYTIC	BASHLYKS*	BASOPHIL	BASTINADOED
BARRETTES	BARYTON	BASHO	BASOPHILE*	BASTINADOES
BARRICADE	BARYTONE	BASIC	BASOPHILES*	BASTINADOING
BARRICADED	BARYTONES	BASICALLY	BASOPHILS	BASTING
BARRICADES	BARYTONS	BASICITIES	BASQUE	BASTINGS
BARRICADING	BAS	BASICITY	BASQUED	BASTION
BARRICADO	BASAL	BASICS	BASQUES	BASTIONED
BARRICADOED	BASALLY*	BASIDIA	BASQUINE	BASTIONS
BARRICADOES	BASALT	BASIDIAL	BASQUINES	BASTLE
BARRICADOING	BASALTES*	BASIDIUM	BASS	BASTLES
BARRICADOS	BASALTIC	BASIFIED*	BASSE	BASTO
BARRICO	BASALTS	BASIFIER*	BASSED	BASTOS
BARRICOES	BASAN	BASIFIERS*	BASSER	BASTS
BARRICOS	BASANITE	BASIFIES*	BASSES	BASUCO
BARRIER	BASANITES	BASIFIXED	BASSEST	BASUCOS
BARRIERED	BASANS	BASIFUGAL	BASSET	BAT
BARRIERING	BASCULE	BASIFY*	BASSETED	BATABLE
BARRIERS	BASCULES	BASIFYING*	BASSETING	BATATA
BARRING	BASE	BASIL	BASSETS	BATATAS
BARRINGS	BASEBALL	BASILAR	BASSETT*	BATBOY*
BARRIO	BASEBALLS	BASILARY*	BASSETTED*	BATBOYS*
BARRIOS	BASEBAND	BASILIC*	BASSETTING*	BATCH
BARRISTER	BASEBOARD	BASILICA	BASSETTS*	BATCHED
BARRISTERS	BASEBOARDS	BASILICAE*	BASSI	BATCHER*
BARROOM*	BASEBORN*	BASILICAL	BASSIER	BATCHERS*
BARROOMS*	BASED	BASILICAN	BASSIEST	BATCHES
BARROW	BASELARD	BASILICAS	BASSINET	BATCHING
BARROWS	BASELARDS	BASILICON	BASSINETS	BATCHINGS
BARRULET	BASELESS	BASILICONS	BASSING	BATE
BARRULETS	BASELINE*	BASILISK	BASSIST	BATEAU
BARS	BASELINER	BASILISKS	BASSISTS	BATEAUX
BARSTOOL*	BASELINERS	BASILS	BASSLY*	BATED
BARSTOOLS*	BASELINES*	BASIN	BASSNESS*	BATELESS
BARTEND*	BASELY	BASINAL*	BASSNESSES*	BATELEUR
BARTENDED*	BASEMAN	BASINED*	BASSO	BATELEURS
BARTENDER	BASEMEN	BASINET	BASSOON	BATEMENT
BARTENDERS	BASEMENT	BASINETS	BASSOONS	BATEMENTS
BARTENDING*	BASEMENTS	BASINFUL	BASSOS	BATES
BARTENDS*	BASENESS	BASINFULS	BASSWOOD	BATFISH
BARTER	BASENESSES	BASING	BASSWOODS	BATFISHES
BARTERED	BASENJI	BASINS	BASSY	BATFOWL*
BARTERER	BASENJIS	BASION*	BAST	BATFOWLED*
BARTERERS	BASEPLATE	BASIONS*	BASTA	BATFOWLING*
BARTERING	BASEPLATES	BASIPETAL	BASTARD	BATFOWLS*

BATH	BATRACHIA	BATTLES	BAWCOCK	BAYT
BATHCUBE	BATS	BATTLING	BAWCOCKS	BAYTED
BATHCUBES	BATSMAN	BATTOLOGIES	BAWD	BAYTING
BATHE	BATSMEN	BATTOLOGY	BAWDIER	BAYTS
BATHED	BATSWING	BATTS	BAWDIES	BAYWOOD*
BATHER	BATSWOMAN	BATTU*	BAWDIEST	BAYWOODS*
BATHERS	BATSWOMEN	BATTUE	BAWDILY	BAZAAR
BATHES	BATT	BATTUES	BAWDINESS	BAZAARS
BATHETIC	BATTA	BATTUTA	BAWDINESSES	BAZAR
BATHHOUSE	BATTALIA	BATTUTAS	BAWDKIN	BAZARS
BATHHOUSES	BATTALIAS	BATTY	BAWDKINS	BAZAZZ
BATHING	BATTALION	BATWING*	BAWDRIC*	BAZAZZES
BATHLESS*	BATTALIONS	BATWOMAN	BAWDRICS*	BAZOO*
BATHMAT*	BATTAS	BATWOMEN	BAWDRIES	BAZOOKA
BATHMATS*	BATTEAU*	BAUBEE*	BAWDRY	BAZOOKAS
BATHMIC	BATTEAUX*	BAUBEES*	BAWDS	BAZOOMS*
BATHMISM	BATTED	BAUBLE	BAWDY	BAZOOS*
BATHMISMS	BATTEL	BAUBLES	BAWL	BAZOUKI
BATHOLITE	BATTELED	BAUBLING	BAWLED	BAZOUKIS
BATHOLITES	BATTELER	BAUCHLE	BAWLER	BDELLIUM
BATHOLITH	BATTELERS	BAUCHLED	BAWLERS	BDELLIUMS
BATHOLITHS	BATTELING	BAUCHLES	BAWLEY	BE
BATHORSE	BATTELLED	BAUCHLING	BAWLEYS	BEACH
BATHORSES	BATTELLING	BAUD	BAWLING	BEACHBOY*
BATHOS	BATTELS	BAUDEKIN	BAWLINGS	BEACHBOYS*
BATHOSES	BATTEMENT	BAUDEKINS	BAWLS	BEACHCOMB*
BATHROBE	BATTEMENTS	BAUDRIC	BAWN	BEACHCOMBED*
BATHROBES	BATTEN	BAUDRICK	BAWNS	BEACHCOMBING*
BATHROOM	BATTENED	BAUDRICKE	BAWR	BEACHCOMBS*
BATHROOMS	BATTENER*	BAUDRICKES	BAWRS	BEACHED
BATHS	BATTENERS*	BAUDRICKS	BAWSUNT*	BEACHES
BATHTUB	BATTENING	BAUDRICS	BAWTIE*	BEACHGOER*
BATHTUBS	BATTENINGS	BAUDRONS	BAWTIES*	BEACHGOERS*
BATHWATER*	BATTENS	BAUDRONSES	BAWTY*	BEACHHEAD
BATHWATERS*	BATTER	BAUDS	BAXTER	BEACHHEADS
BATHYAL	BATTERED	BAUERA	BAXTERS	BEACHIER
BATHYBIUS	BATTERER	BAUERAS	BAY	BEACHIEST
BATHYBIUSES	BATTERERS	BAUHINIA	BAYADEER*	BEACHING
BATHYLITE	BATTERIE	BAUHINIAS	BAYADEERS*	BEACHSIDE*
BATHYLITES	BATTERIES	BAUK	BAYADERE	BEACHWEAR*
BATHYLITH	BATTERING	BAUKED	BAYADERES	BEACHY
BATHYLITHS	BATTERO	BAUKING	BAYAMO*	BEACON
BATIK	BATTEROS	BAUKS	BAYAMOS*	BEACONED
BATIKS	BATTERS	BAULK	BAYARD	BEACONING
BATING	BATTERY	BAULKED	BAYARDS	BEACONS
BATISTE	BATTIER	BAULKIER*	BAYBERRIES	BEAD
BATISTES	BATTIEST	BAULKIEST*	BAYBERRY	BEADED
BATLER	BATTIK*	BAULKING	BAYE	BEADIER
BATLERS	BATTIKS*	BAULKS	BAYED	BEADIEST
BATLET	BATTILL	BAULKY*	BAYES	BEADILY*
BATLETS	BATTILLED	BAUR	BAYING	BEADING
BATLIKE*	BATTILLING	BAURS	BAYLE	BEADINGS
BATMAN	BATTILLS	BAUSOND	BAYLES	BEADLE
BATMEN	BATTINESS*	BAUXITE	BAYMAN*	BEADLEDOM
BATOLOGIES	BATTINESSES*	BAUXITES	BAYMEN*	BEADLEDOMS
BATOLOGY	BATTING	BAUXITIC	BAYONET	BEADLES
BATON	BATTINGS	BAVARDAGE	BAYONETED	BEADLIKE*
BATONED	BATTLE	BAVARDAGES	BAYONETING	BEADMAN
BATONING	BATTLEBUS	BAVIN	BAYONETS	BEADMEN
BATONS	BATTLEBUSES	BAVINS	BAYONETTED*	BEADROLL*
BATOON	BATTLEBUSSES	BAWBEE	BAYONETTING*	BEADROLLS*
BATOONED	BATTLED	BAWBEES	BAYOU	BEADS
BATOONING	BATTLER	BAWBLE	BAYOUS	BEADSMAN
BATOONS	BATTLERS	BAWBLES	BAYS	BEADSMEN

The Chambers Dictionary is the authority for many longer words; see Introduction, page ix

BEADWORK*	BEARBERRIES*	BEATLESS*	BECARPET*	BECLOWNED*
BEADWORKS*	BEARBERRY*	BEATNIK	BECARPETED*	BECLOWNING*
BEADY	BEARBINE	BEATNIKS	BECARPETING*	BECLOWNS*
BEAGLE	BEARBINES	BEATS	BECARPETS*	BECOME
BEAGLED	BEARCAT*	BEAU	BECASSE	BECOMES
BEAGLER	BEARCATS*	BEAUCOUP*	BECASSES	BECOMING
BEAGLERS	BEARD	BEAUFET	BECAUSE	BECOMINGS*
BEAGLES	BEARDED	BEAUFETS	BECCACCIA	BECOWARD*
BEAGLING	BEARDIE	BEAUFFET	BECCACCIAS	BECOWARDED*
BEAGLINGS	BEARDIES	BEAUFFETS	BECCAFICO	BECOWARDING*
BEAK	BEARDING	BEAUFIN	BECCAFICOS	BECOWARDS*
BEAKED	BEARDLESS	BEAUFINS	BECHALK*	BECQUEREL
BEAKER	BEARDS	BEAUISH	BECHALKED*	BECQUERELS
BEAKERS	BEARE	BEAUS*	BECHALKING*	BECRAWL*
BEAKIER	BEARED	BEAUT	BECHALKS*	BECRAWLED*
BEAKIEST	BEARER	BEAUTEOUS	BECHAMEL	BECRAWLING*
BEAKLESS*	BEARERS	BEAUTIED	BECHAMELS	BECRAWLS*
BEAKLIKE*	BEARES	BEAUTIES	BECHANCE	BECRIME*
BEAKS	BEARHUG*	BEAUTIFIED	BECHANCED	BECRIMED*
BEAKY	BEARHUGS*	BEAUTIFIES	BECHANCES	BECRIMES*
BEAM	BEARING	BEAUTIFUL	BECHANCING	BECRIMING*
BEAMED	BEARINGS	BEAUTIFY	BECHARM	BECROWD*
BEAMER	BEARISH	BEAUTIFYING	BECHARMED	BECROWDED*
BEAMERS	BEARISHLY	BEAUTS	BECHARMING	BECROWDING*
BEAMIER	BEARLIKE*	BEAUTY	BECHARMS	BECROWDS*
BEAMIEST	BEARNAISE	BEAUTYING	BECK	BECRUST*
BEAMILY	BEARNAISES	BEAUX	BECKE	BECRUSTED*
BEAMINESS	BEARS	BEAUXITE	BECKED	BECRUSTING*
BEAMINESSES	BEARSKIN	BEAUXITES	BECKES	BECRUSTS*
BEAMING	BEARSKINS	BEAVER	BECKET	BECUDGEL*
BEAMINGLY	BEARWARD	BEAVERED	BECKETS	BECUDGELED*
BEAMINGS	BEARWARDS	BEAVERIES	BECKING	BECUDGELING*
BEAMISH	BEARWOOD*	BEAVERING*	BECKON	BECUDGELLED*
BEAMISHLY*	BEARWOODS*	BEAVERS	BECKONED	BECUDGELLING*
BEAMLESS	BEAST	BEAVERY	BECKONER*	BECUDGELS*
BEAMLET	BEASTHOOD	BEBEERINE	BECKONERS*	BECURL
BEAMLETS	BEASTHOODS	BEBEERINES	BECKONING	BECURLED
BEAMLIKE*	BEASTIE	BEBEERU	BECKONS	BECURLING
BEAMS	BEASTIES	BEBEERUS	BECKS	BECURLS
BEAMY	BEASTILY	BEBLOOD*	BECLAMOR*	BECURSE*
BEAN	BEASTINGS	BEBLOODED*	BECLAMORED*	BECURSED*
BEANBAG	BEASTLIER	BEBLOODING*	BECLAMORING*	BECURSES*
BEANBAGS	BEASTLIEST	BEBLOODS*	BECLAMORS*	BECURSING*
BEANBALL*	BEASTLIKE	BEBOP	BECLASP*	BECURST*
BEANBALLS*	BEASTLY	BEBOPPED	BECLASPED*	BED
BEANED	BEASTS	BEBOPPER*	BECLASPING*	BEDABBLE
BEANERIES	BEAT	BEBOPPERS*	BECLASPS*	BEDABBLED
BEANERY	BEATABLE	BEBOPPING	BECLOAK*	BEDABBLES
BEANFEAST	BEATEN	BEBOPS	BECLOAKED*	BEDABBLING
BEANFEASTS	BEATER	BEBUNG	BECLOAKING*	BEDAD
BEANIE	BEATERS	BEBUNGS	BECLOAKS*	BEDAGGLE
BEANIES	BEATH	BECALL	BECLOG*	BEDAGGLED
BEANING	BEATHED	BECALLED	BECLOGGED*	BEDAGGLES
BEANLIKE*	BEATHING	BECALLING	BECLOGGING*	BEDAGGLING
BEANO	BEATHS	BECALLS	BECLOGS*	BEDAMN*
BEANOS	BEATIFIC	BECALM	BECLOTHE*	BEDAMNED*
BEANPOLE	BEATIFIED	BECALMED	BECLOTHED*	BEDAMNING*
BEANPOLES	BEATIFIES	BECALMING	BECLOTHES*	BEDAMNS*
BEANS	BEATIFY	BECALMS	BECLOTHING*	BEDARKEN
BEANSTALK	BEATIFYING	BECAME	BECLOUD	BEDARKENED
BEANSTALKS	BEATING	BECAP*	BECLOUDED	BEDARKENING
BEAR	BEATINGS	BECAPPED*	BECLOUDING	BEDARKENS
BEARABLE	BEATITUDE	BECAPPING*	BECLOUDS	BEDASH
BEARABLY	BEATITUDES	BECAPS*	BECLOWN*	BEDASHED

BEDASHES	BEDFELLOWS	BEDRAPE*	BEDUCKS	BEEGAHS
BEDASHING	BEDFRAME*	BEDRAPED*	BEDUIN	BEEHIVE
BEDAUB	BEDFRAMES*	BEDRAPES*	BEDUINS	BEEHIVES
BEDAUBED	BEDGOWN*	BEDRAPING*	BEDUMB*	BEEKEEPER
BEDAUBING	BEDGOWNS*	BEDRENCH	BEDUMBED*	BEEKEEPERS
BEDAUBS	BEDIAPER*	BEDRENCHED	BEDUMBING*	BEELIKE*
BEDAWIN	BEDIAPERED*	BEDRENCHES	BEDUMBS*	BEELINE
BEDAWINS	BEDIAPERING*	BEDRENCHING	BEDUNCE*	BEELINED*
BEDAZE	BEDIAPERS*	BEDRID	BEDUNCED*	BEELINES
BEDAZED	BEDIDE	BEDRIDDEN	BEDUNCES*	BEELINING*
BEDAZES	BEDIGHT	BEDRIGHT	BEDUNCING*	BEEN
BEDAZING	BEDIGHTED*	BEDRIGHTS	BEDUNG	BEENAH
BEDAZZLE	BEDIGHTING	BEDRIVEL*	BEDUNGED	BEENAHS
BEDAZZLED	BEDIGHTS	BEDRIVELED*	BEDUNGING	BEEP
BEDAZZLES	BEDIM	BEDRIVELING*	BEDUNGS	BEEPED
BEDAZZLING	BEDIMMED	BEDRIVELLED*	BEDUST	BEEPER
BEDBUG	BEDIMMING	BEDRIVELLING*	BEDUSTED	BEEPERS
BEDBUGS	BEDIMMINGS	BEDRIVELS*	BEDUSTING	BEEPING
BEDCHAIR*	BEDIMPLE*	BEDROCK	BEDUSTS	BEEPS
BEDCHAIRS*	BEDIMPLED*	BEDROCKS	BEDWARD	BEER
BEDCOVER	BEDIMPLES*	BEDROLL*	BEDWARDS	BEERAGE
BEDCOVERS	BEDIMPLING*	BEDROLLS*	BEDWARF	BEERAGES
BEDDABLE	BEDIMS	BEDROOM	BEDWARFED	BEERHALL
BEDDED	BEDIRTIED*	BEDROOMED*	BEDWARFING	BEERHALLS
BEDDER	BEDIRTIES*	BEDROOMS	BEDWARFS	BEERIER
BEDDERS	BEDIRTY*	BEDROP	BEDYDE	BEERIEST
BEDDING	BEDIRTYING*	BEDROPPED	BEDYE	BEERINESS
BEDDINGS	BEDIZEN	BEDROPPING	BEDYED	BEERINESSES
BEDE	BEDIZENED	BEDROPS	BEDYEING	BEERS
BEDEAFEN	BEDIZENING	BEDROPT	BEDYES	BEERY
BEDEAFENED	BEDIZENS	BEDRUG*	BEE	BEES
BEDEAFENING	BEDLAM	BEDRUGGED*	BEEBEE*	BEESOME
BEDEAFENS	BEDLAMISM	BEDRUGGING*	BEEBEES*	BEESTINGS
BEDECK	BEDLAMISMS	BEDRUGS*	BEEBREAD*	BEESWAX
BEDECKED	BEDLAMITE	BEDS	BEEBREADS*	BEESWAXED
BEDECKING	BEDLAMITES	BEDSHEET*	BEECH	BEESWAXES
BEDECKS	BEDLAMP*	BEDSHEETS*	BEECHEN	BEESWAXING
BEDEGUAR	BEDLAMPS*	BEDSIDE	BEECHES	BEESWING
BEDEGUARS	BEDLAMS	BEDSIDES	BEECHIER*	BEESWINGS
BEDEL	BEDLESS*	BEDSIT*	BEECHIEST*	BEET
BEDELL	BEDLIKE*	BEDSITS*	BEECHNUT*	BEETED
BEDELLS	BEDMAKER	BEDSOCKS	BEECHNUTS*	BEETING
BEDELS	BEDMAKERS	BEDSONIA*	BEECHY*	BEETLE
BEDELSHIP	BEDMATE*	BEDSONIAS*	BEEF	BEETLED
BEDELSHIPS	BEDMATES*	BEDSORE	BEEFALO	BEETLER*
BEDEMAN	BEDOTTED*	BEDSORES	BEEFALOES	BEETLERS*
BEDEMEN	BEDOUIN	BEDSPREAD	BEEFALOS	BEETLES
BEDERAL	BEDOUINS	BEDSPREADS	BEEFCAKE	BEETLING
BEDERALS	BEDPAN	BEDSPRING*	BEEFCAKES	BEETROOT
BEDES	BEDPANS	BEDSPRINGS*	BEEFEATER	BEETROOTS
BEDESMAN	BEDPLATE*	BEDSTAND*	BEEFEATERS	BEETS
BEDESMEN	BEDPLATES*	BEDSTANDS*	BEEFED	BEEVES
BEDEVIL	BEDPOST	BEDSTEAD	BEEFIER	BEEYARD*
BEDEVILED*	BEDPOSTS	BEDSTEADS	BEEFIEST	BEEYARDS*
BEDEVILING*	BEDQUILT*	BEDSTRAW	BEEFILY*	BEEZER*
BEDEVILLED	BEDQUILTS*	BEDSTRAWS	BEEFING	BEEZERS*
BEDEVILLING	BEDRAGGLE	BEDTICK	BEEFLESS*	BEFALL
BEDEVILS	BEDRAGGLED	BEDTICKS	BEEFS	BEFALLEN
BEDEW	BEDRAGGLES	BEDTIME	BEEFSTEAK	BEFALLING
BEDEWED	BEDRAGGLING	BEDTIMES	BEEFSTEAKS	BEFALLS
BEDEWING	BEDRAIL*	BEDU*	BEEFWOOD*	BEFANA
BEDEWS	BEDRAILS*	BEDUCK	BEEFWOODS*	BEFANAS
BEDFAST	BEDRAL	BEDUCKED	BEEFY	BEFELD
BEDFELLOW	BEDRALS	BEDUCKING	BEEGAH	BEFELL

The Chambers Dictionary is the authority for many longer words; see Introduction, page ix

BEFFANA	BEFRINGES	BEGIRDLE*	BEGUINAGE	BEHOTES
BEFFANAS	BEFRINGING	BEGIRDLED*	BEGUINAGES	BEHOTING
BEFINGER*	BEFUDDLE	BEGIRDLES*	BEGUINE	BEHOVE
BEFINGERED*	BEFUDDLED	BEGIRDLING*	BEGUINES	BEHOVED
BEFINGERING*	BEFUDDLES	BEGIRDS	BEGUINS	BEHOVEFUL
BEFINGERS*	BEFUDDLING	BEGIRT	BEGULF*	BEHOVELY
BEFINNED	BEG	BEGLAD*	BEGULFED*	BEHOVES
BEFIT	BEGAD	BEGLADDED*	BEGULFING*	BEHOVING
BEFITS	BEGALL*	BEGLADDING*	BEGULFS*	BEHOWL
BEFITTED	BEGALLED*	BEGLADS*	BEGUM	BEHOWLED
BEFITTING	BEGALLING*	BEGLAMOR*	BEGUMS	BEHOWLS
BEFLAG*	BEGALLS*	BEGLAMORED*	BEGUN	BEIGE
BEFLAGGED*	BEGAN	BEGLAMORING*	BEGUNK	BEIGEL
BEFLAGGING*	BEGAR	BEGLAMORS*	BEGUNKED	BEIGELS
BEFLAGS*	BEGARS	BEGLAMOUR	BEGUNKING	BEIGES
BEFLEA*	BEGAT	BEGLAMOURED	BEGUNKS	BEIGNET
BEFLEAED*	BEGAZE*	BEGLAMOURING	BEHALF	BEIGNETS
BEFLEAING*	BEGAZED*	BEGLAMOURS	BEHALVES	BEIGY*
BEFLEAS*	BEGAZES*	BEGLERBEG	BEHAPPEN	BEIN
BEFLECK*	BEGAZING*	BEGLERBEGS	BEHAPPENED	BEING
BEFLECKED*	BEGEM	BEGLOOM	BEHAPPENING	BEINGLESS
BEFLECKING*	BEGEMMED	BEGLOOMED	BEHAPPENS	BEINGNESS
BEFLECKS*	BEGEMMING	BEGLOOMING	BEHATTED	BEINGNESSES
BEFLOWER	BEGEMS	BEGLOOMS	BEHAVE	BEINGS
BEFLOWERED	BEGET	BEGNAW	BEHAVED	BEINKED
BEFLOWERING	BEGETS	BEGNAWED	BEHAVER*	BEINNESS
BEFLOWERS	BEGETTER	BEGNAWING	BEHAVERS*	BEINNESSES
BEFLUM	BEGETTERS	BEGNAWS	BEHAVES	BEJABERS
BEFLUMMED	BEGETTING	BEGO	BEHAVING	BEJADE
BEFLUMMING	BEGGAR	BEGOES	BEHAVIOR	BEJADED
BEFLUMS	BEGGARDOM	BEGOING	BEHAVIORS	BEJADES
BEFOAM	BEGGARDOMS	BEGONE	BEHAVIOUR	BEJADING
BEFOAMED	BEGGARED	BEGONIA	BEHAVIOURS	BEJANT
BEFOAMING	BEGGARIES	BEGONIAS	BEHEAD	BEJANTS
BEFOAMS	BEGGARING	BEGORAH*	BEHEADAL	BEJEEZUS*
BEFOG	BEGGARLY	BEGORED	BEHEADALS	BEJESUIT
BEFOGGED	BEGGARS	BEGORRA	BEHEADED	BEJESUITED
BEFOGGING	BEGGARY	BEGORRAH	BEHEADING	BEJESUITING
BEFOGS	BEGGED	BEGOT	BEHEADINGS	BEJESUITS
BEFOOL	BEGGING	BEGOTTEN	BEHEADS	BEJESUS*
BEFOOLED	BEGGINGLY	BEGRIM*	BEHELD	BEJEWEL
BEFOOLING	BEGGINGS	BEGRIME	BEHEMOTH	BEJEWELED*
BEFOOLS	BEGHARD	BEGRIMED	BEHEMOTHS	BEJEWELING*
BEFORE	BEGHARDS	BEGRIMES	BEHEST	BEJEWELLED
BEFORTUNE	BEGIFT	BEGRIMING	BEHESTS	BEJEWELLING
BEFORTUNED	BEGIFTED	BEGRIMMED*	BEHIGHT	BEJEWELS
BEFORTUNES	BEGIFTING	BEGRIMMING*	BEHIGHTING	BEJUMBLE*
BEFORTUNING	BEGIFTS	BEGRIMS*	BEHIGHTS	BEJUMBLED*
BEFOUL	BEGILD	BEGROAN*	BEHIND	BEJUMBLES*
BEFOULED	BEGILDED	BEGROANED*	BEHINDS	BEJUMBLING*
BEFOULER*	BEGILDING	BEGROANING*	BEHOLD	BEKAH
BEFOULERS*	BEGILDS	BEGROANS*	BEHOLDEN	BEKAHS
BEFOULING	BEGILT	BEGRUDGE	BEHOLDER	BEKISS
BEFOULS	BEGIN	BEGRUDGED	BEHOLDERS	BEKISSED
BEFRET*	BEGINNE	BEGRUDGES	BEHOLDING	BEKISSES
BEFRETS*	BEGINNER	BEGRUDGING	BEHOLDINGS	BEKISSING
BEFRETTED*	BEGINNERS	BEGS	BEHOLDS	BEKNAVE
BEFRETTING*	BEGINNES	BEGUILE	BEHOOF	BEKNAVED
BEFRIEND	BEGINNING	BEGUILED	BEHOOFS	BEKNAVES
BEFRIENDED	BEGINNINGS	BEGUILER	BEHOOVE	BEKNAVING
BEFRIENDING	BEGINS	BEGUILERS	BEHOOVED	BEKNIGHT*
BEFRIENDS	BEGIRD	BEGUILES	BEHOOVES	BEKNIGHTED*
BEFRINGE	BEGIRDED	BEGUILING	BEHOOVING	BEKNIGHTING*
BEFRINGED	BEGIRDING	BEGUIN	BEHOTE	

BEKNIGHTS*	BELEES	BELLOWERS	BEMADDEN*	BEMONSTERED
BEKNOT*	BELEMNITE	BELLOWING	BEMADDENED*	BEMONSTERING
BEKNOTS*	BELEMNITES	BELLOWS	BEMADDENING*	BEMONSTERS
BEKNOTTED*	BELFRIED	BELLPULL*	BEMADDENS*	BEMOUTH
BEKNOTTING*	BELFRIES	BELLPULLS*	BEMADDING	BEMOUTHED
BEKNOWN	BELFRY	BELLPUSH	BEMADS	BEMOUTHING
BEL	BELGA	BELLPUSHES	BEMAS	BEMOUTHS
BELABOR	BELGARD	BELLS	BEMATA	BEMUD
BELABORED	BELGARDS	BELLWORT	BEMAUL	BEMUDDED
BELABORING	BELGAS	BELLWORTS	BEMAULED	BEMUDDING
BELABORS	BELIE	BELLY	BEMAULING	BEMUDDLE
BELABOUR	BELIED	BELLYACHE*	BEMAULS	BEMUDDLED
BELABOURED	BELIEF	BELLYACHED*	BEMAZED	BEMUDDLES
BELABOURING	BELIEFS	BELLYACHES*	BEMBEX	BEMUDDLING
BELABOURS	BELIER	BELLYACHING*	BEMBEXES	BEMUDS
BELACE	BELIERS	BELLYBAND*	BEMBIX	BEMUFFLE
BELACED	BELIES	BELLYBANDS*	BEMBIXES	BEMUFFLED
BELACES	BELIEVE	BELLYFUL	BEMEAN	BEMUFFLES
BELACING	BELIEVED	BELLYFULS	BEMEANED	BEMUFFLING
BELADIED*	BELIEVER	BELLYING	BEMEANING	BEMURMUR*
BELADIES*	BELIEVERS	BELLYINGS	BEMEANS	BEMURMURED*
BELADY*	BELIEVES	BELOMANCIES	BEMEANT	BEMURMURING*
BELADYING*	BELIEVING	BELOMANCY	BEMEDAL	BEMURMURS*
BELAH	BELIKE	BELONG	BEMEDALED*	BEMUSE
BELAHS	BELIQUOR*	BELONGED	BEMEDALLED	BEMUSED
BELAMIES	BELIQUORED*	BELONGER	BEMEDALLING	BEMUSEDLY*
BELAMOURE	BELIQUORING*	BELONGERS	BEMEDALS	BEMUSES
BELAMOURES	BELIQUORS*	BELONGING	BEMETE	BEMUSING
BELAMY	BELITTLE	BELONGINGS	BEMETED	BEMUZZLE*
BELATE	BELITTLED	BELONGS	BEMETES	BEMUZZLED*
BELATED	BELITTLER*	BELOVE	BEMETING	BEMUZZLES*
BELATEDLY	BELITTLERS*	BELOVED	BEMINGLE*	BEMUZZLING*
BELATES	BELITTLES	BELOVEDS	BEMINGLED*	BEN
BELATING	BELITTLING	BELOVES	BEMINGLES*	BENAME
BELAUD	BELIVE	BELOVING	BEMINGLING*	BENAMED
BELAUDED	BELL	BELOW	BEMIRE	BENAMES
BELAUDING	BELLBIND	BELOWS*	BEMIRED	BENAMING
BELAUDS	BELLBINDS	BELS	BEMIRES	BENCH
BELAY	BELLBIRD*	BELT	BEMIRING	BENCHED
BELAYED	BELLBIRDS*	BELTED	BEMIST*	BENCHER
BELAYING	BELLBOY*	BELTER	BEMISTED*	BENCHERS
BELAYS	BELLBOYS*	BELTERS	BEMISTING*	BENCHES
BELCH	BELLCOTE	BELTING	BEMISTS*	BENCHING
BELCHED	BELLCOTES	BELTINGS	BEMIX*	BENCHLAND*
BELCHER	BELLE	BELTLESS*	BEMIXED*	BENCHLANDS*
BELCHERS	BELLED	BELTLINE*	BEMIXES*	BENCHMARK
BELCHES	BELLEEK*	BELTLINES*	BEMIXING*	BENCHMARKS
BELCHING	BELLEEKS*	BELTMAN	BEMIXT*	BEND
BELDAM	BELLES	BELTMEN	BEMOAN	BENDABLE*
BELDAME	BELLETER	BELTS	BEMOANED	BENDAY*
BELDAMES	BELLETERS	BELTWAY	BEMOANER	BENDAYED*
BELDAMS	BELLHOP	BELTWAYS	BEMOANERS	BENDAYING*
BELEAGUER	BELLHOPS	BELUGA	BEMOANING	BENDAYS*
BELEAGUERED	BELLIBONE	BELUGAS	BEMOANINGS	BENDED
BELEAGUERING	BELLIBONES	BELVEDERE	BEMOANS	BENDEE
BELEAGUERS	BELLICOSE	BELVEDERES	BEMOCK	BENDEES*
BELEAP*	BELLIED	BELYING	BEMOCKED	BENDER
BELEAPED*	BELLIES	BEMA	BEMOCKING	BENDERS
BELEAPING*	BELLING	BEMAD	BEMOCKS	BENDIER
BELEAPS*	BELLMAN	BEMADAM*	BEMOIL	BENDIEST
BELEAPT*	BELLMEN	BEMADAMED*	BEMOILED	BENDING
BELEE	BELLOW	BEMADAMING*	BEMOILING	BENDINGLY
BELEED	BELLOWED	BEMADAMS*	BEMOILS	BENDINGS
BELEEING	BELLOWER	BEMADDED	BEMONSTER	BENDLET

BENDLETS	BENITIER	BENZYL	BEQUEATHS	BERGMEHL
BENDS	BENITIERS	BENZYLIC*	BEQUEST	BERGMEHLS
BENDWAYS*	BENJ	BENZYLS	BEQUESTS	BERGOMASK
BENDWISE	BENJAMIN	BEPAINT	BERAKE*	BERGOMASKS
BENDY	BENJAMINS	BEPAINTED	BERAKED*	BERGS
BENDYS*	BENJES	BEPAINTING	BERAKES*	BERGYLT
BENE	BENNE	BEPAINTS	BERAKING*	BERGYLTS
BENEATH	BENNES	BEPAT	BERASCAL*	BERHYME*
BENEDICK*	BENNET	BEPATCHED	BERASCALED*	BERHYMED*
BENEDICKS*	BENNETS	BEPATS	BERASCALING*	BERHYMES*
BENEDICT	BENNI	BEPATTED	BERASCALS*	BERHYMING*
BENEDICTS*	BENNIES	BEPATTING	BERATE	BERIBERI
BENEDIGHT	BENNIS	BEPEARL	BERATED	BERIBERIS
BENEFACT	BENNY	BEPEARLED	BERATES	BERIME*
BENEFACTED	BENOMYL*	BEPEARLING	BERATING	BERIMED*
BENEFACTING	BENOMYLS*	BEPEARLS	BERAY	BERIMES*
BENEFACTS	BENS	BEPELT	BERAYED	BERIMING*
BENEFIC	BENT	BEPELTED	BERAYING	BERINGED*
BENEFICE	BENTHAL*	BEPELTING	BERAYS	BERK
BENEFICED	BENTHIC	BEPELTS	BERBERIN*	BERKELIUM
BENEFICES	BENTHOAL	BEPEPPER	BERBERINE	BERKELIUMS
BENEFICING*	BENTHONIC	BEPEPPERED	BERBERINES	BERKS
BENEFIT	BENTHOS	BEPEPPERING	BERBERINS*	BERLEY
BENEFITED	BENTHOSES	BEPEPPERS	BERBERIS	BERLEYS
BENEFITER*	BENTIER	BEPESTER	BERBERISES	BERLIN
BENEFITERS*	BENTIEST	BEPESTERED	BERCEAU	BERLINE
BENEFITING	BENTONITE	BEPESTERING	BERCEAUX	BERLINES
BENEFITS	BENTONITES	BEPESTERS	BERCEUSE	BERLINS
BENEFITTED	BENTS	BEPIMPLE*	BERCEUSES	BERM
BENEFITTING	BENTWOOD	BEPIMPLED*	BERDACHE	BERME*
BENEMPT	BENTWOODS	BEPIMPLES*	BERDACHES	BERMES*
BENEMPTED*	BENTY	BEPIMPLING*	BERDASH	BERMS
BENES	BENUMB	BEPITIED	BERDASHES	BERMUDAS*
BENET	BENUMBED	BEPITIES	BERE	BERNICLE*
BENETS	BENUMBING	BEPITY	BEREAVE	BERNICLES*
BENETTED	BENUMBS	BEPITYING	BEREAVED	BEROB
BENETTING	BENZAL	BEPLASTER	BEREAVEN	BEROBBED
BENGALINE	BENZALS	BEPLASTERED	BEREAVER*	BEROBBING
BENGALINES	BENZENE	BEPLASTERING	BEREAVERS*	BEROBED*
BENI	BENZENES	BEPLASTERS	BEREAVES	BEROBS
BENIGHT	BENZENOID*	BEPLUMED	BEREAVING	BEROUGED*
BENIGHTED	BENZIDIN*	BEPOMMEL	BEREFT	BERRET
BENIGHTEN	BENZIDINE	BEPOMMELLED	BERES	BERRETS
BENIGHTENED	BENZIDINES	BEPOMMELLING	BERET	BERRETTA*
BENIGHTENING	BENZIDINS*	BEPOMMELS	BERETS	BERRETTAS*
BENIGHTENINGS	BENZIL	BEPOWDER	BERETTA*	BERRIED
BENIGHTENS	BENZILS	BEPOWDERED	BERETTAS*	BERRIES
BENIGHTER	BENZIN*	BEPOWDERING	BERG	BERRY
BENIGHTERS	BENZINE	BEPOWDERS	BERGAMA	BERRYING
BENIGHTING	BENZINES	BEPRAISE	BERGAMAS	BERRYINGS
BENIGHTINGS	BENZINS*	BEPRAISED	BERGAMASK	BERRYLIKE*
BENIGHTS	BENZOATE	BEPRAISES	BERGAMASKS	BERSEEM*
BENIGN	BENZOATES	BEPRAISING	BERGAMOT	BERSEEMS*
BENIGNANT	BENZOIC	BEPROSE	BERGAMOTS	BERSERK
BENIGNER	BENZOIN	BEPROSED	BERGANDER	BERSERKER
BENIGNEST	BENZOINS	BEPROSES	BERGANDERS	BERSERKERS
BENIGNITIES	BENZOL	BEPROSING	BERGENIA	BERSERKLY
BENIGNITY	BENZOLE	BEPUFF	BERGENIAS	BERSERKS
BENIGNLY	BENZOLES	BEPUFFED	BERGERE	BERTH
BENIS	BENZOLINE	BEPUFFING	BERGERES	BERTHA
BENISEED	BENZOLINES	BEPUFFS	BERGFALL	BERTHAGE
BENISEEDS	BENZOLS	BEQUEATH	BERGFALLS	BERTHAGES
BENISON	BENZOYL	BEQUEATHED	BERGHAAN	BERTHAS
BENISONS	BENZOYLS	BEQUEATHING	BERGHAANS	BERTHE

BERTHED	BESETTING	BESLUBBER	BESPAKE	BESTEADING
BERTHES	BESHADOW	BESLUBBERED	BESPANGLE	BESTEADS
BERTHING	BESHADOWED	BESLUBBERING	BESPANGLED	BESTED
BERTHS	BESHADOWING	BESLUBBERS	BESPANGLES	BESTIAL
BERYL	BESHADOWS	BESMEAR	BESPANGLING	BESTIALLY*
BERYLINE*	BESHAME	BESMEARED	BESPAT	BESTIALS
BERYLLIA	BESHAMED	BESMEARING	BESPATE	BESTIARIES
BERYLLIAS	BESHAMES	BESMEARS	BESPATTER	BESTIARY
BERYLLIUM	BESHAMING	BESMILE*	BESPATTERED	BESTICK
BERYLLIUMS	BESHINE	BESMILED*	BESPATTERING	BESTICKING
BERYLS	BESHINES	BESMILES*	BESPATTERS	BESTICKS
BESAINT	BESHINING	BESMILING*	BESPEAK	BESTILL
BESAINTED	BESHIVER*	BESMIRCH	BESPEAKING	BESTILLED
BESAINTING	BESHIVERED*	BESMIRCHED	BESPEAKS	BESTILLING
BESAINTS	BESHIVERING*	BESMIRCHES	BESPECKLE	BESTILLS
BESANG	BESHIVERS*	BESMIRCHING	BESPECKLED	BESTING
BESAT	BESHONE	BESMOKE*	BESPECKLES	BESTIR
BESAW	BESHOUT*	BESMOKED*	BESPECKLING	BESTIRRED
BESCATTER	BESHOUTED*	BESMOKES*	BESPED	BESTIRRING
BESCATTERED	BESHOUTING*	BESMOKING*	BESPEED	BESTIRS
BESCATTERING	BESHOUTS*	BESMOOTH*	BESPEEDING	BESTORM
BESCATTERS	BESHREW	BESMOOTHED*	BESPEEDS	BESTORMED
BESCORCH*	BESHREWED	BESMOOTHING*	BESPICE	BESTORMING
BESCORCHED*	BESHREWING	BESMOOTHS*	BESPICED	BESTORMS
BESCORCHES*	BESHREWS	BESMUDGE*	BESPICES	BESTOW
BESCORCHING*	BESHROUD*	BESMUDGED*	BESPICING	BESTOWAL
BESCOUR*	BESHROUDED*	BESMUDGES*	BESPIT	BESTOWALS
BESCOURED*	BESHROUDING*	BESMUDGING*	BESPITS	BESTOWED
BESCOURING*	BESHROUDS*	BESMUT	BESPITTING	BESTOWER
BESCOURS*	BESIDE	BESMUTCH	BESPOKE	BESTOWERS
BESCRAWL	BESIDES	BESMUTCHED	BESPOKEN	BESTOWING
BESCRAWLED	BESIEGE	BESMUTCHES	BESPORT	BESTOWS
BESCRAWLING	BESIEGED	BESMUTCHING	BESPORTED	BESTREAK
BESCRAWLS	BESIEGER	BESMUTS	BESPORTING	BESTREAKED
BESCREEN	BESIEGERS	BESMUTTED	BESPORTS	BESTREAKING
BESCREENED	BESIEGES	BESMUTTING	BESPOT	BESTREAKS
BESCREENING	BESIEGING	BESNOW*	BESPOTS	BESTREW
BESCREENS	BESIEGINGS	BESNOWED*	BESPOTTED	BESTREWED
BESEE	BESIGH	BESNOWING*	BESPOTTING	BESTREWING
BESEECH	BESIGHED	BESNOWS*	BESPOUSE*	BESTREWN
BESEECHED	BESIGHING	BESOGNIO	BESPOUSED*	BESTREWS
BESEECHER	BESIGHS	BESOGNIOS	BESPOUSES*	BESTRID
BESEECHERS	BESING	BESOIN	BESPOUSING*	BESTRIDDEN
BESEECHES	BESINGING	BESOINS	BESPOUT	BESTRIDE
BESEECHING	BESINGS	BESOM	BESPOUTED	BESTRIDES
BESEECHINGS	BESIT	BESOMED	BESPOUTING	BESTRIDING
BESEEING	BESITS	BESOMING	BESPOUTS	BESTRODE
BESEEKE	BESITTING	BESOMS	BESPREAD	BESTROW*
BESEEKES	BESLAVE	BESONIAN	BESPREADING	BESTROWED*
BESEEKING	BESLAVED	BESONIANS	BESPREADS	BESTROWING*
BESEEM	BESLAVER	BESOOTHE*	BESPRENT	BESTROWN
BESEEMED	BESLAVERED	BESOOTHED*	BEST	BESTROWS*
BESEEMING	BESLAVERING	BESOOTHES*	BESTAD	BESTS
BESEEMINGS	BESLAVERS	BESOOTHING*	BESTADDE	BESTUCK
BESEEMLY	BESLAVES	BESORT	BESTAIN	BESTUD
BESEEMS	BESLAVING	BESORTED	BESTAINED	BESTUDDED
BESEEN	BESLIME*	BESORTING	BESTAINING	BESTUDDING
BESEES	BESLIMED*	BESORTS	BESTAINS	BESTUDS
BESET	BESLIMES*	BESOT	BESTAR	BESUITED
BESETMENT	BESLIMING*	BESOTS	BESTARRED	BESUNG
BESETMENTS	BESLOBBER	BESOTTED	BESTARRING	BESWARM*
BESETS	BESLOBBERED	BESOTTING	BESTARS	BESWARMED*
BESETTER	BESLOBBERING	BESOUGHT	BESTEAD	BESWARMING*
BESETTERS	BESLOBBERS	BESOULED	BESTEADED	BESWARMS*

The Chambers Dictionary is the authority for many longer words; see Introduction, page ix

BET	BETHWACKED	BETTED	BEWEARY*	BEZILS*
BETA	BETHWACKING	BETTER	BEWEARYING*	BEZIQUE
BETACISM	BETHWACKS	BETTERED	BEWEEP	BEZIQUES
BETACISMS	BETID	BETTERING	BEWEEPING	BEZOAR
BETAINE	BETIDE	BETTERINGS	BEWEEPS	BEZOARDIC
BETAINES	BETIDED	BETTERS	BEWENT	BEZOARS
BETAKE	BETIDES	BETTIES	BEWEPT	BEZONIAN
BETAKEN	BETIDING	BETTING	BEWET	BEZONIANS
BETAKES	BETIGHT	BETTINGS	BEWETS	BEZZANT*
BETAKING	BETIME	BETTOR	BEWETTED	BEZZANTS*
BETAS	BETIMED	BETTORS	BEWETTING	BEZZLE
BETATRON	BETIMES	BETTY	BEWHORE	BEZZLED
BETATRONS	BETIMING	BETUMBLED	BEWHORED	BEZZLES
BETATTER*	BETING	BETWEEN	BEWHORES	BEZZLING
BETATTERED*	BETISE	BETWEENS	BEWHORING	BHAGEE
BETATTERING*	BETISES	BETWIXT	BEWIG	BHAGEES
BETATTERS*	BETITLE	BEUNCLED*	BEWIGGED	BHAJAN
BETAXED*	BETITLED	BEURRE	BEWIGGING	BHAJANS
BETE	BETITLES	BEURRES	BEWIGS	BHAJEE
BETED	BETITLING	BEVATRON	BEWILDER	BHAJEES
BETEEM	BETOIL	BEVATRONS	BEWILDERED	BHAKTA*
BETEEME	BETOILED	BEVEL	BEWILDERING	BHAKTAS*
BETEEMED	BETOILING	BEVELED*	BEWILDERS	BHAKTI
BETEEMES	BETOILS	BEVELER*	BEWINGED*	BHAKTIS
BETEEMING	BETOKEN	BEVELERS*	BEWITCH	BHANG
BETEEMS	BETOKENED	BEVELING*	BEWITCHED	BHANGRA
BETEL	BETOKENING	BEVELLED	BEWITCHES	BHANGRAS
BETELNUT*	BETOKENS	BEVELLER	BEWITCHING	BHANGS
BETELNUTS*	BETON	BEVELLERS	BEWORM*	BHARAL
BETELS	BETONIES	BEVELLING	BEWORMED*	BHARALS
BETES	BETONS	BEVELLINGS	BEWORMING*	BHEESTIE
BETH	BETONY	BEVELMENT	BEWORMS*	BHEESTIES
BETHANK*	BETOOK	BEVELMENTS	BEWORRIED*	BHEESTY
BETHANKED*	BETOSS	BEVELS	BEWORRIES*	BHEL
BETHANKING*	BETOSSED	BEVER	BEWORRY*	BHELS
BETHANKIT	BETOSSES	BEVERAGE	BEWORRYING*	BHINDI
BETHANKITS	BETOSSING	BEVERAGES	BEWRAP*	BHINDIS
BETHANKS*	BETRAY	BEVERS	BEWRAPPED*	BHISTEE
BETHEL	BETRAYAL	BEVIES	BEWRAPPING*	BHISTEES
BETHELS	BETRAYALS	BEVOMIT*	BEWRAPS*	BHISTI
BETHESDA	BETRAYED	BEVOMITED*	BEWRAPT*	BHISTIE*
BETHESDAS	BETRAYER	BEVOMITING*	BEWRAY	BHISTIES*
BETHINK	BETRAYERS	BEVOMITS*	BEWRAYED	BHISTIS
BETHINKING	BETRAYING	BEVOR*	BEWRAYER*	BHOOT*
BETHINKS	BETRAYS	BEVORS*	BEWRAYERS*	BHOOTS*
BETHORN*	BETREAD	BEVUE	BEWRAYING	BHUT*
BETHORNED*	BETREADING	BEVUES	BEWRAYS	BHUTS*
BETHORNING*	BETREADS	BEVVIED	BEY	BI
BETHORNS*	BETRIM	BEVVIES	BEYLIC*	BIACETYL*
BETHOUGHT	BETRIMMED	BEVVY	BEYLICS*	BIACETYLS*
BETHRALL	BETRIMMING	BEWAIL	BEYLIK*	BIALI*
BETHRALLED	BETRIMS	BEWAILED	BEYLIKS*	BIALIS*
BETHRALLING	BETROD	BEWAILER*	BEYOND	BIALY*
BETHRALLS	BETRODDEN	BEWAILERS*	BEYONDS	BIALYS*
BETHS	BETROTH	BEWAILING	BEYS	BIANNUAL
BETHUMB	BETROTHAL	BEWAILINGS	BEZ	BIANNUALS
BETHUMBED	BETROTHALS	BEWAILS	BEZANT	BIAS
BETHUMBING	BETROTHED	BEWARE	BEZANTS	BIASED
BETHUMBS	BETROTHEDS	BEWARED	BEZAZZ	BIASEDLY*
BETHUMP	BETROTHING	BEWARES	BEZAZZES	BIASES
BETHUMPED	BETROTHS	BEWARING	BEZEL	BIASING
BETHUMPING	BETS	BEWEARIED*	BEZELS	BIASINGS
BETHUMPS	BETTA*	BEWEARIES*	BEZES	BIASNESS*
BETHWACK	BETTAS*		BEZIL*	BIASNESSES*

Words marked with an asterisk are from OTCWL

BIASSED	BICOLOUR*	BIENNIALS	BIGGETY*	BIKINIS
BIASSES	BICOLOURS*	BIENNIUM*	BIGGIE	BILABIAL
BIASSING	BICONCAVE	BIENNIUMS*	BIGGIES	BILABIALS
BIATHLETE	BICONVEX	BIER	BIGGIN	BILABIATE
BIATHLETES	BICORN	BIERS	BIGGING	BILANDER
BIATHLON	BICORNE	BIESTINGS	BIGGINGS*	BILANDERS
BIATHLONS	BICORNES	BIFACE*	BIGGINS	BILATERAL
BIAXAL	BICORNS	BIFACES*	BIGGISH	BILAYER*
BIAXIAL	BICRON*	BIFACIAL	BIGGITY*	BILAYERS*
BIAXIALLY*	BICRONS*	BIFARIOUS	BIGGS	BILBERRIES
BIB	BICUSPID	BIFF	BIGGY	BILBERRY
BIBACIOUS	BICUSPIDS	BIFFED	BIGHA	BILBO
BIBASIC*	BICYCLE	BIFFIES*	BIGHAS	BILBOA*
BIBATION	BICYCLED	BIFFIN	BIGHEAD*	BILBOAS*
BIBATIONS	BICYCLER*	BIFFING	BIGHEADED	BILBOES
BIBB*	BICYCLERS*	BIFFINS	BIGHEADS*	BILBOS
BIBBED	BICYCLES	BIFFS	BIGHORN	BILE
BIBBER	BICYCLIC*	BIFFY*	BIGHORNS	BILES
BIBBERIES*	BICYCLING	BIFID	BIGHT	BILGE
BIBBERS	BICYCLIST	BIFIDITIES*	BIGHTED*	BILGED
BIBBERY*	BICYCLISTS	BIFIDITY*	BIGHTING*	BILGES
BIBBING	BID	BIFIDLY*	BIGHTS	BILGIER
BIBBS*	BIDARKA	BIFILAR	BIGLY*	BILGIEST
BIBCOCK	BIDARKAS	BIFILARLY*	BIGMOUTH	BILGING
BIBCOCKS	BIDARKEE*	BIFLEX*	BIGMOUTHS	BILGY
BIBELOT	BIDARKEES*	BIFOCAL	BIGNESS	BILHARZIA
BIBELOTS	BIDDABLE	BIFOCALS	BIGNESSES	BILHARZIAS
BIBLE	BIDDABLY*	BIFOLD	BIGNONIA	BILIAN
BIBLES	BIDDEN	BIFOLIATE	BIGNONIAS	BILIANS
BIBLESS*	BIDDER	BIFORATE*	BIGOT	BILIARIES
BIBLICAL	BIDDERS	BIFORKED*	BIGOTED	BILIARY
BIBLICISM	BIDDIES	BIFORM	BIGOTEDLY*	BILIMBI
BIBLICISMS	BIDDING	BIFORMED*	BIGOTRIES	BILIMBING
BIBLICIST	BIDDINGS	BIFURCATE	BIGOTRY	BILIMBINGS
BIBLICISTS	BIDDY	BIFURCATED	BIGOTS	BILIMBIS
BIBLIKE*	BIDE	BIFURCATES	BIGS	BILINEAR*
BIBLIOTIC*	BIDED	BIFURCATING	BIGUANIDE	BILINGUAL
BIBLIST	BIDENT	BIG	BIGUANIDES	BILINGUALS*
BIBLISTS	BIDENTAL	BIGA	BIGWIG	BILIOUS
BIBS	BIDENTALS	BIGAE	BIGWIGS	BILIOUSLY
BIBULOUS	BIDENTATE	BIGAMIES	BIHOURLY*	BILIRUBIN
BICAMERAL	BIDENTS	BIGAMIST	BIJECTION	BILIRUBINS
BICARB	BIDER*	BIGAMISTS	BIJECTIONS	BILITERAL
BICARBS	BIDERS*	BIGAMOUS	BIJECTIVE*	BILK
BICAUDAL*	BIDES	BIGAMY	BIJOU	BILKED
BICCIES	BIDET	BIGARADE	BIJOUS*	BILKER
BICCY	BIDETS	BIGARADES	BIJOUX	BILKERS
BICE	BIDING	BIGAROON*	BIJUGATE*	BILKING
BICEPS	BIDINGS	BIGAROONS*	BIJUGOUS*	BILKS
BICEPSES	BIDON	BIGEMINAL*	BIJWONER	BILL
BICES	BIDONS	BIGEMINIES*	BIJWONERS	BILLABLE*
BICHORD	BIDS	BIGEMINY*	BIKE	BILLABONG
BICHROME*	BIELD	BIGENER	BIKED	BILLABONGS
BICIPITAL	BIELDED	BIGENERIC	BIKER	BILLBOARD
BICKER	BIELDIER	BIGENERS	BIKERS	BILLBOARDED*
BICKERED	BIELDIEST	BIGEYE*	BIKES	BILLBOARDING*
BICKERER*	BIELDING	BIGEYES*	BIKEWAY	BILLBOARDS
BICKERERS*	BIELDS	BIGFEET	BIKEWAYS	BILLBOOK
BICKERING	BIELDY	BIGFOOT	BIKIE	BILLBOOKS
BICKERS	BIEN	BIGFOOTS*	BIKIES	BILLBUG*
BICOASTAL	BIENNALE*	BIGG	BIKING	BILLBUGS*
BICOLOR*	BIENNALES*	BIGGED	BIKINGS	BILLED
BICOLORED*	BIENNIA*	BIGGER	BIKINI	BILLER*
BICOLORS*	BIENNIAL	BIGGEST	BIKINIED*	BILLERS*

BILLET	BIMBOES*	BINMEN	BIOLOGISTS	BIOTICAL*
BILLETED	BIMBOS	BINNACLE	BIOLOGY	BIOTICS*
BILLETER*	BIMENSAL*	BINNACLES	BIOLYSES	BIOTIN
BILLETERS*	BIMESTER*	BINNED	BIOLYSIS	BIOTINS
BILLETING	BIMESTERS*	BINNING	BIOLYTIC*	BIOTITE
BILLETS	BIMETAL*	BINOCLE	BIOMASS	BIOTITES
BILLFISH*	BIMETALS*	BINOCLES	BIOMASSES	BIOTITIC*
BILLFISHES*	BIMETHYL*	BINOCS*	BIOME	BIOTOPE
BILLFOLD	BIMETHYLS*	BINOCULAR	BIOMES	BIOTOPES
BILLFOLDS	BIMODAL	BINOCULARS	BIOMETRIC	BIOTOXIN*
BILLHEAD	BIMONTHLIES*	BINOMIAL	BIOMETRICS	BIOTOXINS*
BILLHEADS	BIMONTHLY	BINOMIALS	BIOMETRIES	BIOTRON*
BILLHOOK	BIMORPH*	BINOMINAL	BIOMETRY	BIOTRONS*
BILLHOOKS	BIMORPHS*	BINS	BIOMINING	BIOTYPE
BILLIARD	BIN	BINT	BIOMININGS	BIOTYPES
BILLIARDS	BINAL*	BINTS	BIOMORPH	BIOTYPIC*
BILLIE	BINARIES	BINTURONG	BIOMORPHS	BIOVULAR*
BILLIES	BINARY	BINTURONGS	BIONIC	BIPACK*
BILLING	BINATE	BIO	BIONICS	BIPACKS*
BILLINGS	BINATELY*	BIOACTIVE*	BIONOMIC	BIPAROUS
BILLION	BINAURAL	BIOASSAY	BIONOMICS	BIPARTED*
BILLIONS	BIND	BIOASSAYED*	BIONOMIES*	BIPARTITE
BILLIONTH	BINDABLE*	BIOASSAYING*	BIONOMY*	BIPARTY*
BILLIONTHS	BINDER	BIOASSAYS	BIONT	BIPED
BILLMAN	BINDERIES	BIOBLAST	BIONTIC	BIPEDAL
BILLMEN	BINDERS	BIOBLASTS	BIONTS	BIPEDALLY*
BILLON	BINDERY	BIOCHIP*	BIOPARENT	BIPEDS
BILLONS	BINDI*	BIOCHIPS*	BIOPARENTS	BIPHASIC
BILLOW	BINDING	BIOCIDAL	BIOPHOR	BIPHENYL
BILLOWED	BINDINGLY*	BIOCIDE	BIOPHORE	BIPHENYLS
BILLOWIER	BINDINGS	BIOCIDES	BIOPHORES	BIPINNATE
BILLOWIEST	BINDIS*	BIOCLEAN*	BIOPHORS	BIPLANE
BILLOWING	BINDLE*	BIOCYCLE*	BIOPIC	BIPLANES
BILLOWS	BINDLES*	BIOCYCLES*	BIOPICS	BIPOD
BILLOWY	BINDS	BIODATA	BIOPLASM	BIPODS
BILLS	BINDWEED	BIOETHIC*	BIOPLASMS	BIPOLAR
BILLY	BINDWEEDS	BIOETHICS	BIOPLAST	BIPYRAMID
BILLYBOY	BINE	BIOG	BIOPLASTS	BIPYRAMIDS
BILLYBOYS	BINERVATE	BIOGAS	BIOPSIC*	BIRACIAL*
BILLYCAN*	BINES	BIOGASES	BIOPSIED*	BIRADIAL*
BILLYCANS*	BING	BIOGASSES*	BIOPSIES	BIRAMOSE*
BILLYCOCK	BINGE	BIOGEN	BIOPSY	BIRAMOUS
BILLYCOCKS	BINGED	BIOGENIC	BIOPSYING*	BIRCH
BILOBAR	BINGEING	BIOGENIES	BIOPTIC*	BIRCHED
BILOBATE	BINGER	BIOGENOUS	BIORHYTHM*	BIRCHEN
BILOBED	BINGERS	BIOGENS	BIORHYTHMS*	BIRCHES
BILOBULAR	BINGES	BIOGENY	BIOS	BIRCHING
BILOCULAR	BINGHI	BIOGRAPH	BIOSAFETIES*	BIRD
BILSTED*	BINGHIS	BIOGRAPHED	BIOSAFETY*	BIRDBATH
BILSTEDS*	BINGIES	BIOGRAPHIES	BIOSCOPE	BIRDBATHS
BILTONG	BINGING	BIOGRAPHING	BIOSCOPES	BIRDBRAIN*
BILTONGS	BINGLE	BIOGRAPHS	BIOSCOPIES*	BIRDBRAINS*
BIMA*	BINGLED	BIOGRAPHY	BIOSCOPY*	BIRDCAGE
BIMAH*	BINGLES	BIOGS	BIOSENSOR	BIRDCAGES
BIMAHS*	BINGLING	BIOHAZARD	BIOSENSORS	BIRDCALL
BIMANAL	BINGO	BIOHAZARDS	BIOSOCIAL*	BIRDCALLS
BIMANOUS	BINGOS	BIOHERM*	BIOSPHERE	BIRDED
BIMANUAL	BINGS	BIOHERMS*	BIOSPHERES	BIRDER
BIMAS*	BINGY	BIOLOGIC*	BIOSTABLE	BIRDERS
BIMBASHI	BINIT*	BIOLOGICS*	BIOTA	BIRDFARM*
BIMBASHIS	BINITS*	BIOLOGIES	BIOTAS	BIRDFARMS*
BIMBETTE	BINK	BIOLOGISM*	BIOTECH*	BIRDHOUSE*
BIMBETTES	BINKS	BIOLOGISMS*	BIOTECHS*	BIRDHOUSES*
BIMBO	BINMAN	BIOLOGIST	BIOTIC	BIRDIE

BIRDIED	BIRSY	BISONTINE*	BITTE	BIZARRE
BIRDIEING	BIRTH	BISQUE	BITTED	BIZARRELY*
BIRDIES	BIRTHDAY	BISQUES	BITTEN	BIZARRES*
BIRDING	BIRTHDAYS	BISSON	BITTER	BIZAZZ
BIRDINGS	BIRTHDOM	BISTABLE	BITTERED*	BIZAZZES
BIRDLIKE	BIRTHDOMS	BISTATE*	BITTERER	BIZCACHA
BIRDLIME*	BIRTHED	BISTER	BITTEREST	BIZCACHAS
BIRDLIMED*	BIRTHING	BISTERED*	BITTERING*	BIZE*
BIRDLIMES*	BIRTHINGS	BISTERS	BITTERISH	BIZES*
BIRDLIMING*	BIRTHMARK	BISTORT	BITTERLY	BIZNAGA*
BIRDMAN	BIRTHMARKS	BISTORTS	BITTERN	BIZNAGAS*
BIRDMEN	BIRTHRATE*	BISTOURIES	BITTERNS	BIZONAL
BIRDS	BIRTHRATES*	BISTOURY	BITTERS	BIZONE
BIRDSEED	BIRTHROOT*	BISTRE	BITTIE	BIZONES
BIRDSEEDS	BIRTHROOTS*	BISTRED	BITTIER	BIZZES
BIRDSEYE*	BIRTHS	BISTRES	BITTIES	BLAB
BIRDSEYES*	BIRTHWORT	BISTRO	BITTIEST	BLABBED
BIRDSHOT	BIRTHWORTS	BISTROIC*	BITTING	BLABBER
BIRDSHOTS	BIRYANI	BISTROS	BITTINGS*	BLABBERED*
BIRDSONG	BIRYANIS	BISULCATE	BITTOCK	BLABBERING*
BIRDSONGS	BIS	BISULFATE*	BITTOCKS	BLABBERS
BIRDWING	BISCACHA	BISULFATES*	BITTOR	BLABBING
BIRDWINGS	BISCACHAS	BISULFIDE*	BITTORS	BLABBINGS
BIREME	BISCUIT	BISULFIDES*	BITTOUR	BLABBY*
BIREMES	BISCUITS	BISULFITE*	BITTOURS	BLABS
BIRETTA	BISCUITY	BISULFITES*	BITTS	BLACK
BIRETTAS	BISE	BIT	BITTUR	BLACKBALL
BIRIYANI	BISECT	BITABLE*	BITTURS	BLACKBALLED
BIRIYANIS	BISECTED	BITCH	BITTY	BLACKBALLING
BIRK	BISECTING	BITCHED	BITUMED	BLACKBALLINGS
BIRKEN	BISECTION	BITCHERIES	BITUMEN	BLACKBALLS
BIRKIE	BISECTIONS	BITCHERY	BITUMENS	BLACKBAND
BIRKIER	BISECTOR	BITCHES	BIUNIQUE*	BLACKBANDS
BIRKIES	BISECTORS	BITCHIER	BIVALENCE	BLACKBIRD
BIRKIEST	BISECTS	BITCHIEST	BIVALENCES	BLACKBIRDED*
BIRKS	BISERIAL	BITCHILY	BIVALENCIES	BLACKBIRDING*
BIRL	BISERRATE	BITCHING	BIVALENCY	BLACKBIRDS
BIRLE	BISES	BITCHY	BIVALENT	BLACKBODIES*
BIRLED	BISEXUAL	BITE	BIVALENTS	BLACKBODY*
BIRLER	BISEXUALS	BITEABLE*	BIVALVE	BLACKBOY
BIRLERS	BISH	BITER	BIVALVED*	BLACKBOYS
BIRLES	BISHES	BITERS	BIVALVES	BLACKBUCK
BIRLIEMAN	BISHOP	BITES	BIVARIANT	BLACKBUCKS
BIRLIEMEN	BISHOPDOM	BITESIZE	BIVARIANTS	BLACKCAP
BIRLING	BISHOPDOMS	BITEWING*	BIVARIATE	BLACKCAPS
BIRLINGS	BISHOPED	BITEWINGS*	BIVARIATES	BLACKCOCK
BIRLINN	BISHOPESS	BITING	BIVIA	BLACKCOCKS
BIRLINNS	BISHOPESSES	BITINGLY*	BIVINYL*	BLACKED
BIRLS	BISHOPING	BITINGS	BIVINYLS*	BLACKEN
BIRR	BISHOPRIC	BITLESS	BIVIOUS	BLACKENED
BIRRED	BISHOPRICS	BITMAP	BIVIUM	BLACKENER*
BIRRETTA*	BISHOPS	BITMAPS	BIVOUAC	BLACKENERS*
BIRRETTAS*	BISK	BITO	BIVOUACKED	BLACKENING
BIRRING	BISKS	BITONAL	BIVOUACKING	BLACKENS
BIRROTCH*	BISMAR	BITOS	BIVOUACKS*	BLACKER
BIRRS	BISMARS	BITS	BIVOUACS	BLACKEST
BIRSE	BISMILLAH	BITSIER	BIVVIED	BLACKFACE
BIRSES	BISMUTH	BITSIEST	BIVVIES	BLACKFACES
BIRSIER	BISMUTHIC*	BITSTOCK*	BIVVY	BLACKFIN*
BIRSIEST	BISMUTHS	BITSTOCKS*	BIVVYING	BLACKFINS*
BIRSLE	BISNAGA*	BITSY	BIWEEKLIES*	BLACKFISH
BIRSLED	BISNAGAS*	BITT	BIWEEKLY*	BLACKFISHES
BIRSLES	BISON	BITTACLE	BIYEARLY*	BLACKFLIES*
BIRSLING	BISONS	BITTACLES	BIZ	BLACKFLY*

BLACKGAME BLAEBERRY BLANKETING BLATANCIES* BLEAK
BLACKGAMES BLAER BLANKETINGS BLATANCY* BLEAKER
BLACKGUM* BLAES BLANKETS BLATANT BLEAKEST
BLACKGUMS* BLAEST BLANKETY BLATANTLY BLEAKISH*
BLACKHEAD BLAG BLANKIES BLATE BLEAKLY
BLACKHEADS BLAGGED BLANKING BLATER BLEAKNESS
BLACKING BLAGGER BLANKINGS BLATEST BLEAKNESSES
BLACKINGS BLAGGERS BLANKLY BLATHER BLEAKS
BLACKISH BLAGGING BLANKNESS BLATHERED BLEAKY
BLACKJACK BLAGS BLANKNESSES BLATHERER BLEAR
BLACKJACKED BLAGUE BLANKS BLATHERERS BLEARED
BLACKJACKING BLAGUES BLANKY BLATHERING BLEARER
BLACKJACKS BLAGUEUR BLANQUET BLATHERS BLEAREST
BLACKLAND* BLAGUEURS BLANQUETS BLATS BLEAREYED
BLACKLANDS* BLAH BLARE BLATT BLEARIER
BLACKLEAD BLAHED BLARED BLATTANT BLEARIEST
BLACKLEADS BLAHING BLARES BLATTED BLEARILY
BLACKLEG BLAHS BLARING BLATTER BLEARING
BLACKLEGGED BLAIN BLARNEY BLATTERED BLEARS
BLACKLEGGING BLAINS BLARNEYED BLATTERING BLEARY
BLACKLEGS BLAISE BLARNEYING BLATTERS BLEAT
BLACKLIST BLAIZE BLARNEYS BLATTING BLEATED
BLACKLISTED BLAM* BLASE BLATTS BLEATER
BLACKLISTING BLAMABLE BLASH BLAUBOK BLEATERS
BLACKLISTINGS BLAMABLY BLASHES BLAUBOKS BLEATING
BLACKLISTS BLAME BLASHIER BLAUD BLEATINGS
BLACKLY BLAMEABLE BLASHIEST BLAUDED BLEATS
BLACKMAIL BLAMEABLY BLASHY BLAUDING BLEB
BLACKMAILED BLAMED BLASPHEME BLAUDS BLEBBY*
BLACKMAILING BLAMEFUL BLASPHEMED BLAW* BLEBS
BLACKMAILS BLAMELESS BLASPHEMES BLAWED* BLED
BLACKNESS BLAMER* BLASPHEMIES BLAWING* BLEE
BLACKNESSES BLAMERS* BLASPHEMING BLAWN* BLEED
BLACKOUT BLAMES BLASPHEMY BLAWORT BLEEDER
BLACKOUTS BLAMING BLAST BLAWORTS BLEEDERS
BLACKPOLL* BLAMS* BLASTED BLAWS* BLEEDING
BLACKPOLLS* BLANCH BLASTEMA BLAY BLEEDINGS
BLACKS BLANCHED BLASTEMAL* BLAYS BLEEDS
BLACKTAIL* BLANCHER* BLASTEMAS BLAZE BLEEP
BLACKTAILS* BLANCHERS* BLASTEMATA BLAZED BLEEPED
BLACKTOP BLANCHES BLASTER BLAZER BLEEPER
BLACKTOPPED* BLANCHING BLASTERS BLAZERED BLEEPERS
BLACKTOPPING* BLANCO BLASTIE* BLAZERS BLEEPING
BLACKTOPS BLANCOED BLASTIER* BLAZES BLEEPS
BLACKWASH BLANCOING BLASTIES* BLAZING BLEES
BLACKWASHES BLANCOS BLASTIEST* BLAZINGLY* BLELLUM*
BLACKWOOD BLAND BLASTING BLAZON BLELLUMS*
BLACKWOODS BLANDER BLASTINGS BLAZONED BLEMISH
BLAD BLANDEST BLASTMENT BLAZONER BLEMISHED
BLADDED BLANDISH BLASTMENTS BLAZONERS BLEMISHES
BLADDER BLANDISHED BLASTOFF* BLAZONING BLEMISHING
BLADDERED BLANDISHES BLASTOFFS* BLAZONINGS* BLENCH
BLADDERS BLANDISHING BLASTOID BLAZONRIES BLENCHED
BLADDERY BLANDLY BLASTOIDS BLAZONRY BLENCHER*
BLADDING BLANDNESS BLASTOMA* BLAZONS BLENCHERS*
BLADE BLANDNESSES BLASTOMAS* BLEACH BLENCHES
BLADED BLANDS BLASTOMATA* BLEACHED BLENCHING
BLADELIKE* BLANK BLASTS BLEACHER BLEND
BLADES BLANKED BLASTULA BLEACHERIES BLENDE
BLADEWORK BLANKER BLASTULAE BLEACHERS BLENDED
BLADEWORKS BLANKEST BLASTULAR BLEACHERY BLENDER
BLADS BLANKET BLASTULAS BLEACHES BLENDERS
BLAE BLANKETED BLASTY* BLEACHING BLENDES
BLAEBERRIES BLANKETIES BLAT BLEACHINGS BLENDING

BLENDINGS	BLINDFISHES	BLITZED	BLOODBATH*	BLOT
BLENDS	BLINDFOLD	BLITZES	BLOODBATHS*	BLOTCH
BLENNIES	BLINDFOLDED	BLITZING	BLOODED	BLOTCHED
BLENNY	BLINDFOLDING	BLIVE	BLOODFIN*	BLOTCHES
BLENT	BLINDFOLDS	BLIZZARD	BLOODFINS*	BLOTCHIER
BLESBOK	BLINDING	BLIZZARDS	BLOODHEAT	BLOTCHIEST
BLESBOKS	BLINDINGS	BLIZZARDY	BLOODHEATS	BLOTCHILY*
BLESBUCK*	BLINDLESS	BLOAT	BLOODIED	BLOTCHING
BLESBUCKS*	BLINDLY	BLOATED	BLOODIER	BLOTCHINGS
BLESS	BLINDNESS	BLOATER	BLOODIES	BLOTCHY
BLESSED	BLINDNESSES	BLOATERS	BLOODIEST	BLOTLESS*
BLESSEDER	BLINDS	BLOATING	BLOODILY	BLOTS
BLESSEDEST	BLINDSIDE*	BLOATINGS	BLOODING	BLOTTED
BLESSEDLY	BLINDSIDED*	BLOATS	BLOODINGS*	BLOTTER
BLESSER*	BLINDSIDES*	BLOATWARE	BLOODLESS	BLOTTERS
BLESSERS*	BLINDSIDING*	BLOATWARES	BLOODLINE*	BLOTTIER
BLESSES	BLINDWORM	BLOB	BLOODLINES*	BLOTTIEST
BLESSING	BLINDWORMS	BLOBBED	BLOODLUST	BLOTTING
BLESSINGS	BLINI	BLOBBING	BLOODLUSTS	BLOTTINGS
BLEST	BLINIS	BLOBS	BLOODRED*	BLOTTO
BLET	BLINK	BLOC	BLOODROOT	BLOTTY
BLETHER	BLINKARD	BLOCK	BLOODROOTS	BLOUBOK
BLETHERED	BLINKARDS	BLOCKADE	BLOODS	BLOUBOKS
BLETHERER	BLINKED	BLOCKADED	BLOODSHED	BLOUSE
BLETHERERS	BLINKER	BLOCKADER*	BLOODSHEDS	BLOUSED
BLETHERING	BLINKERED	BLOCKADERS*	BLOODSHOT	BLOUSES
BLETHERINGS	BLINKERING	BLOCKADES	BLOODWOOD	BLOUSIER*
BLETHERS	BLINKERS	BLOCKADING	BLOODWOODS	BLOUSIEST*
BLETS	BLINKING	BLOCKAGE	BLOODWORM*	BLOUSILY*
BLETTED	BLINKS	BLOCKAGES	BLOODWORMS*	BLOUSING
BLETTING	BLINNED	BLOCKED	BLOODY	BLOUSON
BLEUATRE	BLINNING	BLOCKER	BLOODYING	BLOUSONS
BLEW	BLINS	BLOCKERS	BLOOEY*	BLOUSY*
BLEWART	BLINTZ	BLOCKHEAD	BLOOIE*	BLOVIATE*
BLEWARTS	BLINTZE	BLOCKHEADS	BLOOM	BLOVIATED*
BLEWITS	BLINTZES	BLOCKHOLE	BLOOMED	BLOVIATES*
BLEWITSES	BLIP	BLOCKHOLES	BLOOMER	BLOVIATING*
BLEY	BLIPPED	BLOCKIER	BLOOMERIES	BLOW
BLEYS	BLIPPING	BLOCKIEST	BLOOMERS	BLOWBACK*
BLIGHT	BLIPS	BLOCKING	BLOOMERY	BLOWBACKS*
BLIGHTED	BLISS	BLOCKINGS	BLOOMIER	BLOWBALL
BLIGHTER	BLISSED*	BLOCKISH	BLOOMIEST	BLOWBALLS
BLIGHTERS	BLISSES	BLOCKS	BLOOMING	BLOWBY*
BLIGHTIES	BLISSFUL	BLOCKWORK	BLOOMLESS	BLOWBYS*
BLIGHTING	BLISSING*	BLOCKWORKS	BLOOMS	BLOWDOWN
BLIGHTINGS	BLISSLESS	BLOCKY	BLOOMY	BLOWDOWNS
BLIGHTS	BLIST	BLOCS	BLOOP	BLOWED
BLIGHTY	BLISTER	BLOKE	BLOOPED	BLOWER
BLIMBING	BLISTERED	BLOKEDOM	BLOOPER	BLOWERS
BLIMBINGS	BLISTERIER	BLOKEDOMS	BLOOPERS	BLOWFISH
BLIMEY	BLISTERIEST	BLOKEISH	BLOOPING	BLOWFISHES
BLIMP	BLISTERING	BLOKES	BLOOPS	BLOWFLIES
BLIMPISH	BLISTERS	BLOKEY	BLOOSME	BLOWFLY
BLIMPS	BLISTERY	BLOKIER	BLOOSMED	BLOWGUN
BLIMY	BLITE	BLOKIEST	BLOOSMES	BLOWGUNS
BLIN	BLITES	BLONCKET	BLOOSMING	BLOWHARD
BLIND	BLITHE	BLOND	BLORE	BLOWHARDS
BLINDAGE	BLITHELY	BLONDE	BLORES	BLOWHOLE
BLINDAGES	BLITHER	BLONDER	BLOSSOM	BLOWHOLES
BLINDED	BLITHERED	BLONDES	BLOSSOMED	BLOWIE
BLINDER	BLITHERING	BLONDEST	BLOSSOMING	BLOWIER
BLINDERS	BLITHERS	BLONDISH*	BLOSSOMINGS	BLOWIES
BLINDEST	BLITHEST	BLONDS	BLOSSOMS	BLOWIEST
BLINDFISH	BLITZ	BLOOD	BLOSSOMY	BLOWING

The Chambers Dictionary is the authority for many longer words; see Introduction, page ix

BLOWJOB
BLOWJOBS
BLOWLAMP
BLOWLAMPS
BLOWN
BLOWOFF*
BLOWOFFS*
BLOWOUT*
BLOWOUTS*
BLOWPIPE
BLOWPIPES
BLOWS
BLOWSE
BLOWSED
BLOWSES
BLOWSIER
BLOWSIEST
BLOWSILY*
BLOWSY
BLOWTORCH
BLOWTORCHES
BLOWTUBE*
BLOWTUBES*
BLOWUP*
BLOWUPS*
BLOWY
BLOWZE
BLOWZED
BLOWZES
BLOWZIER
BLOWZIEST
BLOWZILY*
BLOWZY
BLUB
BLUBBED
BLUBBER
BLUBBERED
BLUBBERING
BLUBBERS
BLUBBERY*
BLUBBING
BLUBS
BLUCHER
BLUCHERS
BLUDE
BLUDES
BLUDGE
BLUDGED
BLUDGEON
BLUDGEONED
BLUDGEONING
BLUDGEONS
BLUDGER
BLUDGERS
BLUDGES
BLUDGING
BLUDIE
BLUDIER
BLUDIEST
BLUDY
BLUE
BLUEBACK
BLUEBACKS
BLUEBALL*

BLUEBALLS*
BLUEBEARD
BLUEBEARDS
BLUEBELL
BLUEBELLS
BLUEBERRIES
BLUEBERRY
BLUEBILL*
BLUEBILLS*
BLUEBIRD
BLUEBIRDS
BLUEBOOK*
BLUEBOOKS*
BLUEBUCK
BLUEBUCKS
BLUECAP
BLUECAPS
BLUECOAT
BLUECOATS
BLUED
BLUEFIN*
BLUEFINS*
BLUEFISH
BLUEFISHES
BLUEGILL*
BLUEGILLS*
BLUEGOWN
BLUEGOWNS
BLUEGRASS
BLUEGRASSES
BLUEGUM*
BLUEGUMS*
BLUEHEAD*
BLUEHEADS*
BLUEING
BLUEINGS
BLUEISH*
BLUEJACK*
BLUEJACKS*
BLUEJAY*
BLUEJAYS*
BLUELINE*
BLUELINES*
BLUELY
BLUENESS
BLUENESSES
BLUENOSE
BLUENOSES
BLUEPOINT*
BLUEPOINTS*
BLUEPRINT
BLUEPRINTED
BLUEPRINTING
BLUEPRINTS
BLUER
BLUES
BLUESHIFT*
BLUESHIFTS*
BLUESIER
BLUESIEST
BLUESMAN*
BLUESMEN*
BLUEST
BLUESTEM*

BLUESTEMS*
BLUESTONE
BLUESTONES
BLUESY
BLUET*
BLUETICK*
BLUETICKS*
BLUETS*
BLUETTE
BLUETTES
BLUEWEED
BLUEWEEDS
BLUEWING
BLUEWINGS
BLUEWOOD*
BLUEWOODS*
BLUEY
BLUEYS
BLUFF
BLUFFED
BLUFFER
BLUFFERS
BLUFFEST
BLUFFING
BLUFFLY
BLUFFNESS
BLUFFNESSES
BLUFFS
BLUGGIER
BLUGGIEST
BLUGGY
BLUID
BLUIDIER
BLUIDIEST
BLUIDS
BLUIDY
BLUIER
BLUIEST
BLUING
BLUINGS
BLUISH
BLUME*
BLUMED*
BLUMES*
BLUMING*
BLUNDER
BLUNDERED
BLUNDERER
BLUNDERERS
BLUNDERING
BLUNDERINGS
BLUNDERS
BLUNGE
BLUNGED
BLUNGER
BLUNGERS
BLUNGES
BLUNGING
BLUNK
BLUNKED
BLUNKER
BLUNKERS
BLUNKING
BLUNKS

BLUNT
BLUNTED
BLUNTER
BLUNTEST
BLUNTING
BLUNTISH
BLUNTLY
BLUNTNESS
BLUNTNESSES
BLUNTS
BLUR
BLURB
BLURBED
BLURBING
BLURBS
BLURRED
BLURRIER*
BLURRIEST*
BLURRILY*
BLURRING
BLURRY*
BLURS
BLURT
BLURTED
BLURTER*
BLURTERS*
BLURTING
BLURTINGS
BLURTS
BLUSH
BLUSHED
BLUSHER
BLUSHERS
BLUSHES
BLUSHET
BLUSHETS
BLUSHFUL
BLUSHING
BLUSHINGS
BLUSHLESS
BLUSTER
BLUSTERED
BLUSTERER
BLUSTERERS
BLUSTERIER
BLUSTERIEST
BLUSTERING
BLUSTERINGS
BLUSTERS
BLUSTERY
BLUSTROUS
BLUTWURST
BLUTWURSTS
BLYPE*
BLYPES*
BO
BOA
BOAK
BOAKED
BOAKING
BOAKS
BOAR
BOARD
BOARDED

BOARDER
BOARDERS
BOARDING
BOARDINGS
BOARDLIKE*
BOARDMAN*
BOARDMEN*
BOARDROOM
BOARDROOMS
BOARDS
BOARDWALK
BOARDWALKS
BOARFISH
BOARFISHES
BOARISH
BOARS
BOART
BOARTS
BOAS
BOAST
BOASTED
BOASTER
BOASTERS
BOASTFUL
BOASTING
BOASTINGS
BOASTLESS
BOASTS
BOAT
BOATABLE*
BOATBILL
BOATBILLS
BOATED
BOATEL
BOATELS
BOATER
BOATERS
BOATFUL*
BOATFULS*
BOATHOOK*
BOATHOOKS*
BOATHOUSE
BOATHOUSES
BOATIE
BOATIES
BOATING
BOATINGS
BOATLIKE*
BOATLOAD*
BOATLOADS*
BOATMAN
BOATMEN
BOATS
BOATSMAN*
BOATSMEN*
BOATSWAIN
BOATSWAINS
BOATTAIL
BOATTAILS
BOATYARD*
BOATYARDS*
BOB
BOBA
BOBAC

Words marked with an asterisk are from OTCWL

BOBACS
BOBAK
BOBAKS
BOBAS
BOBBED
BOBBER*
BOBBERIES
BOBBERS*
BOBBERY
BOBBIES
BOBBIN
BOBBINET
BOBBINETS
BOBBING
BOBBINS
BOBBISH
BOBBITT
BOBBITTED
BOBBITTING
BOBBITTS
BOBBLE
BOBBLED
BOBBLES
BOBBLIER
BOBBLIEST
BOBBLING
BOBBLY
BOBBY
BOBBYSOCK
BOBBYSOCKS
BOBCAT
BOBCATS
BOBECHE*
BOBECHES*
BOBOLINK
BOBOLINKS
BOBS
BOBSLED
BOBSLEDDED*
BOBSLEDDING*
BOBSLEDS
BOBSLEIGH
BOBSLEIGHS
BOBSTAY*
BOBSTAYS
BOBTAIL
BOBTAILED
BOBTAILING
BOBTAILS
BOBWHEEL
BOBWHEELS
BOBWHITE*
BOBWHITES*
BOBWIG
BOBWIGS
BOCACCIO*
BOCACCIOS*
BOCAGE
BOCAGES
BOCCA
BOCCAS
BOCCE*
BOCCES*
BOCCI*

BOCCIA*
BOCCIAS*
BOCCIE*
BOCCIES*
BOCCIS*
BOCHE
BOCHES
BOCK
BOCKED
BOCKING
BOCKS
BOD
BODACH
BODACHS
BODACIOUS
BODDLE
BODDLES
BODE
BODED
BODEFUL
BODEGA
BODEGAS
BODEGUERO
BODEGUEROS
BODEMENT
BODEMENTS
BODES
BODGE
BODGED
BODGER
BODGERS
BODGES
BODGIE
BODGIER
BODGIES
BODGIEST
BODGING
BODHRAN
BODHRANS
BODICE
BODICES
BODIED
BODIES
BODIKIN
BODIKINS
BODILESS
BODILY
BODING
BODINGLY*
BODINGS
BODKIN
BODKINS
BODLE
BODLES
BODRAG
BODRAGS
BODS
BODY
BODYCHECK*
BODYCHECKED*
BODYCHECKING*
BODYCHECKS*
BODYGUARD
BODYGUARDS

BODYING
BODYLINE
BODYLINES
BODYSHELL
BODYSHELLS
BODYSUIT
BODYSUITS
BODYSURF*
BODYSURFED*
BODYSURFING*
BODYSURFS*
BODYWORK
BODYWORKS
BOEHMITE*
BOEHMITES*
BOEREWORS
BOEREWORSES
BOFF
BOFFED
BOFFIN
BOFFING
BOFFINS
BOFFO*
BOFFOLA*
BOFFOLAS*
BOFFOS*
BOFFS
BOG
BOGAN
BOGANS
BOGBEAN
BOGBEANS
BOGEY
BOGEYED
BOGEYING
BOGEYISM
BOGEYISMS
BOGEYMAN*
BOGEYMEN*
BOGEYS
BOGGARD
BOGGARDS
BOGGART
BOGGARTS
BOGGED
BOGGIER
BOGGIEST
BOGGINESS
BOGGINESSES
BOGGING
BOGGISH*
BOGGLE
BOGGLED
BOGGLER
BOGGLERS
BOGGLES
BOGGLING
BOGGY
BOGIE
BOGIES
BOGLAND
BOGLANDS
BOGLE
BOGLES

BOGOAK
BOGOAKS
BOGONG
BOGONGS
BOGS
BOGUS
BOGWOOD*
BOGWOODS*
BOGY
BOGYISM
BOGYISMS
BOGYMAN*
BOGYMEN*
BOH
BOHEA
BOHEAS
BOHEMIA*
BOHEMIAN*
BOHEMIANS*
BOHEMIAS*
BOHS
BOHUNK
BOHUNKS
BOIL
BOILABLE*
BOILED
BOILER
BOILERIES
BOILERS
BOILERY
BOILING
BOILINGS
BOILOFF*
BOILOFFS*
BOILS
BOING
BOINGED
BOINGING
BOINGS
BOINK
BOINKED
BOINKING
BOINKS
BOISERIE*
BOISERIES*
BOITE*
BOITES*
BOK
BOKE
BOKED
BOKES
BOKING
BOKO
BOKOS
BOKS
BOLA*
BOLAR*
BOLAS
BOLASES
BOLD
BOLDEN
BOLDENED
BOLDENING
BOLDENS

BOLDER
BOLDEST
BOLDFACE*
BOLDFACED*
BOLDFACES*
BOLDFACING*
BOLDLY
BOLDNESS
BOLDNESSES
BOLDS
BOLE
BOLECTION
BOLECTIONS
BOLERO
BOLEROS
BOLES
BOLETE*
BOLETES*
BOLETI
BOLETUS
BOLETUSES
BOLIDE
BOLIDES
BOLIVAR
BOLIVARES
BOLIVARS
BOLIVIA*
BOLIVIANO
BOLIVIANOS
BOLIVIAS*
BOLIX
BOLIXED
BOLIXES
BOLIXING
BOLL
BOLLARD
BOLLARDS
BOLLED
BOLLEN
BOLLETRIE
BOLLETRIES
BOLLING
BOLLIX
BOLLIXED
BOLLIXES
BOLLIXING
BOLLOCK
BOLLOCKED
BOLLOCKING
BOLLOCKINGS
BOLLOCKS
BOLLOCKSED
BOLLOCKSES
BOLLOCKSING
BOLLOX*
BOLLOXED*
BOLLOXES*
BOLLOXING*
BOLLS
BOLLWORM*
BOLLWORMS*
BOLO
BOLOGNA*
BOLOGNAS*

The Chambers Dictionary is the authority for many longer words; see Introduction, page ix

BOLOMETER	BOMBES	BONDMAN	BONITAS*	BOOBYISM
BOLOMETERS	BOMBESIN*	BONDMEN	BONITO	BOOBYISMS
BOLOMETRIES	BOMBESINS*	BONDS	BONITOES*	BOODIE
BOLOMETRY	BOMBILATE	BONDSMAN	BONITOS	BOODIED
BOLONEY	BOMBILATED	BONDSMEN	BONJOUR	BOODIES
BOLONEYS	BOMBILATES	BONDSTONE	BONK	BOODLE
BOLOS	BOMBILATING	BONDSTONES	BONKED	BOODLED*
BOLSHEVIK	BOMBINATE	BONDUC	BONKERS	BOODLER*
BOLSHEVIKS	BOMBINATED	BONDUCS	BONKING	BOODLERS*
BOLSHIE	BOMBINATES	BONDWOMAN	BONKS	BOODLES
BOLSHIER	BOMBINATING	BONDWOMEN	BONNE	BOODLING*
BOLSHIES	BOMBING	BONE	BONNES	BOODY
BOLSHIEST	BOMBINGS*	BONED	BONNET	BOODYING
BOLSHY	BOMBLET	BONEFISH*	BONNETED	BOOED
BOLSON*	BOMBLETS	BONEFISHES*	BONNETING	BOOGER*
BOLSONS*	BOMBLOAD*	BONEHEAD	BONNETS	BOOGERMAN*
BOLSTER	BOMBLOADS*	BONEHEADS	BONNIBELL	BOOGERMEN*
BOLSTERED	BOMBO	BONELESS	BONNIBELLS	BOOGERS*
BOLSTERER*	BOMBORA	BONEMEAL*	BONNIE	BOOGEY*
BOLSTERERS*	BOMBORAS	BONEMEALS*	BONNIER	BOOGEYED*
BOLSTERING	BOMBOS	BONER	BONNIES	BOOGEYING*
BOLSTERINGS	BOMBPROOF*	BONERS	BONNIEST	BOOGEYMAN*
BOLSTERS	BOMBS	BONES	BONNILY	BOOGEYMEN*
BOLT	BOMBSHELL	BONESET	BONNINESS	BOOGEYS*
BOLTED	BOMBSHELLS	BONESETS	BONNINESSES	BOOGIE
BOLTER	BOMBSIGHT*	BONEY*	BONNOCK*	BOOGIED
BOLTERS	BOMBSIGHTS*	BONEYARD	BONNOCKS*	BOOGIEING
BOLTHEAD	BOMBSITE	BONEYARDS	BONNY	BOOGIES
BOLTHEADS	BOMBSITES	BONFIRE	BONSAI	BOOGY*
BOLTHOLE	BOMBYCID	BONFIRES	BONSAIS	BOOGYING*
BOLTHOLES	BOMBYCIDS	BONG	BONSELLA	BOOGYMAN*
BOLTING	BOMBYX*	BONGED	BONSELLAS	BOOGYMEN*
BOLTINGS	BOMBYXES*	BONGING	BONSOIR	BOOH
BOLTONIA*	BON	BONGO	BONSPELL*	BOOHED
BOLTONIAS*	BONA	BONGOES*	BONSPELLS*	BOOHING
BOLTROPE*	BONACI*	BONGOIST*	BONSPIEL	BOOHOO*
BOLTROPES*	BONACIS*	BONGOISTS*	BONSPIELS	BOOHOOED*
BOLTS	BONAMANI	BONGOS	BONTEBOK	BOOHOOING*
BOLUS	BONAMANO	BONGRACE	BONTEBOKS	BOOHOOS*
BOLUSES	BONAMIA	BONGRACES	BONUS	BOOHS
BOMA	BONAMIAS	BONGS	BONUSES	BOOING
BOMAS	BONANZA	BONHOMIE	BONXIE	BOOK
BOMB	BONANZAS	BONHOMIES	BONXIES	BOOKABLE
BOMBARD	BONASSUS	BONHOMMIE	BONY	BOOKCASE
BOMBARDED	BONASSUSES	BONHOMMIES	BONZA	BOOKCASES
BOMBARDING	BONASUS	BONHOMOUS	BONZE	BOOKED
BOMBARDON	BONASUSES	BONIBELL	BONZER	BOOKEND*
BOMBARDONS	BONBON	BONIBELLS	BONZES	BOOKENDS*
BOMBARDS	BONBONS	BONIE	BOO	BOOKER*
BOMBASINE	BONCE	BONIER	BOOB	BOOKERS*
BOMBASINES	BONCES	BONIEST	BOOBED	BOOKFUL
BOMBAST	BOND	BONIFACE	BOOBIE*	BOOKFULS*
BOMBASTED	BONDABLE*	BONIFACES	BOOBIES	BOOKIE
BOMBASTIC	BONDAGE	BONILASSE	BOOBING	BOOKIER
BOMBASTING	BONDAGER	BONILASSES	BOOBISH*	BOOKIES
BOMBASTS	BONDAGERS	BONINESS	BOOBOISIE*	BOOKIEST
BOMBAX	BONDAGES	BONINESSES	BOOBOISIES*	BOOKING
BOMBAXES	BONDED	BONING	BOOBOO	BOOKINGS
BOMBAZINE	BONDER	BONINGS	BOOBOOK	BOOKISH
BOMBAZINES	BONDERS	BONISM	BOOBOOKS	BOOKISHLY*
BOMBE	BONDING	BONISMS	BOOBOOS	BOOKLAND
BOMBED	BONDINGS	BONIST	BOOBS	BOOKLANDS
BOMBER	BONDMAID	BONISTS	BOOBY	BOOKLESS
BOMBERS	BONDMAIDS	BONITA*	BOOBYISH	BOOKLET

BOOKLETS
BOOKLICE
BOOKLORE
BOOKLORES
BOOKLOUSE
BOOKMAKER
BOOKMAKERS
BOOKMAN
BOOKMARK
BOOKMARKS
BOOKMEN
BOOKPLATE
BOOKPLATES
BOOKRACK*
BOOKRACKS*
BOOKREST
BOOKRESTS
BOOKS
BOOKSHELF
BOOKSHELVES
BOOKSHOP
BOOKSHOPS
BOOKSIE
BOOKSIER
BOOKSIEST
BOOKSTALL
BOOKSTALLS
BOOKSTAND
BOOKSTANDS
BOOKSTORE
BOOKSTORES
BOOKSY
BOOKWORK
BOOKWORKS
BOOKWORM
BOOKWORMS
BOOKY
BOOL
BOOLS
BOOM
BOOMBOX*
BOOMBOXES*
BOOMED
BOOMER
BOOMERANG
BOOMERANGED
BOOMERANGING
BOOMERANGS
BOOMERS
BOOMIER*
BOOMIEST*
BOOMING
BOOMINGS
BOOMKIN*
BOOMKINS*
BOOMLET
BOOMLETS
BOOMS
BOOMSLANG
BOOMSLANGS
BOOMTOWN*
BOOMTOWNS*
BOOMY*
BOON

BOONDOCK*
BOONDOCKS
BOONG
BOONGS
BOONIES*
BOONS
BOOR
BOORD
BOORDE
BOORDES
BOORDS
BOORISH
BOORISHLY
BOORKA
BOORKAS
BOORS
BOORTREE
BOORTREES
BOOS
BOOSE
BOOSED
BOOSES
BOOSING
BOOST
BOOSTED
BOOSTER
BOOSTERS
BOOSTING
BOOSTS
BOOT
BOOTABLE
BOOTBLACK
BOOTBLACKS
BOOTED
BOOTEE
BOOTEES
BOOTERIES*
BOOTERY*
BOOTH
BOOTHOSE
BOOTHS
BOOTIE*
BOOTIES
BOOTIKIN
BOOTIKINS
BOOTING
BOOTJACK*
BOOTJACKS*
BOOTLACE
BOOTLACES
BOOTLAST
BOOTLASTS
BOOTLEG
BOOTLEGGED
BOOTLEGGING
BOOTLEGGINGS
BOOTLEGS
BOOTLESS
BOOTLICK
BOOTLICKED
BOOTLICKING
BOOTLICKINGS
BOOTLICKS
BOOTMAKER

BOOTMAKERS
BOOTS
BOOTSTRAP
BOOTSTRAPPED
BOOTSTRAPPING
BOOTSTRAPS
BOOTY
BOOZE
BOOZED
BOOZER
BOOZERS
BOOZES
BOOZEY
BOOZIER
BOOZIEST
BOOZILY
BOOZINESS
BOOZINESSES
BOOZING
BOOZY
BOP
BOPEEP*
BOPEEPS*
BOPPED
BOPPER
BOPPERS
BOPPING
BOPS
BOR
BORA
BORACES*
BORACHIO
BORACHIOS
BORACIC
BORACITE
BORACITES
BORAGE
BORAGES
BORAK
BORAKS
BORAL*
BORALS*
BORANE
BORANES
BORAS
BORATE
BORATED*
BORATES
BORATING*
BORAX
BORAXES
BORAZON
BORAZONS
BORD
BORDAR
BORDARS
BORDE
BORDEAUX*
BORDEL
BORDELLO
BORDELLOS
BORDELS
BORDER
BORDEREAU

BORDEREAUX
BORDERED
BORDERER
BORDERERS
BORDERING
BORDERS
BORDES
BORDS
BORDURE
BORDURES
BORE
BOREAL
BORECOLE
BORECOLES
BORED
BOREDOM
BOREDOMS
BOREE
BOREEN
BOREENS
BOREES
BOREHOLE
BOREHOLES
BOREL
BORER
BORERS
BORES
BORESCOPE*
BORESCOPES*
BORESOME*
BORGHETTO
BORGHETTOS
BORGO
BORGOS
BORIC
BORIDE
BORIDES
BORING
BORINGLY
BORINGS
BORN
BORNE
BORNEOL*
BORNEOLS*
BORNITE
BORNITES
BORON
BORONIA
BORONIAS
BORONIC*
BORONS
BOROUGH
BOROUGHS
BORREL
BORRELL
BORROW
BORROWED
BORROWER
BORROWERS
BORROWING
BORROWINGS
BORROWS
BORS
BORSCH

BORSCHES
BORSCHT
BORSCHTS
BORSHT*
BORSHTS*
BORSTAL
BORSTALL
BORSTALLS
BORSTALS
BORT
BORTS
BORTSCH
BORTSCHES
BORTY*
BORTZ*
BORTZES*
BORZOI
BORZOIS
BOS
BOSBOK
BOSBOKS
BOSCAGE
BOSCAGES
BOSCHBOK
BOSCHBOKS
BOSCHE
BOSCHES
BOSCHVELD
BOSCHVELDS
BOSH
BOSHBOK*
BOSHBOKS*
BOSHES
BOSHTA
BOSHTER
BOSHVARK*
BOSHVARKS*
BOSK
BOSKAGE
BOSKAGES
BOSKER
BOSKET
BOSKETS
BOSKIER
BOSKIEST
BOSKINESS
BOSKINESSES
BOSKS
BOSKY
BOSOM
BOSOMED
BOSOMIER
BOSOMIEST
BOSOMING
BOSOMS
BOSOMY
BOSON
BOSONS
BOSQUE*
BOSQUES*
BOSQUET
BOSQUETS
BOSS
BOSSDOM*

BOSSDOMS*	BOTHAN	BOUBOUS*	BOUNCY	BOUSIER
BOSSED	BOTHANS	BOUCHE	BOUND	BOUSIEST
BOSSER	BOTHER	BOUCHEE	BOUNDARIES	BOUSING
BOSSES	BOTHERED	BOUCHEES	BOUNDARY	BOUSOUKI*
BOSSEST	BOTHERING	BOUCHES	BOUNDED	BOUSOUKIA*
BOSSIER	BOTHERS	BOUCLE	BOUNDEN	BOUSOUKIS*
BOSSIES*	BOTHIE	BOUCLES	BOUNDER	BOUSY
BOSSIEST	BOTHIES	BOUDERIE	BOUNDERS	BOUT
BOSSILY	BOTHOLE	BOUDERIES	BOUNDING	BOUTADE
BOSSINESS	BOTHOLES	BOUDOIR	BOUNDLESS	BOUTADES
BOSSINESSES	BOTHRIA*	BOUDOIRS	BOUNDS	BOUTIQUE
BOSSING	BOTHRIUM*	BOUFFANT	BOUNED	BOUTIQUES
BOSSISM*	BOTHRIUMS*	BOUFFANTS*	BOUNING	BOUTON
BOSSISMS*	BOTHY	BOUFFE*	BOUNS	BOUTONNE
BOSSY	BOTHYMAN	BOUFFES*	BOUNTEOUS	BOUTONNEE
BOSTANGI	BOTHYMEN	BOUGE	BOUNTIED*	BOUTONS
BOSTANGIS	BOTONE	BOUGED	BOUNTIES	BOUTS
BOSTON	BOTONEE*	BOUGES	BOUNTIFUL	BOUVIER*
BOSTONS	BOTONNEE*	BOUGET	BOUNTREE	BOUVIERS*
BOSTRYX	BOTRYOID	BOUGETS	BOUNTREES	BOUZOUKI
BOSTRYXES	BOTRYOSE	BOUGH	BOUNTY	BOUZOUKIA*
BOSUN	BOTRYTIS*	BOUGHED*	BOUNTYHED	BOUZOUKIS
BOSUNS	BOTRYTISES*	BOUGHPOT	BOUNTYHEDS	BOVATE
BOT	BOTS	BOUGHPOTS	BOUQUET	BOVATES
BOTA*	BOTT	BOUGHS	BOUQUETS	BOVID
BOTANIC	BOTTE	BOUGHT	BOURASQUE	BOVIDS
BOTANICA*	BOTTED	BOUGHTEN	BOURASQUES	BOVINE
BOTANICAL	BOTTEGA	BOUGHTS	BOURBON	BOVINELY
BOTANICALS	BOTTEGAS	BOUGIE	BOURBONS	BOVINES
BOTANICAS*	BOTTES	BOUGIES	BOURD	BOVINITIES*
BOTANIES	BOTTIES	BOUGING	BOURDER	BOVINITY*
BOTANISE	BOTTINE	BOUILLI	BOURDERS	BOVVER
BOTANISED	BOTTINES	BOUILLIS	BOURDON	BOVVERS
BOTANISES	BOTTING	BOUILLON	BOURDONS	BOW
BOTANISING	BOTTLE	BOUILLONS	BOURDS	BOWAT
BOTANIST	BOTTLED	BOUK	BOURG	BOWATS
BOTANISTS	BOTTLEFUL	BOUKS	BOURGEOIS	BOWBENT
BOTANIZE	BOTTLEFULS	BOULDER	BOURGEOISES	BOWED
BOTANIZED	BOTTLER	BOULDERED*	BOURGEON	BOWEL
BOTANIZES	BOTTLERS	BOULDERS	BOURGEONED	BOWELED*
BOTANIZING	BOTTLES	BOULDERY*	BOURGEONING	BOWELING*
BOTANY	BOTTLING	BOULE	BOURGEONS	BOWELLED
BOTARGO	BOTTLINGS*	BOULES	BOURGS	BOWELLESS*
BOTARGOES	BOTTOM	BOULEVARD	BOURKHA	BOWELLING
BOTARGOS	BOTTOMED	BOULEVARDS	BOURKHAS	BOWELS
BOTAS*	BOTTOMER*	BOULLE	BOURLAW	BOWER
BOTCH	BOTTOMERS*	BOULLES	BOURLAWS	BOWERBIRD*
BOTCHED	BOTTOMING	BOULT	BOURN	BOWERBIRDS*
BOTCHER	BOTTOMRIES	BOULTED	BOURNE	BOWERED
BOTCHERIES	BOTTOMRY	BOULTER	BOURNES	BOWERIES
BOTCHERS	BOTTOMS	BOULTERS	BOURNS	BOWERING
BOTCHERY	BOTTONY	BOULTING	BOURREE	BOWERS
BOTCHES	BOTTS	BOULTINGS	BOURREES	BOWERY
BOTCHIER	BOTTY	BOULTS	BOURRIDE*	BOWES
BOTCHIEST	BOTULIN*	BOUN	BOURRIDES*	BOWET
BOTCHILY*	BOTULINAL*	BOUNCE	BOURSE	BOWETS
BOTCHING	BOTULINS*	BOUNCED	BOURSES	BOWFIN
BOTCHINGS	BOTULINUM*	BOUNCER	BOURSIER	BOWFINS
BOTCHY	BOTULINUMS*	BOUNCERS	BOURSIERS	BOWFRONT*
BOTEL	BOTULINUS*	BOUNCES	BOURTREE	BOWGET
BOTELS	BOTULINUSES*	BOUNCIER	BOURTREES	BOWGETS
BOTFLIES	BOTULISM	BOUNCIEST	BOUSE	BOWHEAD
BOTFLY	BOTULISMS	BOUNCILY	BOUSED	BOWHEADS
BOTH	BOUBOU*	BOUNCING	BOUSES	BOWING

Words marked with an asterisk are from OTCWL

BOWINGLY*
BOWINGS
BOWKNOT
BOWKNOTS
BOWL
BOWLDER
BOWLDERS
BOWLED
BOWLEG*
BOWLEGGED*
BOWLEGS*
BOWLER
BOWLERS
BOWLESS*
BOWLFUL
BOWLFULS
BOWLIKE*
BOWLINE
BOWLINES
BOWLING
BOWLINGS
BOWLLIKE*
BOWLS
BOWMAN
BOWMEN
BOWNE
BOWNED
BOWNES
BOWNING
BOWPOT
BOWPOTS
BOWR
BOWRS
BOWS
BOWSE
BOWSED
BOWSER
BOWSERS
BOWSES
BOWSHOT
BOWSHOTS
BOWSING
BOWSPRIT
BOWSPRITS
BOWSTRING
BOWSTRINGED
BOWSTRINGING
BOWSTRINGS
BOWSTRUNG
BOWWOW
BOWWOWED*
BOWWOWING*
BOWWOWS
BOWYANG
BOWYANGS
BOWYER
BOWYERS
BOX
BOXBERRIES*
BOXBERRY*
BOXBOARD*
BOXBOARDS*
BOXCAR
BOXCARS

BOXED
BOXEN
BOXER
BOXERCISE
BOXERCISES
BOXERS
BOXES
BOXFISH*
BOXFISHES*
BOXFUL
BOXFULS
BOXHAUL*
BOXHAULED*
BOXHAULING*
BOXHAULS*
BOXIER
BOXIEST
BOXINESS
BOXINESSES
BOXING
BOXINGS
BOXKEEPER
BOXKEEPERS
BOXLIKE*
BOXROOM
BOXROOMS
BOXTHORN*
BOXTHORNS*
BOXWALLAH
BOXWALLAHS
BOXWOOD
BOXWOODS
BOXY
BOY
BOYAR
BOYARD*
BOYARDS*
BOYARISM*
BOYARISMS*
BOYARS
BOYAU
BOYAUX
BOYCHICK*
BOYCHICKS*
BOYCHIK*
BOYCHIKS*
BOYCOTT
BOYCOTTED
BOYCOTTER
BOYCOTTERS
BOYCOTTING
BOYCOTTS
BOYED
BOYFRIEND
BOYFRIENDS
BOYG
BOYGS
BOYHOOD
BOYHOODS
BOYING
BOYISH
BOYISHLY
BOYLA*
BOYLAS*

BOYO
BOYOS
BOYS
BOZO
BOZOS
BOZZETTI
BOZZETTO
BRA
BRABBLE
BRABBLED
BRABBLER*
BRABBLERS*
BRABBLES
BRABBLING
BRACCATE
BRACCIA
BRACCIO
BRACE
BRACED
BRACELET
BRACELETS
BRACER
BRACERO*
BRACEROS*
BRACERS
BRACES
BRACH
BRACHES
BRACHET
BRACHETS
BRACHIA
BRACHIAL
BRACHIALS*
BRACHIATE
BRACHIATED
BRACHIATES
BRACHIATING
BRACHIUM
BRACHS*
BRACING
BRACINGLY*
BRACINGS*
BRACIOLA*
BRACIOLAS*
BRACIOLE*
BRACIOLES*
BRACK
BRACKEN
BRACKENS
BRACKET
BRACKETED
BRACKETING
BRACKETS
BRACKISH
BRACKS
BRACONID*
BRACONIDS*
BRACT
BRACTEAL
BRACTEATE
BRACTEATES
BRACTED*
BRACTEOLE
BRACTEOLES

BRACTLESS
BRACTLET
BRACTLETS
BRACTS
BRAD
BRADAWL
BRADAWLS
BRADDED*
BRADDING*
BRADOON*
BRADOONS*
BRADS
BRAE
BRAES
BRAG
BRAGGART
BRAGGARTS
BRAGGED
BRAGGER*
BRAGGERS*
BRAGGEST*
BRAGGIER*
BRAGGIEST*
BRAGGING
BRAGGY*
BRAGLY
BRAGS
BRAHMA*
BRAHMAS*
BRAID
BRAIDE
BRAIDED
BRAIDER
BRAIDERS*
BRAIDEST
BRAIDING
BRAIDINGS
BRAIDS
BRAIL
BRAILED
BRAILING
BRAILLE*
BRAILLED*
BRAILLER
BRAILLERS
BRAILLES*
BRAILLING*
BRAILLIST*
BRAILLISTS*
BRAILS
BRAIN
BRAINBOX
BRAINBOXES
BRAINCASE
BRAINCASES
BRAINED
BRAINIER
BRAINIEST
BRAINILY*
BRAINING
BRAINISH
BRAINLESS
BRAINPAN
BRAINPANS

BRAINS
BRAINSICK
BRAINWASH
BRAINWASHED
BRAINWASHES
BRAINWASHING
BRAINWASHINGS
BRAINY
BRAIRD
BRAIRDED
BRAIRDING
BRAIRDS
BRAISE
BRAISED
BRAISES
BRAISING
BRAIZE
BRAIZES
BRAKE
BRAKEAGE*
BRAKEAGES*
BRAKED
BRAKELESS
BRAKEMAN
BRAKEMEN
BRAKES
BRAKIER
BRAKIEST
BRAKING
BRAKY
BRALESS
BRAMBLE
BRAMBLED
BRAMBLES
BRAMBLIER
BRAMBLIEST
BRAMBLING
BRAMBLINGS
BRAMBLY
BRAME
BRAMES
BRAN
BRANCARD
BRANCARDS
BRANCH
BRANCHED
BRANCHER
BRANCHERIES
BRANCHERS
BRANCHERY
BRANCHES
BRANCHIA
BRANCHIAE
BRANCHIAL
BRANCHIER
BRANCHIEST
BRANCHING
BRANCHINGS
BRANCHLET
BRANCHLETS
BRANCHY
BRAND
BRANDADE
BRANDADES

BRANDED	BRASHING	BRATWURST	BRAZA*	BREAKEVENS*
BRANDER	BRASHLY*	BRATWURSTS	BRAZAS*	BREAKFAST
BRANDERED	BRASHNESS*	BRAUNCH	BRAZE	BREAKFASTED
BRANDERING	BRASHNESSES*	BRAUNCHED	BRAZED	BREAKFASTING
BRANDERS	BRASHY	BRAUNCHES	BRAZELESS	BREAKFASTS
BRANDIED	BRASIER	BRAUNCHING	BRAZEN	BREAKING
BRANDIES	BRASIERS	BRAUNITE	BRAZENED	BREAKINGS
BRANDING	BRASIL*	BRAUNITES	BRAZENING	BREAKNECK
BRANDISE	BRASILIN*	BRAVA	BRAZENLY	BREAKOUT*
BRANDISES	BRASILINS*	BRAVADO	BRAZENRIES	BREAKOUTS*
BRANDISH	BRASILS*	BRAVADOED	BRAZENRY	BREAKS
BRANDISHED	BRASS	BRAVADOES	BRAZENS	BREAKTIME
BRANDISHES	BRASSAGE*	BRAVADOING	BRAZER*	BREAKTIMES
BRANDISHING	BRASSAGES*	BRAVADOS	BRAZERS*	BREAKUP*
BRANDLING	BRASSARD	BRAVAS*	BRAZES	BREAKUPS*
BRANDLINGS	BRASSARDS	BRAVE	BRAZIER	BREAM
BRANDRETH	BRASSART	BRAVED	BRAZIERS	BREAMED
BRANDRETHS	BRASSARTS	BRAVELY	BRAZIL	BREAMING
BRANDS	BRASSED*	BRAVER	BRAZILEIN	BREAMS
BRANDY	BRASSERIE	BRAVERIES	BRAZILEINS	BREARE
BRANDYING*	BRASSERIES	BRAVERS*	BRAZILIN	BREARES
BRANGLE	BRASSES	BRAVERY	BRAZILINS	BREASKIT
BRANGLED	BRASSET	BRAVES	BRAZILS	BREASKITS
BRANGLES	BRASSETS	BRAVEST	BRAZING	BREAST
BRANGLING	BRASSICA	BRAVI	BREACH	BREASTED
BRANGLINGS	BRASSICAS	BRAVING	BREACHED	BREASTING
BRANK	BRASSIE	BRAVO	BREACHER*	BREASTPIN
BRANKED	BRASSIER	BRAVOED*	BREACHERS*	BREASTPINS
BRANKIER	BRASSIERE	BRAVOES	BREACHES	BREASTS
BRANKIEST	BRASSIERES	BRAVOING*	BREACHING	BREATH
BRANKING	BRASSIES	BRAVOS	BREAD	BREATHE
BRANKS	BRASSIEST	BRAVURA	BREADBOX*	BREATHED
BRANKY	BRASSILY	BRAVURAS	BREADBOXES*	BREATHER
BRANLE	BRASSING*	BRAVURE*	BREADED	BREATHERS
BRANLES	BRASSISH*	BRAW	BREADHEAD	BREATHES
BRANNED*	BRASSY	BRAWER	BREADHEADS	BREATHFUL
BRANNER*	BRAST	BRAWEST	BREADING	BREATHIER
BRANNERS*	BRASTING	BRAWL	BREADLINE	BREATHIEST
BRANNIER	BRASTS	BRAWLED	BREADLINES	BREATHILY
BRANNIEST	BRAT	BRAWLER	BREADNUT	BREATHING
BRANNIGAN*	BRATCHET	BRAWLERS	BREADNUTS	BREATHINGS
BRANNIGANS*	BRATCHETS	BRAWLIE*	BREADROOM	BREATHS
BRANNING*	BRATLING	BRAWLIER	BREADROOMS	BREATHY
BRANNY	BRATLINGS	BRAWLIEST	BREADROOT	BRECCIA
BRANS	BRATPACK	BRAWLING	BREADROOTS	BRECCIAL*
BRANSLE	BRATS	BRAWLINGS	BREADS	BRECCIAS
BRANSLES	BRATTICE	BRAWLS	BREADTH	BRECCIATE*
BRANT*	BRATTICED	BRAWLY	BREADTHS	BRECCIATED*
BRANTAIL*	BRATTICES	BRAWN	BREADY*	BRECCIATES*
BRANTAILS*	BRATTICING	BRAWNED	BREAK	BRECCIATING*
BRANTLE	BRATTICINGS	BRAWNIER	BREAKABLE	BRECHAM
BRANTLES	BRATTIER	BRAWNIEST	BREAKABLES	BRECHAMS
BRANTS*	BRATTIEST	BRAWNILY*	BREAKAGE	BRECHAN*
BRAS	BRATTISH	BRAWNS	BREAKAGES	BRECHANS*
BRASERO	BRATTISHED	BRAWNY	BREAKAWAY	BRED
BRASEROS	BRATTISHES	BRAWS	BREAKAWAYS	BREDE
BRASES	BRATTISHING	BRAXIES	BREAKBACK	BREDED
BRASH	BRATTISHINGS	BRAXY	BREAKBEAT	BREDES
BRASHED	BRATTLE	BRAY	BREAKBEATS	BREDING
BRASHER	BRATTLED	BRAYED	BREAKDOWN	BREE
BRASHES	BRATTLES	BRAYER	BREAKDOWNS	BREECH
BRASHEST	BRATTLING	BRAYERS	BREAKER	BREECHED
BRASHIER	BRATTLINGS	BRAYING	BREAKERS	BREECHES
BRASHIEST	BRATTY	BRAYS	BREAKEVEN*	BREECHING

BREECHINGS	BREVETE	BRICKLES*	BRIERIEST	BRINERS*
BREED	BREVETED	BRICKS	BRIERS	BRINES
BREEDER	BREVETING	BRICKWALL	BRIERY	BRING
BREEDERS	BREVETS	BRICKWALLS	BRIES*	BRINGDOWN*
BREEDING	BREVETTED	BRICKWORK	BRIG	BRINGDOWNS*
BREEDINGS	BREVETTING	BRICKWORKS	BRIGADE	BRINGER
BREEDS	BREVIARIES	BRICKY	BRIGADED	BRINGERS
BREEKS	BREVIARY	BRICKYARD	BRIGADES	BRINGING
BREEM	BREVIATE	BRICKYARDS	BRIGADIER	BRINGINGS
BREER	BREVIATES	BRICOLAGE*	BRIGADIERS	BRINGS
BREERED	BREVIER	BRICOLAGES*	BRIGADING	BRINIER
BREERING	BREVIERS	BRICOLE	BRIGALOW	BRINIES*
BREERS	BREVITIES	BRICOLES	BRIGALOWS	BRINIEST
BREES	BREVITY	BRIDAL	BRIGAND	BRININESS
BREESE	BREW	BRIDALLY*	BRIGANDRIES	BRININESSES
BREESES	BREWAGE	BRIDALS	BRIGANDRY	BRINING
BREEZE	BREWAGES	BRIDE	BRIGANDS	BRINISH
BREEZED	BREWED	BRIDECAKE	BRIGHT	BRINJAL
BREEZES	BREWER	BRIDECAKES	BRIGHTEN	BRINJALS
BREEZEWAY	BREWERIES	BRIDED	BRIGHTENED	BRINJARRIES
BREEZEWAYS	BREWERS	BRIDEMAID	BRIGHTENING	BRINJARRY
BREEZIER	BREWERY	BRIDEMAIDS	BRIGHTENS	BRINK
BREEZIEST	BREWING	BRIDEMAN	BRIGHTER	BRINKMAN
BREEZILY	BREWINGS	BRIDEMEN	BRIGHTEST	BRINKMEN
BREEZING	BREWIS	BRIDES	BRIGHTLY	BRINKS
BREEZY	BREWISES	BRIDESMAN	BRIGHTS*	BRINS*
BREGMA	BREWPUB	BRIDESMEN	BRIGS	BRINY
BREGMATA	BREWPUBS	BRIDEWELL	BRIGUE	BRIO
BREGMATE*	BREWS	BRIDEWELLS	BRIGUED	BRIOCHE
BREGMATIC	BREWSTER	BRIDGABLE	BRIGUES	BRIOCHES
BREHON	BREWSTERS	BRIDGE	BRIGUING	BRIOLETTE*
BREHONS	BRIAR	BRIDGED	BRIGUINGS	BRIOLETTES*
BRELOQUE	BRIARD*	BRIDGES	BRILL	BRIONIES
BRELOQUES	BRIARDS*	BRIDGING	BRILLER	BRIONY
BREME	BRIARED	BRIDGINGS	BRILLEST	BRIOS
BREN	BRIARS	BRIDIE	BRILLIANT	BRIQUET
BRENNE	BRIARY*	BRIDIES	BRILLIANTED	BRIQUETS
BRENNES	BRIBABLE*	BRIDING	BRILLIANTING	BRIQUETTE
BRENNING	BRIBE	BRIDLE	BRILLIANTS	BRIQUETTED
BRENS	BRIBED	BRIDLED	BRILLS	BRIQUETTES
BRENT	BRIBEE*	BRIDLER	BRIM	BRIQUETTING
BRENTER	BRIBEES*	BRIDLERS	BRIMFUL	BRIS*
BRENTEST	BRIBER	BRIDLES	BRIMFULL*	BRISANCE*
BRENTS*	BRIBERIES	BRIDLING	BRIMING	BRISANCES*
BRER	BRIBERS	BRIDOON	BRIMINGS	BRISANT*
BRERE	BRIBERY	BRIDOONS	BRIMLESS	BRISE
BRERES	BRIBES	BRIE*	BRIMMED	BRISES
BRERS	BRIBING	BRIEF	BRIMMER	BRISK
BRETASCHE	BRICABRAC	BRIEFCASE	BRIMMERS	BRISKED
BRETASCHES	BRICABRACS	BRIEFCASES	BRIMMING	BRISKEN
BRETESSE	BRICK	BRIEFED	BRIMS	BRISKENED
BRETESSES	BRICKBAT	BRIEFER	BRIMSTONE	BRISKENING
BRETHREN	BRICKBATS	BRIEFERS*	BRIMSTONES	BRISKENS
BRETON	BRICKCLAY	BRIEFEST	BRIMSTONY	BRISKER
BRETONS	BRICKCLAYS	BRIEFING	BRIN*	BRISKEST
BRETTICE	BRICKED	BRIEFINGS	BRINDED	BRISKET
BRETTICED	BRICKEN	BRIEFLESS	BRINDISI	BRISKETS
BRETTICES	BRICKIE	BRIEFLY	BRINDISIS	BRISKING
BRETTICING	BRICKIER	BRIEFNESS	BRINDLE	BRISKISH
BREVE	BRICKIES	BRIEFNESSES	BRINDLED	BRISKLY
BREVES	BRICKIEST	BRIEFS	BRINDLES	BRISKNESS
BREVET	BRICKING	BRIER	BRINE	BRISKNESSES
BREVETCIES*	BRICKINGS	BRIERED	BRINED	BRISKS
BREVETCY*	BRICKLE	BRIERIER	BRINER*	BRISKY

The Chambers Dictionary is the authority for many longer words; see Introduction, page ix

BRISLING	BROADLOOM	BROGH	BROMIDE	BROODED
BRISLINGS	BROADLOOMS*	BROGHS	BROMIDES	BROODER
BRISSES*	BROADLY	BROGS	BROMIDIC	BROODERS
BRISTLE	BROADNESS	BROGUE	BROMIDS*	BROODIER
BRISTLED	BROADNESSES	BROGUEISH	BROMIN*	BROODIEST
BRISTLES	BROADS	BROGUERIES*	BROMINATE*	BROODILY*
BRISTLIER	BROADSIDE	BROGUERY*	BROMINATED*	BROODING
BRISTLIEST	BROADSIDED*	BROGUES	BROMINATES*	BROODMARE*
BRISTLING	BROADSIDES	BROGUISH	BROMINATING*	BROODMARES*
BRISTLY	BROADSIDING*	BROIDER	BROMINE	BROODS
BRISTOL*	BROADTAIL	BROIDERED	BROMINES	BROODY
BRISTOLS	BROADTAILS	BROIDERER	BROMINISM	BROOK
BRISURE	BROADWAY	BROIDERERS	BROMINISMS	BROOKED
BRISURES	BROADWAYS	BROIDERIES	BROMINS*	BROOKIE*
BRIT	BROADWISE	BROIDERING	BROMISM	BROOKIES*
BRITCHES	BROCADE	BROIDERINGS	BROMISMS	BROOKING
BRITS	BROCADED	BROIDERS	BROMIZE*	BROOKITE
BRITSCHKA	BROCADES	BROIDERY	BROMIZED*	BROOKITES
BRITSCHKAS	BROCADING*	BROIL	BROMIZES*	BROOKLET
BRITSKA	BROCAGE	BROILED	BROMIZING*	BROOKLETS
BRITSKAS	BROCAGES	BROILER	BROMMER	BROOKLIME
BRITT*	BROCARD	BROILERS	BROMMERS	BROOKLIMES
BRITTLE	BROCARDS	BROILING	BROMO*	BROOKS
BRITTLED*	BROCATEL	BROILS	BROMOFORM	BROOKWEED
BRITTLELY	BROCATELS	BROKAGE	BROMOFORMS	BROOKWEEDS
BRITTLER	BROCCOLI	BROKAGES	BROMOS*	BROOL
BRITTLES	BROCCOLIS	BROKE	BRONC*	BROOLS
BRITTLEST	BROCH	BROKED	BRONCHI	BROOM
BRITTLING*	BROCHAN	BROKEN	BRONCHIA	BROOMBALL
BRITTLY	BROCHANS	BROKENLY	BRONCHIAL	BROOMBALLS
BRITTS*	BROCHE	BROKER	BRONCHIUM*	BROOMCORN*
BRITZKA	BROCHED	BROKERAGE	BRONCHO	BROOMCORNS*
BRITZKAS	BROCHES	BROKERAGES	BRONCHOS	BROOMED
BRITZSKA	BROCHETTE	BROKERED	BRONCHUS	BROOMIER
BRITZSKAS	BROCHETTES	BROKERIES	BRONCO	BROOMIEST
BRIZE	BROCHING	BROKERING	BRONCOS	BROOMING
BRIZES	BROCHS	BROKERINGS*	BRONCS*	BROOMRAPE
BRO	BROCHURE	BROKERS	BROND	BROOMRAPES
BROACH	BROCHURES	BROKERY	BRONDS	BROOMS
BROACHED	BROCK	BROKES	BRONDYRON	BROOMY
BROACHER	BROCKAGE	BROKING	BRONDYRONS	BROOS
BROACHERS	BROCKAGES	BROKINGS	BRONZE	BROOSE
BROACHES	BROCKED	BROLGA	BRONZED	BROOSES
BROACHING	BROCKET	BROLGAS	BRONZEN	BROS
BROAD	BROCKETS	BROLLIES	BRONZER	BROSE
BROADAX*	BROCKIT	BROLLY	BRONZERS	BROSES
BROADAXE*	BROCKRAM	BROMAL*	BRONZES	BROSY*
BROADAXES*	BROCKRAMS	BROMALS*	BRONZIER	BROTH
BROADBAND	BROCKS	BROMATE	BRONZIEST	BROTHEL
BROADBILL	BROCOLI*	BROMATED*	BRONZIFIED	BROTHELS
BROADBILLS	BROCOLIS*	BROMATES	BRONZIFIES	BROTHER
BROADCAST	BROD	BROMATING*	BRONZIFY	BROTHERED*
BROADCASTED	BRODDED	BROME*	BRONZIFYING	BROTHERING*
BROADCASTING	BRODDING	BROMELAIN	BRONZING	BROTHERLY
BROADCASTINGS	BRODEKIN	BROMELAINS	BRONZINGS	BROTHERS
BROADCASTS	BRODEKINS	BROMELIA	BRONZITE	BROTHS
BROADEN	BRODKIN	BROMELIAD	BRONZITES	BROTHY*
BROADENED	BRODKINS	BROMELIADS	BRONZY	BROUGH
BROADENING	BRODS	BROMELIAS	BROO	BROUGHAM
BROADENS	BROG	BROMELIN	BROOCH	BROUGHAMS
BROADER	BROGAN	BROMELINS	BROOCHED	BROUGHS
BROADEST	BROGANS	BROMES*	BROOCHES	BROUGHT
BROADISH	BROGGED	BROMIC	BROOCHING	BROUHAHA
BROADLEAF*	BROGGING	BROMID*	BROOD	BROUHAHAS

Words marked with an asterisk are from OTCWL

BROUZE	BRUHAHA	BRUSHOFF*	BRYOZOANS*	BUCKED
BROUZES	BRUHAHAS	BRUSHOFFS*	BUAT	BUCKEEN
BROW	BRUILZIE	BRUSHUP*	BUATS	BUCKEENS
BROWBAND	BRUILZIES	BRUSHUPS*	BUAZE	BUCKER
BROWBANDS	BRUIN*	BRUSHWOOD	BUAZES	BUCKEROO
BROWBEAT	BRUINS*	BRUSHWOODS	BUB	BUCKEROOS
BROWBEATEN	BRUISE	BRUSHWORK	BUBA	BUCKERS
BROWBEATING	BRUISED	BRUSHWORKS	BUBAL	BUCKET
BROWBEATINGS	BRUISER	BRUSHY	BUBALE*	BUCKETED
BROWBEATS	BRUISERS	BRUSK*	BUBALES*	BUCKETFUL
BROWED*	BRUISES	BRUSKER*	BUBALINE	BUCKETFULS
BROWLESS	BRUISING	BRUSKEST*	BUBALIS	BUCKETING
BROWN	BRUISINGS	BRUSQUE	BUBALISES	BUCKETINGS
BROWNED	BRUIT	BRUSQUELY	BUBALS	BUCKETS
BROWNER	BRUITED	BRUSQUER	BUBAS	BUCKETSFUL*
BROWNEST	BRUITER*	BRUSQUEST	BUBBIES	BUCKEYE*
BROWNIE	BRUITERS*	BRUST	BUBBLE	BUCKEYES*
BROWNIER	BRUITING	BRUSTING	BUBBLED	BUCKHORN
BROWNIES	BRUITS	BRUSTS	BUBBLEGUM*	BUCKHORNS
BROWNIEST	BRULE	BRUT	BUBBLEGUMS*	BUCKHOUND
BROWNING	BRULOT*	BRUTAL	BUBBLER*	BUCKHOUNDS
BROWNINGS	BRULOTS*	BRUTALISE	BUBBLERS*	BUCKIE
BROWNISH	BRULYIE	BRUTALISED	BUBBLES	BUCKIES
BROWNNESS	BRULYIES	BRUTALISES	BUBBLIER	BUCKING
BROWNNESSES	BRULZIE	BRUTALISING	BUBBLIES	BUCKINGS
BROWNNOSE*	BRULZIES	BRUTALISM	BUBBLIEST	BUCKISH
BROWNNOSED*	BRUMAL	BRUTALISMS	BUBBLING	BUCKISHLY
BROWNNOSES*	BRUMBIES	BRUTALIST	BUBBLY	BUCKLE
BROWNNOSING*	BRUMBY	BRUTALISTS	BUBBY	BUCKLED
BROWNOUT	BRUME	BRUTALITIES	BUBINGA	BUCKLER
BROWNOUTS	BRUMES	BRUTALITY	BUBINGAS	BUCKLERED
BROWNS	BRUMMAGEM	BRUTALIZE	BUBO	BUCKLERING
BROWNY	BRUMMAGEMS	BRUTALIZED	BUBOED*	BUCKLERS
BROWRIDGE*	BRUMMER	BRUTALIZES	BUBOES	BUCKLES
BROWRIDGES*	BRUMMERS	BRUTALIZING	BUBONIC	BUCKLING
BROWS	BRUMOUS	BRUTALLY	BUBS	BUCKLINGS
BROWSE	BRUNCH	BRUTE	BUBUKLE	BUCKO
BROWSED	BRUNCHED*	BRUTED	BUBUKLES	BUCKOES
BROWSER	BRUNCHES	BRUTELIKE	BUCCAL	BUCKRA
BROWSERS	BRUNCHING*	BRUTELY*	BUCCALLY*	BUCKRAKE
BROWSES	BRUNET	BRUTENESS	BUCCANEER	BUCKRAKES
BROWSIER	BRUNETS	BRUTENESSES	BUCCANEERED	BUCKRAM
BROWSIEST	BRUNETTE	BRUTER	BUCCANEERING	BUCKRAMED
BROWSING	BRUNETTES	BRUTERS	BUCCANEERINGS	BUCKRAMING
BROWSINGS	BRUNIZEM*	BRUTES	BUCCANEERS	BUCKRAMS
BROWST	BRUNIZEMS*	BRUTIFIED	BUCCANIER	BUCKRAS
BROWSTS	BRUNT	BRUTIFIES	BUCCANIERED	BUCKS
BROWSY	BRUNTED	BRUTIFY	BUCCANIERING	BUCKSAW
BRR*	BRUNTING	BRUTIFYING	BUCCANIERS	BUCKSAWS
BRRR	BRUNTS	BRUTING	BUCCINA	BUCKSHEE
BRUCELLA*	BRUSH	BRUTINGS	BUCCINAS	BUCKSHEES*
BRUCELLAE*	BRUSHBACK*	BRUTISH	BUCELLAS	BUCKSHISH
BRUCELLAS*	BRUSHBACKS*	BRUTISHLY	BUCELLASES	BUCKSHISHED
BRUCHID	BRUSHED	BRUTISM*	BUCHU	BUCKSHISHES
BRUCHIDS	BRUSHER	BRUTISMS*	BUCHUS	BUCKSHISHING
BRUCIN*	BRUSHERS	BRUXISM	BUCK	BUCKSHOT
BRUCINE	BRUSHES	BRUXISMS	BUCKAROO	BUCKSHOTS
BRUCINES	BRUSHFIRE*	BRYOLOGIES	BUCKAROOS	BUCKSKIN
BRUCINS*	BRUSHIER	BRYOLOGY	BUCKAYRO	BUCKSKINS
BRUCITE	BRUSHIEST	BRYONIES	BUCKAYROS	BUCKSOM
BRUCITES	BRUSHING	BRYONY	BUCKBEAN	BUCKTAIL*
BRUCKLE	BRUSHINGS	BRYOPHYTE	BUCKBEANS	BUCKTAILS*
BRUGH*	BRUSHLAND*	BRYOPHYTES	BUCKBOARD	BUCKTEETH
BRUGHS*	BRUSHLANDS*	BRYOZOAN*	BUCKBOARDS	BUCKTHORN

BUCKTHORNS	BUFFABLE*	BUGLER	BULBOSITY	BULLDOGS
BUCKTOOTH	BUFFALO	BUGLERS	BULBOUS	BULLDOZE
BUCKU	BUFFALOED	BUGLES	BULBOUSLY	BULLDOZED
BUCKUS	BUFFALOES	BUGLET	BULBS	BULLDOZER
BUCKWHEAT	BUFFALOING	BUGLETS	BULBUL	BULLDOZERS
BUCKWHEATS	BUFFALOS*	BUGLEWEED*	BULBULS	BULLDOZES
BUCKYBALL	BUFFE	BUGLEWEEDS*	BULGE	BULLDOZING
BUCKYBALLS	BUFFED	BUGLING	BULGED	BULLDUST
BUCOLIC	BUFFER	BUGLOSS	BULGER	BULLDUSTS
BUCOLICAL	BUFFERED	BUGLOSSES	BULGERS	BULLED
BUCOLICS	BUFFERING	BUGONG	BULGES	BULLER
BUD	BUFFERS	BUGONGS	BULGHUR	BULLERED
BUDDED	BUFFET	BUGS	BULGHURS	BULLERING
BUDDER*	BUFFETED	BUGSEED*	BULGIER	BULLERS
BUDDERS*	BUFFETER*	BUGSEEDS*	BULGIEST	BULLET
BUDDHA	BUFFETERS*	BUGSHA*	BULGINE	BULLETED*
BUDDHAS	BUFFETING	BUGSHAS*	BULGINES	BULLETIN
BUDDIED*	BUFFETINGS	BUGWORT	BULGINESS	BULLETINED*
BUDDIER	BUFFETS	BUGWORTS	BULGINESSES	BULLETING*
BUDDIES	BUFFI	BUHL	BULGING	BULLETINING*
BUDDIEST	BUFFIER*	BUHLS	BULGINGLY	BULLETINS
BUDDING	BUFFIEST*	BUHLWORK*	BULGUR	BULLETRIE
BUDDINGS	BUFFING	BUHLWORKS*	BULGURS	BULLETRIES
BUDDLE	BUFFINGS	BUHR*	BULGY	BULLETS
BUDDLED	BUFFO	BUHRS*	BULIMIA	BULLFIGHT
BUDDLEIA	BUFFOON	BUHRSTONE	BULIMIAC*	BULLFIGHTS
BUDDLEIAS	BUFFOONS	BUHRSTONES	BULIMIAS	BULLFINCH
BUDDLES	BUFFOS*	BUIK	BULIMIC	BULLFINCHES
BUDDLING	BUFFS	BUIKS	BULIMICS	BULLFROG
BUDDY	BUFFY*	BUILD	BULIMIES	BULLFROGS
BUDDYING*	BUFO	BUILDABLE*	BULIMUS	BULLGINE
BUDGE	BUFOS	BUILDED	BULIMUSES	BULLGINES
BUDGED	BUG	BUILDER	BULIMY	BULLHEAD
BUDGER	BUGABOO	BUILDERS	BULK	BULLHEADS
BUDGEREE	BUGABOOS	BUILDING	BULKAGE*	BULLHORN*
BUDGERO	BUGBANE	BUILDINGS	BULKAGES*	BULLHORNS*
BUDGEROS	BUGBANES	BUILDS	BULKED	BULLIED
BUDGEROW	BUGBEAR	BUILDUP*	BULKER	BULLIER
BUDGEROWS	BUGBEARS	BUILDUPS*	BULKERS	BULLIES
BUDGERS	BUGEYE*	BUILT	BULKHEAD	BULLIEST
BUDGES	BUGEYES*	BUIRDLIER	BULKHEADS	BULLING
BUDGET	BUGGAN	BUIRDLIEST	BULKIER	BULLINGS
BUDGETARY	BUGGANE	BUIRDLY	BULKIEST	BULLION
BUDGETED	BUGGANES	BUIST	BULKILY	BULLIONS
BUDGETEER*	BUGGANS	BUISTED	BULKINESS	BULLISH
BUDGETEERS*	BUGGED	BUISTING	BULKINESSES	BULLISHLY
BUDGETER*	BUGGER	BUISTS	BULKING	BULLNECK*
BUDGETERS*	BUGGERED	BUKE	BULKS	BULLNECKS*
BUDGETING	BUGGERIES	BUKES	BULKY	BULLNOSE
BUDGETS	BUGGERING	BUKSHEE	BULL	BULLNOSES
BUDGIE	BUGGERS	BUKSHEES	BULLA	BULLOCK
BUDGIES	BUGGERY	BUKSHI	BULLACE	BULLOCKED
BUDGING	BUGGIER	BUKSHIS	BULLACES	BULLOCKIES
BUDLESS	BUGGIES	BULB	BULLAE	BULLOCKING
BUDLIKE*	BUGGIEST	BULBAR	BULLARIES	BULLOCKS
BUDMASH	BUGGIN	BULBED	BULLARY	BULLOCKY
BUDMASHES	BUGGING	BULBEL	BULLATE	BULLOUS*
BUDO	BUGGINS	BULBELS	BULLBAR	BULLPEN*
BUDOS	BUGGY	BULBIL	BULLBARS	BULLPENS*
BUDS	BUGHOUSE	BULBILS	BULLBAT	BULLPOUT*
BUDWORM	BUGHOUSES	BULBING	BULLBATS	BULLPOUTS*
BUDWORMS	BUGLE	BULBLET*	BULLDOG	BULLRING*
BUFF	BUGLED	BULBLETS*	BULLDOGGED	BULLRINGS*
BUFFA		BULBOSITIES	BULLDOGGING	BULLRUSH*

BULLRUSHES* BUMKINS BUNCOMBE BUNKERS BUQSHA*
BULLS BUMMALO BUNCOMBES BUNKHOUSE BUQSHAS*
BULLSHIT BUMMALOTI BUNCOS BUNKHOUSES BUR
BULLSHITS BUMMALOTIS BUND BUNKING BURA*
BULLSHITTED BUMMAREE BUNDED BUNKMATE* BURAN
BULLSHITTING BUMMAREES BUNDING BUNKMATES* BURANS
BULLSHITTINGS BUMMED BUNDIST* BUNKO BURAS*
BULLSHOT* BUMMEL BUNDISTS* BUNKOED BURBLE
BULLSHOTS* BUMMELS BUNDLE BUNKOING BURBLED
BULLWEED* BUMMER BUNDLED BUNKOS BURBLER
BULLWEEDS* BUMMERS BUNDLER* BUNKS BURBLERS
BULLWHACK BUMMEST BUNDLERS* BUNKUM BURBLES
BULLWHACKED BUMMING BUNDLES BUNKUMS BURBLIER*
BULLWHACKING BUMMLE BUNDLING BUNN* BURBLIEST*
BULLWHACKS BUMMLED BUNDLINGS BUNNIA BURBLING
BULLWHIP BUMMLES BUNDOBUST BUNNIAS BURBLINGS
BULLWHIPPED BUMMLING BUNDOBUSTS BUNNIES BURBLY*
BULLWHIPPING BUMMOCK BUNDOOK BUNNS* BURBOT
BULLWHIPS BUMMOCKS BUNDOOKS BUNNY BURBOTS
BULLY BUMP BUNDS BUNODONT BURBS*
BULLYBOY* BUMPED BUNDT* BUNRAKU BURD
BULLYBOYS* BUMPER BUNDTS* BUNRAKUS BURDASH
BULLYING BUMPERED BUNDU BUNS BURDASHES
BULLYISM BUMPERING BUNDUS BUNSEN BURDEN
BULLYISMS BUMPERS BUNG BUNSENS BURDENED
BULLYRAG BUMPH BUNGALOID BUNT BURDENER*
BULLYRAGGED BUMPHS BUNGALOIDS BUNTAL BURDENERS*
BULLYRAGGING BUMPIER BUNGALOW BUNTALS BURDENING
BULLYRAGS BUMPIEST BUNGALOWS BUNTED BURDENOUS
BULRUSH BUMPILY BUNGED BUNTER BURDENS
BULRUSHES BUMPINESS BUNGEE BUNTERS BURDIE
BULRUSHY BUMPINESSES BUNGEES BUNTIER BURDIES
BULSE BUMPING BUNGEY BUNTIEST BURDOCK
BULSES BUMPINGS BUNGEYS BUNTING BURDOCKS
BULWARK BUMPKIN BUNGHOLE BUNTINGS BURDS
BULWARKED BUMPKINLY* BUNGHOLES BUNTLINE BUREAU
BULWARKING BUMPKINS BUNGIE BUNTLINES BUREAUS
BULWARKS BUMPOLOGIES BUNGIES BUNTS BUREAUX
BUM BUMPOLOGY BUNGING BUNTY BURET
BUMALO BUMPS BUNGLE BUNYA BURETS
BUMALOTI BUMPTIOUS BUNGLED BUNYAS BURETTE
BUMALOTIS BUMPY BUNGLER BUNYIP BURETTES
BUMBAG BUMS BUNGLERS BUNYIPS BURG
BUMBAGS BUMSUCKER BUNGLES BUONAMANI BURGAGE
BUMBAZE BUMSUCKERS BUNGLING BUONAMANO BURGAGES
BUMBAZED BUN BUNGLINGS BUOY BURGANET
BUMBAZES BUNA BUNGS BUOYAGE BURGANETS
BUMBAZING BUNAS BUNGY BUOYAGES BURGEE
BUMBLE BUNCE BUNIA BUOYANCE BURGEES
BUMBLEBEE* BUNCED BUNIAS BUOYANCES BURGEON
BUMBLEBEES* BUNCES BUNION BUOYANCIES BURGEONED
BUMBLED BUNCH BUNIONS BUOYANCY BURGEONING
BUMBLER BUNCHED BUNJE BUOYANT BURGEONS
BUMBLERS BUNCHES BUNJEE BUOYANTLY* BURGER
BUMBLES BUNCHIER BUNJEES BUOYED BURGERS
BUMBLING BUNCHIEST BUNJES BUOYING BURGESS
BUMBLINGS BUNCHILY* BUNJIE BUOYS BURGESSES
BUMBO BUNCHING BUNJIES BUPLEVER BURGH
BUMBOAT* BUNCHINGS BUNJY BUPLEVERS BURGHAL
BUMBOATS* BUNCHY BUNK BUPPIE* BURGHER
BUMBOS BUNCING BUNKED BUPPIES BURGHERS
BUMF BUNCO BUNKER BUPPY BURGHS
BUMFS BUNCOED BUNKERED BUPRESTID BURGHUL
BUMKIN BUNCOING BUNKERING BUPRESTIDS BURGHULS

BURGLAR	BURLEYS	BURRITO	BUSHBUCK*	BUSIED
BURGLARED	BURLIER	BURRITOS	BUSHBUCKS*	BUSIER
BURGLARIES	BURLIEST	BURRO	BUSHCRAFT	BUSIES
BURGLARING	BURLILY*	BURROS	BUSHCRAFTS	BUSIEST
BURGLARS	BURLINESS	BURROW	BUSHED	BUSILY
BURGLARY	BURLINESSES	BURROWED	BUSHEL	BUSINESS
BURGLE	BURLING	BURROWER*	BUSHELED*	BUSINESSES
BURGLED	BURLS	BURROWERS*	BUSHELER*	BUSING
BURGLES	BURLY	BURROWING	BUSHELERS*	BUSINGS
BURGLING	BURN	BURROWS	BUSHELING*	BUSK
BURGONET	BURNABLE*	BURRS	BUSHELLED	BUSKED
BURGONETS	BURNABLES*	BURRSTONE	BUSHELLER	BUSKER
BURGOO	BURNED	BURRSTONES	BUSHELLERS	BUSKERS
BURGOOS	BURNER	BURRY	BUSHELLING	BUSKET
BURGOUT*	BURNERS	BURS	BUSHELLINGS	BUSKETS
BURGOUTS*	BURNET	BURSA	BUSHELMAN	BUSKIN
BURGRAVE	BURNETS	BURSAE	BUSHELMEN	BUSKINED
BURGRAVES	BURNIE*	BURSAL	BUSHELS	BUSKING
BURGS	BURNIES*	BURSAR	BUSHER*	BUSKINGS
BURGUNDIES	BURNING	BURSARIAL	BUSHERS*	BUSKINS
BURGUNDY	BURNINGLY	BURSARIES	BUSHES	BUSKS
BURHEL	BURNINGS	BURSARS	BUSHFIRE	BUSKY
BURHELS	BURNISH	BURSARY	BUSHFIRES	BUSLOAD*
BURIAL	BURNISHED	BURSAS*	BUSHGOAT*	BUSLOADS*
BURIALS	BURNISHER	BURSATE*	BUSHGOATS*	BUSMAN
BURIED	BURNISHERS	BURSE	BUSHIDO	BUSMEN
BURIER*	BURNISHES	BURSEED*	BUSHIDOS	BUSS
BURIERS*	BURNISHING	BURSEEDS*	BUSHIER	BUSSED
BURIES	BURNISHINGS	BURSERA*	BUSHIES	BUSSES
BURIN	BURNOOSE*	BURSES	BUSHIEST	BUSSING
BURINIST	BURNOOSED*	BURSIFORM	BUSHILY*	BUSSINGS
BURINISTS	BURNOOSES*	BURSITIS	BUSHINESS	BUSSU
BURINS	BURNOUS	BURSITISES	BUSHINESSES	BUSSUS
BURITI	BURNOUSE	BURST	BUSHING	BUST
BURITIS	BURNOUSES	BURSTED	BUSHINGS	BUSTARD
BURK	BURNOUT*	BURSTEN	BUSHLAND*	BUSTARDS
BURKA	BURNOUTS*	BURSTER	BUSHLANDS*	BUSTED
BURKAS	BURNS	BURSTERS	BUSHLESS*	BUSTEE
BURKE	BURNSIDE	BURSTING	BUSHLIKE*	BUSTEES
BURKED	BURNSIDES	BURSTONE*	BUSHMAN	BUSTER
BURKER*	BURNT	BURSTONES*	BUSHMEN	BUSTERS
BURKERS*	BUROO	BURSTS	BUSHPIG*	BUSTIC*
BURKES	BUROOS	BURTHEN	BUSHPIGS*	BUSTICS*
BURKING	BURP	BURTHENED	BUSHTIT*	BUSTIER
BURKITE*	BURPED	BURTHENING	BUSHTITS*	BUSTIERS
BURKITES*	BURPING	BURTHENS	BUSHVELD	BUSTIEST
BURKS	BURPS	BURTON	BUSHVELDS	BUSTING
BURL	BURQA	BURTONS	BUSHWA*	BUSTINGS
BURLADERO*	BURQAS	BURWEED	BUSHWAH*	BUSTLE
BURLADEROS*	BURR	BURWEEDS	BUSHWAHS*	BUSTLED
BURLAP	BURRAWANG	BURY	BUSHWALK	BUSTLER
BURLAPS	BURRAWANGS	BURYING	BUSHWALKED	BUSTLERS
BURLED	BURRED	BUS	BUSHWALKING	BUSTLES
BURLER	BURREL	BUSBAR*	BUSHWALKINGS	BUSTLINE*
BURLERS	BURRELL	BUSBARS*	BUSHWALKS	BUSTLINES*
BURLESK*	BURRELLS	BUSBIES	BUSHWAS*	BUSTLING
BURLESKS*	BURRELS	BUSBOY	BUSHWHACK	BUSTS
BURLESQUE	BURRER*	BUSBOYS	BUSHWHACKED	BUSTY
BURLESQUED	BURRERS*	BUSBY	BUSHWHACKING	BUSULFAN*
BURLESQUES	BURRHEL	BUSED	BUSHWHACKINGS	BUSULFANS*
BURLESQUING	BURRHELS	BUSES	BUSHWHACKS	BUSY
BURLETTA	BURRIER	BUSGIRL	BUSHWOMAN	BUSYBODIED
BURLETTAS	BURRIEST	BUSGIRLS	BUSHWOMEN	BUSYBODIES
BURLEY	BURRING	BUSH	BUSHY	BUSYBODY

Words marked with an asterisk are from OTCWL

BUSYBODYING
BUSYING
BUSYNESS
BUSYNESSES
BUSYWORK*
BUSYWORKS*
BUT
BUTADIENE
BUTADIENES
BUTANE
BUTANES
BUTANOL
BUTANOLS
BUTANONE*
BUTANONES*
BUTCH
BUTCHER
BUTCHERED
BUTCHERIES
BUTCHERING
BUTCHERINGS
BUTCHERLY
BUTCHERS
BUTCHERY
BUTCHES
BUTCHEST
BUTCHING
BUTCHINGS
BUTE
BUTENE
BUTENES
BUTEO*
BUTEOS*
BUTES
BUTLE*
BUTLED*
BUTLER
BUTLERAGE
BUTLERAGES
BUTLERED
BUTLERIES
BUTLERING
BUTLERS
BUTLERY
BUTLES*
BUTLING*
BUTMENT
BUTMENTS
BUTS
BUTT
BUTTALS*
BUTTE

BUTTED
BUTTER
BUTTERBUR
BUTTERBURS
BUTTERCUP
BUTTERCUPS
BUTTERED
BUTTERFAT*
BUTTERFATS*
BUTTERFLIED*
BUTTERFLIES
BUTTERFLY
BUTTERFLYING*
BUTTERIER
BUTTERIES
BUTTERIEST
BUTTERINE
BUTTERINES
BUTTERING
BUTTERNUT
BUTTERNUTS
BUTTERS
BUTTERY
BUTTES
BUTTIES
BUTTING
BUTTINSKI*
BUTTINSKIES*
BUTTINSKY*
BUTTLE
BUTTLED
BUTTLES
BUTTLING
BUTTOCK
BUTTOCKED
BUTTOCKING
BUTTOCKS
BUTTON
BUTTONED
BUTTONER*
BUTTONERS*
BUTTONING
BUTTONS
BUTTONY
BUTTRESS
BUTTRESSED
BUTTRESSES
BUTTRESSING
BUTTS
BUTTSTOCK*
BUTTSTOCKS*
BUTTY

BUTTYMAN
BUTTYMEN
BUTUT*
BUTUTS*
BUTYL
BUTYLATE*
BUTYLATED*
BUTYLATES*
BUTYLATING*
BUTYLENE
BUTYLENES
BUTYLS
BUTYRAL*
BUTYRALS*
BUTYRATE
BUTYRATES
BUTYRIC
BUTYRIN*
BUTYRINS*
BUTYROUS*
BUTYRYL*
BUTYRYLS*
BUVETTE
BUVETTES
BUXOM
BUXOMER
BUXOMEST
BUXOMLY*
BUXOMNESS
BUXOMNESSES
BUY
BUYABLE
BUYABLES
BUYBACK*
BUYBACKS*
BUYER
BUYERS
BUYING
BUYOUT*
BUYOUTS*
BUYS
BUZUKI*
BUZUKIA*
BUZUKIS*
BUZZ
BUZZARD
BUZZARDS
BUZZED
BUZZER
BUZZERS
BUZZES
BUZZIER

BUZZIEST
BUZZING
BUZZINGLY
BUZZINGS
BUZZWIG*
BUZZWIGS*
BUZZWORD
BUZZWORDS
BUZZY
BWANA
BWANAS
BWAZI
BWAZIS
BY
BYCATCH
BYCATCHES
BYCOKET
BYCOKETS
BYE
BYELAW*
BYELAWS*
BYES
BYGONE
BYGONES
BYKE
BYKED
BYKES
BYKING
BYLANDER
BYLANDERS
BYLAW
BYLAWS
BYLINE
BYLINED*
BYLINER*
BYLINERS*
BYLINES
BYLINING*
BYLIVE
BYNAME
BYNAMES
BYNEMPT
BYPASS
BYPASSED
BYPASSES
BYPASSING
BYPAST*
BYPATH
BYPATHS
BYPLACE
BYPLACES
BYPLAY*

BYPLAYS*
BYRE
BYREMAN
BYREMEN
BYRES
BYREWOMAN
BYREWOMEN
BYRL*
BYRLADY
BYRLAKIN
BYRLAW
BYRLAWS
BYRLED*
BYRLING*
BYRLS*
BYRNIE
BYRNIES
BYROAD
BYROADS
BYROOM
BYROOMS
BYS
BYSSAL
BYSSI
BYSSINE
BYSSOID
BYSSUS
BYSSUSES
BYSTANDER
BYSTANDERS
BYSTREET*
BYSTREETS*
BYTALK*
BYTALKS*
BYTE
BYTES
BYTOWNITE
BYTOWNITES
BYWAY
BYWAYS
BYWONER
BYWONERS
BYWORD
BYWORDS
BYWORK*
BYWORKS*
BYZANT
BYZANTINE*
BYZANTS

C

CAATINGA
CAATINGAS
CAB
CABA
CABAL
CABALA
CABALAS
CABALETTA
CABALETTAS
CABALETTE
CABALISM
CABALISMS
CABALIST
CABALISTS
CABALLED
CABALLER
CABALLERO
CABALLEROS
CABALLERS
CABALLINE
CABALLING
CABALS
CABANA
CABANAS
CABARET
CABARETS
CABAS
CABBAGE
CABBAGED
CABBAGES
CABBAGING
CABBAGY
CABBALA
CABBALAH*
CABBALAHS*
CABBALAS
CABBALISM
CABBALISMS
CABBALIST
CABBALISTS
CABBED*
CABBIE
CABBIES
CABBING*
CABBY
CABDRIVER*
CABDRIVERS*
CABER
CABERNET*
CABERNETS*
CABERS
CABESTRO*
CABESTROS*
CABEZON*
CABEZONE*

CABEZONES*
CABEZONS*
CABILDO*
CABILDOS*
CABIN
CABINED
CABINET
CABINETRIES*
CABINETRY*
CABINETS
CABINING
CABINS
CABLE
CABLED
CABLEGRAM
CABLEGRAMS
CABLES
CABLET
CABLETS
CABLEWAY
CABLEWAYS
CABLING
CABLINGS
CABMAN
CABMEN
CABOB
CABOBBED
CABOBBING
CABOBS
CABOC
CABOCEER
CABOCEERS
CABOCHED
CABOCHON
CABOCHONS
CABOCS
CABOMBA*
CABOMBAS*
CABOODLE
CABOODLES
CABOOSE
CABOOSES
CABOSHED
CABOTAGE
CABOTAGES
CABRE
CABRESTA*
CABRESTAS*
CABRESTO*
CABRESTOS*
CABRETTA
CABRETTAS
CABRIE
CABRIES
CABRILLA*

CABRILLAS*
CABRIOLE
CABRIOLES
CABRIOLET
CABRIOLETS
CABRIT
CABRITS
CABS
CABSTAND*
CABSTANDS*
CACA*
CACAFOGO
CACAFOGOS
CACAFUEGO
CACAFUEGOS
CACAO
CACAOS
CACAS*
CACHAEMIA
CACHAEMIAS
CACHAEMIC
CACHALOT
CACHALOTS
CACHE
CACHECTIC
CACHED
CACHEPOT
CACHEPOTS
CACHES
CACHET
CACHETED*
CACHETING*
CACHETS
CACHEXIA
CACHEXIAS
CACHEXIC*
CACHEXIES
CACHEXY
CACHING
CACHOLONG
CACHOLONGS
CACHOLOT
CACHOLOTS
CACHOU
CACHOUS
CACHUCHA
CACHUCHAS
CACIQUE
CACIQUES
CACIQUISM
CACIQUISMS
CACKLE
CACKLED
CACKLER
CACKLERS

CACKLES
CACKLING
CACODEMON
CACODEMONS
CACODOXIES
CACODOXY
CACODYL
CACODYLIC
CACODYLS
CACOEPIES
CACOEPY
CACOETHES
CACOLET
CACOLETS
CACOLOGIES
CACOLOGY
CACOMIXL
CACOMIXLS
CACOON
CACOONS
CACOPHONIES
CACOPHONY
CACOTOPIA
CACOTOPIAS
CACTI
CACTIFORM
CACTOID*
CACTUS
CACTUSES
CACUMEN
CACUMINA
CACUMINAL
CAD
CADASTER*
CADASTERS*
CADASTRAL
CADASTRE
CADASTRES
CADAVER
CADAVERIC
CADAVERS
CADDICE
CADDICES
CADDIE
CADDIED
CADDIES
CADDIS
CADDISES
CADDISH
CADDISHLY*
CADDY
CADDYING
CADDYSS
CADDYSSES
CADE

CADEAU
CADEAUX
CADEE
CADEES
CADELLE
CADELLES
CADENCE
CADENCED
CADENCES
CADENCIES
CADENCING*
CADENCY
CADENT
CADENTIAL
CADENZA
CADENZAS
CADES
CADET
CADETS
CADETSHIP
CADETSHIPS
CADGE
CADGED
CADGER
CADGERS
CADGES
CADGIER
CADGIEST
CADGING
CADGY
CADI
CADIE
CADIES
CADIS
CADMIC*
CADMIUM
CADMIUMS
CADRANS
CADRANSES
CADRE
CADRES
CADS
CADUAC
CADUACS
CADUCEAN
CADUCEI
CADUCEUS
CADUCITIES
CADUCITY
CADUCOUS
CAECA
CAECAL
CAECALLY*
CAECILIAN
CAECILIANS

CAECITIS	CAGILY	CAJOLING	CALCANEAN	CALDRONS
CAECITISES	CAGINESS	CAJON*	CALCANEI	CALECHE*
CAECUM	CAGINESSES	CAJONES*	CALCANEUM	CALECHES*
CAEOMA*	CAGING	CAJUN	CALCANEUS	CALEFIED
CAEOMAS*	CAGOT	CAJUPUT	CALCAR	CALEFIES
CAERULE	CAGOTS	CAJUPUTS	CALCARATE	CALEFY
CAERULEAN	CAGOUL	CAKE	CALCARIA	CALEFYING
CAESAR	CAGOULE	CAKED	CALCARINE	CALEMBOUR
CAESAREAN*	CAGOULES	CAKES	CALCARS	CALEMBOURS
CAESAREANS*	CAGOULS	CAKEWALK	CALCEATE	CALENDAL*
CAESARIAN*	CAGY	CAKEWALKED	CALCEATED	CALENDAR
CAESARIANS*	CAGYNESS	CAKEWALKING	CALCEATES	CALENDARED
CAESARS	CAGYNESSES	CAKEWALKS	CALCEATING	CALENDARING
CAESE	CAHIER	CAKEY	CALCED	CALENDARS
CAESIOUS	CAHIERS	CAKIER	CALCEDONIES	CALENDER
CAESIUM	CAHOOT	CAKIEST	CALCEDONY	CALENDERED
CAESIUMS	CAHOOTS	CAKING	CALCES	CALENDERING
CAESTUS	CAHOW*	CAKINGS	CALCIC	CALENDERINGS
CAESTUSES	CAHOWS*	CAKY	CALCICOLE	CALENDERS
CAESURA	CAID*	CALABASH	CALCICOLES	CALENDRER
CAESURAE	CAIDS*	CALABASHES	CALCIFIC	CALENDRERS
CAESURAL	CAILLACH	CALABOOSE	CALCIFIED	CALENDRIC
CAESURAS	CAILLACHS	CALABOOSES	CALCIFIES	CALENDRIES
CAESURIC*	CAILLE	CALABRESE	CALCIFUGE	CALENDRY
CAFARD	CAILLEACH	CALABRESES	CALCIFUGES	CALENDS
CAFARDS	CAILLEACHS	CALADIUM	CALCIFY	CALENDULA
CAFE	CAILLES	CALADIUMS	CALCIFYING	CALENDULAS
CAFES	CAILLIACH	CALAMANCO	CALCIMINE	CALENTURE
CAFETERIA	CAILLIACHS	CALAMANCOES	CALCIMINED	CALENTURES
CAFETERIAS	CAIMAC	CALAMANCOS	CALCIMINES	CALESA*
CAFETIERE	CAIMACAM	CALAMAR*	CALCIMINING	CALESAS*
CAFETIERES	CAIMACAMS	CALAMARI	CALCINE	CALF
CAFF	CAIMACS	CALAMARIES	CALCINED	CALFDOZER
CAFFEIN	CAIMAN	CALAMARIS*	CALCINES	CALFDOZERS
CAFFEINE	CAIMANS	CALAMARS*	CALCINING	CALFLESS
CAFFEINES	CAIN	CALAMARY	CALCITE	CALFLICK
CAFFEINS	CAINS	CALAMI	CALCITES	CALFLICKS
CAFFEISM	CAIQUE	CALAMINE	CALCITIC*	CALFLIKE*
CAFFEISMS	CAIQUES	CALAMINED*	CALCIUM	CALFS
CAFFILA	CAIRD	CALAMINES	CALCIUMS	CALFSKIN
CAFFILAS	CAIRDS	CALAMINING*	CALCRETE	CALFSKINS
CAFFS	CAIRN	CALAMINT	CALCRETES	CALIATOUR
CAFILA	CAIRNED	CALAMINTS	CALCSPAR	CALIATOURS
CAFILAS	CAIRNGORM	CALAMITE	CALCSPARS	CALIBER
CAFTAN	CAIRNGORMS	CALAMITES	CALCTUFA*	CALIBERED
CAFTANS	CAIRNS	CALAMITIES	CALCTUFAS*	CALIBERS
CAGE	CAIRNY*	CALAMITY	CALCTUFF*	CALIBRATE
CAGEBIRD	CAISSON	CALAMUS	CALCTUFFS*	CALIBRATED
CAGEBIRDS	CAISSONS	CALANDO	CALCULAR	CALIBRATES
CAGED	CAITIFF	CALANDRIA	CALCULARY	CALIBRATING
CAGEFUL*	CAITIFFS	CALANDRIAS	CALCULATE	CALIBRE
CAGEFULS*	CAITIVE	CALANTHE	CALCULATED	CALIBRED
CAGELING	CAITIVES	CALANTHES	CALCULATES	CALIBRES
CAGELINGS	CAJAPUT*	CALASH	CALCULATING	CALICES
CAGER*	CAJAPUTS*	CALASHES	CALCULI	CALICHE
CAGERS*	CAJEPUT	CALATHEA	CALCULOSE	CALICHES
CAGES	CAJEPUTS	CALATHEAS	CALCULOUS	CALICLE
CAGEWORK	CAJOLE	CALATHI	CALCULUS	CALICLES
CAGEWORKS	CAJOLED	CALATHOS*	CALCULUSES	CALICO
CAGEY	CAJOLER	CALATHUS	CALDARIA	CALICOES
CAGEYNESS	CAJOLERIES	CALAVANCE	CALDARIUM	CALICOS
CAGEYNESSES	CAJOLERS	CALAVANCES	CALDERA	CALID
CAGIER	CAJOLERY	CALCANEA	CALDERAS	CALIDITIES
CAGIEST	CAJOLES	CALCANEAL	CALDRON	CALIDITY

The Chambers Dictionary is the authority for many longer words; see Introduction, page ix

CALIF	CALLIOPES	CALOYER	CALYPTER*	CAMELEONS
CALIFATE*	CALLIPEE*	CALOYERS	CALYPTERA	CAMELIA*
CALIFATES*	CALLIPEES*	CALP	CALYPTERAS	CAMELIAS*
CALIFS	CALLIPER	CALPA	CALYPTERS*	CAMELID
CALIGO	CALLIPERED	CALPAC	CALYPTRA	CAMELIDS
CALIGOES	CALLIPERING	CALPACK	CALYPTRAS	CAMELINE
CALIGOS	CALLIPERS	CALPACKS	CALYX	CAMELINES
CALIMA	CALLOSE*	CALPACS	CALYXES	CAMELISH
CALIMAS	CALLOSES*	CALPAS	CALZONE	CAMELLIA
CALIOLOGIES	CALLOSITIES	CALPS	CALZONES	CAMELLIAS
CALIOLOGY	CALLOSITY	CALQUE	CALZONI	CAMELOID
CALIPASH	CALLOUS	CALQUED	CAM	CAMELOIDS
CALIPASHES	CALLOUSED*	CALQUES	CAMAIEU	CAMELOT
CALIPEE	CALLOUSES*	CALQUING	CAMAIEUX	CAMELOTS
CALIPEES	CALLOUSING*	CALTHA	CAMAIL*	CAMELRIES
CALIPER	CALLOUSLY	CALTHAS	CAMAILED*	CAMELRY
CALIPERED*	CALLOW	CALTHROP	CAMAILS*	CAMELS
CALIPERING*	CALLOWER	CALTHROPS	CAMAN	CAMEO
CALIPERS	CALLOWEST	CALTRAP	CAMANACHD	CAMEOED*
CALIPH	CALLOWS	CALTRAPS	CAMANACHDS	CAMEOING*
CALIPHAL	CALLS	CALTROP	CAMANS	CAMEOS
CALIPHATE	CALLUNA	CALTROPS	CAMARILLA	CAMERA
CALIPHATES	CALLUNAS	CALUMBA	CAMARILLAS	CAMERAE
CALIPHS	CALLUS	CALUMBAS	CAMARON	CAMERAL
CALISAYA	CALLUSED*	CALUMET	CAMARONS	CAMERAMAN
CALISAYAS	CALLUSES	CALUMETS	CAMAS	CAMERAMEN
CALIVER	CALLUSING*	CALUMNIES	CAMASES	CAMERAS
CALIVERS	CALM	CALUMNY	CAMASH	CAMERATED
CALIX	CALMANT	CALUTRON	CAMASHES	CAMES
CALK	CALMANTS	CALUTRONS	CAMASS	CAMESE
CALKED	CALMATIVE	CALVADOS*	CAMASSES	CAMESES
CALKER	CALMATIVES	CALVADOSES*	CAMBER	CAMION
CALKERS	CALMED	CALVARIA	CAMBERED	CAMIONS
CALKIN	CALMER	CALVARIAS	CAMBERING	CAMIS
CALKING	CALMEST	CALVARIES	CAMBERINGS	CAMISA*
CALKINS	CALMIER	CALVARIUM*	CAMBERS	CAMISADE
CALKS	CALMIEST	CALVARY	CAMBIA	CAMISADES
CALL	CALMING	CALVE	CAMBIAL	CAMISADO
CALLA	CALMLY	CALVED	CAMBIFORM	CAMISADOES*
CALLABLE*	CALMNESS	CALVER	CAMBISM	CAMISADOS
CALLALOO*	CALMNESSES	CALVERED	CAMBISMS	CAMISAS*
CALLALOOS*	CALMS	CALVERING	CAMBIST	CAMISE
CALLAN	CALMSTONE	CALVERS	CAMBISTRIES	CAMISES
CALLANS	CALMSTONES	CALVES	CAMBISTRY	CAMISIA*
CALLANT	CALMY	CALVING	CAMBISTS	CAMISIAS*
CALLANTS	CALO*	CALVITIES	CAMBIUM	CAMISOLE
CALLAS	CALOMEL	CALX	CAMBIUMS	CAMISOLES
CALLBACK*	CALOMELS	CALXES	CAMBOGE	CAMLET
CALLBACKS*	CALORIC	CALYCATE*	CAMBOGES	CAMLETS
CALLBOY*	CALORICS	CALYCEAL*	CAMBOGIA*	CAMMED
CALLBOYS*	CALORIE	CALYCES	CAMBOGIAS*	CAMMING
CALLED	CALORIES	CALYCINAL	CAMBREL	CAMOGIE
CALLER	CALORIFIC	CALYCINE	CAMBRELS	CAMOGIES
CALLERS	CALORIST	CALYCLE	CAMBRIC	CAMOMILE
CALLET	CALORISTS	CALYCLED	CAMBRICS	CAMOMILES
CALLETS	CALORIZE*	CALYCLES	CAMCORDER	CAMORRA
CALLID	CALORIZED*	CALYCOID	CAMCORDERS	CAMORRAS
CALLIDITIES	CALORIZES*	CALYCULE	CAME	CAMOTE
CALLIDITY	CALORIZING*	CALYCULES	CAMEL	CAMOTES
CALLIGRAM	CALORY	CALYCULI	CAMELBACK	CAMOUFLET
CALLIGRAMS	CALOTTE	CALYCULUS	CAMELBACKS	CAMOUFLETS
CALLING	CALOTTES	CALYPSO	CAMELEER	CAMP
CALLINGS	CALOTYPE	CALYPSOES*	CAMELEERS	CAMPAGNA
CALLIOPE	CALOTYPES	CALYPSOS	CAMELEON	CAMPAGNAS

Words marked with an asterisk are from OTCWL

CAMPAGNE*	CAMPOREES	CANBANKS	CANDOCKS	CANKERING
CAMPAIGN	CAMPOS	CANCAN	CANDOR	CANKEROUS
CAMPAIGNED	CAMPS	CANCANS	CANDORS	CANKERS
CAMPAIGNING	CAMPSITE	CANCEL	CANDOUR	CANKERY
CAMPAIGNS	CAMPSITES	CANCELED*	CANDOURS	CANN
CAMPANA	CAMPUS	CANCELEER	CANDY	CANNA
CAMPANAS	CAMPUSED*	CANCELEERED	CANDYING	CANNABIC
CAMPANERO	CAMPUSES	CANCELEERING	CANDYTUFT	CANNABIN
CAMPANEROS	CAMPUSING*	CANCELEERS	CANDYTUFTS	CANNABINS
CAMPANILE	CAMPY	CANCELER*	CANE	CANNABIS
CAMPANILES	CAMS	CANCELERS*	CANEBRAKE	CANNABISES
CAMPANILI	CAMSHAFT	CANCELIER	CANEBRAKES	CANNACH
CAMPANIST	CAMSHAFTS	CANCELIERED	CANED	CANNACHS
CAMPANISTS	CAMSHEUGH	CANCELIERING	CANEFRUIT	CANNAE
CAMPANULA	CAMSHO	CANCELIERS	CANEFRUITS	CANNAS
CAMPANULAS	CAMSHOCH	CANCELING*	CANEH	CANNED
CAMPCRAFT*	CAMSTAIRY	CANCELLED	CANEHS	CANNEL
CAMPCRAFTS*	CAMSTANE	CANCELLER*	CANELLA	CANNELON*
CAMPEADOR	CAMSTANES	CANCELLERS*	CANELLAS	CANNELONS*
CAMPEADORS	CAMSTEARY	CANCELLI	CANELLINI	CANNELS
CAMPED	CAMSTONE	CANCELLING	CANEPHOR	CANNELURE
CAMPER	CAMSTONES	CANCELS	CANEPHORA	CANNELURES
CAMPERS	CAMUS	CANCER	CANEPHORAS	CANNER
CAMPESINO	CAMUSES	CANCERATE	CANEPHORE	CANNERIES
CAMPESINOS	CAMWOOD	CANCERATED	CANEPHORES	CANNERS
CAMPEST	CAMWOODS	CANCERATES	CANEPHORS	CANNERY
CAMPFIRE	CAN	CANCERATING	CANER*	CANNIBAL
CAMPFIRES	CANADA	CANCEROUS	CANERS*	CANNIBALS
CAMPHANE	CANADAS	CANCERS	CANES	CANNIE*
CAMPHANES	CANAIGRE	CANCHA*	CANESCENT	CANNIER
CAMPHENE	CANAIGRES	CANCHAS*	CANEWARE*	CANNIEST
CAMPHENES	CANAILLE	CANCRINE	CANEWARES*	CANNIKIN
CAMPHINE	CANAILLES	CANCROID	CANFIELD	CANNIKINS
CAMPHINES	CANAKIN	CANCROIDS	CANFIELDS	CANNILY
CAMPHIRE	CANAKINS	CANDELA	CANFUL	CANNINESS
CAMPHIRES	CANAL	CANDELAS	CANFULS	CANNINESSES
CAMPHOL*	CANALED*	CANDENT	CANG	CANNING
CAMPHOLS*	CANALING*	CANDID	CANGLE	CANNINGS*
CAMPHOR	CANALISE	CANDIDA	CANGLED	CANNISTER*
CAMPHORIC	CANALISED	CANDIDACIES	CANGLES	CANNISTERS*
CAMPHORS	CANALISES	CANDIDACY	CANGLING	CANNOLI*
CAMPI*	CANALISING	CANDIDAL	CANGS	CANNON
CAMPIER	CANALIZE	CANDIDAS	CANGUE	CANNONADE
CAMPIEST	CANALIZED	CANDIDATE	CANGUES	CANNONADED
CAMPILY*	CANALIZES	CANDIDATES	CANICULAR	CANNONADES
CAMPINESS*	CANALIZING	CANDIDER	CANID	CANNONADING
CAMPINESSES*	CANALLED*	CANDIDEST	CANIDS	CANNONED
CAMPING	CANALLER*	CANDIDLY	CANIER	CANNONEER
CAMPINGS*	CANALLERS*	CANDIDS*	CANIEST	CANNONEERS
CAMPION	CANALLING*	CANDIE	CANIKIN	CANNONIER
CAMPIONS	CANALS	CANDIED	CANIKINS	CANNONIERS
CAMPLE	CANAPE	CANDIES	CANINE	CANNONING
CAMPLED	CANAPES	CANDLE	CANINES	CANNONRIES
CAMPLES	CANARD	CANDLED	CANING	CANNONRY
CAMPLING	CANARDS	CANDLELIT*	CANINGS	CANNONS
CAMPLY	CANARIED	CANDLENUT	CANINITIES	CANNOT
CAMPNESS	CANARIES	CANDLENUTS	CANINITY	CANNS
CAMPNESSES	CANARY	CANDLEPIN*	CANISTER	CANNULA
CAMPO	CANARYING	CANDLEPINS*	CANISTERED	CANNULAE
CAMPODEID	CANASTA	CANDLER*	CANISTERING	CANNULAR
CAMPODEIDS	CANASTAS	CANDLERS*	CANISTERS	CANNULAS
CAMPONG*	CANASTER	CANDLES	CANITIES	CANNULATE
CAMPONGS*	CANASTERS	CANDLING	CANKER	CANNY
CAMPOREE	CANBANK	CANDOCK	CANKERED	CANOE

CANOEABLE*	CANTERED	CANTOS	CAPELETS	CAPOEIRAS
CANOED	CANTERING	CANTRAIP*	CAPELIN	CAPON
CANOEING	CANTERS	CANTRAIPS*	CAPELINE	CAPONATA*
CANOEINGS	CANTEST	CANTRAP*	CAPELINES	CAPONATAS*
CANOEIST	CANTHAL*	CANTRAPS*	CAPELINS	CAPONIER
CANOEISTS	CANTHARI	CANTRED	CAPELLET	CAPONIERE
CANOES	CANTHARID	CANTREDS	CAPELLETS	CAPONIERES
CANOLA*	CANTHARIDES	CANTREF	CAPELLINE	CAPONIERS
CANON	CANTHARIDS	CANTREFS	CAPELLINES	CAPONISE
CANONESS	CANTHARIS	CANTRIP	CAPER	CAPONISED
CANONESSES	CANTHARUS	CANTRIPS	CAPERED	CAPONISES
CANONIC	CANTHI	CANTS	CAPERER	CAPONISING
CANONICAL	CANTHOOK	CANTUS	CAPERERS	CAPONIZE
CANONICALS	CANTHOOKS	CANTY	CAPERING	CAPONIZED
CANONISE	CANTHUS	CANULA	CAPERS	CAPONIZES
CANONISED	CANTIC*	CANULAE	CAPES	CAPONIZING
CANONISES	CANTICLE	CANULAS	CAPESKIN	CAPONS
CANONISING	CANTICLES	CANULATE*	CAPESKINS	CAPORAL
CANONIST	CANTICO	CANULATED*	CAPEWORK	CAPORALS
CANONISTS	CANTICOED	CANULATES*	CAPEWORKS	CAPOS
CANONIZE	CANTICOING	CANULATING*	CAPFUL*	CAPOT
CANONIZED	CANTICOS	CANVAS	CAPFULS*	CAPOTASTO
CANONIZES	CANTICOY	CANVASED	CAPH*	CAPOTASTOS
CANONIZING	CANTICOYED	CANVASER*	CAPHS*	CAPOTE
CANONRIES	CANTICOYING	CANVASERS*	CAPI	CAPOTES
CANONRY	CANTICOYS	CANVASES	CAPIAS	CAPOTS
CANONS	CANTICUM	CANVASING	CAPIASES	CAPOTTED
CANOODLE	CANTICUMS	CANVASS	CAPILLARIES	CAPOTTING
CANOODLED	CANTIER	CANVASSED	CAPILLARY	CAPOUCH
CANOODLES	CANTIEST	CANVASSER	CAPING	CAPOUCHES
CANOODLING	CANTILENA	CANVASSERS	CAPITA	CAPPED
CANOPIED	CANTILENAS	CANVASSES	CAPITAL	CAPPER
CANOPIES	CANTINA	CANVASSING	CAPITALLY	CAPPERS
CANOPY	CANTINAS	CANY	CAPITALS	CAPPING
CANOPYING	CANTINESS	CANYON	CAPITAN	CAPPINGS
CANOROUS	CANTINESSES	CANYONS	CAPITANI	CAPRATE
CANS	CANTING	CANZONA	CAPITANO	CAPRATES
CANSFUL*	CANTINGS	CANZONAS	CAPITANOS	CAPRIC
CANSO*	CANTION	CANZONE	CAPITANS	CAPRICCI
CANSOS*	CANTIONS	CANZONES*	CAPITATE	CAPRICCIO
CANST	CANTLE	CANZONET	CAPITAYN	CAPRICCIOS
CANSTICK	CANTLED	CANZONETS	CAPITAYNS	CAPRICE
CANSTICKS	CANTLES	CANZONI	CAPITELLA	CAPRICES
CANT	CANTLET	CAP	CAPITOL*	CAPRID
CANTABANK	CANTLETS	CAPA	CAPITOLS*	CAPRIDS
CANTABANKS	CANTLING	CAPABLE	CAPITULA	CAPRIFIED
CANTABILE	CANTO	CAPABLER	CAPITULAR	CAPRIFIES
CANTABILES	CANTON	CAPABLEST	CAPITULARS	CAPRIFIG
CANTALA	CANTONAL	CAPABLY	CAPITULUM	CAPRIFIGS
CANTALAS	CANTONED	CAPACIOUS	CAPIZ	CAPRIFOIL
CANTALOUP	CANTONING	CAPACITIES	CAPIZES	CAPRIFOILS
CANTALOUPS	CANTONISE	CAPACITOR	CAPLE	CAPRIFOLE
CANTAR	CANTONISED	CAPACITORS	CAPLES	CAPRIFOLES
CANTARS	CANTONISES	CAPACITY	CAPLESS*	CAPRIFORM
CANTATA	CANTONISING	CAPARISON	CAPLET	CAPRIFY
CANTATAS	CANTONIZE	CAPARISONED	CAPLETS	CAPRIFYING
CANTATE	CANTONIZED	CAPARISONING	CAPLIN	CAPRINE
CANTATES	CANTONIZES	CAPARISONS	CAPLINS	CAPRIOLE
CANTDOG	CANTONIZING	CAPAS	CAPMAKER*	CAPRIOLED
CANTDOGS	CANTONS	CAPE	CAPMAKERS*	CAPRIOLES
CANTED	CANTOR	CAPED	CAPO	CAPRIOLING
CANTEEN	CANTORIAL	CAPELAN*	CAPOCCHIA	CAPRIS*
CANTEENS	CANTORIS	CAPELANS*	CAPOCCHIAS	CAPROATE
CANTER	CANTORS	CAPELET	CAPOEIRA	CAPROATES

CAPROCK*
CAPROCKS*
CAPROIC
CAPRYLATE
CAPRYLATES
CAPRYLIC
CAPS
CAPSAICIN
CAPSAICINS
CAPSICIN*
CAPSICINS*
CAPSICUM
CAPSICUMS
CAPSID
CAPSIDAL*
CAPSIDS
CAPSIZAL
CAPSIZALS
CAPSIZE
CAPSIZED
CAPSIZES
CAPSIZING
CAPSOMER*
CAPSOMERS*
CAPSTAN
CAPSTANS
CAPSTONE
CAPSTONES
CAPSULAR
CAPSULARY
CAPSULATE
CAPSULE
CAPSULED*
CAPSULES
CAPSULING*
CAPSULISE
CAPSULISED
CAPSULISES
CAPSULISING
CAPSULIZE
CAPSULIZED
CAPSULIZES
CAPSULIZING
CAPTAIN
CAPTAINCIES
CAPTAINCY
CAPTAINED
CAPTAINING
CAPTAINRIES
CAPTAINRY
CAPTAINS
CAPTAN
CAPTANS
CAPTION
CAPTIONED
CAPTIONING
CAPTIONS
CAPTIOUS
CAPTIVATE
CAPTIVATED
CAPTIVATES
CAPTIVATING
CAPTIVE
CAPTIVED

CAPTIVES
CAPTIVING
CAPTIVITIES
CAPTIVITY
CAPTOPRIL*
CAPTOPRILS*
CAPTOR
CAPTORS
CAPTURE
CAPTURED
CAPTURER
CAPTURERS
CAPTURES
CAPTURING
CAPUCCIO
CAPUCCIOS
CAPUCHE
CAPUCHED*
CAPUCHES
CAPUCHIN
CAPUCHINS
CAPUERA
CAPUERAS
CAPUL
CAPULS
CAPUT
CAPYBARA
CAPYBARAS
CAR
CARABAO
CARABAOS
CARABID
CARABIDS
CARABIN
CARABINE
CARABINER
CARABINERS
CARABINES
CARABINS
CARACAL
CARACALS
CARACARA
CARACARAS
CARACK
CARACKS
CARACOL
CARACOLE
CARACOLED
CARACOLES
CARACOLING
CARACOLLED
CARACOLLING
CARACOLS
CARACT
CARACTS
CARACUL
CARACULS
CARAFE
CARAFES
CARAGANA*
CARAGANAS*
CARAGEEN*
CARAGEENS*
CARAMBA

CARAMBOLA
CARAMBOLAS
CARAMBOLE
CARAMBOLED
CARAMBOLES
CARAMBOLING
CARAMEL
CARAMELLED
CARAMELLING
CARAMELS
CARANGID
CARANGIDS
CARANGOID
CARANGOIDS
CARANNA
CARANNAS
CARAP
CARAPACE
CARAPACES
CARAPAX*
CARAPAXES*
CARAPS
CARASSOW*
CARASSOWS*
CARAT
CARATE*
CARATES*
CARATS
CARAUNA
CARAUNAS
CARAVAN
CARAVANCE
CARAVANCES
CARAVANED
CARAVANER
CARAVANERS
CARAVANING
CARAVANNED
CARAVANNING
CARAVANS
CARAVEL
CARAVELS
CARAWAY
CARAWAYS
CARB
CARBACHOL
CARBACHOLS
CARBAMATE
CARBAMATES
CARBAMIC*
CARBAMIDE
CARBAMIDES
CARBAMINO*
CARBAMYL*
CARBAMYLS*
CARBANION
CARBANIONS
CARBARN*
CARBARNS*
CARBARYL
CARBARYLS
CARBAZOLE
CARBAZOLES
CARBIDE

CARBIDES
CARBIES
CARBINE
CARBINEER
CARBINEERS
CARBINES
CARBINIER
CARBINIERS
CARBINOL*
CARBINOLS*
CARBO*
CARBOLIC
CARBOLICS
CARBON
CARBONADE
CARBONADES
CARBONADO
CARBONADOED
CARBONADOES
CARBONADOING
CARBONADOS
CARBONARA
CARBONARAS
CARBONATE
CARBONATED
CARBONATES
CARBONATING
CARBONIC
CARBONISE
CARBONISED
CARBONISES
CARBONISING
CARBONIZE
CARBONIZED
CARBONIZES
CARBONIZING
CARBONS
CARBONYL
CARBONYLS
CARBORA*
CARBORAS*
CARBOS*
CARBOXYL
CARBOXYLS
CARBOY
CARBOYED*
CARBOYS
CARBS
CARBUNCLE
CARBUNCLES
CARBURATE
CARBURATED
CARBURATES
CARBURATING
CARBURET
CARBURETED*
CARBURETING*
CARBURETS
CARBURETTED
CARBURETTING
CARBURISE
CARBURISED
CARBURISES
CARBURISING

CARBURIZE
CARBURIZED
CARBURIZES
CARBURIZING
CARBY
CARCAJOU
CARCAJOUS
CARCAKE
CARCAKES
CARCANET
CARCANETS
CARCASE
CARCASED
CARCASES
CARCASING
CARCASS
CARCASSED
CARCASSES
CARCASSING
CARCEL*
CARCELS*
CARCERAL
CARCINOID*
CARCINOIDS*
CARCINOMA
CARCINOMAS
CARCINOMATA
CARD
CARDAMINE
CARDAMINES
CARDAMOM
CARDAMOMS
CARDAMON
CARDAMONS
CARDAMUM
CARDAMUMS
CARDBOARD
CARDBOARDS
CARDCASE
CARDCASES
CARDECU
CARDECUE
CARDECUES
CARDECUS
CARDED
CARDER
CARDERS
CARDI
CARDIA*
CARDIAC
CARDIACAL
CARDIACS
CARDIAE*
CARDIALGIES
CARDIALGY
CARDIAS*
CARDIES
CARDIGAN
CARDIGANS
CARDINAL
CARDINALS
CARDING
CARDINGS*
CARDIOID

CARDIOIDS
CARDIS
CARDITIC*
CARDITIS
CARDITISES
CARDOON
CARDOONS
CARDPHONE
CARDPHONES
CARDPUNCH
CARDPUNCHES
CARDS
CARDSHARP*
CARDSHARPS*
CARDUUS
CARDUUSES
CARDY
CARE
CARED
CAREEN
CAREENAGE
CAREENAGES
CAREENED
CAREENER*
CAREENERS*
CAREENING
CAREENS
CAREER
CAREERED
CAREERER*
CAREERERS*
CAREERING
CAREERISM
CAREERISMS
CAREERIST
CAREERISTS
CAREERS
CAREFREE
CAREFUL
CAREFULLER*
CAREFULLEST*
CAREFULLY
CAREGIVER*
CAREGIVERS*
CARELESS
CAREME
CAREMES
CARER
CARERS
CARES
CARESS
CARESSED
CARESSER*
CARESSERS*
CARESSES
CARESSING
CARESSINGS
CARESSIVE
CARET
CARETAKE
CARETAKEN
CARETAKER
CARETAKERS
CARETAKES

CARETAKING
CARETOOK
CARETS
CAREWORN
CAREX
CARFARE
CARFARES
CARFAX
CARFAXES
CARFOX
CARFOXES
CARFUFFLE
CARFUFFLED
CARFUFFLES
CARFUFFLING
CARFUL*
CARFULS*
CARGEESE
CARGO
CARGOED
CARGOES
CARGOING
CARGOOSE
CARGOS*
CARHOP*
CARHOPS*
CARIACOU
CARIACOUS
CARIAMA
CARIAMAS
CARIBE
CARIBES
CARIBOU
CARIBOUS
CARICES
CARIED*
CARIERE
CARIERES
CARIES
CARILLON
CARILLONED
CARILLONING
CARILLONNED*
CARILLONNING*
CARILLONS
CARINA
CARINAE
CARINAL*
CARINAS
CARINATE
CARINATED*
CARING
CARIOCA
CARIOCAS
CARIOLE
CARIOLES
CARIOUS
CARITAS
CARITASES*
CARITATES
CARJACK
CARJACKED
CARJACKER
CARJACKERS

CARJACKING
CARJACKINGS
CARJACKS
CARJACOU
CARJACOUS
CARK
CARKED
CARKING
CARKS
CARL
CARLE*
CARLES*
CARLESS*
CARLIN*
CARLINE
CARLINES
CARLING
CARLINGS
CARLINS*
CARLISH
CARLOAD
CARLOADS
CARLOCK
CARLOCKS
CARLOT
CARLOTS
CARLS
CARMAKER*
CARMAKERS*
CARMAN
CARMELITE
CARMELITES
CARMEN
CARMINE
CARMINES
CARN*
CARNAGE
CARNAGES
CARNAHUBA
CARNAHUBAS
CARNAL
CARNALISE
CARNALISED
CARNALISES
CARNALISING
CARNALISM
CARNALISMS
CARNALIST
CARNALISTS
CARNALITIES
CARNALITY
CARNALIZE
CARNALIZED
CARNALIZES
CARNALIZING
CARNALLED
CARNALLING
CARNALLY
CARNALS
CARNATION
CARNATIONS
CARNAUBA
CARNAUBAS
CARNELIAN

CARNELIANS
CARNEOUS
CARNET
CARNETS
CARNEY
CARNEYED
CARNEYING
CARNEYS
CARNIE*
CARNIED
CARNIER
CARNIES
CARNIEST
CARNIFEX
CARNIFEXES
CARNIFIED
CARNIFIES
CARNIFY
CARNIFYING
CARNITINE*
CARNITINES*
CARNIVAL
CARNIVALS
CARNIVORA*
CARNIVORE
CARNIVORES
CARNOSE
CARNOSITIES
CARNOSITY
CARNOTITE
CARNOTITES
CARNS*
CARNY
CARNYING
CAROACH*
CAROACHES*
CAROB
CAROBS
CAROCH*
CAROCHE
CAROCHES
CAROL
CAROLED*
CAROLER*
CAROLERS*
CAROLI
CAROLING*
CAROLLED
CAROLLER
CAROLLERS
CAROLLING
CAROLS
CAROLUS
CAROLUSES
CAROM
CAROMED
CAROMEL
CAROMELLED
CAROMELLING
CAROMELS
CAROMING
CAROMS
CAROTENE
CAROTENES

CAROTID
CAROTIDS*
CAROTIN
CAROTINS
CAROUSAL
CAROUSALS
CAROUSE
CAROUSED
CAROUSEL
CAROUSELS
CAROUSER
CAROUSERS
CAROUSES
CAROUSING
CARP
CARPACCIO
CARPACCIOS
CARPAL
CARPALE*
CARPALIA*
CARPALS
CARPARK
CARPARKS
CARPED
CARPEL
CARPELS
CARPENTER
CARPENTERED
CARPENTERING
CARPENTERS
CARPENTRIES
CARPENTRY
CARPER
CARPERS
CARPET
CARPETBAG
CARPETBAGS
CARPETED
CARPETING
CARPETINGS
CARPETS
CARPI
CARPING
CARPINGLY
CARPINGS
CARPOLOGIES
CARPOLOGY
CARPOOL*
CARPOOLED*
CARPOOLER*
CARPOOLERS*
CARPOOLING*
CARPOOLS*
CARPORT
CARPORTS
CARPS
CARPUS
CARR
CARRACK
CARRACKS
CARRACT
CARRACTS
CARRAGEEN
CARRAGEENS

CARRAT
CARRATS
CARRAWAY
CARRAWAYS
CARRECT
CARRECTS
CARREFOUR*
CARREFOURS*
CARREL
CARRELL
CARRELLS
CARRELS
CARRIAGE
CARRIAGES
CARRIED
CARRIER
CARRIERS
CARRIES
CARRIOLE
CARRIOLES
CARRION
CARRIONS
CARRITCH
CARRITCHES
CARROCH*
CARROCHES*
CARROM*
CARROMED*
CARROMING*
CARROMS*
CARRONADE
CARRONADES
CARROT
CARROTIER
CARROTIEST
CARROTIN*
CARROTINS*
CARROTS
CARROTTOP*
CARROTTOPS*
CARROTY
CARROUSEL
CARROUSELS
CARRS
CARRY
CARRYALL
CARRYALLS
CARRYBACK*
CARRYBACKS*
CARRYCOT
CARRYCOTS
CARRYING
CARRYON*
CARRYONS*
CARRYOUT*
CARRYOUTS*
CARRYOVER*
CARRYOVERS*
CARRYTALE
CARRYTALES
CARS
CARSE
CARSES
CARSEY

CARSEYS
CARSICK*
CART
CARTA
CARTABLE*
CARTAGE
CARTAGES
CARTAS
CARTE
CARTED
CARTEL
CARTELISE
CARTELISED
CARTELISES
CARTELISING
CARTELISM
CARTELISMS
CARTELIST
CARTELISTS
CARTELIZE
CARTELIZED
CARTELIZES
CARTELIZING
CARTELS
CARTER
CARTERS
CARTES
CARTILAGE
CARTILAGES
CARTING
CARTLOAD
CARTLOADS
CARTOGRAM
CARTOGRAMS
CARTOLOGIES
CARTOLOGY
CARTON
CARTONAGE
CARTONAGES
CARTONED
CARTONING
CARTONS
CARTOON
CARTOONED
CARTOONING
CARTOONS
CARTOONY*
CARTOP*
CARTOPPER*
CARTOPPERS*
CARTOUCH
CARTOUCHE
CARTOUCHES
CARTRIDGE
CARTRIDGES
CARTROAD
CARTROADS
CARTS
CARTULARIES
CARTULARY
CARTWAY
CARTWAYS
CARTWHEEL
CARTWHEELED

CARTWHEELING
CARTWHEELS
CARUCAGE
CARUCAGES
CARUCATE
CARUCATES
CARUNCLE
CARUNCLES
CARVACROL
CARVACROLS
CARVE
CARVED
CARVEL
CARVELS
CARVEN
CARVER
CARVERIES
CARVERS
CARVERY
CARVES
CARVIES
CARVING
CARVINGS
CARVY
CARWASH*
CARWASHES*
CARYATIC
CARYATID
CARYATIDES
CARYATIDS
CARYOPSES
CARYOPSIDES
CARYOPSIS
CARYOTIN*
CARYOTINS*
CASA
CASABA*
CASABAS*
CASAS
CASAVA*
CASAVAS*
CASBAH
CASBAHS
CASCABEL
CASCABELS
CASCABLE*
CASCABLES*
CASCADE
CASCADED
CASCADES
CASCADING
CASCADURA
CASCADURAS
CASCARA
CASCARAS
CASCHROM
CASCHROMS
CASCO
CASCOS
CASE
CASEASE*
CASEASES*
CASEATE*
CASEATED*

CASEATES*
CASEATING*
CASEATION
CASEATIONS
CASEBOOK
CASEBOOKS
CASED
CASEFIED*
CASEFIES*
CASEFY*
CASEFYING*
CASEIC*
CASEIN
CASEINATE*
CASEINATES*
CASEINS
CASELOAD*
CASELOADS*
CASEMAKER
CASEMAKERS
CASEMAN
CASEMATE
CASEMATED
CASEMATES
CASEMEN
CASEMENT
CASEMENTS
CASEOSE*
CASEOSES*
CASEOUS
CASERN
CASERNE
CASERNES
CASERNS
CASES
CASETTE*
CASETTES*
CASEWORK
CASEWORKS
CASEWORM*
CASEWORMS*
CASH
CASHABLE*
CASHAW
CASHAWS
CASHBOOK*
CASHBOOKS*
CASHBOX*
CASHBOXES*
CASHED
CASHES
CASHEW
CASHEWS
CASHIER
CASHIERED
CASHIERER
CASHIERERS
CASHIERING
CASHIERINGS
CASHIERS
CASHING
CASHLESS
CASHMERE
CASHMERES

CASHOO*
CASHOOS*
CASHPOINT
CASHPOINTS
CASIMERE
CASIMERES
CASIMIRE*
CASIMIRES*
CASING
CASINGS
CASINI*
CASINO
CASINOS
CASITA*
CASITAS*
CASK
CASKED
CASKET
CASKETED*
CASKETING*
CASKETS
CASKING
CASKS
CASKSTAND
CASKSTANDS
CASKY*
CASQUE
CASQUED*
CASQUES
CASSABA*
CASSABAS*
CASSAREEP
CASSAREEPS
CASSARIPE
CASSARIPES
CASSATA
CASSATAS
CASSATION
CASSATIONS
CASSAVA
CASSAVAS
CASSEROLE
CASSEROLED
CASSEROLES
CASSEROLING
CASSETTE
CASSETTES
CASSIA
CASSIAS
CASSIMERE
CASSIMERES
CASSINGLE
CASSINGLES
CASSINO
CASSINOS
CASSIS
CASSISES
CASSOCK
CASSOCKED
CASSOCKS
CASSONADE
CASSONADES
CASSONE
CASSONES

CASSOULET	CASUALLY	CATAMENIA	CATCHPOLL	CATERWAULING
CASSOULETS	CASUALS	CATAMITE	CATCHPOLLS	CATERWAULINGS
CASSOWARIES	CASUALTIES	CATAMITES	CATCHT	CATERWAULS
CASSOWARY	CASUALTY	CATAMOUNT	CATCHUP	CATES
CAST	CASUARINA	CATAMOUNTS	CATCHUPS	CATFACE*
CASTABLE*	CASUARINAS	CATAPAN	CATCHWEED	CATFACES*
CASTANET	CASUIST	CATAPANS	CATCHWEEDS	CATFACING*
CASTANETS	CASUISTIC	CATAPHORA*	CATCHWORD	CATFACINGS*
CASTAWAY	CASUISTRIES	CATAPHORAS*	CATCHWORDS	CATFALL*
CASTAWAYS	CASUISTRY	CATAPHYLL	CATCHY	CATFALLS*
CASTE	CASUISTS	CATAPHYLLS	CATCLAW*	CATFIGHT*
CASTED	CASUS*	CATAPLASM	CATCLAWS*	CATFIGHTS*
CASTEISM*	CAT	CATAPLASMS	CATE	CATFISH
CASTEISMS*	CATABASES	CATAPLEXIES	CATECHIN*	CATFISHES
CASTELESS	CATABASIS	CATAPLEXY	CATECHINS*	CATGUT
CASTELLA	CATABOLIC	CATAPULT	CATECHISE	CATGUTS
CASTELLAN	CATACLASM	CATAPULTED	CATECHISED	CATHARISE
CASTELLANS	CATACLASMS	CATAPULTING	CATECHISES	CATHARISED
CASTELLUM	CATACLYSM	CATAPULTS	CATECHISING	CATHARISES
CASTELLUMS	CATACLYSMS	CATARACT	CATECHISINGS	CATHARISING
CASTER	CATACOMB	CATARACTS	CATECHISM	CATHARIZE
CASTERS	CATACOMBS	CATARHINE	CATECHISMS	CATHARIZED
CASTES	CATAFALCO	CATARRH	CATECHIST	CATHARIZES
CASTIGATE	CATAFALCOES	CATARRHAL	CATECHISTS	CATHARIZING
CASTIGATED	CATALASE	CATARRHS	CATECHIZE	CATHARSES
CASTIGATES	CATALASES	CATASTA	CATECHIZED	CATHARSIS
CASTIGATING	CATALATIC*	CATASTAS	CATECHIZES	CATHARTIC
CASTING	CATALEPSIES	CATATONIA	CATECHIZING	CATHARTICS
CASTINGS	CATALEPSY	CATATONIAS	CATECHIZINGS	CATHEAD
CASTLE	CATALEXES	CATATONIC	CATECHOL	CATHEADS
CASTLED	CATALEXIS	CATATONICS	CATECHOLS	CATHECT*
CASTLES	CATALO	CATATONIES	CATECHU	CATHECTED*
CASTLING	CATALOES	CATATONY	CATECHUS	CATHECTIC
CASTOCK	CATALOG	CATAWBA	CATEGORIC	CATHECTING*
CASTOCKS	CATALOGED	CATAWBAS	CATEGORIES	CATHECTS*
CASTOFF*	CATALOGER	CATBIRD	CATEGORY	CATHEDRA
CASTOFFS*	CATALOGERS	CATBIRDS	CATELOG	CATHEDRAE*
CASTOR	CATALOGING	CATBOAT	CATELOGS	CATHEDRAL
CASTOREUM	CATALOGS	CATBOATS	CATENA	CATHEDRALS
CASTOREUMS	CATALOGUE	CATBRIER*	CATENAE	CATHEDRAS
CASTORIES	CATALOGUED	CATBRIERS*	CATENANE	CATHEPSIN*
CASTORS	CATALOGUES	CATCALL	CATENANES	CATHEPSINS*
CASTORY	CATALOGUING	CATCALLED	CATENARIES	CATHETER
CASTRAL	CATALOS	CATCALLING	CATENARY	CATHETERS
CASTRATE	CATALPA	CATCALLS	CATENAS	CATHETUS
CASTRATED	CATALPAS	CATCH	CATENATE	CATHETUSES
CASTRATES	CATALYSE	CATCHABLE	CATENATED	CATHEXES
CASTRATI	CATALYSED	CATCHALL*	CATENATES	CATHEXIS
CASTRATING	CATALYSER	CATCHALLS*	CATENATING	CATHISMA
CASTRATO	CATALYSERS	CATCHED	CATENOID*	CATHISMAS
CASTRATOR*	CATALYSES	CATCHEN	CATENOIDS*	CATHODAL
CASTRATORS*	CATALYSING	CATCHER	CATER	CATHODE
CASTS	CATALYSIS	CATCHERS	CATERAN	CATHODES
CASUAL	CATALYST	CATCHES	CATERANS	CATHODIC
CASUALISE	CATALYSTS	CATCHFLIES	CATERED	CATHOLE
CASUALISED	CATALYTIC	CATCHFLY	CATERER	CATHOLES
CASUALISES	CATALYZE	CATCHIER	CATERERS	CATHOLIC
CASUALISING	CATALYZED	CATCHIEST	CATERESS	CATHOLICS*
CASUALISM	CATALYZER	CATCHING	CATERESSES	CATHOOD
CASUALISMS	CATALYZERS	CATCHINGS	CATERING	CATHOODS
CASUALIZE	CATALYZES	CATCHMENT	CATERINGS	CATHOUSE
CASUALIZED	CATALYZING	CATCHMENTS	CATERS	CATHOUSES
CASUALIZES	CATAMARAN	CATCHPOLE	CATERWAUL	CATION
CASUALIZING	CATAMARANS	CATCHPOLES	CATERWAULED	CATIONIC*

Words marked with an asterisk are from OTCWL

CATIONS	CAUCHEMAR	CAUMSTONE	CAUTIONS	CAVIER
CATKIN	CAUCHEMARS	CAUMSTONES	CAUTIOUS	CAVIERS
CATKINS	CAUCUS	CAUP	CAUVES	CAVIES
CATLIKE	CAUCUSED	CAUPS	CAVALCADE	CAVIL
CATLIN*	CAUCUSES	CAUSA	CAVALCADED	CAVILED*
CATLING	CAUCUSING	CAUSABLE*	CAVALCADES	CAVILER*
CATLINGS	CAUCUSSED*	CAUSAE	CAVALCADING	CAVILERS*
CATLINS*	CAUCUSSES*	CAUSAL	CAVALERO*	CAVILING*
CATMINT	CAUCUSSING*	CAUSALGIA*	CAVALEROS*	CAVILLED
CATMINTS	CAUDAD	CAUSALGIAS*	CAVALETTI*	CAVILLER
CATNAP	CAUDAL	CAUSALGIC*	CAVALIER	CAVILLERS
CATNAPER*	CAUDALLY*	CAUSALITIES	CAVALIERED	CAVILLING
CATNAPERS*	CAUDATE	CAUSALITY	CAVALIERING	CAVILLINGS
CATNAPPED*	CAUDATED	CAUSALLY	CAVALIERS	CAVILS
CATNAPPER*	CAUDATES*	CAUSALS*	CAVALLA	CAVING
CATNAPPERS*	CAUDEX	CAUSATION	CAVALLAS	CAVINGS
CATNAPPING*	CAUDEXES	CAUSATIONS	CAVALLIES	CAVITARY*
CATNAPS	CAUDICES	CAUSATIVE	CAVALLY	CAVITATE
CATNEP	CAUDICLE	CAUSATIVES	CAVALRIES	CAVITATED
CATNEPS	CAUDICLES	CAUSE	CAVALRY	CAVITATES
CATNIP	CAUDILLO	CAUSED	CAVASS	CAVITATING
CATNIPS	CAUDILLOS	CAUSELESS	CAVASSES	CAVITIED
CATOPTRIC	CAUDLE	CAUSEN	CAVATINA	CAVITIES
CATOPTRICS	CAUDLED	CAUSER	CAVATINAS	CAVITY
CATS	CAUDLES	CAUSERIE	CAVATINE*	CAVORT
CATSKIN	CAUDLING	CAUSERIES	CAVE	CAVORTED
CATSKINS	CAUDRON	CAUSERS	CAVEAT	CAVORTER*
CATSPAW*	CAUDRONS	CAUSES	CAVEATED*	CAVORTERS*
CATSPAWS*	CAUF	CAUSEWAY	CAVEATING*	CAVORTING
CATSUIT	CAUGHT	CAUSEWAYED	CAVEATOR*	CAVORTS
CATSUITS	CAUK	CAUSEWAYING*	CAVEATORS*	CAVY
CATSUP	CAUKER	CAUSEWAYS	CAVEATS	CAW
CATSUPS	CAUKERS	CAUSEY	CAVED	CAWED
CATTABU	CAUKS	CAUSEYED	CAVEFISH*	CAWING
CATTABUS	CAUL	CAUSEYS	CAVEFISHES*	CAWINGS
CATTAIL*	CAULD	CAUSING	CAVEL	CAWK
CATTAILS*	CAULDER	CAUSTIC	CAVELIKE*	CAWKER
CATTALO	CAULDEST	CAUSTICS	CAVELS	CAWKERS
CATTALOES	CAULDRIFE	CAUTEL	CAVEMAN	CAWKS
CATTALOS	CAULDRON	CAUTELOUS	CAVEMEN	CAWS
CATTED	CAULDRONS	CAUTELS	CAVENDISH	CAXON
CATTERIES	CAULDS	CAUTER	CAVENDISHES	CAXONS
CATTERY	CAULES	CAUTERANT	CAVER	CAY
CATTIE*	CAULICLE	CAUTERANTS	CAVERN	CAYENNE
CATTIER	CAULICLES	CAUTERIES	CAVERNED	CAYENNED
CATTIES	CAULICULI	CAUTERISE	CAVERNING	CAYENNES
CATTIEST	CAULIFORM	CAUTERISED	CAVERNOUS	CAYMAN
CATTILY	CAULINARY	CAUTERISES	CAVERNS	CAYMANS
CATTINESS	CAULINE	CAUTERISING	CAVERS	CAYS
CATTINESSES	CAULIS	CAUTERISM	CAVES	CAYUSE
CATTING	CAULK	CAUTERISMS	CAVESSON	CAYUSES
CATTISH	CAULKED	CAUTERIZE	CAVESSONS	CAZIQUE
CATTISHLY	CAULKER	CAUTERIZED	CAVETTI	CAZIQUES
CATTLE	CAULKERS	CAUTERIZES	CAVETTO	CEANOTHUS
CATTLEMAN	CAULKING	CAUTERIZING	CAVETTOS*	CEANOTHUSES
CATTLEMEN	CAULKINGS	CAUTERS	CAVIAR	CEAS
CATTLEYA	CAULKS	CAUTERY	CAVIARE	CEASE
CATTLEYAS	CAULOME	CAUTION	CAVIARES	CEASED
CATTY	CAULOMES	CAUTIONED	CAVIARIE	CEASELESS
CATWALK*	CAULS	CAUTIONER	CAVIARIES	CEASES
CATWALKS*	CAUM	CAUTIONERS	CAVIARS	CEASING
CATWORKS	CAUMED	CAUTIONING	CAVICORN	CEASINGS
CATWORM	CAUMING	CAUTIONRIES	CAVICORNS	CEAZE
CATWORMS	CAUMS	CAUTIONRY	CAVIE	CEAZED

The Chambers Dictionary is the authority for many longer words; see Introduction, page ix

CEAZES
CEAZING
CEBADILLA
CEBADILLAS
CEBID*
CEBIDS*
CEBOID*
CEBOIDS*
CECA
CECAL
CECALLY*
CECILS
CECITIES
CECITIS
CECITISES
CECITY
CECROPIA
CECROPIAS
CECUM
CEDAR
CEDARBIRD*
CEDARBIRDS*
CEDARED
CEDARN
CEDARS
CEDARWOOD
CEDARWOODS
CEDE
CEDED
CEDER*
CEDERS*
CEDES
CEDI
CEDILLA
CEDILLAS
CEDING
CEDIS
CEDRATE
CEDRATES
CEDRINE
CEDULA
CEDULAS
CEE
CEES
CEIBA*
CEIBAS*
CEIL
CEILED
CEILER*
CEILERS*
CEILI
CEILIDH
CEILIDHS
CEILING
CEILINGED
CEILINGS
CEILIS
CEILS
CEINTURE
CEINTURES
CEL
CELADON
CELADONS
CELANDINE

CELANDINES
CELEB*
CELEBRANT
CELEBRANTS
CELEBRATE
CELEBRATED
CELEBRATES
CELEBRATING
CELEBRITIES
CELEBRITY
CELEBS*
CELERIAC
CELERIACS
CELERIES
CELERITIES
CELERITY
CELERY
CELESTA
CELESTAS
CELESTE
CELESTES
CELESTIAL
CELESTIALS
CELESTINE
CELESTINES
CELESTITE
CELESTITES
CELIAC
CELIACS
CELIBACIES
CELIBACY
CELIBATE
CELIBATES
CELL
CELLA
CELLAE
CELLAR
CELLARAGE
CELLARAGES
CELLARED
CELLARER
CELLARERS
CELLARET
CELLARETS
CELLARING
CELLARIST
CELLARISTS
CELLARMAN
CELLARMEN
CELLAROUS
CELLARS
CELLED
CELLI*
CELLING*
CELLIST
CELLISTS
CELLMATE*
CELLMATES*
CELLO
CELLOIDIN*
CELLOIDINS*
CELLOS
CELLOSE
CELLOSES

CELLPHONE
CELLPHONES
CELLS
CELLULAR
CELLULASE
CELLULASES
CELLULE
CELLULES
CELLULITE
CELLULITES
CELLULOID
CELLULOIDS
CELLULOSE
CELLULOSES
CELOM
CELOMATA*
CELOMS
CELOSIA*
CELOSIAS*
CELS
CELSITUDE
CELSITUDES
CELT
CELTS
CEMBALI
CEMBALIST
CEMBALISTS
CEMBALO
CEMBALOS
CEMBRA
CEMBRAS
CEMENT
CEMENTA
CEMENTED
CEMENTER
CEMENTERS
CEMENTING
CEMENTITE
CEMENTITES
CEMENTS
CEMENTUM
CEMETERIES
CEMETERY
CEMITARE
CEMITARES
CENACLE
CENACLES
CENDRE
CENOBITE
CENOBITES
CENOBITIC*
CENOTAPH
CENOTAPHS
CENOTE
CENOTES
CENS
CENSE
CENSED
CENSER
CENSERS
CENSES
CENSING
CENSOR

CENSORED
CENSORIAL
CENSORIAN
CENSORING
CENSORS
CENSUAL
CENSURE
CENSURED
CENSURER*
CENSURERS*
CENSURES
CENSURING
CENSUS
CENSUSED
CENSUSES
CENSUSING
CENT
CENTAGE
CENTAGES
CENTAL
CENTALS
CENTARE
CENTARES
CENTAUR
CENTAUREA
CENTAUREAS
CENTAURIES
CENTAURS
CENTAURY
CENTAVO
CENTAVOS
CENTENARIES
CENTENARY
CENTENIER
CENTENIERS
CENTER
CENTERED
CENTERING
CENTERINGS
CENTERS
CENTESES
CENTESIMI*
CENTESIMO
CENTESIMOS
CENTESIS
CENTIARE
CENTIARES
CENTIGRAM
CENTIGRAMS
CENTILE*
CENTILES*
CENTIME
CENTIMES
CENTIMO
CENTIMOS
CENTINEL
CENTINELL
CENTINELLS
CENTINELS
CENTIPEDE
CENTIPEDES
CENTNER
CENTNERS
CENTO

CENTOIST
CENTOISTS
CENTONATE
CENTONEL
CENTONELL
CENTONELLS
CENTONELS
CENTONES
CENTONIST
CENTONISTS
CENTOS
CENTRA
CENTRAL
CENTRALER*
CENTRALEST*
CENTRALLY
CENTRALS*
CENTRE
CENTRED
CENTREING
CENTREINGS
CENTRES
CENTRIC
CENTRICAL
CENTRIES
CENTRING
CENTRINGS
CENTRIOLE
CENTRIOLES
CENTRISM
CENTRISMS
CENTRIST
CENTRISTS
CENTRODE
CENTRODES
CENTROID
CENTROIDS
CENTRUM
CENTRUMS
CENTRY
CENTS
CENTUM
CENTUMS
CENTUMVIR
CENTUMVIRI
CENTUPLE
CENTUPLED
CENTUPLES
CENTUPLING
CENTURIAL
CENTURIES
CENTURION
CENTURIONS
CENTURY
CEORL
CEORLISH*
CEORLS
CEP
CEPACEOUS
CEPE*
CEPES*
CEPHALAD
CEPHALATE
CEPHALIC

CEPHALICS	CEREMONIES	CERULEAN	CESURAL	CHADS
CEPHALIN	CEREMONY	CERULEANS*	CESURAS	CHAETA
CEPHALINS	CEREOUS	CERULEIN	CESURE	CHAETAE
CEPHALOUS	CERES	CERULEINS	CESURES	CHAETAL*
CEPHEID*	CERESIN	CERULEOUS	CETACEAN	CHAETODON
CEPHEIDS*	CERESINE	CERUMEN	CETACEANS	CHAETODONS
CEPS	CERESINES	CERUMENS	CETACEOUS	CHAETOPOD
CERACEOUS	CERESINS	CERUSE	CETANE	CHAETOPODS
CERAMAL	CEREUS	CERUSES	CETANES	CHAFE
CERAMALS	CEREUSES	CERUSITE	CETE	CHAFED
CERAMIC	CERGE	CERUSITES	CETERACH	CHAFER
CERAMICS	CERGES	CERUSSITE	CETERACHS	CHAFERS
CERAMIST	CERIA	CERUSSITES	CETES	CHAFES
CERAMISTS	CERIAS	CERVELAS*	CETOLOGIES	CHAFF
CERASIN	CERIC	CERVELASES*	CETOLOGY	CHAFFED
CERASINS	CERING	CERVELAT	CETYL	CHAFFER
CERASTES	CERIPH	CERVELATS	CETYLS	CHAFFERED
CERASTIUM	CERIPHS	CERVICAL	CETYWALL	CHAFFERER
CERASTIUMS	CERISE	CERVICES	CETYWALLS	CHAFFERERS
CERATE	CERISES	CERVID	CEVADILLA	CHAFFERIES
CERATED	CERITE	CERVIDS	CEVADILLAS	CHAFFERING
CERATES	CERITES	CERVINE	CEVAPCICI	CHAFFERS
CERATIN*	CERIUM	CERVIX	CEVICHE	CHAFFERY
CERATINS*	CERIUMS	CERVIXES	CEVICHES	CHAFFIER
CERATITIS	CERMET	CESAREAN*	CEYLANITE	CHAFFIEST
CERATITISES	CERMETS	CESAREANS*	CEYLANITES	CHAFFINCH
CERATODUS	CERNE	CESAREVNA	CEYLONITE	CHAFFINCHES
CERATODUSES	CERNED	CESAREVNAS	CEYLONITES	CHAFFING
CERATOID	CERNES	CESARIAN*	CH	CHAFFINGS
CERBEREAN	CERNING	CESARIANS*	CHA	CHAFFRON
CERBERIAN	CERNUOUS	CESIUM	CHABAZITE	CHAFFRONS
CERCAL	CERO*	CESIUMS	CHABAZITES	CHAFFS
CERCARIA	CEROGRAPH	CESPITOSE	CHABLIS*	CHAFFY
CERCARIAE	CEROGRAPHS	CESS	CHABOUK	CHAFING
CERCARIAL*	CEROMANCIES	CESSATION	CHABOUKS	CHAFT
CERCARIAN	CEROMANCY	CESSATIONS	CHABUK*	CHAFTS
CERCARIAS*	CEROON	CESSE	CHABUKS*	CHAGAN
CERCI	CEROONS	CESSED	CHACE	CHAGANS
CERCIS*	CEROS*	CESSER	CHACED	CHAGRIN
CERCISES*	CEROTIC*	CESSERS	CHACES	CHAGRINED
CERCUS	CEROTYPE	CESSES	CHACING	CHAGRINING
CERE	CEROTYPES	CESSING	CHACK	CHAGRINNED*
CEREAL	CEROUS	CESSION	CHACKED	CHAGRINNING*
CEREALIST	CERRIAL	CESSIONS	CHACKING	CHAGRINS
CEREALISTS	CERRIS	CESSPIT	CHACKS	CHAI
CEREALS	CERRISES	CESSPITS	CHACMA	CHAIN
CEREBELLA	CERT	CESSPOOL	CHACMAS	CHAINE
CEREBELLUM*	CERTAIN	CESSPOOLS	CHACO	CHAINED
CEREBELLUMS*	CERTAINER*	CESTA*	CHACOES	CHAINES
CEREBRA	CERTAINEST*	CESTAS*	CHACONNE	CHAINING
CEREBRAL	CERTAINLY	CESTI	CHACONNES	CHAINLESS
CEREBRALS*	CERTAINTIES	CESTODE	CHACOS	CHAINLET
CEREBRATE	CERTAINTY	CESTODES	CHAD	CHAINLETS
CEREBRATED	CERTES	CESTOI*	CHADAR	CHAINMAN
CEREBRATES	CERTIFIED	CESTOID	CHADARIM*	CHAINMEN
CEREBRATING	CERTIFIER	CESTOIDS	CHADARS	CHAINS
CEREBRIC	CERTIFIERS	CESTOS	CHADDAR	CHAINSAW
CEREBRUM	CERTIFIES	CESTOSES	CHADDARS	CHAINSAWED*
CEREBRUMS	CERTIFY	CESTUI	CHADDOR	CHAINSAWING*
CERECLOTH	CERTIFYING	CESTUIS	CHADDORS	CHAINSAWS
CERECLOTHS	CERTITUDE	CESTUS	CHADLESS*	CHAINSHOT
CERED	CERTITUDES	CESTUSES*	CHADOR	CHAINSHOTS
CEREMENT	CERTS	CESURA	CHADORS	CHAINWORK
CEREMENTS	CERULE	CESURAE	CHADRI*	CHAINWORKS

The Chambers Dictionary is the authority for many longer words; see Introduction, page ix

CHAIR	CHALLANING	CHAMMYING*	CHANFRONS*	CHAPEAUS*
CHAIRDAYS	CHALLANS	CHAMOIS	CHANG*	CHAPEAUX
CHAIRED	CHALLAS*	CHAMOISED*	CHANGE	CHAPEL
CHAIRING	CHALLENGE	CHAMOISES*	CHANGED	CHAPELESS
CHAIRLIFT	CHALLENGED	CHAMOISING*	CHANGEFUL	CHAPELRIES
CHAIRLIFTS	CHALLENGES	CHAMOIX*	CHANGER	CHAPELRY
CHAIRMAN	CHALLENGING	CHAMOMILE	CHANGERS	CHAPELS
CHAIRMANED*	CHALLIE	CHAMOMILES	CHANGES	CHAPERON
CHAIRMANING*	CHALLIES	CHAMP	CHANGING	CHAPERONE
CHAIRMANNED*	CHALLIS	CHAMPAC	CHANGS*	CHAPERONED
CHAIRMANNING*	CHALLISES	CHAMPACS	CHANK	CHAPERONES
CHAIRMANS*	CHALLOT*	CHAMPAGNE	CHANKS	CHAPERONING
CHAIRMEN	CHALLOTH*	CHAMPAGNES	CHANNEL	CHAPERONS
CHAIRS	CHALLY*	CHAMPAIGN	CHANNELED*	CHAPES
CHAIS	CHALONE	CHAMPAIGNS	CHANNELER	CHAPESS
CHAISE	CHALONES	CHAMPAK	CHANNELERS	CHAPESSES
CHAISES	CHALONIC	CHAMPAKS	CHANNELING*	CHAPITER
CHAKRA	CHALOT*	CHAMPART	CHANNELLED	CHAPITERS
CHAKRAS	CHALOTH*	CHAMPARTS	CHANNELLING	CHAPKA
CHAL	CHALS	CHAMPED	CHANNELS	CHAPKAS
CHALAH*	CHALUMEAU	CHAMPER*	CHANNER	CHAPLAIN
CHALAHS*	CHALUMEAUX	CHAMPERS	CHANNERS	CHAPLAINS
CHALAN	CHALUTZ	CHAMPERTIES	CHANOYU	CHAPLESS
CHALANED	CHALUTZES	CHAMPERTY	CHANOYUS	CHAPLET
CHALANING	CHALUTZIM	CHAMPING	CHANSON	CHAPLETED
CHALANS	CHALYBEAN	CHAMPION	CHANSONS	CHAPLETS
CHALAZA	CHALYBITE	CHAMPIONED	CHANT	CHAPMAN
CHALAZAE	CHALYBITES	CHAMPIONING	CHANTAGE	CHAPMEN
CHALAZAL*	CHAM	CHAMPIONS	CHANTAGES	CHAPPAL
CHALAZAS	CHAMADE	CHAMPLEVE	CHANTED	CHAPPALS
CHALAZIA	CHAMADES	CHAMPLEVES	CHANTER	CHAPPATI*
CHALAZION	CHAMBER	CHAMPS	CHANTERS	CHAPPATIS*
CHALAZIONS*	CHAMBERED	CHAMPY*	CHANTEUSE	CHAPPED
CHALCID	CHAMBERER	CHAMS	CHANTEUSES	CHAPPESS
CHALCIDS	CHAMBERERS	CHANCE	CHANTEY	CHAPPESSES
CHALCOGEN*	CHAMBERING	CHANCED	CHANTEYS	CHAPPIE
CHALCOGENS*	CHAMBERINGS	CHANCEFUL	CHANTIE	CHAPPIER
CHALDER	CHAMBERS	CHANCEL	CHANTIES	CHAPPIES
CHALDERS	CHAMBRAY	CHANCELS	CHANTING	CHAPPIEST
CHALDRON	CHAMBRAYS	CHANCER	CHANTOR	CHAPPING
CHALDRONS	CHAMBRE	CHANCERIES	CHANTORS	CHAPPY
CHALEH*	CHAMELEON	CHANCERS	CHANTRESS	CHAPRASSI
CHALEHS*	CHAMELEONS	CHANCERY	CHANTRESSES	CHAPRASSIES
CHALET	CHAMELOT	CHANCES	CHANTRIES	CHAPRASSIS
CHALETS	CHAMELOTS	CHANCEY	CHANTRY	CHAPRASSY
CHALICE	CHAMFER	CHANCIER	CHANTS	CHAPS
CHALICED	CHAMFERED	CHANCIEST	CHANTY	CHAPSTICK
CHALICES	CHAMFERING	CHANCILY*	CHAO*	CHAPSTICKS
CHALK	CHAMFERS	CHANCING	CHAOLOGIES	CHAPT*
CHALKED	CHAMFRAIN	CHANCRE	CHAOLOGY	CHAPTER
CHALKFACE	CHAMFRAINS	CHANCRES	CHAOS	CHAPTERED
CHALKFACES	CHAMFRON	CHANCROID	CHAOSES	CHAPTERING
CHALKIER	CHAMFRONS	CHANCROIDS	CHAOTIC	CHAPTERS
CHALKIEST	CHAMISAL	CHANCROUS	CHAP	CHAPTREL
CHALKING	CHAMISALS	CHANCY	CHAPARRAL	CHAPTRELS
CHALKPIT	CHAMISE	CHANDELLE	CHAPARRALS	CHAQUETA*
CHALKPITS	CHAMISES	CHANDELLED	CHAPATI	CHAQUETAS*
CHALKS	CHAMISO	CHANDELLES	CHAPATIS	CHAR
CHALKY	CHAMISOS	CHANDELLING	CHAPATTI	CHARA
CHALLA*	CHAMLET	CHANDLER	CHAPATTIS	CHARABANC
CHALLAH	CHAMLETS	CHANDLERIES	CHAPBOOK	CHARABANCS
CHALLAHS	CHAMMIED*	CHANDLERS	CHAPBOOKS	CHARACID
CHALLAN	CHAMMIES	CHANDLERY	CHAPE	CHARACIDS
CHALLANED	CHAMMY	CHANFRON*	CHAPEAU	CHARACIN

CHARACINS	CHARKING	CHARTISM	CHATEAUX	CHAUNTS
CHARACT	CHARKS	CHARTISMS	CHATELAIN	CHAUSSES
CHARACTER	CHARLADIES	CHARTIST	CHATELAINS	CHAUSSURE*
CHARACTERED	CHARLADY	CHARTISTS	CHATLINE	CHAUSSURES*
CHARACTERING	CHARLATAN	CHARTLESS	CHATLINES	CHAUVIN
CHARACTERS	CHARLATANS	CHARTS	CHATON	CHAUVINS
CHARACTS	CHARLEY	CHARWOMAN	CHATONS	CHAVE
CHARADE	CHARLEYS	CHARWOMEN	CHATOYANT	CHAVENDER
CHARADES	CHARLIE	CHARY	CHATOYANTS*	CHAVENDERS
CHARANGO	CHARLIES	CHAS	CHATS	CHAW
CHARANGOS	CHARLOCK	CHASE	CHATTA	CHAWBACON
CHARAS	CHARLOCKS	CHASED	CHATTAS	CHAWBACONS
CHARASES	CHARLOTTE	CHASEPORT	CHATTED	CHAWDRON
CHARBROIL	CHARLOTTES	CHASEPORTS	CHATTEL	CHAWDRONS
CHARBROILED	CHARM	CHASER	CHATTELS	CHAWED
CHARBROILING	CHARMED	CHASERS	CHATTER	CHAWER*
CHARBROILS	CHARMER	CHASES	CHATTERED	CHAWERS*
CHARCOAL	CHARMERS	CHASING	CHATTERER	CHAWING
CHARCOALED	CHARMEUSE	CHASINGS	CHATTERERS	CHAWS
CHARCOALING	CHARMEUSES	CHASM	CHATTERING	CHAY
CHARCOALS	CHARMFUL	CHASMAL	CHATTERINGS	CHAYA
CHARD	CHARMING	CHASMED	CHATTERS	CHAYAS
CHARDS	CHARMINGER*	CHASMIC	CHATTERY*	CHAYOTE
CHARE	CHARMINGEST*	CHASMIER	CHATTI	CHAYOTES
CHARED	CHARMLESS	CHASMIEST	CHATTIER	CHAYROOT
CHARES	CHARMS	CHASMS	CHATTIES	CHAYROOTS
CHARET	CHARNECO	CHASMY	CHATTIEST	CHAYS
CHARETS	CHARNECOS	CHASSE	CHATTILY*	CHAZAN
CHARGE	CHARNEL	CHASSED*	CHATTING	CHAZANIM
CHARGED	CHARNELS	CHASSEED	CHATTIS	CHAZANS
CHARGEFUL	CHAROSET	CHASSEING	CHATTY	CHAZZAN*
CHARGER	CHAROSETH	CHASSEPOT	CHAUFE	CHAZZANIM*
CHARGERS	CHAROSETHS	CHASSEPOTS	CHAUFED	CHAZZANS*
CHARGES	CHAROSETS	CHASSES	CHAUFER	CHAZZEN*
CHARGING	CHARPAI*	CHASSEUR	CHAUFERS	CHAZZENIM*
CHARGRILL	CHARPAIS*	CHASSEURS	CHAUFES	CHAZZENS*
CHARGRILLED	CHARPIE	CHASSIS	CHAUFF	CHE
CHARGRILLING	CHARPIES	CHASTE	CHAUFFED	CHEAP
CHARGRILLS	CHARPOY	CHASTELY	CHAUFFER	CHEAPEN
CHARIER	CHARPOYS	CHASTEN	CHAUFFERS	CHEAPENED
CHARIEST	CHARQUI	CHASTENED	CHAUFFEUR	CHEAPENER
CHARILY	CHARQUID*	CHASTENER	CHAUFFEURED	CHEAPENERS
CHARINESS	CHARQUIS	CHASTENERS	CHAUFFEURING	CHEAPENING
CHARINESSES	CHARR	CHASTENING	CHAUFFEURS	CHEAPENS
CHARING	CHARRED	CHASTENS	CHAUFFING	CHEAPER
CHARIOT	CHARRIER	CHASTER	CHAUFFS	CHEAPEST
CHARIOTED	CHARRIEST	CHASTEST	CHAUFING	CHEAPIE
CHARIOTING	CHARRING	CHASTISE	CHAUMER	CHEAPIES
CHARIOTS	CHARRO*	CHASTISED	CHAUMERS	CHEAPISH*
CHARISM	CHARROS*	CHASTISER*	CHAUNCE	CHEAPJACK*
CHARISMA	CHARRS	CHASTISERS*	CHAUNCED	CHEAPJACKS*
CHARISMAS	CHARRY	CHASTISES	CHAUNCES	CHEAPLY
CHARISMATA*	CHARS	CHASTISING	CHAUNCING	CHEAPNESS
CHARISMS	CHART	CHASTITIES	CHAUNGE	CHEAPNESSES
CHARITIES	CHARTA	CHASTITY	CHAUNGED	CHEAPO
CHARITY	CHARTAS	CHASUBLE	CHAUNGES	CHEAPOS*
CHARIVARI	CHARTED	CHASUBLES	CHAUNGING	CHEAPS
CHARIVARIS	CHARTER	CHAT	CHAUNT	CHEAPY
CHARK	CHARTERED	CHATCHKA*	CHAUNTED	CHEAT
CHARKA	CHARTERER	CHATCHKAS*	CHAUNTER	CHEATED
CHARKAS	CHARTERERS	CHATCHKE*	CHAUNTERS	CHEATER
CHARKED	CHARTERING	CHATCHKES*	CHAUNTING	CHEATERIES
CHARKHA	CHARTERS	CHATEAU	CHAUNTRIES	CHEATERS
CHARKHAS	CHARTING	CHATEAUS*	CHAUNTRY	CHEATERY

CHEATING
CHEATINGS
CHEATS
CHEBEC*
CHEBECS*
CHECHAKO
CHECHAKOES
CHECHAKOS
CHECHAQUA
CHECHAQUAS
CHECHAQUO
CHECHAQUOS
CHECHIA
CHECHIAS
CHECK
CHECKABLE*
CHECKBOOK
CHECKBOOKS
CHECKED
CHECKER
CHECKERED
CHECKERING*
CHECKERS
CHECKING
CHECKLESS*
CHECKLIST
CHECKLISTS
CHECKMARK*
CHECKMARKED*
CHECKMARKING*
CHECKMARKS*
CHECKMATE
CHECKMATED
CHECKMATES
CHECKMATING
CHECKOFF*
CHECKOFFS*
CHECKOUT
CHECKOUTS
CHECKRAIL
CHECKRAILS
CHECKREIN
CHECKREINS
CHECKROOM
CHECKROOMS
CHECKROW*
CHECKROWED*
CHECKROWING*
CHECKROWS*
CHECKS
CHECKSUM
CHECKSUMS
CHECKUP*
CHECKUPS*
CHECKY
CHEDDAR*
CHEDDARS*
CHEDDITE
CHEDDITES
CHEDER*
CHEDERS*
CHEDITE*
CHEDITES*
CHEECHAKO

CHEECHAKOES
CHEECHAKOS
CHEEK
CHEEKBONE
CHEEKBONES
CHEEKED
CHEEKFUL*
CHEEKFULS*
CHEEKIER
CHEEKIEST
CHEEKILY
CHEEKING
CHEEKS
CHEEKY
CHEEP
CHEEPED
CHEEPER
CHEEPERS
CHEEPING
CHEEPS
CHEER
CHEERED
CHEERER
CHEERERS
CHEERFUL
CHEERFULLER
CHEERFULLEST
CHEERIER
CHEERIEST
CHEERILY
CHEERING
CHEERIO
CHEERIOS
CHEERLEAD*
CHEERLEADING*
CHEERLEADS*
CHEERLED*
CHEERLESS
CHEERLY
CHEERO*
CHEEROS*
CHEERS
CHEERY
CHEESE
CHEESED
CHEESES
CHEESEVAT
CHEESEVATS
CHEESIER
CHEESIEST
CHEESILY*
CHEESING
CHEESY
CHEETAH
CHEETAHS
CHEEWINK
CHEEWINKS
CHEF
CHEFDOM*
CHEFDOMS*
CHEFFED*
CHEFFING*
CHEFS
CHEGOE*

CHEGOES*
CHEILITIS
CHEILITISES
CHEKA
CHEKAS
CHEKIST
CHEKISTS
CHELA
CHELAE
CHELAS
CHELASHIP
CHELASHIPS
CHELATE
CHELATED
CHELATES
CHELATING
CHELATION
CHELATIONS
CHELATOR
CHELATORS
CHELICERA
CHELICERAE
CHELIFORM
CHELIPED
CHELIPEDS
CHELOID
CHELOIDAL
CHELOIDS
CHELONE
CHELONES
CHELONIAN
CHELONIANS
CHEMIC
CHEMICAL
CHEMICALS
CHEMICKED
CHEMICKING
CHEMICS
CHEMISE
CHEMISES
CHEMISM
CHEMISMS
CHEMISORB*
CHEMISORBED*
CHEMISORBING*
CHEMISORBS*
CHEMIST
CHEMISTRIES
CHEMISTRY
CHEMISTS
CHEMITYPE
CHEMITYPES
CHEMITYPIES
CHEMITYPY
CHEMMIES
CHEMMY
CHEMO*
CHEMOS*
CHEMOSTAT
CHEMOSTATS
CHEMURGIC
CHEMURGIES
CHEMURGY
CHENAR

CHENARS
CHENET
CHENETS
CHENILLE
CHENILLES
CHENIX
CHENIXES
CHENOPOD
CHENOPODS
CHEONGSAM
CHEONGSAMS
CHEQUE
CHEQUER
CHEQUERED
CHEQUERING
CHEQUERS
CHEQUES
CHEQUY
CHER
CHERALITE
CHERALITES
CHERE
CHERIMOYA
CHERIMOYAS
CHERISH
CHERISHED
CHERISHER*
CHERISHERS*
CHERISHES
CHERISHING
CHERNOZEM
CHERNOZEMS
CHEROOT
CHEROOTS
CHERRIED
CHERRIER
CHERRIES
CHERRIEST
CHERRY
CHERRYING
CHERT
CHERTIER
CHERTIEST
CHERTS
CHERTY
CHERUB
CHERUBIC
CHERUBIM
CHERUBIMS
CHERUBIN
CHERUBINS
CHERUBS
CHERUP
CHERUPED
CHERUPING
CHERUPS
CHERVIL
CHERVILS
CHESIL
CHESILS
CHESNUT
CHESNUTS
CHESS
CHESSEL

CHESSELS
CHESSES
CHESSMAN
CHESSMEN
CHEST
CHESTED
CHESTFUL
CHESTFULS
CHESTIER
CHESTIEST
CHESTING
CHESTNUT
CHESTNUTS
CHESTS
CHESTY
CHETAH
CHETAHS
CHETH*
CHETHS*
CHETNIK
CHETNIKS
CHETRUM*
CHETRUMS*
CHEVALET
CHEVALETS
CHEVALIER
CHEVALIERS
CHEVELURE
CHEVELURES
CHEVEN
CHEVENS
CHEVEREL
CHEVERELS
CHEVERIL
CHEVERILS
CHEVERON
CHEVERONS
CHEVERYE
CHEVERYES
CHEVET
CHEVETS
CHEVIED
CHEVIES
CHEVILLE
CHEVILLES
CHEVIN
CHEVINS
CHEVIOT*
CHEVIOTS*
CHEVRE
CHEVRES
CHEVRETTE
CHEVRETTES
CHEVRON
CHEVRONED
CHEVRONS
CHEVRONY
CHEVY
CHEVYING
CHEW
CHEWABLE
CHEWED
CHEWER
CHEWERS

Words marked with an asterisk are from OTCWL

CHEWET	CHICHA	CHIEFSHIPS	CHILIDOG*	CHIMP
CHEWETS	CHICHAS	CHIEFTAIN	CHILIDOGS*	CHIMPS
CHEWIE	CHICHES	CHIEFTAINS	CHILIES*	CHIN
CHEWIER	CHICHI	CHIEL	CHILIOI	CHINA
CHEWIES	CHICHIS	CHIELD	CHILIOIS	CHINAMPA
CHEWIEST	CHICK	CHIELDS	CHILIS	CHINAMPAS
CHEWING	CHICKADEE	CHIELS	CHILL	CHINAR
CHEWINK	CHICKADEES	CHIFFON	CHILLADA	CHINAROOT
CHEWINKS	CHICKAREE	CHIFFONS	CHILLADAS	CHINAROOTS
CHEWS	CHICKAREES	CHIGETAI*	CHILLED	CHINARS
CHEWY	CHICKEE*	CHIGETAIS*	CHILLER	CHINAS
CHEZ	CHICKEES*	CHIGGER	CHILLERS	CHINAWARE
CHI	CHICKEN	CHIGGERS	CHILLEST	CHINAWARES
CHIA*	CHICKENED	CHIGNON	CHILLI	CHINBONE*
CHIACK	CHICKENING	CHIGNONS	CHILLIER	CHINBONES*
CHIACKED	CHICKENS	CHIGOE	CHILLIES	CHINCAPIN
CHIACKING	CHICKLING	CHIGOES	CHILLIEST	CHINCAPINS
CHIACKINGS	CHICKLINGS	CHIGRE	CHILLILY	CHINCH
CHIACKS	CHICKORIES*	CHIGRES	CHILLING	CHINCHES
CHIAO	CHICKORY*	CHIHUAHUA	CHILLINGS	CHINCHIER*
CHIAREZZA	CHICKPEA	CHIHUAHUAS	CHILLIS	CHINCHIEST*
CHIAREZZE	CHICKPEAS	CHIK	CHILLNESS	CHINCHY*
CHIAS*	CHICKS	CHIKARA	CHILLNESSES	CHINCOUGH
CHIASM	CHICKWEED	CHIKARAS	CHILLS	CHINCOUGHS
CHIASMA	CHICKWEEDS	CHIKHOR	CHILLUM	CHINDIT
CHIASMAL*	CHICLE	CHIKHORS	CHILLUMS	CHINDITS
CHIASMAS	CHICLES	CHIKOR	CHILLY	CHINE
CHIASMATA	CHICLY	CHIKORS	CHILOPOD	CHINED
CHIASMI	CHICNESS*	CHIKS	CHILOPODS	CHINES
CHIASMIC*	CHICNESSES*	CHILBLAIN	CHIMAERA	CHINESE
CHIASMS	CHICO	CHILBLAINS	CHIMAERAS	CHINING
CHIASMUS	CHICON	CHILD	CHIMAERIC*	CHINK
CHIASTIC	CHICONS	CHILDBED	CHIMAR*	CHINKAPIN
CHIAUS	CHICORIES	CHILDBEDS	CHIMARS*	CHINKAPINS
CHIAUSED	CHICORY	CHILDE	CHIMB	CHINKARA
CHIAUSES	CHICOS	CHILDED	CHIMBLEY*	CHINKARAS
CHIAUSING	CHICS	CHILDER	CHIMBLEYS*	CHINKED
CHIBOL	CHID	CHILDES*	CHIMBLIES*	CHINKIE
CHIBOLS	CHIDDEN	CHILDHOOD	CHIMBLY*	CHINKIER
CHIBOUK	CHIDE	CHILDHOODS	CHIMBS	CHINKIES
CHIBOUKS	CHIDED	CHILDING	CHIME	CHINKIEST
CHIBOUQUE	CHIDER	CHILDISH	CHIMED	CHINKING
CHIBOUQUES	CHIDERS	CHILDLESS	CHIMER	CHINKS
CHIC	CHIDES	CHILDLIER*	CHIMERA	CHINKY
CHICA	CHIDING	CHILDLIEST*	CHIMERAS	CHINLESS
CHICANA	CHIDINGS	CHILDLIKE	CHIMERE	CHINNED
CHICANAS	CHIDLINGS	CHILDLY	CHIMERES	CHINNING
CHICANE	CHIEF	CHILDNESS	CHIMERIC	CHINO
CHICANED	CHIEFDOM	CHILDNESSES	CHIMERID	CHINONE*
CHICANER	CHIEFDOMS	CHILDREN	CHIMERIDS	CHINONES*
CHICANERIES	CHIEFER	CHILDS	CHIMERISM	CHINOOK
CHICANERS	CHIEFERIES	CHILE	CHIMERISMS	CHINOOKS
CHICANERY	CHIEFERY	CHILES	CHIMERS	CHINOS
CHICANES	CHIEFESS	CHILI	CHIMES	CHINOVNIK
CHICANING	CHIEFESSES	CHILIAD	CHIMING	CHINOVNIKS
CHICANINGS	CHIEFEST	CHILIADS	CHIMLA*	CHINS
CHICANO	CHIEFLESS	CHILIAGON	CHIMLAS*	CHINSTRAP
CHICANOS	CHIEFLING	CHILIAGONS	CHIMLEY	CHINSTRAPS
CHICAS	CHIEFLINGS	CHILIARCH	CHIMLEYS	CHINTS*
CHICCORIES	CHIEFLY	CHILIARCHS	CHIMNEY	CHINTSES*
CHICCORY	CHIEFRIES	CHILIASM	CHIMNEYED	CHINTZ
CHICER	CHIEFRY	CHILIASMS	CHIMNEYING	CHINTZES
CHICEST	CHIEFS	CHILIAST	CHIMNEYS	CHINTZIER
CHICH	CHIEFSHIP	CHILIASTS	CHIMO	CHINTZIEST

The Chambers Dictionary is the authority for many longer words; see Introduction, page ix

CHINTZY	CHIRPERS	CHITTY	CHLORITE	CHOKERS
CHINWAG	CHIRPIER	CHIV	CHLORITES	CHOKES
CHINWAGGED	CHIRPIEST	CHIVALRIC	CHLORITIC	CHOKEY
CHINWAGGING	CHIRPILY	CHIVALRIES	CHLOROSES	CHOKEYS
CHINWAGS	CHIRPING	CHIVALRY	CHLOROSIS	CHOKIDAR
CHIP	CHIRPS	CHIVAREE	CHLOROTIC	CHOKIDARS
CHIPBOARD	CHIRPY	CHIVAREED*	CHLOROUS	CHOKIER
CHIPBOARDS	CHIRR	CHIVAREEING*	CHOANA	CHOKIES
CHIPMUCK	CHIRRE	CHIVAREES	CHOANAE	CHOKIEST
CHIPMUCKS	CHIRRED	CHIVARI*	CHOBDAR	CHOKING
CHIPMUNK	CHIRRES	CHIVARIED*	CHOBDARS	CHOKINGLY*
CHIPMUNKS	CHIRRING	CHIVARIES*	CHOC	CHOKO
CHIPOCHIA	CHIRRS	CHIVARIING*	CHOCCIER	CHOKOS
CHIPOCHIAS	CHIRRUP	CHIVE	CHOCCIES	CHOKRA
CHIPOLATA	CHIRRUPED	CHIVED	CHOCCIEST	CHOKRAS
CHIPOLATAS	CHIRRUPING	CHIVES	CHOCCY	CHOKRI
CHIPPED	CHIRRUPS	CHIVIED	CHOCHO	CHOKRIS
CHIPPER	CHIRRUPY	CHIVIES	CHOCHOS	CHOKY
CHIPPERED*	CHIRT	CHIVING	CHOCK	CHOLAEMIA
CHIPPERING*	CHIRTED	CHIVS	CHOCKED	CHOLAEMIAS
CHIPPERS	CHIRTING	CHIVVED	CHOCKER	CHOLAEMIC
CHIPPIE	CHIRTS	CHIVVIED	CHOCKFUL*	CHOLATE*
CHIPPIER	CHIS	CHIVVIES	CHOCKING	CHOLATES*
CHIPPIES	CHISEL	CHIVVING	CHOCKO	CHOLECYST
CHIPPIEST	CHISELED*	CHIVVY	CHOCKOS	CHOLECYSTS
CHIPPING	CHISELER*	CHIVVYING	CHOCKS	CHOLELITH
CHIPPINGS	CHISELERS*	CHIVY	CHOCO	CHOLELITHS
CHIPPY	CHISELING*	CHIVYING	CHOCOLATE	CHOLEMIA
CHIPS	CHISELLED	CHIYOGAMI	CHOCOLATES	CHOLEMIAS
CHIPSET	CHISELLER	CHIYOGAMIS	CHOCOLATIER	CHOLENT
CHIPSETS	CHISELLERS	CHIZ	CHOCOLATIEST	CHOLENTS
CHIRAGRA	CHISELLING	CHIZZ	CHOCOLATY	CHOLER
CHIRAGRAS	CHISELLINGS	CHIZZED	CHOCOS	CHOLERA
CHIRAGRIC	CHISELS	CHIZZES	CHOCS	CHOLERAIC
CHIRAL	CHIT	CHIZZING	CHOCTAW	CHOLERAS
CHIRALITIES	CHITAL	CHLAMYDES	CHOCTAWS	CHOLERIC
CHIRALITY	CHITALS	CHLAMYDIA	CHODE	CHOLERS
CHIRIMOYA	CHITCHAT	CHLAMYDIAE*	CHOENIX	CHOLI
CHIRIMOYAS	CHITCHATS	CHLAMYDIAS	CHOENIXES	CHOLIAMB
CHIRK	CHITCHATTED	CHLAMYS	CHOICE	CHOLIAMBS
CHIRKED	CHITCHATTING	CHLAMYSES	CHOICEFUL	CHOLIC
CHIRKER*	CHITIN	CHLOASMA	CHOICELY	CHOLINE
CHIRKEST*	CHITINOID	CHLOASMATA	CHOICER	CHOLINES
CHIRKING	CHITINOUS	CHLORACNE	CHOICES	CHOLIS
CHIRKS	CHITINS	CHLORACNES	CHOICEST	CHOLLA*
CHIRL	CHITLIN*	CHLORAL	CHOIR	CHOLLAS*
CHIRLED	CHITLING*	CHLORALS	CHOIRBOY	CHOLO*
CHIRLING	CHITLINGS	CHLORATE	CHOIRBOYS	CHOLOS*
CHIRLS	CHITLINS*	CHLORATES	CHOIRED	CHOLTRIES
CHIRM	CHITON	CHLORDAN	CHOIRGIRL	CHOLTRY
CHIRMED	CHITONS	CHLORDANE	CHOIRGIRLS	CHOMP
CHIRMING	CHITOSAN*	CHLORDANES	CHOIRING	CHOMPED
CHIRMS	CHITOSANS*	CHLORDANS	CHOIRMAN	CHOMPER*
CHIRO*	CHITS	CHLORELLA	CHOIRMEN	CHOMPERS*
CHIROLOGIES	CHITTED	CHLORELLAS	CHOIRS	CHOMPING
CHIROLOGY	CHITTER	CHLORIC	CHOKE	CHOMPS
CHIRONOMIES	CHITTERED	CHLORID*	CHOKEBORE	CHON
CHIRONOMY	CHITTERING	CHLORIDE	CHOKEBORES	CHONDRAL
CHIROPODIES	CHITTERINGS	CHLORIDES	CHOKECOIL	CHONDRE
CHIROPODY	CHITTERS	CHLORIDS*	CHOKECOILS	CHONDRES
CHIROS*	CHITTIER	CHLORIN	CHOKED	CHONDRI
CHIRP	CHITTIES	CHLORINE	CHOKEDAMP	CHONDRIFIED
CHIRPED	CHITTIEST	CHLORINES	CHOKEDAMPS	CHONDRIFIES
CHIRPER	CHITTING	CHLORINS	CHOKER	CHONDRIFY

Words marked with an asterisk are from OTCWL

CHONDRIFYING	CHORDA	CHORTLES	CHRISMALS	CHRONICLING
CHONDRIN	CHORDAE	CHORTLING	CHRISMON*	CHRONICS
CHONDRINS	CHORDAL	CHORUS	CHRISMONS*	CHRONON
CHONDRITE	CHORDATE	CHORUSED	CHRISMS	CHRONONS
CHONDRITES	CHORDATES	CHORUSES	CHRISOM	CHRYSALID
CHONDROID	CHORDED*	CHORUSING	CHRISOMS	CHRYSALIDES
CHONDRULE	CHORDEE	CHORUSSED*	CHRISTEN	CHRYSALIDS
CHONDRULES	CHORDEES	CHORUSSES*	CHRISTENED	CHRYSALIS
CHONDRUS	CHORDING	CHORUSSING*	CHRISTENING	CHRYSALISES
CHONS	CHORDINGS	CHOSE	CHRISTENINGS	CHRYSANTH
CHOOF	CHORDS	CHOSEN	CHRISTENS	CHRYSANTHS
CHOOFED	CHORE	CHOSES	CHRISTIE	CHTHONIAN
CHOOFING	CHOREA	CHOTA	CHRISTIES	CHTHONIC
CHOOFS	CHOREAL*	CHOTT	CHRISTOM	CHUB
CHOOK	CHOREAS	CHOTTS	CHRISTOMS	CHUBASCO*
CHOOKIE	CHORED*	CHOU	CHRISTY	CHUBASCOS*
CHOOKIES	CHOREE	CHOUGH	CHROMA	CHUBBIER
CHOOKS	CHOREES	CHOUGHS	CHROMAKEY	CHUBBIEST
CHOOM	CHOREGI	CHOULTRIES	CHROMAKEYS	CHUBBILY*
CHOOMS	CHOREGIC	CHOULTRY	CHROMAS	CHUBBY
CHOOSE	CHOREGUS	CHOUNTER	CHROMATE	CHUBS
CHOOSER	CHOREGUSES	CHOUNTERED	CHROMATES	CHUCK
CHOOSERS	CHOREIC	CHOUNTERING	CHROMATIC	CHUCKED
CHOOSES	CHOREMAN*	CHOUNTERS	CHROMATICS	CHUCKHOLE
CHOOSEY	CHOREMEN*	CHOUSE	CHROMATID	CHUCKHOLES
CHOOSIER	CHOREOID*	CHOUSED	CHROMATIDS	CHUCKIE
CHOOSIEST	CHORES	CHOUSER*	CHROMATIN	CHUCKIES
CHOOSING	CHOREUS	CHOUSERS*	CHROMATINS	CHUCKING
CHOOSY	CHOREUSES	CHOUSES	CHROME	CHUCKLE
CHOP	CHORIA	CHOUSH*	CHROMED	CHUCKLED
CHOPHOUSE	CHORIAL	CHOUSHES*	CHROMEL	CHUCKLER*
CHOPHOUSES	CHORIAMB	CHOUSING	CHROMELS	CHUCKLERS*
CHOPIN	CHORIAMBI	CHOUT	CHROMENE	CHUCKLES
CHOPINE	CHORIAMBS	CHOUTS	CHROMENES	CHUCKLING
CHOPINES	CHORIC	CHOUX	CHROMES	CHUCKLINGS
CHOPINS	CHORINE	CHOW	CHROMIC	CHUCKS
CHOPLOGIC	CHORINES	CHOWCHOW*	CHROMIDE*	CHUCKY*
CHOPLOGICS	CHORING*	CHOWCHOWS*	CHROMIDES*	CHUDDAH
CHOPPED	CHORIOID	CHOWDER	CHROMIDIA	CHUDDAHS
CHOPPER	CHORIOIDS	CHOWDERED*	CHROMING	CHUDDAR
CHOPPERED*	CHORION	CHOWDERING*	CHROMINGS*	CHUDDARS
CHOPPERING*	CHORIONIC	CHOWDERS	CHROMITE	CHUDDER*
CHOPPERS	CHORIONS*	CHOWED*	CHROMITES	CHUDDERS*
CHOPPIER	CHORISES	CHOWHOUND*	CHROMIUM	CHUDDIES
CHOPPIEST	CHORISIS	CHOWHOUNDS*	CHROMIUMS	CHUDDY
CHOPPILY*	CHORISM	CHOWING*	CHROMIZE*	CHUFA
CHOPPING	CHORISMS	CHOWKIDAR	CHROMIZED*	CHUFAS
CHOPPINGS	CHORIST	CHOWKIDARS	CHROMIZES*	CHUFF
CHOPPY	CHORISTER	CHOWRI	CHROMIZING*	CHUFFED
CHOPS	CHORISTERS	CHOWRIES	CHROMO	CHUFFER*
CHOPSTICK	CHORISTS	CHOWRIS	CHROMOGEN	CHUFFEST*
CHOPSTICKS	CHORIZO	CHOWRY	CHROMOGENS	CHUFFIER
CHORAGI	CHORIZONT	CHOWS	CHROMOS	CHUFFIEST
CHORAGIC	CHORIZONTS	CHOWSE*	CHROMOUS*	CHUFFING
CHORAGUS	CHORIZOS	CHOWSED*	CHROMYL*	CHUFFS
CHORAGUSES	CHOROID	CHOWSES*	CHROMYLS*	CHUFFY
CHORAL	CHOROIDAL*	CHOWSING*	CHRONAXIE	CHUG
CHORALE	CHOROIDS	CHOWTIME*	CHRONAXIES	CHUGALUG*
CHORALES	CHOROLOGIES	CHOWTIMES*	CHRONAXY*	CHUGALUGGED*
CHORALIST	CHOROLOGY	CHRESARD*	CHRONIC	CHUGALUGGING*
CHORALISTS	CHORTLE	CHRESARDS*	CHRONICAL	CHUGALUGS*
CHORALLY	CHORTLED	CHRISM	CHRONICLE	CHUGGED
CHORALS	CHORTLER*	CHRISMA*	CHRONICLED	CHUGGER*
CHORD	CHORTLERS*	CHRISMAL	CHRONICLES	CHUGGERS*

The Chambers Dictionary is the authority for many longer words; see Introduction, page ix

CHUGGING	CHURCHED	CHYLIFY	CICHLIDAE*	CILIUM
CHUGS	CHURCHES	CHYLIFYING	CICHLIDS	CILL
CHUKAR	CHURCHIER	CHYLOUS*	CICHLOID	CILLS
CHUKARS	CHURCHIEST	CHYLURIA	CICINNUS	CIMAR
CHUKKA	CHURCHING	CHYLURIAS	CICINNUSES	CIMARS
CHUKKAR*	CHURCHINGS	CHYME	CICISBEI	CIMBALOM
CHUKKARS*	CHURCHISM	CHYMES	CICISBEO	CIMBALOMS
CHUKKAS	CHURCHISMS	CHYMIC*	CICISBEOS*	CIMELIA
CHUKKER	CHURCHLIER	CHYMICS*	CICLATON	CIMEX
CHUKKERS	CHURCHLIEST	CHYMIFIED	CICLATONS	CIMICES
CHUKOR	CHURCHLY	CHYMIFIES	CICLATOUN	CIMIER
CHUKORS	CHURCHMAN	CHYMIFY	CICLATOUNS	CIMIERS
CHUM	CHURCHMEN	CHYMIFYING	CICOREE*	CIMINITE
CHUMLEY	CHURCHWAY	CHYMIST*	CICOREES*	CIMINITES
CHUMLEYS	CHURCHWAYS	CHYMISTRIES	CICUTA	CIMOLITE
CHUMMAGE	CHURCHY	CHYMISTRY	CICUTAS	CIMOLITES
CHUMMAGES	CHURIDARS	CHYMISTS*	CID	CINCH
CHUMMED	CHURINGA	CHYMOSIN*	CIDARIS	CINCHED
CHUMMIER	CHURINGAS	CHYMOSINS*	CIDARISES	CINCHES
CHUMMIES	CHURL	CHYMOUS	CIDE	CINCHING
CHUMMIEST	CHURLISH	CHYND	CIDED	CINCHINGS
CHUMMILY*	CHURLS	CHYPRE	CIDER	CINCHONA
CHUMMING	CHURN	CHYPRES	CIDERKIN	CINCHONAS
CHUMMY	CHURNED	CIABATTA	CIDERKINS	CINCHONIC
CHUMP	CHURNER*	CIABATTAS	CIDERS	CINCINNUS
CHUMPED*	CHURNERS*	CIABATTE	CIDERY	CINCINNUSES
CHUMPING	CHURNING	CIAO	CIDES	CINCT
CHUMPINGS	CHURNINGS	CIAOS	CIDING	CINCTURE
CHUMPS	CHURNMILK	CIBATION	CIDS	CINCTURED
CHUMS	CHURNMILKS	CIBATIONS	CIEL	CINCTURES
CHUMSHIP*	CHURNS	CIBOL	CIELED	CINCTURING
CHUMSHIPS*	CHURR	CIBOLS	CIELING	CINDER
CHUNDER	CHURRED	CIBORIA	CIELINGS	CINDERED
CHUNDERED	CHURRING	CIBORIUM	CIELS	CINDERING
CHUNDERING	CHURRS	CIBOULE*	CIERGE	CINDERS
CHUNDERS	CHURRUS	CIBOULES*	CIERGES	CINDERY
CHUNK	CHURRUSES	CICADA	CIG	CINE*
CHUNKED*	CHUSE	CICADAE*	CIGAR	CINEAST
CHUNKIER	CHUSES	CICADAS	CIGARET*	CINEASTE
CHUNKIEST	CHUSING	CICALA	CIGARETS*	CINEASTES
CHUNKILY*	CHUT	CICALAS	CIGARETTE	CINEASTS
CHUNKING	CHUTE	CICALE*	CIGARETTES	CINEMA
CHUNKINGS	CHUTED*	CICATRICE	CIGARILLO	CINEMAS
CHUNKS	CHUTES	CICATRICES	CIGARILLOS	CINEMATIC
CHUNKY	CHUTING*	CICATRISE	CIGARS	CINEOL
CHUNNEL	CHUTIST	CICATRISED	CIGGIE	CINEOLE
CHUNNELS	CHUTISTS	CICATRISES	CIGGIES	CINEOLES
CHUNNER	CHUTNEE*	CICATRISING	CIGGY	CINEOLS
CHUNNERED	CHUTNEES*	CICATRIX	CIGS	CINEPHILE
CHUNNERING	CHUTNEY	CICATRIXES	CIGUATERA*	CINEPHILES
CHUNNERS	CHUTNEYS	CICATRIZE	CIGUATERAS*	CINEPLEX
CHUNTER	CHUTZPA*	CICATRIZED	CILANTRO	CINEPLEXES
CHUNTERED	CHUTZPAH	CICATRIZES	CILANTROS	CINERAMIC
CHUNTERING	CHUTZPAHS	CICATRIZING	CILIA	CINERARIA
CHUNTERS	CHUTZPAS*	CICELIES	CILIARY	CINERARIAS
CHUPATI	CHYACK	CICELY	CILIATE	CINERARIUM*
CHUPATIS	CHYACKED	CICERO	CILIATED*	CINERARY
CHUPATTI	CHYACKING	CICERONE	CILIATES	CINERATOR
CHUPATTIS	CHYACKS	CICERONED	CILIATION*	CINERATORS
CHUPPAH	CHYLDE	CICERONEING	CILIATIONS*	CINEREA
CHUPPAHS	CHYLE	CICERONES	CILICE	CINEREAL
CHUPRASSIES	CHYLES	CICERONI	CILICES	CINEREAS
CHUPRASSY	CHYLIFIED	CICEROS	CILICIOUS	CINEREOUS
CHURCH	CHYLIFIES	CICHLID	CILIOLATE	CINERIN

Words marked with an asterisk are from OTCWL

CINERINS	CIRCULATES	CISTUSES	CITRINS	CLACKBOX
CINES*	CIRCULATING	CISTVAEN	CITRON	CLACKBOXES
CINGULA	CIRCULATINGS	CISTVAENS	CITRONS	CLACKDISH
CINGULATE*	CIRCUS	CIT	CITROUS	CLACKDISHES
CINGULUM	CIRCUSES	CITABLE	CITRUS	CLACKED
CINNABAR	CIRCUSSY	CITADEL	CITRUSES	CLACKER
CINNABARS	CIRCUSY	CITADELS	CITRUSY*	CLACKERS
CINNAMIC	CIRE	CITAL	CITS	CLACKING
CINNAMON	CIRES	CITALS	CITTERN	CLACKS
CINNAMONS	CIRL	CITATION	CITTERNS	CLAD
CINNAMYL*	CIRLS	CITATIONS	CITY	CLADDED
CINNAMYLS*	CIRQUE	CITATOR*	CITYFIED	CLADDER
CINQUAIN	CIRQUES	CITATORS*	CITYFIES	CLADDERS
CINQUAINS	CIRRATE	CITATORY	CITYFY	CLADDING
CINQUE	CIRRHOPOD	CITE	CITYFYING	CLADDINGS
CINQUES	CIRRHOPODS	CITEABLE	CITYSCAPE	CLADE
CION	CIRRHOSES	CITED	CITYSCAPES	CLADES
CIONS	CIRRHOSIS	CITER	CITYWARD*	CLADISM
CIOPPINO*	CIRRHOTIC	CITERS	CITYWIDE*	CLADISMS
CIOPPINOS*	CIRRHOTICS*	CITES	CIVE	CLADIST
CIPHER	CIRRI	CITESS	CIVES	CLADISTIC
CIPHERED	CIRRIFORM	CITESSES	CIVET	CLADISTICS
CIPHERING	CIRRIPED	CITHARA	CIVETS	CLADISTS
CIPHERINGS	CIRRIPEDE	CITHARAS	CIVIC	CLADODE
CIPHERS	CIRRIPEDES	CITHARIST	CIVICALLY	CLADODES
CIPHONIES*	CIRRIPEDS	CITHARISTS	CIVICISM*	CLADODIAL*
CIPHONY*	CIRROSE	CITHER	CIVICISMS*	CLADOGRAM
CIPOLIN	CIRROUS	CITHERN	CIVICS	CLADOGRAMS
CIPOLINS	CIRRUS	CITHERNS	CIVIE*	CLADS
CIPOLLINO	CIRSOID	CITHERS	CIVIES*	CLAES
CIPOLLINOS	CIS*	CITHREN*	CIVIL	CLAG
CIPPI	CISALPINE	CITHRENS*	CIVILIAN	CLAGGED
CIPPUS	CISCO	CITIED*	CIVILIANS	CLAGGIER
CIRCA	CISCOES	CITIES	CIVILISE	CLAGGIEST
CIRCADIAN	CISCOS	CITIFIED	CIVILISED	CLAGGING
CIRCAR	CISELEUR	CITIFIES	CIVILISER	CLAGGY
CIRCARS	CISELEURS	CITIFY	CIVILISERS	CLAGS
CIRCINATE	CISELURE	CITIFYING	CIVILISES	CLAIM
CIRCITER	CISELURES	CITIGRADE	CIVILISING	CLAIMABLE
CIRCLE	CISLUNAR	CITING	CIVILIST	CLAIMANT
CIRCLED	CISPADANE	CITIZEN	CIVILISTS	CLAIMANTS
CIRCLER	CISPLATIN	CITIZENLY*	CIVILITIES	CLAIMED
CIRCLERS	CISPLATINS	CITIZENRIES	CIVILITY	CLAIMER
CIRCLES	CISSIER	CITIZENRY	CIVILIZE	CLAIMERS
CIRCLET	CISSIES	CITIZENS	CIVILIZED	CLAIMING
CIRCLETS	CISSIEST	CITO	CIVILIZER	CLAIMS
CIRCLING	CISSOID	CITOLA*	CIVILIZERS	CLAM
CIRCLINGS	CISSOIDS	CITOLAS*	CIVILIZES	CLAMANCIES
CIRCLIP	CISSUS	CITOLE	CIVILIZING	CLAMANCY
CIRCLIPS	CISSUSES	CITOLES	CIVILLY	CLAMANT
CIRCS	CISSY	CITRAL*	CIVISM	CLAMANTLY
CIRCUIT	CIST	CITRALS*	CIVISMS	CLAMBAKE
CIRCUITAL*	CISTED	CITRANGE	CIVVIES	CLAMBAKES
CIRCUITED	CISTERN	CITRANGES	CIVVY	CLAMBE
CIRCUITIES	CISTERNA	CITRATE	CIZERS	CLAMBER
CIRCUITING	CISTERNAE	CITRATED*	CLABBER	CLAMBERED
CIRCUITRIES	CISTERNAL*	CITRATES	CLABBERED*	CLAMBERER*
CIRCUITRY	CISTERNS	CITREOUS	CLABBERING*	CLAMBERERS*
CIRCUITS	CISTIC	CITRIC	CLABBERS	CLAMBERING
CIRCUITY	CISTRON	CITRIN	CLACH*	CLAMBERS
CIRCULAR	CISTRONIC*	CITRINE	CLACHAN	CLAME
CIRCULARS	CISTRONS	CITRINES	CLACHANS	CLAMES
CIRCULATE	CISTS	CITRININ*	CLACHS*	CLAMMED
CIRCULATED	CISTUS	CITRININS*	CLACK	CLAMMER*

CLAMMERS*	CLAPBOARD	CLARSACHS	CLATCHES	CLAW
CLAMMIER	CLAPBOARDED*	CLART	CLATCHING	CLAWBACK
CLAMMIEST	CLAPBOARDING*	CLARTED	CLATHRATE	CLAWBACKS
CLAMMILY	CLAPBOARDS	CLARTIER	CLATHRATES*	CLAWED
CLAMMING	CLAPBREAD	CLARTIEST	CLATS	CLAWER*
CLAMMY	CLAPBREADS	CLARTING	CLATTED	CLAWERS*
CLAMOR	CLAPDISH	CLARTS	CLATTER	CLAWING
CLAMORED	CLAPDISHES	CLARTY	CLATTERED	CLAWLESS
CLAMORER*	CLAPNET	CLARY	CLATTERER	CLAWLIKE*
CLAMORERS*	CLAPNETS	CLASH	CLATTERERS	CLAWS
CLAMORING	CLAPPED	CLASHED	CLATTERING	CLAXON*
CLAMOROUS	CLAPPER	CLASHER	CLATTERS	CLAXONS*
CLAMORS	CLAPPERED	CLASHERS	CLATTERY	CLAY
CLAMOUR	CLAPPERING	CLASHES	CLATTING	CLAYBANK*
CLAMOURED	CLAPPERINGS	CLASHING	CLAUCHT	CLAYBANKS*
CLAMOURER	CLAPPERS	CLASHINGS	CLAUCHTED	CLAYED
CLAMOURERS	CLAPPING	CLASP	CLAUCHTING	CLAYEY
CLAMOURING	CLAPPINGS	CLASPED	CLAUCHTS	CLAYIER
CLAMOURS	CLAPS	CLASPER	CLAUGHT	CLAYIEST
CLAMP	CLAPT*	CLASPERS	CLAUGHTED	CLAYING
CLAMPDOWN	CLAPTRAP	CLASPING	CLAUGHTING	CLAYISH
CLAMPDOWNS	CLAPTRAPS	CLASPINGS	CLAUGHTS	CLAYLIKE*
CLAMPED	CLAQUE	CLASPS	CLAUSAL	CLAYMORE
CLAMPER	CLAQUER*	CLASPT*	CLAUSE	CLAYMORES
CLAMPERED	CLAQUERS*	CLASS	CLAUSES	CLAYPAN
CLAMPERING	CLAQUES	CLASSABLE	CLAUSTRA	CLAYPANS
CLAMPERS	CLAQUEUR	CLASSED	CLAUSTRAL	CLAYS
CLAMPING	CLAQUEURS	CLASSER*	CLAUSTRUM	CLAYTONIA
CLAMPS	CLARAIN	CLASSERS*	CLAUSULA	CLAYTONIAS
CLAMS	CLARAINS	CLASSES	CLAUSULAE	CLAYWARE*
CLAMSHELL	CLARENCE	CLASSIBLE	CLAUSULAR	CLAYWARES*
CLAMSHELLS	CLARENCES	CLASSIC	CLAUT	CLEAN
CLAMWORM*	CLARENDON	CLASSICAL	CLAUTED	CLEANABLE*
CLAMWORMS*	CLARENDONS	CLASSICO*	CLAUTING	CLEANED
CLAN	CLARET	CLASSICS	CLAUTS	CLEANER
CLANG	CLARETED	CLASSIER	CLAVATE	CLEANERS
CLANGBOX	CLARETING	CLASSIEST	CLAVATED	CLEANEST
CLANGBOXES	CLARETS	CLASSIFIC	CLAVATION	CLEANING
CLANGED	CLARIES	CLASSIFIED	CLAVATIONS	CLEANINGS
CLANGER	CLARIFIED	CLASSIFIES	CLAVE	CLEANLIER
CLANGERS	CLARIFIER	CLASSIFY	CLAVECIN	CLEANLIEST
CLANGING	CLARIFIERS	CLASSIFYING	CLAVECINS	CLEANLY
CLANGINGS	CLARIFIES	CLASSILY*	CLAVER	CLEANNESS
CLANGOR	CLARIFY	CLASSING	CLAVERED	CLEANNESSES
CLANGORED	CLARIFYING	CLASSIS	CLAVERING	CLEANS
CLANGORING	CLARINET	CLASSISM	CLAVERS	CLEANSE
CLANGORS	CLARINETS	CLASSISMS	CLAVES	CLEANSED
CLANGOUR	CLARINI	CLASSIST	CLAVI*	CLEANSER
CLANGOURED	CLARINO	CLASSISTS*	CLAVICLE	CLEANSERS
CLANGOURING	CLARINOS	CLASSLESS	CLAVICLES	CLEANSES
CLANGOURS	CLARION	CLASSMAN	CLAVICORN	CLEANSING
CLANGS	CLARIONED*	CLASSMATE	CLAVICORNS	CLEANSINGS
CLANK	CLARIONET	CLASSMATES	CLAVICULA	CLEANSKIN
CLANKED	CLARIONETS	CLASSMEN	CLAVICULAE	CLEANSKINS
CLANKING	CLARIONING*	CLASSROOM	CLAVIE	CLEANUP*
CLANKINGS	CLARIONS	CLASSROOMS	CLAVIER	CLEANUPS*
CLANKS	CLARITIES	CLASSY	CLAVIERS	CLEAR
CLANNISH	CLARITY	CLAST*	CLAVIES	CLEARABLE*
CLANS	CLARKIA	CLASTIC	CLAVIFORM	CLEARAGE
CLANSHIP	CLARKIAS	CLASTICS*	CLAVIGER	CLEARAGES
CLANSHIPS	CLARO	CLASTS	CLAVIGERS	CLEARANCE
CLANSMAN	CLAROES	CLAT	CLAVIS	CLEARANCES
CLANSMEN	CLAROS	CLATCH	CLAVULATE	CLEARCOLE
CLAP	CLARSACH	CLATCHED	CLAVUS*	CLEARCOLES

CLEARED	CLEMMED	CLEUGH	CLIMATES	CLINKS
CLEARER	CLEMMING	CLEUGHS	CLIMATIC	CLINOAXES
CLEARERS	CLEMS	CLEVE	CLIMATING	CLINOAXIS
CLEAREST	CLENCH	CLEVEITE	CLIMATISE	CLINQUANT
CLEARING	CLENCHED	CLEVEITES	CLIMATISED	CLINQUANTS
CLEARINGS	CLENCHER*	CLEVER	CLIMATISES	CLINT
CLEARLY	CLENCHERS*	CLEVERER	CLIMATISING	CLINTONIA*
CLEARNESS	CLENCHES	CLEVEREST	CLIMATIZE	CLINTONIAS*
CLEARNESSES	CLENCHING	CLEVERISH	CLIMATIZED	CLINTS
CLEARS	CLEOME*	CLEVERLY	CLIMATIZES	CLIP
CLEARSKIN	CLEOMES*	CLEVES	CLIMATIZING	CLIPART
CLEARSKINS	CLEPE	CLEVIS	CLIMATURE	CLIPARTS
CLEARWAY	CLEPED	CLEVISES	CLIMATURES	CLIPBOARD
CLEARWAYS	CLEPES	CLEW	CLIMAX	CLIPBOARDS
CLEARWING	CLEPING	CLEWED	CLIMAXED	CLIPE
CLEARWINGS	CLEPSYDRA	CLEWING	CLIMAXES	CLIPED
CLEAT	CLEPSYDRAE*	CLEWS	CLIMAXING	CLIPES
CLEATED	CLEPSYDRAS	CLIANTHUS	CLIMB	CLIPING
CLEATING	CLEPT*	CLIANTHUSES	CLIMBABLE	CLIPPED
CLEATS	CLERECOLE	CLICHE	CLIMBED	CLIPPER
CLEAVABLE	CLERECOLES	CLICHED*	CLIMBER	CLIPPERS
CLEAVAGE	CLERGIES	CLICHEED	CLIMBERS	CLIPPIE
CLEAVAGES	CLERGY	CLICHES	CLIMBING	CLIPPIES
CLEAVE	CLERGYMAN	CLICK	CLIMBINGS	CLIPPING
CLEAVED	CLERGYMEN	CLICKED	CLIMBS	CLIPPINGS
CLEAVER	CLERIC	CLICKER	CLIME	CLIPS
CLEAVERS	CLERICAL	CLICKERS	CLIMES	CLIPSHEET*
CLEAVES	CLERICALS	CLICKET	CLINAL*	CLIPSHEETS*
CLEAVING	CLERICATE	CLICKETED	CLINALLY*	CLIPT
CLEAVINGS	CLERICATES	CLICKETING	CLINAMEN	CLIQUE
CLECHE	CLERICITIES	CLICKETS	CLINAMENS	CLIQUED*
CLECK	CLERICITY	CLICKING	CLINCH	CLIQUES
CLECKED	CLERICS	CLICKINGS	CLINCHED	CLIQUEY
CLECKING	CLERID*	CLICKS	CLINCHER	CLIQUIER
CLECKINGS	CLERIDS*	CLIED	CLINCHERS	CLIQUIEST
CLECKS	CLERIHEW	CLIENT	CLINCHES	CLIQUING*
CLEEK	CLERIHEWS	CLIENTAGE	CLINCHING	CLIQUISH
CLEEKED	CLERISIES	CLIENTAGES	CLINE	CLIQUISM
CLEEKING	CLERISY	CLIENTAL	CLINES	CLIQUISMS
CLEEKIT	CLERK	CLIENTELE	CLING	CLIQUY
CLEEKS	CLERKDOM	CLIENTELES	CLINGED*	CLITELLA
CLEEP	CLERKDOMS	CLIENTS	CLINGER	CLITELLAR
CLEEPED	CLERKED	CLIES	CLINGERS	CLITELLUM
CLEEPING	CLERKESS	CLIFF	CLINGFILM	CLITHRAL
CLEEPS	CLERKESSES	CLIFFED	CLINGFILMS	CLITIC
CLEEVE	CLERKING	CLIFFHANG	CLINGIER	CLITICS
CLEEVES	CLERKISH	CLIFFHANGING	CLINGIEST	CLITORAL
CLEF	CLERKLIER*	CLIFFHANGINGS	CLINGING	CLITORIC*
CLEFS	CLERKLIEST*	CLIFFHANGS	CLINGS	CLITORIDES*
CLEFT	CLERKLIKE	CLIFFHUNG	CLINGY	CLITORIS
CLEFTED*	CLERKLING	CLIFFIER	CLINIC	CLITORISES
CLEFTING*	CLERKLINGS	CLIFFIEST	CLINICAL	CLITTER
CLEFTS	CLERKLY	CLIFFS	CLINICIAN	CLITTERED
CLEG	CLERKS	CLIFFY	CLINICIANS	CLITTERING
CLEGS	CLERKSHIP	CLIFT	CLINICS	CLITTERS
CLEIDOIC	CLERKSHIPS	CLIFTED	CLINIQUE	CLIVERS
CLEITHRAL	CLERUCH	CLIFTIER	CLINIQUES	CLIVIA
CLEM	CLERUCHIA	CLIFTIEST	CLINK	CLIVIAS
CLEMATIS	CLERUCHIAS	CLIFTS	CLINKED	CLOACA
CLEMATISES	CLERUCHIES	CLIFTY	CLINKER	CLOACAE
CLEMENCIES	CLERUCHS	CLIMACTIC	CLINKERED*	CLOACAL
CLEMENCY	CLERUCHY	CLIMATAL	CLINKERING*	CLOACALIN
CLEMENT	CLEUCH	CLIMATE	CLINKERS	CLOACAS*
CLEMENTLY	CLEUCHS	CLIMATED	CLINKING	CLOACINAL

CLOAK
CLOAKED
CLOAKING
CLOAKROOM
CLOAKROOMS
CLOAKS
CLOAM
CLOAMS
CLOBBER
CLOBBERED
CLOBBERING
CLOBBERS
CLOCHARD
CLOCHARDS
CLOCHE
CLOCHES
CLOCK
CLOCKED
CLOCKER
CLOCKERS
CLOCKING
CLOCKINGS
CLOCKLIKE*
CLOCKS
CLOCKWISE
CLOCKWORK
CLOCKWORKS
CLOD
CLODDED
CLODDIER
CLODDIEST
CLODDING
CLODDISH
CLODDY
CLODLY
CLODPATE
CLODPATED
CLODPATES
CLODPOLE
CLODPOLES
CLODPOLL
CLODPOLLS
CLODS
CLOFF
CLOFFS
CLOG
CLOGDANCE
CLOGDANCES
CLOGGED
CLOGGER
CLOGGERS
CLOGGIER
CLOGGIEST
CLOGGING
CLOGGY
CLOGS
CLOISON
CLOISONNE
CLOISONNES
CLOISONS
CLOISTER
CLOISTERED
CLOISTERING
CLOISTERS

CLOISTRAL
CLOKE
CLOKED
CLOKES
CLOKING
CLOMB
CLOMP
CLOMPED
CLOMPING
CLOMPS
CLON*
CLONAL
CLONALLY
CLONE
CLONED
CLONER*
CLONERS*
CLONES
CLONIC
CLONICITIES
CLONICITY
CLONIDINE*
CLONIDINES*
CLONING
CLONINGS*
CLONISM*
CLONISMS*
CLONK
CLONKED
CLONKING
CLONKS
CLONS*
CLONUS
CLONUSES
CLOOP
CLOOPS
CLOOT
CLOOTS
CLOP
CLOPPED
CLOPPING
CLOPS
CLOQUE
CLOQUES
CLOSABLE*
CLOSE
CLOSEABLE*
CLOSED
CLOSEDOWN
CLOSEDOWNS
CLOSEHEAD
CLOSEHEADS
CLOSELY
CLOSENESS
CLOSENESSES
CLOSEOUT*
CLOSEOUTS*
CLOSER
CLOSERS
CLOSES
CLOSEST
CLOSET
CLOSETED
CLOSETFUL*

CLOSETFULS*
CLOSETING
CLOSETS
CLOSING
CLOSINGS
CLOSURE
CLOSURED
CLOSURES
CLOSURING
CLOT
CLOTBUR
CLOTBURS
CLOTE
CLOTEBUR
CLOTEBURS
CLOTES
CLOTH
CLOTHE
CLOTHED
CLOTHES
CLOTHIER
CLOTHIERS
CLOTHING
CLOTHINGS
CLOTHS
CLOTPOLL
CLOTPOLLS
CLOTS
CLOTTED
CLOTTER
CLOTTERED
CLOTTERING
CLOTTERS
CLOTTIER
CLOTTIEST
CLOTTING
CLOTTINGS
CLOTTY
CLOTURE
CLOTURED
CLOTURES
CLOTURING
CLOU
CLOUD
CLOUDAGE
CLOUDAGES
CLOUDED
CLOUDIER
CLOUDIEST
CLOUDILY
CLOUDING
CLOUDINGS
CLOUDLAND
CLOUDLANDS
CLOUDLESS
CLOUDLET
CLOUDLETS
CLOUDS
CLOUDTOWN
CLOUDTOWNS
CLOUDY
CLOUGH
CLOUGHS
CLOUR

CLOURED
CLOURING
CLOURS
CLOUS
CLOUT
CLOUTED
CLOUTER
CLOUTERLY
CLOUTERS
CLOUTING
CLOUTS
CLOVE
CLOVEN
CLOVEPINK
CLOVEPINKS
CLOVER
CLOVERED
CLOVERS
CLOVERY
CLOVES
CLOW
CLOWDER
CLOWDERS
CLOWN
CLOWNED
CLOWNERIES
CLOWNERY
CLOWNING
CLOWNINGS
CLOWNISH
CLOWNS
CLOWS
CLOY
CLOYE
CLOYED
CLOYES
CLOYING
CLOYINGLY*
CLOYLESS
CLOYMENT
CLOYMENTS
CLOYS
CLOYSOME
CLOZE
CLOZES*
CLUB
CLUBABLE
CLUBBABLE
CLUBBED
CLUBBER
CLUBBERS
CLUBBIER
CLUBBIEST
CLUBBING
CLUBBINGS
CLUBBISH
CLUBBISM
CLUBBISMS
CLUBBIST
CLUBBISTS
CLUBBY
CLUBFEET*
CLUBFOOT*
CLUBHAND*

CLUBHANDS*
CLUBHAUL*
CLUBHAULED*
CLUBHAULING*
CLUBHAULS*
CLUBHOUSE
CLUBHOUSES
CLUBLAND
CLUBLANDS
CLUBMAN
CLUBMEN
CLUBROOM
CLUBROOMS
CLUBROOT
CLUBROOTS
CLUBRUSH
CLUBRUSHES
CLUBS
CLUBWOMAN
CLUBWOMEN
CLUCK
CLUCKED
CLUCKIER
CLUCKIEST
CLUCKING
CLUCKS
CLUCKY
CLUDGIE
CLUDGIES
CLUE
CLUED
CLUEING
CLUELESS
CLUES
CLUING
CLUMBER
CLUMBERS
CLUMP
CLUMPED
CLUMPER
CLUMPERS
CLUMPIER
CLUMPIEST
CLUMPING
CLUMPISH*
CLUMPS
CLUMPY
CLUMSIER
CLUMSIEST
CLUMSILY
CLUMSY
CLUNCH
CLUNCHES
CLUNG
CLUNK
CLUNKED
CLUNKER*
CLUNKERS*
CLUNKIER
CLUNKIEST
CLUNKING
CLUNKS
CLUNKY
CLUPEID

Words marked with an asterisk are from OTCWL

CLUPEIDS	COACTED	COALHOLE*	COARSE	COAUTHOR*
CLUPEOID	COACTING	COALHOLES*	COARSELY	COAUTHORED*
CLUPEOIDS	COACTION	COALHOUSE	COARSEN	COAUTHORING*
CLUSIA	COACTIONS	COALHOUSES	COARSENED	COAUTHORS*
CLUSIAS	COACTIVE	COALIER	COARSENING	COAX
CLUSTER	COACTOR*	COALIEST	COARSENS	COAXAL*
CLUSTERED	COACTORS*	COALIFIED*	COARSER	COAXED
CLUSTERING	COACTS	COALIFIES*	COARSEST	COAXER
CLUSTERS	COADAPTED	COALIFY*	COARSISH	COAXERS
CLUSTERY	COADJUTOR	COALIFYING*	COASSIST*	COAXES
CLUTCH	COADJUTORS	COALING	COASSISTED*	COAXIAL
CLUTCHED	COADMIRE*	COALISE	COASSISTING*	COAXIALLY
CLUTCHES	COADMIRED*	COALISED	COASSISTS*	COAXING
CLUTCHING	COADMIRES*	COALISES	COASSUME*	COAXINGLY
CLUTCHY*	COADMIRING*	COALISING	COASSUMED*	COB
CLUTTER	COADMIT*	COALITION	COASSUMES*	COBALAMIN
CLUTTERED	COADMITS*	COALITIONS	COASSUMING*	COBALAMINS
CLUTTERING	COADMITTED*	COALIZE	COAST	COBALT
CLUTTERS	COADMITTING*	COALIZED	COASTAL	COBALTIC
CLUTTERY*	COADUNATE	COALIZES	COASTED	COBALTINE*
CLY	COADUNATED	COALIZING	COASTER	COBALTINES*
CLYING	COADUNATES	COALLESS*	COASTERS	COBALTITE
CLYPE	COADUNATING	COALMAN	COASTING	COBALTITES
CLYPEAL	COAEVAL*	COALMEN	COASTINGS	COBALTOUS*
CLYPEATE	COAEVALS*	COALMINE	COASTLAND*	COBALTS
CLYPED	COAGENCIES*	COALMINER	COASTLANDS*	COBB
CLYPEI	COAGENCY*	COALMINERS	COASTLINE	COBBED
CLYPES	COAGENT*	COALMINES	COASTLINES	COBBER
CLYPEUS	COAGENTS*	COALPIT	COASTS	COBBERS
CLYPING	COAGULA	COALPITS	COASTWARD	COBBIER
CLYSTER	COAGULANT	COALS	COASTWARDS	COBBIEST
CLYSTERS	COAGULANTS	COALSACK*	COASTWISE	COBBING
CNEMIAL	COAGULASE	COALSACKS*	COAT	COBBLE
CNIDA	COAGULASES	COALSHED*	COATDRESS*	COBBLED
CNIDAE	COAGULATE	COALSHEDS*	COATDRESSES*	COBBLER
CNIDARIAN	COAGULATED	COALTAR	COATE	COBBLERIES
CNIDARIANS	COAGULATES	COALTARS	COATED	COBBLERS
COACH	COAGULATING	COALY	COATEE	COBBLERY
COACHABLE*	COAGULUM	COALYARD*	COATEES	COBBLES
COACHDOG	COAGULUMS*	COALYARDS*	COATER	COBBLING
COACHDOGS	COAITA	COAMING	COATERS	COBBLINGS
COACHED	COAITAS	COAMINGS	COATES	COBBS
COACHEE	COAL	COANCHOR*	COATI	COBBY
COACHEES	COALA*	COANCHORED*	COATING	COBIA
COACHER	COALAS*	COANCHORING*	COATINGS	COBIAS
COACHERS	COALBALL	COANCHORS*	COATIS	COBLE
COACHES	COALBALLS	COANNEX*	COATLESS	COBLES
COACHIES	COALBIN*	COANNEXED*	COATRACK	COBLOAF
COACHING	COALBINS*	COANNEXES*	COATRACKS	COBLOAVES
COACHINGS	COALBOX*	COANNEXING*	COATROOM*	COBNUT
COACHLINE	COALBOXES*	COAPPEAR*	COATROOMS*	COBNUTS
COACHLINES	COALED	COAPPEARED*	COATS	COBRA
COACHLOAD	COALER	COAPPEARING*	COATSTAND	COBRAS
COACHLOADS	COALERS	COAPPEARS*	COATSTANDS	COBRIC
COACHMAN	COALESCE	COAPT	COATTAIL*	COBRIFORM
COACHMEN	COALESCED	COAPTED	COATTAILS*	COBS
COACHWHIP	COALESCES	COAPTING	COATTEND*	COBURG
COACHWHIPS	COALESCING	COAPTS	COATTENDED*	COBURGS
COACHWOOD	COALFACE	COARB	COATTENDING*	COBWEB
COACHWOODS	COALFACES	COARBS	COATTENDS*	COBWEBBED
COACHWORK	COALFIELD	COARCTATE	COATTEST*	COBWEBBIER
COACHWORKS	COALFIELDS	COARCTATED	COATTESTED*	COBWEBBIEST
COACHY	COALFISH	COARCTATES	COATTESTING*	COBWEBBING
COACT	COALFISHES	COARCTATING	COATTESTS*	COBWEBBY

The Chambers Dictionary is the authority for many longer words; see Introduction, page ix

COBWEBS	COCHLEATE	COCKMATCHES	COCOPANS	CODER
COBZA	COCINERA*	COCKNEY	COCOPLUM	CODERIVE*
COBZAS	COCINERAS*	COCKNEYFIED	COCOPLUMS	CODERIVED*
COCA	COCK	COCKNEYFIES	COCOS	CODERIVES*
COCAIN*	COCKADE	COCKNEYFY	COCOTTE	CODERIVING*
COCAINE	COCKADED*	COCKNEYFYING	COCOTTES	CODERS
COCAINES	COCKADES	COCKNEYS	COCOUNSEL*	CODES
COCAINISE	COCKAMAMY*	COCKNIFIED	COCOUNSELED*	CODESIGN*
COCAINISED	COCKAPOO*	COCKNIFIES	COCOUNSELING*	CODESIGNED*
COCAINISES	COCKAPOOS*	COCKNIFY	COCOUNSELLED*	CODESIGNING*
COCAINISING	COCKATEEL	COCKNIFYING	COCOUNSELLING*	CODESIGNS*
COCAINISM	COCKATEELS	COCKPIT	COCOUNSELS*	CODETTA
COCAINISMS	COCKATIEL	COCKPITS	COCOYAM*	CODETTAS
COCAINIST	COCKATIELS	COCKROACH	COCOYAMS*	CODEVELOP*
COCAINISTS	COCKATOO	COCKROACHES	COCREATE*	CODEVELOPED*
COCAINIZE	COCKATOOS	COCKS	COCREATED*	CODEVELOPING*
COCAINIZED	COCKBILL*	COCKSCOMB	COCREATES*	CODEVELOPS*
COCAINIZES	COCKBILLED*	COCKSCOMBS	COCREATING*	CODEX
COCAINIZING	COCKBILLING*	COCKSFOOT	COCREATOR*	CODFISH
COCAINS*	COCKBILLS*	COCKSFOOTS	COCREATORS*	CODFISHES
COCAPTAIN*	COCKBIRD	COCKSHIES	COCTILE	CODGER
COCAPTAINED*	COCKBIRDS	COCKSHOT	COCTION	CODGERS
COCAPTAINING*	COCKBOAT	COCKSHOTS	COCTIONS	CODICES
COCAPTAINS*	COCKBOATS	COCKSHUT	COCULTURE	CODICIL
COCAS	COCKCROW*	COCKSHUTS	COCULTURED	CODICILS
COCCAL	COCKCROWS*	COCKSHY	COCULTURES	CODIFIED
COCCI	COCKED	COCKSIER	COCULTURING	CODIFIER
COCCIC*	COCKER	COCKSIEST	COCURATOR*	CODIFIERS
COCCID	COCKERED	COCKSPUR	COCURATORS*	CODIFIES
COCCIDIA	COCKEREL	COCKSPURS	COCUSWOOD	CODIFY
COCCIDIUM	COCKERELS	COCKSURE	COCUSWOODS	CODIFYING
COCCIDS	COCKERING	COCKSWAIN	COD	CODILLA
COCCO	COCKERS	COCKSWAINED	CODA	CODILLAS
COCCOID	COCKET	COCKSWAINING	CODABLE*	CODILLE
COCCOIDS*	COCKETS	COCKSWAINS	CODAS	CODILLES
COCCOLITE	COCKEYE	COCKSY	CODDED	CODING
COCCOLITES	COCKEYED	COCKTAIL	CODDER	CODINGS
COCCOLITH	COCKEYES	COCKTAILED*	CODDERS	CODIRECT*
COCCOLITHS	COCKFIGHT	COCKTAILING*	CODDING	CODIRECTED*
COCCOS	COCKFIGHTS	COCKTAILS	CODDLE	CODIRECTING*
COCCOUS*	COCKHORSE	COCKUP*	CODDLED	CODIRECTS*
COCCUS	COCKHORSES	COCKUPS*	CODDLER*	CODIST
COCCYGEAL	COCKIER	COCKY	CODDLERS*	CODISTS
COCCYGES	COCKIES	COCO	CODDLES	CODLIN
COCCYGIAN	COCKIEST	COCOA	CODDLING	CODLING
COCCYX	COCKILY	COCOANUT	CODE	CODLINGS
COCCYXES*	COCKINESS	COCOANUTS	CODEBOOK	CODLINS
COCH	COCKINESSES	COCOAS	CODEBOOKS	CODON
COCHAIR*	COCKING	COCOBOLA*	CODEBTOR*	CODONS
COCHAIRED*	COCKISH*	COCOBOLAS*	CODEBTORS*	CODPIECE
COCHAIRING*	COCKLAIRD	COCOBOLO*	CODEC*	CODPIECES
COCHAIRS*	COCKLAIRDS	COCOBOLOS*	CODECS*	CODRIVE*
COCHES	COCKLE	COCOMAT*	CODED	CODRIVEN*
COCHIN*	COCKLEBUR	COCOMATS*	CODEIA*	CODRIVER*
COCHINEAL	COCKLEBURS	COCONUT	CODEIAS*	CODRIVERS*
COCHINEALS	COCKLED	COCONUTS	CODEIN*	CODRIVES*
COCHINS*	COCKLEMAN	COCOON	CODEINA*	CODRIVING*
COCHLEA	COCKLEMEN	COCOONED	CODEINAS*	CODROVE*
COCHLEAE	COCKLES	COCOONERIES	CODEINE	CODS
COCHLEAR	COCKLIKE*	COCOONERY	CODEINES	COED
COCHLEARE	COCKLING	COCOONING	CODEINS*	COEDIT*
COCHLEARES	COCKLOFT	COCOONINGS	CODELESS*	COEDITED*
COCHLEARS	COCKLOFTS	COCOONS	CODEN*	COEDITING*
COCHLEAS*	COCKMATCH	COCOPAN	CODENS*	COEDITOR*

Words marked with an asterisk are from OTCWL

COEDITORS*	COEQUATES*	COFFINITES	COGNITION	COHIBITED
COEDITS*	COEQUATING*	COFFINS	COGNITIONS	COHIBITING
COEDS	COERCE	COFFLE	COGNITIVE	COHIBITS
COEFFECT*	COERCED	COFFLED*	COGNIZANT	COHO
COEFFECTS*	COERCER*	COFFLES	COGNIZE	COHOBATE
COEHORN	COERCERS*	COFFLING*	COGNIZED	COHOBATED
COEHORNS	COERCES	COFFRET	COGNIZER*	COHOBATES
COELIAC	COERCIBLE	COFFRETS	COGNIZERS*	COHOBATING
COELIACS	COERCIBLY	COFFS	COGNIZES	COHOE
COELOM	COERCING	COFINANCE*	COGNIZING	COHOES
COELOMATA*	COERCION	COFINANCED*	COGNOMEN	COHOG
COELOMATE	COERCIONS	COFINANCES*	COGNOMENS	COHOGS
COELOMATES	COERCIVE	COFINANCING*	COGNOMINA	COHOLDER*
COELOME	COERECT*	COFOUND*	COGNOSCE	COHOLDERS*
COELOMES	COERECTED*	COFOUNDED*	COGNOSCED	COHORN
COELOMIC	COERECTING*	COFOUNDER*	COGNOSCES	COHORNS
COELOMS	COERECTS*	COFOUNDERS*	COGNOSCING	COHORT
COELOSTAT	COESITE*	COFOUNDING*	COGNOVIT	COHORTS
COELOSTATS	COESITES*	COFOUNDS*	COGNOVITS	COHOS
COEMBODIED*	COETERNAL	COFT	COGON*	COHOSH*
COEMBODIES*	COEVAL	COG	COGONS*	COHOSHES*
COEMBODY*	COEVALITIES*	COGENCE	COGS	COHOST*
COEMBODYING*	COEVALITY*	COGENCES	COGUE	COHOSTED*
COEMPLOY*	COEVALLY*	COGENCIES	COGUES	COHOSTESS*
COEMPLOYED*	COEVALS	COGENCY	COGWAY*	COHOSTESSED*
COEMPLOYING*	COEVOLVE*	COGENER	COGWAYS*	COHOSTESSES*
COEMPLOYS*	COEVOLVED*	COGENERS	COGWHEEL	COHOSTESSING*
COEMPT*	COEVOLVES*	COGENT	COGWHEELS	COHOSTING*
COEMPTED*	COEVOLVING*	COGENTLY	COHAB	COHOSTS*
COEMPTING*	COEXERT*	COGGED	COHABIT	COHUNE
COEMPTION	COEXERTED*	COGGER	COHABITED	COHUNES
COEMPTIONS	COEXERTING*	COGGERS	COHABITEE	COHYPONYM
COEMPTS*	COEXERTS*	COGGIE	COHABITEES	COHYPONYMS
COENACT*	COEXIST	COGGIES	COHABITING	COIF
COENACTED*	COEXISTED	COGGING	COHABITOR	COIFED
COENACTING*	COEXISTING	COGGINGS	COHABITORS	COIFFE*
COENACTS*	COEXISTS	COGGLE	COHABITS	COIFFED*
COENAMOR*	COEXTEND	COGGLED	COHABS	COIFFES*
COENAMORED*	COEXTENDED	COGGLES	COHEAD*	COIFFEUR
COENAMORING*	COEXTENDING	COGGLIER	COHEADED*	COIFFEURS
COENAMORS*	COEXTENDS	COGGLIEST	COHEADING*	COIFFEUSE
COENDURE*	COFACTOR	COGGLING	COHEADS*	COIFFEUSES
COENDURED*	COFACTORS	COGGLY	COHEIR	COIFFING*
COENDURES*	COFEATURE*	COGIE	COHEIRESS	COIFFURE
COENDURING*	COFEATURED*	COGIES	COHEIRESSES	COIFFURED
COENOBIA	COFEATURES*	COGITABLE	COHEIRS	COIFFURES
COENOBITE	COFEATURING*	COGITATE	COHERE	COIFFURING
COENOBITES	COFF	COGITATED	COHERED	COIFING
COENOBIUM	COFFED	COGITATES	COHERENCE	COIFS
COENOCYTE	COFFEE	COGITATING	COHERENCES	COIGN
COENOCYTES	COFFEEPOT*	COGITO*	COHERENCIES	COIGNE
COENOSARC	COFFEEPOTS*	COGITOS*	COHERENCY	COIGNED
COENOSARCS	COFFEES	COGNAC*	COHERENT	COIGNES
COENURE*	COFFER	COGNACS*	COHERER	COIGNING
COENURES*	COFFERDAM	COGNATE	COHERERS	COIGNS
COENURI	COFFERDAMS	COGNATELY*	COHERES	COIL
COENURUS	COFFERED	COGNATES	COHERING	COILED
COENZYME	COFFERING	COGNATION	COHERITOR	COILER*
COENZYMES	COFFERS	COGNATIONS	COHERITORS	COILERS*
COEQUAL	COFFIN	COGNISANT	COHESIBLE	COILING
COEQUALLY	COFFINED	COGNISE	COHESION	COILS
COEQUALS	COFFING	COGNISED	COHESIONS	COIN
COEQUATE*	COFFINING	COGNISES	COHESIVE	COINABLE*
COEQUATED*	COFFINITE	COGNISING	COHIBIT	COINAGE

The Chambers Dictionary is the authority for many longer words; see Introduction, page ix

COINAGES	COKIEST	COLICKY	COLLEENS	COLLOQUIES
COINCIDE	COKING	COLICROOT*	COLLEGE	COLLOQUING
COINCIDED	COKY	COLICROOTS*	COLLEGER	COLLOQUIUM*
COINCIDES	COL	COLICS	COLLEGERS	COLLOQUIUMS*
COINCIDING	COLA	COLIES*	COLLEGES	COLLOQUY
COINED	COLANDER	COLIFORM	COLLEGIA	COLLOQUYING
COINER	COLANDERS	COLIFORMS	COLLEGIAL	COLLOTYPE
COINERS	COLAS	COLIN	COLLEGIAN	COLLOTYPES
COINFER*	COLCANNON	COLINEAR*	COLLEGIANS	COLLS
COINFERRED*	COLCANNONS	COLINS	COLLEGIUM	COLLUDE
COINFERRING*	COLCHICA	COLIPHAGE*	COLLEGIUMS	COLLUDED
COINFERS*	COLCHICUM	COLIPHAGES*	COLLET	COLLUDER
COINHERE	COLCHICUMS	COLISEUM	COLLETED*	COLLUDERS
COINHERED	COLCOTHAR	COLISEUMS	COLLETING*	COLLUDES
COINHERES	COLCOTHARS	COLISTIN*	COLLETS	COLLUDING
COINHERING	COLD	COLISTINS*	COLLICULI	COLLUSION
COINING	COLDBLOOD	COLITIC*	COLLIDE	COLLUSIONS
COININGS	COLDBLOODS	COLITIS	COLLIDED	COLLUSIVE
COINMATE*	COLDCOCK*	COLITISES	COLLIDER	COLLUVIA*
COINMATES*	COLDCOCKED*	COLL	COLLIDERS	COLLUVIAL*
COINS	COLDCOCKING*	COLLAGE	COLLIDES	COLLUVIES
COINSURE*	COLDCOCKS*	COLLAGED*	COLLIDING	COLLUVIUM*
COINSURED*	COLDER	COLLAGEN	COLLIE	COLLUVIUMS*
COINSURER*	COLDEST	COLLAGENS	COLLIED	COLLY
COINSURERS*	COLDHOUSE	COLLAGES	COLLIER	COLLYING
COINSURES*	COLDHOUSES	COLLAGING*	COLLIERIES	COLLYRIA
COINSURING*	COLDISH	COLLAGIST	COLLIERS	COLLYRIUM
COINTER*	COLDLY	COLLAGISTS	COLLIERY	COLLYRIUMS
COINTERRED*	COLDNESS	COLLAPSAR	COLLIES	COLOBI
COINTERRING*	COLDNESSES	COLLAPSARS	COLLIGATE	COLOBID
COINTERS*	COLDS	COLLAPSE	COLLIGATED	COLOBOMA
COINVENT*	COLE	COLLAPSED	COLLIGATES	COLOBOMATA
COINVENTED*	COLEAD*	COLLAPSES	COLLIGATING	COLOBUS
COINVENTING*	COLEADER*	COLLAPSING	COLLIMATE	COLOBUSES
COINVENTS*	COLEADERS*	COLLAR	COLLIMATED	COLOCATE*
COIR	COLEADING*	COLLARD	COLLIMATES	COLOCATED*
COIRS	COLEADS*	COLLARDS	COLLIMATING	COLOCATES*
COISTREL	COLECTOMIES	COLLARED	COLLINEAR	COLOCATING*
COISTRELS	COLECTOMY	COLLARET*	COLLING	COLOCYNTH
COISTRIL	COLED*	COLLARETS*	COLLINGS	COLOCYNTHS
COISTRILS	COLES	COLLARING	COLLINS	COLOG
COIT	COLESEED	COLLARS	COLLINSES	COLOGNE
COITAL	COLESEEDS	COLLATE	COLLISION	COLOGNED*
COITALLY*	COLESLAW	COLLATED	COLLISIONS	COLOGNES
COITION	COLESLAWS	COLLATES	COLLOCATE	COLOGS
COITIONAL*	COLESSEE*	COLLATING	COLLOCATED	COLON
COITIONS	COLESSEES*	COLLATION	COLLOCATES	COLONE*
COITS	COLESSOR*	COLLATIONS	COLLOCATING	COLONEL
COITUS	COLESSORS*	COLLATIVE	COLLODION	COLONELCIES
COITUSES	COLEUS	COLLATOR	COLLODIONS	COLONELCY
COJOIN	COLEUSES	COLLATORS	COLLOGUE	COLONELS
COJOINED	COLEWORT	COLLEAGUE	COLLOGUED	COLONES
COJOINING	COLEWORTS	COLLEAGUED	COLLOGUES	COLONI*
COJOINS	COLEY	COLLEAGUES	COLLOGUING	COLONIAL
COJONES	COLEYS	COLLEAGUING	COLLOID	COLONIALS
COKE	COLIBRI	COLLECT	COLLOIDAL	COLONIC
COKED	COLIBRIS	COLLECTED	COLLOIDS	COLONICS
COKEHEAD	COLIC	COLLECTING	COLLOP	COLONIES
COKEHEADS	COLICIN*	COLLECTINGS	COLLOPS	COLONISE
COKERNUT	COLICINE*	COLLECTOR	COLLOQUE	COLONISED
COKERNUTS	COLICINES*	COLLECTORS	COLLOQUED	COLONISES
COKES	COLICINS*	COLLECTS	COLLOQUES	COLONISING
COKESES	COLICKIER	COLLED	COLLOQUIA	COLONIST
COKIER	COLICKIEST	COLLEEN	COLLOQUIED	COLONISTS

COLONITIS	COLOURER	COLUMNS	COMBINGS	COMFORTS
COLONITISES	COLOURERS	COLURE	COMBINING	COMFREY
COLONIZE	COLOURFUL	COLURES	COMBIS	COMFREYS
COLONIZED	COLOURING	COLY*	COMBLE	COMFY
COLONIZER*	COLOURINGS	COLZA	COMBLES	COMIC
COLONIZERS*	COLOURISE	COLZAS	COMBLESS	COMICAL
COLONIZES	COLOURISED	COMA	COMBLIKE*	COMICALLY
COLONIZING	COLOURISES	COMADE*	COMBO	COMICE
COLONNADE	COLOURISING	COMAE	COMBOS	COMICES
COLONNADES	COLOURIST	COMAKE*	COMBRETUM	COMICS
COLONS	COLOURISTS	COMAKER*	COMBRETUMS	COMING
COLONUS*	COLOURIZE	COMAKERS*	COMBS	COMINGLE*
COLONY	COLOURIZED	COMAKES*	COMBUST	COMINGLED*
COLOPHON	COLOURIZES	COMAKING*	COMBUSTED	COMINGLES*
COLOPHONIES	COLOURIZING	COMAL	COMBUSTING	COMINGLING*
COLOPHONS	COLOURMAN	COMANAGE*	COMBUSTOR	COMINGS
COLOPHONY	COLOURMEN	COMANAGED*	COMBUSTORS	COMIQUE
COLOR	COLOURS	COMANAGER*	COMBUSTS	COMIQUES
COLORABLE*	COLOURWAY	COMANAGERS*	COMBWISE	COMITADJI
COLORABLY*	COLOURWAYS	COMANAGES*	COMBY	COMITADJIS
COLORADO*	COLOURY	COMANAGING*	COME	COMITAL
COLORANT	COLPITIS*	COMARB	COMEBACK	COMITATUS
COLORANTS	COLPITISES*	COMARBS	COMEBACKS	COMITATUSES
COLORBRED*	COLS	COMART	COMEDDLE	COMITIA
COLORED	COLT	COMARTS	COMEDDLED	COMITIAL*
COLOREDS*	COLTED	COMAS	COMEDDLES	COMITIES
COLORER*	COLTER	COMATE	COMEDDLING	COMITY
COLORERS*	COLTERS	COMATES	COMEDIAN	COMIX*
COLORFAST*	COLTING	COMATIC*	COMEDIANS	COMMA
COLORFUL*	COLTISH	COMATIK*	COMEDIC	COMMAND
COLORIFIC	COLTISHLY*	COMATIKS*	COMEDIES	COMMANDED
COLORING	COLTS	COMATOSE	COMEDO	COMMANDER
COLORINGS*	COLTSFOOT	COMATULA*	COMEDONES*	COMMANDERS
COLORISM*	COLTSFOOTS	COMATULAE*	COMEDOS	COMMANDING
COLORISMS*	COLTWOOD	COMATULID	COMEDOWN	COMMANDO
COLORIST*	COLTWOODS	COMATULIDS	COMEDOWNS	COMMANDOES*
COLORISTS*	COLUBRIAD	COMB	COMEDY	COMMANDOS
COLORIZE*	COLUBRIADS	COMBAT	COMELIER	COMMANDS
COLORIZED*	COLUBRID	COMBATANT	COMELIEST	COMMAS
COLORIZES*	COLUBRIDS	COMBATANTS	COMELILY*	COMMATA*
COLORIZING*	COLUBRINE	COMBATED	COMELY	COMMENCE
COLORLESS*	COLUGO	COMBATER*	COMEMBER*	COMMENCED
COLORMAN*	COLUGOS	COMBATERS*	COMEMBERS*	COMMENCER*
COLORMEN*	COLUMBARIES	COMBATING	COMER	COMMENCERS*
COLORS	COLUMBARY	COMBATIVE	COMERS	COMMENCES
COLOSSAL	COLUMBATE	COMBATS	COMES	COMMENCING
COLOSSEUM	COLUMBATES	COMBATTED*	COMET	COMMEND
COLOSSEUMS	COLUMBIC	COMBATTING*	COMETARY	COMMENDAM
COLOSSI	COLUMBINE	COMBE	COMETH*	COMMENDAMS
COLOSSUS	COLUMBINES	COMBED	COMETHER	COMMENDED
COLOSSUSES	COLUMBITE	COMBER	COMETHERS	COMMENDER*
COLOSTOMIES	COLUMBITES	COMBERS	COMETIC	COMMENDERS*
COLOSTOMY	COLUMBIUM	COMBES	COMETS	COMMENDING
COLOSTRAL*	COLUMBIUMS	COMBI	COMFIER	COMMENDS
COLOSTRIC	COLUMEL	COMBIER	COMFIEST	COMMENSAL
COLOSTRUM	COLUMELLA	COMBIES	COMFIT	COMMENSALS
COLOSTRUMS	COLUMELLAE	COMBIEST	COMFITS	COMMENT
COLOTOMIES	COLUMELS	COMBINATE	COMFITURE	COMMENTED
COLOTOMY	COLUMN	COMBINE	COMFITURES	COMMENTER
COLOUR	COLUMNAL	COMBINED	COMFORT	COMMENTERS
COLOURANT	COLUMNAR	COMBINER*	COMFORTED	COMMENTING
COLOURANTS	COLUMNED	COMBINERS*	COMFORTER	COMMENTOR
COLOURED	COLUMNIST	COMBINES	COMFORTERS	COMMENTORS
COLOUREDS	COLUMNISTS	COMBING	COMFORTING	COMMENTS

The Chambers Dictionary is the authority for many longer words; see Introduction, page ix

COMMER	COMMONINGS	COMPACTLY	COMPERES	COMPLOT
COMMERCE	COMMONLY	COMPACTOR	COMPERING	COMPLOTS
COMMERCED	COMMONS	COMPACTORS	COMPERS	COMPLOTTED
COMMERCES	COMMORANT	COMPACTS	COMPESCE	COMPLOTTING
COMMERCING	COMMORANTS	COMPADRE	COMPESCED	COMPLUVIA
COMMERE	COMMOS	COMPADRES	COMPESCES	COMPLY
COMMERES	COMMOT	COMPAGE	COMPESCING	COMPLYING
COMMERGE	COMMOTE	COMPAGES	COMPETE	COMPO
COMMERGED	COMMOTES	COMPAND	COMPETED	COMPONE
COMMERGES	COMMOTION	COMPANDED	COMPETENT	COMPONENT
COMMERGING	COMMOTIONS	COMPANDER	COMPETES	COMPONENTS
COMMERS	COMMOTS	COMPANDERS	COMPETING	COMPONY
COMMIE	COMMOVE	COMPANDING	COMPILE	COMPORT
COMMIES	COMMOVED	COMPANDOR	COMPILED	COMPORTED
COMMINATE	COMMOVES	COMPANDORS	COMPILER	COMPORTING
COMMINATED	COMMOVING	COMPANDS	COMPILERS	COMPORTS
COMMINATES	COMMUNAL	COMPANIED	COMPILES	COMPOS
COMMINATING	COMMUNARD	COMPANIES	COMPILING	COMPOSE
COMMINGLE	COMMUNARDS	COMPANING	COMPING	COMPOSED
COMMINGLED	COMMUNE	COMPANION	COMPINGS	COMPOSER
COMMINGLES	COMMUNED	COMPANIONED	COMPITAL	COMPOSERS
COMMINGLING	COMMUNES	COMPANIONING	COMPLAIN	COMPOSES
COMMINUTE	COMMUNING	COMPANIONS	COMPLAINED	COMPOSING
COMMINUTED	COMMUNINGS	COMPANY	COMPLAINING	COMPOSITE
COMMINUTES	COMMUNION	COMPANYING	COMPLAININGS	COMPOSITED
COMMINUTING	COMMUNIONS	COMPARE	COMPLAINS	COMPOSITES
COMMIS	COMMUNISE	COMPARED	COMPLAINT	COMPOSITING
COMMISSAR	COMMUNISED	COMPARER*	COMPLAINTS	COMPOST
COMMISSARS	COMMUNISES	COMPARERS*	COMPLEAT	COMPOSTED
COMMIT	COMMUNISING	COMPARES	COMPLECT	COMPOSTER
COMMITS	COMMUNISM	COMPARING	COMPLECTED	COMPOSTERS
COMMITTAL	COMMUNISMS	COMPART	COMPLECTING	COMPOSTING
COMMITTALS	COMMUNIST	COMPARTED	COMPLECTS	COMPOSTS
COMMITTED	COMMUNISTS	COMPARTING	COMPLETE	COMPOSURE
COMMITTEE	COMMUNITIES	COMPARTS	COMPLETED	COMPOSURES
COMMITTEES	COMMUNITY	COMPASS	COMPLETER	COMPOT
COMMITTING	COMMUNIZE	COMPASSED	COMPLETES	COMPOTE
COMMIX	COMMUNIZED	COMPASSES	COMPLETEST	COMPOTES
COMMIXED	COMMUNIZES	COMPASSING	COMPLETING	COMPOTIER
COMMIXES	COMMUNIZING	COMPASSINGS	COMPLEX	COMPOTIERS
COMMIXING	COMMUTATE	COMPAST	COMPLEXED	COMPOTS
COMMIXT*	COMMUTATED	COMPEAR	COMPLEXER	COMPOUND
COMMO	COMMUTATES	COMPEARED	COMPLEXES	COMPOUNDED
COMMODE	COMMUTATING	COMPEARING	COMPLEXEST	COMPOUNDING
COMMODES	COMMUTE	COMPEARS	COMPLEXING	COMPOUNDS
COMMODIFIED	COMMUTED	COMPED	COMPLEXLY	COMPRADOR
COMMODIFIES	COMMUTER	COMPEER	COMPLEXUS	COMPRADORS
COMMODIFY	COMMUTERS	COMPEERED	COMPLEXUSES	COMPRESS
COMMODIFYING	COMMUTES	COMPEERING	COMPLIANT	COMPRESSED
COMMODITIES	COMMUTING	COMPEERS	COMPLICE	COMPRESSES
COMMODITY	COMMUTUAL	COMPEL	COMPLICES	COMPRESSING
COMMODO	COMMY	COMPELLED	COMPLICIT*	COMPRINT
COMMODORE	COMODO	COMPELLER	COMPLIED	COMPRINTED
COMMODORES	COMONOMER*	COMPELLERS	COMPLIER	COMPRINTING
COMMON	COMONOMERS*	COMPELLING	COMPLIERS	COMPRINTS
COMMONAGE	COMOSE	COMPELS	COMPLIES	COMPRISAL
COMMONAGES	COMOUS	COMPEND	COMPLIN	COMPRISALS
COMMONED	COMP	COMPENDIA	COMPLINE	COMPRISE
COMMONER	COMPACT	COMPENDIUM*	COMPLINES	COMPRISED
COMMONERS	COMPACTED	COMPENDIUMS*	COMPLINS	COMPRISES
COMMONEST	COMPACTER	COMPENDS	COMPLISH	COMPRISING
COMMONEY	COMPACTERS*	COMPER	COMPLISHED	COMPRIZE*
COMMONEYS	COMPACTEST	COMPERE	COMPLISHES	COMPRIZED*
COMMONING	COMPACTING	COMPERED	COMPLISHING	COMPRIZES*

COMPRIZING*
COMPS
COMPT
COMPTABLE
COMPTED
COMPTER
COMPTERS
COMPTIBLE
COMPTING
COMPTROLL
COMPTROLLED
COMPTROLLING
COMPTROLLS
COMPTS
COMPULSE
COMPULSED
COMPULSES
COMPULSING
COMPUTANT
COMPUTANTS
COMPUTE
COMPUTED
COMPUTER
COMPUTERS
COMPUTES
COMPUTING
COMPUTIST
COMPUTISTS
COMRADE
COMRADELY
COMRADERIES*
COMRADERY*
COMRADES
COMS
COMSYMP*
COMSYMPS*
COMTE*
COMTES*
COMUS
COMUSES
CON
CONACRE
CONACRED
CONACRES
CONACRING
CONARIA
CONARIAL
CONARIUM
CONATION
CONATIONS
CONATIVE
CONATUS
CONCAUSE
CONCAUSES
CONCAVE
CONCAVED
CONCAVELY
CONCAVES
CONCAVING
CONCAVITIES
CONCAVITY
CONCEAL
CONCEALED
CONCEALER

CONCEALERS
CONCEALING
CONCEALS
CONCEDE
CONCEDED
CONCEDER
CONCEDERS
CONCEDES
CONCEDING
CONCEDO
CONCEIT
CONCEITED
CONCEITING
CONCEITS
CONCEITY
CONCEIVE
CONCEIVED
CONCEIVER*
CONCEIVERS*
CONCEIVES
CONCEIVING
CONCENT
CONCENTER
CONCENTERED
CONCENTERING
CONCENTERS
CONCENTRE
CONCENTRED
CONCENTRES
CONCENTRING
CONCENTS
CONCENTUS
CONCEPT
CONCEPTI
CONCEPTS
CONCEPTUS
CONCEPTUSES
CONCERN
CONCERNED
CONCERNING
CONCERNS
CONCERT
CONCERTED
CONCERTI
CONCERTING
CONCERTO
CONCERTOS
CONCERTS
CONCETTI
CONCETTO
CONCH
CONCHA
CONCHAE
CONCHAL
CONCHATE
CONCHE
CONCHED
CONCHES
CONCHIE
CONCHIES
CONCHING
CONCHITIS
CONCHITISES
CONCHOID

CONCHOIDS
CONCHS
CONCHY
CONCIERGE
CONCIERGES
CONCILIAR
CONCISE
CONCISED
CONCISELY
CONCISER
CONCISES
CONCISEST
CONCISING
CONCISION
CONCISIONS
CONCLAVE
CONCLAVES
CONCLUDE
CONCLUDED
CONCLUDER*
CONCLUDERS*
CONCLUDES
CONCLUDING
CONCOCT
CONCOCTED
CONCOCTER
CONCOCTERS
CONCOCTING
CONCOCTOR
CONCOCTORS
CONCOCTS
CONCOLOR
CONCORD
CONCORDAT
CONCORDATS
CONCORDED
CONCORDING
CONCORDS
CONCOURS
CONCOURSE
CONCOURSES
CONCREATE
CONCREATED
CONCREATES
CONCREATING
CONCRETE
CONCRETED
CONCRETES
CONCRETING
CONCREW
CONCREWED
CONCREWING
CONCREWS
CONCUBINE
CONCUBINES
CONCUPIES
CONCUPY
CONCUR
CONCURRED
CONCURRING
CONCURS
CONCUSS
CONCUSSED
CONCUSSES

CONCUSSING
CONCYCLIC
COND
CONDEMN
CONDEMNED
CONDEMNER*
CONDEMNERS*
CONDEMNING
CONDEMNOR*
CONDEMNORS*
CONDEMNS
CONDENSE
CONDENSED
CONDENSER
CONDENSERS
CONDENSES
CONDENSING
CONDER
CONDERS
CONDIDDLE
CONDIDDLED
CONDIDDLES
CONDIDDLING
CONDIE
CONDIES
CONDIGN
CONDIGNLY
CONDIMENT
CONDIMENTED
CONDIMENTING
CONDIMENTS
CONDITION
CONDITIONED
CONDITIONING
CONDITIONINGS
CONDITIONS
CONDO
CONDOES*
CONDOLE
CONDOLED
CONDOLENT
CONDOLER*
CONDOLERS*
CONDOLES
CONDOLING
CONDOM
CONDOMS
CONDONE
CONDONED
CONDONER*
CONDONERS*
CONDONES
CONDONING
CONDOR
CONDORES*
CONDORS
CONDOS
CONDUCE
CONDUCED
CONDUCER*
CONDUCERS*
CONDUCES
CONDUCING
CONDUCIVE

CONDUCT
CONDUCTED
CONDUCTI
CONDUCTING
CONDUCTOR
CONDUCTORS
CONDUCTS
CONDUCTUS
CONDUIT
CONDUITS
CONDYLAR
CONDYLE
CONDYLES
CONDYLOID
CONDYLOMA
CONDYLOMAS
CONDYLOMATA
CONE
CONED
CONELRAD*
CONELRADS*
CONENOSE*
CONENOSES*
CONEPATE*
CONEPATES*
CONEPATL*
CONEPATLS*
CONES
CONEY
CONEYS
CONF
CONFAB
CONFABBED
CONFABBING
CONFABS
CONFECT
CONFECTED
CONFECTING
CONFECTS
CONFER
CONFEREE
CONFEREES
CONFERRAL*
CONFERRALS*
CONFERRED
CONFERRER
CONFERRERS
CONFERRING
CONFERS
CONFERVA
CONFERVAE
CONFERVAS
CONFESS
CONFESSED
CONFESSES
CONFESSING
CONFESSOR
CONFESSORS
CONFEST
CONFESTLY
CONFETTI
CONFETTO*
CONFIDANT
CONFIDANTS

CONFIDE	CONFOUNDS	CONGREE	CONJUGANT	CONNOTATING
CONFIDED	CONFRERE	CONGREED	CONJUGANTS	CONNOTE
CONFIDENT	CONFRERES	CONGREEING	CONJUGATE	CONNOTED
CONFIDENTS	CONFRERIE	CONGREES	CONJUGATED	CONNOTES
CONFIDER	CONFRERIES	CONGREET	CONJUGATES	CONNOTING
CONFIDERS	CONFRONT	CONGREETED	CONJUGATING	CONNOTIVE
CONFIDES	CONFRONTE	CONGREETING	CONJUGATINGS	CONNS
CONFIDING	CONFRONTED	CONGREETS	CONJUNCT	CONNUBIAL
CONFIGURE	CONFRONTING	CONGRESS	CONJUNCTS*	CONODONT
CONFIGURED	CONFRONTS	CONGRESSED	CONJURE	CONODONTS
CONFIGURES	CONFS	CONGRESSES	CONJURED	CONOID
CONFIGURING	CONFUSE	CONGRESSING	CONJURER	CONOIDAL
CONFINE	CONFUSED	CONGRUE	CONJURERS	CONOIDIC
CONFINED	CONFUSES	CONGRUED	CONJURES	CONOIDS
CONFINER	CONFUSING	CONGRUENT	CONJURIES	CONOMINEE*
CONFINERS	CONFUSION	CONGRUES	CONJURING	CONOMINEES*
CONFINES	CONFUSIONS	CONGRUING	CONJURINGS	CONQUER
CONFINING	CONFUTE	CONGRUITIES	CONJUROR	CONQUERED
CONFIRM	CONFUTED	CONGRUITY	CONJURORS	CONQUERING
CONFIRMED	CONFUTER*	CONGRUOUS	CONJURY	CONQUEROR
CONFIRMEE	CONFUTERS*	CONI*	CONK	CONQUERORS
CONFIRMEES	CONFUTES	CONIA	CONKED	CONQUERS
CONFIRMER	CONFUTING	CONIAS	CONKER	CONQUEST
CONFIRMERS	CONGA	CONIC	CONKERS	CONQUESTS
CONFIRMING	CONGAED	CONICAL	CONKIER	CONQUIAN*
CONFIRMINGS	CONGAING	CONICALLY	CONKIEST	CONQUIANS*
CONFIRMOR	CONGAS	CONICITIES*	CONKING	CONS
CONFIRMORS	CONGE	CONICITY*	CONKS	CONSCIENT
CONFIRMS	CONGEAL	CONICS	CONKY	CONSCIOUS
CONFISEUR	CONGEALED	CONIDIA	CONN	CONSCIOUSES
CONFISEURS	CONGEALING	CONIDIAL	CONNATE	CONSCRIBE
CONFIT	CONGEALS	CONIDIAN*	CONNATELY*	CONSCRIBED
CONFITEOR	CONGED	CONIDIUM	CONNATION	CONSCRIBES
CONFITEORS	CONGEE	CONIES	CONNATIONS	CONSCRIBING
CONFITS	CONGEED	CONIFER	CONNATURE	CONSCRIPT
CONFITURE	CONGEEING	CONIFERS	CONNATURES	CONSCRIPTED
CONFITURES	CONGEES	CONIFORM	CONNE	CONSCRIPTING
CONFIX	CONGEING	CONIINE	CONNECT	CONSCRIPTS
CONFIXED	CONGENER	CONIINES	CONNECTED	CONSEIL
CONFIXES	CONGENERS	CONIMA	CONNECTER	CONSEILS
CONFIXING	CONGENIAL	CONIMAS	CONNECTERS	CONSENSUS
CONFLATE	CONGENIC	CONIN	CONNECTING	CONSENSUSES
CONFLATED	CONGER	CONINE	CONNECTOR	CONSENT
CONFLATES	CONGERIES	CONINES	CONNECTORS	CONSENTED
CONFLATING	CONGERS	CONING	CONNECTS	CONSENTER*
CONFLICT	CONGES	CONINS	CONNED	CONSENTERS*
CONFLICTED	CONGEST	CONIOSES*	CONNER	CONSENTING
CONFLICTING	CONGESTED	CONIOSIS*	CONNERS	CONSENTS
CONFLICTS	CONGESTING	CONIUM*	CONNES	CONSERVE
CONFLUENT	CONGESTS	CONIUMS*	CONNEXION	CONSERVED
CONFLUENTS	CONGIARIES	CONJECT	CONNEXIONS	CONSERVER
CONFLUX	CONGIARY	CONJECTED	CONNEXIVE	CONSERVERS
CONFLUXES	CONGII	CONJECTING	CONNING	CONSERVES
CONFOCAL	CONGIUS	CONJECTS	CONNINGS	CONSERVING
CONFORM	CONGLOBE	CONJEE	CONNIVE	CONSIDER
CONFORMAL	CONGLOBED	CONJEED	CONNIVED	CONSIDERED
CONFORMED	CONGLOBES	CONJEEING	CONNIVENT	CONSIDERING
CONFORMER	CONGLOBING	CONJEES	CONNIVER	CONSIDERS
CONFORMERS	CONGO	CONJOIN	CONNIVERS	CONSIGN
CONFORMING	CONGOES*	CONJOINED	CONNIVES	CONSIGNED
CONFORMS	CONGOS	CONJOINING	CONNIVING	CONSIGNEE
CONFOUND	CONGOU	CONJOINS	CONNOTATE	CONSIGNEES
CONFOUNDED	CONGOUS	CONJOINT	CONNOTATED	CONSIGNER
CONFOUNDING	CONGRATS	CONJUGAL	CONNOTATES	CONSIGNERS

CONSIGNING	CONSTRUCT	CONTE	CONTOUR	CONUNDRUMS
CONSIGNOR	CONSTRUCTED	CONTECK	CONTOURED	CONURBAN
CONSIGNORS	CONSTRUCTING	CONTECKS	CONTOURING	CONURBIA
CONSIGNS	CONSTRUCTS	CONTEMN	CONTOURS	CONURBIAS
CONSIST	CONSTRUE	CONTEMNED	CONTRA	CONURE
CONSISTED	CONSTRUED	CONTEMNER	CONTRACT	CONURES
CONSISTING	CONSTRUER	CONTEMNERS	CONTRACTED	CONUS*
CONSISTS	CONSTRUERS	CONTEMNING	CONTRACTING	CONVECT*
CONSOCIES	CONSTRUES	CONTEMNOR	CONTRACTS	CONVECTED*
CONSOL*	CONSTRUING	CONTEMNORS	CONTRAIL	CONVECTING*
CONSOLATE	CONSUL	CONTEMNS	CONTRAILS	CONVECTOR
CONSOLATED	CONSULAGE	CONTEMPER	CONTRAIR	CONVECTORS
CONSOLATES	CONSULAGES	CONTEMPERED	CONTRALTI	CONVECTS*
CONSOLATING	CONSULAR	CONTEMPERING	CONTRALTO	CONVENE
CONSOLE	CONSULARS	CONTEMPERS	CONTRALTOS	CONVENED
CONSOLED	CONSULATE	CONTEMPT	CONTRARIED	CONVENER
CONSOLER	CONSULATES	CONTEMPTS	CONTRARIES	CONVENERS
CONSOLERS	CONSULS	CONTEND	CONTRARY	CONVENES
CONSOLES	CONSULT	CONTENDED	CONTRARYING	CONVENING
CONSOLING	CONSULTA	CONTENDER	CONTRAS	CONVENOR
CONSOLS	CONSULTAS	CONTENDERS	CONTRAST	CONVENORS
CONSOLUTE	CONSULTED	CONTENDING	CONTRASTED	CONVENT
CONSOMME	CONSULTEE	CONTENDINGS	CONTRASTING	CONVENTED
CONSOMMES	CONSULTEES	CONTENDS	CONTRASTS	CONVENTING
CONSONANT	CONSULTER	CONTENT	CONTRASTY	CONVENTS
CONSONANTS	CONSULTERS	CONTENTED	CONTRAT	CONVERGE
CONSONOUS	CONSULTING	CONTENTING	CONTRATE	CONVERGED
CONSORT	CONSULTOR	CONTENTS	CONTRATS	CONVERGES
CONSORTED	CONSULTORS	CONTES	CONTRIST	CONVERGING
CONSORTER	CONSULTS	CONTESSA	CONTRISTED	CONVERSE
CONSORTERS	CONSUME	CONTESSAS	CONTRISTING	CONVERSED
CONSORTIA	CONSUMED	CONTEST	CONTRISTS	CONVERSER*
CONSORTING	CONSUMER	CONTESTED	CONTRITE	CONVERSERS*
CONSORTIUM*	CONSUMERS	CONTESTER	CONTRIVE	CONVERSES
CONSORTIUMS*	CONSUMES	CONTESTERS	CONTRIVED	CONVERSING
CONSORTS	CONSUMING	CONTESTING	CONTRIVER	CONVERT
CONSPIRE	CONSUMINGS	CONTESTS	CONTRIVERS	CONVERTED
CONSPIRED	CONSUMPT	CONTEXT	CONTRIVES	CONVERTER
CONSPIRER	CONSUMPTS	CONTEXTS	CONTRIVING	CONVERTERS
CONSPIRERS	CONTACT	CONTICENT	CONTROL	CONVERTING
CONSPIRES	CONTACTED	CONTINENT	CONTROLE	CONVERTOR
CONSPIRING	CONTACTING	CONTINENTS	CONTROLLED	CONVERTORS
CONSTABLE	CONTACTOR	CONTINUA	CONTROLLING	CONVERTS
CONSTABLES	CONTACTORS	CONTINUAL	CONTROLS	CONVEX
CONSTANCIES	CONTACTS	CONTINUE	CONTROUL	CONVEXED
CONSTANCY	CONTADINA	CONTINUED	CONTROULED	CONVEXES
CONSTANT	CONTADINAS	CONTINUER	CONTROULING	CONVEXITIES
CONSTANTS	CONTADINE	CONTINUERS	CONTROULS	CONVEXITY
CONSTATE	CONTADINI	CONTINUES	CONTUMACIES	CONVEXLY
CONSTATED	CONTADINO	CONTINUING	CONTUMACY	CONVEY
CONSTATES	CONTAGIA	CONTINUO	CONTUMELIES	CONVEYAL
CONSTATING	CONTAGION	CONTINUOS	CONTUMELY	CONVEYALS
CONSTER	CONTAGIONS	CONTINUUM	CONTUND	CONVEYED
CONSTERED	CONTAGIUM	CONTINUUMS	CONTUNDED	CONVEYER
CONSTERING	CONTAIN	CONTLINE	CONTUNDING	CONVEYERS
CONSTERS	CONTAINED	CONTLINES	CONTUNDS	CONVEYING
CONSTRAIN	CONTAINER	CONTO	CONTUSE	CONVEYOR
CONSTRAINED	CONTAINERS	CONTORNO	CONTUSED	CONVEYORS
CONSTRAINING	CONTAINING	CONTORNOS	CONTUSES	CONVEYS
CONSTRAINS	CONTAINS	CONTORT	CONTUSING	CONVICT
CONSTRICT	CONTANGO	CONTORTED	CONTUSION	CONVICTED
CONSTRICTED	CONTANGOED	CONTORTING	CONTUSIONS	CONVICTING
CONSTRICTING	CONTANGOING	CONTORTS	CONTUSIVE	CONVICTS
CONSTRICTS	CONTANGOS	CONTOS	CONUNDRUM	CONVINCE

The Chambers Dictionary is the authority for many longer words; see Introduction, page ix

CONVINCED	COOKER	COOMBES	COOTS	COPPED
CONVINCER*	COOKERIES	COOMBS	COP	COPPER
CONVINCERS*	COOKERS	COOMED	COPACETIC	COPPERAH*
CONVINCES	COOKERY	COOMIER	COPAIBA	COPPERAHS*
CONVINCING	COOKEY*	COOMIEST	COPAIBAS	COPPERAS
CONVIVE	COOKEYS*	COOMING	COPAIVA	COPPERASES
CONVIVED	COOKHOUSE	COOMS	COPAIVAS	COPPERED
CONVIVES	COOKHOUSES	COOMY	COPAL	COPPERING
CONVIVIAL	COOKIE	COON	COPALM*	COPPERINGS
CONVIVING	COOKIES	COONCAN	COPALMS*	COPPERISH
CONVO	COOKING	COONCANS	COPALS	COPPERS
CONVOCATE	COOKINGS*	COONDOG	COPARENT*	COPPERY
CONVOCATED	COOKLESS*	COONDOGS	COPARENTS*	COPPICE
CONVOCATES	COOKMAID	COONHOUND	COPARTNER	COPPICED
CONVOCATING	COOKMAIDS	COONHOUNDS	COPARTNERED*	COPPICES
CONVOKE	COOKOUT	COONS	COPARTNERING*	COPPICING
CONVOKED	COOKOUTS	COONSKIN	COPARTNERS	COPPICINGS
CONVOKER*	COOKROOM	COONSKINS	COPASETIC*	COPPIES
CONVOKERS*	COOKROOMS	COONTIE	COPASTOR*	COPPIN
CONVOKES	COOKS	COONTIES	COPASTORS*	COPPING
CONVOKING	COOKSHACK*	COONTY	COPATAINE	COPPINS
CONVOLUTE	COOKSHACKS*	COOP	COPATRIOT	COPPLE
CONVOLUTED*	COOKSHOP*	COOPED	COPATRIOTS	COPPLES
CONVOLUTES*	COOKSHOPS*	COOPER	COPATRON*	COPPRA*
CONVOLUTING*	COOKSTOVE*	COOPERAGE	COPATRONS*	COPPRAS*
CONVOLVE	COOKSTOVES*	COOPERAGES	COPE	COPPY
CONVOLVED	COOKTOP*	COOPERATE	COPECK	COPRA
CONVOLVES	COOKTOPS*	COOPERATED	COPECKS	COPRAH*
CONVOLVING	COOKWARE	COOPERATES	COPED	COPRAHS*
CONVOS	COOKWARES	COOPERATING	COPEMATE	COPRAS
CONVOY	COOKY	COOPERED	COPEMATES	COPREMIA*
CONVOYED	COOL	COOPERIES	COPEN*	COPREMIAS*
CONVOYING	COOLABAH	COOPERING	COPENS*	COPREMIC*
CONVOYS	COOLABAHS	COOPERINGS	COPEPOD	COPRESENT
CONVULSE	COOLAMON	COOPERS	COPEPODS	COPRESENTED*
CONVULSED	COOLAMONS	COOPERY	COPER	COPRESENTING*
CONVULSES	COOLANT	COOPING	COPERED	COPRESENTS*
CONVULSING	COOLANTS	COOPS	COPERING	COPRINCE*
CONY	COOLDOWN*	COOPT	COPERS	COPRINCES*
COO	COOLDOWNS*	COOPTED	COPES	COPRODUCE*
COOCH*	COOLED	COOPTING	COPESETIC*	COPRODUCED*
COOCHES*	COOLER	COOPTION*	COPESTONE	COPRODUCES*
COOCOO*	COOLERS	COOPTIONS*	COPESTONES	COPRODUCING*
COOED	COOLEST	COOPTS	COPIED	COPRODUCT*
COOEE	COOLHOUSE	COORDINAL	COPIER	COPRODUCTS*
COOEED	COOLHOUSES	COOS	COPIERS	COPROLITE
COOEEING	COOLIBAH	COOSEN	COPIES	COPROLITES
COOEES	COOLIBAHS	COOSENED	COPIHUE*	COPROLITH
COOER*	COOLIBAR	COOSENING	COPIHUES*	COPROLITHS
COOERS*	COOLIBARS	COOSENS	COPILOT	COPROLOGIES
COOEY	COOLIE	COOSER	COPILOTS	COPROLOGY
COOEYED	COOLIES	COOSERS	COPING	COPROSMA
COOEYING	COOLING	COOSIN	COPINGS	COPROSMAS
COOEYS	COOLISH	COOSINED	COPIOUS	COPROZOIC
COOF	COOLLY	COOSINING	COPIOUSLY	COPS
COOFS	COOLNESS	COOSINS	COPITA	COPSE
COOING	COOLNESSES	COOST	COPITAS	COPSED
COOINGLY	COOLS	COOT	COPLANAR	COPSES
COOINGS	COOLTH	COOTER*	COPLOT*	COPSEWOOD
COOK	COOLTHS	COOTERS*	COPLOTS*	COPSEWOODS
COOKABLE	COOLY	COOTIE	COPLOTTED*	COPSHOP
COOKBOOK	COOM	COOTIES	COPLOTTING*	COPSHOPS
COOKBOOKS	COOMB	COOTIKIN	COPOLYMER	COPSIER
COOKED	COOMBE	COOTIKINS	COPOLYMERS	COPSIEST

COPSING
COPSY
COPTER
COPTERS
COPUBLISH*
COPUBLISHED*
COPUBLISHES*
COPUBLISHING*
COPULA
COPULAE*
COPULAR
COPULAS
COPULATE
COPULATED
COPULATES
COPULATING
COPURIFIED*
COPURIFIES*
COPURIFY*
COPURIFYING*
COPY
COPYBOOK
COPYBOOKS
COPYBOY*
COPYBOYS*
COPYCAT
COPYCATS
COPYCATTED
COPYCATTING
COPYDESK*
COPYDESKS*
COPYEDIT*
COPYEDITED*
COPYEDITING*
COPYEDITS*
COPYHOLD
COPYHOLDS
COPYING
COPYISM
COPYISMS
COPYIST
COPYISTS
COPYREAD
COPYREADING
COPYREADINGS
COPYREADS
COPYRIGHT
COPYRIGHTED
COPYRIGHTING
COPYRIGHTS
COQUET
COQUETRIES
COQUETRY
COQUETS
COQUETTE
COQUETTED
COQUETTES
COQUETTING
COQUILLA
COQUILLAS
COQUILLE
COQUILLES
COQUINA
COQUINAS

COQUITO
COQUITOS
COR
CORACLE
CORACLES
CORACOID
CORACOIDS
CORAGGIO
CORAGGIOS
CORAL
CORALLA
CORALLINE
CORALLINES
CORALLITE
CORALLITES
CORALLOID
CORALLUM
CORALROOT
CORALROOTS
CORALS
CORALWORT
CORALWORTS
CORAM
CORAMINE
CORAMINES
CORANACH
CORANACHS
CORANTO
CORANTOES
CORANTOS
CORBAN
CORBANS
CORBE
CORBEAU
CORBEAUS
CORBEIL
CORBEILLE
CORBEILLES
CORBEILS
CORBEL
CORBELED
CORBELING
CORBELINGS
CORBELLED
CORBELLING
CORBELLINGS
CORBELS
CORBES
CORBICULA
CORBICULAE
CORBIE
CORBIES
CORBINA*
CORBINAS*
CORBY*
CORCASS
CORCASSES
CORD
CORDAGE
CORDAGES
CORDATE
CORDATELY*
CORDED
CORDELLE*

CORDELLED*
CORDELLES*
CORDELLING*
CORDER*
CORDERS*
CORDGRASS*
CORDGRASSES*
CORDIAL
CORDIALLY
CORDIALS
CORDIFORM
CORDINER
CORDINERS
CORDING
CORDINGS
CORDITE
CORDITES
CORDLESS
CORDLIKE*
CORDOBA
CORDOBAS
CORDON
CORDONED
CORDONING
CORDONS
CORDOTOMIES
CORDOTOMY
CORDOVAN
CORDOVANS
CORDS
CORDUROY
CORDUROYED*
CORDUROYING*
CORDUROYS
CORDWAIN
CORDWAINS
CORDWOOD
CORDWOODS
CORDYLINE
CORDYLINES
CORE
CORED
COREDEEM*
COREDEEMED*
COREDEEMING*
COREDEEMS*
COREGENT
COREGENTS
COREIGN*
COREIGNS*
CORELATE*
CORELATED*
CORELATES*
CORELATING*
CORELESS
CORELLA
CORELLAS
COREMIA*
COREMIUM*
COREOPSIS
COREOPSISES
CORER
CORERS
CORES

COREY
COREYS
CORF
CORFHOUSE
CORFHOUSES
CORGI
CORGIS
CORIA
CORIANDER
CORIANDERS
CORIES
CORING
CORIOUS
CORIUM
CORIUMS
CORIVAL
CORIVALLED
CORIVALLING
CORIVALRIES
CORIVALRY
CORIVALS
CORK
CORKAGE
CORKAGES
CORKBOARD
CORKBOARDS
CORKBORER
CORKBORERS
CORKED
CORKER
CORKERS
CORKIER
CORKIEST
CORKINESS
CORKINESSES
CORKING
CORKIR
CORKIRS
CORKLIKE*
CORKS
CORKSCREW
CORKSCREWED
CORKSCREWING
CORKSCREWS
CORKTREE
CORKTREES
CORKWOOD
CORKWOODS
CORKY
CORM
CORMEL
CORMELS
CORMIDIA
CORMIDIUM
CORMLIKE*
CORMOID*
CORMORANT
CORMORANTS
CORMOUS
CORMS
CORMUS
CORMUSES
CORN
CORNACRE

CORNACRES
CORNAGE
CORNAGES
CORNBALL
CORNBALLS
CORNBORER
CORNBORERS
CORNBRAKE
CORNBRAKES
CORNBRASH
CORNBRASHES
CORNBREAD
CORNBREADS
CORNCAKE*
CORNCAKES*
CORNCOB*
CORNCOBS*
CORNCRAKE
CORNCRAKES
CORNCRIB*
CORNCRIBS*
CORNEA
CORNEAL
CORNEAS
CORNED
CORNEL
CORNELIAN
CORNELIANS
CORNELS
CORNEMUSE
CORNEMUSES
CORNEOUS
CORNER
CORNERED
CORNERING
CORNERMAN*
CORNERMEN*
CORNERS
CORNET
CORNETCIES
CORNETCY
CORNETIST
CORNETISTS
CORNETS
CORNETT
CORNETTI
CORNETTO
CORNETTS
CORNFED*
CORNFIELD
CORNFIELDS
CORNFLAG
CORNFLAGS
CORNFLAKE
CORNFLAKES
CORNFLIES
CORNFLOUR
CORNFLOURS
CORNFLY
CORNHUSK
CORNHUSKS
CORNI
CORNICE
CORNICED

The Chambers Dictionary is the authority for many longer words; see Introduction, page ix

CORNICES
CORNICHE
CORNICHES
CORNICING
CORNICLE
CORNICLES
CORNICULA
CORNIER
CORNIEST
CORNIFIC
CORNIFORM
CORNILY*
CORNINESS*
CORNINESSES*
CORNING
CORNIST
CORNISTS
CORNLAND
CORNLANDS
CORNLOFT
CORNLOFTS
CORNMEAL*
CORNMEALS*
CORNMILL
CORNMILLS
CORNMOTH
CORNMOTHS
CORNO
CORNOPEAN
CORNOPEANS
CORNPIPE
CORNPIPES
CORNPONE*
CORNPONES*
CORNRENT
CORNRENTS
CORNROW
CORNROWED*
CORNROWING*
CORNROWS
CORNS
CORNSTALK
CORNSTALKS
CORNSTONE
CORNSTONES
CORNU
CORNUA
CORNUAL
CORNUS*
CORNUSES*
CORNUTE
CORNUTED
CORNUTES
CORNUTING
CORNUTO
CORNUTOS
CORNWORM
CORNWORMS
CORNY
COROCORE
COROCORES
COROCORO
COROCOROS
CORODIES

CORODY
COROLLA
COROLLARIES
COROLLARY
COROLLAS
COROLLATE*
COROLLINE
CORONA
CORONACH
CORONACHS
CORONAE
CORONAL
CORONALS
CORONARIES
CORONARY
CORONAS
CORONATE
CORONATED
CORONATES*
CORONATING*
CORONEL*
CORONELS*
CORONER
CORONERS
CORONET
CORONETED
CORONETS
CORONIS
CORONISES
CORONIUM
CORONIUMS
CORONOID
COROTATE*
COROTATED*
COROTATES*
COROTATING*
COROZO
COROZOS
CORPORA
CORPORAL
CORPORALS
CORPORAS
CORPORASES
CORPORATE
CORPOREAL
CORPORIFIED
CORPORIFIES
CORPORIFY
CORPORIFYING
CORPOSANT
CORPOSANTS
CORPS
CORPSE
CORPSED
CORPSES
CORPSING
CORPSMAN*
CORPSMEN*
CORPULENT
CORPUS
CORPUSCLE
CORPUSCLES
CORRADE
CORRADED

CORRADES
CORRADING
CORRAL
CORRALLED
CORRALLING
CORRALS
CORRASION
CORRASIONS
CORRASIVE*
CORRECT
CORRECTED
CORRECTER
CORRECTEST
CORRECTING
CORRECTLY
CORRECTOR
CORRECTORS
CORRECTS
CORRELATE
CORRELATED
CORRELATES
CORRELATING
CORRIDA
CORRIDAS
CORRIDOR
CORRIDORS
CORRIE
CORRIES
CORRIGENT
CORRIGENTS
CORRIVAL
CORRIVALLED
CORRIVALLING
CORRIVALS
CORRODE
CORRODED
CORRODENT
CORRODENTS
CORRODES
CORRODIES
CORRODING
CORRODY
CORROSION
CORROSIONS
CORROSIVE
CORROSIVES
CORRUGATE
CORRUGATED
CORRUGATES
CORRUGATING
CORRUPT
CORRUPTED
CORRUPTER
CORRUPTERS
CORRUPTEST
CORRUPTING
CORRUPTLY
CORRUPTOR*
CORRUPTORS*
CORRUPTS
CORS
CORSAC
CORSACS
CORSAGE

CORSAGES
CORSAIR
CORSAIRS
CORSE
CORSELET
CORSELETS
CORSES
CORSET
CORSETED
CORSETIER
CORSETIERS
CORSETING
CORSETRIES
CORSETRY
CORSETS
CORSIVE
CORSIVES
CORSLET
CORSLETED
CORSLETS
CORSNED
CORSNEDS
CORSO
CORSOS
CORTEGE
CORTEGES
CORTEX
CORTEXES
CORTICAL
CORTICATE
CORTICES
CORTICOID
CORTICOIDS
CORTILE
CORTILI
CORTIN*
CORTINS*
CORTISOL
CORTISOLS
CORTISONE
CORTISONES
CORULER*
CORULERS*
CORUNDUM
CORUNDUMS
CORUSCANT
CORUSCATE
CORUSCATED
CORUSCATES
CORUSCATING
CORVEE
CORVEES
CORVES
CORVET
CORVETED
CORVETING
CORVETS
CORVETTE
CORVETTED
CORVETTES
CORVETTING
CORVID
CORVIDS
CORVINA*

CORVINAS*
CORVINE
CORVUS
CORVUSES
CORY
CORYBANT
CORYBANTES
CORYBANTS
CORYDALIS
CORYDALISES
CORYLUS
CORYLUSES
CORYMB
CORYMBED*
CORYMBOSE
CORYMBS
CORYPHAEI
CORYPHAEUS*
CORYPHE
CORYPHEE
CORYPHEES
CORYPHENE
CORYPHENES
CORYPHES
CORYZA
CORYZAL*
CORYZAS
COS
COSCRIPT*
COSCRIPTED*
COSCRIPTING*
COSCRIPTS*
COSE
COSEC
COSECANT
COSECANTS
COSECH
COSECHS
COSECS
COSED
COSEISMAL
COSEISMIC
COSES
COSET
COSETS
COSEY*
COSEYS*
COSH
COSHED
COSHER
COSHERED
COSHERER
COSHERERS
COSHERIES
COSHERING
COSHERINGS
COSHERS
COSHERY
COSHES
COSHING
COSIE*
COSIED*
COSIER
COSIERS

COSIES	COSTAR*	COTHS	COTTUS	COUNSEL
COSIEST	COSTARD	COTHURN	COTTUSES	COUNSELED*
COSIGN*	COSTARDS	COTHURNI	COTWAL	COUNSELEE*
COSIGNED*	COSTARRED*	COTHURNS	COTWALS	COUNSELEES*
COSIGNER*	COSTARRING*	COTHURNUS	COTYLAE	COUNSELING*
COSIGNERS*	COSTARS*	COTICULAR	COTYLE	COUNSELLED
COSIGNING*	COSTATE	COTIDAL	COTYLEDON	COUNSELLING
COSIGNS*	COSTATED	COTILLION	COTYLEDONS	COUNSELLINGS
COSILY	COSTE	COTILLIONS	COTYLES	COUNSELOR
COSINE	COSTEAN	COTILLON	COTYLOID	COUNSELORS
COSINES	COSTEANED	COTILLONS	COTYPE*	COUNSELS
COSINESS	COSTEANING	COTING	COTYPES*	COUNT
COSINESSES	COSTEANINGS	COTINGA	COUCAL	COUNTABLE
COSING	COSTEANS	COTINGAS	COUCALS	COUNTABLY*
COSMEA	COSTED	COTISE	COUCH	COUNTDOWN*
COSMEAS	COSTER	COTISED	COUCHANT	COUNTDOWNS*
COSMESES	COSTERS	COTISES	COUCHE	COUNTED
COSMESIS	COSTES	COTISING	COUCHED	COUNTER
COSMETIC	COSTING	COTLAND	COUCHEE	COUNTERED
COSMETICS	COSTIVE	COTLANDS	COUCHEES	COUNTERING
COSMIC	COSTIVELY	COTQUEAN	COUCHER*	COUNTERS
COSMICAL	COSTLESS*	COTQUEANS	COUCHERS*	COUNTESS
COSMISM	COSTLIER	COTRUSTEE*	COUCHES	COUNTESSES
COSMISMS	COSTLIEST	COTRUSTEES*	COUCHETTE	COUNTIAN*
COSMIST	COSTLY	COTS	COUCHETTES	COUNTIANS*
COSMISTS	COSTMARIES	COTT	COUCHING	COUNTIES
COSMOCRAT	COSTMARY	COTTA	COUCHINGS	COUNTING
COSMOCRATS	COSTREL	COTTABUS	COUDE	COUNTLESS
COSMOGENIES	COSTRELS	COTTABUSES	COUGAR	COUNTLINE
COSMOGENY	COSTS	COTTAE*	COUGARS	COUNTLINES
COSMOGONIES	COSTUME	COTTAGE	COUGH	COUNTRIES
COSMOGONY	COSTUMED	COTTAGED	COUGHED	COUNTROL
COSMOLOGIES	COSTUMER	COTTAGER	COUGHER	COUNTROLLED
COSMOLOGY	COSTUMERIES*	COTTAGERS	COUGHERS	COUNTROLLING
COSMONAUT	COSTUMERS	COTTAGES	COUGHING	COUNTROLS
COSMONAUTS	COSTUMERY*	COTTAGEY	COUGHINGS	COUNTRY
COSMORAMA	COSTUMES	COTTAGING	COUGHS	COUNTS
COSMORAMAS	COSTUMEY*	COTTAGINGS	COUGUAR	COUNTSHIP
COSMOS	COSTUMIER	COTTAR	COUGUARS	COUNTSHIPS
COSMOSES	COSTUMIERS	COTTARS	COULD	COUNTY
COSMOTRON	COSTUMING	COTTAS	COULDEST*	COUP
COSMOTRONS	COSTUS	COTTED	COULDST*	COUPE
COSPHERED	COSTUSES	COTTER	COULEE	COUPED
COSPONSOR	COSY	COTTERED*	COULEES	COUPEE
COSPONSORED	COSYING*	COTTERS	COULIS	COUPEES
COSPONSORING	COT	COTTID	COULISES*	COUPER
COSPONSORS	COTAN*	COTTIDS	COULISSE	COUPERS
COSS	COTANGENT	COTTIER	COULISSES	COUPES
COSSACK*	COTANGENTS	COTTIERS	COULOIR	COUPING
COSSACKS*	COTANS*	COTTISE	COULOIRS	COUPLE
COSSES	COTE	COTTISED	COULOMB	COUPLED
COSSET	COTEAU	COTTISES	COULOMBIC*	COUPLEDOM
COSSETED	COTEAUX	COTTISING	COULOMBS	COUPLEDOMS
COSSETING	COTED	COTTOID	COULTER	COUPLER
COSSETS	COTELETTE	COTTON	COULTERS	COUPLERS
COSSIE	COTELETTES	COTTONADE	COUMARIC	COUPLES
COSSIES	COTELINE	COTTONADES	COUMARIN	COUPLET
COST	COTELINES	COTTONED	COUMARINS	COUPLETS
COSTA	COTENANT	COTTONING	COUMAROU*	COUPLING
COSTAE	COTENANTS	COTTONS	COUMAROUS*	COUPLINGS
COSTAL	COTERIE	COTTONY	COUNCIL	COUPON
COSTALGIA	COTERIES	COTTOWN	COUNCILOR	COUPONING*
COSTALGIAS	COTES	COTTOWNS	COUNCILORS	COUPONINGS*
COSTALS	COTH	COTTS	COUNCILS	COUPONS

The Chambers Dictionary is the authority for many longer words; see Introduction, page ix

COUPS	COURTLY	COVENANTED	COWARDLY	COWLICK
COUPURE	COURTROOM	COVENANTING	COWARDREE	COWLICKS
COUPURES	COURTROOMS	COVENANTS	COWARDREES	COWLING
COUR	COURTS	COVENS	COWARDRIES	COWLINGS
COURAGE	COURTSHIP	COVENT	COWARDRY	COWLS
COURAGES	COURTSHIPS	COVENTS	COWARDS	COWLSTAFF*
COURANT	COURTSIDE*	COVER	COWBANE	COWLSTAFFS*
COURANTE	COURTSIDES*	COVERABLE*	COWBANES	COWLSTAVES*
COURANTES	COURTYARD	COVERAGE	COWBELL	COWMAN
COURANTO*	COURTYARDS	COVERAGES	COWBELLS	COWMEN
COURANTOES*	COUSCOUS	COVERALL	COWBERRIES	COWORKER*
COURANTOS*	COUSCOUSES	COVERALLS	COWBERRY	COWORKERS*
COURANTS	COUSIN	COVERED	COWBIND*	COWP
COURB	COUSINAGE	COVERER*	COWBINDS*	COWPAT
COURBARIL	COUSINAGES	COVERERS*	COWBIRD	COWPATS
COURBARILS	COUSINLY	COVERING	COWBIRDS	COWPEA
COURBED	COUSINRIES	COVERINGS	COWBOY	COWPEAS
COURBETTE	COUSINRY	COVERLESS*	COWBOYS	COWPED
COURBETTES	COUSINS	COVERLET	COWED	COWPIE*
COURBING	COUTEAU*	COVERLETS	COWEDLY*	COWPIES*
COURBS	COUTEAUX*	COVERLID	COWER	COWPING
COURD	COUTER	COVERLIDS	COWERED	COWPLOP*
COURE	COUTERS	COVERS	COWERING	COWPLOPS*
COURED	COUTH	COVERSLIP	COWERS	COWPOKE
COURES	COUTHER	COVERSLIPS	COWFEEDER	COWPOKES
COURGETTE	COUTHEST	COVERT	COWFEEDERS	COWPOX
COURGETTES	COUTHIE	COVERTLY	COWFISH	COWPOXES
COURIER	COUTHIER	COVERTS	COWFISHES	COWPS
COURIERS	COUTHIEST	COVERTURE	COWFLAP*	COWRIE
COURING	COUTHS*	COVERTURES	COWFLAPS*	COWRIES
COURLAN	COUTHY	COVERUP*	COWFLOP*	COWRITE*
COURLANS	COUTIL	COVERUPS*	COWFLOPS*	COWRITES*
COURS	COUTILLE	COVES	COWGIRL	COWRITING*
COURSE	COUTILLES	COVET	COWGIRLS	COWRITTEN*
COURSED	COUTILS	COVETABLE	COWGRASS	COWROTE*
COURSER	COUTURE	COVETED	COWGRASSES	COWRY
COURSERS	COUTURES	COVETER*	COWHAGE	COWS
COURSES	COUTURIER	COVETERS*	COWHAGES	COWSHED
COURSING	COUTURIERS	COVETING	COWHAND	COWSHEDS
COURSINGS	COUVADE	COVETISE	COWHANDS	COWSKIN*
COURT	COUVADES	COVETISES	COWHEARD	COWSKINS*
COURTED	COUVERT	COVETOUS	COWHEARDS	COWSLIP
COURTEOUS	COUVERTS	COVETS	COWHEEL	COWSLIPS
COURTER*	COVALENCE*	COVEY	COWHEELS	COWTREE
COURTERS*	COVALENCES*	COVEYS	COWHERB	COWTREES
COURTESAN	COVALENCIES	COVIN	COWHERBS	COWY*
COURTESANS	COVALENCY	COVING	COWHERD	COX
COURTESIED	COVALENT	COVINGS	COWHERDS	COXA
COURTESIES	COVARIANT	COVINOUS	COWHIDE	COXAE
COURTESY	COVARIANTS	COVINS	COWHIDED	COXAL
COURTESYING	COVARIED	COVYNE	COWHIDES	COXALGIA
COURTEZAN	COVARIES	COVYNES	COWHIDING	COXALGIAS
COURTEZANS	COVARY	COW	COWHOUSE	COXALGIC*
COURTIER	COVARYING	COWAGE	COWHOUSES	COXALGIES*
COURTIERS	COVE	COWAGES	COWIER*	COXALGY*
COURTING	COVED	COWAL	COWIEST*	COXCOMB
COURTINGS	COVELET	COWALS	COWING	COXCOMBIC
COURTLET	COVELETS	COWAN	COWINNER*	COXCOMBRIES
COURTLETS	COVELLINE*	COWANS	COWINNERS*	COXCOMBRY
COURTLIER	COVELLINES*	COWARD	COWISH	COXCOMBS
COURTLIEST	COVELLITE	COWARDED	COWITCH	COXED
COURTLIKE	COVELLITES	COWARDICE	COWITCHES	COXES
COURTLING	COVEN	COWARDICES	COWL	COXIER
COURTLINGS	COVENANT	COWARDING	COWLED	COXIEST

Words marked with an asterisk are from OTCWL

COXINESS
COXINESSES
COXING
COXITIDES*
COXITIS*
COXSWAIN
COXSWAINED
COXSWAINING
COXSWAINS
COXY
COY
COYDOG*
COYDOGS*
COYED
COYER
COYEST
COYING
COYISH
COYISHLY
COYLY
COYNESS
COYNESSES
COYOTE
COYOTES
COYOTILLO
COYOTILLOS
COYPOU*
COYPOUS*
COYPU
COYPUS
COYS*
COYSTREL
COYSTRELS
COYSTRIL
COYSTRILS
COZ
COZE
COZED
COZEN
COZENAGE
COZENAGES
COZENED
COZENER
COZENERS
COZENING
COZENS
COZES
COZEY*
COZEYS*
COZIE*
COZIED*
COZIER
COZIERS
COZIES
COZIEST
COZILY*
COZINESS*
COZINESSES*
COZING
COZY
COZYING*
COZZES
CRAAL*
CRAALED*

CRAALING*
CRAALS*
CRAB
CRABBED
CRABBEDLY
CRABBER
CRABBERS
CRABBIER
CRABBIEST
CRABBILY
CRABBING
CRABBY
CRABGRASS*
CRABGRASSES*
CRABLIKE
CRABMEAT*
CRABMEATS*
CRABS
CRABSTICK
CRABSTICKS
CRABWISE
CRACK
CRACKBACK*
CRACKBACKS*
CRACKDOWN
CRACKDOWNS
CRACKED
CRACKER
CRACKERS
CRACKHEAD
CRACKHEADS
CRACKING
CRACKINGS*
CRACKJAW
CRACKLE
CRACKLED
CRACKLES
CRACKLIER
CRACKLIEST
CRACKLING
CRACKLINGS
CRACKLY
CRACKNEL
CRACKNELS
CRACKPOT
CRACKPOTS
CRACKS
CRACKSMAN
CRACKSMEN
CRACKUP*
CRACKUPS*
CRACKY*
CRACOWE
CRACOWES
CRADLE
CRADLED
CRADLER*
CRADLERS*
CRADLES
CRADLING
CRADLINGS
CRAFT
CRAFTED
CRAFTIER

CRAFTIEST
CRAFTILY
CRAFTING
CRAFTLESS
CRAFTS
CRAFTSMAN
CRAFTSMEN
CRAFTWORK
CRAFTWORKS
CRAFTY
CRAG
CRAGFAST
CRAGGED
CRAGGIER
CRAGGIEST
CRAGGILY*
CRAGGY
CRAGS
CRAGSMAN
CRAGSMEN
CRAIG
CRAIGS
CRAKE
CRAKED
CRAKES
CRAKING
CRAM
CRAMBE*
CRAMBES*
CRAMBO
CRAMBOES
CRAMBOS*
CRAME
CRAMES
CRAMESIES
CRAMESY
CRAMMABLE
CRAMMED
CRAMMER
CRAMMERS
CRAMMING
CRAMOISIE*
CRAMOISIES
CRAMOISY
CRAMP
CRAMPBARK
CRAMPBARKS
CRAMPED
CRAMPET
CRAMPETS
CRAMPIER
CRAMPIEST
CRAMPING
CRAMPIT
CRAMPITS
CRAMPON
CRAMPONS
CRAMPOON*
CRAMPOONS*
CRAMPS
CRAMPY
CRAMS
CRAN
CRANAGE

CRANAGES
CRANBERRIES
CRANBERRY
CRANCH
CRANCHED
CRANCHES
CRANCHING
CRANE
CRANED
CRANEFLIES
CRANEFLY
CRANES
CRANIA
CRANIAL
CRANIALLY*
CRANIATE*
CRANIATES*
CRANING
CRANIUM
CRANIUMS
CRANK
CRANKCASE
CRANKCASES
CRANKED
CRANKER*
CRANKEST*
CRANKIER
CRANKIEST
CRANKILY
CRANKING
CRANKISH*
CRANKLE
CRANKLED
CRANKLES
CRANKLING
CRANKLY*
CRANKNESS
CRANKNESSES
CRANKOUS*
CRANKPIN*
CRANKPINS*
CRANKS
CRANKY
CRANNIED
CRANNIES
CRANNOG
CRANNOGE*
CRANNOGES*
CRANNOGS
CRANNY
CRANNYING
CRANREUCH
CRANREUCHS
CRANS
CRANTS
CRANTSES
CRAP
CRAPE
CRAPED*
CRAPES
CRAPIER
CRAPIEST
CRAPING*
CRAPLE

CRAPLES
CRAPPED
CRAPPER*
CRAPPERS*
CRAPPIE*
CRAPPIER
CRAPPIES*
CRAPPIEST
CRAPPING
CRAPPY
CRAPS
CRAPSHOOT*
CRAPSHOOTS*
CRAPULENT
CRAPULOUS
CRAPY
CRARE
CRARES
CRASES
CRASH
CRASHED
CRASHER*
CRASHERS*
CRASHES
CRASHING
CRASHLAND
CRASHLANDED
CRASHLANDING
CRASHLANDS
CRASHPAD
CRASHPADS
CRASIS
CRASS
CRASSER
CRASSEST
CRASSLY
CRASSNESS
CRASSNESSES
CRATCH
CRATCHES
CRATE
CRATED
CRATER
CRATERED
CRATERING
CRATERLET*
CRATERLETS*
CRATEROUS
CRATERS
CRATES
CRATING
CRATON
CRATONIC*
CRATONS
CRATUR
CRATURS
CRAUNCH
CRAUNCHED
CRAUNCHES
CRAUNCHING
CRAVAT
CRAVATS
CRAVATTED
CRAVATTING

CRAVE
CRAVED
CRAVEN
CRAVENED
CRAVENING
CRAVENLY
CRAVENS
CRAVER
CRAVERS
CRAVES
CRAVING
CRAVINGS
CRAW
CRAWDAD*
CRAWDADS*
CRAWFISH
CRAWFISHED
CRAWFISHES
CRAWFISHING
CRAWL
CRAWLED
CRAWLER
CRAWLERS
CRAWLIER
CRAWLIEST
CRAWLING
CRAWLINGS
CRAWLS
CRAWLWAY*
CRAWLWAYS*
CRAWLY
CRAWS
CRAYER
CRAYERS
CRAYFISH
CRAYFISHES
CRAYON
CRAYONED
CRAYONING
CRAYONIST*
CRAYONISTS*
CRAYONS
CRAZE
CRAZED
CRAZES
CRAZIER
CRAZIES
CRAZIEST
CRAZILY
CRAZINESS
CRAZINESSES
CRAZING
CRAZY
CRAZYWEED*
CRAZYWEEDS*
CREACH
CREACHS
CREAGH
CREAGHS
CREAK
CREAKED
CREAKIER
CREAKIEST
CREAKILY

CREAKING
CREAKS
CREAKY
CREAM
CREAMCUPS*
CREAMED
CREAMER
CREAMERIES
CREAMERS
CREAMERY
CREAMIER
CREAMIEST
CREAMILY*
CREAMING
CREAMLAID
CREAMS
CREAMWARE
CREAMWARES
CREAMWOVE
CREAMY
CREANCE
CREANCES
CREANT
CREASE
CREASED
CREASER
CREASERS
CREASES
CREASIER
CREASIEST
CREASING
CREASOTE
CREASOTED
CREASOTES
CREASOTING
CREASY
CREATABLE
CREATE
CREATED
CREATES
CREATIC
CREATIN
CREATINE
CREATINES
CREATING
CREATINS
CREATION
CREATIONS
CREATIVE
CREATOR
CREATORS
CREATRESS
CREATRESSES
CREATRIX
CREATRIXES
CREATURAL
CREATURE
CREATURES
CRECHE
CRECHES
CRED
CREDAL
CREDENCE
CREDENCES

CREDENDA
CREDENDUM
CREDENT
CREDENZA
CREDENZAS
CREDIBLE
CREDIBLY
CREDIT
CREDITED
CREDITING
CREDITOR
CREDITORS
CREDITS
CREDO
CREDOS
CREDS
CREDULITIES
CREDULITY
CREDULOUS
CREE
CREED
CREEDAL
CREEDS
CREEING
CREEK
CREEKIER
CREEKIEST
CREEKS
CREEKY
CREEL
CREELED*
CREELING*
CREELS
CREEP
CREEPAGE*
CREEPAGES*
CREEPER
CREEPERED
CREEPERS
CREEPIE
CREEPIER
CREEPIES
CREEPIEST
CREEPILY*
CREEPING
CREEPS
CREEPY
CREES
CREESE
CREESED
CREESES
CREESH
CREESHED
CREESHES
CREESHIER
CREESHIEST
CREESHING
CREESHY
CREESING
CREMAINS*
CREMASTER
CREMASTERS
CREMATE
CREMATED

CREMATES
CREMATING
CREMATION
CREMATIONS
CREMATOR
CREMATORIES
CREMATORS
CREMATORY
CREME
CREMES
CREMOCARP
CREMOCARPS
CREMONA
CREMONAS
CREMOR
CREMORNE
CREMORNES
CREMORS
CREMOSIN
CREMSIN
CRENA
CRENAS
CRENATE
CRENATED
CRENATION
CRENATIONS
CRENATURE
CRENATURES
CRENEL
CRENELATE
CRENELATED
CRENELATES
CRENELATING
CRENELED*
CRENELING*
CRENELLE
CRENELLED
CRENELLES
CRENELLING
CRENELS
CRENULATE
CREODONT
CREODONTS
CREOLE
CREOLES
CREOLIAN
CREOLIANS
CREOLISE*
CREOLISED*
CREOLISES*
CREOLISING*
CREOLIST
CREOLISTS
CREOLIZE*
CREOLIZED*
CREOLIZES*
CREOLIZING*
CREOSOL
CREOSOLS
CREOSOTE
CREOSOTED
CREOSOTES
CREOSOTING
CREPANCE

CREPANCES
CREPE
CREPED*
CREPERIE
CREPERIES
CREPES
CREPEY
CREPIER
CREPIEST
CREPINESS
CREPINESSES
CREPING*
CREPITANT
CREPITATE
CREPITATED
CREPITATES
CREPITATING
CREPITUS
CREPITUSES
CREPOLINE
CREPOLINES
CREPON
CREPONS
CREPT
CREPUSCLE
CREPUSCLES
CREPY
CRESCENDI*
CRESCENDO
CRESCENDOED
CRESCENDOES*
CRESCENDOING
CRESCENDOS
CRESCENT
CRESCENTS
CRESCIVE
CRESOL
CRESOLS
CRESS
CRESSES
CRESSET
CRESSETS
CREST
CRESTAL*
CRESTED
CRESTING
CRESTINGS*
CRESTLESS
CRESTON
CRESTONS
CRESTS
CRESYL*
CRESYLIC
CRESYLS*
CRETIC
CRETICS
CRETIN
CRETINISE
CRETINISED
CRETINISES
CRETINISING
CRETINISM
CRETINISMS
CRETINIZE

CRETINIZED
CRETINIZES
CRETINIZING
CRETINOID
CRETINOIDS
CRETINOUS
CRETINS
CRETISM
CRETISMS
CRETONNE
CRETONNES
CREUTZER
CREUTZERS
CREVALLE*
CREVALLES*
CREVASSE
CREVASSED
CREVASSES
CREVASSING
CREVETTE
CREVETTES
CREVICE
CREVICED*
CREVICES
CREW
CREWE
CREWED
CREWEL
CREWELIST
CREWELISTS
CREWELLED
CREWELLING
CREWELS
CREWES
CREWING
CREWLESS*
CREWMAN*
CREWMATE*
CREWMATES*
CREWMEN*
CREWNECK*
CREWNECKS*
CREWS
CRIANT
CRIB
CRIBBAGE
CRIBBAGES
CRIBBED
CRIBBER*
CRIBBERS*
CRIBBING
CRIBBINGS*
CRIBBLE
CRIBBLED
CRIBBLES
CRIBBLING
CRIBELLA
CRIBELLAR
CRIBELLUM
CRIBLE
CRIBRATE
CRIBROSE
CRIBROUS
CRIBS

CRIBWORK
CRIBWORKS
CRICETID
CRICETIDS
CRICK
CRICKED
CRICKET
CRICKETED
CRICKETER
CRICKETERS
CRICKETING
CRICKETINGS
CRICKETS
CRICKEY
CRICKING
CRICKS
CRICKY
CRICOID
CRICOIDS
CRIED
CRIER
CRIERS
CRIES
CRIKEY
CRIM
CRIME
CRIMED
CRIMEFUL
CRIMELESS
CRIMEN
CRIMES
CRIMINA
CRIMINAL
CRIMINALS
CRIMINATE
CRIMINATED
CRIMINATES
CRIMINATING
CRIMINE
CRIMING
CRIMINI
CRIMINOUS
CRIMMER
CRIMMERS
CRIMP
CRIMPED
CRIMPER
CRIMPERS
CRIMPIER
CRIMPIEST
CRIMPING
CRIMPLE
CRIMPLED
CRIMPLES
CRIMPLING
CRIMPS
CRIMPY
CRIMS
CRIMSON
CRIMSONED
CRIMSONING
CRIMSONS
CRINAL
CRINATE

CRINATED
CRINE
CRINED
CRINES
CRINGE
CRINGED
CRINGER
CRINGERS
CRINGES
CRINGING
CRINGINGS
CRINGLE
CRINGLES
CRINING
CRINITE
CRINITES
CRINKLE
CRINKLED
CRINKLES
CRINKLIER
CRINKLIES
CRINKLIEST
CRINKLING
CRINKLY
CRINOID
CRINOIDAL
CRINOIDS
CRINOLINE
CRINOLINES
CRINOSE
CRINUM
CRINUMS
CRIOLLO
CRIOLLOS
CRIPE*
CRIPES
CRIPPLE
CRIPPLED
CRIPPLER*
CRIPPLERS*
CRIPPLES
CRIPPLING
CRIPPLINGS
CRIS*
CRISE
CRISES
CRISIC*
CRISIS
CRISP
CRISPATE
CRISPED
CRISPEN*
CRISPENED*
CRISPENING*
CRISPENS*
CRISPER
CRISPERS
CRISPEST
CRISPIER
CRISPIEST
CRISPILY*
CRISPIN
CRISPING
CRISPINS

CRISPLY
CRISPNESS
CRISPNESSES
CRISPS
CRISPY
CRISSA
CRISSAL*
CRISSUM
CRISTA
CRISTAE
CRISTATE
CRIT
CRITERIA
CRITERION
CRITERIONS*
CRITERIUM*
CRITERIUMS*
CRITH
CRITHS
CRITIC
CRITICAL
CRITICISE
CRITICISED
CRITICISES
CRITICISING
CRITICISM
CRITICISMS
CRITICIZE
CRITICIZED
CRITICIZES
CRITICIZING
CRITICS
CRITIQUE
CRITIQUED
CRITIQUES
CRITIQUING
CRITS
CRITTER
CRITTERS
CRITTUR
CRITTURS
CRIVENS
CRIVVENS
CROAK
CROAKED
CROAKER
CROAKERS
CROAKIER
CROAKIEST
CROAKILY
CROAKING
CROAKINGS
CROAKS
CROAKY
CROC
CROCEATE
CROCEIN
CROCEINE*
CROCEINES*
CROCEINS
CROCEOUS
CROCHE
CROCHES
CROCHET

CROCHETED
CROCHETER*
CROCHETERS*
CROCHETING
CROCHETINGS
CROCHETS
CROCI*
CROCINE*
CROCK
CROCKED
CROCKERIES
CROCKERY
CROCKET
CROCKETED*
CROCKETS
CROCKING
CROCKS
CROCODILE
CROCODILES
CROCOITE
CROCOITES
CROCOSMIA
CROCOSMIAS
CROCS
CROCUS
CROCUSES
CROFT
CROFTER
CROFTERS
CROFTING
CROFTINGS
CROFTS
CROISSANT
CROISSANTS
CROJIK*
CROJIKS*
CROMACK
CROMACKS
CROMB
CROMBED
CROMBING
CROMBS
CROME
CROMED
CROMES
CROMING
CROMLECH
CROMLECHS
CROMORNA
CROMORNAS
CROMORNE
CROMORNES
CRONE
CRONES
CRONET
CRONETS
CRONIES
CRONK
CRONKER
CRONKEST
CRONY
CRONYISM
CRONYISMS
CROODLE

The Chambers Dictionary is the authority for many longer words; see Introduction, page ix

CROODLED	CROSSBANDS	CROSSTIES	CROUTE	CRUCIFIED
CROODLES	CROSSBAR	CROSSTOWN	CROUTES	CRUCIFIER
CROODLING	CROSSBARRED*	CROSSTREE	CROUTON	CRUCIFIERS
CROOK	CROSSBARRING*	CROSSTREES	CROUTONS	CRUCIFIES
CROOKBACK	CROSSBARS	CROSSWALK	CROUTS	CRUCIFIX
CROOKBACKS	CROSSBEAM	CROSSWALKS	CROW	CRUCIFIXES
CROOKED	CROSSBEAMS	CROSSWAY	CROWBAR	CRUCIFORM
CROOKEDER	CROSSBILL	CROSSWAYS	CROWBARRED*	CRUCIFORMS*
CROOKEDEST	CROSSBILLS	CROSSWIND	CROWBARRING*	CRUCIFY
CROOKEDLY	CROSSBIT	CROSSWINDS	CROWBARS	CRUCIFYING
CROOKER	CROSSBITE	CROSSWISE	CROWBERRIES	CRUCK
CROOKERIES*	CROSSBITES	CROSSWORD	CROWBERRY	CRUCKS
CROOKERY*	CROSSBITING	CROSSWORDS	CROWD	CRUD
CROOKEST	CROSSBITTEN	CROSSWORT	CROWDED	CRUDDED
CROOKING	CROSSBOW	CROSSWORTS	CROWDER	CRUDDIER
CROOKNECK*	CROSSBOWS	CROST	CROWDERS	CRUDDIEST
CROOKNECKS*	CROSSBRED	CROSTINI	CROWDIE	CRUDDING
CROOKS	CROSSBREDS*	CROSTINIS	CROWDIES	CRUDDLE
CROON	CROSSBREED*	CROTAL	CROWDING	CRUDDLED
CROONED	CROSSBREEDING*	CROTALA	CROWDS	CRUDDLES
CROONER	CROSSBREEDS*	CROTALINE	CROWDY*	CRUDDLING
CROONERS	CROSSBUCK	CROTALISM	CROWED	CRUDDY
CROONING	CROSSBUCKS	CROTALISMS	CROWER*	CRUDE
CROONINGS	CROSSCUT	CROTALS	CROWERS*	CRUDELY
CROONS	CROSSCUTS	CROTALUM	CROWFEET*	CRUDENESS
CROOVE	CROSSCUTTING	CROTCH	CROWFOOT	CRUDENESSES
CROOVES	CROSSCUTTINGS	CROTCHED	CROWFOOTS	CRUDER
CROP	CROSSE	CROTCHES	CROWING	CRUDES
CROPBOUND	CROSSED	CROTCHET	CROWN	CRUDEST
CROPFUL	CROSSER	CROTCHETIER	CROWNED	CRUDITES
CROPFULL	CROSSERS*	CROTCHETIEST	CROWNER	CRUDITIES
CROPFULS	CROSSES	CROTCHETS	CROWNERS	CRUDITY
CROPLAND	CROSSEST	CROTCHETY	CROWNET	CRUDS
CROPLANDS	CROSSETTE	CROTON	CROWNETS	CRUDY
CROPLESS*	CROSSETTES	CROTONS	CROWNING	CRUE
CROPPED	CROSSFALL	CROTTLE	CROWNINGS	CRUEL
CROPPER	CROSSFALLS	CROTTLES	CROWNLESS	CRUELER*
CROPPERS	CROSSFIRE	CROUCH	CROWNLET	CRUELEST*
CROPPIE*	CROSSFIRES	CROUCHED	CROWNLETS	CRUELLER
CROPPIES	CROSSFISH	CROUCHES	CROWNS	CRUELLEST
CROPPING	CROSSFISHES	CROUCHING	CROWNWORK	CRUELLS
CROPPINGS	CROSSHAIR*	CROUP	CROWNWORKS	CRUELLY
CROPPY	CROSSHAIRS*	CROUPADE	CROWS	CRUELNESS
CROPS	CROSSHEAD	CROUPADES	CROWSTEP*	CRUELNESSES
CROPSICK	CROSSHEADS	CROUPE	CROWSTEPS*	CRUELS
CROQUANTE	CROSSING	CROUPED	CROZE	CRUELTIES
CROQUANTES	CROSSINGS	CROUPER	CROZER*	CRUELTY
CROQUET	CROSSISH	CROUPERS	CROZERS*	CRUES
CROQUETED	CROSSJACK	CROUPES	CROZES	CRUET
CROQUETING	CROSSJACKS	CROUPIER	CROZIER	CRUETS
CROQUETS	CROSSLET	CROUPIERS	CROZIERS	CRUISE
CROQUETTE	CROSSLETS	CROUPIEST	CRU	CRUISED
CROQUETTES	CROSSLY	CROUPILY*	CRUBEEN	CRUISER
CROQUIS	CROSSNESS	CROUPING	CRUBEENS	CRUISERS
CRORE	CROSSNESSES	CROUPON	CRUCES	CRUISES
CRORES	CROSSOVER	CROUPONS	CRUCIAL	CRUISEWAY
CROSIER	CROSSOVERS	CROUPOUS	CRUCIALLY*	CRUISEWAYS
CROSIERED	CROSSROAD	CROUPS	CRUCIAN	CRUISIE
CROSIERS	CROSSROADS	CROUPY	CRUCIANS	CRUISIES
CROSS	CROSSRUFF*	CROUSE	CRUCIATE	CRUISING
CROSSABLE*	CROSSRUFFED*	CROUSELY	CRUCIBLE	CRUISINGS*
CROSSARM*	CROSSRUFFING*	CROUSTADE	CRUCIBLES	CRUIVE
CROSSARMS*	CROSSRUFFS*	CROUSTADES	CRUCIFER	CRUIVES
CROSSBAND	CROSSTIE	CROUT	CRUCIFERS	CRULLER

Words marked with an asterisk are from OTCWL

CRULLERS
CRUMB
CRUMBED
CRUMBER*
CRUMBERS*
CRUMBIER
CRUMBIEST
CRUMBING
CRUMBLE
CRUMBLED
CRUMBLES
CRUMBLIER
CRUMBLIES
CRUMBLIEST
CRUMBLING
CRUMBLY
CRUMBS
CRUMBUM*
CRUMBUMS*
CRUMBY
CRUMEN
CRUMENAL
CRUMENALS
CRUMENS
CRUMHORN
CRUMHORNS
CRUMMACK
CRUMMACKS
CRUMMIE*
CRUMMIER
CRUMMIES
CRUMMIEST
CRUMMOCK
CRUMMOCKS
CRUMMY
CRUMP
CRUMPED
CRUMPER
CRUMPEST
CRUMPET
CRUMPETS
CRUMPIER
CRUMPIEST
CRUMPING
CRUMPLE
CRUMPLED
CRUMPLES
CRUMPLIER*
CRUMPLIEST*
CRUMPLING
CRUMPLINGS
CRUMPLY*
CRUMPS
CRUMPY
CRUNCH
CRUNCHED
CRUNCHER*
CRUNCHERS*
CRUNCHES
CRUNCHIER
CRUNCHIEST
CRUNCHILY*
CRUNCHING
CRUNCHY

CRUNKLE
CRUNKLED
CRUNKLES
CRUNKLING
CRUNODAL*
CRUNODE*
CRUNODES*
CRUOR
CRUORES
CRUORS*
CRUPPER
CRUPPERS
CRURA*
CRURAL
CRUS
CRUSADE
CRUSADED
CRUSADER
CRUSADERS
CRUSADES
CRUSADING
CRUSADO
CRUSADOES*
CRUSADOS
CRUSE
CRUSES
CRUSET
CRUSETS
CRUSH
CRUSHABLE
CRUSHED
CRUSHER
CRUSHERS
CRUSHES
CRUSHING
CRUSIAN
CRUSIANS
CRUSIE
CRUSIES
CRUSILY*
CRUST
CRUSTA
CRUSTACEA*
CRUSTAE
CRUSTAL
CRUSTATE
CRUSTATED
CRUSTED
CRUSTIER
CRUSTIES
CRUSTIEST
CRUSTILY
CRUSTING
CRUSTLESS
CRUSTOSE*
CRUSTS
CRUSTY
CRUSY
CRUTCH
CRUTCHED
CRUTCHES
CRUTCHING
CRUVE
CRUVES

CRUX
CRUXES
CRUZADO
CRUZADOES
CRUZADOS
CRUZEIRO
CRUZEIROS
CRWTH
CRWTHS
CRY
CRYBABIES
CRYBABY
CRYING
CRYINGLY*
CRYINGS
CRYOGEN
CRYOGENIC
CRYOGENICS
CRYOGENIES
CRYOGENS
CRYOGENY
CRYOLITE
CRYOLITES
CRYOMETER
CRYOMETERS
CRYONIC
CRYONICS
CRYOPROBE
CRYOPROBES
CRYOSCOPE
CRYOSCOPES
CRYOSCOPIES
CRYOSCOPY
CRYOSTAT
CRYOSTATS
CRYOTRON
CRYOTRONS
CRYPT
CRYPTADIA
CRYPTAL
CRYPTIC
CRYPTICAL
CRYPTO
CRYPTOGAM
CRYPTOGAMS
CRYPTON
CRYPTONS
CRYPTONYM
CRYPTONYMS
CRYPTOS
CRYPTS
CRYSTAL
CRYSTALS
CSARDAS
CSARDASES
CTENE
CTENES
CTENIDIA*
CTENIDIUM*
CTENIFORM
CTENOID
CUADRILLA
CUADRILLAS
CUB

CUBAGE
CUBAGES
CUBATURE
CUBATURES
CUBBED
CUBBIES
CUBBING
CUBBINGS
CUBBISH
CUBBY
CUBBYHOLE*
CUBBYHOLES*
CUBE
CUBEB
CUBEBS
CUBED
CUBER*
CUBERS*
CUBES
CUBHOOD
CUBHOODS
CUBIC
CUBICA
CUBICAL
CUBICALLY
CUBICAS
CUBICITIES*
CUBICITY*
CUBICLE
CUBICLES
CUBICLY*
CUBICS
CUBICULA*
CUBICULUM*
CUBIFORM
CUBING
CUBISM
CUBISMS
CUBIST
CUBISTIC
CUBISTS
CUBIT
CUBITAL
CUBITS
CUBITUS
CUBITUSES
CUBLESS
CUBOID
CUBOIDAL
CUBOIDS
CUBS
CUCKOLD
CUCKOLDED
CUCKOLDING
CUCKOLDLY
CUCKOLDOM
CUCKOLDOMS
CUCKOLDRIES
CUCKOLDRY
CUCKOLDS
CUCKOO
CUCKOOED*
CUCKOOING*
CUCKOOS

CUCULLATE
CUCUMBER
CUCUMBERS
CUCURBIT
CUCURBITS
CUD
CUDBEAR
CUDBEARS
CUDDEEHIH
CUDDEEHIHS
CUDDEN
CUDDENS
CUDDIE
CUDDIES
CUDDIN
CUDDINS
CUDDLE
CUDDLED
CUDDLER*
CUDDLERS*
CUDDLES
CUDDLIER
CUDDLIEST
CUDDLING
CUDDLY
CUDDY
CUDGEL
CUDGELED*
CUDGELER*
CUDGELERS*
CUDGELING*
CUDGELLED
CUDGELLER
CUDGELLERS
CUDGELLING
CUDGELLINGS
CUDGELS
CUDS
CUDWEED
CUDWEEDS
CUE
CUED
CUEING
CUEIST
CUEISTS
CUES
CUESTA
CUESTAS
CUFF
CUFFED
CUFFIN
CUFFING
CUFFINS
CUFFLE
CUFFLED
CUFFLES
CUFFLESS*
CUFFLING
CUFFO
CUFFS
CUFFUFFLE
CUFFUFFLES
CUIF
CUIFS

CUING	CULLYISM	CUMARIN	CUPBOARDED	CURACIES
CUIRASS	CULLYISMS	CUMARINS	CUPBOARDING	CURACOA
CUIRASSED	CULM	CUMBENT	CUPBOARDS	CURACOAS
CUIRASSES	CULMED	CUMBER	CUPCAKE	CURACY
CUIRASSING	CULMEN	CUMBERED	CUPCAKES	CURAGH*
CUISH	CULMENS	CUMBERER	CUPEL	CURAGHS*
CUISHES	CULMINANT	CUMBERERS	CUPELED	CURARA
CUISINE	CULMINATE	CUMBERING	CUPELER*	CURARAS
CUISINES	CULMINATED	CUMBERS	CUPELERS*	CURARE
CUISINIER	CULMINATES	CUMBRANCE	CUPELING	CURARES
CUISINIERS	CULMINATING	CUMBRANCES	CUPELLED	CURARI
CUISSE	CULMING	CUMBROUS	CUPELLER*	CURARINE
CUISSER	CULMS	CUMEC	CUPELLERS*	CURARINES
CUISSERS	CULOTTE	CUMECS	CUPELLING	CURARIS
CUISSES	CULOTTES	CUMIN	CUPELS	CURARISE
CUIT	CULPA*	CUMINS	CUPFUL	CURARISED
CUITER	CULPABLE	CUMMER	CUPFULS	CURARISES
CUITERED	CULPABLY	CUMMERS	CUPGALL	CURARISING
CUITERING	CULPAE*	CUMMIN	CUPGALLS	CURARIZE
CUITERS	CULPATORY	CUMMINS	CUPHEAD	CURARIZED
CUITIKIN	CULPRIT	CUMQUAT	CUPHEADS	CURARIZES
CUITIKINS	CULPRITS	CUMQUATS	CUPID	CURARIZING
CUITS	CULT	CUMSHAW	CUPIDITIES	CURASSOW
CUITTLE	CULTCH	CUMSHAWS	CUPIDITY	CURASSOWS
CUITTLED	CULTCHES	CUMULATE	CUPIDS	CURAT
CUITTLES	CULTER	CUMULATED	CUPLIKE*	CURATE
CUITTLING	CULTERS	CUMULATES	CUPMAN	CURATED
CUKE*	CULTI*	CUMULATING	CUPMEN	CURATES
CUKES*	CULTIC	CUMULI	CUPOLA	CURATING
CULCH	CULTIGEN	CUMULOSE	CUPOLAED	CURATIVE
CULCHES	CULTIGENS	CUMULOUS*	CUPOLAING	CURATIVES*
CULCHIE	CULTISH	CUMULUS	CUPOLAR	CURATOR
CULCHIES	CULTISHLY*	CUNABULA	CUPOLAS	CURATORS
CULET	CULTISM	CUNCTATOR	CUPOLATED	CURATORY
CULETS	CULTISMS	CUNCTATORS	CUPPA	CURATRIX
CULEX	CULTIST	CUNDIES	CUPPAS	CURATRIXES
CULICES	CULTISTS	CUNDUM*	CUPPED	CURATS
CULICID	CULTIVAR	CUNDUMS*	CUPPER	CURB
CULICIDS	CULTIVARS	CUNDY	CUPPERS	CURBABLE
CULICINE	CULTIVATE	CUNEAL	CUPPIER*	CURBED
CULICINES	CULTIVATED	CUNEATE	CUPPIEST*	CURBER*
CULINARY	CULTIVATES	CUNEATED*	CUPPING	CURBERS*
CULL	CULTIVATING	CUNEATIC	CUPPINGS	CURBING
CULLAY*	CULTLIKE*	CUNEIFORM	CUPPY*	CURBINGS*
CULLAYS*	CULTRATE	CUNEIFORMS	CUPREOUS	CURBLESS
CULLED	CULTRATED	CUNETTE	CUPRIC	CURBS
CULLENDER	CULTS	CUNETTES	CUPRITE	CURBSIDE*
CULLENDERS	CULTURAL	CUNIFORM*	CUPRITES	CURBSIDES*
CULLER	CULTURATI*	CUNIFORMS*	CUPROUS	CURBSTONE
CULLERS	CULTURE	CUNJEVOI	CUPRUM*	CURBSTONES
CULLET	CULTURED	CUNJEVOIS	CUPRUMS*	CURCH
CULLETS	CULTURES	CUNNER	CUPS	CURCHES
CULLIED	CULTURING	CUNNERS	CUPSFUL*	CURCULIO
CULLIES	CULTURIST	CUNNING	CUPULA*	CURCULIOS
CULLING	CULTURISTS	CUNNINGER	CUPULAE*	CURCUMA
CULLINGS	CULTUS	CUNNINGEST	CUPULAR	CURCUMAS
CULLION	CULTUSES	CUNNINGLY	CUPULATE	CURCUMIN
CULLIONLY	CULVER	CUNNINGS	CUPULE	CURCUMINE
CULLIONS	CULVERIN	CUNT	CUPULES	CURCUMINES
CULLIS	CULVERINS	CUNTS	CUR	CURCUMINS
CULLISES	CULVERS	CUP	CURABLE	CURD
CULLS	CULVERT	CUPBEARER	CURABLY*	CURDED
CULLY	CULVERTS	CUPBEARERS	CURACAO	CURDIER
CULLYING	CUM	CUPBOARD	CURACAOS	CURDIEST

Words marked with an asterisk are from OTCWL

CURDINESS
CURDINESSES
CURDING
CURDLE
CURDLED
CURDLER*
CURDLERS*
CURDLES
CURDLING
CURDS
CURDY
CURE
CURED
CURELESS
CURER
CURERS
CURES
CURET*
CURETS*
CURETTAGE
CURETTAGES
CURETTE
CURETTED
CURETTES
CURETTING
CURF*
CURFEW
CURFEWS
CURFS*
CURFUFFLE
CURFUFFLED
CURFUFFLES
CURFUFFLING
CURIA
CURIAE
CURIAL*
CURIALISM
CURIALISMS
CURIALIST
CURIALISTS
CURIAS
CURIE
CURIES
CURIET
CURIETS
CURING
CURIO
CURIOS
CURIOSA
CURIOSITIES
CURIOSITY
CURIOUS
CURIOUSER
CURIOUSEST*
CURIOUSLY
CURITE*
CURITES*
CURIUM
CURIUMS
CURL
CURLED
CURLER
CURLERS
CURLEW

CURLEWS
CURLICUE
CURLICUED*
CURLICUES*
CURLICUING*
CURLIER
CURLIEST
CURLILY*
CURLINESS
CURLINESSES
CURLING
CURLINGS
CURLPAPER
CURLPAPERS
CURLS
CURLY
CURLYCUE*
CURLYCUES*
CURN
CURNEY
CURNIER
CURNIEST
CURNS
CURNY
CURPEL
CURPELS
CURR
CURRACH
CURRACHS
CURRAGH
CURRAGHS
CURRAJONG
CURRAJONGS
CURRAN*
CURRANS*
CURRANT
CURRANTIER
CURRANTIEST
CURRANTS
CURRANTY
CURRAWONG
CURRAWONGS
CURRED
CURRENCIES
CURRENCY
CURRENT
CURRENTLY
CURRENTS
CURRICLE
CURRICLES
CURRICULA
CURRICULUM*
CURRICULUMS*
CURRIE
CURRIED
CURRIER
CURRIERIES*
CURRIERS
CURRIERY*
CURRIES
CURRING
CURRISH
CURRISHLY
CURRS

CURRY
CURRYCOMB
CURRYCOMBED*
CURRYCOMBING*
CURRYCOMBS
CURRYING
CURRYINGS
CURS
CURSAL
CURSE
CURSED
CURSEDER
CURSEDEST
CURSEDLY
CURSENARY
CURSER
CURSERS
CURSES
CURSI
CURSING
CURSINGS
CURSITOR
CURSITORS
CURSITORY
CURSIVE
CURSIVELY
CURSIVES*
CURSOR
CURSORARY
CURSORES
CURSORIAL
CURSORILY
CURSORS
CURSORY
CURST
CURSTNESS
CURSTNESSES
CURSUS
CURT
CURTAIL
CURTAILED
CURTAILER*
CURTAILERS*
CURTAILING
CURTAILS
CURTAIN
CURTAINED
CURTAINING
CURTAINS
CURTAL
CURTALAX
CURTALAXE
CURTALAXES
CURTALS
CURTANA
CURTANAS
CURTATE
CURTATION
CURTATIONS
CURTAXE
CURTAXES
CURTER
CURTESIES
CURTEST

CURTESY
CURTILAGE
CURTILAGES
CURTLY
CURTNESS
CURTNESSES
CURTSEY
CURTSEYED
CURTSEYING
CURTSEYS
CURTSIED
CURTSIES
CURTSY
CURTSYING
CURULE
CURVATE
CURVATED
CURVATION
CURVATIONS
CURVATIVE
CURVATURE
CURVATURES
CURVE
CURVEBALL*
CURVEBALLED*
CURVEBALLING*
CURVEBALLS*
CURVED
CURVEDLY*
CURVES
CURVESOME
CURVET
CURVETED
CURVETING
CURVETS
CURVETTED
CURVETTING
CURVEY*
CURVIER
CURVIEST
CURVIFORM
CURVING
CURVITAL
CURVITIES
CURVITY
CURVY
CUSCUS
CUSCUSES
CUSEC
CUSECS
CUSH
CUSHAT
CUSHATS
CUSHAW
CUSHAWS
CUSHES
CUSHIER
CUSHIEST
CUSHILY*
CUSHION
CUSHIONED
CUSHIONET
CUSHIONETS
CUSHIONING

CUSHIONS
CUSHIONY
CUSHY
CUSK
CUSKS
CUSP
CUSPATE
CUSPATED*
CUSPED
CUSPID
CUSPIDAL
CUSPIDATE
CUSPIDES*
CUSPIDOR
CUSPIDORE
CUSPIDORES
CUSPIDORS
CUSPIDS
CUSPIS*
CUSPS
CUSS
CUSSED
CUSSEDLY*
CUSSER
CUSSERS
CUSSES
CUSSING
CUSSO*
CUSSOS*
CUSSWORD
CUSSWORDS
CUSTARD
CUSTARDS
CUSTARDY*
CUSTOCK
CUSTOCKS
CUSTODE
CUSTODES
CUSTODIAL
CUSTODIAN
CUSTODIANS
CUSTODIER
CUSTODIERS
CUSTODIES
CUSTODY
CUSTOM
CUSTOMARIES
CUSTOMARY
CUSTOMED
CUSTOMER
CUSTOMERS
CUSTOMISE
CUSTOMISED
CUSTOMISES
CUSTOMISING
CUSTOMIZE
CUSTOMIZED
CUSTOMIZES
CUSTOMIZING
CUSTOMS
CUSTOS
CUSTREL
CUSTRELS
CUSTUMAL*

CUSTUMALS*	CUTLERY	CYANIDINGS	CYCLECAR*	CYLINDERED*
CUSTUMARIES	CUTLET	CYANIDS*	CYCLECARS*	CYLINDERING*
CUSTUMARY	CUTLETS	CYANIN	CYCLED	CYLINDERS
CUT	CUTLINE	CYANINE	CYCLER	CYLINDRIC
CUTANEOUS	CUTLINES	CYANINES	CYCLERIES*	CYLIX
CUTAWAY	CUTOFF*	CYANINS	CYCLERS	CYMA
CUTAWAYS	CUTOFFS*	CYANISE	CYCLERY*	CYMAE*
CUTBACK	CUTOUT*	CYANISED	CYCLES	CYMAGRAPH
CUTBACKS	CUTOUTS*	CYANISES	CYCLEWAY	CYMAGRAPHS
CUTBANK*	CUTOVER*	CYANISING	CYCLEWAYS	CYMAR
CUTBANKS*	CUTOVERS*	CYANITE	CYCLIC	CYMARS
CUTCH	CUTPURSE	CYANITES	CYCLICAL	CYMAS
CUTCHA	CUTPURSES	CYANITIC*	CYCLICALS*	CYMATIA
CUTCHERIES	CUTS	CYANIZE	CYCLICISM	CYMATICS
CUTCHERRIES	CUTTABLE*	CYANIZED	CYCLICISMS	CYMATIUM
CUTCHERRY	CUTTAGE*	CYANIZES	CYCLICITIES	CYMBAL
CUTCHERY	CUTTAGES*	CYANIZING	CYCLICITY	CYMBALER*
CUTCHES	CUTTER	CYANO*	CYCLICLY*	CYMBALERS*
CUTDOWN*	CUTTERS	CYANOGEN	CYCLING	CYMBALIST
CUTDOWNS*	CUTTHROAT*	CYANOGENS	CYCLINGS	CYMBALISTS
CUTE	CUTTHROATS*	CYANOSED	CYCLIST	CYMBALO
CUTELY	CUTTIER	CYANOSES	CYCLISTS	CYMBALOES
CUTENESS	CUTTIES	CYANOSIS	CYCLITOL*	CYMBALOM*
CUTENESSES	CUTTIEST	CYANOTIC	CYCLITOLS*	CYMBALOMS*
CUTER	CUTTING	CYANOTYPE	CYCLIZE*	CYMBALOS
CUTES	CUTTINGLY*	CYANOTYPES	CYCLIZED*	CYMBALS
CUTESIE*	CUTTINGS	CYANS	CYCLIZES*	CYMBIDIA
CUTESIER	CUTTLE	CYANURET	CYCLIZINE	CYMBIDIUM
CUTESIEST	CUTTLED*	CYANURETS	CYCLIZINES	CYMBIDIUMS
CUTEST	CUTTLES	CYATHI	CYCLIZING*	CYMBIFORM
CUTESY	CUTTLING*	CYATHIA	CYCLO	CYMBLING*
CUTEY	CUTTO	CYATHIUM	CYCLOID	CYMBLINGS*
CUTEYS	CUTTOE	CYATHUS	CYCLOIDAL	CYME
CUTGLASS	CUTTOES	CYBERCAFE	CYCLOIDS	CYMENE*
CUTGRASS*	CUTTY	CYBERCAFES	CYCLOLITH	CYMENES*
CUTGRASSES*	CUTUP*	CYBERNATE	CYCLOLITHS	CYMES
CUTICLE	CUTUPS*	CYBERNATED	CYCLONAL*	CYMLIN*
CUTICLES	CUTWATER*	CYBERNATES	CYCLONE	CYMLING*
CUTICULA*	CUTWATERS*	CYBERNATING	CYCLONES	CYMLINGS*
CUTICULAE*	CUTWORK	CYBERPET	CYCLONIC	CYMLINS*
CUTICULAR	CUTWORKS	CYBERPETS	CYCLONITE	CYMOGENE*
CUTIE	CUTWORM	CYBERPUNK	CYCLONITES	CYMOGENES*
CUTIES	CUTWORMS	CYBERPUNKS	CYCLOPEAN	CYMOGRAPH
CUTIKIN	CUVEE	CYBERSEX	CYCLOPES	CYMOGRAPHS
CUTIKINS	CUVEES	CYBERSEXES	CYCLOPIAN	CYMOID
CUTIN	CUVETTE	CYBORG	CYCLOPIC	CYMOL*
CUTINISE	CUVETTES	CYBORGS	CYCLOPS	CYMOLS*
CUTINISED	CUZ	CYBRID	CYCLORAMA	CYMOPHANE
CUTINISES	CUZZES	CYBRIDS	CYCLORAMAS	CYMOPHANES
CUTINISING	CWM	CYCAD	CYCLOS	CYMOSE
CUTINIZE	CWMS	CYCADEOID*	CYCLOSES	CYMOSELY*
CUTINIZED	CYAN	CYCADEOIDS*	CYCLOSIS	CYMOUS
CUTINIZES	CYANAMID*	CYCADS	CYCLOTRON	CYNANCHE
CUTINIZING	CYANAMIDE	CYCAS*	CYCLOTRONS	CYNANCHES
CUTINS	CYANAMIDES	CYCASES*	CYCLUS	CYNEGETIC
CUTIS	CYANAMIDS*	CYCASIN*	CYCLUSES	CYNIC
CUTISES	CYANATE	CYCASINS*	CYDER	CYNICAL
CUTLAS*	CYANATES	CYCLAMATE	CYDERS	CYNICALLY
CUTLASES*	CYANIC	CYCLAMATES	CYESES	CYNICISM
CUTLASS	CYANID*	CYCLAMEN	CYESIS	CYNICISMS
CUTLASSES	CYANIDE	CYCLAMENS	CYGNET	CYNICS
CUTLER	CYANIDED	CYCLASE*	CYGNETS	CYNOMOLGI
CUTLERIES	CYANIDES	CYCLASES*	CYLICES	CYNOSURE
CUTLERS	CYANIDING	CYCLE	CYLINDER	CYNOSURES

Words marked with an asterisk are from OTCWL

CYPHER	CYSTEINE	CYSTS	CYTOLOGY	CYTOTOXIN
CYPHERED	CYSTEINES	CYTASE	CYTOLYSES	CYTOTOXINS
CYPHERING	CYSTEINS*	CYTASES	CYTOLYSIN*	CZAPKA
CYPHERS	CYSTIC	CYTASTER*	CYTOLYSINS*	CZAPKAS
CYPRES*	CYSTID	CYTASTERS*	CYTOLYSIS	CZAR
CYPRESES*	CYSTIDEAN	CYTE	CYTOLYTIC*	CZARDAS
CYPRESS	CYSTIDEANS	CYTES	CYTOMETER	CZARDASES
CYPRESSES	CYSTIDS	CYTIDINE*	CYTOMETERS	CZARDOM
CYPRIAN	CYSTIFORM	CYTIDINES*	CYTOMETRIES	CZARDOMS
CYPRIANS	CYSTINE	CYTISI	CYTOMETRY	CZAREVICH
CYPRID	CYSTINES	CYTISINE	CYTON	CZAREVICHES
CYPRIDES	CYSTITIDES*	CYTISINES	CYTONS	CZAREVNA
CYPRIDS	CYSTITIS	CYTISUS	CYTOPENIA	CZAREVNAS
CYPRINE	CYSTITISES	CYTODE	CYTOPENIAS	CZARINA
CYPRINID	CYSTOCARP	CYTODES	CYTOPLASM	CZARINAS
CYPRINIDS	CYSTOCARPS	CYTOGENIES*	CYTOPLASMS	CZARISM
CYPRINOID	CYSTOCELE	CYTOGENY*	CYTOSINE	CZARISMS
CYPRIS	CYSTOCELES	CYTOID	CYTOSINES	CZARIST
CYPRUS	CYSTOID	CYTOKINE	CYTOSOL*	CZARISTS
CYPRUSES	CYSTOIDS	CYTOKINES	CYTOSOLIC*	CZARITSA
CYPSELA	CYSTOLITH	CYTOKININ	CYTOSOLS*	CZARITSAS
CYPSELAE	CYSTOLITHS	CYTOKININS	CYTOSOME	CZARITZA*
CYST	CYSTOTOMIES	CYTOLOGIC*	CYTOSOMES	CZARITZAS*
CYSTEIN*	CYSTOTOMY	CYTOLOGIES	CYTOTOXIC	CZARS

D

DA
DAB
DABBED
DABBER
DABBERS
DABBING
DABBITIES
DABBITY
DABBLE
DABBLED
DABBLER
DABBLERS
DABBLES
DABBLING
DABBLINGS
DABCHICK
DABCHICKS
DABS
DABSTER
DABSTERS
DACE
DACES
DACHA
DACHAS
DACHSHUND
DACHSHUNDS
DACITE
DACITES
DACKER
DACKERED
DACKERING
DACKERS
DACOIT
DACOITAGE
DACOITAGES
DACOITIES
DACOITS
DACOITY
DACTYL
DACTYLAR
DACTYLI*
DACTYLIC
DACTYLICS*
DACTYLIST
DACTYLISTS
DACTYLS
DACTYLUS*
DAD
DADA*
DADAISM*
DADAISMS*
DADAIST*
DADAISTIC*
DADAISTS*
DADAS*

DADDED
DADDIES
DADDING
DADDLE
DADDLED
DADDLES
DADDLING
DADDOCK
DADDOCKS
DADDY
DADO
DADOED
DADOES
DADOING
DADOS
DADS
DAE
DAEDAL
DAEDALIAN
DAEDALIC
DAEING
DAEMON
DAEMONIC
DAEMONS
DAES
DAFF
DAFFED
DAFFIER
DAFFIES
DAFFIEST
DAFFILY*
DAFFING
DAFFINGS
DAFFODIL
DAFFODILS
DAFFS
DAFFY
DAFTAR
DAFTARS
DAFTER
DAFTEST
DAFTIE
DAFTIES
DAFTLY
DAFTNESS
DAFTNESSES
DAG
DAGABA
DAGABAS
DAGGA
DAGGAS
DAGGED
DAGGER
DAGGERED*

DAGGERING*
DAGGERS
DAGGIER
DAGGIEST
DAGGING
DAGGINGS
DAGGLE
DAGGLED
DAGGLES
DAGGLING
DAGGY
DAGLOCK
DAGLOCKS
DAGO
DAGOBA
DAGOBAS
DAGOES
DAGOS
DAGS
DAGWOOD
DAGWOODS
DAH
DAHABEAH*
DAHABEAHS*
DAHABEEAH
DAHABEEAHS
DAHABIAH*
DAHABIAHS*
DAHABIEH
DAHABIEHS
DAHABIYA*
DAHABIYAH
DAHABIYAHS
DAHABIYAS*
DAHABIYEH
DAHABIYEHS
DAHL
DAHLIA
DAHLIAS
DAHLS
DAHOON*
DAHOONS*
DAHS
DAIDLE
DAIDLED
DAIDLES
DAIDLING
DAIKER
DAIKERED
DAIKERING
DAIKERS
DAIKON
DAIKONS
DAILIES
DAILINESS*

DAILINESSES*
DAILY
DAIMEN
DAIMIO
DAIMIOS
DAIMON
DAIMONES*
DAIMONIC
DAIMONS
DAIMYO*
DAIMYOS*
DAINE
DAINED
DAINES
DAINING
DAINT
DAINTIER
DAINTIES
DAINTIEST
DAINTILY
DAINTY
DAIQUIRI
DAIQUIRIS
DAIRIES
DAIRY
DAIRYING
DAIRYINGS
DAIRYMAID
DAIRYMAIDS
DAIRYMAN
DAIRYMEN
DAIS
DAISES
DAISHIKI*
DAISHIKIS*
DAISIED
DAISIES
DAISY
DAK
DAKER
DAKERED
DAKERHEN*
DAKERHENS*
DAKERING
DAKERS
DAKOIT
DAKOITI
DAKOITIES*
DAKOITIS
DAKOITS
DAKOITY*
DAKS
DAL
DALAPON*
DALAPONS*

DALASI*
DALASIS*
DALE
DALEDH*
DALEDHS*
DALES
DALESMAN
DALESMEN
DALETH*
DALETHS*
DALI
DALIS
DALLE
DALLES
DALLIANCE
DALLIANCES
DALLIED
DALLIER
DALLIERS
DALLIES
DALLOP
DALLOPS
DALLY
DALLYING
DALMAHOY
DALMAHOYS
DALMATIAN*
DALMATIANS*
DALMATIC
DALMATICS
DALS
DALT
DALTON
DALTONIC*
DALTONISM
DALTONISMS
DALTONS
DALTS
DAM
DAMAGE
DAMAGED
DAMAGER*
DAMAGERS*
DAMAGES
DAMAGING
DAMAN
DAMANS
DAMAR
DAMARS
DAMASCENE
DAMASCENED
DAMASCENES
DAMASCENING
DAMASCENINGS
DAMASK

DAMASKED	DAMPENED	DANDRUFFS	DANTONING	DARKENING
DAMASKEEN	DAMPENER*	DANDRUFFY*	DANTONS	DARKENS
DAMASKEENED	DAMPENERS*	DANDY	DANTS	DARKER
DAMASKEENING	DAMPENING	DANDYFUNK	DAP	DARKEST
DAMASKEENS	DAMPENS	DANDYFUNKS	DAPHNE	DARKEY
DAMASKIN	DAMPER	DANDYISH	DAPHNES	DARKEYS
DAMASKINED	DAMPERS	DANDYISM	DAPHNIA*	DARKIE
DAMASKING	DAMPEST	DANDYISMS	DAPHNIAS*	DARKIES
DAMASKINING	DAMPIER	DANDYPRAT	DAPHNID	DARKING*
DAMASKINS	DAMPIEST	DANDYPRATS	DAPHNIDS	DARKISH
DAMASKS	DAMPING	DANEGELD	DAPPED	DARKLE
DAMASQUIN	DAMPINGS	DANEGELDS	DAPPER	DARKLED
DAMASQUINED	DAMPISH	DANEGELT	DAPPERER	DARKLES
DAMASQUINING	DAMPLY	DANEGELTS	DAPPEREST	DARKLIER*
DAMASQUINS	DAMPNESS	DANELAGH	DAPPERLY	DARKLIEST*
DAMASSIN	DAMPNESSES	DANELAGHS	DAPPERS	DARKLING
DAMASSINS	DAMPS	DANELAW	DAPPING	DARKLINGS
DAMBOARD	DAMPY	DANELAWS	DAPPLE	DARKLY
DAMBOARDS	DAMS	DANEWEED*	DAPPLED	DARKMANS
DAMBROD	DAMSEL	DANEWEEDS*	DAPPLES	DARKNESS
DAMBRODS	DAMSELFLIES	DANEWORT*	DAPPLING	DARKNESSES
DAME	DAMSELFLY	DANEWORTS*	DAPS	DARKROOM
DAMES	DAMSELS	DANG	DAPSONE	DARKROOMS
DAMEWORT*	DAMSON	DANGED	DAPSONES	DARKS
DAMEWORTS*	DAMSONS	DANGER	DAQUIRI	DARKSOME
DAMFOOL	DAN	DANGERED	DAQUIRIS	DARKY
DAMMAR	DANCE	DANGERING	DARAF	DARLING
DAMMARS	DANCEABLE	DANGEROUS	DARAFS	DARLINGLY*
DAMME	DANCED	DANGERS	DARB*	DARLINGS
DAMMED	DANCER	DANGING	DARBIES	DARN
DAMMER	DANCERS	DANGLE	DARBS*	DARNDEST*
DAMMERS	DANCES	DANGLED	DARCIES	DARNDESTS*
DAMMING	DANCETTE	DANGLER	DARCY	DARNED
DAMMIT	DANCETTEE	DANGLERS	DARCYS	DARNEDER
DAMN	DANCETTES	DANGLES	DARE	DARNEDEST
DAMNABLE	DANCETTY	DANGLIER	DARED	DARNEL
DAMNABLY	DANCING	DANGLIEST	DAREDEVIL*	DARNELS
DAMNATION	DANCINGS	DANGLING	DAREDEVILS*	DARNER
DAMNATIONS	DANDELION	DANGLINGS	DAREFUL	DARNERS
DAMNATORY	DANDELIONS	DANGLY	DARER*	DARNING
DAMNDEST*	DANDER	DANGS	DARERS*	DARNINGS
DAMNDESTS*	DANDERED	DANIO	DARES	DARNS
DAMNED	DANDERING	DANIOS	DARESAY*	DARRAIGN
DAMNEDER	DANDERS	DANISH*	DARG	DARRAIGNE
DAMNEDEST	DANDIACAL	DANK	DARGA	DARRAIGNED
DAMNEDESTS*	DANDIER	DANKER	DARGAS	DARRAIGNES
DAMNER*	DANDIES	DANKEST	DARGLE	DARRAIGNING
DAMNERS*	DANDIEST	DANKISH	DARGLES	DARRAIGNS
DAMNIFIED	DANDIFIED	DANKLY*	DARGS	DARRAIN
DAMNIFIES	DANDIFIES	DANKNESS	DARI	DARRAINE
DAMNIFY	DANDIFY	DANKNESSES	DARIC	DARRAINED
DAMNIFYING	DANDIFYING	DANKS	DARICS	DARRAINES
DAMNING	DANDILY	DANNEBROG	DARING	DARRAINING
DAMNINGLY*	DANDIPRAT	DANNEBROGS	DARINGLY	DARRAINS
DAMNS	DANDIPRATS	DANS	DARINGS	DARRAYN
DAMOISEL	DANDLE	DANSEUR	DARIOLE	DARRAYNED
DAMOISELS	DANDLED	DANSEURS	DARIOLES	DARRAYNING
DAMOSEL	DANDLER	DANSEUSE	DARIS	DARRAYNS
DAMOSELS	DANDLERS	DANSEUSES	DARK	DARRE
DAMOZEL	DANDLES	DANT	DARKED*	DARRED
DAMOZELS	DANDLING	DANTED	DARKEN	DARRES
DAMP	DANDRIFF	DANTING	DARKENED	DARRING
DAMPED	DANDRIFFS	DANTON	DARKENER*	DARSHAN
DAMPEN	DANDRUFF	DANTONED	DARKENERS*	DARSHANS

The Chambers Dictionary is the authority for many longer words; see Introduction, page ix

DART	DATAL	DAUGHTERS	DAWEN*	DAYSMEN
DARTBOARD	DATALLER	DAULT	DAWING	DAYSPRING
DARTBOARDS	DATALLERS	DAULTS	DAWISH	DAYSPRINGS
DARTED	DATALS	DAUNDER	DAWK	DAYSTAR
DARTER	DATARIA	DAUNDERED	DAWKS	DAYSTARS
DARTERS	DATARIAS	DAUNDERING	DAWN	DAYTALE
DARTING	DATARIES	DAUNDERS	DAWNED	DAYTALER
DARTINGLY	DATARY	DAUNER	DAWNER	DAYTALERS
DARTLE	DATCHA*	DAUNERED	DAWNERED	DAYTALES
DARTLED	DATCHAS*	DAUNERING	DAWNERING	DAYTIME
DARTLES	DATE	DAUNERS	DAWNERS	DAYTIMES
DARTLING	DATEABLE	DAUNT	DAWNING	DAYWORK*
DARTRE	DATED	DAUNTED	DAWNINGS	DAYWORKS*
DARTRES	DATEDLY*	DAUNTER	DAWNLIKE*	DAZE
DARTROUS	DATEDNESS*	DAUNTERS	DAWNS	DAZED
DARTS	DATEDNESSES*	DAUNTING	DAWS	DAZEDLY
DARZI	DATELESS	DAUNTLESS	DAWSONITE*	DAZEDNESS*
DARZIS	DATELINE*	DAUNTON	DAWSONITES*	DAZEDNESSES*
DAS	DATELINED*	DAUNTONED	DAWT	DAZER
DASH	DATELINES*	DAUNTONING	DAWTED	DAZERS
DASHBOARD	DATELINING*	DAUNTONS	DAWTIE	DAZES
DASHBOARDS	DATER	DAUNTS	DAWTIES	DAZING
DASHED	DATERS	DAUPHIN	DAWTING	DAZZLE
DASHEEN	DATES	DAUPHINE	DAWTS	DAZZLED
DASHEENS	DATING	DAUPHINES	DAY	DAZZLER
DASHEKI	DATINGS	DAUPHINS	DAYBED*	DAZZLERS
DASHEKIS	DATIVAL	DAUR	DAYBEDS*	DAZZLES
DASHER	DATIVE	DAURED	DAYBOOK*	DAZZLING
DASHERS	DATIVELY*	DAURING	DAYBOOKS*	DAZZLINGS
DASHES	DATIVES	DAURS	DAYBREAK	DE*
DASHI*	DATO*	DAUT	DAYBREAKS	DEACIDIFIED*
DASHIER*	DATOLITE	DAUTED	DAYDREAM	DEACIDIFIES*
DASHIEST*	DATOLITES	DAUTIE	DAYDREAMED	DEACIDIFY*
DASHIKI	DATOS*	DAUTIES	DAYDREAMING	DEACIDIFYING*
DASHIKIS	DATTO*	DAUTING	DAYDREAMS	DEACON
DASHING	DATTOS*	DAUTS	DAYDREAMT	DEACONED*
DASHINGLY	DATUM	DAVEN	DAYFLIES*	DEACONESS
DASHIS*	DATUMS*	DAVENED	DAYFLOWER*	DEACONESSES
DASHPOT*	DATURA	DAVENING	DAYFLOWERS*	DEACONING*
DASHPOTS*	DATURAS	DAVENPORT	DAYFLY*	DEACONRIES
DASHY*	DATURIC*	DAVENPORTS	DAYGLO	DEACONRY
DASSIE	DATURINE	DAVENS	DAYGLOW*	DEACONS
DASSIES	DATURINES	DAVIDIA	DAYGLOWS*	DEAD
DASTARD	DAUB	DAVIDIAS	DAYLIGHT	DEADBEAT*
DASTARDIES	DAUBE	DAVIES*	DAYLIGHTED*	DEADBEATS*
DASTARDLY	DAUBED	DAVIT	DAYLIGHTING*	DEADBOLT*
DASTARDS	DAUBER	DAVITS	DAYLIGHTS	DEADBOLTS*
DASTARDY	DAUBERIES	DAVY*	DAYLILIES*	DEADED
DASYPOD	DAUBERS	DAW	DAYLILY*	DEADEN
DASYPODS	DAUBERY	DAWBRIES	DAYLIT*	DEADENED
DASYURE	DAUBES	DAWBRY	DAYLONG	DEADENER
DASYURES	DAUBIER	DAWCOCK	DAYMARE*	DEADENERS
DATA	DAUBIEST	DAWCOCKS	DAYMARES*	DEADENING
DATABANK	DAUBING	DAWD	DAYMARK	DEADENINGS
DATABANKS	DAUBINGS	DAWDED	DAYMARKS	DEADENS
DATABASE	DAUBRIES*	DAWDING	DAYNT	DEADER
DATABASES	DAUBRY*	DAWDLE	DAYROOM*	DEADERS
DATABLE	DAUBS	DAWDLED	DAYROOMS*	DEADEST
DATABUS	DAUBY	DAWDLER	DAYS	DEADEYE*
DATABUSES	DAUD	DAWDLERS	DAYSACK	DEADEYES*
DATABUSSES	DAUDED	DAWDLES	DAYSACKS	DEADFALL*
DATACOMMS	DAUDING	DAWDLING	DAYSIDE*	DEADFALLS*
DATAGLOVE	DAUDS	DAWDS	DAYSIDES*	DEADHEAD
DATAGLOVES	DAUGHTER	DAWED	DAYSMAN	DEADHEADED

Words marked with an asterisk are from OTCWL

DEADHEADING	DEALING	DEATHLIEST	DEBBY	DEBUGGED
DEADHEADS	DEALINGS	DEATHLIKE	DEBEAK*	DEBUGGER*
DEADHOUSE	DEALS	DEATHLY	DEBEAKED*	DEBUGGERS*
DEADHOUSES	DEALT	DEATHS	DEBEAKING*	DEBUGGING
DEADING	DEAMINASE*	DEATHSMAN	DEBEAKS*	DEBUGS
DEADLIER	DEAMINASES*	DEATHSMEN	DEBEL	DEBUNK
DEADLIEST	DEAMINATE*	DEATHWARD	DEBELLED	DEBUNKED
DEADLIFT*	DEAMINATED*	DEATHWARDS	DEBELLING	DEBUNKER*
DEADLIFTED*	DEAMINATES*	DEATHY	DEBELS	DEBUNKERS*
DEADLIFTING*	DEAMINATING*	DEAVE	DEBENTURE	DEBUNKING
DEADLIFTS*	DEAN	DEAVED	DEBENTURES	DEBUNKS
DEADLIGHT*	DEANED*	DEAVES	DEBILE	DEBUS
DEADLIGHTS*	DEANER	DEAVING	DEBILITIES	DEBUSSED
DEADLINE	DEANERIES	DEAW	DEBILITY	DEBUSSES
DEADLINES	DEANERS	DEAWIE	DEBIT	DEBUSSING
DEADLOCK	DEANERY	DEAWS	DEBITED	DEBUT
DEADLOCKED	DEANING*	DEAWY	DEBITING	DEBUTANT
DEADLOCKING	DEANS	DEB	DEBITOR	DEBUTANTE
DEADLOCKS	DEANSHIP	DEBACLE	DEBITORS	DEBUTANTES
DEADLY	DEANSHIPS	DEBACLES	DEBITS	DEBUTANTS
DEADNESS	DEAR	DEBAG	DEBONAIR	DEBUTED
DEADNESSES	DEARE	DEBAGGED	DEBONE*	DEBUTING
DEADPAN	DEARED	DEBAGGING	DEBONED*	DEBUTS
DEADPANNED*	DEARER	DEBAGGINGS	DEBONER*	DEBYE*
DEADPANNING*	DEARES	DEBAGS	DEBONERS*	DEBYES*
DEADPANS	DEAREST	DEBAR	DEBONES*	DECACHORD
DEADS	DEARIE	DEBARK	DEBONING*	DECACHORDS
DEADSTOCK	DEARIES	DEBARKED	DEBOSH	DECAD
DEADSTOCKS	DEARING	DEBARKING	DEBOSHED	DECADAL
DEADWOOD*	DEARLING	DEBARKS	DEBOSHES	DECADE
DEADWOODS*	DEARLINGS	DEBARMENT	DEBOSHING	DECADENCE
DEAERATE*	DEARLY	DEBARMENTS	DEBOSS	DECADENCES
DEAERATED*	DEARN	DEBARRASS	DEBOSSED	DECADENCIES
DEAERATES*	DEARNESS	DEBARRASSED	DEBOSSES	DECADENCY
DEAERATING*	DEARNESSES	DEBARRASSES	DEBOSSING	DECADENT
DEAERATOR*	DEARNFUL	DEBARRASSING	DEBOUCH	DECADENTS
DEAERATORS*	DEARNLY	DEBARRED	DEBOUCHE	DECADES
DEAF	DEARNS	DEBARRING	DEBOUCHED	DECADS
DEAFEN	DEARTH	DEBARS	DEBOUCHES	DECAF*
DEAFENED	DEARTHS	DEBASE	DEBOUCHING	DECAFF
DEAFENING	DEARY	DEBASED	DEBRIDE	DECAFFS
DEAFENINGS	DEASH*	DEBASER	DEBRIDED	DECAFS*
DEAFENS	DEASHED*	DEBASERS	DEBRIDES	DECAGON
DEAFER	DEASHES*	DEBASES	DEBRIDING	DECAGONAL
DEAFEST	DEASHING*	DEBASING	DEBRIEF	DECAGONS
DEAFISH*	DEASIL	DEBATABLE	DEBRIEFED	DECAGRAM
DEAFLY	DEASILS	DEBATE	DEBRIEFING	DECAGRAMS
DEAFNESS	DEASIUL	DEBATED	DEBRIEFINGS	DECAHEDRA
DEAFNESSES	DEASIULS	DEBATEFUL	DEBRIEFS	DECAHEDRON*
DEAIR*	DEASOIL	DEBATER	DEBRIS	DECAHEDRONS*
DEAIRED*	DEASOILS	DEBATERS	DEBRUISE*	DECAL
DEAIRING*	DEATH	DEBATES	DEBRUISED	DECALCIFIED
DEAIRS*	DEATHBED*	DEBATING	DEBRUISES*	DECALCIFIES
DEAL	DEATHBEDS*	DEBAUCH	DEBRUISING*	DECALCIFY
DEALATE*	DEATHBLOW*	DEBAUCHED	DEBS	DECALCIFYING
DEALATED*	DEATHBLOWS*	DEBAUCHEE	DEBT	DECALITER*
DEALATES*	DEATHCUP*	DEBAUCHEES	DEBTED	DECALITERS*
DEALATION*	DEATHCUPS*	DEBAUCHER	DEBTEE	DECALITRE
DEALATIONS*	DEATHFUL	DEBAUCHERS	DEBTEES	DECALITRES
DEALBATE	DEATHIER	DEBAUCHES	DEBTLESS*	DECALOG*
DEALER	DEATHIEST	DEBAUCHING	DEBTOR	DECALOGS*
DEALERS	DEATHLESS	DEBBIER	DEBTORS	DECALOGUE
DEALFISH	DEATHLIER	DEBBIES	DEBTS	DECALOGUES
DEALFISHES	DEATHLIER	DEBBIEST	DEBUG	DECALS

The Chambers Dictionary is the authority for many longer words; see Introduction, page ix

DECAMETER*	DECEIVER	DECIGRAMS	DECLAIMS	DECOLORED
DECAMETERS*	DECEIVERS	DECILE*	DECLARANT	DECOLORING
DECAMETRE	DECEIVES	DECILES*	DECLARANTS	DECOLORS
DECAMETRES	DECEIVING	DECILITER	DECLARE	DECOLOUR
DECAMP	DECEMVIR	DECILITERS	DECLARED	DECOLOURED
DECAMPED	DECEMVIRI	DECILITRE	DECLARER	DECOLOURING
DECAMPING	DECEMVIRS	DECILITRES	DECLARERS	DECOLOURS
DECAMPS	DECENARIES*	DECILLION	DECLARES	DECOMPLEX
DECANAL	DECENARY*	DECILLIONS	DECLARING	DECOMPOSE
DECANE	DECENCIES	DECIMAL	DECLASS	DECOMPOSED
DECANES	DECENCY	DECIMALLY	DECLASSE	DECOMPOSES
DECANI	DECENNARIES	DECIMALS	DECLASSED	DECOMPOSING
DECANT	DECENNARY	DECIMATE	DECLASSEE	DECONGEST
DECANTATE	DECENNIA	DECIMATED	DECLASSES	DECONGESTED
DECANTATED	DECENNIAL	DECIMATES	DECLASSING	DECONGESTING
DECANTATES	DECENNIALS*	DECIMATING	DECLAW*	DECONGESTS
DECANTATING	DECENNIUM	DECIMATOR	DECLAWED*	DECONTROL
DECANTED	DECENNIUMS	DECIMATORS	DECLAWING*	DECONTROLLED
DECANTER	DECENT	DECIME	DECLAWS*	DECONTROLLING
DECANTERS	DECENTER	DECIMES	DECLINAL	DECONTROLS
DECANTING	DECENTERED*	DECIMETER	DECLINANT	DECOR
DECANTS	DECENTERING*	DECIMETERS	DECLINATE	DECORATE
DECAPOD	DECENTERS*	DECIMETRE	DECLINE	DECORATED
DECAPODAL	DECENTEST	DECIMETRES	DECLINED	DECORATES
DECAPODAN	DECENTLY	DECIPHER	DECLINER*	DECORATING
DECAPODANS*	DECENTRE*	DECIPHERED	DECLINERS*	DECORATOR
DECAPODS	DECENTRED*	DECIPHERING	DECLINES	DECORATORS
DECARB	DECENTRES*	DECIPHERS	DECLINING	DECOROUS
DECARBED	DECENTRING*	DECISION	DECLIVITIES	DECORS
DECARBING	DECEPTION	DECISIONED*	DECLIVITY	DECORUM
DECARBS	DECEPTIONS	DECISIONING*	DECLIVOUS	DECORUMS
DECARE	DECEPTIVE	DECISIONS	DECLUTCH	DECOS*
DECARES	DECEPTORY	DECISIVE	DECLUTCHED	DECOUPAGE
DECASTERE	DECERN	DECISORY	DECLUTCHES	DECOUPAGED*
DECASTERES	DECERNED	DECISTERE	DECLUTCHING	DECOUPAGES
DECASTICH	DECERNING	DECISTERES	DECO	DECOUPAGING*
DECASTICHS	DECERNS	DECK	DECOCT	DECOUPLE
DECASTYLE	DECERTIFIED*	DECKCHAIR	DECOCTED	DECOUPLED
DECASTYLES	DECERTIFIES*	DECKCHAIRS	DECOCTING	DECOUPLES
DECATHLON	DECERTIFY*	DECKED	DECOCTION	DECOUPLING
DECATHLONS	DECERTIFYING*	DECKEL*	DECOCTIONS	DECOUPLINGS
DECAUDATE	DECESSION	DECKELS*	DECOCTIVE	DECOY
DECAUDATED	DECESSIONS	DECKER	DECOCTS	DECOYED
DECAUDATES	DECHEANCE	DECKERS	DECOCTURE	DECOYER*
DECAUDATING	DECHEANCES	DECKHAND*	DECOCTURES	DECOYERS*
DECAY	DECIARE	DECKHANDS*	DECODE	DECOYING
DECAYED	DECIARES	DECKHOUSE	DECODED	DECOYS
DECAYER*	DECIBEL	DECKHOUSES	DECODER	DECREASE
DECAYERS*	DECIBELS	DECKING	DECODERS	DECREASED
DECAYING	DECIDABLE	DECKINGS	DECODES	DECREASES
DECAYS	DECIDE	DECKLE	DECODING	DECREASING
DECCIE	DECIDED	DECKLED	DECOHERER	DECREE
DECCIES	DECIDEDLY	DECKLES	DECOHERERS	DECREED
DECEASE	DECIDER	DECKO	DECOKE	DECREEING
DECEASED	DECIDERS	DECKOED	DECOKED	DECREER*
DECEASES	DECIDES	DECKOING	DECOKES	DECREERS*
DECEASING	DECIDING	DECKOS	DECOKING	DECREES
DECEDENT	DECIDUA	DECKS	DECOLLATE	DECREET
DECEDENTS	DECIDUAE	DECLAIM	DECOLLATED	DECREETS
DECEIT	DECIDUAL	DECLAIMED	DECOLLATES	DECREMENT
DECEITFUL	DECIDUAS	DECLAIMER	DECOLLATING	DECREMENTED
DECEITS	DECIDUATE	DECLAIMERS	DECOLLETE	DECREMENTING
DECEIVE	DECIDUOUS	DECLAIMING	DECOLLETES*	DECREMENTS
DECEIVED	DECIGRAM	DECLAIMINGS	DECOLOR	DECREPIT

Words marked with an asterisk are from OTCWL

DECRETAL	DEDICATES	DEERBERRIES	DEFAULTER	DEFERRING
DECRETALS	DEDICATING	DEERBERRY	DEFAULTERS	DEFERS
DECRETIST	DEDICATOR	DEERE	DEFAULTING	DEFFER
DECRETISTS	DEDICATORS	DEERFLIES*	DEFAULTS	DEFFEST
DECRETIVE	DEDIMUS	DEERFLY*	DEFEAT	DEFFLY
DECRETORY	DEDIMUSES	DEERHORN	DEFEATED	DEFI*
DECREW	DEDUCE	DEERHORNS	DEFEATER*	DEFIANCE
DECREWED	DEDUCED	DEERHOUND*	DEFEATERS*	DEFIANCES
DECREWING	DEDUCES	DEERHOUNDS*	DEFEATING	DEFIANT
DECREWS	DEDUCIBLE	DEERLET	DEFEATISM	DEFIANTLY
DECRIAL	DEDUCING	DEERLETS	DEFEATISMS	DEFICIENT
DECRIALS	DEDUCT	DEERLIKE*	DEFEATIST	DEFICIENTS
DECRIED	DEDUCTED	DEERS*	DEFEATISTS	DEFICIT
DECRIER	DEDUCTING	DEERSKIN	DEFEATS	DEFICITS
DECRIERS	DEDUCTION	DEERSKINS	DEFEATURE	DEFIED
DECRIES	DEDUCTIONS	DEERWEED*	DEFEATURED	DEFIER
DECROWN	DEDUCTIVE	DEERWEEDS*	DEFEATURES	DEFIERS
DECROWNED	DEDUCTS	DEERYARD*	DEFEATURING	DEFIES
DECROWNING	DEE	DEERYARDS*	DEFECATE	DEFILADE
DECROWNS	DEED	DEES	DEFECATED	DEFILADED
DECRY	DEEDED	DEET*	DEFECATES	DEFILADES
DECRYING	DEEDER	DEETS*	DEFECATING	DEFILADING
DECRYPT	DEEDEST	DEEV	DEFECATOR	DEFILE
DECRYPTED	DEEDFUL	DEEVE	DEFECATORS	DEFILED
DECRYPTING	DEEDIER	DEEVED	DEFECT	DEFILER
DECRYPTS	DEEDIEST	DEEVES	DEFECTED	DEFILERS
DECTET	DEEDILY	DEEVING	DEFECTING	DEFILES
DECTETS	DEEDING	DEEVS	DEFECTION	DEFILING
DECUBITI	DEEDLESS	DEEWAN*	DEFECTIONS	DEFINABLE
DECUBITUS	DEEDS	DEEWANS*	DEFECTIVE	DEFINABLY
DECUMAN	DEEDY	DEF	DEFECTIVES	DEFINE
DECUMANS	DEEING	DEFACE	DEFECTOR	DEFINED
DECUMBENT	DEEJAY	DEFACED	DEFECTORS	DEFINER
DECUPLE	DEEJAYED	DEFACER	DEFECTS	DEFINERS
DECUPLED	DEEJAYING	DEFACERS	DEFENCE	DEFINES
DECUPLES	DEEJAYS	DEFACES	DEFENCED	DEFINIENS
DECUPLING	DEEK	DEFACING	DEFENCES	DEFINIENTIA
DECURIA	DEEM	DEFAECATE	DEFEND	DEFINING
DECURIAS	DEEMED	DEFAECATED	DEFENDANT	DEFINITE
DECURIES	DEEMING	DEFAECATES	DEFENDANTS	DEFIS*
DECURION	DEEMS	DEFAECATING	DEFENDED	DEFLATE
DECURIONS	DEEMSTER	DEFALCATE	DEFENDER	DEFLATED
DECURRENT	DEEMSTERS	DEFALCATED	DEFENDERS	DEFLATER
DECURSION	DEEN	DEFALCATES	DEFENDING	DEFLATERS
DECURSIONS	DEENS	DEFALCATING	DEFENDS	DEFLATES
DECURSIVE	DEEP	DEFAME	DEFENSE	DEFLATING
DECURVE	DEEPEN	DEFAMED	DEFENSED*	DEFLATION
DECURVED	DEEPENED	DEFAMER*	DEFENSES	DEFLATIONS
DECURVES	DEEPENER*	DEFAMERS*	DEFENSING*	DEFLATOR
DECURVING	DEEPENERS*	DEFAMES	DEFENSIVE	DEFLATORS
DECURY	DEEPENING	DEFAMING	DEFENSIVES	DEFLEA*
DECUSSATE	DEEPENS	DEFAMINGS	DEFER	DEFLEAED*
DECUSSATED	DEEPER	DEFANG*	DEFERABLE	DEFLEAING*
DECUSSATES	DEEPEST	DEFANGED*	DEFERENCE	DEFLEAS*
DECUSSATING	DEEPFELT	DEFANGING*	DEFERENCES	DEFLECT
DEDAL	DEEPIE	DEFANGS*	DEFERENT	DEFLECTED
DEDALIAN	DEEPIES	DEFAST	DEFERENTS	DEFLECTING
DEDANS	DEEPLY	DEFASTE	DEFERMENT	DEFLECTOR
DEDICANT	DEEPMOST	DEFAT	DEFERMENTS	DEFLECTORS
DEDICANTS	DEEPNESS	DEFATS	DEFERRAL	DEFLECTS
DEDICATE	DEEPNESSES	DEFATTED	DEFERRALS	DEFLEX
DEDICATED	DEEPS	DEFATTING	DEFERRED	DEFLEXED
DEDICATEE	DEEPWATER*	DEFAULT	DEFERRER	DEFLEXES
DEDICATEES	DEER	DEFAULTED	DEFERRERS	DEFLEXING

The Chambers Dictionary is the authority for many longer words; see Introduction, page ix

DEFLEXION	DEFRAUD	DEGASSERS*	DEHORTER	DEJECTA
DEFLEXIONS	DEFRAUDED	DEGASSES	DEHORTERS	DEJECTED
DEFLEXURE	DEFRAUDER	DEGASSING	DEHORTING	DEJECTING
DEFLEXURES	DEFRAUDERS	DEGAUSS	DEHORTS	DEJECTION
DEFLORATE	DEFRAUDING	DEGAUSSED	DEHYDRATE	DEJECTIONS
DEFLORATED	DEFRAUDS	DEGAUSSER*	DEHYDRATED	DEJECTORY
DEFLORATES	DEFRAY	DEGAUSSERS*	DEHYDRATES	DEJECTS
DEFLORATING	DEFRAYAL	DEGAUSSES	DEHYDRATING	DEJEUNE
DEFLOWER	DEFRAYALS	DEGAUSSING	DEI	DEJEUNER
DEFLOWERED	DEFRAYED	DEGENDER	DEICE*	DEJEUNERS
DEFLOWERING	DEFRAYER	DEGENDERED	DEICED*	DEJEUNES
DEFLOWERS	DEFRAYERS	DEGENDERING	DEICER*	DEKAGRAM*
DEFLUENT	DEFRAYING	DEGENDERS	DEICERS*	DEKAGRAMS*
DEFLUXION	DEFRAYS	DEGERM*	DEICES*	DEKALITER*
DEFLUXIONS	DEFREEZE	DEGERMED*	DEICIDAL	DEKALITERS*
DEFOAM*	DEFREEZES	DEGERMING*	DEICIDE	DEKALOGIES
DEFOAMED*	DEFREEZING	DEGERMS*	DEICIDES	DEKALOGY
DEFOAMER*	DEFROCK	DEGLAZE*	DEICING*	DEKAMETER*
DEFOAMERS*	DEFROCKED	DEGLAZED*	DEICTIC	DEKAMETERS*
DEFOAMING*	DEFROCKING	DEGLAZES*	DEICTICS	DEKARE*
DEFOAMS*	DEFROCKS	DEGLAZING*	DEID	DEKARES*
DEFOCUS*	DEFROST	DEGOUT	DEIDER	DEKE*
DEFOCUSED*	DEFROSTED	DEGOUTS	DEIDEST	DEKED*
DEFOCUSES*	DEFROSTER	DEGRADE	DEIDS	DEKES*
DEFOCUSING*	DEFROSTERS	DEGRADED	DEIFIC	DEKING*
DEFOCUSSED*	DEFROSTING	DEGRADER*	DEIFICAL	DEKKO
DEFOCUSSES*	DEFROSTS	DEGRADERS*	DEIFIED	DEKKOED
DEFOCUSSING*	DEFROZE	DEGRADES	DEIFIER	DEKKOING
DEFOG*	DEFROZEN	DEGRADING	DEIFIERS	DEKKOS
DEFOGGED*	DEFT	DEGRAS	DEIFIES	DEL
DEFOGGER*	DEFTER	DEGREASE	DEIFORM	DELAINE
DEFOGGERS*	DEFTEST	DEGREASED	DEIFY	DELAINES
DEFOGGING*	DEFTLY	DEGREASER*	DEIFYING	DELAPSE
DEFOGS*	DEFTNESS	DEGREASERS*	DEIGN	DELAPSED
DEFOLIANT	DEFTNESSES	DEGREASES	DEIGNED	DELAPSES
DEFOLIANTS	DEFUNCT	DEGREASING	DEIGNING	DELAPSING
DEFOLIATE	DEFUNCTS	DEGREE	DEIGNS	DELAPSION
DEFOLIATED	DEFUND*	DEGREED*	DEIL	DELAPSIONS
DEFOLIATES	DEFUNDED*	DEGREES	DEILS	DELATE
DEFOLIATING	DEFUNDING*	DEGUM	DEINOSAUR	DELATED
DEFORCE	DEFUNDS*	DEGUMMED	DEINOSAURS	DELATES
DEFORCED	DEFUSE	DEGUMMING	DEIONIZE*	DELATING
DEFORCES	DEFUSED	DEGUMS	DEIONIZED*	DELATION
DEFORCING	DEFUSES	DEGUST	DEIONIZER*	DELATIONS
DEFOREST	DEFUSING	DEGUSTATE	DEIONIZERS*	DELATOR
DEFORESTED	DEFUZE	DEGUSTATED	DEIONIZES*	DELATORS
DEFORESTING	DEFUZED	DEGUSTATES	DEIONIZING*	DELAY
DEFORESTS	DEFUZES	DEGUSTATING	DEIPAROUS	DELAYED
DEFORM	DEFUZING	DEGUSTED	DEISEAL	DELAYER
DEFORMED	DEFY	DEGUSTING	DEISEALS	DELAYERS
DEFORMER	DEFYING	DEGUSTS	DEISHEAL	DELAYING
DEFORMERS	DEGAGE	DEHISCE	DEISHEALS	DELAYS
DEFORMING	DEGAME*	DEHISCED	DEISM	DELE
DEFORMITIES	DEGAMES*	DEHISCENT	DEISMS	DELEAD*
DEFORMITY	DEGAMI*	DEHISCES	DEIST	DELEADED*
DEFORMS	DEGAMIS*	DEHISCING	DEISTIC	DELEADING*
DEFOUL	DEGARNISH	DEHORN	DEISTICAL	DELEADS*
DEFOULED	DEGARNISHED	DEHORNED	DEISTS	DELEAVE*
DEFOULING	DEGARNISHES	DEHORNER	DEITIES	DELEAVED*
DEFOULS	DEGARNISHING	DEHORNERS	DEITY	DELEAVES*
DEFRAG	DEGAS	DEHORNING	DEIXES	DELEAVING*
DEFRAGGED	DEGASES*	DEHORNS	DEIXIS	DELEBLE
DEFRAGGING	DEGASSED	DEHORT	DEIXISES*	DELED
DEFRAGS	DEGASSER*	DEHORTED	DEJECT	DELEGABLE

DELEGACIES	DELIRIA	DELUSION	DEMEANED	DEMISES
DELEGACY	DELIRIANT	DELUSIONS	DEMEANES	DEMISING
DELEGATE	DELIRIOUS	DELUSIVE	DEMEANING	DEMISS
DELEGATED	DELIRIUM	DELUSORY	DEMEANOR	DEMISSION
DELEGATEE*	DELIRIUMS	DELUSTER*	DEMEANORS	DEMISSIONS
DELEGATEES*	DELIS	DELUSTERED*	DEMEANOUR	DEMISSIVE
DELEGATES	DELIST*	DELUSTERING*	DEMEANOURS	DEMISSLY
DELEGATING	DELISTED*	DELUSTERS*	DEMEANS	DEMIST
DELEGATOR*	DELISTING*	DELUXE*	DEMENT	DEMISTED
DELEGATORS*	DELISTS*	DELVE	DEMENTATE	DEMISTER
DELEING	DELIVER	DELVED	DEMENTATED	DEMISTERS
DELENDA	DELIVERED	DELVER	DEMENTATES	DEMISTING
DELES	DELIVERER	DELVERS	DEMENTATING	DEMISTS
DELETE	DELIVERERS	DELVES	DEMENTED	DEMIT
DELETED	DELIVERIES	DELVING	DEMENTI	DEMITASSE
DELETES	DELIVERING	DEMAGOG*	DEMENTIA	DEMITASSES
DELETING	DELIVERLY	DEMAGOGED*	DEMENTIAL*	DEMITS
DELETION	DELIVERS	DEMAGOGIC	DEMENTIAS	DEMITTED
DELETIONS	DELIVERY	DEMAGOGIES	DEMENTING	DEMITTING
DELETIVE	DELL	DEMAGOGING*	DEMENTIS	DEMIURGE
DELETORY	DELLIES*	DEMAGOGS*	DEMENTS	DEMIURGES
DELF	DELLS	DEMAGOGUE	DEMERARA	DEMIURGIC
DELFS	DELLY*	DEMAGOGUED*	DEMERARAS	DEMIURGUS
DELFT	DELOPE	DEMAGOGUES	DEMERGE	DEMIURGUSES
DELFTS	DELOPED	DEMAGOGUING*	DEMERGED	DEMIVOLT*
DELFTWARE*	DELOPES	DEMAGOGY	DEMERGER	DEMIVOLTS*
DELFTWARES*	DELOPING	DEMAIN	DEMERGERED*	DEMIWORLD*
DELI	DELOUSE	DEMAINE	DEMERGERING*	DEMIWORLDS*
DELIBATE	DELOUSED	DEMAINES	DEMERGERS	DEMO
DELIBATED	DELOUSER*	DEMAINS	DEMERGES	DEMOB
DELIBATES	DELOUSERS*	DEMAN	DEMERGING	DEMOBBED
DELIBATING	DELOUSES	DEMAND	DEMERIT	DEMOBBING
DELIBLE	DELOUSING	DEMANDANT	DEMERITED*	DEMOBS
DELICACIES	DELPH	DEMANDANTS	DEMERITING*	DEMOCRACIES
DELICACY	DELPHIC	DEMANDED	DEMERITS	DEMOCRACY
DELICATE	DELPHIN	DEMANDER	DEMERSAL	DEMOCRAT
DELICATES	DELPHINIA	DEMANDERS	DEMERSE	DEMOCRATIES
DELICE	DELPHS	DEMANDING	DEMERSED	DEMOCRATS
DELICES	DELS	DEMANDS	DEMERSES	DEMOCRATY
DELICIOUS	DELT	DEMANNED	DEMERSING	DEMODE
DELICT	DELTA	DEMANNING	DEMERSION	DEMODED
DELICTS	DELTAIC	DEMANNINGS	DEMERSIONS	DEMOLISH
DELIGHT	DELTAS	DEMANS	DEMES	DEMOLISHED
DELIGHTED	DELTIC*	DEMANTOID*	DEMESNE	DEMOLISHES
DELIGHTER*	DELTOID	DEMANTOIDS*	DEMESNES	DEMOLISHING
DELIGHTERS*	DELTOIDEI*	DEMARCATE	DEMETON*	DEMOLOGIES
DELIGHTING	DELTOIDEUS*	DEMARCATED	DEMETONS*	DEMOLOGY
DELIGHTS	DELTOIDS	DEMARCATES	DEMIC	DEMON
DELIME*	DELTS	DEMARCATING	DEMIES	DEMONESS
DELIMED*	DELUBRUM	DEMARCHE	DEMIGOD	DEMONESSES
DELIMES*	DELUBRUMS	DEMARCHES	DEMIGODS	DEMONIAC
DELIMING*	DELUDABLE	DEMARK	DEMIJOHN	DEMONIACS
DELIMIT	DELUDE	DEMARKED	DEMIJOHNS	DEMONIAN
DELIMITED	DELUDED	DEMARKING	DEMILUNE*	DEMONIC
DELIMITER	DELUDER	DEMARKS	DEMILUNES*	DEMONICAL*
DELIMITERS	DELUDERS	DEMAST*	DEMIMONDE*	DEMONISE
DELIMITING	DELUDES	DEMASTED*	DEMIMONDES*	DEMONISED
DELIMITS	DELUDING	DEMASTING*	DEMIPIQUE	DEMONISES
DELINEATE	DELUGE	DEMASTS*	DEMIPIQUES	DEMONISING
DELINEATED	DELUGED	DEMAYNE	DEMIREP	DEMONISM
DELINEATES	DELUGES	DEMAYNES	DEMIREPS	DEMONISMS
DELINEATING	DELUGING	DEME	DEMISABLE	DEMONIST
DELIQUIUM	DELUNDUNG	DEMEAN	DEMISE	DEMONISTS
DELIQUIUMS	DELUNDUNGS	DEMEANE	DEMISED	DEMONIZE

DEMONIZED	DENAY	DENOTES	DENTOID	DEPARTEE*
DEMONIZES	DENAYED	DENOTING	DENTS	DEPARTEES*
DEMONIZING	DENAYING	DENOTIVE*	DENTULOUS*	DEPARTER
DEMONRIES	DENAYS	DENOUNCE	DENTURAL*	DEPARTERS
DEMONRY	DENAZIFIED	DENOUNCED	DENTURE	DEPARTING
DEMONS	DENAZIFIES	DENOUNCER	DENTURES	DEPARTINGS
DEMOS	DENAZIFY	DENOUNCERS	DENTURIST*	DEPARTS
DEMOSES	DENAZIFYING	DENOUNCES	DENTURISTS*	DEPARTURE
DEMOTE	DENDRITE	DENOUNCING	DENUDATE	DEPARTURES
DEMOTED	DENDRITES	DENS	DENUDATED	DEPASTURE
DEMOTES	DENDRITIC	DENSE	DENUDATES	DEPASTURED
DEMOTIC	DENDROID	DENSELY	DENUDATING	DEPASTURES
DEMOTICS*	DENDRON	DENSENESS	DENUDE	DEPASTURING
DEMOTING	DENDRONS	DENSENESSES	DENUDED	DEPECHE
DEMOTION	DENE	DENSER	DENUDER*	DEPECHES
DEMOTIONS	DENERVATE*	DENSEST	DENUDERS*	DEPEINCT
DEMOTIST	DENERVATED*	DENSIFIED	DENUDES	DEPEINCTED
DEMOTISTS	DENERVATES*	DENSIFIER	DENUDING	DEPEINCTING
DEMOUNT	DENERVATING*	DENSIFIERS	DENY	DEPEINCTS
DEMOUNTED	DENES	DENSIFIES	DENYING	DEPEND
DEMOUNTING	DENET	DENSIFY	DENYINGLY	DEPENDANT
DEMOUNTS	DENETS	DENSIFYING	DEODAND	DEPENDANTS
DEMPSTER	DENETTED	DENSITIES	DEODANDS	DEPENDED
DEMPSTERS	DENETTING	DENSITY	DEODAR	DEPENDENT
DEMPT	DENGUE	DENT	DEODARA*	DEPENDENTS
DEMULCENT	DENGUES	DENTAL	DEODARAS*	DEPENDING
DEMULCENTS	DENIABLE	DENTALIA	DEODARS	DEPENDS
DEMULSIFIED	DENIABLY	DENTALIUM	DEODATE	DEPERM*
DEMULSIFIES	DENIAL	DENTALIUMS	DEODATES	DEPERMED*
DEMULSIFY	DENIALS	DENTALLY*	DEODORANT	DEPERMING*
DEMULSIFYING	DENIED	DENTALS	DEODORANTS	DEPERMS*
DEMUR	DENIER	DENTARIA	DEODORISE	DEPICT
DEMURE	DENIERS	DENTARIAS	DEODORISED	DEPICTED
DEMURED	DENIES	DENTARIES	DEODORISES	DEPICTER
DEMURELY	DENIGRATE	DENTARY	DEODORISING	DEPICTERS
DEMURER	DENIGRATED	DENTATE	DEODORIZE	DEPICTING
DEMURES	DENIGRATES	DENTATED	DEODORIZED	DEPICTION
DEMUREST	DENIGRATING	DENTATION	DEODORIZES	DEPICTIONS
DEMURING	DENIM	DENTATIONS	DEODORIZING	DEPICTIVE
DEMURRAGE	DENIMS	DENTED	DEONTIC	DEPICTOR
DEMURRAGES	DENITRATE	DENTEL	DEONTICS	DEPICTORS
DEMURRAL	DENITRATED	DENTELLE	DEORBIT*	DEPICTS
DEMURRALS	DENITRATES	DENTELLES	DEORBITED*	DEPICTURE
DEMURRED	DENITRATING	DENTELS	DEORBITING*	DEPICTURED
DEMURRER	DENITRIFIED	DENTEX	DEORBITS*	DEPICTURES
DEMURRERS	DENITRIFIES	DENTEXES	DEOXIDATE	DEPICTURING
DEMURRING	DENITRIFY	DENTICLE	DEOXIDATED	DEPILATE
DEMURS	DENITRIFYING	DENTICLES	DEOXIDATES	DEPILATED
DEMY	DENIZEN	DENTIFORM	DEOXIDATING	DEPILATES
DEMYSHIP	DENIZENED	DENTIL	DEOXIDISE	DEPILATING
DEMYSHIPS	DENIZENING	DENTILED*	DEOXIDISED	DEPILATOR
DEMYSTIFIED	DENIZENS	DENTILS	DEOXIDISES	DEPILATORS
DEMYSTIFIES	DENNED	DENTIN	DEOXIDISING	DEPLANE
DEMYSTIFY	DENNET	DENTINAL*	DEOXIDIZE	DEPLANED
DEMYSTIFYING	DENNETS	DENTINE	DEOXIDIZED	DEPLANES
DEN	DENNING	DENTINES	DEOXIDIZES	DEPLANING
DENARIES	DENOMINAL*	DENTING	DEOXIDIZING	DEPLETE
DENARII	DENOTABLE	DENTINS	DEOXY*	DEPLETED
DENARIUS	DENOTATE	DENTIST	DEPAINT	DEPLETES
DENARY	DENOTATED	DENTISTRIES	DEPAINTED	DEPLETING
DENATURE	DENOTATES	DENTISTRY	DEPAINTING	DEPLETION
DENATURED	DENOTATING	DENTISTS	DEPAINTS	DEPLETIONS
DENATURES	DENOTE	DENTITION	DEPART	DEPLETIVE
DENATURING	DENOTED	DENTITIONS	DEPARTED	DEPLETORY

Words marked with an asterisk are from OTCWL

DEPLORE
DEPLORED
DEPLORER*
DEPLORERS*
DEPLORES
DEPLORING
DEPLOY
DEPLOYED
DEPLOYING
DEPLOYS
DEPLUME
DEPLUMED
DEPLUMES
DEPLUMING
DEPOLISH*
DEPOLISHED*
DEPOLISHES*
DEPOLISHING*
DEPONE
DEPONED
DEPONENT
DEPONENTS
DEPONES
DEPONING
DEPORT
DEPORTED
DEPORTEE
DEPORTEES
DEPORTING
DEPORTS
DEPOSABLE
DEPOSAL
DEPOSALS
DEPOSE
DEPOSED
DEPOSER
DEPOSERS
DEPOSES
DEPOSING
DEPOSIT
DEPOSITED
DEPOSITING
DEPOSITOR
DEPOSITORS
DEPOSITS
DEPOT
DEPOTS
DEPRAVE
DEPRAVED
DEPRAVER*
DEPRAVERS*
DEPRAVES
DEPRAVING
DEPRAVITIES
DEPRAVITY
DEPRECATE
DEPRECATED
DEPRECATES
DEPRECATING
DEPREDATE
DEPREDATED
DEPREDATES
DEPREDATING
DEPREHEND

DEPREHENDED
DEPREHENDING
DEPREHENDS
DEPRESS
DEPRESSED
DEPRESSES
DEPRESSING
DEPRESSOR
DEPRESSORS
DEPRIVAL
DEPRIVALS
DEPRIVE
DEPRIVED
DEPRIVER*
DEPRIVERS*
DEPRIVES
DEPRIVING
DEPROGRAM
DEPROGRAMED*
DEPROGRAMING*
DEPROGRAMMED
DEPROGRAMMING
DEPROGRAMS
DEPSIDE
DEPSIDES
DEPTH
DEPTHLESS
DEPTHS
DEPURANT
DEPURANTS
DEPURATE
DEPURATED
DEPURATES
DEPURATING
DEPURATOR
DEPURATORS
DEPUTE
DEPUTED
DEPUTES
DEPUTIES
DEPUTING
DEPUTISE
DEPUTISED
DEPUTISES
DEPUTISING
DEPUTIZE
DEPUTIZED
DEPUTIZES
DEPUTIZING
DEPUTY
DERACINE
DERAIGN
DERAIGNED
DERAIGNING
DERAIGNS
DERAIL
DERAILED
DERAILER
DERAILERS
DERAILING
DERAILS
DERANGE
DERANGED
DERANGES

DERANGING
DERAT*
DERATE
DERATED
DERATES
DERATING
DERATINGS
DERATION
DERATIONED
DERATIONING
DERATIONS
DERATS*
DERATTED*
DERATTING*
DERAY
DERAYED
DERAYING
DERAYS
DERBIES
DERBY
DERE
DERED
DERELICT
DERELICTS
DEREPRESS*
DEREPRESSED*
DEREPRESSES*
DEREPRESSING*
DERES
DERHAM
DERHAMS
DERIDE
DERIDED
DERIDER
DERIDERS
DERIDES
DERIDING
DERIG
DERIGGED
DERIGGING
DERIGS
DERING
DERINGER*
DERINGERS*
DERISIBLE
DERISION
DERISIONS
DERISIVE
DERISORY
DERIVABLE
DERIVABLY
DERIVATE
DERIVATES
DERIVE
DERIVED
DERIVER*
DERIVERS*
DERIVES
DERIVING
DERM
DERMA
DERMAL
DERMAS
DERMATIC

DERMATOID
DERMATOME
DERMATOMES
DERMESTID*
DERMESTIDS*
DERMIC
DERMIS
DERMISES
DERMOID
DERMOIDS
DERMS
DERN
DERNFUL
DERNIER
DERNLY
DERNS
DEROGATE
DEROGATED
DEROGATES
DEROGATING
DERRICK
DERRICKED
DERRICKING
DERRICKS
DERRIERE
DERRIERES
DERRIES
DERRINGER
DERRINGERS
DERRIS
DERRISES
DERRY
DERTH
DERTHS
DERV
DERVISH
DERVISHES
DERVS
DESALT
DESALTED
DESALTER*
DESALTERS*
DESALTING
DESALTINGS
DESALTS
DESAND*
DESANDED*
DESANDING*
DESANDS*
DESCALE
DESCALED
DESCALES
DESCALING
DESCANT
DESCANTED
DESCANTING
DESCANTS
DESCEND
DESCENDED
DESCENDER
DESCENDERS
DESCENDING
DESCENDINGS
DESCENDS

DESCENT
DESCENTS
DESCHOOL
DESCHOOLED
DESCHOOLING
DESCHOOLINGS
DESCHOOLS
DESCRIBE
DESCRIBED
DESCRIBER
DESCRIBERS
DESCRIBES
DESCRIBING
DESCRIED
DESCRIER*
DESCRIERS*
DESCRIES
DESCRIVE
DESCRIVED
DESCRIVES
DESCRIVING
DESCRY
DESCRYING
DESECRATE
DESECRATED
DESECRATES
DESECRATING
DESELECT
DESELECTED
DESELECTING
DESELECTS
DESERT
DESERTED
DESERTER
DESERTERS
DESERTIC*
DESERTING
DESERTION
DESERTIONS
DESERTS
DESERVE
DESERVED
DESERVER
DESERVERS
DESERVES
DESERVING
DESERVINGS*
DESEX
DESEXED
DESEXES
DESEXING
DESICCANT
DESICCANTS
DESICCATE
DESICCATED
DESICCATES
DESICCATING
DESIGN
DESIGNATE
DESIGNATED
DESIGNATES
DESIGNATING
DESIGNED
DESIGNEE*

DESIGNEES*	DESOLATORS	DESTAINING*	DETAILS	DETESTED
DESIGNER	DESORB	DESTAINS*	DETAIN	DETESTER*
DESIGNERS	DESORBED	DESTEMPER	DETAINED	DETESTERS*
DESIGNFUL	DESORBING	DESTEMPERED	DETAINEE	DETESTING
DESIGNING	DESORBS	DESTEMPERING	DETAINEES	DETESTS
DESIGNINGS	DESOXY*	DESTEMPERS	DETAINER	DETHRONE
DESIGNS	DESPAIR	DESTINATE	DETAINERS	DETHRONED
DESILVER	DESPAIRED	DESTINATED	DETAINING	DETHRONER
DESILVERED	DESPAIRER*	DESTINATES	DETAINS	DETHRONERS
DESILVERING	DESPAIRERS*	DESTINATING	DETASSEL*	DETHRONES
DESILVERS	DESPAIRING	DESTINE	DETASSELED*	DETHRONING
DESINE	DESPAIRS	DESTINED	DETASSELING*	DETHRONINGS
DESINED	DESPATCH	DESTINES	DETASSELLED*	DETICK*
DESINENCE	DESPATCHED	DESTINIES	DETASSELLING*	DETICKED*
DESINENCES	DESPATCHES	DESTINING	DETASSELS*	DETICKER*
DESINENT	DESPATCHING	DESTINY	DETECT	DETICKERS*
DESINES	DESPERADO	DESTITUTE	DETECTED	DETICKING*
DESINING	DESPERADOES	DESTITUTED	DETECTER*	DETICKS*
DESIPIENT	DESPERADOS	DESTITUTES	DETECTERS*	DETINUE
DESIRABLE	DESPERATE	DESTITUTING	DETECTING	DETINUES
DESIRABLES	DESPIGHT	DESTRIER	DETECTION	DETONABLE*
DESIRABLY	DESPIGHTS	DESTRIERS	DETECTIONS	DETONATE
DESIRE	DESPISAL	DESTROY	DETECTIVE	DETONATED
DESIRED	DESPISALS	DESTROYED	DETECTIVES	DETONATES
DESIRER	DESPISE	DESTROYER	DETECTOR	DETONATING
DESIRERS	DESPISED	DESTROYERS	DETECTORS	DETONATOR
DESIRES	DESPISER	DESTROYING	DETECTS	DETONATORS
DESIRING	DESPISERS	DESTROYS	DETENT	DETORSION
DESIROUS	DESPISES	DESTRUCT	DETENTE	DETORSIONS
DESIST	DESPISING	DESTRUCTED	DETENTES	DETORT
DESISTED	DESPITE	DESTRUCTING	DETENTION	DETORTED
DESISTING	DESPITED*	DESTRUCTS	DETENTIONS	DETORTING
DESISTS	DESPITES	DESUETUDE	DETENTS	DETORTION
DESK	DESPITING*	DESUETUDES	DETENU	DETORTIONS
DESKBOUND	DESPOIL	DESUGAR*	DETENUE	DETORTS
DESKILL	DESPOILED	DESUGARED*	DETENUES	DETOUR
DESKILLED	DESPOILER	DESUGARING*	DETENUS	DETOURED
DESKILLING	DESPOILERS	DESUGARS*	DETER	DETOURING
DESKILLS	DESPOILING	DESULFUR*	DETERGE	DETOURS
DESKMAN*	DESPOILS	DESULFURED*	DETERGED	DETOX
DESKMEN*	DESPOND	DESULFURING*	DETERGENT	DETOXED
DESKS	DESPONDED	DESULFURS*	DETERGENTS	DETOXES
DESKTOP	DESPONDING	DESULPHUR	DETERGER*	DETOXIFIED
DESKTOPS	DESPONDINGS	DESULPHURED	DETERGERS*	DETOXIFIES
DESMAN	DESPONDS	DESULPHURING	DETERGES	DETOXIFY
DESMANS	DESPOT	DESULPHURS	DETERGING	DETOXIFYING
DESMID	DESPOTAT	DESULTORY	DETERMENT	DETOXING
DESMIDS	DESPOTATE	DESYATIN	DETERMENTS	DETRACT
DESMINE	DESPOTATES	DESYATINS	DETERMINE	DETRACTED
DESMINES	DESPOTATS	DESYNE	DETERMINED	DETRACTING
DESMODIUM	DESPOTIC	DESYNED	DETERMINES	DETRACTINGS
DESMODIUMS	DESPOTISM	DESYNES	DETERMINING	DETRACTOR
DESMOID	DESPOTISMS	DESYNING	DETERRED	DETRACTORS
DESMOIDS	DESPOTS	DETACH	DETERRENT	DETRACTS
DESMOSOME	DESPUMATE	DETACHED	DETERRENTS	DETRAIN
DESMOSOMES	DESPUMATED	DETACHER*	DETERRER*	DETRAINED
DESOEUVRE	DESPUMATES	DETACHERS*	DETERRERS*	DETRAINING
DESOLATE	DESPUMATING	DETACHES	DETERRING	DETRAINS
DESOLATED	DESSE	DETACHING	DETERS	DETRAQUE
DESOLATER	DESSERT	DETAIL	DETERSION	DETRAQUEE
DESOLATERS	DESSERTS	DETAILED	DETERSIONS	DETRAQUEES
DESOLATES	DESSES	DETAILER*	DETERSIVE	DETRAQUES
DESOLATING	DESTAIN*	DETAILERS*	DETERSIVES	DETRIMENT
DESOLATOR	DESTAINED*	DETAILING	DETEST	DETRIMENTS

DETRITAL	DEVELLING	DEVIOUSLY	DEWANI	DEXTEROUS
DETRITION	DEVELOP	DEVISABLE	DEWANIS	DEXTERS
DETRITIONS	DEVELOPE	DEVISAL	DEWANNIES	DEXTRAL
LETRITUS	DEVELOPED	DEVISALS	DEWANNY	DEXTRALLY
DETRUDE	DEVELOPER	DEVISE	DEWANS	DEXTRAN
DETRUDED	DEVELOPERS	DEVISED	DEWAR	DEXTRANS
DETRUDES	DEVELOPES	DEVISEE	DEWARS	DEXTRIN
DETRUDING	DEVELOPING	DEVISEES	DEWATER	DEXTRINE
DETRUSION	DEVELOPS	DEVISER	DEWATERED	DEXTRINES
DETRUSIONS	DEVELS	DEVISERS	DEWATERER*	DEXTRINS
DETUNE	DEVERBAL*	DEVISES	DEWATERERS*	DEXTRO*
DETUNED	DEVEST	DEVISING	DEWATERING	DEXTRORSE
DETUNES	DEVESTED	DEVISOR	DEWATERINGS	DEXTROSE
DETUNING	DEVESTING	DEVISORS	DEWATERS	DEXTROSES
DEUCE	DEVESTS	DEVITRIFIED	DEWAX*	DEXTROUS
DEUCED	DEVIANCE	DEVITRIFIES	DEWAXED*	DEXY*
DEUCEDLY	DEVIANCES	DEVITRIFY	DEWAXES*	DEY
DEUCES	DEVIANCIES	DEVITRIFYING	DEWAXING*	DEYS
DEUCING*	DEVIANCY	DEVLING	DEWBERRIES*	DEZINC*
DEUDDARN	DEVIANT	DEVLINGS	DEWBERRY*	DEZINCED*
DEUDDARNS	DEVIANTS	DEVOICE	DEWCLAW*	DEZINCING*
DEUS	DEVIATE .	DEVOICED	DEWCLAWS*	DEZINCKED*
DEUTERATE	DEVIATED	DEVOICES	DEWDROP*	DEZINCKING*
DEUTERATED	DEVIATES	DEVOICING	DEWDROPS*	DEZINCS*
DEUTERATES	DEVIATING	DEVOID	DEWED	DHAK
DEUTERATING	DEVIATION	DEVOIR	DEWFALL*	DHAKS
DEUTERIC*	DEVIATIONS	DEVOIRS	DEWFALLS*	DHAL
DEUTERIDE	DEVIATOR	DEVOLVE	DEWFULL	DHALS
DEUTERIDES	DEVIATORS	DEVOLVED	DEWIER	DHARMA
DEUTERIUM	DEVIATORY	DEVOLVES	DEWIEST	DHARMAS
DEUTERIUMS	DEVICE	DEVOLVING	DEWILY	DHARMIC*
DEUTERON	DEVICEFUL	DEVON*	DEWINESS	DHARMSALA
DEUTERONS	DEVICES	DEVONPORT	DEWINESSES	DHARMSALAS
DEUTON	DEVIL	DEVONPORTS	DEWING	DHARNA
DEUTONS	DEVILDOM	DEVONS*	DEWITT	DHARNAS
DEUTZIA*	DEVILDOMS	DEVORE	DEWITTED	DHOBI
DEUTZIAS*	DEVILED	DEVOT	DEWITTING	DHOBIS
DEV*	DEVILESS	DEVOTE	DEWITTS	DHOL
DEVA	DEVILESSES	DEVOTED	DEWLAP	DHOLE
DEVALL	DEVILET	DEVOTEDLY	DEWLAPPED	DHOLES
DEVALLED	DEVILETS	DEVOTEE	DEWLAPS	DHOLL
DEVALLING	DEVILFISH*	DEVOTEES	DEWLAPT	DHOLLS
DEVALLS	DEVILFISHES*	DEVOTES	DEWLESS*	DHOLS
DEVALUATE	DEVILING	DEVOTING	DEWOOL*	DHOOLIES
DEVALUATED	DEVILINGS	DEVOTION	DEWOOLED*	DHOOLY
DEVALUATES	DEVILISH	DEVOTIONS	DEWOOLING*	DHOORA*
DEVALUATING	DEVILISM	DEVOTS	DEWOOLS*	DHOORAS*
DEVALUE	DEVILISMS	DEVOUR	DEWORM*	DHOOTI
DEVALUED	DEVILKIN	DEVOURED	DEWORMED*	DHOOTIE*
DEVALUES	DEVILKINS	DEVOURER	DEWORMER*	DHOOTIES*
DEVALUING	DEVILLED	DEVOURERS	DEWORMERS*	DHOOTIS
DEVAS	DEVILLING	DEVOURING	DEWORMING*	DHOTI
DEVASTATE	DEVILMENT	DEVOURS	DEWORMS*	DHOTIS
DEVASTATED	DEVILMENTS	DEVOUT	DEWPOINT	DHOURRA*
DEVASTATES	DEVILRIES	DEVOUTER	DEWPOINTS	DHOURRAS*
DEVASTATING	DEVILRY	DEVOUTEST	DEWS	DHOW
DEVEIN*	DEVILS	DEVOUTLY	DEWY	DHOWS
DEVEINED*	DEVILSHIP	DEVS*	DEX*	DHURNA*
DEVEINING*	DEVILSHIPS	DEVVEL	DEXES*	DHURNAS*
DEVEINS*	DEVILTRIES	DEVVELLED	DEXIE*	DHURRA
DEVEL	DEVILTRY	DEVVELLING	DEXIES*	DHURRAS
DEVELED*	DEVILWOOD*	DEVVELS	DEXTER	DHURRIE
DEVELING*	DEVILWOODS*	DEW	DEXTERITIES	DHURRIES
DEVELLED	DEVIOUS	DEWAN	DEXTERITY	DHUTI*

DHUTIS* | DIAGLYPH | DIALOGUES | DIAPHONIES* | DIATHERMIES
DI | DIAGLYPHS | DIALOGUING | DIAPHONY* | DIATHERMY
DIABASE | DIAGNOSE | DIALS | DIAPHRAGM | DIATHESES
DIABASES | DIAGNOSED | DIALYSATE* | DIAPHRAGMS | DIATHESIS
DIABASIC | DIAGNOSES | DIALYSATES* | DIAPHYSES | DIATHETIC
DIABETES | DIAGNOSING | DIALYSE | DIAPHYSIS | DIATOM
DIABETIC | DIAGNOSIS | DIALYSED | DIAPIR | DIATOMIC
DIABETICS | DIAGONAL | DIALYSER | DIAPIRIC | DIATOMIST
DIABLE | DIAGONALS | DIALYSERS | DIAPIRISM | DIATOMISTS
DIABLERIE | DIAGRAM | DIALYSES | DIAPIRISMS | DIATOMITE
DIABLERIES | DIAGRAMED* | DIALYSING | DIAPIRS | DIATOMITES
DIABLERY | DIAGRAMING* | DIALYSIS | DIAPSID* | DIATOMS
DIABLES | DIAGRAMMED* | DIALYTIC | DIAPYESES | DIATONIC
DIABOLIC | DIAGRAMMING* | DIALYZATE* | DIAPYESIS | DIATRETUM
DIABOLISE | DIAGRAMS | DIALYZATES* | DIAPYETIC | DIATRETUMS
DIABOLISED | DIAGRAPH | DIALYZE | DIAPYETICS | DIATRIBE
DIABOLISES | DIAGRAPHS | DIALYZED | DIARCH | DIATRIBES
DIABOLISING | DIAGRID | DIALYZER | DIARCHAL | DIATRON*
DIABOLISM | DIAGRIDS | DIALYZERS | DIARCHIC | DIATRONS*
DIABOLISMS | DIAL | DIALYZES | DIARCHIES | DIATROPIC
DIABOLIST | DIALECT | DIALYZING | DIARCHY | DIAXON
DIABOLISTS | DIALECTAL | DIAMAGNET | DIARIAL | DIAXONS
DIABOLIZE | DIALECTIC | DIAMAGNETS | DIARIAN | DIAZEPAM
DIABOLIZED | DIALECTICS | DIAMANTE | DIARIES | DIAZEPAMS
DIABOLIZES | DIALECTS | DIAMANTES | DIARISE | DIAZEUXES
DIABOLIZING | DIALED | DIAMETER | DIARISED | DIAZEUXIS
DIABOLO | DIALER* | DIAMETERS | DIARISES | DIAZIN*
DIABOLOGIES | DIALERS* | DIAMETRAL | DIARISING | DIAZINE*
DIABOLOGY | DIALING | DIAMETRIC | DIARIST | DIAZINES*
DIABOLOS | DIALINGS* | DIAMIDE* | DIARISTS | DIAZINON*
DIACETYL* | DIALIST | DIAMIDES* | DIARIZE | DIAZINONS*
DIACETYLS* | DIALISTS | DIAMIN* | DIARIZED | DIAZINS*
DIACHRONIES* | DIALLAGE | DIAMINE* | DIARIZES | DIAZO
DIACHRONY* | DIALLAGES | DIAMINES* | DIARIZING | DIAZOES
DIACHYLON | DIALLAGIC | DIAMINS* | DIARRHEA | DIAZOLE*
DIACHYLONS | DIALLED | DIAMOND | DIARRHEAL | DIAZOLES*
DIACHYLUM | DIALLEL* | DIAMONDED | DIARRHEAS | DIAZONIUM*
DIACHYLUMS | DIALLER | DIAMONDING* | DIARRHEIC | DIAZONIUMS*
DIACID | DIALLERS | DIAMONDS | DIARRHOEA | DIAZOS
DIACIDIC* | DIALLING | DIAMYL | DIARRHOEAS | DIAZOTIZE*
DIACIDS* | DIALLINGS | DIANDRIES | DIARY | DIAZOTIZED*
DIACODION | DIALLIST* | DIANDROUS | DIASCOPE | DIAZOTIZES*
DIACODIONS | DIALLISTS* | DIANDRY | DIASCOPES | DIAZOTIZING*
DIACODIUM | DIALOG | DIANODAL | DIASPORA | DIB
DIACODIUMS | DIALOGED | DIANOETIC | DIASPORAS | DIBASIC
DIACONAL | DIALOGER* | DIANTHUS | DIASPORE | DIBBED
DIACONATE | DIALOGERS* | DIANTHUSES | DIASPORES | DIBBER
DIACONATES | DIALOGIC | DIAPASE | DIASTASE | DIBBERS
DIACRITIC | DIALOGING | DIAPASES | DIASTASES | DIBBING
DIACRITICS | DIALOGISE | DIAPASON | DIASTASIC | DIBBLE
DIACT | DIALOGISED | DIAPASONS | DIASTASIS | DIBBLED
DIACTINAL | DIALOGISES | DIAPAUSE | DIASTATIC | DIBBLER
DIACTINE | DIALOGISING | DIAPAUSED* | DIASTEM* | DIBBLERS
DIACTINIC | DIALOGIST | DIAPAUSES | DIASTEMA | DIBBLES
DIADEM | DIALOGISTS | DIAPAUSING* | DIASTEMATA | DIBBLING
DIADEMED | DIALOGITE | DIAPENTE | DIASTEMS* | DIBBS
DIADEMING* | DIALOGITES | DIAPENTES | DIASTER | DIBBUK*
DIADEMS | DIALOGIZE | DIAPER | DIASTERS | DIBBUKIM*
DIADOCHI | DIALOGIZED | DIAPERED | DIASTOLE | DIBBUKS*
DIADROM | DIALOGIZES | DIAPERING | DIASTOLES | DIBBS
DIADROMS | DIALOGIZING | DIAPERINGS | DIASTOLIC | DIBUTYL
DIAERESES | DIALOGS | DIAPERS | DIASTRAL* | DICACIOUS
DIAERESIS | DIALOGUE | DIAPHONE | DIASTYLE | DICACITIES
DIAERETIC* | DIALOGUED | DIAPHONES | DIASTYLES | DICACITY

DICAST	DICKTY	DIDDERING	DIENE	DIFFRACT
DICASTERIES	DICKY	DIDDERS	DIENES	DIFFRACTED
DICASTERY	DICLINIES*	DIDDICOY	DIERESES	DIFFRACTING
DICASTIC	DICLINISM	DIDDICOYS	DIERESIS	DIFFRACTS
DICASTS	DICLINISMS	DIDDIER	DIERETIC*	DIFFUSE
DICE	DICLINOUS	DIDDIES	DIES	DIFFUSED
DICED	DICLINY*	DIDDIEST	DIESEL	DIFFUSELY
DICENTRA	DICOT	DIDDLE	DIESELED*	DIFFUSER
DICENTRAS	DICOTS	DIDDLED	DIESELING*	DIFFUSERS
DICENTRIC*	DICOTYL*	DIDDLER	DIESELINGS*	DIFFUSES
DICENTRICS*	DICOTYLS*	DIDDLERS	DIESELISE	DIFFUSING
DICER	DICROTAL*	DIDDLES	DIESELISED	DIFFUSION
DICERS	DICROTIC	DIDDLEY*	DIESELISES	DIFFUSIONS
DICES	DICROTISM	DIDDLEYS*	DIESELISING	DIFFUSIVE
DICEY	DICROTISMS	DIDDLIES*	DIESELIZE	DIFFUSOR*
DICH	DICROTOUS	DIDDLING	DIESELIZED	DIFFUSORS*
DICHASIA	DICT	DIDDLY*	DIESELIZES	DIG
DICHASIAL	DICTA	DIDDY	DIESELIZING	DIGAMIES
DICHASIUM	DICTATE	DIDELPHIC	DIESELS	DIGAMIST
DICHOGAMIES	DICTATED	DIDELPHID	DIESES	DIGAMISTS
DICHOGAMY	DICTATES	DIDELPHIDS	DIESIS	DIGAMMA
DICHONDRA*	DICTATING	DIDICOI	DIESTER*	DIGAMMAS
DICHONDRAS*	DICTATION	DIDICOIS	DIESTERS*	DIGAMOUS
DICHORD	DICTATIONS	DIDICOY	DIESTOCK*	DIGAMY
DICHORDS	DICTATOR	DIDICOYS	DIESTOCKS*	DIGASTRIC
DICHOTIC*	DICTATORS	DIDIE*	DIESTROUS*	DIGENETIC*
DICHOTOMIES	DICTATORY	DIDIES*	DIESTRUM*	DIGEST
DICHOTOMY	DICTATRIX	DIDO	DIESTRUMS*	DIGESTED
DICHROIC	DICTATRIXES	DIDOES	DIESTRUS	DIGESTER
DICHROISM	DICTATURE	DIDOS	DIESTRUSES	DIGESTERS
DICHROISMS	DICTATURES	DIDRACHM	DIET	DIGESTING
DICHROITE	DICTED	DIDRACHMA	DIETARIAN	DIGESTION
DICHROITES	DICTIER	DIDRACHMAS	DIETARIANS	DIGESTIONS
DICHROMAT	DICTIEST	DIDRACHMS	DIETARIES	DIGESTIVE
DICHROMATS	DICTING	DIDST	DIETARILY*	DIGESTIVES
DICHROMIC	DICTION	DIDY*	DIETARY	DIGESTOR*
DICHT	DICTIONAL*	DIDYMIUM	DIETED	DIGESTORS*
DICHTED	DICTIONS	DIDYMIUMS	DIETER	DIGESTS
DICHTING	DICTS	DIDYMOUS	DIETERS	DIGGABLE
DICHTS	DICTUM	DIDYNAMIES*	DIETETIC	DIGGED
DICIER	DICTUMS*	DIDYNAMY*	DIETETICS	DIGGER
DICIEST	DICTY	DIE	DIETHER*	DIGGERS
DICING	DICTYOGEN	DIEB	DIETHERS*	DIGGING
DICINGS	DICTYOGENS	DIEBACK	DIETHYL	DIGGINGS
DICK	DICUMAROL*	DIEBACKS	DIETICIAN	DIGHT
DICKED*	DICUMAROLS*	DIEBS	DIETICIANS	DIGHTED
DICKENS	DICYCLIC	DIECIOUS*	DIETINE	DIGHTING
DICKENSES*	DICYCLIES*	DIED	DIETINES	DIGHTS
DICKER	DICYCLY*	DIEDRAL	DIETING	DIGIT
DICKERED	DID	DIEDRALS	DIETIST	DIGITAL
DICKERING	DIDACT*	DIEDRE	DIETISTS	DIGITALIN
DICKERS	DIDACTIC	DIEDRES	DIETITIAN	DIGITALINS
DICKEY	DIDACTICS	DIEGESES	DIETITIANS	DIGITALIS
DICKEYS	DIDACTS*	DIEGESIS	DIETS	DIGITALISES
DICKHEAD	DIDACTYL	DIEHARD*	DIFFER	DIGITALLY*
DICKHEADS	DIDACTYLS	DIEHARDS*	DIFFERED	DIGITALS
DICKIE	DIDAKAI	DIEING*	DIFFERENT	DIGITATE
DICKIER	DIDAKAIS	DIEL*	DIFFERING	DIGITATED
DICKIES	DIDAKEI	DIELDRIN	DIFFERS	DIGITISE
DICKIEST	DIDAKEIS	DIELDRINS	DIFFICILE	DIGITISED
DICKING*	DIDAPPER	DIELYTRA	DIFFICULT	DIGITISER
DICKS	DIDAPPERS	DIELYTRAS	DIFFIDENT	DIGITISERS
DICKTIER	DIDDER	DIEMAKER*	DIFFLUENT	DIGITISES
DICKTIEST	DIDDERED	DIEMAKERS*	DIFFORM	DIGITISING

The Chambers Dictionary is the authority for many longer words; see Introduction, page ix

DIGITIZE	DILATANCIES	DIM	DIMWITS	DINKIER
DIGITIZED	DILATANCY	DIMBLE	DIMYARIAN	DINKIES
DIGITIZER	DILATANT	DIMBLES	DIN	DINKIEST
DIGITIZERS	DILATANTS*	DIME	DINAR	DINKING
DIGITIZES	DILATATE*	DIMENSION	DINARCHIES	DINKLY*
DIGITIZING	DILATATOR	DIMENSIONED	DINARCHY	DINKS
DIGITONIN*	DILATATORS	DIMENSIONING	DINARS	DINKUM
DIGITONINS*	DILATE	DIMENSIONS	DINDLE	DINKUMS*
DIGITOXIN*	DILATED	DIMER	DINDLED	DINKY
DIGITOXINS*	DILATER	DIMERIC	DINDLES	DINMONT
DIGITS	DILATERS	DIMERISE	DINDLING	DINMONTS
DIGLOT	DILATES	DIMERISED	DINE	DINNED
DIGLOTS	DILATING	DIMERISES	DINED	DINNER
DIGLYPH	DILATION	DIMERISING	DINER	DINNERED
DIGLYPHS	DILATIONS	DIMERISM	DINERIC*	DINNERING
DIGNIFIED	DILATIVE	DIMERISMS	DINERO*	DINNERS
DIGNIFIES	DILATOR	DIMERIZE	DINEROS*	DINNING
DIGNIFY	DILATORS	DIMERIZED	DINERS	DINNLE
DIGNIFYING	DILATORY	DIMERIZES	DINES	DINNLED
DIGNITARIES	DILDO	DIMERIZING	DINETTE	DINNLES
DIGNITARY	DILDOE	DIMEROUS	DINETTES	DINNLING
DIGNITIES	DILDOES	DIMERS	DINFUL	DINO
DIGNITY	DILDOS	DIMES	DING	DINOMANIA
DIGONAL	DILEMMA	DIMETER	DINGBAT	DINOMANIAS
DIGOXIN*	DILEMMAS	DIMETERS	DINGBATS	DINOS
DIGOXINS*	DILEMMIC*	DIMETHYL	DINGDONG*	DINOSAUR
DIGRAPH	DILIGENCE	DIMETHYLS	DINGDONGED*	DINOSAURS
DIGRAPHIC*	DILIGENCES	DIMETRIC	DINGDONGING*	DINOTHERE
DIGRAPHS	DILIGENT	DIMIDIATE	DINGDONGS*	DINOTHERES
DIGRESS	DILL	DIMIDIATED	DINGE	DINS
DIGRESSED	DILLED*	DIMIDIATES	DINGED	DINT
DIGRESSES	DILLI	DIMIDIATING	DINGER	DINTED
DIGRESSING	DILLIER	DIMINISH	DINGERS	DINTING
DIGS	DILLIES	DIMINISHED	DINGES	DINTS
DIGYNIAN	DILLIEST	DIMINISHES	DINGESES	DIOBOL*
DIGYNOUS	DILLING	DIMINISHING	DINGEY	DIOBOLON*
DIHEDRA	DILLINGS	DIMINISHINGS	DINGEYS	DIOBOLONS*
DIHEDRAL	DILLIS	DIMISSORY	DINGHIES	DIOBOLS*
DIHEDRALS	DILLS	DIMITIES	DINGHY	DIOCESAN
DIHEDRON	DILLY	DIMITY	DINGIER	DIOCESANS
DIHEDRONS	DILUENT	DIMLY	DINGIES	DIOCESE
DIHYBRID	DILUENTS	DIMMABLE*	DINGIEST	DIOCESES
DIHYBRIDS	DILUTABLE	DIMMED	DINGILY*	DIODE
DIHYDRIC	DILUTABLES	DIMMER	DINGINESS	DIODES
DIKA	DILUTE	DIMMERS	DINGINESSES	DIOECIES*
DIKAS	DILUTED	DIMMEST	DINGING	DIOECIOUS
DIKAST	DILUTEE	DIMMING	DINGLE	DIOECISM
DIKASTS	DILUTEES	DIMMISH	DINGLES	DIOECISMS
DIKDIK*	DILUTER	DIMNESS	DINGO	DIOECY*
DIKDIKS*	DILUTERS	DIMNESSES	DINGOES	DIOESTRUS
DIKE	DILUTES	DIMORPH	DINGS	DIOESTRUSES
DIKED	DILUTING	DIMORPHIC	DINGUS	DIOICOUS*
DIKER	DILUTION	DIMORPHS	DINGUSES	DIOL*
DIKERS	DILUTIONS	DIMOUT*	DINGY	DIOLEFIN*
DIKES	DILUTIVE*	DIMOUTS*	DINIC	DIOLEFINS*
DIKEY	DILUTOR	DIMPLE	DINICS	DIOLS*
DIKIER	DILUTORS	DIMPLED	DINING	DIOPSIDE
DIKIEST	DILUVIA	DIMPLES	DINITRO*	DIOPSIDES
DIKING	DILUVIAL	DIMPLIER	DINK	DIOPSIDIC*
DIKKOP	DILUVIAN	DIMPLIEST	DINKED	DIOPTASE
DIKKOPS	DILUVION	DIMPLING	DINKER	DIOPTASES
DIKTAT	DILUVIONS	DIMPLY	DINKEST	DIOPTER
DIKTATS	DILUVIUM	DIMS	DINKEY*	DIOPTERS
DILATABLE	DILUVIUMS	DIMWIT	DINKEYS*	DIOPTRAL*

DIOPTRATE	DIPLOMATA*	DIPTEROSES	DIRKES	DISANCHORING
DIOPTRE	DIPLOMATE	DIPTEROUS	DIRKING	DISANCHORS
DIOPTRES	DIPLOMATED	DIPTYCA*	DIRKS	DISANNEX
DIOPTRIC	DIPLOMATES	DIPTYCAS*	DIRL	DISANNEXED
DIOPTRICS	DIPLOMATING	DIPTYCH	DIRLED	DISANNEXES
DIORAMA	DIPLOMATS	DIPTYCHS	DIRLING	DISANNEXING
DIORAMAS	DIPLON	DIQUAT*	DIRLS	DISANNUL
DIORAMIC	DIPLONS	DIQUATS*	DIRNDL	DISANNULLED
DIORISM	DIPLONT	DIRDAM	DIRNDLS	DISANNULLING
DIORISMS	DIPLONTIC*	DIRDAMS	DIRT	DISANNULLINGS
DIORISTIC	DIPLONTS	DIRDUM	DIRTBAG*	DISANNULS
DIORITE	DIPLOPIA	DIRDUMS	DIRTBAGS*	DISANOINT
DIORITES	DIPLOPIAS	DIRE	DIRTED	DISANOINTED
DIORITIC	DIPLOPIC*	DIRECT	DIRTIED	DISANOINTING
DIOSGENIN	DIPLOPOD*	DIRECTED	DIRTIER	DISANOINTS
DIOSGENINS	DIPLOPODS*	DIRECTER	DIRTIES	DISAPPEAR
DIOTA	DIPLOSES*	DIRECTEST	DIRTIEST	DISAPPEARED
DIOTAS	DIPLOSIS*	DIRECTING	DIRTILY	DISAPPEARING
DIOXAN	DIPLOTENE*	DIRECTION	DIRTINESS	DISAPPEARS
DIOXANE	DIPLOTENES*	DIRECTIONS	DIRTINESSES	DISAPPLIED
DIOXANES	DIPLOZOA	DIRECTIVE	DIRTING	DISAPPLIES
DIOXANS	DIPLOZOON	DIRECTIVES	DIRTS	DISAPPLY
DIOXID*	DIPNET*	DIRECTLY	DIRTY	DISAPPLYING
DIOXIDE	DIPNETS*	DIRECTOR	DIRTYING	DISARM
DIOXIDES	DIPNETTED*	DIRECTORIES	DIS*	DISARMED
DIOXIDS*	DIPNETTING*	DIRECTORS	DISA	DISARMER
DIOXIN	DIPNOAN	DIRECTORY	DISABLE	DISARMERS
DIOXINS	DIPNOANS	DIRECTRICES	DISABLED	DISARMING
DIP	DIPNOOUS	DIRECTRIX	DISABLES	DISARMS
DIPCHICK	DIPODIC*	DIRECTRIXES	DISABLING	DISARRAY
DIPCHICKS	DIPODIES	DIRECTS	DISABUSE	DISARRAYED
DIPEPTIDE	DIPODY	DIREFUL	DISABUSED	DISARRAYING
DIPEPTIDES	DIPOLAR	DIREFULLY	DISABUSES	DISARRAYS
DIPHASE*	DIPOLE	DIRELY*	DISABUSING	DISAS
DIPHASIC*	DIPOLES	DIREMPT	DISACCORD	DISASTER
DIPHENYL	DIPPABLE*	DIREMPTED	DISACCORDED	DISASTERS
DIPHENYLS	DIPPED	DIREMPTING	DISACCORDING	DISATTIRE
DIPHONE	DIPPER	DIREMPTS	DISACCORDS	DISATTIRED
DIPHONES	DIPPERFUL*	DIRENESS	DISADORN	DISATTIRES
DIPHTHONG	DIPPERFULS*	DIRENESSES	DISADORNED	DISATTIRING
DIPHTHONGS	DIPPERS	DIRER	DISADORNING	DISATTUNE
DIPHYSITE	DIPPIER	DIREST	DISADORNS	DISATTUNED
DIPHYSITES	DIPPIEST	DIRGE	DISAFFECT	DISATTUNES
DIPLEGIA	DIPPING	DIRGEFUL*	DISAFFECTED	DISATTUNING
DIPLEGIAS	DIPPINGS	DIRGELIKE*	DISAFFECTING	DISAVOUCH
DIPLEX	DIPPY	DIRGES	DISAFFECTS	DISAVOUCHED
DIPLEXER*	DIPS	DIRHAM	DISAFFIRM	DISAVOUCHES
DIPLEXERS*	DIPSADES	DIRHAMS	DISAFFIRMED	DISAVOUCHING
DIPLOE	DIPSAS	DIRHEM	DISAFFIRMING	DISAVOW
DIPLOES	DIPSO	DIRHEMS	DISAFFIRMS	DISAVOWAL
DIPLOGEN	DIPSOS	DIRIGE	DISAGREE	DISAVOWALS
DIPLOGENS	DIPSTICK	DIRIGENT	DISAGREED	DISAVOWED
DIPLOIC*	DIPSTICKS	DIRIGES	DISAGREEING	DISAVOWING
DIPLOID	DIPT*	DIRIGIBLE	DISAGREES	DISAVOWS
DIPLOIDIES	DIPTERA	DIRIGIBLES	DISALLIED	DISBAND
DIPLOIDS*	DIPTERAL	DIRIGISM	DISALLIES	DISBANDED
DIPLOIDY	DIPTERAN	DIRIGISME	DISALLOW	DISBANDING
DIPLOMA	DIPTERANS	DIRIGISMES	DISALLOWED	DISBANDS
DIPLOMACIES	DIPTERAS	DIRIGISMS	DISALLOWING	DISBAR
DIPLOMACY	DIPTERIST	DIRIGISTE	DISALLOWS	DISBARK
DIPLOMAED	DIPTERISTS	DIRIMENT	DISALLY	DISBARKED
DIPLOMAING	DIPTEROI	DIRK	DISALLYING	DISBARKING
DIPLOMAS	DIPTERON*	DIRKE	DISANCHOR	DISBARKS
DIPLOMAT	DIPTEROS	DIRKED	DISANCHORED	DISBARRED

The Chambers Dictionary is the authority for many longer words; see Introduction, page ix

DISBARRING	DISCASED	DISCOLORS	DISCUSS	DISFAVOR
DISBARS	DISCASES	DISCOLOUR	DISCUSSED	DISFAVORED
DISBELIEF	DISCASING	DISCOLOURED	DISCUSSER*	DISFAVORING
DISBELIEFS	DISCED	DISCOLOURING	DISCUSSERS*	DISFAVORS
DISBENCH	DISCEPT	DISCOLOURS	DISCUSSES	DISFAVOUR
DISBENCHED	DISCEPTED	DISCOMFIT	DISCUSSING	DISFAVOURED
DISBENCHES	DISCEPTING	DISCOMFITED	DISDAIN	DISFAVOURING
DISBENCHING	DISCEPTS	DISCOMFITING	DISDAINED	DISFAVOURS
DISBODIED	DISCERN	DISCOMFITS	DISDAINING	DISFIGURE
DISBOSOM	DISCERNED	DISCOMMON	DISDAINS	DISFIGURED
DISBOSOMED	DISCERNER	DISCOMMONED	DISEASE	DISFIGURES
DISBOSOMING	DISCERNERS	DISCOMMONING	DISEASED	DISFIGURING
DISBOSOMS	DISCERNING	DISCOMMONS	DISEASES	DISFLESH
DISBOUND*	DISCERNS	DISCORD	DISEASING	DISFLESHED
DISBOWEL	DISCERP	DISCORDED	DISEDGE	DISFLESHES
DISBOWELED*	DISCERPED	DISCORDING	DISEDGED	DISFLESHING
DISBOWELING*	DISCERPING	DISCORDS	DISEDGES	DISFLUENT
DISBOWELLED	DISCERPS	DISCOS	DISEDGING	DISFOREST
DISBOWELLING	DISCHARGE	DISCOUNT	DISEMBARK	DISFORESTED
DISBOWELS	DISCHARGED	DISCOUNTED	DISEMBARKED	DISFORESTING
DISBRANCH	DISCHARGES	DISCOUNTING	DISEMBARKING	DISFORESTS
DISBRANCHED	DISCHARGING	DISCOUNTS	DISEMBARKS	DISFORM
DISBRANCHES	DISCHURCH	DISCOURE	DISEMBODIED	DISFORMED
DISBRANCHING	DISCHURCHED	DISCOURED	DISEMBODIES	DISFORMING
DISBUD	DISCHURCHES	DISCOURES	DISEMBODY	DISFORMS
DISBUDDED	DISCHURCHING	DISCOURING	DISEMBODYING	DISFROCK
DISBUDDING	DISCI*	DISCOURSE	DISEMPLOY	DISFROCKED
DISBUDS	DISCIDE	DISCOURSED	DISEMPLOYED	DISFROCKING
DISBURDEN	DISCIDED	DISCOURSES	DISEMPLOYING	DISFROCKS
DISBURDENED	DISCIDES	DISCOURSING	DISEMPLOYS	DISGAVEL
DISBURDENING	DISCIDING	DISCOVER	DISENABLE	DISGAVELLED
DISBURDENS	DISCIFORM*	DISCOVERED	DISENABLED	DISGAVELLING
DISBURSAL	DISCINCT	DISCOVERIES	DISENABLES	DISGAVELS
DISBURSALS	DISCING	DISCOVERING	DISENABLING	DISGEST
DISBURSE	DISCIPLE	DISCOVERS	DISENDOW	DISGESTED
DISBURSED	DISCIPLED	DISCOVERT	DISENDOWED	DISGESTING
DISBURSER*	DISCIPLES	DISCOVERY	DISENDOWING	DISGESTS
DISBURSERS*	DISCIPLING	DISCREDIT	DISENDOWS	DISGODDED
DISBURSES	DISCLAIM	DISCREDITED	DISENGAGE	DISGORGE
DISBURSING	DISCLAIMED	DISCREDITING	DISENGAGED	DISGORGED
DISC	DISCLAIMING	DISCREDITS	DISENGAGES	DISGORGES
DISCAGE	DISCLAIMS	DISCREET	DISENGAGING	DISGORGING
DISCAGED	DISCLIKE*	DISCREETER	DISENROL	DISGOWN
DISCAGES	DISCLIMAX*	DISCREETEST	DISENROLLED	DISGOWNED
DISCAGING	DISCLIMAXES*	DISCRETE	DISENROLLING	DISGOWNING
DISCAL	DISCLOSE	DISCRETER	DISENROLS	DISGOWNS
DISCALCED	DISCLOSED	DISCRETEST	DISENTAIL	DISGRACE
DISCANDIE	DISCLOSER*	DISCROWN	DISENTAILED	DISGRACED
DISCANDIED	DISCLOSERS*	DISCROWNED	DISENTAILING	DISGRACER
DISCANDIES	DISCLOSES	DISCROWNING	DISENTAILS	DISGRACERS
DISCANDY	DISCLOSING	DISCROWNS	DISENTOMB	DISGRACES
DISCANDYING	DISCLOST	DISCS	DISENTOMBED	DISGRACING
DISCANDYINGS	DISCO	DISCUMBER	DISENTOMBING	DISGRADE
DISCANT	DISCOBOLI	DISCUMBERED	DISENTOMBS	DISGRADED
DISCANTED	DISCOED	DISCUMBERING	DISESTEEM	DISGRADES
DISCANTING	DISCOER	DISCUMBERS	DISESTEEMED	DISGRADING
DISCANTS	DISCOERS	DISCURE	DISESTEEMING	DISGUISE
DISCARD	DISCOID	DISCURED	DISESTEEMS	DISGUISED
DISCARDED	DISCOIDAL	DISCURES	DISEUR	DISGUISER
DISCARDER*	DISCOIDS*	DISCURING	DISEURS	DISGUISERS
DISCARDERS*	DISCOING	DISCURSUS	DISEUSE	DISGUISES
DISCARDING	DISCOLOR	DISCURSUSES	DISEUSES	DISGUISING
DISCARDS	DISCOLORED	DISCUS	DISFAME	DISGUISINGS
DISCASE	DISCOLORING	DISCUSES	DISFAMES	DISGUST

DISGUSTED
DISGUSTING
DISGUSTS
DISH
DISHABIT
DISHABITED
DISHABITING
DISHABITS
DISHABLE
DISHABLED
DISHABLES
DISHABLING
DISHALLOW
DISHALLOWED
DISHALLOWING
DISHALLOWS
DISHCLOTH*
DISHCLOTHS*
DISHCLOUT*
DISHCLOUTS*
DISHED
DISHELM
DISHELMED
DISHELMING
DISHELMS
DISHERIT
DISHERITED
DISHERITING
DISHERITS
DISHES
DISHEVEL
DISHEVELED*
DISHEVELING*
DISHEVELLED
DISHEVELLING
DISHEVELS
DISHFUL
DISHFULS
DISHIER
DISHIEST
DISHING
DISHINGS
DISHLIKE*
DISHOME
DISHOMED
DISHOMES
DISHOMING
DISHONEST
DISHONOR
DISHONORED
DISHONORING
DISHONORS
DISHONOUR
DISHONOURED
DISHONOURING
DISHONOURS
DISHORN
DISHORNED
DISHORNING
DISHORNS
DISHORSE
DISHORSED
DISHORSES
DISHORSING

DISHOUSE
DISHOUSED
DISHOUSES
DISHOUSING
DISHPAN*
DISHPANS*
DISHRAG*
DISHRAGS*
DISHTOWEL
DISHTOWELS
DISHUMOUR
DISHUMOURED
DISHUMOURING
DISHUMOURS
DISHWARE*
DISHWARES*
DISHWATER
DISHWATERS
DISHY
DISILLUDE
DISILLUDED
DISILLUDES
DISILLUDING
DISIMMURE
DISIMMURED
DISIMMURES
DISIMMURING
DISINFECT
DISINFECTED
DISINFECTING
DISINFECTS
DISINFEST
DISINFESTED
DISINFESTING
DISINFESTS
DISINHUME
DISINHUMED
DISINHUMES
DISINHUMING
DISINTER
DISINTERRED
DISINTERRING
DISINTERS
DISINURE
DISINURED
DISINURES
DISINURING
DISINVEST
DISINVESTED
DISINVESTING
DISINVESTS
DISINVITE*
DISINVITED*
DISINVITES*
DISINVITING*
DISJASKIT
DISJECT
DISJECTED
DISJECTING
DISJECTS
DISJOIN
DISJOINED
DISJOINING
DISJOINS

DISJOINT
DISJOINTED
DISJOINTING
DISJOINTS
DISJUNCT
DISJUNCTS
DISJUNE
DISJUNES
DISK
DISKED
DISKETTE
DISKETTES
DISKING
DISKLESS
DISKLIKE*
DISKS
DISLEAF
DISLEAFED
DISLEAFING
DISLEAFS
DISLEAL
DISLEAVE
DISLEAVED
DISLEAVES
DISLEAVING
DISLIKE
DISLIKED
DISLIKEN
DISLIKENED
DISLIKENING
DISLIKENS
DISLIKER*
DISLIKERS*
DISLIKES
DISLIKING
DISLIMB
DISLIMBED
DISLIMBING
DISLIMBS
DISLIMN
DISLIMNED
DISLIMNING
DISLIMNS
DISLINK
DISLINKED
DISLINKING
DISLINKS
DISLOAD
DISLOADED
DISLOADING
DISLOADS
DISLOCATE
DISLOCATED
DISLOCATES
DISLOCATING
DISLODGE
DISLODGED
DISLODGES
DISLODGING
DISLOIGN
DISLOIGNED
DISLOIGNING
DISLOIGNS
DISLOYAL

DISLUSTRE
DISLUSTRED
DISLUSTRES
DISLUSTRING
DISMAL
DISMALER*
DISMALEST*
DISMALITIES
DISMALITY
DISMALLER
DISMALLEST
DISMALLY
DISMALS
DISMAN
DISMANNED
DISMANNING
DISMANS
DISMANTLE
DISMANTLED
DISMANTLES
DISMANTLING
DISMASK
DISMASKED
DISMASKING
DISMASKS
DISMAST
DISMASTED
DISMASTING
DISMASTS
DISMAY
DISMAYD
DISMAYED
DISMAYFUL
DISMAYING
DISMAYL
DISMAYLED
DISMAYLING
DISMAYLS
DISMAYS
DISME
DISMEMBER
DISMEMBERED
DISMEMBERING
DISMEMBERS
DISMES
DISMISS
DISMISSAL
DISMISSALS
DISMISSED
DISMISSES
DISMISSING
DISMODED
DISMOUNT
DISMOUNTED
DISMOUNTING
DISMOUNTS
DISNEST
DISNESTED
DISNESTING
DISNESTS
DISOBEY
DISOBEYED
DISOBEYER*
DISOBEYERS*

DISOBEYING
DISOBEYS
DISOBLIGE
DISOBLIGED
DISOBLIGES
DISOBLIGING
DISOMIC*
DISORBED
DISORDER
DISORDERED
DISORDERING
DISORDERS
DISORIENT
DISORIENTED
DISORIENTING
DISORIENTS
DISOWN
DISOWNED
DISOWNER
DISOWNERS
DISOWNING
DISOWNS
DISPACE
DISPACED
DISPACES
DISPACING
DISPARAGE
DISPARAGED
DISPARAGES
DISPARAGING
DISPARATE
DISPARATES
DISPARITIES
DISPARITY
DISPARK
DISPARKED
DISPARKING
DISPARKS
DISPART
DISPARTED
DISPARTING
DISPARTS
DISPATCH
DISPATCHED
DISPATCHES
DISPATCHING
DISPATHIES
DISPATHY
DISPAUPER
DISPAUPERED
DISPAUPERING
DISPAUPERS
DISPEACE
DISPEACES
DISPEL
DISPELLED
DISPELLING
DISPELS
DISPENCE
DISPENCED
DISPENCES
DISPENCING
DISPEND
DISPENDED

The Chambers Dictionary is the authority for many longer words; see Introduction, page ix

DISPENDING	DISPONGED	DISPURSES	DISSEATING	DISSING
DISPENDS	DISPONGES	DISPURSING	DISSEATS	DISSIPATE
DISPENSE	DISPONGING	DISPURVEY	DISSECT	DISSIPATED
DISPENSED	DISPONING	DISPURVEYED	DISSECTED	DISSIPATES
DISPENSER	DISPORT	DISPURVEYING	DISSECTING	DISSIPATING
DISPENSERS	DISPORTED	DISPURVEYS	DISSECTINGS	DISSOCIAL
DISPENSES	DISPORTING	DISPUTANT	DISSECTOR	DISSOLUTE
DISPENSING	DISPORTS	DISPUTANTS	DISSECTORS	DISSOLUTES
DISPEOPLE	DISPOSAL	DISPUTE	DISSECTS	DISSOLVE
DISPEOPLED	DISPOSALS	DISPUTED	DISSED	DISSOLVED
DISPEOPLES	DISPOSE	DISPUTER	DISSEISE	DISSOLVER*
DISPEOPLING	DISPOSED	DISPUTERS	DISSEISED	DISSOLVERS*
DISPERSAL	DISPOSER	DISPUTES	DISSEISES	DISSOLVES
DISPERSALS	DISPOSERS	DISPUTING	DISSEISIN	DISSOLVING
DISPERSE	DISPOSES	DISQUIET	DISSEISING	DISSOLVINGS
DISPERSED	DISPOSING	DISQUIETED	DISSEISINS	DISSONANT
DISPERSER	DISPOSINGS	DISQUIETING	DISSEISOR	DISSUADE
DISPERSERS	DISPOST	DISQUIETS	DISSEISORS	DISSUADED
DISPERSES	DISPOSTED	DISRANK	DISSEIZE	DISSUADER
DISPERSING	DISPOSTING	DISRANKED	DISSEIZED	DISSUADERS
DISPIRIT	DISPOSTS	DISRANKING	DISSEIZES	DISSUADES
DISPIRITED	DISPOSURE	DISRANKS	DISSEIZIN	DISSUADING
DISPIRITING	DISPOSURES	DISRATE	DISSEIZING	DISSUNDER
DISPIRITS	DISPRAD	DISRATED	DISSEIZINS	DISSUNDERED
DISPLACE	DISPRAISE	DISRATES	DISSEIZOR	DISSUNDERING
DISPLACED	DISPRAISED	DISRATING	DISSEIZORS	DISSUNDERS
DISPLACES	DISPRAISES	DISREGARD	DISSEMBLE	DISTAFF
DISPLACING	DISPRAISING	DISREGARDED	DISSEMBLED	DISTAFFS
DISPLANT	DISPREAD	DISREGARDING	DISSEMBLES	DISTAIN
DISPLANTED	DISPREADING	DISREGARDS	DISSEMBLIES	DISTAINED
DISPLANTING	DISPREADS	DISRELISH	DISSEMBLING	DISTAINING
DISPLANTS	DISPRED	DISRELISHED	DISSEMBLINGS	DISTAINS
DISPLAY	DISPREDDEN	DISRELISHES	DISSEMBLY	DISTAL
DISPLAYED	DISPREDDING	DISRELISHING	DISSENSUS*	DISTALLY
DISPLAYER	DISPREDS	DISREPAIR	DISSENSUSES*	DISTANCE
DISPLAYERS	DISPRISON	DISREPAIRS	DISSENT	DISTANCED
DISPLAYING	DISPRISONED	DISREPUTES	DISSENTED	DISTANCES
DISPLAYS	DISPRISONING	DISROBE	DISSENTER	DISTANCING
DISPLE	DISPRISONS	DISROBED	DISSENTERS	DISTANT
DISPLEASE	DISPRIZE	DISROBER*	DISSENTING	DISTANTLY
DISPLEASED	DISPRIZED	DISROBERS*	DISSENTS	DISTASTE
DISPLEASES	DISPRIZES	DISROBES	DISSERT	DISTASTED
DISPLEASING	DISPRIZING	DISROBING	DISSERTED	DISTASTES
DISPLED	DISPROFIT	DISROOT	DISSERTING	DISTASTING
DISPLES	DISPROFITS	DISROOTED	DISSERTS	DISTAVES*
DISPLING	DISPROOF	DISROOTING	DISSERVE	DISTEMPER
DISPLODE	DISPROOFS	DISROOTS	DISSERVED	DISTEMPERED
DISPLODED	DISPROOVE	DISRUPT	DISSERVES	DISTEMPERING
DISPLODES	DISPROOVES	DISRUPTED	DISSERVING	DISTEMPERS
DISPLODING	DISPROOVING	DISRUPTER	DISSES	DISTEND
DISPLUME	DISPROVAL	DISRUPTERS	DISSEVER	DISTENDED
DISPLUMED	DISPROVALS	DISRUPTING	DISSEVERED	DISTENDING
DISPLUMES	DISPROVE	DISRUPTOR	DISSEVERING	DISTENDS
DISPLUMING	DISPROVED	DISRUPTORS	DISSEVERS	DISTENT
DISPONDEE	DISPROVEN	DISRUPTS	DISSHIVER	DISTHENE
DISPONDEES	DISPROVES	DISS	DISSHIVERED	DISTHENES
DISPONE	DISPROVING	DISSAVE*	DISSHIVERING	DISTHRONE
DISPONED	DISPUNGE	DISSAVED*	DISSHIVERS	DISTHRONED
DISPONEE	DISPUNGED	DISSAVES*	DISSIDENT	DISTHRONES
DISPONEES	DISPUNGES	DISSAVING	DISSIDENTS	DISTHRONING
DISPONER	DISPUNGING	DISSAVINGS	DISSIGHT	DISTICH
DISPONERS	DISPURSE	DISSEAT	DISSIGHTS	DISTICHAL
DISPONES	DISPURSED	DISSEATED	DISSIMILE	DISTICHS
DISPONGE			DISSIMILES	DISTIL

DISTILL	DISUNITE	DITROCHEE	DIVERGED	DIVINIFYING
DISTILLED	DISUNITED	DITROCHEES	DIVERGENT	DIVINING
DISTILLER	DISUNITES	DITS	DIVERGES	DIVINISE
DISTILLERS	DISUNITIES	DITSIER	DIVERGING	DIVINISED
DISTILLING	DISUNITING	DITSIEST	DIVERS	DIVINISES
DISTILLINGS	DISUNITY	DITSY	DIVERSE	DIVINISING
DISTILLS	DISUSAGE	DITT	DIVERSED	DIVINITIES
DISTILS	DISUSAGES	DITTANDER	DIVERSELY	DIVINITY
DISTINCT	DISUSE	DITTANDERS	DIVERSES	DIVINIZE
DISTINCTER	DISUSED	DITTANIES	DIVERSIFIED	DIVINIZED
DISTINCTEST	DISUSES	DITTANY	DIVERSIFIES	DIVINIZES
DISTINGUE	DISUSING	DITTAY	DIVERSIFY	DIVINIZING
DISTOME*	DISVALUE	DITTAYS	DIVERSIFYING	DIVIS
DISTOMES*	DISVALUED	DITTED	DIVERSING	DIVISIBLE
DISTORT	DISVALUES	DITTIED	DIVERSION	DIVISIBLY
DISTORTED	DISVALUING	DITTIES	DIVERSIONS	DIVISIM
DISTORTER*	DISVOUCH	DITTING	DIVERSITIES	DIVISION
DISTORTERS*	DISVOUCHED	DITTIT	DIVERSITY	DIVISIONS
DISTORTING	DISVOUCHES	DITTO	DIVERSLY	DIVISIVE
DISTORTS	DISVOUCHING	DITTOED	DIVERT	DIVISOR
DISTRACT	DISYOKE	DITTOING	DIVERTED	DIVISORS
DISTRACTED	DISYOKED	DITTOLOGIES	DIVERTER*	DIVORCE
DISTRACTING	DISYOKES	DITTOLOGY	DIVERTERS*	DIVORCED
DISTRACTS	DISYOKING	DITTOS	DIVERTING	DIVORCEE
DISTRAIL	DIT	DITTS	DIVERTIVE	DIVORCEES
DISTRAILS	DITA	DITTY	DIVERTS	DIVORCER
DISTRAIN	DITAL	DITTYING	DIVES	DIVORCERS
DISTRAINED	DITALS	DITZ*	DIVEST	DIVORCES
DISTRAINING	DITAS	DITZES*	DIVESTED	DIVORCING
DISTRAINS	DITCH	DITZIER	DIVESTING	DIVORCIVE
DISTRAINT	DITCHED	DITZIEST	DIVESTS	DIVOT
DISTRAINTS	DITCHER	DITZY	DIVESTURE	DIVOTS
DISTRAIT	DITCHERS	DIURESES	DIVESTURES	DIVS
DISTRAITE	DITCHES	DIURESIS	DIVI	DIVULGATE
DISTRESS	DITCHING	DIURETIC	DIVIDABLE	DIVULGATED
DISTRESSED	DITE	DIURETICS	DIVIDANT	DIVULGATES
DISTRESSES	DITED	DIURNAL	DIVIDE	DIVULGATING
DISTRESSING	DITES	DIURNALLY	DIVIDED	DIVULGE
DISTRICT	DITHECAL	DIURNALS	DIVIDEDLY	DIVULGED
DISTRICTED	DITHECOUS	DIURON*	DIVIDEND	DIVULGER*
DISTRICTING	DITHEISM	DIURONS*	DIVIDENDS	DIVULGERS*
DISTRICTS	DITHEISMS	DIUTURNAL	DIVIDER	DIVULGES
DISTRUST	DITHEIST	DIV	DIVIDERS	DIVULGING
DISTRUSTED	DITHEISTS	DIVA	DIVIDES	DIVULSION
DISTRUSTING	DITHELETE	DIVAGATE	DIVIDING	DIVULSIONS
DISTRUSTS	DITHELETES	DIVAGATED	DIVIDINGS	DIVULSIVE
DISTUNE	DITHELISM	DIVAGATES	DIVIDIVI	DIVVIED*
DISTUNED	DITHELISMS	DIVAGATING	DIVIDIVIS	DIVVIES
DISTUNES	DITHER	DIVALENCIES	DIVIDUAL	DIVVY
DISTUNING	DITHERED	DIVALENCY	DIVIDUOUS	DIVVYING*
DISTURB	DITHERER	DIVALENT	DIVINATOR	DIWAN
DISTURBED	DITHERERS	DIVALENTS	DIVINATORS	DIWANS
DISTURBER	DITHERIER	DIVAN	DIVINE	DIXI
DISTURBERS	DITHERIEST	DIVANS	DIVINED	DIXIE
DISTURBING	DITHERING	DIVAS	DIVINELY	DIXIES
DISTURBS	DITHERS	DIVE	DIVINER	DIXIT*
DISTYLE	DITHERY	DIVEBOMB*	DIVINERS	DIXITS*
DISTYLES	DITHIOL*	DIVEBOMBED*	DIVINES	DIXY
DISULFID*	DITHYRAMB	DIVEBOMBING*	DIVINEST	DIZAIN
DISULFIDE*	DITHYRAMBS	DIVEBOMBS*	DIVING	DIZAINS
DISULFIDES*	DITING	DIVED	DIVINGS	DIZEN
DISULFIDS*	DITOKOUS	DIVELLENT	DIVINIFIED	DIZENED
DISUNION	DITONE	DIVER	DIVINIFIES	DIZENING
DISUNIONS	DITONES	DIVERGE	DIVINIFY	DIZENS

The Chambers Dictionary is the authority for many longer words; see Introduction, page ix

DIZYGOTIC	DOBSONFLY*	DOCTORATING	DODMAN	DOGFOXES
DIZYGOUS*	DOBSONS*	DOCTORED	DODMANS	DOGGED
DIZZARD	DOBY*	DOCTORESS	DODO	DOGGEDER
DIZZARDS	DOC	DOCTORESSES	DODOES	DOGGEDEST
DIZZIED	DOCENT	DOCTORIAL	DODOISM*	DOGGEDLY
DIZZIER	DOCENTS	DOCTORING	DODOISMS*	DOGGER
DIZZIES	DOCETIC*	DOCTORLY	DODOS	DOGGEREL
DIZZIEST	DOCHMIAC	DOCTORS	DODS	DOGGERELS
DIZZILY	DOCHMII	DOCTRESS	DOE	DOGGERIES
DIZZINESS	DOCHMIUS	DOCTRESSES	DOEK	DOGGERMAN
DIZZINESSES	DOCHMIUSES	DOCTRINAL	DOEKS	DOGGERMEN
DIZZY	DOCHT	DOCTRINE	DOEN	DOGGERS
DIZZYING	DOCIBLE	DOCTRINES	DOER	DOGGERY
DJEBEL	DOCILE	DOCUDRAMA	DOERS	DOGGESS
DJEBELS	DOCILELY*	DOCUDRAMAS	DOES	DOGGESSES
DJELLABA	DOCILER	DOCUMENT	DOESKIN*	DOGGIE
DJELLABAH	DOCILEST	DOCUMENTED	DOESKINS*	DOGGIER
DJELLABAHS	DOCILITIES	DOCUMENTING	DOEST	DOGGIES
DJELLABAS	DOCILITY	DOCUMENTS	DOETH	DOGGIEST
DJIBBAH	DOCIMASIES	DOD	DOFF	DOGGINESS
DJIBBAHS	DOCIMASY	DODDARD	DOFFED	DOGGINESSES
DJIN*	DOCK	DODDED	DOFFER	DOGGING
DJINN	DOCKAGE	DODDER	DOFFERS	DOGGINGS
DJINNI	DOCKAGES	DODDERED	DOFFING	DOGGISH
DJINNS*	DOCKED	DODDERER	DOFFS	DOGGISHLY
DJINNY*	DOCKEN	DODDERERS	DOG	DOGGO
DJINS*	DOCKENS	DODDERIER	DOGARESSA	DOGGONE
DO	DOCKER	DODDERIEST	DOGARESSAS	DOGGONED
DOAB	DOCKERS	DODDERING	DOGATE	DOGGONEDER
DOABLE	DOCKET	DODDERS	DOGATES	DOGGONEDEST
DOABS	DOCKETED	DODDERY	DOGBANE	DOGGONER
DOAT	DOCKETING	DODDIER	DOGBANES	DOGGONES*
DOATED	DOCKETS	DODDIES	DOGBERRIES	DOGGONEST
DOATER	DOCKHAND*	DODDIEST	DOGBERRY	DOGGONING*
DOATERS	DOCKHANDS*	DODDING	DOGBOLT	DOGGREL
DOATING	DOCKING	DODDIPOLL	DOGBOLTS	DOGGRELS
DOATINGS	DOCKINGS	DODDIPOLLS	DOGCART	DOGGY
DOATS	DOCKISE	DODDLE	DOGCARTS	DOGHOLE
DOB	DOCKISED	DODDLES	DOGDAYS	DOGHOLES
DOBBED	DOCKISES	DODDY	DOGDOM*	DOGHOUSE*
DOBBER	DOCKISING	DODDYPOLL	DOGDOMS*	DOGHOUSES*
DOBBERS	DOCKIZE	DODDYPOLLS	DOGE	DOGIE
DOBBIE	DOCKIZED	DODECAGON	DOGEAR*	DOGIES
DOBBIES	DOCKIZES	DODECAGONS	DOGEARED*	DOGLEG*
DOBBIN	DOCKIZING	DODGE	DOGEARING*	DOGLEGGED*
DOBBING	DOCKLAND	DODGEBALL*	DOGEARS*	DOGLEGGING*
DOBBINS	DOCKLANDS	DODGEBALLS*	DOGEATE	DOGLEGS*
DOBBY	DOCKS	DODGED	DOGEATES	DOGLIKE*
DOBCHICK	DOCKSIDE	DODGEM*	DOGEDOM*	DOGMA
DOBCHICKS	DOCKSIDES	DODGEMS	DOGEDOMS*	DOGMAS
DOBHASH	DOCKYARD	DODGER	DOGES	DOGMATA*
DOBHASHES	DOCKYARDS	DODGERIES	DOGESHIP	DOGMATIC
DOBIE*	DOCQUET	DODGERS	DOGESHIPS	DOGMATICS
DOBIES*	DOCQUETED	DODGERY	DOGEY*	DOGMATISE
DOBLA*	DOCQUETING	DODGES	DOGEYS*	DOGMATISED
DOBLAS*	DOCQUETS	DODGIER	DOGFACE*	DOGMATISES
DOBLON*	DOCS	DODGIEST	DOGFACES*	DOGMATISING
DOBLONES*	DOCTOR	DODGINESS*	DOGFIGHT	DOGMATISM
DOBLONS*	DOCTORAL	DODGINESSES*	DOGFIGHTING*	DOGMATISMS
DOBRA*	DOCTORAND	DODGING	DOGFIGHTS	DOGMATIST
DOBRAS*	DOCTORANDS	DODGINGS	DOGFISH	DOGMATISTS
DOBS	DOCTORATE	DODGY	DOGFISHES	DOGMATIZE
DOBSON*	DOCTORATED	DODKIN	DOGFOUGHT*	DOGMATIZED
DOBSONFLIES*	DOCTORATES	DODKINS	DOGFOX	DOGMATIZES

Words marked with an asterisk are from OTCWL

DOGMATIZING
DOGMATORY
DOGNAP*
DOGNAPED*
DOGNAPER*
DOGNAPERS*
DOGNAPING*
DOGNAPPED*
DOGNAPPER*
DOGNAPPERS*
DOGNAPPING*
DOGNAPS*
DOGS
DOGSBODIES
DOGSBODY
DOGSHIP
DOGSHIPS
DOGSHORES
DOGSKIN
DOGSKINS
DOGSLED
DOGSLEDDED*
DOGSLEDDING*
DOGSLEDS
DOGSLEEP
DOGSLEEPS
DOGTEETH
DOGTOOTH
DOGTOWN
DOGTOWNS
DOGTROT
DOGTROTS
DOGTROTTED*
DOGTROTTING*
DOGVANE
DOGVANES
DOGWATCH*
DOGWATCHES*
DOGWOOD
DOGWOODS
DOGY
DOH
DOHS
DOHYO
DOHYOS
DOILED
DOILIES
DOILT
DOILTER
DOILTEST
DOILY
DOING
DOINGS
DOIT
DOITED
DOITIT
DOITKIN
DOITKINS
DOITS
DOJO
DOJOS
DOL*
DOLCE
DOLCES

DOLCI*
DOLDRUMS
DOLE
DOLED
DOLEFUL
DOLEFULLER*
DOLEFULLEST*
DOLEFULLY
DOLENT
DOLERITE
DOLERITES
DOLERITIC
DOLES
DOLESOME
DOLIA
DOLICHOS
DOLICHOSES
DOLICHURI
DOLINA
DOLINAS
DOLINE
DOLINES
DOLING
DOLIUM
DOLL
DOLLAR
DOLLARED
DOLLARS
DOLLDOM
DOLLDOMS
DOLLED
DOLLHOOD
DOLLHOODS
DOLLHOUSE*
DOLLHOUSES*
DOLLIED
DOLLIER
DOLLIERS
DOLLIES
DOLLINESS
DOLLINESSES
DOLLING
DOLLISH
DOLLISHLY*
DOLLOP
DOLLOPED*
DOLLOPING*
DOLLOPS
DOLLS
DOLLY
DOLLYING
DOLMA
DOLMADES
DOLMAN
DOLMANS
DOLMAS
DOLMEN
DOLMENS
DOLOMITE
DOLOMITES
DOLOMITIC
DOLOR
DOLORIFIC
DOLOROSO

DOLOROUS
DOLORS
DOLOUR
DOLOURS
DOLPHIN
DOLPHINET
DOLPHINETS
DOLPHINS
DOLS*
DOLT
DOLTISH
DOLTISHLY
DOLTS
DOM*
DOMAIN
DOMAINAL
DOMAINS
DOMAL
DOMANIAL
DOMATIA
DOMATIUM
DOME
DOMED
DOMELIKE*
DOMES
DOMESDAY*
DOMESDAYS*
DOMESTIC
DOMESTICS
DOMETT
DOMETTS
DOMIC*
DOMICAL
DOMICIL
DOMICILE
DOMICILED
DOMICILES
DOMICILING
DOMICILS
DOMIER
DOMIEST
DOMINANCE
DOMINANCES
DOMINANCIES
DOMINANCY
DOMINANT
DOMINANTS
DOMINATE
DOMINATED
DOMINATES
DOMINATING
DOMINATOR
DOMINATORS
DOMINE*
DOMINEE
DOMINEER
DOMINEERED
DOMINEERING
DOMINEERS
DOMINEES
DOMINES*
DOMING
DOMINICAL

DOMINICKS*
DOMINIE
DOMINIES
DOMINION
DOMINIONS
DOMINIQUE*
DOMINIQUES*
DOMINIUM*
DOMINIUMS*
DOMINO
DOMINOES
DOMINOS
DOMS*
DOMY
DON
DONA
DONAH
DONAHS
DONARIES
DONARY
DONAS
DONATARIES
DONATARY
DONATE
DONATED
DONATES
DONATING
DONATION
DONATIONS
DONATISM
DONATISMS
DONATIVE
DONATIVES
DONATOR
DONATORIES
DONATORS
DONATORY
DONDER
DONDERED
DONDERING
DONDERS
DONE
DONEE
DONEES
DONENESS
DONENESSES
DONG
DONGA
DONGAS
DONGED
DONGING
DONGLE
DONGLES
DONGOLA*
DONGOLAS*
DONGS
DONING
DONINGS
DONJON
DONJONS
DONKEY
DONKEYS
DONNA*
DONNARD

DONNART
DONNAS*
DONNAT
DONNATS
DONNE
DONNED
DONNEE
DONNEES
DONNERD
DONNERED
DONNERT
DONNES
DONNICKER*
DONNICKERS*
DONNIKER*
DONNIKERS*
DONNING
DONNISH
DONNISHLY*
DONNISM
DONNISMS
DONNOT
DONNOTS
DONOR
DONORS
DONS
DONSHIP
DONSHIPS
DONSIE
DONSIER
DONSIEST
DONSY*
DONUT
DONUTS
DONUTTED
DONUTTING
DONZEL
DONZELS
DOO
DOOB
DOOBS
DOOCOT
DOOCOTS
DOODAD
DOODADS
DOODAH
DOODAHS
DOODLE
DOODLEBUG
DOODLEBUGS
DOODLED
DOODLER
DOODLERS
DOODLES
DOODLING
DOOFER
DOOFERS
DOOFUS*
DOOFUSES*
DOOHICKEY*
DOOHICKEYS*
DOOHICKIES*
DOOK
DOOKED

The Chambers Dictionary is the authority for many longer words; see Introduction, page ix

DOOKET	DOORSILL*	DORE*	DORSALLY	DOTAGES
DOOKETS	DOORSILLS*	DOREE	DORSALS	DOTAL
DOOKING	DOORSMAN	DOREES	DORSE	DOTANT
DOOKS	DOORSMEN	DORHAWK	DORSEL	DOTANTS
DOOL	DOORSTEP	DORHAWKS	DORSELS	DOTARD
DOOLALLY	DOORSTEPPED	DORIDOID	DORSER	DOTARDLY*
DOOLE	DOORSTEPPING	DORIDOIDS	DORSERS	DOTARDS
DOOLEE*	DOORSTEPPINGS	DORIES	DORSES	DOTATION
DOOLEES*	DOORSTEPS	DORISE	DORSIFLEX	DOTATIONS
DOOLES	DOORSTONE	DORISED	DORSUM	DOTE
DOOLIE	DOORSTONES	DORISES	DORT	DOTED
DOOLIES	DOORSTOP	DORISING	DORTED	DOTER
DOOLS	DOORSTOPS	DORIZE	DORTER	DOTERS
DOOLY*	DOORWAY	DORIZED	DORTERS	DOTES
DOOM	DOORWAYS	DORIZES	DORTIER	DOTH
DOOMED	DOORYARD*	DORIZING	DORTIEST	DOTIER
DOOMFUL	DOORYARDS*	DORK	DORTING	DOTIEST
DOOMFULLY*	DOOS	DORKIER	DORTOUR	DOTING
DOOMIER	DOOZER*	DORKIEST	DORTOURS	DOTINGLY
DOOMIEST	DOOZERS*	DORKS	DORTS	DOTINGS
DOOMILY*	DOOZIE*	DORKY	DORTY	DOTISH
DOOMING	DOOZIES*	DORLACH	DORY	DOTS
DOOMS	DOOZY*	DORLACHS	DOS	DOTTED
DOOMSAYER	DOP	DORM	DOSAGE	DOTTEL*
DOOMSAYERS	DOPA	DORMANCIES	DOSAGES	DOTTELS*
DOOMSDAY	DOPAMINE	DORMANCY	DOSE	DOTTER*
DOOMSDAYS	DOPAMINES	DORMANT	DOSED	DOTTEREL
DOOMSMAN	DOPANT	DORMANTS	DOSEH	DOTTERELS
DOOMSMEN	DOPANTS	DORMER	DOSEHS	DOTTERS*
DOOMSTER	DOPAS	DORMERS	DOSER*	DOTTIER
DOOMSTERS	DOPATTA	DORMICE	DOSERS*	DOTTIEST
DOOMWATCH	DOPATTAS	DORMIE	DOSES	DOTTILY*
DOOMWATCHED	DOPE	DORMIENT	DOSH	DOTTINESS
DOOMWATCHES	DOPED	DORMIN*	DOSHES	DOTTINESSES
DOOMWATCHING	DOPEHEAD*	DORMINS*	DOSIMETER	DOTTING
DOOMWATCHINGS	DOPEHEADS*	DORMITION	DOSIMETERS	DOTTIPOLL
DOOMY	DOPER	DORMITIONS	DOSIMETRIES	DOTTIPOLLS
DOONA	DOPERS	DORMITIVE	DOSIMETRY	DOTTLE
DOONAS	DOPES	DORMITIVES	DOSING	DOTTLED
DOOR	DOPESTER*	DORMITORIES	DOSIOLOGIES	DOTTLER
DOORBELL	DOPESTERS*	DORMITORY	DOSIOLOGY	DOTTLES
DOORBELLS	DOPEY	DORMOUSE	DOSOLOGIES	DOTTLEST
DOORJAMB*	DOPIER	DORMS	DOSOLOGY	DOTTREL
DOORJAMBS*	DOPIEST	DORMY	DOSS	DOTTRELS
DOORKNOB	DOPINESS	DORNECK*	DOSSAL	DOTTY
DOORKNOBS	DOPINESSES	DORNECKS*	DOSSALS	DOTY
DOORKNOCK	DOPING	DORNICK	DOSSED	DOUANE
DOORKNOCKED	DOPINGS	DORNICKS	DOSSEL	DOUANES
DOORKNOCKING	DOPPED	DORNOCK*	DOSSELS	DOUANIER
DOORKNOCKS	DOPPER	DORNOCKS*	DOSSER	DOUANIERS
DOORLESS*	DOPPERS	DORONICUM	DOSSERET*	DOUAR
DOORMAN*	DOPPIE	DORONICUMS	DOSSERETS*	DOUARS
DOORMAT	DOPPIES	DORP	DOSSERS	DOUBLE
DOORMATS	DOPPING	DORPER*	DOSSES	DOUBLED
DOORMEN*	DOPPINGS	DORPERS*	DOSSHOUSE	DOUBLER
DOORN	DOPS	DORPS	DOSSHOUSES	DOUBLERS
DOORNAIL	DOPY	DORR	DOSSIER	DOUBLES
DOORNAILS	DOR	DORRED	DOSSIERS	DOUBLET
DOORNS	DORAD	DORRING	DOSSIL	DOUBLETON
DOORPLATE*	DORADO	DORRS	DOSSILS	DOUBLETONS
DOORPLATES*	DORADOS	DORS	DOSSING	DOUBLETS
DOORPOST	DORADS	DORSA	DOST	DOUBLING
DOORPOSTS	DORBUG*	DORSAD*	DOT	DOUBLINGS
DOORS	DORBUGS*	DORSAL	DOTAGE	DOUBLOON

DOUBLOONS	DOUPS	DOWAGERS	DOWNER	DOWNSPOUTS
DOUBLURE*	DOUR	DOWAR	DOWNERS	DOWNSTAGE
DOUBLURES*	DOURA	DOWARS	DOWNFALL	DOWNSTAGES*
DOUBLY	DOURAH*	DOWD	DOWNFALLS	DOWNSTAIR
DOUBT	DOURAHS*	DOWDIER	DOWNFIELD*	DOWNSTAIRS
DOUBTABLE	DOURAS	DOWDIES	DOWNFLOW	DOWNSTATE*
DOUBTED	DOURER	DOWDIEST	DOWNFLOWS	DOWNSTATES*
DOUBTER	DOUREST	DOWDILY	DOWNFORCE	DOWNSWING
DOUBTERS	DOURINE	DOWDINESS	DOWNFORCES	DOWNSWINGS
DOUBTFUL	DOURINES	DOWDINESSES	DOWNGRADE	DOWNTICK*
DOUBTFULS	DOURLY	DOWDS	DOWNGRADED	DOWNTICKS*
DOUBTING	DOURNESS	DOWDY	DOWNGRADES	DOWNTIME
DOUBTINGS	DOURNESSES	DOWDYISH	DOWNGRADING	DOWNTIMES
DOUBTLESS	DOUSE	DOWDYISM	DOWNHAUL*	DOWNTOWN*
DOUBTS	DOUSED	DOWDYISMS	DOWNHAULS*	DOWNTOWNS*
DOUC	DOUSER	DOWED	DOWNHILL	DOWNTREND
DOUCE	DOUSERS	DOWEL	DOWNHILLS	DOWNTRENDS
DOUCELY	DOUSES	DOWELED*	DOWNHOLE	DOWNTROD*
DOUCENESS	DOUSING	DOWELING*	DOWNIER	DOWNTURN
DOUCENESSES	DOUT	DOWELLED	DOWNIEST	DOWNTURNS
DOUCEPERE	DOUTED	DOWELLING	DOWNINESS	DOWNWARD
DOUCEPERES	DOUTER	DOWELLINGS	DOWNINESSES	DOWNWARDS
DOUCER	DOUTERS	DOWELS	DOWNING	DOWNWASH*
DOUCEST	DOUTING	DOWER	DOWNLAND	DOWNWASHES*
DOUCET	DOUTS	DOWERED	DOWNLANDS	DOWNWIND
DOUCETS	DOUX*	DOWERIES*	DOWNLINK*	DOWNY
DOUCEUR	DOUZEPER	DOWERING	DOWNLINKS*	DOWP
DOUCEURS	DOUZEPERS	DOWERLESS	DOWNLOAD	DOWPS
DOUCHE	DOVE	DOWERS	DOWNLOADED	DOWRIES
DOUCHED	DOVECOT	DOWERY*	DOWNLOADING	DOWRY
DOUCHES	DOVECOTE*	DOWF	DOWNLOADS	DOWS
DOUCHING	DOVECOTES*	DOWFNESS	DOWNMOST	DOWSABEL*
DOUCINE	DOVECOTS	DOWFNESSES	DOWNPIPE	DOWSABELS*
DOUCINES	DOVED	DOWIE	DOWNPIPES	DOWSE
DOUCS	DOVEISH	DOWIER	DOWNPLAY	DOWSED
DOUGH	DOVEKEY*	DOWIEST	DOWNPLAYED	DOWSER
DOUGHBOY*	DOVEKEYS*	DOWING	DOWNPLAYING	DOWSERS
DOUGHBOYS*	DOVEKIE	DOWITCHER	DOWNPLAYS	DOWSES
DOUGHFACE*	DOVEKIES	DOWITCHERS	DOWNPOUR	DOWSET
DOUGHFACES*	DOVELET	DOWL	DOWNPOURS	DOWSETS
DOUGHIER	DOVELETS	DOWLAS	DOWNRANGE*	DOWSING
DOUGHIEST	DOVELIKE	DOWLASES	DOWNRIGHT	DOWT
DOUGHLIKE*	DOVEN*	DOWLE	DOWNRIVER*	DOWTS
DOUGHNUT	DOVENED*	DOWLES	DOWNRUSH	DOXIE*
DOUGHNUTS	DOVENING*	DOWLNE	DOWNRUSHES	DOXIES
DOUGHNUTTED	DOVENS*	DOWLNES	DOWNS	DOXOLOGIES
DOUGHNUTTING	DOVER	DOWLNEY	DOWNSCALE*	DOXOLOGY
DOUGHNUTTINGS	DOVERED	DOWLS	DOWNSCALED*	DOXY
DOUGHS	DOVERING	DOWN	DOWNSCALES*	DOYEN
DOUGHT	DOVERS	DOWNA	DOWNSCALING*	DOYENNE
DOUGHTIER	DOVES	DOWNBEAT	DOWNSHIFT	DOYENNES
DOUGHTIEST	DOVETAIL	DOWNBEATS	DOWNSHIFTED	DOYENS
DOUGHTILY	DOVETAILED	DOWNBOW	DOWNSHIFTING	DOYLEY
DOUGHTY	DOVETAILING	DOWNBOWS	DOWNSHIFTS	DOYLEYS
DOUGHY	DOVETAILINGS	DOWNBURST	DOWNSIDE	DOYLIES
DOULEIA	DOVETAILS	DOWNBURSTS	DOWNSIDES	DOYLY
DOULEIAS	DOVIE	DOWNCAST	DOWNSIZE	DOZE
DOUM*	DOVIER	DOWNCASTS	DOWNSIZED	DOZED
DOUMA	DOVIEST	DOWNCOME*	DOWNSIZES	DOZEN
DOUMAS	DOVING	DOWNCOMES*	DOWNSIZING	DOZENED
DOUMS*	DOVISH	DOWNCOURT*	DOWNSLIDE*	DOZENING
DOUP	DOW	DOWNDRAFT*	DOWNSLIDES*	DOZENS
DOUPIONI*	DOWABLE	DOWNDRAFTS*	DOWNSLOPE*	DOZENTH
DOUPIONIS*	DOWAGER	DOWNED	DOWNSPOUT	DOZENTHS

The Chambers Dictionary is the authority for many longer words; see Introduction, page ix

DOZER	DRAFTEES	DRAGSTER	DRAPERS	DRAWLING
DOZERS	DRAFTER	DRAGSTERS	DRAPERY	DRAWLS
DOZES	DRAFTERS	DRAIL	DRAPERYING	DRAWLY*
DOZIER	DRAFTIER	DRAILED	DRAPES	DRAWN
DOZIEST	DRAFTIEST	DRAILING	DRAPET	DRAWNWORK*
DOZILY*	DRAFTILY*	DRAILS	DRAPETS	DRAWNWORKS*
DOZINESS	DRAFTING	DRAIN	DRAPEY*	DRAWPLATE*
DOZINESSES	DRAFTINGS*	DRAINABLE	DRAPIER	DRAWPLATES*
DOZING	DRAFTS	DRAINAGE	DRAPIERS	DRAWS
DOZINGS	DRAFTSMAN	DRAINAGES	DRAPING	DRAWSHAVE*
DOZY	DRAFTSMEN	DRAINED	DRAPPED	DRAWSHAVES*
DRAB	DRAFTY	DRAINER	DRAPPIE	DRAWTUBE*
DRABBED	DRAG	DRAINERS	DRAPPIES	DRAWTUBES*
DRABBER	DRAGEE	DRAINING	DRAPPING	DRAY
DRABBERS	DRAGEES	DRAINPIPE	DRAPPY	DRAYAGE
DRABBEST	DRAGGED	DRAINPIPES	DRAPS	DRAYAGES
DRABBET	DRAGGER*	DRAINS	DRASTIC	DRAYED*
DRABBETS	DRAGGERS*	DRAISENE	DRASTICS	DRAYING*
DRABBIER	DRAGGIER	DRAISENES	DRAT	DRAYMAN
DRABBIEST	DRAGGIEST	DRAISINE	DRATCHELL	DRAYMEN
DRABBING	DRAGGING	DRAISINES	DRATCHELLS	DRAYS
DRABBISH	DRAGGLE	DRAKE	DRATS*	DRAZEL
DRABBLE	DRAGGLED	DRAKES	DRATTED	DRAZELS
DRABBLED	DRAGGLES	DRAM	DRATTING*	DREAD
DRABBLER	DRAGGLING	DRAMA	DRAUGHT	DREADED
DRABBLERS	DRAGGY	DRAMAS	DRAUGHTED	DREADER
DRABBLES	DRAGHOUND	DRAMATIC	DRAUGHTER	DREADERS
DRABBLING	DRAGHOUNDS	DRAMATICS	DRAUGHTERS	DREADFUL
DRABBLINGS	DRAGLINE	DRAMATISE	DRAUGHTIER	DREADFULS*
DRABBY	DRAGLINES	DRAMATISED	DRAUGHTIEST	DREADING
DRABETTE	DRAGNET	DRAMATISES	DRAUGHTING	DREADLESS
DRABETTES	DRAGNETS	DRAMATISING	DRAUGHTS	DREADLOCK*
DRABLER	DRAGOMAN	DRAMATIST	DRAUGHTY	DREADLOCKS*
DRABLERS	DRAGOMANS	DRAMATISTS	DRAUNT	DREADLY
DRABLY	DRAGOMEN*	DRAMATIZE	DRAUNTED	DREADS
DRABNESS	DRAGON	DRAMATIZED	DRAUNTING	DREAM
DRABNESSES	DRAGONESS	DRAMATIZES	DRAUNTS	DREAMBOAT
DRABS	DRAGONESSES	DRAMATIZING	DRAVE	DREAMBOATS
DRACAENA*	DRAGONET	DRAMATURG	DRAW	DREAMED
DRACAENAS*	DRAGONETS	DRAMATURGS	DRAWABLE	DREAMER
DRACHM	DRAGONFLIES	DRAMEDIES*	DRAWBACK	DREAMERIES
DRACHMA	DRAGONFLY	DRAMEDY*	DRAWBACKS	DREAMERS
DRACHMAE	DRAGONISE	DRAMMACH	DRAWBAR	DREAMERY
DRACHMAI	DRAGONISED	DRAMMACHS	DRAWBARS	DREAMFUL
DRACHMAS	DRAGONISES	DRAMMED	DRAWBORE*	DREAMHOLE
DRACHMS	DRAGONISH	DRAMMING	DRAWBORES*	DREAMHOLES
DRACONE	DRAGONISING	DRAMMOCK	DRAWDOWN*	DREAMIER
DRACONES	DRAGONISM	DRAMMOCKS	DRAWDOWNS*	DREAMIEST
DRACONIAN	DRAGONISMS	DRAMS	DRAWEE	DREAMILY
DRACONIC	DRAGONIZE	DRAMSHOP*	DRAWEES	DREAMING
DRACONISM	DRAGONIZED	DRAMSHOPS*	DRAWER	DREAMINGS
DRACONISMS	DRAGONIZES	DRANK	DRAWERFUL*	DREAMLAND*
DRACONTIC	DRAGONIZING	DRANT	DRAWERFULS*	DREAMLANDS*
DRAD	DRAGONNE	DRANTED	DRAWERS	DREAMLESS
DRAFF	DRAGONS	DRANTING	DRAWING	DREAMLIKE*
DRAFFIER	DRAGOON	DRANTS	DRAWINGS	DREAMS
DRAFFIEST	DRAGOONED	DRAP	DRAWKNIFE*	DREAMT
DRAFFISH	DRAGOONING	DRAPABLE*	DRAWKNIVES*	DREAMTIME
DRAFFS	DRAGOONS	DRAPE	DRAWL	DREAMTIMES
DRAFFY	DRAGROPE*	DRAPEABLE*	DRAWLED	DREAMY
DRAFT	DRAGROPES*	DRAPED	DRAWLER	DREAR
DRAFTABLE*	DRAGS	DRAPER	DRAWLERS	DREARE
DRAFTED	DRAGSMAN	DRAPERIED	DRAWLIER*	DREARER
DRAFTEE	DRAGSMEN	DRAPERIES	DRAWLIEST*	DREARES

Words marked with an asterisk are from OTCWL

DREAREST	DRESSING	DRILLERS	DROGHERS	DROOGS
DREARIER	DRESSINGS	DRILLING	DROGUE	DROOK
DREARIES*	DRESSMADE	DRILLINGS	DROGUES	DROOKED
DREARIEST	DRESSMAKE	DRILLS	DROGUET	DROOKING
DREARILY	DRESSMAKES	DRILLSHIP	DROGUETS	DROOKINGS
DREARING	DRESSMAKING	DRILLSHIPS	DROICH	DROOKIT
DREARINGS	DRESSMAKINGS	DRILY	DROICHIER	DROOKS
DREARS	DRESSY	DRINK	DROICHIEST	DROOL
DREARY	DREST	DRINKABLE	DROICHS	DROOLED
DRECK	DREVILL	DRINKABLES*	DROICHY	DROOLING
DRECKIER	DREVILLS	DRINKER	DROIL	DROOLS
DRECKIEST	DREW	DRINKERS	DROILED	DROOME
DRECKS	DREY	DRINKING	DROILING	DROOMES
DRECKY	DREYS	DRINKINGS	DROILS	DROOP
DREDGE	DRIB	DRINKS	DROIT	DROOPED
DREDGED	DRIBBED	DRIP	DROITS	DROOPIER
DREDGER	DRIBBER	DRIPLESS*	DROLE	DROOPIEST
DREDGERS	DRIBBERS	DRIPPED	DROLER	DROOPILY
DREDGES	DRIBBING	DRIPPER*	DROLES	DROOPING
DREDGING	DRIBBLE	DRIPPERS*	DROLEST	DROOPS
DREDGINGS*	DRIBBLED	DRIPPIER	DROLL	DROOPY
DREE	DRIBBLER	DRIPPIEST	DROLLED	DROP
DREED	DRIBBLERS	DRIPPING	DROLLER	DROPFLIES
DREEING	DRIBBLES	DRIPPINGS	DROLLERIES	DROPFLY
DREES	DRIBBLET	DRIPPY	DROLLERY	DROPHEAD*
DREG	DRIBBLETS	DRIPS	DROLLEST	DROPHEADS*
DREGGIER	DRIBBLIER	DRIPSTONE*	DROLLING	DROPKICK*
DREGGIEST	DRIBBLIEST	DRIPSTONES*	DROLLINGS	DROPKICKS*
DREGGISH*	DRIBBLING	DRIPT*	DROLLISH	DROPLET
DREGGY	DRIBBLY	DRISHEEN	DROLLNESS	DROPLETS
DREGS	DRIBLET	DRISHEENS	DROLLNESSES	DROPLIGHT*
DREICH	DRIBLETS	DRIVABLE	DROLLS	DROPLIGHTS*
DREICHER	DRIBS	DRIVE	DROLLY	DROPOUT
DREICHEST	DRICE	DRIVEABLE	DROME	DROPOUTS
DREIDEL*	DRICES	DRIVEL	DROMEDARE	DROPPABLE*
DREIDELS*	DRICKSIE	DRIVELED*	DROMEDARES	DROPPED
DREIDL*	DRICKSIER	DRIVELER*	DROMEDARIES	DROPPER
DREIDLS*	DRICKSIEST	DRIVELERS*	DROMEDARY	DROPPERS
DREIGH*	DRIED	DRIVELINE*	DROMES	DROPPING
DREK	DRIEGH*	DRIVELINES*	DROMIC	DROPPINGS
DREKS	DRIER	DRIVELING*	DROMICAL	DROPPLE
DRENCH	DRIERS	DRIVELLED	DROMOI	DROPPLES
DRENCHED	DRIES	DRIVELLER	DROMON	DROPS
DRENCHER	DRIEST	DRIVELLERS	DROMOND	DROPSHOT*
DRENCHERS	DRIFT	DRIVELLING	DROMONDS	DROPSHOTS*
DRENCHES	DRIFTAGE	DRIVELS	DROMONS	DROPSICAL
DRENCHING	DRIFTAGES	DRIVEN	DROMOS	DROPSIED
DRENT	DRIFTED	DRIVER	DRONE	DROPSIES
DREPANIUM	DRIFTER	DRIVERS	DRONED	DROPSTONE
DREPANIUMS	DRIFTERS	DRIVES	DRONER*	DROPSTONES
DRERE	DRIFTIER	DRIVEWAY	DRONERS*	DROPSY
DRERES	DRIFTIEST	DRIVEWAYS	DRONES	DROPT*
DRERIHEAD	DRIFTING	DRIVING	DRONGO	DROPWISE
DRERIHEADS	DRIFTLESS	DRIVINGS*	DRONGOES	DROPWORT*
DRESS	DRIFTPIN	DRIZZLE	DRONGOS	DROPWORTS*
DRESSAGE	DRIFTPINS	DRIZZLED	DRONIER	DROSERA
DRESSAGES	DRIFTS	DRIZZLES	DRONIEST	DROSERAS
DRESSED	DRIFTWOOD	DRIZZLIER	DRONING	DROSHKIES
DRESSER	DRIFTWOODS	DRIZZLIEST	DRONINGLY	DROSHKY
DRESSERS	DRIFTY	DRIZZLING	DRONISH	DROSKIES
DRESSES	DRILL	DRIZZLY	DRONISHLY	DROSKY
DRESSIER	DRILLABLE*	DROGER	DRONY	DROSS
DRESSIEST	DRILLED	DROGERS	DROOG	DROSSES
DRESSILY*	DRILLER	DROGHER	DROOGISH	DROSSIER

The Chambers Dictionary is the authority for many longer words; see Introduction, page ix

DROSSIEST	DRUDGERY	DRUNKARDS	DUALIN	DUCKBILL
DROSSY	DRUDGES	DRUNKEN	DUALINS	DUCKBILLS
DROSTDIES	DRUDGING	DRUNKENLY	DUALISM	DUCKBOARD*
DROSTDY	DRUDGISM	DRUNKER	DUALISMS	DUCKBOARDS*
DROSTDYS	DRUDGISMS	DRUNKEST	DUALIST	DUCKED
DROUGHT	DRUG	DRUNKS	DUALISTIC	DUCKER
DROUGHTIER	DRUGGED	DRUPE	DUALISTS	DUCKERS
DROUGHTIEST	DRUGGER	DRUPEL	DUALITIES	DUCKIE*
DROUGHTS	DRUGGERS	DRUPELET	DUALITY	DUCKIER
DROUGHTY	DRUGGET	DRUPELETS	DUALIZE*	DUCKIES
DROUK	DRUGGETS	DRUPELS	DUALIZED*	DUCKIEST
DROUKED	DRUGGIE	DRUPES	DUALIZES*	DUCKING
DROUKING	DRUGGIER	DRUSE	DUALIZING*	DUCKINGS
DROUKINGS	DRUGGIES	DRUSES	DUALLED	DUCKLING
DROUKIT	DRUGGIEST	DRUSIER	DUALLING	DUCKLINGS
DROUKS	DRUGGING	DRUSIEST	DUALLY	DUCKMOLE
DROUTH	DRUGGIST	DRUSY	DUALS	DUCKMOLES
DROUTHIER	DRUGGISTS	DRUTHERS	DUAN	DUCKPIN*
DROUTHIEST	DRUGGY	DRUXIER	DUANS	DUCKPINS*
DROUTHS	DRUGMAKER*	DRUXIEST	DUAR	DUCKS
DROUTHY	DRUGMAKERS*	DRUXY	DUARCHIES	DUCKSHOVE
DROVE	DRUGS	DRY	DUARCHY	DUCKSHOVED
DROVED*	DRUGSTORE*	DRYABLE*	DUARS	DUCKSHOVES
DROVER	DRUGSTORES*	DRYAD	DUB	DUCKSHOVING
DROVERS	DRUID	DRYADES	DUBBED	DUCKTAIL*
DROVES	DRUIDESS	DRYADIC*	DUBBER*	DUCKTAILS*
DROVING	DRUIDESSES	DRYADS	DUBBERS*	DUCKWALK*
DROVINGS	DRUIDIC	DRYASDUST*	DUBBIN	DUCKWALKED*
DROW	DRUIDICAL	DRYASDUSTS*	DUBBING	DUCKWALKING*
DROWND*	DRUIDISM	DRYBEAT	DUBBINGS	DUCKWALKS*
DROWNDED	DRUIDISMS	DRYBEATEN	DUBBINS	DUCKWEED
DROWNDING*	DRUIDS	DRYBEATING	DUBIETIES	DUCKWEEDS
DROWNDS*	DRUM	DRYBEATS	DUBIETY	DUCKY
DROWNED	DRUMBEAT	DRYER	DUBIOSITIES	DUCT
DROWNER	DRUMBEATS	DRYERS	DUBIOSITY	DUCTAL*
DROWNERS	DRUMBLE	DRYEST*	DUBIOUS	DUCTED
DROWNING	DRUMBLED	DRYING	DUBIOUSLY	DUCTILE
DROWNINGS	DRUMBLES	DRYINGS	DUBITABLE	DUCTILITIES
DROWNS	DRUMBLING	DRYISH	DUBITABLY	DUCTILITY
DROWS	DRUMFIRE	DRYLAND*	DUBITANCIES	DUCTING
DROWSE	DRUMFIRES	DRYLOT*	DUBITANCY	DUCTINGS*
DROWSED	DRUMFISH	DRYLOTS*	DUBITATE	DUCTLESS
DROWSES	DRUMFISHES	DRYLY	DUBITATED	DUCTS
DROWSIER	DRUMHEAD	DRYMOUTH	DUBITATES	DUCTULE*
DROWSIEST	DRUMHEADS	DRYMOUTHS	DUBITATING	DUCTULES*
DROWSIHED	DRUMLIER	DRYNESS	DUBONNET*	DUCTWORK*
DROWSIHEDS	DRUMLIEST	DRYNESSES	DUBONNETS*	DUCTWORKS*
DROWSILY	DRUMLIKE*	DRYPOINT*	DUBS	DUD
DROWSING	DRUMLIN	DRYPOINTS*	DUCAL	DUDDER
DROWSY	DRUMLINS	DRYS*	DUCALLY	DUDDERIES
DRUB	DRUMLY	DRYSALTER	DUCAT	DUDDERS
DRUBBED	DRUMMED	DRYSALTERS	DUCATOON	DUDDERY
DRUBBER*	DRUMMER	DRYSTONE*	DUCATOONS	DUDDIE
DRUBBERS*	DRUMMERS	DRYWALL*	DUCATS	DUDDIER
DRUBBING	DRUMMING	DRYWALLS*	DUCDAME	DUDDIEST
DRUBBINGS	DRUMMOCK	DSO	DUCE	DUDDY
DRUBS	DRUMMOCKS	DSOBO	DUCES	DUDE
DRUCKEN	DRUMROLL*	DSOBOS	DUCHESS	DUDED*
DRUDGE	DRUMROLLS*	DSOMO	DUCHESSE	DUDEEN
DRUDGED	DRUMS	DSOMOS	DUCHESSES	DUDEENS
DRUDGER	DRUMSTICK	DSOS	DUCHIES	DUDES
DRUDGERIES	DRUMSTICKS	DUAD	DUCHY	DUDGEON
DRUDGERS	DRUNK	DUADS	DUCI*	DUDGEONS
	DRUNKARD	DUAL	DUCK	DUDHEEN

DUDHEENS
DUDING*
DUDISH
DUDISHLY*
DUDISM
DUDISMS
DUDS
DUE
DUECENTO*
DUECENTOS*
DUED
DUEFUL
DUEL
DUELED*
DUELER*
DUELERS*
DUELING*
DUELIST*
DUELISTS*
DUELLED
DUELLER
DUELLERS
DUELLI*
DUELLING
DUELLINGS
DUELLIST
DUELLISTS
DUELLO
DUELLOS
DUELS
DUELSOME
DUENDE
DUENDES
DUENESS*
DUENESSES*
DUENNA
DUENNAS
DUES
DUET
DUETS
DUETT
DUETTED
DUETTI
DUETTING
DUETTINO
DUETTINOS
DUETTIST
DUETTISTS
DUETTO
DUETTOS
DUETTS
DUFF
DUFFED
DUFFEL
DUFFELS
DUFFER
DUFFERDOM
DUFFERDOMS
DUFFERISM
DUFFERISMS
DUFFERS
DUFFEST
DUFFING
DUFFINGS

DUFFLE
DUFFLES
DUFFS
DUG
DUGONG
DUGONGS
DUGOUT
DUGOUTS
DUGS
DUI*
DUIKER
DUIKERS
DUING
DUIT*
DUITS*
DUKE
DUKED
DUKEDOM
DUKEDOMS
DUKELING
DUKELINGS
DUKERIES
DUKERY
DUKES
DUKESHIP
DUKESHIPS
DUKING
DULCAMARA
DULCAMARAS
DULCET
DULCETLY*
DULCETS*
DULCIAN
DULCIANA
DULCIANAS
DULCIANS
DULCIFIED
DULCIFIES
DULCIFY
DULCIFYING
DULCIMER
DULCIMERS
DULCIMORE*
DULCIMORES*
DULCINEA*
DULCINEAS*
DULCITE
DULCITES
DULCITOL
DULCITOLS
DULCITUDE
DULCITUDES
DULCOSE
DULCOSES
DULE
DULES
DULIA
DULIAS
DULL
DULLARD
DULLARDS
DULLED
DULLER
DULLEST

DULLIER
DULLIEST
DULLING
DULLISH
DULLISHLY*
DULLNESS
DULLNESSES
DULLS
DULLY
DULNESS
DULNESSES
DULOCRACIES
DULOCRACY
DULOSES
DULOSIS
DULOTIC
DULSE
DULSES
DULY
DUMA
DUMAIST
DUMAISTS
DUMAS
DUMB
DUMBBELL*
DUMBBELLS*
DUMBCANE*
DUMBCANES*
DUMBED
DUMBER
DUMBEST
DUMBFOUND
DUMBFOUNDED
DUMBFOUNDING
DUMBFOUNDS
DUMBHEAD*
DUMBHEADS*
DUMBING
DUMBLY
DUMBNESS
DUMBNESSES
DUMBO
DUMBOS
DUMBS
DUMDUM
DUMDUMS
DUMFOUND
DUMFOUNDED
DUMFOUNDING
DUMFOUNDS
DUMKA
DUMKY
DUMMERER
DUMMERERS
DUMMIED
DUMMIER
DUMMIES
DUMMIEST
DUMMINESS
DUMMINESSES
DUMMKOPF*
DUMMKOPFS*
DUMMY
DUMMYING

DUMOSE
DUMOSITIES
DUMOSITY
DUMOUS
DUMP
DUMPBIN
DUMPBINS
DUMPCART*
DUMPCARTS*
DUMPED
DUMPER
DUMPERS
DUMPIER
DUMPIES
DUMPIEST
DUMPILY*
DUMPINESS
DUMPINESSES
DUMPING
DUMPINGS*
DUMPISH
DUMPISHLY
DUMPLE
DUMPLED
DUMPLES
DUMPLING
DUMPLINGS
DUMPS
DUMPSTER
DUMPSTERS
DUMPY
DUN
DUNAM*
DUNAMS*
DUNCE
DUNCEDOM
DUNCEDOMS
DUNCERIES
DUNCERY
DUNCES
DUNCH
DUNCHED
DUNCHES
DUNCHING
DUNCICAL*
DUNCISH*
DUNDER
DUNDERS
DUNE
DUNELAND*
DUNELANDS*
DUNELIKE*
DUNES
DUNG
DUNGAREE
DUNGAREES
DUNGED
DUNGEON
DUNGEONED
DUNGEONER
DUNGEONERS
DUNGEONING
DUNGEONS
DUNGHILL*

DUNGHILLS*
DUNGIER
DUNGIEST
DUNGING
DUNGMERE
DUNGMERES
DUNGS
DUNGY
DUNITE
DUNITES
DUNITIC*
DUNK
DUNKED
DUNKER
DUNKERS
DUNKING
DUNKS
DUNLIN
DUNLINS
DUNNAGE
DUNNAGES
DUNNAKIN
DUNNAKINS
DUNNART
DUNNARTS
DUNNED
DUNNER
DUNNESS*
DUNNESSES*
DUNNEST
DUNNIER
DUNNIES
DUNNIEST
DUNNING
DUNNINGS
DUNNISH
DUNNITE
DUNNITES
DUNNO
DUNNOCK
DUNNOCKS
DUNNY
DUNS
DUNSH
DUNSHED
DUNSHES
DUNSHING
DUNT
DUNTED
DUNTING
DUNTS
DUO
DUODECIMO
DUODECIMOS
DUODENA
DUODENAL
DUODENARY
DUODENUM
DUODENUMS*
DUOLOG*
DUOLOGS*
DUOLOGUE
DUOLOGUES
DUOMI

DUOMO	DURANTS	DUSKENS	DUUMVIRAL	DWINDLING
DUOMOS	DURAS	DUSKER	DUUMVIRI	DWINE
DUOPOLIES	DURATION	DUSKEST	DUUMVIRS	DWINED
DUOPOLY	DURATIONS	DUSKIER	DUVET	DWINES
DUOPSONIES*	DURATIVE*	DUSKIEST	DUVETINE	DWINING
DUOPSONY*	DURATIVES*	DUSKILY	DUVETINES	DYABLE
DUOS	DURBAR	DUSKINESS	DUVETS	DYAD
DUOTONE	DURBARS	DUSKINESSES	DUVETYN	DYADIC
DUOTONES	DURDUM	DUSKING	DUVETYNE	DYADICS*
DUP	DURDUMS	DUSKISH	DUVETYNES	DYADS
DUPABLE	DURE	DUSKISHLY	DUVETYNS	DYARCHIC*
DUPATTA	DURED	DUSKLY	DUX	DYARCHIES
DUPATTAS	DUREFUL	DUSKNESS	DUXELLES	DYARCHY
DUPE	DURES	DUSKNESSES	DUXES	DYBBUK
DUPED	DURESS	DUSKS	DUYKER	DYBBUKIM
DUPER	DURESSE	DUSKY	DUYKERS	DYBBUKS
DUPERIES	DURESSES	DUST	DVANDVA	DYE
DUPERS	DURGAN	DUSTBIN	DVANDVAS	DYEABLE
DUPERY	DURGANS	DUSTBINS	DVORNIK	DYED
DUPES	DURGIER	DUSTCART	DVORNIKS	DYEING
DUPING	DURGIEST	DUSTCARTS	DWALE	DYEINGS
DUPION	DURGY	DUSTCOVER*	DWALES	DYELINE
DUPIONS	DURIAN	DUSTCOVERS*	DWALM	DYELINES
DUPLE	DURIANS	DUSTED	DWALMED	DYER
DUPLET	DURING	DUSTER	DWALMING	DYERS
DUPLETS	DURION	DUSTERS	DWALMS	DYES
DUPLEX	DURIONS	DUSTHEAP*	DWAM	DYESTER
DUPLEXED*	DURMAST	DUSTHEAPS*	DWAMMED	DYESTERS
DUPLEXER	DURMASTS	DUSTIER	DWAMMING	DYESTUFF
DUPLEXERS	DURN	DUSTIEST	DWAMS	DYESTUFFS
DUPLEXES	DURNDEST*	DUSTILY	DWANG	DYEWEED*
DUPLEXING*	DURNED*	DUSTINESS	DWANGS	DYEWEEDS*
DUPLICAND	DURNEDER*	DUSTINESSES	DWARF	DYEWOOD*
DUPLICANDS	DURNEDEST*	DUSTING	DWARFED	DYEWOODS*
DUPLICATE	DURNING*	DUSTLESS	DWARFER	DYING
DUPLICATED	DURNS	DUSTLIKE*	DWARFEST	DYINGLY
DUPLICATES	DURO	DUSTMAN	DWARFING	DYINGNESS
DUPLICATING	DUROC*	DUSTMEN	DWARFISH	DYINGNESSES
DUPLICITIES	DUROCS*	DUSTOFF*	DWARFISM	DYINGS
DUPLICITY	DUROMETER*	DUSTOFFS*	DWARFISMS	DYKE
DUPLIED	DUROMETERS*	DUSTPAN*	DWARFLIKE*	DYKED
DUPLIES	DUROS	DUSTPANS*	DWARFNESS*	DYKES
DUPLY	DUROY	DUSTPROOF	DWARFNESSES*	DYKEY
DUPLYING	DUROYS	DUSTRAG*	DWARFS	DYKIER
DUPONDII	DURR*	DUSTRAGS*	DWARVES	DYKIEST
DUPONDIUS	DURRA	DUSTS	DWAUM	DYKING
DUPPED	DURRAS	DUSTSHEET	DWAUMED	DYNAMIC
DUPPIES	DURRIE	DUSTSHEETS	DWAUMING	DYNAMICAL
DUPPING	DURRIES	DUSTUP*	DWAUMS	DYNAMICS
DUPPY	DURRS*	DUSTUPS*	DWEEB	DYNAMISE
DUPS	DURST	DUSTY	DWEEBS	DYNAMISED
DURA	DURUKULI	DUTCH	DWELL	DYNAMISES
DURABLE	DURUKULIS	DUTCHES	DWELLED	DYNAMISING
DURABLES	DURUM	DUTCHMAN*	DWELLER	DYNAMISM
DURABLY	DURUMS	DUTCHMEN*	DWELLERS	DYNAMISMS
DURAL	DUSH	DUTEOUS	DWELLING	DYNAMIST
DURALS	DUSHED	DUTEOUSLY	DWELLINGS	DYNAMISTS
DURALUMIN	DUSHES	DUTIABLE	DWELLS	DYNAMITE
DURALUMINS	DUSHING	DUTIED	DWELT	DYNAMITED
DURAMEN	DUSK	DUTIES	DWILE	DYNAMITER
DURAMENS	DUSKED	DUTIFUL	DWILES	DYNAMITERS
DURANCE	DUSKEN	DUTIFULLY	DWINDLE	DYNAMITES
DURANCES	DUSKENED	DUTY	DWINDLED	DYNAMITIC*
DURANT	DUSKENING	DUUMVIR	DWINDLES	DYNAMITING

Words marked with an asterisk are from OTCWL

DYNAMIZE
DYNAMIZED
DYNAMIZES
DYNAMIZING
DYNAMO
DYNAMOS
DYNAMOTOR
DYNAMOTORS
DYNAST
DYNASTIC
DYNASTIES
DYNASTS
DYNASTY
DYNATRON
DYNATRONS
DYNE
DYNEIN*
DYNEL*
DYNELS*
DYNES
DYNODE
DYNODES
DYSCHROA
DYSCHROAS
DYSCHROIA

DYSCHROIAS
DYSCRASIA
DYSCRASIAS
DYSENTERIES
DYSENTERY
DYSGENIC
DYSGENICS
DYSLECTIC
DYSLECTICS
DYSLEXIA
DYSLEXIAS
DYSLEXIC
DYSLEXICS
DYSLOGIES
DYSLOGY
DYSMELIA
DYSMELIAS
DYSMELIC
DYSODIL
DYSODILE
DYSODILES
DYSODILS
DYSODYLE
DYSODYLES
DYSPATHIES

DYSPATHY
DYSPEPSIA
DYSPEPSIAS
DYSPEPSIES
DYSPEPSY
DYSPEPTIC
DYSPEPTICS
DYSPHAGIA
DYSPHAGIAS
DYSPHAGIC
DYSPHAGIES
DYSPHAGY
DYSPHASIA
DYSPHASIAS
DYSPHASIC*
DYSPHASICS*
DYSPHONIA
DYSPHONIAS
DYSPHONIC
DYSPHORIA
DYSPHORIAS
DYSPHORIC
DYSPLASIA
DYSPLASIAS
DYSPNEA

DYSPNEAL
DYSPNEAS
DYSPNEIC
DYSPNOEA
DYSPNOEAL
DYSPNOEAS
DYSPNOEIC
DYSPNOIC*
DYSPRAXIA
DYSPRAXIAS
DYSTAXIA*
DYSTAXIAS*
DYSTECTIC
DYSTHESIA
DYSTHESIAS
DYSTHETIC
DYSTHYMIA
DYSTHYMIAS
DYSTHYMIC
DYSTOCIA
DYSTOCIAS
DYSTONIA
DYSTONIAS
DYSTONIC
DYSTOPIA

DYSTOPIAN
DYSTOPIAS
DYSTROPHIES
DYSTROPHY
DYSURIA
DYSURIAS
DYSURIC
DYSURIES
DYSURY
DYTISCID
DYTISCIDS
DYVOUR
DYVOURIES
DYVOURS
DYVOURY
DZEREN
DZERENS
DZHO
DZHOS
DZIGGETAI
DZIGGETAIS
DZO
DZOS

E

EA
EACH
EACHWHERE
EADISH
EADISHES
EAGER
EAGERER
EAGEREST
EAGERLY
EAGERNESS
EAGERNESSES
EAGERS
EAGLE
EAGLES
EAGLET
EAGLETS
EAGLEWOOD
EAGLEWOODS
EAGRE
EAGRES
EALDORMAN
EALDORMEN
EALE
EALES
EAN
EANED
EANING
EANLING
EANLINGS
EANS
EAR
EARACHE
EARACHES
EARBASH
EARBASHED
EARBASHES
EARBASHING
EARBOB
EARBOBS
EARCON
EARCONS
EARD
EARDED
EARDING
EARDROP
EARDROPS
EARDRUM
EARDRUMS
EARDS
EARED
EARFLAP
EARFLAPS
EARFUL
EARFULS
EARING

EARINGS
EARL
EARLAP
EARLAPS
EARLDOM
EARLDOMS
EARLESS
EARLIER
EARLIES
EARLIEST
EARLINESS
EARLINESSES
EARLOBE
EARLOBES
EARLOCK
EARLOCKS
EARLS
EARLSHIP*
EARLSHIPS*
EARLY
EARLYWOOD*
EARLYWOODS*
EARMARK
EARMARKED
EARMARKING
EARMARKS
EARMUFF*
EARMUFFS
EARN
EARNED
EARNER
EARNERS
EARNEST
EARNESTLY
EARNESTS
EARNING
EARNINGS
EARNS
EARPHONE
EARPHONES
EARPICK
EARPICKS
EARPIECE
EARPIECES
EARPLUG
EARPLUGS
EARRING
EARRINGS
EARS
EARSHOT
EARSHOTS
EARST
EARSTONE*
EARSTONES*
EARTH

EARTHBORN
EARTHED
EARTHEN
EARTHFALL
EARTHFALLS
EARTHFAST
EARTHFLAX
EARTHFLAXES
EARTHIER
EARTHIEST
EARTHILY*
EARTHING
EARTHLIER
EARTHLIES
EARTHLIEST
EARTHLIKE*
EARTHLING
EARTHLINGS
EARTHLY
EARTHMAN
EARTHMEN
EARTHNUT*
EARTHNUTS*
EARTHPEA*
EARTHPEAS*
EARTHRISE*
EARTHRISES*
EARTHS
EARTHSET*
EARTHSETS*
EARTHSTAR*
EARTHSTARS*
EARTHWARD
EARTHWARDS
EARTHWAX
EARTHWAXES
EARTHWOLF
EARTHWOLVES
EARTHWORK
EARTHWORKS
EARTHWORM
EARTHWORMS
EARTHY
EARWAX
EARWAXES
EARWIG
EARWIGGED
EARWIGGING
EARWIGGY
EARWIGS
EARWORM*
EARWORMS*
EAS
EASE
EASED

EASEFUL
EASEFULLY*
EASEL
EASELESS
EASELS
EASEMENT
EASEMENTS
EASES
EASIER
EASIES*
EASIEST
EASILY
EASINESS
EASINESSES
EASING
EASLE
EASLES
EASSEL
EASSIL
EAST
EASTBOUND
EASTED
EASTER
EASTERLIES
EASTERLY
EASTERN
EASTERNER
EASTERNERS
EASTERS*
EASTING
EASTINGS
EASTLAND
EASTLIN
EASTLING
EASTLINGS
EASTLINS
EASTMOST
EASTS
EASTWARD
EASTWARDS
EASY
EASYGOING*
EAT
EATABLE
EATABLES
EATAGE
EATAGES
EATCHE
EATCHES
EATEN
EATER
EATERIES
EATERS
EATERY
EATH

EATHE
EATHLY
EATING
EATINGS
EATS
EAU
EAUS
EAUX
EAVE*
EAVED*
EAVES
EAVESDRIP
EAVESDRIPS
EAVESDROP
EAVESDROPPED
EAVESDROPPING
EAVESDROPPINGS
EAVESDROPS
EBAUCHE
EBAUCHES
EBB
EBBED
EBBET*
EBBETS*
EBBING
EBBLESS
EBBS
EBBTIDE
EBBTIDES
EBENEZER
EBENEZERS
EBENISTE
EBENISTES
EBIONISE
EBIONISED
EBIONISES
EBIONISING
EBIONISM
EBIONISMS
EBIONITIC
EBIONIZE
EBIONIZED
EBIONIZES
EBIONIZING
EBON
EBONICS
EBONIES
EBONISE
EBONISED
EBONISES
EBONISING
EBONIST
EBONISTS
EBONITE
EBONITES

EBONIZE	ECHEVERIA	ECLIPTIC	ECRITOIRES	ECU
EBONIZED	ECHEVERIAS	ECLIPTICS	ECRU	ECUELLE
EBONIZES	ECHIDNA	ECLOGITE	ECRUS	ECUELLES
EBONIZING	ECHIDNAE*	ECLOGITES	ECSTASES	ECUMENIC
EBONS	ECHIDNAS	ECLOGUE	ECSTASIED	ECUMENICS
EBONY	ECHIDNINE	ECLOGUES	ECSTASIES	ECUMENISM
EBRIATE	ECHIDNINES	ECLOSE	ECSTASIS	ECUMENISMS
EBRIATED	ECHINATE	ECLOSED	ECSTASISE	ECUMENIST*
EBRIETIES	ECHINATED	ECLOSES	ECSTASISED	ECUMENISTS*
EBRIETY	ECHING	ECLOSING	ECSTASISES	ECURIE
EBRILLADE	ECHINI	ECLOSION	ECSTASISING	ECURIES
EBRILLADES	ECHINOID	ECLOSIONS	ECSTASIZE	ECUS
EBRIOSE	ECHINOIDS	ECOCIDAL*	ECSTASIZED	ECZEMA
EBRIOSITIES	ECHINUS	ECOCIDE	ECSTASIZES	ECZEMAS
EBRIOSITY	ECHINUSES	ECOCIDES	ECSTASIZING	ED*
EBULLIENT	ECHIUROID*	ECOD	ECSTASY	EDACIOUS
EBURNEAN	ECHIUROIDS*	ECOFREAK	ECSTASYING	EDACITIES
EBURNEOUS	ECHO	ECOFREAKS	ECSTATIC	EDACITY
ECAD	ECHOED	ECOLOGIC	ECSTATICS	EDAPHIC
ECADS	ECHOER	ECOLOGIES	ECTASES	EDDIED
ECARTE	ECHOERS	ECOLOGIST	ECTASIS	EDDIES
ECARTES	ECHOES	ECOLOGISTS	ECTATIC*	EDDISH
ECAUDATE	ECHOEY*	ECOLOGY	ECTHYMA	EDDISHES
ECBOLE	ECHOGRAM	ECONOBOX*	ECTHYMAS	EDDO
ECBOLES	ECHOGRAMS	ECONOBOXES*	ECTHYMATA*	EDDOES
ECBOLIC	ECHOIC	ECONOMIC	ECTOBLAST	EDDY
ECBOLICS	ECHOING	ECONOMICS	ECTOBLASTS	EDDYING
ECCE	ECHOISE	ECONOMIES	ECTOCRINE	EDELWEISS
ECCENTRIC	ECHOISED	ECONOMISE	ECTOCRINES	EDELWEISSES
ECCENTRICS	ECHOISES	ECONOMISED	ECTODERM	EDEMA
ECCLESIA	ECHOISING	ECONOMISES	ECTODERMS	EDEMAS
ECCLESIAE	ECHOISM	ECONOMISING	ECTOGENIC	EDEMATA
ECCLESIAL	ECHOISMS	ECONOMISM	ECTOGENIES	EDEMATOSE
ECCO	ECHOIST	ECONOMISMS	ECTOGENY	EDEMATOUS
ECCRINE	ECHOISTS	ECONOMIST	ECTOMERE*	EDENIC*
ECCRISES	ECHOIZE	ECONOMISTS	ECTOMERES*	EDENTAL
ECCRISIS	ECHOIZED	ECONOMIZE	ECTOMORPH	EDENTATE
ECCRITIC	ECHOIZES	ECONOMIZED	ECTOMORPHS	EDENTATES
ECCRITICS	ECHOIZING	ECONOMIZES	ECTOPHYTE	EDGE
ECDYSES	ECHOLALIA	ECONOMIZING	ECTOPHYTES	EDGEBONE
ECDYSIAL*	ECHOLALIAS	ECONOMY	ECTOPIA	EDGEBONES
ECDYSIAST	ECHOLALIC*	ECONUT	ECTOPIAS	EDGED
ECDYSIASTS	ECHOLESS	ECONUTS	ECTOPIC	EDGELESS
ECDYSIS	ECHOS*	ECOPHOBIA	ECTOPIES	EDGER
ECDYSON*	ECHOVIRUS*	ECOPHOBIAS	ECTOPLASM	EDGERS
ECDYSONE*	ECHOVIRUSES*	ECORCHE	ECTOPLASMS	EDGES
ECDYSONES*	ECHT	ECORCHES	ECTOPY	EDGEWAYS
ECDYSONS*	ECLAIR	ECOSPHERE	ECTOSARC	EDGEWISE
ECESIS*	ECLAIRS	ECOSPHERES	ECTOSARCS	EDGIER
ECESISES*	ECLAMPSIA	ECOSSAISE	ECTOTHERM	EDGIEST
ECH	ECLAMPSIAS	ECOSSAISES	ECTOTHERMS	EDGILY*
ECHAPPE	ECLAMPSIES	ECOSTATE	ECTOZOA	EDGINESS
ECHAPPES	ECLAMPSY	ECOSYSTEM	ECTOZOAN	EDGINESSES
ECHARD*	ECLAMPTIC	ECOSYSTEMS	ECTOZOANS	EDGING
ECHARDS*	ECLAT	ECOTONAL*	ECTOZOIC	EDGINGS
ECHE	ECLATS	ECOTONE*	ECTOZOON	EDGY
ECHED	ECLECTIC	ECOTONES*	ECTROPIC	EDH
ECHELLE*	ECLECTICS	ECOTOXIC	ECTROPION	EDHS
ECHELLES*	ECLIPSE	ECOTYPE	ECTROPIONS	EDIBILITIES
ECHELON	ECLIPSED	ECOTYPES	ECTROPIUM	EDIBILITY
ECHELONED*	ECLIPSES	ECOTYPIC*	ECTROPIUMS	EDIBLE
ECHELONING*	ECLIPSING	ECRASEUR	ECTYPAL	EDIBLES
ECHELONS	ECLIPSIS*	ECRASEURS	ECTYPE	EDICT
ECHES	ECLIPSISES*	ECRITOIRE	ECTYPES	EDICTAL

The Chambers Dictionary is the authority for many longer words; see Introduction, page ix

EDICTALLY	EELGRASSES	EFFICACY	EGENCIES	EGOMANIAC
EDICTS	EELIER	EFFICIENT	EGENCY	EGOMANIACS
EDIFICE	EELIEST	EFFICIENTS	EGER	EGOMANIAS
EDIFICES	EELLIKE*	EFFIERCE	EGERS	EGOS
EDIFICIAL	EELPOUT	EFFIERCED	EGEST	EGOTHEISM
EDIFIED	EELPOUTS	EFFIERCES	EGESTA	EGOTHEISMS
EDIFIER	EELS	EFFIERCING	EGESTED	EGOTISE
EDIFIERS	EELWORM	EFFIGIAL*	EGESTING	EGOTISED
EDIFIES	EELWORMS	EFFIGIES	EGESTION	EGOTISES
EDIFY	EELWRACK	EFFIGY	EGESTIONS	EGOTISING
EDIFYING	EELWRACKS	EFFING	EGESTIVE	EGOTISM
EDILE	EELY	EFFLUENCE	EGESTS	EGOTISMS
EDILES	EEN	EFFLUENCES	EGG	EGOTIST
EDIT	EERIE	EFFLUENT	EGGAR	EGOTISTIC
EDITABLE*	EERIER	EFFLUENTS	EGGARS	EGOTISTS
EDITED	EERIEST	EFFLUVIA	EGGBEATER*	EGOTIZE
EDITING	EERILY	EFFLUVIAL	EGGBEATERS*	EGOTIZED
EDITION	EERINESS	EFFLUVIUM	EGGCUP	EGOTIZES
EDITIONS	EERINESSES	EFFLUVIUMS*	EGGCUPS	EGOTIZING
EDITOR	EERY	EFFLUX	EGGED	EGREGIOUS
EDITORIAL	EEVEN	EFFLUXES	EGGER	EGRESS
EDITORIALS	EEVENS	EFFLUXION	EGGERIES	EGRESSED*
EDITORS	EEVN	EFFLUXIONS	EGGERS	EGRESSES
EDITRESS	EEVNING	EFFORCE	EGGERY	EGRESSING*
EDITRESSES	EEVNINGS	EFFORCED	EGGHEAD	EGRESSION
EDITS	EEVNS	EFFORCES	EGGHEADED*	EGRESSIONS
EDUCABLE	EF	EFFORCING	EGGHEADS	EGRET
EDUCABLES*	EFF	EFFORT	EGGIER	EGRETS
EDUCATE	EFFABLE	EFFORTFUL	EGGIEST	EGYPTIAN*
EDUCATED	EFFACE	EFFORTS	EGGING	EGYPTIANS*
EDUCATES	EFFACED	EFFRAIDE	EGGLER	EH
EDUCATING	EFFACER*	EFFRAY	EGGLERS	EHED
EDUCATION	EFFACERS*	EFFRAYS	EGGLESS*	EHING
EDUCATIONS	EFFACES	EFFS	EGGMASS	EHS
EDUCATIVE	EFFACING	EFFULGE	EGGMASSES	EIDE*
EDUCATOR	EFFECT	EFFULGED	EGGNOG	EIDENT
EDUCATORS	EFFECTED	EFFULGENT	EGGNOGS	EIDER
EDUCATORY	EFFECTER	EFFULGES	EGGPLANT*	EIDERDOWN
EDUCE	EFFECTERS	EFFULGING	EGGPLANTS*	EIDERDOWNS
EDUCED	EFFECTING	EFFUSE	EGGS	EIDERS
EDUCEMENT	EFFECTIVE	EFFUSED	EGGSHELL	EIDETIC
EDUCEMENTS	EFFECTIVES	EFFUSES	EGGSHELLS	EIDETICS
EDUCES	EFFECTOR	EFFUSING	EGGWASH	EIDOGRAPH
EDUCIBLE	EFFECTORS	EFFUSION	EGGWASHES	EIDOGRAPHS
EDUCING	EFFECTS	EFFUSIONS	EGGY	EIDOLA
EDUCT	EFFECTUAL	EFFUSIVE	EGIS	EIDOLIC*
EDUCTION	EFFED	EFS	EGISES	EIDOLON
EDUCTIONS	EFFEIR	EFT	EGLANTINE	EIDOLONS*
EDUCTIVE*	EFFEIRED	EFTEST	EGLANTINES	EIDOS*
EDUCTOR	EFFEIRING	EFTS	EGLATERE	EIGENMODE*
EDUCTORS	EFFEIRS	EFTSOON*	EGLATERES	EIGENMODES*
EDUCTS	EFFENDI	EFTSOONS	EGLOMISE*	EIGENTONE
EDUSKUNTA	EFFENDIS	EGAD	EGMA	EIGENTONES
EDUSKUNTAS	EFFERE	EGADS*	EGMAS	EIGHT
EE	EFFERED	EGAL	EGO	EIGHTEEN
EECH	EFFERENCE	EGALITE*	EGOISM	EIGHTEENS
EECHED	EFFERENCES	EGALITES*	EGOISMS	EIGHTFOIL
EECHES	EFFERENT	EGALITIES	EGOIST	EIGHTFOILS
EECHING	EFFERENTS*	EGALITY	EGOISTIC	EIGHTFOLD
EEK	EFFERES	EGALLY	EGOISTS	EIGHTFOOT
EEL	EFFERING	EGAREMENT	EGOITIES	EIGHTH
EELFARE	EFFETE	EGAREMENTS	EGOITY	EIGHTHLY
EELFARES	EFFETELY	EGENCE	EGOLESS*	EIGHTHS
EELGRASS	EFFICACIES	EGENCES	EGOMANIA	EIGHTIES

EIGHTIETH	EKISTICS	ELATION	ELECTRODES	ELEVENS
EIGHTIETHS	EKKA	ELATIONS	ELECTROED*	ELEVENSES
EIGHTS	EKKAS	ELATIVE	ELECTROING*	ELEVENTH
EIGHTSMAN	EKLOGITE	ELATIVES	ELECTRON	ELEVENTHS
EIGHTSMEN	EKLOGITES	ELBOW	ELECTRONS	ELEVON
EIGHTSOME	EKPHRASES	ELBOWED	ELECTROS	ELEVONS
EIGHTSOMES	EKPHRASIS	ELBOWING	ELECTRUM	ELF
EIGHTVO	EKPWELE	ELBOWROOM*	ELECTRUMS	ELFED
EIGHTVOS	EKPWELES	ELBOWROOMS*	ELECTS	ELFHOOD
EIGHTY	EKTEXINE*	ELBOWS	ELECTUARIES	ELFHOODS
EIGNE	EKTEXINES*	ELCHEE	ELECTUARY	ELFIN
EIK	EKUELE	ELCHEES	ELEDOISIN*	ELFING
EIKED	EL	ELCHI	ELEDOISINS*	ELFINS
EIKING	ELABORATE	ELCHIS	ELEGANCE	ELFISH
EIKON	ELABORATED	ELD	ELEGANCES	ELFISHLY*
EIKONES*	ELABORATES	ELDER	ELEGANCIES	ELFLAND
EIKONS	ELABORATING	ELDERLIES	ELEGANCY	ELFLANDS
EIKS	ELAEOLITE	ELDERLY	ELEGANT	ELFLIKE*
EILDING	ELAEOLITES	ELDERS	ELEGANTLY	ELFLOCK*
EILDINGS	ELAIN*	ELDERSHIP	ELEGIAC	ELFLOCKS
EILDS	ELAINS*	ELDERSHIPS	ELEGIACAL	ELFS
EINE	ELAN	ELDEST	ELEGIACS	ELHI*
EINKORN*	ELANCE	ELDIN	ELEGIAST	ELIAD
EINKORNS*	ELANCED	ELDING	ELEGIASTS	ELIADS
EINSTEIN*	ELANCES	ELDINGS	ELEGIES	ELICIT
EINSTEINS*	ELANCING	ELDINS	ELEGISE	ELICITED
EIRACK	ELAND	ELDRESS*	ELEGISED	ELICITING
EIRACKS	ELANDS	ELDRESSES*	ELEGISES	ELICITOR
EIRENIC	ELANET	ELDRICH*	ELEGISING	ELICITORS
EIRENICON	ELANETS	ELDRITCH	ELEGIST	ELICITS
EIRENICONS	ELANS	ELDS	ELEGISTS	ELIDE
EISEGESES*	ELAPHINE	ELECT	ELEGIT	ELIDED
EISEGESIS*	ELAPID*	ELECTABLE	ELEGITS	ELIDES
EISEL	ELAPIDS*	ELECTED	ELEGIZE	ELIDIBLE*
EISELL	ELAPINE*	ELECTEE*	ELEGIZED	ELIDING
EISELLS	ELAPSE	ELECTEES*	ELEGIZES	ELIGIBLE
EISELS	ELAPSED	ELECTING	ELEGIZING	ELIGIBLES
EISWEIN*	ELAPSES	ELECTION	ELEGY	ELIGIBLY
EISWEINS*	ELAPSING	ELECTIONS	ELEMENT	ELIMINANT
EITHER	ELASTANCE	ELECTIVE	ELEMENTAL	ELIMINANTS
EJACULATE	ELASTANCES	ELECTIVES	ELEMENTALS	ELIMINATE
EJACULATED	ELASTASE	ELECTOR	ELEMENTS	ELIMINATED
EJACULATES	ELASTASES	ELECTORAL	ELEMI	ELIMINATES
EJACULATING	ELASTIC	ELECTORS	ELEMIS	ELIMINATING
EJECT	ELASTICS	ELECTRESS	ELENCH	ELINT*
EJECTA	ELASTIN	ELECTRESSES	ELENCHI	ELINTS*
EJECTABLE*	ELASTINS	ELECTRET	ELENCHIC*	ELISION
EJECTED	ELASTOMER	ELECTRETS	ELENCHS	ELISIONS
EJECTING	ELASTOMERS	ELECTRIC	ELENCHUS	ELITE
EJECTION	ELATE	ELECTRICS	ELENCTIC	ELITES
EJECTIONS	ELATED	ELECTRIFIED	ELEPHANT	ELITISM
EJECTIVE	ELATEDLY	ELECTRIFIES	ELEPHANTS	ELITISMS
EJECTIVES*	ELATER	ELECTRIFY	ELEUTHERI	ELITIST
EJECTMENT	ELATERID*	ELECTRIFYING	ELEVATE	ELITISTS
EJECTMENTS	ELATERIDS*	ELECTRISE	ELEVATED	ELIXIR
EJECTOR	ELATERIN	ELECTRISED	ELEVATEDS*	ELIXIRS
EJECTORS	ELATERINS	ELECTRISES	ELEVATES	ELK
EJECTS	ELATERITE	ELECTRISING	ELEVATING	ELKHOUND
EKE	ELATERITES	ELECTRIZE	ELEVATION	ELKHOUNDS
EKED	ELATERIUM	ELECTRIZED	ELEVATIONS	ELKS
EKES	ELATERIUMS	ELECTRIZES	ELEVATOR	ELL
EKING	ELATERS	ELECTRIZING	ELEVATORS	ELLAGIC
EKISTIC	ELATES	ELECTRO	ELEVATORY	ELLIPSE
	ELATING	ELECTRODE	ELEVEN	ELLIPSES

The Chambers Dictionary is the authority for many longer words; see Introduction, page ix

ELLIPSIS	ELOQUENT	ELVISH	EMBARGOES	EMBLAZE
ELLIPSOID	ELPEE	ELVISHLY*	EMBARGOING	EMBLAZED
ELLIPSOIDS	ELPEES	ELYSIAN*	EMBARK	EMBLAZER*
ELLIPTIC	ELS	ELYTRA	EMBARKED	EMBLAZERS*
ELLOPS	ELSE	ELYTRAL	EMBARKING	EMBLAZES
ELLOPSES	ELSEWHERE	ELYTROID*	EMBARKS	EMBLAZING
ELLS	ELSEWISE	ELYTRON	EMBARRASS	EMBLAZON
ELLWAND	ELSHIN	ELYTROUS*	EMBARRASSED	EMBLAZONED
ELLWANDS	ELSHINS	ELYTRUM	EMBARRASSES	EMBLAZONING
ELM	ELSIN	EM	EMBARRASSING	EMBLAZONS
ELMEN	ELSINS	EMACIATE	EMBARRED	EMBLEM
ELMIER	ELT	EMACIATED	EMBARRING	EMBLEMA
ELMIEST	ELTCHI	EMACIATES	EMBARRINGS	EMBLEMATA
ELMS	ELTCHIS	EMACIATING	EMBARS	EMBLEMED
ELMWOOD	ELTS	EMAIL	EMBASE	EMBLEMING
ELMWOODS	ELUANT	EMAILED	EMBASED	EMBLEMISE
ELMY	ELUANTS	EMAILING	EMBASES	EMBLEMISED
ELOCUTE	ELUATE	EMAILS	EMBASING	EMBLEMISES
ELOCUTED	ELUATES	EMALANGENI	EMBASSADE	EMBLEMISING
ELOCUTES	ELUCIDATE	EMANANT	EMBASSADES	EMBLEMIZE
ELOCUTING	ELUCIDATED	EMANATE	EMBASSAGE	EMBLEMIZED
ELOCUTION	ELUCIDATES	EMANATED	EMBASSAGES	EMBLEMIZES
ELOCUTIONS	ELUCIDATING	EMANATES	EMBASSIES	EMBLEMIZING
ELOCUTORY	ELUDE	EMANATING	EMBASSY	EMBLEMS
ELODEA*	ELUDED	EMANATION	EMBASTE	EMBLIC
ELODEAS*	ELUDER	EMANATIONS	EMBATHE	EMBLICS
ELOGE	ELUDERS	EMANATIST	EMBATHED	EMBLOOM
ELOGES	ELUDES	EMANATISTS	EMBATHES	EMBLOOMED
ELOGIES	ELUDIBLE	EMANATIVE	EMBATHING	EMBLOOMING
ELOGIST	ELUDING	EMANATOR*	EMBATTLE	EMBLOOMS
ELOGISTS	ELUENT	EMANATORS*	EMBATTLED	EMBLOSSOM
ELOGIUM	ELUENTS	EMANATORY	EMBATTLES	EMBLOSSOMED
ELOGIUMS	ELUSION	EMBACE	EMBATTLING	EMBLOSSOMING
ELOGY	ELUSIONS	EMBACES	EMBAY	EMBLOSSOMS
ELOIGN	ELUSIVE	EMBACING	EMBAYED	EMBODIED
ELOIGNED	ELUSIVELY	EMBAIL	EMBAYING	EMBODIER*
ELOIGNER	ELUSORY	EMBAILED	EMBAYLD	EMBODIERS*
ELOIGNERS	ELUTE	EMBAILING	EMBAYMENT	EMBODIES
ELOIGNING	ELUTED	EMBAILS	EMBAYMENTS	EMBODY
ELOIGNS	ELUTES	EMBALE	EMBAYS	EMBODYING
ELOIN	ELUTING	EMBALED	EMBED	EMBOG
ELOINED	ELUTION	EMBALES	EMBEDDED	EMBOGGED
ELOINER	ELUTIONS	EMBALING	EMBEDDING	EMBOGGING
ELOINERS	ELUTOR	EMBALL	EMBEDDINGS	EMBOGS
ELOINING	ELUTORS	EMBALLED	EMBEDMENT	EMBOGUE
ELOINMENT	ELUTRIATE	EMBALLING	EMBEDMENTS	EMBOGUED
ELOINMENTS	ELUTRIATED	EMBALLINGS	EMBEDS	EMBOGUES
ELOINS	ELUTRIATES	EMBALLS	EMBELLISH	EMBOGUING
ELONGATE	ELUTRIATING	EMBALM	EMBELLISHED	EMBOIL
ELONGATED	ELUVIA	EMBALMED	EMBELLISHES	EMBOILED
ELONGATES	ELUVIAL	EMBALMER	EMBELLISHING	EMBOILING
ELONGATING	ELUVIATE*	EMBALMERS	EMBER	EMBOILS
ELOPE	ELUVIATED*	EMBALMING	EMBERS	EMBOLDEN
ELOPED	ELUVIATES*	EMBALMINGS	EMBEZZLE	EMBOLDENED
ELOPEMENT	ELUVIATING*	EMBALMS	EMBEZZLED	EMBOLDENING
ELOPEMENTS	ELUVIUM	EMBANK	EMBEZZLER	EMBOLDENS
ELOPER	ELUVIUMS	EMBANKED	EMBEZZLERS	EMBOLI
ELOPERS	ELVAN	EMBANKER	EMBEZZLES	EMBOLIC
ELOPES	ELVANITE	EMBANKERS	EMBEZZLING	EMBOLIES
ELOPING	ELVANITES	EMBANKING	EMBITTER	EMBOLISM
ELOPS	ELVANS	EMBANKS	EMBITTERED	EMBOLISMS
ELOPSES	ELVER	EMBAR	EMBITTERING	EMBOLUS
ELOQUENCE	ELVERS	EMBARGO	EMBITTERINGS	EMBOLUSES
ELOQUENCES	ELVES	EMBARGOED	EMBITTERS	EMBOLY

Words marked with an asterisk are from OTCWL

EMBORDER	EMBRASURE	EMBUSSED	EMETINE	EMMET
EMBORDERED	EMBRASURES	EMBUSSES	EMETINES	EMMETROPE
EMBORDERING	EMBRAVE	EMBUSSING	EMETINS	EMMETROPES
EMBORDERS	EMBRAVED	EMBUSY	EMEU	EMMETS
EMBOSCATA	EMBRAVES	EMBUSYING	EMEUS	EMMEW
EMBOSCATAS	EMBRAVING	EMCEE	EMEUTE	EMMEWED
EMBOSK*	EMBRAZURE	EMCEED	EMEUTES	EMMEWING
EMBOSKED*	EMBRAZURES	EMCEEING	EMF*	EMMEWS
EMBOSKING*	EMBREAD	EMCEES	EMFS*	EMMOVE
EMBOSKS*	EMBREADED	EME	EMIC*	EMMOVED
EMBOSOM	EMBREADING	EMEER	EMICANT	EMMOVES
EMBOSOMED	EMBREADS	EMEERATE*	EMICATE	EMMOVING
EMBOSOMING	EMBREATHE	EMEERATES*	EMICATED	EMODIN*
EMBOSOMS	EMBREATHED	EMEERS	EMICATES	EMODINS*
EMBOSS	EMBREATHES	EMEND	EMICATING	EMOLLIATE
EMBOSSED	EMBREATHING	EMENDABLE	EMICATION	EMOLLIATED
EMBOSSER	EMBREWE	EMENDALS	EMICATIONS	EMOLLIATES
EMBOSSERS	EMBREWED	EMENDATE	EMICTION	EMOLLIATING
EMBOSSES	EMBREWES	EMENDATED	EMICTIONS	EMOLLIENT
EMBOSSING	EMBREWING	EMENDATES	EMICTORY	EMOLLIENTS
EMBOST	EMBRITTLE	EMENDATING	EMIGRANT	EMOLUMENT
EMBOUND	EMBRITTLED	EMENDATOR	EMIGRANTS	EMOLUMENTS
EMBOUNDED	EMBRITTLES	EMENDATORS	EMIGRATE	EMONG
EMBOUNDING	EMBRITTLING	EMENDED	EMIGRATED	EMONGES
EMBOUNDS	EMBROCATE	EMENDER*	EMIGRATES	EMONGEST
EMBOW	EMBROCATED	EMENDERS*	EMIGRATING	EMONGST
EMBOWED	EMBROCATES	EMENDING	EMIGRE	EMOTE
EMBOWEL	EMBROCATING	EMENDS	EMIGRES	EMOTED
EMBOWELED*	EMBROGLIO	EMERALD	EMINENCE	EMOTER*
EMBOWELING*	EMBROGLIOS	EMERALDS	EMINENCES	EMOTERS*
EMBOWELLED	EMBROIDER	EMERAUDE	EMINENCIES	EMOTES
EMBOWELLING	EMBROIDERED	EMERAUDES	EMINENCY	EMOTICON
EMBOWELS	EMBROIDERING	EMERGE	EMINENT	EMOTICONS
EMBOWER	EMBROIDERS	EMERGED	EMINENTLY	EMOTING
EMBOWERED	EMBROIL	EMERGENCE	EMIR	EMOTION
EMBOWERING	EMBROILED	EMERGENCES	EMIRATE	EMOTIONAL
EMBOWERS	EMBROILING	EMERGENCIES	EMIRATES	EMOTIONS
EMBOWING	EMBROILS	EMERGENCY	EMIRS	EMOTIVE
EMBOWS	EMBROWN	EMERGENT	EMISSARIES	EMOTIVELY*
EMBOX	EMBROWNED	EMERGENTS*	EMISSARY	EMOTIVISM
EMBOXED	EMBROWNING	EMERGES	EMISSILE	EMOTIVISMS
EMBOXES	EMBROWNS	EMERGING	EMISSION	EMOTIVITIES*
EMBOXING	EMBRUE	EMERIED	EMISSIONS	EMOTIVITY*
EMBRACE	EMBRUED	EMERIES	EMISSIVE	EMOVE
EMBRACED	EMBRUES	EMERITA*	EMIT	EMOVED
EMBRACEOR	EMBRUING	EMERITAE*	EMITS	EMOVES
EMBRACEORS	EMBRUTE	EMERITI	EMITTANCE*	EMOVING
EMBRACER	EMBRUTED	EMERITUS	EMITTANCES*	EMPACKET
EMBRACERIES	EMBRUTES	EMEROD*	EMITTED	EMPACKETED
EMBRACERS	EMBRUTING	EMERODS	EMITTER	EMPACKETING
EMBRACERY	EMBRYO	EMEROID*	EMITTERS	EMPACKETS
EMBRACES	EMBRYOID	EMEROIDS*	EMITTING	EMPAESTIC
EMBRACING	EMBRYOIDS	EMERSED	EMMA	EMPAIRE
EMBRACIVE	EMBRYON	EMERSION	EMMARBLE	EMPAIRED
EMBRAID	EMBRYONAL	EMERSIONS	EMMARBLED	EMPAIRES
EMBRAIDED	EMBRYONIC	EMERY	EMMARBLES	EMPAIRING
EMBRAIDING	EMBRYONS	EMERYING	EMMARBLING	EMPALE
EMBRAIDS	EMBRYOS	EMES	EMMAS	EMPALED
EMBRANGLE	EMBRYOTIC	EMESES	EMMER	EMPALER*
EMBRANGLED	EMBUS	EMESIS	EMMERS	EMPALERS*
EMBRANGLES	EMBUSIED	EMETIC	EMMESH	EMPALES
EMBRANGLING	EMBUSIES	EMETICAL	EMMESHED	EMPALING
EMBRASOR	EMBUSQUE	EMETICS	EMMESHES	EMPANADA*
EMBRASORS	EMBUSQUES	EMETIN	EMMESHING	EMPANADAS*

The Chambers Dictionary is the authority for many longer words; see Introduction, page ix

EMPANEL	EMPERIZE	EMPLOYERS	EMPYREANS	ENABLING
EMPANELED*	EMPERIZED	EMPLOYES*	EMPYREUMA	ENACT
EMPANELING*	EMPERIZES	EMPLOYING	EMPYREUMATA	ENACTED
EMPANELLED	EMPERIZING	EMPLOYS	EMS	ENACTING
EMPANELLING	EMPEROR	EMPLUME	EMU	ENACTION
EMPANELS	EMPERORS	EMPLUMED	EMULATE	ENACTIONS
EMPANOPLIED	EMPERY	EMPLUMES	EMULATED	ENACTIVE
EMPANOPLIES	EMPHASES	EMPLUMING	EMULATES	ENACTMENT
EMPANOPLY	EMPHASIS	EMPOISON	EMULATING	ENACTMENTS
EMPANOPLYING	EMPHASISE	EMPOISONED	EMULATION	ENACTOR
EMPARE	EMPHASISED	EMPOISONING	EMULATIONS	ENACTORS
EMPARED	EMPHASISES	EMPOISONS	EMULATIVE	ENACTORY*
EMPARES	EMPHASISING	EMPOLDER	EMULATOR	ENACTS
EMPARING	EMPHASIZE	EMPOLDERED	EMULATORS	ENACTURE
EMPARL	EMPHASIZED	EMPOLDERING	EMULE	ENACTURES
EMPARLED	EMPHASIZES	EMPOLDERS	EMULED	ENALLAGE
EMPARLING	EMPHASIZING	EMPORIA	EMULES	ENALLAGES
EMPARLS	EMPHATIC	EMPORIUM	EMULGE	ENAMEL
EMPART	EMPHLYSES	EMPORIUMS	EMULGED	ENAMELED*
EMPARTED	EMPHLYSIS	EMPOWER	EMULGENCE	ENAMELER*
EMPARTING	EMPHYSEMA	EMPOWERED	EMULGENCES	ENAMELERS*
EMPARTS	EMPHYSEMAS	EMPOWERING	EMULGENT	ENAMELING*
EMPATHIC	EMPIERCE	EMPOWERS	EMULGES	ENAMELIST*
EMPATHIES	EMPIERCED	EMPRESS	EMULGING	ENAMELISTS*
EMPATHISE	EMPIERCES	EMPRESSE	EMULING	ENAMELLED
EMPATHISED	EMPIERCING	EMPRESSES	EMULOUS	ENAMELLER
EMPATHISES	EMPIGHT	EMPRISE	EMULOUSLY	ENAMELLERS
EMPATHISING	EMPIRE	EMPRISES	EMULSIFIED	ENAMELLING
EMPATHIZE	EMPIRES	EMPRIZE*	EMULSIFIES	ENAMELLINGS
EMPATHIZED	EMPIRIC	EMPRIZES*	EMULSIFY	ENAMELS
EMPATHIZES	EMPIRICAL	EMPTIED	EMULSIFYING	ENAMINE*
EMPATHIZING	EMPIRICS	EMPTIER	EMULSIN	ENAMINES*
EMPATHY	EMPLACE	EMPTIERS	EMULSINS	ENAMOR
EMPATRON	EMPLACED	EMPTIES	EMULSION	ENAMORADO
EMPATRONED	EMPLACES	EMPTIEST	EMULSIONS	ENAMORADOS
EMPATRONING	EMPLACING	EMPTILY	EMULSIVE	ENAMORED
EMPATRONS	EMPLANE	EMPTINESS	EMULSOID	ENAMORING
EMPAYRE	EMPLANED	EMPTINESSES	EMULSOIDS	ENAMORS
EMPAYRED	EMPLANES	EMPTINGS*	EMULSOR	ENAMOUR
EMPAYRES	EMPLANING	EMPTINS*	EMULSORS	ENAMOURED
EMPAYRING	EMPLASTER	EMPTION	EMUNCTION	ENAMOURING
EMPEACH	EMPLASTERED	EMPTIONAL	EMUNCTIONS	ENAMOURS
EMPEACHED	EMPLASTERING	EMPTIONS	EMUNCTORIES	ENARCH
EMPEACHES	EMPLASTERS	EMPTY	EMUNCTORY	ENARCHED
EMPEACHING	EMPLASTIC	EMPTYING	EMUNGE	ENARCHES
EMPENNAGE	EMPLASTICS	EMPTYINGS	EMUNGED	ENARCHING
EMPENNAGES	EMPLEACH	EMPTYSES	EMUNGES	ENARM
EMPEOPLE	EMPLEACHED	EMPTYSIS	EMUNGING	ENARMED
EMPEOPLED	EMPLEACHES	EMPURPLE	EMURE	ENARMING
EMPEOPLES	EMPLEACHING	EMPURPLED	EMURED	ENARMS
EMPEOPLING	EMPLECTON	EMPURPLES	EMURES	ENATE
EMPERCE	EMPLECTONS	EMPURPLING	EMURING	ENATES*
EMPERCED	EMPLECTUM	EMPUSA	EMUS	ENATIC*
EMPERCES	EMPLECTUMS	EMPUSAS	EMYD*	ENATION
EMPERCING	EMPLONGE	EMPUSE	EMYDE*	ENATIONS
EMPERIES	EMPLONGED	EMPUSES	EMYDES	ENAUNTER
EMPERISE	EMPLONGES	EMPYEMA	EMYDS*	ENCAENIA
EMPERISED	EMPLONGING	EMPYEMAS	EMYS	ENCAENIAS
EMPERISES	EMPLOY	EMPYEMATA	EN	ENCAGE
EMPERISH	EMPLOYE*	EMPYEMIC	ENABLE	ENCAGED
EMPERISHED	EMPLOYED	EMPYESES	ENABLED	ENCAGES
EMPERISHES	EMPLOYEE	EMPYESIS	ENABLER	ENCAGING
EMPERISHING	EMPLOYEES	EMPYREAL	ENABLERS	ENCALM
EMPERISING	EMPLOYER	EMPYREAN	ENABLES	ENCALMED

ENCALMING	ENCHEERING	ENCOMIA	ENCYSTED	ENDEWS
ENCALMS	ENCHEERS	ENCOMIAST	ENCYSTING	ENDEXINE*
ENCAMP	ENCHILADA	ENCOMIASTS	ENCYSTS	ENDEXINES*
ENCAMPED	ENCHILADAS	ENCOMION	END	ENDGAME
ENCAMPING	ENCHORIAL	ENCOMIUM	ENDAMAGE	ENDGAMES
ENCAMPS	ENCHORIC	ENCOMIUMS	ENDAMAGED	ENDING
ENCANTHIS	ENCIERRO	ENCOMPASS	ENDAMAGES	ENDINGS
ENCANTHISES	ENCIERROS	ENCOMPASSED	ENDAMAGING	ENDIRON
ENCAPSULE*	ENCINA*	ENCOMPASSES	ENDAMEBA*	ENDIRONS
ENCAPSULED*	ENCINAL*	ENCOMPASSING	ENDAMEBAE*	ENDITE
ENCAPSULES*	ENCINAS*	ENCORE	ENDAMEBAS*	ENDITED
ENCAPSULING*	ENCIPHER	ENCORED	ENDAMOEBA	ENDITES
ENCARPUS	ENCIPHERED	ENCORES	ENDAMOEBAE	ENDITING
ENCARPUSES	ENCIPHERING	ENCORING	ENDAMOEBAS	ENDIVE
ENCASE	ENCIPHERS	ENCOUNTER	ENDANGER	ENDIVES
ENCASED	ENCIRCLE	ENCOUNTERED	ENDANGERED	ENDLANG
ENCASES	ENCIRCLED	ENCOUNTERING	ENDANGERING	ENDLEAF*
ENCASH	ENCIRCLES	ENCOUNTERS	ENDANGERS	ENDLEAVES*
ENCASHED	ENCIRCLING	ENCOURAGE	ENDARCH	ENDLESS
ENCASHES	ENCIRCLINGS	ENCOURAGED	ENDARCHIES*	ENDLESSLY
ENCASHING	ENCLASP	ENCOURAGES	ENDARCHY*	ENDLONG
ENCASING	ENCLASPED	ENCOURAGING	ENDART	ENDMOST
ENCAUSTIC	ENCLASPING	ENCOURAGINGS	ENDARTED	ENDNOTE*
ENCAUSTICS	ENCLASPS	ENCRADLE	ENDARTING	ENDNOTES*
ENCAVE	ENCLAVE	ENCRADLED	ENDARTS	ENDOBLAST
ENCAVED	ENCLAVED	ENCRADLES	ENDBRAIN*	ENDOBLASTS
ENCAVES	ENCLAVES	ENCRADLING	ENDBRAINS*	ENDOCARP
ENCAVING	ENCLAVING	ENCRATIES	ENDEAR	ENDOCARPS
ENCEINTE	ENCLISES	ENCRATY	ENDEARED	ENDOCAST*
ENCEINTES	ENCLISIS	ENCREASE	ENDEARING	ENDOCASTS*
ENCEPHALA*	ENCLITIC	ENCREASED	ENDEARS	ENDOCRINE
ENCEPHALON*	ENCLITICS	ENCREASES	ENDEAVOR	ENDOCRINES
ENCHAFE	ENCLOSE	ENCREASING	ENDEAVORED	ENDODERM
ENCHAFED	ENCLOSED	ENCRIMSON	ENDEAVORING	ENDODERMS
ENCHAFES	ENCLOSER	ENCRIMSONED	ENDEAVORS	ENDODYNE
ENCHAFING	ENCLOSERS	ENCRIMSONING	ENDEAVOUR	ENDOERGIC*
ENCHAIN	ENCLOSES	ENCRIMSONS	ENDEAVOURED	ENDOGAMIC
ENCHAINED	ENCLOSING	ENCRINAL	ENDEAVOURING	ENDOGAMIES
ENCHAINING	ENCLOSURE	ENCRINIC	ENDEAVOURS	ENDOGAMY
ENCHAINS	ENCLOSURES	ENCRINITE	ENDECAGON	ENDOGEN
ENCHANT	ENCLOTHE	ENCRINITES	ENDECAGONS	ENDOGENIC
ENCHANTED	ENCLOTHED	ENCROACH	ENDED	ENDOGENIES
ENCHANTER	ENCLOTHES	ENCROACHED	ENDEICTIC	ENDOGENS
ENCHANTERS	ENCLOTHING	ENCROACHES	ENDEIXES	ENDOGENY
ENCHANTING	ENCLOUD	ENCROACHING	ENDEIXIS	ENDOLYMPH
ENCHANTS	ENCLOUDED	ENCRUST	ENDEIXISES	ENDOLYMPHS
ENCHARGE	ENCLOUDING	ENCRUSTED	ENDEMIAL	ENDOMIXES
ENCHARGED	ENCLOUDS	ENCRUSTING	ENDEMIC	ENDOMIXIS
ENCHARGES	ENCODE	ENCRUSTS	ENDEMICAL	ENDOMIXISES
ENCHARGING	ENCODED	ENCRYPT	ENDEMICS	ENDOMORPH
ENCHARM	ENCODER*	ENCRYPTED	ENDEMISM	ENDOMORPHS
ENCHARMED	ENCODERS*	ENCRYPTING	ENDEMISMS	ENDOPHAGIES
ENCHARMING	ENCODES	ENCRYPTS	ENDENIZEN	ENDOPHAGY
ENCHARMS	ENCODING	ENCUMBER	ENDENIZENED	ENDOPHYTE
ENCHASE	ENCOLOUR	ENCUMBERED	ENDENIZENING	ENDOPHYTES
ENCHASED	ENCOLOURED	ENCUMBERING	ENDENIZENS	ENDOPLASM
ENCHASER*	ENCOLOURING	ENCUMBERS	ENDER*	ENDOPLASMS
ENCHASERS*	ENCOLOURS	ENCURTAIN	ENDERMIC	ENDOPOD*
ENCHASES	ENCOLPION	ENCURTAINED	ENDERON	ENDOPODS*
ENCHASING	ENCOLPIONS	ENCURTAINING	ENDERONS	ENDORPHIN
ENCHEASON	ENCOLPIUM	ENCURTAINS	ENDERS*	ENDORPHINS
ENCHEASONS	ENCOLPIUMS	ENCYCLIC	ENDEW	ENDORSE
ENCHEER	ENCOLURE	ENCYCLICS*	ENDEWED	ENDORSED
ENCHEERED	ENCOLURES	ENCYST	ENDEWING	ENDORSEE

The Chambers Dictionary is the authority for many longer words; see Introduction, page ix

ENDORSEES	ENDUNGEONING	ENFEEBLES	ENFORM	ENGIRDING
ENDORSER	ENDUNGEONS	ENFEEBLING	ENFORMED	ENGIRDLE
ENDORSERS	ENDURABLE	ENFELON	ENFORMING	ENGIRDLED
ENDORSES	ENDURABLY	ENFELONED	ENFORMS	ENGIRDLES
ENDORSING	ENDURANCE	ENFELONING	ENFRAME	ENGIRDLING
ENDORSOR*	ENDURANCES	ENFELONS	ENFRAMED	ENGIRDS
ENDORSORS*	ENDURE	ENFEOFF	ENFRAMES	ENGIRT
ENDOSARC	ENDURED	ENFEOFFED	ENFRAMING	ENGISCOPE
ENDOSARCS	ENDURER	ENFEOFFING	ENFREE	ENGISCOPES
ENDOSCOPE	ENDURERS	ENFEOFFS	ENFREED	ENGLISH*
ENDOSCOPES	ENDURES	ENFESTED	ENFREEDOM	ENGLISHED*
ENDOSCOPIES	ENDURING	ENFETTER	ENFREEDOMED	ENGLISHES*
ENDOSCOPY	ENDURO	ENFETTERED	ENFREEDOMING	ENGLISHING*
ENDOSMOS*	ENDUROS	ENFETTERING	ENFREEDOMS	ENGLOBE
ENDOSMOSE	ENDWAYS	ENFETTERS	ENFREEING	ENGLOBED
ENDOSMOSES	ENDWISE	ENFEVER*	ENFREES	ENGLOBES
ENDOSOME*	ENE	ENFEVERED*	ENFREEZE	ENGLOBING
ENDOSOMES*	ENEMA	ENFEVERING*	ENFREEZES	ENGLOOM
ENDOSPERM	ENEMAS	ENFEVERS*	ENFREEZING	ENGLOOMED
ENDOSPERMS	ENEMATA	ENFIERCE	ENFROSEN	ENGLOOMING
ENDOSPORE	ENEMIES	ENFIERCED	ENFROZE	ENGLOOMS
ENDOSPORES	ENEMY	ENFIERCES	ENFROZEN	ENGLUT
ENDOSS	ENERGETIC	ENFIERCING	ENG	ENGLUTS
ENDOSSED	ENERGETICS	ENFILADE	ENGAGE	ENGLUTTED
ENDOSSES	ENERGIC	ENFILADED	ENGAGED	ENGLUTTING
ENDOSSING	ENERGID	ENFILADES	ENGAGER	ENGOBE
ENDOSTEA	ENERGIDS	ENFILADING	ENGAGERS	ENGOBES
ENDOSTEAL	ENERGIES	ENFILED	ENGAGES	ENGORE
ENDOSTEUM	ENERGISE	ENFIRE	ENGAGING	ENGORED
ENDOSTYLE*	ENERGISED	ENFIRED	ENGAOL	ENGORES
ENDOSTYLES*	ENERGISER	ENFIRES	ENGAOLED	ENGORGE
ENDOTHERM*	ENERGISERS	ENFIRING	ENGAOLING	ENGORGED
ENDOTHERMS*	ENERGISES	ENFIX	ENGAOLS	ENGORGES
ENDOTOXIC*	ENERGISING	ENFIXED	ENGARLAND	ENGORGING
ENDOTOXIN*	ENERGIZE	ENFIXES	ENGARLANDED	ENGORING
ENDOTOXINS*	ENERGIZED	ENFIXING	ENGARLANDING	ENGOULED
ENDOW	ENERGIZER	ENFLAME	ENGARLANDS	ENGOUMENT
ENDOWED	ENERGIZERS	ENFLAMED	ENGENDER	ENGOUMENTS
ENDOWER	ENERGIZES	ENFLAMES	ENGENDERED	ENGRACE
ENDOWERS	ENERGIZING	ENFLAMING	ENGENDERING	ENGRACED
ENDOWING	ENERGUMEN	ENFLESH	ENGENDERS	ENGRACES
ENDOWMENT	ENERGUMENS	ENFLESHED	ENGENDURE	ENGRACING
ENDOWMENTS	ENERGY	ENFLESHES	ENGENDURES	ENGRAFF
ENDOWS	ENERVATE	ENFLESHING	ENGILD	ENGRAFFED
ENDOZOA	ENERVATED	ENFLOWER	ENGILDED	ENGRAFFING
ENDOZOIC	ENERVATES	ENFLOWERED	ENGILDING	ENGRAFFS
ENDOZOON	ENERVATING	ENFLOWERING	ENGILDS	ENGRAFT
ENDPAPER*	ENERVE	ENFLOWERS	ENGILT	ENGRAFTED
ENDPAPERS*	ENERVED	ENFOLD	ENGINE	ENGRAFTING
ENDPLATE*	ENERVES	ENFOLDED	ENGINED	ENGRAFTS
ENDPLATES*	ENERVING	ENFOLDER*	ENGINEER	ENGRAIL
ENDPOINT*	ENES	ENFOLDERS*	ENGINEERED	ENGRAILED
ENDPOINTS*	ENEW	ENFOLDING	ENGINEERING	ENGRAILING
ENDRIN*	ENEWED	ENFOLDS	ENGINEERINGS	ENGRAILS
ENDRINS*	ENEWING	ENFORCE	ENGINEERS	ENGRAIN
ENDS	ENEWS	ENFORCED	ENGINER	ENGRAINED
ENDSHIP	ENFACE	ENFORCER	ENGINERIES	ENGRAINER
ENDSHIPS	ENFACED	ENFORCERS	ENGINERS	ENGRAINERS
ENDUE	ENFACES	ENFORCES	ENGINERY	ENGRAINING
ENDUED	ENFACING	ENFORCING	ENGINES	ENGRAINS
ENDUES	ENFANT	ENFOREST	ENGINING	ENGRAM
ENDUING	ENFANTS	ENFORESTED	ENGINOUS*	ENGRAMMA
ENDUNGEON	ENFEEBLE	ENFORESTING	ENGIRD	ENGRAMMAS
ENDUNGEONED	ENFEEBLED	ENFORESTS	ENGIRDED*	ENGRAMME*

Words marked with an asterisk are from OTCWL

ENGRAMMES*	ENHEARTENED	ENLARGER	ENNOBLER*	ENRANCKLE
ENGRAMS	ENHEARTENING	ENLARGERS	ENNOBLERS*	ENRANCKLED
ENGRASP	ENHEARTENS	ENLARGES	ENNOBLES	ENRANCKLES
ENGRASPED	ENHUNGER	ENLARGING	ENNOBLING	ENRANCKLING
ENGRASPING	ENHUNGERED	ENLEVE	ENNUI	ENRANGE
ENGRASPS	ENHUNGERING	ENLIGHT	ENNUIED	ENRANGED
ENGRAVE	ENHUNGERS	ENLIGHTED	ENNUIS	ENRANGES
ENGRAVED	ENHYDRITE	ENLIGHTEN	ENNUYE	ENRANGING
ENGRAVEN	ENHYDRITES	ENLIGHTENED	ENNUYED	ENRANK
ENGRAVER	ENHYDROS	ENLIGHTENING	ENNUYEE*	ENRANKED
ENGRAVERIES	ENHYDROSES	ENLIGHTENS	ENNUYING	ENRANKING
ENGRAVERS	ENHYDROUS	ENLIGHTING	ENODAL	ENRANKS
ENGRAVERY	ENIAC	ENLIGHTS	ENOKI	ENRAPT
ENGRAVES	ENIACS	ENLINK	ENOKIDAKE*	ENRAPTURE
ENGRAVING	ENIGMA	ENLINKED	ENOKIDAKES*	ENRAPTURED
ENGRAVINGS	ENIGMAS	ENLINKING	ENOKIS	ENRAPTURES
ENGRENAGE	ENIGMATA*	ENLINKS	ENOL*	ENRAPTURING
ENGRENAGES	ENIGMATIC	ENLIST	ENOLASE*	ENRAUNGE
ENGRIEVE	ENISLE	ENLISTED	ENOLASES*	ENRAUNGED
ENGRIEVED	ENISLED	ENLISTEE*	ENOLIC*	ENRAUNGES
ENGRIEVES	ENISLES	ENLISTEES*	ENOLOGIES*	ENRAUNGING
ENGRIEVING	ENISLING	ENLISTER*	ENOLOGIST*	ENRAVISH
ENGROOVE	ENJAMB	ENLISTERS*	ENOLOGISTS*	ENRAVISHED
ENGROOVED	ENJAMBED	ENLISTING	ENOLOGY*	ENRAVISHES
ENGROOVES	ENJAMBING	ENLISTS	ENOLS*	ENRAVISHING
ENGROOVING	ENJAMBS	ENLIT	ENOMOTIES	ENRHEUM
ENGROSS	ENJOIN	ENLIVEN	ENOMOTY	ENRHEUMED
ENGROSSED	ENJOINED	ENLIVENED	ENORM	ENRHEUMING
ENGROSSER	ENJOINER	ENLIVENER	ENORMITIES	ENRHEUMS
ENGROSSERS	ENJOINERS	ENLIVENERS	ENORMITY	ENRICH
ENGROSSES	ENJOINING	ENLIVENING	ENORMOUS	ENRICHED
ENGROSSING	ENJOINS	ENLIVENS	ENOSES	ENRICHER*
ENGS	ENJOY	ENLOCK	ENOSIS	ENRICHERS*
ENGUARD	ENJOYABLE	ENLOCKED	ENOSISES*	ENRICHES
ENGUARDED	ENJOYABLY	ENLOCKING	ENOUGH	ENRICHING
ENGUARDING	ENJOYED	ENLOCKS	ENOUGHS	ENRIDGED
ENGUARDS	ENJOYER	ENLUMINE	ENOUNCE	ENRING
ENGULF	ENJOYERS	ENLUMINED	ENOUNCED	ENRINGED
ENGULFED	ENJOYING	ENLUMINES	ENOUNCES	ENRINGING
ENGULFING	ENJOYMENT	ENLUMINING	ENOUNCING	ENRINGS
ENGULFS	ENJOYMENTS	ENMESH	ENOW	ENRIVEN
ENGULPH	ENJOYS	ENMESHED	ENOWS*	ENROBE
ENGULPHED	ENKERNEL	ENMESHES	ENPLANE	ENROBED
ENGULPHING	ENKERNELLED	ENMESHING	ENPLANED	ENROBER*
ENGULPHS	ENKERNELLING	ENMEW	ENPLANES	ENROBERS*
ENGYSCOPE	ENKERNELS	ENMEWED	ENPLANING	ENROBES
ENGYSCOPES	ENKINDLE	ENMEWING	ENPRINT	ENROBING
ENHALO	ENKINDLED	ENMEWS	ENPRINTS	ENROL
ENHALOED	ENKINDLES	ENMITIES	ENQUIRE	ENROLL
ENHALOES	ENKINDLING	ENMITY	ENQUIRED	ENROLLED
ENHALOING	ENLACE	ENMOSSED	ENQUIRER	ENROLLEE*
ENHALOS	ENLACED	ENMOVE	ENQUIRERS	ENROLLEES*
ENHANCE	ENLACES	ENMOVED	ENQUIRES	ENROLLER
ENHANCED	ENLACING	ENMOVES	ENQUIRIES	ENROLLERS
ENHANCER	ENLARD	ENMOVING	ENQUIRING	ENROLLING
ENHANCERS	ENLARDED	ENNAGE	ENQUIRY	ENROLLS
ENHANCES	ENLARDING	ENNAGES	ENRACE	ENROLMENT
ENHANCING	ENLARDS	ENNEAD	ENRACED	ENROLMENTS
ENHANCIVE	ENLARGE	ENNEADIC	ENRACES	ENROLS
ENHEARSE	ENLARGED	ENNEADS	ENRACING	ENROOT
ENHEARSED	ENLARGEN	ENNEAGON	ENRAGE	ENROOTED
ENHEARSES	ENLARGENED	ENNEAGONS	ENRAGED	ENROOTING
ENHEARSING	ENLARGENING	ENNOBLE	ENRAGES	ENROOTS
ENHEARTEN	ENLARGENS	ENNOBLED	ENRAGING	ENROUGH

The Chambers Dictionary is the authority for many longer words; see Introduction, page ix

ENROUGHED
ENROUGHING
ENROUGHS
ENROUND
ENROUNDED
ENROUNDING
ENROUNDS
ENS
ENSAMPLE
ENSAMPLED
ENSAMPLES
ENSAMPLING
ENSATE
ENSCONCE
ENSCONCED
ENSCONCES
ENSCONCING
ENSCROLL*
ENSCROLLED*
ENSCROLLING*
ENSCROLLS*
ENSEAL
ENSEALED
ENSEALING
ENSEALS
ENSEAM
ENSEAMED
ENSEAMING
ENSEAMS
ENSEAR
ENSEARED
ENSEARING
ENSEARS
ENSEMBLE
ENSEMBLES
ENSERF*
ENSERFED*
ENSERFING*
ENSERFS*
ENSEW
ENSEWED
ENSEWING
ENSEWS
ENSHEATH
ENSHEATHE
ENSHEATHED
ENSHEATHES
ENSHEATHING
ENSHEATHS
ENSHELL
ENSHELLED
ENSHELLING
ENSHELLS
ENSHELTER
ENSHELTERED
ENSHELTERING
ENSHELTERS
ENSHIELD
ENSHIELDED
ENSHIELDING
ENSHIELDS
ENSHRINE
ENSHRINED
ENSHRINEE*

ENSHRINEES*
ENSHRINES
ENSHRINING
ENSHROUD
ENSHROUDED
ENSHROUDING
ENSHROUDS
ENSIFORM
ENSIGN
ENSIGNCIES
ENSIGNCY
ENSIGNED
ENSIGNING
ENSIGNS
ENSILAGE
ENSILAGED
ENSILAGEING
ENSILAGES
ENSILAGING
ENSILE
ENSILED
ENSILES
ENSILING
ENSKIED
ENSKIES
ENSKY
ENSKYED*
ENSKYING
ENSLAVE
ENSLAVED
ENSLAVER
ENSLAVERS
ENSLAVES
ENSLAVING
ENSNARE
ENSNARED
ENSNARER*
ENSNARERS*
ENSNARES
ENSNARING
ENSNARL
ENSNARLED
ENSNARLING
ENSNARLS
ENSORCEL*
ENSORCELED*
ENSORCELING*
ENSORCELL
ENSORCELLED
ENSORCELLING
ENSORCELLS
ENSORCELS*
ENSOUL
ENSOULED
ENSOULING
ENSOULS
ENSPHERE
ENSPHERED
ENSPHERES
ENSPHERING
ENSTAMP
ENSTAMPED
ENSTAMPING
ENSTAMPS

ENSTATITE
ENSTATITES
ENSTEEP
ENSTEEPED
ENSTEEPING
ENSTEEPS
ENSTYLE
ENSTYLED
ENSTYLES
ENSTYLING
ENSUE
ENSUED
ENSUES
ENSUING
ENSURE
ENSURED
ENSURER
ENSURERS
ENSURES
ENSURING
ENSWATHE
ENSWATHED
ENSWATHES
ENSWATHING
ENSWEEP
ENSWEEPING
ENSWEEPS
ENSWEPT
ENTAIL
ENTAILED
ENTAILER
ENTAILERS
ENTAILING
ENTAILS
ENTAME
ENTAMEBA*
ENTAMEBAE*
ENTAMEBAS*
ENTAMED
ENTAMES
ENTAMING
ENTAMOEBA
ENTAMOEBAE
ENTAMOEBAS
ENTANGLE
ENTANGLED
ENTANGLER*
ENTANGLERS*
ENTANGLES
ENTANGLING
ENTASES
ENTASIA*
ENTASIAS*
ENTASIS
ENTASTIC*
ENTAYLE
ENTAYLED
ENTAYLES
ENTAYLING
ENTELECHIES
ENTELECHY
ENTELLUS
ENTELLUSES
ENTENDER

ENTENDERED
ENTENDERING
ENTENDERS
ENTENTE
ENTENTES
ENTER
ENTERA
ENTERABLE
ENTERAL
ENTERALLY*
ENTERATE
ENTERED
ENTERER
ENTERERS
ENTERIC
ENTERICS
ENTERING
ENTERINGS
ENTERITIDES*
ENTERITIS
ENTERITISES
ENTERON
ENTERONS*
ENTERS
ENTERTAIN
ENTERTAINED
ENTERTAINING
ENTERTAININGS
ENTERTAINS
ENTERTAKE
ENTERTAKEN
ENTERTAKES
ENTERTAKING
ENTERTOOK
ENTETE
ENTETEE
ENTHALPIES
ENTHALPY
ENTHETIC
ENTHRAL
ENTHRALL
ENTHRALLED
ENTHRALLING
ENTHRALLS
ENTHRALS
ENTHRONE
ENTHRONED
ENTHRONES
ENTHRONING
ENTHUSE
ENTHUSED
ENTHUSES
ENTHUSING
ENTHYMEME
ENTHYMEMES
ENTIA
ENTICE
ENTICED
ENTICER
ENTICERS
ENTICES
ENTICING
ENTICINGS
ENTIRE

ENTIRELY
ENTIRES
ENTIRETIES
ENTIRETY
ENTITIES
ENTITLE
ENTITLED
ENTITLES
ENTITLING
ENTITY
ENTOBLAST
ENTOBLASTS
ENTODERM
ENTODERMS
ENTOIL
ENTOILED
ENTOILING
ENTOILS
ENTOMB
ENTOMBED
ENTOMBING
ENTOMBS
ENTOMIC
ENTOPHYTE
ENTOPHYTES
ENTOPIC
ENTOPROCT*
ENTOPROCTS*
ENTOPTIC
ENTOPTICS
ENTOTIC
ENTOURAGE
ENTOURAGES
ENTOZOA
ENTOZOAL
ENTOZOAN*
ENTOZOANS*
ENTOZOIC
ENTOZOON
ENTRAIL
ENTRAILED
ENTRAILING
ENTRAILS
ENTRAIN
ENTRAINED
ENTRAINER*
ENTRAINERS*
ENTRAINING
ENTRAINS
ENTRALL
ENTRALLES
ENTRAMMEL
ENTRAMMELLED
ENTRAMMELLING
ENTRAMMELS
ENTRANCE
ENTRANCED
ENTRANCES
ENTRANCING
ENTRANT
ENTRANTS
ENTRAP
ENTRAPPED
ENTRAPPER

Words marked with an asterisk are from OTCWL

ENTRAPPERS	ENUMERATES	ENVOIS	EOLITHS	EPHAH
ENTRAPPING	ENUMERATING	ENVOY	EOLOPILE*	EPHAHS
ENTRAPS	ENUNCIATE	ENVOYS	EOLOPILES*	EPHAS
ENTREAT	ENUNCIATED	ENVOYSHIP	EON	EPHEBE
ENTREATED	ENUNCIATES	ENVOYSHIPS	EONIAN*	EPHEBES
ENTREATIES	ENUNCIATING	ENVY	EONISM	EPHEBI
ENTREATING	ENURE	ENVYING	EONISMS	EPHEBIC
ENTREATS	ENURED	ENVYINGLY*	EONS	EPHEBOI*
ENTREATY	ENUREMENT	ENVYINGS	EORL	EPHEBOS
ENTRECHAT	ENUREMENTS	ENWALL	EORLS	EPHEBUS
ENTRECHATS	ENURES	ENWALLED	EOSIN	EPHEDRA
ENTRECOTE	ENURESES	ENWALLING	EOSINE*	EPHEDRAS
ENTRECOTES	ENURESIS	ENWALLOW	EOSINES*	EPHEDRIN*
ENTREE	ENURESISES*	ENWALLOWED	EOSINIC*	EPHEDRINE
ENTREES	ENURETIC	ENWALLOWING	EOSINS	EPHEDRINES
ENTREMES	ENURETICS	ENWALLOWS	EOTHEN	EPHEDRINS*
ENTREMETS	ENURING	ENWALLS	EPACRID	EPHELIDES
ENTRENCH	ENVASSAL	ENWHEEL	EPACRIDS	EPHELIS
ENTRENCHED	ENVASSALLED	ENWHEELED	EPACRIS	EPHEMERA
ENTRENCHES	ENVASSALLING	ENWHEELING	EPACRISES	EPHEMERAE
ENTRENCHING	ENVASSALS	ENWHEELS	EPACT	EPHEMERAL
ENTREPOT	ENVAULT	ENWIND	EPACTS	EPHEMERALS
ENTREPOTS	ENVAULTED	ENWINDING	EPAENETIC	EPHEMERAS
ENTRESOL	ENVAULTING	ENWINDS	EPAGOGE	EPHEMERID
ENTRESOLS	ENVAULTS	ENWOMB	EPAGOGES	EPHEMERIDES
ENTREZ	ENVEIGLE	ENWOMBED	EPAGOGIC	EPHEMERIDS
ENTRIES	ENVEIGLED	ENWOMBING	EPAINETIC	EPHEMERIS
ENTRISM	ENVEIGLES	ENWOMBS	EPANODOS	EPHEMERON
ENTRISMS	ENVEIGLING	ENWOUND	EPANODOSES	EPHIALTES
ENTRIST	ENVELOP	ENWRAP	EPARCH	EPHOD
ENTRISTS	ENVELOPE	ENWRAPPED	EPARCHATE	EPHODS
ENTROLD	ENVELOPED	ENWRAPPING	EPARCHATES	EPHOR
ENTROPIC	ENVELOPES	ENWRAPPINGS	EPARCHIES	EPHORAL*
ENTROPIES	ENVELOPING	ENWRAPS	EPARCHS	EPHORALTIES
ENTROPION	ENVELOPS	ENWREATHE	EPARCHY	EPHORALTY
ENTROPIONS	ENVENOM	ENWREATHED	EPATANT	EPHORATE*
ENTROPIUM	ENVENOMED	ENWREATHES	EPAULE	EPHORATES*
ENTROPIUMS	ENVENOMING	ENWREATHING	EPAULES	EPHORI*
ENTROPY	ENVENOMS	ENZIAN	EPAULET	EPHORS
ENTRUST	ENVERMEIL	ENZIANS	EPAULETS	EPIBLAST
ENTRUSTED	ENVERMEILED	ENZONE	EPAULETTE	EPIBLASTS
ENTRUSTING	ENVERMEILING	ENZONED	EPAULETTES	EPIBOLIC*
ENTRUSTS	ENVERMEILS	ENZONES	EPAXIAL	EPIBOLIES*
ENTRY	ENVIABLE	ENZONING	EPAZOTE*	EPIBOLY*
ENTRYISM	ENVIABLY	ENZOOTIC	EPAZOTES*	EPIC
ENTRYISMS	ENVIED	ENZOOTICS	EPEDAPHIC	EPICAL
ENTRYIST	ENVIER	ENZYM*	EPEE	EPICALLY
ENTRYISTS	ENVIERS	ENZYMATIC	EPEEIST*	EPICALYCES
ENTRYWAY*	ENVIES	ENZYME	EPEEISTS*	EPICALYX
ENTRYWAYS*	ENVIOUS	ENZYMES	EPEES	EPICALYXES
ENTWINE	ENVIOUSLY	ENZYMIC	EPEIRA	EPICANTHI
ENTWINED	ENVIRON	ENZYMS*	EPEIRAS	EPICARDIA*
ENTWINES	ENVIRONED	EOAN	EPEIRIC*	EPICARDIUM*
ENTWINING	ENVIRONING	EOBIONT*	EPEIRID	EPICARP
ENTWIST	ENVIRONS	EOBIONTS*	EPEIRIDS	EPICARPS
ENTWISTED	ENVISAGE	EOHIPPUS*	EPENDYMA*	EPICEDE
ENTWISTING	ENVISAGED	EOHIPPUSES*	EPENDYMAS*	EPICEDES
ENTWISTS	ENVISAGES	EOLIAN*	EPEOLATRIES	EPICEDIA
ENUCLEATE	ENVISAGING	EOLIENNE	EPEOLATRY	EPICEDIAL
ENUCLEATED	ENVISION	EOLIENNES	EPERDU	EPICEDIAN
ENUCLEATES	ENVISIONED	EOLIPILE	EPERDUE	EPICEDIUM
ENUCLEATING	ENVISIONING	EOLIPILES	EPERGNE	EPICENE
ENUMERATE	ENVISIONS	EOLITH	EPERGNES	EPICENES
ENUMERATED	ENVOI	EOLITHIC	EPHA	EPICENISM*

The Chambers Dictionary is the authority for many longer words; see Introduction, page ix

EPICENISMS* EPIGEOUS EPINASTIC EPISTLER EPIZOANS
EPICENTER EPIGON EPINASTIES EPISTLERS EPIZOIC
EPICENTERS EPIGONE EPINASTY EPISTLES EPIZOISM*
EPICENTRE EPIGONES EPINEURAL EPISTLING EPIZOISMS*
EPICENTRES EPIGONI EPINICIAN EPISTOLER EPIZOITE*
EPICIER EPIGONIC* EPINICION EPISTOLERS EPIZOITES*
EPICIERS EPIGONISM* EPINICIONS EPISTOLET EPIZOON
EPICISM EPIGONISMS* EPINIKIAN EPISTOLETS EPIZOOTIC
EPICISMS EPIGONOUS* EPINIKION EPISTOLIC EPIZOOTICS
EPICIST EPIGONS EPINIKIONS EPISTOME* EPIZOOTIES*
EPICISTS EPIGONUS* EPINOSIC EPISTOMES* EPIZOOTY*
EPICLESES EPIGRAM EPIPHANIC EPISTYLE EPOCH
EPICLESIS EPIGRAMS EPIPHANIES* EPISTYLES EPOCHA
EPICLIKE* EPIGRAPH EPIPHANY* EPITAPH EPOCHAL
EPICOTYL EPIGRAPHED EPIPHRAGM EPITAPHED EPOCHALLY*
EPICOTYLS EPIGRAPHIES EPIPHRAGMS EPITAPHER EPOCHAS
EPICRITIC EPIGRAPHING EPIPHYSES EPITAPHERS EPOCHS
EPICS EPIGRAPHS EPIPHYSIS EPITAPHIC EPODE
EPICURE EPIGRAPHY EPIPHYTAL EPITAPHING EPODES
EPICUREAN EPIGYNIES EPIPHYTE EPITAPHS EPODIC
EPICUREANS EPIGYNOUS EPIPHYTES EPITASES EPONYM
EPICURES EPIGYNY EPIPHYTIC EPITASIS EPONYMIC
EPICURISE EPILATE EPIPLOIC EPITAXIAL EPONYMIES*
EPICURISED EPILATED EPIPLOON EPITAXIC* EPONYMOUS
EPICURISES EPILATES EPIPLOONS EPITAXIES EPONYMS
EPICURISING EPILATING EPIPOLIC EPITAXY EPONYMY*
EPICURISM EPILATION EPIPOLISM EPITHELIA EPOPEE
EPICURISMS EPILATIONS EPIPOLISMS EPITHELIUM* EPOPEES
EPICURIZE EPILATOR EPIRRHEMA EPITHEM EPOPOEIA
EPICURIZED EPILATORS EPIRRHEMAS EPITHEMA EPOPOEIAS
EPICURIZES EPILEPSIES EPISCIA* EPITHEMATA EPOPT
EPICURIZING EPILEPSY EPISCIAS* EPITHEMS EPOPTS
EPICYCLE EPILEPTIC EPISCOPAL EPITHESES EPOS
EPICYCLES EPILEPTICS EPISCOPE EPITHESIS EPOSES
EPICYCLIC EPILOBIUM EPISCOPES EPITHET EPOXIDE
EPIDEMIC EPILOBIUMS EPISCOPIES EPITHETED EPOXIDES
EPIDEMICS EPILOG EPISCOPY EPITHETIC EPOXIDIZE*
EPIDERM* EPILOGIC EPISEMON EPITHETING EPOXIDIZED*
EPIDERMAL EPILOGISE EPISEMONS EPITHETON EPOXIDIZES*
EPIDERMIC EPILOGISED EPISODAL EPITHETONS EPOXIDIZING*
EPIDERMIS EPILOGISES EPISODE EPITHETS EPOXIED*
EPIDERMISES EPILOGISING EPISODES EPITOME EPOXIES
EPIDERMS* EPILOGIST EPISODIAL EPITOMES EPOXY
EPIDOSITE EPILOGISTS EPISODIC EPITOMIC EPOXYED*
EPIDOSITES EPILOGIZE EPISOMAL* EPITOMISE EPOXYING*
EPIDOTE EPILOGIZED EPISOME EPITOMISED EPRIS
EPIDOTES EPILOGIZES EPISOMES EPITOMISES EPRISE
EPIDOTIC EPILOGIZING EPISPERM EPITOMISING EPROM
EPIDURAL EPILOGS EPISPERMS EPITOMIST EPROMS
EPIDURALS EPILOGUE EPISPORE EPITOMISTS EPSILON
EPIFAUNA EPILOGUED* EPISPORES EPITOMIZE EPSILONIC*
EPIFAUNAE EPILOGUES EPISTASES EPITOMIZED EPSILONS
EPIFAUNAL* EPILOGUING* EPISTASIES* EPITOMIZES EPSOMITE
EPIFAUNAS EPIMER EPISTASIS EPITOMIZING EPSOMITES
EPIFOCAL EPIMERASE* EPISTASY* EPITONIC EPUISE
EPIGAEAL EPIMERASES* EPISTATIC EPITOPE EPUISEE
EPIGAEAN EPIMERE* EPISTAXES EPITOPES EPULARY
EPIGAEOUS EPIMERES* EPISTAXIS EPITRITE EPULATION
EPIGAMIC EPIMERIC EPISTAXISES EPITRITES EPULATIONS
EPIGEAL EPIMERS EPISTEMIC EPIZEUXES EPULIDES
EPIGEAN EPIMYSIA* EPISTEMICS EPIZEUXIS EPULIS
EPIGEIC* EPIMYSIUM* EPISTERNA EPIZEUXISES EPULISES
EPIGENE EPINAOI* EPISTLE EPIZOA EPULOTIC
EPIGENIC* EPINAOS* EPISTLED EPIZOAN EPULOTICS

EPURATE	EQUIPES	ERECTILE	ERGOTIZED	EROSIONS
EPURATED	EQUIPMENT	ERECTING	ERGOTIZES	EROSIVE
EPURATES	EQUIPMENTS	ERECTION	ERGOTIZING	EROSIVITIES*
EPURATING	EQUIPOISE	ERECTIONS	ERGOTS	EROSIVITY*
EPURATION	EQUIPOISED	ERECTIVE	ERGS	EROSTRATE
EPURATIONS	EQUIPOISES	ERECTLY	ERIACH	EROTEMA
EPYLLION	EQUIPOISING	ERECTNESS	ERIACHS	EROTEMAS
EPYLLIONS	EQUIPPED	ERECTNESSES	ERIC	EROTEME
EQUABLE	EQUIPPER*	ERECTOR	ERICA	EROTEMES
EQUABLY	EQUIPPERS*	ERECTORS	ERICAS	EROTESES
EQUAL	EQUIPPING	ERECTS	ERICK	EROTESIS
EQUALED*	EQUIPS	ERED	ERICKS	EROTETIC
EQUALING*	EQUISETA	ERELONG	ERICOID	EROTIC
EQUALISE	EQUISETIC	EREMIC	ERICS	EROTICA
EQUALISED	EQUISETUM	EREMITAL	ERIGERON	EROTICAL
EQUALISER	EQUISETUMS	EREMITE	ERIGERONS	EROTICISE
EQUALISERS	EQUITABLE	EREMITES	ERING	EROTICISED
EQUALISES	EQUITABLY	EREMITIC	ERINGO	EROTICISES
EQUALISING	EQUITANT	EREMITISM	ERINGOES	EROTICISING
EQUALITIES	EQUITES*	EREMITISMS	ERINGOS	EROTICISM
EQUALITY	EQUITIES	EREMURI*	ERINITE	EROTICISMS
EQUALIZE	EQUITY	EREMURUS*	ERINITES	EROTICIST
EQUALIZED	EQUIVALVE	ERENOW	ERIOMETER	EROTICISTS
EQUALIZER	EQUIVOCAL	EREPSIN	ERIOMETERS	EROTICIZE
EQUALIZERS	EQUIVOKE	EREPSINS	ERIONITE	EROTICIZED
EQUALIZES	EQUIVOKES	ERES	ERIONITES	EROTICIZES
EQUALIZING	EQUIVOQUE	ERETHIC*	ERIOPHYID*	EROTICIZING
EQUALLED	EQUIVOQUES	ERETHISM	ERIOPHYIDS*	EROTICS
EQUALLING	ER	ERETHISMS	ERISTIC	EROTISM
EQUALLY	ERA	ERETHITIC	ERISTICAL	EROTISMS
EQUALNESS	ERADIATE	EREWHILE	ERISTICS*	EROTIZE*
EQUALNESSES	ERADIATED	EREWHILES*	ERK	EROTIZED*
EQUALS	ERADIATES	ERF	ERKS	EROTIZES*
EQUANT	ERADIATING	ERG	ERLKING*	EROTIZING*
EQUANTS	ERADICATE	ERGASTIC*	ERLKINGS*	ERR
EQUATE	ERADICATED	ERGATANER	ERMELIN	ERRABLE
EQUATED	ERADICATES	ERGATANERS	ERMELINS	ERRANCIES*
EQUATES	ERADICATING	ERGATE	ERMINE	ERRANCY*
EQUATING	ERAS	ERGATES	ERMINED	ERRAND
EQUATION	ERASABLE	ERGATIVE	ERMINES	ERRANDS
EQUATIONS	ERASE	ERGATOID	ERN	ERRANT
EQUATOR	ERASED	ERGO	ERNE	ERRANTLY
EQUATORS	ERASEMENT	ERGODIC	ERNED	ERRANTRIES
EQUERRIES	ERASEMENTS	ERGOGRAM	ERNES	ERRANTRY
EQUERRY	ERASER	ERGOGRAMS	ERNING	ERRANTS
EQUID	ERASERS	ERGOGRAPH	ERNS	ERRATA
EQUIDS	ERASES	ERGOGRAPHS	ERODE	ERRATAS*
EQUIMOLAR*	ERASING	ERGOMANIA	ERODED	ERRATIC
EQUINAL	ERASION	ERGOMANIAS	ERODENT	ERRATICAL
EQUINE	ERASIONS	ERGOMETER	ERODENTS	ERRATICS
EQUINELY*	ERASURE	ERGOMETERS	ERODES	ERRATUM
EQUINES*	ERASURES	ERGON	ERODIBLE	ERRED
EQUINIA	ERATHEM	ERGONOMIC	ERODING	ERRHINE
EQUINIAS	ERATHEMS	ERGONOMICS	ERODIUM	ERRHINES
EQUINITIES	ERBIA	ERGONS	ERODIUMS	ERRING
EQUINITY	ERBIAS	ERGOT	EROGENIC	ERRINGLY
EQUINOX	ERBIUM	ERGOTIC*	EROGENOUS	ERRINGS
EQUINOXES	ERBIUMS	ERGOTISE	EROS*	ERRONEOUS
EQUIP	ERE	ERGOTISED	EROSE	ERROR
EQUIPAGE	ERECT	ERGOTISES	EROSELY*	ERRORIST
EQUIPAGED	ERECTABLE*	ERGOTISING	EROSES*	ERRORISTS
EQUIPAGES	ERECTED	ERGOTISM	EROSIBLE*	ERRORLESS*
EQUIPAGING	ERECTER	ERGOTISMS	EROSION	ERRORS
EQUIPE	ERECTERS	ERGOTIZE	EROSIONAL*	ERRS

The Chambers Dictionary is the authority for many longer words; see Introduction, page ix

ERS	ESCALATED	ESCOLAR	ESOPHAGUS	ESSAYIST
ERSATZ	ESCALATES	ESCOLARS	ESOTERIC	ESSAYISTS
ERSATZES	ESCALATING	ESCOPETTE	ESOTERICA	ESSAYS
ERSES	ESCALATOR	ESCOPETTES	ESOTERIES	ESSE
ERST	ESCALATORS	ESCORT	ESOTERISM	ESSENCE
ERSTWHILE	ESCALIER	ESCORTAGE	ESOTERISMS	ESSENCES
ERUCIFORM	ESCALIERS	ESCORTAGES	ESOTERY	ESSENTIAL
ERUCT	ESCALLOP	ESCORTED	ESPADA	ESSENTIALS
ERUCTATE	ESCALLOPED*	ESCORTING	ESPADAS	ESSES
ERUCTATED	ESCALLOPING*	ESCORTS	ESPAGNOLE	ESSIVE
ERUCTATES	ESCALLOPS	ESCOT	ESPAGNOLES	ESSIVES
ERUCTATING	ESCALOP	ESCOTED*	ESPALIER	ESSOIN
ERUCTED	ESCALOPE	ESCOTING*	ESPALIERED	ESSOINER
ERUCTING	ESCALOPED	ESCOTS	ESPALIERING	ESSOINERS
ERUCTS	ESCALOPES	ESCOTTED	ESPALIERS	ESSOINS
ERUDITE	ESCALOPING	ESCOTTING	ESPANOL*	ESSONITE
ERUDITELY	ESCALOPS	ESCRIBANO	ESPANOLES*	ESSONITES
ERUDITES	ESCAPABLE	ESCRIBANOS	ESPARTO	ESSOYNE
ERUDITION	ESCAPADE	ESCRIBE	ESPARTOS	ESSOYNES
ERUDITIONS	ESCAPADES	ESCRIBED	ESPECIAL	EST
ERUGO*	ESCAPADO	ESCRIBES	ESPERANCE	ESTABLISH
ERUGOS*	ESCAPADOES	ESCRIBING	ESPERANCES	ESTABLISHED
ERUMPENT	ESCAPE	ESCROC	ESPIAL	ESTABLISHES
ERUPT	ESCAPED	ESCROCS	ESPIALS	ESTABLISHING
ERUPTED	ESCAPEE	ESCROL	ESPIED	ESTACADE
ERUPTIBLE*	ESCAPEES	ESCROLL	ESPIEGLE	ESTACADES
ERUPTING	ESCAPER	ESCROLLS	ESPIES	ESTAFETTE
ERUPTION	ESCAPERS	ESCROLS	ESPIONAGE	ESTAFETTES
ERUPTIONS	ESCAPES	ESCROW	ESPIONAGES	ESTAMINET
ERUPTIVE	ESCAPING	ESCROWED	ESPLANADE	ESTAMINETS
ERUPTIVES*	ESCAPISM	ESCROWING	ESPLANADES	ESTANCIA
ERUPTS	ESCAPISMS	ESCROWS	ESPOUSAL	ESTANCIAS
ERVALENTA	ESCAPIST	ESCUAGE	ESPOUSALS	ESTATE
ERVALENTAS	ESCAPISTS	ESCUAGES	ESPOUSE	ESTATED
ERVEN	ESCAR*	ESCUDO	ESPOUSED	ESTATES
ERVIL*	ESCARGOT	ESCUDOS	ESPOUSER	ESTATING
ERVILS*	ESCARGOTS	ESCULENT	ESPOUSERS	ESTEEM
ERYNGIUM	ESCAROLE	ESCULENTS	ESPOUSES	ESTEEMED
ERYNGIUMS	ESCAROLES	ESEMPLASIES	ESPOUSING	ESTEEMING
ERYNGO	ESCARP	ESEMPLASY	ESPRESSO	ESTEEMS
ERYNGOES	ESCARPED	ESERINE*	ESPRESSOS	ESTER
ERYNGOS	ESCARPING	ESERINES*	ESPRIT	ESTERASE*
ERYTHEMA	ESCARPS	ESES*	ESPRITS	ESTERASES*
ERYTHEMAL	ESCARS*	ESILE	ESPUMOSO	ESTERIFIED
ERYTHEMAS	ESCHALOT	ESILES	ESPUMOSOS	ESTERIFIES
ERYTHRINA	ESCHALOTS	ESKAR	ESPY	ESTERIFY
ERYTHRINAS	ESCHAR	ESKARS	ESPYING	ESTERIFYING
ERYTHRISM	ESCHARS	ESKER	ESQUIRE	ESTERS
ERYTHRISMS	ESCHEAT	ESKERS	ESQUIRED*	ESTHESES*
ERYTHRITE	ESCHEATED	ESKIES	ESQUIRES	ESTHESIA
ERYTHRITES	ESCHEATING	ESKY	ESQUIRESS	ESTHESIAS
ERYTHROID*	ESCHEATOR	ESLOIN	ESQUIRESSES	ESTHESIS*
ERYTHRON*	ESCHEATORS	ESLOINED	ESQUIRING*	ESTHESISES*
ERYTHRONS*	ESCHEATS	ESLOINING	ESQUISSE	ESTHETE
ES	ESCHEW	ESLOINS	ESQUISSES	ESTHETES
ESCALADE	ESCHEWAL	ESLOYNE	ESS	ESTHETIC*
ESCALADED	ESCHEWALS	ESLOYNED	ESSAY	ESTHETICS*
ESCALADER*	ESCHEWED	ESLOYNES	ESSAYED	ESTIMABLE
ESCALADERS*	ESCHEWER	ESLOYNING	ESSAYER	ESTIMABLY
ESCALADES	ESCHEWERS	ESNE	ESSAYERS	ESTIMATE
ESCALADING	ESCHEWING	ESNECIES	ESSAYETTE	ESTIMATED
ESCALADO	ESCHEWS	ESNECY	ESSAYETTES	ESTIMATES
ESCALADOES	ESCLANDRE	ESNES	ESSAYING	ESTIMATING
ESCALATE	ESCLANDRES	ESOPHAGI	ESSAYISH	ESTIMATOR

ESTIMATORS	ESTRUAL*	ETERNISED	ETHICISMS	ETIOLATING
ESTIVAL	ESTRUM	ETERNISES	ETHICIST	ETIOLIN
ESTIVATE	ESTRUMS	ETERNISING	ETHICISTS	ETIOLINS
ESTIVATED	ESTRUS	ETERNITIES	ETHICIZE	ETIOLOGIC*
ESTIVATES	ESTRUSES	ETERNITY	ETHICIZED	ETIOLOGIES
ESTIVATING	ESTS	ETERNIZE	ETHICIZES	ETIOLOGY
ESTOC	ESTUARIAL	ETERNIZED	ETHICIZING	ETIQUETTE
ESTOCS	ESTUARIAN	ETERNIZES	ETHICS	ETIQUETTES
ESTOILE	ESTUARIES	ETERNIZING	ETHINYL*	ETNA
ESTOILES	ESTUARINE	ETESIAN	ETHINYLS*	ETNAS
ESTOP	ESTUARY	ETESIANS*	ETHION*	ETOILE
ESTOPPAGE	ESURIENCE	ETH	ETHIONINE*	ETOILES
ESTOPPAGES	ESURIENCES	ETHAL	ETHIONINES*	ETOUFFEE*
ESTOPPED	ESURIENCIES	ETHALS	ETHIONS*	ETOUFFEES*
ESTOPPEL	ESURIENCY	ETHANE	ETHIOPS	ETOURDI
ESTOPPELS	ESURIENT	ETHANES	ETHIOPSES	ETOURDIE
ESTOPPING	ET*	ETHANOL	ETHMOID	ETRANGER
ESTOPS	ETA	ETHANOLS	ETHMOIDAL	ETRANGERE
ESTOVER	ETACISM	ETHE	ETHMOIDS*	ETRANGERES
ESTOVERS	ETACISMS	ETHENE	ETHNARCH	ETRANGERS
ESTRADE	ETAERIO	ETHENES	ETHNARCHIES	ETRENNE
ESTRADES	ETAERIOS	ETHEPHON*	ETHNARCHS	ETRENNES
ESTRADIOL	ETAGE	ETHEPHONS*	ETHNARCHY	ETRIER
ESTRADIOLS	ETAGERE	ETHER	ETHNIC	ETRIERS
ESTRAGON*	ETAGERES	ETHERCAP	ETHNICAL	ETTERCAP
ESTRAGONS*	ETAGES	ETHERCAPS	ETHNICISM	ETTERCAPS
ESTRAL	ETALAGE	ETHEREAL	ETHNICISMS	ETTIN
ESTRANGE	ETALAGES	ETHEREOUS	ETHNICITIES	ETTINS
ESTRANGED	ETALON	ETHERIAL	ETHNICITY	ETTLE
ESTRANGER	ETALONS	ETHERIC	ETHNICS	ETTLED
ESTRANGERS	ETAMIN*	ETHERICAL	ETHNOCIDE	ETTLES
ESTRANGES	ETAMINE*	ETHERIFIED	ETHNOCIDES	ETTLING
ESTRANGING	ETAMINES*	ETHERIFIES	ETHNOLOGIES	ETUDE
ESTRAPADE	ETAMINS*	ETHERIFY	ETHNOLOGY	ETUDES
ESTRAPADES	ETAPE	ETHERIFYING	ETHNOS*	ETUI
ESTRAY	ETAPES	ETHERION	ETHNOSES*	ETUIS
ESTRAYED	ETAS	ETHERIONS	ETHOLOGIC	ETWEE
ESTRAYING	ETAT	ETHERISE	ETHOLOGIES	ETWEES
ESTRAYS	ETATISM*	ETHERISED	ETHOLOGY	ETYMA
ESTREAT	ETATISME	ETHERISES	ETHOS	ETYMIC
ESTREATED	ETATISMES	ETHERISH*	ETHOSES	ETYMOLOGIES
ESTREATING	ETATISMS*	ETHERISING	ETHOXIES*	ETYMOLOGY
ESTREATS	ETATIST*	ETHERISM	ETHOXY*	ETYMON
ESTREPE	ETATISTE	ETHERISMS	ETHOXYL*	ETYMONS
ESTREPED	ETATISTES	ETHERIST	ETHOXYLS*	ETYPIC
ESTREPES	ETATS	ETHERISTS	ETHS	ETYPICAL
ESTREPING	ETCETERA	ETHERIZE	ETHYL	EUCAIN
ESTRICH	ETCETERAS	ETHERIZED	ETHYLATE	EUCAINE
ESTRICHES	ETCH	ETHERIZER*	ETHYLATED	EUCAINES
ESTRIDGE	ETCHANT	ETHERIZERS*	ETHYLATES	EUCAINS
ESTRIDGES	ETCHANTS	ETHERIZES	ETHYLATING	EUCALYPT
ESTRILDID	ETCHED	ETHERIZING	ETHYLENE	EUCALYPTI
ESTRILDIDS	ETCHER	ETHERS	ETHYLENES	EUCALYPTS
ESTRIN*	ETCHERS	ETHIC	ETHYLENIC*	EUCALYPTUS*
ESTRINS*	ETCHES	ETHICAL	ETHYLIC*	EUCALYPTUSES*
ESTRIOL*	ETCHING	ETHICALLY	ETHYLS	EUCARYON
ESTRIOLS*	ETCHINGS	ETHICALS	ETHYNE	EUCARYONS
ESTRO	ETEN	ETHICIAN*	ETHYNES	EUCARYOT
ESTROGEN	ETENS	ETHICIANS*	ETHYNYL*	EUCARYOTE
ESTROGENS	ETERNAL	ETHICISE	ETHYNYLS*	EUCARYOTES
ESTRONE*	ETERNALLY	ETHICISED	ETIC*	EUCARYOTS
ESTRONES*	ETERNALS*	ETHICISES	ETIOLATE	EUCHARIS
ESTROS	ETERNE	ETHICISING	ETIOLATED	EUCHARISES
ESTROUS	ETERNISE	ETHICISM	ETIOLATES	EUCHLORIC

The Chambers Dictionary is the authority for many longer words; see Introduction, page ix

EUCHOLOGIES	EULOGIUM	EUPHONIAS	EUROS	EVACUEE
EUCHOLOGY	EULOGIUMS	EUPHONIC	EURYBATH*	EVACUEES
EUCHRE	EULOGIZE	EUPHONIES	EURYBATHS*	EVADABLE
EUCHRED	EULOGIZED	EUPHONISE	EURYOKIES*	EVADE
EUCHRES	EULOGIZER*	EUPHONISED	EURYOKY*	EVADED
EUCHRING	EULOGIZERS*	EUPHONISES	EURYTHERM	EVADER
EUCLASE	EULOGIZES	EUPHONISING	EURYTHERMS	EVADERS
EUCLASES	EULOGIZING	EUPHONISM	EURYTHMIC*	EVADES
EUCLIDEAN*	EULOGY	EUPHONISMS	EURYTHMIES	EVADIBLE*
EUCLIDIAN*	EUMELANIN	EUPHONIUM	EURYTHMY	EVADING
EUCRITE	EUMELANINS	EUPHONIUMS	EURYTOPIC*	EVAGATION
EUCRITES	EUMERISM	EUPHONIZE	EUSOL	EVAGATIONS
EUCRITIC	EUMERISMS	EUPHONIZED	EUSOLS	EVAGINATE
EUCYCLIC	EUNUCH	EUPHONIZES	EUSTACIES	EVAGINATED
EUDAEMON*	EUNUCHISE	EUPHONIZING	EUSTACY	EVAGINATES
EUDAEMONIES	EUNUCHISED	EUPHONS	EUSTASIES	EVAGINATING
EUDAEMONS*	EUNUCHISES	EUPHONY	EUSTASY	EVALUATE
EUDAEMONY	EUNUCHISING	EUPHORBIA	EUSTATIC	EVALUATED
EUDEMON*	EUNUCHISM	EUPHORBIAS	EUSTELE*	EVALUATES
EUDEMONS*	EUNUCHISMS	EUPHORIA	EUSTELES*	EVALUATING
EUDIALYTE	EUNUCHIZE	EUPHORIAS	EUSTYLE	EVALUATOR*
EUDIALYTES	EUNUCHIZED	EUPHORIC	EUSTYLES	EVALUATORS*
EUGE	EUNUCHIZES	EUPHORIES	EUTAXIES	EVANESCE
EUGENIA	EUNUCHIZING	EUPHORY	EUTAXITE	EVANESCED
EUGENIAS	EUNUCHOID	EUPHOTIC*	EUTAXITES	EVANESCES
EUGENIC	EUNUCHOIDS	EUPHRASIES	EUTAXITIC	EVANESCING
EUGENICS	EUNUCHS	EUPHRASY	EUTAXY	EVANGEL
EUGENISM	EUOI	EUPHROE	EUTECTIC	EVANGELIC
EUGENISMS	EUONYMIN	EUPHROES	EUTECTICS	EVANGELIES
EUGENIST	EUONYMINS	EUPHUISE	EUTECTOID	EVANGELS
EUGENISTS	EUONYMUS	EUPHUISED	EUTECTOIDS	EVANGELY
EUGENOL	EUONYMUSES	EUPHUISES	EUTEXIA	EVANISH
EUGENOLS	EUOUAE	EUPHUISING	EUTEXIAS	EVANISHED
EUGH	EUOUAES	EUPHUISM	EUTHANASIES	EVANISHES
EUGHEN	EUPAD	EUPHUISMS	EUTHANASY	EVANISHING
EUGHS	EUPADS	EUPHUIST	EUTHANIZE*	EVANITION
EUGLENA*	EUPATRID	EUPHUISTS	EUTHANIZED*	EVANITIONS
EUGLENAS*	EUPATRIDAE	EUPHUIZE	EUTHANIZES*	EVAPORATE
EUGLENOID*	EUPATRIDS	EUPHUIZED	EUTHANIZING*	EVAPORATED
EUGLENOIDS*	EUPEPSIA	EUPHUIZES	EUTHENICS	EVAPORATES
EUK	EUPEPSIAS	EUPHUIZING	EUTHENIST	EVAPORATING
EUKARYON	EUPEPSIES	EUPLOID*	EUTHENISTS	EVAPORITE
EUKARYONS	EUPEPSY	EUPLOIDIES*	EUTHERIAN	EVAPORITES
EUKARYOT	EUPEPTIC	EUPLOIDS*	EUTHERIANS	EVASIBLE
EUKARYOTE	EUPHAUSID	EUPLOIDY*	EUTHYROID*	EVASION
EUKARYOTES	EUPHAUSIDS	EUPNEA*	EUTRAPELIES	EVASIONS
EUKARYOTS	EUPHEMISE	EUPNEAS*	EUTRAPELY	EVASIVE
EUKED	EUPHEMISED	EUPNEIC*	EUTROPHIC	EVASIVELY
EUKING	EUPHEMISES	EUPNOEA*	EUTROPHIES	EVE
EUKS	EUPHEMISING	EUPNOEAS*	EUTROPHY	EVECTION
EULACHAN	EUPHEMISM	EUPNOEIC*	EUTROPIC	EVECTIONS
EULACHANS	EUPHEMISMS	EUREKA	EUTROPIES	EVEJAR
EULACHON	EUPHEMIST*	EUREKAS	EUTROPOUS	EVEJARS
EULACHONS	EUPHEMISTS*	EURHYTHMIES	EUTROPY	EVEN
EULOGIA	EUPHEMIZE	EURHYTHMY	EUXENITE	EVENED
EULOGIAE*	EUPHEMIZED	EURIPI	EUXENITES	EVENEMENT
EULOGIAS*	EUPHEMIZES	EURIPUS	EVACUANT	EVENEMENTS
EULOGIES	EUPHEMIZING	EURIPUSES	EVACUANTS	EVENER
EULOGISE	EUPHENIC*	EURO	EVACUATE	EVENERS
EULOGISED	EUPHENICS	EUROKIES*	EVACUATED	EVENEST
EULOGISES	EUPHOBIA	EUROKOUS*	EVACUATES	EVENFALL
EULOGISING	EUPHOBIAS	EUROKY*	EVACUATING	EVENFALLS
EULOGIST	EUPHON	EUROPIUM	EVACUATOR	EVENING
EULOGISTS	EUPHONIA	EUROPIUMS	EVACUATORS	EVENINGS

Words marked with an asterisk are from OTCWL

EVENLY	EVIDENCE	EVOLUTE	EXACTRESS	EXCAVATED
EVENNESS	EVIDENCED	EVOLUTED	EXACTRESSES	EXCAVATES
EVENNESSES	EVIDENCES	EVOLUTES	EXACTS	EXCAVATING
EVENS	EVIDENCING	EVOLUTING	EXALT	EXCAVATOR
EVENSONG	EVIDENT	EVOLUTION	EXALTED	EXCAVATORS
EVENSONGS	EVIDENTLY	EVOLUTIONS	EXALTEDLY	EXCEED
EVENT	EVIDENTS	EVOLUTIVE	EXALTER*	EXCEEDED
EVENTED	EVIL	EVOLVABLE	EXALTERS*	EXCEEDER*
EVENTER	EVILDOER*	EVOLVE	EXALTING	EXCEEDERS*
EVENTERS	EVILDOERS*	EVOLVED	EXALTS	EXCEEDING
EVENTFUL	EVILDOING*	EVOLVENT	EXAM	EXCEEDS
EVENTIDE	EVILDOINGS*	EVOLVER	EXAMEN	EXCEL
EVENTIDES	EVILER*	EVOLVERS	EXAMENS	EXCELLED
EVENTING	EVILEST*	EVOLVES	EXAMINANT	EXCELLENT
EVENTINGS	EVILLER	EVOLVING	EXAMINANTS	EXCELLING
EVENTLESS*	EVILLEST	EVONYMUS*	EXAMINATE	EXCELS
EVENTRATE	EVILLY	EVONYMUSES*	EXAMINATES	EXCELSIOR
EVENTRATED	EVILNESS	EVOVAE	EXAMINE	EXCELSIORS
EVENTRATES	EVILNESSES	EVOVAES	EXAMINED	EXCENTRIC
EVENTRATING	EVILS	EVULGATE	EXAMINEE	EXCENTRICS
EVENTS	EVINCE	EVULGATED	EXAMINEES	EXCEPT
EVENTUAL	EVINCED	EVULGATES	EXAMINER	EXCEPTANT
EVENTUATE	EVINCES	EVULGATING	EXAMINERS	EXCEPTANTS
EVENTUATED	EVINCIBLE	EVULSE	EXAMINES	EXCEPTED
EVENTUATES	EVINCIBLY	EVULSED	EXAMINING	EXCEPTING
EVENTUATING	EVINCING	EVULSES	EXAMPLAR	EXCEPTION
EVER	EVINCIVE	EVULSING	EXAMPLARS	EXCEPTIONS
EVERGLADE	EVIRATE	EVULSION	EXAMPLE	EXCEPTIVE
EVERGLADES	EVIRATED	EVULSIONS	EXAMPLED	EXCEPTOR
EVERGREEN	EVIRATES	EVZONE	EXAMPLES	EXCEPTORS
EVERGREENS	EVIRATING	EVZONES	EXAMPLING	EXCEPTS
EVERMORE	EVITABLE	EWE	EXAMS	EXCERPT
EVERSIBLE	EVITATE	EWER	EXANIMATE	EXCERPTA
EVERSION	EVITATED	EWERS	EXANTHEM	EXCERPTED
EVERSIONS	EVITATES	EWES	EXANTHEMA	EXCERPTER*
EVERT	EVITATING	EWEST	EXANTHEMAS*	EXCERPTERS*
EVERTED	EVITATION	EWFTES	EXANTHEMATA	EXCERPTING
EVERTING	EVITATIONS	EWGHEN	EXANTHEMS	EXCERPTINGS
EVERTOR	EVITE	EWHOW	EXARATE	EXCERPTOR
EVERTORS	EVITED	EWK	EXARATION	EXCERPTORS
EVERTS	EVITERNAL	EWKED	EXARATIONS	EXCERPTS
EVERY	EVITES	EWKING	EXARCH	EXCERPTUM
EVERYBODY	EVITING	EWKS	EXARCHAL	EXCESS
EVERYDAY	EVOCABLE	EWT	EXARCHATE	EXCESSED*
EVERYDAYS	EVOCATE	EWTS	EXARCHATES	EXCESSES
EVERYMAN	EVOCATED	EX	EXARCHIES	EXCESSING*
EVERYMEN	EVOCATES	EXACT	EXARCHIST	EXCESSIVE
EVERYONE	EVOCATING	EXACTA*	EXARCHISTS	EXCHANGE
EVERYWAY	EVOCATION	EXACTABLE	EXARCHS	EXCHANGED
EVERYWHEN	EVOCATIONS	EXACTAS*	EXARCHY	EXCHANGER
EVES	EVOCATIVE	EXACTED	EXCAMB	EXCHANGERS
EVET	EVOCATOR	EXACTER	EXCAMBED	EXCHANGES
EVETS	EVOCATORS	EXACTERS	EXCAMBING	EXCHANGING
EVHOE	EVOCATORY	EXACTEST	EXCAMBION	EXCHEAT
EVICT	EVOE	EXACTING	EXCAMBIONS	EXCHEATS
EVICTED	EVOHE	EXACTION	EXCAMBIUM	EXCHEQUER
EVICTEE*	EVOKE	EXACTIONS	EXCAMBIUMS	EXCHEQUERED
EVICTEES*	EVOKED	EXACTLY	EXCAMBS	EXCHEQUERING
EVICTING	EVOKER	EXACTMENT	EXCARNATE	EXCHEQUERS
EVICTION	EVOKERS	EXACTMENTS	EXCARNATED	EXCIDE
EVICTIONS	EVOKES	EXACTNESS	EXCARNATES	EXCIDED
EVICTOR	EVOKING	EXACTNESSES	EXCARNATING	EXCIDES
EVICTORS	EVOLUE	EXACTOR	EXCAUDATE	EXCIDING
EVICTS	EVOLUES	EXACTORS	EXCAVATE	EXCIMER*

EXCIMERS*	EXCRETER	EXECUTORY	EXEUNT	EXILES
EXCIPIENT	EXCRETERS	EXECUTRICES	EXFOLIATE	EXILIAN
EXCIPIENTS	EXCRETES	EXECUTRIES	EXFOLIATED	EXILIC
EXCIPLE*	EXCRETING	EXECUTRIX	EXFOLIATES	EXILING
EXCIPLES*	EXCRETION	EXECUTRIXES	EXFOLIATING	EXILITIES
EXCISABLE	EXCRETIONS	EXECUTRY	EXHALABLE	EXILITY
EXCISE	EXCRETIVE	EXEDRA	EXHALANT	EXIMIOUS
EXCISED	EXCRETORIES	EXEDRAE	EXHALANTS	EXINE
EXCISEMAN	EXCRETORY	EXEEM	EXHALE	EXINES
EXCISEMEN	EXCUBANT	EXEEMED	EXHALED	EXIST
EXCISES	EXCUDIT	EXEEMING	EXHALENT*	EXISTED
EXCISING	EXCULPATE	EXEEMS	EXHALENTS*	EXISTENCE
EXCISION	EXCULPATED	EXEGESES	EXHALES	EXISTENCES
EXCISIONS	EXCULPATES	EXEGESIS	EXHALING	EXISTENT
EXCITABLE	EXCULPATING	EXEGETE	EXHAUST	EXISTENTS*
EXCITANCIES	EXCURRENT	EXEGETES	EXHAUSTED	EXISTING
EXCITANCY	EXCURSE	EXEGETIC	EXHAUSTER	EXISTS
EXCITANT	EXCURSED	EXEGETICS	EXHAUSTERS	EXIT
EXCITANTS	EXCURSES	EXEGETIST	EXHAUSTING	EXITANCE
EXCITE	EXCURSING	EXEGETISTS	EXHAUSTS	EXITANCES
EXCITED	EXCURSION	EXEME	EXHEDRA	EXITED
EXCITEDLY	EXCURSIONED	EXEMED	EXHEDRAE	EXITING
EXCITER	EXCURSIONING	EXEMES	EXHIBIT	EXITLESS*
EXCITERS	EXCURSIONS	EXEMING	EXHIBITED	EXITS
EXCITES	EXCURSIVE	EXEMPLA	EXHIBITER	EXOCARP
EXCITING	EXCURSUS	EXEMPLAR	EXHIBITERS	EXOCARPS
EXCITON	EXCURSUSES	EXEMPLARS	EXHIBITING	EXOCRINE
EXCITONIC*	EXCUSABLE	EXEMPLARY	EXHIBITOR	EXOCRINES
EXCITONS	EXCUSABLY	EXEMPLE	EXHIBITORS	EXOCYCLIC*
EXCITOR	EXCUSAL	EXEMPLES	EXHIBITS	EXODE
EXCITORS	EXCUSALS	EXEMPLIFIED	EXHORT	EXODERM
EXCLAIM	EXCUSE	EXEMPLIFIES	EXHORTED	EXODERMAL
EXCLAIMED	EXCUSED	EXEMPLIFY	EXHORTER	EXODERMIS
EXCLAIMER*	EXCUSER	EXEMPLIFYING	EXHORTERS	EXODERMISES
EXCLAIMERS*	EXCUSERS	EXEMPLUM	EXHORTING	EXODERMS
EXCLAIMING	EXCUSES	EXEMPT	EXHORTS	EXODES
EXCLAIMS	EXCUSING	EXEMPTED	EXHUMATE	EXODIC
EXCLAVE	EXCUSIVE	EXEMPTING	EXHUMATED	EXODIST
EXCLAVES	EXEAT	EXEMPTION	EXHUMATES	EXODISTS
EXCLOSURE	EXEATS	EXEMPTIONS	EXHUMATING	EXODOI*
EXCLOSURES	EXEC*	EXEMPTS	EXHUME	EXODONTIA*
EXCLUDE	EXECRABLE	EXEQUATUR	EXHUMED	EXODONTIAS*
EXCLUDED	EXECRABLY	EXEQUATURS	EXHUMER	EXODOS*
EXCLUDEE	EXECRATE	EXEQUIAL	EXHUMERS	EXODUS
EXCLUDEES	EXECRATED	EXEQUIES	EXHUMES	EXODUSES
EXCLUDER	EXECRATES	EXEQUY	EXHUMING	EXOENZYME
EXCLUDERS	EXECRATING	EXERCISE	EXIES	EXOENZYMES
EXCLUDES	EXECRATOR*	EXERCISED	EXIGEANT	EXOERGIC
EXCLUDING	EXECRATORS*	EXERCISER	EXIGEANTE	EXOGAMIC
EXCLUSION	EXECS*	EXERCISERS	EXIGENCE	EXOGAMIES
EXCLUSIONS	EXECUTANT	EXERCISES	EXIGENCES	EXOGAMOUS
EXCLUSIVE	EXECUTANTS	EXERCISING	EXIGENCIES	EXOGAMY
EXCLUSIVES	EXECUTE	EXERGONIC	EXIGENCY	EXOGEN
EXCLUSORY	EXECUTED	EXERGUAL	EXIGENT	EXOGENOUS
EXCORIATE	EXECUTER	EXERGUE	EXIGENTLY	EXOGENS
EXCORIATED	EXECUTERS	EXERGUES	EXIGENTS	EXOMION
EXCORIATES	EXECUTES	EXERT	EXIGIBLE	EXOMIONS
EXCORIATING	EXECUTING	EXERTED	EXIGUITIES	EXOMIS
EXCREMENT	EXECUTION	EXERTING	EXIGUITY	EXOMISES
EXCREMENTS	EXECUTIONS	EXERTION	EXIGUOUS	EXON
EXCRETA	EXECUTIVE	EXERTIONS	EXILE	EXONERATE
EXCRETAL	EXECUTIVES	EXERTIVE	EXILED	EXONERATED
EXCRETE	EXECUTOR	EXERTS	EXILEMENT	EXONERATES
EXCRETED	EXECUTORS	EXES	EXILEMENTS	EXONERATING

EXONIC	EXPANDOR	EXPERTISM*	EXPLORE	EXPULSIONS
EXONS	EXPANDORS	EXPERTISMS*	EXPLORED	EXPULSIVE
EXONUMIA*	EXPANDS	EXPERTIZE	EXPLORER	EXPUNCT
EXONYM	EXPANSE	EXPERTIZED	EXPLORERS	EXPUNCTED
EXONYMS	EXPANSES	EXPERTIZES	EXPLORES	EXPUNCTING
EXOPHAGIES	EXPANSILE	EXPERTIZING	EXPLORING	EXPUNCTS
EXOPHAGY	EXPANSION	EXPERTLY	EXPLOSION	EXPUNGE
EXOPLASM	EXPANSIONS	EXPERTS	EXPLOSIONS	EXPUNGED
EXOPLASMS	EXPANSIVE	EXPIABLE	EXPLOSIVE	EXPUNGER
EXOPOD	EXPAT	EXPIATE	EXPLOSIVES	EXPUNGERS
EXOPODITE	EXPATIATE	EXPIATED	EXPO	EXPUNGES
EXOPODITES	EXPATIATED	EXPIATES	EXPONENT	EXPUNGING
EXOPODS	EXPATIATES	EXPIATING	EXPONENTS	EXPURGATE
EXORABLE	EXPATIATING	EXPIATION	EXPONIBLE	EXPURGATED
EXORATION	EXPATS	EXPIATIONS	EXPORT	EXPURGATES
EXORATIONS	EXPECT	EXPIATOR	EXPORTED	EXPURGATING
EXORCISE	EXPECTANT	EXPIATORS	EXPORTER	EXPURGE
EXORCISED	EXPECTANTS	EXPIATORY	EXPORTERS	EXPURGED
EXORCISER	EXPECTED	EXPIRABLE	EXPORTING	EXPURGES
EXORCISERS	EXPECTER	EXPIRANT	EXPORTS	EXPURGING
EXORCISES	EXPECTERS	EXPIRANTS	EXPOS	EXQUISITE
EXORCISING	EXPECTING	EXPIRE	EXPOSABLE	EXQUISITES
EXORCISM	EXPECTINGS	EXPIRED	EXPOSAL	EXSCIND
EXORCISMS	EXPECTS	EXPIRER*	EXPOSALS	EXSCINDED
EXORCIST	EXPEDIENT	EXPIRERS*	EXPOSE	EXSCINDING
EXORCISTS	EXPEDIENTS	EXPIRES	EXPOSED	EXSCINDS
EXORCIZE	EXPEDITE	EXPIRIES	EXPOSER	EXSECANT*
EXORCIZED	EXPEDITED	EXPIRING	EXPOSERS	EXSECANTS*
EXORCIZER	EXPEDITER	EXPIRY	EXPOSES	EXSECT
EXORCIZERS	EXPEDITERS	EXPISCATE	EXPOSING	EXSECTED
EXORCIZES	EXPEDITES	EXPISCATED	EXPOSIT*	EXSECTING
EXORCIZING	EXPEDITING	EXPISCATES	EXPOSITED*	EXSECTION
EXORDIA	EXPEDITOR	EXPISCATING	EXPOSITING*	EXSECTIONS
EXORDIAL	EXPEDITORS	EXPLAIN	EXPOSITOR	EXSECTS
EXORDIUM	EXPEL	EXPLAINED	EXPOSITORS	EXSERT
EXORDIUMS	EXPELLANT	EXPLAINER	EXPOSITS*	EXSERTED
EXOSMIC*	EXPELLANTS	EXPLAINERS	EXPOSTURE	EXSERTILE
EXOSMOSE	EXPELLED	EXPLAINING	EXPOSTURES	EXSERTING
EXOSMOSES	EXPELLEE	EXPLAINS	EXPOSURE	EXSERTION
EXOSMOSIS	EXPELLEES	EXPLANT	EXPOSURES	EXSERTIONS
EXOSMOTIC	EXPELLENT	EXPLANTED	EXPOUND	EXSERTS
EXOSPHERE	EXPELLENTS	EXPLANTING	EXPOUNDED	EXSICCANT
EXOSPHERES	EXPELLER*	EXPLANTS	EXPOUNDER	EXSICCATE
EXOSPORAL	EXPELLERS*	EXPLETIVE	EXPOUNDERS	EXSICCATED
EXOSPORE	EXPELLING	EXPLETIVES	EXPOUNDING	EXSICCATES
EXOSPORES	EXPELS	EXPLETORY	EXPOUNDS	EXSICCATING
EXOSTOSES	EXPEND	EXPLICATE	EXPRESS	EXSUCCOUS
EXOSTOSIS	EXPENDED	EXPLICATED	EXPRESSED	EXTANT
EXOTERIC	EXPENDER	EXPLICATES	EXPRESSER*	EXTASIES
EXOTIC	EXPENDERS	EXPLICATING	EXPRESSERS*	EXTASY
EXOTICA	EXPENDING	EXPLICIT	EXPRESSES	EXTATIC
EXOTICISM	EXPENDS	EXPLICITS	EXPRESSING	EXTEMPORE
EXOTICISMS	EXPENSE	EXPLODE	EXPRESSLY	EXTEMPORES
EXOTICS	EXPENSED*	EXPLODED	EXPRESSO	EXTEND
EXOTISM*	EXPENSES	EXPLODER	EXPRESSOS	EXTENDANT
EXOTISMS*	EXPENSING*	EXPLODERS	EXPUGN	EXTENDED
EXOTOXIC	EXPENSIVE	EXPLODES	EXPUGNED	EXTENDER
EXOTOXIN	EXPERT	EXPLODING	EXPUGNING	EXTENDERS
EXOTOXINS	EXPERTED	EXPLOIT	EXPUGNS	EXTENDING
EXPAND	EXPERTING	EXPLOITED	EXPULSE	EXTENDS
EXPANDED	EXPERTISE	EXPLOITER	EXPULSED	EXTENSE
EXPANDER	EXPERTISED	EXPLOITERS	EXPULSES	EXTENSILE
EXPANDERS	EXPERTISES	EXPLOITING	EXPULSING	EXTENSION
EXPANDING	EXPERTISING	EXPLOITS	EXPULSION	EXTENSIONS

The Chambers Dictionary is the authority for many longer words; see Introduction, page ix

EXTENSITIES	EXTORTERS*	EXTRORSAL	EXUVIATES	EYELIKE*
EXTENSITY	EXTORTING	EXTRORSE	EXUVIATING	EYELINER
EXTENSIVE	EXTORTION	EXTROVERT	EXUVIUM*	EYELINERS
EXTENSOR	EXTORTIONS	EXTROVERTED	EYALET	EYEN*
EXTENSORS	EXTORTIVE	EXTROVERTING	EYALETS	EYEPIECE*
EXTENT	EXTORTS	EXTROVERTS	EYAS	EYEPIECES*
EXTENTS	EXTRA	EXTRUDE	EYASES	EYEPOINT*
EXTENUATE	EXTRACT	EXTRUDED	EYE	EYEPOINTS*
EXTENUATED	EXTRACTED	EXTRUDER	EYEABLE*	EYEPOPPER*
EXTENUATES	EXTRACTING	EXTRUDERS	EYEBALL	EYEPOPPERS*
EXTENUATING	EXTRACTOR	EXTRUDES	EYEBALLED	EYER*
EXTENUATINGS	EXTRACTORS	EXTRUDING	EYEBALLING	EYERS*
EXTERIOR	EXTRACTS	EXTRUSION	EYEBALLS	EYES
EXTERIORS	EXTRADITE	EXTRUSIONS	EYEBAR*	EYESHADE
EXTERMINE	EXTRADITED	EXTRUSIVE	EYEBARS*	EYESHADES
EXTERMINED	EXTRADITES	EXTRUSORY	EYEBEAM*	EYESHADOW
EXTERMINES	EXTRADITING	EXTUBATE*	EYEBEAMS*	EYESHADOWS
EXTERMINING	EXTRADOS	EXTUBATED*	EYEBOLT	EYESHOT*
EXTERN	EXTRADOSES	EXTUBATES*	EYEBOLTS	EYESHOTS*
EXTERNAL	EXTRAIT	EXTUBATING*	EYEBRIGHT	EYESIGHT
EXTERNALS	EXTRAITS	EXUBERANT	EYEBRIGHTS	EYESIGHTS
EXTERNAT	EXTRALITIES*	EXUBERATE	EYEBROW	EYESOME*
EXTERNATS	EXTRALITY*	EXUBERATED	EYEBROWED	EYESORE
EXTERNE	EXTRANET	EXUBERATES	EYEBROWING	EYESORES
EXTERNES	EXTRANETS	EXUBERATING	EYEBROWS	EYESPOT*
EXTERNS	EXTRAPOSE	EXUDATE	EYECUP*	EYESPOTS*
EXTINCT	EXTRAPOSED	EXUDATES	EYECUPS*	EYESTALK
EXTINCTED	EXTRAPOSES	EXUDATION	EYED	EYESTALKS
EXTINCTING*	EXTRAPOSING	EXUDATIONS	EYEDNESS*	EYESTONE*
EXTINCTS*	EXTRAS	EXUDATIVE	EYEDNESSES*	EYESTONES*
EXTINE	EXTRAUGHT	EXUDE	EYEDROPS*	EYESTRAIN
EXTINES	EXTRAVERT	EXUDED	EYEFUL	EYESTRAINS
EXTIRP	EXTRAVERTED	EXUDES	EYEFULS	EYETEETH*
EXTIRPATE	EXTRAVERTING	EXUDING	EYEGLASS	EYETOOTH*
EXTIRPATED	EXTRAVERTS	EXUL	EYEGLASSES	EYEWASH*
EXTIRPATES	EXTREAT	EXULS	EYEHOLE*	EYEWASHES*
EXTIRPATING	EXTREATS	EXULT	EYEHOLES*	EYEWATER*
EXTIRPED	EXTREMA*	EXULTANCE	EYEHOOK	EYEWATERS*
EXTIRPING	EXTREME	EXULTANCES	EYEHOOKS	EYEWEAR*
EXTIRPS	EXTREMELY	EXULTANCIES	EYEING	EYEWINK*
EXTOL	EXTREMER	EXULTANCY	EYELASH	EYEWINKS*
EXTOLD	EXTREMES	EXULTANT	EYELASHES	EYING
EXTOLL*	EXTREMEST	EXULTED	EYELESS	EYLIAD
EXTOLLED	EXTREMISM	EXULTING	EYELET	EYLIADS
EXTOLLER	EXTREMISMS	EXULTS	EYELETED	EYNE
EXTOLLERS	EXTREMIST	EXURB	EYELETEER	EYOT
EXTOLLING	EXTREMISTS	EXURBAN	EYELETEERS	EYOTS
EXTOLLS*	EXTREMITIES	EXURBIA	EYELETING	EYRA
EXTOLMENT	EXTREMITY	EXURBIAS	EYELETS	EYRAS
EXTOLMENTS	EXTREMUM*	EXURBS	EYELETTED*	EYRE
EXTOLS	EXTRICATE	EXUVIA*	EYELETTING*	EYRES
EXTORSIVE	EXTRICATED	EXUVIAE	EYELIAD	EYRIE
EXTORT	EXTRICATES	EXUVIAL	EYELIADS	EYRIES
EXTORTED	EXTRICATING	EXUVIATE	EYELID	EYRIR*
EXTORTER*	EXTRINSIC	EXUVIATED	EYELIDS	EYRY

F

FA
FAB
FABACEOUS
FABBER
FABBEST
FABLE
FABLED
FABLER
FABLERS
FABLES
FABLIAU
FABLIAUX
FABLING
FABLINGS
FABRIC
FABRICANT
FABRICANTS
FABRICATE
FABRICATED
FABRICATES
FABRICATING
FABRICKED
FABRICKING
FABRICS
FABULAR
FABULISE
FABULISED
FABULISES
FABULISING
FABULIST
FABULISTS
FABULIZE
FABULIZED
FABULIZES
FABULIZING
FABULOUS
FABURDEN
FABURDENS
FACADE
FACADES
FACE
FACEABLE*
FACECLOTH*
FACECLOTHS*
FACED
FACEDOWN*
FACELESS
FACEMAN
FACEMEN
FACEPLATE*
FACEPLATES*
FACER
FACERS
FACES
FACET

FACETE
FACETED
FACETELY*
FACETIAE
FACETING
FACETIOUS
FACETS
FACETTED*
FACETTING*
FACEUP*
FACIA
FACIAL
FACIALLY
FACIALS
FACIAS
FACIEND*
FACIENDS*
FACIES
FACILE
FACILELY
FACILITIES
FACILITY
FACING
FACINGS
FACONNE
FACONNES
FACSIMILE
FACSIMILED
FACSIMILEING
FACSIMILES
FACT
FACTFUL*
FACTICE
FACTICES
FACTICITIES
FACTICITY
FACTION
FACTIONAL
FACTIONS
FACTIOUS
FACTIS
FACTISES
FACTITIVE
FACTIVE
FACTOID
FACTOIDS
FACTOR
FACTORAGE
FACTORAGES
FACTORED
FACTORIAL
FACTORIALS
FACTORIES
FACTORING
FACTORINGS

FACTORISE
FACTORISED
FACTORISES
FACTORISING
FACTORIZE
FACTORIZED
FACTORIZES
FACTORIZING
FACTORS
FACTORY
FACTOTUM
FACTOTUMS
FACTS
FACTUAL
FACTUALLY*
FACTUM
FACTUMS
FACTURE
FACTURES
FACULA
FACULAE
FACULAR
FACULTIES
FACULTY
FACUNDITIES
FACUNDITY
FAD
FADABLE
FADAISE
FADAISES
FADDIER
FADDIEST
FADDINESS
FADDINESSES
FADDISH
FADDISM
FADDISMS
FADDIST
FADDISTS
FADDLE
FADDLED
FADDLES
FADDLING
FADDY
FADE
FADEAWAY*
FADEAWAYS*
FADED
FADEDLY
FADEDNESS
FADEDNESSES
FADELESS
FADER
FADERS
FADES

FADEUR
FADEURS
FADGE
FADGED
FADGES
FADGING
FADIER
FADIEST
FADING
FADINGS
FADO
FADOS
FADS
FADY
FAECAL
FAECES
FAENA*
FAENAS*
FAERIE
FAERIES
FAERY
FAFF
FAFFED
FAFFING
FAFFS
FAG
FAGACEOUS
FAGGED
FAGGERIES
FAGGERY
FAGGING
FAGGINGS
FAGGOT
FAGGOTED
FAGGOTING
FAGGOTINGS
FAGGOTRIES*
FAGGOTRY*
FAGGOTS
FAGGOTY*
FAGGY*
FAGIN*
FAGINS*
FAGOT
FAGOTED
FAGOTER*
FAGOTERS*
FAGOTING
FAGOTINGS
FAGOTS
FAGOTTI
FAGOTTIST
FAGOTTISTS
FAGOTTO
FAGS

FAH
FAHLBAND
FAHLBANDS
FAHLERZ
FAHLERZES
FAHLORE
FAHLORES
FAHS
FAIBLE
FAIBLES
FAIENCE
FAIENCES
FAIK
FAIKED
FAIKES
FAIKING
FAIKS
FAIL
FAILED
FAILING
FAILINGLY*
FAILINGS
FAILLE
FAILLES
FAILS
FAILURE
FAILURES
FAIN
FAINE
FAINEANCE
FAINEANCES
FAINEANCIES
FAINEANCY
FAINEANT
FAINEANTS
FAINED
FAINER
FAINES
FAINEST
FAINING
FAINITES
FAINLY
FAINNESS
FAINNESSES
FAINS
FAINT
FAINTED
FAINTER
FAINTERS*
FAINTEST
FAINTIER
FAINTIEST
FAINTING
FAINTINGS
FAINTISH

The Chambers Dictionary is the authority for many longer words; see Introduction, page ix

FAINTLY	FAKIR	FALLINGS	FAMING	FANFARONS
FAINTNESS	FAKIRISM	FALLOFF*	FAMISH	FANFOLD
FAINTNESSES	FAKIRISMS	FALLOFFS*	FAMISHED	FANFOLDED*
FAINTS	FAKIRS	FALLOUT	FAMISHES	FANFOLDING*
FAINTY	FALAFEL	FALLOUTS	FAMISHING	FANFOLDS*
FAIR	FALAFELS	FALLOW	FAMOUS	FANG
FAIRED	FALAJ	FALLOWED	FAMOUSED	FANGA*
FAIRER	FALANGISM	FALLOWER	FAMOUSES	FANGAS*
FAIREST	FALANGISMS	FALLOWEST	FAMOUSING	FANGED
FAIRIES	FALANGIST	FALLOWING	FAMOUSLY	FANGING
FAIRILY	FALANGISTS	FALLOWS	FAMULI*	FANGLE
FAIRING	FALBALA	FALLS	FAMULUS	FANGLED
FAIRINGS	FALBALAS	FALSE	FAMULUSES	FANGLES
FAIRISH	FALCADE	FALSED	FAN	FANGLESS
FAIRISHLY*	FALCADES	FALSEHOOD	FANAL	FANGLIKE*
FAIRLEAD*	FALCATE	FALSEHOODS	FANALS	FANGLING
FAIRLEADS*	FALCATED	FALSELY	FANATIC	FANGO
FAIRLY	FALCATION	FALSENESS	FANATICAL	FANGOS
FAIRNESS	FALCATIONS	FALSENESSES	FANATICS	FANGS
FAIRNESSES	FALCES	FALSER	FANCIABLE	FANION
FAIRS	FALCHION	FALSERS	FANCIED	FANIONS
FAIRWAY	FALCHIONS	FALSES	FANCIER	FANJET*
FAIRWAYS	FALCIFORM	FALSEST	FANCIERS	FANJETS*
FAIRY	FALCON	FALSETTO	FANCIES	FANK
FAIRYDOM	FALCONER	FALSETTOS	FANCIEST	FANKLE
FAIRYDOMS	FALCONERS	FALSEWORK	FANCIFIED*	FANKLED
FAIRYHOOD	FALCONET	FALSEWORKS	FANCIFIES*	FANKLES
FAIRYHOODS	FALCONETS	FALSIE*	FANCIFUL	FANKLING
FAIRYISM	FALCONINE	FALSIES	FANCIFY*	FANKS
FAIRYISMS	FALCONRIES	FALSIFIED	FANCIFYING*	FANLIGHT
FAIRYLAND	FALCONRY	FALSIFIER	FANCILESS	FANLIGHTS
FAIRYLANDS	FALCONS	FALSIFIERS	FANCILY*	FANLIKE*
FAIRYLIKE	FALCULA	FALSIFIES	FANCINESS*	FANNED
FAIRYTALE	FALCULAS	FALSIFY	FANCINESSES*	FANNEL
FAIRYTALES	FALCULATE	FALSIFYING	FANCY	FANNELL
FAITH	FALDAGE	FALSING	FANCYING	FANNELLS
FAITHCURE	FALDAGES	FALSISH	FANCYWORK	FANNELS
FAITHCURES	FALDERAL	FALSISM	FANCYWORKS	FANNER
FAITHED	FALDERALS	FALSISMS	FAND	FANNERS
FAITHFUL	FALDEROL*	FALSITIES	FANDANGLE	FANNIES
FAITHFULS*	FALDEROLS*	FALSITY	FANDANGLES	FANNING
FAITHING	FALDETTA	FALTBOAT	FANDANGO	FANNINGS
FAITHLESS	FALDETTAS	FALTBOATS	FANDANGOES	FANNY
FAITHS	FALDSTOOL	FALTER	FANDANGOS	FANO*
FAITOR	FALDSTOOLS	FALTERED	FANDED	FANON
FAITORS	FALL	FALTERER*	FANDING	FANONS
FAITOUR	FALLACIES	FALTERERS*	FANDOM	FANOS*
FAITOURS	FALLACY	FALTERING	FANDOMS	FANS
FAIX	FALLAL	FALTERINGS	FANDS	FANTAD
FAJITA*	FALLALERIES	FALTERS	FANE	FANTADS
FAJITAS	FALLALERY	FALX	FANEGA*	FANTAIL
FAKE	FALLALS	FAME	FANEGADA*	FANTAILED
FAKED	FALLAWAY*	FAMED	FANEGADAS*	FANTAILS
FAKEER*	FALLAWAYS*	FAMELESS	FANEGAS*	FANTASIA
FAKEERS*	FALLBACK*	FAMES	FANES	FANTASIAS
FAKEMENT	FALLBACKS*	FAMILIAL	FANFARADE	FANTASIE*
FAKEMENTS	FALLEN	FAMILIAR	FANFARADES	FANTASIED
FAKER	FALLER	FAMILIARS	FANFARE	FANTASIES
FAKERIES	FALLERS	FAMILIES	FANFARED	FANTASISE
FAKERS	FALLFISH*	FAMILISM	FANFARES	FANTASISED
FAKERY	FALLFISHES*	FAMILISMS	FANFARING	FANTASISES
FAKES	FALLIBLE	FAMILY	FANFARON	FANTASISING
FAKEY*	FALLIBLY	FAMINE	FANFARONA	FANTASIST
FAKING	FALLING	FAMINES	FANFARONAS	FANTASISTS

FANTASIZE	FARCERS*	FARMHAND*	FAS	FASTEST
FANTASIZED	FARCES	FARMHANDS*	FASCES	FASTI
FANTASIZES	FARCEUR	FARMHOUSE	FASCI	FASTIGIUM
FANTASIZING	FARCEURS	FARMHOUSES	FASCIA	FASTIGIUMS
FANTASM	FARCEUSE	FARMING	FASCIAE*	FASTING
FANTASMS	FARCEUSES	FARMINGS	FASCIAL	FASTINGS
FANTASQUE	FARCI	FARMLAND*	FASCIAS	FASTISH
FANTASQUES	FARCICAL	FARMLANDS*	FASCIATE	FASTLY
FANTAST	FARCIE*	FARMOST	FASCIATED	FASTNESS
FANTASTIC	FARCIED	FARMS	FASCICLE	FASTNESSES
FANTASTICS	FARCIES	FARMSTEAD	FASCICLED	FASTS
FANTASTRIES	FARCIFIED	FARMSTEADS	FASCICLES	FASTUOUS
FANTASTRY	FARCIFIES	FARMWIFE*	FASCICULE	FAT
FANTASTS	FARCIFY	FARMWIVES*	FASCICULES	FATAL
FANTASY	FARCIFYING	FARMWORK*	FASCICULI	FATALISM
FANTASYING	FARCIN	FARMWORKS*	FASCICULUS*	FATALISMS
FANTEEG	FARCING	FARMYARD	FASCINATE	FATALIST
FANTEEGS	FARCINGS	FARMYARDS	FASCINATED	FATALISTS
FANTIGUE	FARCINS	FARNESOL	FASCINATES	FATALITIES
FANTIGUES	FARCY	FARNESOLS	FASCINATING	FATALITY
FANTOD	FARD	FARNESS	FASCINE	FATALLY
FANTODS	FARDAGE	FARNESSES	FASCINES	FATBACK*
FANTOM	FARDAGES	FARO	FASCIO	FATBACKS*
FANTOMS	FARDED	FAROS	FASCIOLA	FATBIRD*
FANTOOSH	FARDEL	FAROUCHE	FASCIOLAS	FATBIRDS*
FANUM*	FARDELS	FARRAGO	FASCIOLE	FATE
FANUMS*	FARDEN	FARRAGOES	FASCIOLES	FATED
FANWISE*	FARDENS	FARRAGOS	FASCISM	FATEFUL
FANWORT*	FARDING	FARRAND	FASCISMI	FATEFULLY
FANWORTS*	FARDINGS	FARRANT	FASCISMO	FATES
FANZINE	FARDS	FARRED	FASCISMS	FATHEAD*
FANZINES	FARE	FARREN	FASCIST	FATHEADED*
FAP	FARED	FARRENS	FASCISTA	FATHEADS*
FAQIR*	FARER*	FARRIER	FASCISTI	FATHER
FAQIRS*	FARERS*	FARRIERIES	FASCISTIC	FATHERED
FAQUIR	FARES	FARRIERS	FASCISTS	FATHERING
FAQUIRS	FAREWELL	FARRIERY	FASH	FATHERLY
FAR	FAREWELLED*	FARRING	FASHED	FATHERS
FARAD	FAREWELLING*	FARROW	FASHERIES	FATHOM
FARADAIC*	FAREWELLS	FARROWED	FASHERY	FATHOMED
FARADAY	FARFAL*	FARROWING	FASHES	FATHOMING
FARADAYS	FARFALS*	FARROWS	FASHING	FATHOMS
FARADIC	FARFEL*	FARRUCA	FASHION	FATIDIC*
FARADISE	FARFELS*	FARRUCAS	FASHIONED	FATIDICAL
FARADISED	FARFET	FARS	FASHIONER	FATIGABLE
FARADISES	FARINA	FARSE	FASHIONERS	FATIGATE
FARADISING	FARINAS	FARSED	FASHIONING	FATIGATED
FARADISM	FARING	FARSEEING*	FASHIONS	FATIGATES
FARADISMS	FARINHA*	FARSES	FASHIOUS	FATIGATING
FARADIZE	FARINHAS*	FARSIDE*	FAST	FATIGUE
FARADIZED	FARINOSE	FARSIDES*	FASTBACK	FATIGUED
FARADIZES	FARL	FARSING	FASTBACKS	FATIGUES
FARADIZING	FARLE	FART	FASTBALL	FATIGUING
FARADS	FARLES	FARTED	FASTBALLS	FATING*
FARAND	FARLS	FARTHEL	FASTED	FATISCENT
FARANDINE	FARM	FARTHELS	FASTEN	FATLESS*
FARANDINES	FARMABLE*	FARTHER	FASTENED	FATLIKE*
FARANDOLE	FARMED	FARTHEST	FASTENER	FATLING
FARANDOLES	FARMER	FARTHING	FASTENERS	FATLINGS
FARAWAY	FARMERESS	FARTHINGS	FASTENING	FATLY
FARAWAYS	FARMERESSES	FARTING	FASTENINGS	FATNESS
FARCE	FARMERIES	FARTLEK	FASTENS	FATNESSES
FARCED	FARMERS	FARTLEKS	FASTER	FATS
FARCER*	FARMERY	FARTS	FASTERS	FATSIA

The Chambers Dictionary is the authority for many longer words; see Introduction, page ix

FATSIAS	FAULT	FAVOUR	FEARE	FEBRICULE
FATSO	FAULTED	FAVOURED	FEARED	FEBRICULES
FATSOES	FAULTFUL	FAVOURER	FEARER*	FEBRIFIC
FATSOS	FAULTIER	FAVOURERS	FEARERS*	FEBRIFUGE
FATSTOCK	FAULTIEST	FAVOURING	FEARES	FEBRIFUGES
FATSTOCKS	FAULTILY	FAVOURITE	FEARFUL	FEBRILE
FATTED	FAULTING	FAVOURITES	FEARFULLER*	FEBRILITIES
FATTEN	FAULTLESS	FAVOURS	FEARFULLEST*	FEBRILITY
FATTENED	FAULTS	FAVOUS	FEARFULLY	FECAL
FATTENER	FAULTY	FAVRILE	FEARING	FECES
FATTENERS	FAUN	FAVRILES	FEARLESS	FECHT
FATTENING	FAUNA	FAVUS	FEARLESSLY	FECHTER
FATTENINGS	FAUNAE	FAVUSES	FEARS	FECHTERS
FATTENS	FAUNAL	FAW	FEARSOME	FECHTING
FATTER	FAUNALLY*	FAWN	FEASANCE*	FECHTS
FATTEST	FAUNAS	FAWNED	FEASANCES*	FECIAL
FATTIER	FAUNIST	FAWNER	FEASE*	FECIALS*
FATTIES	FAUNISTIC	FAWNERS	FEASED*	FECIT
FATTIEST	FAUNISTS	FAWNIER*	FEASES*	FECK
FATTILY*	FAUNLIKE*	FAWNIEST*	FEASIBLE	FECKLESS
FATTINESS	FAUNS	FAWNING	FEASIBLY	FECKLY
FATTINESSES	FAURD	FAWNINGLY	FEASING*	FECKS
FATTING	FAUSTIAN	FAWNINGS	FEAST	FECULA
FATTISH	FAUTEUIL	FAWNLIKE*	FEASTED	FECULAE*
FATTISM	FAUTEUILS	FAWNS	FEASTER	FECULAS
FATTISMS	FAUTOR	FAWNY*	FEASTERS	FECULENCE
FATTIST	FAUTORS	FAWS	FEASTFUL	FECULENCES
FATTISTS	FAUVE*	FAX	FEASTING	FECULENCIES
FATTRELS	FAUVES*	FAXED	FEASTINGS	FECULENCY
FATTY	FAUVETTE	FAXES	FEASTS	FECULENT
FATUITIES	FAUVETTES	FAXING	FEAT	FECUND
FATUITOUS	FAUVISM*	FAY	FEATED	FECUNDATE
FATUITY	FAUVISMS*	FAYALITE	FEATEOUS	FECUNDATED
FATUOUS	FAUVIST*	FAYALITES	FEATER*	FECUNDATES
FATUOUSLY*	FAUVISTS*	FAYED	FEATEST*	FECUNDATING
FATWA	FAUX	FAYENCE	FEATHER	FECUNDITIES
FATWAED	FAVA*	FAYENCES	FEATHERED	FECUNDITY
FATWAH	FAVAS*	FAYER	FEATHERIER	FED
FATWAHED	FAVE	FAYEST	FEATHERIEST	FEDARIE
FATWAHING	FAVEL	FAYING	FEATHERING	FEDARIES
FATWAHS	FAVELA	FAYNE	FEATHERINGS	FEDAYEE
FATWAING	FAVELAS	FAYNED	FEATHERS	FEDAYEEN
FATWAS	FAVELL	FAYNES	FEATHERY	FEDELINI
FATWOOD*	FAVELLA*	FAYNING	FEATING	FEDELINIS
FATWOODS*	FAVELLAS*	FAYRE	FEATLIER*	FEDERACIES
FAUBOURG	FAVEOLATE	FAYRES	FEATLIEST*	FEDERACY
FAUBOURGS	FAVER	FAYS	FEATLY	FEDERAL
FAUCAL	FAVES*	FAZE	FEATOUS	FEDERALLY*
FAUCALS*	FAVEST	FAZED	FEATS	FEDERALS
FAUCES	FAVISM	FAZENDA	FEATUOUS	FEDERARIE
FAUCET	FAVISMS	FAZENDAS	FEATURE	FEDERARIES
FAUCETS	FAVONIAN*	FAZES	FEATURED	FEDERARY
FAUCHION	FAVOR	FAZING	FEATURELY	FEDERATE
FAUCHIONS	FAVORABLE	FEAGUE	FEATURES	FEDERATED
FAUCHON	FAVORABLY	FEAGUED	FEATURING	FEDERATES
FAUCHONS	FAVORED	FEAGUES	FEAZE*	FEDERATING
FAUCIAL	FAVORER	FEAGUING	FEAZED*	FEDORA
FAUGH	FAVORERS	FEAL	FEAZES*	FEDORAS
FAULCHIN	FAVORING	FEALED	FEAZING*	FEDS
FAULCHINS	FAVORITE	FEALING	FEBLESSE	FEE
FAULCHION	FAVORITES	FEALS	FEBLESSES	FEEBLE
FAULCHIONS	FAVORLESS	FEALTIES	FEBRICITIES	FEEBLED
FAULD*	FAVORS	FEALTY	FEBRICITY	FEEBLER
FAULDS*	FAVOSE	FEAR	FEBRICULA	FEEBLES
			FEBRICULAS	

Words marked with an asterisk are from OTCWL

FEEBLEST	FEHME	FELLATIONS	FEMERALL	FENESTRAE*
FEEBLING	FEHMIC	FELLATIOS	FEMERALLS	FENESTRAL
FEEBLISH	FEHS*	FELLATOR*	FEMES	FENESTRALS
FEEBLY	FEIGN	FELLATORS*	FEMETARIES	FENESTRAS
FEED	FEIGNED	FELLED	FEMETARY	FENI
FEEDABLE*	FEIGNEDLY	FELLER	FEMINACIES*	FENIS
FEEDBACK	FEIGNER*	FELLERS	FEMINACY*	FENITAR
FEEDBACKS	FEIGNERS*	FELLEST	FEMINAL	FENITARS
FEEDBAG*	FEIGNING	FELLIES	FEMINEITIES	FENKS
FEEDBAGS*	FEIGNINGS	FELLING	FEMINEITY	FENLAND
FEEDBOX*	FEIGNS	FELLNESS	FEMINIE*	FENLANDS
FEEDBOXES*	FEIJOA	FELLNESSES	FEMININE	FENMAN
FEEDER	FEIJOAS	FELLOE	FEMININES	FENMEN
FEEDERS	FEINT	FELLOES	FEMINISE	FENNEC
FEEDHOLE*	FEINTED	FELLOW	FEMINISED	FENNECS
FEEDHOLES*	FEINTER	FELLOWED*	FEMINISES	FENNEL
FEEDING	FEINTEST	FELLOWING*	FEMINISING	FENNELS
FEEDINGS	FEINTING	FELLOWLY	FEMINISM	FENNIER
FEEDLOT	FEINTS	FELLOWMAN*	FEMINISMS	FENNIES
FEEDLOTS	FEIRIE*	FELLOWMEN*	FEMINIST	FENNIEST
FEEDS	FEIS	FELLOWS	FEMINISTS	FENNISH
FEEDSTOCK	FEISEANNA	FELLS	FEMINITIES	FENNY
FEEDSTOCKS	FEIST*	FELLY	FEMINITY	FENS
FEEDSTUFF	FEISTIER	FELON	FEMINIZE	FENT
FEEDSTUFFS	FEISTIEST	FELONIES	FEMINIZED	FENTHION*
FEEING	FEISTS*	FELONIOUS	FEMINIZES	FENTHIONS*
FEEL	FEISTY	FELONOUS	FEMINIZING	FENTS
FEELBAD	FELAFEL	FELONRIES	FEMITER	FENUGREEK
FEELBADS	FELAFELS	FELONRY	FEMITERS	FENUGREEKS
FEELER	FELDGRAU	FELONS	FEMME	FENURON*
FEELERS	FELDGRAUS	FELONY	FEMMES	FENURONS*
FEELESS*	FELDSHER	FELSIC	FEMORA	FEOD
FEELGOOD	FELDSHERS	FELSITE	FEMORAL	FEODAL
FEELGOODS	FELDSPAR	FELSITES	FEMS*	FEODARIES
FEELING	FELDSPARS	FELSITIC	FEMUR	FEODARY
FEELINGLY	FELDSPATH	FELSPAR	FEMURS	FEODS
FEELINGS	FELDSPATHS	FELSPARS	FEN	FEOFF
FEELS	FELICIA	FELSTONE	FENAGLE*	FEOFFED
FEER	FELICIAS	FELSTONES	FENAGLED*	FEOFFEE
FEERED	FELICIFIC	FELT	FENAGLES*	FEOFFEES
FEERIE	FELICITER	FELTED	FENAGLING*	FEOFFER
FEERIES	FELICITIES	FELTER	FENCE	FEOFFERS
FEERIN	FELICITY	FELTERED	FENCED	FEOFFING
FEERING	FELID	FELTERING	FENCELESS	FEOFFMENT
FEERINGS	FELIDS	FELTERS	FENCER	FEOFFMENTS
FEERINS	FELINE	FELTIER	FENCEROW*	FEOFFOR
FEERS	FELINELY*	FELTIEST	FENCEROWS*	FEOFFORS
FEES	FELINES	FELTING	FENCERS	FEOFFS
FEESE	FELINITIES	FELTINGS	FENCES	FER*
FEESED	FELINITY	FELTLIKE*	FENCIBLE	FERACIOUS
FEESES	FELL	FELTS	FENCIBLES	FERACITIES
FEESING	FELLA	FELTY	FENCING	FERACITY
FEET	FELLABLE	FELUCCA	FENCINGS	FERAL
FEETFIRST*	FELLAH	FELUCCAS	FEND	FERALISED
FEETLESS	FELLAHEEN	FELWORT	FENDED	FERALIZED
FEEZE	FELLAHIN	FELWORTS	FENDER	FERBAM*
FEEZED	FELLAHS	FEM*	FENDERED*	FERBAMS*
FEEZES	FELLAS	FEMAL	FENDERS	FERE
FEEZING	FELLATE	FEMALE	FENDIER	FERER
FEGARIES	FELLATED	FEMALES	FENDIEST	FERES
FEGARY	FELLATES	FEMALITIES	FENDING	FEREST
FEGS	FELLATING	FEMALITY	FENDS	FERETORIES
FEH*	FELLATIO	FEMALS	FENDY	FERETORY
FEHM	FELLATION	FEME	FENESTRA	FERIA*

The Chambers Dictionary is the authority for many longer words; see Introduction, page ix

FERIAE*	FERRETERS	FERVIDITIES	FETIALES*	FETTING
FERIAL	FERRETING	FERVIDITY	FETIALIS*	FETTLE
FERIAS*	FERRETINGS*	FERVIDLY	FETIALS*	FETTLED
FERINE	FERRETS	FERVOR*	FETICH	FETTLER
FERITIES	FERRETY	FERVOROUS	FETICHE	FETTLERS
FERITY	FERRIAGE	FERVORS*	FETICHES	FETTLES
FERLIE*	FERRIAGES	FERVOUR	FETICHISE	FETTLING
FERLIED	FERRIC	FERVOURS	FETICHISED	FETTLINGS
FERLIER	FERRIED	FESCUE	FETICHISES	FETTS
FERLIES	FERRIES	FESCUES	FETICHISING	FETTUCINE
FERLIEST	FERRITE	FESS	FETICHISM	FETTUCINES
FERLY	FERRITES	FESSE	FETICHISMS	FETTUCINI
FERLYING	FERRITIC	FESSED	FETICHIST	FETTUCINIS
FERM	FERRITIN	FESSES	FETICHISTS	FETUS
FERMATA	FERRITINS	FESSING	FETICHIZE	FETUSES
FERMATAS	FERROCENE*	FESSWISE*	FETICHIZED	FETWA
FERMATE	FERROCENES*	FEST	FETICHIZES	FETWAS
FERMENT	FERROTYPE	FESTA	FETICHIZING	FEU
FERMENTED	FERROTYPES	FESTAL	FETICIDAL	FEUAR
FERMENTER*	FERROUS	FESTALLY	FETICIDE	FEUARS
FERMENTERS*	FERRUGO	FESTALS	FETICIDES	FEUD
FERMENTING	FERRUGOS	FESTAS	FETID	FEUDAL
FERMENTOR*	FERRULE	FESTER	FETIDER	FEUDALISE
FERMENTORS*	FERRULED*	FESTERED	FETIDEST	FEUDALISED
FERMENTS	FERRULES	FESTERING	FETIDLY*	FEUDALISES
FERMI	FERRULING*	FESTERS	FETIDNESS	FEUDALISING
FERMION	FERRUM*	FESTILOGIES	FETIDNESSES	FEUDALISM
FERMIONS	FERRUMS*	FESTILOGY	FETING	FEUDALISMS
FERMIS	FERRY	FESTINATE	FETISH	FEUDALIST
FERMIUM	FERRYBOAT*	FESTINATED	FETISHES	FEUDALISTS
FERMIUMS	FERRYBOATS*	FESTINATES	FETISHISE	FEUDALITIES
FERMS	FERRYING	FESTINATING	FETISHISED	FEUDALITY
FERN	FERRYMAN	FESTIVAL	FETISHISES	FEUDALIZE
FERNBIRD	FERRYMEN	FESTIVALS	FETISHISING	FEUDALIZED
FERNBIRDS	FERTILE	FESTIVE	FETISHISM	FEUDALIZES
FERNERIES	FERTILELY	FESTIVELY	FETISHISMS	FEUDALIZING
FERNERY	FERTILER	FESTIVITIES	FETISHIST	FEUDALLY
FERNIER	FERTILEST	FESTIVITY	FETISHISTS	FEUDARIES
FERNIEST	FERTILISE	FESTIVOUS	FETISHIZE	FEUDARY
FERNING	FERTILISED	FESTOLOGIES	FETISHIZED	FEUDATORIES
FERNINGS	FERTILISES	FESTOLOGY	FETISHIZES	FEUDATORY
FERNLESS*	FERTILISING	FESTOON	FETISHIZING	FEUDED
FERNLIKE*	FERTILITIES	FESTOONED	FETLOCK	FEUDING
FERNS	FERTILITY	FESTOONING	FETLOCKED	FEUDINGS
FERNSHAW	FERTILIZE	FESTOONS	FETLOCKS	FEUDIST
FERNSHAWS	FERTILIZED	FESTS	FETOLOGIES*	FEUDISTS
FERNTICLE	FERTILIZES	FET	FETOLOGY*	FEUDS
FERNTICLES	FERTILIZING	FETA	FETOR	FEUED
FERNY	FERULA	FETAL	FETORS	FEUILLETE
FEROCIOUS	FERULAE*	FETAS	FETOSCOPE*	FEUILLETES
FEROCITIES	FERULAS	FETATION*	FETOSCOPES*	FEUING
FEROCITY	FERULE	FETATIONS*	FETOSCOPIES	FEUS
FERRATE	FERULED*	FETCH	FETOSCOPY	FEUTRE
FERRATES	FERULES	FETCHED	FETS	FEUTRED
FERREL	FERULING*	FETCHER*	FETT	FEUTRES
FERRELED*	FERVENCIES	FETCHERS*	FETTA	FEUTRING
FERRELING*	FERVENCY	FETCHES	FETTAS	FEVER
FERRELLED*	FERVENT	FETCHING	FETTED	FEVERED
FERRELLING*	FERVENTER	FETE	FETTER	FEVERFEW
FERRELS	FERVENTEST	FETED	FETTERED	FEVERFEWS
FERREOUS	FERVENTLY	FETERITA*	FETTERER*	FEVERING
FERRET	FERVID	FETERITAS*	FETTERERS*	FEVERISH
FERRETED	FERVIDER	FETES	FETTERING	FEVEROUS
FERRETER	FERVIDEST	FETIAL	FETTERS	FEVERS

FEVERWORT*	FIBRE	FICOES*	FIELDERS	FIGHTABLE
FEVERWORTS*	FIBRED	FICOS	FIELDFARE	FIGHTBACK
FEW	FIBREFILL*	FICTILE	FIELDFARES	FIGHTBACKS
FEWER	FIBREFILLS*	FICTION	FIELDING	FIGHTER
FEWEST	FIBRELESS	FICTIONAL	FIELDINGS	FIGHTERS
FEWMET	FIBRES	FICTIONS	FIELDMICE	FIGHTING
FEWMETS	FIBRIFORM	FICTIVE	FIELDS	FIGHTINGS
FEWNESS	FIBRIL	FICTIVELY*	FIELDSMAN	FIGHTS
FEWNESSES	FIBRILLA	FICTOR	FIELDSMEN	FIGMENT
FEWTER	FIBRILLAE	FICTORS	FIELDVOLE	FIGMENTS
FEWTERED	FIBRILLAR	FICUS	FIELDVOLES	FIGO
FEWTERING	FIBRILLIN	FICUSES	FIELDWARD	FIGOS
FEWTERS	FIBRILLINS	FID	FIELDWARDS	FIGS
FEWTRILS	FIBRILS	FIDDIOUS	FIELDWORK	FIGULINE
FEY	FIBRIN	FIDDIOUSED	FIELDWORKS	FIGULINES
FEYED	FIBRINOID*	FIDDIOUSES	FIEND	FIGURABLE
FEYER	FIBRINOIDS*	FIDDIOUSING	FIENDISH	FIGURAL
FEYEST	FIBRINOUS	FIDDLE	FIENDS	FIGURANT
FEYING	FIBRINS	FIDDLED	FIENT	FIGURANTE
FEYLY*	FIBRO	FIDDLER	FIENTS	FIGURANTES
FEYNESS*	FIBROCYTE	FIDDLERS	FIER	FIGURANTS
FEYNESSES*	FIBROCYTES	FIDDLES	FIERCE	FIGURATE
FEYS	FIBROID	FIDDLEY	FIERCELY	FIGURE
FEZ	FIBROIDS	FIDDLEYS	FIERCER	FIGURED
FEZES	FIBROIN	FIDDLIER	FIERCEST	FIGURER*
FEZZED	FIBROINS	FIDDLIEST	FIERE	FIGURERS*
FEZZES	FIBROLINE	FIDDLING	FIERES	FIGURES
FIACRE	FIBROLINES	FIDDLY	FIERIER	FIGURINE
FIACRES	FIBROLITE	FIDEISM	FIERIEST	FIGURINES
FIANCE	FIBROLITES	FIDEISMS	FIERILY	FIGURING
FIANCEE	FIBROMA	FIDEIST	FIERINESS	FIGURIST
FIANCEES	FIBROMAS	FIDEISTIC	FIERINESSES	FIGURISTS
FIANCES	FIBROMATA	FIDEISTS	FIERY	FIGWORT
FIAR	FIBROS	FIDELITIES	FIEST	FIGWORTS
FIARS	FIBROSE	FIDELITY	FIESTA	FIKE
FIASCHI*	FIBROSED	FIDGE	FIESTAS	FIKED
FIASCO	FIBROSES	FIDGED	FIFE	FIKERIES
FIASCOES	FIBROSING	FIDGES	FIFED	FIKERY
FIASCOS	FIBROSIS	FIDGET	FIFER	FIKES
FIAT	FIBROTIC	FIDGETED	FIFERS	FIKIER
FIATED	FIBROUS	FIDGETER*	FIFES	FIKIEST
FIATING	FIBS	FIDGETERS*	FIFING	FIKING
FIATS	FIBSTER	FIDGETIER	FIFTEEN	FIKISH
FIAUNT	FIBSTERS	FIDGETIEST	FIFTEENER	FIKY
FIAUNTS	FIBULA	FIDGETING	FIFTEENERS	FIL
FIB	FIBULAE	FIDGETS	FIFTEENS	FILA*
FIBBED	FIBULAR	FIDGETY	FIFTEENTH	FILABEG
FIBBER	FIBULAS	FIDGING	FIFTEENTHS	FILABEGS
FIBBERIES	FICE*	FIDIBUS	FIFTH	FILACEOUS
FIBBERS	FICES*	FIDIBUSES	FIFTHLY	FILACER
FIBBERY	FICHE	FIDO*	FIFTHS	FILACERS
FIBBING	FICHES	FIDOS*	FIFTIES	FILAGREE
FIBER	FICHU	FIDS	FIFTIETH	FILAGREED*
FIBERED	FICHUS	FIDUCIAL	FIFTIETHS	FILAGREEING*
FIBERFILL*	FICIN*	FIDUCIARIES	FIFTY	FILAGREES
FIBERFILLS*	FICINS*	FIDUCIARY	FIFTYISH	FILAMENT
FIBERIZE*	FICKLE	FIE	FIG	FILAMENTS
FIBERIZED*	FICKLED	FIEF	FIGEATER*	FILANDER
FIBERIZES*	FICKLER	FIEFDOM	FIGEATERS*	FILANDERS
FIBERIZING*	FICKLES	FIEFDOMS	FIGGED	FILAR
FIBERLESS	FICKLEST	FIEFS	FIGGERIES	FILAREE*
FIBERS	FICKLING	FIELD	FIGGERY	FILAREES*
FIBRANNE*	FICKLY*	FIELDED	FIGGING	FILARIA
FIBRANNES*	FICO	FIELDER	FIGHT	FILARIAE*

The Chambers Dictionary is the authority for many longer words; see Introduction, page ix

FILARIAL	FILINGS	FILOPLUME	FINANCED	FINI
FILARIAN*	FILIOQUE	FILOPLUMES	FINANCES	FINIAL
FILARIAS	FILIOQUES	FILOPODIA	FINANCIAL	FINIALED*
FILARIID*	FILISTER*	FILOS	FINANCIER	FINIALS
FILARIIDS*	FILISTERS*	FILOSE	FINANCIERED	FINICAL
FILASSE	FILL	FILOSELLE	FINANCIERING	FINICALLY
FILASSES	FILLE	FILOSELLES	FINANCIERS	FINICKETIER
FILATORIES	FILLED	FILS	FINANCING	FINICKETIEST
FILATORY	FILLER	FILTER	FINANCINGS*	FINICKETY
FILATURE	FILLERS	FILTERED	FINBACK	FINICKIER
FILATURES	FILLES	FILTERER*	FINBACKS	FINICKIEST
FILAZER	FILLET	FILTERERS*	FINCH	FINICKIN*
FILAZERS	FILLETED	FILTERING	FINCHED	FINICKING
FILBERD	FILLETING	FILTERS	FINCHES	FINICKINGS
FILBERDS	FILLETS	FILTH	FIND	FINICKY
FILBERT	FILLIBEG	FILTHIER	FINDABLE*	FINIKIN
FILBERTS	FILLIBEGS	FILTHIEST	FINDER	FINIKING*
FILCH	FILLIES	FILTHILY	FINDERS	FINING
FILCHED	FILLING	FILTHS	FINDING	FININGS
FILCHER	FILLINGS	FILTHY	FINDINGS	FINIS
FILCHERS	FILLIP	FILTRABLE	FINDRAM	FINISES*
FILCHES	FILLIPED	FILTRATE	FINDRAMS	FINISH
FILCHING	FILLIPEEN	FILTRATED	FINDS	FINISHED
FILCHINGS	FILLIPEENS	FILTRATES	FINE	FINISHER
FILE	FILLIPING	FILTRATING	FINEABLE*	FINISHERS
FILEABLE*	FILLIPS	FILUM*	FINED	FINISHES
FILED	FILLISTER	FIMBLE	FINEER	FINISHING
FILEFISH*	FILLISTERS	FIMBLES	FINEERED	FINISHINGS
FILEFISHES*	FILLO*	FIMBRIA	FINEERING	FINITE
FILEMOT	FILLOS*	FIMBRIAE	FINEERS	FINITELY
FILEMOTS	FILLS	FIMBRIAL*	FINEISH	FINITES*
FILENAME	FILLY	FIMBRIATE	FINELESS	FINITUDE
FILENAMES	FILM	FIMBRIATED	FINELY	FINITUDES
FILER	FILMABLE	FIMBRIATES	FINENESS	FINJAN
FILERS	FILMCARD*	FIMBRIATING	FINENESSES	FINJANS
FILES	FILMCARDS*	FIN	FINER	FINK
FILET	FILMDOM	FINABLE	FINERIES	FINKED
FILETED*	FILMDOMS	FINAGLE	FINERS	FINKING
FILETING*	FILMED	FINAGLED	FINERY	FINKS
FILETS	FILMER*	FINAGLER*	FINES	FINLESS
FILFOT	FILMERS*	FINAGLERS*	FINESPUN*	FINLIKE*
FILFOTS	FILMGOER	FINAGLES	FINESSE	FINMARK*
FILIAL	FILMGOERS	FINAGLING	FINESSED	FINMARKS*
FILIALLY	FILMIC	FINAL	FINESSER	FINNAC
FILIATE	FILMIER	FINALE	FINESSERS	FINNACK
FILIATED	FILMIEST	FINALES	FINESSES	FINNACKS
FILIATES	FILMILY*	FINALIS*	FINESSING	FINNACS
FILIATING	FILMINESS	FINALISE	FINESSINGS	FINNAN
FILIATION	FILMINESSES	FINALISED	FINEST	FINNANS
FILIATIONS	FILMING	FINALISES	FINFISH*	FINNED
FILIBEG	FILMISH	FINALISING	FINFISHES*	FINNER
FILIBEGS	FILMLAND	FINALISM	FINFOOT*	FINNERS
FILICIDE	FILMLANDS	FINALISMS	FINFOOTS*	FINNESKO
FILICIDES	FILMMAKER*	FINALIST	FINGAN	FINNICKIER*
FILIFORM	FILMMAKERS*	FINALISTS	FINGANS	FINNICKIEST*
FILIGRAIN	FILMS	FINALITIES	FINGER	FINNICKY*
FILIGRAINS	FILMSET	FINALITY	FINGERED	FINNIER
FILIGRANE	FILMSETS	FINALIZE	FINGERER*	FINNIEST
FILIGRANES	FILMSETTING	FINALIZED	FINGERERS*	FINNING*
FILIGREE	FILMSETTINGS	FINALIZES	FINGERING	FINNMARK*
FILIGREED	FILMSTRIP*	FINALIZING	FINGERINGS	FINNMARKS*
FILIGREEING*	FILMSTRIPS*	FINALLY	FINGERS	FINNOCHIO
FILIGREES	FILMY	FINALS	FINGERTIP	FINNOCHIOS
FILING	FILO	FINANCE	FINGERTIPS	FINNOCK

FINNOCKS	FIREDRAKES*	FIREWATER*	FISH	FISHYBACKS
FINNSKO	FIREFANG*	FIREWATERS*	FISHABLE	FISK
FINNY	FIREFANGED*	FIREWEED	FISHBALL	FISKED
FINO	FIREFANGING*	FIREWEEDS	FISHBALLS	FISKING
FINOCCHIO	FIREFANGS*	FIREWOMAN	FISHBOLT*	FISKS
FINOCCHIOS	FIREFIGHT*	FIREWOMEN	FISHBOLTS*	FISNOMIE
FINOCHIO	FIREFIGHTS*	FIREWOOD	FISHBONE*	FISNOMIES
FINOCHIOS	FIREFLIES	FIREWOODS	FISHBONES*	FISSATE*
FINOS	FIREFLOAT	FIREWORK	FISHBOWL*	FISSILE
FINS	FIREFLOATS	FIREWORKS	FISHBOWLS*	FISSILITIES
FINSKO	FIREFLY	FIREWORM	FISHED	FISSILITY
FIORD	FIREGUARD	FIREWORMS	FISHER	FISSION
FIORDS	FIREGUARDS	FIRING	FISHERIES	FISSIONAL*
FIORIN	FIREHALL*	FIRINGS	FISHERMAN	FISSIONED*
FIORINS	FIREHALLS*	FIRK	FISHERMEN	FISSIONING*
FIORITURA	FIREHOUSE	FIRKED	FISHERS	FISSIONS
FIORITURE	FIREHOUSES	FIRKIN	FISHERY	FISSIPED
FIPPENCE	FIRELESS	FIRKING	FISHES	FISSIPEDE
FIPPENCES	FIRELIGHT	FIRKINS	FISHEYE	FISSIPEDES
FIPPLE	FIRELIGHTS	FIRKS	FISHEYES	FISSIPEDS
FIPPLES	FIRELIT*	FIRLOT	FISHFUL	FISSIVE
FIQUE*	FIRELOCK	FIRLOTS	FISHGIG	FISSLE
FIQUES*	FIRELOCKS	FIRM	FISHGIGS	FISSLED
FIR	FIREMAN	FIRMAMENT	FISHHOOK*	FISSLES
FIRE	FIREMANIC*	FIRMAMENTS	FISHHOOKS*	FISSLING
FIREABLE*	FIREMARK	FIRMAN	FISHIER	FISSURE
FIREARM	FIREMARKS	FIRMANS	FISHIEST	FISSURED
FIREARMS	FIREMEN	FIRMED	FISHIFIED	FISSURES
FIREBACK*	FIREPAN	FIRMER	FISHIFIES	FISSURING
FIREBACKS*	FIREPANS	FIRMERS	FISHIFY	FIST
FIREBALL	FIREPINK*	FIRMEST	FISHIFYING	FISTED
FIREBALLS	FIREPINKS*	FIRMING	FISHILY*	FISTFIGHT*
FIREBASE*	FIREPLACE	FIRMLESS	FISHINESS	FISTFIGHTS*
FIREBASES*	FIREPLACES	FIRMLY	FISHINESSES	FISTFUL
FIREBIRD*	FIREPLUG*	FIRMNESS	FISHING	FISTFULS
FIREBIRDS*	FIREPLUGS*	FIRMNESSES	FISHINGS	FISTIANA
FIREBOAT	FIREPOT	FIRMS	FISHLESS*	FISTIC
FIREBOATS*	FIREPOTS	FIRMWARE	FISHLIKE*	FISTICAL
FIREBOMB*	FIREPOWER*	FIRMWARES	FISHLINE*	FISTICUFF
FIREBOMBED*	FIREPOWERS*	FIRN	FISHLINES*	FISTICUFFS
FIREBOMBING*	FIREPROOF	FIRNS	FISHMEAL*	FISTIER
FIREBOMBS*	FIREPROOFED	FIRRIER	FISHMEALS*	FISTIEST
FIREBOX	FIREPROOFING	FIRRIEST	FISHNET*	FISTING
FIREBOXES	FIREPROOFINGS	FIRRING	FISHNETS*	FISTMELE
FIREBRAND	FIREPROOFS	FIRRINGS	FISHPLATE*	FISTMELES
FIREBRANDS	FIRER	FIRRY	FISHPLATES*	FISTNOTE*
FIREBRAT	FIREROOM*	FIRS	FISHPOLE*	FISTNOTES*
FIREBRATS	FIREROOMS*	FIRST	FISHPOLES*	FISTS
FIREBREAK*	FIRERS	FIRSTBORN*	FISHPOND*	FISTULA
FIREBREAKS*	FIRES	FIRSTBORNS*	FISHPONDS*	FISTULAE
FIREBRICK	FIRESHIP	FIRSTHAND*	FISHSKIN	FISTULAR
FIREBRICKS	FIRESHIPS	FIRSTLING	FISHSKINS	FISTULAS
FIREBUG	FIRESIDE	FIRSTLINGS	FISHTAIL*	FISTULOSE
FIREBUGS	FIRESIDES	FIRSTLY	FISHTAILED*	FISTULOUS
FIRECLAY*	FIRESTONE	FIRSTS	FISHTAILING*	FISTY
FIRECLAYS*	FIRESTONES	FIRTH	FISHTAILS*	FIT
FIRECREST	FIRESTORM*	FIRTHS	FISHWAY*	FITCH
FIRECRESTS	FIRESTORMS*	FISC	FISHWAYS*	FITCHE
FIRED	FIRETHORN	FISCAL	FISHWIFE	FITCHEE
FIREDAMP	FIRETHORNS	FISCALLY	FISHWIVES	FITCHES
FIREDAMPS	FIRETRAP*	FISCALS	FISHWORM*	FITCHET
FIREDOG	FIRETRAPS*	FISCS	FISHWORMS*	FITCHETS
FIREDOGS	FIREWALL	FISGIG	FISHY	FITCHEW
FIREDRAKE*	FIREWALLS	FISGIGS	FISHYBACK	FITCHEWS

The Chambers Dictionary is the authority for many longer words; see Introduction, page ix

FITCHY	FIXURES	FLAGELLIN*	FLAMBEAU	FLANKERED
FITFUL	FIZ	FLAGELLINS*	FLAMBEAUS	FLANKERING
FITFULLY	FIZGIG	FLAGELLUM	FLAMBEAUX	FLANKERS
FITLIER	FIZGIGS	FLAGELLUMS*	FLAMBEE*	FLANKING
FITLIEST	FIZZ	FLAGEOLET	FLAMBEED	FLANKS
FITLY	FIZZED	FLAGEOLETS	FLAMBEEING*	FLANNEL
FITMENT	FIZZEN	FLAGGED	FLAMBES*	FLANNELED*
FITMENTS	FIZZENS	FLAGGER*	FLAME	FLANNELING*
FITNESS	FIZZER	FLAGGERS*	FLAMED	FLANNELLED
FITNESSES	FIZZERS	FLAGGIER	FLAMELESS	FLANNELLING
FITS	FIZZES	FLAGGIEST	FLAMELET	FLANNELLY
FITT	FIZZGIG	FLAGGING	FLAMELETS	FLANNELS
FITTABLE*	FIZZGIGS	FLAGGINGS	FLAMEN	FLANNEN
FITTE	FIZZIER	FLAGGY	FLAMENCO	FLANNENS
FITTED	FIZZIEST	FLAGITATE	FLAMENCOS	FLANS
FITTER	FIZZING	FLAGITATED	FLAMENS	FLAP
FITTERS	FIZZINGS	FLAGITATES	FLAMEOUT	FLAPJACK
FITTES	FIZZLE	FLAGITATING	FLAMEOUTS	FLAPJACKS
FITTEST	FIZZLED	FLAGLESS*	FLAMER*	FLAPLESS*
FITTING	FIZZLES	FLAGMAN*	FLAMERS*	FLAPPABLE
FITTINGLY	FIZZLING	FLAGMEN*	FLAMES	FLAPPED
FITTINGS	FIZZY	FLAGON	FLAMFEW	FLAPPER
FITTS	FJELD*	FLAGONS	FLAMFEWS	FLAPPERS
FIVE	FJELDS*	FLAGPOLE	FLAMIER	FLAPPIER
FIVEFOLD	FJORD	FLAGPOLES	FLAMIEST	FLAPPIEST
FIVEPENCE	FJORDS	FLAGRANCE	FLAMINES	FLAPPING
FIVEPENCES	FLAB	FLAGRANCES	FLAMING	FLAPPINGS
FIVEPENNY	FLABBIER	FLAGRANCIES	FLAMINGLY	FLAPPY
FIVEPIN	FLABBIEST	FLAGRANCY	FLAMINGO	FLAPS
FIVEPINS	FLABBILY	FLAGRANT	FLAMINGOES	FLAPTRACK
FIVER	FLABBY	FLAGS	FLAMINGOS	FLAPTRACKS
FIVERS	FLABELLA	FLAGSHIP	FLAMM	FLARE
FIVES	FLABELLUM	FLAGSHIPS	FLAMMABLE	FLARED
FIX	FLABELLUMS	FLAGSTAFF	FLAMMABLES*	FLARES
FIXABLE	FLABS	FLAGSTAFFS	FLAMMED	FLARIER
FIXATE	FLACCID	FLAGSTAVES*	FLAMMING	FLARIEST
FIXATED	FLACCIDER	FLAGSTICK	FLAMMS	FLARING
FIXATES	FLACCIDEST	FLAGSTICKS	FLAMMULE	FLARINGLY
FIXATIF*	FLACCIDLY	FLAGSTONE	FLAMMULES	FLARY
FIXATIFS*	FLACK	FLAGSTONES	FLAMS	FLASER
FIXATING	FLACKED*	FLAIL	FLAMY	FLASERS
FIXATION	FLACKER	FLAILED	FLAN	FLASH
FIXATIONS	FLACKERED	FLAILING	FLANCARD*	FLASHBACK
FIXATIVE	FLACKERIES*	FLAILS	FLANCARDS*	FLASHBACKED
FIXATIVES	FLACKERING	FLAIR	FLANCH	FLASHBACKING
FIXATURE	FLACKERS	FLAIRS	FLANCHED	FLASHBACKS
FIXATURES	FLACKERY*	FLAK	FLANCHES	FLASHBULB
FIXED	FLACKET	FLAKE	FLANCHING	FLASHBULBS
FIXEDLY	FLACKETS	FLAKED	FLANCHINGS	FLASHCUBE
FIXEDNESS	FLACKING*	FLAKER*	FLANERIE	FLASHCUBES
FIXEDNESSES	FLACKS	FLAKERS*	FLANERIES	FLASHED
FIXER	FLACON	FLAKES	FLANES*	FLASHER
FIXERS	FLACONS	FLAKEY*	FLANEUR	FLASHERS
FIXES	FLAFF	FLAKIER	FLANEURS	FLASHES
FIXING	FLAFFED	FLAKIES	FLANGE	FLASHEST
FIXINGS	FLAFFER	FLAKIEST	FLANGED	FLASHGUN
FIXIT*	FLAFFERED	FLAKILY*	FLANGER*	FLASHGUNS
FIXITIES	FLAFFERING	FLAKINESS	FLANGERS*	FLASHIER
FIXITY	FLAFFERS	FLAKINESSES	FLANGES	FLASHIEST
FIXIVE	FLAFFING	FLAKING	FLANGING	FLASHILY
FIXT*	FLAFFS	FLAKS	FLANK	FLASHING
FIXTURE	FLAG	FLAKY	FLANKED	FLASHINGS
FIXTURES	FLAGELLA	FLAM	FLANKEN*	FLASHLAMP*
FIXURE	FLAGELLAR*	FLAMBE	FLANKER	FLASHLAMPS*

FLASHOVER*
FLASHOVERS*
FLASHTUBE*
FLASHTUBES*
FLASHY
FLASK
FLASKET
FLASKETS
FLASKS
FLAT
FLATBACK
FLATBACKS
FLATBED
FLATBEDS
FLATBOAT
FLATBOATS
FLATCAP*
FLATCAPS*
FLATCAR*
FLATCARS*
FLATFEET*
FLATFISH
FLATFISHES
FLATFOOT*
FLATFOOTED*
FLATFOOTING*
FLATFOOTS*
FLATHEAD
FLATHEADS
FLATIRON
FLATIRONS
FLATLAND*
FLATLANDS*
FLATLET
FLATLETS
FLATLING
FLATLINGS
FLATLONG
FLATLY
FLATMATE
FLATMATES
FLATNESS
FLATNESSES
FLATPACK
FLATPACKS
FLATS
FLATSHARE
FLATSHARES
FLATTED
FLATTEN
FLATTENED
FLATTENER*
FLATTENERS*
FLATTENING
FLATTENS
FLATTER
FLATTERED
FLATTERER
FLATTERERS
FLATTERIES
FLATTERING
FLATTERS
FLATTERY
FLATTEST

FLATTIES
FLATTING
FLATTINGS
FLATTISH
FLATTOP*
FLATTOPS*
FLATTY
FLATULENT
FLATUOUS
FLATUS
FLATUSES
FLATWARE
FLATWARES
FLATWASH*
FLATWASHES*
FLATWAYS
FLATWISE
FLATWORK*
FLATWORKS*
FLATWORM
FLATWORMS
FLAUGHT
FLAUGHTED
FLAUGHTER
FLAUGHTERED
FLAUGHTERING
FLAUGHTERS
FLAUGHTING
FLAUGHTS
FLAUNCH
FLAUNCHED
FLAUNCHES
FLAUNCHING
FLAUNCHINGS
FLAUNE
FLAUNES
FLAUNT
FLAUNTED
FLAUNTER
FLAUNTERS
FLAUNTIER
FLAUNTIEST
FLAUNTING
FLAUNTS
FLAUNTY
FLAUTIST
FLAUTISTS
FLAVANOL*
FLAVANOLS*
FLAVANONE*
FLAVANONES*
FLAVIN
FLAVINE
FLAVINES
FLAVINS
FLAVONE
FLAVONES
FLAVONOID*
FLAVONOIDS*
FLAVONOL*
FLAVONOLS*
FLAVOR
FLAVORED
FLAVORER*

FLAVORERS*
FLAVORFUL*
FLAVORING
FLAVORINGS
FLAVORIST*
FLAVORISTS*
FLAVOROUS
FLAVORS
FLAVORY*
FLAVOURED
FLAVOURING
FLAVOURINGS
FLAVOURS
FLAVOURY*
FLAW
FLAWED
FLAWIER
FLAWIEST
FLAWING
FLAWLESS
FLAWN
FLAWNS
FLAWS
FLAWY
FLAX
FLAXEN
FLAXES
FLAXIER
FLAXIEST
FLAXSEED*
FLAXSEEDS*
FLAXY
FLAY
FLAYED
FLAYER
FLAYERS
FLAYING
FLAYS
FLEA
FLEABAG*
FLEABAGS*
FLEABANE*
FLEABANES*
FLEABITE*
FLEABITES*
FLEAM
FLEAMS
FLEAPIT
FLEAPITS
FLEAS
FLEASOME
FLEAWORT
FLEAWORTS
FLECHE
FLECHES
FLECHETTE
FLECHETTES
FLECK
FLECKED
FLECKER
FLECKERED
FLECKERING
FLECKERS

FLECKING
FLECKLESS
FLECKS
FLECKY*
FLECTION
FLECTIONS
FLED
FLEDGE
FLEDGED
FLEDGES
FLEDGIER
FLEDGIEST
FLEDGING
FLEDGLING
FLEDGLINGS
FLEDGY
FLEE
FLEECE
FLEECED
FLEECER
FLEECERS
FLEECES
FLEECH
FLEECHED
FLEECHES
FLEECHING
FLEECHINGS
FLEECIER
FLEECIEST
FLEECILY*
FLEECING
FLEECY
FLEEING
FLEER
FLEERED
FLEERER
FLEERERS
FLEERING
FLEERINGS
FLEERS
FLEES
FLEET
FLEETED
FLEETER
FLEETEST
FLEETING
FLEETLY
FLEETNESS
FLEETNESSES
FLEETS
FLEG
FLEGGED
FLEGGING
FLEGS
FLEISHIG*
FLEME
FLEMES
FLEMING
FLEMISH
FLEMISHED
FLEMISHES
FLEMISHING
FLEMIT
FLENCH

FLENCHED
FLENCHES
FLENCHING
FLENSE
FLENSED
FLENSER*
FLENSERS*
FLENSES
FLENSING
FLESH
FLESHED
FLESHER
FLESHERS
FLESHES
FLESHHOOD
FLESHHOODS
FLESHIER
FLESHIEST
FLESHING
FLESHINGS
FLESHLESS
FLESHLIER
FLESHLIEST
FLESHLING
FLESHLINGS
FLESHLY
FLESHMENT
FLESHMENTS
FLESHPOT*
FLESHPOTS*
FLESHWORM
FLESHWORMS
FLESHY
FLETCH
FLETCHED
FLETCHER
FLETCHERS
FLETCHES
FLETCHING
FLETCHINGS*
FLETTON
FLETTONS
FLEURET
FLEURETS
FLEURETTE
FLEURETTES
FLEURON
FLEURONS
FLEURY
FLEW
FLEWED
FLEWS
FLEX
FLEXAGON*
FLEXAGONS*
FLEXED
FLEXES
FLEXIBLE
FLEXIBLY
FLEXILE
FLEXING
FLEXION
FLEXIONS
FLEXITIME

FLEXITIMES	FLING	FLITTERED	FLOODED	FLORETS
FLEXOR	FLINGER	FLITTERING	FLOODER*	FLORIATED
FLEXORS	FLINGERS	FLITTERN	FLOODERS*	FLORID
FLEXTIME*	FLINGING	FLITTERNS	FLOODGATE	FLORIDEAN
FLEXTIMES*	FLINGS	FLITTERS	FLOODGATES	FLORIDEANS
FLEXUOSE	FLINKITE*	FLITTING	FLOODING	FLORIDER
FLEXUOUS	FLINKITES*	FLITTINGS	FLOODINGS	FLORIDEST
FLEXURAL	FLINT	FLIVVER	FLOODLIT	FLORIDITIES
FLEXURE	FLINTED*	FLIVVERS	FLOODMARK	FLORIDITY
FLEXURES	FLINTIER	FLIX	FLOODMARKS	FLORIDLY
FLEY	FLINTIEST	FLIXED	FLOODS	FLORIER
FLEYED	FLINTIFIED	FLIXES	FLOODTIDE	FLORIEST
FLEYING	FLINTIFIES	FLIXING	FLOODTIDES	FLORIFORM
FLEYS	FLINTIFY	FLOAT	FLOODWALL	FLORIGEN
FLIC	FLINTIFYING	FLOATABLE	FLOODWALLS	FLORIGENS
FLICHTER	FLINTILY	FLOATAGE	FLOODWAY	FLORIN
FLICHTERED	FLINTING*	FLOATAGES	FLOODWAYS	FLORINS
FLICHTERING	FLINTLIKE*	FLOATANT	FLOOEY*	FLORIST
FLICHTERS	FLINTLOCK	FLOATANTS	FLOOIE*	FLORISTIC
FLICK	FLINTLOCKS	FLOATED	FLOOR	FLORISTICS
FLICKED	FLINTS	FLOATEL	FLOORAGE*	FLORISTRIES
FLICKER	FLINTY	FLOATELS	FLOORAGES*	FLORISTRY
FLICKERED	FLIP	FLOATER	FLOORED	FLORISTS
FLICKERING	FLIPPANCIES	FLOATERS	FLOORER	FLORS
FLICKERS	FLIPPANCY	FLOATIER	FLOORERS	FLORUIT
FLICKERY*	FLIPPANT	FLOATIEST	FLOORHEAD	FLORUITED
FLICKING	FLIPPED	FLOATING	FLOORHEADS	FLORUITING
FLICKS	FLIPPER	FLOATINGS	FLOORING	FLORUITS
FLICS	FLIPPERS	FLOATS	FLOORINGS	FLORY
FLIED*	FLIPPEST	FLOATY	FLOORS	FLOSCULAR
FLIER	FLIPPING	FLOC*	FLOOSIE	FLOSCULE
FLIERS	FLIPPY*	FLOCCED*	FLOOSIES	FLOSCULES
FLIES	FLIPS	FLOCCI	FLOOSY	FLOSH
FLIEST	FLIRT	FLOCCING*	FLOOZIE	FLOSHES
FLIGHT	FLIRTED	FLOCCOSE	FLOOZIES	FLOSS
FLIGHTED	FLIRTER*	FLOCCULAR	FLOOZY	FLOSSED
FLIGHTIER	FLIRTERS*	FLOCCULE	FLOP	FLOSSES
FLIGHTIEST	FLIRTIER	FLOCCULES	FLOPHOUSE	FLOSSIE*
FLIGHTILY	FLIRTIEST	FLOCCULI	FLOPHOUSES	FLOSSIER
FLIGHTING	FLIRTING	FLOCCULUS	FLOPOVER*	FLOSSIES*
FLIGHTS	FLIRTINGS	FLOCCUS	FLOPOVERS*	FLOSSIEST
FLIGHTY	FLIRTISH	FLOCK	FLOPPED	FLOSSILY*
FLIMFLAM*	FLIRTS	FLOCKED	FLOPPER*	FLOSSING
FLIMFLAMMED*	FLIRTY	FLOCKIER*	FLOPPERS*	FLOSSINGS
FLIMFLAMMING*	FLISK	FLOCKIEST*	FLOPPIER	FLOSSY
FLIMFLAMS*	FLISKED	FLOCKING	FLOPPIES	FLOTA
FLIMP	FLISKIER	FLOCKINGS*	FLOPPIEST	FLOTAGE
FLIMPED	FLISKIEST	FLOCKS	FLOPPILY	FLOTAGES
FLIMPING	FLISKING	FLOCKY*	FLOPPING	FLOTANT
FLIMPS	FLISKS	FLOCS*	FLOPPY	FLOTAS
FLIMSIER	FLISKY	FLOE	FLOPS	FLOTATION
FLIMSIES	FLIT	FLOES	FLOPTICAL	FLOTATIONS
FLIMSIEST	FLITCH	FLOG	FLOR	FLOTE
FLIMSILY	FLITCHED*	FLOGGED	FLORA	FLOTEL
FLIMSY	FLITCHES	FLOGGER*	FLORAE	FLOTELS
FLINCH	FLITCHING*	FLOGGERS*	FLORAL	FLOTES
FLINCHED	FLITE	FLOGGING	FLORALLY	FLOTILLA
FLINCHER	FLITED	FLOGGINGS	FLORALS*	FLOTILLAS
FLINCHERS	FLITES	FLOGS	FLORAS	FLOTSAM
FLINCHES	FLITING	FLOKATI	FLOREAT	FLOTSAMS
FLINCHING	FLITT	FLOKATIS	FLOREATED	FLOUNCE
FLINCHINGS	FLITTED	FLONG	FLORENCE	FLOUNCED
FLINDER	FLITTER	FLONGS	FLORENCES	FLOUNCES
FLINDERS			FLOOD	FLORET	FLOUNCIER

FLOUNCIEST
FLOUNCING
FLOUNCINGS
FLOUNCY
FLOUNDER
FLOUNDERED
FLOUNDERING
FLOUNDERS
FLOUR
FLOURED
FLOURIER
FLOURIEST
FLOURING
FLOURISH
FLOURISHED
FLOURISHES
FLOURISHING
FLOURISHY
FLOURLESS*
FLOURS
FLOURY
FLOUSE
FLOUSED
FLOUSES
FLOUSH
FLOUSHED
FLOUSHES
FLOUSHING
FLOUSING
FLOUT
FLOUTED
FLOUTER*
FLOUTERS*
FLOUTING
FLOUTS
FLOW
FLOWAGE
FLOWAGES
FLOWCHART*
FLOWCHARTS*
FLOWED
FLOWER
FLOWERAGE
FLOWERAGES
FLOWERED
FLOWERER
FLOWERERS
FLOWERET
FLOWERETS
FLOWERFUL*
FLOWERIER
FLOWERIEST
FLOWERILY*
FLOWERING
FLOWERINGS
FLOWERPOT
FLOWERPOTS
FLOWERS
FLOWERY
FLOWING
FLOWINGLY
FLOWMETER
FLOWMETERS
FLOWN

FLOWS
FLOWSTONE*
FLOWSTONES*
FLU
FLUATE
FLUATES
FLUB
FLUBBED
FLUBBER*
FLUBBERS*
FLUBBING
FLUBDUB*
FLUBDUBS*
FLUBS
FLUCTUANT
FLUCTUATE
FLUCTUATED
FLUCTUATES
FLUCTUATING
FLUE
FLUED*
FLUELLIN
FLUELLINS
FLUENCE
FLUENCES
FLUENCIES
FLUENCY
FLUENT
FLUENTLY
FLUENTS
FLUERIC*
FLUERICS*
FLUES
FLUEWORK
FLUEWORKS
FLUEY
FLUFF
FLUFFED
FLUFFIER
FLUFFIEST
FLUFFILY*
FLUFFING
FLUFFS
FLUFFY
FLUGEL
FLUGELMAN
FLUGELMEN
FLUGELS
FLUID
FLUIDAL
FLUIDALLY*
FLUIDIC
FLUIDICS
FLUIDIFIED
FLUIDIFIES
FLUIDIFY
FLUIDIFYING
FLUIDISE
FLUIDISED
FLUIDISES
FLUIDISING
FLUIDITIES
FLUIDITY
FLUIDIZE

FLUIDIZED
FLUIDIZER*
FLUIDIZERS*
FLUIDIZES
FLUIDIZING
FLUIDLY*
FLUIDNESS
FLUIDNESSES
FLUIDRAM*
FLUIDRAMS*
FLUIDS
FLUIER
FLUIEST
FLUKE
FLUKED
FLUKES
FLUKEY
FLUKIER
FLUKIEST
FLUKING
FLUKY
FLUME
FLUMED*
FLUMES
FLUMING*
FLUMMERIES
FLUMMERY
FLUMMOX
FLUMMOXED
FLUMMOXES
FLUMMOXING
FLUMP
FLUMPED
FLUMPING
FLUMPS
FLUNG
FLUNK
FLUNKED
FLUNKER*
FLUNKERS*
FLUNKEY
FLUNKEYS
FLUNKIES
FLUNKING
FLUNKS
FLUNKY
FLUOR
FLUORENE*
FLUORENES*
FLUORESCE
FLUORESCED
FLUORESCES
FLUORESCING
FLUORIC
FLUORID*
FLUORIDE
FLUORIDES
FLUORIDS*
FLUORIN*
FLUORINE
FLUORINES
FLUORINS*
FLUORITE
FLUORITES

FLUOROSES
FLUOROSIS
FLUOROTIC*
FLUORS
FLUORSPAR
FLUORSPARS
FLURR
FLURRED
FLURRIED
FLURRIES
FLURRING
FLURRS
FLURRY
FLURRYING
FLUS
FLUSH
FLUSHABLE*
FLUSHED
FLUSHER
FLUSHERS
FLUSHES
FLUSHEST
FLUSHIER
FLUSHIEST
FLUSHING
FLUSHINGS
FLUSHNESS
FLUSHNESSES
FLUSHY
FLUSTER
FLUSTERED
FLUSTERING
FLUSTERS
FLUSTERY
FLUSTRATE
FLUSTRATED
FLUSTRATES
FLUSTRATING
FLUTE
FLUTED
FLUTELIKE*
FLUTER
FLUTERS
FLUTES
FLUTEY*
FLUTIER
FLUTIEST
FLUTINA
FLUTINAS
FLUTING
FLUTINGS
FLUTIST
FLUTISTS
FLUTTER
FLUTTERED
FLUTTERER*
FLUTTERERS*
FLUTTERING
FLUTTERS
FLUTTERY*
FLUTY
FLUVIAL
FLUVIATIC
FLUX

FLUXED
FLUXES
FLUXGATE*
FLUXGATES*
FLUXING
FLUXION
FLUXIONAL
FLUXIONS
FLUXIVE
FLUYT*
FLUYTS*
FLY
FLYABLE
FLYAWAY
FLYAWAYS*
FLYBANE
FLYBANES
FLYBELT
FLYBELTS
FLYBLEW*
FLYBLOW
FLYBLOWING*
FLYBLOWN*
FLYBLOWS
FLYBOAT
FLYBOATS
FLYBOOK
FLYBOOKS
FLYBOY*
FLYBOYS*
FLYBRIDGE*
FLYBRIDGES*
FLYBY*
FLYBYS*
FLYER
FLYERS
FLYEST
FLYING
FLYINGS
FLYLEAF
FLYLEAVES
FLYLESS*
FLYMAKER
FLYMAKERS
FLYMAN*
FLYMEN*
FLYOFF*
FLYOFFS*
FLYOVER
FLYOVERS
FLYPAPER
FLYPAPERS
FLYPAST*
FLYPASTS*
FLYPE
FLYPED
FLYPES
FLYPING
FLYPITCH
FLYPITCHES
FLYSCH
FLYSCHES
FLYSPECK*
FLYSPECKED*

FLYSPECKING*	FOCUSES	FOGHORN	FOLDEROLS	FOLLICLES
FLYSPECKS*	FOCUSING	FOGHORNS	FOLDERS	FOLLIED
FLYTE	FOCUSINGS	FOGIE*	FOLDING	FOLLIES
FLYTED	FOCUSLESS*	FOGIES	FOLDINGS	FOLLIS*
FLYTES	FOCUSSED	FOGLE	FOLDOUT*	FOLLOW
FLYTIER*	FOCUSSES	FOGLES	FOLDOUTS*	FOLLOWED
FLYTIERS*	FOCUSSING	FOGLESS	FOLDS	FOLLOWER
FLYTING	FODDER	FOGMAN	FOLIA	FOLLOWERS
FLYTINGS	FODDERED	FOGMEN	FOLIAGE	FOLLOWING
FLYTRAP	FODDERER	FOGRAM	FOLIAGED	FOLLOWINGS
FLYTRAPS	FODDERERS	FOGRAMITE	FOLIAGES	FOLLOWS
FLYWAY	FODDERING	FOGRAMITES	FOLIAR	FOLLY
FLYWAYS	FODDERINGS	FOGRAMITIES	FOLIATE	FOLLYING
FLYWEIGHT	FODDERS	FOGRAMITY	FOLIATED	FOMENT
FLYWEIGHTS	FODGEL*	FOGRAMS	FOLIATES	FOMENTED
FLYWHEEL	FOE	FOGS	FOLIATING	FOMENTER
FLYWHEELS	FOEDARIE	FOGY	FOLIATION	FOMENTERS
FOAL	FOEDARIES	FOGYDOM	FOLIATIONS	FOMENTING
FOALED	FOEDERATI	FOGYDOMS	FOLIATURE	FOMENTS
FOALFOOT	FOEHN	FOGYISH	FOLIATURES	FOMES
FOALFOOTS	FOEHNS	FOGYISM	FOLIE	FOMITE*
FOALING	FOEMAN	FOGYISMS	FOLIES	FOMITES*
FOALS	FOEMEN	FOH	FOLIO	FON
FOAM	FOEN	FOHN	FOLIOED	FOND
FOAMABLE*	FOES	FOHNS	FOLIOING	FONDA
FOAMED	FOETAL	FOHS	FOLIOLATE	FONDANT
FOAMER*	FOETICIDE	FOIBLE	FOLIOLE	FONDANTS
FOAMERS*	FOETICIDES	FOIBLES	FOLIOLES	FONDAS
FOAMIER	FOETID	FOID	FOLIOLOSE	FONDED
FOAMIEST	FOETIDER	FOIDS	FOLIOS	FONDER
FOAMILY	FOETIDEST	FOIL	FOLIOSE	FONDEST
FOAMINESS	FOETOR	FOILABLE*	FOLIOUS*	FONDING
FOAMINESSES	FOETORS	FOILBORNE	FOLIUM	FONDLE
FOAMING	FOETUS	FOILED	FOLIUMS*	FONDLED
FOAMINGLY	FOETUSES	FOILING	FOLK	FONDLER
FOAMINGS	FOG	FOILINGS	FOLKIE	FONDLERS
FOAMLESS	FOGASH	FOILS	FOLKIES	FONDLES
FOAMLIKE*	FOGASHES	FOILSMAN*	FOLKISH*	FONDLING
FOAMS	FOGBOUND	FOILSMEN*	FOLKLAND	FONDLINGS
FOAMY	FOGBOW*	FOIN	FOLKLANDS	FONDLY
FOB	FOGBOWS*	FOINED	FOLKLIFE*	FONDNESS
FOBBED	FOGDOG*	FOINING	FOLKLIKE*	FONDNESSES
FOBBING	FOGDOGS*	FOININGLY	FOLKLIVES*	FONDS
FOBS	FOGEY	FOINS	FOLKLORE	FONDU*
FOCACCIA	FOGEYDOM	FOISON	FOLKLORES	FONDUE
FOCACCIAS	FOGEYDOMS	FOISONS	FOLKLORIC	FONDUES
FOCAL	FOGEYISH	FOIST	FOLKMOOT	FONDUS*
FOCALISE	FOGEYISM	FOISTED	FOLKMOOTS	FONE
FOCALISED	FOGEYISMS	FOISTER	FOLKMOT*	FONLY
FOCALISES	FOGEYS	FOISTERS	FOLKMOTE*	FONNED
FOCALISING	FOGFRUIT*	FOISTING	FOLKMOTES*	FONNING
FOCALIZE	FOGFRUITS*	FOISTS	FOLKMOTS*	FONS
FOCALIZED	FOGGAGE	FOLACIN	FOLKS	FONT
FOCALIZES	FOGGAGES	FOLACINS	FOLKSIER	FONTAL
FOCALIZING	FOGGED	FOLATE	FOLKSIEST	FONTANEL
FOCALLY	FOGGER	FOLATES	FOLKSILY*	FONTANELS
FOCI	FOGGERS	FOLD	FOLKSY	FONTANGE
FOCIMETER	FOGGIER	FOLDABLE	FOLKTALE*	FONTANGES
FOCIMETERS	FOGGIEST	FOLDAWAY	FOLKTALES*	FONTICULI
FOCUS	FOGGILY	FOLDBOAT	FOLKWAY	FONTINA*
FOCUSABLE*	FOGGINESS	FOLDBOATS	FOLKWAYS	FONTINAS*
FOCUSED	FOGGINESSES	FOLDED	FOLKY*	FONTLET
FOCUSER*	FOGGING	FOLDER	FOLLES*	FONTLETS
FOCUSERS*	FOGGY	FOLDEROL	FOLLICLE	FONTS

Words marked with an asterisk are from OTCWL

FOOD	FOOTIER	FOOTSTEP	FORBEARING	FOREBODE
FOODFUL	FOOTIES	FOOTSTEPS	FORBEARS	FOREBODED
FOODIE	FOOTIEST	FOOTSTONE*	FORBID	FOREBODER
FOODIES	FOOTING	FOOTSTONES*	FORBIDAL*	FOREBODERS
FOODISM	FOOTINGS	FOOTSTOOL	FORBIDALS*	FOREBODES
FOODISMS	FOOTLE	FOOTSTOOLS	FORBIDDAL	FOREBODIES*
FOODLESS	FOOTLED	FOOTSY*	FORBIDDALS	FOREBODING
FOODS	FOOTLER*	FOOTWALL*	FORBIDDEN	FOREBODINGS
FOODSTUFF	FOOTLERS*	FOOTWALLS*	FORBIDDER	FOREBODY*
FOODSTUFFS	FOOTLES	FOOTWAY	FORBIDDERS	FOREBOOM*
FOODWAYS*	FOOTLESS	FOOTWAYS	FORBIDDING	FOREBOOMS*
FOODY	FOOTLIGHT	FOOTWEAR	FORBIDDINGS	FOREBRAIN
FOOFARAW*	FOOTLIGHTS	FOOTWEARS	FORBIDS	FOREBRAINS
FOOFARAWS*	FOOTLIKE*	FOOTWELL	FORBODE	FOREBY
FOOL	FOOTLING	FOOTWELLS*	FORBODED*	FOREBYE*
FOOLED	FOOTLINGS	FOOTWORK	FORBODES	FORECABIN
FOOLERIES	FOOTLOOSE	FOOTWORKS	FORBODING*	FORECABINS
FOOLERY	FOOTMAN	FOOTWORN	FORBORE	FORECAR
FOOLFISH*	FOOTMARK	FOOTY	FORBORNE	FORECARS
FOOLFISHES*	FOOTMARKS	FOOZLE	FORBS	FORECAST
FOOLHARDIER	FOOTMEN	FOOZLED	FORBY	FORECASTED
FOOLHARDIEST	FOOTMUFF	FOOZLER	FORBYE	FORECASTING
FOOLHARDY	FOOTMUFFS	FOOZLERS	FORCAT	FORECASTS
FOOLING	FOOTNOTE	FOOZLES	FORCATS	FORECHECK*
FOOLINGS	FOOTNOTED*	FOOZLING	FORCE	FORECHECKED*
FOOLISH	FOOTNOTES	FOOZLINGS	FORCED	FORECHECKING*
FOOLISHER	FOOTNOTING*	FOP	FORCEDLY	FORECHECKS*
FOOLISHEST	FOOTPACE	FOPLING	FORCEFUL	FORECLOSE
FOOLISHLY	FOOTPACES	FOPLINGS	FORCELESS	FORECLOSED
FOOLPROOF	FOOTPAD	FOPPED*	FORCEMEAT	FORECLOSES
FOOLS	FOOTPADS	FOPPERIES	FORCEMEATS	FORECLOSING
FOOLSCAP	FOOTPAGE	FOPPERY	FORCEPS	FORECLOTH
FOOLSCAPS	FOOTPAGES	FOPPING*	FORCEPSES	FORECLOTHS
FOOT	FOOTPATH	FOPPISH	FORCER	FORECOURT
FOOTAGE	FOOTPATHS	FOPPISHLY	FORCERS	FORECOURTS
FOOTAGES	FOOTPLATE	FOPS	FORCES	FOREDATE
FOOTBALL	FOOTPLATES	FOR	FORCIBLE	FOREDATED
FOOTBALLS	FOOTPOST	FORA	FORCIBLY	FOREDATES
FOOTBAR	FOOTPOSTS	FORAGE	FORCING	FOREDATING
FOOTBARS	FOOTPRINT	FORAGED	FORCIPATE	FOREDECK
FOOTBATH*	FOOTPRINTS	FORAGER	FORCIPES	FOREDECKS
FOOTBATHS*	FOOTRA	FORAGERS	FORD	FOREDID*
FOOTBOARD	FOOTRACE*	FORAGES	FORDABLE	FOREDO*
FOOTBOARDS	FOOTRACES*	FORAGING	FORDED	FOREDOES*
FOOTBOY	FOOTRAS	FORAM*	FORDID	FOREDOING*
FOOTBOYS	FOOTREST	FORAMEN	FORDING	FOREDONE*
FOOTCLOTH	FOOTRESTS	FORAMENS*	FORDLESS*	FOREDOOM
FOOTCLOTHS	FOOTROPE*	FORAMINA	FORDO	FOREDOOMED
FOOTED	FOOTROPES*	FORAMINAL	FORDOES	FOREDOOMING
FOOTER	FOOTROT	FORAMS*	FORDOING	FOREDOOMS
FOOTERS	FOOTROTS	FORANE	FORDONE	FOREFACE*
FOOTFALL	FOOTRULE	FORASMUCH	FORDS	FOREFACES*
FOOTFALLS	FOOTRULES	FORAY	FORE	FOREFEEL
FOOTFAULT	FOOTS	FORAYED	FOREANENT	FOREFEELING
FOOTFAULTED	FOOTSIE*	FORAYER	FOREARM	FOREFEELS
FOOTFAULTING	FOOTSIES*	FORAYERS	FOREARMED	FOREFEET
FOOTFAULTS	FOOTSLOG	FORAYING	FOREARMING	FOREFELT
FOOTGEAR	FOOTSLOGGED	FORAYS	FOREARMS	FOREFEND*
FOOTGEARS	FOOTSLOGGING	FORB	FOREBAY*	FOREFENDED*
FOOTHILL	FOOTSLOGGINGS	FORBAD	FOREBAYS*	FOREFENDING*
FOOTHILLS	FOOTSLOGS	FORBADE	FOREBEAR	FOREFENDS*
FOOTHOLD	FOOTSORE	FORBEAR	FOREBEARS	FOREFOOT
FOOTHOLDS	FOOTSTALK	FORBEARER*	FOREBITT	FOREFRONT
FOOTIE	FOOTSTALKS	FORBEARERS*	FOREBITTS	FOREFRONTS

The Chambers Dictionary is the authority for many longer words; see Introduction, page ix

FOREGLEAM
FOREGLEAMS
FOREGO
FOREGOER
FOREGOERS
FOREGOES
FOREGOING
FOREGOINGS
FOREGONE
FOREGUT
FOREGUTS
FOREHAND
FOREHANDS
FOREHEAD
FOREHEADS
FOREHENT
FOREHENTING
FOREHENTS
FOREHOOF*
FOREHOOFS*
FOREHOOVES*
FOREIGN
FOREIGNER
FOREIGNERS
FOREJUDGE
FOREJUDGED
FOREJUDGES
FOREJUDGING
FOREKING
FOREKINGS
FOREKNEW
FOREKNOW
FOREKNOWING
FOREKNOWN
FOREKNOWS
FOREL
FORELADIES*
FORELADY*
FORELAID
FORELAIN
FORELAND
FORELANDS
FORELAY
FORELAYING
FORELAYS
FORELEG
FORELEGS
FORELEND
FORELENDING
FORELENDS
FORELENT
FORELIE
FORELIES
FORELIFT
FORELIFTED
FORELIFTING
FORELIFTS
FORELIMB
FORELIMBS
FORELOCK
FORELOCKED*
FORELOCKING*
FORELOCKS
FORELS

FORELYING
FOREMAN
FOREMAST
FOREMASTS
FOREMEAN
FOREMEANING
FOREMEANS
FOREMEANT
FOREMEN
FOREMILK*
FOREMILKS*
FOREMOST
FORENAME
FORENAMED
FORENAMES
FORENIGHT
FORENIGHTS
FORENOON
FORENOONS
FORENSIC
FORENSICS
FOREPART
FOREPARTS
FOREPAST
FOREPAW
FOREPAWS
FOREPEAK
FOREPEAKS
FOREPLAN
FOREPLANNED
FOREPLANNING
FOREPLANS
FOREPLAY
FOREPLAYS
FOREPOINT
FOREPOINTED
FOREPOINTING
FOREPOINTS
FORERAN
FORERANK*
FORERANKS*
FOREREACH
FOREREACHED
FOREREACHES
FOREREACHING
FOREREAD
FOREREADING
FOREREADINGS
FOREREADS
FORERUN
FORERUNNING
FORERUNS
FORES
FORESAID
FORESAIL
FORESAILS
FORESAW
FORESAY
FORESAYING
FORESAYS
FORESEE
FORESEEING
FORESEEN
FORESEER*

FORESEERS*
FORESEES
FORESHANK*
FORESHANKS*
FORESHEET*
FORESHEETS*
FORESHEW
FORESHEWED
FORESHEWING
FORESHEWN
FORESHEWS
FORESHIP
FORESHIPS
FORESHOCK
FORESHOCKS
FORESHORE
FORESHORES
FORESHOW
FORESHOWED
FORESHOWING
FORESHOWN
FORESHOWS
FORESIDE
FORESIDES
FORESIGHT
FORESIGHTS
FORESKIN
FORESKINS
FORESKIRT
FORESKIRTS
FORESLACK
FORESLACKED
FORESLACKING
FORESLACKS
FORESLOW
FORESLOWED
FORESLOWING
FORESLOWS
FORESPEAK
FORESPEAKING
FORESPEAKS
FORESPEND
FORESPENDING
FORESPENDS
FORESPENT
FORESPOKE
FORESPOKEN
FOREST
FORESTAGE
FORESTAGES
FORESTAIR
FORESTAIRS
FORESTAL
FORESTALL
FORESTALLED
FORESTALLING
FORESTALLINGS
FORESTALLS
FORESTAY
FORESTAYS
FORESTEAL
FORESTED
FORESTER
FORESTERS

FORESTIAL*
FORESTINE
FORESTING
FORESTRIES
FORESTRY
FORESTS
FORESWEAR*
FORESWEARING*
FORESWEARS*
FORESWORE*
FORESWORN*
FORETASTE
FORETASTED
FORETASTES
FORETASTING
FORETAUGHT
FORETEACH
FORETEACHES
FORETEACHING
FORETEETH
FORETELL
FORETELLING
FORETELLS
FORETHINK
FORETHINKING
FORETHINKS
FORETHOUGHT
FORETHOUGHTS
FORETIME
FORETIMES
FORETOKEN
FORETOKENED
FORETOKENING
FORETOKENINGS
FORETOKENS
FORETOLD
FORETOOTH
FORETOP
FORETOPS
FOREVER
FOREVERS
FOREWARD
FOREWARDS
FOREWARN
FOREWARNED
FOREWARNING
FOREWARNINGS
FOREWARNS
FOREWEIGH
FOREWEIGHED
FOREWEIGHING
FOREWEIGHS
FOREWENT
FOREWIND
FOREWINDS
FOREWING
FOREWINGS
FOREWOMAN
FOREWOMEN
FOREWORD
FOREWORDS
FOREWORN*
FOREYARD*
FOREYARDS*

FORFAIR
FORFAIRED
FORFAIRING
FORFAIRN
FORFAIRS
FORFAITER
FORFAITERS
FORFAULT
FORFAULTS
FORFEIT
FORFEITED
FORFEITER
FORFEITERS
FORFEITING
FORFEITS
FORFEND
FORFENDED
FORFENDING
FORFENDS
FORFEX
FORFEXES
FORFICATE
FORGAT
FORGATHER
FORGATHERED
FORGATHERING
FORGATHERS
FORGAVE
FORGE
FORGEABLE
FORGED
FORGEMAN
FORGEMEN
FORGER
FORGERIES
FORGERS
FORGERY
FORGES
FORGET
FORGETFUL
FORGETIVE
FORGETS
FORGETTER
FORGETTERS
FORGETTING
FORGETTINGS
FORGING
FORGINGS
FORGIVE
FORGIVEN
FORGIVER*
FORGIVERS*
FORGIVES
FORGIVING
FORGO
FORGOER*
FORGOERS*
FORGOES
FORGOING
FORGONE
FORGOT
FORGOTTEN
FORHAILE
FORHAILED

FORHAILES	FORLORNER	FORMULA	FORSLACK	FORTILAGES
FORHAILING	FORLORNEST	FORMULAE	FORSLACKED	FORTING
FORHENT	FORLORNLY	FORMULAIC	FORSLACKING	FORTIS
FORHENTING	FORLORNS	FORMULAR	FORSLACKS	FORTITUDE
FORHENTS	FORM	FORMULARIES	FORSLOE	FORTITUDES
FORHOO	FORMABLE	FORMULARY	FORSLOED	FORTLET
FORHOOED	FORMAL	FORMULAS	FORSLOEING	FORTLETS
FORHOOIE	FORMALIN	FORMULATE	FORSLOES	FORTNIGHT
FORHOOIED	FORMALINS	FORMULATED	FORSLOW	FORTNIGHTS
FORHOOIEING	FORMALISE	FORMULATES	FORSLOWED	FORTRESS
FORHOOIES	FORMALISED	FORMULATING	FORSLOWING	FORTRESSED
FORHOOING	FORMALISES	FORMULISE	FORSLOWS	FORTRESSES
FORHOOS	FORMALISING	FORMULISED	FORSOOK	FORTRESSING
FORHOW	FORMALISM	FORMULISES	FORSOOTH	FORTS
FORHOWED	FORMALISMS	FORMULISING	FORSPEAK	FORTUITIES
FORHOWING	FORMALIST	FORMULISM	FORSPEAKING	FORTUITY
FORHOWS	FORMALISTS	FORMULISMS	FORSPEAKS	FORTUNATE
FORINSEC	FORMALITIES	FORMULIST	FORSPEND	FORTUNE
FORINT	FORMALITY	FORMULISTS	FORSPENDING	FORTUNED
FORINTS	FORMALIZE	FORMULIZE	FORSPENDS	FORTUNES
FORJASKIT	FORMALIZED	FORMULIZED	FORSPENT	FORTUNING
FORJESKIT	FORMALIZES	FORMULIZES	FORSPOKE	FORTUNIZE
FORJUDGE	FORMALIZING	FORMULIZING	FORSPOKEN	FORTUNIZED
FORJUDGED	FORMALLY	FORMWORK	FORSWATT	FORTUNIZES
FORJUDGES	FORMALS*	FORMWORKS	FORSWEAR	FORTUNIZING
FORJUDGING	FORMAMIDE*	FORMYL*	FORSWEARING	FORTY
FORK	FORMAMIDES*	FORMYLS*	FORSWEARS	FORTYISH
FORKBALL*	FORMANT	FORNENST	FORSWINK	FORUM
FORKBALLS*	FORMANTS	FORNENT	FORSWINKED	FORUMS
FORKED	FORMAT	FORNICAL	FORSWINKING	FORWANDER
FORKEDLY	FORMATE	FORNICATE	FORSWINKS	FORWANDERED
FORKER	FORMATED	FORNICATED	FORSWONCK	FORWANDERING
FORKERS	FORMATES	FORNICATES	FORSWORE	FORWANDERS
FORKFUL	FORMATING	FORNICATING	FORSWORN	FORWARD
FORKFULS	FORMATION	FORNICES	FORSWUNK	FORWARDED
FORKHEAD	FORMATIONS	FORNIX	FORSYTHIA	FORWARDER
FORKHEADS	FORMATIVE	FORPET	FORSYTHIAS	FORWARDERS
FORKIER	FORMATIVES	FORPETS	FORT	FORWARDEST
FORKIEST	FORMATS	FORPINE	FORTALICE	FORWARDING
FORKINESS	FORMATTED	FORPINED	FORTALICES	FORWARDINGS
FORKINESSES	FORMATTER	FORPINES	FORTE	FORWARDLY
FORKING	FORMATTERS	FORPINING	FORTED	FORWARDS
FORKLESS*	FORMATTING	FORPIT	FORTES	FORWARN
FORKLIFT*	FORME	FORPITS	FORTH	FORWARNED
FORKLIFTED*	FORMED	FORRAD	FORTHCAME	FORWARNING
FORKLIFTING*	FORMEE*	FORRADER	FORTHCOME	FORWARNS
FORKLIFTS*	FORMER	FORRARDER*	FORTHCOMES	FORWASTE
FORKLIKE*	FORMERLY	FORRAY	FORTHCOMING	FORWASTED
FORKS	FORMERS	FORRAYED	FORTHINK	FORWASTES
FORKSFUL*	FORMES	FORRAYING	FORTHINKING	FORWASTING
FORKTAIL	FORMFUL*	FORRAYS	FORTHINKS	FORWEARIED
FORKTAILS	FORMIATE	FORREN	FORTHOUGHT	FORWEARIES
FORKY	FORMIATES	FORRIT	FORTHWITH	FORWEARY
FORLANA	FORMIC	FORSAID	FORTHY	FORWEARYING
FORLANAS	FORMICANT	FORSAKE	FORTIES	FORWENT
FORLEND	FORMICARIES	FORSAKEN	FORTIETH	FORWHY
FORLENDING	FORMICARY	FORSAKER*	FORTIETHS	FORWORN
FORLENDS	FORMICATE	FORSAKERS*	FORTIFIED	FORZANDI
FORLENT	FORMING	FORSAKES	FORTIFIER	FORZANDO
FORLESE	FORMINGS	FORSAKING	FORTIFIERS	FORZANDOS
FORLESES	FORMLESS	FORSAKINGS	FORTIFIES	FORZATI
FORLESING	FORMOL	FORSAY	FORTIFY	FORZATO
FORLORE	FORMOLS	FORSAYING	FORTIFYING	FORZATOS
FORLORN	FORMS	FORSAYS	FORTILAGE	FOSS

The Chambers Dictionary is the authority for many longer words; see Introduction, page ix

FOSSA	FOUGHT	FOURSES	FOXHOUND	FRACTION
FOSSAE	FOUGHTEN	FOURSOME	FOXHOUNDS	FRACTIONED*
FOSSAS	FOUGHTIER	FOURSOMES	FOXHUNT*	FRACTIONING*
FOSSATE*	FOUGHTIEST	FOURTEEN	FOXHUNTED*	FRACTIONS
FOSSE	FOUGHTY	FOURTEENS	FOXHUNTER*	FRACTIOUS
FOSSED	FOUL	FOURTH	FOXHUNTERS*	FRACTS
FOSSES	FOULARD	FOURTHLY	FOXHUNTING*	FRACTUR*
FOSSETTE	FOULARDS	FOURTHS	FOXHUNTS*	FRACTURE
FOSSETTES	FOULBROOD*	FOUS	FOXIER	FRACTURED
FOSSICK	FOULBROODS*	FOUSSA	FOXIEST	FRACTURES
FOSSICKED	FOULDER	FOUSSAS	FOXILY*	FRACTURING
FOSSICKER	FOULDERED	FOUSTIER	FOXINESS	FRACTURS*
FOSSICKERS	FOULDERING	FOUSTIEST	FOXINESSES	FRACTUS*
FOSSICKING	FOULDERS	FOUSTY	FOXING	FRAE
FOSSICKINGS	FOULE	FOUTER	FOXINGS	FRAENA
FOSSICKS	FOULED	FOUTERED	FOXLIKE*	FRAENUM
FOSSIL	FOULER	FOUTERING	FOXSHARK	FRAENUMS*
FOSSILISE	FOULES	FOUTERS	FOXSHARKS	FRAG
FOSSILISED	FOULEST	FOUTH	FOXSHIP	FRAGGED
FOSSILISES	FOULING	FOUTHS	FOXSHIPS	FRAGGING
FOSSILISING	FOULINGS*	FOUTRA	FOXSKIN*	FRAGGINGS*
FOSSILIZE	FOULLY	FOUTRAS	FOXSKINS*	FRAGILE
FOSSILIZED	FOULMART	FOUTRE	FOXTAIL*	FRAGILELY
FOSSILIZES	FOULMARTS	FOUTRED	FOXTAILS*	FRAGILER
FOSSILIZING	FOULNESS	FOUTRES	FOXTROT	FRAGILEST
FOSSILS	FOULNESSES	FOUTRING	FOXTROTS	FRAGILITIES
FOSSOR	FOULS	FOVEA	FOXTROTTED	FRAGILITY
FOSSORIAL	FOUMART	FOVEAE	FOXTROTTING	FRAGMENT
FOSSORS	FOUMARTS	FOVEAL	FOXY	FRAGMENTED
FOSSULA	FOUND	FOVEAS*	FOY	FRAGMENTING
FOSSULAE	FOUNDED	FOVEATE	FOYER	FRAGMENTS
FOSSULATE	FOUNDER	FOVEATED*	FOYERS	FRAGOR
FOSTER	FOUNDERED	FOVEOLA	FOYLE	FRAGORS
FOSTERAGE	FOUNDERING	FOVEOLAE	FOYLED	FRAGRANCE
FOSTERAGES	FOUNDERS	FOVEOLAR*	FOYLES	FRAGRANCED
FOSTERED	FOUNDING	FOVEOLAS	FOYLING	FRAGRANCES
FOSTERER	FOUNDINGS	FOVEOLE	FOYNE	FRAGRANCIES
FOSTERERS	FOUNDLING	FOVEOLES	FOYNED	FRAGRANCING
FOSTERING	FOUNDLINGS	FOVEOLET*	FOYNES	FRAGRANCY
FOSTERINGS	FOUNDRESS	FOVEOLETS*	FOYNING	FRAGRANT
FOSTERS	FOUNDRESSES	FOWL	FOYS	FRAGS
FOSTRESS	FOUNDRIES	FOWLED	FOZIER	FRAICHEUR
FOSTRESSES	FOUNDRY	FOWLER	FOZIEST	FRAICHEURS
FOTHER	FOUNDS	FOWLERS	FOZINESS	FRAIL
FOTHERED	FOUNT	FOWLING	FOZINESSES	FRAILER
FOTHERING	FOUNTAIN	FOWLINGS	FOZY	FRAILEST
FOTHERS	FOUNTAINED	FOWLPOX*	FRA	FRAILISH
FOU	FOUNTAINING	FOWLPOXES*	FRAB	FRAILLY
FOUAT	FOUNTAINS	FOWLS	FRABBED	FRAILNESS
FOUATS	FOUNTFUL	FOWTH	FRABBING	FRAILNESSES
FOUD	FOUNTS	FOWTHS	FRABBIT	FRAILS
FOUDRIE	FOUR	FOX	FRABJOUS	FRAILTEE
FOUDRIES	FOURCHEE*	FOXBERRIES	FRABS	FRAILTEES
FOUDS	FOURFOLD	FOXBERRY	FRACAS	FRAILTIES
FOUER	FOURGON	FOXED	FRACASES*	FRAILTY
FOUEST	FOURGONS	FOXES	FRACK	FRAIM
FOUET	FOURPENCE	FOXFIRE*	FRACKING	FRAIMS
FOUETS	FOURPENCES	FOXFIRES*	FRACKINGS	FRAISE
FOUETTE	FOURPENNIES	FOXFISH*	FRACT	FRAISED
FOUETTES	FOURPENNY	FOXFISHES*	FRACTAL	FRAISES
FOUGADE	FOURPLEX*	FOXGLOVE	FRACTALS	FRAISING
FOUGADES	FOURPLEXES*	FOXGLOVES	FRACTED	FRAKTUR*
FOUGASSE	FOURS	FOXHOLE	FRACTI*	FRAKTURS*
FOUGASSES	FOURSCORE	FOXHOLES	FRACTING	FRAMABLE*

FRAMBESIA*
FRAMBESIAS*
FRAMBOISE*
FRAMBOISES*
FRAME
FRAMEABLE*
FRAMED
FRAMER
FRAMERS
FRAMES
FRAMEWORK
FRAMEWORKS
FRAMING
FRAMINGS
FRAMPAL
FRAMPLER
FRAMPLERS
FRAMPOLD
FRANC
FRANCHISE
FRANCHISED
FRANCHISES
FRANCHISING
FRANCIUM
FRANCIUMS
FRANCO
FRANCOLIN
FRANCOLINS
FRANCS
FRANGIBLE
FRANGLAIS*
FRANION
FRANIONS
FRANK
FRANKABLE*
FRANKED
FRANKER
FRANKERS*
FRANKEST
FRANKFURT*
FRANKFURTS*
FRANKING
FRANKLIN
FRANKLINS
FRANKLY
FRANKNESS
FRANKNESSES
FRANKS
FRANTIC
FRANTICLY
FRANZIER
FRANZIEST
FRANZY
FRAP
FRAPPANT
FRAPPE
FRAPPED
FRAPPEE
FRAPPES
FRAPPING
FRAPS
FRAS
FRASCATI
FRASCATIS

FRASS
FRASSES
FRAT*
FRATCH
FRATCHES
FRATCHETY
FRATCHIER
FRATCHIEST
FRATCHING
FRATCHY
FRATE
FRATER
FRATERIES
FRATERNAL
FRATERS
FRATERY
FRATI
FRATRIES
FRATRY
FRATS*
FRAU
FRAUD
FRAUDFUL
FRAUDS
FRAUDSMAN
FRAUDSMEN
FRAUDSTER
FRAUDSTERS
FRAUGHT
FRAUGHTED
FRAUGHTER
FRAUGHTEST
FRAUGHTING
FRAUGHTS
FRAULEIN
FRAULEINS
FRAUS
FRAUTAGE
FRAUTAGES
FRAY
FRAYED
FRAYING
FRAYINGS
FRAYS
FRAZIL
FRAZILS
FRAZZLE
FRAZZLED
FRAZZLES
FRAZZLING
FREAK
FREAKED
FREAKFUL
FREAKIER
FREAKIEST
FREAKILY*
FREAKING
FREAKISH
FREAKOUT*
FREAKOUTS*
FREAKS
FREAKY
FRECKLE
FRECKLED

FRECKLES
FRECKLIER
FRECKLIEST
FRECKLING
FRECKLINGS
FRECKLY
FREDAINE
FREDAINES
FREE
FREEBASE
FREEBASED
FREEBASER*
FREEBASERS*
FREEBASES
FREEBASING
FREEBEE
FREEBEES
FREEBIE
FREEBIES
FREEBOARD*
FREEBOARDS*
FREEBOOT*
FREEBOOTED*
FREEBOOTIES
FREEBOOTING*
FREEBOOTS*
FREEBOOTY
FREEBORN
FREED
FREEDMAN
FREEDMEN
FREEDOM
FREEDOMS
FREEFORM*
FREEHAND
FREEHOLD
FREEHOLDS
FREEING
FREELANCE
FREELANCED
FREELANCES
FREELANCING
FREELOAD
FREELOADED
FREELOADING
FREELOADINGS
FREELOADS
FREELY
FREEMAN
FREEMASON
FREEMASONS
FREEMEN
FREENESS
FREENESSES
FREEPHONE
FREEPHONES
FREER
FREERS
FREES
FREESHEET
FREESHEETS
FREESIA
FREESIAS
FREEST

FREESTONE
FREESTONES
FREESTYLE
FREESTYLES
FREET
FREETIER
FREETIEST
FREETS
FREETY
FREEWARE
FREEWARES
FREEWAY
FREEWAYS
FREEWHEEL
FREEWHEELED
FREEWHEELING
FREEWHEELINGS
FREEWHEELS
FREEWILL*
FREEWOMAN
FREEWOMEN
FREEZABLE
FREEZE
FREEZER
FREEZERS
FREEZES
FREEZING
FREEZINGS
FREIGHT
FREIGHTED
FREIGHTER
FREIGHTERS
FREIGHTING
FREIGHTS
FREIT
FREITIER
FREITIEST
FREITS
FREITY
FREMD
FREMDS
FREMIT
FREMITS
FREMITUS
FREMITUSES
FRENA
FRENCH
FRENCHED*
FRENCHES*
FRENCHIFIED*
FRENCHIFIES*
FRENCHIFY*
FRENCHIFYING*
FRENCHING*
FRENETIC
FRENETICS
FRENNE
FRENULA
FRENULUM
FRENULUMS*
FRENUM
FRENUMS*
FRENZICAL
FRENZIED

FRENZIES
FRENZILY*
FRENZY
FRENZYING
FREON
FREONS
FREQUENCE
FREQUENCES
FREQUENCIES
FREQUENCY
FREQUENT
FREQUENTED
FREQUENTER
FREQUENTERS
FREQUENTEST
FREQUENTING
FREQUENTS
FRERE
FRERES
FRESCADE
FRESCADES
FRESCO
FRESCOED
FRESCOER
FRESCOERS
FRESCOES
FRESCOING
FRESCOINGS
FRESCOIST
FRESCOISTS
FRESCOS
FRESH
FRESHED
FRESHEN
FRESHENED
FRESHENER
FRESHENERS
FRESHENING
FRESHENS
FRESHER
FRESHERS
FRESHES
FRESHEST
FRESHET
FRESHETS
FRESHING
FRESHISH
FRESHLY
FRESHMAN
FRESHMEN
FRESHNESS
FRESHNESSES
FRESNEL
FRESNELS
FRET
FRETFUL
FRETFULLY
FRETLESS*
FRETS
FRETSAW
FRETSAWS
FRETSOME*
FRETTED
FRETTER*

The Chambers Dictionary is the authority for many longer words; see Introduction, page ix

FRETTERS*	FRIEZES	FRISEE	FRIVOLLED	FROGLINGS
FRETTIER	FRIEZING	FRISEES	FRIVOLLER*	FROGMAN
FRETTIEST	FRIG	FRISES	FRIVOLLERS*	FROGMARCH
FRETTING	FRIGATE	FRISETTE	FRIVOLLING	FROGMARCHED
FRETTINGS	FRIGATES	FRISETTES	FRIVOLOUS	FROGMARCHES
FRETTY	FRIGATOON	FRISEUR	FRIVOLS	FROGMARCHING
FRETWORK	FRIGATOONS	FRISEURS	FRIZ	FROGMEN
FRETWORKS	FRIGES	FRISK	FRIZE	FROGMOUTH
FRIABLE	FRIGGED	FRISKA	FRIZED*	FROGMOUTHS
FRIAND	FRIGGER	FRISKAS	FRIZER*	FROGS
FRIANDE	FRIGGERS	FRISKED	FRIZERS*	FROIDEUR
FRIANDES	FRIGGING	FRISKER	FRIZES	FROIDEURS
FRIANDS	FRIGGINGS	FRISKERS	FRIZETTE*	FROISE
FRIAR	FRIGHT	FRISKET	FRIZETTES*	FROISES
FRIARBIRD	FRIGHTED	FRISKETS	FRIZING	FROLIC
FRIARBIRDS	FRIGHTEN	FRISKFUL	FRIZZ	FROLICKED
FRIARIES	FRIGHTENED	FRISKIER	FRIZZANTE	FROLICKING
FRIARLY	FRIGHTENING	FRISKIEST	FRIZZED	FROLICKY*
FRIARS	FRIGHTENS	FRISKILY	FRIZZER*	FROLICS
FRIARY	FRIGHTFUL	FRISKING	FRIZZERS*	FROM
FRIBBLE	FRIGHTING	FRISKINGS	FRIZZES	FROMAGE*
FRIBBLED	FRIGHTS	FRISKS	FRIZZIER	FROMAGES*
FRIBBLER	FRIGID	FRISKY	FRIZZIEST	FROMENTIES
FRIBBLERS	FRIGIDER	FRISSON	FRIZZILY*	FROMENTY
FRIBBLES	FRIGIDEST	FRISSONS	FRIZZING	FROND
FRIBBLING	FRIGIDITIES	FRIST	FRIZZLE	FRONDAGE
FRIBBLISH	FRIGIDITY	FRISTED	FRIZZLED	FRONDAGES
FRICADEL	FRIGIDLY	FRISTING	FRIZZLER*	FRONDED
FRICADELS	FRIGOT	FRISTS	FRIZZLERS*	FRONDENT
FRICANDO*	FRIGOTS	FRISURE	FRIZZLES	FRONDEUR
FRICANDOES*	FRIGS	FRISURES	FRIZZLIER	FRONDEURS
FRICASSEE	FRIJOL	FRIT	FRIZZLIEST	FRONDOSE
FRICASSEED	FRIJOLE	FRITFLIES	FRIZZLING	FRONDS
FRICASSEEING	FRIJOLES	FRITFLY	FRIZZLY	FRONS*
FRICASSEES	FRIKKADEL	FRITH	FRIZZY	FRONT
FRICATIVE	FRIKKADELS	FRITHBORH	FRO	FRONTAGE
FRICATIVES	FRILL	FRITHBORHS	FROCK	FRONTAGER
FRICHT	FRILLED	FRITHGILD	FROCKED	FRONTAGERS
FRICHTED	FRILLER*	FRITHGILDS	FROCKING	FRONTAGES
FRICHTING	FRILLERS*	FRITHS	FROCKINGS	FRONTAL
FRICHTS	FRILLIER	FRITS	FROCKLESS	FRONTALLY*
FRICTION	FRILLIES	FRITT*	FROCKS	FRONTALS
FRICTIONS	FRILLIEST	FRITTATA*	FROE*	FRONTED
FRIDGE	FRILLING	FRITTATAS*	FROES*	FRONTER*
FRIDGED	FRILLINGS	FRITTED	FROG	FRONTES*
FRIDGES	FRILLS	FRITTER	FROGBIT	FRONTIER
FRIDGING	FRILLY	FRITTERED	FROGBITS	FRONTIERED
FRIED	FRINGE	FRITTERER	FROGEYE*	FRONTIERING
FRIEDCAKE	FRINGED	FRITTERERS	FROGEYED*	FRONTIERS
FRIEDCAKES	FRINGES	FRITTERING	FROGEYES*	FRONTING
FRIEND	FRINGIER	FRITTERS	FROGFISH*	FRONTLESS
FRIENDED	FRINGIEST	FRITTING	FROGFISHES*	FRONTLET
FRIENDING	FRINGING	FRITTS*	FROGGED	FRONTLETS
FRIENDINGS	FRINGY	FRITURE	FROGGERIES	FRONTLINE*
FRIENDLIER	FRIPON	FRITURES	FROGGERY	FRONTMAN
FRIENDLIES	FRIPONS	FRITZ*	FROGGIER	FRONTMEN
FRIENDLIEST	FRIPPER	FRITZES*	FROGGIEST	FRONTON
FRIENDLY	FRIPPERER	FRIVOL	FROGGING	FRONTONS
FRIENDS	FRIPPERERS	FRIVOLED*	FROGGINGS	FRONTOON
FRIER	FRIPPERIES	FRIVOLER*	FROGGY	FRONTOONS
FRIERS	FRIPPERS	FRIVOLERS*	FROGLET	FRONTS
FRIES	FRIPPERY	FRIVOLING*	FROGLETS	FRONTWARD
FRIEZE	FRIS	FRIVOLITIES	FROGLIKE*	FRONTWARDS
FRIEZED	FRISE*	FRIVOLITY	FROGLING	FRONTWAYS

FRONTWISE	FROWNING	FRUITERY	FUBBED	FUELWOODS*
FRORE	FROWNS	FRUITFUL	FUBBERIES	FUERO
FROREN	FROWS	FRUITFULLER*	FUBBERY	FUEROS
FRORN	FROWSIER	FRUITFULLEST*	FUBBIER	FUFF
FRORNE	FROWSIEST	FRUITIER	FUBBIEST	FUFFED
FRORY	FROWST	FRUITIEST	FUBBING	FUFFIER
FROSH*	FROWSTED	FRUITILY*	FUBBY	FUFFIEST
FROST	FROWSTER	FRUITING	FUBS	FUFFING
FROSTBIT	FROWSTERS	FRUITINGS	FUBSIER	FUFFS
FROSTBITE	FROWSTIER	FRUITION	FUBSIEST	FUFFY
FROSTBITES	FROWSTIEST	FRUITIONS	FUBSY	FUG
FROSTBITING	FROWSTING	FRUITIVE	FUCHSIA	FUGACIOUS
FROSTBITTEN	FROWSTS	FRUITLESS	FUCHSIAS	FUGACITIES
FROSTED	FROWSTY	FRUITLET	FUCHSIN*	FUGACITY
FROSTEDS*	FROWSY	FRUITLETS	FUCHSINE	FUGAL
FROSTIER	FROWY	FRUITS	FUCHSINES	FUGALLY
FROSTIEST	FROWZIER	FRUITWOOD	FUCHSINS*	FUGATO
FROSTILY	FROWZIEST	FRUITWOODS	FUCHSITE	FUGATOS
FROSTING	FROWZILY*	FRUITY	FUCHSITES	FUGGED
FROSTINGS	FROWZY	FRUMENTIES	FUCI	FUGGIER
FROSTLESS	FROZE	FRUMENTY	FUCK	FUGGIEST
FROSTLIKE	FROZEN	FRUMP	FUCKED	FUGGILY*
FROSTS	FROZENLY*	FRUMPED	FUCKER	FUGGING
FROSTWORK	FRUCTANS	FRUMPIER	FUCKERS	FUGGY
FROSTWORKS	FRUCTED	FRUMPIEST	FUCKING	FUGHETTA
FROSTY	FRUCTIFIED	FRUMPILY*	FUCKINGS	FUGHETTAS
FROTH	FRUCTIFIES	FRUMPING	FUCKS	FUGIE
FROTHED	FRUCTIFY	FRUMPISH	FUCKUP*	FUGIES
FROTHERIES	FRUCTIFYING	FRUMPLE	FUCKUPS*	FUGIO*
FROTHERY	FRUCTIVE	FRUMPLED	FUCOID	FUGIOS*
FROTHIER	FRUCTOSE	FRUMPLES	FUCOIDAL	FUGITIVE
FROTHIEST	FRUCTOSES	FRUMPLING	FUCOIDS	FUGITIVES
FROTHILY	FRUCTUARIES	FRUMPS	FUCOSE*	FUGLE
FROTHING	FRUCTUARY	FRUMPY	FUCOSES*	FUGLED
FROTHLESS	FRUCTUATE	FRUSH	FUCOUS*	FUGLEMAN
FROTHS	FRUCTUATED	FRUSHED	FUCUS	FUGLEMEN
FROTHY	FRUCTUATES	FRUSHES	FUCUSED	FUGLES
FROTTAGE	FRUCTUATING	FRUSHING	FUCUSES	FUGLING
FROTTAGES	FRUCTUOUS	FRUST	FUD	FUGS
FROTTEUR	FRUG*	FRUSTA	FUDDLE	FUGU*
FROTTEURS	FRUGAL	FRUSTRATE	FUDDLED	FUGUE
FROUFROU*	FRUGALIST	FRUSTRATED	FUDDLER	FUGUED*
FROUFROUS*	FRUGALISTS	FRUSTRATES	FUDDLERS	FUGUES
FROUGHIER	FRUGALITIES	FRUSTRATING	FUDDLES	FUGUING*
FROUGHIEST	FRUGALITY	FRUSTS	FUDDLING	FUGUIST
FROUGHY	FRUGALLY	FRUSTULE	FUDDLINGS	FUGUISTS
FROUNCE	FRUGGED*	FRUSTULES	FUDGE	FUGUS*
FROUNCED	FRUGGING*	FRUSTUM	FUDGED	FUHRER*
FROUNCES	FRUGIVORE*	FRUSTUMS	FUDGES	FUHRERS*
FROUNCING	FRUGIVORES*	FRUTEX	FUDGING	FUJI*
FROUZIER*	FRUGS*	FRUTICES	FUDS	FUJIS*
FROUZIEST*	FRUICT	FRUTICOSE	FUEHRER*	FULCRA
FROUZY*	FRUICTS	FRUTIFIED	FUEHRERS*	FULCRATE
FROW	FRUIT	FRUTIFIES	FUEL	FULCRUM
FROWARD	FRUITAGE	FRUTIFY	FUELED*	FULCRUMS
FROWARDLY	FRUITAGES	FRUTIFYING	FUELER*	FULFIL
FROWARDS	FRUITCAKE	FRY	FUELERS*	FULFILL
FROWIE	FRUITCAKES	FRYER	FUELING*	FULFILLED
FROWIER	FRUITED	FRYERS	FUELLED	FULFILLER
FROWIEST	FRUITER	FRYING	FUELLER	FULFILLERS
FROWN	FRUITERER	FRYINGS	FUELLERS	FULFILLING
FROWNED	FRUITERERS	FRYPAN*	FUELLING	FULFILLINGS
FROWNER*	FRUITERIES	FRYPANS*	FUELS	FULFILLS
FROWNERS*	FRUITERS	FUB	FUELWOOD*	FULFILS

The Chambers Dictionary is the authority for many longer words; see Introduction, page ix

FULGENCIES	FULSOME	FUMY	FUNICULUS	FURCATED
FULGENCY	FULSOMELY	FUN	FUNK	FURCATES*
FULGENT	FULSOMER	FUNBOARD	FUNKED	FURCATING*
FULGENTLY	FULSOMEST	FUNBOARDS	FUNKER*	FURCATION
FULGID	FULVID	FUNCTION	FUNKERS*	FURCATIONS
FULGOR	FULVOUS	FUNCTIONED	FUNKHOLE	FURCRAEA*
FULGOROUS	FUM	FUNCTIONING	FUNKHOLES	FURCRAEAS*
FULGORS	FUMADO	FUNCTIONS	FUNKIA	FURCULA
FULGOUR	FUMADOES	FUNCTOR*	FUNKIAS	FURCULAE
FULGOURS	FUMADOS	FUNCTORS*	FUNKIER	FURCULAR
FULGURAL	FUMAGE	FUND	FUNKIEST	FURCULUM*
FULGURANT	FUMAGES	FUNDABLE	FUNKINESS	FURDER
FULGURATE	FUMARASE*	FUNDAMENT	FUNKINESSES	FUREUR
FULGURATED	FUMARASES*	FUNDAMENTS	FUNKING	FUREURS
FULGURATES	FUMARATE*	FUNDED	FUNKS	FURFAIR
FULGURATING	FUMARATES*	FUNDER	FUNKY	FURFAIRS
FULGURITE	FUMARIC*	FUNDERS	FUNNED	FURFUR
FULGURITES	FUMAROLE	FUNDI	FUNNEL	FURFURAL
FULGUROUS	FUMAROLES	FUNDIC*	FUNNELED*	FURFURALS
FULHAM	FUMAROLIC	FUNDIE	FUNNELING*	FURFURAN
FULHAMS	FUMATORIA	FUNDIES	FUNNELLED	FURFURANS
FULL	FUMATORIES	FUNDING	FUNNELLING	FURFURES*
FULLAGE	FUMATORY	FUNDINGS	FUNNELS	FURFUROL
FULLAGES	FUMBLE	FUNDIS	FUNNER	FURFUROLE
FULLAM	FUMBLED	FUNDLESS	FUNNEST	FURFUROLES
FULLAMS	FUMBLER	FUNDS	FUNNIER	FURFUROLS
FULLAN	FUMBLERS	FUNDUS	FUNNIES	FURFUROUS
FULLANS	FUMBLES	FUNDY	FUNNIEST	FURFURS
FULLBACK	FUMBLING	FUNEBRAL	FUNNILY	FURIBUND
FULLBACKS	FUME	FUNEBRE	FUNNINESS	FURIES
FULLED	FUMED	FUNEBRIAL	FUNNINESSES	FURIOSITIES
FULLER	FUMELESS*	FUNERAL	FUNNING	FURIOSITY
FULLERED*	FUMELIKE*	FUNERALS	FUNNY	FURIOSO
FULLERENE	FUMER*	FUNERARY	FUNNYMAN*	FURIOSOS
FULLERENES	FUMEROLE	FUNEREAL	FUNNYMEN*	FURIOUS
FULLERIES*	FUMEROLES	FUNEST	FUNS	FURIOUSLY
FULLERING*	FUMERS*	FUNFAIR	FUNSTER	FURL
FULLERS	FUMES	FUNFAIRS	FUNSTERS	FURLABLE*
FULLERY*	FUMET	FUNG	FUR	FURLANA
FULLEST	FUMETS	FUNGAL	FURACIOUS	FURLANAS
FULLFACE*	FUMETTE	FUNGALS*	FURACITIES	FURLED
FULLFACES*	FUMETTES	FUNGI	FURACITY	FURLER*
FULLING	FUMETTI	FUNGIBLE*	FURAL	FURLERS*
FULLISH	FUMETTO	FUNGIBLES	FURALS	FURLESS*
FULLNESS	FUMIER	FUNGIC*	FURAN	FURLING
FULLNESSES	FUMIEST	FUNGICIDE	FURANE	FURLONG
FULLS	FUMIGANT	FUNGICIDES	FURANES	FURLONGS
FULLY	FUMIGANTS	FUNGIFORM	FURANOSE*	FURLOUGH
FULMAR	FUMIGATE	FUNGO*	FURANOSES*	FURLOUGHED
FULMARS	FUMIGATED	FUNGOES*	FURANS	FURLOUGHING
FULMINANT	FUMIGATES	FUNGOID	FURBEARER*	FURLOUGHS
FULMINANTS	FUMIGATING	FUNGOIDAL	FURBEARERS*	FURLS
FULMINATE	FUMIGATOR	FUNGOIDS*	FURBELOW	FURMENTIES
FULMINATED	FUMIGATORS	FUNGOSITIES	FURBELOWED	FURMENTY
FULMINATES	FUMING	FUNGOSITY	FURBELOWING	FURMETIES
FULMINATING	FUMINGLY*	FUNGOUS	FURBELOWS	FURMETY
FULMINE	FUMITORIES	FUNGS	FURBISH	FURMITIES
FULMINED	FUMITORY	FUNGUS	FURBISHED	FURMITY
FULMINES	FUMOSITIES	FUNGUSES	FURBISHER	FURNACE
FULMINIC*	FUMOSITY	FUNICLE	FURBISHERS	FURNACED
FULMINING	FUMOUS	FUNICLES	FURBISHES	FURNACES
FULMINOUS	FUMS	FUNICULAR	FURBISHING	FURNACING
FULNESS	FUMULI*	FUNICULARS*	FURCAL	FURNIMENT
FULNESSES	FUMULUS*	FUNICULI	FURCATE	FURNIMENTS

FURNISH	FURS	FUSILE	FUSTIGATES	FUTZED*
FURNISHED	FURTH	FUSILEER	FUSTIGATING	FUTZES*
FURNISHER	FURTHER	FUSILEERS	FUSTILUGS	FUTZING*
FURNISHERS	FURTHERED	FUSILIER	FUSTILY	FUZE
FURNISHES	FURTHERER	FUSILIERS	FUSTINESS	FUZED*
FURNISHING	FURTHERERS	FUSILLADE	FUSTINESSES	FUZEE
FURNISHINGS	FURTHERING	FUSILLADES	FUSTING	FUZEES
FURNITURE	FURTHERS	FUSILLI	FUSTOC	FUZES
FURNITURES	FURTHEST	FUSILLIS*	FUSTOCS	FUZIL*
FUROL	FURTIVE	FUSILS	FUSTS	FUZILS*
FUROLE	FURTIVELY	FUSING	FUSTY	FUZING*
FUROLES	FURUNCLE	FUSION	FUSULINID*	FUZZ
FUROLS	FURUNCLES	FUSIONISM	FUSULINIDS*	FUZZED
FUROR	FURY	FUSIONISMS	FUTCHEL	FUZZES
FURORE	FURZE	FUSIONIST	FUTCHELS	FUZZIER
FURORES	FURZES	FUSIONISTS	FUTHARC*	FUZZIEST
FURORS	FURZIER	FUSIONS	FUTHARCS*	FUZZILY
FURPHIES	FURZIEST	FUSS	FUTHARK	FUZZINESS
FURPHY	FURZY	FUSSED	FUTHARKS	FUZZINESSES
FURR	FUSAIN	FUSSER	FUTHORC	FUZZING
FURRED	FUSAINS	FUSSERS	FUTHORCS	FUZZLE
FURRIER	FUSAROL	FUSSES	FUTHORK	FUZZLED
FURRIERIES	FUSAROLE	FUSSIER	FUTHORKS	FUZZLES
FURRIERS	FUSAROLES	FUSSIEST	FUTILE	FUZZLING
FURRIERY	FUSAROLS	FUSSILY	FUTILELY	FUZZY
FURRIES	FUSC	FUSSINESS	FUTILER	FY
FURRIEST	FUSCOUS	FUSSINESSES	FUTILEST	FYCE*
FURRILY*	FUSE	FUSSING	FUTILITIES	FYCES*
FURRINER*	FUSED	FUSSPOT*	FUTILITY	FYKE
FURRINERS*	FUSEE	FUSSPOTS*	FUTON	FYKED
FURRINESS	FUSEES	FUSSY	FUTONS	FYKES
FURRINESSES	FUSEL*	FUST	FUTTOCK	FYKING
FURRING	FUSELAGE	FUSTED	FUTTOCKS	FYLE
FURRINGS	FUSELAGES	FUSTET	FUTURAL*	FYLES
FURROW	FUSELESS*	FUSTETS	FUTURE	FYLFOT
FURROWED	FUSELS*	FUSTIAN	FUTURES	FYLFOTS
FURROWER*	FUSES	FUSTIANS	FUTURISM	FYNBOS
FURROWERS*	FUSHION	FUSTIC	FUTURISMS	FYNBOSES
FURROWING	FUSHIONS	FUSTICS	FUTURIST	FYRD
FURROWS	FUSIBLE	FUSTIER	FUTURISTS	FYRDS
FURROWY	FUSIBLY*	FUSTIEST	FUTURITIES	FYTTE
FURRS	FUSIFORM	FUSTIGATE	FUTURITY	FYTTES
FURRY	FUSIL	FUSTIGATED	FUTZ*	

G

GAB
GABARDINE
GABARDINES
GABBARD
GABBARDS
GABBART
GABBARTS
GABBED
GABBER
GABBERS
GABBIER
GABBIEST
GABBING
GABBLE
GABBLED
GABBLER
GABBLERS
GABBLES
GABBLING
GABBLINGS
GABBRO
GABBROIC
GABBROID
GABBROS
GABBY
GABELLE
GABELLED*
GABELLER
GABELLERS
GABELLES
GABERDINE
GABERDINES
GABFEST
GABFESTS
GABIES
GABION
GABIONADE
GABIONADES
GABIONAGE
GABIONAGES
GABIONED
GABIONS
GABLE
GABLED
GABLES
GABLET
GABLETS
GABLING*
GABNASH
GABNASHES
GABOON*
GABOONS*
GABS
GABY
GAD

GADABOUT
GADABOUTS
GADARENE*
GADDED
GADDER
GADDERS
GADDI*
GADDING
GADDIS*
GADE
GADES
GADFLIES
GADFLY
GADGE
GADGES
GADGET
GADGETEER
GADGETEERS
GADGETRIES
GADGETRY
GADGETS
GADGETY*
GADGIE
GADGIES
GADI
GADID*
GADIDS*
GADIS
GADJE
GADJES
GADLING
GADLINGS
GADOID
GADOIDS
GADROON
GADROONED
GADROONING*
GADROONS
GADS
GADSMAN
GADSMEN
GADSO
GADSOS
GADWALL
GADWALLS
GADZOOKS
GAE
GAED
GAEING*
GAELICISE
GAELICISED
GAELICISES
GAELICISING
GAELICISM
GAELICISMS

GAELICIZE
GAELICIZED
GAELICIZES
GAELICIZING
GAEN*
GAES
GAFF
GAFFE
GAFFED
GAFFER
GAFFERS
GAFFES
GAFFING
GAFFINGS
GAFFS
GAG
GAGA
GAGAKU
GAGAKUS
GAGE
GAGED
GAGER*
GAGERS*
GAGES
GAGGED
GAGGER
GAGGERS
GAGGING
GAGGLE
GAGGLED
GAGGLES
GAGGLING
GAGGLINGS
GAGING
GAGMAN
GAGMEN
GAGS
GAGSTER
GAGSTERS
GAHNITE
GAHNITES
GAID
GAIDS
GAIETIES
GAIETY
GAIJIN
GAILLARD
GAILLARDE
GAILY
GAIN
GAINABLE
GAINED
GAINER
GAINERS
GAINEST

GAINFUL
GAINFULLY
GAINING
GAININGS
GAINLESS
GAINLIER
GAINLIEST
GAINLY
GAINS
GAINSAID
GAINSAY
GAINSAYER
GAINSAYERS
GAINSAYING
GAINSAYINGS
GAINSAYS
GAINST*
GAIR
GAIRFOWL
GAIRFOWLS
GAIRS
GAIT
GAITED
GAITER
GAITERS
GAITING
GAITS
GAITT
GAITTS
GAJO
GAJOS
GAL
GALA
GALABEA
GALABEAH
GALABEAHS
GALABEAS
GALABIA
GALABIAH
GALABIAHS
GALABIAS
GALABIEH*
GALABIEHS*
GALABIYA*
GALABIYAS*
GALACTIC
GALACTOSE
GALACTOSES
GALAGE
GALAGES
GALAGO
GALAGOS
GALAH
GALAHS
GALANGA

GALANGAL
GALANGALS
GALANGAS
GALANT
GALANTINE
GALANTINES
GALAPAGO
GALAPAGOS
GALAS
GALATEA
GALATEAS
GALAVANT*
GALAVANTED*
GALAVANTING*
GALAVANTS*
GALAX*
GALAXES*
GALAXIES
GALAXY
GALBANUM
GALBANUMS
GALDRAGON
GALDRAGONS
GALE
GALEA
GALEAE
GALEAS
GALEATE
GALEATED
GALENA
GALENAS
GALENGALE
GALENGALES
GALENIC*
GALENICAL*
GALENICALS*
GALENITE
GALENITES
GALENOID
GALERE
GALERES
GALES
GALETTE
GALETTES
GALILEE
GALILEES
GALINGALE
GALINGALES
GALIONGEE
GALIONGEES
GALIOT
GALIOTS
GALIPOT
GALIPOTS
GALIVANT*

Words marked with an asterisk are from OTCWL

GALIVANTED*	GALLICIZE	GALLOW	GALVANISMS	GAMBOLLING
GALIVANTING*	GALLICIZED	GALLOWED	GALVANIST	GAMBOLS
GALIVANTS*	GALLICIZES	GALLOWING	GALVANISTS	GAMBOS
GALL	GALLICIZING	GALLOWS	GALVANIZE	GAMBREL
GALLABEA	GALLIED	GALLOWSES	GALVANIZED	GAMBRELS
GALLABEAH	GALLIES	GALLS	GALVANIZES	GAMBROON
GALLABEAHS	GALLINAZO	GALLSTONE	GALVANIZING	GAMBROONS
GALLABEAS	GALLINAZOS	GALLSTONES	GALYAC*	GAMBS
GALLABIA	GALLING	GALLUMPH	GALYACS*	GAMBUSIA*
GALLABIAH	GALLINGLY	GALLUMPHED	GALYAK*	GAMBUSIAS*
GALLABIAHS	GALLINULE	GALLUMPHING	GALYAKS*	GAME
GALLABIAS	GALLINULES	GALLUMPHS	GAM	GAMECOCK
GALLABIEH	GALLIOT	GALLUS	GAMA*	GAMECOCKS
GALLABIEHS	GALLIOTS	GALLUSED*	GAMAS*	GAMED
GALLABIYA	GALLIPOT	GALLUSES	GAMASH	GAMELAN
GALLABIYAS	GALLIPOTS	GALLY	GAMASHES	GAMELANS
GALLAMINE*	GALLISE	GALLYING	GAMAY	GAMELIKE*
GALLAMINES*	GALLISED	GALOCHE	GAMAYS	GAMELY
GALLANT	GALLISES	GALOCHED	GAMB	GAMENESS
GALLANTED*	GALLISING	GALOCHES	GAMBA	GAMENESSES
GALLANTER	GALLISISE	GALOCHING	GAMBADE*	GAMER
GALLANTEST	GALLISISED	GALOOT	GAMBADES*	GAMERS*
GALLANTING*	GALLISISES	GALOOTS	GAMBADO	GAMES
GALLANTLY	GALLISISING	GALOP	GAMBADOED	GAMESIER
GALLANTRIES	GALLISIZE	GALOPADE*	GAMBADOES	GAMESIEST
GALLANTRY	GALLISIZED	GALOPADES*	GAMBADOING	GAMESMAN*
GALLANTS	GALLISIZES	GALOPED	GAMBADOS	GAMESMEN*
GALLATE	GALLISIZING	GALOPIN	GAMBAS	GAMESOME
GALLATES	GALLIUM	GALOPING	GAMBE*	GAMEST
GALLEASS	GALLIUMS	GALOPINS	GAMBES*	GAMESTER
GALLEASSES	GALLIVANT	GALOPPED	GAMBESON	GAMESTERS
GALLED	GALLIVANTED	GALOPPING	GAMBESONS	GAMESY
GALLEIN*	GALLIVANTING	GALOPS	GAMBET	GAMETAL
GALLEINS*	GALLIVANTS	GALORE	GAMBETS	GAMETE
GALLEON	GALLIVAT	GALORES*	GAMBETTA	GAMETES
GALLEONS	GALLIVATS	GALOSH	GAMBETTAS	GAMETIC
GALLERIA	GALLIWASP	GALOSHE*	GAMBIA*	GAMEY
GALLERIAS	GALLIWASPS	GALOSHED	GAMBIAS*	GAMIC
GALLERIED	GALLIZE	GALOSHES	GAMBIER	GAMIER
GALLERIES	GALLIZED	GALOSHING	GAMBIERS	GAMIEST
GALLERY	GALLIZES	GALOWSES	GAMBIR	GAMILY*
GALLERYING	GALLIZING	GALRAVAGE	GAMBIRS	GAMIN
GALLET	GALLNUT	GALRAVAGED	GAMBIST	GAMINE
GALLETA*	GALLNUTS	GALRAVAGES	GAMBISTS	GAMINERIE
GALLETAS*	GALLON	GALRAVAGING	GAMBIT	GAMINERIES
GALLETED	GALLONAGE	GALS	GAMBITED	GAMINES
GALLETING	GALLONAGES	GALTONIA	GAMBITING	GAMINESS
GALLETS	GALLONS	GALTONIAS	GAMBITS	GAMINESSES
GALLEY	GALLOON	GALUMPH	GAMBLE	GAMING
GALLEYS	GALLOONED	GALUMPHED	GAMBLED	GAMINGS
GALLFLIES	GALLOONS	GALUMPHER	GAMBLER	GAMINS
GALLFLY	GALLOOT*	GALUMPHERS	GAMBLERS	GAMMA
GALLIARD	GALLOOTS*	GALUMPHING	GAMBLES	GAMMADIA
GALLIARDS	GALLOP	GALUMPHS	GAMBLING	GAMMADION
GALLIASS	GALLOPADE	GALUT	GAMBLINGS	GAMMAS
GALLIASSES	GALLOPADED	GALUTH	GAMBO	GAMMATIA
GALLIC	GALLOPADES	GALUTHS	GAMBOGE	GAMMATION
GALLICAN*	GALLOPADING	GALUTS	GAMBOGES	GAMME
GALLICISE	GALLOPED	GALVANIC	GAMBOGIAN	GAMMED
GALLICISED	GALLOPER	GALVANISE	GAMBOGIC	GAMMER
GALLICISES	GALLOPERS	GALVANISED	GAMBOL	GAMMERS
GALLICISING	GALLOPING	GALVANISES	GAMBOLED*	GAMMES
GALLICISM	GALLOPS	GALVANISING	GAMBOLING*	GAMMIER
GALLICISMS	GALLOUS*	GALVANISM	GAMBOLLED	GAMMIEST

The Chambers Dictionary is the authority for many longer words; see Introduction, page ix

GAMMING
GAMMOCK
GAMMOCKED
GAMMOCKING
GAMMOCKS
GAMMON
GAMMONED
GAMMONER
GAMMONERS
GAMMONING
GAMMONINGS
GAMMONS
GAMMY
GAMODEME*
GAMODEMES*
GAMP
GAMPISH
GAMPS
GAMS
GAMUT
GAMUTS
GAMY
GAMYNESS
GAMYNESSES
GAN
GANACHE*
GANACHES*
GANCH
GANCHED
GANCHES
GANCHING
GANDER
GANDERED*
GANDERING*
GANDERISM
GANDERISMS
GANDERS
GANE
GANEF*
GANEFS*
GANEV*
GANEVS*
GANG
GANGBANG*
GANGBANGS*
GANGBOARD
GANGBOARDS
GANGED
GANGER
GANGERS
GANGING
GANGINGS
GANGLAND
GANGLANDS
GANGLIA
GANGLIAL*
GANGLIAR
GANGLIATE
GANGLIER
GANGLIEST
GANGLING
GANGLION
GANGLIONS
GANGLY

GANGPLANK
GANGPLANKS
GANGPLOW*
GANGPLOWS*
GANGREL
GANGRELS
GANGRENE
GANGRENED
GANGRENES
GANGRENING
GANGS
GANGSMAN
GANGSMEN
GANGSTA
GANGSTAS
GANGSTER
GANGSTERS
GANGUE
GANGUES
GANGWAY
GANGWAYS
GANISTER
GANISTERS
GANJA
GANJAH*
GANJAHS*
GANJAS
GANNET
GANNETRIES
GANNETRY
GANNETS
GANNISTER
GANNISTERS
GANOF*
GANOFS*
GANOID
GANOIDS
GANOIN
GANOINE
GANOINES
GANOINS
GANSEY
GANSEYS
GANT
GANTED
GANTELOPE*
GANTELOPES*
GANTING
GANTLET
GANTLETED*
GANTLETING*
GANTLETS
GANTLINE
GANTLINES
GANTLOPE
GANTLOPES
GANTRIES
GANTRY
GANTS
GANYMEDE*
GANYMEDES*
GAOL
GAOLED
GAOLER

GAOLERESS
GAOLERESSES
GAOLERS
GAOLING
GAOLS
GAP
GAPE
GAPED
GAPER
GAPERS
GAPES
GAPESEED
GAPESEEDS
GAPEWORM
GAPEWORMS
GAPING
GAPINGLY
GAPINGS
GAPO
GAPOS
GAPOSIS*
GAPOSISES*
GAPPED
GAPPIER
GAPPIEST
GAPPING
GAPPY
GAPS
GAPY*
GAR
GARAGE
GARAGED
GARAGEMAN*
GARAGEMEN*
GARAGES
GARAGING
GARAGINGS
GARAGIST
GARAGISTE
GARAGISTES
GARAGISTS
GARB
GARBAGE
GARBAGES
GARBANZO
GARBANZOS
GARBE
GARBED
GARBES
GARBING
GARBLE
GARBLED
GARBLER
GARBLERS
GARBLES
GARBLESS*
GARBLING
GARBLINGS
GARBO
GARBOARD
GARBOARDS
GARBOIL
GARBOILS
GARBOLOGIES

GARBOLOGY
GARBOS
GARBS
GARBURE
GARBURES
GARCINIA
GARCINIAS
GARCON
GARCONS
GARDA
GARDAI
GARDANT
GARDANTS
GARDEN
GARDENED
GARDENER
GARDENERS
GARDENFUL*
GARDENFULS*
GARDENIA
GARDENIAS
GARDENING
GARDENINGS
GARDENS
GARDEROBE
GARDEROBES
GARDYLOO
GARDYLOOS
GARE
GAREFOWL
GAREFOWLS
GARFISH
GARFISHES
GARGANEY
GARGANEYS
GARGARISE
GARGARISED
GARGARISES
GARGARISING
GARGARISM
GARGARISMS
GARGARIZE
GARGARIZED
GARGARIZES
GARGARIZING
GARGET
GARGETS
GARGETY
GARGLE
GARGLED
GARGLER*
GARGLERS*
GARGLES
GARGLING
GARGOYLE
GARGOYLED*
GARGOYLES
GARIAL
GARIALS
GARIBALDI
GARIBALDIS
GARIGUE
GARIGUES
GARISH

GARISHED
GARISHES
GARISHING
GARISHLY
GARJAN
GARJANS
GARLAND
GARLANDED
GARLANDING
GARLANDRIES
GARLANDRY
GARLANDS
GARLIC
GARLICKED*
GARLICKIER
GARLICKIEST
GARLICKY
GARLICS
GARMENT
GARMENTED
GARMENTING
GARMENTS
GARNER
GARNERED
GARNERING
GARNERS
GARNET
GARNETS
GARNI
GARNISH
GARNISHED
GARNISHEE
GARNISHEED
GARNISHEEING
GARNISHEES
GARNISHER
GARNISHERS
GARNISHES
GARNISHING
GARNISHINGS
GARNISHRIES
GARNISHRY
GARNITURE
GARNITURES
GAROTE*
GAROTED*
GAROTES*
GAROTING*
GAROTTE
GAROTTED
GAROTTER
GAROTTERS
GAROTTES
GAROTTING
GAROTTINGS
GARPIKE
GARPIKES
GARRAN
GARRANS
GARRE
GARRED
GARRES
GARRET
GARRETED

GARRETEER	GASCONISM	GASPIEST	GATEHOUSES	GAUFRES
GARRETEERS	GASCONISMS	GASPINESS	GATELEG	GAUGE
GARRETS	GASCONS	GASPINESSES	GATELESS	GAUGEABLE
GARRIGUE	GASEITIES	GASPING	GATELIKE*	GAUGED
GARRIGUES	GASEITY	GASPINGLY	GATEMAN	GAUGER
GARRING	GASELIER	GASPINGS	GATEMEN	GAUGERS
GARRISON	GASELIERS	GASPS	GATEPOST	GAUGES
GARRISONED	GASEOUS	GASPY	GATEPOSTS	GAUGING
GARRISONING	GASES	GASSED	GATES	GAUGINGS
GARRISONS	GASFIELD	GASSER	GATEWAY	GAUJE
GARRON	GASFIELDS	GASSERS	GATEWAYS	GAUJES
GARRONS	GASH	GASSES	GATH	GAULEITER
GARROT	GASHED	GASSIER	GATHER	GAULEITERS
GARROTE	GASHER	GASSIEST	GATHERED	GAULT
GARROTED	GASHES	GASSILY*	GATHERER	GAULTER
GARROTER*	GASHEST	GASSINESS	GATHERERS	GAULTERS
GARROTERS*	GASHFUL	GASSINESSES	GATHERING	GAULTS
GARROTES	GASHING	GASSING	GATHERINGS	GAUM
GARROTING	GASHLY	GASSINGS	GATHERS	GAUMED
GARROTS	GASHOLDER	GASSY	GATHS	GAUMIER
GARROTTE	GASHOLDERS	GAST	GATING	GAUMIEST
GARROTTED	GASHOUSE*	GASTED	GATINGS	GAUMING
GARROTTER	GASHOUSES*	GASTER	GATOR*	GAUMLESS
GARROTTERS	GASIFIED	GASTERS	GATORS*	GAUMS
GARROTTES	GASIFIER	GASTFULL	GATS	GAUMY
GARROTTING	GASIFIERS	GASTIGHT*	GAU	GAUN
GARROTTINGS	GASIFIES	GASTING	GAUCHE	GAUNCH
GARRULITIES	GASIFORM	GASTNESS	GAUCHELY*	GAUNCHED
GARRULITY	GASIFY	GASTNESSE	GAUCHER	GAUNCHES
GARRULOUS	GASIFYING	GASTNESSES	GAUCHERIE	GAUNCHING
GARRYA	GASKET	GASTRAEA	GAUCHERIES	GAUNT
GARRYAS	GASKETS	GASTRAEAS	GAUCHESCO	GAUNTED
GARRYOWEN	GASKIN	GASTRAEUM	GAUCHEST	GAUNTER
GARRYOWENS	GASKING*	GASTRAEUMS	GAUCHO	GAUNTEST
GARS	GASKINGS*	GASTRAL*	GAUCHOS	GAUNTING
GART	GASKINS	GASTREA*	GAUCIE	GAUNTLET
GARTER	GASLESS*	GASTREAS*	GAUCIER	GAUNTLETED*
GARTERED	GASLIGHT	GASTRIC	GAUCIEST	GAUNTLETING*
GARTERING	GASLIGHTS	GASTRIN	GAUCY	GAUNTLETS
GARTERS	GASLIT	GASTRINS	GAUD	GAUNTLY
GARTH	GASMAN	GASTRITIDES*	GAUDEAMUS	GAUNTNESS
GARTHS	GASMEN	GASTRITIS	GAUDEAMUSES	GAUNTNESSES
GARUDA	GASOGENE	GASTRITISES	GAUDED	GAUNTREE
GARUDAS	GASOGENES	GASTROPOD	GAUDERIES	GAUNTREES
GARUM	GASOHOL	GASTROPODS	GAUDERY	GAUNTRIES
GARUMS	GASOHOLS	GASTRULA	GAUDGIE	GAUNTRY
GARVEY*	GASOLENE	GASTRULAE	GAUDGIES	GAUNTS
GARVEYS*	GASOLENES	GASTRULAR*	GAUDIER	GAUP
GARVIE	GASOLIER	GASTRULAS	GAUDIES	GAUPED
GARVIES	GASOLIERS	GASTS	GAUDIEST	GAUPER
GARVOCK	GASOLINE	GASWORKS*	GAUDILY	GAUPERS
GARVOCKS	GASOLINES	GAT	GAUDINESS	GAUPING
GAS	GASOLINIC*	GATE	GAUDINESSES	GAUPS
GASAHOL	GASOMETER	GATEAU	GAUDING	GAUPUS
GASAHOLS	GASOMETERS	GATEAUS	GAUDS	GAUPUSES
GASALIER	GASOMETRIES	GATEAUX	GAUDY	GAUR
GASALIERS	GASOMETRY	GATECRASH	GAUFER	GAURS
GASBAG	GASP	GATECRASHED	GAUFERS	GAUS
GASBAGS	GASPED	GATECRASHES	GAUFFER	GAUSS
GASCON	GASPER	GATECRASHING	GAUFFERED	GAUSSES
GASCONADE	GASPEREAU	GATED	GAUFFERING	GAUSSIAN
GASCONADED	GASPEREAUS	GATEFOLD	GAUFFERINGS	GAUZE
GASCONADES	GASPERS	GATEFOLDS	GAUFFERS	GAUZELIKE*
GASCONADING	GASPIER	GATEHOUSE	GAUFRE	GAUZES

The Chambers Dictionary is the authority for many longer words; see Introduction, page ix

GAUZIER	GAYAL	GAZUMPS	GEES	GELS
GAUZIEST	GAYALS	GAZUNDER	GEESE	GELSEMIA*
GAUZILY*	GAYER	GAZUNDERED	GEEST*	GELSEMINE
GAUZINESS	GAYEST	GAZUNDERING	GEESTS*	GELSEMINES
GAUZINESSES	GAYETIES*	GAZUNDERS	GEEZ*	GELSEMIUM
GAUZY	GAYETY*	GAZY	GEEZER	GELSEMIUMS
GAVAGE	GAYLY*	GEAL	GEEZERS	GELT
GAVAGES	GAYNESS	GEALED	GEFUFFLE	GELTS
GAVE	GAYNESSES	GEALING	GEFUFFLED	GEM
GAVEL	GAYS	GEALOUS	GEFUFFLES	GEMATRIA
GAVELED*	GAYSOME	GEALOUSIES	GEFUFFLING	GEMATRIAS
GAVELING*	GAYWINGS*	GEALOUSY	GEISHA	GEMEL
GAVELKIND	GAZABO*	GEALS	GEISHAS	GEMELS
GAVELKINDS	GAZABOES*	GEAN	GEIST	GEMFISH
GAVELLED*	GAZABOS*	GEANS	GEISTS	GEMFISHES
GAVELLING*	GAZAL	GEAR	GEIT	GEMINAL*
GAVELMAN	GAZALS	GEARBOX	GEITS	GEMINALLY*
GAVELMEN	GAZANIA	GEARBOXES	GEL	GEMINATE
GAVELOCK	GAZANIAS	GEARCASE*	GELABLE*	GEMINATED
GAVELOCKS	GAZAR	GEARCASES*	GELADA	GEMINATES
GAVELS	GAZARS	GEARE	GELADAS	GEMINATING
GAVIAL	GAZE	GEARED	GELANT*	GEMINI
GAVIALS	GAZEBO	GEARES	GELANTS*	GEMINIES
GAVOT*	GAZEBOES	GEARING	GELASTIC	GEMINOUS
GAVOTS*	GAZEBOS	GEARINGS	GELATE*	GEMINY
GAVOTTE	GAZED	GEARLESS	GELATED*	GEMLIKE*
GAVOTTED*	GAZEFUL	GEARS	GELATES*	GEMMA
GAVOTTES	GAZEHOUND*	GEARSHIFT	GELATI	GEMMAE
GAVOTTING*	GAZEHOUNDS*	GEARSHIFTS	GELATIN	GEMMAN
GAWCIER	GAZELLE	GEARWHEEL	GELATINE	GEMMATE
GAWCIEST	GAZELLES	GEARWHEELS	GELATINES	GEMMATED
GAWCY	GAZEMENT	GEASON	GELATING*	GEMMATES
GAWD	GAZEMENTS	GEAT	GELATINS	GEMMATING
GAWDS	GAZER	GEATS	GELATION	GEMMATION
GAWK	GAZERS	GEBUR	GELATIONS	GEMMATIONS
GAWKED	GAZES	GEBURS	GELATO	GEMMATIVE
GAWKER	GAZETTE	GECK	GELATOS*	GEMMED
GAWKERS	GAZETTED	GECKED	GELD	GEMMEN
GAWKIER	GAZETTEER	GECKING	GELDED	GEMMEOUS
GAWKIES	GAZETTEERED	GECKO	GELDER	GEMMERIES
GAWKIEST	GAZETTEERING	GECKOES	GELDERS	GEMMERY
GAWKIHOOD	GAZETTEERS	GECKOS	GELDING	GEMMIER
GAWKIHOODS	GAZETTES	GECKS	GELDINGS	GEMMIEST
GAWKILY*	GAZETTING	GED	GELDS	GEMMILY*
GAWKINESS	GAZIER	GEDDIT	GELEE*	GEMMING
GAWKINESSES	GAZIEST	GEDS	GELEES*	GEMMOLOGIES
GAWKING	GAZING	GEE	GELID	GEMMOLOGY
GAWKISH*	GAZOGENE	GEEBUNG	GELIDER	GEMMULE
GAWKISHLY*	GAZOGENES	GEEBUNGS	GELIDEST	GEMMULES
GAWKS	GAZON	GEECHEE	GELIDITIES	GEMMY
GAWKY	GAZONS	GEECHEES	GELIDITY	GEMOLOGIES
GAWP	GAZOO	GEED	GELIDLY	GEMOLOGY
GAWPED	GAZOOKA	GEEGAW	GELIDNESS	GEMONY
GAWPER	GAZOOKAS	GEEGAWS	GELIDNESSES	GEMOT
GAWPERS	GAZOON	GEEING	GELIGNITE	GEMOTE*
GAWPING	GAZOONS	GEEK	GELIGNITES	GEMOTES*
GAWPS	GAZOOS	GEEKIER	GELLANT*	GEMOTS
GAWPUS	GAZPACHO	GEEKIEST	GELLANTS*	GEMS
GAWPUSES	GAZPACHOS	GEEKS	GELLED	GEMSBOK
GAWSIE*	GAZUMP	GEEKY	GELLIES	GEMSBOKS
GAWSIER	GAZUMPED	GEEP	GELLING	GEMSBUCK*
GAWSIEST	GAZUMPER*	GEEPOUND*	GELLY	GEMSBUCKS*
GAWSY	GAZUMPERS*	GEEPOUNDS*	GELOSIES	GEMSHORN
GAY	GAZUMPING	GEEPS	GELOSY	GEMSHORNS

GEMSTONE
GEMSTONES
GEMUTLICH
GEN
GENA
GENAL
GENAPPE
GENAPPES
GENAS
GENDARME
GENDARMES
GENDER
GENDERED
GENDERING
GENDERS
GENE
GENEALOGIES
GENEALOGY
GENERA
GENERABLE
GENERAL
GENERALE
GENERALIA
GENERALLED
GENERALLING
GENERALLY
GENERALS
GENERANT
GENERANTS
GENERATE
GENERATED
GENERATES
GENERATING
GENERATOR
GENERATORS
GENERIC
GENERICAL
GENERICS
GENEROUS
GENES
GENESES
GENESIS
GENET
GENETIC
GENETICAL
GENETICS
GENETRICES
GENETRIX
GENETRIXES
GENETS
GENETTE
GENETTES
GENEVA
GENEVAS
GENIAL
GENIALISE
GENIALISED
GENIALISES
GENIALISING
GENIALITIES
GENIALITY
GENIALIZE
GENIALIZED
GENIALIZES

GENIALIZING
GENIALLY
GENIC
GENICALLY*
GENIE
GENIES
GENII
GENIP
GENIPAP
GENIPAPS
GENIPS
GENISTA
GENISTAS
GENITAL
GENITALIA
GENITALIC
GENITALLY*
GENITALS
GENITIVAL
GENITIVE
GENITIVES
GENITOR
GENITORS
GENITRICES
GENITRIX
GENITRIXES
GENITURE
GENITURES
GENIUS
GENIUSES
GENIZAH
GENIZAHS
GENLOCK
GENLOCKS
GENNEL
GENNELS
GENNET
GENNETS
GENOA
GENOAS
GENOCIDAL
GENOCIDE
GENOCIDES
GENOISE*
GENOISES*
GENOM
GENOME
GENOMES
GENOMIC*
GENOMS
GENOTYPE
GENOTYPES
GENOTYPIC
GENRE
GENRES
GENRO*
GENROS*
GENS
GENSDARMES
GENSENG*
GENSENGS*
GENT
GENTEEL
GENTEELER

GENTEELEST
GENTEELLY
GENTES
GENTIAN
GENTIANS
GENTIER
GENTIEST
GENTIL*
GENTILE
GENTILES
GENTILIC
GENTILISE
GENTILISED
GENTILISES
GENTILISH
GENTILISING
GENTILISM
GENTILISMS
GENTILITIES
GENTILITY
GENTILIZE
GENTILIZED
GENTILIZES
GENTILIZING
GENTLE
GENTLED
GENTLEMAN
GENTLEMEN
GENTLER
GENTLES
GENTLEST
GENTLING
GENTLY
GENTOO
GENTOOS
GENTRICE
GENTRICES
GENTRIES
GENTRIFIED
GENTRIFIES
GENTRIFY
GENTRIFYING
GENTRY
GENTS
GENTY
GENU
GENUA*
GENUFLECT
GENUFLECTED
GENUFLECTING
GENUFLECTS
GENUINE
GENUINELY
GENUS
GENUSES
GEO
GEOBOTANIES*
GEOBOTANY*
GEOCARPIC
GEOCARPIES
GEOCARPY
GEODE
GEODES
GEODESIC

GEODESICS
GEODESIES
GEODESIST
GEODESISTS
GEODESY
GEODETIC
GEODETICS
GEODIC
GEODUCK*
GEODUCKS*
GEOFACT
GEOFACTS
GEOGENIES
GEOGENY
GEOGNOSES
GEOGNOSIES
GEOGNOSIS
GEOGNOST
GEOGNOSTS
GEOGNOSY
GEOGONIC
GEOGONIES
GEOGONY
GEOGRAPHIES
GEOGRAPHY
GEOID
GEOIDAL
GEOIDS
GEOLATRIES
GEOLATRY
GEOLOGER
GEOLOGERS
GEOLOGIAN
GEOLOGIANS
GEOLOGIC
GEOLOGIES
GEOLOGISE
GEOLOGISED
GEOLOGISES
GEOLOGISING
GEOLOGIST
GEOLOGISTS
GEOLOGIZE
GEOLOGIZED
GEOLOGIZES
GEOLOGIZING
GEOLOGY
GEOMANCER
GEOMANCERS
GEOMANCIES
GEOMANCY
GEOMANT
GEOMANTIC
GEOMANTS
GEOMETER
GEOMETERS
GEOMETRIC
GEOMETRID
GEOMETRIDS
GEOMETRIES
GEOMETRY
GEOMYOID
GEOPHAGIES
GEOPHAGY

GEOPHILIC
GEOPHONE
GEOPHONES
GEOPHYTE
GEOPHYTES
GEOPHYTIC
GEOPONIC
GEOPONICS
GEOPROBE*
GEOPROBES*
GEORGETTE
GEORGETTES
GEORGIC
GEORGICS
GEOS
GEOSPHERE
GEOSPHERES
GEOSTATIC
GEOSTATICS
GEOTACTIC
GEOTAXES
GEOTAXIS
GEOTROPIC
GERAH
GERAHS
GERANIAL*
GERANIALS*
GERANIOL
GERANIOLS
GERANIUM
GERANIUMS
GERARDIA*
GERARDIAS*
GERBE
GERBERA
GERBERAS
GERBES
GERBIL
GERBILLE
GERBILLES
GERBILS
GERE
GERENT
GERENTS
GERENUK
GERENUKS
GERES
GERFALCON
GERFALCONS
GERIATRIC
GERIATRICS
GERLE
GERLES
GERM
GERMAIN
GERMAINE
GERMAINES
GERMAINS
GERMAN
GERMANDER
GERMANDERS
GERMANE
GERMANELY
GERMANIC*

GERMANIUM	GESTATING	GHAT	GHOULS	GIDDAP
GERMANIUMS	GESTATION	GHATS	GHYLL	GIDDIED
GERMANIZE*	GESTATIONS	GHAUT	GHYLLS	GIDDIER
GERMANIZED*	GESTATIVE	GHAUTS	GI	GIDDIES
GERMANIZES*	GESTATORY	GHAZAL	GIAMBEUX	GIDDIEST
GERMANIZING*	GESTE	GHAZALS	GIANT	GIDDILY
GERMANS	GESTES	GHAZEL	GIANTESS	GIDDINESS
GERMED	GESTIC	GHAZELS	GIANTESSES	GIDDINESSES
GERMEN	GESTICAL*	GHAZI	GIANTHOOD	GIDDUP
GERMENS	GESTS	GHAZIES*	GIANTHOODS	GIDDY
GERMFREE*	GESTURAL	GHAZIS	GIANTISM	GIDDYAP*
GERMICIDE	GESTURE	GHEE	GIANTISMS	GIDDYING
GERMICIDES	GESTURED	GHEES	GIANTLIER	GIDDYUP*
GERMIER*	GESTURER*	GHERAO	GIANTLIEST	GIDGEE
GERMIEST*	GESTURERS*	GHERAOED	GIANTLIKE*	GIDGEES
GERMIN	GESTURES	GHERAOES*	GIANTLY	GIDJEE
GERMINA*	GESTURING	GHERAOING	GIANTRIES	GIDJEES
GERMINAL	GET	GHERAOS	GIANTRY	GIDS
GERMINANT	GETA	GHERKIN	GIANTS	GIE
GERMINATE	GETABLE*	GHERKINS	GIANTSHIP	GIED
GERMINATED	GETAS	GHESSE	GIANTSHIPS	GIEING
GERMINATES	GETATABLE*	GHESSED	GIAOUR	GIEN
GERMINATING	GETAWAY	GHESSES	GIAOURS	GIES
GERMING	GETAWAYS	GHESSING	GIB	GIF
GERMINS	GETS	GHEST	GIBBED	GIFT
GERMPROOF*	GETTABLE	GHETTO	GIBBER	GIFTED
GERMS	GETTER	GHETTOED*	GIBBERED	GIFTEDLY
GERMY*	GETTERED	GHETTOES	GIBBERING	GIFTING
GERNE	GETTERING	GHETTOING*	GIBBERISH	GIFTLESS*
GERNED	GETTERINGS	GHETTOISE	GIBBERISHES	GIFTS
GERNES	GETTERS	GHETTOISED	GIBBERS	GIFTSHOP
GERNING	GETTING	GHETTOISES	GIBBET	GIFTSHOPS
GERONTIC	GETTINGS	GHETTOISING	GIBBETED	GIFTWARE*
GEROPIGA	GETUP*	GHETTOIZE	GIBBETING	GIFTWARES*
GEROPIGAS	GETUPS*	GHETTOIZED	GIBBETS	GIG
GERTCHA	GEUM	GHETTOIZES	GIBBETTED*	GIGA
GERUND	GEUMS	GHETTOIZING	GIBBETTING*	GIGABIT*
GERUNDIAL	GEWGAW	GHETTOS	GIBBING	GIGABITS*
GERUNDIVE	GEWGAWS	GHI	GIBBON	GIGABYTE
GERUNDIVES	GEY	GHIBLI*	GIBBONS	GIGABYTES
GERUNDS	GEYAN	GHIBLIS*	GIBBOSE	GIGAFLOP
GESNERIA	GEYER	GHILGAI	GIBBOSITIES	GIGAFLOPS
GESNERIAD*	GEYEST	GHILGAIS	GIBBOSITY	GIGAHERTZ
GESNERIADS*	GEYSER	GHILLIE	GIBBOUS	GIGAHERTZES
GESNERIAS	GEYSERITE	GHILLIED	GIBBOUSLY	GIGANTEAN
GESSAMINE	GEYSERITES	GHILLIES	GIBBSITE	GIGANTIC
GESSAMINES	GEYSERS	GHILLYING	GIBBSITES	GIGANTISM
GESSE	GHARIAL	GHIS	GIBE	GIGANTISMS
GESSED	GHARIALS	GHOST	GIBED	GIGAS
GESSES	GHARRI	GHOSTED	GIBEL	GIGATON*
GESSING	GHARRIES	GHOSTIER	GIBELS	GIGATONS*
GESSO	GHARRIS	GHOSTIEST	GIBER	GIGAWATT
GESSOED*	GHARRY	GHOSTING	GIBERS	GIGAWATTS
GESSOES	GHAST	GHOSTINGS	GIBES	GIGGED
GEST	GHASTED	GHOSTLIER	GIBING	GIGGING
GESTALT	GHASTFUL	GHOSTLIEST	GIBINGLY	GIGGIT
GESTALTEN*	GHASTFULL	GHOSTLIKE	GIBLET	GIGGITED
GESTALTS	GHASTING	GHOSTLY	GIBLETS	GIGGITING
GESTANT	GHASTLIER	GHOSTS	GIBS	GIGGITS
GESTAPO	GHASTLIEST	GHOSTY	GIBSON*	GIGGLE
GESTAPOS	GHASTLY	GHOUL	GIBSONS*	GIGGLED
GESTATE	GHASTNESS	GHOULIE*	GIBUS	GIGGLER
GESTATED	GHASTNESSES	GHOULIES*	GIBUSES	GIGGLERS
GESTATES	GHASTS	GHOULISH	GID	GIGGLES

GIGGLIER	GILLY	GINGAL	GINSHOPS	GIRNEL
GIGGLIEST	GILLYING	GINGALL	GIO	GIRNELS
GIGGLING	GILLYVOR	GINGALLS	GIOCOSO	GIRNER
GIGGLINGS	GILLYVORS	GINGALS	GIOS	GIRNERS
GIGGLY	GILPEY	GINGELEY*	GIP	GIRNIE
GIGHE*	GILPEYS	GINGELEYS*	GIPON*	GIRNIER
GIGLET	GILPIES	GINGELI*	GIPONS*	GIRNIEST
GIGLETS	GILPY	GINGELIES*	GIPPED*	GIRNING
GIGLOT	GILRAVAGE	GINGELIS*	GIPPER*	GIRNS
GIGLOTS	GILRAVAGED	GINGELLI*	GIPPERS*	GIRO
GIGMAN	GILRAVAGES	GINGELLIES	GIPPIES	GIRON
GIGMANITIES	GILRAVAGING	GINGELLIS*	GIPPING*	GIRONIC
GIGMANITY	GILSONITE	GINGELLY	GIPPO	GIRONS
GIGMEN	GILSONITES	GINGELY*	GIPPOS	GIROS
GIGOLO	GILT	GINGER	GIPPY	GIROSOL
GIGOLOS	GILTCUP	GINGERADE	GIPS	GIROSOLS
GIGOT	GILTCUPS	GINGERADES	GIPSEN	GIRR
GIGOTS	GILTHEAD*	GINGERED	GIPSENS	GIRRS
GIGS	GILTHEADS*	GINGERING	GIPSIED	GIRSH*
GIGUE	GILTS	GINGERLY	GIPSIES	GIRSHES*
GIGUES	GILTWOOD	GINGEROUS	GIPSY	GIRT
GILA	GIMBAL	GINGERS	GIPSYING	GIRTED
GILAS	GIMBALED*	GINGERY	GIRAFFE	GIRTH
GILBERT	GIMBALING*	GINGHAM	GIRAFFES	GIRTHED
GILBERTS	GIMBALLED*	GINGHAMS	GIRAFFID	GIRTHING
GILCUP	GIMBALLING*	GINGILI	GIRAFFINE	GIRTHLINE
GILCUPS	GIMBALS	GINGILIS	GIRAFFISH*	GIRTHLINES
GILD	GIMCRACK	GINGILLI*	GIRAFFOID	GIRTHS
GILDED	GIMCRACKS	GINGILLIS*	GIRANDOLA	GIRTING
GILDEN	GIMEL*	GINGIVA*	GIRANDOLAS	GIRTLINE
GILDER	GIMELS*	GINGIVAE*	GIRANDOLE	GIRTLINES
GILDERS	GIMLET	GINGIVAL	GIRANDOLES	GIRTS
GILDHALL*	GIMLETED	GINGKO	GIRASOL	GIS
GILDHALLS*	GIMLETING	GINGKOES	GIRASOLE	GISARME
GILDING	GIMLETS	GINGLE	GIRASOLES	GISARMES
GILDINGS	GIMMAL	GINGLES	GIRASOLS	GISM
GILDS	GIMMALLED	GINGLYMI	GIRD	GISMO
GILET	GIMMALS	GINGLYMUS	GIRDED	GISMOLOGIES
GILETS	GIMME	GINGS	GIRDER	GISMOLOGY
GILGAI	GIMMER	GINHOUSE	GIRDERS	GISMOS
GILGAIS	GIMMERS	GINHOUSES	GIRDING	GISMS
GILGIE	GIMMES	GINK	GIRDINGS	GIST
GILGIES	GIMMICK	GINKGO	GIRDLE	GISTS
GILL	GIMMICKED	GINKGOES	GIRDLED	GIT
GILLAROO	GIMMICKIER	GINKGOS*	GIRDLER	GITANA
GILLAROOS	GIMMICKIEST	GINKS	GIRDLERS	GITANAS
GILLED	GIMMICKING	GINN	GIRDLES	GITANO
GILLER*	GIMMICKRIES	GINNED	GIRDLING	GITANOS
GILLERS*	GIMMICKRY	GINNEL	GIRDS	GITE
GILLET	GIMMICKS	GINNELS	GIRKIN	GITES
GILLETS	GIMMICKY	GINNER	GIRKINS	GITS
GILLFLIRT	GIMMIE*	GINNERIES	GIRL	GITTERN
GILLFLIRTS	GIMMIES*	GINNERS	GIRLHOOD	GITTERNED
GILLIE	GIMMOR	GINNERY	GIRLHOODS	GITTERNING
GILLIED	GIMMORS	GINNIER	GIRLIE	GITTERNS
GILLIES	GIMP	GINNIEST	GIRLIES	GITTIN*
GILLING	GIMPED	GINNING	GIRLISH	GIUST
GILLION	GIMPIER	GINNINGS*	GIRLISHLY	GIUSTED
GILLIONS	GIMPIEST	GINNY	GIRLOND	GIUSTING
GILLNET*	GIMPING	GINORMOUS	GIRLONDS	GIUSTO
GILLNETS*	GIMPS	GINS	GIRLS	GIUSTS
GILLNETTED*	GIMPY	GINSENG	GIRLY	GIVE
GILLNETTING*	GIN	GINSENGS	GIRN	GIVEABLE*
GILLS	GING	GINSHOP	GIRNED	GIVEAWAY

The Chambers Dictionary is the authority for many longer words; see Introduction, page ix

GIVEAWAYS	GLADFUL	GLAMS	GLAUMING	GLEEKS
GIVEBACK*	GLADIATE	GLANCE	GLAUMS	GLEEMAN
GIVEBACKS*	GLADIATOR	GLANCED	GLAUR	GLEEMEN
GIVED	GLADIATORS	GLANCER*	GLAURIER	GLEES
GIVEN	GLADIER	GLANCERS*	GLAURIEST	GLEESOME
GIVENNESS	GLADIEST	GLANCES	GLAURS	GLEET
GIVENNESSES	GLADIOLA*	GLANCING	GLAURY	GLEETED
GIVENS*	GLADIOLAS*	GLANCINGS	GLAZE	GLEETIER
GIVER	GLADIOLE	GLAND	GLAZED	GLEETIEST
GIVERS	GLADIOLES	GLANDERED	GLAZEN	GLEETING
GIVES	GLADIOLI	GLANDERS	GLAZER	GLEETS
GIVING	GLADIOLUS	GLANDES	GLAZERS	GLEETY
GIVINGS	GLADIOLUSES	GLANDLESS*	GLAZES	GLEG
GIZMO	GLADIUS	GLANDS	GLAZIER	GLEGGER
GIZMOLOGIES	GLADIUSES	GLANDULAR	GLAZIERIES*	GLEGGEST
GIZMOLOGY	GLADLIER*	GLANDULE	GLAZIERS	GLEGLY*
GIZMOS	GLADLIEST*	GLANDULES	GLAZIERY*	GLEGNESS*
GIZZ	GLADLY	GLANS	GLAZIEST	GLEGNESSES*
GIZZARD	GLADNESS	GLARE	GLAZING	GLEI
GIZZARDS	GLADNESSES	GLAREAL	GLAZINGS	GLEIS
GIZZEN	GLADS	GLARED	GLAZY	GLEN
GIZZENED	GLADSOME	GLAREOUS	GLEAM	GLENGARRIES
GIZZENING	GLADSOMER*	GLARES	GLEAMED	GLENGARRY
GIZZENS	GLADSOMEST*	GLARIER	GLEAMER*	GLENLIKE*
GIZZES	GLADSTONE*	GLARIEST	GLEAMERS*	GLENOID
GJETOST*	GLADSTONES*	GLARING	GLEAMIER	GLENOIDAL
GJETOSTS*	GLADY	GLARINGLY	GLEAMIEST	GLENOIDS
GJU	GLAIK	GLARY	GLEAMING	GLENS
GJUS	GLAIKET	GLASNOST	GLEAMINGS	GLENT
GLABELLA	GLAIKIT	GLASNOSTS	GLEAMS	GLENTED
GLABELLAE	GLAIKS	GLASS	GLEAMY	GLENTING
GLABELLAR	GLAIR	GLASSED	GLEAN	GLENTS
GLABRATE	GLAIRE*	GLASSEN	GLEANABLE*	GLEY
GLABROUS	GLAIRED	GLASSES	GLEANED	GLEYED
GLACE	GLAIREOUS	GLASSFUL	GLEANER	GLEYING
GLACEED	GLAIRES*	GLASSFULS	GLEANERS	GLEYINGS*
GLACEING	GLAIRIER	GLASSIE*	GLEANING	GLEYS
GLACES	GLAIRIEST	GLASSIER	GLEANINGS	GLIA
GLACIAL	GLAIRIN	GLASSIES*	GLEANS	GLIADIN
GLACIALLY*	GLAIRING	GLASSIEST	GLEAVE	GLIADINE
GLACIALS	GLAIRINS	GLASSIFIED	GLEAVES	GLIADINES
GLACIATE	GLAIRS	GLASSIFIES	GLEBA*	GLIADINS
GLACIATED	GLAIRY	GLASSIFY	GLEBAE*	GLIAL
GLACIATES	GLAIVE	GLASSIFYING	GLEBE	GLIAS
GLACIATING	GLAIVED	GLASSILY	GLEBES	GLIB
GLACIER	GLAIVES	GLASSINE	GLEBOUS	GLIBBED
GLACIERS	GLAM	GLASSINES	GLEBY	GLIBBER
GLACIS	GLAMOR	GLASSING	GLED	GLIBBERY
GLACISES	GLAMORED	GLASSLESS*	GLEDE	GLIBBEST
GLAD	GLAMORING	GLASSLIKE	GLEDES	GLIBBING
GLADDED	GLAMORISE	GLASSMAN	GLEDGE	GLIBLY
GLADDEN	GLAMORISED	GLASSMEN	GLEDGED	GLIBNESS
GLADDENED	GLAMORISES	GLASSWARE	GLEDGES	GLIBNESSES
GLADDENING	GLAMORISING	GLASSWARES	GLEDGING	GLIBS
GLADDENS	GLAMORIZE	GLASSWORK	GLEDS	GLID
GLADDER	GLAMORIZED	GLASSWORKS	GLEE	GLIDDER
GLADDEST	GLAMORIZES	GLASSWORT	GLEED	GLIDDERY
GLADDIE	GLAMORIZING	GLASSWORTS	GLEEDS	GLIDDEST
GLADDIES	GLAMOROUS	GLASSY	GLEEFUL	GLIDE
GLADDING	GLAMORS	GLAUCOMA	GLEEFULLY*	GLIDED
GLADDON	GLAMOUR	GLAUCOMAS	GLEEING	GLIDER
GLADDONS	GLAMOURED	GLAUCOUS	GLEEK	GLIDERS
GLADE	GLAMOURING	GLAUM	GLEEKED	GLIDES
GLADES	GLAMOURS	GLAUMED	GLEEKING	GLIDING

Words marked with an asterisk are from OTCWL

GLIDINGLY	GLITTERIEST	GLOBULITE	GLORIOSAS	GLOZE
GLIDINGS	GLITTERING	GLOBULITES	GLORIOUS	GLOZED
GLIFF	GLITTERINGS	GLOBULOUS	GLORY	GLOZES
GLIFFING	GLITTERS	GLOBY	GLORYING	GLOZING
GLIFFINGS	GLITTERY	GLOCHID*	GLOSS	GLOZINGS
GLIFFS	GLITZ	GLOCHIDIA*	GLOSSA	GLUCAGON
GLIFT	GLITZES	GLOCHIDIUM*	GLOSSAE	GLUCAGONS
GLIFTS	GLITZIER	GLOCHIDS*	GLOSSAL	GLUCAN*
GLIKE	GLITZIEST	GLODE	GLOSSARIES	GLUCANS*
GLIKES	GLITZILY	GLOGG	GLOSSARY	GLUCINA
GLIM	GLITZY	GLOGGS	GLOSSAS	GLUCINAS
GLIME*	GLOAM*	GLOIRE	GLOSSATOR	GLUCINIC*
GLIMED*	GLOAMING	GLOIRES	GLOSSATORS	GLUCINIUM
GLIMES*	GLOAMINGS	GLOM	GLOSSED	GLUCINIUMS
GLIMING*	GLOAMS*	GLOMERA*	GLOSSEME	GLUCINUM
GLIMMER	GLOAT	GLOMERATE	GLOSSEMES	GLUCINUMS
GLIMMERED	GLOATED	GLOMERATED	GLOSSER	GLUCONATE*
GLIMMERING	GLOATER	GLOMERATES	GLOSSERS	GLUCONATES*
GLIMMERINGS	GLOATERS	GLOMERATING	GLOSSES	GLUCOSE
GLIMMERS	GLOATING	GLOMERULE	GLOSSIER	GLUCOSES
GLIMMERY	GLOATS	GLOMERULES	GLOSSIES	GLUCOSIC
GLIMPSE	GLOB	GLOMERULI	GLOSSIEST	GLUCOSIDE
GLIMPSED	GLOBAL	GLOMERULUS*	GLOSSILY	GLUCOSIDES
GLIMPSER*	GLOBALISE	GLOMMED	GLOSSINA	GLUE
GLIMPSERS*	GLOBALISED	GLOMMING	GLOSSINAS	GLUED
GLIMPSES	GLOBALISES	GLOMS	GLOSSING	GLUEING*
GLIMPSING	GLOBALISING	GLOMUS*	GLOSSITIS	GLUELIKE*
GLIMS	GLOBALISM	GLONOIN	GLOSSITISES	GLUEPOT*
GLINT	GLOBALISMS	GLONOINS	GLOSSY	GLUEPOTS*
GLINTED	GLOBALIST*	GLOOM	GLOST*	GLUER
GLINTING	GLOBALISTS*	GLOOMED	GLOSTS*	GLUERS
GLINTS	GLOBALIZE	GLOOMFUL	GLOTTAL	GLUES
GLIOMA	GLOBALIZED	GLOOMIER	GLOTTIC	GLUEY
GLIOMAS	GLOBALIZES	GLOOMIEST	GLOTTIDES	GLUEYNESS
GLIOMATA	GLOBALIZING	GLOOMILY	GLOTTIS	GLUEYNESSES
GLIOSES	GLOBALLY	GLOOMING	GLOTTISES	GLUG
GLIOSIS	GLOBATE	GLOOMINGS	GLOUT	GLUGGED
GLISK	GLOBATED	GLOOMS	GLOUTED	GLUGGING
GLISKS	GLOBBIER	GLOOMY	GLOUTING	GLUGS
GLISSADE	GLOBBIEST	GLOOP	GLOUTS	GLUHWEIN
GLISSADED	GLOBBY	GLOOPED	GLOVE	GLUHWEINS
GLISSADER*	GLOBE	GLOOPIER	GLOVED	GLUIER
GLISSADERS*	GLOBED	GLOOPIEST	GLOVER	GLUIEST
GLISSADES	GLOBEFISH*	GLOOPING	GLOVERS	GLUILY*
GLISSADING	GLOBEFISHES*	GLOOPS	GLOVES	GLUING
GLISSANDI	GLOBES	GLOOPY	GLOVING	GLUISH
GLISSANDO	GLOBIN	GLOP	GLOVINGS	GLUM
GLISSANDOS	GLOBING	GLOPPED*	GLOW	GLUME
GLISTEN	GLOBINS	GLOPPING*	GLOWED	GLUMELLA
GLISTENED	GLOBOID	GLOPPY*	GLOWER	GLUMELLAS
GLISTENING	GLOBOIDS	GLOPS	GLOWERED	GLUMES
GLISTENS	GLOBOSE	GLORIA	GLOWERING	GLUMLY
GLISTER	GLOBOSES	GLORIAS	GLOWERS	GLUMMER
GLISTERED	GLOBOSITIES	GLORIED	GLOWFLIES*	GLUMMEST
GLISTERING	GLOBOSITY	GLORIES	GLOWFLY*	GLUMNESS
GLISTERS	GLOBOUS	GLORIFIED	GLOWING	GLUMNESSES
GLIT	GLOBS	GLORIFIER*	GLOWINGLY	GLUMPIER
GLITCH	GLOBULAR	GLORIFIERS*	GLOWLAMP	GLUMPIEST
GLITCHES	GLOBULE	GLORIFIES	GLOWLAMPS	GLUMPILY*
GLITCHY*	GLOBULES	GLORIFY	GLOWS	GLUMPISH
GLITS	GLOBULET	GLORIFYING	GLOWWORM*	GLUMPS
GLITTER	GLOBULETS	GLORIOLE	GLOWWORMS*	GLUMPY
GLITTERED	GLOBULIN	GLORIOLES	GLOXINIA	GLUNCH*
GLITTERIER	GLOBULINS	GLORIOSA	GLOXINIAS	GLUNCHED*

GLUNCHES*	GLYCYLS*	GNOMISH	GOB	GODHEAD
GLUNCHING*	GLYPH	GNOMIST	GOBAN*	GODHEADS
GLUON	GLYPHIC	GNOMISTS	GOBANG	GODHOOD
GLUONS	GLYPHS	GNOMON	GOBANGS	GODHOODS
GLUT	GLYPTIC	GNOMONIC	GOBANS*	GODLESS
GLUTAEAL	GLYPTICS	GNOMONICS	GOBBED	GODLESSLY
GLUTAEI	GMELINITE	GNOMONS	GOBBELINE	GODLIER
GLUTAEUS	GMELINITES	GNOSES	GOBBELINES	GODLIEST
GLUTAMATE	GNAR	GNOSIS	GOBBET	GODLIKE
GLUTAMATES	GNARL	GNOSTIC	GOBBETS	GODLILY
GLUTAMINE	GNARLED	GNOSTICAL	GOBBI	GODLINESS
GLUTAMINES	GNARLIER	GNU	GOBBING	GODLINESSES
GLUTEAL	GNARLIEST	GNUS	GOBBLE	GODLING
GLUTEI	GNARLING	GO	GOBBLED	GODLINGS
GLUTELIN	GNARLS	GOA	GOBBLER	GODLY
GLUTELINS	GNARLY	GOAD	GOBBLERS	GODMOTHER
GLUTEN	GNARR	GOADED	GOBBLES	GODMOTHERS
GLUTENOUS	GNARRED	GOADING	GOBBLING	GODOWN
GLUTENS	GNARRING	GOADLIKE*	GOBBO	GODOWNS
GLUTEUS	GNARRS	GOADS	GOBIES	GODPARENT
GLUTINOUS	GNARS	GOADSMAN	GOBIID	GODPARENTS
GLUTS	GNASH	GOADSMEN	GOBIIDS	GODROON
GLUTTED	GNASHED	GOADSTER	GOBIOID	GODROONED
GLUTTING	GNASHER	GOADSTERS	GOBIOIDS*	GODROONS
GLUTTON	GNASHERS	GOAF	GOBLET	GODS
GLUTTONIES	GNASHES	GOAFS	GOBLETS	GODSEND
GLUTTONS	GNASHING	GOAL	GOBLIN	GODSENDS
GLUTTONY	GNAT	GOALBALL	GOBLINS	GODSHIP
GLYCAN*	GNATHAL	GOALBALLS	GOBO	GODSHIPS
GLYCANS*	GNATHIC	GOALED	GOBOES	GODSO
GLYCERIA	GNATHION*	GOALIE	GOBONEE*	GODSON
GLYCERIAS	GNATHIONS*	GOALIES	GOBONY	GODSONS
GLYCERIC	GNATHITE	GOALING	GOBOS	GODSOS
GLYCERIDE	GNATHITES	GOALLESS	GOBS	GODSPEED
GLYCERIDES	GNATHONIC	GOALMOUTH	GOBSHITE	GODSPEEDS
GLYCERIN	GNATLIKE*	GOALMOUTHS	GOBSHITES	GODWARD
GLYCERINE	GNATLING	GOALPOST	GOBURRA	GODWARDS
GLYCERINES	GNATLINGS	GOALPOSTS	GOBURRAS	GODWIT
GLYCERINS	GNATS	GOALS	GOBY	GODWITS
GLYCEROL	GNATTIER*	GOALWARD*	GOD	GOE
GLYCEROLS	GNATTIEST*	GOANNA	GODCHILD	GOEL
GLYCERYL	GNATTY*	GOANNAS	GODCHILDREN	GOELS
GLYCERYLS	GNAW	GOARY	GODDAM	GOER
GLYCIN	GNAWABLE*	GOAS	GODDAMMED*	GOERS
GLYCINE	GNAWED	GOAT	GODDAMMING*	GOES
GLYCINES	GNAWER	GOATEE	GODDAMN	GOETHITE
GLYCINS	GNAWERS	GOATEED	GODDAMNED	GOETHITES
GLYCOCOLL	GNAWING	GOATEES	GODDAMNING*	GOETIC
GLYCOCOLLS	GNAWINGS*	GOATFISH	GODDAMNS*	GOETIES
GLYCOGEN	GNAWN	GOATFISHES	GODDAMS*	GOETY
GLYCOGENS	GNAWS	GOATHERD	GODDED	GOEY
GLYCOL	GNEISS	GOATHERDS	GODDEN	GOFER
GLYCOLIC	GNEISSES	GOATIER	GODDENS	GOFERS
GLYCOLLIC	GNEISSIC	GOATIEST	GODDESS	GOFF
GLYCOLS	GNEISSOID	GOATISH	GODDESSES	GOFFED
GLYCONIC	GNEISSOSE	GOATLIKE*	GODDING	GOFFER
GLYCONICS	GNOCCHI	GOATLING	GODET	GOFFERED
GLYCOSE	GNOCCHIS	GOATLINGS	GODETIA	GOFFERING
GLYCOSES	GNOMAE	GOATS	GODETIAS	GOFFERINGS
GLYCOSIDE	GNOME	GOATSKIN	GODETS	GOFFERS
GLYCOSIDES	GNOMELIKE*	GOATSKINS	GODFATHER	GOFFING
GLYCOSYL	GNOMES	GOATWEED	GODFATHERED*	GOFFS
GLYCOSYLS	GNOMIC	GOATWEEDS	GODFATHERING*	GOGGLE
GLYCYL*	GNOMICAL*	GOATY	GODFATHERS	GOGGLED

Words marked with an asterisk are from OTCWL

GOGGLER
GOGGLERS
GOGGLES
GOGGLIER
GOGGLIEST
GOGGLING
GOGGLINGS
GOGGLY
GOGLET
GOGLETS
GOGO
GOGOS*
GOIER
GOIEST
GOING
GOINGS
GOITER
GOITERS
GOITRE
GOITRED
GOITRES
GOITROGEN*
GOITROGENS*
GOITROUS
GOLCONDA*
GOLCONDAS*
GOLD
GOLDARN
GOLDARNS*
GOLDBRICK*
GOLDBRICKED*
GOLDBRICKING*
GOLDBRICKS*
GOLDBUG*
GOLDBUGS*
GOLDCREST
GOLDCRESTS
GOLDEN
GOLDENED
GOLDENER
GOLDENEST
GOLDENEYE*
GOLDENEYES*
GOLDENING
GOLDENLY
GOLDENROD
GOLDENRODS
GOLDENS
GOLDER
GOLDEST
GOLDEYE
GOLDEYES
GOLDFIELD
GOLDFIELDS
GOLDFINCH
GOLDFINCHES
GOLDFINNIES
GOLDFINNY
GOLDFISH
GOLDFISHES
GOLDIER
GOLDIEST
GOLDISH
GOLDLESS

GOLDMINER
GOLDMINERS
GOLDS
GOLDSINNIES
GOLDSINNY
GOLDSIZE
GOLDSIZES
GOLDSMITH
GOLDSMITHS
GOLDSPINK
GOLDSPINKS
GOLDSTICK
GOLDSTICKS
GOLDSTONE
GOLDSTONES
GOLDURN*
GOLDURNS*
GOLDY
GOLE
GOLEM
GOLEMS
GOLES
GOLF
GOLFED
GOLFER
GOLFERS
GOLFIANA
GOLFIANAS
GOLFING
GOLFINGS
GOLFS
GOLGOTHA*
GOLGOTHAS*
GOLIARD
GOLIARDIC
GOLIARDIES
GOLIARDS
GOLIARDY
GOLIAS
GOLIASED
GOLIASES
GOLIASING
GOLLAN
GOLLAND
GOLLANDS
GOLLANS
GOLLAR
GOLLARED
GOLLARING
GOLLARS
GOLLER
GOLLERED
GOLLERING
GOLLERS
GOLLIES
GOLLIWOG
GOLLIWOGG*
GOLLIWOGGS*
GOLLIWOGS
GOLLOP
GOLLOPED
GOLLOPING
GOLLOPS
GOLLY

GOLLYWOG
GOLLYWOGS
GOLOMYNKA
GOLOMYNKAS
GOLOSH
GOLOSHE*
GOLOSHED
GOLOSHES
GOLOSHING
GOLOSHOES
GOLP
GOLPE
GOLPES
GOLPS
GOMBEEN
GOMBEENS
GOMBO
GOMBOS
GOMBRO
GOMBROON*
GOMBROONS*
GOMBROS
GOMERAL
GOMERALS
GOMEREL*
GOMERELS*
GOMERIL
GOMERILS
GOMOKU
GOMOKUS
GOMPA
GOMPAS
GOMPHOSES
GOMPHOSIS
GOMUTI
GOMUTIS
GOMUTO
GOMUTOS
GON
GONAD
GONADAL
GONADIAL
GONADIC
GONADS
GONDELAY
GONDELAYS
GONDOLA
GONDOLAS
GONDOLIER
GONDOLIERS
GONE
GONEF*
GONEFS*
GONENESS
GONENESSES
GONER
GONERS
GONFALON
GONFALONS
GONFANON
GONFANONS
GONG
GONGED
GONGING

GONGLIKE*
GONGS
GONGSTER
GONGSTERS
GONIA
GONIATITE
GONIATITES
GONIDIA
GONIDIAL
GONIDIC
GONIDIUM
GONIF*
GONIFF*
GONIFFS*
GONIFS*
GONION
GONIUM*
GONK
GONKS
GONNA
GONOCOCCI
GONOCOCCUS*
GONOCYTE
GONOCYTES
GONOF*
GONOFS*
GONOPH*
GONOPHORE
GONOPHORES
GONOPHS*
GONOPORE*
GONOPORES*
GONORRHEA
GONORRHEAS
GONS
GONYS
GONYSES
GONZO
GOO
GOOBER
GOOBERS
GOOD
GOODBY*
GOODBYE*
GOODBYES*
GOODBYS*
GOODFACED
GOODIE*
GOODIER
GOODIES
GOODIEST
GOODINESS
GOODINESSES
GOODISH
GOODLIER
GOODLIEST
GOODLY
GOODMAN
GOODMEN
GOODNESS
GOODNESSES
GOODNIGHT
GOODNIGHTS
GOODS

GOODSIRE
GOODSIRES
GOODTIME
GOODWIFE
GOODWILL
GOODWILLS
GOODWIVES
GOODY
GOODYEAR
GOODYEARS
GOOEY
GOOEYNESS*
GOOEYNESSES*
GOOF
GOOFBALL
GOOFBALLS
GOOFED
GOOFIER
GOOFIEST
GOOFILY
GOOFINESS
GOOFINESSES
GOOFING
GOOFS
GOOFY
GOOGLE
GOOGLED
GOOGLES
GOOGLIES
GOOGLING
GOOGLY
GOOGOL
GOOGOLS
GOOIER
GOOIEST
GOOK
GOOKS
GOOKY*
GOOL
GOOLD
GOOLDS
GOOLEY
GOOLEYS
GOOLIE
GOOLIES
GOOLS
GOOLY
GOOMBAH*
GOOMBAHS*
GOOMBAY*
GOOMBAYS*
GOON
GOONDA
GOONDAS
GOONEY
GOONEYS
GOONIE*
GOONIES*
GOONS
GOONY*
GOOP
GOOPIER
GOOPIEST
GOOPS

GOOPY	GORGER*	GOS	GOTHICIZE	GOVERNALLS
GOOR	GORGERIN	GOSH	GOTHICIZED	GOVERNED
GOORAL*	GORGERINS	GOSHAWK	GOTHICIZES	GOVERNESS
GOORALS*	GORGERS*	GOSHAWKS	GOTHICIZING	GOVERNESSED
GOOROO	GORGES	GOSHT	GOTHICS*	GOVERNESSES
GOOROOS	GORGET	GOSHTS	GOTHITE	GOVERNESSING
GOORS	GORGETED*	GOSLARITE	GOTHITES	GOVERNING
GOOS	GORGETS	GOSLARITES	GOTTA	GOVERNOR
GOOSANDER	GORGIA	GOSLET	GOTTEN	GOVERNORS
GOOSANDERS	GORGIAS	GOSLETS	GOUACHE	GOVERNS
GOOSE	GORGING	GOSLING	GOUACHES	GOVS
GOOSED	GORGIO	GOSLINGS	GOUGE	GOWAN
GOOSEFISH*	GORGIOS	GOSPEL	GOUGED	GOWANED
GOOSEFISHES*	GORGON	GOSPELER*	GOUGER*	GOWANS
GOOSEFOOT	GORGONEIA	GOSPELERS*	GOUGERE	GOWANY
GOOSEFOOTS	GORGONIAN	GOSPELISE	GOUGERES	GOWD
GOOSEGOB	GORGONIANS	GOSPELISED	GOUGERS*	GOWDER
GOOSEGOBS	GORGONISE	GOSPELISES	GOUGES	GOWDEST
GOOSEGOG	GORGONISED	GOSPELISING	GOUGING	GOWDS
GOOSEGOGS	GORGONISES	GOSPELIZE	GOUJEERS	GOWDSPINK
GOOSEHERD	GORGONISING	GOSPELIZED	GOUJONS	GOWDSPINKS
GOOSEHERDS	GORGONIZE	GOSPELIZES	GOUK	GOWF
GOOSENECK*	GORGONIZED	GOSPELIZING	GOUKS	GOWFED
GOOSENECKS*	GORGONIZES	GOSPELLED	GOULASH	GOWFER
GOOSERIES	GORGONIZING	GOSPELLER	GOULASHES	GOWFERS
GOOSERY	GORGONS	GOSPELLERS	GOURA	GOWFING
GOOSES	GORHEN*	GOSPELLING	GOURAMI	GOWFS
GOOSEY	GORHENS*	GOSPELS	GOURAMIES*	GOWK
GOOSEYS	GORIER	GOSPODAR	GOURAMIS	GOWKS
GOOSIER	GORIEST	GOSPODARS	GOURAS	GOWL
GOOSIES	GORILLA	GOSPORT*	GOURD	GOWLAN
GOOSIEST	GORILLAS	GOSPORTS*	GOURDE	GOWLAND
GOOSING	GORILLIAN	GOSSAMER	GOURDES	GOWLANDS
GOOSY	GORILLINE	GOSSAMERS	GOURDIER	GOWLANS
GOPAK	GORILLOID	GOSSAMERY	GOURDIEST	GOWLED
GOPAKS	GORILY	GOSSAN	GOURDS	GOWLING
GOPHER	GORINESS	GOSSANS	GOURDY	GOWLS
GOPHERED	GORINESSES	GOSSE	GOURMAND	GOWN
GOPHERING	GORING	GOSSES	GOURMANDS	GOWNBOY
GOPHERS	GORINGS	GOSSIB	GOURMET	GOWNBOYS
GOPURA	GORM	GOSSIBS	GOURMETS	GOWNED
GOPURAM	GORMAND	GOSSIP	GOUSTIER	GOWNING
GOPURAMS	GORMANDS	GOSSIPED	GOUSTIEST	GOWNMAN
GOPURAS	GORMED	GOSSIPER*	GOUSTROUS	GOWNMEN
GOR*	GORMIER	GOSSIPERS*	GOUSTY	GOWNS
GORAL	GORMIEST	GOSSIPING	GOUT	GOWNSMAN
GORALS	GORMING	GOSSIPINGS	GOUTFLIES	GOWNSMEN
GORAMIES	GORMLESS	GOSSIPPED*	GOUTFLY	GOWPEN
GORAMY	GORMS	GOSSIPPING*	GOUTIER	GOWPENFUL
GORBELLIES*	GORMY	GOSSIPRIES	GOUTIEST	GOWPENFULS
GORBELLY*	GORP	GOSSIPRY	GOUTILY*	GOWPENS
GORBLIMEY	GORPED	GOSSIPS	GOUTINESS	GOX*
GORBLIMY	GORPING	GOSSIPY	GOUTINESSES	GOXES*
GORCOCK	GORPS	GOSSOON	GOUTS	GOY
GORCOCKS	GORSE	GOSSOONS	GOUTTE	GOYIM
GORCROW	GORSEDD	GOSSYPINE	GOUTTES	GOYISCH
GORCROWS	GORSEDDS	GOSSYPOL	GOUTWEED	GOYISH
GORE	GORSES	GOSSYPOLS	GOUTWEEDS	GOYS
GORED	GORSIER	GOT	GOUTWORT	GOZZAN
GORES	GORSIEST	GOTHIC	GOUTWORTS	GOZZANS
GORGE	GORSOON	GOTHICISE	GOUTY	GRAAL
GORGED	GORSOONS	GOTHICISED	GOV	GRAALS
GORGEDLY*	GORSY	GOTHICISES	GOVERN	GRAB
GORGEOUS	GORY	GOTHICISING	GOVERNALL	GRABBED

Words marked with an asterisk are from OTCWL

GRABBER	GRADINS	GRALLOCH	GRANDMA	GRANTSMEN*
GRABBERS	GRADS	GRALLOCHED	GRANDMAMA	GRANULAR
GRABBIER*	GRADUAL	GRALLOCHING	GRANDMAMAS	GRANULARY
GRABBIEST*	GRADUALLY	GRALLOCHS	GRANDMAS	GRANULATE
GRABBING	GRADUALS	GRAM	GRANDNESS	GRANULATED
GRABBLE	GRADUAND	GRAMA	GRANDNESSES	GRANULATES
GRABBLED	GRADUANDS	GRAMARIES	GRANDPA	GRANULATING
GRABBLER	GRADUATE	GRAMARY	GRANDPAPA	GRANULE
GRABBLERS	GRADUATED	GRAMARYE	GRANDPAPAS	GRANULES
GRABBLES	GRADUATES	GRAMARYES	GRANDPAS	GRANULITE
GRABBLING	GRADUATING	GRAMAS	GRANDS	GRANULITES
GRABBY*	GRADUATOR	GRAMASH	GRANDSIR*	GRANULOMA
GRABEN	GRADUATORS	GRAMASHES	GRANDSIRE	GRANULOMAS
GRABENS	GRADUS	GRAME	GRANDSIRES	GRANULOMATA
GRABS	GRADUSES	GRAMERCIES	GRANDSIRS*	GRANULOSE
GRACE	GRAECIZE*	GRAMERCY	GRANDSON	GRANULOUS
GRACED	GRAECIZED*	GRAMES	GRANDSONS	GRANUM*
GRACEFUL	GRAECIZES*	GRAMMA	GRANFER	GRAPE
GRACEFULLER*	GRAECIZING*	GRAMMAR	GRANFERS	GRAPED
GRACEFULLEST*	GRAFF	GRAMMARS	GRANGE	GRAPELESS
GRACELESS	GRAFFED	GRAMMAS	GRANGER	GRAPELIKE*
GRACES	GRAFFING	GRAMMATIC	GRANGERS	GRAPERIES
GRACILE	GRAFFITI	GRAMME	GRANGES	GRAPERY
GRACILES*	GRAFFITIS	GRAMMES	GRANITA	GRAPES
GRACILIS*	GRAFFITO	GRAMOCHE	GRANITAS	GRAPESEED
GRACILITIES	GRAFFS	GRAMOCHES	GRANITE	GRAPESEEDS
GRACILITY	GRAFT	GRAMP*	GRANITES	GRAPESHOT
GRACING	GRAFTAGE*	GRAMPS*	GRANITIC	GRAPESHOTS
GRACIOSO	GRAFTAGES*	GRAMPUS	GRANITISE	GRAPETREE
GRACIOSOS	GRAFTED	GRAMPUSES	GRANITISED	GRAPETREES
GRACIOUS	GRAFTER	GRAMS	GRANITISES	GRAPEVINE
GRACIOUSES	GRAFTERS	GRAN	GRANITISING	GRAPEVINES
GRACKLE	GRAFTING	GRANA*	GRANITITE	GRAPEY
GRACKLES	GRAFTINGS	GRANARIES	GRANITITES	GRAPH
GRAD	GRAFTS	GRANARY	GRANITIZE	GRAPHED
GRADABLE	GRAHAM*	GRAND	GRANITIZED	GRAPHEME
GRADABLES	GRAHAMS*	GRANDAD	GRANITIZES	GRAPHEMES
GRADATE	GRAIL	GRANDADDIES	GRANITIZING	GRAPHEMIC
GRADATED	GRAILE	GRANDADDY	GRANITOID	GRAPHEMICS
GRADATES	GRAILES	GRANDADS	GRANIVORE	GRAPHIC
GRADATIM	GRAILS	GRANDAM	GRANIVORES	GRAPHICAL
GRADATING	GRAIN	GRANDAME*	GRANNAM	GRAPHICLY
GRADATION	GRAINAGE	GRANDAMES*	GRANNAMS	GRAPHICS
GRADATIONS	GRAINAGES	GRANDAMS	GRANNIE	GRAPHING
GRADATORY	GRAINE	GRANDAUNT*	GRANNIED	GRAPHITE
GRADDAN	GRAINED	GRANDAUNTS*	GRANNIEING	GRAPHITES
GRADDANED	GRAINER	GRANDBABIES*	GRANNIES	GRAPHITIC
GRADDANING	GRAINERS	GRANDBABY*	GRANNY	GRAPHIUM
GRADDANS	GRAINES	GRANDDAD	GRANNYING	GRAPHIUMS
GRADE	GRAINIER	GRANDDADS	GRANOLA	GRAPHS
GRADED	GRAINIEST	GRANDDAM*	GRANOLAS	GRAPIER
GRADELESS*	GRAINING	GRANDDAMS*	GRANS	GRAPIEST
GRADELY	GRAININGS	GRANDE	GRANT	GRAPINESS*
GRADER	GRAINS	GRANDEE	GRANTABLE	GRAPINESSES*
GRADERS	GRAINY	GRANDEES	GRANTED	GRAPING
GRADES	GRAIP	GRANDER	GRANTEE	GRAPLE
GRADIENT	GRAIPS	GRANDEST	GRANTEES	GRAPLES
GRADIENTS	GRAITH	GRANDEUR	GRANTER	GRAPLIN*
GRADIN	GRAITHED	GRANDEURS	GRANTERS	GRAPLINE*
GRADINE	GRAITHING	GRANDIOSE	GRANTING	GRAPLINES*
GRADINES	GRAITHLY	GRANDIOSO*	GRANTOR	GRAPLINS*
GRADING	GRAITHS	GRANDKID*	GRANTORS	GRAPNEL
GRADINI	GRAKLE	GRANDKIDS*	GRANTS	GRAPNELS
GRADINO	GRAKLES	GRANDLY	GRANTSMAN*	GRAPPA

The Chambers Dictionary is the authority for many longer words; see Introduction, page ix

GRAPPAS	GRATINEES*	GRAVITATE	GREASILY	GREENHAND
GRAPPLE	GRATING	GRAVITATED	GREASING	GREENHANDS
GRAPPLED	GRATINGLY	GRAVITATES	GREASY	GREENHEAD*
GRAPPLER*	GRATINGS	GRAVITATING	GREAT	GREENHEADS*
GRAPPLERS*	GRATINS	GRAVITIES	GREATCOAT	GREENHORN
GRAPPLES	GRATIS	GRAVITON	GREATCOATS	GREENHORNS
GRAPPLING	GRATITUDE	GRAVITONS	GREATEN	GREENIE
GRAPPLINGS*	GRATITUDES	GRAVITY	GREATENED	GREENIER
GRAPY	GRATTOIR	GRAVLAKS*	GREATENING	GREENIES
GRASP	GRATTOIRS	GRAVLAX	GREATENS	GREENIEST
GRASPABLE	GRATUITIES	GRAVLAXES	GREATER	GREENING
GRASPED	GRATUITY	GRAVURE	GREATEST	GREENINGS
GRASPER	GRATULANT	GRAVURES	GREATLY	GREENISH
GRASPERS	GRATULATE	GRAVY	GREATNESS	GREENLET
GRASPING	GRATULATED	GRAY	GREATNESSES	GREENLETS
GRASPLESS	GRATULATES	GRAYBACK*	GREATS	GREENLING*
GRASPS	GRATULATING	GRAYBACKS*	GREAVE	GREENLINGS*
GRASS	GRAUNCH	GRAYBEARD*	GREAVED	GREENLY
GRASSED	GRAUNCHED	GRAYBEARDS*	GREAVES	GREENMAIL
GRASSER	GRAUNCHER	GRAYED	GREAVING	GREENMAILED*
GRASSERS	GRAUNCHERS	GRAYER	GREBE	GREENMAILING*
GRASSES	GRAUNCHES	GRAYEST	GREBES	GREENMAILS
GRASSHOOK	GRAUNCHING	GRAYFISH*	GRECE	GREENNESS
GRASSHOOKS	GRAUPEL	GRAYFISHES*	GRECES	GREENNESSES
GRASSIER	GRAUPELS	GRAYFLIES	GRECIAN	GREENROOM
GRASSIEST	GRAVADLAX	GRAYFLY	GRECIANS	GREENROOMS
GRASSILY*	GRAVADLAXES	GRAYING	GRECIZE*	GREENS
GRASSING	GRAVAMEN	GRAYISH*	GRECIZED*	GREENSAND
GRASSINGS	GRAVAMENS*	GRAYLAG*	GRECIZES*	GREENSANDS
GRASSLAND	GRAVAMINA	GRAYLAGS*	GRECIZING*	GREENSICK*
GRASSLANDS	GRAVE	GRAYLE	GRECQUE	GREENTH
GRASSLESS*	GRAVED	GRAYLES	GRECQUES	GREENTHS
GRASSLIKE*	GRAVEL	GRAYLING	GREE	GREENWASH
GRASSROOT*	GRAVELED*	GRAYLINGS	GREECE	GREENWASHED
GRASSUM	GRAVELESS	GRAYLY*	GREECES	GREENWASHES
GRASSUMS	GRAVELING*	GRAYMAIL*	GREED	GREENWASHING
GRASSY	GRAVELLED	GRAYMAILS*	GREEDIER	GREENWAY*
GRASTE	GRAVELLING	GRAYNESS*	GREEDIEST	GREENWAYS*
GRAT	GRAVELLY	GRAYNESSES*	GREEDILY	GREENWEED
GRATE	GRAVELS	GRAYOUT*	GREEDS	GREENWEEDS
GRATED	GRAVELY	GRAYOUTS*	GREEDY	GREENWING*
GRATEFUL	GRAVEN	GRAYS	GREEGREE	GREENWINGS*
GRATEFULLER*	GRAVENESS	GRAYWACKE	GREEGREES	GREENWOOD
GRATEFULLEST*	GRAVENESSES	GRAYWACKES	GREEING	GREENWOODS
GRATER	GRAVER	GRAZABLE*	GREEK*	GREENY
GRATERS	GRAVERS	GRAZE	GREEKING	GREES
GRATES	GRAVES	GRAZEABLE*	GREEKINGS	GREESE
GRATICULE	GRAVESIDE*	GRAZED	GREEN	GREESES
GRATICULES	GRAVESIDES*	GRAZER	GREENBACK	GREESING
GRATIFIED	GRAVEST	GRAZERS	GREENBACKS	GREESINGS
GRATIFIER	GRAVEYARD	GRAZES	GREENBELT*	GREET
GRATIFIERS	GRAVEYARDS	GRAZIER	GREENBELTS*	GREETE
GRATIFIES	GRAVID	GRAZIERS	GREENBUG*	GREETED
GRATIFY	GRAVIDA*	GRAZING	GREENBUGS*	GREETER
GRATIFYING	GRAVIDAE*	GRAZINGS	GREENED	GREETERS
GRATIN	GRAVIDAS*	GRAZIOSO	GREENER	GREETES
GRATINATE	GRAVIDITIES	GREASE	GREENERIES	GREETING
GRATINATED	GRAVIDITY	GREASED	GREENERS	GREETINGS
GRATINATES	GRAVIDLY*	GREASER	GREENERY	GREETS
GRATINATING	GRAVIES	GREASERS	GREENEST	GREFFIER
GRATINE	GRAVING	GREASIER	GREENFLIES	GREFFIERS
GRATINEE	GRAVINGS	GREASIES	GREENFLY	GREGALE
GRATINEED*	GRAVITAS	GREASIEST	GREENGAGE	GREGALES
GRATINEEING*	GRAVITASES		GREENGAGES	GREGARIAN

GREGARINE
GREGARINES
GREGATIM
GREGE
GREGO
GREGOS
GREIGE
GREIGES*
GREIN
GREINED
GREINING
GREINS
GREISEN
GREISENS
GREISLY
GREMIAL
GREMIALS
GREMLIN
GREMLINS
GREMMIE*
GREMMIES*
GREMMY*
GREMOLATA
GREMOLATAS
GREN
GRENADE
GRENADES
GRENADIER
GRENADIERS
GRENADINE
GRENADINES
GRENNED
GRENNING
GRENS
GRESE
GRESES
GRESSING
GRESSINGS
GREVE
GREVES
GREW
GREWED
GREWHOUND
GREWHOUNDS
GREWING
GREWS
GREWSOME*
GREWSOMER*
GREWSOMEST*
GREY
GREYBEARD
GREYBEARDS
GREYED
GREYER
GREYEST
GREYHEN
GREYHENS
GREYHOUND
GREYHOUNDS
GREYING
GREYINGS
GREYISH
GREYLAG*
GREYLAGS*

GREYLY
GREYNESS
GREYNESSES
GREYS
GREYSTONE
GREYSTONES
GREYWACKE
GREYWACKES
GRIBBLE
GRIBBLES
GRICE
GRICER
GRICERS
GRICES
GRICING
GRICINGS
GRID
GRIDDER
GRIDDERS
GRIDDLE
GRIDDLED*
GRIDDLES
GRIDDLING*
GRIDE
GRIDED
GRIDELIN
GRIDELINS
GRIDES
GRIDING
GRIDIRON
GRIDIRONED
GRIDIRONING
GRIDIRONS
GRIDLOCK
GRIDLOCKED*
GRIDLOCKING*
GRIDLOCKS
GRIDS
GRIECE
GRIECED
GRIECES
GRIEF
GRIEFFUL
GRIEFLESS
GRIEFS
GRIESIE
GRIESLY
GRIESY
GRIEVANCE
GRIEVANCES
GRIEVANT*
GRIEVANTS*
GRIEVE
GRIEVED
GRIEVER
GRIEVERS
GRIEVES
GRIEVING
GRIEVOUS
GRIFF
GRIFFE
GRIFFES
GRIFFIN
GRIFFINS

GRIFFON
GRIFFONS
GRIFFS
GRIFT
GRIFTED
GRIFTER
GRIFTERS
GRIFTING
GRIFTS
GRIG
GRIGGED
GRIGGING
GRIGRI
GRIGRIS
GRIGS
GRIKE
GRIKES
GRILL
GRILLADE
GRILLADES
GRILLAGE
GRILLAGES
GRILLE
GRILLED
GRILLER*
GRILLERS*
GRILLES
GRILLING
GRILLINGS
GRILLROOM*
GRILLROOMS*
GRILLS
GRILLWORK
GRILLWORKS
GRILSE
GRILSES
GRIM
GRIMACE
GRIMACED
GRIMACER*
GRIMACERS*
GRIMACES
GRIMACING
GRIMALKIN
GRIMALKINS
GRIME
GRIMED
GRIMES
GRIMIER
GRIMIEST
GRIMILY
GRIMINESS
GRIMINESSES
GRIMING
GRIMLY
GRIMMER
GRIMMEST
GRIMNESS
GRIMNESSES
GRIMOIRE
GRIMOIRES
GRIMY
GRIN
GRINCH*

GRINCHES*
GRIND
GRINDED
GRINDER
GRINDERIES
GRINDERS
GRINDERY
GRINDING
GRINDINGS
GRINDS
GRINGO
GRINGOS
GRINNED
GRINNER
GRINNERS
GRINNING
GRINS
GRIOT
GRIOTS
GRIP
GRIPE
GRIPED
GRIPER
GRIPERS
GRIPES
GRIPEY*
GRIPIER*
GRIPIEST*
GRIPING
GRIPINGLY
GRIPLE
GRIPMAN*
GRIPMEN*
GRIPPE
GRIPPED
GRIPPER
GRIPPERS
GRIPPES
GRIPPIER
GRIPPIEST
GRIPPING
GRIPPLE
GRIPPLES
GRIPPY
GRIPS
GRIPSACK
GRIPSACKS
GRIPT*
GRIPTAPE
GRIPTAPES
GRIPY*
GRIS
GRISAILLE
GRISAILLES
GRISE
GRISED
GRISELY
GRISEOUS
GRISES
GRISETTE
GRISETTES
GRISGRIS
GRISING
GRISKIN

GRISKINS
GRISLED
GRISLIER
GRISLIEST
GRISLY
GRISON
GRISONS
GRIST
GRISTLE
GRISTLES
GRISTLIER
GRISTLIEST
GRISTLY
GRISTMILL*
GRISTMILLS*
GRISTS
GRISY
GRIT
GRITH
GRITHS
GRITS
GRITSTONE
GRITSTONES
GRITTED
GRITTER
GRITTERS
GRITTEST
GRITTIER
GRITTIEST
GRITTILY*
GRITTING
GRITTY
GRIVET
GRIVETS
GRIZE
GRIZES
GRIZZLE
GRIZZLED
GRIZZLER
GRIZZLERS
GRIZZLES
GRIZZLIER
GRIZZLIES
GRIZZLIEST
GRIZZLING
GRIZZLY
GROAN
GROANED
GROANER
GROANERS
GROANFUL
GROANING
GROANINGS
GROANS
GROAT
GROATS
GROCER
GROCERIES
GROCERS
GROCERY
GROCKLE
GROCKLES
GRODIER
GRODIEST

The Chambers Dictionary is the authority for many longer words; see Introduction, page ix

GRODY	GROSCHEN	GROUNDNUT	GROWING	GRUELINGS
GROG	GROSCHENS	GROUNDNUTS	GROWINGLY*	GRUELLED
GROGGED	GROSER	GROUNDOUT*	GROWINGS	GRUELLER*
GROGGERIES	GROSERS	GROUNDOUTS*	GROWL	GRUELLERS*
GROGGERY	GROSERT	GROUNDS	GROWLED	GRUELLING
GROGGIER	GROSERTS	GROUNDSEL	GROWLER	GRUELLINGS
GROGGIEST	GROSET	GROUNDSELS	GROWLERIES	GRUELS
GROGGILY*	GROSETS	GROUP	GROWLERS	GRUES
GROGGING	GROSGRAIN	GROUPABLE	GROWLERY	GRUESOME
GROGGY	GROSGRAINS	GROUPAGE	GROWLIER	GRUESOMER
GROGRAM	GROSS	GROUPAGES	GROWLIEST	GRUESOMEST
GROGRAMS	GROSSART	GROUPED	GROWLING	GRUFE
GROGS	GROSSARTS	GROUPER	GROWLINGS	GRUFES
GROGSHOP*	GROSSED	GROUPERS	GROWLS	GRUFF
GROGSHOPS*	GROSSER	GROUPIE	GROWLY	GRUFFED*
GROIN	GROSSERS*	GROUPIES	GROWN	GRUFFER
GROINED	GROSSES	GROUPING	GROWNUP*	GRUFFEST
GROINING	GROSSEST	GROUPINGS	GROWNUPS*	GRUFFIER*
GROININGS	GROSSING	GROUPIST	GROWS	GRUFFIEST*
GROINS	GROSSLY	GROUPISTS	GROWTH	GRUFFILY*
GROMA	GROSSNESS	GROUPLET	GROWTHIER*	GRUFFING*
GROMAS	GROSSNESSES	GROUPLETS	GROWTHIEST*	GRUFFISH
GROMET	GROSSULAR	GROUPOID*	GROWTHIST	GRUFFLY
GROMETS	GROSSULARS	GROUPOIDS*	GROWTHISTS	GRUFFNESS
GROMMET	GROSZ*	GROUPS	GROWTHS	GRUFFNESSES
GROMMETS	GROSZE*	GROUPWARE	GROWTHY*	GRUFFS*
GROMWELL	GROSZY*	GROUPWARES	GROYNE	GRUFFY*
GROMWELLS	GROT	GROUPY	GROYNES	GRUFTED
GRONE	GROTESQUE	GROUSE	GRUB	GRUGRU*
GRONED	GROTESQUER	GROUSED	GRUBBED	GRUGRUS*
GRONEFULL	GROTESQUES	GROUSER	GRUBBER	GRUIFORM*
GRONES	GROTESQUEST	GROUSERS	GRUBBERS	GRUING
GRONING	GROTS	GROUSES	GRUBBIER	GRUM
GROOF	GROTTIER	GROUSEST	GRUBBIEST	GRUMBLE
GROOFS	GROTTIEST	GROUSING	GRUBBILY*	GRUMBLED
GROOLIER	GROTTO	GROUT	GRUBBING	GRUMBLER
GROOLIEST	GROTTOES	GROUTED	GRUBBLE	GRUMBLERS
GROOLY	GROTTOS	GROUTER	GRUBBLED	GRUMBLES
GROOM	GROTTY	GROUTERS	GRUBBLES	GRUMBLIER
GROOMED	GROUCH	GROUTIER	GRUBBLING	GRUMBLIEST
GROOMER*	GROUCHED	GROUTIEST	GRUBBY	GRUMBLING
GROOMERS*	GROUCHES	GROUTING	GRUBS	GRUMBLINGS
GROOMING	GROUCHIER	GROUTINGS	GRUBSTAKE	GRUMBLY
GROOMS	GROUCHIEST	GROUTS	GRUBSTAKED	GRUME
GROOMSMAN	GROUCHILY	GROUTY	GRUBSTAKES	GRUMES
GROOMSMEN	GROUCHING	GROVE	GRUBSTAKING	GRUMLY
GROOVE	GROUCHY	GROVED*	GRUBWORM*	GRUMMER
GROOVED	GROUF	GROVEL	GRUBWORMS*	GRUMMEST
GROOVER	GROUFS	GROVELED	GRUDGE	GRUMMET
GROOVERS	GROUGH	GROVELER	GRUDGED	GRUMMETS
GROOVES	GROUGHS	GROVELERS	GRUDGEFUL	GRUMNESS
GROOVIER	GROUND	GROVELING	GRUDGER*	GRUMNESSES
GROOVIEST	GROUNDAGE	GROVELLED	GRUDGERS*	GRUMOSE
GROOVING	GROUNDAGES	GROVELLER	GRUDGES	GRUMOUS
GROOVY	GROUNDED	GROVELLERS	GRUDGING	GRUMP
GROPE	GROUNDEN	GROVELLING	GRUDGINGS	GRUMPED
GROPED	GROUNDER	GROVELS	GRUE	GRUMPH
GROPER	GROUNDERS	GROVES	GRUED	GRUMPHED
GROPERS	GROUNDHOG	GROVET	GRUEING	GRUMPHIE
GROPES	GROUNDHOGS	GROVETS	GRUEL	GRUMPHIES
GROPING	GROUNDING	GROW	GRUELED*	GRUMPHING
GROPINGLY	GROUNDINGS	GROWABLE	GRUELER*	GRUMPHS
GROSBEAK	GROUNDMAN	GROWER	GRUELERS*	GRUMPHY*
GROSBEAKS	GROUNDMEN	GROWERS	GRUELING	GRUMPIER

Words marked with an asterisk are from OTCWL

GRUMPIEST	GUAIACOL*	GUARDLESS	GUERNSEYS	GUIDINGS
GRUMPILY	GUAIACOLS*	GUARDRAIL	GUERRILLA	GUIDON
GRUMPING	GUAIACS*	GUARDRAILS	GUERRILLAS	GUIDONS
GRUMPISH*	GUAIACUM	GUARDROOM	GUES	GUIDS
GRUMPS	GUAIACUMS	GUARDROOMS	GUESS	GUILD
GRUMPY	GUAIOCUM*	GUARDS	GUESSABLE	GUILDER
GRUNGE	GUAIOCUMS*	GUARDSHIP	GUESSED	GUILDERS
GRUNGES	GUAN	GUARDSHIPS	GUESSER	GUILDHALL
GRUNGIER	GUANA	GUARDSMAN	GUESSERS	GUILDHALLS
GRUNGIEST	GUANACO	GUARDSMEN	GUESSES	GUILDRIES
GRUNGY	GUANACOS	GUARISH	GUESSING	GUILDRY
GRUNION	GUANAS	GUARISHED	GUESSINGS	GUILDS
GRUNIONS	GUANASE*	GUARISHES	GUESSWORK	GUILDSHIP*
GRUNT	GUANASES*	GUARISHING	GUESSWORKS	GUILDSHIPS*
GRUNTED	GUANAY*	GUARS	GUEST	GUILDSMAN
GRUNTER	GUANAYS*	GUAVA	GUESTED	GUILDSMEN
GRUNTERS	GUANAZOLO	GUAVAS	GUESTEN	GUILE
GRUNTING	GUANAZOLOS	GUAYABERA*	GUESTENED	GUILED
GRUNTINGS	GUANGO	GUAYABERAS*	GUESTENING	GUILEFUL
GRUNTLE	GUANGOS	GUAYULE	GUESTENS	GUILELESS
GRUNTLED	GUANIDIN*	GUAYULES	GUESTING	GUILER
GRUNTLES	GUANIDINE*	GUB	GUESTS	GUILERS
GRUNTLING	GUANIDINES*	GUBBAH	GUESTWISE	GUILES
GRUNTS	GUANIDINS*	GUBBAHS	GUFF	GUILING
GRUPPETTI	GUANIN*	GUBBINS	GUFFAW	GUILLEMET*
GRUPPETTO	GUANINE	GUBBINSES	GUFFAWED	GUILLEMETS*
GRUSHIE*	GUANINES	GUBS	GUFFAWING	GUILLEMOT
GRUTCH	GUANINS*	GUCK	GUFFAWS	GUILLEMOTS
GRUTCHED	GUANO	GUCKIER	GUFFIE	GUILLOCHE
GRUTCHES	GUANOS	GUCKIEST	GUFFIES	GUILLOCHED
GRUTCHING	GUANOSINE*	GUCKS	GUFFS	GUILLOCHES
GRUTTEN	GUANOSINES*	GUCKY	GUGA	GUILLOCHING
GRUYERE*	GUANS	GUDDLE	GUGAS	GUILT
GRUYERES*	GUAR	GUDDLED	GUGGLE	GUILTIER
GRYCE	GUARANA	GUDDLES	GUGGLED	GUILTIEST
GRYCES	GUARANAS	GUDDLING	GUGGLES	GUILTILY
GRYDE	GUARANI	GUDE	GUGGLING	GUILTLESS
GRYDED	GUARANIES	GUDEMAN	GUGLET*	GUILTS
GRYDES	GUARANIS	GUDEMEN	GUGLETS*	GUILTY
GRYDING	GUARANTEE	GUDES	GUICHET	GUIMBARD
GRYESLY	GUARANTEED	GUDESIRE	GUICHETS	GUIMBARDS
GRYESY	GUARANTEEING	GUDESIRES	GUID	GUIMP
GRYFON	GUARANTEES	GUDEWIFE	GUIDABLE	GUIMPE*
GRYFONS	GUARANTIED	GUDEWIVES	GUIDAGE	GUIMPED
GRYKE	GUARANTIES	GUDGEON	GUIDAGES	GUIMPES*
GRYKES	GUARANTOR	GUDGEONED	GUIDANCE	GUIMPING
GRYPE	GUARANTORS	GUDGEONING	GUIDANCES	GUIMPS
GRYPES	GUARANTY	GUDGEONS	GUIDE	GUINEA
GRYPHON	GUARANTYING	GUE	GUIDEBOOK	GUINEAS
GRYPHONS	GUARD	GUENON	GUIDEBOOKS	GUIPURE
GRYPT	GUARDABLE	GUENONS	GUIDED	GUIPURES
GRYSBOK	GUARDAGE	GUERDON	GUIDELESS	GUIRO
GRYSBOKS	GUARDAGES	GUERDONED	GUIDELINE	GUIROS
GRYSELY	GUARDANT	GUERDONING	GUIDELINES	GUISARD
GRYSIE	GUARDANTS	GUERDONS	GUIDEPOST	GUISARDS
GU	GUARDED	GUEREZA	GUIDEPOSTS	GUISE
GUACAMOLE	GUARDEDLY	GUEREZAS	GUIDER	GUISED
GUACAMOLES	GUARDEE	GUERIDON	GUIDERS	GUISER
GUACHARO	GUARDEES	GUERIDONS	GUIDES	GUISERS
GUACHAROES*	GUARDER*	GUERILLA	GUIDESHIP	GUISES
GUACHAROS	GUARDERS*	GUERILLAS	GUIDESHIPS	GUISING
GUACO	GUARDIAN	GUERITE	GUIDEWAY*	GUISINGS
GUACOS	GUARDIANS	GUERITES	GUIDEWAYS*	GUITAR
GUAIAC*	GUARDING	GUERNSEY	GUIDING	GUITARIST

GUITARISTS	GULPS	GUNBOAT	GUNPAPERS*	GURLS
GUITARS	GULPY*	GUNBOATS	GUNPLAY	GURLY
GUITGUIT*	GULS*	GUNCOTTON	GUNPLAYS	GURN
GUITGUITS*	GULY	GUNCOTTONS	GUNPOINT	GURNARD
GUIZER	GUM	GUNDIES	GUNPOINTS	GURNARDS
GUIZERS	GUMBO	GUNDOG*	GUNPORT	GURNED
GUL*	GUMBOIL	GUNDOGS*	GUNPORTS	GURNET
GULA	GUMBOILS	GUNDY	GUNPOWDER	GURNETS
GULAG	GUMBOOT	GUNFIGHT	GUNPOWDERS	GURNEY
GULAGS	GUMBOOTS	GUNFIGHTING	GUNROOM	GURNEYS
GULAR	GUMBOS	GUNFIGHTS	GUNROOMS	GURNING
GULAS	GUMBOTIL*	GUNFIRE	GUNRUNNER	GURNS
GULCH	GUMBOTILS*	GUNFIRES	GUNRUNNERS	GURRAH
GULCHED	GUMDROP	GUNFLINT	GUNS	GURRAHS
GULCHES	GUMDROPS	GUNFLINTS	GUNSEL	GURRIES
GULCHING	GUMLESS*	GUNFOUGHT	GUNSELS	GURRY
GULDEN	GUMLIKE*	GUNGE	GUNSHIP	GURS
GULDENS	GUMMA	GUNGES	GUNSHIPS	GURSH*
GULE	GUMMAS*	GUNGIER	GUNSHOT	GURSHES*
GULES	GUMMATA	GUNGIEST	GUNSHOTS	GURU
GULF	GUMMATOUS	GUNGY	GUNSMITH	GURUDOM
GULFED	GUMMED	GUNHOUSE	GUNSMITHS	GURUDOMS
GULFIER	GUMMER*	GUNHOUSES	GUNSTICK	GURUISM
GULFIEST	GUMMERS*	GUNITE	GUNSTICKS	GURUISMS
GULFING	GUMMIER	GUNITES	GUNSTOCK	GURUS
GULFLIKE*	GUMMIEST	GUNK	GUNSTOCKS	GURUSHIP
GULFS	GUMMINESS	GUNKHOLE*	GUNSTONE	GURUSHIPS
GULFWEED	GUMMINESSES	GUNKHOLED*	GUNSTONES	GUS
GULFWEEDS	GUMMING	GUNKHOLES*	GUNTER	GUSH
GULFY	GUMMINGS	GUNKHOLING*	GUNTERS	GUSHED
GULL	GUMMITE	GUNKS	GUNWALE	GUSHER
GULLABLE	GUMMITES	GUNKY*	GUNWALES	GUSHERS
GULLABLY*	GUMMOSE*	GUNLAYER	GUNYAH	GUSHES
GULLED	GUMMOSES	GUNLAYERS	GUNYAHS	GUSHIER
GULLER	GUMMOSIS	GUNLESS	GUP	GUSHIEST
GULLERIES	GUMMOSITIES	GUNLOCK	GUPPIES	GUSHILY*
GULLERS	GUMMOSITY	GUNLOCKS	GUPPY	GUSHINESS*
GULLERY	GUMMOUS	GUNMAKER	GUPS	GUSHINESSES*
GULLET	GUMMY	GUNMAKERS	GUR	GUSHING
GULLETS	GUMNUT	GUNMAN	GURAMI	GUSHINGLY
GULLEY	GUMNUTS	GUNMEN	GURAMIS	GUSHY
GULLEYED	GUMP	GUNMETAL	GURDWARA	GUSLA
GULLEYING	GUMPED	GUNMETALS	GURDWARAS	GUSLAR
GULLEYS	GUMPHION	GUNNAGE	GURGE	GUSLARS
GULLIBLE	GUMPHIONS	GUNNAGES	GURGED*	GUSLAS
GULLIBLY*	GUMPING	GUNNED	GURGES	GUSLE
GULLIED	GUMPS	GUNNEL	GURGING*	GUSLES
GULLIES	GUMPTION	GUNNELS	GURGLE	GUSLI
GULLING	GUMPTIONS	GUNNEN*	GURGLED	GUSLIS
GULLISH	GUMPTIOUS	GUNNER	GURGLES	GUSSET
GULLS	GUMS	GUNNERA	GURGLET*	GUSSETED
GULLY	GUMSHIELD	GUNNERAS	GURGLETS*	GUSSETING
GULLYING	GUMSHIELDS	GUNNERIES	GURGLING	GUSSETS
GULOSITIES	GUMSHOE	GUNNERS	GURGOYLE	GUSSIE
GULOSITY	GUMSHOED	GUNNERY	GURGOYLES	GUSSIED*
GULP	GUMSHOEING	GUNNIES	GURJUN	GUSSIES
GULPED	GUMSHOES	GUNNING	GURJUNS	GUSSY*
GULPER	GUMTREE*	GUNNINGS	GURL	GUSSYING*
GULPERS	GUMTREES*	GUNNY	GURLED	GUST
GULPH	GUMWEED*	GUNNYBAG*	GURLET	GUSTABLE
GULPHS	GUMWEEDS*	GUNNYBAGS*	GURLETS	GUSTABLES
GULPIER*	GUMWOOD*	GUNNYSACK*	GURLIER	GUSTATION
GULPIEST*	GUMWOODS*	GUNNYSACKS*	GURLIEST	GUSTATIONS
GULPING	GUN	GUNPAPER*	GURLING	GUSTATIVE

GUSTATORY	GUTTERED	GYAL	GYNIE	GYRATION
GUSTED	GUTTERING	GYALS	GYNIES	GYRATIONS
GUSTFUL	GUTTERINGS	GYBE	GYNNEY	GYRATOR*
GUSTIE	GUTTERS	GYBED	GYNNEYS	GYRATORS*
GUSTIER	GUTTERY*	GYBES	GYNNIES	GYRATORY
GUSTIEST	GUTTIER	GYBING	GYNNY	GYRE
GUSTILY*	GUTTIES	GYELD	GYNOCRACIES	GYRED
GUSTINESS	GUTTIEST	GYELDS	GYNOCRACY	GYRENE*
GUSTINESSES	GUTTING	GYLDEN	GYNOECIA	GYRENES*
GUSTING	GUTTLE	GYM	GYNOECIUM	GYRES
GUSTLESS*	GUTTLED	GYMBAL	GYNOPHORE	GYRFALCON
GUSTO	GUTTLER*	GYMBALS	GYNOPHORES	GYRFALCONS
GUSTOES*	GUTTLERS*	GYMKHANA	GYNY	GYRI
GUSTOS	GUTTLES	GYMKHANAS	GYP	GYRING
GUSTS	GUTTLING	GYMMAL	GYPLURE*	GYRO
GUSTY	GUTTURAL	GYMMALS	GYPLURES*	GYROCAR
GUT	GUTTURALS	GYMNASIA	GYPPED	GYROCARS
GUTBUCKET	GUTTY	GYMNASIAL	GYPPER*	GYRODYNE
GUTBUCKETS	GUTZER	GYMNASIC	GYPPERS*	GYRODYNES
GUTCHER	GUTZERS	GYMNASIEN	GYPPIE	GYROIDAL
GUTCHERS	GUV	GYMNASIUM	GYPPIES	GYROLITE
GUTFUL	GUVS	GYMNASIUMS	GYPPING	GYROLITES
GUTFULS	GUY	GYMNAST	GYPPO	GYROMANCIES
GUTLESS	GUYED	GYMNASTIC	GYPPOS	GYROMANCY
GUTLIKE*	GUYING	GYMNASTICS	GYPPY	GYRON
GUTROT	GUYLE	GYMNASTS	GYPS	GYRONIC
GUTROTS	GUYLED	GYMNIC	GYPSEIAN*	GYRONNY
GUTS	GUYLER	GYMNOSOPH	GYPSEOUS	GYRONS
GUTSED	GUYLERS	GYMNOSOPHS	GYPSIED	GYROPLANE
GUTSER	GUYLES	GYMP	GYPSIES	GYROPLANES
GUTSERS	GUYLINE*	GYMPED	GYPSTER*	GYROS
GUTSES	GUYLINES*	GYMPING	GYPSTERS*	GYROSCOPE
GUTSFUL	GUYLING	GYMPS	GYPSUM	GYROSCOPES
GUTSFULS	GUYOT	GYMS	GYPSUMS	GYROSE
GUTSIER	GUYOTS	GYNAE	GYPSY	GYROSTAT
GUTSIEST	GUYS	GYNAECEA*	GYPSYDOM	GYROSTATS
GUTSILY*	GUYSE	GYNAECEUM	GYPSYDOMS	GYROUS
GUTSINESS	GUYSES	GYNAECEUMS	GYPSYING	GYROVAGUE
GUTSINESSES	GUZZLE	GYNAECIA	GYPSYISH*	GYROVAGUES
GUTSING	GUZZLED	GYNAECIUM	GYPSYISM	GYRUS
GUTSY	GUZZLER	GYNAECOID	GYPSYISMS	GYRUSES
GUTTA	GUZZLERS	GYNAES	GYPSYWORT	GYTE
GUTTAE	GUZZLES	GYNANDRIES	GYPSYWORTS	GYTES
GUTTAS	GUZZLING	GYNANDRY	GYRAL	GYTRASH
GUTTATE	GWEDUC*	GYNARCHIES*	GYRALLY	GYTRASHES
GUTTATED	GWEDUCK*	GYNARCHY*	GYRANT	GYVE
GUTTATES	GWEDUCKS*	GYNECIA	GYRASE*	GYVED
GUTTATING	GWEDUCS*	GYNECIC*	GYRASES*	GYVES
GUTTATION	GWINIAD	GYNECIUM	GYRATE	GYVING
GUTTATIONS	GWINIADS	GYNECOID*	GYRATED	
GUTTED	GWYNIAD	GYNIATRIES*	GYRATES	
GUTTER	GWYNIADS	GYNIATRY*	GYRATING	

H

HA
HAAF
HAAFS
HAANEPOOT
HAANEPOOTS
HAAR
HAARS
HABANERA
HABANERAS
HABDABS
HABDALAH*
HABDALAHS*
HABERDINE
HABERDINES
HABERGEON
HABERGEONS
HABILABLE
HABILE
HABIT
HABITABLE
HABITABLY
HABITAN*
HABITANS
HABITANT
HABITANTS
HABITAT
HABITATS
HABITED
HABITING
HABITS
HABITUAL
HABITUALS
HABITUATE
HABITUATED
HABITUATES
HABITUATING
HABITUDE
HABITUDES
HABITUE
HABITUES
HABITUS
HABLE
HABOOB
HABOOBS
HABU*
HABUS*
HACEK
HACEKS
HACENDADO*
HACENDADOS*
HACHIS
HACHURE
HACHURED
HACHURES
HACHURING

HACIENDA
HACIENDAS
HACK
HACKAMORE
HACKAMORES
HACKBERRIES
HACKBERRY
HACKBOLT
HACKBOLTS
HACKBUT
HACKBUTS
HACKED
HACKEE
HACKEES
HACKER
HACKERIES
HACKERS
HACKERY
HACKETTE
HACKETTES
HACKIE*
HACKIES*
HACKING
HACKINGS
HACKLE
HACKLED
HACKLER
HACKLERS
HACKLES
HACKLET
HACKLETS
HACKLIER
HACKLIEST
HACKLING
HACKLY
HACKMAN*
HACKMEN*
HACKNEY
HACKNEYED
HACKNEYING
HACKNEYS
HACKS
HACKSAW*
HACKSAWS*
HACKWORK*
HACKWORKS*
HACQUETON
HACQUETONS
HAD
HADAL
HADARIM*
HADDEN
HADDEST*
HADDIE
HADDIES

HADDING
HADDOCK
HADDOCKS
HADE
HADED
HADES
HADING
HADITH*
HADITHS*
HADJ
HADJEE*
HADJEES*
HADJES
HADJI
HADJIS
HADROME
HADROMES
HADRON
HADRONIC
HADRONS
HADROSAUR
HADROSAURS
HADS
HADST
HAE
HAECCEITIES
HAECCEITY
HAED*
HAEING
HAEM
HAEMAL
HAEMATAL*
HAEMATIC
HAEMATICS*
HAEMATIN
HAEMATINS
HAEMATITE
HAEMATITES
HAEMATOID
HAEMATOMA
HAEMATOMAS
HAEMIC
HAEMIN
HAEMINS
HAEMOCOEL
HAEMOCOELS
HAEMOCYTE
HAEMOCYTES
HAEMOID*
HAEMONIES
HAEMONY
HAEMOSTAT
HAEMOSTATS
HAEMS
HAEN*

HAEREDES*
HAEREMAI
HAERES*
HAES*
HAET
HAETS
HAFF
HAFFET
HAFFETS
HAFFIT
HAFFITS
HAFFLIN
HAFFLINS
HAFFS
HAFIS*
HAFIZ*
HAFNIUM
HAFNIUMS
HAFT
HAFTARA*
HAFTARAH*
HAFTARAHS*
HAFTARAS*
HAFTAROT*
HAFTAROTH*
HAFTED
HAFTER*
HAFTERS*
HAFTING
HAFTORAH*
HAFTORAHS*
HAFTOROT*
HAFTOROTH*
HAFTS
HAG
HAGADIC*
HAGADIST*
HAGADISTS*
HAGBERRIES
HAGBERRY
HAGBOLT
HAGBOLTS
HAGBORN*
HAGBUSH*
HAGBUSHES*
HAGBUT
HAGBUTS
HAGDEN
HAGDENS
HAGDON
HAGDONS
HAGDOWN
HAGDOWNS
HAGFISH
HAGFISHES

HAGG
HAGGADA*
HAGGADAH*
HAGGADAHS*
HAGGADAS*
HAGGADIC*
HAGGADIST*
HAGGADISTS*
HAGGADOT*
HAGGADOTH*
HAGGARD
HAGGARDLY
HAGGARDS
HAGGED
HAGGING
HAGGIS
HAGGISES
HAGGISH
HAGGISHLY
HAGGLE
HAGGLED
HAGGLER
HAGGLERS
HAGGLES
HAGGLING
HAGGS
HAGIARCHIES
HAGIARCHY
HAGIOLOGIES
HAGIOLOGY
HAGLET
HAGLETS
HAGRIDDEN*
HAGRIDE*
HAGRIDES*
HAGRIDING*
HAGRODE*
HAGS
HAH
HAHA*
HAHAS*
HAHNIUM
HAHNIUMS
HAHS*
HAICK
HAICKS
HAIDUK
HAIDUKS
HAIK
HAIKA*
HAIKAI
HAIKS
HAIKU
HAIL
HAILED

HAILER	HAIRPINS	HALCYON	HALITOTIC	HALMA
HAILERS	HAIRS	HALCYONS	HALITOUS	HALMAS
HAILIER	HAIRSPRAY	HALE	HALITUS	HALMS
HAILIEST	HAIRSPRAYS	HALED	HALITUSES	HALO
HAILING	HAIRST	HALENESS	HALL	HALOBIONT
HAILS	HAIRSTED	HALENESSES	HALLAH*	HALOBIONTS
HAILSHOT	HAIRSTING	HALER	HALLAHS*	HALOCLINE*
HAILSHOTS	HAIRSTS	HALERS	HALLAL	HALOCLINES*
HAILSTONE	HAIRSTYLE	HALERU*	HALLALI	HALOED
HAILSTONES	HAIRSTYLES	HALES	HALLALIS	HALOES
HAILSTORM*	HAIRWORK*	HALEST	HALLALLED	HALOGEN
HAILSTORMS*	HAIRWORKS*	HALF	HALLALLING	HALOGENS
HAILY	HAIRWORM*	HALFA	HALLALOO	HALOGETON*
HAIN	HAIRWORMS*	HALFAS	HALLALOOS	HALOGETONS*
HAINCH	HAIRY	HALFBACK*	HALLALS	HALOID
HAINCHED	HAITH	HALFBACKS*	HALLAN	HALOIDS
HAINCHES	HAJ	HALFBEAK*	HALLANS	HALOING
HAINCHING	HAJES	HALFBEAKS*	HALLEL*	HALOLIKE*
HAINED	HAJI	HALFEN	HALLELS*	HALON
HAINING	HAJIS	HALFLIFE*	HALLIAN	HALONS
HAININGS	HAJJ	HALFLIN	HALLIANS	HALOPHILE
HAINS	HAJJES	HALFLING	HALLIARD	HALOPHILES
HAIQUE	HAJJI	HALFLINGS	HALLIARDS	HALOPHILIES
HAIQUES	HAJJIS	HALFLINS	HALLING	HALOPHILY
HAIR	HAKA	HALFLIVES*	HALLINGS	HALOPHOBE
HAIRBALL*	HAKAM	HALFNESS*	HALLION	HALOPHOBES
HAIRBALLS*	HAKAMS	HALFNESSES*	HALLIONS	HALOPHYTE
HAIRBAND*	HAKAS	HALFPACE	HALLMARK	HALOPHYTES
HAIRBANDS*	HAKE	HALFPACES	HALLMARKED	HALOS
HAIRBELL	HAKEEM*	HALFPENCE	HALLMARKING	HALOTHANE
HAIRBELLS	HAKEEMS*	HALFPENNIES	HALLMARKS	HALOTHANES
HAIRBRUSH	HAKES	HALFPENNY	HALLO	HALSE
HAIRBRUSHES	HAKIM	HALFS	HALLOA	HALSED
HAIRCAP*	HAKIMS	HALFTIME*	HALLOAED	HALSER
HAIRCAPS*	HALACHA*	HALFTIMES*	HALLOAING	HALSERS
HAIRCLOTH	HALACHAS*	HALFTONE*	HALLOAS	HALSES
HAIRCLOTHS	HALACHOT*	HALFTONES*	HALLOED	HALSING
HAIRCUT	HALAKAH*	HALFWAY	HALLOES*	HALT
HAIRCUTS	HALAKAHS*	HALFWIT	HALLOING	HALTED
HAIRDO	HALAKHA*	HALFWITS	HALLOO	HALTER
HAIRDOS	HALAKHAS*	HALIBUT	HALLOOED	HALTERE*
HAIRDRIER	HALAKHOT*	HALIBUTS	HALLOOING	HALTERED
HAIRDRIERS	HALAKIC*	HALICORE	HALLOOS	HALTERES
HAIRDRYER	HALAKIST*	HALICORES	HALLOS	HALTERING
HAIRDRYERS	HALAKISTS*	HALID*	HALLOT*	HALTERS
HAIRED	HALAKOTH*	HALIDE	HALLOTH*	HALTING
HAIRGRIP	HALAL	HALIDES	HALLOUMI	HALTINGLY
HAIRGRIPS	HALALA*	HALIDOM	HALLOUMIS	HALTINGS
HAIRIER	HALALAH*	HALIDOME*	HALLOW	HALTLESS*
HAIRIEST	HALALAHS*	HALIDOMES*	HALLOWED	HALTS
HAIRINESS	HALALAS*	HALIDOMS	HALLOWER*	HALUTZ*
HAIRINESSES	HALALLED	HALIDS*	HALLOWERS*	HALUTZIM*
HAIRING	HALALLING	HALIEUTIC	HALLOWING	HALVA
HAIRLESS	HALALS	HALIEUTICS	HALLOWS	HALVAH
HAIRLIKE	HALATION	HALIMOT	HALLS	HALVAHS
HAIRLINE	HALATIONS	HALIMOTE	HALLSTAND	HALVAS
HAIRLINES	HALAVAH	HALIMOTES	HALLSTANDS	HALVE
HAIRLOCK*	HALAVAHS	HALIMOTS	HALLUCES	HALVED
HAIRLOCKS*	HALAZONE*	HALING	HALLUX	HALVER
HAIRNET	HALAZONES*	HALIOTIS	HALLWAY	HALVERS
HAIRNETS	HALBERD	HALITE	HALLWAYS	HALVES
HAIRPIECE	HALBERDS	HALITES	HALLYON	HALVING
HAIRPIECES	HALBERT	HALITOSES	HALLYONS	HALYARD
HAIRPIN	HALBERTS	HALITOSIS	HALM	HALYARDS

The Chambers Dictionary is the authority for many longer words; see Introduction, page ix

HAM
HAMADA*
HAMADAS*
HAMADRYAD
HAMADRYADES
HAMADRYADS
HAMAL
HAMALS
HAMAMELIS
HAMAMELISES
HAMARTIA
HAMARTIAS
HAMATE
HAMATES*
HAMAUL*
HAMAULS*
HAMBLE
HAMBLED
HAMBLES
HAMBLING
HAMBONE*
HAMBONED*
HAMBONES*
HAMBONING*
HAMBURG*
HAMBURGER
HAMBURGERS
HAMBURGS*
HAME
HAMED
HAMES
HAMEWITH
HAMFATTER
HAMFATTERED
HAMFATTERING
HAMFATTERS
HAMING
HAMLET
HAMLETS
HAMMADA*
HAMMADAS*
HAMMAL
HAMMALS
HAMMAM
HAMMAMS
HAMMED
HAMMER
HAMMERED
HAMMERER
HAMMERERS
HAMMERING
HAMMERINGS
HAMMERKOP
HAMMERKOPS
HAMMERMAN
HAMMERMEN
HAMMERS
HAMMERTOE*
HAMMERTOES*
HAMMIER
HAMMIEST
HAMMILY
HAMMINESS*
HAMMINESSES*

HAMMING
HAMMOCK
HAMMOCKS
HAMMY
HAMOSE
HAMOUS
HAMPER
HAMPERED
HAMPERER*
HAMPERERS*
HAMPERING
HAMPERS
HAMPSTER
HAMPSTERS
HAMS
HAMSTER
HAMSTERS
HAMSTRING
HAMSTRINGED
HAMSTRINGING
HAMSTRINGS
HAMSTRUNG
HAMULAR
HAMULATE
HAMULI
HAMULOSE*
HAMULOUS*
HAMULUS
HAMZA
HAMZAH
HAMZAHS
HAMZAS
HAN
HANAP
HANAPER
HANAPERS
HANAPS
HANCE
HANCES
HANCH
HANCHED
HANCHES
HANCHING
HAND
HANDBAG
HANDBAGGED
HANDBAGGING
HANDBAGGINGS
HANDBAGS
HANDBALL
HANDBALLS
HANDBELL
HANDBELLS
HANDBILL
HANDBILLS
HANDBLOWN*
HANDBOOK
HANDBOOKS
HANDBRAKE
HANDBRAKES
HANDCAR
HANDCARS
HANDCART
HANDCARTS

HANDCLAP
HANDCLAPS
HANDCLASP
HANDCLASPS
HANDCRAFT
HANDCRAFTED*
HANDCRAFTING*
HANDCRAFTS
HANDCUFF
HANDCUFFED
HANDCUFFING
HANDCUFFS
HANDED
HANDER
HANDERS
HANDFAST
HANDFASTED
HANDFASTING
HANDFASTINGS
HANDFASTS
HANDFUL
HANDFULS
HANDGRIP
HANDGRIPS
HANDGUN
HANDGUNS
HANDHELD*
HANDHELDS*
HANDHOLD
HANDHOLDS
HANDICAP
HANDICAPPED
HANDICAPPING
HANDICAPS
HANDIER
HANDIEST
HANDILY
HANDINESS
HANDINESSES
HANDING
HANDIWORK
HANDIWORKS
HANDJAR
HANDJARS
HANDLE
HANDLEBAR
HANDLEBARS
HANDLED
HANDLER
HANDLERS
HANDLES
HANDLESS
HANDLIKE*
HANDLING
HANDLINGS
HANDLIST
HANDLISTS
HANDLOOM*
HANDLOOMS*
HANDMADE
HANDMAID
HANDMAIDS
HANDOFF*
HANDOFFS*

HANDOUT
HANDOUTS
HANDOVER
HANDOVERS
HANDPICK*
HANDPICKED*
HANDPICKING*
HANDPICKS*
HANDPLAY
HANDPLAYS
HANDPRESS*
HANDPRESSES*
HANDPRINT*
HANDPRINTS*
HANDRAIL
HANDRAILS
HANDS
HANDSAW
HANDSAWS
HANDSEL
HANDSELED*
HANDSELING*
HANDSELLED
HANDSELLING
HANDSELS
HANDSET
HANDSETS
HANDSEWN*
HANDSFUL*
HANDSHAKE
HANDSHAKES
HANDSOME
HANDSOMER
HANDSOMEST
HANDSPIKE
HANDSPIKES
HANDSTAFF
HANDSTAFFS
HANDSTAND
HANDSTANDS
HANDSTAVES
HANDSTURN
HANDSTURNS
HANDTOWEL
HANDTOWELS
HANDWHEEL*
HANDWHEELS*
HANDWORK
HANDWORKS
HANDWOVEN*
HANDWRIT*
HANDWRITE*
HANDWRITES*
HANDWRITING*
HANDWRITTEN*
HANDWROTE*
HANDY
HANDYMAN
HANDYMEN
HANDYWORK
HANDYWORKS
HANEPOOT
HANEPOOTS
HANG

HANGABLE
HANGAR
HANGARED*
HANGARING*
HANGARS
HANGBIRD
HANGBIRDS
HANGDOG
HANGDOGS
HANGED
HANGER
HANGERS
HANGFIRE
HANGFIRES
HANGING
HANGINGS
HANGMAN
HANGMEN
HANGNAIL
HANGNAILS
HANGNEST
HANGNESTS
HANGOUT
HANGOUTS
HANGOVER
HANGOVERS
HANGS
HANGTAG*
HANGTAGS*
HANGUL*
HANGUP*
HANGUPS*
HANIWA*
HANJAR
HANJARS
HANK
HANKED
HANKER
HANKERED
HANKERER*
HANKERERS*
HANKERING
HANKERINGS
HANKERS
HANKIE
HANKIES
HANKING
HANKS
HANKY
HANSA*
HANSAS*
HANSE*
HANSEL
HANSELED*
HANSELING*
HANSELLED
HANSELLING
HANSELS
HANSES*
HANSOM
HANSOMS
HANT*
HANTED*
HANTING*

HANTLE	HAPTICAL*	HARDENED	HARDY	HARMANS
HANTLES	HAPTICS	HARDENER	HARE	HARMATTAN
HANTS*	HAQUETON	HARDENERS	HAREBELL	HARMATTANS
HANUMAN	HAQUETONS	HARDENING	HAREBELLS	HARMDOING
HANUMANS	HARAM	HARDENINGS	HARED	HARMDOINGS
HAO*	HARAMBEE	HARDENS	HAREEM	HARMED
HAOLE*	HARAMBEES	HARDER	HAREEMS	HARMEL
HAOLES*	HARAMS	HARDEST	HARELD	HARMELS
HAOMA	HARANGUE	HARDFACE	HARELDS	HARMER*
HAOMAS	HARANGUED	HARDFACES	HARELIKE*	HARMERS*
HAP	HARANGUER	HARDGRASS	HARELIP*	HARMFUL
HAPAX*	HARANGUERS	HARDGRASSES	HARELIPS*	HARMFULLY
HAPAXES*	HARANGUES	HARDHACK	HAREM	HARMIN
HAPHAZARD	HARANGUING	HARDHACKS	HAREMS	HARMINE
HAPHAZARDS	HARASS	HARDHAT*	HARES	HARMINES
HAPHTARA*	HARASSED	HARDHATS*	HAREWOOD	HARMING
HAPHTARAS*	HARASSER	HARDHEAD	HAREWOODS	HARMINS
HAPHTAROT*	HARASSERS	HARDHEADS	HARIANA*	HARMLESS
HAPHTAROTH*	HARASSES	HARDIER	HARIANAS*	HARMONIC
HAPLESS	HARASSING	HARDIES*	HARICOT	HARMONICA
HAPLESSLY	HARASSINGS	HARDIEST	HARICOTS	HARMONICAS
HAPLITE*	HARBINGER	HARDIHEAD	HARIGALDS	HARMONICS
HAPLITES*	HARBINGERED	HARDIHEADS	HARIGALS	HARMONIES
HAPLOID	HARBINGERING	HARDIHOOD	HARIJAN*	HARMONISE
HAPLOIDIES	HARBINGERS	HARDIHOODS	HARIJANS*	HARMONISED
HAPLOIDS*	HARBOR	HARDILY	HARIM	HARMONISES
HAPLOIDY	HARBORAGE	HARDIMENT	HARIMS	HARMONISING
HAPLOLOGIES	HARBORAGES	HARDIMENTS	HARING	HARMONIST
HAPLOLOGY	HARBORED	HARDINESS	HARIOLATE	HARMONISTS
HAPLONT*	HARBORER	HARDINESSES	HARIOLATED	HARMONIUM
HAPLONTIC*	HARBORERS	HARDISH	HARIOLATES	HARMONIUMS
HAPLONTS*	HARBORFUL*	HARDLINE	HARIOLATING	HARMONIZE
HAPLOPIA*	HARBORFULS*	HARDLINER	HARISH	HARMONIZED
HAPLOPIAS*	HARBORING	HARDLINERS	HARK	HARMONIZES
HAPLOSES*	HARBORS	HARDLY	HARKED	HARMONIZING
HAPLOSIS*	HARBOUR	HARDNESS	HARKEN	HARMONY
HAPLOTYPE*	HARBOURED	HARDNESSES	HARKENED	HARMOST
HAPLOTYPES*	HARBOURER	HARDNOSE*	HARKENER*	HARMOSTIES
HAPLY	HARBOURERS	HARDNOSED	HARKENERS*	HARMOSTS
HAPPED	HARBOURING	HARDNOSES*	HARKENING	HARMOSTY
HAPPEN	HARBOURS	HARDOKE	HARKENS	HARMOTOME
HAPPENED	HARD	HARDOKES	HARKING	HARMOTOMES
HAPPENING	HARDBACK	HARDPAN*	HARKS	HARMS
HAPPENINGS	HARDBACKS	HARDPANS*	HARL	HARN
HAPPENS	HARDBAG	HARDPARTS	HARLED	HARNESS
HAPPIED	HARDBAGS	HARDS	HARLEQUIN	HARNESSED
HAPPIER	HARDBAKE	HARDSET*	HARLEQUINED	HARNESSES
HAPPIES	HARDBAKES	HARDSHELL	HARLEQUINING	HARNESSING
HAPPIEST	HARDBALL	HARDSHIP	HARLEQUINS	HARNS
HAPPILY	HARDBALLS	HARDSHIPS	HARLING	HARO
HAPPINESS	HARDBEAM	HARDSTAND*	HARLINGS	HAROS
HAPPINESSES	HARDBEAMS	HARDSTANDS*	HARLOT	HAROSET
HAPPING	HARDBOARD	HARDTACK	HARLOTRIES	HAROSETH
HAPPY	HARDBOARDS	HARDTACKS	HARLOTRY	HAROSETHS
HAPPYING	HARDBOOT*	HARDTOP	HARLOTS	HAROSETS
HAPS	HARDBOOTS*	HARDTOPS	HARLS	HARP
HAPTEN	HARDBOUND*	HARDWARE	HARM	HARPED
HAPTENE*	HARDCASE*	HARDWARES	HARMALA	HARPER
HAPTENES*	HARDCORE*	HARDWIRE*	HARMALAS	HARPERS
HAPTENIC*	HARDCOVER*	HARDWIRED*	HARMALIN	HARPIES
HAPTENS	HARDCOVERS*	HARDWIRES*	HARMALINE	HARPIN*
HAPTERON	HARDEDGE*	HARDWIRING*	HARMALINES	HARPING
HAPTERONS	HARDEDGES*	HARDWOOD	HARMALINS	HARPINGS
HAPTIC	HARDEN	HARDWOODS	HARMAN	HARPINS*

The Chambers Dictionary is the authority for many longer words; see Introduction, page ix

HARPIST	HARVEST	HATABLE	HATS	HAUSENS*
HARPISTS	HARVESTED	HATBAND	HATSFUL*	HAUSES
HARPOON	HARVESTER	HATBANDS	HATSTAND	HAUSFRAU
HARPOONED	HARVESTERS	HATBOX	HATSTANDS	HAUSFRAUEN*
HARPOONER	HARVESTING	HATBOXES	HATTED	HAUSFRAUS
HARPOONERS	HARVESTS	HATBRUSH	HATTER	HAUSING
HARPOONING	HAS	HATBRUSHES	HATTERED	HAUSTELLA
HARPOONS	HASH	HATCH	HATTERIA*	HAUSTELLUM*
HARPS	HASHED	HATCHABLE*	HATTERIAS*	HAUSTORIA
HARPY	HASHEESH	HATCHBACK	HATTERING	HAUSTORIUM*
HARQUEBUS	HASHEESHES	HATCHBACKS	HATTERS	HAUT
HARQUEBUSES	HASHES	HATCHECK*	HATTING	HAUTBOIS
HARRIDAN	HASHHEAD*	HATCHED	HATTINGS	HAUTBOY
HARRIDANS	HASHHEADS*	HATCHEL	HATTOCK	HAUTBOYS
HARRIED	HASHIER	HATCHELED*	HATTOCKS	HAUTE
HARRIER	HASHIEST	HATCHELING*	HAUBERK	HAUTEUR
HARRIERS	HASHING	HATCHELLED	HAUBERKS	HAUTEURS
HARRIES	HASHISH	HATCHELLING	HAUD	HAUYNE
HARROW	HASHISHES	HATCHELS	HAUDING	HAUYNES
HARROWED	HASHMARK	HATCHER	HAUDS	HAVARTI*
HARROWER*	HASHMARKS	HATCHERIES	HAUGH	HAVARTIS*
HARROWERS*	HASHY	HATCHERS	HAUGHS	HAVDALAH*
HARROWING	HASK	HATCHERY	HAUGHT	HAVDALAHS*
HARROWS	HASKS	HATCHES	HAUGHTIER	HAVE
HARRUMPH	HASLET	HATCHET	HAUGHTIEST	HAVELOCK
HARRUMPHED	HASLETS	HATCHETS	HAUGHTILY	HAVELOCKS
HARRUMPHING	HASP	HATCHETY	HAUGHTY	HAVEN
HARRUMPHS	HASPED	HATCHING	HAUL	HAVENED
HARRY	HASPING	HATCHINGS	HAULAGE	HAVENING
HARRYING	HASPS	HATCHLING	HAULAGES	HAVENS
HARSH	HASSAR	HATCHLINGS	HAULD	HAVEOUR
HARSHEN	HASSARS	HATCHMENT	HAULDS	HAVEOURS
HARSHENED	HASSEL*	HATCHMENTS	HAULED	HAVER
HARSHENING	HASSELS*	HATCHWAY	HAULER	HAVERED
HARSHENS	HASSLE	HATCHWAYS	HAULERS	HAVEREL
HARSHER	HASSLED	HATE	HAULIER	HAVERELS
HARSHEST	HASSLES	HATEABLE	HAULIERS	HAVERING
HARSHLY	HASSLING	HATED	HAULING	HAVERINGS
HARSHNESS	HASSOCK	HATEFUL	HAULM	HAVERS
HARSHNESSES	HASSOCKS	HATEFULLY	HAULMIER*	HAVERSACK
HARSLET	HASSOCKY	HATELESS	HAULMIEST*	HAVERSACKS
HARSLETS	HAST	HATER	HAULMS	HAVERSINE
HART	HASTA	HATERENT	HAULMY*	HAVERSINES
HARTAL	HASTATE	HATERENTS	HAULS	HAVES
HARTALS	HASTATED	HATERS	HAULST	HAVILDAR
HARTBEES	HASTE	HATES	HAULT	HAVILDARS
HARTBEESES	HASTED	HATFUL	HAULYARD*	HAVING
HARTELY	HASTEFUL*	HATFULS	HAULYARDS*	HAVINGS
HARTEN	HASTEN	HATGUARD	HAUNCH	HAVIOR*
HARTENED	HASTENED	HATGUARDS	HAUNCHED	HAVIORS*
HARTENING	HASTENER	HATH	HAUNCHES	HAVIOUR
HARTENS	HASTENERS	HATING	HAUNCHING	HAVIOURS
HARTLESSE	HASTENING	HATLESS	HAUNT	HAVOC
HARTS	HASTENS	HATLIKE*	HAUNTED	HAVOCKED
HARTSHORN	HASTES	HATMAKER*	HAUNTER	HAVOCKER*
HARTSHORNS	HASTIER	HATMAKERS*	HAUNTERS	HAVOCKERS*
HARUMPH*	HASTIEST	HATPEG	HAUNTING	HAVOCKING
HARUMPHED*	HASTILY	HATPEGS	HAUNTINGS	HAVOCS
HARUMPHING*	HASTINESS	HATPIN	HAUNTS	HAW
HARUMPHS*	HASTINESSES	HATPINS	HAURIANT	HAWBUCK
HARUSPEX	HASTING	HATRACK	HAURIENT	HAWBUCKS
HARUSPICES	HASTINGS	HATRACKS	HAUSE	HAWED
HARUSPICIES	HASTY	HATRED	HAUSED	HAWFINCH
HARUSPICY	HAT	HATREDS	HAUSEN*	HAWFINCHES

HAWING	HAYING	HAZZANIM	HEADLOCK	HEADSTONES
HAWK	HAYINGS	HAZZANS	HEADLOCKS	HEADWATER*
HAWKBELL	HAYLAGE*	HE	HEADLONG	HEADWATERS*
HAWKBELLS	HAYLAGES*	HEAD	HEADMAN	HEADWAY
HAWKBILL*	HAYLE	HEADACHE	HEADMARK	HEADWAYS
HAWKBILLS*	HAYLES	HEADACHES	HEADMARKS	HEADWIND*
HAWKBIT	HAYLOFT	HEADACHIER	HEADMEN	HEADWINDS*
HAWKBITS	HAYLOFTS	HEADACHIEST	HEADMOST	HEADWORD
HAWKED	HAYMAKER	HEADACHY	HEADNOTE	HEADWORDS
HAWKER	HAYMAKERS	HEADAGE	HEADNOTES	HEADWORK
HAWKERS	HAYMAKING	HEADAGES	HEADPEACE	HEADWORKS
HAWKEY	HAYMAKINGS	HEADBAND	HEADPEACES	HEADY
HAWKEYED*	HAYMOW	HEADBANDS	HEADPHONE	HEAL
HAWKEYS	HAYMOWS	HEADBOARD	HEADPHONES	HEALABLE
HAWKIE	HAYRACK*	HEADBOARDS	HEADPIECE	HEALD
HAWKIES	HAYRACKS*	HEADCASE	HEADPIECES	HEALDED
HAWKING	HAYRICK	HEADCASES	HEADPIN*	HEALDING
HAWKINGS	HAYRICKS	HEADCHAIR	HEADPINS*	HEALDS
HAWKISH	HAYRIDE	HEADCHAIRS	HEADRACE	HEALED
HAWKISHLY	HAYRIDES	HEADCLOTH	HEADRACES	HEALER
HAWKIT	HAYS	HEADCLOTHS	HEADRAIL	HEALERS
HAWKLIKE	HAYSEED	HEADDRESS	HEADRAILS	HEALING
HAWKMOTH*	HAYSEEDS	HEADDRESSES	HEADREACH	HEALINGLY
HAWKMOTHS*	HAYSEL	HEADED	HEADREACHED	HEALINGS
HAWKNOSE*	HAYSELS	HEADER	HEADREACHES	HEALS
HAWKNOSES*	HAYSTACK	HEADERS	HEADREACHING	HEALSOME
HAWKS	HAYSTACKS	HEADFAST	HEADREST	HEALTH
HAWKSBILL	HAYWARD	HEADFASTS	HEADRESTS	HEALTHFUL
HAWKSBILLS	HAYWARDS	HEADFIRST*	HEADRIG	HEALTHIER
HAWKSHAW*	HAYWIRE	HEADFISH*	HEADRIGS	HEALTHIEST
HAWKSHAWS*	HAYWIRES	HEADFISHES*	HEADRING	HEALTHILY
HAWKWEED	HAZAN	HEADFRAME	HEADRINGS	HEALTHS
HAWKWEEDS	HAZANIM	HEADFRAMES	HEADROOM	HEALTHY
HAWM	HAZANS	HEADGATE*	HEADROOMS	HEAME
HAWMED	HAZARD	HEADGATES*	HEADROPE	HEAP
HAWMING	HAZARDED	HEADGEAR	HEADROPES	HEAPED
HAWMS	HAZARDING	HEADGEARS	HEADS	HEAPIER
HAWS	HAZARDIZE	HEADHUNT	HEADSAIL*	HEAPIEST
HAWSE	HAZARDIZES	HEADHUNTED	HEADSAILS*	HEAPING
HAWSED	HAZARDOUS	HEADHUNTING	HEADSCARF	HEAPS
HAWSEHOLE	HAZARDRIES	HEADHUNTINGS	HEADSCARVES	HEAPSTEAD
HAWSEHOLES	HAZARDRY	HEADHUNTS	HEADSET	HEAPSTEADS
HAWSEPIPE	HAZARDS	HEADIER	HEADSETS	HEAPY
HAWSEPIPES	HAZE	HEADIEST	HEADSHAKE	HEAR
HAWSER	HAZED	HEADILY	HEADSHAKES	HEARABLE*
HAWSERS	HAZEL	HEADINESS	HEADSHIP	HEARD
HAWSES	HAZELHEN*	HEADINESSES	HEADSHIPS	HEARDS
HAWSING	HAZELHENS*	HEADING	HEADSHOT	HEARE
HAWTHORN	HAZELLY	HEADINGS	HEADSHOTS	HEARER
HAWTHORNS	HAZELNUT	HEADLAMP	HEADSMAN	HEARERS
HAY	HAZELNUTS	HEADLAMPS	HEADSMEN	HEARES
HAYBAND	HAZELS	HEADLAND	HEADSPACE*	HEARIE
HAYBANDS	HAZER	HEADLANDS	HEADSPACES*	HEARING
HAYBOX	HAZERS	HEADLEASE	HEADSTALL	HEARINGS
HAYBOXES	HAZES	HEADLEASES	HEADSTALLS	HEARKEN
HAYCOCK	HAZIER	HEADLESS	HEADSTAND*	HEARKENED
HAYCOCKS	HAZIEST	HEADLIGHT	HEADSTANDS*	HEARKENER
HAYED	HAZILY	HEADLIGHTS	HEADSTAY*	HEARKENERS
HAYER*	HAZINESS	HEADLINE	HEADSTAYS*	HEARKENING
HAYERS*	HAZINESSES	HEADLINED	HEADSTICK	HEARKENS
HAYFIELD	HAZING	HEADLINER	HEADSTICKS	HEARS
HAYFIELDS	HAZINGS	HEADLINERS	HEADSTOCK	HEARSAY
HAYFORK	HAZY	HEADLINES	HEADSTOCKS	HEARSAYS
HAYFORKS	HAZZAN	HEADLINING	HEADSTONE	HEARSE

The Chambers Dictionary is the authority for many longer words; see Introduction, page ix

HEARSED	HEATHEN	HEBRAIZE*	HEDGIER	HEFTY
HEARSES	HEATHENRIES	HEBRAIZED*	HEDGIEST	HEGARI*
HEARSIER	HEATHENRY	HEBRAIZES*	HEDGING	HEGARIS*
HEARSIEST	HEATHENS	HEBRAIZING*	HEDGINGLY*	HEGEMONIC
HEARSING	HEATHER	HECATOMB	HEDGINGS	HEGEMONIES
HEARSY	HEATHERIER	HECATOMBS	HEDGY	HEGEMONY
HEART	HEATHERIEST	HECH	HEDONIC	HEGIRA
HEARTACHE	HEATHERS	HECHT	HEDONICS	HEGIRAS
HEARTACHES	HEATHERY	HECHTING	HEDONISM	HEGUMEN*
HEARTBEAT	HEATHIER	HECHTS	HEDONISMS	HEGUMENE*
HEARTBEATS	HEATHIEST	HECK	HEDONIST	HEGUMENES*
HEARTBURN	HEATHLAND*	HECKLE	HEDONISTS	HEGUMENIES*
HEARTBURNS	HEATHLANDS*	HECKLED	HEDYPHANE	HEGUMENS*
HEARTED	HEATHLESS*	HECKLER	HEDYPHANES	HEGUMENY*
HEARTEN	HEATHLIKE*	HECKLERS	HEED	HEH*
HEARTENED	HEATHS	HECKLES	HEEDED	HEHS*
HEARTENING	HEATHY	HECKLING	HEEDER*	HEID
HEARTENS	HEATING	HECKLINGS	HEEDERS*	HEIDS
HEARTFELT	HEATINGS	HECKS	HEEDFUL	HEIFER
HEARTH	HEATLESS*	HECOGENIN	HEEDFULLY	HEIFERS
HEARTHS	HEATPROOF*	HECOGENINS	HEEDINESS	HEIGH
HEARTIER	HEATS	HECTARE	HEEDINESSES	HEIGHT
HEARTIES	HEATSPOT	HECTARES	HEEDING	HEIGHTEN
HEARTIEST	HEATSPOTS	HECTIC	HEEDLESS	HEIGHTENED
HEARTIKIN	HEAUME	HECTICAL	HEEDS	HEIGHTENING
HEARTIKINS	HEAUMES	HECTICLY*	HEEDY	HEIGHTENS
HEARTILY	HEAVE	HECTICS	HEEHAW	HEIGHTH*
HEARTING	HEAVED	HECTOGRAM	HEEHAWED	HEIGHTHS*
HEARTLAND	HEAVEN	HECTOGRAMS	HEEHAWING	HEIGHTS
HEARTLANDS	HEAVENLIER	HECTOR	HEEHAWS	HEIL
HEARTLESS	HEAVENLIEST	HECTORED	HEEL	HEILED*
HEARTLET	HEAVENLY	HECTORER	HEELBALL*	HEILING*
HEARTLETS	HEAVENS	HECTORERS	HEELBALLS*	HEILS*
HEARTLING	HEAVER	HECTORING	HEELED	HEIMISH*
HEARTLINGS	HEAVERS	HECTORINGS	HEELER	HEINIE*
HEARTLY	HEAVES	HECTORISM	HEELERS	HEINIES*
HEARTPEA	HEAVIER	HECTORISMS	HEELING	HEINOUS
HEARTPEAS	HEAVIES	HECTORLY	HEELINGS	HEINOUSLY
HEARTS	HEAVIEST	HECTORS	HEELLESS*	HEIR
HEARTSEED	HEAVILY	HEDDLE	HEELPIECE*	HEIRDOM
HEARTSEEDS	HEAVINESS	HEDDLED	HEELPIECES*	HEIRDOMS
HEARTSICK*	HEAVINESSES	HEDDLES	HEELPOST*	HEIRED
HEARTSOME	HEAVING	HEDDLING	HEELPOSTS*	HEIRESS
HEARTSORE*	HEAVINGS	HEDER*	HEELS	HEIRESSES
HEARTWOOD	HEAVY	HEDERAL	HEELTAP*	HEIRING
HEARTWOODS	HEAVYSET*	HEDERATED	HEELTAPS*	HEIRLESS
HEARTWORM*	HEBDOMAD	HEDERS*	HEEZE	HEIRLOOM
HEARTWORMS*	HEBDOMADS	HEDGE	HEEZED	HEIRLOOMS
HEARTY	HEBE	HEDGEBILL	HEEZES	HEIRS
HEAST	HEBEN	HEDGEBILLS	HEEZIE	HEIRSHIP
HEASTE	HEBENON	HEDGED	HEEZIES	HEIRSHIPS
HEASTES	HEBENONS	HEDGEHOG	HEEZING	HEISHI*
HEASTS	HEBENS	HEDGEHOGS	HEFT	HEIST
HEAT	HEBES	HEDGEHOP*	HEFTE	HEISTED
HEATABLE*	HEBETANT	HEDGEHOPPED*	HEFTED	HEISTER
HEATED	HEBETATE	HEDGEHOPPING*	HEFTER*	HEISTERS
HEATEDLY*	HEBETATED	HEDGEHOPS*	HEFTERS*	HEISTING
HEATER	HEBETATES	HEDGEPIG	HEFTIER	HEISTS
HEATERS	HEBETATING	HEDGEPIGS	HEFTIEST	HEJAB
HEATH	HEBETIC*	HEDGER	HEFTILY	HEJABS
HEATHBIRD	HEBETUDE	HEDGEROW	HEFTINESS	HEJIRA
HEATHBIRDS	HEBETUDES	HEDGEROWS	HEFTINESSES	HEJIRAS
HEATHCOCK	HEBONA	HEDGERS	HEFTING	HEJRA
HEATHCOCKS	HEBONAS	HEDGES	HEFTS	HEJRAS

Words marked with an asterisk are from OTCWL

HEKTARE*
HEKTARES*
HELCOID
HELD
HELE
HELED
HELENIUM
HELENIUMS
HELES
HELIAC
HELIACAL
HELIAST*
HELIASTS*
HELIBORNE
HELIBUS
HELIBUSES
HELIBUSSES
HELICAL
HELICALLY
HELICES
HELICITIES*
HELICITY*
HELICOID
HELICOIDS*
HELICON
HELICONS
HELICOPT*
HELICOPTED*
HELICOPTING*
HELICOPTS*
HELICTITE
HELICTITES
HELIDECK
HELIDECKS
HELIDROME
HELIDROMES
HELILIFT*
HELILIFTED*
HELILIFTING*
HELILIFTS*
HELIMAN
HELIMEN
HELING
HELIO*
HELIODOR
HELIODORS
HELIOLOGIES
HELIOLOGY
HELIOS*
HELIOSES
HELIOSIS
HELIOSTAT
HELIOSTATS
HELIOTYPE
HELIOTYPES
HELIOTYPIES
HELIOTYPY
HELIOZOAN
HELIOZOANS
HELIOZOIC
HELIPAD
HELIPADS
HELIPILOT
HELIPILOTS

HELIPORT
HELIPORTS
HELISCOOP
HELISCOOPS
HELISTOP
HELISTOPS
HELIUM
HELIUMS
HELIX
HELIXES
HELL
HELLBENT*
HELLBOX*
HELLBOXES*
HELLBROTH*
HELLBROTHS*
HELLCAT*
HELLCATS*
HELLEBORE
HELLEBORES
HELLED
HELLENISE
HELLENISED
HELLENISES
HELLENISING
HELLENIZE
HELLENIZED
HELLENIZES
HELLENIZING
HELLER
HELLERI*
HELLERIES*
HELLERS
HELLERY*
HELLFIRE
HELLFIRES
HELLHOLE*
HELLHOLES*
HELLHOUND
HELLHOUNDS
HELLICAT
HELLICATS
HELLIER
HELLIERS
HELLING
HELLION
HELLIONS
HELLISH
HELLISHLY
HELLKITE*
HELLKITES*
HELLO
HELLOED
HELLOES*
HELLOING
HELLOS
HELLOVA
HELLS
HELLUVA
HELLWARD
HELLWARDS
HELM
HELMED
HELMET

HELMETED
HELMETING*
HELMETS
HELMING
HELMINTH
HELMINTHS
HELMLESS
HELMS
HELMSMAN
HELMSMEN
HELO*
HELOS*
HELOT
HELOTAGE
HELOTAGES
HELOTISM
HELOTISMS
HELOTRIES
HELOTRY
HELOTS
HELP
HELPABLE
HELPDESK
HELPDESKS
HELPED
HELPER
HELPERS
HELPFUL
HELPFULLY*
HELPING
HELPINGS
HELPLESS
HELPLINE
HELPLINES
HELPMATE
HELPMATES
HELPMEET
HELPMEETS
HELPS
HELVE
HELVED
HELVES
HELVETIUM
HELVETIUMS
HELVING
HEM
HEMAGOG*
HEMAGOGS*
HEMAL
HEMATAL*
HEMATEIN*
HEMATEINS*
HEMATIC*
HEMATICS*
HEMATIN*
HEMATINE*
HEMATINES*
HEMATINIC*
HEMATINICS*
HEMATINS*
HEMATITE*
HEMATITES*
HEMATITIC*
HEMATOID*

HEMATOMA*
HEMATOMAS*
HEMATOMATA*
HEMATURIA*
HEMATURIAS*
HEME
HEMELYTRA*
HEMELYTRON*
HEMES
HEMIALGIA
HEMIALGIAS
HEMIC*
HEMICYCLE
HEMICYCLES
HEMIHEDRIES
HEMIHEDRY
HEMIN*
HEMINA
HEMINAS
HEMINS*
HEMIOLA
HEMIOLAS
HEMIOLIA
HEMIOLIAS
HEMIOLIC
HEMIONE
HEMIONES
HEMIONUS
HEMIONUSES
HEMIOPIA
HEMIOPIAS
HEMIOPIC
HEMIOPSIA
HEMIOPSIAS
HEMIPTER*
HEMIPTERS*
HEMISPACE
HEMISPACES
HEMISTICH
HEMISTICHS
HEMITROPE
HEMITROPES
HEMLINE*
HEMLINES*
HEMLOCK
HEMLOCKS
HEMMED
HEMMER*
HEMMERS*
HEMMING
HEMOCOEL*
HEMOCOELS*
HEMOCYTE*
HEMOCYTES*
HEMOID*
HEMOLYMPH*
HEMOLYMPHS*
HEMOLYSES*
HEMOLYSIN*
HEMOLYSINS*
HEMOLYSIS*
HEMOLYTIC*
HEMOLYZE*
HEMOLYZED*

HEMOLYZES*
HEMOLYZING*
HEMOSTAT*
HEMOSTATS*
HEMP
HEMPEN
HEMPIE*
HEMPIER
HEMPIES
HEMPIEST
HEMPLIKE*
HEMPS
HEMPSEED*
HEMPSEEDS*
HEMPWEED*
HEMPWEEDS*
HEMPY
HEMS
HEMSTITCH*
HEMSTITCHED*
HEMSTITCHES*
HEMSTITCHING*
HEN
HENBANE
HENBANES
HENBIT*
HENBITS*
HENCE
HENCHMAN
HENCHMEN
HENCOOP*
HENCOOPS*
HEND
HENDED
HENDIADYS
HENDIADYSES
HENDING
HENDS
HENEQUEN
HENEQUENS
HENEQUIN
HENEQUINS
HENGE
HENGES
HENHOUSE*
HENHOUSES*
HENIQUEN*
HENIQUENS*
HENIQUIN
HENIQUINS
HENLIKE*
HENNA
HENNAED
HENNAING*
HENNAS
HENNED
HENNER
HENNERIES
HENNERS
HENNERY
HENNIER
HENNIES
HENNIEST
HENNIN

The Chambers Dictionary is the authority for many longer words; see Introduction, page ix

HENNING	HEPTARCHY	HERCULEAN	HERISSON	HEROINE
HENNINS	HEPTOSE*	HERCULES*	HERISSONS	HEROINES
HENNY	HEPTOSES*	HERCULESES*	HERITABLE	HEROINISM*
HENOTIC	HER	HERCYNITE	HERITABLY	HEROINISMS*
HENPECK	HERALD	HERCYNITES	HERITAGE	HEROINS
HENPECKED	HERALDED	HERD	HERITAGES	HEROISE
HENPECKING	HERALDIC	HERDBOY	HERITOR	HEROISED
HENPECKS	HERALDING	HERDBOYS	HERITORS	HEROISES
HENRIES	HERALDRIES	HERDED	HERITRESS	HEROISING
HENRY	HERALDRY	HERDEN	HERITRESSES	HEROISM
HENRYS	HERALDS	HERDENS	HERITRICES	HEROISMS
HENS	HERB	HERDER*	HERITRIX	HEROIZE
HENT	HERBAGE	HERDERS*	HERITRIXES	HEROIZED
HENTED*	HERBAGED	HERDESS	HERKOGAMIES	HEROIZES
HENTING	HERBAGES	HERDESSES	HERKOGAMY	HEROIZING
HENTS	HERBAL	HERDIC	HERL	HERON
HEP	HERBALISM	HERDICS	HERLING	HERONRIES
HEPAR	HERBALISMS	HERDING	HERLINGS	HERONRY
HEPARIN	HERBALIST	HERDLIKE*	HERLS	HERONS
HEPARINS	HERBALISTS	HERDMAN	HERM	HERONSEW
HEPARS	HERBALS	HERDMEN	HERMA	HERONSEWS
HEPATIC	HERBAR	HERDS	HERMAE	HERONSHAW
HEPATICA*	HERBARIA	HERDSMAN	HERMAEAN*	HERONSHAWS
HEPATICAE*	HERBARIAN	HERDSMEN	HERMAI*	HEROON
HEPATICAL	HERBARIANS	HERDWICK	HERMANDAD	HEROONS
HEPATICAS*	HERBARIES	HERDWICKS	HERMANDADS	HEROS*
HEPATICS	HERBARIUM	HERE	HERMETIC	HEROSHIP
HEPATISE	HERBARIUMS	HEREABOUT	HERMETICS	HEROSHIPS
HEPATISED	HERBARS	HEREABOUTS	HERMETISM*	HERPES
HEPATISES	HERBARY	HEREAFTER	HERMETISMS*	HERPESES
HEPATISING	HERBED*	HEREAFTERS	HERMETIST*	HERPETIC
HEPATITE	HERBELET	HEREAT	HERMETISTS*	HERPETOID
HEPATITES	HERBELETS	HEREAWAY	HERMIT	HERRIED
HEPATITIDES*	HERBICIDE	HEREAWAYS*	HERMITAGE	HERRIES
HEPATITIS	HERBICIDES	HEREBY	HERMITAGES	HERRIMENT
HEPATITISES	HERBIER	HEREDES*	HERMITESS	HERRIMENTS
HEPATIZE	HERBIEST	HEREDITIES	HERMITESSES	HERRING
HEPATIZED	HERBIST	HEREDITY	HERMITIC*	HERRINGER
HEPATIZES	HERBISTS	HEREFROM	HERMITISM*	HERRINGERS
HEPATIZING	HERBIVORA	HEREIN	HERMITISMS*	HERRINGS
HEPATOMA*	HERBIVORE	HEREINTO*	HERMITRIES*	HERRY
HEPATOMAS*	HERBIVORES	HERENESS	HERMITRY*	HERRYING
HEPATOMATA*	HERBIVORIES	HERENESSES	HERMITS	HERRYMENT
HEPCAT*	HERBIVORY	HEREOF	HERMS	HERRYMENTS
HEPCATS*	HERBLESS	HEREON	HERN	HERS
HEPPER	HERBLET	HERES*	HERNIA	HERSALL
HEPPEST	HERBLETS	HERESIES	HERNIAE	HERSALLS
HEPS	HERBLIKE*	HERESY	HERNIAL	HERSE
HEPSTER	HERBORISE	HERETIC	HERNIAS	HERSED
HEPSTERS	HERBORISED	HERETICAL	HERNIATE*	HERSELF
HEPT	HERBORISES	HERETICS	HERNIATED	HERSES
HEPTAD	HERBORISING	HERETO	HERNIATES*	HERSHIP
HEPTADS	HERBORIST	HERETRICES*	HERNIATING*	HERSHIPS
HEPTAGLOT	HERBORISTS	HERETRIX*	HERNS	HERSTORIES
HEPTAGLOTS	HERBORIZE	HERETRIXES*	HERNSHAW	HERSTORY
HEPTAGON	HERBORIZED	HEREUNDER	HERNSHAWS	HERTZ
HEPTAGONS	HERBORIZES	HEREUNTO	HERO	HERTZES
HEPTANE	HERBORIZING	HEREUPON	HEROE	HERY
HEPTANES	HERBOSE	HEREWITH	HEROES	HERYE
HEPTAPODIES	HERBOUS	HERIED	HEROIC	HERYED
HEPTAPODY	HERBS	HERIES	HEROICAL	HERYES
HEPTARCH	HERBY	HERIOT	HEROICLY	HERYING
HEPTARCHIES	HERCOGAMIES	HERIOTS	HEROICS	HES
HEPTARCHS	HERCOGAMY	HERISSE	HEROIN	HESITANCE

Words marked with an asterisk are from OTCWL

HESITANCES	HEUCH	HEXASTICHS	HICCOUGHS	HIERACIUMS
HESITANCIES	HEUCHS	HEXASTYLE	HICCUP	HIERARCH
HESITANCY	HEUGH	HEXASTYLES	HICCUPED	HIERARCHIES
HESITANT	HEUGHS	HEXED	HICCUPING	HIERARCHS
HESITATE	HEUREKA	HEXENE	HICCUPPED*	HIERARCHY
HESITATED	HEUREKAS	HEXENES	HICCUPPING*	HIERATIC
HESITATER*	HEURETIC	HEXER*	HICCUPS	HIERATICA
HESITATERS*	HEURETICS	HEXEREI*	HICCUPY	HIERATICAS
HESITATES	HEURISM	HEXEREIS*	HICK	HIEROCRAT
HESITATING	HEURISMS	HEXERS*	HICKEY	HIEROCRATS
HESITATOR	HEURISTIC	HEXES	HICKEYS	HIERODULE
HESITATORS	HEURISTICS	HEXING	HICKIES*	HIERODULES
HESP	HEVEA	HEXINGS	HICKISH*	HIEROGRAM
HESPED	HEVEAS	HEXONE*	HICKORIES	HIEROGRAMS
HESPERID	HEW	HEXONES*	HICKORY	HIEROLOGIES
HESPERIDS	HEWABLE*	HEXOSAN*	HICKS	HIEROLOGY
HESPING	HEWED	HEXOSANS*	HICKWALL	HIERURGIES
HESPS	HEWER	HEXOSE	HICKWALLS	HIERURGY
HESSIAN	HEWERS	HEXOSES	HID	HIES
HESSIANS	HEWGH	HEXYL*	HIDABLE*	HIFALUTIN*
HESSITE*	HEWING	HEXYLENE	HIDAGE	HIGGLE
HESSITES*	HEWINGS	HEXYLENES	HIDAGES	HIGGLED
HESSONITE	HEWN	HEXYLS*	HIDALGA	HIGGLER
HESSONITES	HEWS	HEY	HIDALGAS	HIGGLERS
HEST	HEX	HEYDAY	HIDALGO	HIGGLES
HESTERNAL	HEXACHORD	HEYDAYS	HIDALGOS	HIGGLING
HESTS	HEXACHORDS	HEYDEY*	HIDDEN	HIGGLINGS
HET	HEXACT	HEYDEYS*	HIDDENITE	HIGH
HETAERA	HEXACTS	HEYDUCK	HIDDENITES	HIGHBALL
HETAERAE	HEXAD	HEYDUCKS	HIDDENLY	HIGHBALLED
HETAERAS*	HEXADE*	HEYED	HIDDER	HIGHBALLING
HETAERIC*	HEXADES*	HEYING	HIDDERS	HIGHBALLS
HETAERISM	HEXADIC	HEYS	HIDE	HIGHBORN*
HETAERISMS	HEXADS	HI	HIDEAWAY*	HIGHBOY
HETAIRA	HEXAFOIL	HIANT	HIDEAWAYS*	HIGHBOYS
HETAIRAI	HEXAFOILS	HIATAL*	HIDEBOUND*	HIGHBRED*
HETAIRAS	HEXAGLOT	HIATUS	HIDED	HIGHBROW
HETAIRIA	HEXAGON	HIATUSES	HIDELESS*	HIGHBROWS
HETAIRIAS	HEXAGONAL	HIBACHI	HIDEOSITIES	HIGHBUSH*
HETAIRISM	HEXAGONS	HIBACHIS	HIDEOSITY	HIGHCHAIR
HETAIRISMS	HEXAGRAM	HIBAKUSHA	HIDEOUS	HIGHCHAIRS
HETAIRIST	HEXAGRAMS	HIBERNAL	HIDEOUSLY	HIGHED
HETAIRISTS	HEXAHEDRA	HIBERNATE	HIDEOUT	HIGHER
HETE	HEXAHEDRON*	HIBERNATED	HIDEOUTS	HIGHERED
HETERO	HEXAHEDRONS*	HIBERNATES	HIDER	HIGHERING
HETERODOX	HEXAMETER	HIBERNATING	HIDERS	HIGHERS
HETERONYM	HEXAMETERS	HIBERNISE	HIDES	HIGHEST
HETERONYMS	HEXAMINE*	HIBERNISED	HIDING	HIGHFLIER*
HETEROPOD	HEXAMINES*	HIBERNISES	HIDINGS	HIGHFLIERS*
HETEROPODS	HEXANE	HIBERNISING	HIDLING	HIGHFLYER*
HETEROS	HEXANES	HIBERNIZE	HIDLINGS	HIGHFLYERS*
HETEROSES	HEXAPLA	HIBERNIZED	HIDLINS	HIGHING
HETEROSIS	HEXAPLAR	HIBERNIZES	HIDROSES	HIGHISH
HETEROTIC	HEXAPLAS	HIBERNIZING	HIDROSIS	HIGHJACK
HETES	HEXAPLOID	HIBISCUS	HIDROTIC	HIGHJACKED
HETH*	HEXAPLOIDS	HIBISCUSES	HIDROTICS	HIGHJACKING
HETHER	HEXAPOD	HIC	HIE	HIGHJACKS
HETHS*	HEXAPODIES	HICATEE	HIED	HIGHLAND
HETING	HEXAPODS	HICATEES	HIEING	HIGHLANDS
HETMAN	HEXAPODY	HICCATEE	HIELAMAN	HIGHLIFE*
HETMANATE	HEXARCH	HICCATEES	HIELAMANS	HIGHLIFES*
HETMANATES	HEXARCHIES*	HICCOUGH	HIEMAL	HIGHLIGHT
HETMANS	HEXARCHY*	HICCOUGHED	HIEMS	HIGHLIGHTED
HETS	HEXASTICH	HICCOUGHING	HIERACIUM	HIGHLIGHTING

The Chambers Dictionary is the authority for many longer words; see Introduction, page ix

HIGHLIGHTS	HILLFOLK	HINDSIGHTS	HIPPURIC	HISPANISM*
HIGHLY	HILLIER	HINDWARD	HIPPURITE	HISPANISMS*
HIGHMAN	HILLIEST	HINDWING	HIPPURITES	HISPID
HIGHMEN	HILLINESS	HINDWINGS	HIPPUS	HISPIDITIES
HIGHMOST	HILLINESSES	HING	HIPPUSES	HISPIDITY
HIGHNESS	HILLING	HINGE	HIPPY	HISS
HIGHNESSES	HILLMEN	HINGED	HIPPYDOM	HISSED
HIGHROAD	HILLO	HINGER*	HIPPYDOMS	HISSELF*
HIGHROADS	HILLOA*	HINGERS*	HIPS	HISSER*
HIGHS	HILLOAED*	HINGES	HIPSHOT*	HISSERS*
HIGHSPOT*	HILLOAING*	HINGING	HIPSTER	HISSES
HIGHSPOTS*	HILLOAS*	HINGS	HIPSTERS	HISSIES*
HIGHT	HILLOCK	HINNIED	HIPT	HISSING
HIGHTAIL	HILLOCKS	HINNIES	HIRABLE	HISSINGLY
HIGHTAILED	HILLOCKY	HINNY	HIRAGANA	HISSINGS
HIGHTAILING	HILLOED	HINNYING	HIRAGANAS	HISSY*
HIGHTAILS	HILLOES*	HINS	HIRAGE	HIST
HIGHTED*	HILLOING	HINT	HIRAGES	HISTAMIN*
HIGHTH	HILLOS	HINTED	HIRCINE	HISTAMINE
HIGHTHS	HILLS	HINTER*	HIRCOSITIES	HISTAMINES
HIGHTING	HILLSIDE	HINTERS*	HIRCOSITY	HISTAMINS*
HIGHTS	HILLSIDES	HINTING	HIRE	HISTED
HIGHWAY	HILLTOP	HINTINGLY	HIREABLE	HISTIDIN*
HIGHWAYS	HILLTOPS	HINTS	HIREAGE	HISTIDINE
HIJAB	HILLY	HIP	HIREAGES	HISTIDINES
HIJABS	HILT	HIPBONE*	HIRED	HISTIDINS*
HIJACK	HILTED	HIPBONES*	HIRELING	HISTIE
HIJACKED	HILTING	HIPLESS*	HIRELINGS	HISTING
HIJACKER	HILTLESS*	HIPLIKE*	HIRER	HISTIOID
HIJACKERS	HILTS	HIPLINE*	HIRERS	HISTOGEN
HIJACKING	HILUM	HIPLINES*	HIRES	HISTOGENIES
HIJACKS	HILUS	HIPNESS	HIRING	HISTOGENS
HIJINKS	HIM	HIPNESSES	HIRINGS	HISTOGENY
HIJRA	HIMATIA	HIPPARCH	HIRLING	HISTOGRAM
HIJRAH	HIMATION	HIPPARCHS	HIRLINGS	HISTOGRAMS
HIJRAHS	HIMATIONS	HIPPED	HIRPLE	HISTOID
HIJRAS	HIMBO	HIPPEN	HIRPLED	HISTOLOGIES
HIKE	HIMBOS	HIPPENS	HIRPLES	HISTOLOGY
HIKED	HIMSELF	HIPPER	HIRPLING	HISTONE
HIKER	HIN	HIPPEST	HIRRIENT	HISTONES
HIKERS	HIND	HIPPIATRIES	HIRRIENTS	HISTORIAN
HIKES	HINDBERRIES	HIPPIATRY	HIRSEL	HISTORIANS
HIKING	HINDBERRY	HIPPIC	HIRSELED*	HISTORIC
HILA	HINDBRAIN	HIPPIE	HIRSELING*	HISTORIED
HILAR	HINDBRAINS	HIPPIEDOM	HIRSELLED	HISTORIES
HILARIOUS	HINDER	HIPPIEDOMS	HIRSELLING	HISTORIFIED
HILARITIES	HINDERED	HIPPIER	HIRSELS	HISTORIFIES
HILARITY	HINDERER	HIPPIES	HIRSLE	HISTORIFY
HILCH	HINDERERS	HIPPIEST	HIRSLED	HISTORIFYING
HILCHED	HINDERING	HIPPIN	HIRSLES	HISTORISM
HILCHES	HINDERS	HIPPINESS*	HIRSLING	HISTORISMS
HILCHING	HINDFEET	HIPPINESSES*	HIRSTIE	HISTORY
HILD	HINDFOOT	HIPPING	HIRSUTE	HISTORYING
HILDING	HINDGUT*	HIPPINGS	HIRSUTISM	HISTRIO
HILDINGS	HINDGUTS*	HIPPINS	HIRSUTISMS	HISTRION
HILI	HINDHEAD	HIPPISH	HIRUDIN	HISTRIONS
HILL	HINDHEADS	HIPPO	HIRUDINS	HISTRIOS
HILLBILLIES*	HINDLEG	HIPPOCRAS	HIRUNDINE	HISTS
HILLBILLY*	HINDLEGS	HIPPOCRASES	HIS	HIT
HILLCREST*	HINDMOST	HIPPODAME	HISH	HITCH
HILLCRESTS*	HINDRANCE	HIPPODAMES	HISHED	HITCHED
HILLED	HINDRANCES	HIPPOLOGIES	HISHES	HITCHER
HILLER*	HINDS	HIPPOLOGY	HISHING	HITCHERS
HILLERS*	HINDSIGHT	HIPPOS	HISN	HITCHES

HITCHHIKE*	HOARHEADS	HOBJOBBED	HODMAN	HOGNUTS*
HITCHHIKED*	HOARHOUND	HOBJOBBER	HODMANDOD	HOGS
HITCHHIKES*	HOARHOUNDS	HOBJOBBERS	HODMANDODS	HOGSHEAD
HITCHHIKING*	HOARIER	HOBJOBBING	HODMEN	HOGSHEADS
HITCHIER	HOARIEST	HOBJOBBINGS	HODOGRAPH	HOGTIE
HITCHIEST	HOARILY	HOBJOBS	HODOGRAPHS	HOGTIED
HITCHILY	HOARINESS	HOBLIKE*	HODOMETER	HOGTIEING*
HITCHING	HOARINESSES	HOBNAIL	HODOMETERS	HOGTIES
HITCHY	HOARING	HOBNAILED	HODOMETRIES	HOGTYING
HITHE	HOARS	HOBNAILING	HODOMETRY	HOGWARD
HITHER	HOARSE	HOBNAILS	HODOSCOPE	HOGWARDS
HITHERED	HOARSELY	HOBNOB	HODOSCOPES	HOGWASH
HITHERING	HOARSEN	HOBNOBBED	HODS	HOGWASHES
HITHERS	HOARSENED	HOBNOBBER*	HOE	HOGWEED
HITHERTO	HOARSENING	HOBNOBBERS*	HOECAKE*	HOGWEEDS
HITHES	HOARSENS	HOBNOBBING	HOECAKES*	HOH
HITLESS*	HOARSER	HOBNOBBY	HOED	HOHED
HITS	HOARSEST	HOBNOBS	HOEDOWN	HOHING
HITTER	HOARY	HOBO	HOEDOWNS	HOHS
HITTERS	HOAS	HOBODOM	HOEING	HOI
HITTING	HOAST	HOBODOMS	HOELIKE*	HOICK
HIVE	HOASTED	HOBOED	HOER	HOICKED
HIVED	HOASTING	HOBOES	HOERS	HOICKING
HIVELESS	HOASTMAN	HOBOING	HOES	HOICKS
HIVELIKE	HOASTMEN	HOBOISM	HOG	HOICKSED
HIVER	HOASTS	HOBOISMS	HOGAN	HOICKSES
HIVERS	HOATZIN	HOBOS	HOGANS	HOICKSING
HIVES	HOATZINES*	HOBS	HOGBACK	HOIDEN
HIVEWARD	HOATZINS	HOC	HOGBACKS	HOIDENED*
HIVEWARDS	HOAX	HOCK	HOGEN	HOIDENING*
HIVING	HOAXED	HOCKED	HOGENS	HOIDENS
HIYA	HOAXER	HOCKER	HOGFISH*	HOIK
HIZEN	HOAXERS	HOCKERS	HOGFISHES*	HOIKED
HIZENS	HOAXES	HOCKEY	HOGG	HOIKING
HIZZ	HOAXING	HOCKEYS	HOGGED	HOIKS
HIZZED	HOB	HOCKING	HOGGER	HOING
HIZZES	HOBBED*	HOCKS	HOGGEREL	HOISE
HIZZING	HOBBIES	HOCKSHOP*	HOGGERELS	HOISED
HIZZONER*	HOBBING*	HOCKSHOPS*	HOGGERIES	HOISES
HIZZONERS*	HOBBISH	HOCUS	HOGGERS	HOISING
HM*	HOBBIT	HOCUSED	HOGGERY	HOIST
HMM*	HOBBITRIES	HOCUSES	HOGGET	HOISTED
HO	HOBBITRY	HOCUSING	HOGGETS	HOISTER
HOA	HOBBITS	HOCUSSED	HOGGIN	HOISTERS
HOACTZIN	HOBBLE	HOCUSSES	HOGGING	HOISTING
HOACTZINES*	HOBBLED	HOCUSSING	HOGGINGS	HOISTINGS
HOACTZINS	HOBBLER	HOD	HOGGINS	HOISTMAN
HOAED	HOBBLERS	HODAD*	HOGGISH	HOISTMEN
HOAGIE*	HOBBLES	HODADDIES*	HOGGISHLY	HOISTS
HOAGIES*	HOBBLING	HODADDY*	HOGGS	HOISTWAY
HOAGY*	HOBBLINGS	HODADS*	HOGH	HOISTWAYS
HOAING	HOBBY	HODDED	HOGHOOD	HOKE
HOAR	HOBBYISM	HODDEN	HOGHOODS	HOKED
HOARD	HOBBYISMS	HODDENS	HOGHS	HOKES
HOARDED	HOBBYIST	HODDIN*	HOGLIKE*	HOKEY
HOARDER	HOBBYISTS	HODDING	HOGMANAY*	HOKEYNESS*
HOARDERS	HOBBYLESS	HODDINS*	HOGMANAYS*	HOKEYNESSES*
HOARDING	HOBDAY	HODDLE	HOGMANE*	HOKI
HOARDINGS	HOBDAYED	HODDLED	HOGMANES*	HOKIER
HOARDS	HOBDAYING	HODDLES	HOGMENAY*	HOKIEST
HOARED	HOBDAYS	HODDLING	HOGMENAYS*	HOKILY*
HOARFROST*	HOBGOBLIN	HODIERNAL	HOGNOSE*	HOKINESS*
HOARFROSTS*	HOBGOBLINS	HODJA	HOGNOSES*	HOKINESSES*
HOARHEAD	HOBJOB	HODJAS	HOGNUT*	HOKING

HOKIS	HOLLAED*	HOLOTYPES	HOMEMADE*	HOMINIANS*
HOKKU	HOLLAING*	HOLOTYPIC	HOMEMAKER	HOMINID
HOKUM	HOLLAND	HOLOZOIC	HOMEMAKERS	HOMINIDS
HOKUMS	HOLLANDS	HOLP	HOMEOBOX	HOMINIES
HOKYPOKIES*	HOLLAS	HOLPEN	HOMEOBOXES*	HOMININE*
HOKYPOKY*	HOLLER	HOLS	HOMEOMERIES	HOMINIZE*
HOLANDRIC*	HOLLERED	HOLSTEIN*	HOMEOMERY	HOMINIZED*
HOLARD*	HOLLERING	HOLSTEINS*	HOMEOPATH	HOMINIZES*
HOLARDS*	HOLLERS	HOLSTER	HOMEOPATHS	HOMINIZING*
HOLD	HOLLIDAM	HOLSTERED	HOMEOSES	HOMINOID
HOLDABLE*	HOLLIDAMS	HOLSTERS	HOMEOSIS	HOMINOIDS
HOLDALL*	HOLLIES	HOLT	HOMEOTIC	HOMINY
HOLDALLS*	HOLLO	HOLTS	HOMEOWNER	HOMME
HOLDBACK	HOLLOA	HOLY	HOMEOWNERS	HOMMES
HOLDBACKS	HOLLOAED	HOLYDAM	HOMEPORT*	HOMMOCK
HOLDEN	HOLLOAING	HOLYDAME	HOMEPORTED*	HOMMOCKS
HOLDER	HOLLOAS	HOLYDAMES	HOMEPORTING*	HOMMOS*
HOLDERBAT	HOLLOED	HOLYDAMS	HOMEPORTS*	HOMMOSES*
HOLDERBATS	HOLLOES	HOLYDAY*	HOMER	HOMO
HOLDERS	HOLLOING	HOLYDAYS*	HOMERED*	HOMODONT
HOLDFAST	HOLLOO*	HOLYSTONE	HOMERING*	HOMODYNE
HOLDFASTS	HOLLOOED*	HOLYSTONED	HOMEROOM*	HOMOEOBOX
HOLDING	HOLLOOING*	HOLYSTONES	HOMEROOMS*	HOMOEOSES
HOLDINGS	HOLLOOS*	HOLYSTONING	HOMERS	HOMOEOSIS
HOLDOUT	HOLLOS	HOLYTIDE*	HOMES	HOMOEOTIC
HOLDOUTS	HOLLOW	HOLYTIDES*	HOMESICK	HOMOGAMIC
HOLDOVER	HOLLOWARE	HOMAGE	HOMESITE*	HOMOGAMIES
HOLDOVERS	HOLLOWARES	HOMAGED	HOMESITES*	HOMOGAMY
HOLDS	HOLLOWED	HOMAGER	HOMESPUN	HOMOGENIES
HOLDUP*	HOLLOWER	HOMAGERS	HOMESPUNS	HOMOGENY
HOLDUPS*	HOLLOWEST	HOMAGES	HOMESTALL	HOMOGONIES*
HOLE	HOLLOWING	HOMAGING	HOMESTALLS	HOMOGONY*
HOLED	HOLLOWLY	HOMALOID	HOMESTAY*	HOMOGRAFT
HOLELESS*	HOLLOWS	HOMALOIDS	HOMESTAYS*	HOMOGRAFTS
HOLES	HOLLY	HOMBRE	HOMESTEAD	HOMOGRAPH
HOLESOM	HOLLYHOCK	HOMBRES	HOMESTEADED*	HOMOGRAPHS
HOLESOME	HOLLYHOCKS	HOMBURG*	HOMESTEADING*	HOMOLOG
HOLEY	HOLM	HOMBURGS*	HOMESTEADS	HOMOLOGIES
HOLIBUT	HOLMIA	HOME	HOMETOWN*	HOMOLOGS
HOLIBUTS	HOLMIAS	HOMEBODIES*	HOMETOWNS*	HOMOLOGUE
HOLIDAY	HOLMIC	HOMEBODY*	HOMEWARD	HOMOLOGUES
HOLIDAYED	HOLMIUM	HOMEBOUND	HOMEWARDS	HOMOLOGY
HOLIDAYER*	HOLMIUMS	HOMEBOY	HOMEWORK	HOMOLYSES*
HOLIDAYERS*	HOLMS	HOMEBOYS	HOMEWORKS	HOMOLYSIS*
HOLIDAYING	HOLOCAUST	HOMEBRED*	HOMEY	HOMOLYTIC*
HOLIDAYS	HOLOCAUSTS	HOMEBREDS*	HOMEYNESS*	HOMOMORPH
HOLIER	HOLOCRINE	HOMEBUILT*	HOMEYNESSES*	HOMOMORPHS
HOLIES	HOLOGAMIES*	HOMEBUYER	HOMICIDAL	HOMONYM
HOLIEST	HOLOGAMY*	HOMEBUYERS	HOMICIDE	HOMONYMIC
HOLILY	HOLOGRAM	HOMECRAFT	HOMICIDES	HOMONYMIES
HOLINESS	HOLOGRAMS	HOMECRAFTS	HOMIER	HOMONYMS
HOLINESSES	HOLOGRAPH	HOMED	HOMIEST	HOMONYMY
HOLING	HOLOGRAPHED	HOMEFELT	HOMILETIC	HOMOPHILE
HOLINGS	HOLOGRAPHING	HOMEGROWN*	HOMILETICS	HOMOPHILES
HOLISM	HOLOGRAPHS	HOMELAND	HOMILIES	HOMOPHOBE
HOLISMS	HOLOGYNIES*	HOMELANDS	HOMILIST	HOMOPHOBES
HOLIST	HOLOGYNY*	HOMELESS	HOMILISTS	HOMOPHONE
HOLISTIC	HOLOHEDRA	HOMELIER	HOMILY	HOMOPHONES
HOLISTS	HOLOPHOTE	HOMELIEST	HOMINES*	HOMOPHONIES
HOLK*	HOLOPHOTES	HOMELIKE	HOMINESS*	HOMOPHONY
HOLKED*	HOLOPHYTE	HOMELILY	HOMINESSES*	HOMOPHYLIES
HOLKING*	HOLOPHYTES	HOMELY	HOMING	HOMOPHYLY
HOLKS*	HOLOPTIC	HOMELYN	HOMINGS	HOMOPLASIES
HOLLA	HOLOTYPE	HOMELYNS	HOMINIAN*	HOMOPLASY

Words marked with an asterisk are from OTCWL

HOMOPOLAR	HONEYCOMBS	HOODIER*	HOOLACHAN	HOOTS
HOMOS	HONEYDEW*	HOODIES	HOOLACHANS	HOOTY*
HOMOSEX*	HONEYDEWS*	HOODIEST*	HOOLEY	HOOVE
HOMOSEXES*	HONEYED	HOODING	HOOLEYS	HOOVED
HOMOSPORIES*	HONEYFUL*	HOODLESS	HOOLICAN	HOOVEN
HOMOSPORY*	HONEYING	HOODLIKE*	HOOLICANS	HOOVER
HOMOTAXES	HONEYLESS	HOODLUM	HOOLIE*	HOOVERED
HOMOTAXIC	HONEYMOON	HOODLUMS	HOOLIER	HOOVERING
HOMOTAXIS	HONEYMOONED	HOODMAN	HOOLIEST	HOOVERS
HOMOTONIC	HONEYMOONING	HOODMEN	HOOLIGAN	HOOVES
HOMOTONIES	HONEYMOONS	HOODOO	HOOLIGANS	HOOVING
HOMOTONY	HONEYPOT	HOODOOED	HOOLOCK	HOP
HOMOTYPAL	HONEYPOTS	HOODOOING	HOOLOCKS	HOPBIND
HOMOTYPE	HONEYS	HOODOOISM*	HOOLY	HOPBINDS
HOMOTYPES	HONG	HOODOOISMS*	HOON	HOPBINE
HOMOTYPIC	HONGI	HOODOOS	HOONS	HOPBINES
HOMOTYPIES	HONGING	HOODS	HOOP	HOPDOG
HOMOTYPY	HONGIS	HOODWINK	HOOPED	HOPDOGS
HOMOUSIAN	HONGS	HOODWINKED	HOOPER	HOPE
HOMOUSIANS	HONIED	HOODWINKING	HOOPERS	HOPED
HOMUNCLE	HONING	HOODWINKS	HOOPING	HOPEFUL
HOMUNCLES	HONK	HOODY*	HOOPLA*	HOPEFULLY
HOMUNCULE	HONKED	HOOEY	HOOPLAS*	HOPEFULS
HOMUNCULES	HONKER	HOOEYS	HOOPLESS*	HOPELESS
HOMUNCULI	HONKERS	HOOF	HOOPLIKE*	HOPER
HOMUNCULUS*	HONKEY*	HOOFBEAT	HOOPOE	HOPERS
HOMY	HONKEYS*	HOOFBEATS	HOOPOES	HOPES
HON	HONKIE	HOOFED	HOOPOO*	HOPHEAD*
HONAN*	HONKIES	HOOFER	HOOPOOS*	HOPHEADS*
HONANS*	HONKING	HOOFERS	HOOPS	HOPING
HONCHO	HONKS	HOOFING	HOOPSKIRT*	HOPINGLY
HONCHOED*	HONKY	HOOFLESS	HOOPSKIRTS*	HOPLITE
HONCHOING*	HONOR	HOOFLIKE*	HOOPSTER*	HOPLITES
HONCHOS	HONORABLE*	HOOFPRINT	HOOPSTERS*	HOPLITIC*
HOND	HONORABLY*	HOOFPRINTS	HOORAH	HOPLOLOGIES
HONDA*	HONORAND	HOOFROT	HOORAHED	HOPLOLOGY
HONDAS*	HONORANDS	HOOFROTS	HOORAHING	HOPPED
HONDLE*	HONORARIA	HOOFS	HOORAHS	HOPPER
HONDLED*	HONORARIES	HOOK	HOORAY	HOPPERS
HONDLES*	HONORARIUM*	HOOKA	HOORAYED	HOPPIER
HONDLING*	HONORARIUMS*	HOOKAH	HOORAYING	HOPPIEST
HONDS	HONORARY	HOOKAHS	HOORAYS	HOPPING
HONE	HONORED	HOOKAS	HOORD	HOPPINGS
HONED	HONOREE*	HOOKED	HOORDS	HOPPLE
HONER	HONOREES*	HOOKER	HOOROO	HOPPLED
HONERS	HONORER*	HOOKERS	HOOSEGOW	HOPPLES
HONES	HONORERS*	HOOKEY	HOOSEGOWS	HOPPLING
HONEST	HONORIFIC	HOOKEYS	HOOSGOW	HOPPY
HONESTER	HONORIFICS	HOOKIER	HOOSGOWS	HOPS
HONESTEST	HONORING	HOOKIES	HOOSH	HOPSACK
HONESTIES	HONORS	HOOKIEST	HOOSHED	HOPSACKS
HONESTLY	HONOUR	HOOKING	HOOSHES	HOPSCOTCH
HONESTY	HONOURED	HOOKLESS*	HOOSHING	HOPSCOTCHED*
HONEWORT	HONOURER	HOOKLET*	HOOT	HOPSCOTCHES
HONEWORTS	HONOURERS	HOOKLETS*	HOOTCH	HOPSCOTCHING*
HONEY	HONOURING	HOOKLIKE*	HOOTCHES	HOPTOAD*
HONEYBEE*	HONOURS	HOOKNOSE*	HOOTED	HOPTOADS*
HONEYBEES*	HONS	HOOKNOSES*	HOOTER	HORA*
HONEYBUN	HOO	HOOKS	HOOTERS	HORAH*
HONEYBUNS	HOOCH	HOOKUP*	HOOTIER*	HORAHS*
HONEYCOMB	HOOCHES	HOOKUPS*	HOOTIEST*	HORAL
HONEYCOMBED	HOOD	HOOKWORM*	HOOTING	HORARY
HONEYCOMBING	HOODED	HOOKWORMS*	HOOTNANNIES	HORAS*
HONEYCOMBINGS	HOODIE	HOOKY	HOOTNANNY	HORDE

The Chambers Dictionary is the authority for many longer words; see Introduction, page ix

HORDED	HORNS	HORSEMEN	HOSIERS	HOTCHES
HORDEIN	HORNSTONE	HORSEMINT	HOSIERY	HOTCHING
HORDEINS	HORNSTONES	HORSEMINTS	HOSING	HOTCHPOT
HORDEOLA	HORNTAIL	HORSEPLAY	HOSPICE	HOTCHPOTS
HORDEOLUM	HORNTAILS	HORSEPLAYS	HOSPICES	HOTDOG*
HORDES	HORNWORK	HORSEPOND	HOSPITAGE	HOTDOGGED*
HORDING	HORNWORKS	HORSEPONDS	HOSPITAGES	HOTDOGGER*
HORDOCK	HORNWORM	HORSEPOX*	HOSPITAL	HOTDOGGERS*
HORDOCKS	HORNWORMS	HORSEPOXES*	HOSPITALE	HOTDOGGING*
HORE	HORNWORT	HORSES	HOSPITALES	HOTDOGS*
HOREHOUND	HORNWORTS	HORSESHIT*	HOSPITALS	HOTE
HOREHOUNDS	HORNWRACK	HORSESHITS*	HOSPITIA	HOTEL
HORIZON	HORNWRACKS	HORSESHOD*	HOSPITIUM	HOTELDOM*
HORIZONAL*	HORNY	HORSESHOE	HOSPODAR	HOTELDOMS*
HORIZONS	HORNYHEAD	HORSESHOED*	HOSPODARS	HOTELIER
HORKEY	HORNYHEADS	HORSESHOEING*	HOSS	HOTELIERS
HORKEYS	HOROLOGE	HORSESHOES	HOSSES	HOTELMAN*
HORME	HOROLOGER	HORSETAIL	HOST	HOTELMEN*
HORMES	HOROLOGERS	HORSETAILS	HOSTA	HOTELS
HORMONAL	HOROLOGES	HORSEWAY	HOSTAGE	HOTEN
HORMONE	HOROLOGIC	HORSEWAYS	HOSTAGES	HOTFOOT
HORMONES	HOROLOGIES	HORSEWEED*	HOSTAS	HOTFOOTED*
HORMONIC	HOROLOGY	HORSEWEEDS*	HOSTED	HOTFOOTING*
HORN	HOROMETRIES	HORSEWHIP	HOSTEL	HOTFOOTS*
HORNBEAK	HOROMETRY	HORSEWHIPPED	HOSTELED*	HOTHEAD
HORNBEAKS	HOROSCOPE	HORSEWHIPPING	HOSTELER	HOTHEADED
HORNBEAM	HOROSCOPES	HORSEWHIPS	HOSTELERS	HOTHEADS
HORNBEAMS	HOROSCOPIES	HORSEY	HOSTELING*	HOTHOUSE
HORNBILL	HOROSCOPY	HORSIER	HOSTELLED*	HOTHOUSES
HORNBILLS	HORRENT	HORSIEST	HOSTELLER	HOTLINE
HORNBOOK	HORRIBLE	HORSILY*	HOSTELLERS	HOTLINES
HORNBOOKS	HORRIBLES*	HORSINESS	HOSTELLING*	HOTLY
HORNBUG	HORRIBLY	HORSINESSES	HOSTELRIES	HOTNESS
HORNBUGS	HORRID	HORSING	HOSTELRY	HOTNESSES
HORNED	HORRIDER	HORSINGS	HOSTELS	HOTPOT
HORNER	HORRIDEST	HORSON	HOSTESS	HOTPOTS
HORNERS	HORRIDLY	HORSONS	HOSTESSED	HOTPRESS*
HORNET	HORRIFIC	HORST	HOSTESSES	HOTPRESSED*
HORNETS	HORRIFIED	HORSTE*	HOSTESSING	HOTPRESSES*
HORNFELS	HORRIFIES	HORSTES*	HOSTILE	HOTPRESSING*
HORNFUL	HORRIFY	HORSTS	HOSTILELY	HOTROD*
HORNFULS	HORRIFYING	HORSY	HOSTILES*	HOTRODS*
HORNGELD	HORROR	HORTATION	HOSTILITIES	HOTS
HORNGELDS	HORRORS	HORTATIONS	HOSTILITY	HOTSHOT
HORNIER	HORS	HORTATIVE	HOSTING	HOTSHOTS
HORNIEST	HORSE	HORTATORY	HOSTINGS	HOTSPUR*
HORNILY*	HORSEBACK	HOS	HOSTLER	HOTSPURS*
HORNINESS	HORSEBACKS	HOSANNA	HOSTLERS	HOTTED
HORNINESSES	HORSEBEAN*	HOSANNAED*	HOSTLESSE	HOTTENTOT
HORNING	HORSEBEANS*	HOSANNAH*	HOSTLY*	HOTTENTOTS
HORNINGS	HORSECAR	HOSANNAING*	HOSTRIES	HOTTER
HORNISH	HORSECARS	HOSANNAS	HOSTRY	HOTTERED
HORNIST	HORSED	HOSE	HOSTS	HOTTERING
HORNISTS	HORSEFLIES	HOSED	HOT	HOTTERS
HORNITO	HORSEFLY	HOSEL*	HOTBED	HOTTEST
HORNITOS	HORSEHAIR	HOSELS*	HOTBEDS	HOTTIE
HORNLESS	HORSEHAIRS	HOSEMAN	HOTBLOOD*	HOTTIES
HORNLET	HORSEHIDE	HOSEMEN	HOTBLOODS*	HOTTING
HORNLETS	HORSEHIDES	HOSEN	HOTBOX*	HOTTINGS
HORNLIKE*	HORSELESS	HOSEPIPE	HOTBOXES*	HOTTISH
HORNPIPE	HORSELIKE*	HOSEPIPES	HOTCAKE*	HOUDAH
HORNPIPES	HORSEMAN	HOSES	HOTCAKES*	HOUDAHS
HORNPOUT*	HORSEMEAT	HOSIER	HOTCH	HOUDAN
HORNPOUTS*	HORSEMEATS	HOSIERIES	HOTCHED	HOUDANS

HOUF	HOUSEMAN	HOWF	HUBBUB	HUGGING
HOUFED	HOUSEMATE*	HOWFED	HUBBUBOO	HUGS
HOUFF	HOUSEMATES*	HOWFF	HUBBUBOOS	HUGY
HOUFFED	HOUSEMEN	HOWFFED	HUBBUBS	HUH
HOUFFING	HOUSER*	HOWFFING	HUBBY	HUI
HOUFFS	HOUSEROOM	HOWFFS	HUBCAP*	HUIA
HOUFING	HOUSEROOMS	HOWFING	HUBCAPS*	HUIAS
HOUFS	HOUSERS*	HOWFS	HUBRIS	HUIC*
HOUGH	HOUSES	HOWITZER	HUBRISES	HUIPIL*
HOUGHED	HOUSESAT*	HOWITZERS	HUBRISTIC	HUIPILES*
HOUGHING	HOUSESIT*	HOWK	HUBS	HUIPILS*
HOUGHS	HOUSESITS*	HOWKED	HUCK	HUIS
HOUMMOS	HOUSESITTING*	HOWKER	HUCKABACK	HUISACHE*
HOUMMOSES	HOUSETOP	HOWKERS	HUCKABACKS	HUISACHES*
HOUMUS	HOUSETOPS	HOWKING	HUCKLE	HUISSIER
HOUMUSES	HOUSEWIFE	HOWKS	HUCKLES	HUISSIERS
HOUND	HOUSEWIVES	HOWL	HUCKS	HUITAIN
HOUNDED	HOUSEWORK	HOWLED	HUCKSTER	HUITAINS
HOUNDER*	HOUSEWORKS	HOWLER	HUCKSTERED	HULA
HOUNDERS*	HOUSEY	HOWLERS	HUCKSTERIES	HULAS
HOUNDING	HOUSIER	HOWLET	HUCKSTERING	HULE
HOUNDS	HOUSIEST	HOWLETS	HUCKSTERS	HULES
HOUR	HOUSING	HOWLING	HUCKSTERY	HULK
HOURGLASS*	HOUSINGS	HOWLINGLY*	HUDDEN	HULKED*
HOURGLASSES*	HOUSLING	HOWLINGS	HUDDLE	HULKIER
HOURI	HOUT	HOWLS	HUDDLED	HULKIEST
HOURIS	HOUTED	HOWRE	HUDDLER*	HULKING
HOURLONG	HOUTING	HOWRES	HUDDLERS*	HULKS
HOURLY	HOUTINGS	HOWS	HUDDLES	HULKY
HOURPLATE	HOUTS	HOWSO	HUDDLING	HULL
HOURPLATES	HOVE	HOWSOEVER	HUDDUP	HULLED
HOURS	HOVED	HOWTOWDIE	HUE	HULLER*
HOUSE	HOVEL	HOWTOWDIES	HUED	HULLERS*
HOUSEBOAT	HOVELED	HOWZAT	HUELESS	HULLIER
HOUSEBOATS	HOVELING	HOX	HUER	HULLIEST
HOUSEBOY	HOVELLED	HOXED	HUERS	HULLING
HOUSEBOYS	HOVELLER	HOXES	HUES	HULLO
HOUSECARL*	HOVELLERS	HOXING	HUFF	HULLOA*
HOUSECARLS*	HOVELLING	HOY	HUFFED	HULLOAED*
HOUSECOAT	HOVELS	HOYA	HUFFIER	HULLOAING*
HOUSECOATS	HOVEN	HOYAS	HUFFIEST	HULLOAS*
HOUSED	HOVER	HOYDEN	HUFFILY	HULLOED
HOUSEFLIES	HOVERED	HOYDENED*	HUFFINESS	HULLOES*
HOUSEFLY	HOVERER*	HOYDENING*	HUFFINESSES	HULLOING
HOUSEFUL	HOVERERS*	HOYDENISH	HUFFING	HULLOS
HOUSEFULS	HOVERING	HOYDENISM	HUFFISH	HULLS
HOUSEHOLD	HOVERPORT	HOYDENISMS	HUFFISHLY	HULLY
HOUSEHOLDS	HOVERPORTS	HOYDENS	HUFFKIN	HUM
HOUSEKEEP*	HOVERS	HOYED	HUFFKINS	HUMA
HOUSEKEEPING*	HOVES	HOYING	HUFFS	HUMAN
HOUSEKEEPS*	HOVING	HOYLE*	HUFFY	HUMANE
HOUSEKEPT*	HOW	HOYLES*	HUG	HUMANELY
HOUSEL	HOWBE	HOYS	HUGE	HUMANER
HOUSELED*	HOWBEIT	HUANACO	HUGELY	HUMANEST
HOUSELEEK*	HOWDAH	HUANACOS	HUGENESS	HUMANISE
HOUSELEEKS*	HOWDAHS	HUAQUERO	HUGENESSES	HUMANISED
HOUSELESS	HOWDIE	HUAQUEROS	HUGEOUS	HUMANISES
HOUSELING*	HOWDIED*	HUARACHE*	HUGEOUSLY	HUMANISING
HOUSELLED	HOWDIES	HUARACHES*	HUGER	HUMANISM
HOUSELLING	HOWDY	HUARACHO*	HUGEST	HUMANISMS
HOUSELLINGS	HOWDYING*	HUARACHOS*	HUGGABLE	HUMANIST
HOUSELS	HOWE	HUB	HUGGED	HUMANISTS
HOUSEMAID	HOWES	HUBBIES	HUGGER*	HUMANITIES
HOUSEMAIDS	HOWEVER	HUBBLY*	HUGGERS*	HUMANITY

The Chambers Dictionary is the authority for many longer words; see Introduction, page ix

HUMANIZE	HUMFS	HUMORESKS	HUNGERS	HURLY
HUMANIZED	HUMHUM	HUMORFUL*	HUNGOVER*	HURRA
HUMANIZER*	HUMHUMS	HUMORING	HUNGRIER	HURRAED
HUMANIZERS*	HUMIC	HUMORIST	HUNGRIEST	HURRAH
HUMANIZES	HUMID	HUMORISTS	HUNGRILY	HURRAHED
HUMANIZING	HUMIDER	HUMORLESS	HUNGRY	HURRAHING
HUMANKIND	HUMIDEST	HUMOROUS	HUNH*	HURRAHS
HUMANKINDS	HUMIDIFIED	HUMORS	HUNK	HURRAING
HUMANLIKE	HUMIDIFIES	HUMOUR	HUNKER	HURRAS
HUMANLY	HUMIDIFY	HUMOURED	HUNKERED	HURRAY
HUMANNESS	HUMIDIFYING	HUMOURING	HUNKERING	HURRAYED
HUMANNESSES	HUMIDITIES	HUMOURS	HUNKERS	HURRAYING
HUMANOID	HUMIDITY	HUMOUS	HUNKIER	HURRAYS
HUMANOIDS	HUMIDLY	HUMP	HUNKIES	HURRICANE
HUMANS	HUMIDNESS	HUMPBACK	HUNKIEST	HURRICANES
HUMAS	HUMIDNESSES	HUMPBACKS	HUNKS	HURRICANO
HUMATE*	HUMIDOR	HUMPED	HUNKSES	HURRICANOES
HUMATES*	HUMIDORS	HUMPEN	HUNKY	HURRIED
HUMBLE	HUMIFIED	HUMPENS	HUNNISH*	HURRIEDLY
HUMBLED	HUMIFIES	HUMPER	HUNS*	HURRIER*
HUMBLER	HUMIFY	HUMPERS	HUNT	HURRIERS*
HUMBLERS*	HUMIFYING	HUMPH	HUNTABLE*	HURRIES
HUMBLES	HUMILIANT	HUMPHED	HUNTED	HURRY
HUMBLESSE	HUMILIATE	HUMPHING	HUNTEDLY*	HURRYING
HUMBLESSES	HUMILIATED	HUMPHS	HUNTER	HURRYINGS
HUMBLEST	HUMILIATES	HUMPIER	HUNTERS	HURST
HUMBLING	HUMILIATING	HUMPIES	HUNTING	HURSTS
HUMBLINGS	HUMILITIES	HUMPIEST	HUNTINGS	HURT
HUMBLY	HUMILITY	HUMPING	HUNTRESS	HURTER
HUMBUG	HUMITE	HUMPLESS*	HUNTRESSES	HURTERS
HUMBUGGED	HUMITES	HUMPS	HUNTS	HURTFUL
HUMBUGGER	HUMLIE	HUMPTIES	HUNTSMAN	HURTFULLY
HUMBUGGERS	HUMLIES	HUMPTY	HUNTSMEN	HURTING
HUMBUGGING	HUMMABLE	HUMPY	HUP	HURTLE
HUMBUGS	HUMMAUM	HUMS	HUPPAH	HURTLED
HUMBUZZ	HUMMAUMS	HUMSTRUM	HUPPAHS	HURTLES
HUMBUZZES	HUMMED	HUMSTRUMS	HUPPED	HURTLESS
HUMDINGER	HUMMEL	HUMUNGOUS	HUPPING	HURTLING
HUMDINGERS	HUMMELLED	HUMUS	HUPS	HURTS
HUMDRUM	HUMMELLER	HUMUSES	HURCHEON	HUSBAND
HUMDRUMS	HUMMELLERS	HUMUSY	HURCHEONS	HUSBANDED
HUMECT	HUMMELLING	HUMVEE*	HURDEN	HUSBANDER*
HUMECTANT	HUMMELS	HUMVEES*	HURDENS	HUSBANDERS*
HUMECTANTS	HUMMER	HUN*	HURDIES	HUSBANDING
HUMECTATE	HUMMERS	HUNCH	HURDLE	HUSBANDLY
HUMECTATED	HUMMING	HUNCHBACK	HURDLED	HUSBANDRIES
HUMECTATES	HUMMINGS	HUNCHBACKS	HURDLER	HUSBANDRY
HUMECTATING	HUMMOCK	HUNCHED	HURDLERS	HUSBANDS
HUMECTED	HUMMOCKED	HUNCHES	HURDLES	HUSH
HUMECTING	HUMMOCKING*	HUNCHING	HURDLING	HUSHABIED
HUMECTIVE	HUMMOCKS	HUNDRED	HURDLINGS	HUSHABIES
HUMECTIVES	HUMMOCKY	HUNDREDER	HURDS	HUSHABY
HUMECTS	HUMMUM	HUNDREDERS	HURL	HUSHABYING
HUMEFIED	HUMMUMS	HUNDREDOR	HURLBAT	HUSHED
HUMEFIES	HUMMUS	HUNDREDORS	HURLBATS	HUSHEDLY*
HUMEFY	HUMMUSES	HUNDREDS	HURLED	HUSHER
HUMEFYING	HUMOGEN	HUNDREDTH	HURLER	HUSHERED
HUMERAL	HUMOGENS	HUNDREDTHS	HURLERS	HUSHERING
HUMERALS	HUMONGOUS	HUNG	HURLEY	HUSHERS
HUMERI	HUMOR	HUNGER	HURLEYS	HUSHES
HUMERUS	HUMORAL	HUNGERED	HURLIES	HUSHFUL*
HUMF	HUMORALLY	HUNGERFUL	HURLING	HUSHIER
HUMFED	HUMORED	HUNGERING	HURLINGS	HUSHIEST
HUMFING	HUMORESK	HUNGERLY	HURLS	HUSHING

HUSHY	HUZZAS	HYDRAGOGS*	HYDRONAUTS	HYGRISTORS
HUSK	HUZZIES	HYDRANGEA	HYDRONIC*	HYGRODEIK
HUSKED	HUZZY	HYDRANGEAS	HYDRONIUM*	HYGRODEIKS
HUSKER	HWAN*	HYDRANT	HYDRONIUMS*	HYGROLOGIES
HUSKERS	HWYL	HYDRANTH	HYDROPIC	HYGROLOGY
HUSKIER	HWYLS	HYDRANTHS	HYDROPS*	HYGROPHIL
HUSKIES	HYACINE	HYDRANTS	HYDROPSES*	HYGROSTAT
HUSKIEST	HYACINES	HYDRAS	HYDROPSIES	HYGROSTATS
HUSKILY	HYACINTH	HYDRASE*	HYDROPSY	HYING
HUSKINESS	HYACINTHS	HYDRASES*	HYDROPTIC	HYKE
HUSKINESSES	HYAENA	HYDRATE	HYDROPULT	HYKES
HUSKING	HYAENAS	HYDRATED	HYDROPULTS	HYLA*
HUSKINGS	HYAENIC*	HYDRATES	HYDROS	HYLAS*
HUSKLIKE*	HYALIN*	HYDRATING	HYDROSERE*	HYLDING
HUSKS	HYALINE	HYDRATION	HYDROSERES*	HYLDINGS
HUSKY	HYALINES	HYDRATIONS	HYDROSKI	HYLE
HUSO	HYALINISE	HYDRATOR*	HYDROSKIS	HYLEG
HUSOS	HYALINISED	HYDRATORS*	HYDROSOL*	HYLEGS
HUSS	HYALINISES	HYDRAULIC	HYDROSOLS*	HYLES
HUSSAR	HYALINISING	HYDRAULICKED	HYDROSOMA	HYLIC
HUSSARS	HYALINIZE	HYDRAULICKING	HYDROSOMATA	HYLICISM
HUSSES	HYALINIZED	HYDRAULICS	HYDROSOME	HYLICISMS
HUSSIES	HYALINIZES	HYDRAZIDE*	HYDROSOMES	HYLICIST
HUSSIF	HYALINIZING	HYDRAZIDES*	HYDROSTAT	HYLICISTS
HUSSIFS	HYALINS*	HYDRAZINE	HYDROSTATS	HYLISM
HUSSY	HYALITE	HYDRAZINES	HYDROUS	HYLISMS
HUSTINGS	HYALITES	HYDREMIA	HYDROVANE	HYLIST
HUSTLE	HYALOGEN*	HYDREMIAS	HYDROVANES	HYLISTS
HUSTLED	HYALOGENS*	HYDRIA	HYDROXIDE	HYLOBATE
HUSTLER	HYALOID	HYDRIAE	HYDROXIDES	HYLOBATES
HUSTLERS	HYALOIDS*	HYDRIC	HYDROXY	HYLOIST
HUSTLES	HYALONEMA	HYDRID*	HYDROXYL	HYLOISTS
HUSTLING	HYALONEMAS	HYDRIDE	HYDROXYLS	HYLOPHYTE
HUSTLINGS	HYBRID	HYDRIDES	HYDROZOA	HYLOPHYTES
HUSWIFE	HYBRIDISE	HYDRIDS*	HYDROZOAN	HYLOZOIC*
HUSWIFES*	HYBRIDISED	HYDRIODIC	HYDROZOANS	HYLOZOISM
HUSWIVES	HYBRIDISES	HYDRO	HYDROZOON	HYLOZOISMS
HUT	HYBRIDISING	HYDROCELE	HYDYNE	HYLOZOIST
HUTCH	HYBRIDISM	HYDROCELES	HYDYNES	HYLOZOISTS
HUTCHED	HYBRIDISMS	HYDROFOIL	HYE	HYMEN
HUTCHES	HYBRIDITIES	HYDROFOILS	HYED	HYMENAEAL
HUTCHING	HYBRIDITY	HYDROGEL*	HYEING	HYMENAEAN
HUTIA	HYBRIDIZE	HYDROGELS*	HYEN	HYMENAL
HUTIAS	HYBRIDIZED	HYDROGEN	HYENA	HYMENEAL
HUTLIKE*	HYBRIDIZES	HYDROGENS	HYENAS	HYMENEALS
HUTMENT	HYBRIDIZING	HYDROID	HYENIC*	HYMENEAN
HUTMENTS	HYBRIDOMA	HYDROIDS	HYENINE*	HYMENIA
HUTS	HYBRIDOMAS	HYDROLASE*	HYENOID*	HYMENIAL
HUTTED	HYBRIDOUS	HYDROLASES*	HYENS	HYMENIUM
HUTTING	HYBRIDS	HYDROLOGIES	HYES	HYMENIUMS
HUTTINGS	HYBRIS	HYDROLOGY	HYETAL	HYMENS
HUTZPA*	HYBRISES	HYDROLYSE	HYETOLOGIES	HYMN
HUTZPAH	HYDATHODE	HYDROLYSED	HYETOLOGY	HYMNAL
HUTZPAHS	HYDATHODES	HYDROLYSES	HYGEIST*	HYMNALS
HUTZPAS*	HYDATID	HYDROLYSING	HYGEISTS*	HYMNARIES
HUZOOR	HYDATIDS	HYDROLYTE	HYGIEIST*	HYMNARY
HUZOORS	HYDATOID	HYDROLYTES	HYGIEISTS*	HYMNBOOK*
HUZZA	HYDRA	HYDROLYZE	HYGIENE	HYMNBOOKS*
HUZZAED	HYDRACID*	HYDROLYZED	HYGIENES	HYMNED
HUZZAH*	HYDRACIDS*	HYDROLYZES	HYGIENIC	HYMNIC
HUZZAHED*	HYDRAE*	HYDROLYZING	HYGIENICS	HYMNING
HUZZAHING*	HYDRAEMIA	HYDROMEL	HYGIENIST	HYMNIST
HUZZAHS*	HYDRAEMIAS	HYDROMELS	HYGIENISTS	HYMNISTS
HUZZAING	HYDRAGOG*	HYDRONAUT	HYGRISTOR	HYMNLESS*

HYMNLIKE*	HYPERGOLS*	HYPHENIZES	HYPOCAUSTS	HYPOPLOIDS*
HYMNODIES	HYPERLINK	HYPHENIZING	HYPOCIST	HYPOPNEA*
HYMNODIST	HYPERLINKS	HYPHENS	HYPOCISTS	HYPOPNEAS*
HYMNODISTS	HYPERMART	HYPING	HYPOCOTYL	HYPOPYON*
HYMNODY	HYPERMARTS	HYPINOSES	HYPOCOTYLS	HYPOPYONS*
HYMNOLOGIES	HYPERNYM	HYPINOSIS	HYPOCRISIES	HYPOS
HYMNOLOGY	HYPERNYMIES	HYPNIC	HYPOCRISY	HYPOSTOME*
HYMNS	HYPERNYMS	HYPNICS	HYPOCRITE	HYPOSTOMES*
HYNDE	HYPERNYMY	HYPNOGENIES	HYPOCRITES	HYPOSTYLE
HYNDES	HYPERON	HYPNOGENY	HYPODERM	HYPOSTYLES
HYOID	HYPERONS	HYPNOID	HYPODERMA	HYPOTAXES
HYOIDAL*	HYPEROPE*	HYPNOIDAL	HYPODERMAS	HYPOTAXIS
HYOIDEAN*	HYPEROPES*	HYPNOLOGIES	HYPODERMS	HYPOTHEC
HYOIDS*	HYPEROPIA	HYPNOLOGY	HYPOED*	HYPOTHECS
HYOSCINE	HYPEROPIAS	HYPNONE	HYPOGAEA	HYPOTONIA
HYOSCINES	HYPEROPIC*	HYPNONES	HYPOGAEAL	HYPOTONIAS
HYP	HYPERPNEA*	HYPNOSES	HYPOGAEAN	HYPOTONIC
HYPALGIA	HYPERPNEAS*	HYPNOSIS	HYPOGAEUM	HYPOXEMIA
HYPALGIAS	HYPERPURE*	HYPNOTEE	HYPOGEA	HYPOXEMIAS
HYPALLAGE	HYPERS	HYPNOTEES	HYPOGEAL	HYPOXEMIC
HYPALLAGES	HYPERTEXT	HYPNOTIC	HYPOGEAN	HYPOXIA
HYPANTHIA	HYPERTEXTS	HYPNOTICS	HYPOGENE	HYPOXIAS
HYPANTHIUM*	HYPES	HYPNOTISE	HYPOGEOUS	HYPOXIC
HYPATE	HYPHA	HYPNOTISED	HYPOGEUM	HYPPED
HYPATES	HYPHAE	HYPNOTISES	HYPOGYNIES	HYPPING
HYPE	HYPHAL	HYPNOTISING	HYPOGYNY	HYPS
HYPED	HYPHEMIA*	HYPNOTISM	HYPOID	HYPURAL
HYPER	HYPHEMIAS*	HYPNOTISMS	HYPOING*	HYRACES
HYPERACID*	HYPHEN	HYPNOTIST	HYPOMANIA	HYRACOID
HYPERARID*	HYPHENATE	HYPNOTISTS	HYPOMANIAS	HYRACOIDS*
HYPERBOLA	HYPHENATED	HYPNOTIZE	HYPOMANIC	HYRAX
HYPERBOLAE*	HYPHENATES	HYPNOTIZED	HYPOMORPH*	HYRAXES
HYPERBOLAS	HYPHENATING	HYPNOTIZES	HYPOMORPHS*	HYSON
HYPERBOLE	HYPHENED	HYPNOTIZING	HYPONASTIES	HYSONS
HYPERBOLES	HYPHENIC	HYPNOTOID	HYPONASTY	HYSSOP
HYPERCUBE	HYPHENING	HYPNUM	HYPONEA*	HYSSOPS
HYPERCUBES	HYPHENISE	HYPNUMS	HYPONEAS*	HYSTERIA
HYPEREMIA	HYPHENISED	HYPO	HYPONOIA*	HYSTERIAS
HYPEREMIAS	HYPHENISES	HYPOACID*	HYPONOIAS*	HYSTERIC
HYPEREMIC	HYPHENISING	HYPOBLAST	HYPONYM	HYSTERICS
HYPERFINE*	HYPHENISM	HYPOBLASTS	HYPONYMIES	HYSTEROID
HYPERGAMIES	HYPHENISMS	HYPOBOLE	HYPONYMS	HYTE*
HYPERGAMY	HYPHENIZE	HYPOBOLES	HYPONYMY	HYTHE
HYPERGOL*	HYPHENIZED	HYPOCAUST	HYPOPLOID*	HYTHES

I

IAMB	ICEPACK	ICONIFIED	IDEALIZES	IDIOPATHY
IAMBI	ICEPACKS	ICONIFIES	IDEALIZING	IDIOPHONE
IAMBIC	ICER	ICONIFY	IDEALLESS	IDIOPHONES
IAMBICS	ICERS	ICONIFYING	IDEALLY	IDIOPLASM
IAMBIST	ICES	ICONISE	IDEALOGIES*	IDIOPLASMS
IAMBISTS	ICESTONE	ICONISED	IDEALOGUE	IDIOT
IAMBS	ICESTONES	ICONISES	IDEALOGUES	IDIOTCIES
IAMBUS	ICH	ICONISING	IDEALOGY*	IDIOTCY
IAMBUSES	ICHABOD	ICONIZE	IDEALS	IDIOTIC
IANTHINE	ICHED	ICONIZED	IDEAS	IDIOTICAL
IATRIC*	ICHES	ICONIZES	IDEATE	IDIOTICON
IATRICAL*	ICHING	ICONIZING	IDEATED	IDIOTICONS
IATROGENIES	ICHNEUMON	ICONOLOGIES	IDEATES	IDIOTISH
IATROGENY	ICHNEUMONS	ICONOLOGY	IDEATING	IDIOTISM
IBERIS	ICHNITE	ICONOSTAS	IDEATION	IDIOTISMS
IBERISES	ICHNITES	ICONOSTASES	IDEATIONS	IDIOTS
IBEX	ICHNOLITE	ICONS	IDEATIVE	IDLE
IBEXES	ICHNOLITES	ICTAL	IDEE	IDLED
IBICES	ICHNOLOGIES	ICTERIC	IDEES	IDLEHOOD
IBIDEM	ICHNOLOGY	ICTERICAL	IDEM	IDLEHOODS
IBIS	ICHOR	ICTERICALS	IDENTIC	IDLENESS
IBISES	ICHOROUS	ICTERICS	IDENTICAL	IDLENESSES
IBOGAINE*	ICHORS	ICTERID	IDENTIFIED	IDLER
IBOGAINES*	ICHS*	ICTERIDS	IDENTIFIES	IDLERS
IBUPROFEN	ICHTHIC	ICTERINE	IDENTIFY	IDLES
IBUPROFENS	ICHTHYIC	ICTERUS	IDENTIFYING	IDLESSE
ICE	ICHTHYOID	ICTERUSES	IDENTIKIT	IDLESSES
ICEBALL	ICHTHYOIDS	ICTIC	IDENTIKITS	IDLEST
ICEBALLS	ICHTHYS	ICTUS	IDENTITIES	IDLING
ICEBERG	ICHTHYSES	ICTUSES	IDENTITY	IDLY
ICEBERGS	ICICLE	ICY	IDEOGRAM	IDOCRASE
ICEBLINK	ICICLED*	ID	IDEOGRAMS	IDOCRASES
ICEBLINKS	ICICLES	IDANT	IDEOGRAPH	IDOL
ICEBOAT	ICIER	IDANTS	IDEOGRAPHS	IDOLA
ICEBOATER*	ICIEST	IDE	IDEOLOGIC	IDOLATER
ICEBOATERS*	ICILY	IDEA	IDEOLOGIES	IDOLATERS
ICEBOATS	ICINESS	IDEAED	IDEOLOGUE	IDOLATOR
ICEBOUND	ICINESSES	IDEAL	IDEOLOGUES	IDOLATORS
ICEBOX	ICING	IDEALESS	IDEOLOGY	IDOLATRIES
ICEBOXES	ICINGS	IDEALISE	IDEOMOTOR	IDOLATRY
ICECAP	ICK*	IDEALISED	IDEOPHONE	IDOLISE
ICECAPS	ICKER	IDEALISER	IDEOPHONES	IDOLISED
ICED	ICKERS	IDEALISERS	IDES	IDOLISER
ICEFALL*	ICKIER	IDEALISES	IDIOBLAST	IDOLISERS
ICEFALLS*	ICKIEST	IDEALISING	IDIOBLASTS	IDOLISES
ICEFIELD	ICKILY*	IDEALISM	IDIOCIES	IDOLISING
ICEFIELDS	ICKINESS*	IDEALISMS	IDIOCY	IDOLISM
ICEHOUSE*	ICKINESSES*	IDEALIST	IDIOGRAPH	IDOLISMS
ICEHOUSES*	ICKY	IDEALISTS	IDIOGRAPHS	IDOLIST
ICEKHANA*	ICON	IDEALITIES	IDIOLECT	IDOLISTS
ICEKHANAS*	ICONES*	IDEALITY	IDIOLECTS	IDOLIZE
ICELESS*	ICONIC	IDEALIZE	IDIOM	IDOLIZED
ICELIKE*	ICONICAL*	IDEALIZED	IDIOMATIC	IDOLIZER
ICEMAN*	ICONICITIES*	IDEALIZER	IDIOMS	IDOLIZERS
ICEMEN*	ICONICITY*	IDEALIZERS	IDIOPATHIES	IDOLIZES

The Chambers Dictionary is the authority for many longer words; see Introduction, page ix

IDOLIZING	IGNOMIES	ILLAPSE	ILMENITE	IMBATHED
IDOLS	IGNOMINIES	ILLAPSED	ILMENITES	IMBATHES
IDOLUM	IGNOMINY	ILLAPSES	IMAGE	IMBATHING
IDONEITIES*	IGNOMY	ILLAPSING	IMAGEABLE	IMBECILE
IDONEITY*	IGNORABLE	ILLATION	IMAGED	IMBECILES
IDONEOUS*	IGNORAMI*	ILLATIONS	IMAGELESS	IMBECILIC
IDS	IGNORAMUS	ILLATIVE	IMAGER*	IMBED
IDYL	IGNORAMUSES	ILLATIVES	IMAGERIES	IMBEDDED
IDYLIST*	IGNORANCE	ILLEGAL	IMAGERS*	IMBEDDING
IDYLISTS*	IGNORANCES	ILLEGALLY	IMAGERY	IMBEDS
IDYLL	IGNORANT	ILLEGALS*	IMAGES	IMBIBE
IDYLLIAN	IGNORANTS	ILLEGIBLE	IMAGINAL	IMBIBED
IDYLLIC	IGNORE	ILLEGIBLY	IMAGINARIES*	IMBIBER
IDYLLIST	IGNORED	ILLER*	IMAGINARY	IMBIBERS
IDYLLISTS	IGNORER	ILLEST*	IMAGINE	IMBIBES
IDYLLS	IGNORERS	ILLIAD	IMAGINED	IMBIBING
IDYLS	IGNORES	ILLIADS	IMAGINER	IMBITTER
IF	IGNORING	ILLIBERAL	IMAGINERS	IMBITTERED
IFF	IGUANA	ILLICIT	IMAGINES	IMBITTERING
IFFIER	IGUANAS	ILLICITLY	IMAGING	IMBITTERS
IFFIEST	IGUANIAN*	ILLIMITED	IMAGINGS	IMBLAZE*
IFFINESS	IGUANIANS*	ILLINIUM	IMAGINING	IMBLAZED*
IFFINESSES	IGUANID	ILLINIUMS	IMAGININGS	IMBLAZES*
IFFY	IGUANIDS	ILLIPE	IMAGINIST	IMBLAZING*
IFS	IGUANODON	ILLIPES	IMAGINISTS	IMBODIED
IGAD	IGUANODONS	ILLIQUID	IMAGISM	IMBODIES
IGAPO	IHRAM	ILLISION	IMAGISMS	IMBODY
IGAPOS	IHRAMS	ILLISIONS	IMAGIST	IMBODYING
IGARAPE	IJTIHAD	ILLITE	IMAGISTIC	IMBOLDEN*
IGARAPES	IJTIHADS	ILLITES	IMAGISTS	IMBOLDENED*
IGLOO	IKAT	ILLITIC*	IMAGO	IMBOLDENING*
IGLOOS	IKATS	ILLNESS	IMAGOES	IMBOLDENS*
IGLU*	IKEBANA	ILLNESSES	IMAGOS	IMBORDER
IGLUS*	IKEBANAS	ILLOGIC	IMAM	IMBORDERED
IGNARO	IKON	ILLOGICAL	IMAMATE	IMBORDERING
IGNAROES	IKONS	ILLOGICS	IMAMATES	IMBORDERS
IGNAROS	ILEA	ILLS	IMAMS	IMBOSK
IGNATIA*	ILEAC	ILLTH	IMARET	IMBOSKED
IGNATIAS*	ILEAL*	ILLTHS	IMARETS	IMBOSKING
IGNEOUS	ILEITIDES*	ILLUDE	IMARI	IMBOSKS
IGNESCENT	ILEITIS	ILLUDED	IMARIS	IMBOSOM
IGNESCENTS	ILEITISES	ILLUDES	IMAUM	IMBOSOMED
IGNIFIED*	ILEOSTOMIES	ILLUDING	IMAUMS	IMBOSOMING
IGNIFIES*	ILEOSTOMY	ILLUME	IMBALANCE	IMBOSOMS
IGNIFY*	ILEUM	ILLUMED	IMBALANCES	IMBOSS
IGNIFYING*	ILEUS	ILLUMES	IMBALM*	IMBOSSED
IGNITABLE	ILEUSES	ILLUMINE	IMBALMED*	IMBOSSES
IGNITE	ILEX	ILLUMINED	IMBALMER*	IMBOSSING
IGNITED	ILEXES	ILLUMINER	IMBALMERS*	IMBOWER
IGNITER	ILIA	ILLUMINERS	IMBALMING*	IMBOWERED
IGNITERS	ILIAC	ILLUMINES	IMBALMS*	IMBOWERING
IGNITES	ILIACUS	ILLUMING	IMBAR	IMBOWERS
IGNITIBLE	ILIACUSES	ILLUMINING	IMBARK	IMBRANGLE
IGNITING	ILIAD*	ILLUPI	IMBARKED	IMBRANGLED
IGNITION	ILIADS*	ILLUPIS	IMBARKING	IMBRANGLES
IGNITIONS	ILIAL*	ILLUSION	IMBARKS	IMBRANGLING
IGNITOR*	ILICES	ILLUSIONS	IMBARRED	IMBRAST
IGNITORS*	ILIUM	ILLUSIVE	IMBARRING	IMBREX
IGNITRON	ILK	ILLUSORY	IMBARS	IMBRICATE
IGNITRONS	ILKA	ILLUVIA	IMBASE	IMBRICATED
IGNOBLE	ILKADAY	ILLUVIAL	IMBASED	IMBRICATES
IGNOBLER	ILKADAYS	ILLUVIUM	IMBASES	IMBRICATING
IGNOBLEST	ILKS	ILLUVIUMS	IMBASING	IMBRICES
IGNOBLY	ILL	ILLY	IMBATHE	IMBROGLIO

IMBROGLIOS	IMMASKED	IMMODESTY	IMPALAS	IMPEACHERS
IMBROWN	IMMASKING	IMMOLATE	IMPALE	IMPEACHES
IMBROWNED	IMMASKS	IMMOLATED	IMPALED	IMPEACHING
IMBROWNING	IMMATURE	IMMOLATES	IMPALER*	IMPEARL
IMBROWNS	IMMATURES*	IMMOLATING	IMPALERS*	IMPEARLED
IMBRUE	IMMEDIACIES	IMMOLATOR	IMPALES	IMPEARLING
IMBRUED	IMMEDIACY	IMMOLATORS	IMPALING	IMPEARLS
IMBRUES	IMMEDIATE	IMMOMENT	IMPANATE	IMPECCANT
IMBRUING	IMMENSE	IMMORAL	IMPANEL	IMPED
IMBRUTE	IMMENSELY	IMMORALLY	IMPANELED*	IMPEDANCE
IMBRUTED	IMMENSER	IMMORTAL	IMPANELING*	IMPEDANCES
IMBRUTES	IMMENSEST	IMMORTALS	IMPANELLED	IMPEDE
IMBRUTING	IMMENSITIES	IMMOTILE*	IMPANELLING	IMPEDED
IMBUE	IMMENSITY	IMMOVABLE	IMPANELS	IMPEDER*
IMBUED	IMMERGE	IMMOVABLES	IMPANNEL	IMPEDERS*
IMBUES	IMMERGED	IMMOVABLY	IMPANNELLED	IMPEDES
IMBUING	IMMERGES	IMMUNE	IMPANNELLING	IMPEDING
IMBURSE	IMMERGING	IMMUNES	IMPANNELS	IMPEL
IMBURSED	IMMERSE	IMMUNISE	IMPARITIES	IMPELLED
IMBURSES	IMMERSED	IMMUNISED	IMPARITY	IMPELLENT
IMBURSING	IMMERSES	IMMUNISES	IMPARK	IMPELLENTS
IMID*	IMMERSING	IMMUNISING	IMPARKED	IMPELLER
IMIDAZOLE	IMMERSION	IMMUNITIES	IMPARKING	IMPELLERS
IMIDAZOLES	IMMERSIONS	IMMUNITY	IMPARKS	IMPELLING
IMIDE	IMMESH	IMMUNIZE	IMPARL	IMPELLOR*
IMIDES	IMMESHED	IMMUNIZED	IMPARLED	IMPELLORS*
IMIDIC	IMMESHES	IMMUNIZES	IMPARLING	IMPELS
IMIDO*	IMMESHING	IMMUNIZING	IMPARLS	IMPEND
IMIDS*	IMMEW	IMMUNOGEN	IMPART	IMPENDED
IMINE	IMMEWED	IMMUNOGENS	IMPARTED	IMPENDENT
IMINES	IMMEWING	IMMURE	IMPARTER	IMPENDING
IMINO*	IMMEWS	IMMURED	IMPARTERS	IMPENDS
IMITABLE	IMMIES*	IMMURES	IMPARTIAL	IMPENNATE
IMITANCIES	IMMIGRANT	IMMURING	IMPARTING	IMPERATOR
IMITANCY	IMMIGRANTS	IMMUTABLE	IMPARTS	IMPERATORS
IMITANT	IMMIGRATE	IMMUTABLY	IMPASSE	IMPERFECT
IMITANTS	IMMIGRATED	IMMY*	IMPASSES	IMPERFECTS
IMITATE	IMMIGRATES	IMP	IMPASSION	IMPERIA
IMITATED	IMMIGRATING	IMPACABLE	IMPASSIONED	IMPERIAL
IMITATES	IMMINENCE	IMPACT	IMPASSIONING	IMPERIALS
IMITATING	IMMINENCES	IMPACTED	IMPASSIONS	IMPERIL
IMITATION	IMMINENCIES	IMPACTER*	IMPASSIVE	IMPERILED*
IMITATIONS	IMMINENCY	IMPACTERS*	IMPASTE	IMPERILING*
IMITATIVE	IMMINENT	IMPACTING	IMPASTED	IMPERILLED
IMITATOR	IMMINGLE	IMPACTION	IMPASTES	IMPERILLING
IMITATORS	IMMINGLED	IMPACTIONS	IMPASTING	IMPERILS
IMMANACLE	IMMINGLES	IMPACTITE	IMPASTO	IMPERIOUS
IMMANACLED	IMMINGLING	IMPACTITES	IMPASTOED	IMPERIUM
IMMANACLES	IMMINUTE	IMPACTIVE	IMPASTOS	IMPERIUMS*
IMMANACLING	IMMISSION	IMPACTOR*	IMPATIENS	IMPETICOS
IMMANE	IMMISSIONS	IMPACTORS*	IMPATIENT	IMPETICOSSED
IMMANELY	IMMIT	IMPACTS	IMPAVE	IMPETICOSSES
IMMANENCE	IMMITS	IMPAINT	IMPAVED	IMPETICOSSING
IMMANENCES	IMMITTED	IMPAINTED	IMPAVES	IMPETIGINES
IMMANENCIES	IMMITTING	IMPAINTING	IMPAVID	IMPETIGO
IMMANENCY	IMMIX	IMPAINTS	IMPAVIDLY	IMPETIGOS
IMMANENT	IMMIXED	IMPAIR	IMPAVING	IMPETRATE
IMMANITIES	IMMIXES	IMPAIRED	IMPAWN	IMPETRATED
IMMANITY	IMMIXING	IMPAIRER	IMPAWNED	IMPETRATES
IMMANTLE	IMMIXTURE	IMPAIRERS	IMPAWNING	IMPETRATING
IMMANTLED	IMMIXTURES	IMPAIRING	IMPAWNS	IMPETUOUS
IMMANTLES	IMMOBILE	IMPAIRINGS	IMPEACH	IMPETUS
IMMANTLING	IMMODEST	IMPAIRS	IMPEACHED	IMPETUSES
IMMASK	IMMODESTIES	IMPALA	IMPEACHER	IMPHEE*

The Chambers Dictionary is the authority for many longer words; see Introduction, page ix

IMPHEES*	IMPLIES	IMPOSING	IMPROBITIES	INACTION
IMPI	IMPLODE	IMPOST	IMPROBITY	INACTIONS
IMPIES	IMPLODED	IMPOSTED*	IMPROMPTU	INACTIVE
IMPIETIES	IMPLODENT	IMPOSTER	IMPROMPTUS	INAIDABLE
IMPIETY	IMPLODENTS	IMPOSTERS	IMPROPER	INAMORATA
IMPING	IMPLODES	IMPOSTING*	IMPROV	INAMORATAS
IMPINGE	IMPLODING	IMPOSTOR	IMPROVE	INAMORATO
IMPINGED	IMPLORE	IMPOSTORS	IMPROVED	INAMORATOS
IMPINGENT	IMPLORED	IMPOSTS	IMPROVER	INANE
IMPINGER*	IMPLORER	IMPOSTUME	IMPROVERS	INANELY
IMPINGERS*	IMPLORERS	IMPOSTUMES	IMPROVES	INANENESS
IMPINGES	IMPLORES	IMPOSTURE	IMPROVING	INANENESSES
IMPINGING	IMPLORING	IMPOSTURES	IMPROVISE	INANER
IMPINGS*	IMPLOSION	IMPOT	IMPROVISED	INANES*
IMPIOUS	IMPLOSIONS	IMPOTENCE	IMPROVISES	INANEST
IMPIOUSLY	IMPLOSIVE	IMPOTENCES	IMPROVISING	INANIMATE
IMPIS	IMPLOSIVES	IMPOTENCIES	IMPROVS	INANITIES
IMPISH	IMPLUNGE	IMPOTENCY	IMPRUDENT	INANITION
IMPISHLY	IMPLUNGED	IMPOTENT	IMPS	INANITIONS
IMPLANT	IMPLUNGES	IMPOTENTS*	IMPSONITE	INANITY
IMPLANTED	IMPLUNGING	IMPOTS	IMPSONITES	INAPT
IMPLANTER*	IMPLUVIA	IMPOUND	IMPUDENCE	INAPTLY
IMPLANTERS*	IMPLUVIUM	IMPOUNDED	IMPUDENCES	INAPTNESS
IMPLANTING	IMPLY	IMPOUNDER	IMPUDENT	INAPTNESSES
IMPLANTS	IMPLYING	IMPOUNDERS	IMPUGN	INARABLE
IMPLATE	IMPOCKET	IMPOUNDING	IMPUGNED	INARCH
IMPLATED	IMPOCKETED	IMPOUNDS	IMPUGNER	INARCHED
IMPLATES	IMPOCKETING	IMPOWER*	IMPUGNERS	INARCHES
IMPLATING	IMPOCKETS	IMPOWERED*	IMPUGNING	INARCHING
IMPLEACH	IMPOLDER	IMPOWERING*	IMPUGNS	INARM
IMPLEACHED	IMPOLDERED	IMPOWERS*	IMPULSE	INARMED
IMPLEACHES	IMPOLDERING	IMPRECATE	IMPULSED	INARMING
IMPLEACHING	IMPOLDERS	IMPRECATED	IMPULSES	INARMS
IMPLEAD	IMPOLICIES	IMPRECATES	IMPULSING	INAUDIBLE
IMPLEADED	IMPOLICY	IMPRECATING	IMPULSION	INAUDIBLY
IMPLEADER	IMPOLITE	IMPRECISE	IMPULSIONS	INAUGURAL
IMPLEADERS	IMPOLITER	IMPREGN	IMPULSIVE	INAUGURALS
IMPLEADING	IMPOLITEST	IMPREGNED	IMPUNDULU	INAURATE
IMPLEADS	IMPOLITIC	IMPREGNING	IMPUNDULUS	INBEING
IMPLEDGE	IMPONE	IMPREGNS	IMPUNITIES	INBEINGS
IMPLEDGED	IMPONED	IMPRESA	IMPUNITY	INBENT
IMPLEDGES	IMPONENT	IMPRESARI	IMPURE	INBOARD
IMPLEDGING	IMPONENTS	IMPRESAS	IMPURELY	INBOARDS*
IMPLEMENT	IMPONES	IMPRESE	IMPURER	INBORN
IMPLEMENTED	IMPONING	IMPRESES	IMPUREST	INBOUND
IMPLEMENTING	IMPOROUS*	IMPRESS	IMPURITIES	INBOUNDED*
IMPLEMENTS	IMPORT	IMPRESSE	IMPURITY	INBOUNDING*
IMPLETE	IMPORTANT	IMPRESSED	IMPURPLE	INBOUNDS*
IMPLETED	IMPORTED	IMPRESSES	IMPURPLED	INBREAK
IMPLETES	IMPORTER	IMPRESSING	IMPURPLES	INBREAKS
IMPLETING	IMPORTERS	IMPREST	IMPURPLING	INBREATHE
IMPLETION	IMPORTING	IMPRESTS	IMPUTABLE	INBREATHED
IMPLETIONS	IMPORTS	IMPRIMIS	IMPUTABLY	INBREATHES
IMPLEX	IMPORTUNE	IMPRINT	IMPUTE	INBREATHING
IMPLEXES	IMPORTUNED	IMPRINTED	IMPUTED	INBRED
IMPLEXION	IMPORTUNES	IMPRINTER*	IMPUTER	INBREDS*
IMPLEXIONS	IMPORTUNING	IMPRINTERS*	IMPUTERS	INBREED
IMPLICATE	IMPORTUNINGS	IMPRINTING	IMPUTES	INBREEDING
IMPLICATED	IMPOSABLE	IMPRINTINGS	IMPUTING	INBREEDINGS
IMPLICATES	IMPOSE	IMPRISON	IMSHI	INBREEDS
IMPLICATING	IMPOSED	IMPRISONED	IMSHY	INBRING
IMPLICIT	IMPOSER	IMPRISONING	IN	INBRINGING
IMPLIED	IMPOSERS	IMPRISONS	INABILITIES	INBRINGINGS
IMPLIEDLY	IMPOSES		INABILITY	INBRINGS

INBROUGHT	INCERTAIN	INCLINING	INCREMENTING	INCUS
INBUILT*	INCESSANT	INCLININGS	INCREMENTS	INCUSE
INBURNING	INCEST	INCLIP	INCRETION	INCUSED
INBURST	INCESTS	INCLIPPED	INCRETIONS	INCUSES
INBURSTS	INCH	INCLIPPING	INCROSS	INCUSING
INBY	INCHASE	INCLIPS	INCROSSED	INCUT
INBYE	INCHASED	INCLOSE	INCROSSES	INDABA
INCAGE	INCHASES	INCLOSED	INCROSSING	INDABAS
INCAGED	INCHASING	INCLOSER	INCRUST	INDAGATE
INCAGES	INCHED	INCLOSERS	INCRUSTED	INDAGATED
INCAGING	INCHES	INCLOSES	INCRUSTING	INDAGATES
INCANT*	INCHING	INCLOSING	INCRUSTS	INDAGATING
INCANTED*	INCHMEAL	INCLOSURE	INCUBATE	INDAGATOR
INCANTING*	INCHOATE	INCLOSURES	INCUBATED	INDAGATORS
INCANTS*	INCHOATED	INCLUDE	INCUBATES	INDAMIN*
INCAPABLE	INCHOATES	INCLUDED	INCUBATING	INDAMINE
INCAPABLES	INCHOATING	INCLUDES	INCUBATOR	INDAMINES
INCAPABLY	INCHPIN	INCLUDING	INCUBATORS	INDAMINS*
INCARNATE	INCHPINS	INCLUSION	INCUBI	INDART
INCARNATED	INCHWORM*	INCLUSIONS	INCUBOUS	INDARTED
INCARNATES	INCHWORMS*	INCLUSIVE	INCUBUS	INDARTING
INCARNATING	INCIDENCE	INCOG*	INCUBUSES	INDARTS
INCASE	INCIDENCES	INCOGNITA*	INCUDAL*	INDEBTED
INCASED	INCIDENT	INCOGNITAS*	INCUDATE*	INDECENCIES
INCASES	INCIDENTS	INCOGNITO	INCUDES	INDECENCY
INCASING	INCIPIENT	INCOGNITOS	INCULCATE	INDECENT
INCAUTION	INCIPIT	INCOGS*	INCULCATED	INDECENTER
INCAUTIONS	INCIPITS*	INCOME	INCULCATES	INDECENTEST
INCAVE	INCISAL*	INCOMER	INCULCATING	INDECORUM
INCAVED	INCISE	INCOMERS	INCULPATE	INDECORUMS
INCAVES	INCISED	INCOMES	INCULPATED	INDEED
INCAVI	INCISES	INCOMING	INCULPATES	INDELIBLE
INCAVING	INCISING	INCOMINGS	INCULPATING	INDELIBLY
INCAVO	INCISION	INCOMMODE	INCULT	INDEMNIFIED
INCEDE	INCISIONS	INCOMMODED	INCUMBENT	INDEMNIFIES
INCEDED	INCISIVE	INCOMMODES	INCUMBENTS	INDEMNIFY
INCEDES	INCISOR	INCOMMODING	INCUMBER*	INDEMNIFYING
INCEDING	INCISORS	INCONDITE	INCUMBERED*	INDEMNITIES
INCENSE	INCISORY	INCONIE	INCUMBERING*	INDEMNITY
INCENSED	INCISURE	INCONNU	INCUMBERS*	INDENE
INCENSER	INCISURES	INCONNUE	INCUNABLE	INDENES
INCENSERS	INCITANT	INCONNUES	INCUNABLES	INDENT
INCENSES	INCITANTS	INCONNUS	INCUR	INDENTED
INCENSING	INCITE	INCONY	INCURABLE	INDENTER
INCENSOR	INCITED	INCORPSE	INCURABLES	INDENTERS
INCENSORIES	INCITER	INCORPSED	INCURABLY	INDENTING
INCENSORS	INCITERS	INCORPSES	INCURIOUS	INDENTION
INCENSORY	INCITES	INCORPSING	INCURRED	INDENTIONS
INCENTER*	INCITING	INCORRECT	INCURRENT	INDENTOR*
INCENTERS*	INCIVIL	INCORRUPT	INCURRING	INDENTORS*
INCENTIVE	INCIVISM	INCREASE	INCURS	INDENTS
INCENTIVES	INCIVISMS	INCREASED	INCURSION	INDENTURE
INCENTRE	INCLASP	INCREASER	INCURSIONS	INDENTURED
INCENTRES	INCLASPED	INCREASERS	INCURSIVE	INDENTURES
INCEPT	INCLASPING	INCREASES	INCURVATE	INDENTURING
INCEPTED	INCLASPS	INCREASING	INCURVATED	INDEVOUT*
INCEPTING	INCLE	INCREASINGS	INCURVATES	INDEW
INCEPTION	INCLEMENT	INCREATE	INCURVATING	INDEWED
INCEPTIONS	INCLES	INCREMATE	INCURVE	INDEWING
INCEPTIVE	INCLINE	INCREMATED	INCURVED	INDEWS
INCEPTIVES	INCLINED	INCREMATES	INCURVES	INDEX
INCEPTOR	INCLINER*	INCREMATING	INCURVING	INDEXAL
INCEPTORS	INCLINERS*	INCREMENT	INCURVITIES	INDEXED
INCEPTS	INCLINES	INCREMENTED	INCURVITY	INDEXER

The Chambers Dictionary is the authority for many longer words; see Introduction, page ix

INDEXERS	INDIGOTINS	INDUCIAE	INEBRIATING	INFANCY
INDEXES	INDIRECT	INDUCIBLE	INEBRIETIES	INFANT
INDEXICAL	INDIRUBIN	INDUCING	INEBRIETY	INFANTA
INDEXICALS*	INDIRUBINS	INDUCT	INEBRIOUS	INFANTAS
INDEXING	INDISPOSE	INDUCTED	INEDIBLE	INFANTE
INDEXINGS	INDISPOSED	INDUCTEE	INEDITA*	INFANTES
INDEXLESS	INDISPOSES	INDUCTEES	INEDITED	INFANTILE
INDICAN	INDISPOSING	INDUCTILE	INEFFABLE	INFANTINE
INDICANS	INDITE	INDUCTING	INEFFABLY	INFANTRIES
INDICANT	INDITED	INDUCTION	INELASTIC	INFANTRY
INDICANTS	INDITER	INDUCTIONS	INELEGANT	INFANTS
INDICATE	INDITERS	INDUCTIVE	INEPT	INFARCT
INDICATED	INDITES	INDUCTOR	INEPTER	INFARCTED*
INDICATES	INDITING	INDUCTORS	INEPTEST	INFARCTS
INDICATING	INDIUM	INDUCTS	INEPTLY	INFARE
INDICATOR	INDIUMS	INDUE	INEPTNESS	INFARES
INDICATORS	INDIVIDUA	INDUED	INEPTNESSES	INFATUATE
INDICES	INDOCIBLE	INDUES	INEQUABLE	INFATUATED
INDICIA	INDOCILE	INDUING	INEQUITIES	INFATUATES
INDICIAL	INDOL	INDULGE	INEQUITY	INFATUATING
INDICIAS*	INDOLE	INDULGED	INERM	INFAUNA
INDICIUM	INDOLENCE	INDULGENT	INERMOUS	INFAUNAE
INDICIUMS*	INDOLENCES	INDULGER	INERRABLE	INFAUNAL
INDICT	INDOLENCIES	INDULGERS	INERRABLY	INFAUNAS
INDICTED	INDOLENCY	INDULGES	INERRANCIES	INFAUST
INDICTEE	INDOLENT	INDULGING	INERRANCY	INFECT
INDICTEES	INDOLES	INDULIN	INERRANT	INFECTED
INDICTER*	INDOLS	INDULINE	INERT	INFECTER*
INDICTERS*	INDOOR	INDULINES	INERTER	INFECTERS*
INDICTING	INDOORS	INDULINS	INERTEST	INFECTING
INDICTION	INDORSE	INDULT	INERTIA	INFECTION
INDICTIONS	INDORSED	INDULTS	INERTIAE*	INFECTIONS
INDICTOR*	INDORSEE*	INDUMENTA	INERTIAL	INFECTIVE
INDICTORS*	INDORSEES*	INDUNA	INERTIAS	INFECTOR
INDICTS	INDORSER*	INDUNAS	INERTLY	INFECTORS
INDIE	INDORSERS*	INDURATE	INERTNESS	INFECTS
INDIES	INDORSES	INDURATED	INERTNESSES	INFECUND
INDIGEN*	INDORSING	INDURATES	INERTS*	INFEFT
INDIGENCE	INDORSOR*	INDURATING	INERUDITE	INFEFTED
INDIGENCES	INDORSORS*	INDUSIA	INESSIVE	INFEFTING
INDIGENCIES	INDOW*	INDUSIAL	INESSIVES	INFEFTS
INDIGENCY	INDOWED*	INDUSIATE	INEXACT	INFELT
INDIGENE	INDOWING*	INDUSIUM	INEXACTLY	INFEOFF*
INDIGENES	INDOWS*	INDUSTRIES	INEXPERT	INFEOFFED*
INDIGENS*	INDOXYL	INDUSTRY	INEXPERTS*	INFEOFFING*
INDIGENT	INDOXYLS	INDUVIAE	INFALL	INFEOFFS*
INDIGENTS	INDRAFT	INDUVIAL	INFALLING*	INFER
INDIGEST	INDRAFTS	INDUVIATE	INFALLS	INFERABLE
INDIGESTS	INDRAUGHT	INDWELL	INFAME	INFERE
INDIGN	INDRAUGHTS	INDWELLER	INFAMED	INFERENCE
INDIGNANT	INDRAWN	INDWELLERS	INFAMES	INFERENCES
INDIGNIFIED	INDRENCH	INDWELLING	INFAMIES	INFERIAE
INDIGNIFIES	INDRENCHED	INDWELLINGS	INFAMING	INFERIOR
INDIGNIFY	INDRENCHES	INDWELLS	INFAMISE	INFERIORS
INDIGNIFYING	INDRENCHING	INDWELT	INFAMISED	INFERNAL
INDIGNITIES	INDRI	INEARTH	INFAMISES	INFERNO
INDIGNITY	INDRIS	INEARTHED	INFAMISING	INFERNOS
INDIGNLY*	INDRISES	INEARTHING	INFAMIZE	INFERRED
INDIGO	INDUBIOUS	INEARTHS	INFAMIZED	INFERRER*
INDIGOES	INDUCE	INEBRIANT	INFAMIZES	INFERRERS*
INDIGOID*	INDUCED	INEBRIANTS	INFAMIZING	INFERRING
INDIGOIDS*	INDUCER	INEBRIATE	INFAMOUS	INFERS
INDIGOS	INDUCERS	INEBRIATED	INFAMY	INFERTILE
INDIGOTIN	INDUCES	INEBRIATES	INFANCIES	INFEST

INFESTANT*	INFLATUS	INFRA	INGINE	INHABITING
INFESTANTS*	INFLATUSES	INFRACT	INGINES	INHABITOR
INFESTED	INFLECT	INFRACTED	INGLE	INHABITORS
INFESTER*	INFLECTED	INFRACTING	INGLENEUK	INHABITS
INFESTERS*	INFLECTING	INFRACTOR	INGLENEUKS	INHALANT
INFESTING	INFLECTS	INFRACTORS	INGLENOOK	INHALANTS
INFESTS	INFLEXED	INFRACTS	INGLENOOKS	INHALATOR
INFICETE	INFLEXION	INFRARED	INGLES	INHALATORS
INFIDEL	INFLEXIONS	INFRAREDS	INGLOBE	INHALE
INFIDELS	INFLEXURE	INFRINGE	INGLOBED	INHALED
INFIELD	INFLEXURES	INFRINGED	INGLOBES	INHALER
INFIELDER	INFLICT	INFRINGER*	INGLOBING	INHALERS
INFIELDERS	INFLICTED	INFRINGERS*	INGLUVIAL	INHALES
INFIELDS	INFLICTER	INFRINGES	INGLUVIES	INHALING
INFIGHT*	INFLICTERS	INFRINGING	INGO	INHARMONIES
INFIGHTER*	INFLICTING	INFRUGAL*	INGOES	INHARMONY
INFIGHTERS*	INFLICTOR	INFULA	INGOING	INHAUL
INFIGHTING*	INFLICTORS	INFULAE	INGOINGS	INHAULER
INFIGHTS*	INFLICTS	INFURIATE	INGOT	INHAULERS
INFILL	INFLIGHT*	INFURIATED	INGOTED*	INHAULS
INFILLED	INFLOW	INFURIATES	INGOTING*	INHAUST
INFILLING	INFLOWING	INFURIATING	INGOTS	INHAUSTED
INFILLINGS	INFLOWINGS	INFUSCATE	INGRAFT	INHAUSTING
INFILLS	INFLOWS	INFUSE	INGRAFTED	INHAUSTS
INFIMUM	INFLUENCE	INFUSED	INGRAFTING	INHEARSE
INFIMUMS	INFLUENCED	INFUSER	INGRAFTS	INHEARSED
INFINITE	INFLUENCES	INFUSERS	INGRAIN	INHEARSES
INFINITES	INFLUENCING	INFUSES	INGRAINED	INHEARSING
INFINITIES	INFLUENT	INFUSIBLE	INGRAINING	INHERCE
INFINITY	INFLUENTS	INFUSING	INGRAINS	INHERCED
INFIRM	INFLUENZA	INFUSION	INGRAM	INHERCES
INFIRMARIES	INFLUENZAS	INFUSIONS	INGRATE	INHERCING
INFIRMARY	INFLUX	INFUSIVE	INGRATELY	INHERE
INFIRMED*	INFLUXES	INFUSORIA	INGRATES	INHERED
INFIRMER	INFLUXION	INFUSORY	INGRESS	INHERENCE
INFIRMEST	INFLUXIONS	INGAN	INGRESSES	INHERENCES
INFIRMING*	INFO	INGANS	INGROOVE	INHERENCIES
INFIRMITIES	INFOBAHN	INGATE	INGROOVED	INHERENCY
INFIRMITY	INFOBAHNS	INGATES	INGROOVES	INHERENT
INFIRMLY	INFOLD	INGATHER	INGROOVING	INHERES
INFIRMS*	INFOLDED	INGATHERED	INGROSS	INHERING
INFIX	INFOLDER*	INGATHERING	INGROSSED	INHERIT
INFIXED	INFOLDERS*	INGATHERINGS	INGROSSES	INHERITED
INFIXES	INFOLDING	INGATHERS	INGROSSING	INHERITING
INFIXING	INFOLDS	INGENER	INGROUP	INHERITOR
INFIXION*	INFOMANIA	INGENERS	INGROUPS	INHERITORS
INFIXIONS*	INFOMANIAS	INGENIOUS	INGROWING	INHERITS
INFLAME	INFORCE	INGENIUM	INGROWN	INHESION
INFLAMED	INFORCED	INGENIUMS	INGROWTH	INHESIONS
INFLAMER	INFORCES	INGENU	INGROWTHS	INHIBIN*
INFLAMERS	INFORCING	INGENUE	INGRUM	INHIBINS*
INFLAMES	INFORM	INGENUES	INGUINAL	INHIBIT
INFLAMING	INFORMAL	INGENUITIES	INGULF	INHIBITED
INFLATE	INFORMANT	INGENUITY	INGULFED	INHIBITER
INFLATED	INFORMANTS	INGENUOUS	INGULFING	INHIBITERS
INFLATER*	INFORMED	INGENUS	INGULFS	INHIBITING
INFLATERS*	INFORMER	INGEST	INGULPH	INHIBITOR
INFLATES	INFORMERS	INGESTA	INGULPHED	INHIBITORS
INFLATING	INFORMING	INGESTED	INGULPHING	INHIBITS
INFLATION	INFORMS	INGESTING	INGULPHS	INHOLDER
INFLATIONS	INFORTUNE	INGESTION	INHABIT	INHOLDERS
INFLATIVE	INFORTUNES	INGESTIONS	INHABITED	INHOLDING*
INFLATOR	INFOS	INGESTIVE	INHABITER	INHOLDINGS*
INFLATORS	INFOUGHT*	INGESTS	INHABITERS	INHOOP

The Chambers Dictionary is the authority for many longer words; see Introduction, page ix

INHOOPED	INJURED	INLET	INNS	INQUINATING
INHOOPING	INJURER	INLETS	INNUENDO	INQUIRE
INHOOPS	INJURERS	INLETTING*	INNUENDOED	INQUIRED
INHUMAN	INJURES	INLIER	INNUENDOES	INQUIRER
INHUMANE	INJURIES	INLIERS	INNUENDOING	INQUIRERS
INHUMANLY	INJURING	INLOCK	INNUENDOS	INQUIRES
INHUMATE	INJURIOUS	INLOCKED	INNYARD	INQUIRIES
INHUMATED	INJURY	INLOCKING	INNYARDS	INQUIRING
INHUMATES	INJUSTICE	INLOCKS	INOCULA	INQUIRY
INHUMATING	INJUSTICES	INLY	INOCULANT*	INQUORATE
INHUME	INK	INLYING	INOCULANTS*	INRO
INHUMED	INKBERRIES	INMATE	INOCULATE	INROAD
INHUMER	INKBERRY	INMATES	INOCULATED	INROADS
INHUMERS	INKBLOT*	INMESH	INOCULATES	INRUSH
INHUMES	INKBLOTS*	INMESHED	INOCULATING	INRUSHES
INHUMING	INKED	INMESHES	INOCULUM	INRUSHING
INIA	INKER	INMESHING	INOCULUMS	INRUSHINGS
INIMICAL	INKERS	INMOST	INODOROUS	INS
INION	INKHOLDER	INN	INOPINATE	INSANE
INIQUITIES	INKHOLDERS	INNARDS	INORB	INSANELY
INIQUITY	INKHORN	INNATE	INORBED	INSANER
INISLE	INKHORNS	INNATELY	INORBING	INSANEST
INISLED	INKIER	INNATIVE	INORBS	INSANIE
INISLES	INKIEST	INNED	INORGANIC	INSANIES
INISLING	INKINESS	INNER	INORNATE	INSANITIES
INITIAL	INKINESSES	INNERLY*	INOSITE*	INSANITY
INITIALED	INKING	INNERMOST	INOSITES*	INSATIATE
INITIALING	INKJET*	INNERMOSTS*	INOSITOL	INSATIETIES
INITIALLED	INKLE	INNERS	INOSITOLS	INSATIETY
INITIALLING	INKLED	INNERSOLE*	INOTROPIC	INSCAPE
INITIALLY	INKLES	INNERSOLES*	INPATIENT*	INSCAPES
INITIALS	INKLESS*	INNERVATE	INPATIENTS*	INSCIENCE
INITIATE	INKLIKE*	INNERVATED	INPAYMENT	INSCIENCES
INITIATED	INKLING	INNERVATES	INPAYMENTS	INSCIENT
INITIATES	INKLINGS	INNERVATING	INPHASE	INSCONCE
INITIATING	INKPOT	INNERVE	INPOUR*	INSCONCED
INITIATOR	INKPOTS	INNERVED	INPOURED*	INSCONCES
INITIATORS	INKS	INNERVES	INPOURING	INSCONCING
INJECT	INKSPOT	INNERVING	INPOURINGS	INSCRIBE
INJECTANT*	INKSPOTS	INNERWEAR	INPOURS*	INSCRIBED
INJECTANTS*	INKSTAND	INNERWEARS	INPUT	INSCRIBER
INJECTED	INKSTANDS	INNING	INPUTS	INSCRIBERS
INJECTING	INKSTONE	INNINGS	INPUTTED*	INSCRIBES
INJECTION	INKSTONES	INNKEEPER	INPUTTER	INSCRIBING
INJECTIONS	INKWELL	INNKEEPERS	INPUTTERS	INSCROLL
INJECTIVE*	INKWELLS	INNLESS*	INPUTTING	INSCROLLED
INJECTOR	INKWOOD*	INNOCENCE	INQILAB	INSCROLLING
INJECTORS	INKWOODS*	INNOCENCES	INQILABS	INSCROLLS
INJECTS	INKY	INNOCENCY	INQUERE	INSCULP
INJELLIED	INLACE	INNOCENCIES	INQUERED	INSCULPED
INJELLIES	INLACED	INNOCENT	INQUERES	INSCULPING
INJELLY	INLACES	INNOCENTER*	INQUERING	INSCULPS
INJELLYING	INLACING	INNOCENTEST*	INQUEST	INSCULPT
INJERA	INLAID	INNOCENTS	INQUESTS	INSEAM
INJERAS	INLAND	INNOCUITIES	INQUIET	INSEAMED
INJOINT	INLANDER	INNOCUITY	INQUIETED	INSEAMING
INJOINTED	INLANDERS	INNOCUOUS	INQUIETING	INSEAMS
INJOINTING	INLANDS	INNOVATE	INQUIETLY	INSECT
INJOINTS	INLAY	INNOVATED	INQUIETS	INSECTAN*
INJUNCT	INLAYER	INNOVATES	INQUILINE	INSECTARIES
INJUNCTED	INLAYERS	INNOVATING	INQUILINES	INSECTARY
INJUNCTING	INLAYING	INNOVATOR	INQUINATE	INSECTILE
INJUNCTS	INLAYINGS	INNOVATORS	INQUINATED	INSECTION
INJURE	INLAYS	INNOXIOUS	INQUINATES	INSECTIONS

INSECTS	INSINUATED	INSPIRING	INSULA	INTEGRANDS
INSECURE	INSINUATES	INSPIRIT	INSULAE	INTEGRANT
INSEEM	INSINUATING	INSPIRITED	INSULANT*	INTEGRATE
INSEEMED	INSIPID	INSPIRITING	INSULANTS*	INTEGRATED
INSEEMING	INSIPIDLY	INSPIRITS	INSULAR	INTEGRATES
INSEEMS	INSIPIENT	INSTABLE	INSULARLY	INTEGRATING
INSELBERG	INSIST	INSTAL	INSULARS*	INTEGRITIES
INSELBERGE	INSISTED	INSTALL	INSULAS	INTEGRITY
INSELBERGS*	INSISTENT	INSTALLED	INSULATE	INTELLECT
INSENSATE	INSISTER*	INSTALLER*	INSULATED	INTELLECTS
INSERT	INSISTERS*	INSTALLERS*	INSULATES	INTENABLE
INSERTED	INSISTING	INSTALLING	INSULATING	INTEND
INSERTER	INSISTS	INSTALLS	INSULATOR	INTENDANT
INSERTERS	INSNARE	INSTALS	INSULATORS	INTENDANTS
INSERTING	INSNARED	INSTANCE	INSULIN	INTENDED
INSERTION	INSNARER*	INSTANCED	INSULINS	INTENDEDS
INSERTIONS	INSNARERS*	INSTANCES	INSULSE	INTENDER
INSERTS	INSNARES	INSTANCIES	INSULSITIES	INTENDERED
INSET	INSNARING	INSTANCING	INSULSITY	INTENDERING
INSETS	INSOFAR*	INSTANCY	INSULT	INTENDERS
INSETTED*	INSOLATE	INSTANT	INSULTANT	INTENDING
INSETTER*	INSOLATED	INSTANTER*	INSULTED	INTENDS
INSETTERS*	INSOLATES	INSTANTLY	INSULTER	INTENIBLE
INSETTING	INSOLATING	INSTANTS	INSULTERS	INTENSATE
INSHALLAH	INSOLE	INSTAR	INSULTING	INTENSATED
INSHEATH*	INSOLENCE	INSTARRED	INSULTS	INTENSATES
INSHEATHE	INSOLENCES	INSTARRING	INSURABLE	INTENSATING
INSHEATHED	INSOLENT	INSTARS	INSURANCE	INTENSE
INSHEATHES	INSOLENTS*	INSTATE	INSURANCES	INTENSELY
INSHEATHING	INSOLES	INSTATED	INSURANT	INTENSER
INSHEATHS*	INSOLUBLE	INSTATES	INSURANTS	INTENSEST
INSHELL	INSOLUBLES*	INSTATING	INSURE	INTENSIFIED
INSHELLED	INSOLUBLY	INSTEAD	INSURED	INTENSIFIES
INSHELLING	INSOLVENT	INSTEP	INSUREDS	INTENSIFY
INSHELLS	INSOLVENTS	INSTEPS	INSURER	INTENSIFYING
INSHELTER	INSOMNIA	INSTIGATE	INSURERS	INTENSION
INSHELTERED	INSOMNIAC	INSTIGATED	INSURES	INTENSIONS
INSHELTERING	INSOMNIACS	INSTIGATES	INSURGENT	INTENSITIES
INSHELTERS	INSOMNIAS	INSTIGATING	INSURGENTS	INTENSITY
INSHIP	INSOMUCH	INSTIL	INSURING	INTENSIVE
INSHIPPED	INSOOTH	INSTILL	INSWATHE	INTENSIVES
INSHIPPING	INSOUL	INSTILLED	INSWATHED	INTENT
INSHIPS	INSOULED	INSTILLER*	INSWATHES	INTENTION
INSHORE	INSOULING	INSTILLERS*	INSWATHING	INTENTIONS
INSHRINE	INSOULS	INSTILLING	INSWEPT*	INTENTIVE
INSHRINED	INSPAN	INSTILLS	INSWING	INTENTLY
INSHRINES	INSPANNED	INSTILS	INSWINGER	INTENTS
INSHRINING	INSPANNING	INSTINCT	INSWINGERS	INTER
INSIDE	INSPANS	INSTINCTS	INSWINGS	INTERACT
INSIDER	INSPECT	INSTITUTE	INTACT	INTERACTED
INSIDERS	INSPECTED	INSTITUTED	INTAGLI*	INTERACTING
INSIDES	INSPECTING	INSTITUTES	INTAGLIO	INTERACTS
INSIDIOUS	INSPECTOR	INSTITUTING	INTAGLIOED	INTERAGE*
INSIGHT	INSPECTORS	INSTRESS	INTAGLIOING	INTERBANK
INSIGHTS	INSPECTS	INSTRESSED	INTAGLIOS	INTERBED*
INSIGNE	INSPHERE	INSTRESSES	INTAKE	INTERBEDDED*
INSIGNIA	INSPHERED	INSTRESSING	INTAKES	INTERBEDDING*
INSIGNIAS	INSPHERES	INSTROKE*	INTARSIA	INTERBEDS*
INSINCERE	INSPHERING	INSTROKES*	INTARSIAS	INTERBRED
INSINEW	INSPIRE	INSTRUCT	INTEGER	INTERBREED*
INSINEWED	INSPIRED	INSTRUCTED	INTEGERS	INTERBREEDING*
INSINEWING	INSPIRER	INSTRUCTING	INTEGRAL	INTERBREEDS*
INSINEWS	INSPIRERS	INSTRUCTS	INTEGRALS	INTERCEDE
INSINUATE	INSPIRES	INSUCKEN	INTEGRAND	INTERCEDED

The Chambers Dictionary is the authority for many longer words; see Introduction, page ix

INTERCEDES	INTERFOLDING	INTERLOPED	INTERPRETING	INTERWOUND
INTERCEDING	INTERFOLDS	INTERLOPES	INTERPRETS	INTERWOVE
INTERCELL*	INTERFUSE	INTERLOPING	INTERRAIL	INTERWOVEN*
INTERCEPT	INTERFUSED	INTERLUDE	INTERRAILED	INTERZONE
INTERCEPTED	INTERFUSES	INTERLUDED	INTERRAILING	INTERZONES
INTERCEPTING	INTERFUSING	INTERLUDES	INTERRAILS	INTESTACIES
INTERCEPTS	INTERGANG*	INTERLUDING	INTERRED	INTESTACY
INTERCITY	INTERGREW	INTERMALE*	INTERREGES	INTESTATE
INTERCLAN*	INTERGROW	INTERMENT	INTERREX	INTESTATES
INTERCLUB*	INTERGROWING	INTERMENTS	INTERRING	INTESTINE
INTERCOM	INTERGROWN	INTERMESH*	INTERROW*	INTESTINES
INTERCOMS	INTERGROWS	INTERMESHED*	INTERRUPT	INTHRAL
INTERCROP	INTERIM	INTERMESHES*	INTERRUPTED	INTHRALL
INTERCROPPED	INTERIMS	INTERMESHING*	INTERRUPTING	INTHRALLED
INTERCROPPING	INTERIOR	INTERMIT	INTERRUPTS	INTHRALLING
INTERCROPS	INTERIORS	INTERMITS	INTERS	INTHRALS
INTERCUT	INTERJECT	INTERMITTED	INTERSECT	INTHRONE*
INTERCUTS	INTERJECTED	INTERMITTING	INTERSECTED	INTHRONED*
INTERCUTTING	INTERJECTING	INTERMIX	INTERSECTING	INTHRONES*
INTERDASH	INTERJECTS	INTERMIXED	INTERSECTS	INTHRONING*
INTERDASHED	INTERJOIN	INTERMIXES	INTERSERT	INTI
INTERDASHES	INTERJOINED	INTERMIXING	INTERSERTED	INTIFADA
INTERDASHING	INTERJOINING	INTERMONT*	INTERSERTING	INTIFADAS
INTERDEAL	INTERJOINS	INTERMURE	INTERSERTS	INTIL
INTERDEALING	INTERKNIT	INTERMURED	INTERSEX	INTIMA
INTERDEALS	INTERKNITS	INTERMURES	INTERSEXES	INTIMACIES
INTERDEALT	INTERKNITTED	INTERMURING	INTERTERM*	INTIMACY
INTERDICT	INTERKNITTING	INTERN	INTERTEXT	INTIMAE
INTERDICTED	INTERLACE	INTERNAL	INTERTEXTS	INTIMAL*
INTERDICTING	INTERLACED	INTERNALS	INTERTIE	INTIMAS*
INTERDICTS	INTERLACES	INTERNE	INTERTIES	INTIMATE
INTERDINE	INTERLACING	INTERNED	INTERTILL*	INTIMATED
INTERDINED	INTERLAID	INTERNEE	INTERTILLED*	INTIMATER*
INTERDINES	INTERLAP*	INTERNEES	INTERTILLING*	INTIMATERS*
INTERDINING	INTERLAPPED*	INTERNES	INTERTILLS*	INTIMATES
INTERESS	INTERLAPPING*	INTERNING	INTERUNIT*	INTIMATING
INTERESSE	INTERLAPS*	INTERNIST	INTERVAL	INTIME
INTERESSED	INTERLARD	INTERNISTS	INTERVALE	INTIMISM
INTERESSES	INTERLARDED	INTERNODE	INTERVALES	INTIMISMS
INTERESSING	INTERLARDING	INTERNODES	INTERVALS	INTIMIST
INTEREST	INTERLARDS	INTERNS	INTERVEIN	INTIMISTE
INTERESTED	INTERLAY	INTERPAGE	INTERVEINED	INTIMISTES
INTERESTING	INTERLAYING	INTERPAGED	INTERVEINING	INTIMISTS
INTERESTS	INTERLAYS	INTERPAGES	INTERVEINS	INTIMITIES
INTERFACE	INTERLEAF	INTERPAGING	INTERVENE	INTIMITY
INTERFACED	INTERLEAVES	INTERPLAY	INTERVENED	INTINE
INTERFACES	INTERLEND*	INTERPLAYED*	INTERVENES	INTINES
INTERFACING	INTERLENDING*	INTERPLAYING*	INTERVENING	INTIRE
INTERFACINGS	INTERLENDS*	INTERPLAYS	INTERVIEW	INTIS
INTERFERE	INTERLENT*	INTERPLEAD*	INTERVIEWED	INTITLE*
INTERFERED	INTERLINE	INTERPLEADED*	INTERVIEWING	INTITLED*
INTERFERES	INTERLINED	INTERPLEADING*	INTERVIEWS	INTITLES*
INTERFERING	INTERLINES	INTERPLEADS*	INTERWAR	INTITLING*
INTERFILE*	INTERLINING	INTERPLED	INTERWEAVE*	INTITULE
INTERFILED*	INTERLININGS	INTERPONE	INTERWEAVED*	INTITULED
INTERFILES*	INTERLINK	INTERPONED	INTERWEAVES*	INTITULES
INTERFILING*	INTERLINKED	INTERPONES	INTERWEAVING*	INTITULING
INTERFIRM*	INTERLINKING	INTERPONING	INTERWIND	INTO
INTERFLOW	INTERLINKS	INTERPOSE	INTERWINDING	INTOED
INTERFLOWED	INTERLOCK	INTERPOSED	INTERWINDS	INTOMB
INTERFLOWING	INTERLOCKED	INTERPOSES	INTERWORK	INTOMBED
INTERFLOWS	INTERLOCKING	INTERPOSING	INTERWORKED	INTOMBING
INTERFOLD	INTERLOCKS	INTERPRET	INTERWORKING	INTOMBS
INTERFOLDED	INTERLOPE	INTERPRETED	INTERWORKS	

Words marked with an asterisk are from OTCWL

INTONACO	INTROFYING*	INULA	INVEIGH	INVIRILE*
INTONACOS	INTROIT	INULAS	INVEIGHED	INVISCID*
INTONATE	INTROITS	INULASE	INVEIGHER*	INVISIBLE
INTONATED	INTROITUS	INULASES	INVEIGHERS*	INVISIBLES
INTONATES	INTROITUSES	INULIN	INVEIGHING	INVISIBLY
INTONATING	INTROJECT	INULINS	INVEIGHS	INVITAL*
INTONATOR	INTROJECTED	INUMBRATE	INVEIGLE	INVITE
INTONATORS	INTROJECTING	INUMBRATED	INVEIGLED	INVITED
INTONE	INTROJECTS	INUMBRATES	INVEIGLER	INVITEE
INTONED	INTROLD	INUMBRATING	INVEIGLERS	INVITEES
INTONER	INTROMIT	INUNCTION	INVEIGLES	INVITER
INTONERS	INTROMITS	INUNCTIONS	INVEIGLING	INVITERS
INTONES	INTROMITTED	INUNDANT	INVENIT	INVITES
INTONING	INTROMITTING	INUNDATE	INVENT	INVITING
INTONINGS	INTRON	INUNDATED	INVENTED	INVITINGS
INTORSION	INTRONS	INUNDATES	INVENTER*	INVOCATE*
INTORSIONS	INTRORSE	INUNDATING	INVENTERS*	INVOCATED*
INTORT*	INTROS	INUNDATOR*	INVENTING	INVOCATES*
INTORTED	INTROVERT	INUNDATORS*	INVENTION	INVOCATING*
INTORTING*	INTROVERTED	INURBANE	INVENTIONS	INVOICE
INTORTION	INTROVERTING	INURE	INVENTIVE	INVOICED
INTORTIONS	INTROVERTS	INURED	INVENTOR	INVOICES
INTORTS*	INTRUDE	INUREMENT	INVENTORIED	INVOICING
INTOWN	INTRUDED	INUREMENTS	INVENTORIES	INVOKE
INTRA	INTRUDER	INURES	INVENTORS	INVOKED
INTRADA	INTRUDERS	INURING	INVENTORY	INVOKER*
INTRADAS	INTRUDES	INURN	INVENTORYING	INVOKERS*
INTRADAY*	INTRUDING	INURNED	INVENTS	INVOKES
INTRADOS	INTRUSION	INURNING	INVERITIES*	INVOKING
INTRADOSES	INTRUSIONS	INURNS	INVERITY*	INVOLUCEL
INTRANET	INTRUSIVE	INUSITATE	INVERNESS*	INVOLUCELS
INTRANETS	INTRUSIVES	INUST	INVERNESSES*	INVOLUCRA
INTRANT	INTRUST	INUSTION	INVERSE	INVOLUCRE
INTRANTS	INTRUSTED	INUSTIONS	INVERSELY	INVOLUCRES
INTREAT	INTRUSTING	INUTILE*	INVERSES	INVOLUCRUM*
INTREATED	INTRUSTS	INUTILITIES	INVERSION	INVOLUTE
INTREATING	INTUBATE	INUTILITY	INVERSIONS	INVOLUTED
INTREATS	INTUBATED	INVADE	INVERSIVE	INVOLUTES
INTRENCH	INTUBATES	INVADED	INVERT	INVOLUTING
INTRENCHED	INTUBATING	INVADER	INVERTASE	INVOLVE
INTRENCHES	INTUIT	INVADERS	INVERTASES	INVOLVED
INTRENCHING	INTUITED	INVADES	INVERTED	INVOLVER*
INTREPID	INTUITING	INVADING	INVERTER	INVOLVERS*
INTRICACIES	INTUITION	INVALID	INVERTERS	INVOLVES
INTRICACY	INTUITIONS	INVALIDED	INVERTIN	INVOLVING
INTRICATE	INTUITIVE	INVALIDING	INVERTING	INWALL
INTRIGANT	INTUITS	INVALIDINGS	INVERTINS	INWALLED
INTRIGANTS	INTUMESCE	INVALIDLY	INVERTOR	INWALLING
INTRIGUE	INTUMESCED	INVALIDS	INVERTORS	INWALLS
INTRIGUED	INTUMESCES	INVAR*	INVERTS	INWARD
INTRIGUER	INTUMESCING	INVARIANT	INVEST	INWARDLY
INTRIGUERS	INTURN*	INVARIANTS	INVESTED	INWARDS
INTRIGUES	INTURNED*	INVARS*	INVESTING	INWEAVE
INTRIGUING	INTURNS*	INVASION	INVESTOR	INWEAVED*
INTRINCE	INTUSE	INVASIONS	INVESTORS	INWEAVES
INTRINSIC	INTUSES	INVASIVE	INVESTS	INWEAVING
INTRO	INTWINE	INVEAGLE	INVEXED	INWICK
INTRODUCE	INTWINED	INVEAGLED	INVIABLE	INWICKED
INTRODUCED	INTWINES	INVEAGLES	INVIABLY*	INWICKING
INTRODUCES	INTWINING	INVEAGLING	INVIDIOUS	INWICKS
INTRODUCING	INTWIST	INVECKED	INVIOLACIES*	INWIND
INTROFIED*	INTWISTED	INVECTED	INVIOLACY*	INWINDING
INTROFIES*	INTWISTING	INVECTIVE	INVIOLATE	INWINDS
INTROFY*	INTWISTS	INVECTIVES	INVIOUS	INWIT

INWITH	IODYRITE	IRENIC	IRONER	IRRISORY
INWITS	IODYRITES	IRENICAL	IRONERS	IRRITABLE
INWORK	IOLITE	IRENICISM	IRONES*	IRRITABLY
INWORKED	IOLITES	IRENICISMS	IRONIC	IRRITANCIES
INWORKING	ION	IRENICON	IRONICAL	IRRITANCY
INWORKINGS	IONIC	IRENICONS	IRONIER	IRRITANT
INWORKS	IONICITIES*	IRENICS	IRONIES	IRRITANTS
INWORN	IONICITY*	IRENOLOGIES	IRONIEST	IRRITATE
INWOUND	IONICS*	IRENOLOGY	IRONING	IRRITATED
INWOVE	IONISE	IRES	IRONINGS	IRRITATES
INWOVEN	IONISED	IRID	IRONISE	IRRITATING
INWRAP	IONISER	IRIDAL	IRONISED	IRRITATOR
INWRAPPED	IONISERS	IRIDEAL	IRONISES	IRRITATORS
INWRAPPING	IONISES	IRIDES	IRONISING	IRRUPT
INWRAPS	IONISING	IRIDIAL	IRONIST	IRRUPTED
INWREATHE	IONIUM	IRIDIAN	IRONISTS	IRRUPTING
INWREATHED	IONIUMS	IRIDIC	IRONIZE	IRRUPTION
INWREATHES	IONIZABLE*	IRIDISE	IRONIZED	IRRUPTIONS
INWREATHING	IONIZE	IRIDISED	IRONIZES	IRRUPTIVE
INWROUGHT	IONIZED	IRIDISES	IRONIZING	IRRUPTS
INYALA	IONIZER	IRIDISING	IRONLIKE*	IS
INYALAS	IONIZERS	IRIDIUM	IRONNESS*	ISABEL
IO	IONIZES	IRIDIUMS	IRONNESSES*	ISABELLA
IODATE	IONIZING	IRIDIZE	IRONS	ISABELLAS
IODATED*	IONOGEN*	IRIDIZED	IRONSIDE*	ISABELS
IODATES	IONOGENS*	IRIDIZES	IRONSIDES*	ISAGOGE
IODATING*	IONOMER	IRIDIZING	IRONSMITH	ISAGOGES
IODATION*	IONOMERS	IRIDOLOGIES	IRONSMITHS	ISAGOGIC
IODATIONS*	IONONE	IRIDOLOGY	IRONSTONE	ISAGOGICS
IODIC	IONONES	IRIDOTOMIES	IRONSTONES	ISALLOBAR
IODID*	IONOPAUSE	IRIDOTOMY	IRONWARE	ISALLOBARS
IODIDE	IONOPAUSES	IRIDS	IRONWARES	ISARITHM*
IODIDES	IONOPHORE	IRING*	IRONWEED*	ISARITHMS*
IODIDS*	IONOPHORES	IRIS	IRONWEEDS*	ISATIN
IODIN*	IONS	IRISATE	IRONWOOD	ISATINE
IODINATE*	IOS	IRISATED	IRONWOODS	ISATINES
IODINATED*	IOTA	IRISATES	IRONWORK	ISATINIC*
IODINATES*	IOTACISM*	IRISATING	IRONWORKS	ISATINS
IODINATING*	IOTACISMS*	IRISATION	IRONY	ISBA*
IODINE	IOTAS	IRISATIONS	IRRADIANT	ISBAS*
IODINES	IPECAC	IRISCOPE	IRRADIATE	ISCHAEMIA
IODINS*	IPECACS	IRISCOPES	IRRADIATED	ISCHAEMIAS
IODISE	IPOMOEA	IRISED	IRRADIATES	ISCHAEMIC
IODISED	IPOMOEAS	IRISES	IRRADIATING	ISCHEMIA
IODISES	IPPON	IRISING*	IRREAL*	ISCHEMIAS
IODISING	IPPONS	IRITIC	IRREALITIES	ISCHEMIC
IODISM	IPRINDOLE	IRITIS	IRREALITY	ISCHIA
IODISMS	IPRINDOLES	IRITISES	IRREDENTA*	ISCHIADIC
IODIZE	IRACUND	IRK	IRREDENTAS*	ISCHIAL
IODIZED	IRADE	IRKED	IRREGULAR	ISCHIATIC
IODIZER*	IRADES	IRKING	IRREGULARS	ISCHIUM
IODIZERS*	IRASCIBLE	IRKS	IRRELATED	ISCHURIA
IODIZES	IRASCIBLY	IRKSOME	IRRIDENTA*	ISCHURIAS
IODIZING	IRATE	IRKSOMELY	IRRIDENTAS*	ISENERGIC
IODOFORM	IRATELY	IROKO	IRRIGABLE	ISH
IODOFORMS	IRATENESS*	IROKOS	IRRIGATE	ISHES
IODOPHILE	IRATENESSES*	IRON	IRRIGATED	ISINGLASS
IODOPHOR*	IRATER	IRONBARK	IRRIGATES	ISINGLASSES
IODOPHORS*	IRATEST	IRONBARKS	IRRIGATING	ISLAND
IODOPSIN*	IRE	IRONBOUND*	IRRIGATOR	ISLANDED
IODOPSINS*	IRED*	IRONCLAD*	IRRIGATORS	ISLANDER
IODOUS	IREFUL	IRONCLADS*	IRRIGUOUS	ISLANDERS
IODURET	IREFULLY	IRONE*	IRRISION	ISLANDING
IODURETS	IRELESS*	IRONED	IRRISIONS	ISLANDS

ISLE	ISODOMON	ISOLATORS	ISOSPIN	ITALICISE
ISLED	ISODOMONS	ISOLEAD*	ISOSPINS	ITALICISED
ISLELESS*	ISODOMOUS	ISOLEADS*	ISOSPORIES	ITALICISES
ISLEMAN	ISODOMUM	ISOLINE	ISOSPORY	ITALICISING
ISLEMEN	ISODONT	ISOLINES	ISOSTASIES	ITALICIZE
ISLES	ISODONTAL	ISOLOG*	ISOSTASY	ITALICIZED
ISLESMAN	ISODONTALS	ISOLOGOUS	ISOSTATIC	ITALICIZES
ISLESMEN	ISODONTS	ISOLOGS*	ISOSTERIC	ITALICIZING
ISLET	ISODOSE*	ISOLOGUE	ISOTACH*	ITALICS
ISLETS	ISOENZYME*	ISOLOGUES	ISOTACHS*	ITAS
ISLING	ISOENZYMES*	ISOMER	ISOTACTIC	ITCH
ISM	ISOETES	ISOMERASE	ISOTHERAL	ITCHED
ISMATIC	ISOGAMETE	ISOMERASES	ISOTHERALS	ITCHES
ISMATICAL	ISOGAMETES	ISOMERE	ISOTHERE	ITCHIER
ISMS	ISOGAMIC	ISOMERES	ISOTHERES	ITCHIEST
ISO	ISOGAMIES	ISOMERIC	ISOTHERM	ITCHILY*
ISOBAR	ISOGAMOUS	ISOMERISE	ISOTHERMS	ITCHINESS
ISOBARE	ISOGAMY	ISOMERISED	ISOTONE	ITCHINESSES
ISOBARES	ISOGENEIC*	ISOMERISES	ISOTONES	ITCHING
ISOBARIC	ISOGENIC*	ISOMERISING	ISOTONIC	ITCHINGS*
ISOBARS	ISOGENIES	ISOMERISM	ISOTOPE	ITCHWEED
ISOBASE	ISOGENOUS	ISOMERISMS	ISOTOPES	ITCHWEEDS
ISOBASES	ISOGENY	ISOMERIZE	ISOTOPIC	ITCHY
ISOBATH	ISOGLOSS	ISOMERIZED	ISOTOPIES	ITEM
ISOBATHIC	ISOGLOSSES	ISOMERIZES	ISOTOPY	ITEMED
ISOBATHS	ISOGON	ISOMERIZING	ISOTRON	ITEMING
ISOBRONT	ISOGONAL	ISOMEROUS	ISOTRONS	ITEMISE
ISOBRONTS	ISOGONALS	ISOMERS	ISOTROPIC	ITEMISED
ISOBUTANE*	ISOGONE*	ISOMETRIC	ISOTROPIES	ITEMISES
ISOBUTANES*	ISOGONES*	ISOMETRICS	ISOTROPY	ITEMISING
ISOCHASM	ISOGONIC	ISOMETRIES	ISOTYPE	ITEMIZE
ISOCHASMS	ISOGONICS	ISOMETRY	ISOTYPES	ITEMIZED
ISOCHEIM	ISOGONIES*	ISOMORPH	ISOTYPIC*	ITEMIZER*
ISOCHEIMS	ISOGONS	ISOMORPHS	ISOZYME*	ITEMIZERS*
ISOCHIMAL	ISOGONY*	ISONIAZID	ISOZYMES*	ITEMIZES
ISOCHIMALS	ISOGRAFT*	ISONIAZIDS	ISOZYMIC*	ITEMIZING
ISOCHIME	ISOGRAFTED*	ISONOMIC	ISSEI	ITEMS
ISOCHIMES	ISOGRAFTING*	ISONOMIES	ISSEIS	ITERANCE
ISOCHOR	ISOGRAFTS*	ISONOMOUS	ISSUABLE	ITERANCES
ISOCHORE	ISOGRAM	ISONOMY	ISSUABLY	ITERANT
ISOCHORES	ISOGRAMS	ISOOCTANE*	ISSUANCE	ITERATE
ISOCHORIC	ISOGRAPH*	ISOOCTANES*	ISSUANCES	ITERATED
ISOCHORS	ISOGRAPHS*	ISOPACH*	ISSUANT	ITERATES
ISOCHRON*	ISOGRIV*	ISOPACHS*	ISSUE	ITERATING
ISOCHRONE	ISOGRIVS*	ISOPHOTAL*	ISSUED	ITERATION
ISOCHRONES	ISOHEL	ISOPHOTE*	ISSUELESS	ITERATIONS
ISOCHRONS*	ISOHELS	ISOPHOTES*	ISSUER	ITERATIVE
ISOCLINAL	ISOHYET	ISOPLETH	ISSUERS	ITERUM
ISOCLINALS	ISOHYETAL	ISOPLETHS	ISSUES	ITHER*
ISOCLINE	ISOHYETALS	ISOPOD	ISSUING	ITINERACIES
ISOCLINES	ISOHYETS	ISOPODAN	ISTHMI*	ITINERACY
ISOCLINIC	ISOKONT	ISOPODANS*	ISTHMIAN	ITINERANT
ISOCLINICS	ISOKONTAN	ISOPODOUS	ISTHMIANS*	ITINERANTS
ISOCRACIES	ISOKONTANS	ISOPODS	ISTHMIC*	ITINERARIES
ISOCRACY	ISOKONTS	ISOPOLITIES	ISTHMOID*	ITINERARY
ISOCRATIC	ISOLABLE	ISOPOLITY	ISTHMUS	ITINERATE
ISOCRYMAL	ISOLATE	ISOPRENE	ISTHMUSES	ITINERATED
ISOCRYMALS	ISOLATED	ISOPRENES	ISTLE	ITINERATES
ISOCRYME	ISOLATES	ISOPROPYL	ISTLES	ITINERATING
ISOCRYMES	ISOLATING	ISOPROPYLS	IT	ITS
ISOCYCLIC	ISOLATION	ISOPYCNIC*	ITA	ITSELF
ISODICA	ISOLATIONS	ISOS	ITACISM	IURE
ISODICON	ISOLATIVE	ISOSCELES	ITACISMS	IVIED
ISODOMA	ISOLATOR	ISOSMOTIC*	ITALIC	IVIES

The Chambers Dictionary is the authority for many longer words; see Introduction, page ix

IVORIED	IVRESSE	IXODIASES	IXTLES	IZVESTIYA
IVORIES	IVRESSES	IXODIASIS	IZAR*	IZVESTIYAS
IVORIST	IVY	IXODID*	IZARD	IZZARD
IVORISTS	IVYLIKE*	IXODIDS*	IZARDS	IZZARDS
IVORY	IWIS	IXORA*	IZARS*	IZZAT
IVORYBILL*	IXIA	IXORAS*	IZVESTIA	IZZATS
IVORYBILLS*	IXIAS	IXTLE	IZVESTIAS	

J

JAB	JACKED	JACOBUS	JAGHIR	JALOUSIED
JABBED	JACKEEN	JACOBUSES	JAGHIRDAR	JALOUSIES
JABBER	JACKEENS	JACONET	JAGHIRDARS	JALOUSING
JABBERED	JACKER*	JACONETS	JAGHIRE	JAM
JABBERER	JACKEROO	JACQUARD	JAGHIRES	JAMADAR
JABBERERS	JACKEROOED	JACQUARDS	JAGHIRS	JAMADARS
JABBERING	JACKEROOING	JACQUERIE*	JAGIR	JAMB
JABBERINGS	JACKEROOS	JACQUERIES*	JAGIRS	JAMBALAYA
JABBERS	JACKERS*	JACTATION	JAGLESS*	JAMBALAYAS
JABBING	JACKET	JACTATIONS	JAGRA*	JAMBE
JABBLE	JACKETED	JACULATE	JAGRAS*	JAMBEAU
JABBLED	JACKETING	JACULATED	JAGS	JAMBEAUX
JABBLES	JACKETS	JACULATES	JAGUAR	JAMBED*
JABBLING	JACKFISH*	JACULATING	JAGUARS	JAMBEE
JABERS	JACKFISHES*	JACULATOR	JAIL	JAMBEES
JABIRU	JACKFRUIT*	JACULATORS	JAILBAIT*	JAMBER
JABIRUS	JACKFRUITS*	JACUZZI	JAILBIRD*	JAMBERS
JABORANDI	JACKIES*	JACUZZIS	JAILBIRDS*	JAMBES
JABORANDIS	JACKING	JADE	JAILBREAK*	JAMBEUX
JABOT	JACKKNIFE	JADED	JAILBREAKS*	JAMBIER
JABOTS	JACKKNIFED	JADEDLY	JAILED	JAMBIERS
JABS	JACKKNIFES	JADEDNESS*	JAILER	JAMBING*
JACAL*	JACKKNIFING	JADEDNESSES*	JAILERESS	JAMBIYA
JACALES*	JACKKNIVES	JADEITE	JAILERESSES	JAMBIYAH
JACALS*	JACKLEG*	JADEITES	JAILERS	JAMBIYAHS
JACAMAR	JACKLEGS*	JADERIES	JAILHOUSE	JAMBIYAS
JACAMARS	JACKLIGHT*	JADERY	JAILHOUSES	JAMBO
JACANA	JACKLIGHTS*	JADES	JAILING	JAMBOK
JACANAS	JACKMAN	JADING	JAILOR	JAMBOKKED
JACARANDA	JACKMEN	JADISH	JAILORESS	JAMBOKKING
JACARANDAS	JACKPOT	JADISHLY*	JAILORESSES	JAMBOKS
JACCHUS	JACKPOTS	JADITIC*	JAILORS	JAMBOLAN
JACCHUSES	JACKROLL*	JAEGER	JAILS	JAMBOLANA
JACENT	JACKROLLED*	JAEGERS	JAK	JAMBOLANAS
JACINTH	JACKROLLING	JAG	JAKE	JAMBOLANS
JACINTHE*	JACKROLLS*	JAGER	JAKES	JAMBONE
JACINTHES*	JACKS	JAGERS	JAKESES	JAMBONES
JACINTHS	JACKSCREW*	JAGG*	JAKS	JAMBOOL
JACK	JACKSCREWS*	JAGGARIES*	JALAP	JAMBOOLS
JACKAL	JACKSHAFT	JAGGARY*	JALAPENO	JAMBOREE
JACKALLED	JACKSHAFTS	JAGGED	JALAPENOS	JAMBOREES
JACKALLING	JACKSIE	JAGGEDER	JALAPIC	JAMBOS
JACKALS	JACKSIES	JAGGEDEST	JALAPIN	JAMBS
JACKAROO	JACKSMELT*	JAGGEDLY	JALAPINS	JAMBU
JACKAROOED	JACKSMELTS*	JAGGER	JALAPS	JAMBUL
JACKAROOING	JACKSMITH	JAGGERIES	JALOP*	JAMBULS
JACKAROOS	JACKSMITHS	JAGGERS	JALOPIES	JAMBUS
JACKASS	JACKSTAY*	JAGGERY	JALOPPIES	JAMDANI
JACKASSES	JACKSTAYS*	JAGGHERIES*	JALOPPY	JAMDANIS
JACKBOOT	JACKSTRAW*	JAGGHERY*	JALOPS*	JAMES
JACKBOOTED	JACKSTRAWS*	JAGGIER	JALOPY	JAMESES
JACKBOOTING	JACKSY	JAGGIEST	JALOUSE	JAMJAR
JACKBOOTS	JACKY*	JAGGING	JALOUSED	JAMJARS
JACKDAW	JACOBIN	JAGGS*	JALOUSES	JAMMED
JACKDAWS	JACOBINS	JAGGY	JALOUSIE	JAMMER

The Chambers Dictionary is the authority for many longer words; see Introduction, page ix

JAMMERS	JAPANNER	JAROVIZED*	JAUNDICES	JAYHAWKERS*
JAMMIER	JAPANNERS	JAROVIZES*	JAUNDICING	JAYS
JAMMIES*	JAPANNING	JAROVIZING*	JAUNSE	JAYVEE*
JAMMIEST	JAPANS	JARRAH	JAUNSED	JAYVEES*
JAMMING	JAPE	JARRAHS	JAUNSES	JAYWALK
JAMMY	JAPED	JARRED	JAUNSING	JAYWALKED
JAMPAN	JAPER	JARRING	JAUNT	JAYWALKER
JAMPANEE	JAPERIES*	JARRINGLY	JAUNTED	JAYWALKERS
JAMPANEES	JAPERS	JARRINGS	JAUNTEE	JAYWALKING
JAMPANI	JAPERY*	JARS	JAUNTIE	JAYWALKINGS
JAMPANIS	JAPES	JARSFUL*	JAUNTIER	JAYWALKS
JAMPANS	JAPING	JARTA	JAUNTIES	JAZERANT
JAMPOT	JAPINGLY*	JARTAS	JAUNTIEST	JAZERANTS
JAMPOTS	JAPINGS	JARUL	JAUNTILY	JAZIES
JAMS	JAPONICA	JARULS	JAUNTING	JAZY
JANDAL	JAPONICAS	JARVEY	JAUNTS	JAZZ
JANDALS	JAPPED	JARVEYS	JAUNTY	JAZZED
JANE	JAPPING	JARVIE	JAUP	JAZZER
JANES	JAPS	JARVIES	JAUPED	JAZZERS
JANGLE	JAR	JASEY	JAUPING	JAZZES
JANGLED	JARARACA	JASEYS	JAUPS	JAZZIER
JANGLER	JARARACAS	JASIES	JAVA*	JAZZIEST
JANGLERS	JARARAKA	JASMIN*	JAVAS*	JAZZILY
JANGLES	JARARAKAS	JASMINE	JAVEL	JAZZINESS
JANGLIER	JARFUL	JASMINES	JAVELIN	JAZZINESSES
JANGLIEST	JARFULS	JASMINS*	JAVELINA*	JAZZING
JANGLING	JARGON	JASP	JAVELINAS*	JAZZLIKE*
JANGLINGS	JARGONED	JASPE	JAVELINED*	JAZZMAN
JANGLY	JARGONEER	JASPER	JAVELINING*	JAZZMEN
JANIFORM*	JARGONEERS	JASPERISE	JAVELINS	JAZZY
JANISARIES*	JARGONEL*	JASPERISED	JAVELS	JEALOUS
JANISARY*	JARGONELS*	JASPERISES	JAW	JEALOUSE
JANISSARIES	JARGONING	JASPERISING	JAWAN	JEALOUSED
JANISSARY	JARGONISE	JASPERIZE	JAWANS	JEALOUSES
JANITOR	JARGONISED	JASPERIZED	JAWARI	JEALOUSIES
JANITORS	JARGONISES	JASPERIZES	JAWARIS	JEALOUSING
JANITRESS	JARGONISH*	JASPERIZING	JAWBATION	JEALOUSLY
JANITRESSES	JARGONISING	JASPEROUS	JAWBATIONS	JEALOUSY
JANITRIX	JARGONIST	JASPERS	JAWBONE	JEAN
JANITRIXES	JARGONISTS	JASPERY	JAWBONED	JEANETTE
JANIZAR	JARGONIZE	JASPES	JAWBONER*	JEANETTES
JANIZARIES	JARGONIZED	JASPIDEAN	JAWBONERS*	JEANS
JANIZARS	JARGONIZES	JASPIS	JAWBONES	JEAT
JANIZARY	JARGONIZING	JASPISES	JAWBONING	JEATS
JANKER	JARGONS	JASPS	JAWBONINGS	JEBEL
JANKERS	JARGOON	JASS	JAWBOX	JEBELS
JANN	JARGOONS	JASSES	JAWBOXES	JEE
JANNOCK	JARHEAD*	JASSID*	JAWED	JEED
JANNOCKS	JARHEADS*	JASSIDS*	JAWFALL	JEEING
JANNS	JARINA*	JASY	JAWFALLS	JEEL
JANSKY	JARINAS*	JATAKA	JAWHOLE	JEELED
JANSKYS	JARK	JATAKAS	JAWHOLES	JEELIE
JANTEE	JARKMAN	JATO	JAWING	JEELIED
JANTIER	JARKMEN	JATOS	JAWINGS	JEELIEING
JANTIES	JARKS	JAUK*	JAWLIKE*	JEELIES
JANTIEST	JARL	JAUKED*	JAWLINE*	JEELING
JANTY	JARLDOM*	JAUKING*	JAWLINES*	JEELS
JAP	JARLDOMS*	JAUKS*	JAWS	JEELY
JAPAN	JARLS	JAUNCE	JAY	JEELYING
JAPANIZE*	JAROOL	JAUNCED	JAYBIRD*	JEEP*
JAPANIZED*	JAROOLS	JAUNCES	JAYBIRDS*	JEEPED*
JAPANIZES*	JAROSITE	JAUNCING	JAYGEE*	JEEPERS
JAPANIZING*	JAROSITES	JAUNDICE	JAYGEES*	JEEPING*
JAPANNED	JAROVIZE*	JAUNDICED	JAYHAWKER*	JEEPNEY

JEEPNEYS	JEMMIEST	JERQUINGS	JETPORTS*	JIB
JEEPS*	JEMMINESS	JERREED*	JETS	JIBB*
JEER	JEMMINESSES	JERREEDS*	JETSAM	JIBBAH
JEERED	JEMMY	JERRICAN	JETSAMS	JIBBAHS
JEERER	JEMMYING	JERRICANS	JETSOM	JIBBED
JEERERS	JENNET	JERRID*	JETSOMS	JIBBER
JEERING	JENNETING	JERRIDS*	JETSON	JIBBERED
JEERINGLY	JENNETINGS	JERRIES	JETSONS	JIBBERING
JEERINGS	JENNETS	JERRY	JETSTREAM	JIBBERS
JEERS	JENNIES	JERRYCAN	JETSTREAMS	JIBBING
JEES	JENNY	JERRYCANS	JETTATURA	JIBBINGS
JEEZ*	JEOFAIL	JERSEY	JETTATURAS	JIBBOOM*
JEFE*	JEOFAILS	JERSEYED*	JETTED	JIBBOOMS*
JEFES*	JEON*	JERSEYS	JETTIED	JIBBS*
JEFF	JEOPARD	JESS	JETTIER	JIBE
JEFFED	JEOPARDED	JESSAMIES	JETTIES	JIBED
JEFFING	JEOPARDER	JESSAMINE	JETTIEST	JIBER
JEFFS	JEOPARDERS	JESSAMINES	JETTINESS	JIBERS
JEHAD	JEOPARDIED	JESSAMY	JETTINESSES	JIBES
JEHADS	JEOPARDIES	JESSANT	JETTING	JIBING
JEHU*	JEOPARDING	JESSE*	JETTISON	JIBINGLY*
JEHUS*	JEOPARDS	JESSED	JETTISONED	JIBS
JEJUNA	JEOPARDY	JESSERANT	JETTISONING	JICAMA*
JEJUNAL*	JEOPARDYING	JESSERANTS	JETTISONS	JICAMAS*
JEJUNE	JEQUIRITIES	JESSES	JETTON	JICKAJOG
JEJUNELY	JEQUIRITY	JESSIE	JETTONS	JICKAJOGGED
JEJUNITIES	JERBIL	JESSIES	JETTY	JICKAJOGGING
JEJUNITY	JERBILS	JESSING*	JETTYING	JICKAJOGS
JEJUNUM	JERBOA	JEST	JEU	JIFF
JELAB	JERBOAS	JESTBOOK	JEUNE	JIFFIES
JELABS	JEREED	JESTBOOKS	JEUX	JIFFS
JELL	JEREEDS	JESTED	JEW	JIFFY
JELLABA	JEREMIAD	JESTEE	JEWED	JIG
JELLABAS	JEREMIADS	JESTEES	JEWEL	JIGABOO*
JELLED	JERFALCON	JESTER	JEWELED*	JIGABOOS*
JELLIED	JERFALCONS	JESTERS	JEWELER*	JIGAJIG
JELLIES	JERID	JESTFUL	JEWELERS*	JIGAJIGGED
JELLIFIED	JERIDS	JESTING	JEWELFISH	JIGAJIGGING
JELLIFIES	JERK	JESTINGLY	JEWELFISHES	JIGAJIGS
JELLIFORM	JERKED	JESTINGS	JEWELING*	JIGAJOG
JELLIFY	JERKER	JESTS	JEWELLED	JIGAJOGGED
JELLIFYING	JERKERS	JESUIT*	JEWELLER	JIGAJOGGING
JELLING	JERKIER	JESUITIC*	JEWELLERIES	JIGAJOGS
JELLO	JERKIES	JESUITISM*	JEWELLERS	JIGAMAREE
JELLOS	JERKIEST	JESUITISMS*	JEWELLERY	JIGAMAREES
JELLS	JERKILY*	JESUITRIES*	JEWELLIKE*	JIGGED
JELLY	JERKIN	JESUITRY*	JEWELLING	JIGGER
JELLYBEAN	JERKINESS	JESUITS*	JEWELRIES	JIGGERED
JELLYBEANS	JERKINESSES	JESUS	JEWELRY	JIGGERING
JELLYFISH	JERKING	JET	JEWELS	JIGGERS
JELLYFISHES	JERKINGS	JETBEAD*	JEWELWEED*	JIGGING
JELLYING	JERKINS	JETBEADS*	JEWELWEEDS*	JIGGINGS
JELLYLIKE*	JERKS	JETE	JEWFISH	JIGGISH
JELUTONG	JERKWATER	JETES	JEWFISHES	JIGGLE
JELUTONGS	JERKWATERS	JETFOIL	JEWING	JIGGLED
JEMADAR	JERKY	JETFOILS	JEWS	JIGGLES
JEMADARS	JEROBOAM	JETLIKE*	JEZAIL	JIGGLIER
JEMIDAR	JEROBOAMS	JETLINER	JEZAILS	JIGGLIEST
JEMIDARS	JERQUE	JETLINERS	JEZEBEL*	JIGGLING
JEMIMA	JERQUED	JETON	JEZEBELS*	JIGGLY
JEMIMAS	JERQUER	JETONS	JHALA	JIGGUMBOB
JEMMIED	JERQUERS	JETPLANE	JHALAS	JIGGUMBOBS
JEMMIER	JERQUES	JETPLANES	JIAO	JIGJIG
JEMMIES	JERQUING	JETPORT*	JIAOS	JIGJIGGED

JIGJIGGING	JINGLETS	JIVE	JOCKSTRAP	JOINT
JIGJIGS	JINGLIER	JIVEASS*	JOCKSTRAPS	JOINTED
JIGOT	JINGLIEST	JIVED	JOCKTELEG	JOINTEDLY*
JIGOTS	JINGLING	JIVER	JOCKTELEGS	JOINTER
JIGS	JINGLY	JIVERS	JOCO	JOINTERS
JIGSAW	JINGO	JIVES	JOCOSE	JOINTING
JIGSAWED	JINGOES	JIVEY*	JOCOSELY	JOINTLESS
JIGSAWING	JINGOISH	JIVIER*	JOCOSITIES	JOINTLY
JIGSAWN*	JINGOISM	JIVIEST*	JOCOSITY	JOINTNESS
JIGSAWS	JINGOISMS	JIVING	JOCULAR	JOINTNESSES
JIHAD	JINGOIST	JIZ	JOCULARLY	JOINTRESS
JIHADS	JINGOISTS	JIZZ	JOCULATOR	JOINTRESSES
JILGIE	JINJILI	JIZZES	JOCULATORS	JOINTS
JILGIES	JINJILIS	JNANA	JOCUND	JOINTURE
JILL	JINK	JNANAS	JOCUNDITIES	JOINTURED
JILLAROO	JINKED	JO	JOCUNDITY	JOINTURES
JILLAROOS	JINKER	JOANNA	JOCUNDLY	JOINTURING
JILLET	JINKERS	JOANNAS	JODEL	JOINTWORM
JILLETS	JINKING	JOANNES	JODELLED	JOINTWORMS
JILLFLIRT	JINKS	JOANNESES	JODELLING	JOIST
JILLFLIRTS	JINN	JOB	JODELS	JOISTED
JILLION	JINNEE	JOBATION	JODHPUR*	JOISTING
JILLIONS	JINNI	JOBATIONS	JODHPURS	JOISTS
JILLS	JINNS	JOBBED	JOE	JOJOBA
JILT	JINS*	JOBBER	JOES	JOJOBAS
JILTED	JINX	JOBBERIES	JOEY	JOKE
JILTER*	JINXED	JOBBERS	JOEYS	JOKED
JILTERS*	JINXES	JOBBERY	JOG	JOKER
JILTING	JINXING	JOBBIE	JOGGED	JOKERS
JILTS	JIPIJAPA*	JOBBIES	JOGGER	JOKES
JIMCRACK	JIPIJAPAS*	JOBBING	JOGGERS	JOKESMITH
JIMCRACKS	JIPYAPA	JOBBINGS	JOGGING	JOKESMITHS
JIMINY	JIPYAPAS	JOBCENTRE	JOGGINGS	JOKESOME
JIMJAM	JIRBLE	JOBCENTRES	JOGGLE	JOKESTER*
JIMJAMS	JIRBLED	JOBE	JOGGLED	JOKESTERS*
JIMMIED	JIRBLES	JOBED	JOGGLER*	JOKEY
JIMMIES	JIRBLING	JOBERNOWL	JOGGLERS*	JOKIER
JIMMINY*	JIRD	JOBERNOWLS	JOGGLES	JOKIEST
JIMMY	JIRDS	JOBES	JOGGLING	JOKILY*
JIMMYING	JIRGA	JOBHOLDER*	JOGPANTS	JOKINESS*
JIMP	JIRGAS	JOBHOLDERS*	JOGS	JOKINESSES*
JIMPER	JIRKINET	JOBING	JOGTROT	JOKING
JIMPEST	JIRKINETS	JOBLESS	JOGTROTS	JOKINGLY
JIMPIER	JISM	JOBNAME*	JOHANNES	JOKOL
JIMPIEST	JISMS	JOBNAMES*	JOHANNESES	JOKY
JIMPLY	JISSOM	JOBS	JOHN	JOLE
JIMPNESS	JISSOMS	JOBSHARE	JOHNBOAT*	JOLED
JIMPNESSES	JITNEY	JOBSHARES	JOHNBOATS*	JOLES
JIMPY	JITNEYS	JOBSWORTH	JOHNNIE	JOLING
JIN*	JITTER	JOBSWORTHS	JOHNNIES	JOLL
JINGAL	JITTERBUG	JOCK	JOHNNY	JOLLED
JINGALL*	JITTERBUGGED	JOCKETTE	JOHNS	JOLLEY
JINGALLS*	JITTERBUGGING	JOCKETTES	JOIN	JOLLEYER
JINGALS	JITTERBUGS	JOCKEY	JOINABLE*	JOLLEYERS
JINGBANG	JITTERED	JOCKEYED	JOINDER	JOLLEYING
JINGBANGS	JITTERIER	JOCKEYING	JOINDERS	JOLLEYINGS
JINGKO*	JITTERIEST	JOCKEYISM	JOINED	JOLLEYS
JINGKOES*	JITTERING	JOCKEYISMS	JOINER	JOLLIED
JINGLE	JITTERS	JOCKEYS	JOINERIES	JOLLIER
JINGLED	JITTERY	JOCKNEY	JOINERS	JOLLIES
JINGLER	JIUJITSU*	JOCKNEYS	JOINERY	JOLLIEST
JINGLERS	JIUJITSUS*	JOCKO	JOINING	JOLLIFIED
JINGLES	JIUJUTSU*	JOCKOS	JOININGS	JOLLIFIES
JINGLET	JIUJUTSUS*	JOCKS	JOINS	JOLLIFY

Words marked with an asterisk are from OTCWL

JOLLIFYING
JOLLILY
JOLLIMENT
JOLLIMENTS
JOLLINESS
JOLLINESSES
JOLLING
JOLLITIES
JOLLITY
JOLLS
JOLLY
JOLLYBOAT
JOLLYBOATS
JOLLYER
JOLLYERS
JOLLYHEAD
JOLLYHEADS
JOLLYING
JOLLYINGS
JOLT
JOLTED
JOLTER
JOLTERS
JOLTHEAD
JOLTHEADS
JOLTIER
JOLTIEST
JOLTILY*
JOLTING
JOLTINGLY
JOLTS
JOLTY
JOMO
JOMOS
JONCANOE
JONCANOES
JONES*
JONESES*
JONGLEUR
JONGLEURS
JONQUIL
JONQUILS
JONTIES
JONTY
JOOK
JOOKED
JOOKERIES
JOOKERY
JOOKING
JOOKS
JOR
JORAM
JORAMS
JORDAN
JORDANS
JORDELOO
JORDELOOS
JORS
JORUM
JORUMS
JOSEPH
JOSEPHS
JOSH
JOSHED

JOSHER
JOSHERS
JOSHES
JOSHING
JOSKIN
JOSKINS
JOSS
JOSSER
JOSSERS
JOSSES
JOSTLE
JOSTLED
JOSTLER*
JOSTLERS*
JOSTLES
JOSTLING
JOSTLINGS
JOT
JOTA
JOTAS
JOTS
JOTTED
JOTTER
JOTTERS
JOTTING
JOTTINGS
JOTTY*
JOTUN
JOTUNN
JOTUNNS
JOTUNS
JOUAL
JOUALS
JOUGS
JOUISANCE
JOUISANCES
JOUK
JOUKED
JOUKERIES
JOUKERY
JOUKING
JOUKS
JOULE
JOULED
JOULES
JOULING
JOUNCE
JOUNCED
JOUNCES
JOUNCIER*
JOUNCIEST*
JOUNCING
JOUNCY*
JOUR
JOURNAL
JOURNALLED
JOURNALLING
JOURNALS
JOURNEY
JOURNEYED
JOURNEYER
JOURNEYERS
JOURNEYING
JOURNEYS

JOURNO
JOURNOS
JOURS
JOUST
JOUSTED
JOUSTER
JOUSTERS
JOUSTING
JOUSTS
JOVIAL
JOVIALITIES
JOVIALITY
JOVIALLY
JOVIALTIES*
JOVIALTY*
JOW
JOWAR
JOWARI
JOWARIS
JOWARS
JOWED
JOWING
JOWL
JOWLED
JOWLER
JOWLERS
JOWLIER
JOWLIEST
JOWLING
JOWLS
JOWLY
JOWS
JOY
JOYANCE
JOYANCES
JOYED
JOYFUL
JOYFULLER
JOYFULLEST
JOYFULLY
JOYING
JOYLESS
JOYLESSLY
JOYOUS
JOYOUSLY
JOYPOP*
JOYPOPPED*
JOYPOPPER*
JOYPOPPERS*
JOYPOPPING*
JOYPOPS*
JOYRIDDEN*
JOYRIDE*
JOYRIDER*
JOYRIDERS*
JOYRIDES*
JOYRIDING*
JOYRIDINGS*
JOYRODE*
JOYS
JOYSTICK*
JOYSTICKS*
JUBA
JUBAS

JUBATE
JUBBAH
JUBBAHS
JUBE
JUBES
JUBHAH*
JUBHAHS*
JUBILANCE
JUBILANCES
JUBILANCIES
JUBILANCY
JUBILANT
JUBILATE
JUBILATED
JUBILATES
JUBILATING
JUBILE*
JUBILEE
JUBILEES
JUBILES*
JUD
JUDAS
JUDASES
JUDDER
JUDDERED
JUDDERING
JUDDERS
JUDGE
JUDGED
JUDGEMENT
JUDGEMENTS
JUDGER*
JUDGERS*
JUDGES
JUDGESHIP
JUDGESHIPS
JUDGING
JUDGMATIC*
JUDGMENT
JUDGMENTS
JUDICABLE
JUDICATOR
JUDICATORS
JUDICIAL
JUDICIARIES
JUDICIARY
JUDICIOUS
JUDIES
JUDO
JUDOGI
JUDOGIS
JUDOIST
JUDOISTS
JUDOKA
JUDOKAS
JUDOS
JUDS
JUDY
JUG
JUGA
JUGAL
JUGALS
JUGATE

JUGFULS
JUGGED
JUGGING
JUGGINGS
JUGGINS
JUGGINSES
JUGGLE
JUGGLED
JUGGLER
JUGGLERIES
JUGGLERS
JUGGLERY
JUGGLES
JUGGLING
JUGGLINGS
JUGHEAD
JUGHEADS
JUGLET
JUGLETS
JUGS
JUGSFUL*
JUGULA*
JUGULAR
JUGULARS
JUGULATE
JUGULATED
JUGULATES
JUGULATING
JUGULUM*
JUGUM
JUGUMS*
JUICE
JUICED
JUICEHEAD*
JUICEHEADS*
JUICELESS
JUICER
JUICERS
JUICES
JUICIER
JUICIEST
JUICILY*
JUICINESS
JUICINESSES
JUICING
JUICY
JUJITSU*
JUJITSUS*
JUJU
JUJUBE
JUJUBES
JUJUISM*
JUJUISMS*
JUJUIST*
JUJUISTS*
JUJUS
JUJUTSU*
JUJUTSUS*
JUKE
JUKEBOX*
JUKEBOXES*
JUKED
JUKES
JUKING

JUBA
JUBAS
JUGFUL

The Chambers Dictionary is the authority for many longer words; see Introduction, page ix

JUKSKEI
JUKSKEIS
JULEP
JULEPS
JULIENNE
JULIENNED
JULIENNES
JULIENNING
JUMAR
JUMARRED
JUMARRING
JUMARS
JUMART
JUMARTS
JUMBAL
JUMBALS
JUMBIE
JUMBIES
JUMBLE
JUMBLED
JUMBLER
JUMBLERS
JUMBLES
JUMBLIER
JUMBLIEST
JUMBLING
JUMBLY
JUMBO
JUMBOISE
JUMBOISED
JUMBOISES
JUMBOISING
JUMBOIZE
JUMBOIZED
JUMBOIZES
JUMBOIZING
JUMBOS
JUMBUCK
JUMBUCKS
JUMBY
JUMELLE
JUMELLES
JUMP

JUMPABLE
JUMPED
JUMPER
JUMPERS
JUMPIER
JUMPIEST
JUMPILY
JUMPINESS
JUMPINESSES
JUMPING
JUMPOFF*
JUMPOFFS*
JUMPS
JUMPSUIT*
JUMPSUITS*
JUMPY
JUN*
JUNCATE
JUNCATES
JUNCO
JUNCOES
JUNCOS
JUNCTION
JUNCTIONS
JUNCTURAL*
JUNCTURE
JUNCTURES
JUNCUS
JUNCUSES
JUNEATING
JUNEATINGS
JUNGLE
JUNGLED*
JUNGLES
JUNGLI
JUNGLIER
JUNGLIEST
JUNGLIS
JUNGLIST
JUNGLISTS
JUNGLY
JUNIOR
JUNIORATE*

JUNIORATES*
JUNIORITIES
JUNIORITY
JUNIORS
JUNIPER
JUNIPERS
JUNK
JUNKANOO
JUNKANOOS
JUNKED
JUNKER
JUNKERS
JUNKET
JUNKETED
JUNKETEER
JUNKETEERS
JUNKETER*
JUNKETERS*
JUNKETING
JUNKETINGS
JUNKETS
JUNKIE
JUNKIER
JUNKIES
JUNKIEST
JUNKINESS
JUNKINESSES
JUNKING
JUNKMAN
JUNKMEN
JUNKS
JUNKY
JUNKYARD*
JUNKYARDS*
JUNTA
JUNTAS
JUNTO
JUNTOS
JUPATI
JUPATIS
JUPE*
JUPES*
JUPON

JUPONS
JURA
JURAL
JURALLY
JURANT
JURANTS
JURAT
JURATORY
JURATS
JURE
JUREL*
JURELS*
JURIDIC
JURIDICAL
JURIED*
JURIES
JURIST
JURISTIC
JURISTS
JUROR
JURORS
JURY
JURYING*
JURYMAN
JURYMAST
JURYMASTS
JURYMEN
JURYWOMAN
JURYWOMEN
JUS
JUSSIVE
JUSSIVES
JUST
JUSTED
JUSTER
JUSTERS*
JUSTEST
JUSTICE
JUSTICER
JUSTICERS
JUSTICES
JUSTICIAR
JUSTICIARS

JUSTIFIED
JUSTIFIER
JUSTIFIERS
JUSTIFIES
JUSTIFY
JUSTIFYING
JUSTING
JUSTLE
JUSTLED
JUSTLES
JUSTLING
JUSTLY
JUSTNESS
JUSTNESSES
JUSTS
JUT
JUTE
JUTES
JUTS
JUTTED
JUTTIED
JUTTIES
JUTTING
JUTTINGLY
JUTTY
JUTTYING
JUVE
JUVENAL
JUVENALS
JUVENILE
JUVENILES
JUVENILIA
JUVES
JUXTAPOSE
JUXTAPOSED
JUXTAPOSES
JUXTAPOSING
JYMOLD
JYNX
JYNXES

K

KA
KAAMA
KAAMAS
KAAS*
KAB*
KABAB
KABABBED
KABABBING
KABABS
KABADDI
KABADDIS
KABAKA*
KABAKAS*
KABALA
KABALAS
KABAR*
KABARS*
KABAYA
KABAYAS
KABBALA
KABBALAH
KABBALAHS
KABBALAS
KABELE
KABELES
KABELJOU
KABELJOUS
KABELJOUW
KABELJOUWS
KABIKI*
KABIKIS*
KABOB
KABOBBED
KABOBBING
KABOBS
KABS*
KABUKI
KABUKIS
KACCHA
KACCHAS
KACHA
KACHAHRI
KACHAHRIS
KACHCHA
KACHERI
KACHERIS
KACHINA
KACHINAS
KADDISH*
KADDISHIM*
KADE
KADES
KADI
KADIS
KAE

KAED
KAEING
KAES
KAF*
KAFFIR*
KAFFIRS*
KAFFIYEH
KAFFIYEHS
KAFILA
KAFILAS
KAFIR*
KAFIRS*
KAFS*
KAFTAN
KAFTANS
KAGO
KAGOOL
KAGOOLS
KAGOS
KAGOUL
KAGOULE
KAGOULES
KAGOULS
KAGU*
KAGUS*
KAHAL
KAHALS
KAHAWAI
KAHAWAIS
KAHUNA*
KAHUNAS*
KAI
KAIAK
KAIAKED
KAIAKING
KAIAKS
KAID
KAIDS
KAIE
KAIES
KAIF
KAIFS
KAIKAI
KAIKAIS
KAIL
KAILS
KAILYAIRD
KAILYAIRDS
KAILYARD
KAILYARDS
KAIM
KAIMAKAM
KAIMAKAMS
KAIMS
KAIN

KAING
KAINIT*
KAINITE
KAINITES
KAINITS*
KAINS
KAIS
KAISER
KAISERDOM
KAISERDOMS
KAISERIN
KAISERINS
KAISERISM
KAISERISMS
KAISERS
KAIZEN
KAIZENS
KAJAWAH
KAJAWAHS
KAJEPUT*
KAJEPUTS*
KAKA
KAKAPO
KAKAPOS
KAKAS
KAKEMONO
KAKEMONOS
KAKI
KAKIEMON
KAKIEMONS
KAKIS
KAKODYL
KAKODYLS
KALAM*
KALAMDAN
KALAMDANS
KALAMKARI
KALAMKARIS
KALAMS*
KALANCHOE
KALANCHOES
KALE
KALENDAR
KALENDARED
KALENDARING
KALENDARS
KALENDS
KALES
KALEWIFE*
KALEWIVES*
KALEYARD*
KALEYARDS*
KALI
KALIAN
KALIANS

KALIF
KALIFATE*
KALIFATES*
KALIFS
KALIMBA*
KALIMBAS*
KALINITE
KALINITES
KALIPH*
KALIPHS*
KALIS
KALIUM
KALIUMS
KALLIDIN*
KALLIDINS*
KALLITYPE
KALLITYPES
KALMIA
KALMIAS
KALONG
KALONGS
KALOTYPE
KALOTYPES
KALPA
KALPAK
KALPAKS
KALPAS
KALPIS
KALPISES
KALSOMINE
KALSOMINED
KALSOMINES
KALSOMINING
KALUMPIT
KALUMPITS
KALYPTRA
KALYPTRAS
KAM
KAMA
KAMAAINA*
KAMAAINAS*
KAMACITE
KAMACITES
KAMALA
KAMALAS
KAMAS
KAME
KAMEES
KAMEESES
KAMEEZ
KAMEEZES
KAMELA
KAMELAS
KAMERAD
KAMERADED

KAMERADING
KAMERADS
KAMES
KAMI
KAMICHI
KAMICHIS
KAMIK
KAMIKAZE
KAMIKAZES
KAMIKS
KAMILA
KAMILAS
KAMIS
KAMISES
KAMME
KAMPONG
KAMPONGS
KAMSEEN
KAMSEENS
KAMSIN
KAMSINS
KANA
KANAKA
KANAKAS
KANAMYCIN*
KANAMYCINS*
KANAS
KANBAN*
KANBANS*
KANDIES
KANDY
KANE*
KANEH
KANEHS
KANES*
KANG
KANGA
KANGAROO
KANGAROOED
KANGAROOING
KANGAROOS
KANGAS
KANGHA
KANGHAS
KANGS
KANJI
KANJIS
KANS
KANSES
KANT
KANTAR
KANTARS
KANTED
KANTELA
KANTELAS

KANTELE	KARATS	KASHMIR	KAYAKER*	KECKLINGS
KANTELES	KARITE	KASHMIRS	KAYAKERS*	KECKS
KANTEN	KARITES	KASHRUS	KAYAKING	KECKSES
KANTENS	KARK	KASHRUSES	KAYAKINGS*	KECKSIES
KANTHA	KARKED	KASHRUT	KAYAKS	KECKSY
KANTHAS	KARKING	KASHRUTH	KAYLE	KED
KANTIKOY	KARKS	KASHRUTHS	KAYLES	KEDDAH
KANTIKOYED	KARMA	KASHRUTS	KAYO	KEDDAHS
KANTIKOYING	KARMAS	KAT	KAYOED	KEDGE
KANTIKOYS	KARMIC	KATA	KAYOES	KEDGED
KANTING	KARN*	KATABASES	KAYOING	KEDGER
KANTS	KARNS*	KATABASIS	KAYOINGS	KEDGEREE
KANZU	KAROO*	KATABATIC	KAYOS	KEDGEREES
KANZUS	KAROOS*	KATAKANA	KAYS	KEDGERS
KAOLIANG	KAROSS	KATAKANAS	KAZACHKI*	KEDGES
KAOLIANGS	KAROSSES	KATANA	KAZACHOK*	KEDGIER
KAOLIN	KARRI	KATANAS	KAZATSKI*	KEDGIEST
KAOLINE	KARRIS	KATAS	KAZATSKIES*	KEDGING
KAOLINES	KARROO*	KATCHINA*	KAZATSKY*	KEDGY
KAOLINIC*	KARROOS*	KATCHINAS*	KAZATZKA	KEDS
KAOLINISE	KARSEY	KATCINA*	KAZATZKAS	KEECH
KAOLINISED	KARSEYS	KATCINAS*	KAZI	KEECHES
KAOLINISES	KARSIES	KATHAK	KAZIS	KEEF*
KAOLINISING	KARST	KATHAKALI	KAZOO	KEEFS*
KAOLINITE	KARSTIC	KATHAKALIS	KAZOOS	KEEK
KAOLINITES	KARSTIFIED	KATHAKS	KBAR*	KEEKED
KAOLINIZE	KARSTIFIES	KATHARSES	KBARS*	KEEKER
KAOLINIZED	KARSTIFY	KATHARSIS	KEA	KEEKERS
KAOLINIZES	KARSTIFYING	KATHODAL*	KEAS	KEEKING
KAOLINIZING	KARSTS	KATHODE	KEASAR	KEEKS
KAOLINS	KARSY	KATHODES	KEASARS	KEEL
KAON	KART	KATHODIC*	KEAVIE	KEELAGE
KAONS	KARTER	KATI	KEAVIES	KEELAGES
KAPA*	KARTERS	KATION	KEB	KEELBOAT
KAPAS*	KARTING	KATIONS	KEBAB	KEELBOATS
KAPH*	KARTINGS	KATIPO	KEBABBED	KEELED
KAPHS*	KARTS	KATIPOS	KEBABBING	KEELER
KAPOK	KARYOGAMIES	KATIS	KEBABS	KEELERS
KAPOKS	KARYOGAMY	KATORGA	KEBAR*	KEELHALE*
KAPPA	KARYOGRAM	KATORGAS	KEBARS*	KEELHALED*
KAPPAS	KARYOGRAMS	KATS	KEBBED	KEELHALES*
KAPUT	KARYOLOGIES	KATTI	KEBBIE	KEELHALING*
KAPUTT	KARYOLOGY	KATTIS	KEBBIES	KEELHAUL
KARA	KARYON	KATYDID	KEBBING	KEELHAULED
KARABINER	KARYONS	KATYDIDS	KEBBOCK	KEELHAULING
KARABINERS	KARYOSOME	KAUGH	KEBBOCKS	KEELHAULINGS
KARAISM	KARYOSOMES	KAUGHS	KEBBUCK	KEELHAULS
KARAISMS	KARYOTIN	KAURI	KEBBUCKS	KEELIE
KARAIT	KARYOTINS	KAURIES*	KEBELE	KEELIES
KARAITS	KARYOTYPE	KAURIS	KEBELES	KEELING
KARAKA	KARYOTYPED	KAURY*	KEBLAH	KEELINGS
KARAKAS	KARYOTYPES	KAVA	KEBLAHS	KEELIVINE
KARAKUL	KARYOTYPING	KAVAKAVA*	KEBOB	KEELIVINES
KARAKULS	KARZIES	KAVAKAVAS*	KEBOBBED	KEELLESS*
KARAOKE	KARZY	KAVAS	KEBOBBING	KEELMAN
KARAOKES	KAS	KAVASS	KEBOBS	KEELMEN
KARAS	KASBAH	KAVASSES	KEBS	KEELS
KARAT	KASBAHS	KAW	KECK	KEELSON
KARATE	KASHA	KAWED	KECKED	KEELSONS
KARATEIST	KASHAS	KAWING	KECKING	KEELYVINE
KARATEISTS	KASHER*	KAWS	KECKLE	KEELYVINES
KARATEKA	KASHERED*	KAY	KECKLED	KEEN
KARATEKAS	KASHERING*	KAYAK	KECKLES	KEENED
KARATES	KASHERS*	KAYAKED	KECKLING	KEENER

KEENERS	KELLAUT	KENNING	KERF	KESTS
KEENEST	KELLAUTS	KENNINGS	KERFED*	KET
KEENING	KELLIES	KENO	KERFING*	KETA
KEENINGS	KELLS	KENOS	KERFS	KETAMINE
KEENLY	KELLY	KENOSES	KERFUFFLE	KETAMINES
KEENNESS	KELOID	KENOSIS	KERFUFFLED	KETAS
KEENNESSES	KELOIDAL	KENOSISES*	KERFUFFLES	KETCH
KEENS	KELOIDS	KENOTIC	KERFUFFLING	KETCHES
KEEP	KELP	KENOTRON*	KERMES	KETCHING
KEEPABLE*	KELPED*	KENOTRONS*	KERMESITE	KETCHUP
KEEPER	KELPER	KENS	KERMESITES	KETCHUPS
KEEPERS	KELPERS	KENSPECK	KERMESS*	KETENE*
KEEPING	KELPIE	KENT	KERMESSE	KETENES*
KEEPINGS	KELPIES	KENTED	KERMESSES	KETO*
KEEPNET	KELPING*	KENTIA	KERMIS	KETOGENIC*
KEEPNETS	KELPS	KENTIAS	KERMISES	KETOL*
KEEPS	KELPY	KENTING	KERN	KETOLS*
KEEPSAKE	KELSON	KENTLEDGE	KERNE	KETONE
KEEPSAKES	KELSONS	KENTLEDGES	KERNED	KETONES
KEEPSAKY	KELT	KENTS	KERNEL	KETONIC*
KEESHOND	KELTER	KEP	KERNELED*	KETONURIA
KEESHONDEN	KELTERS	KEPHALIC	KERNELING*	KETONURIAS
KEESHONDS	KELTIE	KEPHALICS	KERNELLED	KETOSE
KEESTER*	KELTIES	KEPHALIN	KERNELLING	KETOSES
KEESTERS*	KELTS	KEPHALINS	KERNELLY	KETOSIS
KEET*	KELTY	KEPHIR	KERNELS	KETOTIC*
KEETS*	KELVIN	KEPHIRS	KERNES	KETS
KEEVE	KELVINS	KEPI	KERNING	KETTLE
KEEVES	KEMB	KEPIS	KERNINGS	KETTLEFUL
KEF	KEMBED	KEPPED*	KERNISH	KETTLEFULS
KEFFEL	KEMBING	KEPPEN*	KERNITE	KETTLES
KEFFELS	KEMBO	KEPPING	KERNITES	KEVEL
KEFFIYEH	KEMBOED	KEPPIT	KERNS	KEVELS
KEFFIYEHS	KEMBOING	KEPS	KEROGEN	KEVIL*
KEFIR	KEMBOS	KEPT	KEROGENS	KEVILS*
KEFIRS	KEMBS	KERAMIC	KEROSENE	KEX
KEFS	KEMP	KERAMICS	KEROSENES	KEXES
KEFUFFLE	KEMPED	KERATIN	KEROSINE	KEY
KEFUFFLED	KEMPER	KERATINS	KEROSINES	KEYBOARD
KEFUFFLES	KEMPERS	KERATITIDES*	KERPLUNK*	KEYBOARDED
KEFUFFLING	KEMPING	KERATITIS	KERPLUNKED*	KEYBOARDING
KEG	KEMPINGS	KERATITISES	KERPLUNKING*	KEYBOARDS
KEGELER*	KEMPLE	KERATOID	KERPLUNKS*	KEYBUGLE
KEGELERS*	KEMPLES	KERATOMA*	KERRIA	KEYBUGLES
KEGLER*	KEMPS	KERATOMAS*	KERRIAS	KEYBUTTON*
KEGLERS*	KEMPT	KERATOMATA*	KERRIES*	KEYBUTTONS*
KEGLING*	KEN	KERATOSE	KERRY*	KEYCARD*
KEGLINGS*	KENAF	KERATOSES	KERSEY	KEYCARDS*
KEGS	KENAFS	KERATOSIS	KERSEYS	KEYED
KEIGHT	KENCH*	KERATOTIC*	KERVE	KEYHOLE
KEIR	KENCHES*	KERB	KERVED	KEYHOLES
KEIRS	KENDO	KERBED*	KERVES	KEYING
KEISTER	KENDOS	KERBING*	KERVING	KEYLESS
KEISTERS	KENNED	KERBS	KERYGMA	KEYLINE
KEITLOA	KENNEL	KERBSIDE	KERYGMAS	KEYLINES
KEITLOAS	KENNELED*	KERBSIDES	KERYGMATA	KEYNOTE
KEKS	KENNELING*	KERBSTONE	KESAR	KEYNOTED
KEKSYE	KENNELLED	KERBSTONES	KESARS	KEYNOTER*
KEKSYES	KENNELLING	KERCHIEF	KESH	KEYNOTERS*
KELEP*	KENNELS	KERCHIEFED	KESHES	KEYNOTES
KELEPS*	KENNER	KERCHIEFING	KEST	KEYNOTING
KELIM	KENNERS	KERCHIEFS	KESTING	KEYPAD
KELIMS	KENNET	KERCHIEVES*	KESTREL	KEYPADS
KELL	KENNETS	KERCHOO*	KESTRELS	KEYPUNCH

The Chambers Dictionary is the authority for many longer words; see Introduction, page ix

KEYPUNCHED
KEYPUNCHES
KEYPUNCHING
KEYS
KEYSET*
KEYSETS*
KEYSTER*
KEYSTERS*
KEYSTONE
KEYSTONED
KEYSTONES
KEYSTONING
KEYSTROKE
KEYSTROKED*
KEYSTROKES
KEYSTROKING*
KEYWAY*
KEYWAYS*
KEYWORD
KEYWORDS
KGOTLA
KGOTLAS
KHADDAR
KHADDARS
KHADI
KHADIS
KHAF*
KHAFS*
KHAKI
KHAKIS
KHALAT
KHALATS
KHALIF
KHALIFA
KHALIFAH
KHALIFAHS
KHALIFAS
KHALIFAT
KHALIFATE
KHALIFATES
KHALIFATS
KHALIFS
KHAMSEEN*
KHAMSEENS*
KHAMSIN
KHAMSINS
KHAN
KHANATE
KHANATES
KHANGA
KHANGAS
KHANJAR
KHANJARS
KHANS
KHANSAMA
KHANSAMAH
KHANSAMAHS
KHANSAMAS
KHANUM
KHANUMS
KHAPH*
KHAPHS*
KHARIF
KHARIFS

KHAT
KHATS
KHAYA
KHAYAS
KHAZEN*
KHAZENIM*
KHAZENS*
KHEDA
KHEDAH*
KHEDAHS*
KHEDAS
KHEDIVA
KHEDIVAL
KHEDIVAS
KHEDIVATE
KHEDIVATES
KHEDIVE
KHEDIVES
KHEDIVIAL
KHET*
KHETH*
KHETHS*
KHETS*
KHI*
KHILAFAT
KHILAFATS
KHILAT
KHILATS
KHILIM
KHILIMS
KHIRKAH*
KHIRKAHS*
KHIS*
KHODJA
KHODJAS
KHOJA
KHOJAS
KHOR
KHORS
KHOTBAH
KHOTBAHS
KHOTBEH
KHOTBEHS
KHOUM*
KHOUMS*
KHUD
KHUDS
KHURTA
KHURTAS
KHUSKHUS
KHUSKHUSES
KHUTBAH
KHUTBAHS
KIANG
KIANGS
KIAUGH
KIAUGHS
KIBBE*
KIBBEH*
KIBBEHS*
KIBBES*
KIBBI*
KIBBIS*
KIBBITZ*

KIBBITZED*
KIBBITZER*
KIBBITZERS*
KIBBITZES*
KIBBITZING*
KIBBLE
KIBBLED
KIBBLES
KIBBLING
KIBBUTZ
KIBBUTZIM
KIBE
KIBEI*
KIBEIS*
KIBES
KIBITKA
KIBITKAS
KIBITZ
KIBITZED
KIBITZER
KIBITZERS
KIBITZES
KIBITZING
KIBLA*
KIBLAH
KIBLAHS
KIBLAS*
KIBOSH
KIBOSHED
KIBOSHES
KIBOSHING
KICK
KICKABLE
KICKBACK
KICKBACKS
KICKBALL
KICKBALLS
KICKBOARD*
KICKBOARDS*
KICKBOXER*
KICKBOXERS*
KICKDOWN
KICKDOWNS
KICKED
KICKER
KICKERS
KICKIER*
KICKIEST*
KICKING
KICKOFF*
KICKOFFS*
KICKS
KICKSHAW
KICKSHAWS
KICKSHAWSES
KICKSTAND
KICKSTANDS
KICKUP*
KICKUPS*
KICKY*
KID
KIDDED
KIDDER
KIDDERS

KIDDIE*
KIDDIED
KIDDIER
KIDDIERS
KIDDIES
KIDDING
KIDDINGLY*
KIDDISH*
KIDDLE
KIDDLES
KIDDO
KIDDOES*
KIDDOS
KIDDUSH
KIDDUSHES
KIDDY
KIDDYING
KIDDYWINK
KIDDYWINKS
KIDEL
KIDELS
KIDGE
KIDGIE
KIDGIER
KIDGIEST
KIDLET
KIDLETS
KIDLIKE*
KIDLING
KIDLINGS
KIDNAP
KIDNAPED*
KIDNAPEE*
KIDNAPEES*
KIDNAPER*
KIDNAPERS*
KIDNAPING*
KIDNAPPED
KIDNAPPEE*
KIDNAPPEES*
KIDNAPPER
KIDNAPPERS
KIDNAPPING
KIDNAPS
KIDNEY
KIDNEYS
KIDOLOGIES
KIDOLOGY
KIDS
KIDSKIN
KIDSKINS
KIDSTAKES
KIDULT
KIDULTS
KIDVID
KIDVIDS
KIEF*
KIEFS*
KIELBASA*
KIELBASAS*
KIELBASI*
KIELBASY*
KIER
KIERIE

KIERIES
KIERS
KIESERITE
KIESERITES
KIESTER*
KIESTERS*
KIEVE
KIEVES
KIF
KIFS
KIGHT
KIGHTS
KIKE
KIKES
KIKOI
KIKOIS
KIKUMON
KIKUMONS
KIKUYU
KIKUYUS
KILD
KILDERKIN
KILDERKINS
KILERG
KILERGS
KILEY
KILEYS
KILIM
KILIMS
KILL
KILLADAR
KILLADARS
KILLAS
KILLASES
KILLCOW
KILLCOWS
KILLCROP
KILLCROPS
KILLDEE
KILLDEER
KILLDEERS
KILLDEES
KILLED
KILLER
KILLERS
KILLICK
KILLICKS
KILLIE*
KILLIES*
KILLIFISH
KILLIFISHES
KILLING
KILLINGLY*
KILLINGS
KILLJOY
KILLJOYS
KILLOCK
KILLOCKS
KILLOGIE
KILLOGIES
KILLS
KILLUT
KILLUTS
KILN

KILNED	KIMMERS	KINGBIRDS*	KINREDS	KIRPAN
KILNING	KIMONO	KINGBOLT*	KINS	KIRPANS
KILNS	KIMONOED*	KINGBOLTS*	KINSFOLK	KIRRI
KILO	KIMONOS	KINGCRAFT	KINSFOLKS	KIRRIS
KILOBAR	KIN	KINGCRAFTS	KINSHIP	KIRS
KILOBARS	KINA	KINGCUP	KINSHIPS	KIRSCH
KILOBASE*	KINAKINA	KINGCUPS	KINSMAN	KIRSCHES
KILOBASES*	KINAKINAS	KINGDOM	KINSMEN	KIRTLE
KILOBAUD*	KINAS	KINGDOMED	KINSWOMAN	KIRTLED
KILOBAUDS*	KINASE	KINGDOMS	KINSWOMEN	KIRTLES
KILOBIT	KINASES	KINGED	KINTLEDGE	KISAN
KILOBITS	KINCHIN	KINGFISH	KINTLEDGES	KISANS
KILOBYTE	KINCHINS	KINGFISHES	KIOSK	KISH
KILOBYTES	KINCOB	KINGHOOD	KIOSKS	KISHES
KILOCYCLE	KINCOBS	KINGHOODS	KIP	KISHKA*
KILOCYCLES	KIND	KINGING	KIPE	KISHKAS*
KILOGAUSS*	KINDA	KINGKLIP	KIPES	KISHKE
KILOGAUSSES*	KINDED	KINGKLIPS	KIPP	KISHKES
KILOGRAM	KINDER	KINGLE	KIPPA	KISMAT*
KILOGRAMS	KINDERS	KINGLES	KIPPAGE	KISMATS*
KILOGRAY	KINDEST	KINGLESS	KIPPAGES	KISMET
KILOGRAYS	KINDIES	KINGLET	KIPPAS	KISMETIC*
KILOHERTZ	KINDING	KINGLETS	KIPPED	KISMETS
KILOHERTZES	KINDLE	KINGLIER	KIPPEN*	KISS
KILOJOULE	KINDLED	KINGLIEST	KIPPER	KISSABLE
KILOJOULES	KINDLER	KINGLIKE*	KIPPERED	KISSABLY*
KILOLITER*	KINDLERS	KINGLING	KIPPERER	KISSAGRAM
KILOLITERS*	KINDLES	KINGLINGS	KIPPERERS	KISSAGRAMS
KILOMETER*	KINDLESS	KINGLY	KIPPERING	KISSED
KILOMETERS*	KINDLIER	KINGMAKER	KIPPERS	KISSEL
KILOMETRE	KINDLIEST	KINGMAKERS	KIPPING	KISSELS
KILOMETRES	KINDLILY	KINGPIN*	KIPPS	KISSER
KILOMOLE*	KINDLING	KINGPINS*	KIPS	KISSERS
KILOMOLES*	KINDLINGS	KINGPOST	KIPSKIN*	KISSES
KILORAD*	KINDLY	KINGPOSTS	KIPSKINS*	KISSING
KILORADS*	KINDNESS	KINGS	KIR	KISSOGRAM
KILOS	KINDNESSES	KINGSHIP	KIRBEH	KISSOGRAMS
KILOTON	KINDRED	KINGSHIPS	KIRBEHS	KISSY*
KILOTONS	KINDREDS	KINGSIDE*	KIRBIGRIP	KIST
KILOVOLT	KINDS	KINGSIDES*	KIRBIGRIPS	KISTED
KILOVOLTS	KINDY	KINGWOOD	KIRIGAMI*	KISTFUL*
KILOWATT	KINE	KINGWOODS	KIRIGAMIS*	KISTFULS*
KILOWATTS	KINEMA	KININ	KIRIMON	KISTING
KILP	KINEMAS	KININS	KIRIMONS	KISTS
KILPS	KINEMATIC	KINK	KIRK	KISTVAEN
KILT	KINEMATICS	KINKAJOU	KIRKED	KISTVAENS
KILTED	KINES*	KINKAJOUS	KIRKING	KIT
KILTER	KINESCOPE	KINKED	KIRKINGS	KITCHEN
KILTERS	KINESCOPED*	KINKIER	KIRKMAN*	KITCHENED
KILTIE	KINESCOPES	KINKIEST	KIRKMEN*	KITCHENER
KILTIES	KINESCOPING*	KINKILY	KIRKS	KITCHENERS
KILTING	KINESES	KINKINESS*	KIRKTON	KITCHENING
KILTINGS*	KINESIC*	KINKINESSES*	KIRKTONS	KITCHENS
KILTS	KINESICS	KINKING	KIRKWARD	KITE
KILTY	KINESIS	KINKLE	KIRKYAIRD	KITED
KIMBO	KINETIC	KINKLES	KIRKYAIRDS	KITELIKE*
KIMBOED	KINETICAL	KINKS	KIRKYARD	KITENGE
KIMBOING	KINETICS	KINKY	KIRKYARDS	KITENGES
KIMBOS	KINETIN*	KINLESS	KIRMESS	KITER*
KIMCHEE*	KINETINS*	KINO	KIRMESSES	KITERS*
KIMCHEES*	KINFOLK	KINONE	KIRN	KITES
KIMCHI	KINFOLKS	KINONES	KIRNED*	KITH
KIMCHIS	KING	KINOS	KIRNING*	KITHARA
KIMMER	KINGBIRD*	KINRED	KIRNS	KITHARAS

KITHE	KLEPHTIC	KNAGGIEST	KNEELERS	KNIVES
KITHED	KLEPHTISM	KNAGGY	KNEELING	KNIVING
KITHES	KLEPHTISMS	KNAGS	KNEELS	KNOB
KITHING	KLEPHTS	KNAIDEL	KNEEPAD*	KNOBBED
KITHS	KLEZMER	KNAIDLOCH	KNEEPADS*	KNOBBER
KITING	KLEZMORIM	KNAP	KNEEPAN*	KNOBBERS
KITINGS	KLINKER	KNAPPED	KNEEPANS*	KNOBBIER
KITLING	KLINKERS	KNAPPER	KNEES	KNOBBIEST
KITLINGS	KLINOSTAT	KNAPPERS	KNEESOCK*	KNOBBLE
KITS	KLINOSTATS	KNAPPING	KNEESOCKS*	KNOBBLED
KITSCH	KLIPDAS	KNAPPLE	KNEIDLACH	KNOBBLES
KITSCHES	KLIPDASES	KNAPPLED	KNELL	KNOBBLIER
KITSCHIER	KLISTER*	KNAPPLES	KNELLED	KNOBBLIEST
KITSCHIEST	KLISTERS*	KNAPPLING	KNELLING	KNOBBLING
KITSCHILY	KLONDIKE	KNAPS	KNELLS	KNOBBLY
KITSCHY	KLONDIKED	KNAPSACK	KNELT	KNOBBY
KITTED	KLONDIKER	KNAPSACKS	KNESSET*	KNOBLIKE*
KITTEL*	KLONDIKERS	KNAPSCAL	KNESSETS*	KNOBS
KITTEN	KLONDIKES	KNAPSCALS	KNEVELL	KNOCK
KITTENED	KLONDIKING	KNAPSCULL	KNEVELLED	KNOCKDOWN*
KITTENING	KLONDYKE	KNAPSCULLS	KNEVELLING	KNOCKDOWNS*
KITTENISH	KLONDYKED	KNAPSKULL	KNEVELLS	KNOCKED
KITTENS	KLONDYKER	KNAPSKULLS	KNEW	KNOCKER
KITTENY	KLONDYKERS	KNAPWEED	KNICKER	KNOCKERS
KITTIES	KLONDYKES	KNAPWEEDS	KNICKERED	KNOCKING
KITTING	KLONDYKING	KNAR	KNICKERS	KNOCKINGS
KITTIWAKE	KLONG*	KNARL	KNICKS	KNOCKOFF*
KITTIWAKES	KLONGS*	KNARLS	KNIFE	KNOCKOFFS*
KITTLE	KLOOCH	KNARRED	KNIFED	KNOCKOUT
KITTLED	KLOOCHES	KNARRING	KNIFELESS	KNOCKOUTS
KITTLER	KLOOCHMAN	KNARRY*	KNIFELIKE*	KNOCKS
KITTLES	KLOOCHMANS	KNARS	KNIFER*	KNOLL
KITTLEST	KLOOCHMEN	KNAUR*	KNIFERS*	KNOLLED
KITTLIER	KLOOF	KNAURS*	KNIFES	KNOLLER*
KITTLIEST	KLOOFS	KNAVE	KNIFING	KNOLLERS*
KITTLING	KLOOTCH	KNAVERIES	KNIFINGS	KNOLLING
KITTLY	KLOOTCHES	KNAVERY	KNIGHT	KNOLLS
KITTUL	KLUDGE	KNAVES	KNIGHTAGE	KNOLLY*
KITTULS	KLUDGES	KNAVESHIP	KNIGHTAGES	KNOP
KITTY	KLUGE*	KNAVESHIPS	KNIGHTED	KNOPPED*
KIVA	KLUGES*	KNAVISH	KNIGHTING	KNOPS
KIVAS	KLUTZ	KNAVISHLY	KNIGHTLIER	KNOSP
KIWI	KLUTZES	KNAWEL	KNIGHTLIEST	KNOSPS
KIWIFRUIT*	KLUTZIER*	KNAWELS	KNIGHTLY	KNOT
KIWIFRUITS*	KLUTZIEST*	KNEAD	KNIGHTS	KNOTGRASS
KIWIS	KLUTZY*	KNEADABLE*	KNIPHOFIA	KNOTGRASSES
KLANG	KLYSTRON	KNEADED	KNIPHOFIAS	KNOTHOLE*
KLANGS	KLYSTRONS	KNEADER	KNISH	KNOTHOLES*
KLATCH	KNACK	KNEADERS	KNISHES	KNOTLESS
KLATCHES	KNACKED*	KNEADING	KNIT	KNOTLIKE*
KLATSCH	KNACKER	KNEADS	KNITCH	KNOTS
KLATSCHES	KNACKERED	KNEE	KNITCHES	KNOTTED
KLAVERN*	KNACKERIES	KNEECAP	KNITS	KNOTTER
KLAVERNS*	KNACKERING	KNEECAPPED	KNITTED	KNOTTERS
KLAVIER	KNACKERS	KNEECAPPING	KNITTER	KNOTTIER
KLAVIERS	KNACKERY	KNEECAPPINGS	KNITTERS	KNOTTIEST
KLAXON	KNACKIER	KNEECAPS	KNITTING	KNOTTILY*
KLAXONED	KNACKIEST	KNEED	KNITTINGS	KNOTTING
KLAXONING	KNACKING*	KNEEHOLE	KNITTLE	KNOTTINGS
KLAXONS	KNACKISH	KNEEHOLES	KNITTLES	KNOTTY
KLEAGLE*	KNACKS	KNEEING	KNITWEAR	KNOTWEED
KLEAGLES*	KNACKY	KNEEL	KNITWEARS	KNOTWEEDS
KLENDUSIC	KNAG	KNEELED	KNIVE	KNOTWORK
KLEPHT	KNAGGIER	KNEELER	KNIVED	KNOTWORKS

Words marked with an asterisk are from OTCWL

KNOUT	KOANS	KOMATIKS	KORE	KOWS
KNOUTED	KOAS	KOMBU	KORERO	KOWTOW
KNOUTING	KOB	KOMBUS	KOREROS	KOWTOWED
ʹNOUTS	KOBAN	KOMISSAR	KORES	KOWTOWER*
KNOW	KOBANG	KOMISSARS	KORFBALL	KOWTOWERS*
KNOWABLE	KOBANGS	KOMITAJI	KORFBALLS	KOWTOWING
KNOWE	KOBANS	KOMITAJIS	KORKIR	KOWTOWS
KNOWER	KOBO*	KOMONDOR*	KORKIRS	KRAAL
KNOWERS	KOBOLD	KOMONDOROCK*	KORMA	KRAALED
KNOWES	KOBOLDS	KOMONDOROK*	KORMAS	KRAALING
KNOWHOW	KOBS	KOMONDORS*	KORORA	KRAALS
KNOWHOWS	KOEL*	KON	KORORAS	KRAB
KNOWING	KOELS*	KOND	KORS*	KRABS
KNOWINGER*	KOFF	KONFYT	KORUN*	KRAFT
KNOWINGEST*	KOFFS	KONFYTS	KORUNA	KRAFTS
KNOWINGLY	KOFTA	KONIMETER	KORUNAS	KRAIT
KNOWINGS*	KOFTAS	KONIMETERS	KORUNY*	KRAITS
KNOWLEDGE	KOFTGAR	KONIOLOGIES	KOS	KRAKEN
KNOWLEDGED	KOFTGARI	KONIOLOGY	KOSES	KRAKENS
KNOWLEDGES	KOFTGARIS	KONISCOPE	KOSHER	KRAKOWIAK
KNOWLEDGING	KOFTGARS	KONISCOPES	KOSHERED	KRAKOWIAKS
KNOWN	KOFTWORK	KONK	KOSHERING	KRAMERIA
KNOWNS	KOFTWORKS	KONKED	KOSHERS	KRAMERIAS
KNOWS	KOHL	KONKING	KOSMOS	KRANG
KNUB	KOHLRABI	KONKS	KOSMOSES	KRANGS
KNUBBIER	KOHLRABIES*	KONNING	KOSS	KRANS
KNUBBIEST	KOHLRABIS	KONS	KOSSES	KRANSES
KNUBBLE	KOHLS	KOODOO	KOTO	KRANTZ
KNUBBLED	KOI	KOODOOS	KOTOS	KRANTZES
KNUBBLES	KOINE	KOOK	KOTOW	KRANZ
KNUBBLIER	KOINES	KOOKED	KOTOWED	KRANZES
KNUBBLIEST	KOKANEE	KOOKIE	KOTOWER*	KRATER
KNUBBLING	KOKANEES	KOOKIER	KOTOWERS*	KRATERS
KNUBBLY	KOKER	KOOKIEST	KOTOWING	KRAUT
KNUBBY	KOKERS	KOOKINESS*	KOTOWS	KRAUTS
KNUBS	KOKRA	KOOKINESSES*	KOTTABOS	KREASOTE
KNUCKLE	KOKRAS	KOOKING	KOTTABOSES	KREASOTED
KNUCKLED	KOKUM	KOOKS	KOTWAL	KREASOTES
KNUCKLER*	KOKUMS	KOOKY	KOTWALS	KREASOTING
KNUCKLERS*	KOLA	KOOLAH	KOULAN	KREATINE
KNUCKLES	KOLACKY*	KOOLAHS	KOULANS	KREATINES
KNUCKLIER	KOLAS	KOORI	KOUMIS*	KREEP*
KNUCKLIEST	KOLBASI*	KOORIS	KOUMISES*	KREEPS*
KNUCKLING	KOLBASIS*	KOP	KOUMISS	KREESE
KNUCKLY	KOLBASSI*	KOPASETIC	KOUMISSES	KREESED
KNUR	KOLBASSIS*	KOPECK	KOUMYS*	KREESES
KNURL	KOLHOZ*	KOPECKS	KOUMYSES*	KREESING
KNURLED	KOLHOZES*	KOPEK*	KOUMYSS*	KREMLIN
KNURLIER	KOLHOZY*	KOPEKS*	KOUMYSSES*	KREMLINS
KNURLIEST	KOLINSKI*	KOPH	KOUPREY	KRENG
KNURLING	KOLINSKIES	KOPHS	KOUPREYS	KRENGS
KNURLINGS	KOLINSKY	KOPJE	KOURBASH	KREOSOTE
KNURLS	KOLKHOS*	KOPJES	KOURBASHED	KREOSOTED
KNURLY	KOLKHOSES*	KOPPA	KOURBASHES	KREOSOTES
KNURR	KOLKHOSY*	KOPPAS	KOURBASHING	KREOSOTING
KNURRS	KOLKHOZ	KOPPIE	KOUROI	KREPLACH
KNURS	KOLKHOZES	KOPPIES	KOUROS	KREUTZER
KNUT	KOLKHOZY*	KOPS	KOUSKOUS	KREUTZERS
KNUTS	KOLKOZ*	KOR*	KOUSKOUSES	KREUZER*
KO	KOLKOZES*	KORA	KOUSSO*	KREUZERS*
KOA	KOLKOZY*	KORAI*	KOUSSOS*	KRILL
KOALA	KOLO	KORAS	KOW	KRILLS
KOALAS	KOLOS	KORAT*	KOWHAI	KRIMMER
KOAN	KOMATIK	KORATS*	KOWHAIS	KRIMMERS

The Chambers Dictionary is the authority for many longer words; see Introduction, page ix

KRIS
KRISED
KRISES
KRISING
KROMESKIES
KROMESKY
KRONA
KRONE
KRONEN
KRONER
KRONOR
KRONUR
KROON*
KROONI*
KROONS*
KRUBI*
KRUBIS*
KRUBUT*
KRUBUTS*
KRULLER
KRULLERS
KRUMHORN
KRUMHORNS
KRUMMHOLZ*
KRUMMHORN
KRUMMHORNS
KRYOLITE*
KRYOLITES*
KRYOLITH*
KRYOLITHS*
KRYOMETER
KRYOMETERS
KRYPSES
KRYPSIS
KRYPTON
KRYPTONS
KRYTRON
KRYTRONS
KSAR
KSARS
KUCHCHA
KUCHEN*

KUDO*
KUDOS
KUDOSES
KUDU
KUDUS
KUDZU
KUDZUS
KUE*
KUES*
KUFIYAH
KUFIYAHS
KUGEL*
KUGELS*
KUKRI
KUKRIS
KUKU
KUKUS
KULAK
KULAKI*
KULAKS
KULAN
KULANS
KULTUR*
KULTURS*
KUMARA
KUMARAS
KUMARI
KUMARIS
KUMISS
KUMISSES
KUMMEL
KUMMELS
KUMQUAT
KUMQUATS
KUMYS*
KUMYSES*
KUNDALINI*
KUNDALINIS*
KUNKAR
KUNKARS
KUNKUR
KUNKURS

KUNZITE
KUNZITES
KURBASH
KURBASHED
KURBASHES
KURBASHING
KURGAN
KURGANS
KURI
KURIS
KURRAJONG
KURRAJONGS
KURRE
KURRES
KURSAAL
KURSAALS
KURTA
KURTAS
KURTOSES
KURTOSIS
KURTOSISES*
KURU
KURUS
KURVEY
KURVEYED
KURVEYING
KURVEYOR
KURVEYORS
KURVEYS
KUSSO*
KUSSOS*
KUTCH
KUTCHA
KUTCHES
KUVASZ*
KUVASZOK*
KUZU
KUZUS
KVAS*
KVASES*
KVASS
KVASSES

KVETCH
KVETCHED
KVETCHER
KVETCHERS
KVETCHES
KVETCHIER*
KVETCHIEST*
KVETCHING
KVETCHY*
KWACHA
KWACHAS
KWANZA
KWANZAS
KWELA
KWELAS
KY
KYACK*
KYACKS*
KYAK*
KYAKS*
KYANG
KYANGS
KYANISE
KYANISED
KYANISES
KYANISING
KYANITE
KYANITES
KYANIZE
KYANIZED
KYANIZES
KYANIZING
KYAR*
KYARS*
KYAT
KYATS
KYBOSH
KYBOSHED
KYBOSHES
KYBOSHING
KYDST
KYE

KYLE
KYLES
KYLICES
KYLIE
KYLIES
KYLIKES*
KYLIN
KYLINS
KYLIX
KYLLOSES
KYLLOSIS
KYLOE
KYLOES
KYMOGRAM
KYMOGRAMS
KYMOGRAPH
KYMOGRAPHS
KYND
KYNDE
KYNDED
KYNDES
KYNDING
KYNDS
KYNE
KYOGEN
KYOGENS
KYPHOSES
KYPHOSIS
KYPHOTIC
KYRIE*
KYRIELLE
KYRIELLES
KYRIES*
KYTE
KYTES
KYTHE
KYTHED
KYTHES
KYTHING
KYU
KYUS

L

LA
LAAGER
LAAGERED
LAAGERING
LAAGERS
LAARI*
LAB
LABARA
LABARUM
LABARUMS
LABDA
LABDACISM
LABDACISMS
LABDANUM
LABDANUMS
LABDAS
LABEL
LABELABLE*
LABELED*
LABELER*
LABELERS*
LABELING*
LABELLA
LABELLED
LABELLER*
LABELLERS*
LABELLING
LABELLOID
LABELLUM
LABELS
LABIA
LABIAL
LABIALISE
LABIALISED
LABIALISES
LABIALISING
LABIALISM
LABIALISMS
LABIALIZE
LABIALIZED
LABIALIZES
LABIALIZING
LABIALLY
LABIALS
LABIATE
LABIATED*
LABIATES
LABILE
LABILITIES
LABILITY
LABIS
LABISES
LABIUM
LABLAB
LABLABS

LABOR
LABORED
LABORER*
LABORERS*
LABORING
LABORIOUS
LABORITE*
LABORITES*
LABORS
LABOUR
LABOURED
LABOURER
LABOURERS
LABOURING
LABOURISM
LABOURISMS
LABOURIST
LABOURISTS
LABOURS
LABRA
LABRADOR*
LABRADORS*
LABRET
LABRETS
LABRID
LABRIDS
LABROID
LABROIDS
LABROSE
LABRUM
LABRUMS*
LABRUSCA*
LABRYS
LABRYSES
LABS
LABURNUM
LABURNUMS
LABYRINTH
LABYRINTHS
LAC
LACCOLITE
LACCOLITES
LACCOLITH
LACCOLITHS
LACE
LACEBARK
LACEBARKS
LACED
LACELESS*
LACELIKE*
LACER*
LACERABLE
LACERANT
LACERATE
LACERATED

LACERATES
LACERATING
LACERS*
LACERTIAN
LACERTID*
LACERTIDS*
LACERTINE
LACES
LACET
LACETS
LACEWING
LACEWINGS
LACEWOOD*
LACEWOODS*
LACEWORK*
LACEWORKS*
LACEY
LACHES
LACHESES
LACHRYMAL
LACHRYMALS
LACIER
LACIEST
LACILY*
LACINESS*
LACINESSES*
LACING
LACINGS
LACINIA
LACINIAE
LACINIATE
LACK
LACKADAY
LACKED
LACKER
LACKERED
LACKERING
LACKERS
LACKEY
LACKEYED
LACKEYING
LACKEYS
LACKING
LACKLAND
LACKLANDS
LACKS
LACMUS
LACMUSES
LACONIC
LACONICAL
LACONISM
LACONISMS
LACQUER
LACQUERED
LACQUERER

LACQUERERS
LACQUERING
LACQUERINGS
LACQUERS
LACQUEY
LACQUEYED
LACQUEYING
LACQUEYS
LACRIMAL
LACRIMALS
LACRIMOSO
LACROSSE
LACROSSES
LACRYMAL
LACRYMALS
LACS
LACTAM*
LACTAMS*
LACTARIAN
LACTARIANS
LACTARY*
LACTASE
LACTASES
LACTATE
LACTATED
LACTATES
LACTATING
LACTATION
LACTATIONS
LACTEAL
LACTEALS
LACTEAN*
LACTEOUS
LACTIC
LACTIFIC
LACTONE
LACTONES
LACTONIC*
LACTOSE
LACTOSES
LACUNA
LACUNAE
LACUNAL
LACUNAR
LACUNARIA
LACUNARS
LACUNARY
LACUNAS*
LACUNATE
LACUNE*
LACUNES*
LACUNOSE
LACY
LAD
LADANUM

LADANUMS
LADDER
LADDERED
LADDERING
LADDERS
LADDERY
LADDIE
LADDIES
LADDISH
LADE
LADED
LADEN
LADENED*
LADENING*
LADENS*
LADER*
LADERS*
LADES
LADETTE
LADETTES
LADIES
LADIFIED
LADIFIES
LADIFY
LADIFYING
LADING
LADINGS
LADINO*
LADINOS*
LADLE
LADLED
LADLEFUL
LADLEFULS
LADLER*
LADLERS*
LADLES
LADLING
LADRON*
LADRONE
LADRONES
LADRONS*
LADS
LADY
LADYBIRD
LADYBIRDS
LADYBUG
LADYBUGS
LADYCOW
LADYCOWS
LADYFIED
LADYFIES
LADYFISH*
LADYFISHES*
LADYFLIES
LADYFLY

LADYFY	LAGOONS	LAIRIZED	LAMANTIN	LAMENT
LADYFYING	LAGRIMOSO	LAIRIZES	LAMANTINS	LAMENTED
LADYHOOD	LAGS	LAIRIZING	LAMAS	LAMENTER*
LADYHOODS	LAGUNA*	LAIRS	LAMASERAI	LAMENTERS*
LADYISH	LAGUNAS*	LAIRY	LAMASERAIS	LAMENTING
LADYISM	LAGUNE	LAISSE	LAMASERIES	LAMENTINGS
LADYISMS	LAGUNES	LAISSES	LAMASERY	LAMENTS
LADYKIN	LAH	LAITANCE	LAMB	LAMER
LADYKINS	LAHAR	LAITANCES	LAMBADA	LAMES
LADYLIKE	LAHARS	LAITH	LAMBADAS	LAMEST
LADYLOVE*	LAHS	LAITHLY*	LAMBAST	LAMETER
LADYLOVES*	LAIC	LAITIES	LAMBASTE	LAMETERS
LADYPALM*	LAICAL	LAITY	LAMBASTED	LAMIA
LADYPALMS*	LAICALLY*	LAKE	LAMBASTES	LAMIAE
LADYSHIP	LAICH*	LAKED	LAMBASTING	LAMIAS
LADYSHIPS	LAICHS*	LAKEFRONT*	LAMBASTS	LAMIGER
LAER	LAICISE	LAKEFRONTS*	LAMBDA	LAMIGERS
LAERED	LAICISED	LAKELAND	LAMBDAS	LAMINA
LAERING	LAICISES	LAKELANDS	LAMBDOID	LAMINABLE
LAERS	LAICISING	LAKELET	LAMBED	LAMINAE
LAESIE	LAICISM*	LAKELETS	LAMBENCIES	LAMINAL*
LAETARE	LAICISMS*	LAKELIKE*	LAMBENCY	LAMINAR
LAETARES	LAICITIES	LAKEPORT*	LAMBENT	LAMINARIA*
LAETRILE*	LAICITY	LAKEPORTS*	LAMBENTLY	LAMINARIAS*
LAETRILES*	LAICIZE	LAKER	LAMBER	LAMINARIN*
LAEVIGATE	LAICIZED	LAKERS	LAMBERS	LAMINARINS*
LAEVIGATED	LAICIZES	LAKES	LAMBERT	LAMINARY
LAEVIGATES	LAICIZING	LAKESHORE*	LAMBERTS	LAMINAS*
LAEVIGATING	LAICS	LAKESHORES*	LAMBIE	LAMINATE
LAEVO*	LAID	LAKESIDE	LAMBIER*	LAMINATED
LAEVULOSE	LAIDED	LAKESIDES	LAMBIES	LAMINATES
LAEVULOSES	LAIDING	LAKH	LAMBIEST*	LAMINATING
LAG	LAIDLY	LAKHS	LAMBING	LAMINATOR
LAGAN	LAIDS	LAKIER	LAMBITIVE	LAMINATORS
LAGANS	LAIGH	LAKIEST	LAMBITIVES	LAMING
LAGENA	LAIGHER	LAKIN	LAMBKILL*	LAMINGTON
LAGENAS	LAIGHEST	LAKING	LAMBKILLS*	LAMINGTONS
LAGEND*	LAIGHS	LAKINGS*	LAMBKIN	LAMINITIS
LAGENDS*	LAIK	LAKINS	LAMBKINS	LAMINITISES
LAGER	LAIKA	LAKISH	LAMBLIKE*	LAMINOSE
LAGERED*	LAIKAS	LAKY	LAMBLING	LAMINOUS*
LAGERING*	LAIKED	LALANG	LAMBLINGS	LAMISH
LAGERS	LAIKER	LALANGS	LAMBOYS	LAMISTER*
LAGGARD	LAIKERS	LALDIE	LAMBS	LAMISTERS*
LAGGARDLY*	LAIKING	LALDIES	LAMBSKIN	LAMITER
LAGGARDS	LAIKS	LALDY	LAMBSKINS	LAMITERS
LAGGED	LAIN	LALL*	LAMBY*	LAMMED
LAGGEN	LAIR	LALLAN	LAME	LAMMER
LAGGENS	LAIRAGE	LALLAND*	LAMEBRAIN*	LAMMERS
LAGGER	LAIRAGES	LALLANDS*	LAMEBRAINS*	LAMMIE
LAGGERS	LAIRD	LALLANS	LAMED	LAMMIES
LAGGIN	LAIRDLY*	LALLATION	LAMEDH*	LAMMIGER
LAGGING	LAIRDS	LALLATIONS	LAMEDHS*	LAMMIGERS
LAGGINGLY	LAIRDSHIP	LALLED*	LAMEDS*	LAMMING
LAGGINGS	LAIRDSHIPS	LALLING	LAMELLA	LAMMINGS
LAGGINS	LAIRED	LALLINGS	LAMELLAE	LAMMY
LAGNAPPE	LAIRIER	LALLS*	LAMELLAR	LAMP
LAGNAPPES	LAIRIEST	LALLYGAG	LAMELLAS*	LAMPAD
LAGNIAPPE	LAIRING	LALLYGAGGED	LAMELLATE	LAMPADARIES
LAGNIAPPES	LAIRISED	LALLYGAGGING	LAMELLOID	LAMPADARY
LAGOMORPH	LAIRISE	LALLYGAGS	LAMELLOSE	LAMPADIST
LAGOMORPHS	LAIRISES	LAM	LAMELY	LAMPADISTS
LAGOON	LAIRISING	LAMA	LAMENESS	LAMPADS
LAGOONAL	LAIRIZE	LAMAISTIC	LAMENESSES	LAMPAS

LAMPASES
LAMPASSE
LAMPASSES
LAMPBLACK*
LAMPBLACKS*
LAMPED
LAMPERN
LAMPERNS
LAMPERS
LAMPERSES
LAMPHOLE
LAMPHOLES
LAMPING
LAMPINGS
LAMPION
LAMPIONS
LAMPLIGHT
LAMPLIGHTS
LAMPOON
LAMPOONED
LAMPOONER
LAMPOONERS
LAMPOONING
LAMPOONS
LAMPPOST
LAMPPOSTS
LAMPREY
LAMPREYS
LAMPS
LAMPSHADE
LAMPSHADES
LAMPSHELL*
LAMPSHELLS*
LAMPUKA
LAMPUKAS
LAMPUKI
LAMPUKIS
LAMPYRID*
LAMPYRIDS*
LAMS
LAMSTER*
LAMSTERS*
LANA
LANAI*
LANAIS*
LANAS
LANATE
LANATED*
LANCE
LANCED
LANCEGAY
LANCEGAYS
LANCELET
LANCELETS
LANCEOLAR
LANCER
LANCERS
LANCES
LANCET
LANCETED
LANCETS
LANCEWOOD*
LANCEWOODS*
LANCH

LANCHED
LANCHES
LANCHING
LANCIERS*
LANCIFORM
LANCINATE
LANCINATED
LANCINATES
LANCINATING
LANCING
LAND
LANDAMMAN
LANDAMMANS
LANDAU
LANDAULET
LANDAULETS
LANDAUS
LANDDAMNE
LANDDAMNED
LANDDAMNES
LANDDAMNING
LANDDROS
LANDDROSES
LANDDROST
LANDDROSTS
LANDE
LANDED
LANDER
LANDERS
LANDES
LANDFALL
LANDFALLS
LANDFILL
LANDFILLS
LANDFORCE
LANDFORCES
LANDFORM
LANDFORMS
LANDGRAB*
LANDGRABS*
LANDGRAVE
LANDGRAVES
LANDING
LANDINGS
LANDLADIES
LANDLADY
LANDLER
LANDLERS
LANDLESS
LANDLINE*
LANDLINES*
LANDLOPER
LANDLOPERS
LANDLORD
LANDLORDS
LANDMAN
LANDMARK
LANDMARKS
LANDMASS
LANDMASSES
LANDMEN
LANDOWNER
LANDOWNERS
LANDRACE

LANDRACES
LANDRAIL
LANDRAILS
LANDS
LANDSCAPE
LANDSCAPED
LANDSCAPES
LANDSCAPING
LANDSIDE
LANDSIDES
LANDSKIP
LANDSKIPPED
LANDSKIPPING
LANDSKIPS
LANDSLEIT*
LANDSLID*
LANDSLIDE
LANDSLIDES
LANDSLIDING*
LANDSLIP
LANDSLIPS
LANDSMAN
LANDSMEN
LANDWARD
LANDWARDS
LANDWIND
LANDWINDS
LANE
LANELY*
LANES
LANEWAY
LANEWAYS
LANG
LANGAHA
LANGAHAS
LANGER
LANGEST
LANGLAUF
LANGLAUFS
LANGLEY*
LANGLEYS*
LANGOUSTE
LANGOUSTES
LANGRAGE
LANGRAGES
LANGREL
LANGRELS
LANGRIDGE
LANGRIDGES
LANGSHAN*
LANGSHANS*
LANGSPEL
LANGSPELS
LANGSPIEL
LANGSPIELS
LANGSYNE*
LANGSYNES*
LANGUAGE
LANGUAGED
LANGUAGES
LANGUAGING
LANGUE
LANGUED
LANGUES

LANGUET
LANGUETS
LANGUETTE
LANGUETTES
LANGUID
LANGUIDLY
LANGUISH
LANGUISHED
LANGUISHES
LANGUISHING
LANGUISHINGS
LANGUOR
LANGUORS
LANGUR
LANGURS
LANIARD
LANIARDS
LANIARIES*
LANIARY
LANITAL*
LANITALS*
LANK
LANKED
LANKER
LANKEST
LANKIER
LANKIEST
LANKILY
LANKINESS
LANKINESSES
LANKING
LANKLY
LANKNESS
LANKNESSES
LANKS
LANKY
LANNER
LANNERET
LANNERETS
LANNERS
LANOLIN
LANOLINE
LANOLINES
LANOLINS
LANOSE
LANOSITIES*
LANOSITY*
LANT
LANTANA
LANTANAS
LANTERLOO
LANTERLOOS
LANTERN
LANTERNED
LANTERNING
LANTERNS
LANTHANUM
LANTHANUMS
LANTHORN
LANTHORNS
LANTS
LANTSKIP
LANTSKIPS
LANUGO

LANUGOS
LANX
LANYARD
LANYARDS
LAP
LAPBOARD*
LAPBOARDS*
LAPDOG
LAPDOGS
LAPEL
LAPELED*
LAPELLED
LAPELS
LAPFUL
LAPFULS
LAPHELD
LAPIDARIES
LAPIDARY
LAPIDATE
LAPIDATED
LAPIDATES
LAPIDATING
LAPIDEOUS
LAPIDES*
LAPIDIFIC
LAPIDIFIED
LAPIDIFIES
LAPIDIFY
LAPIDIFYING
LAPIDIST*
LAPIDISTS*
LAPILLI
LAPILLUS*
LAPIN*
LAPINS*
LAPIS
LAPISES
LAPJE
LAPJES
LAPPED
LAPPEL
LAPPELS
LAPPER
LAPPERED
LAPPERING
LAPPERS
LAPPET
LAPPETED
LAPPETS
LAPPIE
LAPPIES
LAPPING
LAPPINGS
LAPS
LAPSABLE
LAPSANG
LAPSANGS
LAPSE
LAPSED
LAPSER*
LAPSERS*
LAPSES
LAPSIBLE*
LAPSING

The Chambers Dictionary is the authority for many longer words; see Introduction, page ix

LAPSTONE	LARGHETTO	LARYNGEALS*	LASTS	LATHERED
LAPSTONES	LARGHETTOS	LARYNGES	LAT	LATHERER*
LAPSTRAKE	LARGISH	LARYNX	LATAKIA*	LATHERERS*
LAPSTRAKES	LARGITION	LARYNXES	LATAKIAS*	LATHERIER
LAPSTREAK	LARGITIONS	LAS	LATCH	LATHERIEST
LAPSTREAKS	LARGO	LASAGNA	LATCHED	LATHERING
LAPSUS	LARGOS	LASAGNAS	LATCHES	LATHERS
LAPTOP	LARI*	LASAGNE	LATCHET	LATHERY
LAPTOPS	LARIAT	LASAGNES	LATCHETS	LATHES
LAPWING	LARIATED*	LASCAR	LATCHING	LATHI
LAPWINGS	LARIATING*	LASCARS	LATCHKEY	LATHIER
LAPWORK	LARIATS	LASE	LATCHKEYS	LATHIEST
LAPWORKS	LARINE	LASED	LATE	LATHING
LAQUEARIA	LARIS*	LASER	LATECOMER*	LATHINGS
LAR	LARK	LASERS	LATECOMERS*	LATHIS
LARBOARD	LARKED	LASERWORT	LATED	LATHLIKE
LARBOARDS	LARKER	LASERWORTS	LATEEN	LATHS
LARCENER	LARKERS	LASES	LATEENER*	LATHWORK*
LARCENERS	LARKIER	LASH	LATEENERS*	LATHWORKS*
LARCENIES	LARKIEST	LASHED	LATEENS	LATHY
LARCENIST	LARKINESS	LASHER	LATEN	LATHYRISM
LARCENISTS	LARKINESSES	LASHERS	LATENCE	LATHYRISMS
LARCENOUS	LARKING	LASHES	LATENCES	LATHYRUS
LARCENY	LARKISH	LASHING	LATENCIES	LATHYRUSES
LARCH	LARKS	LASHINGS	LATENCY	LATI*
LARCHEN	LARKSOME*	LASHINS*	LATENED	LATICES
LARCHES	LARKSPUR	LASHKAR	LATENESS	LATICIFER*
LARD	LARKSPURS	LASHKARS	LATENESSES	LATICIFERS*
LARDALITE	LARKY	LASING	LATENING	LATICLAVE
LARDALITES	LARMIER	LASINGS	LATENS	LATICLAVES
LARDED	LARMIERS	LASKET	LATENT	LATIFONDI
LARDER	LARN	LASKETS	LATENTLY	LATIGO*
LARDERER	LARNAKES	LASQUE	LATENTS*	LATIGOES*
LARDERERS	LARNAX	LASQUES	LATER	LATIGOS*
LARDERS	LARNED	LASS	LATERAD*	LATINITIES*
LARDIER	LARNING	LASSES	LATERAL	LATINITY*
LARDIEST	LARNS	LASSI	LATERALED*	LATINIZE*
LARDING	LAROID	LASSIE	LATERALING*	LATINIZED*
LARDLIKE*	LARRIGAN	LASSIES	LATERALLY	LATINIZES*
LARDON	LARRIGANS	LASSIS	LATERALS	LATINIZING*
LARDONS	LARRIKIN	LASSITUDE	LATERITE	LATINO*
LARDOON	LARRIKINS	LASSITUDES	LATERITES	LATINOS*
LARDOONS	LARRUP	LASSLORN	LATERITIC	LATISH
LARDS	LARRUPED	LASSO	LATERIZE*	LATITANCIES
LARDY	LARRUPER*	LASSOCK	LATERIZED*	LATITANCY
LARE	LARRUPERS*	LASSOCKS	LATERIZES*	LATITANT
LAREE*	LARRUPING	LASSOED	LATERIZING*	LATITAT
LAREES*	LARRUPS	LASSOER*	LATESCENT	LATITATS
LARES	LARS*	LASSOERS*	LATEST	LATITUDE
LARGANDO*	LARUM	LASSOES	LATESTS	LATITUDES
LARGE	LARUMS	LASSOING	LATEWAKE	LATKE
LARGELY	LARVA	LASSOS	LATEWAKES	LATKES
LARGEN	LARVAE	LASSU	LATEWOOD*	LATOSOL*
LARGENED	LARVAL	LASSUS	LATEWOODS*	LATOSOLIC*
LARGENESS	LARVAS*	LAST	LATEX	LATOSOLS*
LARGENESSES	LARVATE	LASTAGE	LATEXES	LATRANT
LARGENING	LARVATED	LASTAGES	LATH	LATRATION
LARGENS	LARVICIDE	LASTED	LATHE	LATRATIONS
LARGER	LARVICIDES	LASTER	LATHED	LATRIA
LARGES	LARVIFORM	LASTERS	LATHEE	LATRIAS
LARGESS	LARVIKITE	LASTING	LATHEES	LATRINE
LARGESSE	LARVIKITES	LASTINGLY	LATHEN	LATRINES
LARGESSES	LARYNGAL	LASTINGS	LATHER	LATROCINIES
LARGEST	LARYNGEAL	LASTLY	LATHER	LATROCINY

LATRON	LAUNCHERS	LAVENDERED	LAWNIER	LAYOVERS*
LATRONS	LAUNCHES	LAVENDERING	LAWNIEST	LAYPEOPLE*
LATS	LAUNCHING	LAVENDERS	LAWNMOWER	LAYPERSON
LATTE*	LAUNCHPAD*	LAVER	LAWNMOWERS	LAYPERSONS
LATTEN	LAUNCHPADS*	LAVEROCK	LAWNS	LAYS
LATTENS	LAUNCING	LAVEROCKED	LAWNY	LAYSTALL
LATTER	LAUND	LAVEROCKING	LAWS	LAYSTALLS
LATTERLY	LAUNDER	LAVEROCKS	LAWSUIT	LAYTIME
LATTES*	LAUNDERED	LAVERS	LAWSUITS	LAYTIMES
LATTICE	LAUNDERER	LAVES	LAWYER	LAYUP*
LATTICED	LAUNDERERS	LAVING	LAWYERED*	LAYUPS*
LATTICES	LAUNDERING	LAVISH	LAWYERING*	LAYWOMAN
LATTICING	LAUNDERS	LAVISHED	LAWYERINGS*	LAYWOMEN
LATTICINI	LAUNDRESS	LAVISHER	LAWYERLY	LAZAR
LATTICINO	LAUNDRESSES	LAVISHERS*	LAWYERS	LAZARET
LATTIN*	LAUNDRIES	LAVISHES	LAX	LAZARETS
LATTINS*	LAUNDRY	LAVISHEST	LAXATION*	LAZARETTE*
LAUAN*	LAUNDS	LAVISHING	LAXATIONS*	LAZARETTES*
LAUANS*	LAURA	LAVISHLY	LAXATIVE	LAZARETTO
LAUCH	LAURAE*	LAVOLT	LAXATIVES	LAZARETTOS
LAUCHING	LAURAS	LAVOLTA	LAXATOR	LAZARS
LAUCHS	LAUREATE	LAVOLTAED	LAXATORS	LAZE
LAUD	LAUREATED	LAVOLTAING	LAXER	LAZED
LAUDABLE	LAUREATES	LAVOLTAS	LAXES	LAZES
LAUDABLY	LAUREATING	LAVOLTED	LAXEST	LAZIED*
LAUDANUM	LAUREL	LAVOLTING	LAXISM	LAZIER
LAUDANUMS	LAURELED*	LAVOLTS	LAXISMS	LAZIES*
LAUDATION	LAURELING*	LAVRA	LAXIST	LAZIEST
LAUDATIONS	LAURELLED	LAVRAS	LAXISTS	LAZILY
LAUDATIVE	LAURELLING*	LAVROCK*	LAXITIES	LAZINESS
LAUDATIVES	LAURELS	LAVROCKS*	LAXITY	LAZINESSES
LAUDATOR*	LAUWINE	LAVS	LAXLY	LAZING
LAUDATORIES	LAUWINES	LAW	LAXNESS	LAZO
LAUDATORS*	LAV	LAWBOOK*	LAXNESSES	LAZOED
LAUDATORY	LAVA	LAWBOOKS*	LAY	LAZOES
LAUDED	LAVABO	LAWED	LAYABOUT	LAZOING
LAUDER	LAVABOES	LAWER	LAYABOUTS	LAZOS
LAUDERS	LAVABOS	LAWEST	LAYAWAY	LAZULI*
LAUDING	LAVAFORM	LAWFUL	LAYAWAYS	LAZULIS*
LAUDS	LAVAGE	LAWFULLY	LAYBACK	LAZULITE
LAUF	LAVAGES	LAWGIVER*	LAYBACKED	LAZULITES
LAUFS	LAVALAVA*	LAWGIVERS*	LAYBACKING	LAZURITE
LAUGH	LAVALAVAS*	LAWIN	LAYBACKS	LAZURITES
LAUGHABLE	LAVALIER*	LAWINE*	LAYED*	LAZY
LAUGHABLY	LAVALIERE	LAWINES*	LAYER	LAZYBONES*
LAUGHED	LAVALIERES	LAWING	LAYERAGE*	LAZYING*
LAUGHER	LAVALIERS*	LAWINGS	LAYERAGES*	LAZYISH*
LAUGHERS	LAVALIKE*	LAWINS	LAYERED	LAZZARONE
LAUGHFUL	LAVAS	LAWK	LAYERING	LAZZARONI
LAUGHIER	LAVATERA	LAWKS	LAYERINGS	LAZZI
LAUGHIEST	LAVATERAS	LAWLAND	LAYERS	LAZZO
LAUGHING	LAVATION	LAWLANDS	LAYETTE	LEA
LAUGHINGS	LAVATIONS	LAWLESS	LAYETTES	LEACH
LAUGHS	LAVATORIES	LAWLESSLY	LAYING	LEACHABLE*
LAUGHSOME	LAVATORY	LAWLIKE*	LAYINGS	LEACHATE
LAUGHTER	LAVE	LAWMAKER*	LAYLOCK	LEACHATES
LAUGHTERS	LAVED	LAWMAKERS*	LAYLOCKS	LEACHED
LAUGHY	LAVEER	LAWMAKING*	LAYMAN	LEACHER*
LAUNCE	LAVEERED	LAWMAKINGS*	LAYMEN	LEACHERS*
LAUNCED	LAVEERING	LAWMAN	LAYOFF*	LEACHES
LAUNCES	LAVEERS	LAWMEN	LAYOFFS*	LEACHIER
LAUNCH	LAVEMENT	LAWMONGER	LAYOUT	LEACHIEST
LAUNCHED	LAVEMENTS	LAWMONGERS	LAYOUTS	LEACHING
LAUNCHER	LAVENDER	LAWN	LAYOVER*	LEACHINGS

LEACHOUR
LEACHOURS
LEACHTUB
LEACHTUBS
LEACHY
LEAD
LEADED
LEADEN
LEADENED
LEADENING
LEADENLY
LEADENS
LEADER
LEADERENE
LEADERENES
LEADERS
LEADIER
LEADIEST
LEADING
LEADINGS
LEADLESS
LEADMAN*
LEADMEN*
LEADOFF*
LEADOFFS*
LEADPLANT*
LEADPLANTS*
LEADS
LEADSCREW*
LEADSCREWS*
LEADSMAN
LEADSMEN
LEADWORK*
LEADWORKS*
LEADWORT*
LEADWORTS*
LEADY
LEAF
LEAFAGE
LEAFAGES
LEAFBUD
LEAFBUDS
LEAFED
LEAFERIES
LEAFERY
LEAFIER
LEAFIEST
LEAFINESS
LEAFINESSES
LEAFING
LEAFLESS
LEAFLET
LEAFLETED
LEAFLETING
LEAFLETS
LEAFLETTED
LEAFLETTING
LEAFLIKE
LEAFS
LEAFSTALK*
LEAFSTALKS*
LEAFWORM*
LEAFWORMS*
LEAFY

LEAGUE
LEAGUED
LEAGUER
LEAGUERED
LEAGUERING
LEAGUERS
LEAGUES
LEAGUING
LEAK
LEAKAGE
LEAKAGES
LEAKED
LEAKER
LEAKERS
LEAKIER
LEAKIEST
LEAKILY*
LEAKINESS
LEAKINESSES
LEAKING
LEAKLESS*
LEAKPROOF*
LEAKS
LEAKY
LEAL
LEALLY
LEALTIES
LEALTY
LEAM
LEAMED
LEAMING
LEAMS
LEAN
LEANED
LEANER
LEANERS*
LEANEST
LEANING
LEANINGS
LEANLY
LEANNESS
LEANNESSES
LEANS
LEANT
LEANY
LEAP
LEAPED
LEAPER
LEAPEROUS
LEAPERS
LEAPFROG*
LEAPFROGGED*
LEAPFROGGING*
LEAPFROGS*
LEAPING
LEAPOROUS
LEAPROUS
LEAPS
LEAPT
LEAR
LEARE
LEARED
LEARES
LEARIER

LEARIEST
LEARING
LEARN
LEARNABLE
LEARNED
LEARNEDLY
LEARNER
LEARNERS
LEARNING
LEARNINGS
LEARNS
LEARNT
LEARS
LEARY
LEAS
LEASABLE
LEASE
LEASEBACK
LEASEBACKS
LEASED
LEASEHOLD
LEASEHOLDS
LEASER
LEASERS
LEASES
LEASH
LEASHED
LEASHES
LEASHING
LEASING
LEASINGS
LEASOW
LEASOWE
LEASOWED
LEASOWES
LEASOWING
LEASOWS
LEAST
LEASTS
LEASTWAYS
LEASTWISE
LEASURE
LEASURES
LEAT
LEATHER
LEATHERED
LEATHERIER
LEATHERIEST
LEATHERING
LEATHERINGS
LEATHERN
LEATHERS
LEATHERY
LEATS
LEAVE
LEAVED
LEAVEN
LEAVENED
LEAVENING
LEAVENINGS
LEAVENOUS
LEAVENS
LEAVER
LEAVERS

LEAVES
LEAVIER
LEAVIEST
LEAVING
LEAVINGS
LEAVY
LEAZE
LEAZES
LEBBEK
LEBBEKS
LEBEN*
LEBENS*
LECANORA
LECANORAS
LECH
LECHAYIM*
LECHAYIMS*
LECHED
LECHER
LECHERED
LECHERIES
LECHERING
LECHEROUS
LECHERS
LECHERY
LECHES
LECHING
LECHWE
LECHWES
LECITHIN
LECITHINS
LECTERN
LECTERNS
LECTIN
LECTINS
LECTION
LECTIONS
LECTOR
LECTORATE
LECTORATES
LECTORS
LECTOTYPE*
LECTOTYPES*
LECTRESS
LECTRESSES
LECTURE
LECTURED
LECTURER
LECTURERS
LECTURES
LECTURING
LECTURN
LECTURNS
LECYTHI
LECYTHIS*
LECYTHUS
LED
LEDDEN
LEDDENS
LEDGE
LEDGER
LEDGERED
LEDGERING
LEDGERS

LEDGES
LEDGIER
LEDGIEST
LEDGY
LEDUM
LEDUMS
LEE
LEEAR
LEEARS
LEEBOARD*
LEEBOARDS*
LEECH
LEECHDOM
LEECHDOMS
LEECHED
LEECHEE
LEECHEES
LEECHES
LEECHING
LEECHLIKE*
LEED
LEEING
LEEK
LEEKS
LEEP
LEEPED
LEEPING
LEEPS
LEER
LEERED
LEERIER
LEERIEST
LEERILY*
LEERING
LEERINGLY
LEERINGS
LEERS
LEERY
LEES
LEESE
LEESES
LEESING
LEET
LEETLE
LEETS
LEEWARD
LEEWARDS
LEEWAY
LEEWAYS
LEFT
LEFTE
LEFTER
LEFTEST
LEFTIE
LEFTIES
LEFTISH
LEFTISM
LEFTISMS
LEFTIST
LEFTISTS
LEFTOVER
LEFTOVERS
LEFTS
LEFTWARD

Words marked with an asterisk are from OTCWL

LEFTWARDS
LEFTWING*
LEFTY
LEG
LEGACIES
LEGACY
LEGAL
LEGALESE
LEGALESES
LEGALISE
LEGALISED
LEGALISES
LEGALISING
LEGALISM
LEGALISMS
LEGALIST
LEGALISTS
LEGALITIES
LEGALITY
LEGALIZE
LEGALIZED
LEGALIZER*
LEGALIZERS*
LEGALIZES
LEGALIZING
LEGALLY
LEGALS*
LEGATARIES
LEGATARY
LEGATE
LEGATED*
LEGATEE
LEGATEES
LEGATES
LEGATINE
LEGATING*
LEGATION
LEGATIONS
LEGATO
LEGATOR
LEGATORS
LEGATOS
LEGEND
LEGENDARIES
LEGENDARY
LEGENDIST
LEGENDISTS
LEGENDRIES
LEGENDRY
LEGENDS
LEGER
LEGERING
LEGERINGS
LEGERITIES
LEGERITY
LEGERS
LEGES
LEGGE
LEGGED
LEGGER
LEGGERS
LEGGES
LEGGIER
LEGGIERO*

LEGGIEST
LEGGIN*
LEGGINESS
LEGGINESSES
LEGGING
LEGGINGS
LEGGINS*
LEGGISM
LEGGISMS
LEGGY
LEGHORN
LEGHORNS
LEGIBLE
LEGIBLY
LEGION
LEGIONARIES
LEGIONARY
LEGIONED
LEGIONS
LEGISLATE
LEGISLATED
LEGISLATES
LEGISLATING
LEGIST
LEGISTS
LEGIT
LEGITIM
LEGITIMS
LEGITS*
LEGLAN
LEGLANS
LEGLEN
LEGLENS
LEGLESS
LEGLET
LEGLETS
LEGLIKE*
LEGLIN
LEGLINS
LEGMAN*
LEGMEN*
LEGONG*
LEGONGS*
LEGROOM
LEGROOMS
LEGS
LEGUME
LEGUMES
LEGUMIN
LEGUMINS
LEGWEAR
LEGWEARS
LEGWORK
LEGWORKS
LEHAYIM*
LEHAYIMS*
LEHR
LEHRJAHRE
LEHRS
LEHUA*
LEHUAS*
LEI
LEIDGER
LEIDGERS

LEIGER
LEIGERS
LEIPOA
LEIPOAS
LEIR
LEIRED
LEIRING
LEIRS
LEIS
LEISH
LEISHER
LEISHEST
LEISLER
LEISLERS
LEISTER
LEISTERED
LEISTERING
LEISTERS
LEISURE
LEISURED
LEISURELY
LEISURES
LEISURING
LEITMOTIF
LEITMOTIFS
LEITMOTIV
LEITMOTIVS
LEK
LEKE
LEKKED
LEKKING
LEKKINGS
LEKS
LEKU*
LEKVAR*
LEKVARS*
LEKYTHI*
LEKYTHOI
LEKYTHOS
LEKYTHUS*
LEMAN
LEMANS
LEME
LEMED
LEMEL
LEMELS
LEMES
LEMING
LEMMA
LEMMAS
LEMMATA
LEMMATISE
LEMMATISED
LEMMATISES
LEMMATISING
LEMMATIZE
LEMMATIZED
LEMMATIZES
LEMMATIZING
LEMMING
LEMMINGS
LEMNISCAL*
LEMNISCI*
LEMNISCUS*

LEMON
LEMONADE
LEMONADES
LEMONED
LEMONFISH
LEMONFISHES
LEMONIER
LEMONIEST
LEMONING
LEMONISH*
LEMONS
LEMONY
LEMPIRA
LEMPIRAS
LEMUR
LEMURES
LEMURIAN
LEMURIANS
LEMURINE
LEMURINES
LEMUROID
LEMUROIDS
LEMURS
LEND
LENDABLE*
LENDER
LENDERS
LENDING
LENDINGS
LENDS
LENES
LENG
LENGED
LENGER
LENGEST
LENGING
LENGS
LENGTH
LENGTHEN
LENGTHENED
LENGTHENING
LENGTHENS
LENGTHFUL
LENGTHIER
LENGTHIEST
LENGTHILY
LENGTHS
LENGTHY
LENIENCE
LENIENCES
LENIENCIES
LENIENCY
LENIENT
LENIENTLY
LENIENTS
LENIFIED
LENIFIES
LENIFY
LENIFYING
LENIS
LENITIES
LENITION
LENITIONS
LENITIVE

LENITIVES
LENITY
LENO
LENOS
LENS
LENSE*
LENSED*
LENSES
LENSING*
LENSLESS*
LENSMAN
LENSMEN
LENT
LENTANDO
LENTEN
LENTI
LENTIC
LENTICEL
LENTICELS
LENTICLE
LENTICLES
LENTICULE*
LENTICULES*
LENTIFORM
LENTIGINES
LENTIGO
LENTIL
LENTILS
LENTISK
LENTISKS
LENTO
LENTOID
LENTOR
LENTORS
LENTOS
LENTOUS
LENVOY
LENVOYS
LEONE
LEONES
LEONINE
LEOPARD
LEOPARDS
LEOTARD
LEOTARDED*
LEOTARDS
LEP
LEPER
LEPERS
LEPID
LEPIDOTE
LEPIDOTES*
LEPORID*
LEPORIDAE*
LEPORIDS*
LEPORINE
LEPPED
LEPPING
LEPRA
LEPRAS
LEPROSE
LEPROSERIES
LEPROSERY
LEPROSIES

The Chambers Dictionary is the authority for many longer words; see Introduction, page ix

LEPROSITIES	LETDOWN*	LEUCOTOMIES	LEVERET	LEXEMIC*
LEPROSITY	LETDOWNS*	LEUCOTOMY	LEVERETS	LEXES
LEPROSY	LETHAL	LEUD*	LEVERING	LEXICA*
LEPROTIC*	LETHALITIES	LEUDES*	LEVERS	LEXICAL
LEPROUS	LETHALITY	LEUDS*	LEVIABLE	LEXICALLY
LEPROUSLY*	LETHALLY	LEUGH	LEVIATHAN	LEXICON
LEPS	LETHALS*	LEUGHEN	LEVIATHANS	LEXICONS
LEPT*	LETHARGIC	LEUKAEMIA	LEVIED	LEXIGRAM
LEPTA	LETHARGIES	LEUKAEMIAS	LEVIER*	LEXIGRAMS
LEPTOME	LETHARGY	LEUKEMIA	LEVIERS*	LEXIS
LEPTOMES	LETHE*	LEUKEMIAS	LEVIES	LEXISES
LEPTON	LETHEAN	LEUKEMIC*	LEVIGABLE	LEY
LEPTONIC	LETHEE	LEUKEMICS*	LEVIGATE	LEYS
LEPTONS	LETHEES	LEUKEMOID*	LEVIGATED	LEZ
LEPTOSOME	LETHES*	LEUKOCYTE*	LEVIGATES	LEZES
LEPTOSOMES	LETHIED	LEUKOCYTES*	LEVIGATING	LEZZ
LEPTOTENE	LETS	LEUKOMA*	LEVIN	LEZZES
LEPTOTENES	LETTABLE	LEUKOMAS*	LEVINS	LEZZIE*
LERE	LETTED	LEUKON*	LEVIRATE	LEZZIES
LERED	LETTER	LEUKONS*	LEVIRATES	LEZZY
LERES	LETTERBOX	LEUKOSES*	LEVIRATIC*	LI
LERING	LETTERBOXES	LEUKOSIS*	LEVIS	LIABILITIES
LERNAEAN	LETTERED	LEUKOTIC*	LEVITATE	LIABILITY
LERNEAN	LETTERER	LEUKOTOMIES*	LEVITATED	LIABLE
LERP	LETTERERS	LEUKOTOMY*	LEVITATES	LIAISE
LERPS	LETTERING	LEV	LEVITATING	LIAISED
LES	LETTERINGS	LEVA	LEVITE	LIAISES
LESBIAN	LETTERMAN*	LEVANT	LEVITES	LIAISING
LESBIANS	LETTERMEN*	LEVANTED	LEVITIC	LIAISON
LESBIC	LETTERN	LEVANTER	LEVITICAL	LIAISONS
LESBO	LETTERNS	LEVANTERS	LEVITIES	LIANA
LESBOS	LETTERS	LEVANTINE	LEVITY	LIANAS
LESES	LETTING	LEVANTINES	LEVO*	LIANE
LESION	LETTINGS	LEVANTING	LEVODOPA*	LIANES
LESIONED*	LETTRE	LEVANTS	LEVODOPAS*	LIANG
LESIONS	LETTRES	LEVATOR	LEVOGYRE*	LIANGS
LESPEDEZA*	LETTUCE	LEVATORES*	LEVULIN*	LIANOID
LESPEDEZAS*	LETTUCES	LEVATORS	LEVULINS*	LIAR
LESS	LETUP*	LEVE	LEVULOSE	LIARD
LESSEE	LETUPS*	LEVEE	LEVULOSES	LIARDS
LESSEES	LEU	LEVEED	LEVY	LIARS
LESSEN	LEUCAEMIA	LEVEEING	LEVYING	LIART
LESSENED	LEUCAEMIAS	LEVEES	LEW	LIB
LESSENING	LEUCAEMIC	LEVEL	LEWD	LIBANT
LESSENS	LEUCEMIA*	LEVELED*	LEWDER	LIBATE
LESSER	LEUCEMIAS*	LEVELER*	LEWDEST	LIBATED
LESSES	LEUCEMIC*	LEVELERS*	LEWDLY	LIBATES
LESSON	LEUCH	LEVELING*	LEWDNESS	LIBATING
LESSONED	LEUCHEN	LEVELLED	LEWDNESSES	LIBATION
LESSONING	LEUCIN	LEVELLER	LEWDSBIES	LIBATIONS
LESSONINGS	LEUCINE	LEVELLERS	LEWDSBY	LIBATORY
LESSONS	LEUCINES	LEVELLEST	LEWDSTER	LIBBARD
LESSOR	LEUCINS	LEVELLING	LEWDSTERS	LIBBARDS
LESSORS	LEUCITE	LEVELLINGS	LEWIS	LIBBED
LEST	LEUCITES	LEVELLY*	LEWISES	LIBBER
LESTED	LEUCITIC	LEVELNESS*	LEWISIA	LIBBERS
LESTING	LEUCOCYTE	LEVELNESSES*	LEWISIAS	LIBBING
LESTS	LEUCOCYTES	LEVELS	LEWISITE	LIBECCHIO
LET	LEUCOMA	LEVER	LEWISITES	LIBECCHIOS
LETCH	LEUCOMAS	LEVERAGE	LEWISSON	LIBECCIO
LETCHED	LEUCOSIN	LEVERAGED	LEWISSONS	LIBECCIOS
LETCHES	LEUCOSINS	LEVERAGES	LEX	LIBEL
LETCHING	LEUCOTOME	LEVERAGING	LEXEME	LIBELANT
LETCHINGS	LEUCOTOMES	LEVERED	LEXEMES	LIBELANTS

LIBELED	LIBRETTO	LICIT	LIEVEST	LIGATING
LIBELEE	LIBRETTOS	LICITLY	LIFE	LIGATION
LIBELEES	LIBRI*	LICK	LIFEBELT	LIGATIONS
LIBELER	LIBRIFORM*	LICKED	LIFEBELTS	LIGATIVE*
LIBELERS	LIBS	LICKER	LIFEBLOOD*	LIGATURE
LIBELING	LICE	LICKERISH	LIFEBLOODS*	LIGATURED
LIBELINGS	LICENCE	LICKERS	LIFEBOAT	LIGATURES
LIBELIST*	LICENCED	LICKING	LIFEBOATS	LIGATURING
LIBELISTS*	LICENCEE*	LICKINGS	LIFEBUOY	LIGER
LIBELLANT	LICENCEES*	LICKPENNIES	LIFEBUOYS	LIGERS
LIBELLANTS	LICENCER*	LICKPENNY	LIFEFUL	LIGGE
LIBELLED	LICENCERS*	LICKS	LIFEGUARD	LIGGED
LIBELLEE	LICENCES	LICKSPIT*	LIFEGUARDED*	LIGGEN
LIBELLEES	LICENCING	LICKSPITS*	LIFEGUARDING*	LIGGER
LIBELLER	LICENSE	LICORICE	LIFEGUARDS	LIGGERS
LIBELLERS	LICENSED	LICORICES	LIFEHOLD	LIGGES
LIBELLING	LICENSEE	LICTOR	LIFELESS	LIGGING
LIBELLINGS	LICENSEES	LICTORS	LIFELIKE	LIGGINGS
LIBELLOUS	LICENSER	LID	LIFELINE	LIGHT
LIBELOUS	LICENSERS	LIDAR*	LIFELINES	LIGHTBULB*
LIBELS	LICENSES	LIDARS*	LIFELONG	LIGHTBULBS*
LIBER	LICENSING	LIDDED	LIFER	LIGHTED
LIBERAL	LICENSOR	LIDDING*	LIFERS	LIGHTEN
LIBERALLY	LICENSORS	LIDGER	LIFESAVER*	LIGHTENED
LIBERALS	LICENSURE	LIDGERS	LIFESAVERS*	LIGHTENER*
LIBERATE	LICENSURES	LIDLESS	LIFESOME	LIGHTENERS*
LIBERATED	LICENTE*	LIDO	LIFESPAN	LIGHTENING
LIBERATES	LICH	LIDOCAINE	LIFESPANS	LIGHTENINGS
LIBERATING	LICHANOS	LIDOCAINES	LIFESTYLE	LIGHTENS
LIBERATOR	LICHANOSES	LIDOS	LIFESTYLES	LIGHTER
LIBERATORS	LICHEE	LIDS	LIFETIME	LIGHTERED*
LIBERO	LICHEES	LIE	LIFETIMES	LIGHTERING*
LIBEROS	LICHEN	LIED	LIFEWAY*	LIGHTERS
LIBERS	LICHENED	LIEDER	LIFEWAYS*	LIGHTEST
LIBERTIES	LICHENIN	LIEF	LIFEWORK*	LIGHTFACE*
LIBERTINE	LICHENING*	LIEFER	LIFEWORKS*	LIGHTFACES*
LIBERTINES	LICHENINS	LIEFEST	LIFT	LIGHTFAST*
LIBERTY	LICHENISM	LIEFLY*	LIFTABLE	LIGHTFUL
LIBIDINAL	LICHENISMS	LIEFS	LIFTBACK	LIGHTING
LIBIDO	LICHENIST	LIEGE	LIFTBACKS	LIGHTINGS
LIBIDOS	LICHENISTS	LIEGEDOM	LIFTED	LIGHTISH
LIBKEN	LICHENOID	LIEGEDOMS	LIFTER	LIGHTLESS
LIBKENS	LICHENOSE	LIEGELESS	LIFTERS	LIGHTLIED
LIBLAB*	LICHENOUS	LIEGEMAN	LIFTGATE*	LIGHTLIES
LIBLABS*	LICHENS	LIEGEMEN	LIFTGATES*	LIGHTLY
LIBRA	LICHES	LIEGER	LIFTING	LIGHTLYING
LIBRAE	LICHGATE	LIEGERS	LIFTMAN*	LIGHTNESS
LIBRAIRE	LICHGATES	LIEGES	LIFTMEN*	LIGHTNESSES
LIBRAIRES	LICHI	LIEN	LIFTOFF*	LIGHTNING
LIBRAIRIE	LICHIS	LIENABLE*	LIFTOFFS*	LIGHTNINGED*
LIBRAIRIES	LICHT	LIENAL	LIFTS	LIGHTNINGS
LIBRARIAN	LICHTED	LIENS	LIFULL	LIGHTS
LIBRARIANS	LICHTER	LIENTERIC	LIG	LIGHTSHIP
LIBRARIES	LICHTEST	LIENTERIES	LIGAMENT	LIGHTSHIPS
LIBRARY	LICHTING	LIENTERY	LIGAMENTS	LIGHTSOME
LIBRAS	LICHTLIED	LIER	LIGAN	LIGHTWOOD*
LIBRATE	LICHTLIES	LIERNE	LIGAND	LIGHTWOODS*
LIBRATED	LICHTLY	LIERNES	LIGANDS	LIGNAGE
LIBRATES	LICHTLYING	LIERS	LIGANS	LIGNAGES
LIBRATING	LICHTS	LIES	LIGASE	LIGNALOES
LIBRATION	LICHWAKE	LIEU	LIGASES	LIGNE
LIBRATIONS	LICHWAKES	LIEUS	LIGATE	LIGNEOUS
LIBRATORY	LICHWAY	LIEVE	LIGATED	LIGNES
LIBRETTI	LICHWAYS	LIEVER	LIGATES	LIGNIFIED

The Chambers Dictionary is the authority for many longer words; see Introduction, page ix

LIGNIFIES	LILLIPUTS*	LIMELIGHT	LIMOSES	LINDIES*
LIGNIFORM	LILLS	LIMELIGHTED	LIMOSIS	LINDS
LIGNIFY	LILO	LIMELIGHTING	LIMOUS	LINDWORM
LIGNIFYING	LILOS	LIMELIGHTS	LIMOUSINE	LINDWORMS
LIGNIN	LILT	LIMELIT	LIMOUSINES	LINDY*
LIGNINS	LILTED	LIMEN	LIMP	LINE
LIGNITE	LILTING	LIMENS	LIMPA*	LINEABLE*
LIGNITES	LILTINGLY*	LIMEPIT	LIMPAS*	LINEAGE
LIGNITIC	LILTS	LIMEPITS	LIMPED	LINEAGES
LIGNOSE	LILY	LIMERICK	LIMPER	LINEAL
LIGNOSES	LILYLIKE*	LIMERICKS	LIMPERS*	LINEALITIES
LIGNUM	LIMA	LIMES	LIMPEST	LINEALITY
LIGNUMS	LIMACEL	LIMESTONE	LIMPET	LINEALLY
LIGROIN	LIMACELS	LIMESTONES	LIMPETS	LINEAMENT
LIGROINE*	LIMACEOUS	LIMEWASH	LIMPID	LINEAMENTS
LIGROINES*	LIMACES	LIMEWASHES	LIMPIDITIES	LINEAR
LIGROINS	LIMACINE	LIMEWATER	LIMPIDITY	LINEARISE*
LIGS	LIMACON	LIMEWATERS	LIMPIDLY	LINEARISED*
LIGULA	LIMACONS	LIMEY	LIMPING	LINEARISES*
LIGULAE	LIMAIL	LIMEYS	LIMPINGLY	LINEARISING*
LIGULAR	LIMAILS	LIMIER	LIMPINGS	LINEARITIES
LIGULAS	LIMAN*	LIMIEST	LIMPKIN	LINEARITY
LIGULATE	LIMANS*	LIMINA*	LIMPKINS	LINEARIZE*
LIGULE	LIMAS	LIMINAL	LIMPLY	LINEARIZED*
LIGULES	LIMATION	LIMINESS	LIMPNESS	LINEARIZES*
LIGULOID	LIMATIONS	LIMINESSES	LIMPNESSES	LINEARIZING*
LIGURE	LIMAX	LIMING	LIMPS	LINEARLY
LIGURES	LIMB	LIMINGS	LIMPSEY*	LINEATE
LIKABLE	LIMBA*	LIMIT	LIMPSIER*	LINEATED
LIKE	LIMBAS*	LIMITABLE	LIMPSIEST*	LINEATION
LIKEABLE	LIMBATE	LIMITARY	LIMPSY*	LINEATIONS
LIKED	LIMBEC	LIMITED	LIMULI	LINEBRED*
LIKELIER	LIMBECK	LIMITEDLY	LIMULOID*	LINECUT*
LIKELIEST	LIMBECKS	LIMITEDS	LIMULOIDS*	LINECUTS*
LIKELY	LIMBECS	LIMITER	LIMULUS	LINED
LIKEN	LIMBED	LIMITERS	LIMULUSES	LINELESS*
LIKENED	LIMBER	LIMITES	LIMY	LINELIKE*
LIKENESS	LIMBERED	LIMITING	LIN	LINEMAN
LIKENESSES	LIMBERER*	LIMITINGS	LINABLE*	LINEMEN
LIKENING	LIMBEREST*	LIMITLESS	LINAC	LINEN
LIKENS	LIMBERING	LIMITS	LINACS	LINENS
LIKER	LIMBERLY*	LIMMA	LINAGE	LINENY*
LIKERS	LIMBERS	LIMMAS	LINAGES	LINEOLATE
LIKES	LIMBI*	LIMMER	LINALOL*	LINER
LIKEST*	LIMBIC	LIMMERS	LINALOLS*	LINERLESS*
LIKEWAKE	LIMBIER*	LIMN	LINALOOL	LINERS
LIKEWAKES	LIMBIEST*	LIMNAEID	LINALOOLS	LINES
LIKEWALK	LIMBING	LIMNAEIDS	LINCH	LINESMAN
LIKEWALKS	LIMBLESS	LIMNED	LINCHES	LINESMEN
LIKEWISE	LIMBMEAL	LIMNER	LINCHET	LINEUP*
LIKIN	LIMBO	LIMNERS	LINCHETS	LINEUPS*
LIKING	LIMBOS	LIMNETIC	LINCHPIN	LINEY
LIKINGS	LIMBOUS	LIMNIC*	LINCHPINS	LING
LIKINS	LIMBS	LIMNING	LINCRUSTA	LINGA
LIKUTA*	LIMBUS*	LIMNOLOGIES	LINCRUSTAS	LINGAM
LILAC	LIMBUSES*	LIMNOLOGY	LINCTURE	LINGAMS
LILACS	LIMBY*	LIMNS	LINCTURES	LINGAS
LILANGENI	LIME	LIMO	LINCTUS	LINGCOD*
LILIED	LIMEADE	LIMONENE*	LINCTUSES	LINGCODS*
LILIES	LIMEADES	LIMONENES*	LIND	LINGEL
LILL	LIMED	LIMONITE	LINDANE	LINGELS
LILLED	LIMEKILN	LIMONITES	LINDANES	LINGER
LILLING	LIMEKILNS	LIMONITIC	LINDEN	LINGERED
LILLIPUT*	LIMELESS*	LIMOS	LINDENS	LINGERER

LINGERERS	LINKS	LIONCEL	LIPPENING	LIQUOR
LINGERIE	LINKSMAN*	LIONCELLE	LIPPENS	LIQUORED
LINGERIES	LINKSMEN*	LIONCELLES	LIPPER*	LIQUORICE
LINGERING	LINKSTER	LIONCELS	LIPPERED*	LIQUORICES
LINGERINGS	LINKSTERS	LIONEL	LIPPERING*	LIQUORING
LINGERS	LINKUP*	LIONELS	LIPPERS*	LIQUORISH
LINGIER	LINKUPS*	LIONESS	LIPPIE	LIQUORS
LINGIEST	LINKWORK	LIONESSES	LIPPIER	LIRA
LINGLE	LINKWORKS	LIONET	LIPPIES	LIRAS
LINGLES	LINKY*	LIONETS	LIPPIEST	LIRE
LINGO	LINN	LIONFISH*	LIPPING	LIRI*
LINGOES	LINNED	LIONFISHES*	LIPPINGS*	LIRIPIPE
LINGOT	LINNET	LIONISE	LIPPITUDE	LIRIPIPES
LINGOTS	LINNETS	LIONISED	LIPPITUDES	LIRIPOOP
LINGS	LINNEY	LIONISER*	LIPPY	LIRIPOOPS
LINGSTER	LINNEYS	LIONISERS*	LIPS	LIRK
LINGSTERS	LINNIES	LIONISES	LIPSTICK	LIRKED
LINGUA	LINNING	LIONISING	LIPSTICKED	LIRKING
LINGUAE	LINNS	LIONISM	LIPSTICKING	LIRKS
LINGUAL	LINNY	LIONISMS	LIPSTICKS	LIROT*
LINGUALLY	LINO	LIONIZE	LIQUABLE	LIROTH*
LINGUALS*	LINOCUT	LIONIZED	LIQUATE	LIS
LINGUAS	LINOCUTS	LIONIZER*	LIQUATED	LISENTE*
LINGUINE	LINOLEATE*	LIONIZERS*	LIQUATES	LISK
LINGUINES*	LINOLEATES*	LIONIZES	LIQUATING	LISKS
LINGUINI	LINOLEUM	LIONIZING	LIQUATION	LISLE
LINGUINIS*	LINOLEUMS	LIONLIKE	LIQUATIONS	LISLES
LINGUIST	LINOS	LIONLY	LIQUEFIED	LISP
LINGUISTS	LINS	LIONS	LIQUEFIER	LISPED
LINGULA	LINSANG	LIP	LIQUEFIERS	LISPER
LINGULAE	LINSANGS	LIPARITE	LIQUEFIES	LISPERS
LINGULAR	LINSEED	LIPARITES	LIQUEFY	LISPING
LINGULAS	LINSEEDS	LIPASE	LIQUEFYING	LISPINGLY
LINGULATE	LINSEY	LIPASES	LIQUESCE	LISPINGS
LINGY	LINSEYS	LIPECTOMIES	LIQUESCED	LISPOUND
LINHAY	LINSTOCK	LIPECTOMY	LIQUESCES	LISPOUNDS
LINHAYS	LINSTOCKS	LIPID	LIQUESCING	LISPS
LINIER	LINT	LIPIDE	LIQUEUR	LISPUND
LINIEST	LINTEL	LIPIDES	LIQUEURED	LISPUNDS
LINIMENT	LINTELLED	LIPIDIC*	LIQUEURING	LISSES
LINIMENTS	LINTELS	LIPIDS	LIQUEURS	LISSOM
LININ	LINTER	LIPIN*	LIQUID	LISSOME
LINING	LINTERS	LIPINS*	LIQUIDATE	LISSOMELY
LININGS	LINTIE	LIPLESS	LIQUIDATED	LISSOMLY
LININS	LINTIER	LIPLIKE	LIQUIDATES	LIST
LINISH	LINTIES	LIPOCYTE*	LIQUIDATING	LISTABLE*
LINISHED	LINTIEST	LIPOCYTES*	LIQUIDISE	LISTED
LINISHER	LINTLESS*	LIPOGRAM	LIQUIDISED	LISTEE*
LINISHERS	LINTOL*	LIPOGRAMS	LIQUIDISES	LISTEES*
LINISHES	LINTOLS*	LIPOID	LIQUIDISING	LISTEL
LINISHING	LINTS	LIPOIDAL*	LIQUIDITIES	LISTELS
LINISHINGS	LINTSEED	LIPOIDS	LIQUIDITY	LISTEN
LINK	LINTSEEDS	LIPOLYSES*	LIQUIDIZE	LISTENED
LINKABLE	LINTSTOCK	LIPOLYSIS*	LIQUIDIZED	LISTENER
LINKAGE	LINTSTOCKS	LIPOLYTIC*	LIQUIDIZES	LISTENERS
LINKAGES	LINTWHITE	LIPOMA	LIQUIDIZING	LISTENING
LINKBOY	LINTWHITES	LIPOMAS*	LIQUIDLY	LISTENS
LINKBOYS	LINTY	LIPOMATA	LIQUIDS	LISTER
LINKED	LINUM*	LIPOSOMAL	LIQUIDUS	LISTERIA
LINKER	LINUMS*	LIPOSOME	LIQUIDUSES	LISTERIAS
LINKERS	LINURON*	LIPOSOMES	LIQUIFIED*	LISTERS
LINKING	LINURONS*	LIPPED	LIQUIFIES*	LISTETH
LINKMAN	LINY	LIPPEN	LIQUIFY*	LISTFUL
LINKMEN	LION	LIPPENED	LIQUIFYING*	LISTING

The Chambers Dictionary is the authority for many longer words; see Introduction, page ix

LISTINGS	LITHO	LITURGIC	LIVINGS	LOANBACK
LISTLESS	LITHOCYST	LITURGICS	LIVOR	LOANBACKS
LISTS	LITHOCYSTS	LITURGIES	LIVORS	LOANED
LIT	LITHOED*	LITURGIST	LIVRAISON	LOANER*
LITAI*	LITHOID	LITURGISTS	LIVRAISONS	LOANERS*
LITANIES	LITHOIDAL	LITURGY	LIVRE	LOANING
LITANY	LITHOING*	LITUUS	LIVRES	LOANINGS
LITAS*	LITHOLOGIES	LITUUSES	LIVYER*	LOANS
LITCHI	LITHOLOGY	LIVABLE	LIVYERS*	LOANWORD*
LITCHIS	LITHOPONE	LIVE	LIXIVIA	LOANWORDS*
LITE	LITHOPONES	LIVEABLE	LIXIVIAL	LOAST
LITED	LITHOS	LIVED	LIXIVIATE	LOATH
LITER	LITHOSOL*	LIVELIER	LIXIVIATED	LOATHE
LITERACIES	LITHOSOLS*	LIVELIEST	LIXIVIATES	LOATHED
LITERACY	LITHOTOME	LIVELILY	LIXIVIATING	LOATHER
LITERAL	LITHOTOMES	LIVELOD	LIXIVIOUS	LOATHERS
LITERALLY	LITHOTOMIES	LIVELODS	LIXIVIUM	LOATHES
LITERALS	LITHOTOMY	LIVELONG	LIXIVIUMS	LOATHEST
LITERARY	LITHS	LIVELONGS	LIZARD	LOATHFUL
LITERATE	LITIGABLE	LIVELOOD	LIZARDS	LOATHING
LITERATES	LITIGANT	LIVELOODS	LLAMA	LOATHINGS
LITERATI	LITIGANTS	LIVELY	LLAMAS	LOATHLY
LITERATIM	LITIGATE	LIVEN	LLANERO	LOATHNESS*
LITERATO	LITIGATED	LIVENED	LLANEROS	LOATHNESSES*
LITERATOR	LITIGATES	LIVENER	LLANO	LOATHSOME
LITERATORS	LITIGATING	LIVENERS	LLANOS	LOATHY
LITERATUS	LITIGATOR*	LIVENESS*	LO	LOAVE
LITEROSE	LITIGATORS*	LIVENESSES*	LOACH	LOAVED
LITERS	LITIGIOUS	LIVENING	LOACHES	LOAVES
LITES	LITING	LIVENS	LOAD	LOAVING
LITH	LITMUS	LIVER	LOADED	LOB
LITHARGE	LITMUSES	LIVERIED	LOADEN	LOBAR
LITHARGES	LITORAL*	LIVERIES	LOADENED	LOBATE
LITHATE	LITOTES	LIVERISH	LOADENING	LOBATED*
LITHATES	LITOTIC*	LIVERS	LOADENS	LOBATELY*
LITHE	LITRE	LIVERWING	LOADER	LOBATION
LITHED	LITRES	LIVERWINGS	LOADERS	LOBATIONS
LITHELY	LITS*	LIVERWORT	LOADING	LOBBED
LITHEMIA*	LITTEN	LIVERWORTS	LOADINGS	LOBBER*
LITHEMIAS*	LITTER	LIVERY	LOADS	LOBBERS*
LITHEMIC*	LITTERBAG*	LIVERYMAN	LOADSTAR	LOBBIED
LITHENESS	LITTERBAGS*	LIVERYMEN	LOADSTARS	LOBBIES
LITHENESSES	LITTERBUG*	LIVES	LOADSTONE	LOBBING
LITHER	LITTERBUGS*	LIVEST	LOADSTONES	LOBBY
LITHERLY	LITTERED	LIVESTOCK	LOAF	LOBBYER
LITHES	LITTERER*	LIVESTOCKS	LOAFED	LOBBYERS
LITHESOME	LITTERERS*	LIVETRAP*	LOAFER	LOBBYGOW*
LITHEST	LITTERING	LIVETRAPPED*	LOAFERISH	LOBBYGOWS*
LITHIA	LITTERS	LIVETRAPPING*	LOAFERS	LOBBYING
LITHIAS	LITTERY	LIVETRAPS*	LOAFING	LOBBYINGS
LITHIASES	LITTLE	LIVEWARE	LOAFINGS	LOBBYISM*
LITHIASIS	LITTLEANE	LIVEWARES	LOAFS	LOBBYISMS*
LITHIC	LITTLEANES	LIVID	LOAM	LOBBYIST
LITHIFIED*	LITTLER	LIVIDER	LOAMED	LOBBYISTS
LITHIFIES*	LITTLES	LIVIDEST	LOAMIER	LOBE
LITHIFY*	LITTLEST	LIVIDITIES	LOAMIEST	LOBECTOMIES
LITHIFYING*	LITTLIN	LIVIDITY	LOAMINESS	LOBECTOMY
LITHING	LITTLING	LIVIDLY	LOAMINESSES	LOBED
LITHISTID	LITTLINGS	LIVIDNESS	LOAMING	LOBEFIN*
LITHISTIDS	LITTLINS	LIVIDNESSES	LOAMLESS*	LOBEFINS*
LITHITE	LITTLISH*	LIVIER*	LOAMS	LOBELET
LITHITES	LITTORAL	LIVIERS*	LOAMY	LOBELETS
LITHIUM	LITTORALS	LIVING	LOAN	LOBELIA
LITHIUMS	LITU*	LIVINGLY*	LOANABLE	LOBELIAS

Words marked with an asterisk are from OTCWL

LOBELINE	LOCATERS*	LOCOING*	LODICULE	LOGICIZE
LOBELINES	LOCATES	LOCOISM*	LODICULES	LOGICIZED
LOBES	LOCATING	LOCOISMS*	LODS	LOGICIZES
LOBI	LOCATION	LOCOMAN	LOESS	LOGICIZING
LOBING	LOCATIONS	LOCOMEN	LOESSAL*	LOGICS
LOBINGS	LOCATIVE	LOCOMOTE	LOESSES	LOGIE
LOBIPED	LOCATIVES	LOCOMOTED	LOESSIAL*	LOGIER
LOBLOLLIES	LOCATOR*	LOCOMOTES	LOFT	LOGIES
LOBLOLLY	LOCATORS*	LOCOMOTING	LOFTED	LOGIEST
LOBO	LOCELLATE	LOCOMOTOR	LOFTER	LOGILY*
LOBOS	LOCH	LOCOMOTORS	LOFTERS	LOGIN
LOBOSE	LOCHAN	LOCOPLANT	LOFTIER	LOGINESS*
LOBOTOMIES	LOCHANS	LOCOPLANTS	LOFTIEST	LOGINESSES*
LOBOTOMY	LOCHIA	LOCOS	LOFTILY	LOGINS
LOBS	LOCHIAL	LOCOWEED	LOFTINESS	LOGION
LOBSCOUSE	LOCHS	LOCOWEEDS	LOFTINESSES	LOGIONS*
LOBSCOUSES	LOCI	LOCULAR	LOFTING	LOGISTIC
LOBSTER	LOCK	LOCULATE	LOFTLESS*	LOGISTICS
LOBSTERED*	LOCKABLE	LOCULE	LOFTLIKE*	LOGJAM*
LOBSTERING*	LOCKAGE	LOCULED*	LOFTS	LOGJAMS*
LOBSTERS	LOCKAGES	LOCULES	LOFTY	LOGJUICE
LOBSTICK*	LOCKAWAY	LOCULI	LOG	LOGJUICES
LOBSTICKS*	LOCKAWAYS	LOCULUS	LOGAN	LOGLINE
LOBULAR	LOCKBOX*	LOCUM	LOGANIA	LOGLINES
LOBULATE	LOCKBOXES*	LOCUMS	LOGANIAS	LOGLOG
LOBULATED	LOCKDOWN*	LOCUPLETE	LOGANS	LOGLOGS
LOBULE	LOCKDOWNS*	LOCUS	LOGAOEDIC	LOGNORMAL*
LOBULES	LOCKED	LOCUST	LOGAOEDICS*	LOGO
LOBULI	LOCKER	LOCUSTA	LOGARITHM	LOGOFF
LOBULOSE*	LOCKERS	LOCUSTAE	LOGARITHMS	LOGOFFS
LOBULUS	LOCKET	LOCUSTAL*	LOGBOARD	LOGOGRAM
LOBUS	LOCKETS	LOCUSTED	LOGBOARDS	LOGOGRAMS
LOBWORM	LOCKFAST	LOCUSTING	LOGBOOK	LOGOGRAPH
LOBWORMS	LOCKFUL	LOCUSTS	LOGBOOKS	LOGOGRAPHS
LOCA*	LOCKFULS	LOCUTION	LOGE	LOGOGRIPH
LOCAL	LOCKHOUSE	LOCUTIONS	LOGES	LOGOGRIPHS
LOCALE	LOCKHOUSES	LOCUTORIES	LOGGAT	LOGOI*
LOCALES	LOCKING	LOCUTORY	LOGGATS	LOGOMACH*
LOCALISE	LOCKJAW	LOD	LOGGED	LOGOMACHIES
LOCALISED	LOCKJAWS	LODE	LOGGER	LOGOMACHS*
LOCALISER	LOCKMAN	LODEN	LOGGERS	LOGOMACHY
LOCALISERS	LOCKMEN	LODENS	LOGGETS*	LOGON
LOCALISES	LOCKNUT*	LODES	LOGGIA	LOGONS
LOCALISING	LOCKNUTS*	LODESMAN	LOGGIAS	LOGOPEDIC
LOCALISM	LOCKOUT	LODESMEN	LOGGIE	LOGOPHILE
LOCALISMS	LOCKOUTS	LODESTAR	LOGGIER*	LOGOPHILES
LOCALIST	LOCKPICK	LODESTARS	LOGGIEST*	LOGORRHEA
LOCALISTS	LOCKPICKS	LODESTONE	LOGGING	LOGORRHEAS
LOCALITE*	LOCKRAM	LODESTONES	LOGGINGS	LOGOS
LOCALITES*	LOCKS	LODGE	LOGGY*	LOGOTHETE
LOCALITIES	LOCKSMAN	LODGED	LOGIA	LOGOTHETES
LOCALITY	LOCKSMEN	LODGEMENT	LOGIC	LOGOTYPE
LOCALIZE	LOCKSMITH	LODGEMENTS	LOGICAL	LOGOTYPES
LOCALIZED	LOCKSMITHS	LODGEPOLE	LOGICALLY	LOGOTYPIES*
LOCALIZER	LOCKSTEP	LODGEPOLES	LOGICIAN	LOGOTYPY*
LOCALIZERS	LOCKSTEPS	LODGER	LOGICIANS	LOGOUT
LOCALIZES	LOCKUP*	LODGERS	LOGICISE	LOGOUTS
LOCALIZING	LOCKUPS*	LODGES	LOGICISED	LOGROLL*
LOCALLY	LOCO	LODGING	LOGICISES	LOGROLLED*
LOCALS	LOCOED	LODGINGS	LOGICISING	LOGROLLER*
LOCATABLE	LOCOES	LODGMENT	LOGICISM	LOGROLLERS*
LOCATE	LOCOFOCO	LODGMENTS	LOGICISMS	LOGROLLING*
LOCATED	LOCOFOCOS	LODICULA	LOGICIST	LOGROLLS*
LOCATER*		LODICULAE	LOGICISTS	LOGS

The Chambers Dictionary is the authority for many longer words; see Introduction, page ix

LOGWAY*	LOMENTUM	LONGLY	LOONINESS	LOPPIEST*
LOGWAYS*	LOMENTUMS*	LONGNESS	LOONINESSES	LOPPING
LOGWOOD	LOMES	LONGNESSES	LOONING	LOPPINGS
LOGWOODS	LOMING	LONGS	LOONINGS	LOPPY*
LOGY	LOMPISH	LONGSHIP	LOONS	LOPS
LOID	LONE	LONGSHIPS	LOONY	LOPSIDED
LOIDED	LONELIER	LONGSHORE	LOOP	LOPSTICK*
LOIDING	LONELIEST	LONGSOME	LOOPED	LOPSTICKS*
LOIDS	LONELILY*	LONGSPUR*	LOOPER	LOQUACITIES
LOIN	LONELY	LONGSPURS*	LOOPERS	LOQUACITY
LOINCLOTH	LONENESS	LONGTIME*	LOOPHOLE	LOQUAT
LOINCLOTHS	LONENESSES	LONGUEUR	LOOPHOLED	LOQUATS
LOINS	LONER	LONGUEURS	LOOPHOLES	LOQUITUR
LOIPE	LONERS	LONGWALL	LOOPHOLING	LOR
LOIPEN	LONESOME	LONGWALLS	LOOPIER	LORAL
LOIR	LONESOMES	LONGWAYS	LOOPIEST	LORAN
LOIRS	LONG	LONGWISE	LOOPING	LORANS
LOITER	LONGA	LONICERA	LOOPINGS	LORATE
LOITERED	LONGAEVAL	LONICERAS	LOOPS	LORAZEPAM
LOITERER	LONGAN	LOO	LOOPY	LORAZEPAMS
LOITERERS	LONGANS	LOOBIER	LOOR	LORCHA
LOITERING	LONGAS	LOOBIES	LOORD	LORCHAS
LOITERINGS	LONGBOAT	LOOBIEST	LOORDS	LORD
LOITERS	LONGBOATS	LOOBILY	LOOS	LORDED
LOKE	LONGBOW	LOOBY	LOOSE	LORDING
LOKES	LONGBOWS	LOOED	LOOSED	LORDINGS
LOKSHEN	LONGCLOTH	LOOEY*	LOOSELY	LORDKIN
LOLIGO	LONGCLOTHS	LOOEYS*	LOOSEN	LORDKINS
LOLIGOS	LONGE	LOOF	LOOSENED	LORDLESS
LOLIUM	LONGED	LOOFA	LOOSENER	LORDLIER
LOLIUMS	LONGEING	LOOFAH	LOOSENERS	LORDLIEST
LOLL	LONGER	LOOFAHS	LOOSENESS	LORDLIKE*
LOLLED	LONGERON	LOOFAS	LOOSENESSES	LORDLING
LOLLER	LONGERONS	LOOFFUL	LOOSENING	LORDLINGS
LOLLERS	LONGERS*	LOOFFULS	LOOSENS	LORDLY
LOLLIES	LONGES	LOOFS	LOOSER	LORDOMA*
LOLLING	LONGEST	LOOIE*	LOOSES	LORDOMAS*
LOLLINGLY	LONGEVAL	LOOIES*	LOOSEST	LORDOSES
LOLLIPOP	LONGEVITIES	LOOING	LOOSING	LORDOSIS
LOLLIPOPS	LONGEVITY	LOOK	LOOT	LORDOTIC
LOLLOP	LONGEVOUS	LOOKDOWN*	LOOTED	LORDS
LOLLOPED	LONGHAIR*	LOOKDOWNS*	LOOTEN	LORDSHIP
LOLLOPING	LONGHAIRS*	LOOKED	LOOTER	LORDSHIPS
LOLLOPS	LONGHAND	LOOKER	LOOTERS	LORDY
LOLLS	LONGHANDS	LOOKERS	LOOTING	LORE
LOLLY	LONGHEAD*	LOOKING	LOOTINGS	LOREAL*
LOLLYGAG	LONGHEADS*	LOOKISM	LOOTS	LOREL
LOLLYGAGGED	LONGHORN	LOOKISMS	LOOVES	LORELS
LOLLYGAGGING	LONGHORNS	LOOKOUT	LOP	LORES
LOLLYGAGS	LONGHOUSE	LOOKOUTS	LOPE	LORETTE
LOLLYPOP*	LONGHOUSES	LOOKS	LOPED	LORETTES
LOLLYPOPS*	LONGICORN	LOOKUP*	LOPER	LORGNETTE
LOLOG	LONGICORNS	LOOKUPS*	LOPERS	LORGNETTES
LOLOGS	LONGIES*	LOOM	LOPES	LORGNON
LOMA	LONGING	LOOMED	LOPGRASS	LORGNONS
LOMAS	LONGINGLY	LOOMING	LOPGRASSES	LORIC
LOMATA	LONGINGS	LOOMS	LOPHODONT	LORICA
LOME	LONGISH	LOON	LOPING	LORICAE
LOMED	LONGITUDE	LOONEY*	LOPPED	LORICATE
LOMEIN*	LONGITUDES	LOONEYS*	LOPPER	LORICATED
LOMEINS*	LONGLEAF*	LOONIE	LOPPERED	LORICATES
LOMENT	LONGLEAVES*	LOONIER	LOPPERING	LORICATING
LOMENTA	LONGLINE*	LOONIES	LOPPERS	LORICS
LOMENTS	LONGLINES*	LOONIEST	LOPPIER*	LORIES

LORIKEET	LOTOS	LOUPIT	LOVEMAKER	LOWLIGHTING
LORIKEETS	LOTOSES	LOUPS	LOVEMAKERS	LOWLIGHTS
LORIMER	LOTS	LOUR	LOVER	LOWLIHEAD
LORIMERS	LOTTE*	LOURE	LOVERED	LOWLIHEADS
LORINER	LOTTED	LOURED	LOVERLESS	LOWLILY
LORINERS	LOTTERIES	LOURES	LOVERLY	LOWLINESS
LORING	LOTTERY	LOURIER	LOVERS	LOWLINESSES
LORINGS	LOTTES*	LOURIEST	LOVES	LOWLIVES*
LORIOT	LOTTING	LOURING	LOVESICK	LOWLY
LORIOTS	LOTTO	LOURINGLY	LOVESOME	LOWN
LORIS	LOTTOS	LOURINGS	LOVEVINE*	LOWND
LORISES	LOTUS	LOURS	LOVEVINES*	LOWNDED
LORN	LOTUSES	LOURY	LOVEY	LOWNDING
LORNNESS*	LOTUSLAND*	LOUSE	LOVEYS	LOWNDS
LORNNESSES*	LOTUSLANDS*	LOUSED	LOVING	LOWNE
LORRELL	LOUCHE	LOUSES	LOVINGLY	LOWNED
LORRELLS	LOUCHELY	LOUSEWORT*	LOVINGS	LOWNES
LORRIES	LOUD	LOUSEWORTS*	LOW	LOWNESS
LORRY	LOUDEN	LOUSIER	LOWAN	LOWNESSES
LORY	LOUDENED	LOUSIEST	LOWANS	LOWNING
LOS	LOUDENING	LOUSILY	LOWBALL*	LOWNS
LOSABLE	LOUDENS	LOUSINESS	LOWBALLED*	LOWRIDER*
LOSE	LOUDER	LOUSINESSES	LOWBALLING*	LOWRIDERS*
LOSED	LOUDEST	LOUSING	LOWBALLS*	LOWS
LOSEL	LOUDISH	LOUSY	LOWBORN*	LOWSE
LOSELS	LOUDLIER*	LOUT	LOWBOY	LOWSER
LOSEN	LOUDLIEST*	LOUTED	LOWBOYS	LOWSES
LOSER	LOUDLY	LOUTING	LOWBRED*	LOWSEST
LOSERS	LOUDMOUTH	LOUTISH	LOWBROW*	LOWSING
LOSES	LOUDMOUTHS	LOUTISHLY	LOWBROWS*	LOWSIT
LOSH	LOUDNESS	LOUTS	LOWDOWN*	LOWT
LOSING	LOUDNESSES	LOUVER	LOWDOWNS*	LOWTED
LOSINGLY	LOUGH	LOUVERED	LOWE	LOWTING
LOSINGS	LOUGHS	LOUVERS	LOWED	LOWTS
LOSS	LOUIE*	LOUVRE	LOWER	LOWVELD
LOSSES	LOUIES*	LOUVRED	LOWERCASE*	LOWVELDS
LOSSIER	LOUIS	LOUVRES	LOWERCASED*	LOX
LOSSIEST	LOUN	LOVABLE	LOWERCASES*	LOXED*
LOSSMAKER	LOUND	LOVABLY*	LOWERCASING*	LOXES
LOSSMAKERS	LOUNDED	LOVAGE	LOWERED	LOXING*
LOSSY	LOUNDER	LOVAGES	LOWERIER	LOXODROME
LOST	LOUNDERED	LOVAT	LOWERIEST	LOXODROMES
LOSTNESS*	LOUNDERING	LOVATS	LOWERING	LOXODROMIES
LOSTNESSES*	LOUNDERINGS	LOVE	LOWERINGS	LOXODROMY
LOT	LOUNDERS	LOVEABLE	LOWERMOST	LOXYGEN
LOTA	LOUNDING	LOVEABLY*	LOWERS	LOXYGENS
LOTAH	LOUNDS	LOVEBIRD	LOWERY	LOY
LOTAHS	LOUNED	LOVEBIRDS	LOWES	LOYAL
LOTAS	LOUNGE	LOVEBITE	LOWEST	LOYALER*
LOTE	LOUNGED	LOVEBITES	LOWING	LOYALEST*
LOTES	LOUNGER	LOVEBUG*	LOWINGS	LOYALISM*
LOTH	LOUNGERS	LOVEBUGS*	LOWISH*	LOYALISMS*
LOTHARIO*	LOUNGES	LOVED	LOWLAND	LOYALIST
LOTHARIOS*	LOUNGING	LOVELESS	LOWLANDER	LOYALISTS
LOTHEFULL	LOUNGINGS	LOVELIER	LOWLANDERS	LOYALLER
LOTHER	LOUNGY*	LOVELIES	LOWLANDS	LOYALLEST
LOTHEST	LOUNING	LOVELIEST	LOWLIER	LOYALLY
LOTHFULL	LOUNS	LOVELIGHT	LOWLIEST	LOYALTIES
LOTHSOME*	LOUP	LOVELIGHTS	LOWLIFE*	LOYALTY
LOTI*	LOUPE	LOVELILY	LOWLIFER*	LOYS
LOTIC	LOUPED	LOVELOCK	LOWLIFERS*	LOZELL
LOTION	LOUPEN	LOVELOCKS	LOWLIFES*	LOZELLS
LOTIONS	LOUPES	LOVELORN	LOWLIGHT	LOZEN
LOTO	LOUPING	LOVELY	LOWLIGHTED	LOZENGE

LOZENGED	LUCKINESS	LUGSAIL	LUMINING	LUNCHERS
LOZENGES	LUCKINESSES	LUGSAILS	LUMINISM*	LUNCHES
LOZENGY	LUCKING*	LUGWORM	LUMINISMS*	LUNCHING
LOZENS	LUCKLESS	LUGWORMS	LUMINIST	LUNCHROOM*
LUAU	LUCKS	LUIT	LUMINISTS	LUNCHROOMS*
LUAUS	LUCKY	LUITEN	LUMINOUS	LUNCHTIME*
LUBBARD	LUCRATIVE	LUKE	LUMME	LUNCHTIMES*
LUBBARDS	LUCRE	LUKEWARM	LUMMIER	LUNE
LUBBER	LUCRES	LULIBUB	LUMMIEST	LUNES
LUBBERLY	LUCTATION	LULIBUBS	LUMMOX	LUNET*
LUBBERS	LUCTATIONS	LULL	LUMMOXES	LUNETS*
LUBE*	LUCUBRATE	LULLABIED	LUMMY	LUNETTE
LUBES*	LUCUBRATED	LULLABIES	LUMP	LUNETTES
LUBFISH	LUCUBRATES	LULLABY	LUMPED	LUNG
LUBFISHES	LUCUBRATING	LULLABYING	LUMPEN	LUNGAN*
LUBRA	LUCULENT	LULLED	LUMPENLY	LUNGANS*
LUBRAS	LUCUMA	LULLING	LUMPENS*	LUNGE
LUBRIC	LUCUMAS	LULLS	LUMPER	LUNGED
LUBRICAL	LUCUMO	LULU	LUMPERS	LUNGEE*
LUBRICANT	LUCUMONES	LULUS	LUMPFISH	LUNGEES*
LUBRICANTS	LUCUMOS	LUM	LUMPFISHES	LUNGEING
LUBRICATE	LUD	LUMBAGO	LUMPIER	LUNGER*
LUBRICATED	LUDE*	LUMBAGOS	LUMPIEST	LUNGERS*
LUBRICATES	LUDES*	LUMBANG	LUMPILY	LUNGES
LUBRICATING	LUDIC	LUMBANGS	LUMPINESS	LUNGFISH*
LUBRICITIES	LUDICALLY	LUMBAR	LUMPINESSES	LUNGFISHES*
LUBRICITY	LUDICROUS	LUMBARS*	LUMPING	LUNGFUL
LUBRICOUS	LUDO	LUMBER	LUMPISH	LUNGFULS
LUCARNE	LUDOS	LUMBERED	LUMPISHLY	LUNGI
LUCARNES	LUDS	LUMBERER	LUMPKIN	LUNGIE
LUCE	LUDSHIP	LUMBERERS	LUMPKINS	LUNGIES
LUCENCE*	LUDSHIPS	LUMBERING	LUMPS	LUNGING
LUCENCES*	LUES	LUMBERINGS	LUMPY	LUNGIS
LUCENCIES	LUETIC	LUMBERLY	LUMS	LUNGS
LUCENCY	LUETICS*	LUMBERMAN	LUNA	LUNGWORM*
LUCENT	LUFF	LUMBERMEN	LUNACIES	LUNGWORMS*
LUCENTLY*	LUFFA	LUMBERS	LUNACY	LUNGWORT
LUCERN	LUFFAS	LUMBRICAL	LUNANAUT	LUNGWORTS
LUCERNE	LUFFED	LUMBRICALS	LUNANAUTS	LUNGYI*
LUCERNES	LUFFING	LUMBRICI	LUNAR	LUNGYIS*
LUCERNS	LUFFS	LUMBRICUS	LUNARIAN	LUNIER*
LUCES	LUG	LUMBRICUSES	LUNARIANS	LUNIES*
LUCID	LUGE	LUMEN	LUNARIES	LUNIEST*
LUCIDER	LUGED	LUMENAL	LUNARIST	LUNISOLAR
LUCIDEST	LUGEING	LUMENS	LUNARISTS	LUNITIDAL
LUCIDITIES	LUGEINGS	LUMINA	LUNARNAUT	LUNK*
LUCIDITY	LUGER	LUMINAIRE	LUNARNAUTS	LUNKER
LUCIDLY	LUGERS	LUMINAIRES	LUNARS	LUNKERS
LUCIDNESS	LUGES	LUMINAL	LUNARY	LUNKHEAD
LUCIDNESSES	LUGGABLE	LUMINANCE	LUNAS	LUNKHEADS
LUCIFER	LUGGABLES	LUMINANCES	LUNATE	LUNKS*
LUCIFERIN	LUGGAGE	LUMINANT	LUNATED	LUNT
LUCIFERINS	LUGGAGES	LUMINANTS	LUNATELY*	LUNTED
LUCIFERS	LUGGED	LUMINARIA*	LUNATIC	LUNTING
LUCIGEN	LUGGER	LUMINARIAS*	LUNATICS	LUNTS
LUCIGENS	LUGGERS	LUMINARIES	LUNATION	LUNULA
LUCK	LUGGIE	LUMINARY	LUNATIONS	LUNULAE
LUCKED*	LUGGIES	LUMINE	LUNCH	LUNULAR
LUCKEN	LUGGING	LUMINED	LUNCHED	LUNULATE
LUCKIE	LUGHOLE	LUMINES	LUNCHEON	LUNULATED
LUCKIER	LUGHOLES	LUMINESCE	LUNCHEONED	LUNULE
LUCKIES	LUGING	LUMINESCED	LUNCHEONING	LUNULES
LUCKIEST	LUGINGS	LUMINESCES	LUNCHEONS	LUNY*
LUCKILY	LUGS	LUMINESCING	LUNCHER	LUNYIE

LUNYIES
LUPANAR*
LUPANARS*
LUPIN
LUPINE
LUPINES
LUPINS
LUPOUS*
LUPPEN
LUPULIN
LUPULINE
LUPULINIC
LUPULINS
LUPUS
LUPUSES
LUR
LURCH
LURCHED
LURCHER
LURCHERS
LURCHES
LURCHING
LURDAN
LURDANE
LURDANES
LURDANS
LURDEN
LURDENS
LURE
LURED
LURER*
LURERS*
LURES
LURGI
LURGIES
LURGIS
LURGY
LURID
LURIDER
LURIDEST
LURIDLY
LURIDNESS
LURIDNESSES
LURING
LURK
LURKED
LURKER
LURKERS
LURKING
LURKINGS
LURKS
LURRIES
LURRY
LURS
LURVE
LURVES
LUSCIOUS
LUSH
LUSHED
LUSHER
LUSHERS
LUSHES
LUSHEST
LUSHIER

LUSHIEST
LUSHING
LUSHLY
LUSHNESS
LUSHNESSES
LUSHY
LUSK
LUSKED
LUSKING
LUSKISH
LUSKS
LUST
LUSTED
LUSTER
LUSTERED
LUSTERING
LUSTERS
LUSTFUL
LUSTFULLY
LUSTICK
LUSTIER
LUSTIEST
LUSTIHEAD
LUSTIHEADS
LUSTIHOOD
LUSTIHOODS
LUSTILY
LUSTINESS
LUSTINESSES
LUSTING
LUSTIQUE
LUSTLESS
LUSTRA
LUSTRAL
LUSTRATE
LUSTRATED
LUSTRATES
LUSTRATING
LUSTRE
LUSTRED
LUSTRES
LUSTRINE
LUSTRINES
LUSTRING
LUSTRINGS
LUSTROUS
LUSTRUM
LUSTRUMS
LUSTS
LUSTY
LUSUS*
LUSUSES*
LUTANIST
LUTANISTS
LUTE
LUTEA*
LUTEAL
LUTECIUM
LUTECIUMS
LUTED
LUTEFISK*
LUTEFISKS*
LUTEIN
LUTEINISE

LUTEINISED
LUTEINISES
LUTEINISING
LUTEINIZE
LUTEINIZED
LUTEINIZES
LUTEINIZING
LUTEINS
LUTENIST
LUTENISTS
LUTEOLIN
LUTEOLINS
LUTEOLOUS
LUTEOUS
LUTER
LUTERS
LUTES
LUTESCENT
LUTETIUM
LUTETIUMS
LUTEUM*
LUTHERN
LUTHERNS
LUTHIER
LUTHIERS
LUTING
LUTINGS
LUTIST
LUTISTS
LUTTEN
LUTZ
LUTZES
LUV
LUVS
LUVVIE
LUVVIES
LUVVY
LUX
LUXATE
LUXATED
LUXATES
LUXATING
LUXATION
LUXATIONS
LUXE
LUXES
LUXMETER
LUXMETERS
LUXURIANT
LUXURIATE
LUXURIATED
LUXURIATES
LUXURIATING
LUXURIES
LUXURIOUS
LUXURIST
LUXURISTS
LUXURY
LUZ
LUZERN
LUZERNS
LUZZES
LWEI*
LWEIS*

LYAM
LYAMS
LYARD*
LYART
LYASE*
LYASES*
LYCEA*
LYCEE
LYCEES
LYCEUM
LYCEUMS
LYCHEE
LYCHEES
LYCHGATE
LYCHGATES
LYCHNIS
LYCHNISES
LYCOPENE*
LYCOPENES*
LYCOPOD
LYCOPODS
LYDDITE
LYDDITES
LYE
LYES
LYFULL
LYING
LYINGLY
LYINGS
LYKEWAKE
LYKEWAKES
LYKEWALK
LYKEWALKS
LYM
LYME
LYMES
LYMITER
LYMITERS
LYMPH
LYMPHAD
LYMPHADS
LYMPHATIC
LYMPHATICS
LYMPHOID
LYMPHOMA
LYMPHOMAS
LYMPHOMATA
LYMPHS
LYMS
LYNAGE
LYNAGES
LYNCEAN
LYNCH
LYNCHED
LYNCHER*
LYNCHERS*
LYNCHES
LYNCHET
LYNCHETS
LYNCHING
LYNCHINGS*
LYNCHPIN
LYNCHPINS
LYNE

LYNES
LYNX
LYNXES
LYOMEROUS
LYONNAISE
LYOPHIL
LYOPHILE
LYOPHILED*
LYOPHILIC
LYOPHOBE
LYOPHOBIC
LYRATE
LYRATED
LYRATELY*
LYRE
LYREBIRD*
LYREBIRDS*
LYRES
LYRIC
LYRICAL
LYRICALLY
LYRICISE*
LYRICISED*
LYRICISES*
LYRICISING*
LYRICISM
LYRICISMS
LYRICIST
LYRICISTS
LYRICIZE*
LYRICIZED*
LYRICIZES*
LYRICIZING*
LYRICON
LYRICONS
LYRICS
LYRIFORM
LYRISM
LYRISMS
LYRIST
LYRISTS
LYSATE*
LYSATES*
LYSE
LYSED
LYSERGIDE
LYSERGIDES
LYSES
LYSIGENIC
LYSIMETER
LYSIMETERS
LYSIN
LYSINE
LYSINES
LYSING
LYSINS
LYSIS
LYSOGEN*
LYSOGENIC*
LYSOGENIES*
LYSOGENS*
LYSOGENY*
LYSOL
LYSOLS

The Chambers Dictionary is the authority for many longer words; see Introduction, page ix

LYSOSOMAL*	LYSOZYMES	LYTED	LYTIC*	LYTTAE
LYSOSOME	LYSSA	LYTES	LYTICALLY*	LYTTAS
LYSOSOMES	LYSSAS	LYTHE	LYTING	
LYSOZYME	LYTE	LYTHES	LYTTA	

M

MA
MAA
MAAED
MAAING
MAAR
MAARS
MAAS
MAATJES
MABE*
MABES*
MAC
MACABER*
MACABRE
MACACO
MACACOS
MACADAM
MACADAMIA
MACADAMIAS
MACADAMS
MACAHUBA
MACAHUBAS
MACALLUM
MACALLUMS
MACAQUE
MACAQUES
MACARISE
MACARISED
MACARISES
MACARISING
MACARISM
MACARISMS
MACARIZE
MACARIZED
MACARIZES
MACARIZING
MACARONI
MACARONIC
MACARONICS
MACARONIES
MACARONIS
MACAROON
MACAROONS
MACASSAR
MACASSARS
MACAW
MACAWS
MACCABAW*
MACCABAWS*
MACCABOY*
MACCABOYS*
MACCHIA*
MACCHIE
MACCOBOY*
MACCOBOYS*
MACE

MACED
MACEDOINE
MACEDOINES
MACER
MACERATE
MACERATED
MACERATES
MACERATING
MACERATOR
MACERATORS
MACERS
MACES
MACH*
MACHAIR
MACHAIRS
MACHAN
MACHANS
MACHE*
MACHES*
MACHETE
MACHETES
MACHINATE
MACHINATED
MACHINATES
MACHINATING
MACHINE
MACHINED
MACHINERIES
MACHINERY
MACHINES
MACHINING
MACHINIST
MACHINISTS
MACHISMO
MACHISMOS
MACHMETER
MACHMETERS
MACHO
MACHOS
MACHREE
MACHREES
MACHS*
MACHZOR
MACHZORIM
MACHZORS*
MACING
MACINTOSH
MACINTOSHES
MACK
MACKEREL
MACKERELS
MACKINAW
MACKINAWS
MACKLE
MACKLED

MACKLES
MACKLING
MACKS
MACLE
MACLED
MACLES
MACON
MACONS
MACOYA
MACOYAS
MACRAME
MACRAMES
MACRAMI
MACRAMIS
MACRO
MACROBIAN
MACROCODE
MACROCODES
MACROCOPIES
MACROCOPY
MACROCOSM
MACROCOSMS
MACROCYTE
MACROCYTES
MACRODOME
MACRODOMES
MACROLOGIES
MACROLOGY
MACROMERE*
MACROMERES*
MACRON
MACRONS
MACROPOD
MACROPODS
MACROS
MACRURAL
MACRURAN*
MACRURANS*
MACRUROUS
MACS
MACTATION
MACTATIONS
MACULA
MACULAE
MACULAR
MACULAS*
MACULATE
MACULATED
MACULATES
MACULATING
MACULE
MACULED*
MACULES
MACULING*
MACULOSE

MACUMBA*
MACUMBAS*
MAD
MADAM
MADAME
MADAMED
MADAMES*
MADAMING
MADAMS
MADAROSES
MADAROSIS
MADBRAIN
MADCAP
MADCAPS
MADDED
MADDEN
MADDENED
MADDENING
MADDENS
MADDER
MADDERS
MADDEST
MADDING
MADDINGLY
MADDISH*
MADDOCK
MADDOCKS
MADE
MADEFIED
MADEFIES
MADEFY
MADEFYING
MADEIRA*
MADEIRAS*
MADELEINE
MADELEINES
MADERISE
MADERISED
MADERISES
MADERISING
MADERIZE
MADERIZED
MADERIZES
MADERIZING
MADGE
MADGES
MADHOUSE
MADHOUSES
MADID
MADLING
MADLINGS
MADLY
MADMAN
MADMEN
MADNESS

MADNESSES
MADONNA*
MADONNAS*
MADOQUA
MADOQUAS
MADRAS
MADRASA
MADRASAH
MADRASAHS
MADRASAS
MADRASES
MADRASSA
MADRASSAH
MADRASSAHS
MADRASSAS
MADRE*
MADREPORE
MADREPORES
MADRES*
MADRIGAL
MADRIGALS
MADRILENE*
MADRILENES*
MADRONA
MADRONAS
MADRONE
MADRONES
MADRONO
MADRONOS
MADS
MADURO*
MADUROS*
MADWOMAN
MADWOMEN
MADWORT
MADWORTS
MADZOON
MADZOONS
MAE
MAELID
MAELIDS
MAELSTROM
MAELSTROMS
MAENAD
MAENADES*
MAENADIC
MAENADS
MAES*
MAESTOSO
MAESTOSOS*
MAESTRI
MAESTRO
MAESTROS
MAFFIA
MAFFIAS

The Chambers Dictionary is the authority for many longer words; see Introduction, page ix

MAFFICK	MAGISTERY	MAGNOXES	MAIDHOOD	MAIN
MAFFICKED	MAGISTRAL	MAGNUM	MAIDHOODS	MAINBOOM
MAFFICKER	MAGISTRALS	MAGNUMS	MAIDING	MAINBOOMS
MAFFICKERS	MAGLEV	MAGOT	MAIDISH	MAINBRACE
MAFFICKING	MAGLEVS*	MAGOTS	MAIDISM	MAINBRACES
MAFFICKINGS	MAGMA	MAGPIE	MAIDISMS	MAINDOOR
MAFFICKS	MAGMAS	MAGPIES	MAIDLESS	MAINDOORS
MAFFLED	MAGMATA	MAGS	MAIDS	MAINED
MAFFLIN	MAGMATIC	MAGSMAN	MAIEUTIC	MAINER
MAFFLING	MAGNALIUM	MAGSMEN	MAIEUTICS	MAINEST
MAFFLINGS	MAGNALIUMS	MAGUEY	MAIGRE	MAINFRAME
MAFFLINS	MAGNATE	MAGUEYS	MAIGRES	MAINFRAMES
MAFIA	MAGNATES	MAGUS	MAIHEM*	MAINING
MAFIAS	MAGNES	MAGYAR	MAIHEMS*	MAINLAND
MAFIC	MAGNESES	MAHARAJA	MAIK	MAINLANDS
MAFICS	MAGNESIA	MAHARAJAH	MAIKO	MAINLINE
MAFIOSI	MAGNESIAN	MAHARAJAHS	MAIKOS	MAINLINED
MAFIOSO	MAGNESIAS	MAHARAJAS	MAIKS	MAINLINER
MAFTIR*	MAGNESIC*	MAHARANEE	MAIL	MAINLINERS
MAFTIRS*	MAGNESITE	MAHARANEES	MAILABLE	MAINLINES
MAG	MAGNESITES	MAHARANI	MAILBAG	MAINLINING
MAGALOG	MAGNESIUM	MAHARANIS	MAILBAGS	MAINLININGS
MAGALOGS	MAGNESIUMS	MAHARISHI	MAILBOX	MAINLY
MAGAZINE	MAGNET	MAHARISHIS	MAILBOXES	MAINMAST
MAGAZINES	MAGNETIC	MAHATMA	MAILE	MAINMASTS
MAGDALEN	MAGNETICS	MAHATMAS	MAILED	MAINOR
MAGDALENE	MAGNETISE	MAHIMAHI*	MAILER	MAINORS
MAGDALENES	MAGNETISED	MAHJONG*	MAILERS	MAINOUR
MAGDALENS	MAGNETISES	MAHJONGG*	MAILES	MAINOURS
MAGE	MAGNETISING	MAHJONGGS*	MAILGRAM	MAINPRISE
MAGENTA	MAGNETISM	MAHJONGS*	MAILGRAMMED	MAINPRISES
MAGENTAS	MAGNETISMS	MAHLSTICK	MAILGRAMMING	MAINS
MAGES	MAGNETIST	MAHLSTICKS	MAILGRAMS	MAINSAIL
MAGESHIP	MAGNETISTS	MAHMAL	MAILING	MAINSAILS
MAGESHIPS	MAGNETITE	MAHMALS	MAILINGS	MAINSHEET
MAGG	MAGNETITES	MAHOE	MAILL*	MAINSHEETS
MAGGED	MAGNETIZE	MAHOES	MAILLESS*	MAINSTAY
MAGGING	MAGNETIZED	MAHOGANIES	MAILLOT	MAINSTAYS
MAGGOT	MAGNETIZES	MAHOGANY	MAILLOTS	MAINTAIN
MAGGOTIER	MAGNETIZING	MAHONIA	MAILLS*	MAINTAINED
MAGGOTIEST	MAGNETO	MAHONIAS	MAILMAN	MAINTAINING
MAGGOTS	MAGNETON	MAHOUT	MAILMEN	MAINTAINS
MAGGOTY	MAGNETONS	MAHOUTS	MAILMERGE	MAINTOP
MAGGS	MAGNETOS	MAHSEER	MAILMERGED	MAINTOPS
MAGI	MAGNETRON	MAHSEERS	MAILMERGES	MAINYARD
MAGIAN	MAGNETRONS	MAHSIR	MAILMERGING	MAINYARDS
MAGIANISM	MAGNETS	MAHSIRS	MAILROOM	MAIOLICA
MAGIANISMS	MAGNIFIC	MAHUA	MAILROOMS	MAIOLICAS
MAGIANS	MAGNIFICO	MAHUANG*	MAILS	MAIR
MAGIC	MAGNIFICOES	MAHUANGS*	MAILSACK	MAIRE
MAGICAL	MAGNIFICOS*	MAHUAS	MAILSACKS	MAIRES
MAGICALLY	MAGNIFIED	MAHWA	MAILSHOT	MAIRS
MAGICIAN	MAGNIFIER	MAHWAS	MAILSHOTS	MAISE
MAGICIANS	MAGNIFIERS	MAHZOR	MAILSHOTTED	MAISES
MAGICKED	MAGNIFIES	MAHZORIM	MAILSHOTTING	MAIST
MAGICKING	MAGNIFY	MAHZORS*	MAILVAN	MAISTER
MAGICS	MAGNIFYING	MAID	MAILVANS	MAISTERED
MAGILP	MAGNITUDE	MAIDAN	MAIM	MAISTERING
MAGILPS	MAGNITUDES	MAIDANS	MAIMED	MAISTERS
MAGISM	MAGNOLIA	MAIDED	MAIMER*	MAISTRIES
MAGISMS	MAGNOLIAS	MAIDEN	MAIMERS*	MAISTRING
MAGISTER	MAGNON	MAIDENISH	MAIMING	MAISTRINGS
MAGISTERIES	MAGNONS	MAIDENLY	MAIMINGS	MAISTRY
MAGISTERS	MAGNOX	MAIDENS	MAIMS	MAISTS*

MAIZE
MAIZES
MAJAGUA*
MAJAGUAS*
MAJESTIC
MAJESTIES
MAJESTY
MAJLIS
MAJLISES
MAJOLICA
MAJOLICAS
MAJOR
MAJORAT
MAJORATS
MAJORDOMO*
MAJORDOMOS*
MAJORED
MAJORETTE
MAJORETTES
MAJORING
MAJORITIES
MAJORITY
MAJORLY*
MAJORS
MAJORSHIP
MAJORSHIPS
MAJUSCULE
MAJUSCULES
MAK
MAKABLE
MAKAR
MAKARS
MAKE
MAKEABLE
MAKEBATE
MAKEBATES
MAKEFAST*
MAKEFASTS*
MAKELESS
MAKEOVER
MAKEOVERS
MAKER
MAKEREADIES*
MAKEREADY*
MAKERS
MAKES
MAKESHIFT
MAKESHIFTS
MAKEUP*
MAKEUPS*
MAKIMONO
MAKIMONOS
MAKING
MAKINGS
MAKO
MAKOS
MAKS
MAKUTA*
MAL
MALACCA*
MALACCAS*
MALACHITE
MALACHITES
MALACIA

MALACIAS
MALADIES
MALADROIT
MALADY
MALAGUENA
MALAGUENAS
MALAISE
MALAISES
MALAMUTE
MALAMUTES
MALANDER
MALANDERS
MALANGA*
MALANGAS*
MALAPERT
MALAPERTS*
MALAPROP*
MALAPROPS*
MALAR
MALARIA
MALARIAL
MALARIAN
MALARIAS
MALARIOUS
MALARKEY
MALARKEYS
MALARKIES
MALARKY
MALAROMA*
MALAROMAS*
MALARS
MALATE
MALATES
MALATHION*
MALATHIONS*
MALAX
MALAXAGE
MALAXAGES
MALAXATE
MALAXATED
MALAXATES
MALAXATING
MALAXATOR
MALAXATORS
MALAXED
MALAXES
MALAXING
MALE
MALEATE
MALEATES
MALEDICT
MALEDICTED
MALEDICTING
MALEDICTS
MALEFFECT
MALEFFECTS
MALEFIC
MALEFICE
MALEFICES
MALEIC
MALEMIUT*
MALEMIUTS*
MALEMUTE
MALEMUTES

MALENESS*
MALENESSES*
MALENGINE
MALENGINES
MALES
MALFED*
MALFORMED
MALGRADO
MALGRE
MALGRED
MALGRES
MALGRING
MALI
MALIC
MALICE
MALICED
MALICES
MALICHO
MALICHOS
MALICING
MALICIOUS
MALIGN
MALIGNANT
MALIGNANTS
MALIGNED
MALIGNER
MALIGNERS
MALIGNING
MALIGNITIES
MALIGNITY
MALIGNLY
MALIGNS
MALIHINI*
MALIHINIS*
MALIK
MALIKS
MALINE*
MALINES*
MALINGER
MALINGERED
MALINGERIES
MALINGERING
MALINGERS
MALINGERY
MALIS
MALISM
MALISMS
MALISON
MALISONS
MALIST
MALKIN
MALKINS
MALL
MALLAM
MALLAMS
MALLANDER
MALLANDERS
MALLARD
MALLARDS
MALLEABLE
MALLEATE
MALLEATED
MALLEATES
MALLEATING

MALLECHO
MALLECHOS
MALLED
MALLEE
MALLEES
MALLEI
MALLEMUCK
MALLEMUCKS
MALLENDER
MALLENDERS
MALLEOLAR
MALLEOLI
MALLEOLUS
MALLEOLUSES
MALLET
MALLETS
MALLEUS
MALLEUSES
MALLING
MALLOW
MALLOWS
MALLS
MALM
MALMAG
MALMAGS
MALMIER*
MALMIEST*
MALMS
MALMSEY
MALMSEYS
MALMSTONE
MALMSTONES
MALMY*
MALODOR*
MALODORS*
MALODOUR
MALODOURS
MALONATE
MALONATES
MALOTI*
MALPOSED*
MALS
MALSTICK
MALSTICKS
MALT
MALTALENT
MALTALENTS
MALTASE
MALTASES
MALTED
MALTEDS*
MALTHA
MALTHAS
MALTIER
MALTIEST
MALTING
MALTINGS
MALTMAN
MALTMEN
MALTOL*
MALTOLS*
MALTOSE
MALTOSES
MALTREAT

MALTREATED
MALTREATING
MALTREATS
MALTS
MALTSTER
MALTSTERS
MALTWORM
MALTWORMS
MALTY
MALVA
MALVAS
MALVASIA
MALVASIAS
MALVESIE
MALVESIES
MALVOISIE
MALVOISIES
MAM
MAMA
MAMALIGA*
MAMALIGAS*
MAMAS
MAMBA
MAMBAS
MAMBO
MAMBOED
MAMBOES*
MAMBOING
MAMBOS
MAMEE
MAMEES
MAMELON
MAMELONS
MAMELUCO
MAMELUCOS
MAMELUKE*
MAMELUKES*
MAMEY*
MAMEYES*
MAMEYS*
MAMIE*
MAMIES*
MAMILLA
MAMILLAE
MAMILLAR
MAMILLARY
MAMILLATE
MAMLUK*
MAMLUKS*
MAMMA
MAMMAE
MAMMAL
MAMMALIAN
MAMMALIANS*
MAMMALOGIES
MAMMALOGY
MAMMALS
MAMMARY
MAMMAS
MAMMATE
MAMMATI*
MAMMATUS*
MAMMEE
MAMMEES

The Chambers Dictionary is the authority for many longer words; see Introduction, page ix

MAMMER	MANATOID*	MANDRAKE	MANGING	MANIHOCS
MAMMERED	MANCALA	MANDRAKES	MANGLE	MANIHOT*
MAMMERING	MANCALAS	MANDREL	MANGLED	MANIHOTS*
MAMMERS	MANCANDO	MANDRELS	MANGLER	MANIKIN
MAMMET	MANCHE	MANDRIL	MANGLERS	MANIKINS
MAMMETRIES	MANCHES	MANDRILL	MANGLES	MANILA
MAMMETRY	MANCHET	MANDRILLS	MANGLING	MANILAS
MAMMETS	MANCHETS	MANDRILS	MANGO	MANILLA
MAMMEY*	MANCIPATE	MANDUCATE	MANGOES	MANILLAS
MAMMEYS*	MANCIPATED	MANDUCATED	MANGOLD	MANILLE
MAMMIE*	MANCIPATES	MANDUCATES	MANGOLDS	MANILLES
MAMMIES	MANCIPATING	MANDUCATING	MANGONEL	MANIOC
MAMMIFER	MANCIPLE	MANDYLION	MANGONELS	MANIOCA*
MAMMIFERS	MANCIPLES	MANDYLIONS	MANGOS*	MANIOCAS*
MAMMIFORM	MANCUS	MANE	MANGOSTAN	MANIOCS
MAMMILLA	MANCUSES	MANED	MANGOSTANS	MANIPLE
MAMMILLAE	MAND	MANEGE	MANGOUSTE	MANIPLES
MAMMITIDES*	MANDALA	MANEGED	MANGOUSTES	MANIPLIES
MAMMITIS*	MANDALAS	MANEGES	MANGROVE	MANIPULAR
MAMMOCK	MANDALIC*	MANEGING	MANGROVES	MANIPULARS
MAMMOCKED	MANDAMUS	MANEH	MANGS	MANIS
MAMMOCKING	MANDAMUSED*	MANEHS	MANGY	MANITO
MAMMOCKS	MANDAMUSES	MANELESS	MANHANDLE	MANITOS
MAMMOGRAM	MANDAMUSING*	MANENT	MANHANDLED	MANITOU
MAMMOGRAMS	MANDARIN	MANES	MANHANDLES	MANITOUS
MAMMON	MANDARINE	MANET	MANHANDLING	MANITU*
MAMMONISH	MANDARINES	MANEUVER	MANHATTAN*	MANITUS*
MAMMONISM	MANDARINS	MANEUVERED	MANHATTANS*	MANJACK
MAMMONISMS	MANDATARIES	MANEUVERING	MANHOLE	MANJACKS
MAMMONIST	MANDATARY	MANEUVERS	MANHOLES	MANKIER
MAMMONISTS	MANDATE	MANFUL	MANHOOD	MANKIEST
MAMMONITE	MANDATED	MANFULLY	MANHOODS	MANKIND
MAMMONITES	MANDATES	MANG	MANHUNT	MANKINDS
MAMMONS	MANDATING	MANGA	MANHUNTS	MANKY
MAMMOTH	MANDATOR	MANGABEY	MANI	MANLESS*
MAMMOTHS	MANDATORIES	MANGABEYS	MANIA	MANLIER
MAMMY	MANDATORS	MANGABIES*	MANIAC	MANLIEST
MAMS	MANDATORY	MANGABY*	MANIACAL	MANLIKE*
MAMSELLE	MANDIBLE	MANGAL	MANIACS	MANLILY*
MAMSELLES	MANDIBLES	MANGALS	MANIAS	MANLINESS
MAMZER	MANDILION	MANGANATE	MANIC	MANLINESSES
MAMZERIM	MANDILIONS	MANGANATES	MANICALLY	MANLY
MAMZERS	MANDIOC	MANGANESE	MANICOTTI*	MANMADE*
MAN	MANDIOCA	MANGANESES	MANICS*	MANNA
MANA	MANDIOCAS	MANGANIC	MANICURE	MANNAN*
MANACLE	MANDIOCCA	MANGANITE	MANICURED	MANNANS*
MANACLED	MANDIOCCAS	MANGANITES	MANICURES	MANNAS
MANACLES	MANDIOCS	MANGANOUS	MANICURING	MANNED
MANACLING	MANDIR	MANGAS	MANIES	MANNEQUIN
MANAGE	MANDIRA	MANGE	MANIFEST	MANNEQUINS
MANAGED	MANDIRAS	MANGED	MANIFESTED	MANNER
MANAGER	MANDIRS	MANGEL	MANIFESTING	MANNERED
MANAGERS	MANDOLA	MANGELS	MANIFESTO	MANNERISM
MANAGES	MANDOLAS	MANGER	MANIFESTOED	MANNERISMS
MANAGING	MANDOLIN	MANGERS	MANIFESTOES	MANNERIST
MANAKIN	MANDOLINE	MANGES	MANIFESTOING	MANNERISTS
MANAKINS	MANDOLINES	MANGETOUT	MANIFESTOS	MANNERLY
MANANA	MANDOLINS	MANGETOUTS	MANIFESTS	MANNERS
MANANAS	MANDOM	MANGEY	MANIFOLD	MANNIKIN
MANAS	MANDOMS	MANGIER	MANIFOLDED	MANNIKINS
MANATEE	MANDORA	MANGIEST	MANIFOLDING	MANNING
MANATEES	MANDORAS	MANGILY*	MANIFOLDS	MANNISH
MANATI	MANDORLA	MANGINESS	MANIFORM	MANNISHLY*
MANATIS	MANDORLAS	MANGINESSES	MANIHOC	MANNITE

MANNITES	MANTICORA	MANWISE*	MARASMUS	MARDIER
MANNITIC*	MANTICORAS	MANY	MARASMUSES	MARDIES
MANNITOL	MANTICORE	MANYATA	MARATHON	MARDIEST
MANNITOLS	MANTICORES	MANYATAS	MARATHONS	MARDY
MANNOSE	MANTID	MANYATTA	MARAUD	MARDYING
MANNOSES	MANTIDS	MANYATTAS	MARAUDED	MARE
MANO	MANTIES	MANYFOLD	MARAUDER	MAREMMA
MANOAO	MANTILLA	MANYPLIES	MARAUDERS	MAREMMAS
MANOAOS	MANTILLAS	MANZANITA	MARAUDING	MAREMME*
MANOEUVRE	MANTIS	MANZANITAS	MARAUDS	MARENGO*
MANOEUVRED	MANTISES	MANZELLO	MARAVEDI	MARES
MANOEUVRES	MANTISSA	MANZELLOS	MARAVEDIS	MARESCHAL
MANOEUVRING	MANTISSAS	MAORMOR	MARBLE	MARESCHALS
MANOMETER	MANTLE	MAORMORS	MARBLED	MARG
MANOMETERS	MANTLED	MAP	MARBLEISE*	MARGARIC
MANOMETRIES	MANTLES	MAPLE	MARBLEISED*	MARGARIN
MANOMETRY	MANTLET	MAPLES	MARBLEISES*	MARGARINE
MANOR	MANTLETS	MAPLIKE*	MARBLEISING*	MARGARINES
MANORIAL	MANTLING	MAPMAKER*	MARBLEIZE*	MARGARINS
MANORS	MANTLINGS	MAPMAKERS*	MARBLEIZED*	MARGARITA
MANOS	MANTO	MAPMAKING*	MARBLEIZES*	MARGARITAS
MANPACK	MANTOES	MAPMAKINGS*	MARBLEIZING*	MARGARITE
MANPACKS	MANTOS	MAPPABLE*	MARBLER	MARGARITES
MANPOWER	MANTRA	MAPPED	MARBLERS	MARGAY
MANPOWERS	MANTRAM	MAPPEMOND	MARBLES	MARGAYS
MANQUE	MANTRAMS	MAPPEMONDS	MARBLIER	MARGE
MANRED	MANTRAP	MAPPER	MARBLIEST	MARGENT
MANREDS	MANTRAPS	MAPPERIES	MARBLING	MARGENTED
MANRENT	MANTRAS	MAPPERS	MARBLINGS	MARGENTING
MANRENTS	MANTRIC*	MAPPERY	MARBLY	MARGENTS
MANRIDER	MANTUA	MAPPING	MARC	MARGES
MANRIDERS	MANTUAS	MAPPINGS	MARCASITE	MARGIN
MANRIDING	MANTY	MAPPIST	MARCASITES	MARGINAL
MANROPE*	MANUAL	MAPPISTS	MARCATO	MARGINALS
MANROPES*	MANUALLY	MAPS	MARCEL	MARGINATE
MANS	MANUALS	MAPSTICK	MARCELLA	MARGINATED*
MANSARD	MANUARY*	MAPSTICKS	MARCELLAS	MARGINATES*
MANSARDED*	MANUBRIA	MAPWISE	MARCELLED	MARGINATING*
MANSARDS	MANUBRIAL	MAQUETTE	MARCELLING	MARGINED
MANSE	MANUBRIUM	MAQUETTES	MARCELS	MARGINING
MANSES	MANUBRIUMS*	MAQUI	MARCH	MARGINS
MANSHIFT	MANUKA	MAQUIS	MARCHED	MARGOSA
MANSHIFTS	MANUKAS	MAQUISARD	MARCHEN*	MARGOSAS
MANSION	MANUL	MAQUISARDS	MARCHER	MARGRAVE
MANSIONS	MANULS	MAR	MARCHERS	MARGRAVES
MANSLAYER*	MANUMEA	MARA	MARCHES	MARGS
MANSLAYERS*	MANUMEAS	MARABOU	MARCHESA	MARIA
MANSONRIES	MANUMIT	MARABOUS	MARCHESAS	MARIACHI
MANSONRY	MANUMITS	MARABOUT	MARCHESE	MARIACHIS
MANSUETE	MANUMITTED	MARABOUTS	MARCHESES	MARIALITE
MANSWORN	MANUMITTING	MARACA	MARCHESI	MARIALITES
MANTA	MANURANCE	MARACAS	MARCHING	MARID
MANTAS	MANURANCES	MARAE	MARCHLIKE*	MARIDS
MANTEAU	MANURE	MARAES	MARCHMAN	MARIES
MANTEAUS	MANURED	MARAGING	MARCHMEN	MARIGOLD
MANTEAUX	MANURER	MARAGINGS	MARCHPANE	MARIGOLDS
MANTEEL	MANURERS	MARAH	MARCHPANES	MARIGRAM
MANTEELS	MANURES	MARAHS	MARCONI	MARIGRAMS
MANTEL	MANURIAL	MARANTA*	MARCONIED	MARIGRAPH
MANTELET	MANURING	MARANTAS*	MARCONIING	MARIGRAPHS
MANTELETS	MANURINGS	MARAS	MARCONIS	MARIHUANA
MANTELS	MANUS	MARASCA*	MARCS	MARIHUANAS
MANTES*	MANWARD*	MARASCAS*	MARD	MARIJUANA
MANTIC	MANWARDS*	MARASMIC	MARDIED	MARIJUANAS

The Chambers Dictionary is the authority for many longer words; see Introduction, page ix

MARIMBA	MARKMEN	MAROONINGS	MARSHALING*	MARTYRIZE
MARIMBAS	MARKS	MAROONS	MARSHALL*	MARTYRIZED
MARIMBIST*	MARKSMAN	MAROQUIN	MARSHALLED	MARTYRIZES
MARIMBISTS*	MARKSMEN	MAROQUINS	MARSHALLING	MARTYRIZING
MARINA	MARKUP*	MAROR	MARSHALLINGS	MARTYRLY*
MARINADE	MARKUPS*	MARORS	MARSHALLS*	MARTYRS
MARINADED	MARL	MARPLOT	MARSHALS	MARTYRY
MARINADES	MARLE	MARPLOTS	MARSHES	MARVEL
MARINADING	MARLED	MARQUE	MARSHIER	MARVELED*
MARINARA*	MARLES	MARQUEE	MARSHIEST	MARVELING*
MARINARAS*	MARLIER	MARQUEES	MARSHLAND	MARVELLED
MARINAS	MARLIEST	MARQUES	MARSHLANDS	MARVELLING
MARINATE	MARLIN	MARQUESS	MARSHWORT	MARVELOUS*
MARINATED	MARLINE	MARQUESSES	MARSHWORTS	MARVELS
MARINATES	MARLINES	MARQUETRIES	MARSHY	MARVER
MARINATING	MARLING	MARQUETRY	MARSPORT	MARVERED
MARINE	MARLINGS	MARQUIS	MARSPORTS	MARVERING
MARINER	MARLINS	MARQUISE	MARSQUAKE	MARVERS
MARINERA	MARLITE*	MARQUISES	MARSQUAKES	MARVY*
MARINERAS	MARLITES*	MARRAM	MARSUPIA	MARXISANT
MARINERS	MARLITIC*	MARRAMS	MARSUPIAL	MARY
MARINES	MARLS	MARRANO*	MARSUPIALS	MARYBUD
MARINIERE	MARLSTONE	MARRANOS*	MARSUPIUM	MARYBUDS
MARIPOSA	MARLSTONES	MARRED	MARSUPIUMS	MARYJANE*
MARIPOSAS	MARLY	MARRELS	MART	MARYJANES*
MARISCHAL	MARM	MARRER*	MARTAGON	MARZIPAN
MARISCHALLED	MARMALADE	MARRERS*	MARTAGONS	MARZIPANS
MARISCHALLING	MARMALADES	MARRIAGE	MARTED	MAS
MARISCHALS	MARMARISE	MARRIAGES	MARTEL	MASA
MARISH	MARMARISED	MARRIED	MARTELLED	MASALA
MARISHES	MARMARISES	MARRIEDS*	MARTELLING	MASALAS
MARITAGE	MARMARISING	MARRIER	MARTELLO	MASAS
MARITAGES	MARMARIZE	MARRIERS	MARTELLOS	MASCARA
MARITAL	MARMARIZED	MARRIES	MARTELS	MASCARAED*
MARITALLY	MARMARIZES	MARRING	MARTEN	MASCARAING*
MARITIME	MARMARIZING	MARRON*	MARTENS	MASCARAS
MARJORAM	MARMELISE	MARRONS*	MARTEXT	MASCARON
MARJORAMS	MARMELISED	MARROW	MARTEXTS	MASCARONS
MARK	MARMELISES	MARROWED	MARTIAL	MASCLE
MARKDOWN*	MARMELISING	MARROWFAT	MARTIALLY	MASCLED
MARKDOWNS*	MARMELIZE	MARROWFATS	MARTIAN*	MASCLES
MARKED	MARMELIZED	MARROWING	MARTIANS*	MASCON
MARKEDLY	MARMELIZES	MARROWISH	MARTIN	MASCONS
MARKER	MARMELIZING	MARROWS	MARTINET	MASCOT
MARKERS	MARMITE	MARROWSKIED	MARTINETS	MASCOTS
MARKET	MARMITES	MARROWSKIES	MARTING	MASCULINE
MARKETED	MARMOREAL	MARROWSKY	MARTINI	MASCULINES
MARKETEER	MARMOREAN*	MARROWSKYING	MARTINIS	MASCULY
MARKETEERS	MARMOSE	MARROWY	MARTINS	MASE
MARKETER	MARMOSES	MARRUM	MARTLET	MASED
MARKETERS	MARMOSET	MARRUMS	MARTLETS	MASER
MARKETING	MARMOSETS	MARRY	MARTS	MASERS
MARKETINGS	MARMOT	MARRYING	MARTYR	MASES
MARKETS	MARMOTS	MARRYINGS	MARTYRDOM	MASH
MARKHOOR*	MARMS	MARS	MARTYRDOMS	MASHALLAH
MARKHOORS*	MAROCAIN	MARSALA*	MARTYRED	MASHED
MARKHOR	MAROCAINS	MARSALAS*	MARTYRIA	MASHER
MARKHORS	MARON	MARSE*	MARTYRIES	MASHERS
MARKING	MARONS	MARSES*	MARTYRING	MASHES
MARKINGS	MAROON	MARSH	MARTYRISE	MASHIE
MARKKA	MAROONED	MARSHAL	MARTYRISED	MASHIER
MARKKAA	MAROONER	MARSHALCIES	MARTYRISES	MASHIES
MARKKAS	MAROONERS	MARSHALCY	MARTYRISING	MASHIEST
MARKMAN	MAROONING	MARSHALED*	MARTYRIUM	MASHING

Words marked with an asterisk are from OTCWL

MASHINGS	MASSAGIST	MASTICHE*	MATCHWOOD	MATRIARCH
MASHLAM	MASSAGISTS	MASTICHES*	MATCHWOODS	MATRIARCHS
MASHLAMS	MASSAS	MASTICHS	MATE	MATRIC
MASHLIM	MASSCULT*	MASTICOT	MATED	MATRICE
MASHLIMS	MASSCULTS*	MASTICOTS	MATELASSE	MATRICES
MASHLIN	MASSE	MASTICS	MATELASSES	MATRICIDE
MASHLINS	MASSED	MASTIER	MATELESS	MATRICIDES
MASHLOCH	MASSEDLY*	MASTIEST	MATELOT	MATRICS
MASHLOCHS	MASSES	MASTIFF	MATELOTE	MATRICULA
MASHLUM	MASSETER	MASTIFFS	MATELOTES	MATRICULAS
MASHLUMS	MASSETERS	MASTING	MATELOTS	MATRILINIES
MASHMAN	MASSEUR	MASTITIC*	MATER	MATRILINY
MASHMEN	MASSEURS	MASTITIDES*	MATERIAL	MATRIMONIES
MASHUA	MASSEUSE	MASTITIS	MATERIALS	MATRIMONY
MASHUAS	MASSEUSES	MASTITISES	MATERIEL	MATRIX
MASHY	MASSICOT	MASTIX*	MATERIELS	MATRIXES
MASING	MASSICOTS	MASTIXES*	MATERNAL	MATRON
MASJID	MASSIER	MASTLESS	MATERNITIES	MATRONAGE
MASJIDS	MASSIEST	MASTLIKE*	MATERNITY	MATRONAGES
MASK	MASSIF	MASTODON	MATERS	MATRONAL
MASKABLE*	MASSIFS	MASTODONS	MATES	MATRONISE
MASKED	MASSINESS	MASTODONT*	MATESHIP	MATRONISED
MASKEG*	MASSINESSES	MASTODONTS*	MATESHIPS	MATRONISES
MASKEGS*	MASSING	MASTOID	MATEY	MATRONISING
MASKER	MASSIVE	MASTOIDAL	MATEYNESS	MATRONIZE
MASKERS	MASSIVELY	MASTOIDS	MATEYNESSES	MATRONIZED
MASKING	MASSLESS*	MASTS	MATEYS*	MATRONIZES
MASKINGS*	MASSOOLA	MASTY	MATFELON	MATRONIZING
MASKLIKE*	MASSOOLAS	MASU	MATFELONS	MATRONLY
MASKS	MASSY	MASULA	MATGRASS	MATRONS
MASLIN	MASSYMORE	MASULAS	MATGRASSES	MATROSS
MASLINS	MASSYMORES	MASURIUM	MATH	MATROSSES
MASOCHISM	MAST	MASURIUMS	MATHESES	MATS
MASOCHISMS	MASTABA	MASUS	MATHESIS	MATSAH*
MASOCHIST	MASTABAH*	MAT	MATHS	MATSAHS*
MASOCHISTS	MASTABAHS*	MATACHIN	MATICO	MATSURI
MASON	MASTABAS	MATACHINA	MATICOS	MATSURIS
MASONED	MASTED	MATACHINAS	MATIER	MATT
MASONIC	MASTER	MATACHINI	MATIEST	MATTAMORE
MASONING	MASTERATE	MATADOR	MATILDA*	MATTAMORES
MASONRIED	MASTERATES	MATADORA	MATILDAS*	MATTE
MASONRIES	MASTERDOM	MATADORAS	MATILY	MATTED
MASONRY	MASTERDOMS	MATADORE	MATIN	MATTEDLY*
MASONS	MASTERED	MATADORES	MATINAL	MATTER
MASOOLAH	MASTERFUL	MATADORS	MATINEE	MATTERED
MASOOLAHS	MASTERIES	MATAMATA	MATINEES	MATTERFUL
MASQUE	MASTERING	MATAMATAS	MATINESS	MATTERING
MASQUER	MASTERINGS	MATAMBALA*	MATINESSES	MATTERS
MASQUERS	MASTERLY	MATCH	MATING	MATTERY
MASQUES	MASTERS	MATCHABLE	MATINGS*	MATTES
MASS	MASTERY	MATCHBOOK*	MATINS	MATTIE
MASSA	MASTFUL	MATCHBOOKS*	MATJES	MATTIES
MASSACRE	MASTHEAD	MATCHBOX	MATLESS*	MATTIN*
MASSACRED	MASTHEADED	MATCHBOXES	MATLO	MATTING
MASSACRER*	MASTHEADING	MATCHED	MATLOS	MATTINGS
MASSACRERS*	MASTHEADS	MATCHER	MATLOW	MATTINS
MASSACRES	MASTHOUSE	MATCHERS	MATLOWS	MATTOCK
MASSACRING	MASTHOUSES	MATCHES	MATOKE	MATTOCKS
MASSAGE	MASTIC	MATCHING	MATOKES	MATTOID
MASSAGED	MASTICATE	MATCHLESS	MATOOKE	MATTOIDS
MASSAGER*	MASTICATED	MATCHLOCK	MATOOKES	MATTRASS*
MASSAGERS*	MASTICATES	MATCHLOCKS	MATRASS	MATTRASSES*
MASSAGES	MASTICATING	MATCHUP*	MATRASSES	MATTRESS
MASSAGING	MASTICH	MATCHUPS*	MATRES*	MATTRESSES

MATTS*	MAUNDERERS	MAWPUS	MAYFLIES	MAZURKAS
MATURABLE	MAUNDERING	MAWPUSES	MAYFLOWER	MAZUT
MATURATE	MAUNDERINGS	MAWR	MAYFLOWERS	MAZUTS
MATURATED	MAUNDERS	MAWRS	MAYFLY	MAZY
MATURATES	MAUNDIES	MAWS	MAYHAP	MAZZARD
MATURATING	MAUNDING	MAWSEED	MAYHEM	MAZZARDS
MATURE	MAUNDS	MAWSEEDS	MAYHEMS	MBAQANGA
MATURED	MAUNDY	MAWTHER	MAYING	MBAQANGAS
MATURELY	MAUNGIER	MAWTHERS	MAYINGS	MBIRA
MATURER	MAUNGIEST	MAX	MAYO*	MBIRAS
MATURES	MAUNGY	MAXES	MAYOR	ME
MATUREST	MAUNNA	MAXI	MAYORAL	MEACOCK
MATURING	MAUSOLEA*	MAXICOAT*	MAYORALTIES	MEACOCKS
MATURITIES	MAUSOLEAN	MAXICOATS*	MAYORALTY	MEAD
MATURITY	MAUSOLEUM	MAXILLA	MAYORESS	MEADOW
MATUTINAL	MAUSOLEUMS	MAXILLAE	MAYORESSES	MEADOWS
MATUTINE	MAUT*	MAXILLARIES	MAYORS	MEADOWY
MATWEED	MAUTHER	MAXILLARY	MAYORSHIP	MEADS
MATWEEDS	MAUTHERS	MAXILLAS*	MAYORSHIPS	MEAGER*
MATY	MAUTS*	MAXILLULA	MAYOS*	MEAGERLY*
MATZA	MAUVAIS	MAXILLULAE	MAYPOLE	MEAGRE
MATZAH	MAUVAISE	MAXIM	MAYPOLES	MEAGRELY
MATZAHS	MAUVE	MAXIMA	MAYPOP*	MEAGRER
MATZAS	MAUVEIN	MAXIMAL	MAYPOPS*	MEAGRES
MATZO	MAUVEINE	MAXIMALLY	MAYS	MEAGREST
MATZOH	MAUVEINES	MAXIMALS*	MAYST	MEAL
MATZOHS*	MAUVEINS	MAXIMIN	MAYSTER	MEALED
MATZOON	MAUVER	MAXIMINS	MAYSTERS	MEALER
MATZOONS	MAUVES	MAXIMISE	MAYVIN*	MEALERS
MATZOS	MAUVEST	MAXIMISED	MAYVINS*	MEALIE
MATZOT	MAUVIN	MAXIMISES	MAYWEED	MEALIER
MATZOTH	MAUVINE	MAXIMISING	MAYWEEDS	MEALIES
MAUD	MAUVINES	MAXIMIST	MAZAEDIA*	MEALIEST
MAUDLIN	MAUVINS	MAXIMISTS	MAZAEDIUM*	MEALINESS
MAUDS	MAVEN	MAXIMITE*	MAZARD	MEALINESSES
MAUGER*	MAVENS	MAXIMITES*	MAZARDS	MEALING
MAUGRE	MAVERICK	MAXIMIZE	MAZARINE	MEALLESS*
MAUGRED	MAVERICKED	MAXIMIZED	MAZARINES	MEALS
MAUGRES	MAVERICKING	MAXIMIZER*	MAZE	MEALTIME
MAUGRING	MAVERICKS	MAXIMIZERS*	MAZED	MEALTIMES
MAUL	MAVIE*	MAXIMIZES	MAZEDLY*	MEALWORM
MAULED	MAVIES*	MAXIMIZING	MAZEFUL	MEALWORMS
MAULER*	MAVIN	MAXIMS	MAZELIKE*	MEALY
MAULERS	MAVINS	MAXIMUM	MAZELTOV	MEALYBUG*
MAULGRE	MAVIS	MAXIMUMS*	MAZEMENT	MEALYBUGS*
MAULGRED	MAVISES	MAXIS	MAZEMENTS	MEAN
MAULGRES	MAW	MAXIXE	MAZER	MEANDER
MAULGRING	MAWBOUND	MAXIXES	MAZERS	MEANDERED
MAULING	MAWED*	MAXWELL	MAZES	MEANDERING
MAULS	MAWING*	MAXWELLS	MAZHBI	MEANDERS
MAULSTICK	MAWK	MAY	MAZHBIS	MEANDRIAN
MAULSTICKS	MAWKIER	MAYA	MAZIER	MEANDROUS
MAULVI	MAWKIEST	MAYAN*	MAZIEST	MEANE
MAULVIS	MAWKIN	MAYAPPLE*	MAZILY	MEANED
MAUMET	MAWKINS	MAYAPPLES*	MAZINESS	MEANER
MAUMETRIES	MAWKISH	MAYAS	MAZINESSES	MEANERS*
MAUMETRY	MAWKISHLY	MAYBE	MAZING	MEANES
MAUMETS	MAWKS	MAYBES	MAZOURKA*	MEANEST
MAUN	MAWKY	MAYBUSH*	MAZOURKAS*	MEANIE
MAUND	MAWMET	MAYBUSHES*	MAZOUT	MEANIES
MAUNDED	MAWMETRIES	MAYDAY	MAZOUTS	MEANING
MAUNDER	MAWMETRY	MAYDAYS	MAZUMA	MEANINGLY
MAUNDERED	MAWMETS	MAYED	MAZUMAS	MEANINGS
MAUNDERER	MAWN*	MAYEST	MAZURKA	MEANLY

MEANNESS	MECHANISE	MEDIAD*	MEDINA	MEETINGS
MEANNESSES	MECHANISED	MEDIAE	MEDINAS	MEETLY
MEANS	MECHANISES	MEDIAEVAL	MEDIOCRE	MEETNESS
MEANT	MECHANISING	MEDIAEVALS*	MEDITATE	MEETNESSES
MEANTIME	MECHANISM	MEDIAL	MEDITATED	MEETS
MEANTIMES	MECHANISMS	MEDIALLY	MEDITATES	MEG
MEANWHILE	MECHANIST	MEDIALS	MEDITATING	MEGA
MEANWHILES	MECHANISTS	MEDIAN	MEDITATOR*	MEGABAR
MEANY	MECHANIZE	MEDIANLY*	MEDITATORS*	MEGABARS
MEARE	MECHANIZED	MEDIANS	MEDIUM	MEGABIT
MEARES	MECHANIZES	MEDIANT	MEDIUMS	MEGABITS
MEARING	MECHANIZING	MEDIANTS	MEDIUS	MEGABUCK
MEASE	MECLIZINE*	MEDIAS*	MEDIUSES	MEGABUCKS
MEASED	MECLIZINES*	MEDIATE	MEDLAR	MEGABYTE
MEASES	MECONATE	MEDIATED	MEDLARS	MEGABYTES
MEASING	MECONATES	MEDIATELY	MEDLE	MEGACITIES
MEASLE	MECONIC	MEDIATES	MEDLED	MEGACITY
MEASLED	MECONIN	MEDIATING	MEDLES	MEGACURIE
MEASLES	MECONINS	MEDIATION	MEDLEY	MEGACURIES
MEASLIER	MECONIUM	MEDIATIONS	MEDLEYS	MEGACYCLE
MEASLIEST	MECONIUMS	MEDIATISE	MEDLING	MEGACYCLES
MEASLING	MED*	MEDIATISED	MEDRESSEH	MEGADEAL*
MEASLY	MEDACCA	MEDIATISES	MEDRESSEHS	MEGADEALS*
MEASURE	MEDACCAS	MEDIATISING	MEDULLA	MEGADEATH
MEASURED	MEDAEWART	MEDIATIVE	MEDULLAE	MEGADEATHS
MEASURER	MEDAEWARTS	MEDIATIZE	MEDULLAR	MEGADOSE
MEASURERS	MEDAILLON*	MEDIATIZED	MEDULLARY	MEGADOSES
MEASURES	MEDAILLONS*	MEDIATIZES	MEDULLAS	MEGADYNE
MEASURING	MEDAKA	MEDIATIZING	MEDULLATE	MEGADYNES
MEASURINGS	MEDAKAS	MEDIATOR	MEDUSA	MEGAFARAD
MEAT	MEDAL	MEDIATORS	MEDUSAE	MEGAFARADS
MEATAL	MEDALED	MEDIATORY	MEDUSAL*	MEGAFAUNA
MEATBALL	MEDALET	MEDIATRICES	MEDUSAN	MEGAFAUNAE
MEATBALLS	MEDALETS	MEDIATRIX	MEDUSANS	MEGAFAUNAS
MEATED*	MEDALING	MEDIATRIXES*	MEDUSAS	MEGAFLOP
MEATH	MEDALIST	MEDIC	MEDUSOID	MEGAFLOPS
MEATHE	MEDALISTS	MEDICABLE	MEDUSOIDS	MEGAFLORA
MEATHEAD	MEDALLED	MEDICAID	MEED	MEGAFLORAE
MEATHEADS	MEDALLIC	MEDICAIDS	MEEDS	MEGAFLORAS
MEATHES	MEDALLING	MEDICAL	MEEK	MEGAFOG
MEATHS	MEDALLION	MEDICALLY	MEEKEN	MEGAFOGS
MEATIER	MEDALLIONED	MEDICALS	MEEKENED	MEGAGAUSS
MEATIEST	MEDALLIONING	MEDICARE	MEEKENING	MEGAGAUSSES
MEATILY	MEDALLIONS	MEDICARES	MEEKENS	MEGAHERTZ
MEATINESS	MEDALLIST	MEDICATE	MEEKER	MEGAHERTZES
MEATINESSES	MEDALLISTS	MEDICATED	MEEKEST	MEGAHIT*
MEATLESS	MEDALS	MEDICATES	MEEKLY	MEGAHITS*
MEATLOAF*	MEDCINAL	MEDICATING	MEEKNESS	MEGAJOULE
MEATLOAVES*	MEDDLE	MEDICINAL	MEEKNESSES	MEGAJOULES
MEATMAN*	MEDDLED	MEDICINALS*	MEEMIE	MEGALITH
MEATMEN*	MEDDLER	MEDICINE	MEEMIES	MEGALITHS
MEATS	MEDDLERS	MEDICINED	MEER	MEGALOPS*
MEATUS	MEDDLES	MEDICINER	MEERCAT	MEGALOPSES*
MEATUSES	MEDDLING	MEDICINERS	MEERCATS	MEGAPHONE
MEATY	MEDDLINGS	MEDICINES	MEERED	MEGAPHONED
MEAWES	MEDEVAC*	MEDICINING	MEERING	MEGAPHONES
MEAZEL	MEDEVACKED*	MEDICK	MEERKAT	MEGAPHONING
MEAZELS	MEDEVACKING*	MEDICKS	MEERKATS	MEGAPOD*
MEBOS	MEDEVACS*	MEDICO	MEERS	MEGAPODE
MEBOSES	MEDFLIES	MEDICOS	MEET	MEGAPODES
MECCA*	MEDFLY	MEDICS	MEETER	MEGAPODS*
MECCAS*	MEDIA	MEDIEVAL	MEETERS*	MEGARA
MECHANIC	MEDIACIES	MEDIEVALS*	MEETEST	MEGARAD
MECHANICS	MEDIACY	MEDII	MEETING	MEGARADS

The Chambers Dictionary is the authority for many longer words; see Introduction, page ix

MEGARON
MEGARONS
MEGASCOPE
MEGASCOPES
MEGASPORE
MEGASPORES
MEGASS
MEGASSE
MEGASSES
MEGASTAR
MEGASTARS
MEGASTORE
MEGASTORES
MEGATON
MEGATONS
MEGAVOLT
MEGAVOLTS
MEGAWATT
MEGAWATTS
MEGILLAH
MEGILLAHS
MEGILLOTH
MEGILP
MEGILPH*
MEGILPHS*
MEGILPS
MEGOHM
MEGOHMS
MEGRIM
MEGRIMS
MEGS
MEIKLE*
MEIN
MEINED
MEINEY
MEINEYS
MEINIE
MEINIES
MEINING
MEINS
MEINT
MEINY
MEIOFAUNA
MEIONITE
MEIONITES
MEIOSES
MEIOSIS
MEIOTIC
MEISHI
MEISHIS
MEISTER
MEISTERS
MEITH
MEITHS
MEJLIS
MEJLISES
MEKOMETER
MEKOMETERS
MEL
MELA
MELAMDIM*
MELAMED*
MELAMINE
MELAMINES

MELAMPODE
MELAMPODES
MELANGE
MELANGES
MELANIAN*
MELANIC
MELANICS*
MELANIN
MELANINS
MELANISM
MELANISMS
MELANIST*
MELANISTS*
MELANITE
MELANITES
MELANITIC*
MELANIZE*
MELANIZED*
MELANIZES*
MELANIZING*
MELANO
MELANOID*
MELANOIDS*
MELANOMA
MELANOMAS
MELANOMATA
MELANOS
MELANOSES
MELANOSIS
MELANOTIC
MELANOUS
MELANURIA
MELANURIAS
MELANURIC
MELAPHYRE
MELAPHYRES
MELAS
MELATONIN
MELATONINS
MELD
MELDED
MELDER
MELDERS
MELDING
MELDS
MELEE
MELEES
MELIC
MELICS
MELIK
MELIKS
MELILITE
MELILITES
MELILOT
MELILOTS
MELINITE
MELINITES
MELIORATE
MELIORATED
MELIORATES
MELIORATING
MELIORISM
MELIORISMS
MELIORIST

MELIORISTS
MELIORITIES
MELIORITY
MELISMA
MELISMAS
MELISMATA
MELL
MELLAY
MELLAYS
MELLED
MELLIFIC*
MELLING
MELLITE
MELLITES
MELLITIC
MELLOTRON*
MELLOTRONS*
MELLOW
MELLOWED
MELLOWER
MELLOWEST
MELLOWING
MELLOWLY
MELLOWS
MELLOWY
MELLS
MELOCOTON
MELOCOTONS
MELODEON
MELODEONS
MELODIA*
MELODIAS*
MELODIC
MELODICA
MELODICAS
MELODICS
MELODIES
MELODION
MELODIONS
MELODIOUS
MELODISE
MELODISED
MELODISES
MELODISING
MELODIST
MELODISTS
MELODIZE
MELODIZED
MELODIZER*
MELODIZERS*
MELODIZES
MELODIZING
MELODRAMA
MELODRAMAS
MELODRAME
MELODRAMES
MELODY
MELOID*
MELOIDS*
MELOMANIA
MELOMANIAS
MELOMANIC
MELON
MELONS

MELPHALAN*
MELPHALANS*
MELS
MELT
MELTABLE*
MELTAGE*
MELTAGES*
MELTDOWN
MELTDOWNS
MELTED
MELTER*
MELTERS*
MELTIER
MELTIEST
MELTING
MELTINGLY
MELTINGS
MELTITH
MELTITHS
MELTON
MELTONS
MELTS
MELTWATER*
MELTWATERS*
MELTY
MEM*
MEMBER
MEMBERED
MEMBERS
MEMBRAL
MEMBRANE
MEMBRANED*
MEMBRANES
MEME
MEMENTO
MEMENTOES
MEMENTOS
MEMES
MEMO
MEMOIR
MEMOIRISM
MEMOIRISMS
MEMOIRIST
MEMOIRISTS
MEMOIRS
MEMORABLE
MEMORABLY
MEMORANDA
MEMORANDUM*
MEMORANDUMS*
MEMORIAL
MEMORIALS
MEMORIES
MEMORISE
MEMORISED
MEMORISES
MEMORISING
MEMORITER
MEMORIZE
MEMORIZED
MEMORIZER*
MEMORIZERS*
MEMORIZES
MEMORIZING

MEMORY
MEMOS
MEMS*
MEMSAHIB*
MEMSAHIBS*
MEN
MENACE
MENACED
MENACER
MENACERS
MENACES
MENACING
MENAD*
MENADIONE
MENADIONES
MENADS*
MENAGE
MENAGED
MENAGERIE
MENAGERIES
MENAGES
MENAGING
MENARCHE
MENARCHES
MENAZON*
MENAZONS*
MEND
MENDABLE*
MENDACITIES
MENDACITY
MENDED
MENDER
MENDERS
MENDICANT
MENDICANTS
MENDICITIES
MENDICITY
MENDIGO*
MENDIGOS*
MENDING
MENDINGS
MENDS
MENE
MENED
MENEER
MENEERS
MENES
MENFOLK
MENFOLKS
MENG
MENGE
MENGED
MENGES
MENGING
MENGS
MENHADEN
MENHADENS
MENHIR
MENHIRS
MENIAL
MENIALLY*
MENIALS
MENING
MENINGEAL

MENINGES	MENTHOLS	MERCHANTINGS	MERGING	MEROSOME
MENINX	MENTICIDE	MERCHANTS	MERI	MEROSOMES
MENISCAL*	MENTICIDES	MERCHET	MERICARP	MEROZOITE
MENISCI	MENTION	MERCHETS	MERICARPS	MEROZOITES
MENISCOID	MENTIONED	MERCHILD	MERIDIAN	MERPEOPLE
MENISCUS	MENTIONER*	MERCHILDREN	MERIDIANS	MERPEOPLES
MENISCUSES	MENTIONERS*	MERCIABLE	MERIL	MERRIER
MENO*	MENTIONING	MERCIES	MERILS	MERRIES
MENOLOGIES	MENTIONS	MERCIFIDE	MERIMAKE	MERRIEST
MENOLOGY	MENTO	MERCIFIED	MERIMAKES	MERRILY
MENOMINEE	MENTOR	MERCIFIES	MERING	MERRIMENT
MENOMINEES	MENTORED*	MERCIFUL	MERINGUE	MERRIMENTS
MENOMINI	MENTORIAL	MERCIFY	MERINGUES	MERRINESS
MENOMINIS	MENTORING	MERCIFYING	MERINO	MERRINESSES
MENOPAUSE	MENTORINGS	MERCILESS	MERINOS	MERRY
MENOPAUSES	MENTORS	MERCS	MERIS	MERRYMAN
MENOPOME	MENTOS	MERCURATE	MERISES*	MERRYMEN
MENOPOMES	MENTUM	MERCURATED	MERISIS*	MERSALYL
MENORAH	MENU	MERCURATES	MERISM	MERSALYLS
MENORAHS	MENUISIER	MERCURATING	MERISMS	MERSE
MENORRHEA	MENUISIERS	MERCURIAL	MERISTEM	MERSES
MENORRHEAS	MENUS	MERCURIALS	MERISTEMS	MERSION
MENSA*	MENYIE	MERCURIC	MERISTIC	MERSIONS
MENSAE*	MENYIES	MERCURIES	MERIT	MERYCISM
MENSAL	MEOU*	MERCURISE	MERITED	MERYCISMS
MENSAS*	MEOUED*	MERCURISED	MERITING	MES
MENSCH	MEOUING*	MERCURISES	MERITS	MESA
MENSCHEN*	MEOUS*	MERCURISING	MERK	MESAIL
MENSCHES	MEOW	MERCURIZE	MERKIN	MESAILS
MENSE	MEOWED	MERCURIZED	MERKINS	MESAL
MENSED	MEOWING	MERCURIZES	MERKS	MESALLY
MENSEFUL	MEOWS	MERCURIZING	MERL	MESARAIC
MENSELESS	MEPACRINE	MERCUROUS	MERLE	MESARCH
MENSES	MEPACRINES	MERCURY	MERLES	MESAS
MENSH	MEPHITIC	MERCY	MERLIN	MESCAL
MENSHED	MEPHITIS	MERDE*	MERLING	MESCALIN
MENSHES	MEPHITISES	MERDES*	MERLINGS	MESCALINE*
MENSHING	MEPHITISM	MERE	MERLINS	MESCALINES*
MENSING	MEPHITISMS	MERED	MERLON	MESCALINS
MENSTRUA	MERBROMIN*	MEREL	MERLONS	MESCALISM
MENSTRUAL	MERBROMINS*	MERELL	MERLOT*	MESCALISMS
MENSTRUUM	MERC	MERELLS	MERLOTS*	MESCALS
MENSTRUUMS	MERCAPTAN	MERELS	MERLS	MESCLUM
MENSUAL	MERCAPTANS	MERELY	MERMAID	MESCLUMS
MENSURAL	MERCAPTO*	MERENGUE	MERMAIDEN	MESCLUN
MENSWEAR	MERCAT	MERENGUES	MERMAIDENS	MESCLUNS
MENSWEARS	MERCATS	MERER	MERMAIDS	MESDAMES
MENT	MERCENARIES	MERES	MERMAN	MESE
MENTA	MERCENARY	MERESMAN	MERMEN	MESEEMED*
MENTAL	MERCER	MERESMEN	MEROCRINE*	MESEEMETH*
MENTALISM	MERCERIES	MEREST	MEROGONIES	MESEEMS*
MENTALISMS	MERCERISE	MERESTONE	MEROGONY	MESEL
MENTALIST	MERCERISED	MERESTONES	MEROISTIC	MESELED
MENTALISTS	MERCERISES	MERFOLK	MEROME	MESELS
MENTALITIES	MERCERISING	MERFOLKS	MEROMES	MESENTERA
MENTALITY	MERCERIZE	MERGANSER	MERONYM	MESENTERIES
MENTALLY	MERCERIZED	MERGANSERS	MERONYMIES	MESENTERON*
MENTATION	MERCERIZES	MERGE	MERONYMS	MESENTERY
MENTATIONS	MERCERIZING	MERGED	MERONYMY	MESES
MENTEE	MERCERS	MERGENCE	MEROPIA*	MESETA
MENTEES	MERCERY	MERGENCES	MEROPIAS*	MESETAS
MENTHENE*	MERCHANT	MERGER	MEROPIC*	MESH
MENTHENES*	MERCHANTED	MERGERS	MEROPIDAN	MESHED
MENTHOL	MERCHANTING	MERGES	MEROPIDANS	MESHES

The Chambers Dictionary is the authority for many longer words; see Introduction, page ix

MESHIER	MESOSOMES*	MET	METAPLASMS	METHINK
MESHIEST	MESOTRON	META*	METAPLOT	METHINKETH
MESHING	MESOTRONS	METABASES	METATARSI	METHINKS
MESHINGS	MESPRISE	METABASIS	METATARSUS*	METHOD
MESHUGA	MESPRISES	METABATIC	METATE	METHODIC
MESHUGAAS	MESPRIZE	METABOLIC	METATES	METHODISE
MESHUGAASEN	MESPRIZES	METACARPI	METAXYLEM*	METHODISED
MESHUGAH*	MESQUIN	METACARPUS*	METAXYLEMS*	METHODISES
MESHUGGA	MESQUINE	METAGE	METAYAGE	METHODISING
MESHUGGAH*	MESQUIT	METAGES	METAYAGES	METHODISM*
MESHUGGE	MESQUITE	METAIRIE	METAYER	METHODISMS*
MESHWORK*	MESQUITES	METAIRIES	METAYERS	METHODIST
MESHWORKS*	MESQUITS	METAL	METAZOA	METHODISTS
MESHY	MESS	METALED	METAZOAL*	METHODIZE
MESIAL	MESSAGE	METALING	METAZOAN	METHODIZED
MESIALLY	MESSAGED	METALISE*	METAZOANS	METHODIZES
MESIAN	MESSAGES	METALISED*	METAZOIC	METHODIZING
MESIC	MESSAGING	METALISES*	METAZOON	METHODS
MESMERIC	MESSAGINGS	METALISING*	METCAST	METHOUGHT
MESMERISE	MESSALINE*	METALIST	METCASTS	METHOXY*
MESMERISED	MESSALINES*	METALISTS	METE	METHOXYL*
MESMERISES	MESSAN	METALIZE	METED	METHS
MESMERISING	MESSANS	METALIZED	METEOR	METHYL
MESMERISM	MESSED	METALIZES	METEORIC	METHYLAL*
MESMERISMS	MESSENGER	METALIZING	METEORISM	METHYLALS*
MESMERIST	MESSENGERED	METALLED	METEORISMS	METHYLASE*
MESMERISTS	MESSENGERING	METALLIC	METEORIST	METHYLASES*
MESMERIZE	MESSENGERS	METALLICS*	METEORISTS	METHYLATE
MESMERIZED	MESSES	METALLINE	METEORITE	METHYLATED
MESMERIZES	MESSIAH	METALLING	METEORITES	METHYLATES
MESMERIZING	MESSIAHS	METALLINGS	METEOROID	METHYLATING
MESNALTIES*	MESSIANIC	METALLISE	METEOROIDS	METHYLENE
MESNALTY*	MESSIAS	METALLISED	METEOROUS	METHYLENES
MESNE	MESSIASES	METALLISES	METEORS	METHYLIC
MESNES*	MESSIER	METALLISING	METEPA*	METHYLS
MESOBLAST	MESSIEST	METALLIST	METEPAS*	METHYSES
MESOBLASTS	MESSIEURS	METALLISTS	METER	METHYSIS
MESOCARP	MESSILY	METALLIZE	METERAGE*	METHYSTIC
MESOCARPS	MESSINESS	METALLIZED	METERAGES*	METIC
MESODERM	MESSINESSES	METALLIZES	METERED	METICAIS*
MESODERMS	MESSING	METALLIZING	METERING	METICAL
MESOGLEA*	MESSMAN*	METALLOID	METERS	METICALS
MESOGLEAS*	MESSMATE	METALLOIDS	METES	METICS
MESOGLOEA	MESSMATES	METALLY	METESTICK	METIER
MESOGLOEAS	MESSMEN*	METALMARK*	METESTICKS	METIERS
MESOLITE	MESSUAGE	METALMARKS*	METESTRUS*	METIF
MESOLITES	MESSUAGES	METALS	METESTRUSES*	METIFS
MESOMERE*	MESSY	METALWARE	METEWAND	METING
MESOMERES*	MESTEE	METALWARES	METEWANDS	METIS
MESOMORPH	MESTEES	METALWORK	METEYARD	METISSE
MESOMORPHS	MESTESO*	METALWORKS	METEYARDS	METISSES
MESON	MESTESOES*	METAMER	METH*	METOL
MESONIC	MESTESOS*	METAMERE	METHADON	METOLS
MESONS	MESTINO*	METAMERES	METHADONE	METONYM
MESOPAUSE*	MESTINOES*	METAMERIC	METHADONES	METONYMIC
MESOPAUSES*	MESTINOS*	METAMERS	METHADONS	METONYMIES
MESOPHYL*	MESTIZA	METANOIA	METHANAL	METONYMS
MESOPHYLL	MESTIZAS	METANOIAS	METHANALS	METONYMY
MESOPHYLLS	MESTIZO	METAPELET	METHANE	METOPAE
MESOPHYLS*	MESTIZOES*	METAPHASE	METHANES	METOPE
MESOPHYTE	MESTIZOS	METAPHASES	METHANOL	METOPES
MESOPHYTES	MESTO	METAPHOR	METHANOLS	METOPIC
MESOSCALE*	MESTRANOL*	METAPHORS	METHEGLIN	METOPISM
MESOSOME*	MESTRANOLS*	METAPLASM	METHEGLINS	METOPISMS

METOPON	MEWING	MIAUL	MICROCAR	MICROS
METOPONS	MEWL	MIAULED	MICROCARD	MICROSOME
METOPRYL	MEWLED	MIAULING	MICROCARDS	MICROSOMES
METOPRYLS	MEWLER*	MIAULS	MICROCARS	MICROTOME
METRE	MEWLERS*	MIB*	MICROCHIP	MICROTOMES
METRED	MEWLING	MIBS*	MICROCHIPS	MICROTOMIES
METRES	MEWLS	MICA	MICROCODE	MICROTOMY
METRIC	MEWS	MICACEOUS	MICROCODES	MICROTONE
METRICAL	MEWSED	MICAS	MICROCOPIED	MICROTONES
METRICATE	MEWSES	MICATE	MICROCOPIES	MICROVOLT*
METRICATED	MEWSING	MICATED	MICROCOPY	MICROVOLTS*
METRICATES	MEYNT	MICATES	MICROCOPYING	MICROWATT*
METRICATING	MEZAIL	MICATING	MICROCOPYINGS	MICROWATTS*
METRICIAN	MEZAILS	MICAWBER*	MICROCOSM	MICROWAVE
METRICIANS	MEZCAL*	MICAWBERS*	MICROCOSMS	MICROWAVED
METRICISE	MEZCALS*	MICE	MICROCYTE	MICROWAVES
METRICISED	MEZE	MICELL*	MICROCYTES	MICROWAVING
METRICISES	MEZEREON	MICELLA	MICRODOT	MICROWIRE
METRICISING	MEZEREONS	MICELLAE	MICRODOTS	MICROWIRES
METRICIST	MEZEREUM	MICELLAR	MICROFILM	MICRURGIES
METRICISTS	MEZEREUMS	MICELLE	MICROFILMED	MICRURGY
METRICIZE	MEZES	MICELLES	MICROFILMING	MICTION
METRICIZED	MEZQUIT*	MICELLS*	MICROFILMS	MICTIONS
METRICIZES	MEZQUITE*	MICHE	MICROFORM	MICTURATE
METRICIZING	MEZQUITES*	MICHED	MICROFORMS	MICTURATED
METRICS	MEZQUITS*	MICHER	MICROGRAM	MICTURATES
METRIFIED*	MEZUZA	MICHERS	MICROGRAMS	MICTURATING
METRIFIER	MEZUZAH	MICHES	MICROHM*	MID
METRIFIERS	MEZUZAHS	MICHING	MICROHMS*	MIDAIR
METRIFIES*	MEZUZAS*	MICHINGS	MICROINCH*	MIDAIRS
METRIFY*	MEZUZOT*	MICK	MICROINCHES*	MIDBRAIN
METRIFYING*	MEZUZOTH	MICKEY	MICROLITE	MIDBRAINS
METRING	MEZZANINE	MICKEYED	MICROLITES	MIDCOURSE*
METRIST	MEZZANINES	MICKEYING	MICROLITH	MIDCULT*
METRISTS	MEZZE	MICKEYS	MICROLITHS	MIDCULTS*
METRITIS	MEZZES	MICKIES	MICROLOGIES	MIDDAY
METRITISES	MEZZO	MICKLE	MICROLOGY	MIDDAYS
METRO	MEZZOS	MICKLER*	MICROLUCES*	MIDDEN
METROLOGIES	MEZZOTINT	MICKLES	MICROLUX*	MIDDENS
METROLOGY	MEZZOTINTS	MICKLEST*	MICROLUXES*	MIDDEST
METRONOME	MGANGA	MICKS	MICROMERE*	MIDDIES
METRONOMES	MGANGAS	MICKY	MICROMERES*	MIDDLE
METROPLEX	MHO	MICO	MICROMESH	MIDDLED
METROPLEXES	MHORR	MICOS	MICROMESHES	MIDDLEMAN
METROS	MHORRS	MICRA	MICROMHO*	MIDDLEMEN
METS	MHOS	MICRIFIED*	MICROMHOS*	MIDDLER*
METTLE	MI	MICRIFIES*	MICROMINI*	MIDDLERS*
METTLED	MIAOU*	MICRIFY*	MICROMINIS*	MIDDLES
METTLES	MIAOUED*	MICRIFYING*	MICROMOLE*	MIDDLING
METUMP*	MIAOUING*	MICRO	MICROMOLES*	MIDDLINGS
METUMPS*	MIAOUS*	MICROBAR	MICRON	MIDDORSAL*
MEU	MIAOW	MICROBARS	MICRONIZE*	MIDDY
MEUNIERE	MIAOWED	MICROBE	MICRONIZED*	MIDFIELD
MEUS	MIAOWING	MICROBEAM*	MICRONIZES*	MIDFIELDS
MEUSE	MIAOWS	MICROBEAMS*	MICRONIZING*	MIDGE
MEUSED	MIASM	MICROBES	MICRONS	MIDGES
MEUSES	MIASMA	MICROBIAL	MICROPORE	MIDGET
MEUSING	MIASMAL	MICROBIAN	MICROPORES	MIDGETS
MEVE	MIASMAS	MICROBIC	MICROPSIA	MIDGUT*
MEVED	MIASMATA	MICROBREW*	MICROPSIAS	MIDGUTS*
MEVES	MIASMATIC	MICROBREWS*	MICROPUMP	MIDI
MEVING	MIASMIC	MICROBUS	MICROPUMPS	MIDINETTE
MEW	MIASMOUS	MICROBUSES	MICROPYLE	MIDINETTES
MEWED	MIASMS	MICROBUSSES	MICROPYLES	MIDIRON

The Chambers Dictionary is the authority for many longer words; see Introduction, page ix

MIDIRONS	MIDWINTER*	MIKES	MILITARIA	MILLEPEDS
MIDIS	MIDWINTERS*	MIKING*	MILITARIES	MILLEPORE
MIDLAND	MIDWIVE	MIKRA	MILITARY	MILLEPORES
MIDLANDS	MIDWIVED	MIKRON	MILITATE	MILLER
MIDLEG*	MIDWIVES	MIKRONS	MILITATED	MILLERITE
MIDLEGS*	MIDWIVING	MIKVAH*	MILITATES	MILLERITES
MIDLIFE*	MIDYEAR*	MIKVAHS*	MILITATING	MILLERS
MIDLINE*	MIDYEARS*	MIKVEH*	MILITIA	MILLES
MIDLINES*	MIEN	MIKVEHS*	MILITIAS	MILLET
MIDLIVES*	MIENS	MIKVOTH*	MILIUM*	MILLETS
MIDMONTH*	MIEVE	MIL	MILK	MILLIARD
MIDMONTHS*	MIEVED	MILADI	MILKED	MILLIARDS
MIDMOST	MIEVES	MILADIES	MILKEN	MILLIARE
MIDMOSTS	MIEVING	MILADIS	MILKER	MILLIARES
MIDNIGHT	MIFF	MILADY	MILKERS	MILLIARIES
MIDNIGHTS	MIFFED	MILAGE	MILKFISH	MILLIARY
MIDNOON	MIFFIER	MILAGES	MILKFISHES	MILLIBAR
MIDNOONS	MIFFIEST	MILCH	MILKIER	MILLIBARS
MIDPOINT*	MIFFILY	MILCHIG*	MILKIEST	MILLIEME
MIDPOINTS*	MIFFINESS	MILD	MILKILY	MILLIEMES
MIDRANGE*	MIFFINESSES	MILDEN	MILKINESS	MILLIER*
MIDRANGES*	MIFFING	MILDENED	MILKINESSES	MILLIERS*
MIDRASH*	MIFFS	MILDENING	MILKING	MILLIGAL*
MIDRASHIC*	MIFFY	MILDENS	MILKINGS	MILLIGALS*
MIDRASHIM*	MIG*	MILDER	MILKLESS	MILLIGRAM*
MIDRASHOTH*	MIGG*	MILDEST	MILKLIKE	MILLIGRAMS*
MIDRIB	MIGGLE*	MILDEW	MILKMAID	MILLILUCES*
MIDRIBS	MIGGLES*	MILDEWED	MILKMAIDS	MILLILUX*
MIDRIFF	MIGGS*	MILDEWING	MILKMAN	MILLILUXES*
MIDRIFFS	MIGHT	MILDEWS	MILKMEN	MILLIME
MIDS	MIGHTEST	MILDEWY	MILKO	MILLIMES
MIDSHIP	MIGHTFUL	MILDLY	MILKOS	MILLIMHO*
MIDSHIPS	MIGHTIER	MILDNESS	MILKS	MILLIMHOS*
MIDSIZE	MIGHTIEST	MILDNESSES	MILKSHED*	MILLIMOLE
MIDSIZED*	MIGHTILY	MILDS	MILKSHEDS*	MILLIMOLES
MIDSOLE*	MIGHTS	MILE	MILKSOP*	MILLINE*
MIDSOLES*	MIGHTST	MILEAGE	MILKSOPS*	MILLINER
MIDSPACE*	MIGHTY	MILEAGES	MILKWEED*	MILLINERIES
MIDSPACES*	MIGNON	MILEPOST*	MILKWEEDS*	MILLINERS
MIDST	MIGNONNE	MILEPOSTS*	MILKWOOD	MILLINERY
MIDSTORIES*	MIGNONS*	MILER	MILKWOODS	MILLINES*
MIDSTORY*	MIGRAINE	MILERS	MILKWORT	MILLING
MIDSTREAM	MIGRAINES	MILES	MILKWORTS	MILLINGS
MIDSTREAMS	MIGRANT	MILESIMO*	MILKY	MILLIOHM*
MIDSTS	MIGRANTS	MILESIMOS*	MILL	MILLIOHMS*
MIDSUMMER	MIGRATE	MILESTONE	MILLABLE*	MILLION
MIDSUMMERS	MIGRATED	MILESTONES	MILLAGE*	MILLIONS
MIDTERM	MIGRATES	MILFOIL	MILLAGES*	MILLIONTH
MIDTERMS	MIGRATING	MILFOILS	MILLBOARD	MILLIONTHS
MIDTOWN*	MIGRATION	MILIA*	MILLBOARDS	MILLIPED
MIDTOWNS*	MIGRATIONS	MILIARIA	MILLCAKE*	MILLIPEDE
MIDWATCH*	MIGRATOR	MILIARIAL*	MILLCAKES*	MILLIPEDES
MIDWATCHES*	MIGRATORS	MILIARIAS	MILLDAM	MILLIPEDS
MIDWAY	MIGRATORY	MILIARY	MILLDAMS	MILLIREM
MIDWAYS	MIGS*	MILIEU	MILLE	MILLIREMS
MIDWEEK*	MIHRAB	MILIEUS	MILLED	MILLIVOLT*
MIDWEEKLY*	MIHRABS	MILIEUX	MILLENARIES	MILLIVOLTS*
MIDWEEKS*	MIJNHEER*	MILITANCE*	MILLENARY	MILLIWATT*
MIDWIFE	MIJNHEERS*	MILITANCES*	MILLENNIA	MILLIWATTS*
MIDWIFED	MIKADO	MILITANCIES	MILLENNIUM*	MILLOCRAT
MIDWIFERIES	MIKADOS	MILITANCY	MILLENNIUMS*	MILLOCRATS
MIDWIFERY	MIKE	MILITANT	MILLEPED	MILLPOND
MIDWIVES	MIKED*	MILITANTS	MILLEPEDE	MILLPONDS
MIDWIFING		MILITAR	MILLEPEDES	MILLRACE

MILLRACES
MILLRIND
MILLRINDS
MILLRUN
MILLRUNS
MILLS
MILLSCALE
MILLSCALES
MILLSTONE
MILLSTONES
MILLTAIL
MILLTAILS
MILLWORK*
MILLWORKS*
MILNEB*
MILNEBS*
MILO
MILOMETER
MILOMETERS
MILOR
MILORD
MILORDS
MILORS
MILOS
MILPA*
MILPAS*
MILREIS
MILS
MILSEY
MILSEYS
MILT
MILTED
MILTER
MILTERS
MILTIER*
MILTIEST*
MILTING
MILTONIA
MILTONIAS
MILTS
MILTY*
MILTZ
MILTZES
MILVINE
MIM
MIMBAR
MIMBARS
MIME
MIMED
MIMEO*
MIMEOED*
MIMEOING*
MIMEOS*
MIMER
MIMERS
MIMES
MIMESES
MIMESIS
MIMESISES*
MIMESTER
MIMESTERS
MIMETIC
MIMETICAL
MIMETITE

MIMETITES
MIMIC
MIMICAL
MIMICKED
MIMICKER
MIMICKERS
MIMICKING
MIMICRIES
MIMICRY
MIMICS
MIMING
MIMMER
MIMMEST
MIMMICK
MIMMICKED
MIMMICKING
MIMMICKS
MIMOSA
MIMOSAS
MIMSEY
MIMSIER
MIMSIEST
MIMSY
MIMULUS
MIMULUSES
MINA
MINABLE*
MINACIOUS
MINACITIES
MINACITY
MINAE
MINAR
MINARET
MINARETS
MINARS
MINAS
MINATORY
MINBAR
MINBARS
MINCE
MINCED
MINCEMEAT
MINCEMEATS
MINCER
MINCERS
MINCES
MINCEUR
MINCIER*
MINCIEST*
MINCING
MINCINGLY
MINCINGS
MINCY*
MIND
MINDED
MINDER
MINDERS
MINDFUCK
MINDFUCKS
MINDFUL
MINDFULLY
MINDING
MINDINGS
MINDLESS

MINDS
MINDSET
MINDSETS
MINE
MINEABLE*
MINED
MINEFIELD
MINEFIELDS
MINELAYER*
MINELAYERS*
MINEOLA
MINEOLAS
MINER
MINERAL
MINERALS
MINERS
MINES
MINESTONE
MINESTONES
MINETTE
MINETTES
MINEVER
MINEVERS
MING
MINGE
MINGED
MINGES
MINGIER
MINGIEST
MINGIN
MINGINESS
MINGINESSES
MINGING
MINGLE
MINGLED
MINGLER
MINGLERS
MINGLES
MINGLING
MINGLINGS
MINGS
MINGY
MINI
MINIATE
MINIATED
MINIATES
MINIATING
MINIATION
MINIATIONS
MINIATURE
MINIATURED
MINIATURES
MINIATURING
MINIBAR
MINIBARS
MINIBIKE
MINIBIKER*
MINIBIKERS*
MINIBIKES
MINIBREAK
MINIBREAKS
MINIBUS
MINIBUSES
MINIBUSSES

MINICAB
MINICABS
MINICAM
MINICAMP*
MINICAMPS*
MINICAMS
MINICAR*
MINICARS*
MINIDISK
MINIDISKS
MINIER
MINIEST
MINIFIED
MINIFIES
MINIFY
MINIFYING
MINIKIN
MINIKINS
MINILAB*
MINILABS*
MINIM
MINIMA
MINIMAL
MINIMALLY*
MINIMALS*
MINIMAX
MINIMAXED
MINIMAXES
MINIMAXING
MINIMENT
MINIMENTS
MINIMILL*
MINIMILLS*
MINIMISE
MINIMISED
MINIMISES
MINIMISING
MINIMISM
MINIMISMS
MINIMIST
MINIMISTS
MINIMIZE
MINIMIZED
MINIMIZER*
MINIMIZERS*
MINIMIZES
MINIMIZING
MINIMS
MINIMUM
MINIMUMS*
MINIMUS
MINIMUSES
MINING
MININGS
MINION
MINIONS
MINIPARK*
MINIPARKS*
MINIPILL
MINIPILLS
MINIRUGBIES
MINIRUGBY
MINIS
MINISCULE

MINISCULES
MINISH
MINISHED
MINISHES
MINISHING
MINISKI*
MINISKIRT
MINISKIRTS
MINISKIS*
MINISTATE*
MINISTATES*
MINISTER
MINISTERED
MINISTERING
MINISTERS
MINISTRIES
MINISTRY
MINIUM
MINIUMS
MINIVAN*
MINIVANS*
MINIVER
MINIVERS
MINIVET
MINIVETS
MINK
MINKE
MINKES
MINKS
MINNEOLA
MINNEOLAS
MINNICK
MINNICKED
MINNICKING
MINNICKS
MINNIE
MINNIES
MINNOCK
MINNOCKED
MINNOCKING
MINNOCKS
MINNOW
MINNOWS
MINNY*
MINO
MINOR
MINORCA*
MINORCAS*
MINORED
MINORING
MINORITIES
MINORITY
MINORS
MINORSHIP
MINORSHIPS
MINOS
MINOXIDIL*
MINOXIDILS*
MINSHUKU
MINSHUKUS
MINSTER
MINSTERS
MINSTREL
MINSTRELS

MINT	MIRE	MISADJUSTS*	MISBECOME	MISCEGEN
MINTAGE	MIRED	MISADVISE	MISBECOMES	MISCEGENE
MINTAGES	MIREPOIX	MISADVISED	MISBECOMING	MISCEGENES
MINTED	MIRES	MISADVISES	MISBEGAN*	MISCEGENS
MINTER	MIREX*	MISADVISING	MISBEGIN*	MISCEGINE
MINTERS	MIREXES*	MISAGENT*	MISBEGINNING*	MISCEGINES
MINTIER	MIRI	MISAGENTS*	MISBEGINS*	MISCHANCE
MINTIEST	MIRIER	MISAIM	MISBEGOT	MISCHANCED
MINTING	MIRIEST	MISAIMED	MISBEGUN*	MISCHANCES
MINTS	MIRIFIC	MISAIMING	MISBEHAVE	MISCHANCING
MINTY	MIRIFICAL	MISAIMS	MISBEHAVED	MISCHANCY
MINUEND	MIRIN	MISALIGN	MISBEHAVES	MISCHARGE
MINUENDS	MIRINESS	MISALIGNED	MISBEHAVING	MISCHARGED
MINUET	MIRINESSES	MISALIGNING	MISBELIEF	MISCHARGES
MINUETS	MIRING	MISALIGNS	MISBELIEFS	MISCHARGING
MINUS	MIRINS	MISALLEGE	MISBESEEM	MISCHIEF
MINUSCULE	MIRITI	MISALLEGED	MISBESEEMED	MISCHIEFED
MINUSCULES	MIRITIS	MISALLEGES	MISBESEEMING	MISCHIEFING
MINUSES	MIRK	MISALLEGING	MISBESEEMS	MISCHIEFS
MINUTE	MIRKER	MISALLIED	MISBESTOW	MISCHOICE*
MINUTED	MIRKEST	MISALLIES	MISBESTOWED	MISCHOICES*
MINUTELY	MIRKIER*	MISALLOT	MISBESTOWING	MISCIBLE
MINUTEMAN	MIRKIEST*	MISALLOTS	MISBESTOWS	MISCITE*
MINUTEMEN	MIRKILY*	MISALLOTTED	MISBIAS*	MISCITED*
MINUTER	MIRKS	MISALLOTTING	MISBIASED*	MISCITES*
MINUTES	MIRKY*	MISALLY	MISBIASES*	MISCITING*
MINUTEST	MIRLIER	MISALLYING	MISBIASING*	MISCLAIM*
MINUTIA	MIRLIEST	MISALTER*	MISBIASSED*	MISCLAIMED*
MINUTIAE	MIRLIGOES	MISALTERED*	MISBIASSES*	MISCLAIMING*
MINUTIAL*	MIRLITON	MISALTERING*	MISBIASSING*	MISCLAIMS*
MINUTING	MIRLITONS	MISALTERS*	MISBILL*	MISCLASS*
MINUTIOSE	MIRLY	MISANDRIES	MISBILLED*	MISCLASSED*
MINX	MIRROR	MISANDRY	MISBILLING*	MISCLASSES*
MINXES	MIRRORED	MISAPPLIED	MISBILLS*	MISCLASSING*
MINXISH*	MIRRORING	MISAPPLIES	MISBIND*	MISCODE*
MINY	MIRRORS	MISAPPLY	MISBINDING*	MISCODED*
MINYAN	MIRS	MISAPPLYING	MISBINDS*	MISCODES*
MINYANIM	MIRTH	MISARRAY	MISBIRTH	MISCODING*
MINYANS	MIRTHFUL	MISARRAYS	MISBIRTHS	MISCOIN*
MIOMBO	MIRTHLESS	MISASSAY*	MISBORN	MISCOINED*
MIOMBOS	MIRTHS	MISASSAYED*	MISBOUND*	MISCOINING*
MIOSES	MIRV	MISASSAYING*	MISBRAND*	MISCOINS*
MIOSIS	MIRVED	MISASSAYS*	MISBRANDED*	MISCOLOR
MIOTIC	MIRVING	MISASSIGN	MISBRANDING*	MISCOLORED
MIOTICS	MIRVS	MISASSIGNED	MISBRANDS*	MISCOLORING
MIQUELET*	MIRY	MISASSIGNING	MISBUILD*	MISCOLORS
MIQUELETS*	MIRZA*	MISASSIGNS	MISBUILDING*	MISCOLOUR
MIR	MIRZAS*	MISATE*	MISBUILDS*	MISCOLOURED
MIRABELLE	MIS	MISATONE*	MISBUILT*	MISCOLOURING
MIRABELLES	MISACT*	MISATONED*	MISBUTTON*	MISCOLOURS
MIRABILIA	MISACTED*	MISATONES*	MISBUTTONED*	MISCOOK*
MIRABILIS	MISACTING*	MISATONING*	MISBUTTONING*	MISCOOKED*
MIRABILISES	MISACTS*	MISAUNTER	MISBUTTONS*	MISCOOKING*
MIRABLE	MISADAPT*	MISAUNTERS	MISCALL	MISCOOKS*
MIRACIDIA	MISADAPTED*	MISAVER*	MISCALLED	MISCOPIED
MIRACIDIUM*	MISADAPTING*	MISAVERRED*	MISCALLING	MISCOPIES
MIRACLE	MISADAPTS*	MISAVERRING*	MISCALLS	MISCOPY
MIRACLES	MISADD*	MISAVERS*	MISCARRIED	MISCOPYING
MIRADOR	MISADDED*	MISAVISED	MISCARRIES	MISCOUNT
MIRADORS	MISADDING*	MISAWARD*	MISCARRY	MISCOUNTED
MIRAGE	MISADDS*	MISAWARDED*	MISCARRYING	MISCOUNTING
MIRAGES	MISADJUST*	MISAWARDING*	MISCAST	MISCOUNTS
MIRBANE	MISADJUSTED*	MISAWARDS*	MISCASTING	MISCREANT
MIRBANES	MISADJUSTING*	MISBECAME	MISCASTS	MISCREANTS

Words marked with an asterisk are from OTCWL

MISCREATE	MISDONE	MISESTEEMS	MISGIVES	MISHITS
MISCREATED*	MISDONNE	MISEVENT*	MISGIVING	MISHITTING
MISCREATES*	MISDOUBT	MISEVENTS*	MISGIVINGS	MISHMASH
MISCREATING*	MISDOUBTED	MISFAITH	MISGO	MISHMASHES
MISCREDIT	MISDOUBTING	MISFAITHS	MISGOES	MISHMEE
MISCREDITED	MISDOUBTS	MISFALL	MISGOING	MISHMEES
MISCREDITING	MISDRAW	MISFALLEN	MISGONE	MISHMI
MISCREDITS	MISDRAWING	MISFALLING	MISGOTTEN	MISHMIS
MISCREED	MISDRAWINGS	MISFALLS	MISGOVERN	MISHMOSH*
MISCREEDS	MISDRAWN	MISFALNE	MISGOVERNED	MISHMOSHES*
MISCUE	MISDRAWS	MISFARE	MISGOVERNING	MISINFER*
MISCUED	MISDREAD	MISFARED	MISGOVERNS	MISINFERRED*
MISCUEING	MISDREADS	MISFARES	MISGRADE*	MISINFERRING*
MISCUES	MISDREW	MISFARING	MISGRADED*	MISINFERS*
MISCUING	MISDRIVE*	MISFARINGS	MISGRADES*	MISINFORM
MISCUT*	MISDRIVEN*	MISFEASOR	MISGRADING*	MISINFORMED
MISCUTS*	MISDRIVES*	MISFEASORS	MISGRAFF	MISINFORMING
MISCUTTING*	MISDRIVING*	MISFED	MISGRAFT	MISINFORMS
MISDATE	MISDROVE*	MISFEED	MISGRAFTED	MISINTEND
MISDATED	MISE	MISFEEDING	MISGRAFTING	MISINTENDED
MISDATES	MISEASE	MISFEEDS	MISGRAFTS	MISINTENDING
MISDATING	MISEASES	MISFEIGN	MISGREW*	MISINTENDS
MISDEAL	MISEAT*	MISFEIGNED	MISGROW*	MISINTER*
MISDEALING	MISEATEN*	MISFEIGNING	MISGROWING*	MISINTERRED*
MISDEALS	MISEATING*	MISFEIGNS	MISGROWN*	MISINTERRING*
MISDEALT	MISEATS*	MISFELL	MISGROWS*	MISINTERS*
MISDEED	MISEDIT*	MISFIELD	MISGROWTH	MISJOIN
MISDEEDS	MISEDITED*	MISFIELDED	MISGROWTHS	MISJOINED
MISDEEM	MISEDITING*	MISFIELDING	MISGUESS*	MISJOINING
MISDEEMED	MISEDITS*	MISFIELDS	MISGUESSED*	MISJOINS
MISDEEMING	MISEMPLOY	MISFILE	MISGUESSES*	MISJUDGE
MISDEEMINGS	MISEMPLOYED	MISFILED	MISGUESSING*	MISJUDGED
MISDEEMS	MISEMPLOYING	MISFILES	MISGUGGLE	MISJUDGES
MISDEFINE*	MISEMPLOYS	MISFILING	MISGUGGLED	MISJUDGING
MISDEFINED*	MISENROL*	MISFIRE	MISGUGGLES	MISKAL*
MISDEFINES*	MISENROLL*	MISFIRED	MISGUGGLING	MISKALS*
MISDEFINING*	MISENROLLED*	MISFIRES	MISGUIDE	MISKEEP*
MISDEMEAN	MISENROLLING*	MISFIRING	MISGUIDED	MISKEEPING*
MISDEMEANED	MISENROLS*	MISFIT	MISGUIDER	MISKEEPS*
MISDEMEANING	MISENROLS*	MISFITS	MISGUIDERS	MISKEN
MISDEMEANS	MISENTER*	MISFITTED	MISGUIDES	MISKENNED
MISDEMPT	MISENTERED*	MISFITTING	MISGUIDING	MISKENNING
MISDESERT	MISENTERING*	MISFOCUS*	MISHANDLE	MISKENS
MISDESERTS	MISENTERS*	MISFOCUSED*	MISHANDLED	MISKENT
MISDIAL	MISENTRIES	MISFOCUSES*	MISHANDLES	MISKEPT*
MISDIALED	MISENTRY	MISFOCUSING*	MISHANDLING	MISKEY
MISDIALING	MISER	MISFOCUSSED*	MISHANTER	MISKEYED
MISDIALLED	MISERABLE	MISFOCUSSES*	MISHANTERS	MISKEYING
MISDIALLING	MISERABLES	MISFOCUSSING*	MISHAP	MISKEYS
MISDIALS	MISERABLY	MISFORM	MISHAPPED	MISKICK*
MISDID	MISERE	MISFORMED	MISHAPPEN	MISKICKED*
MISDIET	MISERERE	MISFORMING	MISHAPPENED	MISKICKING*
MISDIETS	MISERERES	MISFORMS	MISHAPPENING	MISKICKS*
MISDIGHT	MISERES	MISFRAME*	MISHAPPENS	MISKNEW
MISDIRECT	MISERIES	MISFRAMED*	MISHAPPING	MISKNOW
MISDIRECTED	MISERLIER	MISFRAMES*	MISHAPS	MISKNOWING
MISDIRECTING	MISERLIEST	MISFRAMING*	MISHAPT	MISKNOWN
MISDIRECTS	MISERLY	MISGAUGE*	MISHEAR	MISKNOWS
MISDO	MISERS	MISGAUGED*	MISHEARD	MISLABEL*
MISDOER	MISERY	MISGAUGES*	MISHEARING	MISLABELED*
MISDOERS	MISES	MISGAUGING*	MISHEARS	MISLABELING*
MISDOES	MISESTEEM	MISGAVE	MISHEGAAS	MISLABELLED*
MISDOING	MISESTEEMED	MISGIVE	MISHEGAASEN	MISLABELLING*
MISDOINGS	MISESTEEMING	MISGIVEN	MISHIT	MISLABELS*

MISLABOR*	MISMADE	MISORIENTS*	MISPRAISES	MISREPORTING
MISLABORED*	MISMAKE	MISOS	MISPRAISING	MISREPORTS
MISLABORING*	MISMAKES	MISPAGE*	MISPRICE*	MISROUTE
MISLABORS*	MISMAKING	MISPAGED*	MISPRICED*	MISROUTED
MISLAID	MISMANAGE	MISPAGES*	MISPRICES*	MISROUTEING
MISLAIN*	MISMANAGED	MISPAGING*	MISPRICING*	MISROUTES
MISLAY	MISMANAGES	MISPAINT*	MISPRINT	MISROUTING
MISLAYER*	MISMANAGING	MISPAINTED*	MISPRINTED	MISRULE
MISLAYERS*	MISMARK*	MISPAINTING*	MISPRINTING	MISRULED
MISLAYING	MISMARKED*	MISPAINTS*	MISPRINTS	MISRULES
MISLAYS	MISMARKING*	MISPARSE*	MISPRISE	MISRULING
MISLEAD	MISMARKS*	MISPARSED*	MISPRISED	MISS
MISLEADER	MISMARRIED	MISPARSES*	MISPRISES	MISSA
MISLEADERS	MISMARRIES	MISPARSING*	MISPRISING	MISSABLE
MISLEADING	MISMARRY	MISPART*	MISPRIZE	MISSAE
MISLEADS	MISMARRYING	MISPARTED*	MISPRIZED	MISSAID
MISLEARED	MISMATCH	MISPARTING*	MISPRIZES	MISSAL
MISLEARN*	MISMATCHED	MISPARTS*	MISPRIZING	MISSALS
MISLEARNED*	MISMATCHES	MISPATCH*	MISPROUD	MISSAW
MISLEARNING*	MISMATCHING	MISPATCHED*	MISQUOTE	MISSAY
MISLEARNS*	MISMATE	MISPATCHES*	MISQUOTED	MISSAYING
MISLEARNT*	MISMATED	MISPATCHING*	MISQUOTES	MISSAYINGS
MISLED	MISMATES	MISPEN*	MISQUOTING	MISSAYS
MISLEEKE	MISMATING	MISPENNED*	MISRAISE*	MISSEAT*
MISLEEKED	MISMEET*	MISPENNING*	MISRAISED*	MISSEATED*
MISLEEKES	MISMEETING*	MISPENS*	MISRAISES*	MISSEATING*
MISLEEKING	MISMEETS*	MISPICKEL	MISRAISING*	MISSEATS*
MISLETOE	MISMET*	MISPICKELS	MISRATE	MISSED
MISLETOES	MISMETRE	MISPLACE	MISRATED	MISSEE
MISLIE*	MISMETRED	MISPLACED	MISRATES	MISSEEING
MISLIES*	MISMETRES	MISPLACES	MISRATING	MISSEEM
MISLIGHT	MISMETRING	MISPLACING	MISREAD	MISSEEMED
MISLIGHTED	MISMOVE*	MISPLAN*	MISREADING	MISSEEMING
MISLIGHTING	MISMOVED*	MISPLANNED*	MISREADINGS	MISSEEMINGS
MISLIGHTS	MISMOVES*	MISPLANNING*	MISREADS	MISSEEMS
MISLIKE	MISMOVING*	MISPLANS*	MISRECKON	MISSEEN
MISLIKED	MISNAME	MISPLANT*	MISRECKONED	MISSEES
MISLIKER	MISNAMED	MISPLANTED*	MISRECKONING	MISSEL
MISLIKERS	MISNAMES	MISPLANTING*	MISRECKONINGS	MISSELS
MISLIKES	MISNAMING	MISPLANTS*	MISRECKONS	MISSEND
MISLIKING	MISNOMER	MISPLAY	MISRECORD*	MISSENDING
MISLIKINGS	MISNOMERED	MISPLAYED	MISRECORDED*	MISSENDS
MISLIPPEN	MISNOMERING	MISPLAYING	MISRECORDING*	MISSENSE*
MISLIPPENED	MISNOMERS	MISPLAYS	MISRECORDS*	MISSENSES*
MISLIPPENING	MISO	MISPLEAD	MISREFER*	MISSENT
MISLIPPENS	MISOCLERE	MISPLEADED	MISREFERRED*	MISSES
MISLIT	MISOGAMIES	MISPLEADING	MISREFERRING*	MISSET
MISLIVE	MISOGAMY	MISPLEADINGS	MISREFERS*	MISSETS
MISLIVED	MISOGYNIC*	MISPLEADS	MISREGARD	MISSETTING
MISLIVES	MISOGYNIES	MISPLEASE	MISREGARDS	MISSHAPE
MISLIVING	MISOGYNY	MISPLEASED	MISRELATE	MISSHAPED
MISLOCATE*	MISOLOGIES	MISPLEASES	MISRELATED	MISSHAPEN
MISLOCATED*	MISOLOGY	MISPLEASING	MISRELATES	MISSHAPES
MISLOCATES*	MISONEISM	MISPLED	MISRELATING	MISSHAPING
MISLOCATING*	MISONEISMS	MISPOINT	MISRELIED*	MISSHOD*
MISLODGE*	MISONEIST	MISPOINTED	MISRELIES*	MISSHOOD
MISLODGED*	MISONEISTS	MISPOINTING	MISRELY*	MISSHOODS
MISLODGES*	MISORDER	MISPOINTS	MISRELYING*	MISSIER
MISLODGING*	MISORDERED	MISPOISE*	MISRENDER*	MISSIES
MISLUCK	MISORDERING	MISPOISED*	MISRENDERED*	MISSIEST
MISLUCKED	MISORDERS	MISPOISES*	MISRENDERING*	MISSILE
MISLUCKING	MISORIENT*	MISPOISING*	MISRENDERS*	MISSILEER*
MISLUCKS	MISORIENTED*	MISPRAISE	MISREPORT	MISSILEERS*
MISLYING*	MISORIENTING*	MISPRAISED	MISREPORTED	MISSILERIES

MISSILERY	MISSTOPPING*	MISTHROWN*	MISTUNE	MITES
MISSILES	MISSTOPS*	MISTHROWS*	MISTUNED	MITHER
MISSILRIES	MISSTRICKEN*	MISTICO	MISTUNES	MITHERED
MISSILRY	MISSTRIKE*	MISTICOS	MISTUNING	MITHERING
MISSING	MISSTRIKES*	MISTIER	MISTUTOR*	MITHERS
MISSINGLY	MISSTRIKING*	MISTIEST	MISTUTORED*	MITICIDAL
MISSION	MISSTRUCK*	MISTIGRIS	MISTUTORING*	MITICIDE
MISSIONED	MISSTYLE*	MISTIGRISES	MISTUTORS*	MITICIDES
MISSIONER	MISSTYLED*	MISTILY	MISTY	MITIER
MISSIONERS	MISSTYLES*	MISTIME	MISTYPE*	MITIEST
MISSIONING	MISSTYLING*	MISTIMED	MISTYPED*	MITIGABLE
MISSIONS	MISSUIT	MISTIMES	MISTYPES*	MITIGANT
MISSIS	MISSUITED	MISTIMING	MISTYPING*	MITIGATE
MISSISES	MISSUITING	MISTINESS	MISUNION*	MITIGATED
MISSISH	MISSUITS	MISTINESSES	MISUNIONS*	MITIGATES
MISSIVE	MISSUS	MISTING	MISUSAGE	MITIGATING
MISSIVES	MISSUSES	MISTINGS	MISUSAGES	MITIGATOR
MISSORT*	MISSY	MISTITLE	MISUSE	MITIGATORS
MISSORTED*	MIST	MISTITLED	MISUSED	MITIS*
MISSORTING*	MISTAKE	MISTITLES	MISUSER	MITISES*
MISSORTS*	MISTAKEN	MISTITLING	MISUSERS	MITOGEN
MISSOUND*	MISTAKER*	MISTLE	MISUSES	MITOGENIC
MISSOUNDED*	MISTAKERS*	MISTLED	MISUSING	MITOGENS
MISSOUNDING*	MISTAKES	MISTLES	MISUST	MITOMYCIN*
MISSOUNDS*	MISTAKING	MISTLETOE	MISVALUE*	MITOMYCINS*
MISSOUT*	MISTAKINGS	MISTLETOES	MISVALUED*	MITOSES
MISSOUTS*	MISTAUGHT	MISTLING	MISVALUES*	MITOSIS
MISSPACE*	MISTBOW*	MISTOLD	MISVALUING*	MITOTIC
MISSPACED*	MISTBOWS*	MISTOOK	MISWEEN	MITRAILLE
MISSPACES*	MISTEACH	MISTOUCH*	MISWEENED	MITRAILLES
MISSPACING*	MISTEACHES	MISTOUCHED*	MISWEENING	MITRAL
MISSPEAK	MISTEACHING	MISTOUCHES*	MISWEENS	MITRE
MISSPEAKING	MISTED	MISTOUCHING*	MISWEND	MITRED
MISSPEAKS	MISTELL	MISTRACE*	MISWENDING	MITRES
MISSPELL	MISTELLING	MISTRACED*	MISWENDS	MITREWORT*
MISSPELLED	MISTELLS	MISTRACES*	MISWENT	MITREWORTS*
MISSPELLING	MISTEMPER	MISTRACING*	MISWORD	MITRIFORM
MISSPELLINGS	MISTEMPERED	MISTRAIN*	MISWORDED	MITRING
MISSPELLS	MISTEMPERING	MISTRAINED*	MISWORDING	MITSVAH*
MISSPELT	MISTEMPERS	MISTRAINING*	MISWORDINGS	MITSVAHS*
MISSPEND	MISTEND*	MISTRAINS*	MISWORDS	MITSVOTH*
MISSPENDING	MISTENDED*	MISTRAL	MISWRIT*	MITT
MISSPENDS	MISTENDING*	MISTRALS	MISWRITE	MITTEN
MISSPENT	MISTENDS*	MISTREAT	MISWRITES	MITTENED
MISSPOKE	MISTER	MISTREATED	MISWRITING	MITTENS
MISSPOKEN	MISTERED	MISTREATING	MISWRITTEN	MITTIMUS
MISSTART*	MISTERIES	MISTREATS	MISWROTE	MITTIMUSES
MISSTARTED*	MISTERING	MISTRESS	MISYOKE	MITTS
MISSTARTING*	MISTERM	MISTRESSED	MISYOKED	MITY
MISSTARTS*	MISTERMED	MISTRESSES	MISYOKES	MITZVAH
MISSTATE	MISTERMING	MISTRESSING	MISYOKING	MITZVAHS
MISSTATED	MISTERMS	MISTRIAL	MITCH	MITZVOTH
MISSTATES	MISTERS	MISTRIALS	MITCHED	MIURUS
MISSTATING	MISTERY	MISTRUST	MITCHES	MIURUSES
MISSTEER*	MISTEUK*	MISTRUSTED	MITCHING	MIX
MISSTEERED*	MISTFUL	MISTRUSTING	MITE	MIXABLE
MISSTEERING*	MISTHINK	MISTRUSTS	MITER	MIXED
MISSTEERS*	MISTHINKING	MISTRUTH*	MITERED	MIXEDLY
MISSTEP	MISTHINKS	MISTRUTHS*	MITERER*	MIXEDNESS
MISSTEPPED	MISTHOUGHT	MISTRYST	MITERERS*	MIXEDNESSES
MISSTEPPING	MISTHOUGHTS	MISTRYSTED	MITERING	MIXEN
MISSTEPS	MISTHREW*	MISTRYSTING	MITERS	MIXENS
MISSTOP*	MISTHROW*	MISTRYSTS	MITERWORT*	MIXER
MISSTOPPED*	MISTHROWING*	MISTS	MITERWORTS*	MIXERS

The Chambers Dictionary is the authority for many longer words; see Introduction, page ix

MIXES	MOBBER*	MOCKADO	MODERATOR	MODULATOR
MIXIBLE*	MOBBERS*	MOCKADOES	MODERATORS	MODULATORS
MIXIER	MOBBIE	MOCKAGE	MODERATOS	MODULE
MIXIEST	MOBBIES	MOCKAGES	MODERN	MODULES
MIXING	MOBBING	MOCKED	MODERNE*	MODULI
MIXOLOGIES*	MOBBINGS	MOCKER	MODERNER	MODULO
MIXOLOGY*	MOBBISH	MOCKERIES	MODERNEST	MODULUS
MIXT	MOBBLE	MOCKERNUT	MODERNISE	MODUS
MIXTION	MOBBLED	MOCKERNUTS	MODERNISED	MOE
MIXTIONS	MOBBLES	MOCKERS	MODERNISES	MOELLON
MIXTURE	MOBBLING	MOCKERY	MODERNISING	MOELLONS
MIXTURES	MOBBY	MOCKING	MODERNISM	MOES
MIXUP*	MOBCAP*	MOCKINGLY	MODERNISMS	MOFETTE
MIXUPS*	MOBCAPS*	MOCKINGS	MODERNIST	MOFETTES
MIXY	MOBILE	MOCKS	MODERNISTS	MOFFETTE*
MIZ	MOBILES	MOCKUP*	MODERNITIES	MOFFETTES*
MIZEN	MOBILISE	MOCKUPS*	MODERNITY	MOFUSSIL
MIZENS	MOBILISED	MOCOCK	MODERNIZE	MOFUSSILS
MIZMAZE	MOBILISER	MOCOCKS	MODERNIZED	MOG
MIZMAZES	MOBILISERS	MOCS*	MODERNIZES	MOGGAN
MIZZ	MOBILISES	MOCUCK	MODERNIZING	MOGGANS
MIZZEN	MOBILISING	MOCUCKS	MODERNLY	MOGGED*
MIZZENS	MOBILITIES	MOCUDDUM	MODERNS	MOGGIE
MIZZES	MOBILITY	MOCUDDUMS	MODERS	MOGGIES
MIZZLE	MOBILIZE	MOD	MODES	MOGGING*
MIZZLED	MOBILIZED	MODAL	MODEST	MOGGY
MIZZLES	MOBILIZER	MODALISM	MODESTER	MOGS
MIZZLIER	MOBILIZERS	MODALISMS	MODESTEST	MOGUL
MIZZLIEST	MOBILIZES	MODALIST	MODESTIES	MOGULED
MIZZLING	MOBILIZING	MODALISTS	MODESTLY	MOGULS
MIZZLINGS	MOBLE	MODALITIES	MODESTY	MOHAIR
MIZZLY	MOBLED	MODALITY	MODI	MOHAIRS
MIZZONITE	MOBLES	MODALLY	MODICA*	MOHALIM*
MIZZONITES	MOBLING	MODALS	MODICUM	MOHAWK
MM*	MOBOCRACIES	MODE	MODICUMS	MOHAWKS
MNA	MOBOCRACY	MODEL	MODIFIED	MOHEL
MNAS	MOBOCRAT	MODELED	MODIFIER	MOHELIM*
MNEME	MOBOCRATS	MODELER	MODIFIERS	MOHELS
MNEMES	MOBS	MODELERS	MODIFIES	MOHR
MNEMIC	MOBSMAN	MODELING	MODIFY	MOHRS
MNEMON	MOBSMEN	MODELINGS	MODIFYING	MOHUR
MNEMONIC	MOBSTER	MODELIST*	MODII	MOHURS
MNEMONICS	MOBSTERS	MODELISTS*	MODILLION	MOI
MNEMONIST	MOC*	MODELLED	MODILLIONS	MOIDER
MNEMONISTS	MOCASSIN	MODELLER	MODIOLAR	MOIDERED
MNEMONS	MOCASSINS	MODELLERS	MODIOLI	MOIDERING
MO	MOCCASIN	MODELLI	MODIOLUS	MOIDERS
MOA	MOCCASINS	MODELLING	MODIOLUSES	MOIDORE
MOAN	MOCH	MODELLINGS	MODISH	MOIDORES
MOANED	MOCHA	MODELLO	MODISHLY	MOIETIES
MOANER	MOCHAS	MODELLOS	MODIST	MOIETY
MOANERS	MOCHELL	MODELS	MODISTE	MOIL
MOANFUL	MOCHELLS	MODEM	MODISTES	MOILED
MOANFULLY	MOCHIE	MODEMED	MODISTS	MOILER
MOANING	MOCHIER	MODEMING	MODIUS	MOILERS
MOANS	MOCHIEST	MODEMS	MODIWORT	MOILING
MOAS	MOCHILA*	MODENA	MODIWORTS	MOILINGLY*
MOAT	MOCHILAS*	MODENAS	MODS	MOILS
MOATED	MOCHINESS	MODER	MODULAR	MOINEAU
MOATING	MOCHINESSES	MODERATE	MODULARLY*	MOINEAUS
MOATLIKE*	MOCHS	MODERATED	MODULATE	MOIRA*
MOATS	MOCHY	MODERATES	MODULATED	MOIRAI*
MOB	MOCK	MODERATING	MODULATES	MOIRE
MOBBED	MOCKABLE	MODERATO	MODULATING	MOIRES

MOISER
MOISERS
MOIST
MOISTED
MOISTEN
MOISTENED
MOISTENER*
MOISTENERS*
MOISTENING
MOISTENS
MOISTER
MOISTEST
MOISTFUL*
MOISTIFIED
MOISTIFIES
MOISTIFY
MOISTIFYING
MOISTING
MOISTLY
MOISTNESS
MOISTNESSES
MOISTS
MOISTURE
MOISTURES
MOIT
MOITHER
MOITHERED
MOITHERING
MOITHERS
MOITS
MOJARRA*
MOJARRAS*
MOJO
MOJOES
MOJOS
MOKADDAM
MOKADDAMS
MOKE
MOKES
MOKI
MOKIS
MOKO
MOKOS
MOL*
MOLA
MOLAL
MOLALITIES
MOLALITY
MOLAR
MOLARITIES
MOLARITY
MOLARS
MOLAS
MOLASSES
MOLASSESES*
MOLD
MOLDABLE*
MOLDBOARD*
MOLDBOARDS*
MOLDED
MOLDER*
MOLDERED*
MOLDERING*
MOLDERS*

MOLDIER*
MOLDIEST*
MOLDINESS*
MOLDINESSES*
MOLDING
MOLDINGS*
MOLDS
MOLDWARP
MOLDWARPS
MOLDY*
MOLE
MOLECAST
MOLECASTS
MOLECULAR
MOLECULE
MOLECULES
MOLEHILL
MOLEHILLS
MOLEHUNT
MOLEHUNTS
MOLERAT
MOLERATS
MOLES
MOLESKIN
MOLESKINS
MOLEST
MOLESTED
MOLESTER
MOLESTERS
MOLESTFUL
MOLESTING
MOLESTS
MOLIES
MOLIMEN
MOLIMENS
MOLINE
MOLINES
MOLINET
MOLINETS
MOLL
MOLLA
MOLLAH
MOLLAHS
MOLLAS
MOLLIE
MOLLIES
MOLLIFIED
MOLLIFIER
MOLLIFIERS
MOLLIFIES
MOLLIFY
MOLLIFYING
MOLLITIES
MOLLS
MOLLUSC
MOLLUSCAN
MOLLUSCS
MOLLUSK
MOLLUSKAN
MOLLUSKS
MOLLY
MOLLYMAWK
MOLLYMAWKS
MOLOCH

MOLOCHISE
MOLOCHISED
MOLOCHISES
MOLOCHISING
MOLOCHIZE
MOLOCHIZED
MOLOCHIZES
MOLOCHIZING
MOLOCHS
MOLOSSI
MOLOSSUS
MOLS*
MOLT
MOLTED
MOLTEN
MOLTENLY
MOLTER*
MOLTERS*
MOLTING
MOLTO
MOLTS
MOLY
MOLYBDATE
MOLYBDATES
MOLYBDIC
MOLYBDOUS
MOM
MOME
MOMENT
MOMENTA
MOMENTANY
MOMENTARY
MOMENTLY
MOMENTO*
MOMENTOES*
MOMENTOS*
MOMENTOUS
MOMENTS
MOMENTUM
MOMENTUMS*
MOMES
MOMI*
MOMISM*
MOMISMS*
MOMMA
MOMMAS
MOMMET
MOMMETS
MOMMIES
MOMMY
MOMS
MOMSER*
MOMSERS*
MOMUS*
MOMUSES*
MOMZER
MOMZERIM
MOMZERS
MON
MONA
MONACHAL
MONACHISM
MONACHISMS
MONACHIST

MONACID
MONACIDS*
MONACT
MONACTINE
MONAD
MONADAL*
MONADES
MONADIC
MONADICAL
MONADISM
MONADISMS
MONADNOCK
MONADNOCKS
MONADS
MONAL
MONALS
MONANDRIES
MONANDRY
MONARCH
MONARCHAL
MONARCHIC
MONARCHIES
MONARCHS
MONARCHY
MONARDA
MONARDAS
MONAS
MONASES
MONASTERIES
MONASTERY
MONASTIC
MONASTICS
MONATOMIC
MONAUL
MONAULS
MONAURAL
MONAXIAL
MONAXON
MONAXONIC
MONAXONS
MONAZITE
MONAZITES
MONDAIN
MONDAINE
MONDAINES
MONDAINS
MONDE*
MONDES*
MONDIAL
MONDO
MONDOS*
MONECIAN*
MONECIOUS
MONELLIN*
MONELLINS*
MONER
MONERA
MONERAN*
MONERANS*
MONERGISM
MONERGISMS
MONERON
MONETARY
MONETH

MONETHS
MONETISE
MONETISED
MONETISES
MONETISING
MONETIZE
MONETIZED
MONETIZES
MONETIZING
MONEY
MONEYBAG*
MONEYBAGS
MONEYED
MONEYER
MONEYERS
MONEYLESS
MONEYMAN
MONEYMEN
MONEYS
MONEYWORT
MONEYWORTS
MONG
MONGCORN
MONGCORNS
MONGEESE*
MONGER
MONGERED*
MONGERIES
MONGERING
MONGERINGS
MONGERS
MONGERY
MONGO*
MONGOE*
MONGOES*
MONGOL
MONGOLISM
MONGOLISMS
MONGOLOID
MONGOLOIDS
MONGOLS
MONGOOSE
MONGOOSES
MONGOS*
MONGREL
MONGRELLY
MONGRELS
MONGS
MONGST*
MONIAL
MONIALS
MONICKER
MONICKERS
MONIE*
MONIED
MONIES
MONIKER
MONIKERS
MONILIA
MONILIAS
MONIMENT
MONIMENTS
MONIPLIES
MONISH*

MONISHED* MONOCULAR MONOLOGUES MONOSTELES* MONTHLIES
MONISHES* MONOCULARS* MONOLOGY MONOSTELIES* MONTHLING
MONISHING* MONOCYTE MONOMACHIES MONOSTELY* MONTHLINGS
MONISM MONOCYTES MONOMACHY MONOSTICH MONTHLONG*
MONISMS MONOCYTIC* MONOMANIA MONOSTICHS MONTHLY
MONIST MONODIC MONOMANIAS MONOSTYLE MONTHS
MONISTIC MONODICAL MONOMARK MONOSY MONTICLE
MONISTS MONODIES MONOMARKS MONOTINT MONTICLES
MONITION MONODIST MONOMER MONOTINTS MONTICULE
MONITIONS MONODISTS MONOMERIC MONOTONE MONTICULES
MONITIVE MONODONT MONOMERS MONOTONED MONTIES
MONITOR MONODRAMA MONOMETER MONOTONES MONTRE
MONITORED MONODRAMAS MONOMETERS MONOTONIC MONTRES
MONITORIES* MONODY MONOMIAL MONOTONIES MONTURE
MONITORING MONOECIES* MONOMIALS MONOTONING MONTURES
MONITORS MONOECISM MONOMODE MONOTONY MONTY
MONITORY MONOECISMS MONOPHAGIES MONOTREME MONUMENT
MONITRESS MONOECY* MONOPHAGY MONOTREMES MONUMENTED
MONITRESSES MONOESTER* MONOPHASE MONOTROCH MONUMENTING
MONK MONOESTERS* MONOPHONIES MONOTROCHS MONUMENTS
MONKERIES MONOFIL MONOPHONY MONOTYPE MONURON*
MONKERY MONOFILS MONOPHYLIES* MONOTYPES MONURONS*
MONKEY MONOFUEL* MONOPHYLY* MONOTYPIC MONY
MONKEYED MONOFUELS* MONOPITCH MONOVULAR* MONYPLIES
MONKEYING MONOGAMIC MONOPLANE MONOXIDE MONZONITE
MONKEYISH MONOGAMIES MONOPLANES MONOXIDES MONZONITES
MONKEYISM MONOGAMY MONOPLOID* MONOXYLON MOO
MONKEYISMS MONOGENIC MONOPLOIDS* MONOXYLONS MOOCH
MONKEYPOD* MONOGENIES MONOPOD MONS* MOOCHED
MONKEYPODS* MONOGENY MONOPODE MONSIEUR MOOCHER
MONKEYS MONOGERM* MONOPODES MONSIGNOR* MOOCHERS
MONKFISH MONOGLOT MONOPODIA MONSIGNORI* MOOCHES
MONKFISHES MONOGLOTS MONOPODIES* MONSIGNORS* MOOCHING
MONKHOOD MONOGONIES MONOPODS MONSOON MOOD
MONKHOODS MONOGONY MONOPODY* MONSOONAL MOODIED
MONKISH MONOGRAM MONOPOLE MONSOONS MOODIER
MONKS MONOGRAMED* MONOPOLES MONSTER MOODIES
MONKSHOOD MONOGRAMING* MONOPOLIES MONSTERA MOODIEST
MONKSHOODS MONOGRAMMED* MONOPOLY MONSTERAS MOODILY
MONO MONOGRAMMING* MONOPSONIES MONSTERS MOODINESS
MONOACID MONOGRAMS MONOPSONY MONSTROUS MOODINESSES
MONOACIDS* MONOGRAPH MONOPTERA MONTADALE* MOODS
MONOAMINE MONOGRAPHED MONOPTOTE MONTADALES* MOODY
MONOAMINES MONOGRAPHING MONOPTOTES MONTAGE MOODYING
MONOBASIC MONOGRAPHS MONOPULSE MONTAGED MOOED
MONOCARP MONOGYNIES MONOPULSES MONTAGES MOOI
MONOCARPS MONOGYNY MONORAIL MONTAGING MOOING
MONOCEROS MONOHULL MONORAILS MONTANE MOOK
MONOCEROSES MONOHULLS MONORCHID MONTANES* MOOKS
MONOCHORD MONOKINI MONORCHIDS* MONTANT MOOKTAR
MONOCHORDS MONOKINIS MONORHINE MONTANTO MOOKTARS
MONOCLE MONOLATER MONORHYME MONTANTOS MOOL
MONOCLED MONOLATERS MONORHYMES MONTANTS MOOLA
MONOCLES MONOLATRIES MONOS MONTARIA MOOLAH
MONOCLINE MONOLATRY MONOSES MONTARIAS MOOLAHS
MONOCLINES MONOLAYER MONOSIES MONTE MOOLAS
MONOCOQUE MONOLAYERS MONOSIS MONTEITH MOOLED
MONOCOQUES MONOLITH MONOSOME* MONTEITHS MOOLEY*
MONOCOT MONOLITHS MONOSOMES* MONTEM MOOLEYS*
MONOCOTS MONOLOG* MONOSOMIC* MONTEMS MOOLI
MONOCRACIES MONOLOGIC MONOSOMICS* MONTERO MOOLIES
MONOCRACY MONOLOGIES MONOSOMIES* MONTEROS MOOLING
MONOCRAT MONOLOGS* MONOSOMY* MONTES MOOLIS
MONOCRATS MONOLOGUE MONOSTELE* MONTH MOOLS

Words marked with an asterisk are from OTCWL

MOOLY	MOONSHINES	MOOVES	MORALISES	MORELLO
MOON	MOONSHINY	MOOVING	MORALISING	MORELLOS
MOONBEAM	MOONSHOT	MOP	MORALISM	MORELS
MOONBEAMS	MOONSHOTS	MOPANE	MORALISMS	MORENDO
MOONBLIND	MOONSTONE	MOPANES	MORALIST	MOREOVER
MOONBOW*	MOONSTONES	MOPANI	MORALISTS	MOREPORK
MOONBOWS*	MOONWALK	MOPANIS	MORALITIES	MOREPORKS
MOONCALF	MOONWALKED	MOPBOARD	MORALITY	MORES
MOONCALVES	MOONWALKING	MOPBOARDS	MORALIZE	MORESQUE*
MOONDUST*	MOONWALKS	MOPE	MORALIZED	MORESQUES*
MOONDUSTS*	MOONWARD*	MOPED	MORALIZER	MORGAN*
MOONED	MOONWORT	MOPEDS	MORALIZERS	MORGANITE
MOONER	MOONWORTS	MOPEHAWK	MORALIZES	MORGANITES
MOONERS	MOONY	MOPEHAWKS	MORALIZING	MORGANS*
MOONEYE	MOOP	MOPER	MORALL	MORGAY
MOONEYES	MOOPED	MOPERIES*	MORALLED	MORGAYS
MOONFACE	MOOPING	MOPERS	MORALLER	MORGEN
MOONFACED*	MOOPS	MOPERY*	MORALLERS	MORGENS
MOONFACES	MOOR	MOPES	MORALLING	MORGUE
MOONFISH*	MOORAGE	MOPEY	MORALLS	MORGUES
MOONFISHES*	MOORAGES	MOPHEAD	MORALLY	MORIA
MOONIER	MOORCOCK	MOPHEADS	MORALS	MORIAS
MOONIES	MOORCOCKS	MOPIER	MORAS	MORIBUND
MOONIEST	MOORED	MOPIEST	MORASS	MORICHE
MOONILY*	MOORFOWL	MOPING	MORASSES	MORICHES
MOONING	MOORFOWLS	MOPINGLY	MORASSY	MORION
MOONISH	MOORHEN	MOPISH	MORAT	MORIONS
MOONISHLY*	MOORHENS	MOPISHLY	MORATORIA	MORISCO
MOONLESS	MOORIER	MOPOKE	MORATORIUM*	MORISCOES
MOONLET	MOORIEST	MOPOKES	MORATORIUMS*	MORISCOS
MOONLETS	MOORILL	MOPPED	MORATORY	MORISH
MOONLIGHT	MOORILLS	MOPPER	MORATS	MORKIN
MOONLIGHTED	MOORING	MOPPERS	MORAY	MORKINS
MOONLIGHTING	MOORINGS	MOPPET	MORAYS	MORLING
MOONLIGHTINGS	MOORISH	MOPPETS	MORBID	MORLINGS
MOONLIGHTS	MOORLAND	MOPPIER	MORBIDER	MORMAOR
MOONLIKE*	MOORLANDS	MOPPIEST	MORBIDEST	MORMAORS
MOONLIT	MOORLOG	MOPPING	MORBIDITIES	MORN
MOONPHASE	MOORLOGS	MOPPY	MORBIDITY	MORNAY
MOONPHASES	MOORMAN	MOPS	MORBIDLY	MORNAYS
MOONPORT*	MOORMEN	MOPSIES	MORBIFIC	MORNE
MOONPORTS*	MOORS	MOPSTICK	MORBILLI	MORNED
MOONQUAKE	MOORVA	MOPSTICKS	MORBUS	MORNES
MOONQUAKES	MOORVAS	MOPSY	MORBUSES	MORNING
MOONRAKER	MOORWORT*	MOPUS	MORCEAU	MORNINGS
MOONRAKERS	MOORWORTS*	MOPUSES	MORCEAUX	MORNS
MOONRISE	MOORY	MOPY	MORDACITIES	MOROCCO
MOONRISES	MOOS	MOQUETTE	MORDACITY	MOROCCOS
MOONROCK	MOOSE	MOQUETTES	MORDANCIES	MORON
MOONROCKS	MOOSEYARD	MOR	MORDANCY	MORONIC
MOONROOF	MOOSEYARDS	MORA	MORDANT	MORONISM*
MOONROOFS	MOOT	MORACEOUS	MORDANTED	MORONISMS*
MOONS	MOOTABLE	MORAE*	MORDANTING	MORONITIES*
MOONSAIL	MOOTED	MORAINAL	MORDANTLY	MORONITY*
MOONSAILS	MOOTER	MORAINE	MORDANTS	MORONS
MOONSCAPE	MOOTERS	MORAINES	MORDENT	MOROSE
MOONSCAPES	MOOTEST	MORAINIC	MORDENTS	MOROSELY
MOONSEED	MOOTING	MORAL	MORE	MOROSER
MOONSEEDS	MOOTINGS	MORALE	MOREEN	MOROSEST
MOONSET	MOOTMAN	MORALES	MOREENS	MOROSITIES
MOONSETS	MOOTMEN	MORALISE	MOREISH	MOROSITY
MOONSHEE	MOOTS	MORALISED	MOREL	MORPH
MOONSHEES	MOOVE	MORALISER	MORELLE*	MORPHEAN
MOONSHINE	MOOVED	MORALISERS	MORELLES*	MORPHED

The Chambers Dictionary is the authority for many longer words; see Introduction, page ix

MORPHEME	MORTALLY	MOSAICS	MOTES	MOTLEYS
MORPHEMES	MORTALS	MOSASAUR*	MOTET	MOTLIER
MORPHEMIC	MORTAR	MOSASAURS*	MOTETS	MOTLIEST
MORPHEMICS	MORTARED	MOSCHATE*	MOTETT	MOTMOT
MORPHETIC	MORTARING	MOSCHATEL	MOTETTIST	MOTMOTS
MORPHEW	MORTARS	MOSCHATELS	MOTETTISTS	MOTOCROSS
MORPHEWS	MORTARY*	MOSE	MOTETTS	MOTOCROSSES
MORPHIA	MORTBELL	MOSED	MOTEY	MOTOR
MORPHIAS	MORTBELLS	MOSES	MOTH	MOTORABLE
MORPHIC	MORTCLOTH	MOSEY	MOTHBALL	MOTORAIL
MORPHIN*	MORTCLOTHS	MOSEYED	MOTHBALLED	MOTORAILS
MORPHINE	MORTGAGE	MOSEYING	MOTHBALLING	MOTORBIKE
MORPHINES	MORTGAGED	MOSEYS	MOTHBALLS	MOTORBIKED*
MORPHING	MORTGAGEE	MOSHAV	MOTHED	MOTORBIKES
MORPHINGS	MORTGAGEES	MOSHAVIM	MOTHER	MOTORBIKING*
MORPHINS*	MORTGAGER	MOSHING	MOTHERED	MOTORBOAT
MORPHO	MORTGAGERS	MOSHINGS	MOTHERING	MOTORBOATS
MORPHOGEN*	MORTGAGES	MOSING	MOTHERINGS	MOTORBUS*
MORPHOGENS*	MORTGAGING	MOSK*	MOTHERLY	MOTORBUSES*
MORPHOS	MORTGAGOR	MOSKONFYT	MOTHERS	MOTORBUSES*
MORPHOSES	MORTGAGORS	MOSKONFYTS	MOTHERY	MOTORBUSSES*
MORPHOSIS	MORTICE	MOSKS*	MOTHIER	MOTORCADE
MORPHOTIC	MORTICED	MOSLINGS	MOTHIEST	MOTORCADED*
MORPHS	MORTICER	MOSQUE	MOTHLIKE*	MOTORCADES
MORRA	MORTICERS	MOSQUES	MOTHPROOF	MOTORCADING*
MORRAS	MORTICES	MOSQUITO	MOTHPROOFED	MOTORCAR*
MORRHUA	MORTICIAN	MOSQUITOES	MOTHPROOFING	MOTORCARS*
MORRHUAS	MORTICIANS	MOSQUITOS	MOTHPROOFS	MOTORDOM*
MORRICE	MORTICING	MOSS	MOTHS	MOTORDOMS*
MORRICES	MORTIFIC	MOSSBACK	MOTHY	MOTORED
MORRION	MORTIFIED	MOSSBACKS	MOTIER	MOTORIAL
MORRIONS	MORTIFIER	MOSSED	MOTIEST	MOTORIC*
MORRIS	MORTIFIERS	MOSSER*	MOTIF	MOTORING
MORRISED	MORTIFIES	MOSSERS*	MOTIFIC*	MOTORINGS*
MORRISES	MORTIFY	MOSSES	MOTIFS	MOTORISE
MORRISING	MORTIFYING	MOSSIE	MOTILE	MOTORISED
MORRO	MORTIFYINGS	MOSSIER	MOTILES	MOTORISES
MORROS	MORTISE	MOSSIES	MOTILITIES	MOTORISING
MORROW	MORTISED	MOSSIEST	MOTILITY	MOTORIST
MORROWS	MORTISER	MOSSINESS	MOTION	MOTORISTS
MORS	MORTISERS	MOSSINESSES	MOTIONAL	MOTORIUM
MORSAL	MORTISES	MOSSING	MOTIONED	MOTORIUMS
MORSE	MORTISING	MOSSLAND	MOTIONER*	MOTORIZE
MORSEL	MORTLING	MOSSLANDS	MOTIONERS*	MOTORIZED
MORSELED*	MORTLINGS	MOSSLIKE*	MOTIONING	MOTORIZES
MORSELING*	MORTMAIN	MOSSO*	MOTIONIST	MOTORIZING
MORSELLED	MORTMAINS	MOSSPLANT	MOTIONISTS	MOTORLESS*
MORSELLING	MORTS	MOSSPLANTS	MOTIONS	MOTORMAN
MORSELS	MORTUARIES	MOSSY	MOTIVATE	MOTORMEN
MORSES	MORTUARY	MOST	MOTIVATED	MOTORS
MORSURE	MORULA	MOSTE*	MOTIVATES	MOTORWAY
MORSURES	MORULAE	MOSTEST*	MOTIVATING	MOTORWAYS
MORT	MORULAR	MOSTESTS*	MOTIVATOR	MOTORY
MORTAL	MORULAS*	MOSTLY	MOTIVATORS	MOTOSCAFI
MORTALISE	MORWONG	MOSTS	MOTIVE	MOTOSCAFO
MORTALISED	MORWONGS	MOSTWHAT	MOTIVED	MOTS
MORTALISES	MOS*	MOT	MOTIVES	MOTSER
MORTALISING	MOSAIC	MOTE	MOTIVIC*	MOTSERS
MORTALITIES	MOSAICISM	MOTED	MOTIVING	MOTT
MORTALITY	MOSAICISMS	MOTEL	MOTIVITIES	MOTTE
MORTALIZE	MOSAICIST	MOTELIER	MOTIVITY	MOTTES
MORTALIZED	MOSAICISTS	MOTELIERS	MOTLEY	MOTTIER
MORTALIZES	MOSAICKED*	MOTELS	MOTLEYER	MOTTIEST
MORTALIZING	MOSAICKING*	MOTEN	MOTLEYEST	MOTTLE
				MOTTLED

Words marked with an asterisk are from OTCWL

MOTTLER*	MOULT	MOUSILY*	MOVED	MOZETTA
MOTTLERS*	MOULTED	MOUSINESS*	MOVELESS	MOZETTAS
MOTTLES	MOULTEN	MOUSINESSES*	MOVEMENT	MOZETTE*
MOTTLING	MOULTER*	MOUSING	MOVEMENTS	MOZING
MOTTLINGS	MOULTERS*	MOUSINGS	MOVER	MOZO*
MOTTO	MOULTING	MOUSLE	MOVERS	MOZOS*
MOTTOED	MOULTINGS	MOUSLED	MOVES	MOZZ
MOTTOES	MOULTS	MOUSLES	MOVIE	MOZZES
MOTTOS*	MOUND	MOUSLING	MOVIEDOM*	MOZZETTA
MOTTS	MOUNDED	MOUSME	MOVIEDOMS*	MOZZETTAS
MOTTY	MOUNDING	MOUSMEE	MOVIEGOER	MOZZETTE*
MOTU	MOUNDS	MOUSMEES	MOVIEGOERS	MOZZIE
MOTUCA	MOUNSEER	MOUSMES	MOVIELAND	MOZZIES
MOTUCAS	MOUNSEERS	MOUSSAKA	MOVIELANDS	MOZZLE
MOTUS	MOUNT	MOUSSAKAS	MOVIEOLA*	MOZZLES
MOTZA	MOUNTABLE*	MOUSSE	MOVIEOLAS*	MPRET
MOTZAS	MOUNTAIN	MOUSSED*	MOVIES	MPRETS
MOU	MOUNTAINS	MOUSSES	MOVING	MRIDAMGAM
MOUCH	MOUNTAINY*	MOUSSING*	MOVINGLY	MRIDAMGAMS
MOUCHARD	MOUNTANT	MOUST	MOVIOLA*	MRIDANG
MOUCHARDS	MOUNTANTS	MOUSTACHE	MOVIOLAS*	MRIDANGA
MOUCHED	MOUNTED	MOUSTACHES	MOW	MRIDANGAM
MOUCHER	MOUNTER	MOUSTED	MOWA	MRIDANGAMS
MOUCHERS	MOUNTERS	MOUSTING	MOWAS	MRIDANGAS
MOUCHES	MOUNTING	MOUSTS	MOWBURN	MRIDANGS
MOUCHING	MOUNTINGS	MOUSY	MOWBURNED	MU
MOUCHOIR	MOUNTS	MOUTAN	MOWBURNING	MUCATE
MOUCHOIRS	MOUP	MOUTANS	MOWBURNS	MUCATES
MOUDIWART	MOUPED	MOUTER	MOWBURNT	MUCH
MOUDIWARTS	MOUPING	MOUTERED	MOWDIWART	MUCHACHO*
MOUDIWORT	MOUPS	MOUTERER	MOWDIWARTS	MUCHACHOS*
MOUDIWORTS	MOURN	MOUTERERS	MOWDIWORT	MUCHEL
MOUE	MOURNED	MOUTERING	MOWDIWORTS	MUCHELL
MOUES	MOURNER	MOUTERS	MOWED	MUCHELLS
MOUFFLON	MOURNERS	MOUTH	MOWER	MUCHELS
MOUFFLONS	MOURNFUL	MOUTHABLE	MOWERS	MUCHES
MOUFLON	MOURNFULLER*	MOUTHED	MOWING	MUCHLY
MOUFLONS	MOURNFULLEST*	MOUTHER	MOWINGS	MUCHNESS
MOUGHT	MOURNING	MOUTHERS	MOWN	MUCHNESSES
MOUILLE	MOURNINGS	MOUTHFEEL	MOWRA	MUCID
MOUJIK	MOURNIVAL	MOUTHFEELS	MOWRAS	MUCIDITIES*
MOUJIKS	MOURNIVALS	MOUTHFUL	MOWS	MUCIDITY*
MOULAGE	MOURNS	MOUTHFULS	MOXA	MUCIGEN
MOULAGES	MOUS	MOUTHIER	MOXAS	MUCIGENS
MOULD	MOUSAKA	MOUTHIEST	MOXIE	MUCILAGE
MOULDABLE	MOUSAKAS	MOUTHILY*	MOXIES	MUCILAGES
MOULDED	MOUSE	MOUTHING	MOY	MUCIN
MOULDER	MOUSED	MOUTHLESS	MOYA	MUCINOID*
MOULDERED	MOUSEKIN	MOUTHLIKE*	MOYAS	MUCINOUS*
MOULDERING	MOUSEKINS	MOUTHPART*	MOYGASHEL	MUCINS
MOULDERS	MOUSER	MOUTHPARTS*	MOYGASHELS	MUCK
MOULDIER	MOUSERIES	MOUTHS	MOYITIES	MUCKED
MOULDIEST	MOUSERS	MOUTHWASH	MOYITY	MUCKENDER
MOULDING	MOUSERY	MOUTHWASHES	MOYL	MUCKENDERS
MOULDINGS	MOUSES	MOUTHY	MOYLE	MUCKER
MOULDS	MOUSETRAP*	MOUTON	MOYLED	MUCKERED
MOULDWARP	MOUSETRAPPED*	MOUTONS	MOYLES	MUCKERING
MOULDWARPS	MOUSETRAPPING*	MOVABLE	MOYLING	MUCKERS
MOULDY	MOUSETRAPS*	MOVABLES	MOYLS	MUCKHEAP
MOULIN	MOUSEY	MOVABLY	MOYS	MUCKHEAPS
MOULINET	MOUSIE	MOVE	MOZ	MUCKIER
MOULINETS	MOUSIER	MOVEABLE	MOZE	MUCKIEST
MOULINS	MOUSIES	MOVEABLES	MOZED	MUCKILY*
MOULS	MOUSIEST	MOVEABLY	MOZES	MUCKINESS

The Chambers Dictionary is the authority for many longer words; see Introduction, page ix

MUCKINESSES	MUDDLERS	MUENSTERS	MUIDS	MULLER
MUCKING	MUDDLES	MUESLI	MUIL	MULLERS
MUCKLE	MUDDLING	MUESLIS	MUILS	MULLET
MUCKLES	MUDDLY*	MUEZZIN	MUIR	MULLETS
MUCKLUCK	MUDDY	MUEZZINS	MUIRBURN	MULLEY
MUCKLUCKS	MUDDYING	MUFF	MUIRBURNS	MULLEYS
MUCKRAKE*	MUDEJAR	MUFFED	MUIRS	MULLIGAN
MUCKRAKED*	MUDEJARES	MUFFETTEE	MUIST	MULLIGANS
MUCKRAKER*	MUDFISH	MUFFETTEES	MUISTED	MULLING
MUCKRAKERS*	MUDFISHES	MUFFIN	MUISTING	MULLION
MUCKRAKES*	MUDFLAP	MUFFINEER	MUISTS	MULLIONED
MUCKRAKING*	MUDFLAPS	MUFFINEERS	MUJAHEDIN	MULLIONING*
MUCKS	MUDFLAT	MUFFING	MUJAHIDIN	MULLIONS
MUCKSWEAT	MUDFLATS	MUFFINS	MUJIK	MULLITE*
MUCKSWEATS	MUDFLOW*	MUFFISH	MUJIKS	MULLITES*
MUCKWORM*	MUDFLOWS*	MUFFLE	MUKHTAR	MULLOCK
MUCKWORMS*	MUDGE	MUFFLED	MUKHTARS	MULLOCKS
MUCKY	MUDGED	MUFFLER	MUKLUK	MULLOCKY*
MUCLUC	MUDGER	MUFFLERED*	MUKLUKS	MULLOWAY
MUCLUCS	MUDGERS	MUFFLERS	MUKTUK*	MULLOWAYS
MUCOID	MUDGES	MUFFLES	MUKTUKS*	MULLS
MUCOIDAL*	MUDGING	MUFFLING	MULATTA	MULMUL
MUCOIDS*	MUDGUARD	MUFFS	MULATTAS	MULMULL
MUCOLYTIC*	MUDGUARDS	MUFLON	MULATTO	MULMULLS
MUCOR	MUDHOLE	MUFLONS	MULATTOES	MULMULS
MUCORS	MUDHOLES	MUFTI	MULATTOS	MULSE
MUCOSA	MUDHOOK	MUFTIS	MULBERRIES	MULSES
MUCOSAE	MUDHOOKS	MUG	MULBERRY	MULSH
MUCOSAL*	MUDIR	MUGEARITE	MULCH	MULSHED
MUCOSAS*	MUDIRIA	MUGEARITES	MULCHED	MULSHES
MUCOSE*	MUDIRIAS	MUGFUL	MULCHES	MULSHING
MUCOSITIES	MUDIRIEH	MUGFULS	MULCHING	MULTEITIES
MUCOSITY	MUDIRIEHS	MUGG*	MULCT	MULTEITY
MUCOUS	MUDIRS	MUGGAR*	MULCTED	MULTIAGE*
MUCRO	MUDLARK	MUGGARS*	MULCTING	MULTIATOM*
MUCRONATE	MUDLARKED	MUGGED	MULCTS	MULTIBAND*
MUCRONES	MUDLARKING	MUGGEE	MULE	MULTIBANK*
MUCROS	MUDLARKS	MUGGEES	MULED*	MULTICAR*
MUCULENT	MUDLOGGER	MUGGER	MULES	MULTICELL*
MUCUS	MUDLOGGERS	MUGGERS	MULETA*	MULTICITY*
MUCUSES	MUDPACK	MUGGIER	MULETAS*	MULTICOPY*
MUD	MUDPACKS	MUGGIEST	MULETEER	MULTIDRUG*
MUDBATH	MUDPUPPIES	MUGGILY*	MULETEERS	MULTIFID
MUDBATHS	MUDPUPPY	MUGGINESS	MULEY	MULTIFIL
MUDCAP*	MUDRA	MUGGINESSES	MULEYS	MULTIFILS
MUDCAPPED*	MUDRAS	MUGGING	MULGA	MULTIFOIL
MUDCAPPING*	MUDROCK*	MUGGINGS	MULGAS	MULTIFOILS
MUDCAPS*	MUDROCKS*	MUGGINS	MULING*	MULTIFOLD*
MUDCAT	MUDROOM*	MUGGINSES	MULISH	MULTIFORM
MUDCATS	MUDROOMS*	MUGGISH	MULISHLY	MULTIFORMS
MUDDED	MUDS	MUGGS*	MULL	MULTIGERM*
MUDDER	MUDSCOW	MUGGUR*	MULLA*	MULTIGRID*
MUDDERS	MUDSCOWS	MUGGURS*	MULLAH	MULTIGYM
MUDDIED	MUDSILL*	MUGGY	MULLAHISM*	MULTIGYMS
MUDDIER	MUDSILLS*	MUGS	MULLAHISMS*	MULTIHUED*
MUDDIES	MUDSLIDE	MUGSHOT	MULLAHS	MULTIHULL
MUDDIEST	MUDSLIDES	MUGSHOTS	MULLARKIES	MULTIHULLS
MUDDILY	MUDSTONE	MUGWORT	MULLARKY	MULTIJET*
MUDDINESS	MUDSTONES	MUGWORTS	MULLAS*	MULTILANE*
MUDDINESSES	MUDWORT	MUGWUMP	MULLED	MULTILINE*
MUDDING	MUDWORTS	MUGWUMPS	MULLEIN	MULTIMODE
MUDDLE	MUEDDIN	MUHLIES*	MULLEINS	MULTIPACK
MUDDLED	MUEDDINS	MUHLY*	MULLEN*	MULTIPACKS
MUDDLER	MUENSTER	MUID	MULLENS*	MULTIPAGE*

Words marked with an asterisk are from OTCWL

MULTIPARA	MUMMICHOGS*	MUNICIPAL	MURDEROUS	MURR*
MULTIPARAE	MUMMIED	MUNICIPALS*	MURDERS	MURRA
MULTIPARAS	MUMMIES	MUNIFIED	MURE	MURRAIN
MULTIPART*	MUMMIFIED	MUNIFIES	MURED	MURRAINED
MULTIPATH*	MUMMIFIES	MUNIFY	MUREIN*	MURRAINS
MULTIPED	MUMMIFORM	MUNIFYING	MUREINS*	MURRAM
MULTIPEDE	MUMMIFY	MUNIMENT	MURENA	MURRAMS
MULTIPEDES	MUMMIFYING	MUNIMENTS	MURENAS	MURRAS
MULTIPEDS	MUMMING	MUNIS*	MURES	MURRAY
MULTIPION*	MUMMINGS	MUNITE	MUREX	MURRAYS
MULTIPLE	MUMMOCK	MUNITED	MUREXES	MURRE
MULTIPLES	MUMMOCKS	MUNITES	MURGEON	MURRELET
MULTIPLET	MUMMS	MUNITING	MURGEONED	MURRELETS
MULTIPLETS	MUMMY	MUNITION	MURGEONING	MURREN
MULTIPLEX	MUMMYING	MUNITIONED	MURGEONS	MURRENS
MULTIPLEXED	MUMP	MUNITIONING	MURIATE	MURRES
MULTIPLEXES	MUMPED	MUNITIONS	MURIATED	MURREY
MULTIPLEXING	MUMPER	MUNNION	MURIATES	MURREYS
MULTIPLIED	MUMPERS	MUNNIONS	MURIATIC	MURRHA
MULTIPLIES	MUMPING	MUNS*	MURICATE	MURRHAS
MULTIPLY	MUMPISH	MUNSHI	MURICATED	MURRHINE
MULTIPLYING	MUMPISHLY	MUNSHIS	MURICES	MURRIES
MULTIPOLE*	MUMPS	MUNSTER	MURID*	MURRIN
MULTIROOM*	MUMPSIMUS	MUNSTERS	MURIDS*	MURRINE
MULTISITE*	MUMPSIMUSES	MUNT	MURIFORM	MURRINS
MULTISIZE*	MUMS	MUNTIN	MURINE	MURRION
MULTISTEP*	MUMSIER	MUNTING	MURINES	MURRIONS
MULTITON*	MUMSIEST	MUNTINGS	MURING	MURRS*
MULTITONE*	MUMSY	MUNTINS	MURK	MURRY
MULTITUDE	MUMU*	MUNTJAC	MURKER	MURTHER
MULTITUDES	MUMUS*	MUNTJACS	MURKEST	MURTHERED
MULTIUNIT*	MUN	MUNTJAK	MURKIER	MURTHERER
MULTIUSE*	MUNCH	MUNTJAKS	MURKIEST	MURTHERERS
MULTIUSER	MUNCHED	MUNTS	MURKILY	MURTHERING
MULTIWALL*	MUNCHER	MUNTU	MURKINESS	MURTHERS
MULTIYEAR*	MUNCHERS	MUNTUS	MURKINESSES	MURVA
MULTUM	MUNCHES	MUON	MURKISH	MURVAS
MULTUMS	MUNCHIES*	MUONIC	MURKLY*	MUS
MULTURE	MUNCHING	MUONIUM	MURKS	MUSACEOUS
MULTURED	MUNCHKIN	MUONIUMS	MURKSOME	MUSANG
MULTURER	MUNCHKINS	MUONS	MURKY	MUSANGS
MULTURERS	MUNDANE	MUQADDAM	MURL	MUSCA*
MULTURES	MUNDANELY	MUQADDAMS	MURLAIN	MUSCADEL
MULTURING	MUNDANER	MURA*	MURLAINS	MUSCADELS
MUM	MUNDANEST	MURAENA	MURLAN	MUSCADET*
MUMBLE	MUNDANITIES	MURAENAS	MURLANS	MUSCADETS*
MUMBLED	MUNDANITY	MURAENID*	MURLED	MUSCADIN
MUMBLER	MUNDIC	MURAENIDS*	MURLIER	MUSCADINE
MUMBLERS	MUNDICS	MURAGE	MURLIEST	MUSCADINES
MUMBLES	MUNDIFIED	MURAGES	MURLIN	MUSCADINS
MUMBLING	MUNDIFIES	MURAL	MURLING	MUSCAE*
MUMBLINGS	MUNDIFY	MURALIST	MURLINS	MUSCARINE
MUMBLY*	MUNDIFYING	MURALISTS	MURLS	MUSCARINES
MUMCHANCE	MUNDUNGO*	MURALS	MURLY	MUSCAT
MUMCHANCES	MUNDUNGOS*	MURAS*	MURMUR	MUSCATEL
MUMM	MUNDUNGUS	MURDER	MURMURED	MUSCATELS
MUMMED	MUNDUNGUSES	MURDERED	MURMURER	MUSCATS
MUMMER	MUNGCORN	MURDEREE	MURMURERS	MUSCID
MUMMERIES	MUNGCORNS	MURDEREES	MURMURING	MUSCIDS
MUMMERS	MUNGO	MURDERER	MURMURINGS	MUSCLE
MUMMERY	MUNGOOSE	MURDERERS	MURMUROUS	MUSCLED
MUMMIA	MUNGOOSES	MURDERESS	MURMURS	MUSCLEMAN
MUMMIAS	MUNGOS	MURDERESSES	MURPHIES	MUSCLEMEN
MUMMICHOG*	MUNI*	MURDERING	MURPHY	MUSCLES

MUSCLIER	MUSIMON	MUSSIER	MUTCHES	MUTUALITY
MUSCLIEST	MUSIMONS	MUSSIEST	MUTCHKIN	MUTUALIZE
MUSCLING	MUSING	MUSSILY*	MUTCHKINS	MUTUALIZED
MUSCLINGS	MUSINGLY	MUSSINESS	MUTE	MUTUALIZES
MUSCLY	MUSINGS	MUSSINESSES	MUTED	MUTUALIZING
MUSCOID	MUSIT	MUSSING	MUTEDLY*	MUTUALLY
MUSCOLOGIES	MUSITS	MUSSITATE	MUTELY	MUTUALS
MUSCOLOGY	MUSIVE	MUSSITATED	MUTENESS	MUTUCA
MUSCONE	MUSJID*	MUSSITATES	MUTENESSES	MUTUCAS
MUSCONES	MUSJIDS*	MUSSITATING	MUTER	MUTUEL*
MUSCOSE	MUSK	MUSSY	MUTES	MUTUELS*
MUSCOVADO	MUSKED	MUST	MUTEST	MUTULAR*
MUSCOVADOS	MUSKEG	MUSTACHE	MUTI	MUTULE
MUSCOVITE	MUSKEGS	MUSTACHED*	MUTICOUS	MUTULES
MUSCOVITES	MUSKET	MUSTACHES	MUTILATE	MUTUUM
MUSCULAR	MUSKETEER	MUSTACHIO	MUTILATED	MUTUUMS
MUSCULOUS	MUSKETEERS	MUSTACHIOS	MUTILATES	MUUMUU*
MUSE	MUSKETOON	MUSTANG	MUTILATING	MUUMUUS*
MUSED	MUSKETOONS	MUSTANGS	MUTILATOR	MUX
MUSEFUL	MUSKETRIES	MUSTARD	MUTILATORS	MUXED
MUSEFULLY	MUSKETRY	MUSTARDS	MUTINE	MUXES
MUSEOLOGIES	MUSKETS	MUSTARDY*	MUTINED	MUXING
MUSEOLOGY	MUSKIE*	MUSTED	MUTINEER	MUZAKY
MUSER	MUSKIER	MUSTEE	MUTINEERED	MUZHIK
MUSERS	MUSKIES*	MUSTEES	MUTINEERING	MUZHIKS
MUSES	MUSKIEST	MUSTELINE	MUTINEERS	MUZJIK*
MUSET	MUSKILY	MUSTELINES	MUTINES	MUZJIKS*
MUSETS	MUSKINESS	MUSTER	MUTING	MUZZIER
MUSETTE	MUSKINESSES	MUSTERED	MUTINIED	MUZZIEST
MUSETTES	MUSKING	MUSTERER	MUTINIES	MUZZILY
MUSEUM	MUSKIT*	MUSTERERS	MUTINING	MUZZINESS
MUSEUMS	MUSKITS*	MUSTERING	MUTINOUS	MUZZINESSES
MUSH	MUSKLE	MUSTERS	MUTINY	MUZZLE
MUSHA	MUSKLES	MUSTH	MUTINYING	MUZZLED
MUSHED	MUSKMELON*	MUSTHS	MUTIS	MUZZLER
MUSHER	MUSKMELONS*	MUSTIER	MUTISM	MUZZLERS
MUSHERS	MUSKONE	MUSTIEST	MUTISMS	MUZZLES
MUSHES	MUSKONES	MUSTILY	MUTON	MUZZLING
MUSHIER	MUSKRAT	MUSTINESS	MUTONS	MUZZY
MUSHIEST	MUSKRATS	MUSTINESSES	MUTOSCOPE	MVULE
MUSHILY	MUSKS	MUSTING	MUTOSCOPES	MVULES
MUSHINESS	MUSKY	MUSTS	MUTS*	MY
MUSHINESSES	MUSLIN	MUSTY	MUTT	MYAL
MUSHING	MUSLINED	MUT*	MUTTER	MYALGIA
MUSHMOUTH	MUSLINET	MUTABLE	MUTTERED	MYALGIAS
MUSHMOUTHS	MUSLINETS	MUTABLY	MUTTERER	MYALGIC
MUSHROOM	MUSLINS	MUTAGEN	MUTTERERS	MYALISM
MUSHROOMED	MUSMON	MUTAGENIC	MUTTERING	MYALISMS
MUSHROOMING	MUSMONS	MUTAGENS	MUTTERINGS	MYALL
MUSHROOMS	MUSO	MUTANDA	MUTTERS	MYALLS
MUSHY	MUSOS	MUTANDUM	MUTTON	MYASES*
MUSIC	MUSPIKE*	MUTANT	MUTTONS	MYASIS*
MUSICAL	MUSPIKES*	MUTANTS	MUTTONY	MYCELE*
MUSICALE	MUSQUASH	MUTASE*	MUTTS	MYCELES*
MUSICALES	MUSQUASHES	MUTASES*	MUTUAL	MYCELIA
MUSICALLY	MUSROL	MUTATE	MUTUALISE	MYCELIAL
MUSICALS	MUSROLS	MUTATED	MUTUALISED	MYCELIAN*
MUSICIAN	MUSS	MUTATES	MUTUALISES	MYCELIUM
MUSICIANS	MUSSE	MUTATING	MUTUALISING	MYCELOID*
MUSICKED	MUSSED	MUTATION	MUTUALISM	MYCETES
MUSICKER	MUSSEL	MUTATIONS	MUTUALISMS	MYCETOMA
MUSICKERS	MUSSELLED	MUTATIVE	MUTUALIST*	MYCETOMAS
MUSICKING	MUSSELS	MUTATORY	MUTUALISTS*	MYCETOMATA
MUSICS	MUSSES	MUTCH	MUTUALITIES	MYCOFLORA*

Words marked with an asterisk are from OTCWL

MYCOFLORAE*
MYCOFLORAS*
MYCOLOGIC
MYCOLOGIES
MYCOLOGY
MYCOPHAGIES
MYCOPHAGY
MYCOPHILE*
MYCOPHILES*
MYCORHIZA
MYCORHIZAS
MYCOSES
MYCOSIS
MYCOTIC
MYCOTOXIN
MYCOTOXINS
MYDRIASES
MYDRIASIS
MYDRIATIC
MYDRIATICS
MYELIN
MYELINE*
MYELINES*
MYELINIC*
MYELINS
MYELITIDES*
MYELITIS
MYELITISES
MYELOCYTE*
MYELOCYTES*
MYELOID
MYELOMA
MYELOMAS
MYELOMATA
MYELON
MYELONS
MYGALE
MYGALES
MYIASES
MYIASIS
MYLODON
MYLODONS
MYLODONT
MYLODONTS
MYLOHYOID
MYLOHYOIDS
MYLONITE
MYLONITES

MYLONITIC
MYNA
MYNAH
MYNAHS
MYNAS
MYNHEER
MYNHEERS
MYOBLAST
MYOBLASTS
MYOCARDIA*
MYOCARDIUM*
MYOCLONIC*
MYOCLONUS*
MYOCLONUSES*
MYOFIBRIL
MYOFIBRILS
MYOGEN
MYOGENIC
MYOGENS
MYOGLOBIN
MYOGLOBINS
MYOGRAM
MYOGRAMS
MYOGRAPH
MYOGRAPHIES
MYOGRAPHS
MYOGRAPHY
MYOID
MYOLOGIC*
MYOLOGIES
MYOLOGIST
MYOLOGISTS
MYOLOGY
MYOMA
MYOMANCIES
MYOMANCY
MYOMANTIC
MYOMAS
MYOMATA
MYOMATOUS*
MYONEURAL*
MYOPATHIC*
MYOPATHIES*
MYOPATHY*
MYOPE
MYOPES
MYOPIA
MYOPIAS

MYOPIC
MYOPICS
MYOPIES*
MYOPS
MYOPSES
MYOPY*
MYOSCOPE*
MYOSCOPES*
MYOSES
MYOSIN
MYOSINS
MYOSIS
MYOSITIS
MYOSITISES
MYOSOTE
MYOSOTES
MYOSOTIS
MYOSOTISES
MYOTIC*
MYOTICS*
MYOTOME*
MYOTOMES*
MYOTONIA
MYOTONIAS
MYOTONIC*
MYOTUBE
MYOTUBES
MYRBANE
MYRBANES
MYRIAD
MYRIADS
MYRIADTH
MYRIADTHS
MYRIAPOD
MYRIAPODS
MYRICA*
MYRICAS*
MYRINGA
MYRINGAS
MYRIOPOD
MYRIOPODS
MYRIORAMA
MYRIORAMAS
MYRISTIC
MYRMECOID
MYRMIDON
MYRMIDONS
MYROBALAN

MYROBALANS
MYRRH
MYRRHIC
MYRRHINE
MYRRHOL
MYRRHOLS
MYRRHS
MYRTLE
MYRTLES
MYSELF
MYSID*
MYSIDS*
MYSOST*
MYSOSTS*
MYSTAGOG*
MYSTAGOGIES
MYSTAGOGS*
MYSTAGOGY
MYSTERIES
MYSTERY
MYSTIC
MYSTICAL
MYSTICISM
MYSTICISMS
MYSTICLY*
MYSTICS
MYSTIFIED
MYSTIFIER
MYSTIFIERS
MYSTIFIES
MYSTIFY
MYSTIFYING
MYSTIQUE
MYSTIQUES
MYTH
MYTHI
MYTHIC
MYTHICAL
MYTHICISE
MYTHICISED
MYTHICISES
MYTHICISING
MYTHICISM
MYTHICISMS
MYTHICIST
MYTHICISTS
MYTHICIZE
MYTHICIZED

MYTHICIZES
MYTHICIZING
MYTHIER*
MYTHIEST*
MYTHISE
MYTHISED
MYTHISES
MYTHISING
MYTHISM
MYTHISMS
MYTHIST
MYTHISTS
MYTHIZE
MYTHIZED
MYTHIZES
MYTHIZING
MYTHMAKER*
MYTHMAKERS*
MYTHOI
MYTHOLOGIES
MYTHOLOGY
MYTHOMANE
MYTHOMANES
MYTHOPOET
MYTHOPOETS
MYTHOS
MYTHS
MYTHUS
MYTHY*
MYTILOID
MYXEDEMA
MYXEDEMAS
MYXEDEMIC
MYXOCYTE*
MYXOCYTES*
MYXOEDEMA
MYXOEDEMAS
MYXOID*
MYXOMA
MYXOMAS*
MYXOMATA
MYXOVIRAL*
MYXOVIRUS
MYXOVIRUSES
MZEE
MZEES
MZUNGU
MZUNGUS

N

NA
NAAM
NAAMS
NAAN
NAANS
NAARTJE
NAARTJES
NAB
NABBED
NABBER
NABBERS
NABBING
NABE*
NABES*
NABIS*
NABK
NABKS
NABLA
NABLAS
NABOB
NABOBERIES*
NABOBERY*
NABOBESS*
NABOBESSES*
NABOBISH*
NABOBISM*
NABOBISMS*
NABOBS
NABS
NACARAT
NACARATS
NACELLE
NACELLES
NACH
NACHAS*
NACHE
NACHES
NACHO
NACHOS
NACHTMAAL
NACHTMAALS
NACKET
NACKETS
NACRE
NACRED
NACREOUS
NACRES
NACRITE
NACRITES
NACROUS
NADA
NADAS
NADIR
NADIRAL*
NADIRS

NAE
NAEBODIES
NAEBODY
NAETHING
NAETHINGS
NAEVE
NAEVES
NAEVI
NAEVOID
NAEVUS
NAFF
NAFFING
NAFFLY
NAFFNESS
NAFFNESSES
NAFFS
NAG
NAGA
NAGANA
NAGANAS
NAGAPIE
NAGAPIES
NAGARI
NAGARIS
NAGAS
NAGGED
NAGGER
NAGGERS
NAGGIER
NAGGIEST
NAGGING
NAGGINGLY*
NAGGY
NAGMAAL
NAGMAALS
NAGOR
NAGORS
NAGS
NAH*
NAHAL
NAHALS
NAIAD
NAIADES
NAIADS
NAIANT
NAIF
NAIFER
NAIFEST
NAIFS*
NAIK
NAIKS
NAIL
NAILBRUSH*
NAILBRUSHES*
NAILED

NAILER
NAILERIES
NAILERS
NAILERY
NAILFOLD*
NAILFOLDS*
NAILHEAD*
NAILHEADS*
NAILING
NAILINGS
NAILLESS
NAILS
NAILSET*
NAILSETS*
NAIN
NAINSELL
NAINSELLS
NAINSOOK
NAINSOOKS
NAIRA
NAIRAS
NAISSANT
NAIVE
NAIVELY
NAIVENESS
NAIVENESSES
NAIVER
NAIVES*
NAIVEST
NAIVETE
NAIVETES
NAIVETIES
NAIVETY
NAIVIST
NAKED
NAKEDER
NAKEDEST
NAKEDLY
NAKEDNESS
NAKEDNESSES
NAKER
NAKERS
NALA
NALAS
NALED*
NALEDS*
NALLA
NALLAH
NALLAHS
NALLAS
NALOXONE
NALOXONES
NAM
NAMABLE
NAMASKAR

NAMASKARS
NAMASTE
NAMASTES
NAME
NAMEABLE
NAMED
NAMELESS
NAMELY
NAMEPLATE*
NAMEPLATES*
NAMER
NAMERS
NAMES
NAMESAKE
NAMESAKES
NAMETAG*
NAMETAGS*
NAMETAPE
NAMETAPES
NAMING
NAMINGS
NAMS
NAN
NANA
NANAS
NANCE
NANCES
NANCIES
NANCY
NANDIN*
NANDINA*
NANDINAS*
NANDINE
NANDINES
NANDINS*
NANDOO
NANDOOS
NANDU
NANDUS
NANISM
NANISMS
NANKEEN
NANKEENS
NANKIN
NANKINS
NANNA
NANNAS
NANNIE*
NANNIED
NANNIES
NANNY
NANNYGAI
NANNYGAIS
NANNYGHAI
NANNYGHAIS

NANNYING
NANNYISH
NANOGRAM
NANOGRAMS
NANOMETER*
NANOMETERS*
NANOMETRE
NANOMETRES
NANOTESLA*
NANOTESLAS*
NANOWATT*
NANOWATTS*
NANS
NAOI
NAOS
NAOSES
NAP
NAPA
NAPALM
NAPALMED
NAPALMING
NAPALMS
NAPAS
NAPE
NAPERIES
NAPERY
NAPES
NAPHTHA
NAPHTHAS
NAPHTHENE
NAPHTHENES
NAPHTHOL
NAPHTHOLS
NAPHTHYL*
NAPHTHYLS*
NAPHTOL*
NAPHTOLS*
NAPIFORM
NAPKIN
NAPKINS
NAPLESS
NAPOLEON
NAPOLEONS
NAPOO
NAPOOED
NAPOOING
NAPOOS
NAPPA
NAPPAS
NAPPE
NAPPED
NAPPER
NAPPERS
NAPPES
NAPPIE*

Words marked with an asterisk are from OTCWL

NAPPIER	NARGILEH	NASALIZE	NATIVITY	NAUTICAL
NAPPIES	NARGILEHS	NASALIZED	NATRIUM	NAUTICS
NAPPIEST	NARGILES	NASALIZES	NATRIUMS	NAUTILI
NAPPINESS	NARGILIES	NASALIZING	NATROLITE	NAUTILOID*
NAPPINESSES	NARGILLIES	NASALLY	NATROLITES	NAUTILOIDS*
NAPPING	NARGILLY	NASALS	NATRON	NAUTILUS
NAPPY	NARGILY	NASARD	NATRONS	NAUTILUSES
NAPRON	NARIAL	NASARDS	NATS	NAVAID
NAPRONS	NARIC*	NASCENCE	NATTER	NAVAIDS
NAPS	NARICORN	NASCENCES	NATTERED	NAVAL
NARAS	NARICORNS	NASCENCIES	NATTERER	NAVALISM
NARASES	NARINE	NASCENCY	NATTERERS	NAVALISMS
NARC	NARIS*	NASCENT	NATTERING	NAVALLY*
NARCEEN	NARK	NASEBERRIES	NATTERS	NAVAR*
NARCEENS	NARKED	NASEBERRY	NATTERY	NAVARCH
NARCEIN*	NARKIER	NASHGAB	NATTIER	NAVARCHIES
NARCEINE	NARKIEST	NASHGABS	NATTIEST	NAVARCHS
NARCEINES	NARKING	NASIAL*	NATTILY	NAVARCHY
NARCEINS*	NARKS	NASION	NATTINESS	NAVARHO
NARCISM*	NARKY	NASIONS	NATTINESSES	NAVARHOS
NARCISMS*	NARQUOIS	NASTALIK	NATTY	NAVARIN
NARCISSI	NARRAS	NASTALIKS	NATURA	NAVARINS
NARCISSUS	NARRASES	NASTIC	NATURAE	NAVARS*
NARCISSUSES	NARRATE	NASTIER	NATURAL	NAVE
NARCIST*	NARRATED	NASTIES	NATURALLY	NAVEL
NARCISTS*	NARRATER*	NASTIEST	NATURALS	NAVELS
NARCO	NARRATERS*	NASTILY	NATURE	NAVELWORT
NARCOS	NARRATES	NASTINESS	NATURED	NAVELWORTS
NARCOSE*	NARRATING	NASTINESSES	NATURES	NAVES
NARCOSES	NARRATION	NASTY	NATURING	NAVETTE
NARCOSIS	NARRATIONS	NASUTE	NATURISM	NAVETTES
NARCOTIC	NARRATIVE	NASUTES	NATURISMS	NAVEW
NARCOTICS	NARRATIVES	NAT	NATURIST	NAVEWS
NARCOTINE	NARRATOR	NATAL	NATURISTS	NAVICERT
NARCOTINES	NARRATORS	NATALITIES	NAUGHT	NAVICERTS
NARCOTISE	NARRATORY	NATALITY	NAUGHTIER	NAVICULA
NARCOTISED	NARRE	NATANT	NAUGHTIES	NAVICULAR
NARCOTISES	NARROW	NATANTLY*	NAUGHTIEST	NAVICULARS
NARCOTISING	NARROWED	NATATION	NAUGHTILY	NAVICULAS
NARCOTISM	NARROWER	NATATIONS	NAUGHTS	NAVIES
NARCOTISMS	NARROWEST	NATATORIA	NAUGHTY	NAVIGABLE
NARCOTIST	NARROWING	NATATORIUM*	NAUMACHIA	NAVIGABLY
NARCOTISTS	NARROWINGS	NATATORIUMS*	NAUMACHIAE	NAVIGATE
NARCOTIZE	NARROWLY	NATATORY	NAUMACHIAS	NAVIGATED
NARCOTIZED	NARROWS	NATCH	NAUMACHIES	NAVIGATES
NARCOTIZES	NARTHEX	NATCHES	NAUMACHY	NAVIGATING
NARCOTIZING	NARTHEXES	NATES	NAUNT	NAVIGATOR
NARCS	NARTJIE	NATHELESS	NAUNTS	NAVIGATORS
NARD	NARTJIES	NATHEMO	NAUPLIAL*	NAVVIED
NARDED	NARWAL*	NATHEMORE	NAUPLII	NAVVIES
NARDINE*	NARWALS*	NATHLESS	NAUPLIOID	NAVVY
NARDING	NARWHAL	NATIFORM	NAUPLIUS	NAVVYING
NARDOO	NARWHALE*	NATION	NAUSEA	NAVY
NARDOOS	NARWHALES*	NATIONAL	NAUSEANT	NAW*
NARDS	NARWHALS	NATIONALS	NAUSEANTS	NAWAB
NARE	NARY	NATIONS	NAUSEAS	NAWABS
NARES	NAS	NATIVE	NAUSEATE	NAY
NARGHILE	NASAL	NATIVELY	NAUSEATED	NAYS
NARGHILES	NASALISE	NATIVES	NAUSEATES	NAYSAYER*
NARGHILIES	NASALISED	NATIVISM	NAUSEATING	NAYSAYERS*
NARGHILLIES	NASALISES	NATIVISMS	NAUSEOUS	NAYTHLES
NARGHILLY	NASALISING	NATIVIST	NAUTCH	NAYWARD
NARGHILY	NASALITIES	NATIVISTS	NAUTCHES	NAYWARDS
NARGILE	NASALITY	NATIVITIES	NAUTIC	NAYWORD

The Chambers Dictionary is the authority for many longer words; see Introduction, page ix

NAYWORDS	NEBBISHY*	NECKLESS*	NEEDER	NEGATIVED
NAZE	NEBBUK	NECKLET	NEEDERS	NEGATIVES
NAZES	NEBBUKS	NECKLETS	NEEDFIRE	NEGATIVING
NAZI*	NEBECK	NECKLIKE*	NEEDFIRES	NEGATON*
NAZIFIED*	NEBECKS	NECKLINE	NEEDFUL	NEGATONS*
NAZIFIES*	NEBEK	NECKLINES	NEEDFULLY	NEGATOR*
NAZIFY*	NEBEKS	NECKPIECE	NEEDFULS*	NEGATORS*
NAZIFYING*	NEBEL	NECKPIECES	NEEDIER	NEGATORY
NAZIR	NEBELS	NECKS	NEEDIEST	NEGATRON
NAZIRS	NEBENKERN*	NECKTIE	NEEDILY	NEGATRONS
NAZIS*	NEBENKERNS*	NECKTIES	NEEDINESS	NEGLECT
NE	NEBISH	NECKVERSE	NEEDINESSES	NEGLECTED
NEAFE	NEBISHES	NECKVERSES	NEEDING	NEGLECTER
NEAFES	NEBRIS	NECKWEAR	NEEDLE	NEGLECTERS
NEAFFE	NEBRISES	NECKWEARS	NEEDLED	NEGLECTING
NEAFFES	NEBS	NECKWEED	NEEDLEFUL	NEGLECTS
NEAL	NEBULA	NECKWEEDS	NEEDLEFULS	NEGLIGE
NEALED	NEBULAE	NECROLOGIES	NEEDLER	NEGLIGEE
NEALING	NEBULAR	NECROLOGY	NEEDLERS	NEGLIGEES
NEALS	NEBULAS	NECROPHIL	NEEDLES	NEGLIGENT
NEANIC	NEBULE	NECROPHILS	NEEDLESS	NEGLIGES
NEAP	NEBULES	NECROPOLEIS*	NEEDLIER	NEGOCIANT
NEAPED	NEBULISE	NECROPOLES*	NEEDLIEST	NEGOCIANTS
NEAPING	NEBULISED	NECROPOLI*	NEEDLING	NEGOTIANT
NEAPS	NEBULISER	NECROPOLIS*	NEEDLINGS*	NEGOTIANTS
NEAR	NEBULISERS	NECROPOLISES*	NEEDLY	NEGOTIATE
NEARBY*	NEBULISES	NECROPSIED*	NEEDMENT	NEGOTIATED
NEARED	NEBULISING	NECROPSIES	NEEDMENTS	NEGOTIATES
NEARER	NEBULIUM	NECROPSY	NEEDS	NEGOTIATING
NEAREST	NEBULIUMS	NECROPSYING*	NEEDY	NEGRESS
NEARING	NEBULIZE	NECROSE	NEELD	NEGRESSES
NEARLIER*	NEBULIZED	NECROSED	NEELDS	NEGRITUDE
NEARLIEST*	NEBULIZER	NECROSES	NEELE	NEGRITUDES
NEARLY	NEBULIZERS	NECROSING	NEELES	NEGRO
NEARNESS	NEBULIZES	NECROSIS	NEEM	NEGROES
NEARNESSES	NEBULIZING	NECROTIC	NEEMB	NEGROHEAD
NEARS	NEBULOSE*	NECROTISE	NEEMBS	NEGROHEADS
NEARSHORE*	NEBULOUS	NECROTISED	NEEMS	NEGROID
NEARSIDE	NEBULY	NECROTISES	NEEP	NEGROIDAL
NEARSIDES	NECESSARIES	NECROTISING	NEEPS	NEGROIDS
NEAT	NECESSARY	NECROTIZE	NEESBERRIES	NEGROISM
NEATEN	NECESSITIES	NECROTIZED	NEESBERRY	NEGROISMS
NEATENED	NECESSITY	NECROTIZES	NEESE	NEGRONI*
NEATENING	NECK	NECROTIZING	NEESED	NEGRONIS*
NEATENS	NECKATEE	NECROTOMIES	NEESES	NEGROPHIL
NEATER	NECKATEES	NECROTOMY	NEESING	NEGROPHILS
NEATEST	NECKBAND	NECTAR	NEEZE	NEGUS
NEATH	NECKBANDS	NECTAREAL	NEEZED	NEGUSES
NEATHERD*	NECKBEEF	NECTAREAN	NEEZES	NEIF
NEATHERDS*	NECKBEEFS	NECTARED	NEEZING	NEIFS
NEATLY	NECKCLOTH	NECTARIAL	NEF	NEIGH
NEATNESS	NECKCLOTHS	NECTARIES	NEFANDOUS	NEIGHBOR
NEATNESSES	NECKED	NECTARINE	NEFARIOUS	NEIGHBORED
NEATS*	NECKER*	NECTARINES	NEFAST	NEIGHBORING
NEB	NECKERS*	NECTAROUS	NEFS	NEIGHBORS
NEBBED	NECKGEAR	NECTARS	NEGATE	NEIGHBOUR
NEBBICH	NECKGEARS	NECTARY	NEGATED	NEIGHBOURED
NEBBICHS	NECKING	NED	NEGATER*	NEIGHBOURING
NEBBING	NECKINGS	NEDDIES	NEGATERS*	NEIGHBOURS
NEBBISH	NECKLACE	NEDDY	NEGATES	NEIGHED
NEBBISHE	NECKLACED	NEDS	NEGATING	NEIGHING
NEBBISHER	NECKLACES	NEE	NEGATION	NEIGHS
NEBBISHERS	NECKLACING	NEED	NEGATIONS	NEIST
NEBBISHES	NECKLACINGS	NEEDED	NEGATIVE	NEITHER

Words marked with an asterisk are from OTCWL

NEIVE	NEOLOGISED	NEOTERIZES	NERDY	NEST
NEIVES	NEOLOGISES	NEOTERIZING	NEREID	NESTABLE*
NEK	NEOLOGISING	NEOTOXIN	NEREIDES	NESTED
NEKS	NEOLOGISM	NEOTOXINS	NEREIDS	NESTER
NEKTON	NEOLOGISMS	NEOTYPE*	NEREIS*	NESTERS
NEKTONIC*	NEOLOGIST	NEOTYPES*	NERINE	NESTFUL
NEKTONS	NEOLOGISTS	NEP	NERINES	NESTFULS
NELIES	NEOLOGIZE	NEPENTHE	NERITE	NESTING
NELIS	NEOLOGIZED	NEPENTHES	NERITES	NESTINGS
NELLIE*	NEOLOGIZES	NEPER	NERITIC	NESTLE
NELLIES	NEOLOGIZING	NEPERS	NERK	NESTLED
NELLY	NEOLOGY	NEPETA	NERKA	NESTLER*
NELSON	NEOMORPH*	NEPETAS	NERKAS	NESTLERS*
NELSONS	NEOMORPHS*	NEPHALISM	NERKS	NESTLES
NELUMBIUM	NEOMYCIN	NEPHALISMS	NEROL*	NESTLIKE
NELUMBIUMS	NEOMYCINS	NEPHALIST	NEROLI	NESTLING
NELUMBO	NEON	NEPHALISTS	NEROLIS	NESTLINGS
NELUMBOS	NEONATAL	NEPHELINE	NEROLS*	NESTOR*
NEMA*	NEONATE	NEPHELINES	NERTS*	NESTORS*
NEMAS*	NEONATES	NEPHELITE	NERTZ*	NESTS
NEMATIC	NEONED*	NEPHELITES	NERVAL	NET
NEMATODE	NEONOMIAN	NEPHEW	NERVATE	NETBALL
NEMATODES	NEONOMIANS	NEPHEWS	NERVATION	NETBALLS
NEMATOID	NEONS	NEPHOGRAM	NERVATIONS	NETE
NEMERTEAN	NEOPAGAN	NEPHOGRAMS	NERVATURE	NETES
NEMERTEANS	NEOPAGANS	NEPHOLOGIES	NERVATURES	NETFUL
NEMERTIAN	NEOPHILE	NEPHOLOGY	NERVE	NETFULS
NEMERTIANS	NEOPHILES	NEPHRALGIES	NERVED	NETHELESS
NEMERTINE	NEOPHILIA	NEPHRALGY	NERVELESS	NETHER
NEMERTINES	NEOPHILIAS	NEPHRIC	NERVELET	NETIZEN
NEMESES	NEOPHOBE	NEPHRIDIA	NERVELETS	NETIZENS
NEMESIA	NEOPHOBES	NEPHRIDIUM*	NERVER	NETLESS*
NEMESIAS	NEOPHOBIA	NEPHRISM*	NERVERS	NETLIKE*
NEMESIS	NEOPHOBIAS	NEPHRISMS*	NERVES	NETMINDER*
NEMN	NEOPHOBIC	NEPHRITE	NERVIER	NETMINDERS*
NEMNED	NEOPHYTE	NEPHRITES	NERVIEST	NETOP*
NEMNING	NEOPHYTES	NEPHRITIC	NERVILY	NETOPS*
NEMNS	NEOPHYTIC	NEPHRITICS	NERVINE	NETS
NEMOPHILA	NEOPILINA	NEPHRITIDES*	NERVINES	NETSUKE
NEMOPHILAS	NEOPILINAS	NEPHRITIS	NERVINESS	NETSUKES
NEMORAL	NEOPLASIA*	NEPHRITISES	NERVINESSES	NETT
NEMOROUS	NEOPLASIAS*	NEPHROID	NERVING	NETTABLE*
NEMPT	NEOPLASM	NEPHRON	NERVINGS*	NETTED
NENE	NEOPLASMS	NEPHRONS	NERVOSITIES*	NETTER*
NENES	NEOPRENE	NEPHROSES	NERVOSITY*	NETTERS*
NENNIGAI	NEOPRENES	NEPHROSIS	NERVOUS	NETTIER
NENNIGAIS	NEOTEINIA	NEPHROTIC	NERVOUSLY	NETTIEST
NENUPHAR	NEOTEINIAS	NEPHROTICS*	NERVULAR	NETTING
NENUPHARS	NEOTENIC	NEPIONIC	NERVULE	NETTINGS
NEOBLAST	NEOTENIES	NEPIT	NERVULES	NETTLE
NEOBLASTS	NEOTENOUS	NEPITS	NERVURE	NETTLED
NEOCORTEX*	NEOTENY	NEPOTIC	NERVURES	NETTLER*
NEOCORTEXES*	NEOTERIC	NEPOTISM	NERVY	NETTLERS*
NEOCORTICES*	NEOTERICS	NEPOTISMS	NESCIENCE	NETTLES
NEODYMIUM	NEOTERISE	NEPOTIST	NESCIENCES	NETTLIER
NEODYMIUMS	NEOTERISED	NEPOTISTS	NESCIENT	NETTLIEST
NEOLITH	NEOTERISES	NEPS	NESCIENTS*	NETTLING
NEOLITHIC*	NEOTERISING	NEPTUNIUM	NESH	NETTLY
NEOLITHS	NEOTERISM	NEPTUNIUMS	NESHER	NETTS
NEOLOGIAN	NEOTERISMS	NERD	NESHEST	NETTY
NEOLOGIANS	NEOTERIST	NERDIER	NESHNESS	NETWORK
NEOLOGIC	NEOTERISTS	NERDIEST	NESHNESSES	NETWORKED
NEOLOGIES	NEOTERIZE	NERDISH*	NESS	NETWORKER
NEOLOGISE	NEOTERIZED	NERDS	NESSES	NETWORKERS

The Chambers Dictionary is the authority for many longer words; see Introduction, page ix

NETWORKING
NETWORKINGS
NETWORKS
NEUK
NEUKS
NEUM
NEUMATIC*
NEUME
NEUMES
NEUMIC*
NEUMS
NEURAL
NEURALGIA
NEURALGIAS
NEURALGIC
NEURALLY
NEURATION
NEURATIONS
NEURAXON*
NEURAXONS*
NEURILITIES
NEURILITY
NEURINE
NEURINES
NEURISM
NEURISMS
NEURITE
NEURITES
NEURITIC
NEURITICS
NEURITIDES*
NEURITIS
NEURITISES
NEUROCHIP
NEUROCHIPS
NEUROGLIA
NEUROGLIAS
NEUROGRAM
NEUROGRAMS
NEUROID*
NEUROLOGIES
NEUROLOGY
NEUROMA
NEUROMAS
NEUROMATA
NEURON
NEURONAL
NEURONE
NEURONES
NEURONIC
NEURONS
NEUROPATH
NEUROPATHS
NEUROPIL
NEUROPILS
NEUROSAL*
NEUROSES
NEUROSIS
NEUROTIC
NEUROTICS
NEUROTOMIES
NEUROTOMY
NEURULA*
NEURULAE*

NEURULAS*
NEUSTON
NEUSTONS
NEUTER
NEUTERED
NEUTERING
NEUTERS
NEUTRAL
NEUTRALLY
NEUTRALS
NEUTRETTO
NEUTRETTOS
NEUTRINO
NEUTRINOS
NEUTRON
NEUTRONIC*
NEUTRONS
NEVE
NEVEL
NEVELLED
NEVELLING
NEVELS
NEVER
NEVERMORE
NEVES
NEVI
NEVOID*
NEVUS
NEW
NEWBIE
NEWBIES
NEWBORN
NEWBORNS*
NEWCOME
NEWCOMER
NEWCOMERS
NEWED
NEWEL
NEWELL
NEWELLED
NEWELLS
NEWELS
NEWER
NEWEST
NEWFANGLE
NEWFOUND*
NEWIE*
NEWIES*
NEWING
NEWISH
NEWISHLY
NEWLY
NEWLYWED*
NEWLYWEDS*
NEWMARKET
NEWMARKETS
NEWMOWN*
NEWNESS
NEWNESSES
NEWS
NEWSAGENT
NEWSAGENTS
NEWSBOY
NEWSBOYS

NEWSBREAK*
NEWSBREAKS*
NEWSCAST
NEWSCASTS
NEWSED
NEWSES
NEWSFLASH
NEWSFLASHES
NEWSGIRL
NEWSGIRLS
NEWSGROUP
NEWSGROUPS
NEWSHAWK
NEWSHAWKS
NEWSHOUND
NEWSHOUNDS
NEWSIE*
NEWSIER
NEWSIES
NEWSIEST
NEWSINESS
NEWSINESSES
NEWSING
NEWSLESS
NEWSMAN
NEWSMEN
NEWSPAPER
NEWSPAPERED*
NEWSPAPERING*
NEWSPAPERS
NEWSPEAK
NEWSPEAKS
NEWSPRINT
NEWSPRINTS
NEWSREEL
NEWSREELS
NEWSROOM
NEWSROOMS
NEWSSTAND*
NEWSSTANDS*
NEWSTRADE
NEWSTRADES
NEWSWIRE
NEWSWIRES
NEWSWOMAN
NEWSWOMEN
NEWSY
NEWT
NEWTON
NEWTONS
NEWTS
NEXT
NEXTDOOR*
NEXTLY
NEXTNESS
NEXTNESSES
NEXTS
NEXUS
NEXUSES*
NGAIO
NGAIOS
NGANA
NGANAS
NGULTRUM

NGULTRUMS
NGWEE
NHANDU
NHANDUS
NIACIN
NIACINS
NIAISERIE
NIAISERIES
NIALAMIDE*
NIALAMIDES*
NIB
NIBBED
NIBBING
NIBBLE
NIBBLED
NIBBLER
NIBBLERS
NIBBLES
NIBBLING
NIBBLINGS
NIBLICK
NIBLICKS
NIBLIKE*
NIBS
NICAD
NICADS
NICCOLITE
NICCOLITES
NICE
NICEISH
NICELY
NICENESS
NICENESSES
NICER
NICEST
NICETIES
NICETY
NICHE
NICHED
NICHER
NICHERED
NICHERING
NICHERS
NICHES
NICHING
NICISH
NICK
NICKAR
NICKARS
NICKED
NICKEL
NICKELED
NICKELIC
NICKELINE
NICKELINES
NICKELING
NICKELISE
NICKELISED
NICKELISES
NICKELISING
NICKELIZE
NICKELIZED
NICKELIZES
NICKELIZING

NICKELLED
NICKELLING
NICKELOUS
NICKELS
NICKER
NICKERED
NICKERING
NICKERS
NICKING
NICKLE*
NICKLED*
NICKLES*
NICKLING*
NICKNACK*
NICKNACKS*
NICKNAME
NICKNAMED
NICKNAMER*
NICKNAMERS*
NICKNAMES
NICKNAMING
NICKPOINT
NICKPOINTS
NICKS
NICKSTICK
NICKSTICKS
NICKUM
NICKUMS
NICOL
NICOLS
NICOMPOOP
NICOMPOOPS
NICOTIAN
NICOTIANA
NICOTIANAS
NICOTIANS
NICOTIN*
NICOTINE
NICOTINED
NICOTINES
NICOTINIC
NICOTINS*
NICTATE
NICTATED
NICTATES
NICTATING
NICTATION
NICTATIONS
NICTITATE
NICTITATED
NICTITATES
NICTITATING
NID
NIDAL
NIDAMENTA
NIDATION
NIDATIONS
NIDDERING
NIDDERINGS
NIDE
NIDED*
NIDERING
NIDERINGS
NIDERLING

NIDERLINGS	NIGGARD	NIGHTLY	NIMBUS	NIP
NIDES	NIGGARDED	NIGHTMARE	NIMBUSED	NIPA
NIDGET	NIGGARDING	NIGHTMARES	NIMBUSES	NIPAS
NIDGETS	NIGGARDLY	NIGHTMARY	NIMBYISM	NIPCHEESE
NIDI	NIGGARDS	NIGHTS	NIMBYISMS	NIPCHEESES
NIDIFIED	NIGGER	NIGHTSIDE*	NIMIETIES	NIPPED
NIDIFIES	NIGGERDOM	NIGHTSIDES*	NIMIETY	NIPPER
NIDIFY	NIGGERDOMS	NIGHTSPOT	NIMIOUS	NIPPERED
NIDIFYING	NIGGERED	NIGHTSPOTS	NIMMED	NIPPERING
NIDING	NIGGERING	NIGHTTIME*	NIMMER	NIPPERKIN
NIDINGS	NIGGERISH	NIGHTTIMES*	NIMMERS	NIPPERKINS
NIDOR	NIGGERISM	NIGHTWARD	NIMMING	NIPPERS
NIDOROUS	NIGGERISMS	NIGHTWEAR	NIMONIC	NIPPIER
NIDORS	NIGGERS	NIGHTWEARS	NIMROD*	NIPPIEST
NIDS	NIGGERY	NIGHTY	NIMRODS*	NIPPILY
NIDUS	NIGGLE	NIGRICANT	NIMS	NIPPINESS
NIDUSES*	NIGGLED	NIGRIFIED	NINCOM	NIPPINESSES
NIE	NIGGLER	NIGRIFIES	NINCOMS	NIPPING
NIECE	NIGGLERS	NIGRIFY	NINCUM	NIPPINGLY
NIECES	NIGGLES	NIGRIFYING	NINCUMS	NIPPLE
NIED	NIGGLIER	NIGRITUDE	NINE	NIPPLED
NIEF	NIGGLIEST	NIGRITUDES	NINEBARK*	NIPPLES
NIEFS	NIGGLING	NIGROSIN	NINEBARKS*	NIPPLING
NIELLATED	NIGGLINGS	NIGROSINE	NINEFOLD	NIPPY
NIELLI	NIGGLY	NIGROSINES	NINEHOLES	NIPS
NIELLIST	NIGH	NIGROSINS	NINEPENCE	NIPTER
NIELLISTS	NIGHED	NIHIL	NINEPENCES	NIPTERS
NIELLO	NIGHER*	NIHILISM	NINEPENNIES	NIRAMIAI
NIELLOED	NIGHEST	NIHILISMS	NINEPENNY	NIRAMIAIS
NIELLOING	NIGHING	NIHILIST	NINEPIN	NIRL
NIELLOS	NIGHLY	NIHILISTS	NINEPINS	NIRLED
NIES	NIGHNESS	NIHILITIES	NINES	NIRLIE
NIEVE	NIGHNESSES	NIHILITY	NINESCORE	NIRLIER
NIEVEFUL	NIGHS	NIHILS	NINESCORES	NIRLIEST
NIEVEFULS	NIGHT	NIHONGA	NINETEEN	NIRLING
NIEVES	NIGHTBIRD	NIHONGAS	NINETEENS	NIRLIT
NIFE	NIGHTBIRDS	NIKAU	NINETIES	NIRLS
NIFES	NIGHTCAP	NIKAUS	NINETIETH	NIRLY
NIFF	NIGHTCAPS	NIL	NINETIETHS	NIRVANA
NIFFED	NIGHTCLUB	NILGAI	NINETY	NIRVANAS
NIFFER	NIGHTCLUBBED*	NILGAIS	NINHYDRIN*	NIRVANIC*
NIFFERED	NIGHTCLUBBING*	NILGAU	NINHYDRINS*	NIS
NIFFERING	NIGHTCLUBS	NILGAUS	NINJA	NISBERRIES
NIFFERS	NIGHTED	NILGHAI*	NINJAS	NISBERRY
NIFFIER	NIGHTFALL	NILGHAIS*	NINJITSU	NISEI
NIFFIEST	NIGHTFALLS	NILGHAU*	NINJITSUS	NISEIS
NIFFING	NIGHTFIRE	NILGHAUS*	NINJUTSU	NISI
NIFFNAFF	NIGHTFIRES	NILL	NINJUTSUS	NISSE
NIFFNAFFED	NIGHTGEAR	NILLED	NINNIES	NISSES
NIFFNAFFING	NIGHTGEARS	NILLING	NINNY	NISUS
NIFFNAFFS	NIGHTGLOW*	NILLS	NINNYISH*	NIT
NIFFS	NIGHTGLOWS*	NILPOTENT*	NINON	NITCHIE*
NIFFY	NIGHTGOWN	NILS	NINONS	NITCHIES*
NIFTIER	NIGHTGOWNS	NIM	NINTH	NITE
NIFTIES*	NIGHTHAWK	NIMB	NINTHLY	NITER
NIFTIEST	NIGHTHAWKS	NIMBED	NINTHS	NITERIE
NIFTILY	NIGHTIE	NIMBI	NIOBATE	NITERIES
NIFTINESS	NIGHTIES	NIMBLE	NIOBATES	NITERS
NIFTINESSES	NIGHTJAR	NIMBLER	NIOBIC	NITERY
NIFTY	NIGHTJARS	NIMBLESSE	NIOBITE	NITES
NIGELLA	NIGHTLESS	NIMBLESSES	NIOBITES	NITHING
NIGELLAS	NIGHTLIFE	NIMBLEST	NIOBIUM	NITHINGS
NIGER	NIGHTLIFES	NIMBLY	NIOBIUMS	NITID
NIGERS	NIGHTLONG	NIMBS	NIOBOUS	NITINOL*

The Chambers Dictionary is the authority for many longer words; see Introduction, page ix

NITINOLS*	NITWITTED	NOCKING	NODULES	NOMADIES
NITON	NIVAL	NOCKS	NODULOSE	NOMADISE
NITONS	NIVEOUS	NOCTILIO	NODULOUS	NOMADISED
NITPICK*	NIX	NOCTILIOS	NODUS	NOMADISES
NITPICKED*	NIXE*	NOCTILUCA	NOEL	NOMADISING
NITPICKER*	NIXED	NOCTILUCAE	NOELS	NOMADISM
NITPICKERS*	NIXES	NOCTUA	NOES	NOMADISMS
NITPICKIER*	NIXIE	NOCTUARIES	NOESES	NOMADIZE
NITPICKIEST*	NIXIES	NOCTUARY	NOESIS	NOMADIZED
NITPICKING*	NIXING	NOCTUAS	NOESISES*	NOMADIZES
NITPICKS*	NIXY	NOCTUID	NOETIC	NOMADIZING
NITPICKY*	NIZAM	NOCTUIDS	NOG	NOMADS
NITRATE	NIZAMATE*	NOCTULE	NOGAKU	NOMADY
NITRATED	NIZAMATES*	NOCTULES	NOGG	NOMARCH
NITRATES	NIZAMS	NOCTUOID*	NOGGED	NOMARCHIES
NITRATINE	NO	NOCTURN	NOGGIN	NOMARCHS
NITRATINES	NOB	NOCTURNAL	NOGGING	NOMARCHY
NITRATING	NOBBIER	NOCTURNALS	NOGGINGS	NOMAS
NITRATION	NOBBIEST	NOCTURNE	NOGGINS	NOMBLES
NITRATIONS	NOBBILY	NOCTURNES	NOGGS	NOMBRIL
NITRATOR*	NOBBINESS	NOCTURNS	NOGS	NOMBRILS
NITRATORS*	NOBBINESSES	NOCUOUS	NOH	NOME
NITRE	NOBBLE	NOCUOUSLY	NOHOW	NOMEN
NITRES	NOBBLED	NOD	NOHOWISH	NOMES
NITRIC	NOBBLER	NODAL	NOIL	NOMIC
NITRID*	NOBBLERS	NODALISE	NOILS	NOMINA
NITRIDE	NOBBLES	NODALISED	NOILY*	NOMINABLE
NITRIDED	NOBBLING	NODALISES	NOINT	NOMINAL
NITRIDES	NOBBUT	NODALISING	NOINTED	NOMINALLY
NITRIDING	NOBBY	NODALITIES	NOINTING	NOMINALS
NITRIDINGS	NOBELIUM	NODALITY	NOINTS	NOMINATE
NITRIDS*	NOBELIUMS	NODALIZE	NOIR*	NOMINATED
NITRIFIED	NOBILESSE	NODALIZED	NOIRISH*	NOMINATES
NITRIFIER*	NOBILESSES	NODALIZES	NOIRS*	NOMINATING
NITRIFIERS*	NOBILIARY	NODALIZING	NOISE	NOMINATOR
NITRIFIES	NOBILITIES	NODALLY	NOISED	NOMINATORS
NITRIFY	NOBILITY	NODATED	NOISEFUL	NOMINEE
NITRIFYING	NOBLE	NODATION	NOISELESS	NOMINEES
NITRIL*	NOBLEMAN	NODATIONS	NOISES	NOMISM
NITRILE	NOBLEMEN	NODDED	NOISETTE	NOMISMS
NITRILES	NOBLENESS	NODDER	NOISETTES	NOMISTIC
NITRILS*	NOBLENESSES	NODDERS	NOISIER	NOMOCRACIES
NITRITE	NOBLER	NODDIES	NOISIEST	NOMOCRACY
NITRITES	NOBLES	NODDING	NOISILY	NOMOGENIES
NITRO*	NOBLESSE	NODDINGLY	NOISINESS	NOMOGENY
NITROGEN	NOBLESSES	NODDINGS	NOISINESSES	NOMOGRAM
NITROGENS	NOBLEST	NODDLE	NOISING	NOMOGRAMS
NITROLIC*	NOBLY	NODDLED	NOISOME	NOMOGRAPH
NITROS*	NOBODIES	NODDLES	NOISOMELY	NOMOGRAPHS
NITROSO	NOBODY	NODDLING	NOISY	NOMOI
NITROSYL	NOBS	NODDY	NOLE	NOMOLOGIES
NITROSYLS*	NOCAKE	NODE	NOLES	NOMOLOGY
NITROUS	NOCAKES	NODES	NOLITION	NOMOS
NITROXYL	NOCENT	NODI	NOLITIONS	NOMOTHETE
NITROXYLS	NOCENTLY	NODICAL	NOLL	NOMOTHETES
NITRY	NOCENTS	NODOSE	NOLLS	NOMS
NITRYL	NOCHEL	NODOSITIES	NOLO*	NON
NITRYLS	NOCHELLED	NODOSITY	NOLOS*	NONA*
NITS	NOCHELLING	NODOUS	NOM	NONACID*
NITTIER	NOCHELS	NODS	NOMA	NONACIDIC*
NITTIEST	NOCK	NODULAR	NOMAD	NONACIDS*
NITTY	NOCKED	NODULATED	NOMADE	NONACTING*
NITWIT	NOCKET	NODULE	NOMADES	NONACTION*
NITWITS	NOCKETS	NODULED	NOMADIC	NONACTIONS*

NONACTOR*	NONCOMS*	NONFAMILIES*	NONJURY*	NONPAREILS
NONACTORS*	NONCONCUR*	NONFAMILY*	NONKOSHER*	NONPAROUS
NONADDICT*	NONCONCURRED*	NONFAN*	NONLABOR*	NONPARTY*
NONADDICTS*	NONCONCURRING*	NONFANS*	NONLAWYER*	NONPAST*
NONADULT*	NONCONCURS*	NONFARM*	NONLAWYERS*	NONPASTS*
NONADULTS*	NONCOUNTY*	NONFARMER*	NONLEADED*	NONPAYING*
NONAGE	NONCREDIT*	NONFARMERS*	NONLEAFY*	NONPEAK*
NONAGED	NONCRIME*	NONFAT*	NONLEAGUE*	NONPERSON*
NONAGES	NONCRIMES*	NONFATAL*	NONLEGAL*	NONPERSONS*
NONAGON	NONCRISES*	NONFATTY*	NONLEGUME*	NONPLANAR*
NONAGONAL	NONCRISIS*	NONFINAL*	NONLEGUMES*	NONPLAY*
NONAGONS	NONCYCLIC*	NONFINITE*	NONLETHAL*	NONPLAYS*
NONANE	NONDAIRY*	NONFLUID*	NONLIFE*	NONPLUS
NONANES	NONDANCE*	NONFLUIDS*	NONLINEAL*	NONPLUSED
NONANIMAL*	NONDANCER*	NONFLYING*	NONLINEAR*	NONPLUSES
NONANSWER*	NONDANCERS*	NONFOCAL*	NONLIQUID*	NONPLUSING
NONANSWERS*	NONDANCES*	NONFOOD*	NONLIQUIDS*	NONPLUSSED
NONARABLE*	NONDEGREE*	NONFORMAL*	NONLIVES*	NONPLUSSES
NONART*	NONDESERT*	NONFOSSIL*	NONLIVING*	NONPLUSSING
NONARTIST*	NONDOCTOR*	NONFROZEN*	NONLOCAL*	NONPOETIC*
NONARTISTS*	NONDOCTORS*	NONFUEL*	NONLOCALS*	NONPOINT*
NONARTS*	NONDOLLAR*	NONG	NONMAJOR*	NONPOLAR
NONARY	NONDRIVER*	NONGAME*	NONMAJORS*	NONPOLICE*
NONAS*	NONDRIVERS*	NONGAY*	NONMAN*	NONPOOR*
NONATOMIC*	NONDRUG*	NONGAYS*	NONMANUAL*	NONPOROUS*
NONAUTHOR*	NONE	NONGHETTO*	NONMARKET*	NONPRINT*
NONAUTHORS*	NONEDIBLE*	NONGLARE*	NONMEAT*	NONPROFIT*
NONBANK*	NONEGO*	NONGOLFER*	NONMEMBER*	NONPROFITS*
NONBANKS*	NONEGOS*	NONGOLFERS*	NONMEMBERS*	NONPROS*
NONBASIC*	NONELECT*	NONGRADED*	NONMEN*	NONPROSSED*
NONBEING*	NONELITE*	NONGREASY*	NONMENTAL*	NONPROSSES*
NONBEINGS*	NONEMPTY*	NONGREEN*	NONMETAL*	NONPROSSING*
NONBELIEF*	NONENDING*	NONGROWTH*	NONMETALS*	NONPUBLIC*
NONBELIEFS*	NONENERGY*	NONGS	NONMETRIC*	NONQUOTA*
NONBINARY*	NONENTITIES	NONGUEST*	NONMETRO*	NONRACIAL*
NONBITING*	NONENTITY	NONGUESTS*	NONMOBILE*	NONRANDOM*
NONBLACK*	NONENTRIES*	NONGUILT*	NONMODAL*	NONRATED*
NONBLACKS*	NONENTRY*	NONGUILTS*	NONMONEY*	NONREADER*
NONBODIES*	NONEQUAL*	NONHARDY*	NONMORAL*	NONREADERS*
NONBODY*	NONEQUALS*	NONHEME*	NONMOTILE*	NONRIGID*
NONBONDED*	NONEROTIC*	NONHERO*	NONMOVING*	NONRIOTER*
NONBOOK*	NONES	NONHEROES*	NONMUSIC*	NONRIOTERS*
NONBOOKS*	NONESUCH	NONHOME*	NONMUSICS*	NONRIVAL*
NONBRAND*	NONESUCHES	NONHUMAN*	NONMUTANT*	NONRIVALS*
NONBUYING*	NONET	NONHUNTER*	NONMUTANTS*	NONROYAL*
NONCAKING*	NONETHNIC*	NONHUNTERS*	NONNATIVE*	NONRUBBER*
NONCAMPUS*	NONETS	NONIDEAL*	NONNATIVES*	NONRULING*
NONCAREER*	NONETTE	NONILLION	NONNAVAL*	NONRURAL*
NONCASH*	NONETTES	NONILLIONS	NONNEWS*	NONSALINE*
NONCASUAL*	NONETTI	NONIMAGE*	NONNIES	NONSCHOOL*
NONCAUSAL*	NONETTO	NONIMMUNE*	NONNOVEL*	NONSECURE*
NONCE	NONETTOS	NONIMPACT*	NONNOVELS*	NONSELF*
NONCES	NONEVENT*	NONINJURY*	NONNY	NONSELVES*
NONCHURCH*	NONEVENTS*	NONINSECT*	NONOBESE*	NONSENSE
NONCLASS*	NONEXEMPT*	NONINSECTS*	NONOHMIC*	NONSENSES
NONCLASSES*	NONEXOTIC*	NONIONIC*	NONOILY*	NONSEXIST*
NONCLING*	NONEXPERT*	NONIRON*	NONOWNER*	NONSEXUAL*
NONCOITAL*	NONEXPERTS*	NONISSUE*	NONOWNERS*	NONSHRINK*
NONCOKING*	NONEXTANT*	NONISSUES*	NONPAGAN*	NONSIGNER*
NONCOLA*	NONFACT*	NONJOINER*	NONPAGANS*	NONSIGNERS*
NONCOLOR*	NONFACTOR*	NONJOINERS*	NONPAID*	NONSKATER*
NONCOLORS*	NONFACTORS*	NONJURING	NONPAPAL*	NONSKATERS*
NONCOM*	NONFACTS*	NONJUROR	NONPAR*	NONSKED*
NONCOMBAT*	NONFADING*	NONJURORS	NONPAREIL	NONSKEDS*

The Chambers Dictionary is the authority for many longer words; see Introduction, page ix

NONSKID*	NONVIRGINS*	NOOSERS*	NORTHERING	NOSING
NONSKIER*	NONVISUAL*	NOOSES	NORTHERLIES	NOSINGS
NONSKIERS*	NONVOCAL*	NOOSING	NORTHERLY	NOSODE
NONSLIP*	NONVOTER*	NOOSPHERE	NORTHERN	NOSODES
NONSMOKER*	NONVOTERS*	NOOSPHERES	NORTHERNS	NOSOLOGIC*
NONSMOKERS*	NONVOTING*	NOPAL	NORTHERS	NOSOLOGIES
NONSOCIAL*	NONWAR*	NOPALS	NORTHING	NOSOLOGY
NONSOLAR*	NONWARS*	NOPE	NORTHINGS	NOSTALGIA
NONSOLID*	NONWHITE*	NOR	NORTHLAND	NOSTALGIAS
NONSOLIDS*	NONWHITES*	NORDIC*	NORTHLANDS	NOSTALGIC
NONSPEECH*	NONWOODY*	NORI	NORTHMOST	NOSTALGICS*
NONSTEADY*	NONWORD*	NORIA	NORTHS	NOSTOC
NONSTICK*	NONWORDS*	NORIAS	NORTHWARD	NOSTOCS
NONSTOP*	NONWORK*	NORIMON	NORTHWARDS	NOSTOI
NONSTORIES*	NONWORKER*	NORIMONS	NORTHWEST*	NOSTOLOGIES
NONSTORY*	NONWORKERS*	NORIS	NORTHWESTS*	NOSTOLOGY
NONSTYLE*	NONWOVEN*	NORITE	NORWARD	NOSTOS
NONSTYLES*	NONWOVENS*	NORITES	NORWARDS	NOSTRIL
NONSUCH	NONWRITER*	NORITIC*	NOS	NOSTRILS
NONSUCHES	NONWRITERS*	NORK	NOSE	NOSTRUM
NONSUGAR*	NONYL*	NORKS	NOSEAN	NOSTRUMS
NONSUGARS*	NONYLS*	NORLAND	NOSEANS	NOSY
NONSUIT	NONZERO*	NORLANDS	NOSEBAG	NOT
NONSUITED	NOO*	NORM	NOSEBAGS	NOTA
NONSUITING	NOODGE*	NORMA	NOSEBAND	NOTABILIA
NONSUITS	NOODGED*	NORMAL	NOSEBANDS	NOTABLE
NONSYSTEM*	NOODGES*	NORMALCIES	NOSEBLEED	NOTABLES
NONSYSTEMS*	NOODGING*	NORMALCY	NOSEBLEEDS	NOTABLY
NONTARGET*	NOODLE	NORMALISE	NOSED	NOTAEUM
NONTARIFF*	NOODLED	NORMALISED	NOSEDIVE	NOTAEUMS
NONTAX*	NOODLEDOM	NORMALISES	NOSEDIVED	NOTAL
NONTAXES*	NOODLEDOMS	NORMALISING	NOSEDIVES	NOTANDA
NONTHEIST*	NOODLES	NORMALITIES	NOSEDIVING	NOTANDUM
NONTHEISTS*	NOODLING	NORMALITY	NOSEGAY	NOTAPHILIES
NONTIDAL*	NOOK	NORMALIZE	NOSEGAYS	NOTAPHILY
NONTITLE*	NOOKIE	NORMALIZED	NOSEGUARD*	NOTARIAL
NONTONAL*	NOOKIER	NORMALIZES	NOSEGUARDS*	NOTARIES
NONTOXIC*	NOOKIES	NORMALIZING	NOSELESS	NOTARISE
NONTRUMP*	NOOKIEST	NORMALLY	NOSELIKE*	NOTARISED
NONTRUTH*	NOOKLIKE*	NORMALS	NOSELITE	NOTARISES
NONTRUTHS*	NOOKS	NORMAN	NOSELITES	NOTARISING
NONUNION*	NOOKY	NORMANDE*	NOSEPIECE*	NOTARIZE
NONUNIONS*	NOOLOGIES	NORMANS	NOSEPIECES*	NOTARIZED
NONUNIQUE*	NOOLOGY	NORMAS	NOSER	NOTARIZES
NONUPLE	NOOMETRIES	NORMATIVE	NOSERS	NOTARIZING
NONUPLES*	NOOMETRY	NORMED*	NOSES	NOTARY
NONUPLET	NOON	NORMLESS*	NOSEWHEEL*	NOTATE
NONUPLETS	NOONDAY	NORMS	NOSEWHEELS*	NOTATED
NONURBAN*	NOONDAYS	NORSEL	NOSEY	NOTATES
NONURGENT*	NOONED	NORSELLED	NOSEYS	NOTATING
NONUSE*	NOONER	NORSELLER	NOSH	NOTATION
NONUSER*	NOONERS	NORSELLERS	NOSHED	NOTATIONS
NONUSERS*	NOONING	NORSELLING	NOSHER	NOTCH
NONUSES*	NOONINGS	NORSELS	NOSHERIES	NOTCHBACK
NONUSING*	NOONS	NORTENA	NOSHERS	NOTCHBACKS
NONVALID*	NOONTIDE	NORTENAS	NOSHERY	NOTCHED
NONVECTOR*	NOONTIDES	NORTENO	NOSHES	NOTCHEL
NONVECTORS*	NOONTIME	NORTENOS	NOSHING	NOTCHELLED
NONVERBAL*	NOONTIMES	NORTH	NOSIER	NOTCHELLING
NONVIABLE*	NOOP	NORTHEAST*	NOSIES	NOTCHELS
NONVIEWER*	NOOPS	NORTHEASTS*	NOSIEST	NOTCHER
NONVIEWERS*	NOOSE	NORTHED	NOSILY	NOTCHERS
NONVIRAL*	NOOSED	NORTHER	NOSINESS	NOTCHES
NONVIRGIN*	NOOSER*	NORTHERED	NOSINESSES	NOTCHIER

NOTCHIEST	NOULD	NOVELISES	NOXAL	NUCLEASES
NOTCHING	NOULDE	NOVELISH	NOXES	NUCLEATE
NOTCHINGS	NOULE	NOVELISING	NOXIOUS	NUCLEATED
NOTCHY	NOULES	NOVELISM	NOXIOUSLY	NUCLEATES
NOTE	NOULS	NOVELISMS	NOY	NUCLEATING
NOTEBOOK	NOUMENA	NOVELIST	NOYADE	NUCLEATOR
NOTEBOOKS	NOUMENAL	NOVELISTS	NOYADES	NUCLEATORS
NOTECASE	NOUMENON	NOVELIZE	NOYANCE	NUCLEI
NOTECASES	NOUN	NOVELIZED	NOYANCES	NUCLEIDE
NOTED	NOUNAL	NOVELIZER	NOYAU	NUCLEIDES
NOTEDLY	NOUNALLY*	NOVELIZERS	NOYAUS	NUCLEIN
NOTEDNESS	NOUNIER	NOVELIZES	NOYED	NUCLEINS
NOTEDNESSES	NOUNIEST	NOVELIZING	NOYES	NUCLEOID*
NOTELESS	NOUNLESS*	NOVELLA	NOYESES	NUCLEOIDS*
NOTELET	NOUNS	NOVELLAE	NOYING	NUCLEOLAR
NOTELETS	NOUNY	NOVELLAS	NOYOUS	NUCLEOLE
NOTEPAD*	NOUP	NOVELLE	NOYS	NUCLEOLES
NOTEPADS*	NOUPS	NOVELLY*	NOYSOME	NUCLEOLI
NOTEPAPER	NOURICE	NOVELS	NOZZER	NUCLEOLUS
NOTEPAPERS	NOURICES	NOVELTIES	NOZZERS	NUCLEON
NOTER	NOURISH	NOVELTY	NOZZLE	NUCLEONIC*
NOTERS	NOURISHED	NOVENA	NOZZLES	NUCLEONS
NOTES	NOURISHER	NOVENAE*	NTH	NUCLEUS
NOTHER*	NOURISHERS	NOVENARIES	NU	NUCLEUSES*
NOTHING	NOURISHES	NOVENARY	NUANCE	NUCLIDE
NOTHINGS	NOURISHING	NOVENAS	NUANCED	NUCLIDES
NOTICE	NOURITURE	NOVENNIAL	NUANCES	NUCLIDIC*
NOTICED	NOURITURES	NOVERCAL	NUANCING	NUCULE
NOTICER*	NOURSLE	NOVERINT	NUB	NUCULES
NOTICERS*	NOURSLED	NOVERINTS	NUBBED	NUDATION
NOTICES	NOURSLES	NOVICE	NUBBIER	NUDATIONS
NOTICING	NOURSLING	NOVICES	NUBBIEST	NUDE
NOTIFIED	NOUS	NOVICIATE	NUBBIN	NUDELY
NOTIFIER	NOUSELL	NOVICIATES	NUBBING	NUDENESS
NOTIFIERS	NOUSELLED	NOVITIATE	NUBBINS	NUDENESSES
NOTIFIES	NOUSELLING	NOVITIATES	NUBBLE	NUDER
NOTIFY	NOUSELLS	NOVITIES	NUBBLED	NUDES
NOTIFYING	NOUSES	NOVITY	NUBBLES	NUDEST
NOTING	NOUSLE	NOVOCAINE*	NUBBLIER	NUDGE
NOTION	NOUSLED	NOVOCAINES*	NUBBLIEST	NUDGED
NOTIONAL	NOUSLES	NOVODAMUS	NUBBLING	NUDGER
NOTIONIST	NOUSLING	NOVODAMUSES	NUBBLY	NUDGERS
NOTIONISTS	NOUT	NOVUM	NUBBY	NUDGES
NOTIONS	NOUVEAU	NOVUMS	NUBECULA	NUDGING
NOTITIA	NOUVELLE	NOW	NUBECULAE	NUDICAUL
NOTITIAE	NOUVELLES	NOWADAYS	NUBIA	NUDIE
NOTITIAS	NOVA	NOWAY	NUBIAS	NUDIES
NOTOCHORD	NOVAE	NOWAYS	NUBIFORM	NUDISM
NOTOCHORDS	NOVALIA	NOWED	NUBILE	NUDISMS
NOTORIETIES	NOVALIKE*	NOWHENCE	NUBILITIES	NUDIST
NOTORIETY	NOVAS	NOWHERE	NUBILITY	NUDISTS
NOTORIOUS	NOVATION	NOWHERES	NUBILOSE*	NUDITIES
NOTORNIS	NOVATIONS	NOWHITHER	NUBILOUS	NUDITY
NOTORNISES	NOVEL	NOWISE	NUBS	NUDNICK*
NOTOUR	NOVELDOM	NOWL	NUCELLAR	NUDNICKS*
NOTT	NOVELDOMS	NOWLS	NUCELLI	NUDNIK
NOTTURNI*	NOVELESE	NOWN	NUCELLUS	NUDNIKS
NOTTURNO*	NOVELESES	NOWNESS	NUCHA	NUDZH*
NOTUM	NOVELETTE	NOWNESSES	NUCHAE	NUDZHED*
NOUGAT	NOVELETTES	NOWS	NUCHAL	NUDZHES*
NOUGATS	NOVELISE	NOWT	NUCHALS*	NUDZHING*
NOUGHT	NOVELISED	NOWTS	NUCLEAL	NUFF
NOUGHTS	NOVELISER	NOWY	NUCLEAR	NUFFIN
NOUL	NOVELISERS	NOX	NUCLEASE	NUFFINS

The Chambers Dictionary is the authority for many longer words; see Introduction, page ix

NUFFS
NUGAE
NUGATORY
NUGGAR
NUGGARS
NUGGET
NUGGETS
NUGGETY
NUISANCE
NUISANCER
NUISANCERS
NUISANCES
NUKE
NUKED
NUKES
NUKING
NULL
NULLA
NULLAH
NULLAHS
NULLAS
NULLED
NULLIFIED
NULLIFIER
NULLIFIERS
NULLIFIES
NULLIFY
NULLIFYING
NULLING
NULLINGS
NULLIPARA
NULLIPARAE
NULLIPARAS
NULLIPORE
NULLIPORES
NULLITIES
NULLITY
NULLNESS
NULLNESSES
NULLS
NUMB
NUMBAT
NUMBATS
NUMBED
NUMBER
NUMBERED
NUMBERER
NUMBERERS
NUMBERING
NUMBERS
NUMBEST
NUMBFISH*
NUMBFISHES*
NUMBING
NUMBINGLY
NUMBLES
NUMBLY
NUMBNESS
NUMBNESSES
NUMBS
NUMBSKULL
NUMBSKULLS
NUMDAH
NUMDAHS

NUMEN
NUMERABLE
NUMERABLY
NUMERACIES
NUMERACY
NUMERAIRE
NUMERAIRES
NUMERAL
NUMERALLY
NUMERALS
NUMERARY
NUMERATE
NUMERATED
NUMERATES
NUMERATING
NUMERATOR
NUMERATORS
NUMERIC
NUMERICAL
NUMERICS*
NUMEROUS
NUMINA
NUMINOUS
NUMINOUSES
NUMMARY
NUMMULAR
NUMMULARY
NUMMULINE
NUMMULITE
NUMMULITES
NUMNAH
NUMNAHS
NUMPTIES
NUMPTY
NUMSKULL
NUMSKULLS
NUN
NUNATAK
NUNATAKER
NUNATAKS
NUNCHAKU
NUNCHAKUS
NUNCHEON
NUNCHEONS
NUNCIO
NUNCIOS
NUNCLE
NUNCLES
NUNCUPATE
NUNCUPATED
NUNCUPATES
NUNCUPATING
NUNDINAL
NUNDINE
NUNDINES
NUNHOOD
NUNHOODS
NUNLIKE*
NUNNATION
NUNNATIONS
NUNNERIES
NUNNERY
NUNNISH
NUNS

NUNSHIP
NUNSHIPS
NUPTIAL
NUPTIALS
NUR
NURAGHE
NURAGHI
NURAGHIC
NURD
NURDLE
NURDLED
NURDLES
NURDLING
NURDS
NURHAG
NURHAGS
NURL
NURLED
NURLING
NURLS
NURR
NURRS
NURS
NURSE
NURSED
NURSELIKE
NURSELING
NURSELINGS
NURSEMAID
NURSEMAIDED
NURSEMAIDING
NURSEMAIDS
NURSER
NURSERIES
NURSERS
NURSERY
NURSES
NURSING
NURSINGS
NURSLE
NURSLED
NURSLES
NURSLING
NURSLINGS
NURTURAL
NURTURANT
NURTURE
NURTURED
NURTURER
NURTURERS
NURTURES
NURTURING
NUS
NUT
NUTANT
NUTARIAN
NUTARIANS
NUTATE
NUTATED
NUTATES
NUTATING
NUTATION
NUTATIONS
NUTBROWN*

NUTBUTTER
NUTBUTTERS
NUTCASE
NUTCASES
NUTGALL
NUTGALLS
NUTGRASS*
NUTGRASSES*
NUTHATCH
NUTHATCHES
NUTHOUSE
NUTHOUSES
NUTJOBBER
NUTJOBBERS
NUTLET
NUTLETS
NUTLIKE
NUTMEAL
NUTMEALS
NUTMEAT*
NUTMEATS*
NUTMEG
NUTMEGGED
NUTMEGGING
NUTMEGGY
NUTMEGS
NUTPECKER
NUTPECKERS
NUTPICK*
NUTPICKS*
NUTRIA
NUTRIAS
NUTRIENT
NUTRIENTS
NUTRIMENT
NUTRIMENTS
NUTRITION
NUTRITIONS
NUTRITIVE
NUTRITIVES
NUTS
NUTSEDGE*
NUTSEDGES*
NUTSHELL
NUTSHELLS
NUTSIER*
NUTSIEST*
NUTSY*
NUTTED
NUTTER
NUTTERIES
NUTTERS
NUTTERY
NUTTIER
NUTTIEST
NUTTILY
NUTTINESS
NUTTINESSES
NUTTING
NUTTINGS
NUTTY
NUTWOOD
NUTWOODS
NUZZER

NUZZERS
NUZZLE
NUZZLED
NUZZLER*
NUZZLERS*
NUZZLES
NUZZLING
NY
NYAFF
NYAFFED
NYAFFING
NYAFFS
NYALA
NYALAS
NYANZA
NYANZAS
NYAS
NYASES
NYBBLE
NYBBLES
NYCTALOPES
NYCTALOPS
NYE
NYED
NYES
NYING
NYLGHAI*
NYLGHAIS*
NYLGHAU
NYLGHAUS
NYLON
NYLONS
NYMPH
NYMPHA*
NYMPHAE
NYMPHAEA
NYMPHAEUM
NYMPHAEUMS
NYMPHAL
NYMPHALID
NYMPHALIDS
NYMPHEAN
NYMPHET
NYMPHETS
NYMPHETTE*
NYMPHETTES*
NYMPHIC
NYMPHICAL
NYMPHISH
NYMPHLIKE
NYMPHLY
NYMPHO
NYMPHOS
NYMPHS
NYS
NYSSA
NYSSAS
NYSTAGMIC
NYSTAGMUS
NYSTAGMUSES
NYSTATIN
NYSTATINS

Words marked with an asterisk are from OTCWL

O

OAF	OATERS	OBELISING	OBJECTIVE	OBLIVIOUS
OAFISH	OATH	OBELISK	OBJECTIVES	OBLONG
OAFISHLY*	OATHABLE	OBELISKS	OBJECTOR	OBLONGLY*
OAFS	OATHS	OBELISM*	OBJECTORS	OBLONGS
OAK	OATLIKE*	OBELISMS*	OBJECTS	OBLOQUIES
OAKEN	OATMEAL	OBELIZE	OBJET	OBLOQUY
OAKENSHAW	OATMEALS	OBELIZED	OBJETS	OBNOXIOUS
OAKENSHAWS	OATS	OBELIZES	OBJURE	OBO
OAKER	OAVES	OBELIZING	OBJURED	OBOE
OAKERS	OB	OBELUS	OBJURES	OBOES
OAKIER	OBA	OBES*	OBJURGATE	OBOIST
OAKIEST	OBANG	OBESE	OBJURGATED	OBOISTS
OAKLEAF	OBANGS	OBESELY*	OBJURGATES	OBOL
OAKLEAVES	OBAS	OBESENESS	OBJURGATING	OBOLARY
OAKLIKE*	OBBLIGATI	OBESENESSES	OBJURING	OBOLE*
OAKLING	OBBLIGATO	OBESER	OBLAST	OBOLES*
OAKLINGS	OBBLIGATOS	OBESEST	OBLASTI*	OBOLI
OAKMOSS*	OBCONIC	OBESITIES	OBLASTS	OBOLS
OAKMOSSES*	OBCONICAL	OBESITY	OBLATE	OBOLUS
OAKS	OBCORDATE	OBEY	OBLATELY*	OBOS
OAKUM	OBDURACIES	OBEYABLE*	OBLATES	OBOVATE
OAKUMS	OBDURACY	OBEYED	OBLATION	OBOVATELY
OAKY	OBDURATE	OBEYER	OBLATIONS	OBOVOID
OAR	OBDURATED	OBEYERS	OBLATORY	OBREPTION
OARAGE	OBDURATES	OBEYING	OBLIGANT	OBREPTIONS
OARAGES	OBDURATING	OBEYS	OBLIGANTS	OBS
OARED	OBDURE	OBFUSCATE	OBLIGATE	OBSCENE
OARFISH*	OBDURED	OBFUSCATED	OBLIGATED	OBSCENELY
OARFISHES*	OBDURES	OBFUSCATES	OBLIGATES	OBSCENER
OARIER	OBDURING	OBFUSCATING	OBLIGATI	OBSCENEST
OARIEST	OBE*	OBI	OBLIGATING	OBSCENITIES
OARING	OBEAH	OBIA	OBLIGATO	OBSCENITY
OARLESS	OBEAHED	OBIAS	OBLIGATOS	OBSCURANT
OARLIKE*	OBEAHING	OBIED	OBLIGE	OBSCURANTS
OARLOCK*	OBEAHISM	OBIING	OBLIGED	OBSCURE
OARLOCKS*	OBEAHISMS	OBIISM	OBLIGEE	OBSCURED
OARS	OBEAHS	OBIISMS	OBLIGEES	OBSCURELY
OARSMAN	OBECHE	OBIIT	OBLIGER*	OBSCURER
OARSMEN	OBECHES	OBIS	OBLIGERS*	OBSCURERS
OARSWOMAN	OBEDIENCE	OBIT	OBLIGES	OBSCURES
OARSWOMEN	OBEDIENCES	OBITAL	OBLIGING	OBSCUREST
OARWEED	OBEDIENT	OBITER	OBLIGOR	OBSCURING
OARWEEDS	OBEISANCE	OBITS	OBLIGORS	OBSCURITIES
OARY	OBEISANCES	OBITUAL	OBLIQUE	OBSCURITY
OASES	OBEISANT	OBITUARIES	OBLIQUED	OBSECRATE
OASIS	OBEISM	OBITUARY	OBLIQUELY	OBSECRATED
OAST	OBEISMS	OBJECT	OBLIQUER	OBSECRATES
OASTHOUSE*	OBELI	OBJECTED	OBLIQUES	OBSECRATING
OASTHOUSES*	OBELIA	OBJECTIFIED	OBLIQUEST	OBSEQUENT
OASTS	OBELIAS*	OBJECTIFIES	OBLIQUID	OBSEQUIAL
OAT	OBELION	OBJECTIFY	OBLIQUING	OBSEQUIE
OATCAKE	OBELISCAL	OBJECTIFYING	OBLIQUITIES	OBSEQUIES
OATCAKES	OBELISE	OBJECTING	OBLIQUITY	OBSEQUY
OATEN	OBELISED	OBJECTION	OBLIVION	OBSERVANT
OATER	OBELISES	OBJECTIONS	OBLIVIONS	OBSERVANTS

OBSERVE	OBTENTIONS	OCARINAS	OCCURS	OCTAHEDRA
OBSERVED	OBTEST	OCAS	OCEAN	OCTAHEDRON*
OBSERVER	OBTESTED	OCCAM	OCEANARIA	OCTAHEDRONS*
OBSERVERS	OBTESTING	OCCAMIES	OCEANARIUM*	OCTAL
OBSERVES	OBTESTS	OCCAMS	OCEANARIUMS*	OCTALS
OBSERVING	OBTRUDE	OCCAMY	OCEANAUT	OCTAMETER
OBSESS	OBTRUDED	OCCASION	OCEANAUTS	OCTAMETERS
OBSESSED	OBTRUDER	OCCASIONED	OCEANIC	OCTAN*
OBSESSES	OBTRUDERS	OCCASIONING	OCEANID	OCTANE
OBSESSING	OBTRUDES	OCCASIONS	OCEANIDES	OCTANES
OBSESSION	OBTRUDING	OCCIDENT	OCEANIDS	OCTANGLE*
OBSESSIONS	OBTRUDINGS	OCCIDENTS	OCEANS	OCTANGLES*
OBSESSIVE	OBTRUSION	OCCIPITA*	OCELLAR	OCTANOL*
OBSESSIVES*	OBTRUSIONS	OCCIPITAL	OCELLATE	OCTANOLS*
OBSESSOR*	OBTRUSIVE	OCCIPITALS	OCELLATED	OCTANS*
OBSESSORS*	OBTUND	OCCIPUT	OCELLI	OCTANT
OBSIDIAN	OBTUNDED	OCCIPUTS	OCELLUS	OCTANTAL
OBSIDIANS	OBTUNDENT	OCCLUDE	OCELOID	OCTANTS
OBSIGN	OBTUNDENTS	OCCLUDED	OCELOT	OCTAPLA
OBSIGNATE	OBTUNDING	OCCLUDENT	OCELOTS	OCTAPLAS
OBSIGNATED	OBTUNDS	OCCLUDENTS	OCH	OCTAPLOID
OBSIGNATES	OBTURATE	OCCLUDER	OCHE	OCTAPLOIDS
OBSIGNATING	OBTURATED	OCCLUDERS	OCHER	OCTAPODIC
OBSIGNED	OBTURATES	OCCLUDES	OCHERED	OCTAPODIES
OBSIGNING	OBTURATING	OCCLUDING	OCHERING	OCTAPODY
OBSIGNS	OBTURATOR	OCCLUSAL	OCHEROUS	OCTARCHIES*
OBSOLESCE	OBTURATORS	OCCLUSION	OCHERS	OCTARCHY*
OBSOLESCED	OBTUSE	OCCLUSIONS	OCHERY	OCTAROON
OBSOLESCES	OBTUSELY	OCCLUSIVE	OCHES	OCTAROONS
OBSOLESCING	OBTUSER	OCCLUSIVES	OCHIDORE	OCTAS
OBSOLETE	OBTUSEST	OCCLUSOR	OCHIDORES	OCTASTICH
OBSOLETED*	OBTUSITIES	OCCLUSORS	OCHLOCRAT	OCTASTICHS
OBSOLETES*	OBTUSITY	OCCULT	OCHLOCRATS	OCTASTYLE
OBSOLETING*	OBUMBRATE	OCCULTED	OCHONE	OCTASTYLES
OBSTACLE	OBUMBRATED	OCCULTER*	OCHRE	OCTAVAL
OBSTACLES	OBUMBRATES	OCCULTERS*	OCHREA	OCTAVE
OBSTETRIC	OBUMBRATING	OCCULTING	OCHREAE	OCTAVES
OBSTETRICS	OBVENTION	OCCULTISM	OCHREATE	OCTAVO
OBSTINACIES	OBVENTIONS	OCCULTISMS	OCHRED	OCTAVOS
OBSTINACY	OBVERSE	OCCULTIST	OCHREOUS	OCTENNIAL
OBSTINATE	OBVERSELY	OCCULTISTS	OCHRES	OCTET
OBSTRUCT	OBVERSES	OCCULTLY	OCHREY	OCTETS
OBSTRUCTED	OBVERSION	OCCULTS	OCHRING	OCTETT
OBSTRUCTING	OBVERSIONS	OCCUPANCE	OCHROID	OCTETTE
OBSTRUCTS	OBVERT	OCCUPANCES	OCHROUS	OCTETTES
OBSTRUENT	OBVERTED	OCCUPANCIES	OCHRY	OCTETTS
OBSTRUENTS	OBVERTING	OCCUPANCY	OCKER	OCTILLION
OBTAIN	OBVERTS	OCCUPANT	OCKERISM	OCTILLIONS
OBTAINED	OBVIABLE*	OCCUPANTS	OCKERISMS	OCTOFID
OBTAINER	OBVIATE	OCCUPATE	OCKERS	OCTOHEDRA
OBTAINERS	OBVIATED	OCCUPATED	OCOTILLO	OCTONARIES
OBTAINING	OBVIATES	OCCUPATES	OCOTILLOS	OCTONARII
OBTAINS	OBVIATING	OCCUPATING	OCREA	OCTONARY
OBTECT	OBVIATION	OCCUPIED	OCREAE	OCTOPI
OBTECTED	OBVIATIONS	OCCUPIER	OCREATE	OCTOPLOID
OBTEMPER	OBVIATOR*	OCCUPIERS	OCTA	OCTOPLOIDS
OBTEMPERED	OBVIATORS*	OCCUPIES	OCTACHORD	OCTOPOD
OBTEMPERING	OBVIOUS	OCCUPY	OCTACHORDS	OCTOPODES
OBTEMPERS	OBVIOUSLY	OCCUPYING	OCTAD	OCTOPODS
OBTEND	OBVOLUTE	OCCUR	OCTADIC	OCTOPUS
OBTENDED	OBVOLUTED	OCCURRED	OCTADS	OCTOPUSES
OBTENDING	OBVOLVENT	OCCURRENT	OCTAGON	OCTOPUSH
OBTENDS	OCA	OCCURRENTS	OCTAGONAL	OCTOPUSHES
OBTENTION	OCARINA	OCCURRING	OCTAGONS	OCTOROON

OCTOROONS	ODEONS	OE	OFFCUT	OFFPUT
OCTOSTYLE	ODES	OECIST	OFFCUTS	OFFPUTS
OCTOSTYLES	ODEUM	OECISTS	OFFED	OFFRAMP*
OCTOTHORP*	ODEUMS	OECOLOGIES	OFFENCE	OFFRAMPS*
OCTOTHORPS*	ODIC	OECOLOGY	OFFENCES	OFFS
OCTROI	ODIOUS	OECUMENIC	OFFEND	OFFSADDLE
OCTROIS	ODIOUSLY	OEDEMA	OFFENDED	OFFSADDLED
OCTUOR	ODISM	OEDEMAS	OFFENDER	OFFSADDLES
OCTUORS	ODISMS	OEDEMATA	OFFENDERS	OFFSADDLING
OCTUPLE	ODIST	OEDIPAL*	OFFENDING	OFFSCREEN*
OCTUPLED	ODISTS	OEDIPALLY*	OFFENDS	OFFSCUM
OCTUPLES	ODIUM	OEDIPEAN*	OFFENSE	OFFSCUMS
OCTUPLET	ODIUMS	OEILLADE	OFFENSES	OFFSEASON
OCTUPLETS	ODOGRAPH	OEILLADES	OFFENSIVE	OFFSEASONS
OCTUPLEX*	ODOGRAPHS	OENANTHIC	OFFENSIVES	OFFSET
OCTUPLING	ODOMETER	OENOLOGIES	OFFER	OFFSETS
OCTUPLY*	ODOMETERS	OENOLOGY	OFFERABLE	OFFSETTING
OCTYL*	ODOMETRIES	OENOMANCIES	OFFERED	OFFSHOOT
OCTYLS*	ODOMETRY	OENOMANCY	OFFEREE	OFFSHOOTS
OCULAR	ODONATE*	OENOMANIA	OFFEREES	OFFSHORE
OCULARIST	ODONATES*	OENOMANIAS	OFFERER	OFFSIDE
OCULARISTS	ODONATIST	OENOMEL	OFFERERS	OFFSIDER
OCULARLY	ODONATISTS	OENOMELS	OFFERING	OFFSIDERS
OCULARS	ODONTALGIES	OENOMETER	OFFERINGS	OFFSIDES
OCULATE	ODONTALGY	OENOMETERS	OFFEROR	OFFSPRING
OCULATED	ODONTIC	OENOPHIL	OFFERORS	OFFSPRINGS
OCULI	ODONTIST	OENOPHILE	OFFERS	OFFSTAGE*
OCULIST	ODONTISTS	OENOPHILES	OFFERTORIES	OFFSTAGES*
OCULISTS	ODONTOID	OENOPHILIES	OFFERTORY	OFFTAKE
OCULUS	ODONTOIDS*	OENOPHILS	OFFHAND	OFFTAKES
OD	ODONTOMA	OENOPHILY	OFFHANDED	OFFTRACK*
ODA	ODONTOMAS	OERLIKON	OFFICE	OFLAG
ODAL	ODONTOMATA	OERLIKONS	OFFICER	OFLAGS
ODALIQUE	ODOR	OERSTED	OFFICERED	OFT
ODALIQUES	ODORANT	OERSTEDS	OFFICERING	OFTEN
ODALISK	ODORANTS	OES	OFFICERS	OFTENER
ODALISKS	ODORATE	OESOPHAGI	OFFICES	OFTENEST
ODALISQUE	ODORED*	OESOPHAGUS*	OFFICIAL	OFTENNESS
ODALISQUES	ODORFUL*	OESTRAL	OFFICIALS	OFTENNESSES
ODALLER	ODORIZE*	OESTRIN*	OFFICIANT	OFTER*
ODALLERS	ODORIZED*	OESTRINS*	OFFICIANTS	OFTEST*
ODALS	ODORIZES*	OESTRIOL*	OFFICIARIES*	OFTTIMES
ODAS	ODORIZING*	OESTRIOLS*	OFFICIARY*	OGAM
ODD	ODORLESS*	OESTROGEN	OFFICIATE	OGAMIC
ODDBALL	ODOROUS	OESTROGENS	OFFICIATED	OGAMS
ODDBALLS	ODOROUSLY	OESTRONE*	OFFICIATES	OGDOAD
ODDER	ODORS	OESTRONES*	OFFICIATING	OGDOADS
ODDEST	ODOUR	OESTROUS	OFFICINAL	OGEE
ODDISH	ODOURED	OESTRUM	OFFICIOUS	OGEES
ODDITIES	ODOURFUL*	OESTRUMS	OFFING	OGGIN
ODDITY	ODOURLESS	OESTRUS	OFFINGS	OGGINS
ODDLY	ODOURS	OESTRUSES	OFFISH	OGHAM
ODDMENT	ODS	OEUVRE	OFFISHLY*	OGHAMIC
ODDMENTS	ODSO	OEUVRES	OFFKEY*	OGHAMIST*
ODDNESS	ODSOS	OF	OFFLINE	OGHAMISTS*
ODDNESSES	ODYL	OFAY	OFFLOAD	OGHAMS
ODDS	ODYLE	OFAYS	OFFLOADED	OGIVAL
ODDSMAKER*	ODYLES	OFF	OFFLOADING	OGIVE
ODDSMAKERS*	ODYLISM	OFFAL	OFFLOADS	OGIVES
ODDSMAN	ODYLISMS	OFFALS	OFFPEAK	OGLE
ODDSMEN	ODYLS	OFFBEAT	OFFPRINT	OGLED
ODE	ODYSSEY	OFFBEATS	OFFPRINTED*	OGLER
ODEA	ODYSSEYS	OFFCAST*	OFFPRINTING*	OGLERS
ODEON	ODZOOKS	OFFCASTS*	OFFPRINTS	OGLES

The Chambers Dictionary is the authority for many longer words; see Introduction, page ix

OGLING	OILLET	OLDEST	OLIGARCH	OMBRE
OGLINGS	OILLETS	OLDIE	OLIGARCHIES	OMBRELLA
OGMIC	OILMAN	OLDIES	OLIGARCHS	OMBRELLAS
OGRE	OILMEN	OLDISH	OLIGARCHY	OMBRES
OGREISH	OILNUT	OLDNESS	OLIGIST	OMBROPHIL
OGREISM*	OILNUTS	OLDNESSES	OLIGISTS	OMBROPHILS
OGREISMS*	OILPAPER*	OLDS	OLIGOMER*	OMBU
OGRES	OILPAPERS*	OLDSQUAW	OLIGOMERS*	OMBUDSMAN
OGRESS	OILPROOF*	OLDSQUAWS	OLIGOPOLIES	OMBUDSMEN
OGRESSES	OILS	OLDSTER	OLIGOPOLY	OMBUS
OGRISH	OILSEED*	OLDSTERS	OLIGURIA	OMEGA
OGRISHLY*	OILSEEDS*	OLDSTYLE*	OLIGURIAS	OMEGAS
OGRISM*	OILSKIN	OLDSTYLES*	OLIO	OMELET
OGRISMS*	OILSKINS	OLDWIFE*	OLIOS	OMELETS
OH	OILSTONE	OLDWIVES*	OLIPHANT	OMELETTE
OHED*	OILSTONES	OLDY	OLIPHANTS	OMELETTES
OHIA*	OILTIGHT*	OLE	OLITORIES	OMEN
OHIAS*	OILWAY*	OLEA*	OLITORY	OMENED
OHING*	OILWAYS*	OLEACEOUS	OLIVARY	OMENING
OHM	OILY	OLEANDER	OLIVE	OMENS
OHMAGE	OINK	OLEANDERS	OLIVENITE	OMENTA
OHMAGES	OINKED	OLEARIA	OLIVENITES	OMENTAL
OHMIC	OINKING	OLEARIAS	OLIVER	OMENTUM
OHMICALLY*	OINKS	OLEASTER	OLIVERS	OMENTUMS*
OHMMETER	OINOLOGIES*	OLEASTERS	OLIVES	OMER
OHMMETERS	OINOLOGY*	OLEATE	OLIVET	OMERS
OHMS	OINOMEL*	OLEATES	OLIVETS	OMERTA
OHO	OINOMELS*	OLECRANAL	OLIVINE	OMERTAS
OHONE	OINT	OLECRANON	OLIVINES	OMICRON
OHOS	OINTED	OLECRANONS	OLIVINIC*	OMICRONS
OHS*	OINTING	OLEFIANT	OLLA	OMIKRON*
OI	OINTMENT	OLEFIN	OLLAMH	OMIKRONS*
OIDIA	OINTMENTS	OLEFINE	OLLAMHS	OMINOUS
OIDIUM	OINTS	OLEFINES	OLLAS	OMINOUSLY
OIK	OITICICA	OLEFINIC*	OLLAV	OMISSIBLE
OIKIST	OITICICAS	OLEFINS	OLLAVS	OMISSION
OIKISTS	OJIME	OLEIC	OLM	OMISSIONS
OIKS	OJIMES	OLEIN	OLMS	OMISSIVE
OIL	OKA*	OLEINE*	OLOGIES	OMIT
OILBIRD*	OKAPI	OLEINES*	OLOGIST*	OMITS
OILBIRDS*	OKAPIS	OLEINS	OLOGISTS*	OMITTANCE
OILCAMP*	OKAS*	OLENT	OLOGY	OMITTANCES
OILCAMPS*	OKAY	OLEO	OLOLIUQUI*	OMITTED
OILCAN	OKAYED	OLEOGRAPH	OLOLIUQUIS*	OMITTER
OILCANS	OKAYING	OLEOGRAPHS	OLOROSO	OMITTERS
OILCLOTH	OKAYS	OLEORESIN*	OLOROSOS	OMITTING
OILCLOTHS	OKE	OLEORESINS*	OLPAE	OMLAH
OILCUP*	OKEH*	OLEOS	OLPE	OMLAHS
OILCUPS*	OKEHS*	OLES*	OLPES	OMMATEA
OILED	OKES	OLEUM	OLYCOOK	OMMATEUM
OILER	OKEYDOKE*	OLEUMS	OLYCOOKS	OMMATIDIA
OILERIES	OKEYDOKEY*	OLFACT	OLYKOEK	OMMATIDIUM*
OILERS	OKIMONO	OLFACTED	OLYKOEKS	OMNEITIES
OILERY	OKIMONOS	OLFACTING	OLYMPIAD	OMNEITY
OILFIELD	OKRA	OLFACTION	OLYMPIADS	OMNIANA
OILFIELDS	OKRAS	OLFACTIONS	OLYMPICS	OMNIARCH*
OILHOLE*	OKTA	OLFACTIVE	OM	OMNIARCHS*
OILHOLES*	OKTAS	OLFACTORY	OMADHAUN	OMNIBUS
OILIER	OLD	OLFACTS	OMADHAUNS	OMNIBUSES
OILIEST	OLDEN	OLIBANUM	OMASA	OMNIETIES
OILILY	OLDENED	OLIBANUMS	OMASAL	OMNIETY
OILINESS	OLDENING	OLID	OMASUM	OMNIFIC
OILINESSES	OLDENS	OLIGAEMIA	OMBER*	OMNIFIED
OILING	OLDER	OLIGAEMIAS	OMBERS*	OMNIFIES

OMNIFORM	ONCOMICE	ONNED	OOGAMETE*	OORALIS*
OMNIFY	ONCOMING	ONNING	OOGAMETES*	OORIAL
OMNIFYING	ONCOMINGS	ONOMASTIC	OOGAMIES	OORIALS
OMNIMODE*	ONCOMOUSE	ONOMASTICS	OOGAMOUS	OORIE
OMNIRANGE*	ONCOST	ONRUSH	OOGAMY	OORIER
OMNIRANGES*	ONCOSTMAN	ONRUSHES	OOGENESES	OORIEST
OMNIUM	ONCOSTMEN	ONRUSHING*	OOGENESIS	OOS
OMNIUMS	ONCOSTS	ONS	OOGENETIC	OOSE
OMNIVORA*	ONCOTOMIES	ONSET	OOGENIES	OOSES
OMNIVORE	ONCOTOMY	ONSETS	OOGENY	OOSIER
OMNIVORES	ONCUS	ONSETTER	OOGONIA	OOSIEST
OMNIVORIES	ONDATRA	ONSETTERS	OOGONIAL	OOSPERM*
OMNIVORY	ONDATRAS	ONSETTING	OOGONIUM	OOSPERMS*
OMOHYOID	ONDINE	ONSETTINGS	OOGONIUMS*	OOSPHERE
OMOHYOIDS	ONDINES	ONSHORE	OOH	OOSPHERES
OMOPHAGIA	ONDING	ONSIDE	OOHED	OOSPORE
OMOPHAGIAS	ONDINGS	ONSIDES	OOHING	OOSPORES
OMOPHAGIC	ONDOGRAM*	ONSLAUGHT	OOHS	OOSPORIC*
OMOPHAGIES	ONDOGRAMS*	ONSLAUGHTS	OOIDAL	OOSY
OMOPHAGY	ONE	ONST	OOLACHAN*	OOT*
OMOPHORIA	ONEFOLD	ONSTAGE*	OOLACHANS*	OOTHECA*
OMOPLATE	ONEIRIC	ONSTEAD	OOLAKAN	OOTHECAE*
OMOPLATES	ONELY	ONSTEADS	OOLAKANS	OOTHECAL*
OMPHACITE	ONENESS	ONSTREAM*	OOLITE	OOTID*
OMPHACITES	ONENESSES	ONTIC*	OOLITES	OOTIDS*
OMPHALI	ONER	ONTICALLY*	OOLITH*	OOTS*
OMPHALIC	ONERIER*	ONTO	OOLITHS*	OOZE
OMPHALOID	ONERIEST*	ONTOGENIC	OOLITIC	OOZED
OMPHALOS	ONEROUS	ONTOGENIES	OOLOGIC*	OOZES
OMRAH	ONEROUSLY	ONTOGENY	OOLOGIES	OOZIER
OMRAHS	ONERS	ONTOLOGIC	OOLOGIST	OOZIEST
OMS	ONERY*	ONTOLOGIES	OOLOGISTS	OOZILY
ON	ONES	ONTOLOGY	OOLOGY	OOZINESS
ONAGER	ONESELF	ONUS	OOLONG	OOZINESSES
ONAGERS	ONETIME*	ONUSES	OOLONGS	OOZING
ONAGRI*	ONEYER	ONWARD	OOM	OOZY
ONANISM	ONEYERS	ONWARDLY	OOMIAC	OP
ONANISMS	ONEYRE	ONWARDS	OOMIACK	OPACIFIED*
ONANIST	ONEYRES	ONYCHA	OOMIACKS	OPACIFIES*
ONANISTIC	ONFALL	ONYCHAS	OOMIACS	OPACIFY*
ONANISTS	ONFALLS	ONYCHIA	OOMIAK	OPACIFYING*
ONBOARD	ONFLOW	ONYCHIAS	OOMIAKS	OPACITIES
ONCE	ONFLOWS	ONYCHITE	OOMPAH	OPACITY
ONCER	ONGOING	ONYCHITES	OOMPAHED	OPACOUS
ONCERS	ONGOINGS	ONYCHITIS	OOMPAHING	OPAH
ONCES	ONION	ONYCHITISES	OOMPAHS	OPAHS
ONCIDIUM	ONIONED	ONYCHIUM	OOMPH	OPAL
ONCIDIUMS	ONIONIER	ONYCHIUMS	OOMPHS	OPALED
ONCOGEN	ONIONIEST	ONYMOUS	OOMS	OPALESCE*
ONCOGENE	ONIONING	ONYX	OON	OPALESCED*
ONCOGENES	ONIONS	ONYXES	OONS	OPALESCES*
ONCOGENIC	ONIONSKIN*	OO	OONT	OPALESCING*
ONCOGENS	ONIONSKINS*	OOBIT	OONTS	OPALINE
ONCOLOGIC*	ONIONY	OOBITS	OOP	OPALINES
ONCOLOGIES	ONIRIC	OOCYST*	OOPED	OPALISED
ONCOLOGY	ONISCOID	OOCYSTS*	OOPHORON	OPALIZED
ONCOLYSES	ONIUM*	OOCYTE	OOPHORONS	OPALS
ONCOLYSIS	ONKUS	OOCYTES	OOPHYTE	OPAQUE
ONCOLYTIC	ONLIEST	OODLES	OOPHYTES	OPAQUED
ONCOLYTICS	ONLINE	OODLINS	OOPHYTIC*	OPAQUELY
ONCOME	ONLOOKER	OOF	OOPING	OPAQUER
ONCOMES	ONLOOKERS	OOFS	OOPS	OPAQUES
ONCOMETER	ONLOOKING	OOFTISH	OOR	OPAQUEST
ONCOMETERS	ONLY	OOFTISHES	OORALI*	OPAQUING

The Chambers Dictionary is the authority for many longer words; see Introduction, page ix

OPCODE	OPHIOLITE	OPPOSED	OPTIME	ORACLED
OPCODES	OPHIOLITES	OPPOSER	OPTIMES	ORACLES
OPE	OPHIOLOGIES	OPPOSERS	OPTIMISE	ORACLING
OPED	OPHIOLOGY	OPPOSES	OPTIMISED	ORACULAR
OPEN	OPHITE	OPPOSING	OPTIMISES	ORACULOUS
OPENABLE	OPHITES	OPPOSITE	OPTIMISING	ORACY
OPENCAST*	OPHITIC	OPPOSITES	OPTIMISM	ORAD*
OPENED	OPHIURA	OPPRESS	OPTIMISMS	ORAGIOUS
OPENER	OPHIURAN	OPPRESSED	OPTIMIST	ORAL
OPENERS	OPHIURANS	OPPRESSES	OPTIMISTS	ORALISM
OPENEST	OPHIURAS	OPPRESSING	OPTIMIZE	ORALISMS
OPENING	OPHIURID	OPPRESSOR	OPTIMIZED	ORALIST*
OPENINGS	OPHIURIDS	OPPRESSORS	OPTIMIZER*	ORALISTS*
OPENLY	OPHIUROID	OPPUGN	OPTIMIZERS*	ORALITIES
OPENNESS	OPHIUROIDS	OPPUGNANT	OPTIMIZES	ORALITY
OPENNESSES	OPIATE	OPPUGNANTS	OPTIMIZING	ORALLY
OPENS	OPIATED	OPPUGNED	OPTIMUM	ORALS
OPENWORK	OPIATES	OPPUGNER	OPTIMUMS*	ORANG
OPENWORKS	OPIATING	OPPUGNERS	OPTING	ORANGE
OPEPE	OPIFICER	OPPUGNING	OPTION	ORANGEADE
OPEPES	OPIFICERS	OPPUGNS	OPTIONAL	ORANGEADES
OPERA	OPINABLE	OPS	OPTIONALS*	ORANGER
OPERABLE	OPINE	OPSIMATH	OPTIONED*	ORANGERIE*
OPERABLY*	OPINED	OPSIMATHIES	OPTIONEE*	ORANGERIES
OPERAGOER*	OPINES	OPSIMATHS	OPTIONEES*	ORANGERY
OPERAGOERS*	OPING	OPSIMATHY	OPTIONING*	ORANGES
OPERAND	OPINICUS	OPSIN*	OPTIONS	ORANGEST
OPERANDS	OPINICUSES	OPSINS*	OPTOLOGIES	ORANGEY
OPERANT	OPINING	OPSOMANIA	OPTOLOGY	ORANGIER
OPERANTLY*	OPINION	OPSOMANIAS	OPTOMETER	ORANGIEST
OPERANTS	OPINIONED	OPSONIC	OPTOMETERS	ORANGISH*
OPERAS	OPINIONS	OPSONIFIED*	OPTOMETRIES	ORANGS
OPERATE	OPIOID	OPSONIFIES*	OPTOMETRY	ORANGUTAN*
OPERATED	OPIOIDS*	OPSONIFY*	OPTOPHONE	ORANGUTANS*
OPERATES	OPIUM	OPSONIFYING*	OPTOPHONES	ORANGY*
OPERATIC	OPIUMISM	OPSONIN	OPTRONICS	ORANT
OPERATICS*	OPIUMISMS	OPSONINS	OPTS	ORANTS
OPERATING	OPIUMS	OPSONIUM	OPULENCE	ORARIA
OPERATION	OPOBALSAM	OPSONIUMS	OPULENCES	ORARIAN
OPERATIONS	OPOBALSAMS	OPSONIZE*	OPULENCIES*	ORARIANS
OPERATIVE	OPODELDOC	OPSONIZED*	OPULENCY*	ORARION
OPERATIVES	OPODELDOCS	OPSONIZES*	OPULENT	ORARIONS
OPERATOR	OPOPANAX	OPSONIZING*	OPULENTLY	ORARIUM
OPERATORS	OPOPANAXES	OPT	OPULUS	ORARIUMS
OPERCELE*	OPORICE	OPTANT	OPULUSES	ORATE
OPERCELES*	OPORICES	OPTANTS	OPUNTIA	ORATED
OPERCULA	OPOSSUM	OPTATIVE	OPUNTIAS	ORATES
OPERCULAR	OPOSSUMS	OPTATIVES	OPUS	ORATING
OPERCULARS*	OPPIDAN	OPTED	OPUSCLE	ORATION
OPERCULE*	OPPIDANS	OPTER	OPUSCLES	ORATIONS
OPERCULES*	OPPILANT*	OPTERS	OPUSCULA	ORATOR
OPERCULUM	OPPILATE	OPTIC	OPUSCULE	ORATORIAL
OPERCULUMS*	OPPILATED	OPTICAL	OPUSCULES	ORATORIAN
OPERETTA	OPPILATES	OPTICALLY	OPUSCULUM	ORATORIANS
OPERETTAS	OPPILATING	OPTICIAN	OPUSES	ORATORIES
OPERON	OPPO	OPTICIANS	OQUASSA*	ORATORIO
OPERONS	OPPONENCIES	OPTICIST*	OQUASSAS*	ORATORIOS
OPEROSE	OPPONENCY	OPTICISTS*	OR	ORATORS
OPEROSELY	OPPONENT	OPTICS	ORA*	ORATORY
OPEROSITIES	OPPONENTS	OPTIMA	ORACH	ORATRESS
OPEROSITY	OPPORTUNE	OPTIMAL	ORACHE	ORATRESSES
OPES	OPPOS	OPTIMALLY	ORACHES	ORATRICES*
OPHIDIAN	OPPOSABLE	OPTIMATE	ORACIES	ORATRIX
OPHIDIANS	OPPOSE	OPTIMATES	ORACLE	ORATRIXES

Words marked with an asterisk are from OTCWL

ORB	ORDAINING	OREOLOGY	ORGIAS	ORILLION
ORBED	ORDAINS	OREPEARCH	ORGIAST	ORILLIONS
ORBICULAR	ORDALIAN	OREPEARCHED	ORGIASTIC	ORINASAL*
ORBIER	ORDALIUM	OREPEARCHES	ORGIASTS	ORINASALS*
ORBIEST	ORDALIUMS	OREPEARCHING	ORGIC	ORIOLE
ORBING	ORDEAL	ORES	ORGIES	ORIOLES
ORBIT	ORDEALS	ORESTUNCK	ORGILLOUS	ORISON
ORBITA	ORDER	OREWEED	ORGONE	ORISONS
ORBITAL	ORDERABLE*	OREWEEDS	ORGONES	ORLE
ORBITALS	ORDERED	OREXIS	ORGUE	ORLEANS
ORBITAS	ORDERER	OREXISES	ORGUES	ORLEANSES
ORBITED	ORDERERS	ORF	ORGULOUS	ORLES
ORBITER	ORDERING	ORFE	ORGY	ORLOP
ORBITERS	ORDERINGS	ORFES	ORIBATID*	ORLOPS
ORBITIES	ORDERLESS	ORFRAY*	ORIBATIDS*	ORMER
ORBITING	ORDERLIES	ORFRAYS*	ORIBI	ORMERS
ORBITS	ORDERLY	ORFS	ORIBIS	ORMOLU
ORBITY	ORDERS	ORGAN	ORICALCHE	ORMOLUS
ORBS	ORDINAIRE	ORGANA	ORICALCHES	ORNAMENT
ORBY	ORDINAIRES	ORGANDIE	ORICHALC	ORNAMENTED
ORC	ORDINAL	ORGANDIES	ORICHALCS	ORNAMENTING
ORCA	ORDINALS	ORGANDY*	ORIEL	ORNAMENTS
ORCAS	ORDINANCE	ORGANELLE	ORIELLED	ORNATE
ORCEIN	ORDINANCES	ORGANELLES	ORIELS	ORNATELY
ORCEINS	ORDINAND	ORGANIC	ORIENCIES	ORNATER
ORCHARD	ORDINANDS	ORGANICAL	ORIENCY	ORNATEST
ORCHARDS	ORDINANT	ORGANICS*	ORIENT	ORNERIER*
ORCHAT	ORDINANTS	ORGANISE	ORIENTAL	ORNERIEST*
ORCHATS	ORDINAR	ORGANISED	ORIENTALS	ORNERY
ORCHEL	ORDINARIER*	ORGANISER	ORIENTATE	ORNIS
ORCHELLA	ORDINARIES	ORGANISERS	ORIENTATED	ORNISES
ORCHELLAS	ORDINARIEST*	ORGANISES	ORIENTATES	ORNITHES*
ORCHELS	ORDINARS	ORGANISING	ORIENTATING	ORNITHIC
ORCHESES	ORDINARY	ORGANISM	ORIENTED	ORNITHINE*
ORCHESIS	ORDINATE	ORGANISMS	ORIENTEER	ORNITHINES*
ORCHESTIC	ORDINATED	ORGANIST	ORIENTEERED	ORNITHOID
ORCHESTICS	ORDINATES	ORGANISTS	ORIENTEERING	OROGEN
ORCHESTRA	ORDINATING	ORGANITIES	ORIENTEERINGS	OROGENIC
ORCHESTRAS	ORDINEE	ORGANITY	ORIENTEERS	OROGENIES
ORCHID	ORDINEES	ORGANIZE	ORIENTING	OROGENS
ORCHIDIST	ORDINES*	ORGANIZED	ORIENTS	OROGENY
ORCHIDISTS	ORDNANCE	ORGANIZER	ORIFEX	OROGRAPHIES
ORCHIDS	ORDNANCES	ORGANIZERS	ORIFEXES	OROGRAPHY
ORCHIL	ORDO*	ORGANIZES	ORIFICE	OROIDE
ORCHILLA	ORDOS*	ORGANIZING	ORIFICES	OROIDES
ORCHILLAS	ORDS	ORGANON	ORIFICIAL	OROLOGIES
ORCHILS	ORDURE	ORGANONS*	ORIFLAMME	OROLOGIST
ORCHIS	ORDURES	ORGANS	ORIFLAMMES	OROLOGISTS
ORCHISES	ORDUROUS	ORGANUM	ORIGAMI	OROLOGY
ORCHITIC	ORE	ORGANUMS*	ORIGAMIS	OROMETER*
ORCHITIS	OREAD	ORGANZA	ORIGAN	OROMETERS*
ORCHITISES	OREADES	ORGANZAS	ORIGANE	OROPESA
ORCIN	OREADS	ORGANZINE	ORIGANES	OROPESAS
ORCINE	ORECROWE	ORGANZINES	ORIGANS	OROROTUND
ORCINES	ORECROWED	ORGASM	ORIGANUM	OROTUND
ORCINOL	ORECROWES	ORGASMED	ORIGANUMS	ORPHAN
ORCINOLS	ORECROWING	ORGASMIC	ORIGIN	ORPHANAGE
ORCINS	ORECTIC	ORGASMING	ORIGINAL	ORPHANAGES
ORCS	ORECTIVE*	ORGASMS	ORIGINALS	ORPHANED
ORD	OREGANO	ORGASTIC	ORIGINATE	ORPHANING
ORDAIN	OREGANOS	ORGEAT	ORIGINATED	ORPHANISM
ORDAINED	OREIDE	ORGEATS	ORIGINATES	ORPHANISMS
ORDAINER	OREIDES	ORGIA	ORIGINATING	ORPHANS
ORDAINERS	OREOLOGIES	ORGIAC*	ORIGINS	ORPHARION

The Chambers Dictionary is the authority for many longer words; see Introduction, page ix

ORPHARIONS	ORZOS	OSMOTIC	OSTEOSES*	OTHERNESSES
ORPHIC*	OS	OSMOUS	OSTEOSIS*	OTHERS
ORPHICAL*	OSAR*	OSMUND	OSTEOSISES*	OTHERWISE
ORPHREY	OSCHEAL	OSMUNDA	OSTEOTOME	OTIC
ORPHREYS	OSCILLATE	OSMUNDAS	OSTEOTOMES	OTIOSE
ORPIMENT	OSCILLATED	OSMUNDS	OSTEOTOMIES	OTIOSELY*
ORPIMENTS	OSCILLATES	OSNABURG	OSTEOTOMY	OTIOSITIES
ORPIN	OSCILLATING	OSNABURGS	OSTIA	OTIOSITY
ORPINE	OSCINE	OSPREY	OSTIAL	OTITIC*
ORPINES	OSCINES*	OSPREYS	OSTIARIES	OTITIDES*
ORPINS	OSCININE	OSSA	OSTIARY	OTITIS
ORRA	OSCITANCIES	OSSARIUM	OSTIATE	OTITISES
ORRERIES	OSCITANCY	OSSARIUMS	OSTINATO	OTOCYST
ORRERY	OSCITANT	OSSEIN	OSTINATOS	OTOCYSTIC*
ORRICE*	OSCITATE	OSSEINS	OSTIOLAR*	OTOCYSTS
ORRICES*	OSCITATED	OSSELET	OSTIOLATE	OTOLITH
ORRIS	OSCITATES	OSSELETS	OSTIOLE	OTOLITHIC*
ORRISES	OSCITATING	OSSEOUS	OSTIOLES	OTOLITHS
ORRISROOT*	OSCULA	OSSETER	OSTIUM	OTOLOGIES
ORRISROOTS*	OSCULANT	OSSETERS	OSTLER	OTOLOGIST
ORS	OSCULAR	OSSIA	OSTLERESS	OTOLOGISTS
ORSEILLE	OSCULATE	OSSICLE	OSTLERESSES	OTOLOGY
ORSEILLES	OSCULATED	OSSICLES	OSTLERS	OTORRHOEA
ORSELLIC	OSCULATES	OSSICULAR	OSTMARK*	OTORRHOEAS
ORT	OSCULATING	OSSIFIC	OSTMARKS*	OTOSCOPE
ORTANIQUE	OSCULE	OSSIFIED	OSTOMIES*	OTOSCOPES
ORTANIQUES	OSCULES	OSSIFIER*	OSTOMY*	OTOSCOPIES*
ORTHIAN	OSCULUM	OSSIFIERS*	OSTOSES*	OTOSCOPY*
ORTHICON	OSE*	OSSIFIES	OSTOSIS*	OTOTOXIC*
ORTHICONS	OSES*	OSSIFRAGA	OSTOSISES*	OTTAR
ORTHO	OSHAC	OSSIFRAGAS	OSTRACA	OTTARS
ORTHOAXES	OSHACS	OSSIFRAGE	OSTRACEAN	OTTAVA
ORTHOAXIS	OSIER	OSSIFRAGES	OSTRACISE	OTTAVAS
ORTHODOX	OSIERED	OSSIFY	OSTRACISED	OTTAVINO
ORTHODOXES*	OSIERIES	OSSIFYING	OSTRACISES	OTTAVINOS
ORTHODOXIES	OSIERS	OSSUARIES	OSTRACISING	OTTER
ORTHODOXY	OSIERY	OSSUARY	OSTRACISM	OTTERED
ORTHOEPIC	OSMATE	OSTEAL	OSTRACISMS	OTTERING
ORTHOEPIES	OSMATES	OSTEITIC*	OSTRACIZE	OTTERS
ORTHOEPY	OSMATIC*	OSTEITIDES*	OSTRACIZED	OTTO
ORTHOPEDIES	OSMETERIA	OSTEITIS	OSTRACIZES	OTTOMAN
ORTHOPEDY	OSMETERIUM*	OSTEITISES	OSTRACIZING	OTTOMANS
ORTHOPOD	OSMIATE	OSTENSIVE	OSTRACOD	OTTOS
ORTHOPODS	OSMIATES	OSTENSORIES	OSTRACODE*	OTTRELITE
ORTHOPTIC	OSMIC	OSTENSORY	OSTRACODES*	OTTRELITES
ORTHOPTICS	OSMICS*	OSTENT	OSTRACODS	OU
ORTHOS	OSMIOUS	OSTENTS	OSTRACON	OUABAIN
ORTHOSES	OSMIUM	OSTEOCYTE*	OSTRAKA	OUABAINS
ORTHOSIS	OSMIUMS	OSTEOCYTES*	OSTRAKON	OUAKARI
ORTHOTIC	OSMOL*	OSTEODERM	OSTREGER	OUAKARIS
ORTHOTICS	OSMOLAL*	OSTEODERMS	OSTREGERS	OUBIT
ORTHOTIST	OSMOLAR*	OSTEOGEN	OSTRICH	OUBITS
ORTHOTISTS	OSMOLE*	OSTEOGENIES	OSTRICHES	OUBLIETTE
ORTHOTONE	OSMOLES*	OSTEOGENS	OTAKU	OUBLIETTES
ORTHROS	OSMOLS*	OSTEOGENY	OTALGIA	OUCH
ORTHROSES	OSMOMETER	OSTEOID	OTALGIAS	OUCHED*
ORTOLAN	OSMOMETERS	OSTEOIDS*	OTALGIC*	OUCHES
ORTOLANS	OSMOMETRIES	OSTEOLOGIES	OTALGIES	OUCHING*
ORTS	OSMOMETRY	OSTEOLOGY	OTALGY	OUCHT
ORVAL	OSMOSE	OSTEOMA	OTARIES	OUCHTS
ORVALS	OSMOSED	OSTEOMAS	OTARINE	OUD
ORYX	OSMOSES	OSTEOMATA	OTARY	OUDS
ORYXES	OSMOSING	OSTEOPATH	OTHER	OUGHLIED
ORZO	OSMOSIS	OSTEOPATHS	OTHERNESS	OUGHLIES

OUGHLY	OUSELS	OUTBITCHING*	OUTBUILD*	OUTCLASSED
OUGHLYING	OUST	OUTBLAZE*	OUTBUILDING*	OUTCLASSES
OUGHT	OUSTED	OUTBLAZED*	OUTBUILDS*	OUTCLASSING
OUGHTED*	OUSTER	OUTBLAZES*	OUTBUILT*	OUTCLIMB*
OUGHTING*	OUSTERS	OUTBLAZING*	OUTBULK*	OUTCLIMBED*
OUGHTNESS	OUSTING	OUTBLEAT*	OUTBULKED*	OUTCLIMBING*
OUGHTNESSES	OUSTITI	OUTBLEATED*	OUTBULKING*	OUTCLIMBS*
OUGHTS	OUSTITIS	OUTBLEATING*	OUTBULKS*	OUTCLOMB*
OUGLIE	OUSTS	OUTBLEATS*	OUTBULLIED*	OUTCOACH*
OUGLIED	OUT	OUTBLESS*	OUTBULLIES*	OUTCOACHED*
OUGLIEING	OUTACT*	OUTBLESSED*	OUTBULLY*	OUTCOACHES*
OUGLIES	OUTACTED*	OUTBLESSES*	OUTBULLYING*	OUTCOACHING*
OUGUIYA*	OUTACTING*	OUTBLESSING*	OUTBURN	OUTCOME
OUIJA	OUTACTS*	OUTBLOOM*	OUTBURNED	OUTCOMES
OUIJAS	OUTADD*	OUTBLOOMED*	OUTBURNING	OUTCOOK*
OUISTITI	OUTADDED*	OUTBLOOMING*	OUTBURNS	OUTCOOKED*
OUISTITIS	OUTADDING*	OUTBLOOMS*	OUTBURNT	OUTCOOKING*
OUK	OUTADDS*	OUTBLUFF*	OUTBURST	OUTCOOKS*
OUKS	OUTAGE	OUTBLUFFED*	OUTBURSTING	OUTCOUNT*
OULACHON	OUTAGES	OUTBLUFFING*	OUTBURSTS	OUTCOUNTED*
OULACHONS	OUTARGUE*	OUTBLUFFS*	OUTBUY*	OUTCOUNTING*
OULAKAN	OUTARGUED*	OUTBLUSH*	OUTBUYING*	OUTCOUNTS*
OULAKANS	OUTARGUES*	OUTBLUSHED*	OUTBUYS*	OUTCRAFTIED
OULD	OUTARGUING*	OUTBLUSHES*	OUTBY	OUTCRAFTIES
OULDER	OUTASK*	OUTBLUSHING*	OUTBYE	OUTCRAFTY
OULDEST	OUTASKED*	OUTBOARD	OUTCAPER*	OUTCRAFTYING
OULK	OUTASKING*	OUTBOARDS*	OUTCAPERED*	OUTCRAWL*
OULKS	OUTASKS*	OUTBOAST*	OUTCAPERING*	OUTCRAWLED*
OULONG	OUTATE	OUTBOASTED*	OUTCAPERS*	OUTCRAWLING*
OULONGS	OUTBACK	OUTBOASTING*	OUTCAST	OUTCRAWLS*
OUNCE	OUTBACKER	OUTBOASTS*	OUTCASTE	OUTCRIED
OUNCES	OUTBACKERS	OUTBOUGHT*	OUTCASTED	OUTCRIES
OUNDY	OUTBACKS	OUTBOUND	OUTCASTES	OUTCROP
OUP	OUTBAKE*	OUTBOUNDS	OUTCASTING	OUTCROPPED
OUPED	OUTBAKED*	OUTBOX	OUTCASTS	OUTCROPPING
OUPH	OUTBAKES*	OUTBOXED	OUTCATCH*	OUTCROPS
OUPHE	OUTBAKING*	OUTBOXES	OUTCATCHES*	OUTCROSS
OUPHES	OUTBAR	OUTBOXING	OUTCATCHING*	OUTCROSSED
OUPHS	OUTBARK*	OUTBRAG	OUTCAUGHT*	OUTCROSSES
OUPING	OUTBARKED*	OUTBRAGGED	OUTCAVIL*	OUTCROSSING
OUPS	OUTBARKING*	OUTBRAGGING	OUTCAVILED*	OUTCROSSINGS
OUR	OUTBARKS*	OUTBRAGS	OUTCAVILING*	OUTCROW*
OURALI	OUTBARRED	OUTBRAVE	OUTCAVILLED*	OUTCROWED*
OURALIS	OUTBARRING	OUTBRAVED	OUTCAVILLING*	OUTCROWING*
OURANG*	OUTBARS	OUTBRAVES	OUTCAVILS*	OUTCROWS*
OURANGS*	OUTBAWL*	OUTBRAVING	OUTCHARGE*	OUTCRY
OURARI	OUTBAWLED*	OUTBRAWL*	OUTCHARGED*	OUTCRYING
OURARIS	OUTBAWLING*	OUTBRAWLED*	OUTCHARGES*	OUTCURSE*
OUREBI	OUTBAWLS*	OUTBRAWLING*	OUTCHARGING*	OUTCURSED*
OUREBIS	OUTBEAM*	OUTBRAWLS*	OUTCHARM*	OUTCURSES*
OURIE	OUTBEAMED*	OUTBREAK	OUTCHARMED*	OUTCURSING*
OURIER	OUTBEAMING*	OUTBREAKING	OUTCHARMING*	OUTCURVE*
OURIEST	OUTBEAMS*	OUTBREAKS	OUTCHARMS*	OUTCURVES*
OURN	OUTBEG*	OUTBRED	OUTCHEAT*	OUTDANCE
OUROBOROS	OUTBEGGED*	OUTBREED	OUTCHEATED*	OUTDANCED
OUROBOROSES	OUTBEGGING*	OUTBREEDING	OUTCHEATING*	OUTDANCES
OUROLOGIES	OUTBEGS*	OUTBREEDINGS	OUTCHEATS*	OUTDANCING
OUROLOGY	OUTBID	OUTBREEDS	OUTCHID*	OUTDARE
OUROSCOPIES	OUTBIDDEN*	OUTBRIBE*	OUTCHIDDEN*	OUTDARED
OUROSCOPY	OUTBIDDING	OUTBRIBED*	OUTCHIDE*	OUTDARES
OURS	OUTBIDS	OUTBRIBES*	OUTCHIDED*	OUTDARING
OURSELF	OUTBITCH*	OUTBRIBING*	OUTCHIDES*	OUTDATE
OURSELVES	OUTBITCHED*	OUTBROKE	OUTCHIDING*	OUTDATED
OUSEL	OUTBITCHES*	OUTBROKEN	OUTCLASS	OUTDATES

The Chambers Dictionary is the authority for many longer words; see Introduction, page ix

OUTDATING	OUTDUELS*	OUTFIGURED*	OUTFUMBLED*	OUTGUIDED*
OUTDAZZLE*	OUTDURE	OUTFIGURES*	OUTFUMBLES*	OUTGUIDES*
OUTDAZZLED*	OUTDURED	OUTFIGURING*	OUTFUMBLING*	OUTGUIDING*
OUTDAZZLES*	OUTDURES	OUTFIND*	OUTGAIN*	OUTGUN
OUTDAZZLING*	OUTDURING	OUTFINDING*	OUTGAINED*	OUTGUNNED
OUTDEBATE*	OUTDWELL	OUTFINDS*	OUTGAINING*	OUTGUNNING
OUTDEBATED*	OUTDWELLED	OUTFIRE*	OUTGAINS*	OUTGUNS
OUTDEBATES*	OUTDWELLING	OUTFIRED*	OUTGAS	OUTGUSH
OUTDEBATING*	OUTDWELLS	OUTFIRES*	OUTGASSED	OUTGUSHED
OUTDESIGN*	OUTDWELT	OUTFIRING*	OUTGASSES	OUTGUSHES
OUTDESIGNED*	OUTEARN*	OUTFISH*	OUTGASSING	OUTGUSHING
OUTDESIGNING*	OUTEARNED*	OUTFISHED*	OUTGASSINGS	OUTHAUL
OUTDESIGNS*	OUTEARNING*	OUTFISHES*	OUTGATE	OUTHAULER
OUTDID	OUTEARNS*	OUTFISHING*	OUTGATES	OUTHAULERS
OUTDO	OUTEAT	OUTFIT	OUTGAVE	OUTHAULS
OUTDODGE*	OUTEATEN	OUTFITS	OUTGIVE	OUTHEAR*
OUTDODGED*	OUTEATING	OUTFITTED	OUTGIVEN	OUTHEARD*
OUTDODGES*	OUTEATS	OUTFITTER	OUTGIVES	OUTHEARING*
OUTDODGING*	OUTECHO*	OUTFITTERS	OUTGIVING	OUTHEARS*
OUTDOER*	OUTECHOED*	OUTFITTING	OUTGIVINGS	OUTHER
OUTDOERS*	OUTECHOES*	OUTFITTINGS	OUTGLARE	OUTHIRE
OUTDOES	OUTECHOING*	OUTFLANK	OUTGLARED	OUTHIRED
OUTDOING	OUTED	OUTFLANKED	OUTGLARES	OUTHIRES
OUTDONE	OUTEDGE	OUTFLANKING	OUTGLARING	OUTHIRING
OUTDOOR	OUTEDGES	OUTFLANKS	OUTGLOW*	OUTHIT
OUTDOORS	OUTER	OUTFLASH	OUTGLOWED*	OUTHITS
OUTDOORSY	OUTERCOAT*	OUTFLASHED	OUTGLOWING*	OUTHITTING
OUTDRAG*	OUTERCOATS*	OUTFLASHES	OUTGLOWS*	OUTHOMER*
OUTDRAGGED*	OUTERMOST	OUTFLASHING	OUTGNAW*	OUTHOMERED*
OUTDRAGGING*	OUTERS	OUTFLEW	OUTGNAWED*	OUTHOMERING*
OUTDRAGS*	OUTERWEAR	OUTFLIES	OUTGNAWING*	OUTHOMERS*
OUTDRANK	OUTERWEARS	OUTFLING	OUTGNAWN*	OUTHOUSE
OUTDRAW*	OUTFABLE*	OUTFLINGS	OUTGNAWS*	OUTHOUSES
OUTDRAWING*	OUTFABLED*	OUTFLOW	OUTGO	OUTHOWL*
OUTDRAWN*	OUTFABLES*	OUTFLOWED	OUTGOER	OUTHOWLED*
OUTDRAWS*	OUTFABLING*	OUTFLOWING	OUTGOERS	OUTHOWLING*
OUTDREAM*	OUTFACE	OUTFLOWINGS	OUTGOES	OUTHOWLS*
OUTDREAMED*	OUTFACED	OUTFLOWN	OUTGOING	OUTHUMOR*
OUTDREAMING*	OUTFACES	OUTFLOWS	OUTGOINGS	OUTHUMORED*
OUTDREAMS*	OUTFACING	OUTFLUSH	OUTGONE	OUTHUMORING*
OUTDREAMT*	OUTFALL	OUTFLUSHED	OUTGREW	OUTHUMORS*
OUTDRESS*	OUTFALLS	OUTFLUSHES	OUTGRIN*	OUTHUNT*
OUTDRESSED*	OUTFAST*	OUTFLUSHING	OUTGRINNED*	OUTHUNTED*
OUTDRESSES*	OUTFASTED*	OUTFLY	OUTGRINNING*	OUTHUNTING*
OUTDRESSING*	OUTFASTING*	OUTFLYING	OUTGRINS*	OUTHUNTS*
OUTDREW*	OUTFASTS*	OUTFOOL*	OUTGROSS*	OUTHUSTLE*
OUTDRINK	OUTFAWN*	OUTFOOLED*	OUTGROSSED*	OUTHUSTLED*
OUTDRINKING	OUTFAWNED*	OUTFOOLING*	OUTGROSSES*	OUTHUSTLES*
OUTDRINKS	OUTFAWNING*	OUTFOOLS*	OUTGROSSING*	OUTHUSTLING*
OUTDRIVE	OUTFAWNS*	OUTFOOT	OUTGROUP*	OUTHYRE
OUTDRIVEN	OUTFEAST*	OUTFOOTED	OUTGROUPS*	OUTHYRED
OUTDRIVES	OUTFEASTED*	OUTFOOTING	OUTGROW	OUTHYRES
OUTDRIVING	OUTFEASTING*	OUTFOOTS	OUTGROWING	OUTHYRING
OUTDROP*	OUTFEASTS*	OUTFOUGHT	OUTGROWN	OUTING
OUTDROPPED*	OUTFEEL*	OUTFOUND*	OUTGROWS	OUTINGS
OUTDROPPING*	OUTFEELING*	OUTFOX	OUTGROWTH	OUTJEST
OUTDROPS*	OUTFEELS*	OUTFOXED	OUTGROWTHS	OUTJESTED
OUTDROVE	OUTFELT*	OUTFOXES	OUTGUARD	OUTJESTING
OUTDRUNK	OUTFIELD	OUTFOXING	OUTGUARDS	OUTJESTS
OUTDUEL*	OUTFIELDS	OUTFROWN	OUTGUESS*	OUTJET
OUTDUELED*	OUTFIGHT	OUTFROWNED	OUTGUESSED*	OUTJETS
OUTDUELING*	OUTFIGHTING	OUTFROWNING	OUTGUESSES*	OUTJINX*
OUTDUELLED*	OUTFIGHTS	OUTFROWNS	OUTGUESSING*	OUTJINXED*
OUTDUELLING*	OUTFIGURE*	OUTFUMBLE*	OUTGUIDE*	OUTJINXES*

Words marked with an asterisk are from OTCWL

OUTJINXING*	OUTLEAPING	OUTMOVE	OUTPLAYING	OUTPUNCHING*
OUTJOCKEY	OUTLEAPS	OUTMOVED	OUTPLAYS	OUTPUSH*
OUTJOCKEYED	OUTLEAPT	OUTMOVES	OUTPLOD*	OUTPUSHED*
OUTJOCKEYING	OUTLEARN	OUTMOVING	OUTPLODDED*	OUTPUSHES*
OUTJOCKEYS	OUTLEARNED	OUTMUSCLE*	OUTPLODDING*	OUTPUSHING*
OUTJUMP	OUTLEARNING	OUTMUSCLED*	OUTPLODS*	OUTPUT
OUTJUMPED	OUTLEARNS	OUTMUSCLES*	OUTPLOT*	OUTPUTS
OUTJUMPING	OUTLEARNT	OUTMUSCLING*	OUTPLOTS*	OUTPUTTED*
OUTJUMPS	OUTLER	OUTNAME	OUTPLOTTED*	OUTPUTTING
OUTJUT	OUTLERS	OUTNAMED	OUTPLOTTING*	OUTQUOTE*
OUTJUTS	OUTLET	OUTNAMES	OUTPOINT	OUTQUOTED*
OUTJUTTED*	OUTLETS	OUTNAMING	OUTPOINTED	OUTQUOTES*
OUTJUTTING*	OUTLIE	OUTNESS	OUTPOINTING	OUTQUOTING*
OUTKEEP*	OUTLIED	OUTNESSES	OUTPOINTS	OUTRACE
OUTKEEPING*	OUTLIER	OUTNIGHT	OUTPOLL*	OUTRACED
OUTKEEPS*	OUTLIERS	OUTNIGHTED	OUTPOLLED*	OUTRACES
OUTKEPT*	OUTLIES	OUTNIGHTING	OUTPOLLING*	OUTRACING
OUTKICK*	OUTLINE	OUTNIGHTS	OUTPOLLS*	OUTRAGE
OUTKICKED*	OUTLINEAR	OUTNUMBER	OUTPORT	OUTRAGED
OUTKICKING*	OUTLINED	OUTNUMBERED	OUTPORTS	OUTRAGES
OUTKICKS*	OUTLINER*	OUTNUMBERING	OUTPOST	OUTRAGING
OUTKILL*	OUTLINERS*	OUTNUMBERS	OUTPOSTS	OUTRAIGNE
OUTKILLED*	OUTLINES	OUTPACE	OUTPOUR	OUTRAIGNED
OUTKILLING*	OUTLINING	OUTPACED	OUTPOURED	OUTRAIGNES
OUTKILLS*	OUTLIVE	OUTPACES	OUTPOURER	OUTRAIGNING
OUTKISS*	OUTLIVED	OUTPACING	OUTPOURERS	OUTRAISE*
OUTKISSED*	OUTLIVER*	OUTPAINT*	OUTPOURING	OUTRAISED*
OUTKISSES*	OUTLIVERS*	OUTPAINTED*	OUTPOURINGS	OUTRAISES*
OUTKISSING*	OUTLIVES	OUTPAINTING*	OUTPOURS	OUTRAISING*
OUTLAID	OUTLIVING	OUTPAINTS*	OUTPOWER	OUTRAN
OUTLAIN	OUTLOOK	OUTPART	OUTPOWERED	OUTRANCE
OUTLAND	OUTLOOKED	OUTPARTS	OUTPOWERING	OUTRANCES
OUTLANDER	OUTLOOKING	OUTPASS*	OUTPOWERS	OUTRANG*
OUTLANDERS	OUTLOOKS	OUTPASSED*	OUTPRAY	OUTRANGE*
OUTLANDS	OUTLOVE*	OUTPASSES*	OUTPRAYED	OUTRANGED*
OUTLASH	OUTLOVED*	OUTPASSING*	OUTPRAYING	OUTRANGES*
OUTLASHES	OUTLOVES*	OUTPEEP	OUTPRAYS	OUTRANGING*
OUTLAST	OUTLOVING*	OUTPEEPED	OUTPREACH*	OUTRANK
OUTLASTED	OUTLUSTRE	OUTPEEPING	OUTPREACHED*	OUTRANKED
OUTLASTING	OUTLUSTRED	OUTPEEPS	OUTPREACHES*	OUTRANKING
OUTLASTS	OUTLUSTRES	OUTPEER	OUTPREACHING*	OUTRANKS
OUTLAUGH*	OUTLUSTRING	OUTPEERED	OUTPREEN*	OUTRATE
OUTLAUGHED*	OUTLYING	OUTPEERING	OUTPREENED*	OUTRATED
OUTLAUGHING*	OUTMAN	OUTPEERS	OUTPREENING*	OUTRATES
OUTLAUGHS*	OUTMANNED	OUTPITCH*	OUTPREENS*	OUTRATING
OUTLAUNCE	OUTMANNING	OUTPITCHED*	OUTPRESS*	OUTRAVE*
OUTLAUNCED	OUTMANS	OUTPITCHES*	OUTPRESSED*	OUTRAVED*
OUTLAUNCES	OUTMANTLE	OUTPITCHING*	OUTPRESSES*	OUTRAVES*
OUTLAUNCH	OUTMANTLED	OUTPITIED*	OUTPRESSING*	OUTRAVING*
OUTLAUNCHED	OUTMANTLES	OUTPITIES*	OUTPRICE	OUTRE
OUTLAUNCHES	OUTMANTLING	OUTPITY*	OUTPRICED	OUTREACH
OUTLAUNCHING	OUTMARCH	OUTPITYING*	OUTPRICES	OUTREACHED
OUTLAUNCING	OUTMARCHED	OUTPLACE	OUTPRICING	OUTREACHES
OUTLAW	OUTMARCHES	OUTPLACED	OUTPRIZE	OUTREACHING
OUTLAWED	OUTMARCHING	OUTPLACER	OUTPRIZED	OUTREAD*
OUTLAWING	OUTMATCH	OUTPLACERS	OUTPRIZES	OUTREADING*
OUTLAWRIES	OUTMATCHED	OUTPLACES	OUTPRIZING	OUTREADS*
OUTLAWRY	OUTMATCHES	OUTPLACING	OUTPULL*	OUTRED
OUTLAWS	OUTMATCHING	OUTPLAN*	OUTPULLED*	OUTREDDED
OUTLAY	OUTMODE	OUTPLANNED*	OUTPULLING*	OUTREDDEN
OUTLAYING	OUTMODED	OUTPLANNING*	OUTPULLS*	OUTREDDENED
OUTLAYS	OUTMODES	OUTPLANS*	OUTPUNCH*	OUTREDDENING
OUTLEAP	OUTMODING	OUTPLAY	OUTPUNCHED*	OUTREDDENS
OUTLEAPED	OUTMOST	OUTPLAYED	OUTPUNCHES*	OUTREDDING

The Chambers Dictionary is the authority for many longer words; see Introduction, page ix

OUTREDS	OUTRUSHES	OUTSHOUTED*	OUTSPAN	OUTSTEPPING
OUTREIGN	OUTRUSHING	OUTSHOUTING*	OUTSPANNED	OUTSTEPS
OUTREIGNED	OUTS	OUTSHOUTS*	OUTSPANNING	OUTSTOOD
OUTREIGNING	OUTSAIL	OUTSIDE	OUTSPANS	OUTSTRAIN
OUTREIGNS	OUTSAILED	OUTSIDER	OUTSPEAK	OUTSTRAINED
OUTRELIEF	OUTSAILING	OUTSIDERS	OUTSPEAKING	OUTSTRAINING
OUTRELIEFS	OUTSAILS	OUTSIDES	OUTSPEAKS	OUTSTRAINS
OUTREMER	OUTSANG*	OUTSIGHT	OUTSPED*	OUTSTRIDDEN*
OUTREMERS	OUTSAT	OUTSIGHTS	OUTSPEED*	OUTSTRIDE*
OUTRIDDEN	OUTSAVOR*	OUTSIN*	OUTSPEEDED*	OUTSTRIDES*
OUTRIDE	OUTSAVORED*	OUTSING*	OUTSPEEDING*	OUTSTRIDING*
OUTRIDER	OUTSAVORING*	OUTSINGING*	OUTSPEEDS*	OUTSTRIKE
OUTRIDERS	OUTSAVORS*	OUTSINGS*	OUTSPELL*	OUTSTRIKES
OUTRIDES	OUTSAW*	OUTSINNED*	OUTSPELLED*	OUTSTRIKING
OUTRIDING	OUTSCHEME*	OUTSINNING*	OUTSPELLING*	OUTSTRIP
OUTRIGGER	OUTSCHEMED*	OUTSINS*	OUTSPELLS*	OUTSTRIPPED
OUTRIGGERS	OUTSCHEMES*	OUTSIT	OUTSPELT*	OUTSTRIPPING
OUTRIGHT	OUTSCHEMING*	OUTSITS	OUTSPEND	OUTSTRIPS
OUTRING*	OUTSCOLD	OUTSITTING	OUTSPENDING	OUTSTRODE*
OUTRINGING*	OUTSCOLDED	OUTSIZE	OUTSPENDS	OUTSTRUCK
OUTRINGS*	OUTSCOLDING	OUTSIZED	OUTSPENT	OUTSTUDIED*
OUTRIVAL	OUTSCOLDS	OUTSIZES	OUTSPOKE	OUTSTUDIES*
OUTRIVALED*	OUTSCOOP*	OUTSKATE*	OUTSPOKEN	OUTSTUDY*
OUTRIVALING*	OUTSCOOPED*	OUTSKATED*	OUTSPORT	OUTSTUDYING*
OUTRIVALLED	OUTSCOOPING*	OUTSKATES*	OUTSPORTED	OUTSTUNT*
OUTRIVALLING	OUTSCOOPS*	OUTSKATING*	OUTSPORTING	OUTSTUNTED*
OUTRIVALS	OUTSCORE*	OUTSKIRT*	OUTSPORTS	OUTSTUNTING*
OUTROAR	OUTSCORED*	OUTSKIRTS	OUTSPRANG	OUTSTUNTS*
OUTROARED	OUTSCORES*	OUTSLEEP	OUTSPREAD	OUTSULK*
OUTROARING	OUTSCORING*	OUTSLEEPING	OUTSPREADING	OUTSULKED*
OUTROARS	OUTSCORN	OUTSLEEPS	OUTSPREADS	OUTSULKING*
OUTROCK*	OUTSCORNED	OUTSLEPT	OUTSPRING	OUTSULKS*
OUTROCKED*	OUTSCORNING	OUTSLICK*	OUTSPRINGING	OUTSUM
OUTROCKING*	OUTSCORNS	OUTSLICKED*	OUTSPRINGS	OUTSUMMED
OUTROCKS*	OUTSEE*	OUTSLICKING*	OUTSPRINT*	OUTSUMMING
OUTRODE	OUTSEEING*	OUTSLICKS*	OUTSPRINTED*	OUTSUMS
OUTROLL*	OUTSEEN*	OUTSMART	OUTSPRINTING*	OUTSUNG*
OUTROLLED*	OUTSEES*	OUTSMARTED	OUTSPRINTS*	OUTSWAM
OUTROLLING*	OUTSELL	OUTSMARTING	OUTSPRUNG	OUTSWARE*
OUTROLLS*	OUTSELLING	OUTSMARTS	OUTSTAND	OUTSWEAR
OUTROOP	OUTSELLS	OUTSMILE*	OUTSTANDING	OUTSWEARING
OUTROOPER	OUTSERT*	OUTSMILED*	OUTSTANDS	OUTSWEARS
OUTROOPERS	OUTSERTS*	OUTSMILES*	OUTSTARE	OUTSWELL
OUTROOPS	OUTSERVE*	OUTSMILING*	OUTSTARED	OUTSWELLED
OUTROOT	OUTSERVED*	OUTSMOKE*	OUTSTARES	OUTSWELLING
OUTROOTED	OUTSERVES*	OUTSMOKED*	OUTSTARING	OUTSWELLS
OUTROOTING	OUTSERVING*	OUTSMOKES*	OUTSTART*	OUTSWIM
OUTROOTS	OUTSET	OUTSMOKING*	OUTSTARTED*	OUTSWIMMING
OUTROPE	OUTSETS	OUTSNORE*	OUTSTARTING*	OUTSWIMS
OUTROPER	OUTSHAME*	OUTSNORED*	OUTSTARTS*	OUTSWING
OUTROPERS	OUTSHAMED*	OUTSNORES*	OUTSTATE*	OUTSWINGS
OUTROPES	OUTSHAMES*	OUTSNORING*	OUTSTATED*	OUTSWOLLEN
OUTROW*	OUTSHAMING*	OUTSOAR	OUTSTATES*	OUTSWORE
OUTROWED*	OUTSHINE	OUTSOARED	OUTSTATING*	OUTSWORN
OUTROWING*	OUTSHINED*	OUTSOARING	OUTSTAY	OUTSWUM
OUTROWS*	OUTSHINES	OUTSOARS	OUTSTAYED	OUTTAKE
OUTRUN	OUTSHINING	OUTSOLD	OUTSTAYING	OUTTAKEN
OUTRUNG*	OUTSHONE	OUTSOLE	OUTSTAYS	OUTTAKES
OUTRUNNER	OUTSHOOT	OUTSOLES	OUTSTEER*	OUTTAKING
OUTRUNNERS	OUTSHOOTING	OUTSOURCE	OUTSTEERED*	OUTTALK
OUTRUNNING	OUTSHOOTS	OUTSOURCED	OUTSTEERING*	OUTTALKED
OUTRUNS	OUTSHOT	OUTSOURCES	OUTSTEERS*	OUTTALKING
OUTRUSH	OUTSHOTS	OUTSOURCING	OUTSTEP	OUTTALKS
OUTRUSHED	OUTSHOUT*	OUTSOURCINGS	OUTSTEPPED	OUTTASK*

OUTTASKED* OUTVALUING OUTWEIGHING OUTWRITES* OVENWARE
OUTTASKING* OUTVAUNT* OUTWEIGHS OUTWRITING* OVENWARES
OUTTASKS* OUTVAUNTED* OUTWELL OUTWRITTEN* OVENWOOD
OUTTELL OUTVAUNTING* OUTWELLED OUTWROTE* OVENWOODS
OUTTELLING OUTVAUNTS* OUTWELLING OUTWROUGHT OVER
OUTTELLS OUTVENOM OUTWELLS OUTYELL* OVERABLE*
OUTTHANK* OUTVENOMED OUTWENT OUTYELLED* OVERACT
OUTTHANKED* OUTVENOMING OUTWEPT OUTYELLING* OVERACTED
OUTTHANKING* OUTVENOMS OUTWHIRL* OUTYELLS* OVERACTING
OUTTHANKS* OUTVIE OUTWHIRLED* OUTYELP* OVERACTS
OUTTHINK OUTVIED OUTWHIRLING* OUTYELPED* OVERAGE
OUTTHINKING OUTVIES OUTWHIRLS* OUTYELPING* OVERAGED*
OUTTHINKS OUTVOICE OUTWICK OUTYELPS* OVERAGES
OUTTHOUGHT OUTVOICED OUTWICKED OUTYIELD* OVERALERT*
OUTTHREW* OUTVOICES OUTWICKING OUTYIELDED* OVERALL
OUTTHROB* OUTVOICING OUTWICKS OUTYIELDING* OVERALLED
OUTTHROBBED* OUTVOTE OUTWILE* OUTYIELDS* OVERALLS
OUTTHROBBING* OUTVOTED OUTWILED* OUVERT OVERAPT*
OUTTHROBS* OUTVOTER OUTWILES* OUVERTE OVERARCH
OUTTHROW* OUTVOTERS OUTWILING* OUVRAGE OVERARCHED
OUTTHROWING* OUTVOTES OUTWILL* OUVRAGES OVERARCHES
OUTTHROWN* OUTVOTING OUTWILLED* OUVRIER OVERARCHING
OUTTHROWS* OUTVYING OUTWILLING* OUVRIERE OVERARM
OUTTOLD OUTWAIT* OUTWILLS* OUVRIERES OVERATE
OUTTONGUE OUTWAITED* OUTWIN OUVRIERS OVERAWE
OUTTONGUED OUTWAITING* OUTWIND OUZEL OVERAWED
OUTTONGUES OUTWAITS* OUTWINDED* OUZELS OVERAWES
OUTTONGUING OUTWALK OUTWINDING OUZO OVERAWING
OUTTOOK OUTWALKED OUTWINDS OUZOS OVERBAKE*
OUTTOP OUTWALKING OUTWING OVA OVERBAKED*
OUTTOPPED OUTWALKS OUTWINGED OVAL OVERBAKES*
OUTTOPPING OUTWAR* OUTWINGING OVALBUMIN OVERBAKING
OUTTOPS OUTWARD OUTWINGS OVALBUMINS OVERBEAR
OUTTOWER* OUTWARDLY OUTWINNING OVALITIES* OVERBEARING
OUTTOWERED* OUTWARDS OUTWINS OVALITY* OVERBEARS
OUTTOWERING* OUTWARRED* OUTWISH* OVALLY OVERBEAT
OUTTOWERS* OUTWARRING* OUTWISHED* OVALNESS* OVERBEATEN
OUTTRADE* OUTWARS* OUTWISHES* OVALNESSES* OVERBEATING
OUTTRADED* OUTWASH OUTWISHING* OVALS OVERBEATS
OUTTRADES* OUTWASHES OUTWIT OVARIAL* OVERBED*
OUTTRADING* OUTWASTE* OUTWITH OVARIAN OVERBET*
OUTTRAVEL OUTWASTED* OUTWITS OVARIES OVERBETS*
OUTTRAVELED OUTWASTES* OUTWITTED OVARIOLE OVERBETTED*
OUTTRAVELING OUTWASTING* OUTWITTING OVARIOLES OVERBETTING*
OUTTRAVELLED OUTWATCH OUTWON OVARIOUS OVERBID
OUTTRAVELLING OUTWATCHED OUTWORE OVARITIDES* OVERBIDDEN*
OUTTRAVELS OUTWATCHES OUTWORK OVARITIS OVERBIDDING
OUTTRICK* OUTWATCHING OUTWORKED* OVARITISES OVERBIDDINGS
OUTTRICKED* OUTWEAR OUTWORKER OVARY OVERBIDS
OUTTRICKING* OUTWEARIED OUTWORKERS OVATE OVERBIG*
OUTTRICKS* OUTWEARIES OUTWORKING OVATED OVERBILL*
OUTTROT* OUTWEARING OUTWORKS OVATELY* OVERBILLED*
OUTTROTS* OUTWEARS OUTWORN OVATES OVERBILLING*
OUTTROTTED* OUTWEARY OUTWORTH OVATING OVERBILLS*
OUTTROTTING* OUTWEARYING OUTWORTHED OVATION OVERBITE
OUTTRUMP* OUTWEED OUTWORTHING OVATIONS OVERBITES
OUTTRUMPED* OUTWEEDED OUTWORTHS OVATOR OVERBLEW
OUTTRUMPING* OUTWEEDING OUTWOUND OVATORS OVERBLOW
OUTTRUMPS* OUTWEEDS OUTWREST OVEN OVERBLOWING
OUTTURN OUTWEEP OUTWRESTED OVENBIRD* OVERBLOWN
OUTTURNS OUTWEEPING OUTWRESTING OVENBIRDS* OVERBLOWS
OUTVALUE OUTWEEPS OUTWRESTS OVENLIKE* OVERBOARD
OUTVALUED OUTWEIGH OUTWRIT* OVENPROOF* OVERBOIL
OUTVALUES OUTWEIGHED OUTWRITE* OVENS OVERBOILED

OVERBOILING	OVERCAUGHT	OVERCRAWS	OVERDRIVES	OVERFELL
OVERBOILS	OVERCHECK	OVERCROP	OVERDRIVING	OVERFILL
OVERBOLD	OVERCHECKS	OVERCROPPED	OVERDROVE	OVERFILLED
OVERBOOK	OVERCHILL*	OVERCROPPING	OVERDRUNK*	OVERFILLING
OVERBOOKED	OVERCHILLED*	OVERCROPS	OVERDRY*	OVERFILLS
OVERBOOKING	OVERCHILLING*	OVERCROW	OVERDRYING*	OVERFINE
OVERBOOKS	OVERCHILLS*	OVERCROWD	OVERDUB*	OVERFISH
OVERBORE	OVERCLAD	OVERCROWDED	OVERDUBBED*	OVERFISHED
OVERBORN*	OVERCLAIM*	OVERCROWDING	OVERDUBBING*	OVERFISHES
OVERBORNE	OVERCLAIMED*	OVERCROWDINGS	OVERDUBS*	OVERFISHING
OVERBOUGHT	OVERCLAIMING*	OVERCROWDS	OVERDUE	OVERFLEW
OVERBOUND	OVERCLAIMS*	OVERCROWED	OVERDUST	OVERFLIES
OVERBOUNDED	OVERCLEAN*	OVERCROWING	OVERDUSTED	OVERFLOW
OVERBOUNDING	OVERCLEANED*	OVERCROWS	OVERDUSTING	OVERFLOWED
OVERBOUNDS	OVERCLEANING*	OVERCURE*	OVERDUSTS	OVERFLOWING
OVERBRED*	OVERCLEANS*	OVERCURED*	OVERDYE	OVERFLOWINGS
OVERBRIEF*	OVERCLEAR*	OVERCURES*	OVERDYED	OVERFLOWN
OVERBRIM	OVERCLEARED*	OVERCURING*	OVERDYEING	OVERFLOWS
OVERBRIMMED	OVERCLEARING*	OVERCUT*	OVERDYES	OVERFLUSH
OVERBRIMMING	OVERCLEARS*	OVERCUTS*	OVEREAGER*	OVERFLUSHES
OVERBRIMS	OVERCLOUD	OVERCUTTING*	OVEREASY*	OVERFLY
OVERBROAD*	OVERCLOUDED	OVERDARE*	OVEREAT	OVERFLYING
OVERBROW	OVERCLOUDING	OVERDARED*	OVEREATEN	OVERFOCUS*
OVERBROWED	OVERCLOUDS	OVERDARES*	OVEREATER*	OVERFOCUSED*
OVERBROWING	OVERCLOY	OVERDARING*	OVEREATERS*	OVERFOCUSES*
OVERBROWS	OVERCLOYED	OVERDATED	OVEREATING	OVERFOCUSING*
OVERBUILD	OVERCLOYING	OVERDEAR*	OVEREATS	OVERFOCUSSED*
OVERBUILDING	OVERCLOYS	OVERDECK*	OVERED	OVERFOCUSSES*
OVERBUILDS	OVERCOACH*	OVERDECKED*	OVEREDIT*	OVERFOCUSSING*
OVERBUILT	OVERCOACHED*	OVERDECKING*	OVEREDITED*	OVERFOLD
OVERBULK	OVERCOACHES*	OVERDECKS*	OVEREDITING*	OVERFOLDED
OVERBULKED	OVERCOACHING*	OVERDID	OVEREDITS*	OVERFOLDING
OVERBULKING	OVERCOAT	OVERDIGHT	OVEREMOTE*	OVERFOLDS
OVERBULKS	OVERCOATS	OVERDO	OVEREMOTED*	OVERFOND
OVERBURN	OVERCOLD*	OVERDOER	OVEREMOTES*	OVERFOUL*
OVERBURNED	OVERCOME	OVERDOERS	OVEREMOTING*	OVERFREE
OVERBURNING	OVERCOMER*	OVERDOES	OVEREXERT	OVERFULL
OVERBURNS	OVERCOMERS*	OVERDOG*	OVEREXERTED	OVERFUND
OVERBURNT	OVERCOMES	OVERDOGS*	OVEREXERTING	OVERFUNDED
OVERBUSIED	OVERCOMING	OVERDOING	OVEREXERTS	OVERFUNDING
OVERBUSIES	OVERCOOK	OVERDONE	OVEREYE	OVERFUNDINGS
OVERBUSY	OVERCOOKED	OVERDOSE	OVEREYED	OVERFUNDS
OVERBUSYING	OVERCOOKING	OVERDOSED	OVEREYEING	OVERFUSSY*
OVERBUY	OVERCOOKS	OVERDOSES	OVEREYES	OVERGALL
OVERBUYING	OVERCOOL*	OVERDOSING	OVEREYING	OVERGALLED
OVERBUYS	OVERCOOLED*	OVERDRAFT	OVERFALL	OVERGALLING
OVERBY	OVERCOOLING*	OVERDRAFTS	OVERFALLEN	OVERGALLS
OVERCALL	OVERCOOLS*	OVERDRANK*	OVERFALLING	OVERGANG
OVERCALLED	OVERCOUNT	OVERDRAW	OVERFALLS	OVERGANGING
OVERCALLING	OVERCOUNTED	OVERDRAWING	OVERFAR	OVERGANGS
OVERCALLS	OVERCOUNTING	OVERDRAWN	OVERFAST*	OVERGAVE
OVERCAME	OVERCOUNTS	OVERDRAWS	OVERFAT*	OVERGET
OVERCARRIED	OVERCOVER	OVERDRESS	OVERFAVOR*	OVERGETS
OVERCARRIES	OVERCOVERED	OVERDRESSED	OVERFAVORED*	OVERGETTING
OVERCARRY	OVERCOVERING	OVERDRESSES	OVERFAVORING*	OVERGILD*
OVERCARRYING	OVERCOVERS	OVERDRESSING	OVERFAVORS*	OVERGILDED*
OVERCAST	OVERCOY*	OVERDREW	OVERFEAR*	OVERGILDING*
OVERCASTED*	OVERCRAM*	OVERDRIED*	OVERFEARED*	OVERGILDS*
OVERCASTING	OVERCRAMMED*	OVERDRIES*	OVERFEARING*	OVERGILT*
OVERCASTINGS	OVERCRAMMING*	OVERDRINK*	OVERFEARS*	OVERGIRD*
OVERCASTS	OVERCRAMS*	OVERDRINKING*	OVERFED	OVERGIRDED*
OVERCATCH	OVERCRAW	OVERDRINKS*	OVERFEED	OVERGIRDING*
OVERCATCHES	OVERCRAWED	OVERDRIVE	OVERFEEDING	OVERGIRDS*
OVERCATCHING	OVERCRAWING	OVERDRIVEN	OVERFEEDS	OVERGIRT*

OVERGIVE	OVERHANG	OVERJOY	OVERLENDING	OVERMELTS*
OVERGIVEN	OVERHANGING	OVERJOYED	OVERLENDS	OVERMEN
OVERGIVES	OVERHANGS	OVERJOYING	OVERLENT	OVERMERRY
OVERGIVING	OVERHAPPY	OVERJOYS	OVERLET*	OVERMILD*
OVERGLAD*	OVERHARD*	OVERJUMP	OVERLETS*	OVERMILK*
OVERGLAZE	OVERHASTE	OVERJUMPED	OVERLETTING*	OVERMILKED*
OVERGLAZED	OVERHASTES	OVERJUMPING	OVERLEWD*	OVERMILKING*
OVERGLAZES	OVERHASTY	OVERJUMPS	OVERLIE	OVERMILKS*
OVERGLAZING	OVERHATE*	OVERJUST*	OVERLIER	OVERMINE*
OVERGLOOM	OVERHATED*	OVERKEEN*	OVERLIERS	OVERMINED*
OVERGLOOMED	OVERHATES*	OVERKEEP	OVERLIES	OVERMINES*
OVERGLOOMING	OVERHATING*	OVERKEEPING	OVERLIGHT*	OVERMINING*
OVERGLOOMS	OVERHAUL	OVERKEEPS	OVERLIGHTED*	OVERMIX*
OVERGO	OVERHAULED	OVERKEPT	OVERLIGHTING*	OVERMIXED*
OVERGOAD*	OVERHAULING	OVERKEST	OVERLIGHTS*	OVERMIXES*
OVERGOADED*	OVERHAULS	OVERKILL	OVERLIT*	OVERMIXING*
OVERGOADING*	OVERHEAD	OVERKILLED*	OVERLIVE	OVERMOUNT
OVERGOADS*	OVERHEADS	OVERKILLING*	OVERLIVED	OVERMOUNTED
OVERGOES	OVERHEAP*	OVERKILLS	OVERLIVES	OVERMOUNTING
OVERGOING	OVERHEAPED*	OVERKIND	OVERLIVING	OVERMOUNTS
OVERGOINGS	OVERHEAPING*	OVERKING	OVERLOAD	OVERMUCH
OVERGONE	OVERHEAPS*	OVERKINGS	OVERLOADED	OVERMUCHES*
OVERGORGE	OVERHEAR	OVERKNEE	OVERLOADING	OVERNAME
OVERGORGED	OVERHEARD	OVERLABOR*	OVERLOADS	OVERNAMED
OVERGORGES	OVERHEARING	OVERLABORED*	OVERLOCK	OVERNAMES
OVERGORGING	OVERHEARS	OVERLABORING*	OVERLOCKED	OVERNAMING
OVERGOT	OVERHEAT	OVERLABORS*	OVERLOCKING	OVERNEAR*
OVERGRAIN	OVERHEATED	OVERLADE	OVERLOCKINGS	OVERNEAT
OVERGRAINED	OVERHEATING	OVERLADED	OVERLOCKS	OVERNET
OVERGRAINING	OVERHEATINGS	OVERLADEN	OVERLONG	OVERNETS
OVERGRAINS	OVERHEATS	OVERLADES	OVERLOOK	OVERNETTED
OVERGRASS	OVERHELD	OVERLADING	OVERLOOKED	OVERNETTING
OVERGRASSED	OVERHENT	OVERLAID	OVERLOOKING	OVERNEW*
OVERGRASSES	OVERHENTING	OVERLAIN	OVERLOOKS	OVERNICE
OVERGRASSING	OVERHENTS	OVERLAND	OVERLORD	OVERNIGHT
OVERGRAZE	OVERHIGH*	OVERLANDED	OVERLORDED	OVERNIGHTED*
OVERGRAZED	OVERHIT	OVERLANDING	OVERLORDING	OVERNIGHTING*
OVERGRAZES	OVERHITS	OVERLANDS	OVERLORDS	OVERNIGHTS
OVERGRAZING	OVERHITTING	OVERLAP	OVERLOUD	OVERPAGE
OVERGRAZINGS	OVERHOLD	OVERLAPPED	OVERLOVE*	OVERPAID
OVERGREAT	OVERHOLDING	OVERLAPPING	OVERLOVED*	OVERPAINT
OVERGREEN	OVERHOLDS	OVERLAPS	OVERLOVES*	OVERPAINTED
OVERGREENED	OVERHOLY*	OVERLARD	OVERLOVING*	OVERPAINTING
OVERGREENING	OVERHOPE*	OVERLARDED	OVERLUSH*	OVERPAINTS
OVERGREENS	OVERHOPED*	OVERLARDING	OVERLUSTY	OVERPART
OVERGREW	OVERHOPES*	OVERLARDS	OVERLY	OVERPARTED
OVERGROW	OVERHOPING*	OVERLARGE*	OVERLYING	OVERPARTING
OVERGROWING	OVERHOT*	OVERLATE*	OVERMAN	OVERPARTS
OVERGROWN	OVERHUNG	OVERLAX*	OVERMANNED	OVERPASS
OVERGROWS	OVERHUNT*	OVERLAY	OVERMANNING	OVERPASSED
OVERHAILE	OVERHUNTED*	OVERLAYING	OVERMANS	OVERPASSES
OVERHAILED	OVERHUNTING*	OVERLAYINGS	OVERMANY*	OVERPASSING
OVERHAILES	OVERHUNTS*	OVERLAYS	OVERMAST	OVERPAST
OVERHAILING	OVERHYPE	OVERLEAF	OVERMASTED	OVERPAY
OVERHAIR	OVERHYPED	OVERLEAP	OVERMASTING	OVERPAYING
OVERHAIRS	OVERHYPES	OVERLEAPED	OVERMASTS	OVERPAYS
OVERHALE	OVERHYPING	OVERLEAPING	OVERMATCH	OVERPEDAL
OVERHALED	OVERIDLE*	OVERLEAPS	OVERMATCHED	OVERPEDALED
OVERHALES	OVERING	OVERLEAPT	OVERMATCHES	OVERPEDALING
OVERHALING	OVERINKED	OVERLEARN*	OVERMATCHING	OVERPEDALLED
OVERHAND	OVERISSUE	OVERLEARNED*	OVERMEEK*	OVERPEDALLING
OVERHANDED	OVERISSUED	OVERLEARNING*	OVERMELT*	OVERPEDALS
OVERHANDING	OVERISSUES	OVERLEARNS*	OVERMELTED*	OVERPEER
OVERHANDS	OVERISSUING	OVERLEND	OVERMELTING*	OVERPEERED

The Chambers Dictionary is the authority for many longer words; see Introduction, page ix

OVERPEERING	OVERPRIZING	OVERRUFFS	OVERSHADING	OVERSPILLS
OVERPEERS	OVERPROOF	OVERRULE	OVERSHINE	OVERSPIN
OVERPERCH	OVERPROUD	OVERRULED	OVERSHINES	OVERSPINS
OVERPERCHED	OVERPUMP*	OVERRULER	OVERSHINING	OVERSTAFF
OVERPERCHES	OVERPUMPED*	OVERRULERS	OVERSHIRT	OVERSTAFFED
OVERPERCHING	OVERPUMPING*	OVERRULES	OVERSHIRTS	OVERSTAFFING
OVERPERT*	OVERPUMPS*	OVERRULING	OVERSHOE	OVERSTAFFS
OVERPITCH	OVERRACK	OVERRULINGS	OVERSHOES	OVERSTAIN
OVERPITCHED	OVERRACKED	OVERRUN	OVERSHONE	OVERSTAINED
OVERPITCHES	OVERRACKING	OVERRUNNING	OVERSHOOT	OVERSTAINING
OVERPITCHING	OVERRACKS	OVERRUNS	OVERSHOOTING	OVERSTAINS
OVERPLAID*	OVERRAKE	OVERS	OVERSHOOTS	OVERSTAND
OVERPLAIDS*	OVERRAKED	OVERSAD*	OVERSHOT	OVERSTANDING
OVERPLAN*	OVERRAKES	OVERSAIL	OVERSHOTS*	OVERSTANDS
OVERPLANNED*	OVERRAKING	OVERSAILED	OVERSICK*	OVERSTANK
OVERPLANNING*	OVERRAN	OVERSAILING	OVERSIDE	OVERSTARE
OVERPLANS*	OVERRANK	OVERSAILS	OVERSIDES*	OVERSTARED
OVERPLANT*	OVERRASH	OVERSALE*	OVERSIGHT	OVERSTARES
OVERPLANTED*	OVERRATE	OVERSALES*	OVERSIGHTS	OVERSTARING
OVERPLANTING*	OVERRATED	OVERSALT*	OVERSIZE	OVERSTATE
OVERPLANTS*	OVERRATES	OVERSALTED*	OVERSIZED	OVERSTATED
OVERPLAST	OVERRATING	OVERSALTING*	OVERSIZES	OVERSTATES
OVERPLAY	OVERRAUGHT	OVERSALTS*	OVERSIZING	OVERSTATING
OVERPLAYED	OVERREACH	OVERSAUCE*	OVERSKIP	OVERSTAY
OVERPLAYING	OVERREACHED	OVERSAUCED*	OVERSKIPPED	OVERSTAYED
OVERPLAYS	OVERREACHES	OVERSAUCES*	OVERSKIPPING	OVERSTAYING
OVERPLIED	OVERREACHING	OVERSAUCING*	OVERSKIPS	OVERSTAYS
OVERPLIES	OVERREACT	OVERSAVE*	OVERSKIRT	OVERSTEER
OVERPLOT*	OVERREACTED	OVERSAVED*	OVERSKIRTS	OVERSTEERED
OVERPLOTS*	OVERREACTING	OVERSAVES*	OVERSLEEP	OVERSTEERING
OVERPLOTTED*	OVERREACTS	OVERSAVING*	OVERSLEEPING	OVERSTEERS
OVERPLOTTING*	OVERREAD	OVERSAW	OVERSLEEPS	OVERSTEP
OVERPLUS	OVERREADING	OVERSCALE*	OVERSLEPT	OVERSTEPPED
OVERPLUSES	OVERREADS	OVERSCORE	OVERSLIP	OVERSTEPPING
OVERPLUSSES	OVERRED	OVERSCORED	OVERSLIPPED	OVERSTEPS
OVERPLY	OVERREDDED	OVERSCORES	OVERSLIPPING	OVERSTINK
OVERPLYING	OVERREDDING	OVERSCORING	OVERSLIPS	OVERSTINKING
OVERPOISE	OVERREDS	OVERSEA	OVERSLIPT*	OVERSTINKS
OVERPOISED	OVERREN	OVERSEAS	OVERSLOW*	OVERSTIR*
OVERPOISES	OVERRENNING	OVERSEE	OVERSMAN	OVERSTIRRED*
OVERPOISING	OVERRENS	OVERSEED*	OVERSMEN	OVERSTIRRING*
OVERPOST	OVERRICH*	OVERSEEDED*	OVERSMOKE*	OVERSTIRS*
OVERPOSTED	OVERRIDDEN	OVERSEEDING*	OVERSMOKED*	OVERSTOCK
OVERPOSTING	OVERRIDE	OVERSEEDS*	OVERSMOKES*	OVERSTOCKED
OVERPOSTS	OVERRIDER	OVERSEEING	OVERSMOKING*	OVERSTOCKING
OVERPOWER	OVERRIDERS	OVERSEEN	OVERSOAK*	OVERSTOCKS
OVERPOWERED	OVERRIDES	OVERSEER	OVERSOAKED*	OVERSTOOD
OVERPOWERING	OVERRIDING	OVERSEERS	OVERSOAKING*	OVERSTORIES*
OVERPOWERS	OVERRIFE*	OVERSEES	OVERSOAKS*	OVERSTORY*
OVERPRESS	OVERRIGID*	OVERSELL	OVERSOFT*	OVERSTREW
OVERPRESSED	OVERRIPE	OVERSELLING	OVERSOLD	OVERSTREWED
OVERPRESSES	OVERRIPEN	OVERSELLS	OVERSOON*	OVERSTREWING
OVERPRESSING	OVERRIPENED	OVERSET	OVERSOUL	OVERSTREWN
OVERPRICE	OVERRIPENING	OVERSETS	OVERSOULS	OVERSTREWS
OVERPRICED	OVERRIPENS	OVERSETTING	OVERSOW	OVERSTUDIED
OVERPRICES	OVERROAST	OVERSEW	OVERSOWED	OVERSTUDIES
OVERPRICING	OVERROASTED	OVERSEWED	OVERSOWING	OVERSTUDY
OVERPRINT	OVERROASTING	OVERSEWING	OVERSOWN	OVERSTUDYING
OVERPRINTED	OVERROASTS	OVERSEWN	OVERSOWS	OVERSTUFF
OVERPRINTING	OVERRODE	OVERSEWS	OVERSPEND	OVERSTUFFED
OVERPRINTS	OVERRUDE*	OVERSEXED	OVERSPENDING	OVERSTUFFING
OVERPRIZE	OVERRUFF	OVERSHADE	OVERSPENDS	OVERSTUFFS
OVERPRIZED	OVERRUFFED	OVERSHADED	OVERSPENT	OVERSTUNK
OVERPRIZES	OVERRUFFING	OVERSHADES	OVERSPILL	OVERSUDS*

Words marked with an asterisk are from OTCWL

OVERSUDSED*	OVERTHROWS	OVERTURED	OVERWEIGHING	OVIPARITY
OVERSUDSES*	OVERTIME	OVERTURES	OVERWEIGHS	OVIPAROUS
OVERSUDSING*	OVERTIMED	OVERTURING	OVERWENT	OVIPOSIT
OVERSUP*	OVERTIMER	OVERTURN	OVERWET*	OVIPOSITED
OVERSUPPED*	OVERTIMERS	OVERTURNED	OVERWETS*	OVIPOSITING
OVERSUPPING*	OVERTIMES	OVERTURNING	OVERWETTED*	OVIPOSITS
OVERSUPS*	OVERTIMING	OVERTURNS	OVERWETTING*	OVIRAPTOR
OVERSURE*	OVERTIP*	OVERTYPE	OVERWHELM	OVIRAPTORS
OVERSWAM	OVERTIPPED*	OVERTYPED	OVERWHELMING	OVISAC
OVERSWAY	OVERTIPPING*	OVERTYPES	OVERWHELMINGS	OVISACS
OVERSWAYED	OVERTIPS*	OVERTYPING	OVERWHELMS	OVIST
OVERSWAYING	OVERTIRE	OVERURGE*	OVERWIDE*	OVISTS
OVERSWAYS	OVERTIRED	OVERURGED*	OVERWILY*	OVOID
OVERSWEAR	OVERTIRES	OVERURGES*	OVERWIND	OVOIDAL
OVERSWEARING	OVERTIRING	OVERURGING*	OVERWINDING	OVOIDS
OVERSWEARS	OVERTLY	OVERUSE	OVERWINDS	OVOLI
OVERSWEET*	OVERTNESS*	OVERUSED	OVERWING	OVOLO
OVERSWELL	OVERTNESSES*	OVERUSES	OVERWINGED	OVOLOS*
OVERSWELLED	OVERTOIL	OVERUSING	OVERWINGING	OVONIC*
OVERSWELLING	OVERTOILED	OVERVALUE	OVERWINGS	OVONICS*
OVERSWELLS	OVERTOILING	OVERVALUED	OVERWISE	OVOTESTES
OVERSWIM	OVERTOILS	OVERVALUES	OVERWORD	OVOTESTIS
OVERSWIMMING	OVERTONE	OVERVALUING	OVERWORDS	OVULAR
OVERSWIMS	OVERTONES	OVERVEIL	OVERWORE	OVULARY*
OVERSWING*	OVERTOOK	OVERVEILED	OVERWORK	OVULATE
OVERSWINGING*	OVERTOP	OVERVEILING	OVERWORKED	OVULATED
OVERSWINGS*	OVERTOPPED	OVERVEILS	OVERWORKING	OVULATES
OVERSWOLLEN	OVERTOPPING	OVERVIEW	OVERWORKS	OVULATING
OVERSWORE	OVERTOPS	OVERVIEWS	OVERWORN	OVULATION
OVERSWORN	OVERTOWER	OVERVIVID*	OVERWOUND	OVULATIONS
OVERSWUM	OVERTOWERED	OVERVOTE*	OVERWREST	OVULATORY*
OVERSWUNG*	OVERTOWERING	OVERVOTED*	OVERWRESTED	OVULE
OVERT	OVERTOWERS	OVERVOTES*	OVERWRESTING	OVULES
OVERTAKE	OVERTRADE*	OVERVOTING*	OVERWRESTS	OVUM
OVERTAKEN	OVERTRADED*	OVERWARM*	OVERWRITE	OW
OVERTAKES	OVERTRADES*	OVERWARMED*	OVERWRITES	OWCHE
OVERTAKING	OVERTRADING*	OVERWARMING*	OVERWRITING	OWCHES
OVERTALK	OVERTRAIN	OVERWARMS*	OVERWRITTEN	OWE
OVERTALKED	OVERTRAINED	OVERWARY*	OVERWROTE	OWED
OVERTALKING	OVERTRAINING	OVERWASH	OVERWROUGHT	OWELTIES
OVERTALKS	OVERTRAINS	OVERWASHES	OVERYEAR	OWELTY
OVERTAME*	OVERTREAT*	OVERWATCH	OVERYEARED	OWER
OVERTART*	OVERTREATED*	OVERWATCHED	OVERYEARING	OWERBY
OVERTASK	OVERTREATING*	OVERWATCHES	OVERYEARS	OWERLOUP
OVERTASKED	OVERTREATS*	OVERWATCHING	OVERZEAL*	OWERLOUPEN
OVERTASKING	OVERTRICK	OVERWATER*	OVERZEALS*	OWERLOUPING
OVERTASKS	OVERTRICKS	OVERWATERED*	OVIBOS	OWERLOUPIT
OVERTAX	OVERTRIM*	OVERWATERING*	OVIBOSES	OWERLOUPS
OVERTAXED	OVERTRIMMED*	OVERWATERS*	OVIBOVINE	OWES
OVERTAXES	OVERTRIMMING*	OVERWEAK*	OVICIDAL*	OWING
OVERTAXING	OVERTRIMS*	OVERWEAR	OVICIDE	OWL
OVERTEEM	OVERTRIP	OVERWEARIED	OVICIDES	OWLED
OVERTEEMED	OVERTRIPPED	OVERWEARIES	OVIDUCAL	OWLER
OVERTEEMING	OVERTRIPPING	OVERWEARING	OVIDUCT	OWLERIES
OVERTEEMS	OVERTRIPS	OVERWEARS	OVIDUCTAL	OWLERS
OVERTHIN*	OVERTRUMP	OVERWEARY	OVIDUCTS	OWLERY
OVERTHINK*	OVERTRUMPED	OVERWEARYING	OVIFEROUS	OWLET
OVERTHINKING*	OVERTRUMPING	OVERWEEN	OVIFORM	OWLETS
OVERTHINKS*	OVERTRUMPS	OVERWEENED	OVIGEROUS	OWLIER
OVERTHOUGHT*	OVERTRUST	OVERWEENING	OVINE	OWLIEST
OVERTHREW	OVERTRUSTED	OVERWEENINGS	OVINES*	OWLING
OVERTHROW	OVERTRUSTING	OVERWEENS	OVIPARA*	OWLISH
OVERTHROWING	OVERTRUSTS	OVERWEIGH	OVIPARITIES	OWLISHLY*
OVERTHROWN	OVERTURE	OVERWEIGHED	OVIPARITIES	OWLLIKE*

The Chambers Dictionary is the authority for many longer words; see Introduction, page ix

OWLS	OXBLOODS	OXIDISES	OXYGENIC*	OYSTERED*
OWLY	OXBOW*	OXIDISING	OXYGENISE	OYSTERER*
OWN	OXBOWS*	OXIDIZE	OXYGENISED	OYSTERERS*
OWNABLE*	OXCART*	OXIDIZED	OXYGENISES	OYSTERING*
OWNED	OXCARTS*	OXIDIZER	OXYGENISING	OYSTERINGS*
OWNER	OXEN	OXIDIZERS	OXYGENIZE	OYSTERMAN*
OWNERLESS	OXER	OXIDIZES	OXYGENIZED	OYSTERMEN*
OWNERS	OXERS	OXIDIZING	OXYGENIZES	OYSTERS
OWNERSHIP	OXES*	OXIDS*	OXYGENIZING	OYSTRIGE
OWNERSHIPS	OXEYE*	OXIM*	OXYGENOUS	OYSTRIGES
OWNING	OXEYES*	OXIME	OXYGENS	OZAENA
OWNS	OXFORD	OXIMES	OXYMEL	OZAENAS
OWRE	OXFORDS	OXIMETER	OXYMELS	OZEKI
OWRECOME	OXGANG	OXIMETERS	OXYMORA*	OZEKIS
OWRECOMES	OXGANGS	OXIMS*	OXYMORON	OZOCERITE
OWRELAY	OXGATE	OXLAND	OXYMORONS	OZOCERITES
OWRELAYS	OXGATES	OXLANDS	OXYPHIL*	OZOKERITE
OWRES	OXHEAD	OXLIP	OXYPHILE*	OZOKERITES
OWREWORD	OXHEADS	OXLIPS	OXYPHILES*	OZONATE*
OWREWORDS	OXHEART*	OXO*	OXYPHILIC*	OZONATED*
OWRIE	OXHEARTS*	OXONIUM	OXYPHILS*	OZONATES*
OWRIER	OXID*	OXONIUMS	OXYSALT*	OZONATING*
OWRIEST	OXIDABLE*	OXPECKER*	OXYSALTS*	OZONATION
OWSE*	OXIDANT	OXPECKERS*	OXYSOME*	OZONATIONS
OWSEN	OXIDANTS	OXSLIP	OXYSOMES*	OZONE
OWT	OXIDASE	OXSLIPS	OXYTOCIC	OZONES
OWTS	OXIDASES	OXTAIL	OXYTOCICS	OZONIC*
OX	OXIDASIC*	OXTAILS	OXYTOCIN	OZONIDE*
OXACILLIN*	OXIDATE	OXTER	OXYTOCINS	OZONIDES*
OXACILLINS*	OXIDATED	OXTERED	OXYTONE	OZONISE
OXALATE	OXIDATES	OXTERING	OXYTONES	OZONISED
OXALATED*	OXIDATING	OXTERS	OY	OZONISER
OXALATES	OXIDATION	OXTONGUE*	OYE	OZONISERS
OXALATING*	OXIDATIONS	OXTONGUES*	OYER	OZONISES
OXALIC	OXIDATIVE*	OXY*	OYERS	OZONISING
OXALIS	OXIDE	OXYACID*	OYES	OZONIZE
OXALISES	OXIDES	OXYACIDS*	OYESES	OZONIZED
OXAZEPAM*	OXIDIC*	OXYGEN	OYESSES*	OZONIZER
OXAZEPAMS*	OXIDISE	OXYGENATE	OYEZ	OZONIZERS
OXAZINE	OXIDISED	OXYGENATED	OYEZES	OZONIZES
OXAZINES	OXIDISER	OXYGENATES	OYS	OZONIZING
OXBLOOD	OXIDISERS	OXYGENATING	OYSTER	OZONOUS*

P

PA
PABLUM*
PABLUMS*
PABOUCHE
PABOUCHES
PABULAR
PABULOUS
PABULUM
PABULUMS
PAC*
PACA
PACABLE
PACAS
PACATION
PACATIONS
PACE
PACED
PACEMAKER
PACEMAKERS
PACER
PACERS
PACES
PACEY
PACHA
PACHADOM*
PACHADOMS*
PACHAK
PACHAKS
PACHALIC
PACHALICS
PACHAS
PACHINKO
PACHINKOS
PACHISI
PACHISIS
PACHOULI*
PACHOULIS*
PACHUCO*
PACHUCOS*
PACHYDERM
PACHYDERMS
PACHYTENE*
PACHYTENES*
PACIER
PACIEST
PACIFIC
PACIFICAL
PACIFIED
PACIFIER
PACIFIERS
PACIFIES
PACIFISM
PACIFISMS
PACIFIST
PACIFISTS

PACIFY
PACIFYING
PACING
PACK
PACKABLE*
PACKAGE
PACKAGED
PACKAGER
PACKAGERS
PACKAGES
PACKAGING
PACKAGINGS
PACKBOARD*
PACKBOARDS*
PACKED
PACKER
PACKERS
PACKET
PACKETED
PACKETING
PACKETS
PACKFONG
PACKFONGS
PACKHORSE*
PACKHORSES*
PACKING
PACKINGS
PACKLY*
PACKMAN
PACKMEN
PACKNESS*
PACKNESSES*
PACKS
PACKSACK*
PACKSACKS*
PACKSHEET
PACKSHEETS
PACKSTAFF
PACKSTAFFS
PACKWAX*
PACKWAXES*
PACKWAY
PACKWAYS
PACO
PACOS
PACS*
PACT
PACTA
PACTION
PACTIONAL
PACTIONED
PACTIONING
PACTIONS
PACTS
PACTUM

PACY
PAD
PADANG
PADANGS
PADAUK
PADAUKS
PADDED
PADDER
PADDERS
PADDIES
PADDING
PADDINGS
PADDLE
PADDLED
PADDLER
PADDLERS
PADDLES
PADDLING
PADDLINGS
PADDOCK
PADDOCKED*
PADDOCKING*
PADDOCKS
PADDY
PADELLA
PADELLAS
PADEMELON
PADEMELONS
PADERERO
PADEREROES
PADEREROS
PADI*
PADIS*
PADISHAH
PADISHAHS
PADLE
PADLES
PADLOCK
PADLOCKED
PADLOCKING
PADLOCKS
PADMA
PADMAS
PADNAG*
PADNAGS*
PADOUK
PADOUKS
PADRE
PADRES
PADRI*
PADRONE
PADRONES*
PADRONI
PADS
PADSAW

PADSAWS
PADSHAH*
PADSHAHS*
PADUASOY
PADUASOYS
PADYMELON
PADYMELONS
PAEAN
PAEANISM*
PAEANISMS*
PAEANS
PAEDERAST
PAEDERASTS
PAEDEUTIC
PAEDEUTICS
PAEDIATRIES
PAEDIATRY
PAEDOLOGIES
PAEDOLOGY
PAELLA
PAELLAS
PAENULA
PAENULAE
PAENULAS
PAEON
PAEONIC
PAEONICS
PAEONIES
PAEONS
PAEONY
PAESAN*
PAESANI*
PAESANO*
PAESANOS*
PAESANS*
PAGAN
PAGANDOM*
PAGANDOMS*
PAGANISE
PAGANISED
PAGANISES
PAGANISH
PAGANISING
PAGANISM
PAGANISMS
PAGANIST*
PAGANISTS*
PAGANIZE
PAGANIZED
PAGANIZER*
PAGANIZERS*
PAGANIZES
PAGANIZING
PAGANS
PAGE

PAGEANT
PAGEANTRIES
PAGEANTRY
PAGEANTS
PAGEBOY*
PAGEBOYS*
PAGED
PAGEHOOD
PAGEHOODS
PAGER
PAGERS
PAGES
PAGINAL
PAGINATE
PAGINATED
PAGINATES
PAGINATING
PAGING
PAGINGS
PAGLE
PAGLES
PAGOD
PAGODA
PAGODAS
PAGODS
PAGRI
PAGRIS
PAGURIAN
PAGURIANS
PAGURID
PAGURIDS
PAH
PAHLAVI*
PAHLAVIS*
PAHOEHOE
PAHOEHOES
PAHS
PAID
PAIDEUTIC
PAIDEUTICS
PAIDLE
PAIDLES
PAIGLE
PAIGLES
PAIK
PAIKED
PAIKING
PAIKS
PAIL
PAILFUL
PAILFULS
PAILLARD*
PAILLARDS*
PAILLASSE
PAILLASSES

The Chambers Dictionary is the authority for many longer words; see Introduction, page ix

PAILLETTE	PAISLEYS	PALAVERER	PALISADOED	PALMARY
PAILLETTES	PAITRICK	PALAVERERS	PALISADOES	PALMATE
PAILLON	PAITRICKS	PALAVERING	PALISADOING	PALMATED
PAILLONS	PAJAMA*	PALAVERS	PALISH	PALMATELY
PAILS	PAJAMAED*	PALAY	PALKEE	PALMATION
PAILSFUL*	PAJAMAS	PALAYS	PALKEES	PALMATIONS
PAIN	PAJOCK	PALAZZI	PALKI	PALMED
PAINCH*	PAJOCKE	PALAZZO	PALKIS	PALMER
PAINCHES*	PAJOCKES	PALAZZOS*	PALL	PALMERS
PAINED	PAJOCKS	PALE	PALLA	PALMETTE
PAINFUL	PAKAPOO	PALEA	PALLADIA*	PALMETTES
PAINFULLER	PAKAPOOS	PALEAE	PALLADIC	PALMETTO
PAINFULLEST	PAKEHA	PALEAL*	PALLADIUM	PALMETTOES
PAINFULLY	PAKEHAS	PALEBUCK	PALLADIUMS	PALMETTOS
PAINIM	PAKFONG	PALEBUCKS	PALLADOUS	PALMFUL
PAINIMS	PAKFONGS	PALED	PALLAE	PALMFULS
PAINING	PAKKA	PALEFACE	PALLAH	PALMHOUSE
PAINLESS	PAKORA	PALEFACES	PALLAHS	PALMHOUSES
PAINS	PAKORAS	PALELY	PALLED	PALMIE
PAINT	PAKTONG	PALEMPORE	PALLET	PALMIER
PAINTABLE	PAKTONGS	PALEMPORES	PALLETED	PALMIES
PAINTBALL	PAL	PALENESS	PALLETISE	PALMIEST
PAINTBALLS	PALABRA	PALENESSES	PALLETISED	PALMIET
PAINTED	PALABRAS	PALEOSOL*	PALLETISES	PALMIETS
PAINTER	PALACE	PALEOSOLS*	PALLETISING	PALMING
PAINTERLY	PALACED*	PALER	PALLETIZE	PALMIPED
PAINTERS	PALACES	PALES	PALLETIZED	PALMIPEDE
PAINTIER	PALADIN	PALEST	PALLETIZES	PALMIPEDES
PAINTIEST	PALADINS	PALESTRA	PALLETIZING	PALMIPEDS
PAINTING	PALAESTRA	PALESTRAE	PALLETS	PALMIST
PAINTINGS	PALAESTRAE	PALESTRAS	PALLETTE*	PALMISTRIES
PAINTRESS	PALAESTRAS	PALET	PALLETTES*	PALMISTRY
PAINTRESSES	PALAFITTE	PALETOT	PALLIA	PALMISTS
PAINTS	PALAFITTES	PALETOTS	PALLIAL	PALMITATE
PAINTURE	PALAGI	PALETS	PALLIARD	PALMITATES
PAINTURES	PALAGIS	PALETTE	PALLIARDS	PALMITIN
PAINTWORK*	PALAIS*	PALETTES	PALLIASSE	PALMITINS
PAINTWORKS*	PALAMA	PALEWAYS*	PALLIASSES	PALMLIKE*
PAINTY	PALAMAE	PALEWISE	PALLIATE	PALMS
PAIOCK	PALAMATE	PALFREY	PALLIATED	PALMTOP
PAIOCKE	PALAMINO	PALFREYED	PALLIATES	PALMTOPS
PAIOCKES	PALAMINOS	PALFREYS	PALLIATING	PALMY
PAIOCKS	PALAMPORE	PALIER	PALLIATOR*	PALMYRA
PAIR	PALAMPORES	PALIEST	PALLIATORS*	PALMYRAS
PAIRE	PALANKEEN	PALIFORM	PALLID	PALOLO
PAIRED	PALANKEENS	PALIKAR*	PALLIDER	PALOLOS
PAIRES	PALANQUIN	PALIKARS*	PALLIDEST	PALOMINO
PAIRIAL	PALANQUINS	PALILALIA	PALLIDITIES	PALOMINOS
PAIRIALS	PALAS	PALILALIAS	PALLIDITY	PALOOKA
PAIRING	PALASES	PALILLOGIES	PALLIDLY	PALOOKAS
PAIRINGS	PALATABLE	PALILLOGY	PALLIER	PALOVERDE*
PAIRS	PALATABLY	PALIMONIES	PALLIEST	PALOVERDES*
PAIRWISE	PALATAL	PALIMONY	PALLING	PALP
PAIS	PALATALLY*	PALING	PALLIUM	PALPABLE
PAISA	PALATALS	PALINGS	PALLIUMS*	PALPABLY
PAISAN*	PALATE	PALINODE	PALLONE	PALPAL
PAISANA*	PALATED	PALINODES	PALLONES	PALPATE
PAISANAS*	PALATES	PALINODIES	PALLOR	PALPATED
PAISANO	PALATIAL	PALINODY	PALLORS	PALPATES
PAISANOS	PALATINE	PALISADE	PALLS	PALPATING
PAISANS*	PALATINES	PALISADED	PALLY	PALPATION
PAISAS	PALATING	PALISADES	PALM	PALPATIONS
PAISE	PALAVER	PALISADING	PALMAR	PALPATOR*
PAISLEY	PALAVERED	PALISADO	PALMARIAN	PALPATORS*

PALPEBRA*	PAMS	PANDER	PANFRY*	PANNAGES
PALPEBRAE*	PAN	PANDERED	PANFRYING*	PANNE
PALPEBRAL	PANACEA	PANDERER*	PANFUL	PANNED
PALPED	PANACEAN	PANDERERS*	PANFULS	PANNELLED
PALPI	PANACEAS	PANDERESS	PANG	PANNES
PALPING	PANACHAEA	PANDERESSES	PANGA	PANNICK
PALPITANT	PANACHAEAS	PANDERING	PANGAMIC	PANNICKS
PALPITATE	PANACHE	PANDERISM	PANGAMIES	PANNICLE
PALPITATED	PANACHES	PANDERISMS	PANGAMY	PANNICLES
PALPITATES	PANADA	PANDERLY	PANGAS	PANNIER
PALPITATING	PANADAS	PANDEROUS	PANGED	PANNIERED
PALPS	PANAMA	PANDERS	PANGEN	PANNIERS
PALPUS	PANAMAS	PANDIED	PANGENE	PANNIKEL
PALS	PANARIES	PANDIES	PANGENES	PANNIKELL
PALSGRAVE	PANARY	PANDIT	PANGENS	PANNIKELLS
PALSGRAVES	PANATELA*	PANDITS	PANGING	PANNIKELS
PALSHIP*	PANATELAS*	PANDOOR	PANGLESS	PANNIKIN
PALSHIPS*	PANATELLA	PANDOORS	PANGOLIN	PANNIKINS
PALSIED	PANATELLAS	PANDORA	PANGOLINS	PANNING
PALSIER	PANAX	PANDORAS	PANGRAM	PANNINGS
PALSIES	PANAXES	PANDORE	PANGRAMS	PANNOSE
PALSIEST	PANBROIL*	PANDORES	PANGS	PANNUS
PALSTAFF	PANBROILED*	PANDOUR	PANHANDLE	PANNUSES
PALSTAFFS	PANBROILING*	PANDOURS	PANHANDLED	PANOCHA
PALSTAVE	PANBROILS*	PANDOWDIES	PANHANDLES	PANOCHAS
PALSTAVES	PANCAKE	PANDOWDY	PANHANDLING	PANOCHE*
PALSY	PANCAKED	PANDS	PANHUMAN*	PANOCHES*
PALSYING	PANCAKES	PANDURA	PANIC	PANOISTIC
PALTER	PANCAKING	PANDURAS	PANICK	PANOPLIED
PALTERED	PANCE	PANDURATE	PANICKED	PANOPLIES
PALTERER	PANCES	PANDY	PANICKIER	PANOPLY
PALTERERS	PANCETTA*	PANDYING	PANICKIEST	PANOPTIC
PALTERING	PANCETTAS*	PANE	PANICKING	PANORAMA
PALTERS	PANCHAX	PANED	PANICKS	PANORAMAS
PALTRIER	PANCHAXES	PANEGOISM	PANICKY	PANORAMIC
PALTRIEST	PANCHAYAT	PANEGOISMS	PANICLE	PANPIPE*
PALTRILY	PANCHAYATS	PANEGYRIC	PANICLED	PANPIPES*
PALTRY	PANCHEON	PANEGYRICS	PANICLES	PANS
PALUDAL	PANCHEONS	PANEGYRIES	PANICS	PANSEXUAL
PALUDIC	PANCHION	PANEGYRY	PANICUM*	PANSIED
PALUDINAL	PANCHIONS	PANEITIES	PANICUMS*	PANSIES
PALUDINE	PANCOSMIC	PANEITY	PANIER*	PANSOPHIC
PALUDISM	PANCRATIC	PANEL	PANIERS*	PANSOPHIES
PALUDISMS	PANCREAS	PANELED*	PANIM	PANSOPHY
PALUDOSE	PANCREASES	PANELING*	PANIMS	PANSPERMIES
PALUDOUS	PAND	PANELINGS*	PANING	PANSPERMY
PALUSTRAL	PANDA	PANELIST*	PANISC	PANSY
PALY	PANDANI*	PANELISTS*	PANISCS	PANT
PAM	PANDANUS*	PANELLED	PANISK	PANTABLE
PAMPA	PANDANUSES*	PANELLING	PANISKS	PANTABLES
PAMPAS	PANDAR	PANELLINGS	PANISLAM	PANTAGAMIES
PAMPASES	PANDARED	PANELLIST	PANISLAMS	PANTAGAMY
PAMPEAN	PANDARING	PANELLISTS	PANJANDRA*	PANTALEON
PAMPEANS*	PANDARS	PANELS	PANJANDRUM*	PANTALEONS
PAMPER	PANDAS	PANES	PANJANDRUMS*	PANTALETS
PAMPERED	PANDATION	PANETELA*	PANLOGISM	PANTALON
PAMPERER	PANDATIONS	PANETELAS*	PANLOGISMS	PANTALONE*
PAMPERERS	PANDECT	PANETTONE	PANMICTIC	PANTALONES*
PAMPERING	PANDECTS	PANETTONES*	PANMIXES*	PANTALONS
PAMPERO	PANDEMIA	PANETTONI	PANMIXIA	PANTALOON
PAMPEROS	PANDEMIAN	PANFISH*	PANMIXIAS	PANTALOONS
PAMPERS	PANDEMIAS	PANFISHES*	PANMIXIS	PANTDRESS*
PAMPHLET	PANDEMIC	PANFRIED*	PANMIXISES	PANTDRESSES*
PAMPHLETS	PANDEMICS	PANFRIES*	PANNAGE	PANTED

The Chambers Dictionary is the authority for many longer words; see Introduction, page ix

PANTER	PAPAINS	PAPILLOTES	PARABOLIC	PARAGOGUES
PANTERS	PAPAL	PAPILLOUS	PARABRAKE	PARAGON
PANTHEISM	PAPALISE	PAPILLULE	PARABRAKES	PARAGONED
PANTHEISMS	PAPALISED	PAPILLULES	PARACHOR*	PARAGONING
PANTHEIST	PAPALISES	PAPISH	PARACHORS*	PARAGONS
PANTHEISTS	PAPALISING	PAPISHER	PARACHUTE	PARAGRAM
PANTHENOL	PAPALISM	PAPISHERS	PARACHUTED	PARAGRAMS
PANTHENOLS	PAPALISMS	PAPISHES	PARACHUTES	PARAGRAPH
PANTHEON*	PAPALIST	PAPISM	PARACHUTING	PARAGRAPHED
PANTHEONS*	PAPALISTS	PAPISMS	PARACLETE	PARAGRAPHING
PANTHER	PAPALIZE	PAPIST	PARACLETES	PARAGRAPHS
PANTHERS	PAPALIZED	PAPISTIC	PARACME	PARAKEET
PANTIE*	PAPALIZES	PAPISTRIES	PARACMES	PARAKEETS
PANTIES	PAPALIZING	PAPISTRY	PARACUSES	PARAKITE*
PANTIHOSE	PAPALLY	PAPISTS	PARACUSIS	PARAKITES*
PANTILE	PAPARAZZI	PAPOOSE	PARADE	PARALALIA
PANTILED	PAPARAZZO	PAPOOSES	PARADED	PARALALIAS
PANTILES	PAPAS	PAPPADOM	PARADER*	PARALEGAL
PANTILING	PAPAW	PAPPADOMS	PARADERS*	PARALEGALS
PANTILINGS	PAPAWS	PAPPED	PARADES	PARALEXIA
PANTINE	PAPAYA	PAPPI*	PARADIGM	PARALEXIAS
PANTINES	PAPAYAN*	PAPPIER	PARADIGMS	PARALLAX
PANTING	PAPAYAS	PAPPIES	PARADING	PARALLAXES
PANTINGLY	PAPE	PAPPIEST	PARADISAL	PARALLEL
PANTINGS	PAPER	PAPPING	PARADISE	PARALLELED
PANTLER	PAPERBACK	PAPPOOSE	PARADISES	PARALLELING
PANTLERS	PAPERBACKED	PAPPOOSES	PARADISIC	PARALLELINGS
PANTO	PAPERBACKING	PAPPOSE	PARADOR	PARALLELLED*
PANTOFFLE	PAPERBACKS	PAPPOUS	PARADORES	PARALLELLING*
PANTOFFLES	PAPERBOY*	PAPPUS	PARADORS*	PARALLELS
PANTOFLE	PAPERBOYS*	PAPPUSES	PARADOS	PARALOGIA
PANTOFLES	PAPERED	PAPPY	PARADOSES	PARALOGIAS
PANTOMIME	PAPERER	PAPRICA*	PARADOX	PARALOGIES
PANTOMIMED*	PAPERERS	PAPRICAS*	PARADOXAL	PARALOGY
PANTOMIMES	PAPERIER	PAPRIKA	PARADOXER	PARALYSE
PANTOMIMING*	PAPERIEST	PAPRIKAS	PARADOXERS	PARALYSED
PANTON	PAPERING	PAPS	PARADOXES	PARALYSER
PANTONS	PAPERINGS	PAPULA	PARADOXIES	PARALYSERS
PANTOS	PAPERLESS	PAPULAE	PARADOXY	PARALYSES
PANTOUFLE	PAPERS	PAPULAR	PARADROP	PARALYSING
PANTOUFLES	PAPERWARE	PAPULE	PARADROPPED*	PARALYSIS
PANTOUM	PAPERWARES	PAPULES	PARADROPPING*	PARALYTIC
PANTOUMS	PAPERWORK	PAPULOSE	PARADROPS	PARALYTICS
PANTRIES	PAPERWORKS	PAPULOUS	PARAFFIN	PARALYZE
PANTROPIC*	PAPERY	PAPYRAL*	PARAFFINE	PARALYZED
PANTRY	PAPES	PAPYRI	PARAFFINED	PARALYZER
PANTRYMAN	PAPETERIE	PAPYRIAN*	PARAFFINES	PARALYZERS
PANTRYMEN	PAPETERIES	PAPYRINE*	PARAFFINING	PARALYZES
PANTS	PAPHIAN*	PAPYRUS	PARAFFINS	PARALYZING
PANTSUIT*	PAPHIANS*	PAPYRUSES*	PARAFFINY	PARAMATTA
PANTSUITS*	PAPILIO	PAR	PARAFFLE	PARAMATTAS
PANTUN	PAPILIOS	PARA	PARAFFLES	PARAMECIA
PANTUNS	PAPILLA	PARABASES	PARAFLE	PARAMECIUM*
PANTY*	PAPILLAE	PARABASIS	PARAFLES	PARAMECIUMS*
PANZER	PAPILLAR	PARABEMA	PARAFOIL	PARAMEDIC
PANZERS	PAPILLARY	PARABEMATA	PARAFOILS	PARAMEDICS
PAOLI	PAPILLATE	PARABLE	PARAFORM*	PARAMENT
PAOLO	PAPILLOMA	PARABLED	PARAFORMS*	PARAMENTA*
PAP	PAPILLOMAS	PARABLES	PARAGE	PARAMENTS
PAPA	PAPILLOMATA	PARABLING	PARAGES	PARAMESE
PAPABLE	PAPILLON	PARABOLA	PARAGOGE	PARAMESES
PAPACIES	PAPILLONS	PARABOLAS	PARAGOGES	PARAMETER
PAPACY	PAPILLOSE	PARABOLE	PARAGOGIC	PARAMETERS
PAPAIN	PAPILLOTE	PARABOLES	PARAGOGUE	PARAMO

Words marked with an asterisk are from OTCWL

PARAMORPH
PARAMORPHS
PARAMOS
PARAMOUNT
PARAMOUNTS
PARAMOUR
PARAMOURS
PARAMYLUM*
PARAMYLUMS*
PARANETE
PARANETES
PARANG
PARANGS
PARANOEA
PARANOEAS
PARANOEIC
PARANOEICS
PARANOIA
PARANOIAC
PARANOIACS
PARANOIAS
PARANOIC
PARANOICS
PARANOID
PARANOIDS*
PARANYM
PARANYMPH
PARANYMPHS
PARANYMS
PARAPET
PARAPETED
PARAPETS
PARAPH
PARAPHED
PARAPHING
PARAPHS
PARAPODIA
PARAPODIUM*
PARAQUAT*
PARAQUATS*
PARAQUET*
PARAQUETS*
PARAQUITO
PARAQUITOS
PARARHYME
PARARHYMES
PARAS
PARASANG
PARASANGS
PARASCEVE
PARASCEVES
PARASHAH*
PARASHIOTH*
PARASHOTH*
PARASITE
PARASITES
PARASITIC
PARASOL
PARASOLS
PARATAXES
PARATAXIS
PARATHA
PARATHAS
PARATHION*

PARATHIONS*
PARATONIC
PARATROOP*
PARAVAIL
PARAVANE
PARAVANES
PARAVANT
PARAVAUNT
PARAWING*
PARAWINGS*
PARAZOA
PARAZOAN
PARAZOANS
PARAZOON
PARBOIL
PARBOILED
PARBOILING
PARBOILS
PARBREAK
PARBREAKED
PARBREAKING
PARBREAKS
PARBUCKLE
PARBUCKLED
PARBUCKLES
PARBUCKLING
PARCEL
PARCELED*
PARCELING*
PARCELLED
PARCELLING
PARCELS
PARCENARIES
PARCENARY
PARCENER
PARCENERS
PARCH
PARCHED
PARCHEDLY
PARCHEESI
PARCHEESIS
PARCHES
PARCHESI
PARCHESIS
PARCHING
PARCHISI*
PARCHISIS*
PARCHMENT
PARCHMENTS
PARCIMONIES
PARCIMONY
PARCLOSE
PARCLOSES
PARD
PARDAH*
PARDAHS*
PARDAL
PARDALE
PARDALES
PARDALIS
PARDALISES
PARDALS
PARDED
PARDEE*

PARDI
PARDIE
PARDINE
PARDNER
PARDNERS
PARDON
PARDONED
PARDONER
PARDONERS
PARDONING
PARDONINGS
PARDONS
PARDS
PARDY
PARE
PARECIOUS
PARECISM*
PARECISMS*
PARED
PAREGORIC
PAREGORICS
PAREIRA
PAREIRAS
PARELLA
PARELLAS
PARELLE
PARELLES
PARENESES
PARENESIS
PARENT
PARENTAGE
PARENTAGES
PARENTAL
PARENTED
PARENTING
PARENTINGS
PARENTS
PAREO
PAREOS
PARER
PARERGA
PARERGON
PARERS
PARES
PARESES
PARESIS
PARETIC
PARETICS*
PAREU
PAREUS
PAREVE*
PARFAIT
PARFAITS
PARFLECHE
PARFLECHES
PARFLESH*
PARFLESHES*
PARFOCAL*
PARGANA
PARGANAS
PARGASITE
PARGASITES
PARGE
PARGED

PARGES
PARGET
PARGETED
PARGETER
PARGETERS
PARGETING
PARGETINGS
PARGETS
PARGETTED
PARGETTING
PARGETTINGS
PARGING
PARGINGS*
PARGO*
PARGOS*
PARGYLINE*
PARGYLINES*
PARHELIA
PARHELIC
PARHELION
PARHYPATE
PARHYPATES
PARIAH
PARIAHS
PARIAL
PARIALS
PARIAN*
PARIANS*
PARIES*
PARIETAL
PARIETALS
PARIETES*
PARING
PARINGS
PARIS*
PARISCHAN
PARISCHANS
PARISES*
PARISH
PARISHEN
PARISHENS
PARISHES
PARISON
PARISONS
PARITIES
PARITOR
PARITORS
PARITY
PARK
PARKA
PARKAS
PARKED
PARKEE
PARKEES
PARKER
PARKERS
PARKI
PARKIE
PARKIER
PARKIES
PARKIEST
PARKIN
PARKING
PARKINGS

PARKINS
PARKIS
PARKISH
PARKLAND
PARKLANDS
PARKLIKE
PARKLY
PARKS
PARKWARD
PARKWARDS
PARKWAY
PARKWAYS
PARKY
PARLANCE
PARLANCES
PARLANDO
PARLANTE*
PARLAY
PARLAYED
PARLAYING
PARLAYS
PARLE
PARLED
PARLES
PARLEY
PARLEYED
PARLEYER*
PARLEYERS*
PARLEYING
PARLEYS
PARLEYVOO
PARLEYVOOED
PARLEYVOOING
PARLEYVOOS
PARLIES
PARLING
PARLOR
PARLORS
PARLOUR
PARLOURS
PARLOUS
PARLOUSLY*
PARLY
PAROCHIAL
PAROCHIN
PAROCHINE
PAROCHINES
PAROCHINS
PARODIC
PARODICAL
PARODIED
PARODIES
PARODIST
PARODISTS
PARODOI*
PARODOS*
PARODY
PARODYING
PAROEMIA
PAROEMIAC
PAROEMIACS
PAROEMIAL
PAROEMIAS
PAROICOUS

PAROL	PARRIED	PARTERRE	PARURES	PASSAMENT
PAROLE	PARRIES	PARTERRES	PARVE*	PASSAMENTED
PAROLED	PARRING*	PARTERS	PARVENU	PASSAMENTING
PAROLEE	PARRITCH	PARTI	PARVENUE*	PASSAMENTS
PAROLEES	PARRITCHES	PARTIAL	PARVENUS	PASSANT
PAROLES	PARROCK	PARTIALLY	PARVIS	PASSATA
PAROLING	PARROCKED	PARTIALS	PARVISE	PASSATAS
PAROLS*	PARROCKING	PARTIBLE	PARVISES	PASSBAND*
PARONYM	PARROCKS	PARTICLE	PARVO*	PASSBANDS*
PARONYMIES	PARROKET*	PARTICLES	PARVOLIN*	PASSBOOK*
PARONYMS	PARROKETS*	PARTIED	PARVOLINS*	PASSBOOKS*
PARONYMY	PARROQUET	PARTIER*	PARVOS*	PASSE
PAROQUET	PARROQUETS	PARTIERS*	PAS	PASSED
PAROQUETS	PARROT	PARTIES	PASCAL	PASSEE
PAROTIC	PARROTED	PARTIM	PASCALS	PASSEL*
PAROTID	PARROTER	PARTING	PASCHAL	PASSELS*
PAROTIDS	PARROTERS	PARTINGS	PASCHALS*	PASSEMENT
PAROTIS	PARROTING	PARTIS	PASCUAL	PASSEMENTED
PAROTISES	PARROTRIES	PARTISAN	PASE*	PASSEMENTING
PAROTITIS	PARROTRY	PARTISANS	PASEAR	PASSEMENTS
PAROTITISES	PARROTS	PARTITA	PASEARED	PASSENGER
PAROTOID*	PARROTY	PARTITAS	PASEARING	PASSENGERS
PAROTOIDS*	PARRS	PARTITE	PASEARS	PASSEPIED
PAROUS*	PARRY	PARTITION	PASEO	PASSEPIEDS
PAROUSIA	PARRYING	PARTITIONED	PASEOS	PASSER
PAROUSIAS	PARS	PARTITIONING	PASES*	PASSERBY*
PAROXYSM	PARSABLE*	PARTITIONS	PASH	PASSERINE
PAROXYSMS	PARSE	PARTITIVE	PASHA	PASSERINES
PARP	PARSEC	PARTITIVES	PASHADOM*	PASSERS
PARPANE	PARSECS	PARTITURA	PASHADOMS*	PASSERSBY*
PARPANES	PARSED	PARTITURAS	PASHALIC*	PASSES
PARPED	PARSER	PARTIZAN	PASHALICS*	PASSIBLE
PARPEN	PARSERS	PARTIZANS	PASHALIK	PASSIBLY
PARPEND	PARSES	PARTLET	PASHALIKS	PASSIM
PARPENDS	PARSIMONIES	PARTLETS	PASHAS	PASSING
PARPENS	PARSIMONY	PARTLY	PASHED	PASSINGS
PARPENT	PARSING	PARTNER	PASHES	PASSION
PARPENTS	PARSINGS	PARTNERED	PASHIM	PASSIONAL
PARPING	PARSLEY	PARTNERING	PASHIMS	PASSIONALS
PARPOINT	PARSLEYED*	PARTNERS	PASHING	PASSIONED
PARPOINTS	PARSLEYS	PARTON	PASHM	PASSIONING
PARPS	PARSLIED*	PARTONS	PASHMINA	PASSIONS
PARQUET	PARSNEP	PARTOOK	PASHMINAS	PASSIVATE
PARQUETED	PARSNEPS	PARTRIDGE	PASHMS	PASSIVATED
PARQUETING	PARSNIP	PARTRIDGES	PASPALUM	PASSIVATES
PARQUETRIES	PARSNIPS	PARTS	PASPALUMS	PASSIVATING
PARQUETRY	PARSON	PARTURE	PASPIES	PASSIVE
PARQUETS	PARSONAGE	PARTURES	PASPY	PASSIVELY
PARQUETTED	PARSONAGES	PARTWAY*	PASQUIL*	PASSIVES
PARQUETTING	PARSONIC	PARTWORK	PASQUILER	PASSIVISM
PARR	PARSONISH	PARTWORKS	PASQUILERS	PASSIVISMS
PARRAKEET	PARSONS	PARTY	PASQUILS*	PASSIVIST
PARRAKEETS	PART	PARTYER*	PASS	PASSIVISTS
PARRAL	PARTAKE	PARTYERS*	PASSABLE	PASSIVITIES
PARRALS	PARTAKEN	PARTYGOER	PASSABLY	PASSIVITY
PARRED*	PARTAKER	PARTYGOERS	PASSADE	PASSKEY
PARREL	PARTAKERS	PARTYING	PASSADES	PASSKEYS
PARRELS	PARTAKES	PARTYISM	PASSADO	PASSLESS
PARRHESIA	PARTAKING	PARTYISMS	PASSADOES	PASSMAN
PARRHESIAS	PARTAKINGS	PARULIS	PASSADOS	PASSMEN
PARRICIDE	PARTAN	PARULISES	PASSAGE	PASSMENT
PARRICIDES	PARTANS	PARURA*	PASSAGED	PASSMENTED
PARRIDGE*	PARTED	PARURAS*	PASSAGES	PASSMENTING
PARRIDGES*	PARTER	PARURE	PASSAGING	PASSMENTS

PASSOUT	PASTORED*	PATENT	PATINIZED*	PATRONLY*
PASSOUTS	PASTORING*	PATENTED	PATINIZES*	PATRONNE
PASSOVER*	PASTORLY	PATENTEE	PATINIZING*	PATRONNES
PASSOVERS*	PASTORS	PATENTEES	PATINS	PATRONS
PASSPORT	PASTRAMI	PATENTING	PATIO	PATROON
PASSPORTS	PASTRAMIS	PATENTLY	PATIOS	PATROONS
PASSUS	PASTRIES	PATENTOR	PATISSIER*	PATS
PASSUSES	PASTROMI*	PATENTORS	PATISSIERS*	PATSIES
PASSWORD	PASTROMIS*	PATENTS	PATLY	PATSY
PASSWORDS	PASTRY	PATER	PATNESS	PATTAMAR*
PAST	PASTS	PATERA	PATNESSES	PATTAMARS*
PASTA	PASTURAGE	PATERAE	PATOIS	PATTE
PASTANCE	PASTURAGES	PATERCOVE	PATONCE	PATTED
PASTANCES	PASTURAL	PATERCOVES	PATRIAL	PATTEE
PASTAS	PASTURE	PATERERO	PATRIALS	PATTEN
PASTE	PASTURED	PATEREROES	PATRIARCH	PATTENED
PASTED	PASTURER*	PATEREROS	PATRIARCHS	PATTENING
PASTEDOWN*	PASTURERS*	PATERNAL	PATRIATE	PATTENS
PASTEDOWNS*	PASTURES	PATERNITIES	PATRIATED	PATTER
PASTEL	PASTURING	PATERNITY	PATRIATES	PATTERED
PASTELIST*	PASTY	PATERS	PATRIATING	PATTERER
PASTELISTS*	PAT	PATES	PATRICIAN	PATTERERS
PASTELS	PATACA	PATH	PATRICIANS	PATTERING
PASTER	PATACAS	PATHED	PATRICIDE	PATTERN
PASTERN	PATAGIA	PATHETIC	PATRICIDES	PATTERNED
PASTERNS	PATAGIAL	PATHETICS	PATRICK	PATTERNING
PASTERS	PATAGIUM	PATHIC	PATRICKS	PATTERNS
PASTES	PATAMAR	PATHICS	PATRICO	PATTERS
PASTEUP*	PATAMARS	PATHING	PATRICOES	PATTES
PASTEUPS*	PATBALL	PATHLESS	PATRILINIES	PATTIE*
PASTICCI	PATBALLS	PATHOGEN	PATRILINY	PATTIES
PASTICCIO	PATCH	PATHOGENIES	PATRIMONIES	PATTING
PASTICCIOS*	PATCHABLE	PATHOGENS	PATRIMONY	PATTLE
PASTICHE	PATCHED	PATHOGENY	PATRIOT	PATTLES
PASTICHES	PATCHER	PATHOLOGIES	PATRIOTIC	PATTY
PASTIE*	PATCHERIES	PATHOLOGY	PATRIOTS	PATTYPAN*
PASTIER	PATCHERS	PATHOS	PATRISTIC	PATTYPANS*
PASTIES	PATCHERY	PATHOSES	PATRISTICS	PATULENT*
PASTIEST	PATCHES	PATHS	PATRO	PATULIN
PASTIL	PATCHIER	PATHWAY	PATROL	PATULINS
PASTILLE	PATCHIEST	PATHWAYS	PATROLLED	PATULOUS
PASTILLES	PATCHILY	PATIBLE	PATROLLER	PATY*
PASTILS	PATCHING	PATIENCE	PATROLLERS	PATZER
PASTIME	PATCHINGS	PATIENCES	PATROLLING	PATZERS
PASTIMES	PATCHOCKE	PATIENT	PATROLMAN	PAUA
PASTINA*	PATCHOCKES	PATIENTED	PATROLMEN	PAUAS
PASTINAS*	PATCHOULI	PATIENTER	PATROLOGIES	PAUCITIES
PASTINESS	PATCHOULIES	PATIENTEST	PATROLOGY	PAUCITY
PASTINESSES	PATCHOULIS	PATIENTING	PATROLS	PAUGHTIER
PASTING	PATCHOULY	PATIENTLY	PATRON	PAUGHTIEST
PASTINGS	PATCHWORK	PATIENTS	PATRONAGE	PAUGHTY
PASTIS	PATCHWORKS	PATIN	PATRONAGED	PAUL
PASTISES	PATCHY	PATINA	PATRONAGES	PAULDRON
PASTLESS*	PATE	PATINAE*	PATRONAGING	PAULDRONS
PASTNESS*	PATED	PATINAS	PATRONAL	PAULIN*
PASTNESSES*	PATELLA	PATINATE*	PATRONESS	PAULINS*
PASTOR	PATELLAE	PATINATED	PATRONESSES	PAULOWNIA
PASTORAL	PATELLAR	PATINATES*	PATRONISE	PAULOWNIAS
PASTORALE	PATELLAS	PATINATING*	PATRONISED	PAULS
PASTORALES	PATELLATE	PATINE	PATRONISES	PAUNCE
PASTORALI	PATEN	PATINED	PATRONISING	PAUNCES
PASTORALS	PATENCIES	PATINES	PATRONIZE	PAUNCH
PASTORATE	PATENCY	PATINING*	PATRONIZED	PAUNCHED
PASTORATES	PATENS	PATINIZE*	PATRONIZES	PAUNCHES

The Chambers Dictionary is the authority for many longer words; see Introduction, page ix

PAUNCHIER	PAVIOUR	PAYABLES*	PEACETIME	PEARLED
PAUNCHIEST	PAVIOURS	PAYABLY*	PEACETIMES	PEARLER
PAUNCHING	PAVIS	PAYBACK	PEACH	PEARLERS
PAUNCHY	PAVISE	PAYBACKS	PEACHED	PEARLIER
PAUPER	PAVISER*	PAYCHECK*	PEACHER	PEARLIES
PAUPERED*	PAVISERS*	PAYCHECKS*	PEACHERS	PEARLIEST
PAUPERESS	PAVISES	PAYDAY*	PEACHES	PEARLIN
PAUPERESSES	PAVLOVA	PAYDAYS*	PEACHIER	PEARLING
PAUPERING*	PAVLOVAS	PAYED	PEACHIEST	PEARLINGS
PAUPERISE	PAVONAZZO	PAYEE	PEACHING	PEARLINS
PAUPERISED	PAVONAZZOS	PAYEES	PEACHY	PEARLISED
PAUPERISES	PAVONE	PAYER	PEACING	PEARLITE
PAUPERISING	PAVONES	PAYERS	PEACOAT*	PEARLITES
PAUPERISM	PAVONIAN	PAYFONE	PEACOATS*	PEARLITIC
PAUPERISMS	PAVONINE	PAYFONES	PEACOCK	PEARLIZED
PAUPERIZE	PAW	PAYGRADE*	PEACOCKED	PEARLS
PAUPERIZED	PAWA	PAYGRADES*	PEACOCKIER*	PEARLWORT
PAUPERIZES	PAWAS	PAYING	PEACOCKIEST*	PEARLWORTS
PAUPERIZING	PAWAW	PAYINGS	PEACOCKING	PEARLY
PAUPERS	PAWAWED	PAYLOAD*	PEACOCKS	PEARMAIN
PAUPIETTE*	PAWAWING	PAYLOADS*	PEACOCKY	PEARMAINS
PAUPIETTES*	PAWAWS	PAYMASTER	PEACOD	PEARS
PAUSAL	PAWED	PAYMASTERS	PEACODS	PEARST
PAUSE	PAWER*	PAYMENT	PEAFOWL	PEART
PAUSED	PAWERS*	PAYMENTS	PEAFOWLS	PEARTER
PAUSEFUL	PAWING	PAYNIM	PEAG	PEARTEST
PAUSELESS	PAWK	PAYNIMRIES	PEAGE*	PEARTLY
PAUSER	PAWKIER	PAYNIMRY	PEAGES*	PEAS
PAUSERS	PAWKIEST	PAYNIMS	PEAGS	PEASANT
PAUSES	PAWKILY	PAYOFF*	PEAHEN*	PEASANTRIES
PAUSING	PAWKINESS	PAYOFFS*	PEAHENS*	PEASANTRY
PAUSINGLY	PAWKINESSES	PAYOLA	PEAK	PEASANTS
PAUSINGS	PAWKS	PAYOLAS	PEAKED	PEASANTY
PAVAGE	PAWKY	PAYOR*	PEAKIER	PEASCOD
PAVAGES	PAWL	PAYORS*	PEAKIEST	PEASCODS
PAVAN	PAWLS	PAYOUT*	PEAKING	PEASE
PAVANE	PAWN	PAYOUTS*	PEAKISH*	PEASECOD
PAVANES	PAWNABLE*	PAYROLL	PEAKLESS*	PEASECODS
PAVANS	PAWNAGE*	PAYROLLS	PEAKLIKE*	PEASED
PAVE	PAWNAGES*	PAYS	PEAKS	PEASEN*
PAVED	PAWNCE	PAYSAGE	PEAKY	PEASES
PAVEED*	PAWNCES	PAYSAGES	PEAL	PEASEWEEP
PAVEMENT	PAWNED	PAYSAGIST	PEALED	PEASEWEEPS
PAVEMENTED	PAWNEE	PAYSAGISTS	PEALIKE*	PEASING
PAVEMENTING	PAWNEES	PAYSD	PEALING	PEASON
PAVEMENTS	PAWNER	PAYSLIP	PEALS	PEAT
PAVEN	PAWNERS	PAYSLIPS	PEAN	PEATARIES
PAVENS	PAWNING	PAZAZZ	PEANED	PEATARY
PAVER	PAWNOR*	PAZAZZES	PEANING	PEATERIES
PAVERS	PAWNORS*	PE*	PEANS	PEATERY
PAVES	PAWNS	PEA	PEANUT	PEATIER
PAVID	PAWNSHOP	PEABERRIES	PEANUTS	PEATIEST
PAVILION	PAWNSHOPS	PEABERRY	PEAPOD	PEATMAN
PAVILIONED	PAWPAW	PEACE	PEAPODS	PEATMEN
PAVILIONING	PAWPAWS	PEACEABLE	PEAR	PEATS
PAVILIONS	PAWS	PEACEABLY	PEARCE	PEATSHIP
PAVILLON*	PAX	PEACED	PEARCED	PEATSHIPS
PAVILLONS*	PAXES	PEACEFUL	PEARCES	PEATY
PAVIN	PAXIUBA	PEACEFULLER*	PEARCING	PEAVEY
PAVING	PAXIUBAS	PEACEFULLEST*	PEARE	PEAVEYS
PAVINGS	PAXWAX	PEACELESS	PEARES	PEAVIES
PAVINS	PAXWAXES	PEACENIK	PEARL	PEAVY
PAVIOR	PAY	PEACENIKS	PEARLASH*	PEAZE
PAVIORS	PAYABLE	PEACES	PEARLASHES*	PEAZED

PEAZES
PEAZING
PEBA
PEBAS
PEBBLE
PEBBLED
PEBBLES
PEBBLIER
PEBBLIEST
PEBBLING
PEBBLINGS
PEBBLY
PEBRINE
PEBRINES
PEC
PECAN
PECANS
PECCABLE
PECCANCIES
PECCANCY
PECCANT
PECCANTLY
PECCARIES
PECCARY
PECCAVI
PECCAVIS
PECH
PECHAN*
PECHANS*
PECHED
PECHING
PECHS
PECK
PECKE
PECKED
PECKER
PECKERS
PECKES
PECKIER*
PECKIEST*
PECKING
PECKINGS
PECKISH
PECKS
PECKY*
PECORINI*
PECORINO*
PECORINOS*
PECS
PECTASE*
PECTASES*
PECTATE*
PECTATES*
PECTEN
PECTENS*
PECTIC
PECTIN
PECTINAL
PECTINATE
PECTINEAL
PECTINES
PECTINS
PECTISE
PECTISED

PECTISES
PECTISING
PECTIZE
PECTIZED
PECTIZES
PECTIZING
PECTOLITE
PECTOLITES
PECTORAL
PECTORALS
PECTOSE
PECTOSES
PECULATE
PECULATED
PECULATES
PECULATING
PECULATOR
PECULATORS
PECULIA
PECULIAR
PECULIARS
PECULIUM
PECUNIARY
PECUNIOUS
PED
PEDAGOG*
PEDAGOGIC
PEDAGOGICS
PEDAGOGIES
PEDAGOGS*
PEDAGOGUE
PEDAGOGUED
PEDAGOGUES
PEDAGOGUING
PEDAGOGY
PEDAL
PEDALED
PEDALFER*
PEDALFERS*
PEDALIER
PEDALIERS
PEDALING
PEDALLED
PEDALLER
PEDALLERS
PEDALLING
PEDALLINGS
PEDALO
PEDALOES
PEDALOS
PEDALS
PEDANT
PEDANTIC
PEDANTISE
PEDANTISED
PEDANTISES
PEDANTISING
PEDANTISM
PEDANTISMS
PEDANTIZE
PEDANTIZED
PEDANTIZES
PEDANTIZING
PEDANTRIES

PEDANTRY
PEDANTS
PEDATE
PEDATELY
PEDATIFID
PEDDER
PEDDERS
PEDDLE
PEDDLED
PEDDLER
PEDDLERIES*
PEDDLERS
PEDDLERY*
PEDDLES
PEDDLING
PEDDLINGS
PEDERAST
PEDERASTIES
PEDERASTS
PEDERASTY
PEDERERO
PEDEREROES
PEDEREROS
PEDES*
PEDESES
PEDESIS
PEDESTAL
PEDESTALED*
PEDESTALING*
PEDESTALLED
PEDESTALLING
PEDESTALS
PEDETIC
PEDIATRIC*
PEDICAB
PEDICABS
PEDICEL
PEDICELS
PEDICLE
PEDICLED
PEDICLES
PEDICULAR
PEDICULI
PEDICULUS
PEDICURE
PEDICURED
PEDICURES
PEDICURING
PEDIFORM*
PEDIGREE
PEDIGREED
PEDIGREES
PEDIMENT
PEDIMENTS
PEDIPALP
PEDIPALPI
PEDIPALPS
PEDLAR
PEDLARIES
PEDLARS
PEDLARY
PEDLER*
PEDLERIES*
PEDLERS*

PEDLERY*
PEDOCAL*
PEDOCALIC*
PEDOCALS*
PEDOGENIC*
PEDOLOGIC*
PEDOLOGIES
PEDOLOGY
PEDOMETER
PEDOMETERS
PEDOPHILE*
PEDOPHILES*
PEDRAIL
PEDRAILS
PEDRERO
PEDREROES
PEDREROS
PEDRO
PEDROS
PEDS
PEDUNCLE
PEDUNCLED*
PEDUNCLES
PEE
PEEBEEN*
PEEBEENS*
PEECE
PEECES
PEED
PEEING
PEEK
PEEKABO
PEEKABOO
PEEKABOOS
PEEKABOS
PEEKED
PEEKING
PEEKS
PEEL
PEELABLE*
PEELED
PEELER
PEELERS
PEELING
PEELINGS
PEELS
PEEN
PEENED
PEENGE
PEENGED
PEENGEING
PEENGES
PEENGING
PEENING
PEENS
PEEOY
PEEOYS
PEEP
PEEPE
PEEPED
PEEPER
PEEPERS
PEEPES
PEEPHOLE*

PEEPHOLES*
PEEPING
PEEPS
PEEPSHOW*
PEEPSHOWS*
PEEPUL
PEEPULS
PEER
PEERAGE
PEERAGES
PEERED
PEERESS
PEERESSES
PEERIE
PEERIER
PEERIES
PEERIEST
PEERING
PEERLESS
PEERS
PEERY
PEES
PEESWEEP
PEESWEEPS
PEETWEET
PEETWEETS
PEEVE
PEEVED
PEEVER
PEEVERS
PEEVES
PEEVING
PEEVISH
PEEVISHLY
PEEWEE
PEEWEES
PEEWIT
PEEWITS
PEG
PEGASUS
PEGASUSES
PEGBOARD
PEGBOARDS
PEGBOX*
PEGBOXES*
PEGGED
PEGGIES
PEGGING
PEGGINGS
PEGGY
PEGH
PEGHED
PEGHING
PEGHS
PEGLESS*
PEGLIKE*
PEGMATITE
PEGMATITES
PEGS
PEH*
PEHS*
PEIGNOIR
PEIGNOIRS
PEIN

PEINCT	PELLAGRIN	PELTERED	PENCILLER	PENILE
PEINCTED	PELLAGRINS	PELTERING	PENCILLERS	PENILLION
PEINCTING	PELLET	PELTERS	PENCILLING	PENING
PEINCTS	PELLETAL*	PELTING	PENCILLINGS	PENINSULA
PEINED	PELLETED	PELTINGLY	PENCILS	PENINSULAS
PEINING	PELLETIFIED	PELTINGS	PENCRAFT	PENIS
PEINS	PELLETIFIES	PELTRIES	PENCRAFTS	PENISES
PEIRASTIC	PELLETIFY	PELTRY	PEND	PENISTONE
PEISE	PELLETIFYING	PELTS	PENDANT	PENISTONES
PEISED	PELLETING	PELVES	PENDANTS	PENITENCE
PEISES	PELLETISE	PELVIC	PENDED	PENITENCES
PEISHWA	PELLETISED	PELVICS*	PENDENCIES	PENITENCIES
PEISHWAH	PELLETISES	PELVIFORM	PENDENCY	PENITENCY
PEISHWAHS	PELLETISING	PELVIS	PENDENT	PENITENT
PEISHWAS	PELLETIZE	PELVISES	PENDENTLY	PENITENTS
PEISING	PELLETIZED	PEMBINA*	PENDENTS	PENK
PEIZE	PELLETIZES	PEMBINAS*	PENDICLE	PENKNIFE
PEIZED	PELLETIZING	PEMBROKE	PENDICLER	PENKNIVES
PEIZES	PELLETS	PEMBROKES	PENDICLERS	PENKS
PEIZING	PELLICLE	PEMICAN	PENDICLES	PENLIGHT
PEJORATE	PELLICLES	PEMICANS	PENDING	PENLIGHTS
PEJORATED	PELLITORIES	PEMMICAN	PENDRAGON	PENLITE*
PEJORATES	PELLITORY	PEMMICANS	PENDRAGONS	PENLITES*
PEJORATING	PELLMELL*	PEMOLINE	PENDS	PENMAN
PEKAN	PELLMELLS*	PEMOLINES	PENDULAR	PENMEN
PEKANS	PELLOCK	PEMPHIGUS	PENDULATE	PENNA
PEKE	PELLOCKS	PEMPHIGUSES	PENDULATED	PENNAE
PEKES	PELLS	PEMPHIX*	PENDULATES	PENNAL
PEKIN*	PELLUCID	PEMPHIXES*	PENDULATING	PENNALISM
PEKINS*	PELMA	PEN	PENDULINE	PENNALISMS
PEKOE	PELMANISM	PENAL	PENDULOUS	PENNALS
PEKOES	PELMANISMS	PENALISE	PENDULUM	PENNAME*
PELA	PELMAS	PENALISED	PENDULUMS	PENNAMES*
PELAGE	PELMATIC	PENALISES	PENE	PENNANT
PELAGES	PELMET	PENALISING	PENED	PENNANTS
PELAGIAL*	PELMETS	PENALITIES*	PENEPLAIN	PENNATE
PELAGIAN	PELOID	PENALITY*	PENEPLAINS	PENNATED*
PELAGIANS	PELOIDS	PENALIZE	PENEPLANE	PENNATULA
PELAGIC	PELOLOGIES	PENALIZED	PENEPLANES	PENNATULAE
PELAS	PELOLOGY	PENALIZES	PENES	PENNATULAS
PELE	PELON*	PENALIZING	PENETRANT	PENNE
PELECYPOD*	PELORIA	PENALLY	PENETRANTS	PENNED
PELECYPODS*	PELORIAN*	PENALTIES	PENETRATE	PENNEECH
PELERINE	PELORIAS	PENALTY	PENETRATED	PENNEECHS
PELERINES	PELORIC	PENANCE	PENETRATES	PENNEECK
PELES	PELORIES	PENANCED	PENETRATING	PENNEECKS
PELF	PELORISED	PENANCES	PENFOLD	PENNER
PELFS	PELORISM	PENANCING	PENFOLDS	PENNERS
PELHAM	PELORISMS	PENANG*	PENFUL	PENNES
PELHAMS	PELORIZED	PENANGS*	PENFULS	PENNI*
PELICAN	PELORUS	PENATES	PENGO*	PENNIA*
PELICANS	PELORUSES	PENCE	PENGOS*	PENNIED
PELISSE	PELORY	PENCEL	PENGUIN	PENNIES
PELISSES	PELOTA	PENCELS	PENGUINRIES	PENNIFORM
PELITE	PELOTAS	PENCES	PENGUINRY	PENNILESS
PELITES	PELT	PENCHANT	PENGUINS	PENNILL
PELITIC	PELTA	PENCHANTS	PENHOLDER	PENNINE
PELL	PELTAE	PENCIL	PENHOLDERS	PENNINES
PELLACH	PELTAS	PENCILED*	PENI	PENNING
PELLACHS	PELTAST	PENCILER*	PENIAL	PENNINITE
PELLACK	PELTASTS	PENCILERS*	PENICIL*	PENNINITES
PELLACKS	PELTATE	PENCILING*	PENICILS*	PENNIS*
PELLAGRA	PELTED	PENCILINGS*	PENIE	PENNON
PELLAGRAS	PELTER	PENCILLED	PENIES	PENNONCEL

PENNONCELS
PENNONED
PENNONS
PENNY
PENNYFEE
PENNYFEES
PENNYLAND
PENNYLANDS
PENNYWORT*
PENNYWORTS*
PENOCHE*
PENOCHES*
PENOLOGIES
PENOLOGY
PENONCEL
PENONCELS
PENPOINT*
PENPOINTS*
PENS
PENSEE
PENSEES
PENSEL
PENSELS
PENSIL
PENSILE
PENSILITIES
PENSILITY
PENSILS
PENSION
PENSIONE*
PENSIONED
PENSIONER
PENSIONERS
PENSIONES*
PENSIONING
PENSIONS
PENSIVE
PENSIVELY
PENSTEMON
PENSTEMONS
PENSTER*
PENSTERS*
PENSTOCK
PENSTOCKS
PENSUM
PENSUMS
PENT
PENTACLE
PENTACLES
PENTACT
PENTACTS
PENTAD
PENTADIC
PENTADS
PENTAGON
PENTAGONS
PENTAGRAM
PENTAGRAMS
PENTALOGIES
PENTALOGY
PENTALPHA
PENTALPHAS
PENTAMERIES
PENTAMERY

PENTANE
PENTANES
PENTANGLE
PENTANGLES
PENTANOL*
PENTANOLS*
PENTAPODIES
PENTAPODY
PENTARCH
PENTARCHIES
PENTARCHS
PENTARCHY
PENTATHLA
PENTEL
PENTELS
PENTENE
PENTENES
PENTHIA
PENTHIAS
PENTHOUSE
PENTHOUSED
PENTHOUSES
PENTHOUSING
PENTICE
PENTICED
PENTICES
PENTICING
PENTISE
PENTISED
PENTISES
PENTISING
PENTODE
PENTODES
PENTOMIC
PENTOSAN
PENTOSANE
PENTOSANES
PENTOSANS
PENTOSE
PENTOSES
PENTOXIDE
PENTOXIDES
PENTROOF
PENTROOFS
PENTS
PENTYL*
PENTYLENE
PENTYLENES
PENTYLS*
PENUCHE
PENUCHES
PENUCHI
PENUCHIS
PENUCHLE
PENUCHLES
PENUCKLE*
PENUCKLES*
PENULT
PENULTIMA
PENULTIMAS
PENULTS
PENUMBRA
PENUMBRAE*
PENUMBRAL

PENUMBRAS
PENURIES
PENURIOUS
PENURY
PENWOMAN
PENWOMEN
PEON
PEONAGE
PEONAGES
PEONES*
PEONIES
PEONISM
PEONISMS
PEONS
PEONY
PEOPLE
PEOPLED
PEOPLER*
PEOPLERS*
PEOPLES
PEOPLING
PEP
PEPERINO
PEPERINOS
PEPEROMIA
PEPEROMIAS
PEPERONI
PEPERONIS
PEPFUL
PEPINO
PEPINOS
PEPLA
PEPLOS
PEPLOSES
PEPLUM
PEPLUMED*
PEPLUMS
PEPLUS
PEPLUSES
PEPO
PEPONIDA*
PEPONIDAS*
PEPONIUM*
PEPONIUMS*
PEPOS
PEPPED
PEPPER
PEPPERBOX*
PEPPERBOXES*
PEPPERED
PEPPERER
PEPPERERS
PEPPERIER
PEPPERIEST
PEPPERING
PEPPERINGS
PEPPERONI
PEPPERONIS
PEPPERS
PEPPERY
PEPPIER
PEPPIEST
PEPPILY*
PEPPINESS*

PEPPINESSES*
PEPPING
PEPPY
PEPS
PEPSIN
PEPSINATE
PEPSINATED
PEPSINATES
PEPSINATING
PEPSINE
PEPSINES
PEPSINS
PEPTIC
PEPTICITIES
PEPTICITY
PEPTICS
PEPTID*
PEPTIDASE
PEPTIDASES
PEPTIDE
PEPTIDES
PEPTIDIC*
PEPTIDS*
PEPTISE
PEPTISED
PEPTISES
PEPTISING
PEPTIZE
PEPTIZED
PEPTIZER*
PEPTIZERS*
PEPTIZES
PEPTIZING
PEPTONE
PEPTONES
PEPTONIC*
PEPTONISE
PEPTONISED
PEPTONISES
PEPTONISING
PEPTONIZE
PEPTONIZED
PEPTONIZES
PEPTONIZING
PER
PERACID*
PERACIDS*
PERACUTE
PERAEA
PERAEON
PERAEONS
PERAEOPOD
PERAEOPODS
PERAI
PERAIS
PERBORATE*
PERBORATES*
PERCALE
PERCALES
PERCALINE
PERCALINES
PERCASE
PERCE
PERCEABLE

PERCEANT
PERCED
PERCEIVE
PERCEIVED
PERCEIVER
PERCEIVERS
PERCEIVES
PERCEIVING
PERCEIVINGS
PERCEN
PERCENT*
PERCENTAL
PERCENTS*
PERCEPT
PERCEPTS
PERCES
PERCH
PERCHANCE
PERCHED
PERCHER
PERCHERON
PERCHERONS
PERCHERS
PERCHERY
PERCHES
PERCHING
PERCHINGS
PERCIFORM
PERCINE
PERCING
PERCOCT
PERCOID
PERCOIDS*
PERCOLATE
PERCOLATED
PERCOLATES
PERCOLATING
PERCOLIN
PERCOLINS
PERCUSS
PERCUSSED
PERCUSSES
PERCUSSING
PERCUSSOR
PERCUSSORS
PERDENDO
PERDIE
PERDITION
PERDITIONS
PERDU
PERDUE
PERDUES
PERDURE
PERDURED
PERDURES
PERDURING
PERDUS
PERDY
PERE
PEREA*
PEREGAL
PEREGALS
PEREGRIN*
PEREGRINE

PEREGRINES	PERFUMING	PERIGEAN	PERIPHERY	PERKS
PEREGRINS*	PERFUMY	PERIGEE	PERIPLAST	PERKY
PEREIA	PERFUSATE	PERIGEES	PERIPLASTS	PERLITE
PEREION	PERFUSATES	PERIGON	PERIPLUS	PERLITES
PEREIOPOD	PERFUSE	PERIGONE	PERIPLUSES	PERLITIC
PEREIOPODS	PERFUSED	PERIGONES	PERIPROCT	PERLOUS
PEREIRA	PERFUSES	PERIGONIA	PERIPROCTS	PERM
PEREIRAS	PERFUSING	PERIGONS	PERIPTER*	PERMALLOY
PERENNATE	PERFUSION	PERIGYNIES	PERIPTERIES	PERMALLOYS
PERENNATED	PERFUSIONS	PERIGYNY	PERIPTERS*	PERMANENT
PERENNATES	PERFUSIVE	PERIHELIA	PERIPTERY	PERMANENTS*
PERENNATING	PERGOLA	PERIHELION*	PERIQUE	PERMEABLE
PERENNIAL	PERGOLAS	PERIKARYA	PERIQUES	PERMEABLY
PERENNIALS	PERGUNNAH	PERIKARYON*	PERIS	PERMEANCE
PERENNITIES	PERGUNNAHS	PERIL	PERISARC	PERMEANCES
PERENNITY	PERHAPS	PERILED*	PERISARCS	PERMEANT*
PEREON*	PERHAPSES*	PERILING*	PERISCIAN	PERMEASE
PEREOPOD*	PERI	PERILLA*	PERISCIANS	PERMEASES
PEREOPODS*	PERIAGUA	PERILLAS*	PERISCOPE	PERMEATE
PERES	PERIAGUAS	PERILLED	PERISCOPES	PERMEATED
PERFAY	PERIAKTOI	PERILLING	PERISH	PERMEATES
PERFECT	PERIAKTOS	PERILOUS	PERISHED	PERMEATING
PERFECTA	PERIANTH	PERILS	PERISHER	PERMED
PERFECTAS	PERIANTHS	PERILUNE	PERISHERS	PERMING
PERFECTED	PERIAPT	PERILUNES	PERISHES	PERMIT
PERFECTER	PERIAPTS	PERILYMPH	PERISHING	PERMITS
PERFECTERS	PERIBLAST	PERILYMPHS	PERISPERM	PERMITTED
PERFECTEST	PERIBLASTS	PERIMETER	PERISPERMS	PERMITTEE*
PERFECTI	PERIBLEM	PERIMETERS	PERISTOME	PERMITTEES*
PERFECTING	PERIBLEMS	PERIMETRIES	PERISTOMES	PERMITTER
PERFECTLY	PERIBOLI	PERIMETRY	PERISTYLE	PERMITTERS
PERFECTO	PERIBOLOI	PERIMORPH	PERISTYLES	PERMITTING
PERFECTOR	PERIBOLOS	PERIMORPHS	PERITI	PERMS
PERFECTORS	PERIBOLUS	PERIMYSIA*	PERITONEA	PERMUTATE
PERFECTOS	PERICARP	PERIMYSIUM*	PERITONEUM*	PERMUTATED
PERFECTS	PERICARPS	PERINAEUM	PERITONEUMS*	PERMUTATES
PERFERVID	PERICLASE	PERINAEUMS	PERITRICH	PERMUTATING
PERFERVOR	PERICLASES	PERINATAL	PERITRICHA	PERMUTE
PERFERVORS	PERICLINE	PERINEA	PERITUS	PERMUTED
PERFET	PERICLINES	PERINEAL	PERIWIG	PERMUTES
PERFIDIES	PERICON	PERINEUM	PERIWIGGED	PERMUTING
PERFIDY	PERICONES	PERINEUMS	PERIWIGGING	PERN
PERFORANS	PERICOPAE*	PERIOD	PERIWIGS	PERNANCIES
PERFORANSES	PERICOPE	PERIODATE	PERJINK	PERNANCY
PERFORANT	PERICOPES	PERIODATES	PERJURE	PERNS
PERFORATE	PERICRANIES	PERIODED	PERJURED	PERONE
PERFORATED	PERICRANY	PERIODIC	PERJURER	PERONEAL
PERFORATES	PERICYCLE	PERIODID*	PERJURERS	PERONES
PERFORATING	PERICYCLES	PERIODIDS*	PERJURES	PERONEUS
PERFORCE	PERIDERM	PERIODING	PERJURIES	PERONEUSES
PERFORM	PERIDERMS	PERIODS	PERJURING	PERORAL*
PERFORMED	PERIDIA	PERIOST	PERJUROUS	PERORALLY*
PERFORMER	PERIDIAL	PERIOSTEA	PERJURY	PERORATE
PERFORMERS	PERIDINIA	PERIOSTEUM*	PERK	PERORATED
PERFORMING	PERIDIUM	PERIOSTS	PERKED	PERORATES
PERFORMINGS	PERIDIUMS	PERIOTIC	PERKIER	PERORATING
PERFORMS	PERIDOT	PERIOTICS	PERKIEST	PEROVSKIA
PERFUME	PERIDOTE	PERIPATUS	PERKILY	PEROVSKIAS
PERFUMED	PERIDOTES	PERIPATUSES	PERKIN	PEROXID*
PERFUMER	PERIDOTIC	PERIPETIA	PERKINESS	PEROXIDE
PERFUMERIES	PERIDOTS	PERIPETIAS	PERKINESSES	PEROXIDED
PERFUMERS	PERIDROME	PERIPETIES	PERKING	PEROXIDES
PERFUMERY	PERIDROMES	PERIPETY	PERKINS	PEROXIDIC*
PERFUMES	PERIGEAL	PERIPHERIES	PERKISH*	PEROXIDING

Words marked with an asterisk are from OTCWL

PEROXIDS*	PERSONALS*	PERTURBED	PESETAS	PETARA
PEROXY*	PERSONAS	PERTURBER	PESEWA	PETARAS
PERPEND	PERSONATE	PERTURBERS	PESEWAS	PETARD
PERPENDED	PERSONATED	PERTURBING	PESHWA	PETARDS
PERPENDING	PERSONATES	PERTURBS	PESHWAS	PETARIES
PERPENDS	PERSONATING	PERTUSATE	PESKIER	PETARS
PERPENT	PERSONATINGS	PERTUSE	PESKIEST	PETARY
PERPENTS	PERSONIFIED	PERTUSED	PESKILY	PETASOS*
PERPETUAL	PERSONIFIES	PERTUSION	PESKY	PETASOSES*
PERPETUALS	PERSONIFY	PERTUSIONS	PESO	PETASUS
PERPLEX	PERSONIFYING	PERTUSSAL	PESOS	PETASUSES
PERPLEXED	PERSONISE	PERTUSSIS	PESSARIES	PETAURINE
PERPLEXES	PERSONISED	PERTUSSISES	PESSARY	PETAURIST
PERPLEXING	PERSONISES	PERUKE	PESSIMA	PETAURISTS
PERRADIAL	PERSONISING	PERUKED	PESSIMAL	PETCHARIES
PERRADII	PERSONIZE	PERUKES	PESSIMISM	PETCHARY
PERRADIUS	PERSONIZED	PERUSAL	PESSIMISMS	PETCOCK
PERRIER	PERSONIZES	PERUSALS	PESSIMIST	PETCOCKS
PERRIERS	PERSONIZING	PERUSE	PESSIMISTS	PETECHIA
PERRIES	PERSONNEL	PERUSED	PESSIMUM	PETECHIAE
PERRON	PERSONNELS	PERUSER	PEST	PETECHIAL
PERRONS	PERSONS	PERUSERS	PESTER	PETER
PERRUQUE	PERSPIRE	PERUSES	PESTERED	PETERED
PERRUQUES	PERSPIRED	PERUSING	PESTERER	PETERING
PERRY	PERSPIRES	PERV	PESTERERS	PETERMAN
PERSALT*	PERSPIRING	PERVADE	PESTERING	PETERMEN
PERSALTS*	PERSPIRY*	PERVADED	PESTEROUS	PETERS
PERSANT	PERST	PERVADER*	PESTERS	PETERSHAM
PERSAUNT	PERSUADE	PERVADERS*	PESTFUL	PETERSHAMS
PERSE	PERSUADED	PERVADES	PESTHOLE*	PETHER
PERSECUTE	PERSUADER	PERVADING	PESTHOLES*	PETHERS
PERSECUTED	PERSUADERS	PERVASION	PESTHOUSE	PETHIDINE
PERSECUTES	PERSUADES	PERVASIONS	PESTHOUSES	PETHIDINES
PERSECUTING	PERSUADING	PERVASIVE	PESTICIDE	PETILLANT
PERSEITIES	PERSUE	PERVE	PESTICIDES	PETIOLAR
PERSEITY	PERSUED	PERVED	PESTIER*	PETIOLATE
PERSELINE	PERSUES	PERVERSE	PESTIEST*	PETIOLE
PERSELINES	PERSUING	PERVERSER	PESTILENT	PETIOLED
PERSES	PERSWADE	PERVERSEST	PESTLE	PETIOLES
PERSEVERE	PERSWADED	PERVERT	PESTLED	PETIOLULE
PERSEVERED	PERSWADES	PERVERTED	PESTLES	PETIOLULES
PERSEVERES	PERSWADING	PERVERTER	PESTLING	PETIT
PERSEVERING	PERT	PERVERTERS	PESTO	PETITE
PERSICO	PERTAIN	PERVERTING	PESTOLOGIES	PETITES*
PERSICOS	PERTAINED	PERVERTS	PESTOLOGY	PETITION
PERSICOT	PERTAINING	PERVES	PESTOS	PETITIONED
PERSICOTS	PERTAINS	PERVIATE	PESTS	PETITIONING
PERSIENNE	PERTAKE	PERVIATED	PESTY*	PETITIONINGS
PERSIENNES	PERTAKEN	PERVIATES	PET	PETITIONS
PERSIMMON	PERTAKES	PERVIATING	PETAL	PETITORY
PERSIMMONS	PERTAKING	PERVICACIES	PETALED*	PETNAP*
PERSING	PERTER	PERVICACY	PETALINE	PETNAPPED*
PERSIST	PERTEST	PERVING	PETALISM	PETNAPPING*
PERSISTED	PERTHITE	PERVIOUS	PETALISMS	PETNAPS*
PERSISTER*	PERTHITES	PERVS	PETALLED	PETRALE*
PERSISTERS*	PERTHITIC	PES*	PETALLIKE*	PETRALES*
PERSISTING	PERTINENT	PESADE	PETALODIES	PETRARIES
PERSISTS	PERTINENTS	PESADES	PETALODY	PETRARY
PERSON	PERTLY	PESANT	PETALOID	PETRE
PERSONA	PERTNESS	PESANTE	PETALOUS	PETREL
PERSONAE	PERTNESSES	PESANTS	PETALS	PETRELS
PERSONAGE	PERTOOK	PESAUNT	PETANQUE	PETRES
PERSONAGES	PERTS	PESAUNTS	PETANQUES	PETRIFIC
PERSONAL	PERTURB	PESETA	PETAR	PETRIFIED

The Chambers Dictionary is the authority for many longer words; see Introduction, page ix

PETRIFIES	PETUNTZE	PHALANGER	PHASELESS	PHENOGAM
PETRIFY	PETUNTZES	PHALANGERS	PHASEOLIN	PHENOGAMS
PETRIFYING	PEW	PHALANGES	PHASEOLINS	PHENOL
PETROGRAM	PEWEE*	PHALANGID	PHASEOUT*	PHENOLATE
PETROGRAMS	PEWEES*	PHALANGIDS	PHASEOUTS*	PHENOLATES
PETROL	PEWHOLDER*	PHALANX	PHASES	PHENOLIC
PETROLAGE	PEWHOLDERS*	PHALANXES	PHASIC	PHENOLICS*
PETROLAGES	PEWIT	PHALAROPE	PHASING	PHENOLOGIES
PETROLEUM	PEWITS	PHALAROPES	PHASIS	PHENOLOGY
PETROLEUMS	PEWS	PHALLI	PHASMID	PHENOLS
PETROLEUR	PEWTER	PHALLIC	PHASMIDS	PHENOM
PETROLEURS	PEWTERER	PHALLIN	PHAT	PHENOMENA
PETROLIC	PEWTERERS	PHALLINS	PHATIC	PHENOMENAS*
PETROLLED	PEWTERS	PHALLISM	PHATTER	PHENOMENON*
PETROLLING	PEYOTE	PHALLISMS	PHATTEST	PHENOMENONS*
PETROLOGIES	PEYOTES	PHALLIST*	PHEASANT	PHENOMS
PETROLOGY	PEYOTISM	PHALLISTS*	PHEASANTS	PHENOTYPE
PETROLS	PEYOTISMS	PHALLOID	PHEAZAR	PHENOTYPED
PETRONEL	PEYOTIST	PHALLUS	PHEAZARS	PHENOTYPES
PETRONELS	PEYOTISTS	PHALLUSES	PHEER	PHENOTYPING
PETROSAL	PEYOTL*	PHANG	PHEERE	PHENOXIDE*
PETROSALS	PEYOTLS*	PHANGED	PHEERES	PHENOXIDES*
PETROUS	PEYSE	PHANGING	PHEERS	PHENOXY*
PETS	PEYSED	PHANGS	PHEESE	PHENYL
PETSAI*	PEYSES	PHANSIGAR	PHEESED	PHENYLIC
PETSAIS*	PEYSING	PHANSIGARS	PHEESES	PHENYLS
PETTED	PEYTRAL*	PHANTASIED	PHEESING	PHENYTOIN*
PETTEDLY	PEYTRALS*	PHANTASIES	PHEEZE	PHENYTOINS*
PETTER	PEYTREL*	PHANTASIM	PHEEZED	PHEON
PETTERS	PEYTRELS*	PHANTASIMS	PHEEZES	PHEONS
PETTI*	PEZANT	PHANTASM	PHEEZING	PHEROMONE
PETTICOAT	PEZANTS	PHANTASMA	PHELLEM	PHEROMONES
PETTICOATS	PEZIZOID	PHANTASMATA	PHELLEMS	PHESE
PETTIER	PFENNIG	PHANTASMS	PHELLOGEN	PHESED
PETTIES	PFENNIGE	PHANTAST*	PHELLOGENS	PHESES
PETTIEST	PFENNIGS	PHANTASTS*	PHELLOID	PHESING
PETTIFOG	PFENNING	PHANTASY	PHELONIA*	PHEW
PETTIFOGGED	PFENNINGS	PHANTASYING	PHELONION	PHI
PETTIFOGGING	PFFT*	PHANTOM	PHELONIONS	PHIAL
PETTIFOGGINGS	PFUI*	PHANTOMS	PHENACITE	PHIALLED
PETTIFOGS	PH	PHANTOMY	PHENACITES	PHIALLING
PETTILY	PHACELIA	PHANTOSME	PHENAKISM	PHIALS
PETTINESS	PHACELIAS	PHANTOSMES	PHENAKISMS	PHILABEG
PETTINESSES	PHACOID	PHARAOH*	PHENAKITE	PHILABEGS
PETTING	PHACOIDAL	PHARAOHS*	PHENAKITES	PHILAMOT
PETTINGS	PHACOLITE	PHARAONIC	PHENATE	PHILAMOTS
PETTISH	PHACOLITES	PHARE	PHENATES	PHILANDER
PETTISHLY	PHACOLITH	PHARES	PHENAZIN*	PHILANDERED
PETTITOES	PHACOLITHS	PHARISAIC	PHENAZINE*	PHILANDERING
PETTLE	PHAEIC	PHARISEE*	PHENAZINES*	PHILANDERS
PETTLED	PHAEISM	PHARISEES*	PHENAZINS*	PHILATELIES
PETTLES	PHAEISMS	PHARMACIES	PHENE	PHILATELY
PETTLING	PHAENOGAM	PHARMACY	PHENES	PHILHORSE
PETTO*	PHAENOGAMS	PHAROS	PHENETIC	PHILHORSES
PETTY	PHAETON	PHAROSES	PHENETICS	PHILIBEG
PETULANCE	PHAETONS	PHARYNGAL	PHENETOL*	PHILIBEGS
PETULANCES	PHAGE	PHARYNGES	PHENETOLS*	PHILIPPIC
PETULANCIES	PHAGEDENA	PHARYNX	PHENGITE	PHILIPPICS
PETULANCY	PHAGEDENAS	PHARYNXES	PHENGITES	PHILISTIA*
PETULANT	PHAGES	PHASE	PHENIC	PHILLABEG
PETUNIA	PHAGOCYTE	PHASEAL*	PHENIX*	PHILLABEGS
PETUNIAS	PHAGOCYTES	PHASED	PHENIXES*	PHILLIBEG
PETUNTSE	PHALANGAL	PHASEDOWN*	PHENOCOPIES*	PHILLIBEGS
PETUNTSES	PHALANGE	PHASEDOWNS*	PHENOCOPY*	PHILOGYNIES

Words marked with an asterisk are from OTCWL

PHILOGYNY	PHOCINE	PHONOLITE	PHOTOCOPYINGS	PHRASAL
PHILOLOGIES	PHOEBE	PHONOLITES	PHOTOED	PHRASALLY*
PHILOLOGY	PHOEBES	PHONOLOGIES	PHOTOFIT	PHRASE
PHILOMATH	PHOEBUS*	PHONOLOGY	PHOTOFITS	PHRASED
PHILOMATHS	PHOEBUSES*	PHONON	PHOTOG*	PHRASEMAN
PHILOMEL*	PHOENIX	PHONONS	PHOTOGEN	PHRASEMEN
PHILOMELS*	PHOENIXES	PHONOPORE	PHOTOGENE	PHRASER
PHILOMOT	PHOH	PHONOPORES	PHOTOGENES	PHRASERS
PHILOMOTS	PHOHS	PHONOS*	PHOTOGENIES	PHRASES
PHILOPENA	PHOLADES	PHONOTYPE	PHOTOGENS	PHRASIER
PHILOPENAS	PHOLAS	PHONOTYPED	PHOTOGENY	PHRASIEST
PHILTER	PHON	PHONOTYPES	PHOTOGRAM	PHRASING
PHILTERED*	PHONAL	PHONOTYPIES	PHOTOGRAMS	PHRASINGS
PHILTERING*	PHONATE	PHONOTYPING	PHOTOGS*	PHRASY
PHILTERS	PHONATED	PHONOTYPY	PHOTOING	PHRATRAL*
PHILTRA*	PHONATES	PHONS	PHOTOLYSE	PHRATRIC*
PHILTRE	PHONATING	PHONY	PHOTOLYSED	PHRATRIES
PHILTRED*	PHONATION	PHONYING	PHOTOLYSES	PHRATRY
PHILTRES	PHONATIONS	PHOOEY	PHOTOLYSING	PHREAK
PHILTRING*	PHONATORY	PHORATE*	PHOTOLYZE*	PHREAKING
PHILTRUM*	PHONE	PHORATES*	PHOTOLYZED*	PHREAKINGS
PHIMOSES	PHONECARD	PHORMINGES	PHOTOLYZES*	PHREAKS
PHIMOSIS	PHONECARDS	PHORMINX	PHOTOLYZING*	PHREATIC
PHIMOTIC*	PHONED	PHORMIUM	PHOTOMAP*	PHRENESES
PHINNOCK	PHONEME	PHORMIUMS	PHOTOMAPPED*	PHRENESIS
PHINNOCKS	PHONEMES	PHORONID*	PHOTOMAPPING*	PHRENETIC
PHIS	PHONEMIC	PHORONIDS*	PHOTOMAPS*	PHRENETICS
PHISNOMIES	PHONEMICS	PHOS	PHOTOMASK*	PHRENIC
PHISNOMY	PHONER	PHOSGENE	PHOTOMASKS*	PHRENISM
PHIZ	PHONERS	PHOSGENES	PHOTON	PHRENISMS
PHIZES*	PHONES	PHOSPHATE	PHOTONIC*	PHRENITIC
PHIZOG	PHONETIC	PHOSPHATED	PHOTONICS	PHRENITIS
PHIZOGS	PHONETICS	PHOSPHATES	PHOTONS	PHRENITISES
PHIZZES	PHONETISE	PHOSPHATING	PHOTOPHIL	PHRENSIED
PHLEBITIDES*	PHONETISED	PHOSPHENE	PHOTOPHILS	PHRENSIES
PHLEBITIS	PHONETISES	PHOSPHENES	PHOTOPIA	PHRENSY
PHLEBITISES	PHONETISING	PHOSPHID*	PHOTOPIAS	PHRENSYING
PHLEGM	PHONETISM	PHOSPHIDE	PHOTOPIC	PHRENTICK
PHLEGMIER	PHONETISMS	PHOSPHIDES	PHOTOPLAY*	PHS
PHLEGMIEST	PHONETIST	PHOSPHIDS*	PHOTOPLAYS*	PHT*
PHLEGMON	PHONETISTS	PHOSPHIN*	PHOTOPSIA	PHTHALATE
PHLEGMONS	PHONETIZE	PHOSPHINE	PHOTOPSIAS	PHTHALATES
PHLEGMS	PHONETIZED	PHOSPHINES	PHOTOPSIES	PHTHALEIN
PHLEGMY	PHONETIZES	PHOSPHINS*	PHOTOPSY	PHTHALEINS
PHLOEM	PHONETIZING	PHOSPHITE	PHOTOS	PHTHALIC
PHLOEMS	PHONEY	PHOSPHITES	PHOTOSET*	PHTHALIN
PHLOMIS	PHONEYED	PHOSPHOR	PHOTOSETS*	PHTHALINS
PHLOMISES	PHONEYING	PHOSPHORE*	PHOTOSETTING*	PHTHISES
PHLOX	PHONEYS	PHOSPHORES*	PHOTOSTAT*	PHTHISIC
PHLOXES	PHONIC	PHOSPHORS	PHOTOSTATED*	PHTHISICS
PHLYCTENA	PHONICS	PHOT	PHOTOSTATING*	PHTHISIS
PHLYCTENAE	PHONIED	PHOTIC	PHOTOSTATS*	PHUT
PHO	PHONIER	PHOTICS	PHOTOSTATTED*	PHUTS
PHOBIA	PHONIES	PHOTINIA	PHOTOSTATTING*	PHUTTED
PHOBIAS	PHONIEST	PHOTINIAS	PHOTOTUBE*	PHUTTING
PHOBIC	PHONILY*	PHOTISM	PHOTOTUBES*	PHYCOCYAN
PHOBICS	PHONINESS	PHOTISMS	PHOTOTYPE	PHYCOCYANS
PHOBISM	PHONINESSES	PHOTO	PHOTOTYPED	PHYCOLOGIES
PHOBISMS	PHONING	PHOTOCELL	PHOTOTYPES	PHYCOLOGY
PHOBIST	PHONMETER	PHOTOCELLS	PHOTOTYPIES	PHYLA
PHOBISTS	PHONMETERS	PHOTOCOPIED	PHOTOTYPING	PHYLAE
PHOCA	PHONO*	PHOTOCOPIES	PHOTOTYPY	PHYLAR*
PHOCAE	PHONOGRAM	PHOTOCOPY	PHOTS	PHYLARCH
PHOCAS	PHONOGRAMS	PHOTOCOPYING	PHPHT*	PHYLARCHIES

The Chambers Dictionary is the authority for many longer words; see Introduction, page ix

PHYLARCHS	PHYTOL*	PIBROCHS	PICKBACK	PICOLINS*
PHYLARCHY	PHYTOLOGIES	PIC	PICKBACKS	PICOMOLE*
PHYLAXIS*	PHYTOLOGY	PICA	PICKED	PICOMOLES*
PHYLAXISES*	PHYTOLS*	PICACHO*	PICKEER	PICOT
PHYLE	PHYTON	PICACHOS*	PICKEERED	PICOTE
PHYLESES*	PHYTONIC*	PICADOR	PICKEERER	PICOTED
PHYLESIS*	PHYTONS	PICADORES*	PICKEERERS	PICOTEE
PHYLESISES*	PHYTOSES	PICADORS	PICKEERING	PICOTEES
PHYLETIC	PHYTOSIS	PICAL*	PICKEERS	PICOTING
PHYLIC*	PHYTOTOMIES	PICAMAR	PICKER	PICOTITE
PHYLLARIES	PHYTOTOMY	PICAMARS	PICKEREL	PICOTITES
PHYLLARY	PHYTOTRON	PICANINNIES*	PICKERELS	PICOTS
PHYLLITE	PHYTOTRONS	PICANINNY*	PICKERIES	PICQUET
PHYLLITES	PI	PICARA*	PICKERS	PICQUETED
PHYLLO	PIA	PICARAS*	PICKERY	PICQUETING
PHYLLODE	PIACEVOLE	PICARIAN	PICKET	PICQUETS
PHYLLODES	PIACULAR	PICARIANS	PICKETED	PICRA
PHYLLODIA*	PIAFFE	PICARO*	PICKETER	PICRAS
PHYLLODIES	PIAFFED	PICAROON	PICKETERS	PICRATE
PHYLLODIUM*	PIAFFER	PICAROONED*	PICKETING	PICRATED*
PHYLLODY	PIAFFERS	PICAROONING*	PICKETS	PICRATES
PHYLLOID	PIAFFES	PICAROONS	PICKIER	PICRIC
PHYLLOIDS*	PIAFFING	PICAROS*	PICKIEST	PICRITE
PHYLLOME	PIAL*	PICAS	PICKING	PICRITES
PHYLLOMES	PIAN*	PICAYUNE	PICKINGS	PICRITIC*
PHYLLOPOD	PIANETTE	PICAYUNES	PICKLE	PICS
PHYLLOPODS	PIANETTES	PICCADELL	PICKLED	PICTARNIE
PHYLLOS	PIANIC*	PICCADELLS	PICKLER	PICTARNIES
PHYLOGENIES	PIANINO	PICCADILL	PICKLERS	PICTOGRAM
PHYLOGENY	PIANINOS	PICCADILLS	PICKLES	PICTOGRAMS
PHYLON*	PIANISM	PICCANIN	PICKLING	PICTORIAL
PHYLUM	PIANISMS	PICCANINS	PICKLOCK	PICTORIALS
PHYSALIA	PIANIST	PICCIES	PICKLOCKS	PICTURAL
PHYSALIAS	PIANISTE	PICCOLO	PICKMAW	PICTURALS
PHYSALIS	PIANISTES	PICCOLOS	PICKMAWS	PICTURE
PHYSALISES	PIANISTIC	PICCY	PICKOFF*	PICTURED
PHYSED*	PIANISTS	PICE	PICKOFFS*	PICTURES
PHYSEDS*	PIANO	PICENE	PICKPROOF*	PICTURING
PHYSES*	PIANOLIST	PICENES	PICKS	PICTURIZE*
PHYSETER	PIANOLISTS	PICEOUS	PICKTHANK*	PICTURIZED*
PHYSETERS	PIANOS	PICHURIM	PICKTHANKS*	PICTURIZES*
PHYSIC	PIANS*	PICHURIMS	PICKUP*	PICTURIZING*
PHYSICAL	PIARIST	PICIFORM*	PICKUPS*	PICUL
PHYSICALS	PIARISTS	PICINE	PICKWICK*	PICULS
PHYSICIAN	PIAS	PICK	PICKWICKS*	PIDDLE
PHYSICIANS	PIASABA*	PICKABACK	PICKY	PIDDLED
PHYSICISM	PIASABAS*	PICKABACKED*	PICLORAM*	PIDDLER
PHYSICISMS	PIASAVA*	PICKABACKING*	PICLORAMS*	PIDDLERS
PHYSICIST	PIASAVAS*	PICKABACKS	PICNIC	PIDDLES
PHYSICISTS	PIASSABA	PICKADELL	PICNICKED	PIDDLING
PHYSICKED	PIASSABAS	PICKADELLS	PICNICKER	PIDDLY*
PHYSICKING	PIASSAVA	PICKADIL*	PICNICKERS	PIDDOCK
PHYSICKY	PIASSAVAS	PICKADILL	PICNICKING	PIDDOCKS
PHYSICS	PIASTER*	PICKADILLS	PICNICKY	PIDGEON
PHYSIO	PIASTERS*	PICKADILS*	PICNICS	PIDGEONS
PHYSIOS	PIASTRE	PICKAPACK	PICOCURIE	PIDGIN
PHYSIQUE	PIASTRES	PICKAPACKS	PICOCURIES	PIDGINIZE*
PHYSIQUES	PIAZZA	PICKAROON*	PICOFARAD*	PIDGINIZED*
PHYSIS*	PIAZZAS	PICKAROONS*	PICOFARADS*	PIDGINIZES*
PHYTANE*	PIAZZE*	PICKAX*	PICOGRAM*	PIDGINIZING*
PHYTANES*	PIAZZIAN	PICKAXE	PICOGRAMS*	PIDGINS
PHYTOGENIES	PIBAL*	PICKAXED*	PICOLIN*	PIE
PHYTOGENY	PIBALS*	PICKAXES	PICOLINE*	PIEBALD
PHYTOID*	PIBROCH	PICKAXING*	PICOLINES*	PIEBALDS

PIECE	PIERT	PIGLET	PIKAKE*	PILFERED
PIECED	PIES	PIGLETS	PIKAKES*	PILFERER
PIECELESS	PIET	PIGLIKE*	PIKAS	PILFERERS
PIECEMEAL	PIETA	PIGLING	PIKE	PILFERIES
PIECEMEALED	PIETAS	PIGLINGS	PIKED	PILFERING
PIECEMEALING	PIETIES	PIGMAEAN	PIKELET	PILFERINGS
PIECEMEALS	PIETISM	PIGMEAN	PIKELETS	PILFERS
PIECEN	PIETISMS	PIGMEAT	PIKEMAN	PILFERY
PIECENED	PIETIST	PIGMEATS	PIKEMEN	PILGARLIC*
PIECENER	PIETISTIC	PIGMENT	PIKER	PILGARLICS*
PIECENERS	PIETISTS	PIGMENTAL	PIKERS	PILGRIM
PIECENING	PIETS	PIGMENTED	PIKES	PILGRIMER
PIECENS	PIETY	PIGMENTING*	PIKESTAFF	PILGRIMERS
PIECER	PIEZO	PIGMENTS	PIKESTAFFS	PILGRIMS
PIECERS	PIFFERARI	PIGMIES	PIKESTAVES*	PILHORSE
PIECES	PIFFERARO	PIGMOID	PIKI*	PILHORSES
PIECEWISE*	PIFFERO	PIGMY	PIKING	PILI
PIECEWORK*	PIFFEROS	PIGNERATE	PIKIS*	PILIFORM
PIECEWORKS*	PIFFLE	PIGNERATED	PIKUL	PILING
PIECING	PIFFLED	PIGNERATES	PIKULS	PILINGS
PIECINGS*	PIFFLER	PIGNERATING	PILA	PILIS
PIECRUST	PIFFLERS	PIGNOLI*	PILAF*	PILL
PIECRUSTS	PIFFLES	PIGNOLIA*	PILAFF	PILLAGE
PIED	PIFFLING	PIGNOLIAS*	PILAFFS	PILLAGED
PIEDFORT*	PIG	PIGNOLIS*	PILAFS*	PILLAGER
PIEDFORTS*	PIGBOAT	PIGNORA*	PILAR*	PILLAGERS
PIEDISH	PIGBOATS	PIGNORATE	PILASTER	PILLAGES
PIEDISHES	PIGEON	PIGNORATED	PILASTERS	PILLAGING
PIEDMONT	PIGEONED	PIGNORATES	PILAU	PILLAR
PIEDMONTS	PIGEONING	PIGNORATING	PILAUS	PILLARED*
PIEDNESS	PIGEONITE*	PIGNUS*	PILAW	PILLARING*
PIEDNESSES	PIGEONITES*	PIGNUT	PILAWS	PILLARIST
PIEFORT*	PIGEONRIES	PIGNUTS	PILCH	PILLARISTS
PIEFORTS*	PIGEONRY	PIGOUT*	PILCHARD	PILLARS
PIEING	PIGEONS	PIGOUTS*	PILCHARDS	PILLAU
PIEMAN	PIGFEED	PIGPEN	PILCHER	PILLAUS
PIEMEN	PIGFEEDS	PIGPENS	PILCHERS	PILLBOX*
PIEND	PIGFISH*	PIGS	PILCHES	PILLBOXES*
PIENDS	PIGFISHES*	PIGSCONCE	PILCORN	PILLED
PIEPLANT*	PIGGED	PIGSCONCES	PILCORNS	PILLHEAD
PIEPLANTS*	PIGGERIES	PIGSKIN	PILCROW	PILLHEADS
PIEPOWDER	PIGGERY	PIGSKINS	PILCROWS	PILLICOCK
PIEPOWDERS	PIGGIE	PIGSNEY	PILE	PILLICOCKS
PIER	PIGGIER	PIGSNEYS	PILEA	PILLING
PIERAGE	PIGGIES	PIGSNIE	PILEATE	PILLINGS
PIERAGES	PIGGIEST	PIGSNIES	PILEATED	PILLION
PIERCE	PIGGIN	PIGSNY	PILED	PILLIONED
PIERCED	PIGGING	PIGSTICK*	PILEI	PILLIONING
PIERCER	PIGGINGS	PIGSTICKED*	PILELESS*	PILLIONS
PIERCERS	PIGGINS	PIGSTICKING*	PILEOUS	PILLOCK
PIERCES	PIGGISH	PIGSTICKS*	PILER	PILLOCKS
PIERCING	PIGGISHLY	PIGSTIES	PILERS	PILLORIED
PIERCINGS	PIGGY	PIGSTY	PILES	PILLORIES
PIERID	PIGGYBACK	PIGSWILL	PILEUM	PILLORISE
PIERIDINE	PIGGYBACKED*	PIGSWILLS	PILEUP*	PILLORISED
PIERIDS	PIGGYBACKING*	PIGTAIL	PILEUPS*	PILLORISES
PIEROGI*	PIGGYBACKS	PIGTAILED*	PILEUS	PILLORISING
PIEROGIES*	PIGHEADED	PIGTAILS	PILEWORK	PILLORIZE
PIERRETTE	PIGHT	PIGWASH	PILEWORKS	PILLORIZED
PIERRETTES	PIGHTED	PIGWASHES	PILEWORT	PILLORIZES
PIERROT	PIGHTING	PIGWEED	PILEWORTS	PILLORIZING
PIERROTS	PIGHTLE	PIGWEEDS	PILFER	PILLORY
PIERS	PIGHTLES	PIING*	PILFERAGE	PILLORYING
PIERST	PIGHTS	PIKA	PILFERAGES	PILLOW

The Chambers Dictionary is the authority for many longer words; see Introduction, page ix

PILLOWED	PINAFORES	PINES	PINKERS*	PINOCHLE
PILLOWING	PINAKOID	PINESAP*	PINKERTON	PINOCHLES
PILLOWS	PINAKOIDS	PINESAPS*	PINKERTONS	PINOCLE
PILLOWY	PINANG*	PINETA	PINKEST	PINOCLES
PILLS	PINANGS*	PINETUM	PINKEY*	PINOCYTIC*
PILLWORM	PINAS	PINEWOOD	PINKEYE*	PINOLE
PILLWORMS	PINASTER	PINEWOODS	PINKEYES*	PINOLES
PILLWORT	PINASTERS	PINEY	PINKEYS*	PINON
PILLWORTS	PINATA	PINFISH	PINKIE	PINONES*
PILOSE	PINATAS	PINFISHES	PINKIER	PINONS
PILOSITIES	PINBALL	PINFOLD	PINKIES	PINOT
PILOSITY	PINBALLS	PINFOLDED	PINKIEST	PINOTS
PILOT	PINBONE*	PINFOLDING	PINKINESS	PINPOINT
PILOTAGE	PINBONES*	PINFOLDS	PINKINESSES	PINPOINTED
PILOTAGES	PINCASE	PING	PINKING	PINPOINTING
PILOTED	PINCASES	PINGED	PINKINGS	PINPOINTS
PILOTING	PINCER	PINGER	PINKISH	PINPRICK*
PILOTINGS*	PINCERED	PINGERS	PINKLY*	PINPRICKED*
PILOTIS	PINCERING	PINGING	PINKNESS	PINPRICKING*
PILOTLESS	PINCERS	PINGLE	PINKNESSES	PINPRICKS*
PILOTMAN	PINCH	PINGLED	PINKO	PINS
PILOTMEN	PINCHBECK	PINGLER	PINKOES	PINSCHER*
PILOTS	PINCHBECKS	PINGLERS	PINKOS	PINSCHERS*
PILOUS	PINCHBUG*	PINGLES	PINKROOT	PINSETTER*
PILOW	PINCHBUGS*	PINGLING	PINKROOTS	PINSETTERS*
PILOWS	PINCHCOCK	PINGO	PINKS	PINSTRIPE*
PILSENER	PINCHCOCKS	PINGOES	PINKY	PINSTRIPES*
PILSENERS	PINCHECK*	PINGOS	PINNA	PINT
PILSNER	PINCHECKS*	PINGRASS*	PINNACE	PINTA
PILSNERS	PINCHED	PINGRASSES*	PINNACES	PINTABLE
PILULA	PINCHER	PINGS	PINNACLE	PINTABLES
PILULAR	PINCHERS	PINGUEFIED	PINNACLED	PINTADA*
PILULAS	PINCHES	PINGUEFIES	PINNACLES	PINTADAS*
PILULE	PINCHFIST	PINGUEFY	PINNACLING	PINTADO
PILULES	PINCHFISTS	PINGUEFYING	PINNAE	PINTADOES*
PILUM	PINCHGUT	PINGUID	PINNAL*	PINTADOS
PILUS	PINCHGUTS	PINGUIN	PINNAS*	PINTAIL
PILY*	PINCHING	PINGUINS	PINNATE	PINTAILED
PIMA*	PINCHINGS	PINHEAD	PINNATED	PINTAILS
PIMAS*	PINDAREE	PINHEADED*	PINNATELY	PINTANO*
PIMENT	PINDAREES	PINHEADS	PINNED	PINTANOS*
PIMENTO	PINDARI	PINHOLE	PINNER	PINTAS
PIMENTOS	PINDARIS	PINHOLES	PINNERS	PINTLE
PIMENTS	PINDER	PINHOOKER	PINNET	PINTLES
PIMIENTO	PINDERS	PINHOOKERS	PINNETS	PINTO
PIMIENTOS	PINDLING*	PINIER	PINNIE	PINTOES*
PIMP	PINDOWN	PINIES	PINNIES	PINTOS
PIMPED	PINDOWNS	PINIEST	PINNING	PINTS
PIMPERNEL	PINE	PINING	PINNINGS	PINTSIZE*
PIMPERNELS	PINEAL	PINION	PINNIPED	PINUP*
PIMPING	PINEALS*	PINIONED	PINNIPEDE	PINUPS*
PIMPLE	PINEAPPLE	PINIONING	PINNIPEDES	PINWALE*
PIMPLED	PINEAPPLES	PINIONS	PINNIPEDS	PINWALES*
PIMPLES	PINECONE*	PINITE	PINNOCK	PINWEED*
PIMPLIER	PINECONES*	PINITES	PINNOCKS	PINWEEDS*
PIMPLIEST	PINED	PINITOL*	PINNOED	PINWHEEL*
PIMPLY	PINEDROPS*	PINITOLS*	PINNULA	PINWHEELED*
PIMPS	PINELAND*	PINK	PINNULAE*	PINWHEELING*
PIN	PINELANDS*	PINKED	PINNULAR*	PINWHEELS*
PINA	PINELIKE*	PINKEN*	PINNULAS	PINWORK*
PINACOID	PINENE*	PINKENED*	PINNULATE	PINWORKS*
PINACOIDS	PINENES*	PINKENING*	PINNULE	PINWORM*
PINAFORE	PINERIES	PINKENS*	PINNULES	PINWORMS*
PINAFORED	PINERY	PINKER	PINNY	PINXIT

Words marked with an asterisk are from OTCWL

PINY	PIPERS	PIRANA	PISES	PITARAHS
PINYIN*	PIPES	PIRANAS	PISH	PITARAS
PINYON*	PIPESTEM*	PIRANHA	PISHED	PITAS
PINYONS*	PIPESTEMS*	PIRANHAS	PISHES	PITCH
PIOLET	PIPESTONE	PIRARUCU	PISHING	PITCHED
PIOLETS	PIPESTONES	PIRARUCUS	PISHOGE*	PITCHER
PION	PIPET*	PIRATE	PISHOGES*	PITCHERS
PIONED	PIPETS*	PIRATED	PISHOGUE	PITCHES
PIONEER	PIPETTE	PIRATES	PISHOGUES	PITCHFORK
PIONEERED	PIPETTED	PIRATIC	PISIFORM	PITCHFORKED
PIONEERING	PIPETTES	PIRATICAL	PISIFORMS	PITCHFORKING
PIONEERS	PIPETTING	PIRATING	PISKIES	PITCHFORKS
PIONER	PIPEWORK	PIRAYA	PISKY	PITCHIER
PIONERS	PIPEWORKS	PIRAYAS	PISMIRE	PITCHIEST
PIONEY	PIPEWORT	PIRIFORM*	PISMIRES	PITCHILY*
PIONEYS	PIPEWORTS	PIRL	PISO*	PITCHING
PIONIC	PIPI	PIRLICUE	PISOLITE	PITCHINGS
PIONIES	PIPIER	PIRLICUED	PISOLITES	PITCHMAN
PIONING	PIPIEST	PIRLICUES	PISOLITIC	PITCHMEN
PIONINGS	PIPINESS*	PIRLICUING	PISOS*	PITCHOUT*
PIONS	PIPINESSES*	PIRLS	PISS	PITCHOUTS*
PIONY	PIPING	PIRN	PISSANT*	PITCHPINE
PIOSITIES*	PIPINGLY*	PIRNIE	PISSANTS*	PITCHPINES
PIOSITY*	PIPINGS	PIRNIES	PISSED	PITCHPIPE
PIOTED	PIPIS	PIRNIT	PISSER*	PITCHPIPES
PIOUS	PIPIT	PIRNS	PISSERS*	PITCHPOLE*
PIOUSLY	PIPITS	PIROG*	PISSES	PITCHPOLED*
PIOUSNESS*	PIPKIN	PIROGEN*	PISSHEAD	PITCHPOLES*
PIOUSNESSES*	PIPKINS	PIROGHI*	PISSHEADS	PITCHPOLING*
PIOY	PIPLESS	PIROGI*	PISSING	PITCHY
PIOYE	PIPPED	PIROGIES*	PISSOIR	PITEOUS
PIOYES	PIPPIER	PIROGUE	PISSOIRS	PITEOUSLY
PIOYS	PIPPIEST	PIROGUES	PISTACHE*	PITFALL
PIP	PIPPIN	PIROJKI*	PISTACHES*	PITFALLS
PIPA	PIPPING	PIROPLASM*	PISTACHIO	PITH
PIPAGE	PIPPINS	PIROPLASMS*	PISTACHIOS	PITHBALL
PIPAGES	PIPPY	PIROQUE*	PISTAREEN	PITHBALLS
PIPAL	PIPS	PIROQUES*	PISTAREENS	PITHEAD
PIPALS	PIPSQUEAK	PIROSHKI	PISTE	PITHEADS
PIPAS	PIPSQUEAKS	PIROUETTE	PISTES	PITHECOID
PIPE	PIPUL	PIROUETTED	PISTIL	PITHED
PIPEAGE*	PIPULS	PIROUETTES	PISTILS	PITHFUL
PIPEAGES*	PIPY	PIROUETTING	PISTOL	PITHIER
PIPECLAY	PIQUANCE*	PIROZHKI	PISTOLE	PITHIEST
PIPECLAYED	PIQUANCES*	PIROZHOK*	PISTOLED*	PITHILY
PIPECLAYING	PIQUANCIES	PIRS	PISTOLEER	PITHINESS
PIPECLAYS	PIQUANCY	PIS	PISTOLEERS	PITHINESSES
PIPED	PIQUANT	PISCARIES	PISTOLES	PITHING
PIPEFISH	PIQUANTLY	PISCARY	PISTOLET	PITHLESS
PIPEFISHES	PIQUE	PISCATOR	PISTOLETS	PITHLIKE
PIPEFUL	PIQUED	PISCATORS	PISTOLING*	PITHOI
PIPEFULS	PIQUES	PISCATORY	PISTOLLED	PITHOS
PIPELESS	PIQUET	PISCATRIX	PISTOLLING	PITHS
PIPELIKE	PIQUETED	PISCATRIXES	PISTOLS	PITHY
PIPELINE	PIQUETING	PISCIFORM	PISTON	PITIABLE
PIPELINED*	PIQUETS	PISCINA	PISTONS	PITIABLY
PIPELINES	PIQUING	PISCINAE	PIT	PITIED
PIPELINING*	PIR	PISCINAL*	PITA	PITIER
PIPER	PIRACIES	PISCINAS	PITAPAT	PITIERS
PIPERIC	PIRACY	PISCINE	PITAPATS	PITIES
PIPERINE	PIRAGUA	PISCINES	PITAPATTED	PITIFUL
PIPERINES	PIRAGUAS	PISCO*	PITAPATTING	PITIFULLER*
PIPERONAL	PIRAI	PISCOS*	PITARA	PITIFULLEST*
PIPERONALS	PIRAIS	PISE	PITARAH	PITIFULLY

The Chambers Dictionary is the authority for many longer words; see Introduction, page ix

PITILESS	PIXINESS*	PLACETS	PLAINNESSES	PLANISH
PITMAN	PIXINESSES*	PLACID	PLAINS	PLANISHED
PITMANS*	PIXY	PLACIDER	PLAINSMAN	PLANISHER
PITMEN	PIXYISH*	PLACIDEST	PLAINSMEN	PLANISHERS
PITON	PIZAZZ	PLACIDITIES	PLAINSONG	PLANISHES
PITONS	PIZAZZES	PLACIDITY	PLAINSONGS	PLANISHING
PITPROP	PIZAZZY*	PLACIDLY	PLAINT	PLANK
PITPROPS	PIZE	PLACING	PLAINTEXT*	PLANKED
PITS	PIZES	PLACINGS	PLAINTEXTS*	PLANKING
PITSAW*	PIZZA	PLACIT	PLAINTFUL	PLANKINGS
PITSAWS*	PIZZAIOLA	PLACITA	PLAINTIFF	PLANKS
PITTA	PIZZALIKE*	PLACITORY	PLAINTIFFS	PLANKTER*
PITTANCE	PIZZAS	PLACITS	PLAINTIVE	PLANKTERS*
PITTANCES	PIZZERIA	PLACITUM	PLAINTS	PLANKTON
PITTAS	PIZZERIAS	PLACK	PLAINWORK	PLANKTONS
PITTED	PIZZICATI*	PLACKET	PLAINWORKS	PLANLESS
PITTEN	PIZZICATO	PLACKETS	PLAISTER	PLANNED
PITTER	PIZZICATOS	PLACKLESS	PLAISTERED*	PLANNER
PITTERED	PIZZLE	PLACKS	PLAISTERING*	PLANNERS
PITTERING	PIZZLES	PLACODERM	PLAISTERS	PLANNING
PITTERS	PLACABLE	PLACODERMS	PLAIT	PLANNINGS
PITTING	PLACABLY	PLACOID	PLAITED	PLANOSOL*
PITTINGS	PLACARD	PLACOIDS*	PLAITER	PLANOSOLS*
PITTITE	PLACARDED	PLAFOND	PLAITERS	PLANS
PITTITES	PLACARDING	PLAFONDS	PLAITING	PLANT
PITUITA	PLACARDS	PLAGAL	PLAITINGS	PLANTA
PITUITARIES*	PLACATE	PLAGE	PLAITS	PLANTABLE
PITUITARY	PLACATED	PLAGES	PLAN	PLANTAGE
PITUITAS	PLACATER*	PLAGIARIES	PLANAR	PLANTAGES
PITUITE	PLACATERS*	PLAGIARY	PLANARIA*	PLANTAIN
PITUITES	PLACATES	PLAGIUM	PLANARIAN	PLANTAINS
PITUITRIN	PLACATING	PLAGIUMS	PLANARIANS	PLANTAR
PITUITRINS	PLACATION	PLAGUE	PLANARIAS*	PLANTAS
PITURI	PLACATIONS	PLAGUED	PLANARITIES*	PLANTED
PITURIS	PLACATIVE*	PLAGUER*	PLANARITY*	PLANTER
PITY	PLACATORY	PLAGUERS*	PLANATE*	PLANTERS
PITYING	PLACCAT	PLAGUES	PLANATION	PLANTING
PITYINGLY	PLACCATE	PLAGUEY	PLANATIONS	PLANTINGS
PITYROID	PLACCATES	PLAGUIER	PLANCH	PLANTLESS
PIU	PLACCATS	PLAGUIEST	PLANCHE*	PLANTLET
PIUM	PLACE	PLAGUILY	PLANCHED	PLANTLETS
PIUMS	PLACEABLE*	PLAGUING	PLANCHES	PLANTLIKE*
PIUPIU	PLACEBO	PLAGUY	PLANCHET	PLANTLING
PIUPIUS	PLACEBOES	PLAICE	PLANCHETS	PLANTLINGS
PIVOT	PLACEBOS	PLAICES	PLANCHING	PLANTS
PIVOTABLE*	PLACED	PLAID	PLANE	PLANTSMAN
PIVOTAL	PLACEKICK*	PLAIDED	PLANED	PLANTSMEN
PIVOTALLY	PLACEKICKED*	PLAIDING	PLANELOAD*	PLANTULE
PIVOTED	PLACEKICKING*	PLAIDINGS	PLANELOADS*	PLANTULES
PIVOTER	PLACEKICKS*	PLAIDMAN	PLANER	PLANULA
PIVOTERS	PLACELESS	PLAIDMEN	PLANERS	PLANULAE
PIVOTING	PLACEMAN	PLAIDS	PLANES	PLANULAR
PIVOTINGS	PLACEMEN	PLAIN	PLANET	PLANULOID
PIVOTMAN*	PLACEMENT	PLAINANT	PLANETARY	PLANURIA
PIVOTMEN*	PLACEMENTS	PLAINANTS	PLANETIC	PLANURIAS
PIVOTS	PLACENTA	PLAINED	PLANETOID	PLANURIES
PIX	PLACENTAE	PLAINER	PLANETOIDS	PLANURY
PIXEL	PLACENTAL	PLAINEST	PLANETS	PLANXTIES
PIXELS	PLACENTALS	PLAINFUL	PLANFORM*	PLANXTY
PIXES	PLACENTAS	PLAINING	PLANFORMS*	PLAP
PIXIE	PLACER	PLAININGS	PLANGENCIES	PLAPPED
PIXIEISH*	PLACERS	PLAINISH	PLANGENCY	PLAPPING
PIXIES	PLACES	PLAINLY	PLANGENT	PLAPS
PIXILATED	PLACET	PLAINNESS	PLANING	PLAQUE

Words marked with an asterisk are from OTCWL

PLAQUES
PLAQUETTE
PLAQUETTES
PLASH
PLASHED
PLASHER*
PLASHERS*
PLASHES
PLASHET
PLASHETS
PLASHIER
PLASHIEST
PLASHING
PLASHINGS
PLASHY
PLASM
PLASMA
PLASMAGEL*
PLASMAGELS*
PLASMAS
PLASMASOL*
PLASMASOLS*
PLASMATIC
PLASMIC
PLASMID
PLASMIDS
PLASMIN
PLASMINS
PLASMODIA
PLASMODIUM*
PLASMOID*
PLASMOIDS*
PLASMON*
PLASMONS*
PLASMS
PLAST
PLASTE
PLASTER
PLASTERED
PLASTERER
PLASTERERS
PLASTERING
PLASTERINGS
PLASTERS
PLASTERY
PLASTIC
PLASTICKY
PLASTICS
PLASTID
PLASTIDS
PLASTIQUE
PLASTIQUES
PLASTISOL
PLASTISOLS
PLASTRAL
PLASTRON
PLASTRONS
PLASTRUM*
PLASTRUMS*
PLAT
PLATAN
PLATANE
PLATANES
PLATANNA

PLATANNAS
PLATANS
PLATBAND
PLATBANDS
PLATE
PLATEASM
PLATEASMS
PLATEAU
PLATEAUED
PLATEAUING
PLATEAUS
PLATEAUX
PLATED
PLATEFUL
PLATEFULS
PLATELET
PLATELETS
PLATELIKE*
PLATEMAN
PLATEMARK
PLATEMARKS
PLATEMEN
PLATEN
PLATENS
PLATER
PLATERS
PLATES
PLATESFUL*
PLATFORM
PLATFORMED
PLATFORMING
PLATFORMINGS
PLATFORMS
PLATIER
PLATIES*
PLATIEST
PLATINA
PLATINAS
PLATING
PLATINGS
PLATINIC
PLATINISE
PLATINISED
PLATINISES
PLATINISING
PLATINIZE
PLATINIZED
PLATINIZES
PLATINIZING
PLATINOID
PLATINOIDS
PLATINOUS
PLATINUM
PLATINUMS
PLATITUDE
PLATITUDES
PLATONIC
PLATONICS
PLATOON
PLATOONED*
PLATOONING*
PLATOONS
PLATS
PLATTED

PLATTER
PLATTERS
PLATTING
PLATTINGS
PLATY
PLATYFISH*
PLATYFISHES*
PLATYPI*
PLATYPUS
PLATYPUSES
PLATYS*
PLATYSMA
PLATYSMAS
PLAUDIT
PLAUDITE
PLAUDITS
PLAUSIBLE
PLAUSIBLY
PLAUSIVE
PLAUSTRAL
PLAY
PLAYA
PLAYABLE
PLAYACT*
PLAYACTED*
PLAYACTING*
PLAYACTS*
PLAYAS
PLAYBACK
PLAYBACKS
PLAYBILL
PLAYBILLS
PLAYBOOK
PLAYBOOKS
PLAYBOY
PLAYBOYS
PLAYBUS
PLAYBUSES
PLAYBUSSES
PLAYDATE*
PLAYDATES*
PLAYDAY*
PLAYDAYS*
PLAYDOWN*
PLAYDOWNS*
PLAYED
PLAYER
PLAYERS
PLAYFIELD*
PLAYFIELDS*
PLAYFUL
PLAYFULLY
PLAYGIRL
PLAYGIRLS
PLAYGOER*
PLAYGOERS*
PLAYGROUP
PLAYGROUPS
PLAYHOUSE
PLAYHOUSES
PLAYING
PLAYLAND*
PLAYLANDS*
PLAYLESS*

PLAYLET
PLAYLETS
PLAYLIKE*
PLAYLIST*
PLAYLISTS*
PLAYMAKER*
PLAYMAKERS*
PLAYMATE
PLAYMATES
PLAYOFF*
PLAYOFFS*
PLAYPEN
PLAYPENS
PLAYROOM
PLAYROOMS
PLAYS
PLAYSOME
PLAYSUIT
PLAYSUITS
PLAYTHING
PLAYTHINGS
PLAYTIME
PLAYTIMES
PLAYWEAR*
PLAZA
PLAZAS
PLEA
PLEACH
PLEACHED
PLEACHES
PLEACHING
PLEAD
PLEADABLE
PLEADED
PLEADER
PLEADERS
PLEADING
PLEADINGS
PLEADS
PLEAED
PLEAING
PLEAS
PLEASANCE
PLEASANCES
PLEASANT
PLEASANTER
PLEASANTEST
PLEASE
PLEASED
PLEASEMAN
PLEASEMEN
PLEASER
PLEASERS
PLEASES
PLEASETH
PLEASING
PLEASINGS
PLEASURE
PLEASURED
PLEASURER
PLEASURERS
PLEASURES
PLEASURING
PLEAT

PLEATED
PLEATER
PLEATERS
PLEATING
PLEATLESS*
PLEATS
PLEB
PLEBBIER
PLEBBIEST
PLEBBY
PLEBE*
PLEBEAN
PLEBEIAN
PLEBEIANS
PLEBES
PLEBIFIED
PLEBIFIES
PLEBIFY
PLEBIFYING
PLEBS
PLECTRA
PLECTRE
PLECTRES
PLECTRON
PLECTRONS
PLECTRUM
PLECTRUMS
PLED
PLEDGE
PLEDGED
PLEDGEE
PLEDGEES
PLEDGEOR
PLEDGEORS
PLEDGER
PLEDGERS
PLEDGES
PLEDGET
PLEDGETS
PLEDGING
PLEDGOR
PLEDGORS
PLEIAD*
PLEIADES*
PLEIADS*
PLEIOMERIES
PLEIOMERY
PLENA
PLENARILY
PLENARTIES
PLENARTY
PLENARY
PLENCH*
PLENCHES*
PLENILUNE
PLENILUNES
PLENIPO
PLENIPOES
PLENIPOS
PLENISH
PLENISHED
PLENISHES
PLENISHING
PLENISHINGS

The Chambers Dictionary is the authority for many longer words; see Introduction, page ix

PLENISM*	PLIANCIES	PLODDERS	PLOUGHER	PLUGGED
PLENISMS*	PLIANCY	PLODDING	PLOUGHERS	PLUGGER
PLENIST	PLIANT	PLODDINGS	PLOUGHING	PLUGGERS
PLENISTS	PLIANTLY	PLODS	PLOUGHINGS	PLUGGING
PLENITUDE	PLICA	PLOIDIES	PLOUGHMAN	PLUGGINGS
PLENITUDES	PLICAE	PLOIDY	PLOUGHMEN	PLUGLESS*
PLENTEOUS	PLICAL	PLONG	PLOUGHS	PLUGOLA*
PLENTIES	PLICATE	PLONGD	PLOUK	PLUGOLAS*
PLENTIFUL	PLICATED	PLONGE	PLOUKIE	PLUGS
PLENTY	PLICATELY	PLONGED	PLOUKIER	PLUGUGLIES*
PLENUM	PLICATES	PLONGES	PLOUKIEST	PLUGUGLY*
PLENUMS	PLICATING	PLONGING	PLOUKS	PLUM
PLEON	PLICATION	PLONGS	PLOUTER	PLUMAGE
PLEONASM	PLICATIONS	PLONK	PLOUTERED	PLUMAGED
PLEONASMS	PLICATURE	PLONKED	PLOUTERING	PLUMAGES
PLEONAST	PLICATURES	PLONKER	PLOUTERS	PLUMATE
PLEONASTE	PLIE	PLONKERS	PLOVER	PLUMB
PLEONASTES	PLIED	PLONKIER	PLOVERS	PLUMBAGO
PLEONASTS	PLIER	PLONKIEST	PLOVERY	PLUMBAGOS
PLEONEXIA	PLIERS	PLONKING	PLOW	PLUMBATE
PLEONEXIAS	PLIES	PLONKINGS	PLOWABLE*	PLUMBATES
PLEONS	PLIGHT	PLONKS	PLOWBACK*	PLUMBED
PLEOPOD	PLIGHTED	PLONKY	PLOWBACKS*	PLUMBEOUS
PLEOPODS	PLIGHTER	PLOOK	PLOWBOY*	PLUMBER
PLEROMA	PLIGHTERS	PLOOKIE	PLOWBOYS*	PLUMBERIES
PLEROMAS	PLIGHTFUL	PLOOKIER	PLOWED	PLUMBERS
PLEROME	PLIGHTING	PLOOKIEST	PLOWER*	PLUMBERY
PLEROMES	PLIGHTS	PLOOKS	PLOWERS*	PLUMBIC
PLESH	PLIM	PLOP	PLOWHEAD*	PLUMBING
PLESHES	PLIMMED	PLOPPED	PLOWHEADS*	PLUMBINGS
PLESSOR	PLIMMING	PLOPPING	PLOWING	PLUMBISM
PLESSORS	PLIMS	PLOPS	PLOWLAND*	PLUMBISMS
PLETHORA	PLIMSOL*	PLOSION	PLOWLANDS*	PLUMBITE
PLETHORAS	PLIMSOLE	PLOSIONS	PLOWMAN*	PLUMBITES
PLETHORIC	PLIMSOLES	PLOSIVE	PLOWMEN*	PLUMBLESS
PLEUCH	PLIMSOLL	PLOSIVES	PLOWS	PLUMBOUS
PLEUCHS	PLIMSOLLS	PLOT	PLOWSHARE*	PLUMBS
PLEUGH	PLIMSOLS*	PLOTFUL	PLOWSHARES*	PLUMBUM
PLEUGHS	PLING	PLOTLESS	PLOWTER	PLUMBUMS
PLEURA	PLINGS	PLOTLINE*	PLOWTERED	PLUMCOT
PLEURAE	PLINK	PLOTLINES*	PLOWTERING	PLUMCOTS
PLEURAL	PLINKED	PLOTS	PLOWTERS	PLUMDAMAS
PLEURAS*	PLINKER*	PLOTTAGE*	PLOY	PLUMDAMASES
PLEURISIES	PLINKERS*	PLOTTAGES*	PLOYED*	PLUME
PLEURISY	PLINKING	PLOTTED	PLOYING*	PLUMED
PLEURITIC	PLINKS	PLOTTER	PLOYS	PLUMELESS
PLEURITICS	PLINTH	PLOTTERED	PLUCK	PLUMELET
PLEURITIS	PLINTHS	PLOTTERING	PLUCKED	PLUMELETS
PLEURITISES	PLIOSAUR	PLOTTERS	PLUCKER	PLUMERIA*
PLEURON	PLIOSAURS	PLOTTIE	PLUCKERS	PLUMERIAS*
PLEUSTON*	PLIOTRON*	PLOTTIER*	PLUCKIER	PLUMERIES
PLEUSTONS*	PLIOTRONS*	PLOTTIES	PLUCKIEST	PLUMERY
PLEW*	PLISKIE	PLOTTIEST*	PLUCKILY	PLUMES
PLEWS*	PLISKIES	PLOTTING	PLUCKING	PLUMIER
PLEXAL*	PLISKY*	PLOTTINGS	PLUCKS	PLUMIEST
PLEXIFORM	PLISSE	PLOTTY	PLUCKY	PLUMING
PLEXOR	PLISSES*	PLOTZ*	PLUFF	PLUMIPED
PLEXORS	PLOAT	PLOTZED*	PLUFFED	PLUMIPEDS*
PLEXURE	PLOATED	PLOTZES*	PLUFFIER	PLUMIST
PLEXURES	PLOATING	PLOTZING*	PLUFFIEST	PLUMISTS
PLEXUS	PLOATS	PLOUGH	PLUFFING	PLUMLIKE*
PLEXUSES	PLOD	PLOUGHBOY	PLUFFS	PLUMMET
PLIABLE	PLODDED	PLOUGHBOYS	PLUFFY	PLUMMETED
PLIABLY	PLODDER	PLOUGHED	PLUG	PLUMMETING

PLUMMETS	PLURALIZE	PNEUMATICS	PODAGRAS	POESY
PLUMMIER	PLURALIZED	PNEUMONIA	PODAGRIC	POESYING
PLUMMIEST	PLURALIZES	PNEUMONIAS	PODAGROUS	POET
PLUMMY	PLURALIZING	PNEUMONIC	PODAL	POETASTER
PLUMOSE	PLURALLY	PNEUMONICS	PODALIC	POETASTERS
PLUMOUS	PLURALS	PO	PODARGUS	POETASTRIES
PLUMP	PLURIPARA	POA	PODARGUSES	POETASTRY
PLUMPED	PLURIPARAE	POACEOUS	PODDED	POETESS
PLUMPEN	PLURIPARAS	POACH	PODDIER	POETESSES
PLUMPENED	PLURISIE	POACHED	PODDIES	POETIC
PLUMPENING	PLURISIES	POACHER	PODDIEST	POETICAL
PLUMPENS	PLUS	POACHERS	PODDING	POETICALS
PLUMPER	PLUSAGE	POACHES	PODDY	POETICISE
PLUMPERS	PLUSAGES	POACHIER	PODESTA	POETICISED
PLUMPEST	PLUSED	POACHIEST	PODESTAS	POETICISES
PLUMPIE	PLUSES	POACHING	PODEX	POETICISING
PLUMPIER	PLUSH	POACHINGS	PODEXES	POETICISM
PLUMPIEST	PLUSHER	POACHY	PODGE	POETICISMS
PLUMPING	PLUSHES	POAKA	PODGES	POETICIZE
PLUMPISH	PLUSHEST	POAKAS	PODGIER	POETICIZED
PLUMPLY	PLUSHIER	POAKE	PODGIEST	POETICIZES
PLUMPNESS	PLUSHIEST	POAKES	PODGILY*	POETICIZING
PLUMPNESSES	PLUSHILY*	POAS	PODGINESS	POETICS
PLUMPS	PLUSHLY*	POCHARD	PODGINESSES	POETICULE
PLUMPY	PLUSHNESS*	POCHARDS	PODGY	POETICULES
PLUMS	PLUSHNESSES*	POCHAY	PODIA	POETISE
PLUMULA	PLUSHY	POCHAYS	PODIAL	POETISED
PLUMULAE	PLUSING	POCHETTE	PODIATRIC*	POETISER*
PLUMULAR	PLUSSAGE	POCHETTES	PODIATRIES	POETISERS*
PLUMULATE	PLUSSAGES	POCHOIR	PODIATRY	POETISES
PLUMULE	PLUSSED	POCHOIRS	PODITE	POETISING
PLUMULES	PLUSSES	POCK	PODITES	POETIZE
PLUMULOSE	PLUSSING	POCKARD	PODITIC*	POETIZED
PLUMY	PLUTEAL	POCKARDS	PODIUM	POETIZER*
PLUNDER	PLUTEI*	POCKED	PODIUMS*	POETIZERS*
PLUNDERED	PLUTEUS	POCKET	PODLEY	POETIZES
PLUNDERER	PLUTEUSES	POCKETED	PODLEYS	POETIZING
PLUNDERERS	PLUTOCRAT	POCKETER*	PODLIKE*	POETLESS*
PLUNDERING	PLUTOCRATS	POCKETERS*	PODOCARP	POETLIKE*
PLUNDERS	PLUTOLOGIES	POCKETFUL	PODOCARPS	POETRESSE
PLUNGE	PLUTOLOGY	POCKETFULS	PODOLOGIES	POETRESSES
PLUNGED	PLUTON	POCKETING	PODOLOGY	POETRIES
PLUNGER	PLUTONIAN*	POCKETS	PODOMERE*	POETRY
PLUNGERS	PLUTONIC	POCKETSFUL*	PODOMERES*	POETS
PLUNGES	PLUTONIUM	POCKIER	PODS	POETSHIP
PLUNGING	PLUTONIUMS	POCKIEST	PODSOL	POETSHIPS
PLUNGINGS	PLUTONOMIES	POCKILY*	PODSOLIC	POFFLE
PLUNK	PLUTONOMY	POCKING*	PODSOLS	POFFLES
PLUNKED	PLUTONS	POCKMANKIES	PODZOL	POGEY*
PLUNKER	PLUVIAL	POCKMANKY	PODZOLIC*	POGEYS*
PLUNKERS	PLUVIALS	POCKMARK	PODZOLIZE*	POGGE
PLUNKING	PLUVIAN*	POCKMARKED*	PODZOLIZED*	POGGES
PLUNKS	PLUVIOSE	POCKMARKING*	PODZOLIZES*	POGIES*
PLURAL	PLUVIOUS	POCKMARKS	PODZOLIZING*	POGO
PLURALISE	PLY	POCKPIT	PODZOLS	POGOED
PLURALISED	PLYER*	POCKPITS	POECHORE*	POGOING
PLURALISES	PLYERS*	POCKS	POECHORES*	POGONIA*
PLURALISING	PLYING	POCKY	POEM	POGONIAS*
PLURALISM	PLYINGLY*	POCO	POEMATIC	POGONIP*
PLURALISMS	PLYWOOD	POCOSIN*	POEMS	POGONIPS*
PLURALIST	PLYWOODS	POCOSINS*	POENOLOGIES	POGOS
PLURALISTS	PNEUMA	POD	POENOLOGY	POGROM
PLURALITIES	PNEUMAS	PODAGRA	POESIED	POGROMED*
PLURALITY	PNEUMATIC	PODAGRAL	POESIES	POGROMING*

The Chambers Dictionary is the authority for many longer words; see Introduction, page ix

POGROMIST*	POISSON	POLECATS	POLITICKED	POLLOCK
POGROMISTS*	POISSONS	POLED	POLITICKING	POLLOCKS
POGROMS	POITREL	POLEIS*	POLITICKINGS	POLLS
POGY*	POITRELS	POLELESS*	POLITICKS	POLLSTER
POH	POKAL	POLEMARCH	POLITICLY	POLLSTERS
POI	POKALS	POLEMARCHS	POLITICO	POLLUSION
POIGNADO	POKE	POLEMIC	POLITICOES	POLLUSIONS
POIGNADOES	POKEBERRIES	POLEMICAL	POLITICOS	POLLUTANT
POIGNANCE*	POKEBERRY	POLEMICS	POLITICS	POLLUTANTS
POIGNANCES*	POKED	POLEMISE	POLITIES	POLLUTE
POIGNANCIES	POKEFUL	POLEMISED	POLITIQUE	POLLUTED
POIGNANCY	POKEFULS	POLEMISES	POLITIQUES	POLLUTER
POIGNANT	POKER	POLEMISING	POLITY	POLLUTERS
POILU	POKERISH	POLEMIST	POLK	POLLUTES
POILUS	POKEROOT*	POLEMISTS	POLKA	POLLUTING
POINADO	POKEROOTS*	POLEMIZE	POLKAED*	POLLUTION
POINADOES	POKERS	POLEMIZED	POLKAING*	POLLUTIONS
POINCIANA	POKES	POLEMIZES	POLKAS	POLLUTIVE
POINCIANAS	POKEWEED	POLEMIZING	POLKED	POLLY
POIND	POKEWEEDS	POLENTA	POLKING	POLLYANNA
POINDED	POKEY	POLENTAS	POLKS	POLLYANNAS
POINDER	POKEYS	POLER	POLL	POLLYWIG
POINDERS	POKIER	POLERS	POLLACK	POLLYWIGS
POINDING	POKIES	POLES	POLLACKS	POLLYWOG
POINDINGS	POKIEST	POLESTAR*	POLLAN	POLLYWOGS
POINDS	POKILY*	POLESTARS*	POLLANS	POLO
POINT	POKINESS*	POLEWARD*	POLLARD	POLOIDAL
POINTE	POKINESSES*	POLEY	POLLARDED	POLOIST
POINTED	POKING	POLEYN	POLLARDING	POLOISTS
POINTEDLY	POKY	POLEYNS	POLLARDS	POLONAISE
POINTEL	POL*	POLEYS	POLLED	POLONAISES
POINTELLE*	POLACCA	POLIANITE	POLLEE*	POLONIE
POINTELLES*	POLACCAS	POLIANITES	POLLEES*	POLONIES
POINTELS	POLACRE	POLICE	POLLEN	POLONISE
POINTER	POLACRES	POLICED	POLLENED	POLONISED
POINTERS	POLAR	POLICEMAN	POLLENING	POLONISES
POINTES	POLARISE	POLICEMEN	POLLENS	POLONISING
POINTIER	POLARISED	POLICES	POLLENT	POLONISM
POINTIEST	POLARISER	POLICIES	POLLER	POLONISMS
POINTILLE	POLARISERS	POLICING	POLLERS	POLONIUM
POINTING	POLARISES	POLICY	POLLEX	POLONIUMS
POINTINGS	POLARISING	POLING	POLLICAL	POLONIZE
POINTLESS	POLARITIES	POLINGS	POLLICES	POLONIZED
POINTMAN*	POLARITY	POLIO	POLLICIE	POLONIZES
POINTMEN*	POLARIZE	POLIOS	POLLICIES	POLONIZING
POINTS	POLARIZED	POLIS*	POLLICY	POLONY
POINTSMAN	POLARIZER	POLISH	POLLIES	POLOS
POINTSMEN	POLARIZERS	POLISHED	POLLINATE	POLS*
POINTY	POLARIZES	POLISHER	POLLINATED	POLT
POIS	POLARIZING	POLISHERS	POLLINATES	POLTED
POISE	POLARON	POLISHES	POLLINATING	POLTFEET
POISED	POLARONS	POLISHING	POLLING	POLTFOOT
POISER	POLARS	POLISHINGS	POLLINGS	POLTING
POISERS	POLDER	POLITBURO*	POLLINIA	POLTROON
POISES	POLDERED	POLITBUROS*	POLLINIC	POLTROONS
POISHA*	POLDERING	POLITE	POLLINIUM	POLTS
POISING	POLDERS	POLITELY	POLLIST*	POLVERINE
POISON	POLE	POLITER	POLLISTS*	POLVERINES
POISONED	POLEAX*	POLITESSE	POLLIWIG	POLY
POISONER	POLEAXE*	POLITESSES	POLLIWIGS	POLYACID
POISONERS	POLEAXED*	POLITEST	POLLIWOG	POLYACT
POISONING	POLEAXES*	POLITIC	POLLIWOGS	POLYAMIDE
POISONOUS	POLEAXING*	POLITICAL	POLLMAN	POLYAMIDES
POISONS	POLECAT	POLITICK	POLLMEN	POLYAMINE*

POLYAMINES*	POLYMER	POLYSEME	POMMELLING	PONDERATING
POLYANDRIES	POLYMERIC	POLYSEMES	POMMELS	PONDERED
POLYANDRY	POLYMERIES	POLYSEMIES	POMMETTY	PONDERER
POLYANTHA*	POLYMERS	POLYSEMY	POMMIE*	PONDERERS
POLYANTHAS*	POLYMERY	POLYSOME	POMMIES	PONDERING
POLYANTHI*	POLYMORPH	POLYSOMES	POMMY	PONDEROSA*
POLYANTHUS*	POLYMORPHS	POLYSOMIES	POMOERIUM	PONDEROSAS*
POLYANTHUSES*	POLYMYXIN*	POLYSOMY	POMOERIUMS	PONDEROUS
POLYARCH	POLYMYXINS*	POLYSTYLE	POMOLOGIES	PONDERS
POLYARCHIES	POLYNIA	POLYTENE	POMOLOGY	PONDING
POLYARCHY	POLYNIAS	POLYTENIES*	POMP	PONDOK
POLYAXIAL	POLYNYA	POLYTENY*	POMPADOUR	PONDOKKIE
POLYAXIALS	POLYNYAS	POLYTHENE	POMPADOURS	PONDOKKIES
POLYAXON	POLYNYI*	POLYTHENES	POMPANO	PONDOKS
POLYAXONS	POLYOMA	POLYTONAL	POMPANOS	PONDS
POLYBASIC	POLYOMAS	POLYTYPE*	POMPELO	PONDWEED
POLYBRID*	POLYOMINO	POLYTYPES*	POMPELOS	PONDWEEDS
POLYBRIDS*	POLYOMINOS	POLYTYPIC	POMPEY	PONE
POLYCONIC	POLYONYM	POLYURIA	POMPEYED	PONENT
POLYCOT*	POLYONYMIES	POLYURIAS	POMPEYING	PONES
POLYCOTS*	POLYONYMS	POLYURIC*	POMPEYS	PONEY
POLYENE*	POLYONYMY	POLYVINYL	POMPHOLYX	PONEYS
POLYENES*	POLYP	POLYVINYLS	POMPHOLYXES	PONG
POLYENIC*	POLYPARIES	POLYWATER	POMPIER	PONGA
POLYESTER	POLYPARY	POLYWATERS	POMPION	PONGAS
POLYESTERS	POLYPE	POLYZOA	POMPIONS	PONGED
POLYGALA	POLYPES	POLYZOAN	POMPOM	PONGEE
POLYGALAS	POLYPHAGIES	POLYZOANS	POMPOMS	PONGEES
POLYGAM	POLYPHAGY	POLYZOARIES	POMPON	PONGID
POLYGAMIC	POLYPHASE	POLYZOARY	POMPONS	PONGIDS
POLYGAMIES	POLYPHON	POLYZOIC	POMPOON	PONGIER
POLYGAMS	POLYPHONE	POLYZONAL	POMPOONS	PONGIEST
POLYGAMY	POLYPHONES	POLYZOOID	POMPOSITIES	PONGING
POLYGENE	POLYPHONIES	POLYZOON	POMPOSITY	PONGO
POLYGENES	POLYPHONS	POM	POMPOUS	PONGOES
POLYGENIC	POLYPHONY	POMACE	POMPOUSLY	PONGOS
POLYGENIES	POLYPI	POMACEOUS	POMPS	PONGS
POLYGENY	POLYPIDE	POMACES	POMROY	PONGY
POLYGLOT	POLYPIDES	POMADE	POMROYS	PONIARD
POLYGLOTS	POLYPIDOM	POMADED	POMS	PONIARDED
POLYGLOTT	POLYPIDOMS	POMADES	POMWATER	PONIARDING
POLYGLOTTS	POLYPINE	POMADING	POMWATERS	PONIARDS
POLYGON	POLYPITE	POMANDER	PONCE	PONIED
POLYGONAL	POLYPITES	POMANDERS	PONCEAU	PONIES
POLYGONIES	POLYPLOID	POMATO	PONCEAUS	PONK
POLYGONS	POLYPLOIDS*	POMATOES	PONCEAUX	PONKED
POLYGONUM	POLYPNEA*	POMATUM	PONCED	PONKING
POLYGONUMS	POLYPNEAS*	POMATUMS	PONCES	PONKS
POLYGONY	POLYPOD	POMBE	PONCEY	PONS
POLYGRAPH	POLYPODIES	POMBES	PONCHO	PONT
POLYGRAPHS	POLYPODS	POME	PONCHOS	PONTAGE
POLYGYNIES	POLYPODY	POMELO	PONCIER	PONTAGES
POLYGYNY	POLYPOID	POMELOS	PONCIEST	PONTAL
POLYHEDRA	POLYPORE*	POMEROY	PONCING	PONTES
POLYHEDRON*	POLYPORES*	POMEROYS	PONCY	PONTIANAC
POLYHEDRONS*	POLYPOSES	POMES	POND	PONTIANACS
POLYLEMMA	POLYPOSIS	POMFRET	PONDAGE	PONTIANAK
POLYLEMMAS	POLYPOUS	POMFRETS	PONDAGES	PONTIANAKS
POLYMASTIES	POLYPS	POMMEE*	PONDED	PONTIC
POLYMASTY	POLYPTYCH	POMMEL	PONDER	PONTIE
POLYMATH	POLYPTYCHS	POMMELE	PONDERAL	PONTIES
POLYMATHIES	POLYPUS	POMMELED*	PONDERATE	PONTIFEX
POLYMATHS	POLYPUSES*	POMMELING*	PONDERATED	PONTIFF
POLYMATHY	POLYS	POMMELLED	PONDERATES	PONTIFFS

The Chambers Dictionary is the authority for many longer words; see Introduction, page ix

PONTIFIC	POOJAHS	POPADUM	POPPLY	PORK
PONTIFICE	POOJAS	POPADUMS	POPPY	PORKER
PONTIFICES	POOK	POPCORN	POPPYCOCK	PORKERS
PONTIFIED	POOKA	POPCORNS	POPPYCOCKS	PORKIER
PONTIFIES	POOKAS	POPE	POPPYHEAD*	PORKIES
PONTIFY	POOKING	POPEDOM	POPPYHEADS*	PORKIEST
PONTIFYING	POOKIT	POPEDOMS	POPRIN	PORKLING
PONTIL	POOKS	POPEHOOD	POPRINS	PORKLINGS
PONTILE	POOL	POPEHOODS	POPS	PORKPIE*
PONTILES	POOLED	POPELESS*	POPSIE*	PORKPIES*
PONTILS	POOLHALL*	POPELIKE*	POPSIES	PORKS
PONTINE*	POOLHALLS*	POPELING	POPSY	PORKWOOD*
PONTLEVIS	POOLING	POPELINGS	POPULACE	PORKWOODS*
PONTLEVISES	POOLROOM*	POPERIES	POPULACES	PORKY
PONTON	POOLROOMS*	POPERIN	POPULAR	PORN
PONTONEER	POOLS	POPERINS	POPULARLY	PORNIER*
PONTONEERS	POOLSIDE	POPERY	POPULARS	PORNIEST*
PONTONIER	POOLSIDES	POPES	POPULATE	PORNO
PONTONIERS	POON	POPESHIP	POPULATED	PORNOMAG
PONTONS	POONAC	POPESHIPS	POPULATES	PORNOMAGS
PONTOON	POONACS	POPEYED*	POPULATING	PORNOS
PONTOONED	POONCE	POPGUN*	POPULISM	PORNS
PONTOONER	POONCES	POPGUNS*	POPULISMS	PORNY*
PONTOONERS	POONS	POPINJAY	POPULIST	POROGAMIC
PONTOONING	POONTANG	POPINJAYS	POPULISTS	POROGAMIES
PONTOONS	POONTANGS	POPISH	POPULOUS	POROGAMY
PONTS	POOP	POPISHLY	PORAL	POROMERIC
PONTY	POOPED	POPJOY	PORBEAGLE	POROSCOPE
PONY	POOPING	POPJOYED	PORBEAGLES	POROSCOPES
PONYING	POOPS	POPJOYING	PORCELAIN	POROSCOPIES
PONYSKIN	POOR	POPJOYS	PORCELAINS	POROSCOPY
PONYSKINS	POORER	POPLAR	PORCH	POROSE
PONYTAIL	POOREST	POPLARS	PORCHES	POROSES
PONYTAILS	POORHOUSE	POPLIN	PORCINE	POROSIS
POO	POORHOUSES	POPLINS	PORCINI*	POROSITIES
POOCH	POORI	POPLITEAL	PORCINO*	POROSITY
POOCHED*	POORIS	POPLITIC	PORCPISCE	POROUS
POOCHES	POORISH	POPOVER	PORCPISCES	POROUSLY*
POOCHING*	POORLIER	POPOVERS	PORCUPINE	PORPESS
POOD	POORLIEST	POPPA	PORCUPINES	PORPESSE
POODLE	POORLY	POPPADUM	PORE	PORPESSES
POODLES	POORNESS	POPPADUMS	PORED	PORPHYRIA
POODS	POORNESSES	POPPAS	PORER	PORPHYRIAS
POOED	POORT	POPPED	PORERS	PORPHYRIES
POOF	POORTITH	POPPER	PORES	PORPHYRIN
POOFIER	POORTITHS	POPPERING	PORGE	PORPHYRINS
POOFIEST	POORTS	POPPERINGS	PORGED	PORPHYRIO
POOFS	POORWILL	POPPERS	PORGES	PORPHYRIOS
POOFTAH	POORWILLS	POPPET	PORGIE	PORPHYRY
POOFTAHS	POOS	POPPETS	PORGIES	PORPOISE
POOFTER	POOT	POPPIED	PORGING	PORPOISED
POOFTERS	POOTED	POPPIER	PORGY	PORPOISES
POOFY	POOTER	POPPIES	PORIER	PORPOISING
POOGYE	POOTERS	POPPIEST	PORIEST	PORPORATE
POOGYEE	POOTING	POPPING	PORIFER	PORRECT
POOGYEES	POOTS	POPPISH	PORIFERAL	PORRECTED
POOGYES	POOVE	POPPIT	PORIFERAN	PORRECTING
POOH	POOVERIES	POPPITS	PORIFERS	PORRECTS
POOHED*	POOVERY	POPPLE	PORINESS	PORRENGER
POOHING*	POOVES	POPPLED	PORINESSES	PORRENGERS
POOHS*	POOVIER	POPPLES	PORING	PORRIDGE
POOING	POOVIEST	POPPLIER	PORISM	PORRIDGES
POOJA	POOVY	POPPLIEST	PORISMS	PORRIDGY*
POOJAH	POP	POPPLING	PORISTIC	PORRIGO

Words marked with an asterisk are from OTCWL

PORRIGOS	PORTIER	POSED	POSSIBLER*	POSTFACE
PORRINGER	PORTIERE	POSER	POSSIBLES	POSTFACES
PORRINGERS	PORTIERES	POSERS	POSSIBLEST*	POSTFAULT*
PORT	PORTIEST	POSES	POSSIBLY	POSTFIRE*
PORTA	PORTIGUE	POSEUR	POSSIE	POSTFIX
PORTABLE	PORTIGUES	POSEURS	POSSIES	POSTFIXED
PORTABLES	PORTING	POSEUSE	POSSING	POSTFIXES
PORTABLY*	PORTION	POSEUSES	POSSUM	POSTFIXING
PORTAGE	PORTIONED	POSEY	POSSUMED	POSTFORM*
PORTAGED*	PORTIONER	POSH	POSSUMING	POSTFORMED*
PORTAGES	PORTIONERS	POSHED	POSSUMS	POSTFORMING*
PORTAGING*	PORTIONING	POSHER	POST	POSTFORMS*
PORTAGUE	PORTIONS	POSHES	POSTAGE	POSTGAME*
PORTAGUES	PORTLAND	POSHEST	POSTAGES	POSTHASTE
PORTAL	PORTLANDS	POSHING	POSTAL	POSTHASTES
PORTALED*	PORTLAST	POSHLY	POSTALLY	POSTHEAT*
PORTALS	PORTLASTS	POSHNESS	POSTALS	POSTHEATS*
PORTANCE	PORTLESS*	POSHNESSES	POSTANAL*	POSTHOLE*
PORTANCES	PORTLIER	POSHTEEN	POSTAXIAL*	POSTHOLES*
PORTAPACK*	PORTLIEST	POSHTEENS	POSTBAG	POSTHORSE
PORTAPACKS*	PORTLY	POSIER	POSTBAGS	POSTHORSES
PORTAPAK*	PORTMAN	POSIES	POSTBASE*	POSTHOUSE
PORTAPAKS*	PORTMEN	POSIEST	POSTBOX	POSTHOUSES
PORTAS	PORTOISE	POSIGRADE	POSTBOXES	POSTICHE
PORTASES	PORTOISES	POSING	POSTBOY*	POSTICHES
PORTATE	PORTOLAN	POSINGLY	POSTBOYS*	POSTICOUS
PORTATILE	PORTOLANI	POSINGS	POSTBURN*	POSTIE
PORTATIVE	PORTOLANO	POSIT	POSTBUS	POSTIES
PORTATIVES	PORTOLANOS	POSITED	POSTBUSES	POSTIL
PORTED	PORTOLANS	POSITING	POSTBUSSES	POSTILION
PORTEND	PORTOUS	POSITION	POSTCARD	POSTILIONS
PORTENDED	PORTOUSES	POSITIONED	POSTCARDED	POSTILLED
PORTENDING	PORTRAIT	POSITIONING	POSTCARDING	POSTILLER
PORTENDS	PORTRAITED	POSITIONS	POSTCARDS	POSTILLERS
PORTENT	PORTRAITING	POSITIVE	POSTCAVA	POSTILLING
PORTENTS	PORTRAITS	POSITIVER*	POSTCAVAE	POSTILS
PORTEOUS	PORTRAY	POSITIVES	POSTCAVAL*	POSTIN*
PORTEOUSES	PORTRAYAL	POSITIVEST*	POSTCODE	POSTING
PORTER	PORTRAYALS	POSITON	POSTCODED	POSTINGS
PORTERAGE	PORTRAYED	POSITONS	POSTCODES	POSTINS*
PORTERAGES	PORTRAYER	POSITRON	POSTCODING	POSTIQUE*
PORTERED*	PORTRAYERS	POSITRONS	POSTCOUP*	POSTIQUES*
PORTERESS	PORTRAYING	POSITS	POSTCRASH*	POSTLUDE
PORTERESSES	PORTRAYS	POSNET	POSTDATE	POSTLUDES
PORTERING*	PORTREEVE	POSNETS	POSTDATED	POSTMAN
PORTERLY	PORTREEVES	POSOLOGIES	POSTDATES	POSTMARK
PORTERS	PORTRESS	POSOLOGY	POSTDATING	POSTMARKED*
PORTESS	PORTRESSES	POSS	POSTDIVE*	POSTMARKING*
PORTESSE	PORTS	POSSE	POSTDOC*	POSTMARKS
PORTESSES	PORTULACA	POSSED	POSTDOCS*	POSTMEN
PORTFOLIO	PORTULACAS	POSSER	POSTDRUG*	POSTNASAL
PORTFOLIOS	PORTULAN	POSSERS	POSTED	POSTNATAL
PORTHOLE	PORTULANS	POSSES	POSTEEN	POSTNATI
PORTHOLES	PORTY	POSSESS	POSTEENS	POSTORAL
PORTHORS	PORWIGGLE	POSSESSED	POSTER	POSTPAID*
PORTHORSES	PORWIGGLES	POSSESSES	POSTERED	POSTPONE
PORTHOS	PORY	POSSESSING	POSTERING	POSTPONED
PORTHOSES	POS	POSSESSOR	POSTERIOR	POSTPONER
PORTHOUSE	POSADA	POSSESSORS	POSTERIORS	POSTPONERS
PORTHOUSES	POSADAS	POSSET	POSTERITIES	POSTPONES
PORTICO	POSAUNE	POSSETED	POSTERITY	POSTPONING
PORTICOED	POSAUNES	POSSETING	POSTERN	POSTPOSE
PORTICOES	POSE	POSSETS	POSTERNS	POSTPOSED
PORTICOS	POSEABLE	POSSIBLE	POSTERS	POSTPOSES

POSTPOSING	POTBOILER*	POTHOUSES	POTTERING	POULDRES
POSTRACE*	POTBOILERS*	POTHUNTER*	POTTERINGS	POULDRON
POSTRIDER	POTBOILING*	POTHUNTERS*	POTTERS	POULDRONS
POSTRIDERS	POTBOILS*	POTICARIES	POTTERY	POULE
POSTRIOT*	POTBOY	POTICARY	POTTIER	POULES
POSTS	POTBOYS	POTICHE	POTTIES	POULP
POSTSHOW*	POTCH	POTICHES	POTTIEST	POULPE
POSTSYNC*	POTCHE	POTIN	POTTINESS	POULPES
POSTSYNCED*	POTCHED	POTING	POTTINESSES	POULPS
POSTSYNCING*	POTCHER	POTINS	POTTING	POULT
POSTSYNCS*	POTCHERS	POTION	POTTINGAR	POULTER
POSTTAX*	POTCHES	POTIONS	POTTINGARS	POULTERER
POSTTEEN*	POTCHING	POTLACH	POTTINGER	POULTERERS
POSTTEST*	POTE	POTLACHE*	POTTINGERS	POULTERS
POSTTESTS*	POTED	POTLACHES	POTTLE	POULTFEET
POSTTRIAL*	POTEEN	POTLATCH	POTTLES	POULTFOOT
POSTULANT	POTEENS	POTLATCHED*	POTTO	POULTICE
POSTULANTS	POTENCE	POTLATCHES	POTTOS	POULTICED
POSTULATA	POTENCES	POTLATCHING*	POTTS	POULTICES
POSTULATE	POTENCIES	POTLIKE*	POTTY	POULTICING
POSTULATED	POTENCY	POTLINE*	POTZER*	POULTRIES
POSTULATES	POTENT	POTLINES*	POTZERS*	POULTRY
POSTULATING	POTENTATE	POTLUCK*	POUCH	POULTS
POSTURAL	POTENTATES	POTLUCKS*	POUCHED	POUNCE
POSTURE	POTENTIAL	POTMAN	POUCHES	POUNCED
POSTURED	POTENTIALS	POTMEN	POUCHFUL	POUNCER*
POSTURER	POTENTISE	POTOMETER	POUCHFULS	POUNCERS*
POSTURERS	POTENTISED	POTOMETERS	POUCHIER	POUNCES
POSTURES	POTENTISES	POTOO	POUCHIEST	POUNCET
POSTURING	POTENTISING	POTOOS	POUCHING	POUNCETS
POSTURIST	POTENTIZE	POTOROO	POUCHY	POUNCHING
POSTURISTS	POTENTIZED	POTOROOS	POUDER	POUNCING
POSTWAR	POTENTIZES	POTPIE*	POUDERS	POUND
POSTWOMAN	POTENTIZING	POTPIES*	POUDRE	POUNDAGE
POSTWOMEN	POTENTLY	POTPOURRI	POUDRES	POUNDAGES
POSY	POTENTS	POTPOURRIS	POUF	POUNDAL
POT	POTES	POTS	POUFED	POUNDALS
POTABLE	POTFUL	POTSHARD	POUFF*	POUNDED
POTABLES	POTFULS	POTSHARDS	POUFFE	POUNDER
POTAGE	POTGUN	POTSHARE	POUFFED	POUNDERS
POTAGER	POTGUNS	POTSHARES	POUFFES	POUNDING
POTAGERS	POTHEAD*	POTSHERD	POUFFING	POUNDS
POTAGES	POTHEADS*	POTSHERDS	POUFFS*	POUPE
POTAMIC	POTHECARIES	POTSHOP	POUFING	POUPED
POTASH	POTHECARY	POTSHOPS	POUFS	POUPES
POTASHED	POTHEEN	POTSHOT*	POUFTAH	POUPING
POTASHES	POTHEENS	POTSHOTS*	POUFTAHS	POUPT
POTASHING	POTHER	POTSHOTTING*	POUFTER	POUR
POTASS	POTHERB*	POTSIE*	POUFTERS	POURABLE
POTASSA	POTHERBS*	POTSIES*	POUK	POURBOIRE
POTASSAS	POTHERED	POTSTONE	POUKE	POURBOIRES
POTASSES	POTHERING	POTSTONES	POUKES	POURED
POTASSIC	POTHERS	POTSY*	POUKING	POURER
POTASSIUM	POTHERY	POTT	POUKIT	POURERS
POTASSIUMS	POTHOLE	POTTAGE	POUKS	POURIE
POTATION	POTHOLED	POTTAGES	POULAINE	POURIES
POTATIONS	POTHOLER	POTTED	POULAINES	POURING
POTATO	POTHOLERS	POTTEEN*	POULARD	POURINGLY*
POTATOES	POTHOLES	POTTEENS*	POULARDE*	POURINGS
POTATORY	POTHOLING	POTTER	POULARDES*	POURPOINT
POTBELLIES*	POTHOLINGS	POTTERED	POULARDS	POURPOINTS
POTBELLY*	POTHOOK	POTTERER	POULDER	POURS
POTBOIL*	POTHOOKS	POTTERERS	POULDERS	POURSEW
POTBOILED*	POTHOUSE	POTTERIES	POULDRE	POURSEWED

POURSEWING	POWELLIZE	POYSONED	PRAESIDIUMS*	PRAOS*
POURSEWS	POWELLIZED	POYSONING	PRAETOR	PRASE
POURSUE	POWELLIZES	POYSONS	PRAETORS	PRASES
POURSUED	POWELLIZING	POZ	PRAGMATIC	PRAT
POURSUES	POWER	POZZ	PRAGMATICS	PRATE
POURSUING	POWERBOAT	POZZIES	PRAHU	PRATED
POURSUIT	POWERBOATS	POZZOLAN*	PRAHUS	PRATER
POURSUITS	POWERED	POZZOLANA	PRAIRIE	PRATERS
POURSUITT	POWERFUL	POZZOLANAS	PRAIRIED	PRATES
POURSUITTS	POWERING	POZZOLANS*	PRAIRIES	PRATFALL
POURTRAHED	POWERLESS	POZZY	PRAISE	PRATFALLEN
POURTRAY	POWERPLAY	PRAAM	PRAISEACH	PRATFALLING
POURTRAYD	POWERPLAYS	PRAAMS	PRAISEACHS	PRATFALLS
POURTRAYED	POWERS	PRABBLE	PRAISED	PRATFELL
POURTRAYING	POWIN	PRABBLES	PRAISEFUL	PRATIE
POURTRAYS	POWINS	PRACTIC	PRAISER	PRATIES
POUSOWDIE	POWN	PRACTICAL	PRAISERS	PRATING
POUSOWDIES	POWND	PRACTICALS	PRAISES	PRATINGLY
POUSSE	POWNDED	PRACTICE	PRAISING	PRATINGS
POUSSES	POWNDING	PRACTICED	PRAISINGS	PRATIQUE
POUSSETTE	POWNDS	PRACTICER*	PRALINE	PRATIQUES
POUSSETTED	POWNEY	PRACTICERS*	PRALINES	PRATS
POUSSETTES	POWNEYS	PRACTICES	PRAM	PRATT
POUSSETTING	POWNIE	PRACTICING	PRAMS	PRATTED
POUSSIE*	POWNIES	PRACTICK	PRANA	PRATTING
POUSSIES*	POWNS	PRACTICKS	PRANAS	PRATTLE
POUSSIN	POWNY	PRACTICS	PRANAYAMA	PRATTLED
POUSSINS	POWRE	PRACTICUM	PRANAYAMAS	PRATTLER
POUT	POWRED	PRACTICUMS	PRANCE	PRATTLERS
POUTED	POWRES	PRACTIQUE	PRANCED	PRATTLES
POUTER	POWRING	PRACTIQUES	PRANCER	PRATTLING
POUTERS	POWS	PRACTISE	PRANCERS	PRATTS
POUTFUL*	POWSOWDIES	PRACTISED	PRANCES	PRATY
POUTHER	POWSOWDY	PRACTISER	PRANCING	PRAU
POUTHERED	POWTER	PRACTISERS	PRANCINGS	PRAUNCE
POUTHERING	POWTERED	PRACTISES	PRANCK	PRAUNCED
POUTHERS	POWTERING	PRACTISING	PRANCKE	PRAUNCES
POUTIER	POWTERS	PRACTIVE	PRANCKED	PRAUNCING
POUTIEST	POWWAW	PRACTOLOL	PRANCKES	PRAUS
POUTING	POWWOW	PRACTOLOLS	PRANCKING	PRAVITIES
POUTINGLY	POWWOWED	PRAD	PRANCKS	PRAVITY
POUTINGS	POWWOWING	PRADS	PRANDIAL	PRAWLE
POUTS	POWWOWS	PRAEAMBLE	PRANG	PRAWLES
POUTY	POX	PRAEAMBLES	PRANGED	PRAWLIN
POVERTIES	POXED	PRAECAVA	PRANGING	PRAWLINS
POVERTY	POXES	PRAECAVAE	PRANGS	PRAWN
POW	POXIER	PRAECIPE*	PRANK	PRAWNED
POWAN	POXIEST	PRAECIPES*	PRANKED	PRAWNER*
POWANS	POXING	PRAECOCES	PRANKFUL	PRAWNERS*
POWDER	POXVIRUS	PRAEDIAL	PRANKIER	PRAWNING
POWDERED	POXVIRUSES	PRAEDIALS	PRANKIEST	PRAWNS
POWDERER*	POXY	PRAEFECT	PRANKING	PRAXES
POWDERERS*	POYNANT	PRAEFECTS	PRANKINGS	PRAXIS
POWDERIER	POYNT	PRAELECT*	PRANKISH	PRAXISES*
POWDERIEST	POYNTED	PRAELECTED*	PRANKLE	PRAY
POWDERING	POYNTING	PRAELECTING*	PRANKLED	PRAYED
POWDERS	POYNTS	PRAELECTS*	PRANKLES	PRAYER
POWDERY	POYOU*	PRAELUDIA	PRANKLING	PRAYERFUL
POWELLISE	POYOUS*	PRAENOMEN	PRANKS	PRAYERS
POWELLISED	POYSE	PRAENOMENS	PRANKSOME	PRAYING
POWELLISES	POYSED	PRAENOMINA	PRANKSTER	PRAYINGLY
POWELLISING	POYSES	PRAESES	PRANKSTERS	PRAYINGS
POWELLITE	POYSING	PRAESIDIA	PRANKY	PRAYS
POWELLITES	POYSON	PRAESIDIUM*	PRAO*	PRE

The Chambers Dictionary is the authority for many longer words; see Introduction, page ix

PREACE	PREATOMIC*	PRECENSORS*	PRECOCITY	PREDESIGNING
PREACED	PREAUDIT*	PRECENT*	PRECODE*	PREDESIGNS
PREACES	PREAUDITS*	PRECENTED*	PRECODED*	PREDEVOTE
PREACH	PREAVER*	PRECENTING*	PRECODES*	PREDIAL
PREACHED	PREAVERRED*	PRECENTOR	PRECODING*	PREDIALS
PREACHER	PREAVERRING*	PRECENTORS	PRECOITAL	PREDICANT
PREACHERS	PREAVERS*	PRECENTS*	PRECONISE	PREDICANTS
PREACHES	PREAXIAL*	PRECEPIT	PRECONISED	PREDICATE
PREACHIER	PREBAKE*	PRECEPITS	PRECONISES	PREDICATED
PREACHIEST	PREBAKED*	PRECEPT	PRECONISING	PREDICATES
PREACHIFIED	PREBAKES*	PRECEPTOR	PRECONIZE	PREDICATING
PREACHIFIES	PREBAKING*	PRECEPTORS	PRECONIZED	PREDICT
PREACHIFY	PREBASAL*	PRECEPTS	PRECONIZES	PREDICTED
PREACHIFYING	PREBATTLE*	PRECESS	PRECONIZING	PREDICTER
PREACHILY	PREBEND	PRECESSED	PRECOOK	PREDICTERS
PREACHING	PREBENDAL	PRECESSES	PRECOOKED	PREDICTING
PREACHINGS	PREBENDS	PRECESSING	PRECOOKING	PREDICTOR
PREACHY	PREBILL*	PRECHECK*	PRECOOKS	PREDICTORS
PREACING	PREBILLED*	PRECHECKED*	PRECOOL	PREDICTS
PREACT*	PREBILLING*	PRECHECKING*	PRECOOLED	PREDIED
PREACTED*	PREBILLS*	PRECHECKS*	PRECOOLING	PREDIES
PREACTING*	PREBIND*	PRECHILL*	PRECOOLS	PREDIGEST
PREACTS*	PREBINDING*	PRECHILLED*	PRECOUP*	PREDIGESTED
PREADAPT*	PREBINDS*	PRECHILLING*	PRECRASH*	PREDIGESTING
PREADAPTED*	PREBIOTIC	PRECHILLS*	PRECREASE*	PREDIGESTS
PREADAPTING*	PREBLESS*	PRECIEUSE	PRECREASED*	PREDIKANT
PREADAPTS*	PREBLESSED*	PRECIEUSES	PRECREASES*	PREDIKANTS
PREADMIT*	PREBLESSES*	PRECIEUX*	PRECREASING*	PREDILECT
PREADMITS*	PREBLESSING*	PRECINCT	PRECRISIS*	PREDINNER*
PREADMITTED*	PREBOIL*	PRECINCTS	PRECURE*	PREDIVE*
PREADMITTING*	PREBOILED*	PRECIOUS	PRECURED*	PREDOOM
PREADOPT*	PREBOILING*	PRECIOUSES	PRECURES*	PREDOOMED
PREADOPTED*	PREBOILS*	PRECIPE*	PRECURING*	PREDOOMING
PREADOPTING*	PREBOOK*	PRECIPES*	PRECURRER	PREDOOMS
PREADOPTS*	PREBOOKED*	PRECIPICE	PRECURRERS	PREDRILL*
PREADULT*	PREBOOKING*	PRECIPICES	PRECURSE	PREDRILLED*
PREAGED*	PREBOOKS*	PRECIS	PRECURSES	PREDRILLING*
PREALLOT*	PREBOOM*	PRECISE	PRECURSOR	PREDRILLS*
PREALLOTS*	PREBORN	PRECISED	PRECURSORS	PREDUSK*
PREALLOTTED*	PREBOUND*	PRECISELY	PRECUT	PREDUSKS*
PREALLOTTING*	PRECANCEL*	PRECISER	PRECUTS	PREDY
PREAMBLE	PRECANCELED*	PRECISES	PRECUTTING	PREDYING
PREAMBLED	PRECANCELING*	PRECISEST	PREDACITIES	PREE
PREAMBLES	PRECANCELLED*	PRECISIAN	PREDACITY	PREED
PREAMBLING	PRECANCELLING*	PRECISIANS	PREDATE	PREEDIT*
PREAMP	PRECANCELS*	PRECISING	PREDATED	PREEDITED*
PREAMPS	PRECAST	PRECISION	PREDATES	PREEDITING*
PREANAL*	PRECASTING*	PRECISIONS	PREDATING	PREEDITS*
PREARM*	PRECASTS*	PRECISIVE	PREDATION	PREEING
PREARMED*	PRECATIVE	PRECITED*	PREDATIONS	PREELECT*
PREARMING*	PRECATORY	PRECLEAN*	PREDATIVE	PREELECTED*
PREARMS*	PRECAVA	PRECLEANED*	PREDATOR	PREELECTING*
PREASE	PRECAVAE	PRECLEANING*	PREDATORS	PREELECTS*
PREASED	PRECAVAL*	PRECLEANS*	PREDATORY	PREEMIE
PREASES	PRECEDE	PRECLEAR*	PREDAWN	PREEMIES
PREASING	PRECEDED	PRECLEARED*	PREDAWNS	PREEMPT*
PREASSE	PRECEDENT	PRECLEARING*	PREDEFINE	PREEMPTED*
PREASSED	PRECEDENTS	PRECLEARS*	PREDEFINED	PREEMPTING*
PREASSES	PRECEDES	PRECLUDE	PREDEFINES	PREEMPTOR*
PREASSIGN*	PRECEDING	PRECLUDED	PREDEFINING	PREEMPTORS*
PREASSIGNED*	PRECEESE	PRECLUDES	PREDELLA	PREEMPTS*
PREASSIGNING*	PRECENSOR*	PRECLUDING	PREDELLAS	PREEN
PREASSIGNS*	PRECENSORED*	PRECOCIAL	PREDESIGN	PREENACT*
PREASSING	PRECENSORING*	PRECOCITIES	PREDESIGNED	PREENACTED*

PREENACTING*
PREENACTS*
PREENED
PREENER*
PREENERS*
PREENING
PREENS
PREERECT*
PREERECTED*
PREERECTING*
PREERECTS*
PREES
PREEVE
PREEVED
PREEVES
PREEVING
PREEXILIC*
PREEXIST*
PREEXISTED*
PREEXISTING*
PREEXISTS*
PREFAB
PREFABBED*
PREFABBING*
PREFABS
PREFACE
PREFACED
PREFACER*
PREFACERS*
PREFACES
PREFACIAL
PREFACING
PREFADE
PREFADED
PREFADES
PREFADING
PREFARD
PREFATORY
PREFECT
PREFECTS
PREFER
PREFERRED
PREFERRER
PREFERRERS
PREFERRING
PREFERS
PREFEUDAL*
PREFIGHT*
PREFIGURE
PREFIGURED
PREFIGURES
PREFIGURING
PREFILE*
PREFILED*
PREFILES*
PREFILING*
PREFILLED*
PREFIRE*
PREFIRED*
PREFIRES*
PREFIRING*
PREFIX
PREFIXAL*
PREFIXED

PREFIXES
PREFIXING
PREFIXION
PREFIXIONS
PREFLAME*
PREFLIGHT
PREFOCUS*
PREFOCUSED*
PREFOCUSES*
PREFOCUSING*
PREFOCUSSED*
PREFOCUSSES*
PREFOCUSSING*
PREFORM
PREFORMAT*
PREFORMATS*
PREFORMATTED*
PREFORMATTING*
PREFORMED
PREFORMING
PREFORMS
PREFRANK*
PREFRANKED*
PREFRANKING*
PREFRANKS*
PREFREEZE*
PREFREEZES*
PREFREEZING*
PREFROZE*
PREFROZEN*
PREGAME*
PREGGERS
PREGNABLE
PREGNANCE
PREGNANCES
PREGNANCIES
PREGNANCY
PREGNANT
PREHALLUCES
PREHALLUX
PREHEAT
PREHEATED
PREHEATER*
PREHEATERS*
PREHEATING
PREHEATS
PREHEND
PREHENDED
PREHENDING
PREHENDS
PREHENSOR
PREHENSORS
PREHIRING*
PREHNITE
PREHNITES
PREHUMAN
PREHUMANS*
PREIF
PREIFE
PREIFES
PREIFS
PREJINK
PREJUDGE
PREJUDGED

PREJUDGER*
PREJUDGERS*
PREJUDGES
PREJUDGING
PREJUDICE
PREJUDICED
PREJUDICES
PREJUDICING
PREJUDIZE
PREJUDIZES
PRELACIES
PRELACY
PRELATE
PRELATES
PRELATESS
PRELATESSES
PRELATIAL
PRELATIC
PRELATIES
PRELATION
PRELATIONS
PRELATISE
PRELATISED
PRELATISES
PRELATISH
PRELATISING
PRELATISM
PRELATISMS
PRELATIST
PRELATISTS
PRELATIZE
PRELATIZED
PRELATIZES
PRELATIZING
PRELATURE
PRELATURES
PRELATY
PRELAUNCH*
PRELECT
PRELECTED
PRELECTING
PRELECTOR
PRELECTORS
PRELECTS
PRELEGAL*
PRELIFE*
PRELIM
PRELIMIT*
PRELIMITED*
PRELIMITING*
PRELIMITS*
PRELIMS
PRELIVES*
PRELUDE
PRELUDED
PRELUDER*
PRELUDERS*
PRELUDES
PRELUDI
PRELUDIAL
PRELUDING
PRELUDIO
PRELUNCH*
PRELUSION*

PRELUSIONS*
PRELUSIVE
PRELUSORY
PREMADE*
PREMAN*
PREMARKET*
PREMATURE
PREMATURES*
PREMEAL*
PREMED
PREMEDIC
PREMEDICS
PREMEDS
PREMEET*
PREMEN*
PREMERGER*
PREMIA
PREMIE
PREMIER
PREMIERE
PREMIERED
PREMIERES
PREMIERING
PREMIERS
PREMIES
PREMISE
PREMISED
PREMISES
PREMISING
PREMISS
PREMISSES
PREMIUM
PREMIUMS
PREMIX
PREMIXED
PREMIXES
PREMIXING
PREMIXT*
PREMODERN*
PREMODIFIED*
PREMODIFIES*
PREMODIFY*
PREMODIFYING*
PREMOLAR
PREMOLARS
PREMOLD*
PREMOLDED*
PREMOLDING*
PREMOLDS*
PREMOLT*
PREMONISH
PREMONISHED
PREMONISHES
PREMONISHING
PREMORAL*
PREMORSE
PREMOSAIC
PREMOTION
PREMOTIONS
PREMOVE
PREMOVED
PREMOVES
PREMOVING
PREMUNE*

PREMY
PRENAME*
PRENAMES*
PRENASAL
PRENASALS
PRENATAL
PRENOMEN*
PRENOMENS*
PRENOMINA*
PRENOON*
PRENOTIFIED
PRENOTIFIES
PRENOTIFY
PRENOTIFYING
PRENOTION
PRENOTIONS
PRENT
PRENTED
PRENTICE
PRENTICED
PRENTICES
PRENTICING
PRENTING
PRENTS
PRENUBILE
PRENUMBER*
PRENUMBERED*
PRENUMBERING*
PRENUMBERS*
PRENZIE
PREOCCUPIED
PREOCCUPIES
PREOCCUPY
PREOCCUPYING
PREOCULAR
PREOPTION
PREOPTIONS
PREORAL
PREORDAIN
PREORDAINED
PREORDAINING
PREORDAINS
PREORDER
PREORDERED
PREORDERING
PREORDERS
PREP
PREPACK
PREPACKED
PREPACKING
PREPACKS
PREPAID
PREPARE
PREPARED
PREPARER
PREPARERS
PREPARES
PREPARING
PREPASTE*
PREPASTED*
PREPASTES*
PREPASTING*
PREPAY
PREPAYING

PREPAYS	PREREVIEW*	PRESENTER	PRESS	PRETASTES*
PREPENSE	PRERINSE*	PRESENTERS	PRESSED	PRETASTING*
PREPENSED	PRERINSES*	PRESENTING	PRESSER	PRETAX*
PREPENSES	PRERIOT*	PRESENTLY	PRESSERS	PRETEEN*
PREPENSING	PREROCK*	PRESENTS	PRESSES	PRETEENS*
PREPILL*	PREROSION	PRESERVE	PRESSFAT	PRETENCE
PREPLACE*	PREROSIONS	PRESERVED	PRESSFATS	PRETENCES
PREPLACED*	PRERUPT	PRESERVER	PRESSFUL	PRETEND
PREPLACES*	PRESA	PRESERVERS	PRESSFULS	PRETENDED
PREPLACING*	PRESAGE	PRESERVES	PRESSIE	PRETENDER
PREPLAN*	PRESAGED	PRESERVING	PRESSIES	PRETENDERS
PREPLANNED*	PRESAGER	PRESES	PRESSING	PRETENDING
PREPLANNING*	PRESAGERS	PRESET	PRESSINGS	PRETENDS
PREPLANS*	PRESAGES	PRESETS	PRESSION	PRETENSE
PREPLANT*	PRESAGING	PRESETTING	PRESSIONS	PRETENSES
PREPOLLEX	PRESALE*	PRESHAPE*	PRESSMAN	PRETERIST
PREPOLLICES	PRESBYOPE	PRESHAPED*	PRESSMARK	PRETERISTS
PREPONE	PRESBYOPES	PRESHAPES*	PRESSMARKS	PRETERIT
PREPONED	PRESBYOPIES	PRESHAPING*	PRESSMEN	PRETERITE
PREPONES	PRESBYOPY	PRESHOW*	PRESSOR	PRETERITES
PREPONING	PRESBYTE	PRESHOWED*	PRESSORS*	PRETERITS
PREPOSE	PRESBYTER	PRESHOWING*	PRESSROOM	PRETERM
PREPOSED	PRESBYTERS	PRESHOWN*	PRESSROOMS	PRETERMIT
PREPOSES	PRESBYTES	PRESHOWS*	PRESSRUN*	PRETERMITS
PREPOSING	PRESBYTIC	PRESHRANK*	PRESSRUNS*	PRETERMITTED
PREPOSTOR	PRESCHOOL	PRESHRINK*	PRESSURE	PRETERMITTING
PREPOSTORS	PRESCHOOLS	PRESHRINKING*	PRESSURED	PRETEST
PREPOTENT	PRESCIENT	PRESHRINKS*	PRESSURES	PRETESTED
PREPPED	PRESCIND	PRESHRUNK*	PRESSURING	PRETESTING
PREPPIE*	PRESCINDED	PRESHRUNKEN*	PRESSWORK	PRETESTS
PREPPIER	PRESCINDING	PRESIDE	PRESSWORKS	PRETEXT
PREPPIES	PRESCINDS	PRESIDED	PREST	PRETEXTED*
PREPPIEST	PRESCIOUS	PRESIDENT	PRESTAMP*	PRETEXTING*
PREPPILY	PRESCORE*	PRESIDENTS	PRESTAMPED*	PRETEXTS
PREPPING	PRESCORED*	PRESIDER*	PRESTAMPING*	PRETOR
PREPPY	PRESCORES*	PRESIDERS*	PRESTAMPS*	PRETORIAN*
PREPREG*	PRESCORING*	PRESIDES	PRESTED	PRETORIANS*
PREPREGS*	PRESCREEN*	PRESIDIA	PRESTER*	PRETORS
PREPRICE*	PRESCREENED*	PRESIDIAL	PRESTERNA	PRETRAIN*
PREPRICED*	PRESCREENING*	PRESIDING	PRESTERS*	PRETRAINED*
PREPRICES*	PRESCREENS*	PRESIDIO	PRESTIGE	PRETRAINING*
PREPRICING*	PRESCRIBE	PRESIDIOS	PRESTIGES	PRETRAINS*
PREPRINT*	PRESCRIBED	PRESIDIUM	PRESTING	PRETRAVEL*
PREPRINTED*	PRESCRIBES	PRESIDIUMS	PRESTO	PRETREAT*
PREPRINTING*	PRESCRIBING	PRESIFT*	PRESTOS	PRETREATED*
PREPRINTS*	PRESCRIPT	PRESIFTED*	PRESTRESS*	PRETREATING*
PREPS	PRESCRIPTS	PRESIFTING*	PRESTRESSED*	PRETREATS*
PREPUCE	PRESCUTA	PRESIFTS*	PRESTRESSES*	PRETRIAL*
PREPUCES	PRESCUTUM	PRESLEEP*	PRESTRESSING*	PRETRIALS*
PREPUNCH*	PRESE	PRESLICE*	PRESTRIKE*	PRETRIM*
PREPUNCHED*	PRESEASON*	PRESLICED*	PRESTS	PRETRIMMED*
PREPUNCHES*	PRESELECT	PRESLICES*	PRESUME	PRETRIMMING*
PREPUNCHING*	PRESELECTED	PRESLICING*	PRESUMED	PRETRIMS*
PREPUPAL*	PRESELECTING	PRESOAK*	PRESUMER	PRETTIED
PREPUTIAL	PRESELECTS	PRESOAKED*	PRESUMERS	PRETTIER
PREQUEL	PRESELL*	PRESOAKING*	PRESUMES	PRETTIES
PREQUELS	PRESELLING*	PRESOAKS*	PRESUMING	PRETTIEST
PRERACE*	PRESELLS*	PRESOLD*	PRESUMMIT*	PRETTIFIED
PRERECORD	PRESENCE	PRESONG*	PRETAPE*	PRETTIFIES
PRERECORDED	PRESENCES	PRESORT*	PRETAPED*	PRETTIFY
PRERECORDING	PRESENT	PRESORTED*	PRETAPES*	PRETTIFYING
PRERECORDS	PRESENTED	PRESORTING*	PRETAPING*	PRETTILY
PRERENAL*	PRESENTEE	PRESORTS*	PRETASTE*	PRETTY
PRERETURN*	PRESENTEES	PRESPLIT*	PRETASTED*	PRETTYING

Words marked with an asterisk are from OTCWL

PRETTYISH	PREWARMS	PRICKLE	PRIMAEVAL	PRIMS
PRETTYISM	PREWARN	PRICKLED	PRIMAGE	PRIMSIE
PRETTYISMS	PREWARNED	PRICKLES	PRIMAGES	PRIMSIER
PRETYPE*	PREWARNING	PRICKLIER	PRIMAL	PRIMSIEST
PRETYPED*	PREWARNS	PRICKLIEST	PRIMALITIES	PRIMULA
PRETYPES*	PREWASH*	PRICKLING	PRIMALITY	PRIMULAS
PRETYPING*	PREWASHED*	PRICKLINGS	PRIMALLY	PRIMULINE
PRETZEL	PREWASHES*	PRICKLY	PRIMARIES	PRIMULINES
PRETZELS	PREWASHING*	PRICKS	PRIMARILY	PRIMUS
PREUNION*	PREWORK*	PRICKWOOD	PRIMARY	PRIMUSES
PREUNIONS*	PREWRAP*	PRICKWOODS	PRIMAS*	PRIMY
PREUNITE*	PREWRAPPED*	PRICKY*	PRIMATAL	PRINCE
PREUNITED*	PREWRAPPING*	PRICY	PRIMATALS*	PRINCED
PREUNITES*	PREWRAPS*	PRIDE	PRIMATE	PRINCEDOM
PREUNITING*	PREWYN	PRIDED	PRIMATES	PRINCEDOMS
PREVAIL	PREWYNS	PRIDEFUL	PRIMATIAL	PRINCEKIN
PREVAILED	PREX	PRIDELESS	PRIMATIC	PRINCEKINS
PREVAILING	PREXES	PRIDES	PRIME	PRINCELET
PREVAILS	PREXIES	PRIDIAN	PRIMED	PRINCELETS
PREVALENT	PREXY	PRIDING	PRIMELY	PRINCELIER
PREVALENTS*	PREY	PRIED	PRIMENESS	PRINCELIEST
PREVE	PREYED	PRIEDIEU*	PRIMENESSES	PRINCELY
PREVED	PREYER*	PRIEDIEUS*	PRIMER	PRINCES
PREVENE	PREYERS*	PRIEDIEUX*	PRIMERO	PRINCESS
PREVENED	PREYFUL	PRIEF	PRIMEROS	PRINCESSE
PREVENES	PREYING	PRIEFE	PRIMERS	PRINCESSES
PREVENING	PREYS	PRIEFES	PRIMES	PRINCING
PREVENT	PREZ*	PRIEFS	PRIMEUR	PRINCIPAL
PREVENTED	PREZES*	PRIER	PRIMEURS	PRINCIPALS
PREVENTER	PREZZIE	PRIERS	PRIMEVAL	PRINCIPE*
PREVENTERS	PREZZIES	PRIES	PRIMI*	PRINCIPI*
PREVENTING	PRIAL	PRIEST	PRIMINE	PRINCIPIA
PREVENTS	PRIALS	PRIESTED	PRIMINES	PRINCIPIUM*
PREVERB	PRIAPEAN*	PRIESTESS	PRIMING	PRINCIPLE
PREVERBAL	PRIAPI*	PRIESTESSES	PRIMINGS	PRINCIPLED
PREVERBS	PRIAPIC	PRIESTING	PRIMIPARA	PRINCIPLES
PREVES	PRIAPISM	PRIESTLIER	PRIMIPARAE	PRINCIPLING
PREVIABLE*	PRIAPISMS	PRIESTLIEST	PRIMIPARAS	PRINCOCK
PREVIEW	PRIAPUS*	PRIESTLY	PRIMITIAE	PRINCOCKS
PREVIEWED	PRIAPUSES*	PRIESTS	PRIMITIAL	PRINCOX
PREVIEWER*	PRIBBLE	PRIEVE	PRIMITIAS	PRINCOXES
PREVIEWERS*	PRIBBLES	PRIEVED	PRIMITIVE	PRINK
PREVIEWING	PRICE	PRIEVES	PRIMITIVES	PRINKED
PREVIEWS	PRICED	PRIEVING	PRIMLY	PRINKER*
PREVING	PRICELESS	PRIG	PRIMMED	PRINKERS*
PREVIOUS	PRICER	PRIGGED	PRIMMER	PRINKING
PREVISE	PRICERS	PRIGGER	PRIMMERS	PRINKS
PREVISED	PRICES	PRIGGERIES	PRIMMEST	PRINT
PREVISES	PRICEY	PRIGGERS	PRIMMING	PRINTABLE
PREVISING	PRICIER	PRIGGERY	PRIMNESS	PRINTED
PREVISION	PRICIEST	PRIGGING	PRIMNESSES	PRINTER
PREVISIONED	PRICINESS	PRIGGINGS	PRIMO	PRINTERIES*
PREVISIONING	PRICINESSES	PRIGGISH	PRIMORDIA	PRINTERS
PREVISIONS	PRICING	PRIGGISM	PRIMORDIUM*	PRINTERY*
PREVISOR*	PRICK	PRIGGISMS	PRIMOS	PRINTHEAD
PREVISORS*	PRICKED	PRIGS	PRIMP	PRINTHEADS
PREVUE	PRICKER	PRILL	PRIMPED	PRINTING
PREVUED	PRICKERS	PRILLED	PRIMPING	PRINTINGS
PREVUES	PRICKET	PRILLING	PRIMPS	PRINTLESS
PREVUING	PRICKETS	PRILLS	PRIMROSE	PRINTOUT
PREWAR*	PRICKIER*	PRIM	PRIMROSED	PRINTOUTS
PREWARM	PRICKIEST*	PRIMA	PRIMROSES	PRINTS
PREWARMED	PRICKING	PRIMACIES	PRIMROSING	PRION
PREWARMING	PRICKINGS	PRIMACY	PRIMROSY	PRIONS

The Chambers Dictionary is the authority for many longer words; see Introduction, page ix

PRIOR	PRIVATION	PROBIOTIC	PROCTITISES	PROFANE
PRIORATE	PRIVATIONS	PROBIOTICS	PROCTOR	PROFANED
PRIORATES	PRIVATISE	PROBIT	PROCTORED*	PROFANELY
PRIORESS	PRIVATISED	PROBITIES	PROCTORING*	PROFANER
PRIORESSES	PRIVATISES	PROBITS	PROCTORS	PROFANERS
PRIORIES	PRIVATISING	PROBITY	PROCURACIES	PROFANES
PRIORITIES	PRIVATISM*	PROBLEM	PROCURACY	PROFANING
PRIORITY	PRIVATISMS*	PROBLEMS	PROCURAL*	PROFANITIES
PRIORLY*	PRIVATIVE	PROBOSCIDES	PROCURALS*	PROFANITY
PRIORS	PRIVATIVES	PROBOSCIS	PROCURE	PROFESS
PRIORSHIP	PRIVATIZE	PROBOSCISES	PROCURED	PROFESSED
PRIORSHIPS	PRIVATIZED	PROBS	PROCURER	PROFESSES
PRIORY	PRIVATIZES	PROCACITIES	PROCURERS	PROFESSING
PRISAGE	PRIVATIZING	PROCACITY	PROCURES	PROFESSOR
PRISAGES	PRIVET	PROCAINE	PROCURESS	PROFESSORS
PRISE	PRIVETS	PROCAINES	PROCURESSES	PROFFER
PRISED	PRIVIER	PROCAMBIA*	PROCUREUR	PROFFERED
PRISER	PRIVIES	PROCAMBIUM*	PROCUREURS	PROFFERER
PRISERE*	PRIVIEST	PROCAMBIUMS*	PROCURING	PROFFERERS
PRISERES*	PRIVILEGE	PROCARP*	PROD	PROFFERING
PRISERS	PRIVILEGED	PROCARPS*	PRODDED	PROFFERS
PRISES	PRIVILEGES	PROCARYON	PRODDER*	PROFILE
PRISING	PRIVILEGING	PROCARYONS	PRODDERS*	PROFILED
PRISM	PRIVILY	PROCEDURE	PRODDING	PROFILER
PRISMATIC	PRIVITIES	PROCEDURES	PRODIGAL	PROFILERS
PRISMOID	PRIVITY	PROCEED	PRODIGALS	PROFILES
PRISMOIDS	PRIVY	PROCEEDED	PRODIGIES	PROFILING
PRISMS	PRIZABLE	PROCEEDER	PRODIGY	PROFILINGS
PRISMY	PRIZE	PROCEEDERS	PRODITOR	PROFILIST
PRISON	PRIZED	PROCEEDING	PRODITORS	PROFILISTS
PRISONED	PRIZEMAN	PROCEEDINGS	PRODITORY	PROFIT
PRISONER	PRIZEMEN	PROCEEDS	PRODNOSE	PROFITED
PRISONERS	PRIZER	PROCERITIES	PRODNOSED	PROFITEER
PRISONING	PRIZERS	PROCERITY	PRODNOSES	PROFITEERED
PRISONOUS	PRIZES	PROCESS	PRODNOSING	PROFITEERING
PRISONS	PRIZING	PROCESSED	PRODROMAL	PROFITEERINGS
PRISS*	PRO	PROCESSES	PRODROMATA*	PROFITEERS
PRISSED*	PROA	PROCESSING	PRODROME	PROFITER
PRISSES*	PROACTIVE	PROCESSOR	PRODROMES	PROFITERS
PRISSIER	PROAS	PROCESSORS	PRODROMI	PROFITING
PRISSIES*	PROB	PROCHAIN*	PRODROMIC	PROFITINGS
PRISSIEST	PROBABLE	PROCHEIN*	PRODROMUS	PROFITS
PRISSILY*	PROBABLES	PROCIDENT	PRODS	PROFLUENT
PRISSING*	PROBABLY	PROCINCT	PRODUCE	PROFORMA
PRISSY	PROBALL	PROCINCTS	PRODUCED	PROFORMAS
PRISTANE	PROBAND	PROCLAIM	PRODUCER	PROFOUND
PRISTANES	PROBANDS	PROCLAIMED	PRODUCERS	PROFOUNDER
PRISTINE	PROBANG	PROCLAIMING	PRODUCES	PROFOUNDEST
PRITHEE	PROBANGS	PROCLAIMS	PRODUCING	PROFOUNDS
PRIVACIES	PROBATE	PROCLISES	PRODUCT	PROFS
PRIVACY	PROBATED	PROCLISIS	PRODUCTS	PROFUSE
PRIVADO	PROBATES	PROCLITIC	PROEM	PROFUSELY
PRIVADOES	PROBATING	PROCLITICS	PROEMBRYO	PROFUSER
PRIVADOS	PROBATION	PROCLIVE	PROEMBRYOS	PROFUSERS
PRIVATE	PROBATIONS	PROCONSUL	PROEMIAL	PROFUSION
PRIVATEER	PROBATIVE	PROCONSULS	PROEMS	PROFUSIONS
PRIVATEERED	PROBATORY	PROCREANT	PROENZYME	PROG
PRIVATEERING	PROBE	PROCREANTS	PROENZYMES	PROGENIES
PRIVATEERINGS	PROBEABLE	PROCREATE	PROESTRUS*	PROGENY
PRIVATEERS	PROBED	PROCREATED	PROESTRUSES*	PROGERIA
PRIVATELY	PROBER	PROCREATES	PROETTE*	PROGERIAS
PRIVATER	PROBERS	PROCREATING	PROETTES*	PROGESTIN
PRIVATES	PROBES	PROCTAL	PROF	PROGESTINS
PRIVATEST	PROBING	PROCTITIS	PROFACE	PROGGED

PROGGER*	PROLACTIN	PROLOGUES	PROMULGE	PROOFING
PROGGERS*	PROLACTINS	PROLOGUING	PROMULGED	PROOFINGS
PROGGING	PROLAMIN	PROLONG	PROMULGES	PROOFLESS
PROGGINS	PROLAMINE	PROLONGE	PROMULGING	PROOFREAD
PROGGINSES	PROLAMINES	PROLONGED	PROMUSCES	PROOFREADING
PROGNOSE*	PROLAMINS	PROLONGER	PROMUSCIDES	PROOFREADINGS
PROGNOSED*	PROLAN*	PROLONGERS	PROMUSCIS	PROOFREADS
PROGNOSES	PROLANS*	PROLONGES	PRONAOI	PROOFROOM*
PROGNOSING*	PROLAPSE	PROLONGING	PRONAOS	PROOFROOMS*
PROGNOSIS	PROLAPSED	PROLONGS	PRONATE	PROOFS
PROGRADE	PROLAPSES	PROLUSION	PRONATED	PROOTIC
PROGRADED	PROLAPSING	PROLUSIONS	PRONATES	PROOTICS
PROGRADES	PROLAPSUS	PROLUSORY	PRONATING	PROP
PROGRADING	PROLAPSUSES	PROM	PRONATION	PROPAGATE
PROGRAM	PROLATE	PROMACHOS	PRONATIONS	PROPAGATED
PROGRAMED*	PROLATED	PROMACHOSES	PRONATOR	PROPAGATES
PROGRAMER*	PROLATELY	PROMENADE	PRONATORES*	PROPAGATING
PROGRAMERS*	PROLATES	PROMENADED	PRONATORS	PROPAGE
PROGRAMING*	PROLATING	PROMENADES	PRONE	PROPAGED
PROGRAMME	PROLATION	PROMENADING	PRONELY	PROPAGES
PROGRAMMED	PROLATIONS	PROMETAL	PRONENESS	PROPAGING
PROGRAMMES	PROLATIVE	PROMETALS	PRONENESSES	PROPAGULA
PROGRAMMING	PROLE	PROMINE*	PRONER	PROPAGULE
PROGRAMMINGS	PROLED	PROMINENT	PRONES	PROPAGULES
PROGRAMS	PROLEG	PROMINES*	PRONEST	PROPALE
PROGRESS	PROLEGS	PROMISE	PRONEUR	PROPALED
PROGRESSED	PROLEPSES	PROMISED	PRONEURS	PROPALES
PROGRESSES	PROLEPSIS	PROMISEE	PRONG	PROPALING
PROGRESSING	PROLEPTIC	PROMISEES	PRONGBUCK	PROPANE
PROGS	PROLER	PROMISER	PRONGBUCKS	PROPANES
PROHIBIT	PROLERS	PROMISERS	PRONGED	PROPANOL
PROHIBITED	PROLES	PROMISES	PRONGHORN	PROPANOLS
PROHIBITING	PROLETARIES	PROMISING	PRONGHORNS	PROPEL
PROHIBITS	PROLETARY	PROMISOR	PRONGING	PROPELLED
PROIGN	PROLICIDE	PROMISORS	PRONGS	PROPELLER
PROIGNED	PROLICIDES	PROMISSOR	PRONK	PROPELLERS
PROIGNING	PROLIFIC	PROMISSORS	PRONKED	PROPELLING
PROIGNS	PROLINE	PROMMER	PRONKING	PROPELLOR*
PROIN	PROLINES	PROMMERS	PRONKS	PROPELLORS*
PROINE	PROLING	PROMO	PRONOTA	PROPELS
PROINED	PROLIX	PROMOS	PRONOTAL	PROPEND
PROINES	PROLIXITIES	PROMOTE	PRONOTUM	PROPENDED
PROINING	PROLIXITY	PROMOTED	PRONOUN	PROPENDING
PROINS	PROLIXLY	PROMOTER	PRONOUNCE	PROPENDS
PROJECT	PROLL	PROMOTERS	PRONOUNCED	PROPENE
PROJECTED	PROLLED	PROMOTES	PRONOUNCES	PROPENES
PROJECTING	PROLLER	PROMOTING	PRONOUNCING	PROPENOL*
PROJECTINGS	PROLLERS	PROMOTION	PRONOUNCINGS	PROPENOLS*
PROJECTOR	PROLLING	PROMOTIONS	PRONOUNS	PROPENSE
PROJECTORS	PROLLS	PROMOTIVE	PRONTO	PROPENYL*
PROJECTS	PROLOG*	PROMOTOR	PRONUCLEI	PROPER
PROJET*	PROLOGED*	PROMOTORS	PRONUCLEUS*	PROPERDIN
PROJETS*	PROLOGING*	PROMPT	PRONUCLEUSES*	PROPERDINS
PROKARYON	PROLOGISE	PROMPTED	PRONUNCIO	PROPERER
PROKARYONS	PROLOGISES	PROMPTER	PRONUNCIOS	PROPEREST
PROKARYOT	PROLOGISING	PROMPTERS	PROO	PROPERLY
PROKARYOTS	PROLOGIZE	PROMPTEST	PROOEMION	PROPERS
PROKE	PROLOGIZED	PROMPTING	PROOEMIONS	PROPERTIED
PROKED	PROLOGIZES	PROMPTINGS	PROOEMIUM	PROPERTIES
PROKER	PROLOGIZING	PROMPTLY	PROOEMIUMS	PROPERTY
PROKERS	PROLOGS*	PROMPTS	PROOF	PROPERTYING
PROKES	PROLOGUE	PROMPTURE	PROOFED	PROPHAGE
PROKING	PROLOGUED	PROMPTURES	PROOFER*	PROPHAGES
PROLABOR*		PROMS	PROOFERS*	PROPHASE

The Chambers Dictionary is the authority for many longer words; see Introduction, page ix

PROPHASES	PROPYLAEUM*	PROSEUCHE	PROTANOPE	PROTISTS
PROPHASIC*	PROPYLENE	PROSIER	PROTANOPES	PROTIUM
PROPHECIES	PROPYLENES	PROSIEST	PROTASES	PROTIUMS
PROPHECY	PROPYLIC	PROSIFIED	PROTASIS	PROTOAVIS
PROPHESIED	PROPYLITE	PROSIFIES	PROTATIC	PROTOAVISES
PROPHESIES	PROPYLITES	PROSIFY	PROTEA	PROTOCOL
PROPHESY	PROPYLON	PROSIFYING	PROTEAN	PROTOCOLED*
PROPHESYING	PROPYLS	PROSILY	PROTEANS*	PROTOCOLING*
PROPHESYINGS	PRORATE	PROSIMIAN	PROTEAS	PROTOCOLLED
PROPHET	PRORATED	PROSIMIANS	PROTEASE	PROTOCOLLING
PROPHETIC	PRORATES	PROSINESS	PROTEASES	PROTOCOLS
PROPHETS	PRORATING	PROSINESSES	PROTECT	PROTODERM*
PROPHYLL	PRORATION	PROSING	PROTECTED	PROTODERMS*
PROPHYLLS	PRORATIONS	PROSINGS	PROTECTING	PROTOGINE
PROPINE	PRORE	PROSIT	PROTECTOR	PROTOGINES
PROPINED	PRORECTOR	PROSO	PROTECTORS	PROTOGYNIES
PROPINES	PRORECTORS	PROSODIAL	PROTECTS	PROTOGYNY
PROPINING	PRORES	PROSODIAN	PROTEGE	PROTON
PROPJET*	PROROGATE	PROSODIANS	PROTEGEE	PROTONATE*
PROPJETS*	PROROGATED	PROSODIC	PROTEGEES	PROTONATED*
PROPMAN*	PROROGATES	PROSODIES	PROTEGES	PROTONATES*
PROPMEN*	PROROGATING	PROSODIST	PROTEI*	PROTONATING*
PROPODEON	PROROGUE	PROSODISTS	PROTEID	PROTONEMA
PROPODEONS	PROROGUED	PROSODY	PROTEIDE*	PROTONEMATA
PROPODEUM	PROROGUES	PROSOMA*	PROTEIDES*	PROTONIC
PROPODEUMS	PROROGUING	PROSOMAL*	PROTEIDS	PROTONS
PROPOLIS	PROS	PROSOMAS*	PROTEIN	PROTOPOD*
PROPOLISES	PROSAIC	PROSOPON	PROTEINIC	PROTOPODS*
PROPONE	PROSAICAL	PROSOPONS	PROTEINS	PROTORE
PROPONED	PROSAISM	PROSOS	PROTEND	PROTORES
PROPONENT	PROSAISMS	PROSPECT	PROTENDED	PROTOSTAR
PROPONENTS	PROSAIST	PROSPECTED	PROTENDING	PROTOSTARS
PROPONES	PROSAISTS	PROSPECTING	PROTENDS	PROTOTYPE
PROPONING	PROSATEUR	PROSPECTINGS	PROTENSE	PROTOTYPED
PROPOSAL	PROSATEURS	PROSPECTS	PROTENSES	PROTOTYPES
PROPOSALS	PROSCRIBE	PROSPER	PROTEOSE	PROTOTYPING
PROPOSE	PROSCRIBED	PROSPERED	PROTEOSES	PROTOXID*
PROPOSED	PROSCRIBES	PROSPERING	PROTEST	PROTOXIDE
PROPOSER	PROSCRIBING	PROSPERS	PROTESTED	PROTOXIDES
PROPOSERS	PROSCRIPT	PROSS*	PROTESTER	PROTOXIDS*
PROPOSES	PROSCRIPTS	PROSSES*	PROTESTERS	PROTOZOA
PROPOSING	PROSE	PROSSIE*	PROTESTING	PROTOZOAL
PROPOSITI*	PROSECT*	PROSSIES*	PROTESTOR	PROTOZOAN
PROPOSITUS*	PROSECTED*	PROST*	PROTESTORS	PROTOZOANS
PROPOUND	PROSECTING*	PROSTATE	PROTESTS	PROTOZOIC
PROPOUNDED	PROSECTOR	PROSTATES	PROTEUS	PROTOZOON
PROPOUNDING	PROSECTORS	PROSTATIC	PROTEUSES	PROTRACT
PROPOUNDS	PROSECTS*	PROSTIE*	PROTHALLI	PROTRACTED
PROPPANT	PROSECUTE	PROSTIES*	PROTHALLUS*	PROTRACTING
PROPPANTS	PROSECUTED	PROSTOMIA*	PROTHALLUSES*	PROTRACTS
PROPPED	PROSECUTES	PROSTOMIUM*	PROTHESES	PROTRUDE
PROPPING	PROSECUTING	PROSTRATE	PROTHESIS	PROTRUDED
PROPRETOR*	PROSED	PROSTRATED	PROTHETIC	PROTRUDES
PROPRETORS*	PROSELYTE	PROSTRATES	PROTHORACES	PROTRUDING
PROPRIETIES	PROSELYTED	PROSTRATING	PROTHORAX	PROTYL
PROPRIETY	PROSELYTES	PROSTYLE	PROTHORAXES	PROTYLE
PROPS	PROSELYTING	PROSTYLES	PROTHYL	PROTYLES
PROPTOSES	PROSEMAN	PROSY	PROTHYLE	PROTYLS
PROPTOSIS	PROSEMEN	PROTAMIN*	PROTHYLES	PROUD
PROPULSOR	PROSER	PROTAMINE	PROTHYLS	PROUDER
PROPULSORS	PROSERS	PROTAMINES	PROTIST	PROUDEST
PROPYL	PROSES	PROTAMINS*	PROTISTAN*	PROUDFUL
PROPYLA	PROSEUCHA	PROTANDRIES	PROTISTANS*	PROUDISH
PROPYLAEA	PROSEUCHAE	PROTANDRY	PROTISTIC	PROUDLY

PROUDNESS
PROUDNESSES
PROUL
PROULED
PROULER
PROULERS
PROULING
PROULS
PROUNION*
PROUSTITE
PROUSTITES
PROVABLE
PROVABLY
PROVAND
PROVANDS
PROVANT
PROVE
PROVEABLE
PROVEABLY
PROVED
PROVEDOR
PROVEDORE
PROVEDORES
PROVEDORS
PROVEN
PROVEND
PROVENDER
PROVENDERED
PROVENDERING
PROVENDERS
PROVENDS
PROVENLY*
PROVER
PROVERB
PROVERBED
PROVERBING
PROVERBS
PROVERS
PROVIANT
PROVIANTS
PROVIDE
PROVIDED
PROVIDENT
PROVIDER
PROVIDERS
PROVIDES
PROVIDING
PROVIDOR
PROVIDORS
PROVINCE
PROVINCES
PROVINE
PROVINED
PROVINES
PROVING
PROVINGS
PROVINING
PROVIRAL
PROVIRUS
PROVIRUSES
PROVISION
PROVISIONED
PROVISIONING

PROVISIONS
PROVISO
PROVISOES
PROVISOR
PROVISORS
PROVISORY
PROVISOS
PROVOCANT
PROVOCANTS
PROVOKE
PROVOKED
PROVOKER
PROVOKERS
PROVOKES
PROVOKING
PROVOLONE*
PROVOLONES*
PROVOST
PROVOSTRIES
PROVOSTRY
PROVOSTS
PROW
PROWAR*
PROWER*
PROWESS
PROWESSED
PROWESSES
PROWEST*
PROWL
PROWLED
PROWLER
PROWLERS
PROWLING
PROWLINGS
PROWLS
PROWS
PROXEMIC*
PROXEMICS*
PROXIES
PROXIMAL
PROXIMATE
PROXIMITIES
PROXIMITY
PROXIMO
PROXY
PROYN
PROYNE
PROYNED
PROYNES
PROYNING
PROYNS
PROZYMITE
PROZYMITES
PRUDE
PRUDENCE
PRUDENCES
PRUDENT
PRUDENTLY
PRUDERIES
PRUDERY
PRUDES
PRUDISH
PRUDISHLY
PRUH

PRUINA
PRUINAS
PRUINE
PRUINES
PRUINOSE
PRUNABLE*
PRUNE
PRUNED
PRUNELLA
PRUNELLAS
PRUNELLE
PRUNELLES
PRUNELLO
PRUNELLOS
PRUNER
PRUNERS
PRUNES
PRUNING
PRUNINGS
PRUNT
PRUNTED
PRUNTS
PRUNUS
PRUNUSES
PRURIENCE
PRURIENCES
PRURIENCIES
PRURIENCY
PRURIENT
PRURIGO
PRURIGOS
PRURITIC
PRURITUS
PRURITUSES
PRUSIK
PRUSIKED
PRUSIKING
PRUSIKS
PRUSSIATE
PRUSSIATES
PRUSSIC
PRUTA*
PRUTAH*
PRUTOT*
PRUTOTH*
PRY
PRYER
PRYERS
PRYING
PRYINGLY
PRYINGS
PRYS
PRYSE
PRYSED
PRYSES
PRYSING
PRYTANEA
PRYTANEUM
PRYTHEE
PSALM
PSALMBOOK*
PSALMBOOKS*
PSALMED*
PSALMIC*

PSALMING*
PSALMIST
PSALMISTS
PSALMODIC
PSALMODIES
PSALMODY
PSALMS
PSALTER
PSALTERIA
PSALTERIES
PSALTERIUM*
PSALTERS
PSALTERY
PSALTRESS
PSALTRESSES
PSALTRIES*
PSALTRY*
PSAMMITE
PSAMMITES
PSAMMITIC
PSAMMON*
PSAMMONS*
PSCHENT
PSCHENTS
PSELLISM
PSELLISMS
PSEPHISM
PSEPHISMS
PSEPHITE
PSEPHITES
PSEPHITIC
PSEUD
PSEUDAXES
PSEUDAXIS
PSEUDERIES
PSEUDERY
PSEUDISH
PSEUDO
PSEUDONYM
PSEUDONYMS
PSEUDOPOD
PSEUDOPODS
PSEUDOS*
PSEUDS
PSHAW
PSHAWED
PSHAWING
PSHAWS
PSI
PSILOCIN
PSILOCINS
PSILOSES
PSILOSIS
PSILOTIC
PSION
PSIONIC
PSIONICS
PSIONS
PSIS
PSOAE*
PSOAI*
PSOAS
PSOASES
PSOATIC*

PSOCID
PSOCIDS
PSORA
PSORALEA*
PSORALEAS*
PSORALEN
PSORALENS
PSORAS
PSORIASES
PSORIASIS
PSORIATIC
PSORIATICS*
PSORIC
PSST
PST
PSYCH
PSYCHE
PSYCHED
PSYCHES
PSYCHIC
PSYCHICAL
PSYCHICS
PSYCHING
PSYCHISM
PSYCHISMS
PSYCHIST
PSYCHISTS
PSYCHO
PSYCHOGAS
PSYCHOGASES
PSYCHOID
PSYCHOIDS
PSYCHOS
PSYCHOSES
PSYCHOSIS
PSYCHOTIC
PSYCHOTICS
PSYCHS
PSYLLA
PSYLLAS
PSYLLID
PSYLLIDS
PSYLLIUM*
PSYLLIUMS*
PSYOP
PSYOPS
PSYWAR
PSYWARS
PTARMIC
PTARMICS
PTARMIGAN
PTARMIGANS
PTERIA
PTERIDINE*
PTERIDINES*
PTERIN
PTERINS
PTERION
PTEROPOD
PTEROPODS
PTEROSAUR
PTEROSAURS
PTERYGIA
PTERYGIAL

PTERYGIALS	PUBLISHES	PUDGE	PUGGAREES	PULDRONS
PTERYGIUM	PUBLISHING	PUDGES	PUGGED	PULE
PTERYGIUMS*	PUBS	PUDGIER	PUGGERIES	PULED
PTERYGOID	PUCCOON	PUDGIEST	PUGGERY	PULER
PTERYGOIDS	PUCCOONS	PUDGILY*	PUGGIE	PULERS
PTERYLA	PUCE	PUDGINESS	PUGGIER	PULES
PTERYLAE	PUCELAGE	PUDGINESSES	PUGGIES	PULI*
PTILOSES	PUCELAGES	PUDGY	PUGGIEST	PULICENE*
PTILOSIS	PUCELLE	PUDIBUND	PUGGING	PULICIDE
PTISAN	PUCELLES	PUDIC	PUGGINGS	PULICIDES
PTISANS	PUCER	PUDICITIES	PUGGISH	PULIER
PTOMAIN*	PUCES	PUDICITY	PUGGLE	PULIEST
PTOMAINE	PUCEST	PUDOR	PUGGLED	PULIK*
PTOMAINES	PUCK	PUDORS	PUGGLES	PULING
PTOMAINS*	PUCKA	PUDS	PUGGLING	PULINGLY
PTOSES	PUCKER	PUDSEY	PUGGREE	PULINGS
PTOSIS	PUCKERED	PUDSIER	PUGGREES	PULIS*
PTOTIC*	PUCKERER*	PUDSIEST	PUGGRIES*	PULK
PTYALIN	PUCKERERS*	PUDSY	PUGGRY*	PULKA
PTYALINS	PUCKERIER*	PUDU	PUGGY	PULKAS
PTYALISE	PUCKERIEST*	PUDUS	PUGH	PULKHA
PTYALISED	PUCKERING	PUEBLO	PUGIL	PULKHAS
PTYALISES	PUCKERS	PUEBLOS	PUGILISM	PULKS
PTYALISING	PUCKERY	PUER	PUGILISMS	PULL
PTYALISM	PUCKFIST	PUERED	PUGILIST	PULLBACK*
PTYALISMS	PUCKFISTS	PUERILE	PUGILISTS	PULLBACKS*
PTYALIZE	PUCKISH	PUERILELY*	PUGILS	PULLED
PTYALIZED	PUCKISHLY*	PUERILISM	PUGMARK*	PULLER
PTYALIZES	PUCKLE	PUERILISMS	PUGMARKS*	PULLERS
PTYALIZING	PUCKLES	PUERILITIES	PUGNACITIES	PULLET
PTYXES	PUCKS	PUERILITY	PUGNACITY	PULLETS
PTYXIS	PUD	PUERING	PUGREE*	PULLEY
PTYXISES	PUDDEN	PUERPERAL	PUGREES*	PULLEYS
PUB	PUDDENING	PUERPERIA*	PUGS	PULLING
PUBERAL	PUDDENINGS	PUERPERIUM*	PUH	PULLMAN*
PUBERTAL	PUDDENS	PUERS	PUIR	PULLMANS*
PUBERTIES	PUDDER	PUFF	PUIRER	PULLOUT*
PUBERTY	PUDDERED	PUFFBALL	PUIREST	PULLOUTS*
PUBES	PUDDERING	PUFFBALLS	PUISNE	PULLOVER
PUBESCENT	PUDDERS	PUFFBIRD	PUISNES	PULLOVERS
PUBIC	PUDDIES	PUFFBIRDS	PUISNY	PULLS
PUBIS	PUDDING	PUFFED	PUISSANCE	PULLULATE
PUBISES	PUDDINGS	PUFFER	PUISSANCES	PULLULATED
PUBLIC	PUDDINGY	PUFFERIES	PUISSANT	PULLULATES
PUBLICAN	PUDDLE	PUFFERS	PUISSAUNT	PULLULATING
PUBLICANS	PUDDLED	PUFFERY	PUJA	PULLUP*
PUBLICISE	PUDDLER	PUFFIER	PUJAH*	PULLUPS*
PUBLICISED	PUDDLERS	PUFFIEST	PUJAHS*	PULMO
PUBLICISES	PUDDLES	PUFFILY	PUJAS	PULMONARY
PUBLICISING	PUDDLIER	PUFFIN	PUKE	PULMONATE
PUBLICIST	PUDDLIEST	PUFFINESS	PUKED	PULMONATES
PUBLICISTS	PUDDLING	PUFFINESSES	PUKEKO	PULMONES
PUBLICITIES	PUDDLINGS	PUFFING	PUKEKOS	PULMONIC
PUBLICITY	PUDDLY	PUFFINGLY	PUKER	PULMONICS
PUBLICIZE	PUDDOCK	PUFFINGS	PUKERS	PULMOTOR*
PUBLICIZED	PUDDOCKS	PUFFINS	PUKES	PULMOTORS*
PUBLICIZES	PUDDY	PUFFS	PUKING	PULP
PUBLICIZING	PUDENCIES	PUFFY	PUKKA	PULPAL*
PUBLICLY	PUDENCY	PUFTALOON	PUKU	PULPALLY*
PUBLICS	PUDENDA	PUFTALOONS	PUKUS	PULPBOARD
PUBLISH	PUDENDAL	PUG	PUL*	PULPBOARDS
PUBLISHED	PUDENDOUS	PUGAREE*	PULA	PULPED
PUBLISHER	PUDENDUM	PUGAREES*	PULAS	PULPER
PUBLISHERS	PUDENT	PUGGAREE	PULDRON	PULPERS

PULPIER	PULSOJETS	PUMICES	PUNCTUATE	PUNKINESS
PULPIEST	PULTAN	PUMICING	PUNCTUATED	PUNKINESSES
PULPIFIED	PULTANS	PUMICITE*	PUNCTUATES	PUNKINS*
PULPIFIES	PULTON	PUMICITES*	PUNCTUATING	PUNKISH*
PULPIFY	PULTONS	PUMIE	PUNCTULE	PUNKS
PULPIFYING	PULTOON	PUMIES	PUNCTULES	PUNKY*
PULPILY	PULTOONS	PUMMEL	PUNCTUM	PUNNED
PULPINESS	PULTUN	PUMMELED*	PUNCTURE	PUNNER
PULPINESSES	PULTUNS	PUMMELING*	PUNCTURED	PUNNERS
PULPING	PULTURE	PUMMELLED	PUNCTURER	PUNNET
PULPIT	PULTURES	PUMMELLING	PUNCTURERS	PUNNETS
PULPITAL*	PULU	PUMMELO*	PUNCTURES	PUNNIER*
PULPITED	PULUS	PUMMELOS*	PUNCTURING	PUNNIEST*
PULPITEER	PULVER	PUMMELS	PUNDIT	PUNNING
PULPITEERS	PULVERED	PUMP	PUNDITIC*	PUNNINGLY
PULPITER	PULVERINE	PUMPED	PUNDITRIES	PUNNINGS
PULPITERS	PULVERINES	PUMPER	PUNDITRY	PUNNY*
PULPITRIES	PULVERING	PUMPERS	PUNDITS	PUNS
PULPITRY	PULVERISE	PUMPHOOD	PUNDONOR	PUNSTER
PULPITS	PULVERISED	PUMPHOODS	PUNDONORES	PUNSTERS
PULPITUM	PULVERISES	PUMPING	PUNG*	PUNT
PULPITUMS	PULVERISING	PUMPION	PUNGA	PUNTED
PULPLESS*	PULVERIZE	PUMPIONS	PUNGAS	PUNTEE
PULPMILL	PULVERIZED	PUMPKIN	PUNGENCE	PUNTEES
PULPMILLS	PULVERIZES	PUMPKINS	PUNGENCES	PUNTER
PULPOUS	PULVERIZING	PUMPLESS*	PUNGENCIES	PUNTERS
PULPS	PULVEROUS	PUMPLIKE*	PUNGENCY	PUNTIES
PULPSTONE	PULVERS	PUMPS	PUNGENT	PUNTING
PULPSTONES	PULVIL	PUMY	PUNGENTLY	PUNTO
PULPWOOD	PULVILIO	PUN	PUNGLE*	PUNTOS
PULPWOODS	PULVILIOS	PUNA	PUNGLED*	PUNTS
PULPY	PULVILLAR	PUNALUA	PUNGLES*	PUNTSMAN
PULQUE	PULVILLE	PUNALUAN	PUNGLING*	PUNTSMEN
PULQUES	PULVILLED	PUNALUAS	PUNGS*	PUNTY
PULS*	PULVILLES	PUNAS	PUNIER	PUNY
PULSANT*	PULVILLI	PUNCE	PUNIEST	PUP
PULSAR	PULVILLING	PUNCED	PUNILY	PUPA
PULSARS	PULVILLIO	PUNCES	PUNINESS	PUPAE
PULSATE	PULVILLIOS	PUNCH	PUNINESSES	PUPAL
PULSATED	PULVILLUS	PUNCHBALL*	PUNISH	PUPARIA
PULSATES	PULVILS	PUNCHBALLS*	PUNISHED	PUPARIAL
PULSATILE	PULVINAR	PUNCHED	PUNISHER	PUPARIUM
PULSATING	PULVINARS	PUNCHEON	PUNISHERS	PUPAS
PULSATION	PULVINATE	PUNCHEONS	PUNISHES	PUPATE
PULSATIONS	PULVINI	PUNCHER	PUNISHING	PUPATED
PULSATIVE	PULVINULE	PUNCHERS	PUNITION	PUPATES
PULSATOR	PULVINULES	PUNCHES	PUNITIONS	PUPATING
PULSATORS	PULVINUS	PUNCHIER	PUNITIVE	PUPATION
PULSATORY	PULWAR	PUNCHIEST	PUNITORY	PUPATIONS
PULSE	PULWARS	PUNCHILY*	PUNK	PUPFISH
PULSED	PULY	PUNCHING	PUNKA	PUPFISHES
PULSEJET	PUMA	PUNCHLESS*	PUNKAH	PUPIL
PULSEJETS	PUMAS	PUNCHY	PUNKAHS	PUPILAGE
PULSELESS	PUMELO	PUNCING	PUNKAS	PUPILAGES
PULSER*	PUMELOS	PUNCTA	PUNKER	PUPILAR
PULSERS*	PUMICATE	PUNCTATE	PUNKERS*	PUPILARY
PULSES	PUMICATED	PUNCTATED	PUNKEST	PUPILLAGE
PULSIDGE	PUMICATES	PUNCTATOR	PUNKEY*	PUPILLAGES
PULSIDGES	PUMICATING	PUNCTATORS	PUNKEYS*	PUPILLAR
PULSIFIC	PUMICE	PUNCTILIO	PUNKIE*	PUPILLARY
PULSING	PUMICED	PUNCTILIOS	PUNKIER*	PUPILLATE
PULSION*	PUMICEOUS	PUNCTO	PUNKIES*	PUPILS
PULSIONS*	PUMICER*	PUNCTOS	PUNKIEST*	PUPILSHIP
PULSOJET	PUMICERS*	PUNCTUAL	PUNKIN*	PUPILSHIPS

The Chambers Dictionary is the authority for many longer words; see Introduction, page ix

PUPPED	PURFLY	PURPIE	PURSUANCES	PUSLED
PUPPET	PURGATION	PURPIES	PURSUANT	PUSLES
PUPPETEER	PURGATIONS	PURPLE	PURSUE	PUSLEY*
PUPPETEERS	PURGATIVE	PURPLED	PURSUED	PUSLEYS*
PUPPETRIES	PURGATIVES	PURPLER	PURSUER	PUSLIKE*
PUPPETRY	PURGATORIES	PURPLES	PURSUERS	PUSLING
PUPPETS	PURGATORY	PURPLEST	PURSUES	PUSS
PUPPIED	PURGE	PURPLIER	PURSUING	PUSSEL
PUPPIES	PURGED	PURPLIEST	PURSUINGS	PUSSELS
PUPPING	PURGER	PURPLING	PURSUIT	PUSSER
PUPPODUM	PURGERS	PURPLISH	PURSUITS	PUSSERS
PUPPODUMS	PURGES	PURPLY	PURSY	PUSSES
PUPPY	PURGING	PURPORT	PURTIER	PUSSIER*
PUPPYDOM	PURGINGS	PURPORTED	PURTIEST	PUSSIES
PUPPYDOMS	PURI	PURPORTING	PURTRAID	PUSSIEST*
PUPPYHOOD	PURIFIED	PURPORTS	PURTRAYD	PUSSLEY*
PUPPYHOODS	PURIFIER	PURPOSE	PURTY	PUSSLEYS*
PUPPYING	PURIFIERS	PURPOSED	PURULENCE	PUSSLIES*
PUPPYISH	PURIFIES	PURPOSELY	PURULENCES	PUSSLIKE*
PUPPYISM	PURIFY	PURPOSES	PURULENCIES	PUSSLY*
PUPPYISMS	PURIFYING	PURPOSING	PURULENCY	PUSSY
PUPPYLIKE*	PURIM	PURPOSIVE	PURULENT	PUSSYCAT*
PUPS	PURIMS	PURPURA	PURVEY	PUSSYCATS*
PUPUNHA	PURIN	PURPURAS	PURVEYED	PUSSYFOOT
PUPUNHAS	PURINE	PURPURE	PURVEYING	PUSSYFOOTED
PUR	PURINES	PURPUREAL	PURVEYOR	PUSSYFOOTING
PURANA*	PURING	PURPURES	PURVEYORS	PUSSYFOOTS
PURANAS*	PURINS	PURPURIC	PURVEYS	PUSSYTOES*
PURANIC*	PURIS	PURPURIN	PURVIEW	PUSTULANT
PURBLIND	PURISM	PURPURINS	PURVIEWS	PUSTULANTS
PURCHASE	PURISMS	PURPY	PUS	PUSTULAR
PURCHASED	PURIST	PURR	PUSES	PUSTULATE
PURCHASER	PURISTIC	PURRED	PUSH	PUSTULATED
PURCHASERS	PURISTS	PURRING	PUSHBALL*	PUSTULATES
PURCHASES	PURITAN	PURRINGLY	PUSHBALLS*	PUSTULATING
PURCHASING	PURITANIC	PURRINGS	PUSHCART*	PUSTULE
PURDA*	PURITANS	PURRS	PUSHCARTS*	PUSTULED*
PURDAH	PURITIES	PURS	PUSHCHAIR*	PUSTULES
PURDAHED	PURITY	PURSE	PUSHCHAIRS*	PUSTULOUS
PURDAHS	PURL	PURSED	PUSHDOWN*	PUT
PURDAS*	PURLED	PURSEFUL	PUSHDOWNS*	PUTAMEN
PURDONIUM	PURLER	PURSEFULS	PUSHED	PUTAMINA
PURDONIUMS	PURLERS	PURSELIKE*	PUSHER	PUTATIVE
PURE	PURLICUE	PURSER	PUSHERS	PUTCHEON
PUREBLOOD*	PURLICUED	PURSERS	PUSHES	PUTCHEONS
PUREBLOODS*	PURLICUES	PURSES	PUSHFUL	PUTCHER
PUREBRED*	PURLICUING	PURSEW	PUSHFULLY	PUTCHERS
PUREBREDS*	PURLIEU	PURSEWED	PUSHIER	PUTCHOCK
PURED	PURLIEUS	PURSEWING	PUSHIEST	PUTCHOCKS
PUREE	PURLIN	PURSEWS	PUSHILY*	PUTCHUK
PUREED	PURLINE	PURSIER	PUSHINESS	PUTCHUKS
PUREEING	PURLINES	PURSIEST	PUSHINESSES	PUTEAL
PUREES	PURLING	PURSILY*	PUSHING	PUTEALS
PURELY	PURLINGS	PURSINESS	PUSHINGLY	PUTELI
PURENESS	PURLINS	PURSINESSES	PUSHOVER*	PUTELIS
PURENESSES	PURLOIN	PURSING	PUSHOVERS*	PUTID
PURER	PURLOINED	PURSLAIN	PUSHPIN*	PUTLOCK
PURES	PURLOINER	PURSLAINS	PUSHPINS*	PUTLOCKS
PUREST	PURLOINERS	PURSLANE	PUSHROD	PUTLOG
PURFLE	PURLOINING	PURSLANES	PUSHRODS	PUTLOGS
PURFLED	PURLOINS	PURSUABLE	PUSHUP*	PUTOFF*
PURFLES	PURLS	PURSUAL	PUSHUPS*	PUTOFFS*
PURFLING	PUROMYCIN*	PURSUALS	PUSHY	PUTOIS
PURFLINGS	PUROMYCINS*	PURSUANCE	PUSLE	PUTON*

Words marked with an asterisk are from OTCWL

PUTONS*
PUTOUT*
PUTOUTS*
PUTREFIED
PUTREFIES
PUTREFY
PUTREFYING
PUTRID
PUTRIDER
PUTRIDEST
PUTRIDITIES
PUTRIDITY
PUTRIDLY
PUTS
PUTSCH
PUTSCHES
PUTSCHIST
PUTSCHISTS
PUTT
PUTTED
PUTTEE
PUTTEES
PUTTEN
PUTTER
PUTTERED
PUTTERER*
PUTTERERS*
PUTTERING
PUTTERS
PUTTI
PUTTIE
PUTTIED
PUTTIER
PUTTIERS
PUTTIES
PUTTING
PUTTINGS
PUTTO
PUTTOCK
PUTTOCKS
PUTTS
PUTTY
PUTTYING
PUTTYLESS*
PUTTYLIKE*
PUTTYROOT*
PUTTYROOTS*
PUTURE
PUTURES
PUTZ
PUTZED*
PUTZES
PUTZING*
PUY
PUYS
PUZEL
PUZELS
PUZZEL
PUZZELS
PUZZLE
PUZZLED
PUZZLEDOM
PUZZLEDOMS
PUZZLER

PUZZLERS
PUZZLES
PUZZLING
PUZZOLANA
PUZZOLANAS
PYA*
PYAEMIA
PYAEMIAS
PYAEMIC
PYAS*
PYAT
PYATS
PYCNIC
PYCNIDIA
PYCNIDIAL*
PYCNIDIUM
PYCNITE
PYCNITES
PYCNON
PYCNONS
PYCNOSES
PYCNOSIS
PYCNOTIC*
PYE
PYEBALD
PYEBALDS
PYEING
PYELITIC
PYELITIS
PYELITISES
PYELOGRAM
PYELOGRAMS
PYEMIA
PYEMIAS
PYEMIC*
PYENGADU
PYENGADUS
PYES
PYET
PYETS
PYGAL
PYGALS
PYGARG
PYGARGS
PYGIDIA
PYGIDIAL
PYGIDIUM
PYGIDIUMS
PYGMAEAN
PYGMEAN
PYGMIES
PYGMOID
PYGMY
PYGMYISH*
PYGMYISM*
PYGMYISMS*
PYGOSTYLE
PYGOSTYLES
PYIC*
PYIN*
PYINS*
PYJAMAED
PYJAMAS
PYKNIC

PYKNICS*
PYKNOSES*
PYKNOSIS*
PYKNOSOME
PYKNOSOMES
PYKNOTIC*
PYLON
PYLONS
PYLORI*
PYLORIC
PYLORUS
PYLORUSES
PYNE
PYNED
PYNES
PYNING
PYODERMA*
PYODERMAS*
PYOGENIC
PYOID
PYONER
PYONERS
PYONINGS
PYORRHEA*
PYORRHEAS*
PYORRHOEA
PYORRHOEAS
PYOSES*
PYOSIS*
PYOT
PYOTS
PYRACANTH
PYRACANTHS
PYRAL
PYRALID
PYRALIDS
PYRALIS
PYRALISES
PYRAMID
PYRAMIDAL
PYRAMIDED
PYRAMIDES
PYRAMIDIA
PYRAMIDIC
PYRAMIDING
PYRAMIDON
PYRAMIDONS
PYRAMIDS
PYRAMIS
PYRAMISES
PYRAN*
PYRANOID*
PYRANOSE*
PYRANOSES*
PYRANS*
PYRE
PYRENE
PYRENEITE
PYRENEITES
PYRENES
PYRENOID
PYRENOIDS
PYRES
PYRETHRIN

PYRETHRINS
PYRETHRUM
PYRETHRUMS
PYRETIC
PYREXIA
PYREXIAL
PYREXIAS
PYREXIC
PYRIC*
PYRIDIC*
PYRIDINE
PYRIDINES
PYRIDOXAL*
PYRIDOXALS*
PYRIDOXIN
PYRIDOXINS
PYRIFORM
PYRITE
PYRITES
PYRITIC
PYRITICAL
PYRITISE
PYRITISED
PYRITISES
PYRITISING
PYRITIZE
PYRITIZED
PYRITIZES
PYRITIZING
PYRITOUS
PYRO
PYROCLAST
PYROCLASTS
PYROGEN
PYROGENIC
PYROGENS
PYROLA*
PYROLAS*
PYROLATER
PYROLATERS
PYROLATRIES
PYROLATRY
PYROLIZE*
PYROLIZED*
PYROLIZES*
PYROLIZING*
PYROLOGIES*
PYROLOGY*
PYROLYSE
PYROLYSED
PYROLYSES
PYROLYSING
PYROLYSIS
PYROLYTIC
PYROLYZE
PYROLYZED
PYROLYZER*
PYROLYZERS*
PYROLYZES
PYROLYZING
PYROMANCIES
PYROMANCY
PYROMANIA
PYROMANIAS

PYROMETER
PYROMETERS
PYROMETRIES
PYROMETRY
PYRONE*
PYRONES*
PYRONINE*
PYRONINES*
PYROPE
PYROPES
PYROPHONE
PYROPHONES
PYROPUS
PYROPUSES
PYROS
PYROSCOPE
PYROSCOPES
PYROSES
PYROSIS
PYROSISES*
PYROSOME
PYROSOMES
PYROSTAT
PYROSTATS
PYROXENE
PYROXENES
PYROXENIC
PYROXYLE
PYROXYLES
PYROXYLIC
PYROXYLIN
PYROXYLINS
PYRRHIC
PYRRHICS
PYRRHOUS
PYRROL*
PYRROLE
PYRROLES
PYRROLIC*
PYRROLS*
PYRUVATE
PYRUVATES
PYTHIUM
PYTHIUMS
PYTHON
PYTHONESS
PYTHONESSES
PYTHONIC
PYTHONS
PYURIA
PYURIAS
PYX
PYXED
PYXES
PYXIDES
PYXIDIA
PYXIDIUM
PYXIE*
PYXIES*
PYXING
PYXIS
PZAZZ
PZAZZES

Q

QABALAH · QABALAHS · QADI · QADIS · QAID* · QAIDS* · QAIMAQAM · QAIMAQAMS · QALAMDAN · QALAMDANS · QANAT · QANATS · QASIDA · QASIDAS · QAT · QATS · QAWWAL · QAWWALI · QAWWALIS · QAWWALS · QI · QIBLA · QIBLAS · QIGONG · QIGONGS · QINDAR · QINDARKA* · QINDARS · QINGHAOSU · QINGHAOSUS · QINTAR · QINTARS · QIS · QIVIUT · QIVIUTS · QOPH · QOPHS · QUA · QUAALUDE* · QUAALUDES* · QUACK · QUACKED · QUACKER · QUACKERIES · QUACKERS · QUACKERY · QUACKING · QUACKISH* · QUACKISM* · QUACKISMS* · QUACKLE · QUACKLED · QUACKLES · QUACKLING · QUACKS

QUAD · QUADDED · QUADDING · QUADPLEX* · QUADPLEXES* · QUADRANS · QUADRANT · QUADRANTES · QUADRANTS · QUADRAT · QUADRATE · QUADRATED · QUADRATES · QUADRATIC · QUADRATICS · QUADRATING · QUADRATS · QUADRATUS · QUADRATUSES · QUADRELLA · QUADRELLAS · QUADRIC · QUADRICS · QUADRIFID · QUADRIGA · QUADRIGAE · QUADRILLE · QUADRILLED · QUADRILLES · QUADRILLING · QUADROON · QUADROONS · QUADRUMAN · QUADRUMANS · QUADRUPED · QUADRUPEDS · QUADRUPLE · QUADRUPLED · QUADRUPLES · QUADRUPLIES · QUADRUPLING · QUADRUPLY · QUADS · QUAERE · QUAERED · QUAEREING · QUAERES · QUAERITUR · QUAESITUM · QUAESITUMS · QUAESTOR · QUAESTORS · QUAFF · QUAFFED · QUAFFER

QUAFFERS · QUAFFING · QUAFFS · QUAG · QUAGGA · QUAGGAS · QUAGGIER · QUAGGIEST · QUAGGY · QUAGMIRE · QUAGMIRED · QUAGMIRES · QUAGMIRIER · QUAGMIRIEST · QUAGMIRING · QUAGMIRY · QUAGS · QUAHAUG · QUAHAUGS · QUAHOG · QUAHOGS · QUAI* · QUAICH · QUAICHES* · QUAICHS · QUAIGH · QUAIGHS · QUAIL · QUAILED · QUAILING · QUAILINGS · QUAILS · QUAINT · QUAINTER · QUAINTEST · QUAINTLY · QUAIR · QUAIRS · QUAIS* · QUAKE · QUAKED · QUAKER · QUAKERS · QUAKES · QUAKIER · QUAKIEST · QUAKILY* · QUAKINESS · QUAKINESSES · QUAKING · QUAKINGLY · QUAKINGS · QUAKY · QUALE · QUALIA

QUALIFIED · QUALIFIER · QUALIFIERS · QUALIFIES · QUALIFY · QUALIFYING · QUALIFYINGS · QUALITIED · QUALITIES · QUALITY · QUALM · QUALMIER · QUALMIEST · QUALMING · QUALMISH · QUALMLESS · QUALMS · QUALMY · QUAMASH · QUAMASHES · QUANDANG · QUANDANGS · QUANDARIES · QUANDARY · QUANDONG · QUANDONGS · QUANGO · QUANGOS · QUANNET · QUANNETS · QUANT · QUANTA · QUANTAL · QUANTED · QUANTIC · QUANTICAL · QUANTICS · QUANTIFIED · QUANTIFIES · QUANTIFY · QUANTIFYING · QUANTILE* · QUANTILES* · QUANTING · QUANTISE · QUANTISED · QUANTISES · QUANTISING · QUANTITIES · QUANTITY · QUANTIZE · QUANTIZED · QUANTIZER* · QUANTIZERS* · QUANTIZES

QUANTIZING · QUANTONG · QUANTONGS · QUANTS · QUANTUM · QUARE · QUARENDEN · QUARENDENS · QUARENDER · QUARENDERS · QUARER · QUAREST · QUARK · QUARKS · QUARREL · QUARRELED* · QUARRELER* · QUARRELERS* · QUARRELING* · QUARRELLED · QUARRELLING · QUARRELLINGS · QUARRELS · QUARRIED · QUARRIER · QUARRIERS · QUARRIES · QUARRY · QUARRYING · QUARRYINGS* · QUARRYMAN · QUARRYMEN · QUART · QUARTAN · QUARTANS · QUARTE · QUARTER · QUARTERED · QUARTERING · QUARTERINGS · QUARTERLIES · QUARTERLY · QUARTERN · QUARTERNS · QUARTERS · QUARTES · QUARTET · QUARTETS · QUARTETT · QUARTETTE · QUARTETTES · QUARTETTI · QUARTETTO · QUARTETTS · QUARTIC

Words marked with an asterisk are from OTCWL

QUARTICS	QUAYSIDE	QUEESTS	QUESTOR	QUICKLIMES
QUARTIER	QUAYSIDES	QUEINT	QUESTORS	QUICKLY
QUARTIERS	QUEACH	QUELCH	QUESTRIST	QUICKNESS
QUARTILE	QUEACHES	QUELCHED	QUESTRISTS	QUICKNESSES
QUARTILES	QUEACHIER	QUELCHES	QUESTS	QUICKS
QUARTO	QUEACHIEST	QUELCHING	QUETCH	QUICKSAND
QUARTOS	QUEACHY	QUELEA	QUETCHED	QUICKSANDS
QUARTS	QUEAN	QUELEAS	QUETCHES	QUICKSET
QUARTZ	QUEANS	QUELL	QUETCHING	QUICKSETS
QUARTZES	QUEASIER	QUELLED	QUETHE	QUICKSTEP
QUARTZIER	QUEASIEST	QUELLER	QUETHES	QUICKSTEPPED
QUARTZIEST	QUEASILY	QUELLERS	QUETHING	QUICKSTEPPING
QUARTZITE	QUEASY	QUELLING	QUETSCH	QUICKSTEPS
QUARTZITES	QUEAZIER	QUELLS	QUETSCHES	QUID
QUARTZOSE	QUEAZIEST	QUEME	QUETZAL	QUIDAM
QUARTZY	QUEAZY	QUEMED	QUETZALES	QUIDAMS
QUASAR	QUEBRACHO	QUEMES	QUETZALS	QUIDDANIES
QUASARS	QUEBRACHOS	QUEMING	QUEUE	QUIDDANY
QUASH	QUEECHIER	QUENA	QUEUED	QUIDDIT
QUASHED	QUEECHIEST	QUENAS	QUEUEING	QUIDDITIES
QUASHEE	QUEECHY	QUENCH	QUEUEINGS	QUIDDITS
QUASHEES	QUEEN	QUENCHED	QUEUER*	QUIDDITY
QUASHER*	QUEENDOM	QUENCHER	QUEUERS*	QUIDDLE
QUASHERS*	QUEENDOMS	QUENCHERS	QUEUES	QUIDDLED
QUASHES	QUEENED	QUENCHES	QUEUING	QUIDDLER
QUASHIE	QUEENHOOD	QUENCHING	QUEUINGS	QUIDDLERS
QUASHIES	QUEENHOODS	QUENCHINGS	QUEY	QUIDDLES
QUASHING	QUEENIE	QUENELLE	QUEYN	QUIDDLING
QUASI	QUEENIER	QUENELLES	QUEYNIE	QUIDNUNC
QUASS*	QUEENIES	QUEP	QUEYNIES	QUIDNUNCS
QUASSES*	QUEENIEST	QUERCETIN	QUEYNS	QUIDS
QUASSIA	QUEENING	QUERCETINS	QUEYS	QUIESCE
QUASSIAS	QUEENINGS	QUERCETUM	QUEZAL*	QUIESCED
QUASSIN*	QUEENITE	QUERCETUMS	QUEZALES*	QUIESCENT
QUASSINS*	QUEENITES	QUERCINE*	QUEZALS*	QUIESCES
QUAT	QUEENLESS	QUERIDA*	QUIBBLE	QUIESCING
QUATCH	QUEENLET	QUERIDAS*	QUIBBLED	QUIET
QUATCHED	QUEENLETS	QUERIED	QUIBBLER	QUIETED
QUATCHES	QUEENLIER	QUERIER*	QUIBBLERS	QUIETEN
QUATCHING	QUEENLIEST	QUERIERS*	QUIBBLES	QUIETENED
QUATE*	QUEENLY	QUERIES	QUIBBLING	QUIETENING
QUATORZE	QUEENS	QUERIMONIES	QUIBBLINGS	QUIETENINGS
QUATORZES	QUEENSHIP	QUERIMONY	QUIBLIN	QUIETENS
QUATRAIN	QUEENSHIPS	QUERIST	QUIBLINS	QUIETER
QUATRAINS	QUEENSIDE*	QUERISTS	QUICH	QUIETERS
QUATRE*	QUEENSIDES*	QUERN	QUICHE	QUIETEST
QUATRES*	QUEENY	QUERNS	QUICHED	QUIETING
QUATS	QUEER	QUERULOUS	QUICHES	QUIETINGS
QUAVER	QUEERCORE	QUERY	QUICHING	QUIETISM
QUAVERED	QUEERCORES	QUERYING	QUICK	QUIETISMS
QUAVERER	QUEERDOM	QUERYINGS	QUICKBEAM	QUIETIST
QUAVERERS	QUEERDOMS	QUEST	QUICKBEAMS	QUIETISTS
QUAVERIER	QUEERED	QUESTANT	QUICKEN	QUIETIVE
QUAVERIEST	QUEERER	QUESTANTS	QUICKENED	QUIETIVES
QUAVERING	QUEEREST	QUESTED	QUICKENER	QUIETLY
QUAVERINGS	QUEERING	QUESTER	QUICKENERS	QUIETNESS
QUAVERS	QUEERISH	QUESTERS	QUICKENING	QUIETNESSES
QUAVERY	QUEERITIES	QUESTING	QUICKENINGS	QUIETS
QUAY	QUEERITY	QUESTINGS	QUICKENS	QUIETSOME
QUAYAGE	QUEERLY	QUESTION	QUICKER	QUIETUDE
QUAYAGES	QUEERNESS	QUESTIONED	QUICKEST	QUIETUDES
QUAYD	QUEERNESSES	QUESTIONING	QUICKIE	QUIETUS
QUAYLIKE*	QUEERS	QUESTIONINGS	QUICKIES	QUIETUSES
QUAYS	QUEEST	QUESTIONS	QUICKLIME	QUIFF

The Chambers Dictionary is the authority for many longer words; see Introduction, page ix

QUIFFS
QUIGHT
QUIGHTED
QUIGHTING
QUIGHTS
QUILL
QUILLAI
QUILLAIA*
QUILLAIAS*
QUILLAIS
QUILLAJA*
QUILLAJAS*
QUILLBACK*
QUILLBACKS*
QUILLED
QUILLET
QUILLETS
QUILLING
QUILLINGS
QUILLMAN
QUILLMEN
QUILLON
QUILLONS
QUILLS
QUILLWORK*
QUILLWORKS*
QUILLWORT
QUILLWORTS
QUILT
QUILTED
QUILTER
QUILTERS
QUILTING
QUILTINGS
QUILTS
QUIM
QUIMS
QUIN
QUINA
QUINARIES
QUINARY
QUINAS
QUINATE
QUINCE
QUINCES
QUINCHE
QUINCHED
QUINCHES
QUINCHING
QUINCUNX
QUINCUNXES
QUINE
QUINELA*
QUINELAS*
QUINELLA
QUINELLAS
QUINES
QUINIC
QUINIDINE
QUINIDINES
QUINIE
QUINIELA*
QUINIELAS*

QUINIES
QUININ*
QUININA*
QUININAS*
QUININE
QUININES
QUININS*
QUINNAT
QUINNATS
QUINOA
QUINOAS
QUINOID
QUINOIDAL
QUINOIDS
QUINOL
QUINOLIN*
QUINOLINE
QUINOLINES
QUINOLINS*
QUINOLONE
QUINOLONES
QUINOLS
QUINONE
QUINONES
QUINONOID
QUINQUINA
QUINQUINAS
QUINS
QUINSIED
QUINSIES
QUINSY
QUINT
QUINTA
QUINTAIN
QUINTAINS
QUINTAL
QUINTALS
QUINTAN
QUINTANS*
QUINTAR*
QUINTARS*
QUINTAS
QUINTE
QUINTES
QUINTET
QUINTETS
QUINTETT
QUINTETTE
QUINTETTES
QUINTETTI
QUINTETTO
QUINTETTS
QUINTIC
QUINTICS*
QUINTILE
QUINTILES
QUINTIN*
QUINTINS*
QUINTROON
QUINTROONS
QUINTS
QUINTUPLE
QUINTUPLED

QUINTUPLES
QUINTUPLING
QUINZE
QUINZES
QUIP
QUIPO
QUIPOS
QUIPPED
QUIPPER*
QUIPPERS*
QUIPPING
QUIPPISH
QUIPPU*
QUIPPUS*
QUIPS
QUIPSTER
QUIPSTERS
QUIPU
QUIPUS
QUIRE
QUIRED
QUIRES
QUIRING
QUIRISTER
QUIRISTERS
QUIRK
QUIRKED
QUIRKIER
QUIRKIEST
QUIRKILY
QUIRKING
QUIRKISH
QUIRKS
QUIRKY
QUIRT
QUIRTED
QUIRTING
QUIRTS
QUISLING
QUISLINGS
QUIST
QUISTS
QUIT
QUITCH
QUITCHED
QUITCHES
QUITCHING
QUITCLAIM
QUITCLAIMED
QUITCLAIMING
QUITCLAIMS
QUITE
QUITED
QUITES
QUITING
QUITRENT*
QUITRENTS*
QUITS
QUITTAL
QUITTALS
QUITTANCE
QUITTANCED
QUITTANCES

QUITTANCING
QUITTED
QUITTER
QUITTERS
QUITTING
QUITTOR
QUITTORS
QUIVER
QUIVERED
QUIVERER*
QUIVERERS*
QUIVERFUL
QUIVERFULS
QUIVERIER
QUIVERIEST
QUIVERING
QUIVERINGS
QUIVERISH
QUIVERS
QUIVERY
QUIXOTE*
QUIXOTES*
QUIXOTIC
QUIXOTISM
QUIXOTISMS
QUIXOTRIES
QUIXOTRY
QUIZ
QUIZZED
QUIZZER
QUIZZERIES
QUIZZERS
QUIZZERY
QUIZZES
QUIZZICAL
QUIZZIFIED
QUIZZIFIES
QUIZZIFY
QUIZZIFYING
QUIZZING
QUIZZINGS
QUOAD
QUOD
QUODDED
QUODDING
QUODLIBET
QUODLIBETS
QUODLIN
QUODLINS
QUODS
QUOHOG*
QUOHOGS*
QUOIF
QUOIFED
QUOIFING
QUOIFS
QUOIN
QUOINED
QUOINING
QUOINS
QUOIST
QUOISTS
QUOIT

QUOITED
QUOITER
QUOITERS
QUOITING
QUOITS
QUOKKA
QUOKKAS
QUOLL
QUOLLS
QUOMODO*
QUOMODOS*
QUONDAM
QUONK
QUONKED
QUONKING
QUONKS
QUOOKE
QUOP
QUOPPED
QUOPPING
QUOPS
QUORATE
QUORUM
QUORUMS
QUOTA
QUOTABLE
QUOTABLY
QUOTAS
QUOTATION
QUOTATIONS
QUOTATIVE
QUOTATIVES
QUOTE
QUOTED
QUOTER
QUOTERS
QUOTES
QUOTH
QUOTHA
QUOTIDIAN
QUOTIDIANS
QUOTIENT
QUOTIENTS
QUOTING
QUOTITION
QUOTITIONS
QUOTUM
QUOTUMS
QURSH*
QURSHES*
QURUSH*
QURUSHES*
QUYTE
QUYTED
QUYTES
QUYTING
QWERTIES
QWERTY
QWERTYS

Words marked with an asterisk are from OTCWL

R

RABANNA
RABANNAS
RABAT
RABATINE
RABATINES
RABATMENT
RABATMENTS
RABATO
RABATOES
RABATOS*
RABATS
RABATTE
RABATTED
RABATTES
RABATTING
RABATTINGS
RABBET
RABBETED
RABBETING
RABBETS
RABBI
RABBIES*
RABBIN
RABBINATE
RABBINATES
RABBINIC
RABBINISM
RABBINISMS
RABBINIST
RABBINISTS
RABBINITE
RABBINITES
RABBINS
RABBIS
RABBIT
RABBITED
RABBITER
RABBITERS
RABBITING
RABBITRIES
RABBITRY
RABBITS
RABBITY
RABBLE
RABBLED
RABBLER
RABBLERS
RABBLES
RABBLING
RABBLINGS
RABBONI
RABBONIS
RABI
RABIC
RABID

RABIDER
RABIDEST
RABIDITIES
RABIDITY
RABIDLY
RABIDNESS
RABIDNESSES
RABIES
RABIETIC*
RABIS
RACA
RACAHOUT
RACAHOUTS
RACCAHOUT
RACCAHOUTS
RACCOON
RACCOONS
RACE
RACECARD
RACECARDS
RACED
RACEGOER
RACEGOERS
RACEGOING
RACEGOINGS
RACEHORSE
RACEHORSES
RACEMATE
RACEMATES
RACEME
RACEMED
RACEMES
RACEMIC
RACEMISE
RACEMISED
RACEMISES
RACEMISING
RACEMISM
RACEMISMS
RACEMIZE
RACEMIZED
RACEMIZES
RACEMIZING
RACEMOID*
RACEMOSE
RACEMOUS*
RACEPATH
RACEPATHS
RACER
RACERS
RACES
RACETRACK
RACETRACKS
RACEWAY
RACEWAYS

RACH
RACHE
RACHES
RACHET*
RACHETS*
RACHIAL
RACHIDES
RACHIDIAL
RACHIDIAN
RACHILLA
RACHILLAE*
RACHILLAS
RACHIS
RACHISES
RACHITIC
RACHITIDES*
RACHITIS
RACHITISES
RACIAL
RACIALISM
RACIALISMS
RACIALIST
RACIALISTS
RACIALLY
RACIATION
RACIATIONS
RACIER
RACIEST
RACILY
RACINESS
RACINESSES
RACING
RACINGS
RACISM
RACISMS
RACIST
RACISTS
RACK
RACKED
RACKER
RACKERS
RACKET
RACKETED
RACKETEER
RACKETEERED
RACKETEERING
RACKETEERINGS
RACKETEERS
RACKETER
RACKETERS
RACKETIER
RACKETIEST
RACKETING
RACKETRIES
RACKETRY

RACKETS
RACKETT
RACKETTS
RACKETY
RACKFUL*
RACKFULS*
RACKING
RACKINGLY*
RACKINGS
RACKLE*
RACKS
RACKWORK
RACKWORKS
RACLETTE
RACLETTES
RACLOIR
RACLOIRS
RACON
RACONS
RACONTEUR
RACONTEURS
RACOON
RACOONS
RACQUET
RACQUETS
RACY
RAD
RADAR
RADARS
RADDED*
RADDER
RADDEST
RADDING*
RADDLE
RADDLED
RADDLEMAN
RADDLEMEN
RADDLES
RADDLING
RADDOCKE
RADDOCKES
RADE
RADGE
RADGER
RADGES
RADGEST
RADIABLE*
RADIAL
RADIALE
RADIALIA
RADIALISE
RADIALISED
RADIALISES
RADIALISING
RADIALITIES

RADIALITY
RADIALIZE
RADIALIZED
RADIALIZES
RADIALIZING
RADIALLY
RADIALS
RADIAN
RADIANCE
RADIANCES
RADIANCIES
RADIANCY
RADIANS
RADIANT
RADIANTLY
RADIANTS
RADIATA
RADIATAS
RADIATE
RADIATED
RADIATELY
RADIATES
RADIATING
RADIATION
RADIATIONS
RADIATIVE
RADIATOR
RADIATORS
RADIATORY
RADICAL
RADICALLY
RADICALS
RADICAND*
RADICANDS*
RADICANT
RADICATE
RADICATED
RADICATES
RADICATING
RADICCHIO
RADICCHIOS
RADICEL
RADICELS
RADICES
RADICLE
RADICLES
RADICULAR
RADICULE
RADICULES
RADII
RADIO
RADIOED
RADIOGRAM
RADIOGRAMS
RADIOING

The Chambers Dictionary is the authority for many longer words; see Introduction, page ix

RADIOLOGIES	RAGBAG	RAGTIMER	RAILROADED	RAIS
RADIOLOGY	RAGBAGS	RAGTIMERS	RAILROADING	RAISABLE
RADIOMAN*	RAGBOLT	RAGTIMES	RAILROADS	RAISE
RADIOMEN*	RAGBOLTS	RAGTOP	RAILS	RAISEABLE
RADIONICS	RAGDE	RAGTOPS	RAILWAY	RAISED
RADIOS	RAGE	RAGULED	RAILWAYS	RAISER
RADIOTHON	RAGED	RAGULY	RAILWOMAN	RAISERS
RADIOTHONS	RAGEE	RAGWEED	RAILWOMEN	RAISES
RADISH	RAGEES	RAGWEEDS	RAIMENT	RAISIN
RADISHES	RAGEFUL	RAGWHEEL	RAIMENTS	RAISING
RADIUM	RAGER	RAGWHEELS	RAIN	RAISINGS
RADIUMS	RAGERS	RAGWORK	RAINBAND	RAISINS
RADIUS	RAGES	RAGWORKS	RAINBANDS	RAISINY*
RADIUSES	RAGG	RAGWORM	RAINBIRD*	RAISONNE
RADIX	RAGGA	RAGWORMS	RAINBIRDS*	RAIT
RADIXES*	RAGGAS	RAGWORT	RAINBOW	RAITA
RADOME	RAGGED	RAGWORTS	RAINBOWED	RAITAS
RADOMES	RAGGEDER	RAH	RAINBOWS	RAITED
RADON	RAGGEDEST	RAHED	RAINBOWY	RAITING
RADONS	RAGGEDLY	RAHING	RAINCHECK	RAITS
RADS	RAGGEDY	RAHS	RAINCHECKS	RAIYAT
RADULA	RAGGEE	RAI	RAINCOAT	RAIYATS
RADULAE	RAGGEES	RAIA*	RAINCOATS	RAJ
RADULAR	RAGGERIES	RAIAS*	RAINDATE	RAJA
RADULAS*	RAGGERY	RAID	RAINDATES	RAJAH
RADULATE	RAGGIER	RAIDED	RAINDROP	RAJAHS
RADWASTE	RAGGIES	RAIDER	RAINDROPS	RAJAHSHIP
RADWASTES	RAGGIEST	RAIDERS	RAINE	RAJAHSHIPS
RAFALE	RAGGING	RAIDING	RAINED	RAJAS
RAFALES	RAGGINGS	RAIDS	RAINES	RAJASHIP
RAFF	RAGGLE	RAIK	RAINFALL	RAJASHIPS
RAFFIA	RAGGLED	RAIKED	RAINFALLS	RAJES
RAFFIAS	RAGGLES	RAIKING	RAINIER	RAKE
RAFFINATE	RAGGLING	RAIKS	RAINIEST	RAKED
RAFFINATES	RAGGS	RAIL	RAINILY*	RAKEE
RAFFINOSE	RAGGY	RAILBED	RAININESS	RAKEES
RAFFINOSES	RAGHEAD	RAILBEDS	RAININESSES	RAKEHELL
RAFFISH	RAGHEADS	RAILBIRD*	RAINING	RAKEHELLS
RAFFISHLY	RAGI	RAILBIRDS*	RAINLESS	RAKEHELLY
RAFFLE	RAGING	RAILBUS	RAINMAKER	RAKEOFF*
RAFFLED	RAGINGLY	RAILBUSES	RAINMAKERS	RAKEOFFS*
RAFFLER	RAGINGS	RAILBUSSES	RAINOUT*	RAKER
RAFFLERS	RAGINI	RAILCAR*	RAINOUTS*	RAKERIES
RAFFLES	RAGINIS	RAILCARD	RAINPROOF	RAKERS
RAFFLESIA*	RAGIS	RAILCARDS	RAINPROOFED	RAKERY
RAFFLESIAS*	RAGLAN	RAILCARS*	RAINPROOFING	RAKES
RAFFLING	RAGLANS	RAILE	RAINPROOFS	RAKESHAME
RAFFS	RAGMAN	RAILED	RAINS	RAKESHAMES
RAFT	RAGMANS	RAILER	RAINSPOUT*	RAKI
RAFTED	RAGMEN	RAILERS	RAINSPOUTS*	RAKING
RAFTER	RAGMENT	RAILES	RAINSTORM	RAKINGS
RAFTERED	RAGMENTS	RAILHEAD	RAINSTORMS	RAKIS
RAFTERING	RAGOUT	RAILHEADS	RAINTIGHT	RAKISH
RAFTERINGS	RAGOUTED	RAILING	RAINWASH*	RAKISHLY
RAFTERS	RAGOUTING	RAILINGLY	RAINWASHED*	RAKSHAS
RAFTING	RAGOUTS	RAILINGS	RAINWASHES*	RAKSHASA
RAFTMAN	RAGPICKER*	RAILLERIES	RAINWASHING*	RAKSHASAS
RAFTMEN	RAGPICKERS*	RAILLERY	RAINWATER	RAKSHASES
RAFTS	RAGS	RAILLESS	RAINWATERS	RAKU
RAFTSMAN	RAGSTONE	RAILLIES	RAINWEAR	RAKUS
RAFTSMEN	RAGSTONES	RAILLY	RAINWEARS	RALE
RAG	RAGTAG	RAILMAN	RAINY	RALES
RAGA	RAGTAGS	RAILMEN	RAIRD	RALLIED
RAGAS	RAGTIME	RAILROAD	RAIRDS	RALLIER

RALLIERS	RAMJETS	RAMSTAM	RANDOMISES	RANSEL
RALLIES	RAMMED	RAMTIL*	RANDOMISING	RANSELS
RALLINE	RAMMER	RAMTILS*	RANDOMIZE	RANSHAKLE
RALLY	RAMMERS	RAMULAR	RANDOMIZED	RANSHAKLED
RALLYE	RAMMIER*	RAMULI	RANDOMIZES	RANSHAKLES
RALLYES	RAMMIES	RAMULOSE	RANDOMIZING	RANSHAKLING
RALLYING	RAMMIEST*	RAMULOUS	RANDOMLY	RANSOM
RALLYINGS	RAMMING	RAMULUS	RANDOMS	RANSOMED
RALLYIST	RAMMISH	RAMUS	RANDON	RANSOMER
RALLYISTS	RAMMY	RAN	RANDONS	RANSOMERS
RALPH*	RAMOSE	RANA	RANDS	RANSOMING
RALPHED*	RAMOSELY*	RANARIAN	RANDY	RANSOMS
RALPHING*	RAMOSITIES*	RANARIUM	RANEE	RANT
RALPHS*	RAMOSITY*	RANARIUMS	RANEES	RANTED
RAM	RAMOUS	RANAS	RANG	RANTER
RAMAKIN	RAMP	RANCE	RANGATIRA	RANTERISM
RAMAKINS	RAMPAGE	RANCED	RANGATIRAS	RANTERISMS
RAMAL	RAMPAGED	RANCEL	RANGE	RANTERS
RAMATE	RAMPAGER*	RANCELS	RANGED	RANTING
RAMBLE	RAMPAGERS*	RANCES	RANGELAND	RANTINGLY
RAMBLED	RAMPAGES	RANCH	RANGELANDS	RANTINGS
RAMBLER	RAMPAGING	RANCHED	RANGER	RANTIPOLE
RAMBLERS	RAMPAGINGS	RANCHER	RANGERS	RANTIPOLED
RAMBLES	RAMPANCIES	RANCHERIA	RANGES	RANTIPOLES
RAMBLING	RAMPANCY	RANCHERIAS	RANGIER	RANTIPOLING
RAMBLINGS	RAMPANT	RANCHERIE	RANGIEST	RANTS
RAMBUTAN	RAMPANTLY	RANCHERIES	RANGINESS	RANULA
RAMBUTANS	RAMPART	RANCHERO	RANGINESSES	RANULAS
RAMCAT	RAMPARTED	RANCHEROS	RANGING	RANUNCULI
RAMCATS	RAMPARTING	RANCHERS	RANGOLI	RANUNCULUS*
RAMEAL	RAMPARTS	RANCHES	RANGOLIS	RANUNCULUSES*
RAMEE	RAMPAUGE	RANCHING	RANGY	RANZEL
RAMEES	RAMPAUGED	RANCHINGS	RANI	RANZELMAN
RAMEKIN	RAMPAUGES	RANCHMAN	RANID*	RANZELMEN
RAMEKINS	RAMPAUGING	RANCHMEN	RANIDS*	RANZELS
RAMEN	RAMPED	RANCHO	RANIFORM	RAOULIA
RAMENS	RAMPER	RANCHOS	RANINE	RAOULIAS
RAMENTA	RAMPERS	RANCID	RANIS	RAP
RAMENTUM	RAMPICK	RANCIDER	RANK	RAPACIOUS
RAMEOUS	RAMPICKED	RANCIDEST	RANKE	RAPACITIES
RAMEQUIN	RAMPICKS	RANCIDITIES	RANKED	RAPACITY
RAMEQUINS	RAMPIKE	RANCIDITY	RANKER	RAPE
RAMET*	RAMPIKES	RANCIDLY*	RANKERS	RAPED
RAMETS*	RAMPING	RANCING	RANKES	RAPER
RAMFEEZLE	RAMPINGS	RANCOR	RANKEST	RAPERS
RAMFEEZLED	RAMPION	RANCORED*	RANKING	RAPES
RAMFEEZLES	RAMPIONS	RANCOROUS	RANKINGS	RAPESEED
RAMFEEZLING	RAMPIRE	RANCORS	RANKISH*	RAPESEEDS
RAMI	RAMPIRED	RANCOUR	RANKLE	RAPHAE*
RAMIE	RAMPIRES	RANCOURS	RANKLED	RAPHANIA
RAMIES	RAMPOLE*	RAND	RANKLES	RAPHANIAS
RAMIFIED	RAMPOLES*	RANDAN	RANKLING	RAPHE
RAMIFIES	RAMPS	RANDANS	RANKLY	RAPHES
RAMIFORM	RAMPSMAN	RANDED	RANKNESS	RAPHIA
RAMIFY	RAMPSMEN	RANDEM	RANKNESSES	RAPHIAS
RAMIFYING	RAMROD	RANDEMS	RANKS	RAPHIDE
RAMILIE*	RAMRODDED	RANDIE	RANPIKE*	RAPHIDES
RAMILIES*	RAMRODDING	RANDIER	RANPIKES*	RAPHIS
RAMILLIE*	RAMRODS	RANDIES	RANSACK	RAPID
RAMILLIES*	RAMS	RANDIEST	RANSACKED	RAPIDER
RAMIN	RAMSHORN*	RANDING	RANSACKER	RAPIDEST
RAMINS	RAMSHORNS*	RANDOM	RANSACKERS	RAPIDITIES
RAMIS	RAMSON	RANDOMISE	RANSACKING	RAPIDITY
RAMJET	RAMSONS	RANDOMISED	RANSACKS	RAPIDLY

The Chambers Dictionary is the authority for many longer words; see Introduction, page ix

RAPIDNESS	RAREFIES	RASPIEST	RATED	RATOONING
RAPIDNESSES	RAREFY	RASPING	RATEL	RATOONS
RAPIDS	RAREFYING	RASPINGLY	RATELS	RATOOS
RAPIER	RARELY	RASPINGS	RATEMETER*	RATOS*
RAPIERED*	RARENESS	RASPISH*	RATEMETERS*	RATPACK
RAPIERS	RARENESSES	RASPS	RATEPAYER	RATPACKS
RAPINE	RARER	RASPY	RATEPAYERS	RATPROOF
RAPINES	RARERIPE*	RASSE	RATER	RATS
RAPING	RARERIPES*	RASSES	RATERS	RATSBANE
RAPINI*	RARES*	RASSLE*	RATES	RATSBANES
RAPIST	RAREST	RASSLED*	RATFINK	RATTAIL*
RAPISTS	RARIFIED*	RASSLES*	RATFINKS	RATTAILS*
RAPLOCH	RARIFIES*	RASSLING*	RATFISH*	RATTAN
RAPLOCHS	RARIFY*	RAST	RATFISHES*	RATTANS
RAPPAREE	RARIFYING*	RASTA	RATH	RATTED
RAPPAREES	RARING	RASTAFARI	RATHE	RATTEEN
RAPPED	RARITIES	RASTER	RATHER	RATTEENS
RAPPEE	RARITY	RASTERISE	RATHEREST	RATTEN
RAPPEES	RAS	RASTERISED	RATHERIPE	RATTENED
RAPPEL	RASBORA*	RASTERISES	RATHERIPES	RATTENER*
RAPPELED*	RASBORAS*	RASTERISING	RATHERISH	RATTENERS*
RAPPELING*	RASCAILLE	RASTERIZE	RATHEST	RATTENING
RAPPELLED	RASCAILLES	RASTERIZED	RATHOLE*	RATTENINGS
RAPPELLING	RASCAL	RASTERIZES	RATHOLES*	RATTENS
RAPPELLINGS	RASCALDOM	RASTERIZING	RATHRIPE	RATTER
RAPPELS	RASCALDOMS	RASTERS	RATHRIPES	RATTERIES
RAPPEN*	RASCALISM	RASTRUM	RATHS	RATTERS
RAPPER	RASCALISMS	RASTRUMS	RATICIDE*	RATTERY
RAPPERS	RASCALITIES	RASURE	RATICIDES*	RATTIER
RAPPING	RASCALITY	RASURES	RATIFIED	RATTIEST
RAPPINGS	RASCALLIEST	RAT	RATIFIER	RATTING
RAPPINI*	RASCALLY	RATA	RATIFIERS	RATTINGS
RAPPORT	RASCALS	RATABLE	RATIFIES	RATTISH
RAPPORTS	RASCASSE	RATABLY	RATIFY	RATTLE
RAPS	RASCASSES	RATAFEE*	RATIFYING	RATTLEBAG
RAPT	RASCHEL	RATAFEES*	RATINE	RATTLEBAGS
RAPTLY	RASCHELS	RATAFIA	RATINES	RATTLED
RAPTNESS*	RASE	RATAFIAS	RATING	RATTLER
RAPTNESSES*	RASED	RATAL*	RATINGS	RATTLERS
RAPTOR	RASER*	RATALS*	RATIO	RATTLES
RAPTORIAL	RASERS*	RATAN	RATION	RATTLIER
RAPTORS	RASES	RATANIES*	RATIONAL	RATTLIEST
RAPTURE	RASH	RATANS	RATIONALE	RATTLIN
RAPTURED	RASHED	RATANY*	RATIONALES	RATTLINE
RAPTURES	RASHER	RATAPLAN	RATIONALS	RATTLINES
RAPTURING	RASHERS	RATAPLANNED*	RATIONED	RATTLING
RAPTURISE	RASHES	RATAPLANNING*	RATIONING	RATTLINGS
RAPTURISED	RASHEST	RATAPLANS	RATIONS	RATTLINS
RAPTURISES	RASHING	RATAS	RATIOS	RATTLY
RAPTURISING	RASHLIKE*	RATATAT*	RATITE	RATTON
RAPTURIST	RASHLY	RATATATS*	RATITES*	RATTONS
RAPTURISTS	RASHNESS	RATBAG	RATLIKE*	RATTOON*
RAPTURIZE	RASHNESSES	RATBAGS	RATLIN	RATTOONED*
RAPTURIZED	RASING	RATCH	RATLINE	RATTOONING*
RAPTURIZES	RASORIAL	RATCHED	RATLINES	RATTOONS*
RAPTURIZING	RASP	RATCHES	RATLING	RATTRAP*
RAPTUROUS	RASPATORIES	RATCHET	RATLINGS	RATTRAPS*
RARE	RASPATORY	RATCHETED	RATLINS	RATTY
RAREBIT	RASPBERRIES	RATCHETING	RATO*	RATU
RAREBITS	RASPBERRY	RATCHETS	RATOO	RATUS
RARED*	RASPED	RATCHING	RATOON	RAUCID
RAREFIED	RASPER	RATE	RATOONED	RAUCITIES*
RAREFIER*	RASPERS	RATEABLE	RATOONER	RAUCITY*
RAREFIERS*	RASPIER	RATEABLY	RATOONERS	RAUCLE

RAUCLER	RAVINGLY	RAZEEING	REACTANCES	READS
RAUCLEST	RAVINGS	RAZEES	REACTANT	READVANCE
RAUCOUS	RAVINING	RAZER*	REACTANTS	READVANCED
RAUCOUSLY	RAVINS	RAZERS*	REACTED	READVANCES
RAUGHT	RAVIOLI	RAZES	REACTING	READVANCING
RAUN	RAVIOLIS	RAZING	REACTION	READVISE
RAUNCH	RAVISH	RAZMATAZ	REACTIONS	READVISED
RAUNCHED	RAVISHED	RAZMATAZES	REACTIVE	READVISES
RAUNCHES	RAVISHER	RAZOO	REACTOR	READVISING
RAUNCHIER	RAVISHERS	RAZOOS	REACTORS	READY
RAUNCHIEST	RAVISHES	RAZOR	REACTS	READYING
RAUNCHILY	RAVISHING	RAZORABLE	REACTUATE	READYMADE*
RAUNCHING	RAW	RAZORBACK*	REACTUATED	READYMADES*
RAUNCHY	RAWBONE	RAZORBACKS*	REACTUATES	REAEDIFIED
RAUNGE	RAWBONED	RAZORBILL*	REACTUATING	REAEDIFIES
RAUNGED	RAWER	RAZORBILLS*	READ	REAEDIFY
RAUNGES	RAWEST	RAZORED*	READABLE	REAEDIFYE
RAUNGING	RAWHEAD	RAZORING*	READABLY	REAEDIFYED
RAUNS	RAWHEADS	RAZORS	READAPT	REAEDIFYES
RAUWOLFIA*	RAWHIDE	RAZURE	READAPTED	REAEDIFYING
RAUWOLFIAS*	RAWHIDED*	RAZURES	READAPTING	REAFFIRM
RAVAGE	RAWHIDES	RAZZ	READAPTS	REAFFIRMED
RAVAGED	RAWHIDING*	RAZZED	READD*	REAFFIRMING
RAVAGER	RAWIN*	RAZZES	READDED*	REAFFIRMS
RAVAGERS	RAWING	RAZZIA	READDICT*	REAFFIX*
RAVAGES	RAWINGS	RAZZIAS	READDICTED*	REAFFIXED*
RAVAGING	RAWINS*	RAZZING	READDICTING*	REAFFIXES*
RAVE	RAWISH	RAZZLE	READDICTS*	REAFFIXING*
RAVED	RAWLY	RAZZLES	READDING*	REAGENCIES
RAVEL	RAWN	RE	READDRESS	REAGENCY
RAVELED*	RAWNESS	REABSORB	READDRESSED	REAGENT
RAVELER*	RAWNESSES	REABSORBED	READDRESSES	REAGENTS
RAVELERS*	RAWNS	REABSORBING	READDRESSING	REAGIN*
RAVELIN	RAWS	REABSORBS	READDS*	REAGINIC*
RAVELING*	RAX	REACCEDE*	READER	REAGINS*
RAVELINGS*	RAXED	REACCEDED*	READERLY*	REAK
RAVELINS	RAXES	REACCEDES*	READERS	REAKED
RAVELLED	RAXING	REACCEDING*	READIED	REAKING
RAVELLER*	RAY	REACCENT*	READIER	REAKS
RAVELLERS*	RAYA*	REACCENTED*	READIES	REAL
RAVELLING	RAYAH	REACCENTING*	READIEST	REALER
RAVELLINGS	RAYAHS	REACCENTS*	READILY	REALES*
RAVELLY*	RAYAS*	REACCEPT*	READINESS	REALEST
RAVELMENT	RAYED	REACCEPTED*	READINESSES	REALGAR
RAVELMENTS	RAYGRASS*	REACCEPTING*	READING	REALGARS
RAVELS	RAYGRASSES*	REACCEPTS*	READINGS	REALIA
RAVEN	RAYING	REACCUSE*	READJUST	REALIGN
RAVENED	RAYLE	REACCUSED*	READJUSTED	REALIGNED
RAVENER	RAYLED	REACCUSES*	READJUSTING	REALIGNING
RAVENERS	RAYLES	REACCUSING*	READJUSTS	REALIGNS
RAVENING	RAYLESS	REACH	READMIT	REALISE
RAVENINGS*	RAYLET	REACHABLE	READMITS	REALISED
RAVENOUS	RAYLETS	REACHED	READMITTED	REALISER
RAVENS	RAYLIKE*	REACHER	READMITTING	REALISERS
RAVER	RAYLING	REACHERS	READOPT	REALISES
RAVERS	RAYNE	REACHES	READOPTED	REALISING
RAVES	RAYNES	REACHING	READOPTS	REALISM
RAVIGOTE*	RAYON	REACHLESS	READORN*	REALISMS
RAVIGOTES*	RAYONS	REACQUIRE	READORNED*	REALIST
RAVIN	RAYS	REACQUIRED	READORNING*	REALISTIC
RAVINE	RAZE	REACQUIRES	READORNS*	REALISTS
RAVINED	RAZED	REACQUIRING	READOUT*	REALITIES
RAVINES	RAZEE	REACT	READOUTS*	REALITY
RAVING	RAZEED	REACTANCE		REALIZE

REALIZED	REANS	REAROUSES	REATAS	REBAPTISING
REALIZER	REANSWER	REAROUSING	REATE	REBAPTISM
REALIZERS	REANSWERED	REARRANGE	REATES	REBAPTISMS
REALIZES	REANSWERING	REARRANGED	REATTACH	REBAPTIZE
REALIZING	REANSWERS	REARRANGES	REATTACHED	REBAPTIZED
REALLIE	REAP	REARRANGING	REATTACHES	REBAPTIZES
REALLIED	REAPABLE*	REARREST	REATTACHING	REBAPTIZING
REALLIES	REAPED	REARRESTED	REATTACK*	REBAR*
REALLOT	REAPER	REARRESTING	REATTACKED*	REBARS*
REALLOTS	REAPERS	REARRESTS	REATTACKING*	REBATE
REALLOTTED	REAPHOOK*	REARS	REATTACKS*	REBATED
REALLOTTING	REAPHOOKS*	REARWARD	REATTAIN	REBATER
REALLY	REAPING	REARWARDS	REATTAINED	REBATERS
REALLYING	REAPPAREL	REASCEND	REATTAINING	REBATES
REALM	REAPPARELLED	REASCENDED	REATTAINS	REBATING
REALMLESS	REAPPARELLING	REASCENDING	REATTEMPT	REBATO
REALMS	REAPPARELS	REASCENDS	REATTEMPTED	REBATOES
REALNESS	REAPPEAR	REASCENT	REATTEMPTING	REBATOS*
REALNESSES	REAPPEARED	REASCENTS	REATTEMPTS	REBBE
REALO	REAPPEARING	REASON	REAVAIL*	REBBES
REALOS	REAPPEARS	REASONED	REAVAILED*	REBBETZIN
REALS	REAPPLIED	REASONER	REAVAILING*	REBBETZINS
REALTER*	REAPPLIES	REASONERS	REAVAILS*	REBEC
REALTERED*	REAPPLY	REASONING	REAVE	REBECK
REALTERING*	REAPPLYING	REASONINGS	REAVED*	REBECKS
REALTERS*	REAPPOINT	REASONS	REAVER	REBECS
REALTIE	REAPPOINTED	REASSAIL*	REAVERS	REBEGAN*
REALTIES	REAPPOINTING	REASSAILED*	REAVES	REBEGIN*
REALTIME	REAPPOINTS	REASSAILING*	REAVING	REBEGINNING*
REALTOR	REAPPROVE*	REASSAILS*	REAVOW*	REBEGINS*
REALTORS	REAPPROVED*	REASSERT	REAVOWED*	REBEGUN*
REALTY	REAPPROVES*	REASSERTED	REAVOWING*	REBEL
REAM	REAPPROVING*	REASSERTING	REAVOWS*	REBELDOM
REAME	REAPS	REASSERTS	REAWAKE	REBELDOMS
REAMED	REAR	REASSESS	REAWAKED	REBELLED
REAMEND	REARED	REASSESSED	REAWAKEN	REBELLER
REAMENDED	REARER	REASSESSES	REAWAKENED	REBELLERS
REAMENDING	REARERS	REASSESSING	REAWAKENING	REBELLING
REAMENDS	REARGUARD	REASSIGN	REAWAKENINGS	REBELLION
REAMER	REARGUARDS	REASSIGNED	REAWAKENS	REBELLIONS
REAMERS	REARGUE*	REASSIGNING	REAWAKES	REBELLOW
REAMES	REARGUED*	REASSIGNS	REAWAKING	REBELLOWED
REAMIER	REARGUES*	REASSORT*	REAWOKE	REBELLOWING
REAMIEST	REARGUING*	REASSORTED*	REAWOKEN	REBELLOWS
REAMING	REARHORSE	REASSORTING*	REB*	REBELS
REAMS	REARHORSES	REASSORTS*	REBACK	REBID
REAMY	REARING	REASSUME	REBACKED	REBIDDEN
REAN	REARISE	REASSUMED	REBACKING	REBIDDING
REANALYZE*	REARISEN	REASSUMES	REBACKS	REBIDS
REANALYZED*	REARISES	REASSUMING	REBADGE	REBILL*
REANALYZES*	REARISING	REASSURE	REBADGED	REBILLED*
REANALYZING*	REARLY	REASSURED	REBADGES	REBILLING*
REANIMATE	REARM	REASSURER	REBADGING	REBILLS*
REANIMATED	REARMED	REASSURERS	REBAIT*	REBIND
REANIMATES	REARMICE	REASSURES	REBAITED*	REBINDING
REANIMATING	REARMING	REASSURING	REBAITING*	REBINDS
REANNEX	REARMOST	REAST	REBAITS*	REBIRTH
REANNEXED	REARMOUSE	REASTED	REBALANCE*	REBIRTHS
REANNEXES	REARMS	REASTIER	REBALANCED*	REBIT
REANNEXING	REAROSE	REASTIEST	REBALANCES*	REBITE
REANOINT*	REAROUSAL	REASTING	REBALANCING*	REBITES
REANOINTED*	REAROUSALS	REASTS	REBAPTISE	REBITING
REANOINTING*	REAROUSE	REASTY	REBAPTISED	REBITTEN
REANOINTS*	REAROUSED	REATA	REBAPTISES	REBLEND*

REBLENDED*	REBRANCHES*	RECAMIER*	RECENCY	RECHEATING
REBLENDING*	REBRANCHING*	RECAMIERS*	RECENSE	RECHEATS
REBLENDS*	REBRED*	RECANE*	RECENSED	RECHECK
REBLOOM	REBREED*	RECANED*	RECENSES	RECHECKED
REBLOOMED	REBREEDING*	RECANES*	RECENSING	RECHECKING
REBLOOMING	REBREEDS*	RECANING*	RECENSION	RECHECKS
REBLOOMS	REBS*	RECANT	RECENSIONS	RECHERCHE
REBLOSSOM	REBUFF	RECANTED	RECENT	RECHEW*
REBLOSSOMED	REBUFFED	RECANTER	RECENTER	RECHEWED*
REBLOSSOMING	REBUFFING	RECANTERS	RECENTEST	RECHEWING*
REBLOSSOMS	REBUFFS	RECANTING	RECENTLY	RECHEWS*
REBOANT	REBUILD	RECANTS	RECENTRE	RECHIE
REBOARD*	REBUILDED*	RECAP	RECENTRED	RECHLESSE
REBOARDED*	REBUILDING	RECAPPED	RECENTRES	RECHOOSE*
REBOARDING*	REBUILDS	RECAPPING	RECENTRING	RECHOOSES*
REBOARDS*	REBUILT	RECAPS	RECEPT	RECHOOSING*
REBOATION	REBUKABLE	RECAPTION	RECEPTION	RECHOSE*
REBOATIONS	REBUKE	RECAPTIONS	RECEPTIONS	RECHOSEN*
REBODIED*	REBUKED	RECAPTOR	RECEPTIVE	RECIPE
REBODIES*	REBUKEFUL	RECAPTORS	RECEPTOR	RECIPES
REBODY*	REBUKER	RECAPTURE	RECEPTORS	RECIPIENT
REBODYING*	REBUKERS	RECAPTURED	RECEPTS	RECIPIENTS
REBOIL	REBUKES	RECAPTURES	RECERTIFIED*	RECIRCLE*
REBOILED	REBUKING	RECAPTURING	RECERTIFIES*	RECIRCLED*
REBOILING	REBURIAL	RECARRIED*	RECERTIFY*	RECIRCLES*
REBOILS	REBURIALS	RECARRIES*	RECERTIFYING*	RECIRCLING*
REBOOK*	REBURIED	RECARRY*	RECESS	RECISION
REBOOKED*	REBURIES	RECARRYING*	RECESSED	RECISIONS
REBOOKING*	REBURY	RECAST	RECESSES	RECIT
REBOOKS*	REBURYING	RECASTING	RECESSING	RECITAL
REBOOT	REBUS	RECASTS	RECESSION	RECITALS
REBOOTED	REBUSES	RECATCH	RECESSIONS	RECITE
REBOOTING	REBUT	RECATCHES	RECESSIVE	RECITED
REBOOTS	REBUTMENT	RECATCHING	RECESSIVES	RECITER
REBOP*	REBUTMENTS	RECAUGHT	RECHANGE*	RECITERS
REBOPS*	REBUTS	RECCE	RECHANGED*	RECITES
REBORE	REBUTTAL	RECCED	RECHANGES*	RECITING
REBORED	REBUTTALS	RECCEED	RECHANGING*	RECITS
REBORES	REBUTTED	RECCEING	RECHANNEL*	RECK
REBORING	REBUTTER	RECCES	RECHANNELED*	RECKAN
REBORN	REBUTTERS	RECCIED	RECHANNELING*	RECKED
REBORROW	REBUTTING	RECCIES	RECHANNELLED*	RECKING
REBORROWED	REBUTTON	RECCO	RECHANNELLING*	RECKLESS
REBORROWING	REBUTTONED	RECCOS	RECHANNELS*	RECKLING
REBORROWS	REBUTTONING	RECCY	RECHARGE	RECKLINGS
REBOTTLE*	REBUTTONS	RECCYING	RECHARGED	RECKON
REBOTTLED*	REBUY*	RECEDE	RECHARGER*	RECKONED
REBOTTLES*	REBUYING*	RECEDED	RECHARGERS*	RECKONER
REBOTTLING*	REBUYS*	RECEDES	RECHARGES	RECKONERS
REBOUGHT*	REC	RECEDING	RECHARGING	RECKONING
REBOUND	RECAL	RECEIPT	RECHART	RECKONINGS
REBOUNDED	RECALESCE	RECEIPTED	RECHARTED	RECKONS
REBOUNDER*	RECALESCED	RECEIPTING	RECHARTER	RECKS
REBOUNDERS*	RECALESCES	RECEIPTS	RECHARTERED	RECLAD*
REBOUNDING	RECALESCING	RECEIVAL	RECHARTERING	RECLAIM
REBOUNDS	RECALL	RECEIVALS	RECHARTERS	RECLAIMED
REBOZO*	RECALLED	RECEIVE	RECHARTING	RECLAIMER
REBOZOS*	RECALLER*	RECEIVED	RECHARTS	RECLAIMERS
REBRACE	RECALLERS*	RECEIVER	RECHATE	RECLAIMING
REBRACED	RECALLING	RECEIVERS	RECHATES	RECLAIMS
REBRACES	RECALLS	RECEIVES	RECHAUFFE	RECLAME
REBRACING	RECALMENT	RECEIVING	RECHAUFFES	RECLAMES
REBRANCH*	RECALMENTS	RECEIVINGS	RECHEAT	RECLASP*
REBRANCHED*	RECALS	RECENCIES	RECHEATED	RECLASPED*

RECLASPING*	RECOINAGE	RECONNECTS	RECOUPLED*	RECS
RECLASPS*	RECOINAGES	RECONQUER	RECOUPLES*	RECTA
RECLEAN*	RECOINED	RECONQUERED	RECOUPLING*	RECTAL
RECLEANED*	RECOINING	RECONQUERING	RECOUPS	RECTALLY
RECLEANING*	RECOINS	RECONQUERS	RECOURE	RECTANGLE
RECLEANS*	RECOLLECT	RECONS*	RECOURED	RECTANGLES
RECLIMB	RECOLLECTED	RECONTACT*	RECOURES	RECTI
RECLIMBED	RECOLLECTING	RECONTACTED*	RECOURING	RECTIFIED
RECLIMBING	RECOLLECTS	RECONTACTING*	RECOURSE	RECTIFIER
RECLIMBS	RECOLLET	RECONTACTS*	RECOURSED	RECTIFIERS
RECLINATE	RECOLLETS	RECONTOUR*	RECOURSES	RECTIFIES
RECLINE	RECOLOR*	RECONTOURED*	RECOURSING	RECTIFY
RECLINED	RECOLORED*	RECONTOURING*	RECOVER	RECTIFYING
RECLINER	RECOLORING*	RECONTOURS*	RECOVERED	RECTION
RECLINERS	RECOLORS*	RECONVENE	RECOVEREE	RECTIONS
RECLINES	RECOMB*	RECONVENED	RECOVERER	RECTITIC
RECLINING	RECOMBED*	RECONVENES	RECOVERERS	RECTITIS
RECLOSE	RECOMBINE	RECONVENING	RECOVERIES	RECTITISES
RECLOSED	RECOMBINED	RECONVERT	RECOVERING	RECTITUDE
RECLOSES	RECOMBINES	RECONVERTED	RECOVEROR	RECTITUDES
RECLOSING	RECOMBING*	RECONVERTING	RECOVERORS	RECTO
RECLOTHE	RECOMBINING	RECONVERTS	RECOVERS	RECTOR
RECLOTHED	RECOMBS*	RECONVEY	RECOVERY	RECTORAL
RECLOTHES	RECOMFORT	RECONVEYED	RECOWER	RECTORATE
RECLOTHING	RECOMFORTED	RECONVEYING	RECOWERED	RECTORATES
RECLUSE	RECOMFORTING	RECONVEYS	RECOWERING	RECTORESS
RECLUSELY	RECOMFORTS	RECONVICT*	RECOWERS	RECTORESSES
RECLUSES	RECOMMEND	RECONVICTED*	RECOYLE	RECTORIAL
RECLUSION	RECOMMENDED	RECONVICTING*	RECOYLED	RECTORIALS
RECLUSIONS	RECOMMENDING	RECONVICTS*	RECOYLES	RECTORIES
RECLUSIVE	RECOMMENDS	RECOOK*	RECOYLING	RECTORS
RECLUSORIES	RECOMMIT	RECOOKED*	RECRATE*	RECTORY
RECLUSORY	RECOMMITS	RECOOKING*	RECRATED*	RECTOS
RECOAL*	RECOMMITTED	RECOOKS*	RECRATES*	RECTRESS
RECOALED*	RECOMMITTING	RECOPIED*	RECRATING*	RECTRESSES
RECOALING*	RECOMPACT	RECOPIES*	RECREANCE	RECTRICES
RECOALS*	RECOMPACTED	RECOPY*	RECREANCES	RECTRIX
RECOCK*	RECOMPACTING	RECOPYING*	RECREANCIES	RECTUM
RECOCKED*	RECOMPACTS	RECORD	RECREANCY	RECTUMS
RECOCKING*	RECOMPILE*	RECORDED	RECREANT	RECTUS
RECOCKS*	RECOMPILED*	RECORDER	RECREANTS	RECUILE
RECODE	RECOMPILES*	RECORDERS	RECREATE	RECUILED
RECODED	RECOMPILING*	RECORDING	RECREATED	RECUILES
RECODES	RECOMPOSE	RECORDINGS	RECREATES	RECUILING
RECODIFIED*	RECOMPOSED	RECORDIST	RECREATING	RECULE
RECODIFIES*	RECOMPOSES	RECORDISTS	RECREMENT	RECULED
RECODIFY*	RECOMPOSING	RECORDS	RECREMENTS	RECULES
RECODIFYING*	RECOMPUTE*	RECORK*	RECROSS	RECULING
RECODING	RECOMPUTED*	RECORKED*	RECROSSED	RECUMBENT
RECOGNISE	RECOMPUTES*	RECORKING*	RECROSSES	RECUR
RECOGNISED	RECOMPUTING*	RECORKS*	RECROSSING	RECURE
RECOGNISES	RECON*	RECOUNT	RECROWN*	RECURED
RECOGNISING	RECONCILE	RECOUNTAL	RECROWNED*	RECURES
RECOGNIZE	RECONCILED	RECOUNTALS	RECROWNING*	RECURING
RECOGNIZED	RECONCILES	RECOUNTED	RECROWNS*	RECURRED
RECOGNIZES	RECONCILING	RECOUNTER*	RECRUIT	RECURRENT
RECOGNIZING	RECONDITE	RECOUNTERS*	RECRUITAL	RECURRING
RECOIL	RECONFIRM	RECOUNTING	RECRUITALS	RECURS
RECOILED	RECONFIRMED	RECOUNTS	RECRUITED	RECURSION
RECOILER	RECONFIRMING	RECOUP	RECRUITER	RECURSIONS
RECOILERS	RECONFIRMS	RECOUPE*	RECRUITERS	RECURSIVE
RECOILING	RECONNECT	RECOUPED	RECRUITING	RECURVE
RECOILS	RECONNECTED	RECOUPING	RECRUITS	RECURVED
RECOIN	RECONNECTING	RECOUPLE*		RECURVES

RECURVING	REDBREASTS	REDEFECTS*	REDID	REDON*
RECUSAL*	REDBRICK	REDEFIED*	REDIGEST*	REDONE
RECUSALS*	REDBRICKS*	REDEFIES*	REDIGESTED*	REDONNED*
RECUSANCE	REDBUD	REDEFINE	REDIGESTING*	REDONNING*
RECUSANCES	REDBUDS	REDEFINED	REDIGESTS*	REDONS*
RECUSANCIES	REDBUG*	REDEFINES	REDING	REDOS
RECUSANCY	REDBUGS*	REDEFINING	REDINGOTE	REDOUBLE
RECUSANT	REDCAP	REDEFY*	REDINGOTES	REDOUBLED
RECUSANTS	REDCAPS	REDEFYING*	REDIP	REDOUBLES
RECUSE	REDCOAT	REDELESS	REDIPPED	REDOUBLING
RECUSED	REDCOATS	REDELIVER	REDIPPING	REDOUBT
RECUSES	REDD	REDELIVERED	REDIPS	REDOUBTED
RECUSING	REDDED*	REDELIVERING	REDIPT*	REDOUBTING
RECUT*	REDDEN	REDELIVERS	REDIRECT	REDOUBTS
RECUTS*	REDDENDA	REDEMAND*	REDIRECTED	REDOUND
RECUTTING*	REDDENDO	REDEMANDED*	REDIRECTING	REDOUNDED
RECYCLATE	REDDENDOS	REDEMANDING*	REDIRECTS	REDOUNDING
RECYCLATES	REDDENDUM	REDEMANDS*	REDISCUSS*	REDOUNDINGS
RECYCLE	REDDENED	REDENIED*	REDISCUSSED*	REDOUNDS
RECYCLED	REDDENING	REDENIES*	REDISCUSSES*	REDOUT*
RECYCLER*	REDDENS	REDENY*	REDISCUSSING*	REDOUTS*
RECYCLERS*	REDDER	REDENYING*	REDISPLAY*	REDOWA
RECYCLES	REDDERS	REDEPLOY	REDISPLAYED*	REDOWAS
RECYCLING	REDDEST	REDEPLOYED	REDISPLAYING*	REDOX
RECYCLIST	REDDIER	REDEPLOYING	REDISPLAYS*	REDOXES*
RECYCLISTS	REDDIEST	REDEPLOYS	REDISPOSE*	REDPOLL
RED	REDDING	REDEPOSIT*	REDISPOSED*	REDPOLLS
REDACT	REDDINGS	REDEPOSITED*	REDISPOSES*	REDRAFT
REDACTED	REDDISH	REDEPOSITING*	REDISPOSING*	REDRAFTED
REDACTING	REDDLE	REDEPOSITS*	REDISTIL	REDRAFTING
REDACTION	REDDLED	REDES	REDISTILL*	REDRAFTS
REDACTIONS	REDDLEMAN	REDESCEND	REDISTILLED	REDRAW
REDACTOR	REDDLEMEN	REDESCENDED	REDISTILLING	REDRAWER*
REDACTORS	REDDLES	REDESCENDING	REDISTILLS*	REDRAWERS*
REDACTS	REDDLING	REDESCENDS	REDISTILS	REDRAWING
REDAMAGE*	REDDS	REDESIGN	REDIVIDE	REDRAWN
REDAMAGED*	REDDY	REDESIGNED	REDIVIDED	REDRAWS
REDAMAGES*	REDE	REDESIGNING	REDIVIDES	REDREAM*
REDAMAGING*	REDEAL	REDESIGNS	REDIVIDING	REDREAMED*
REDAN	REDEALING	REDEVELOP	REDIVIVUS	REDREAMING*
REDANS	REDEALS	REDEVELOPED	REDLEG	REDREAMS*
REDARGUE	REDEALT	REDEVELOPING	REDLEGS	REDREAMT*
REDARGUED	REDEAR*	REDEVELOPS	REDLINE*	REDRESS
REDARGUES	REDEARS*	REDEYE*	REDLINED*	REDRESSED
REDARGUING	REDECIDE*	REDEYES*	REDLINES*	REDRESSER
REDATE	REDECIDED*	REDFIN*	REDLINING*	REDRESSERS
REDATED	REDECIDES*	REDFINS*	REDLY	REDRESSES
REDATES	REDECIDING*	REDFISH	REDNECK	REDRESSING
REDATING	REDECRAFT	REDFISHES	REDNECKED*	REDREW
REDBACK	REDECRAFTS	REDHANDED	REDNECKS	REDRIED*
REDBACKS	REDED*	REDHEAD	REDNESS	REDRIES*
REDBAIT*	REDEEM	REDHEADED*	REDNESSES	REDRILL*
REDBAITED*	REDEEMED	REDHEADS	REDO	REDRILLED*
REDBAITING*	REDEEMER	REDHORSE*	REDOCK*	REDRILLING*
REDBAITS*	REDEEMERS	REDHORSES*	REDOCKED*	REDRILLS*
REDBAY*	REDEEMING	REDIA	REDOCKING*	REDRIVE
REDBAYS*	REDEEMS	REDIAE	REDOCKS*	REDRIVEN
REDBELLIES	REDEFEAT*	REDIAL	REDOES	REDRIVES
REDBELLY	REDEFEATED*	REDIALED	REDOING	REDRIVING
REDBIRD	REDEFEATING*	REDIALING	REDOLENCE	REDROOT
REDBIRDS	REDEFEATS*	REDIALLED	REDOLENCES	REDROOTS
REDBONE*	REDEFECT*	REDIALLING	REDOLENCIES	REDROVE
REDBONES*	REDEFECTED*	REDIALS	REDOLENCY	REDRY*
REDBREAST	REDEFECTING*	REDIAS*	REDOLENT	REDRYING*

REDS	REEARNED*	REEFED	REENDOWED*	REEXPEL*
REDSEAR	REEARNING*	REEFER	REENDOWING*	REEXPELLED*
REDSHANK	REEARNS*	REEFERS	REENDOWS*	REEXPELLING*
REDSHANKS	REEBOK	REEFIER*	REENFORCE*	REEXPELS*
REDSHARE	REEBOKS	REEFIEST*	REENFORCED*	REEXPLORE*
REDSHIFT*	REECH	REEFING	REENFORCES*	REEXPLORED*
REDSHIFTS*	REECHED	REEFINGS	REENFORCING*	REEXPLORES*
REDSHIRE	REECHES	REEFS	REENGAGE*	REEXPLORING*
REDSHIRT*	REECHIE	REEFY*	REENGAGED*	REEXPORT*
REDSHIRTED*	REECHIER	REEJECT*	REENGAGES*	REEXPORTED*
REDSHIRTING*	REECHIEST	REEJECTED*	REENGAGING*	REEXPORTING*
REDSHIRTS*	REECHING	REEJECTING*	REENGRAVE*	REEXPORTS*
REDSHORT	REECHO*	REEJECTS*	REENGRAVED*	REEXPOSE*
REDSKIN	REECHOED*	REEK	REENGRAVES*	REEXPOSED*
REDSKINS	REECHOES*	REEKED	REENGRAVING*	REEXPOSES*
REDSTART	REECHOING*	REEKER*	REENJOY*	REEXPOSING*
REDSTARTS	REECHY	REEKERS*	REENJOYED*	REEXPRESS*
REDSTREAK	REED	REEKIE	REENJOYING*	REEXPRESSED*
REDSTREAKS	REEDBED	REEKIER	REENJOYS*	REEXPRESSES*
REDTAIL*	REEDBEDS	REEKIEST	REENLIST*	REEXPRESSING*
REDTAILS*	REEDBIRD*	REEKING	REENLISTED*	REF
REDTOP	REEDBIRDS*	REEKS	REENLISTING*	REFACE
REDTOPS	REEDBUCK*	REEKY	REENLISTS*	REFACED
REDUB*	REEDBUCKS*	REEL	REENROLL*	REFACES
REDUBBED*	REEDE	REELABLE*	REENROLLED*	REFACING
REDUBBING*	REEDED	REELECT*	REENROLLING*	REFALL*
REDUBS*	REEDEN	REELECTED*	REENROLLS*	REFALLEN*
REDUCE	REEDER	REELECTING*	REENS	REFALLING*
REDUCED	REEDERS	REELECTS*	REENTER*	REFALLS*
REDUCER	REEDES	REELED	REENTERED*	REFASHION
REDUCERS	REEDIER	REELER	REENTERING*	REFASHIONED
REDUCES	REEDIEST	REELERS	REENTERS*	REFASHIONING
REDUCIBLE	REEDIFIED*	REELING	REENTRANT*	REFASHIONS
REDUCIBLY*	REEDIFIES*	REELINGLY	REENTRANTS*	REFASTEN*
REDUCING	REEDIFY*	REELINGS	REENTRIES*	REFASTENED*
REDUCTANT	REEDIFYING*	REELMAN	REENTRY*	REFASTENING*
REDUCTANTS	REEDILY*	REELMEN	REEQUIP*	REFASTENS*
REDUCTASE	REEDINESS	REELS	REEQUIPPED*	REFECT
REDUCTASES	REEDINESSES	REEMBARK*	REEQUIPPING*	REFECTED
REDUCTION	REEDING	REEMBARKED*	REEQUIPS*	REFECTING
REDUCTIONS	REEDINGS	REEMBARKING*	REERECT*	REFECTION
REDUCTIVE	REEDIT*	REEMBARKS*	REERECTED*	REFECTIONS
REDUCTOR*	REEDITED*	REEMBODIED*	REERECTING*	REFECTORIES
REDUCTORS*	REEDITING*	REEMBODIES*	REERECTS*	REFECTORY
REDUIT	REEDITION*	REEMBODY*	REES	REFECTS
REDUITS	REEDITIONS*	REEMBODYING*	REEST	REFED*
REDUNDANT	REEDITS*	REEMERGE*	REESTED	REFEED*
REDUVIID	REEDLIKE*	REEMERGED*	REESTIER	REFEEDING*
REDUVIIDS	REEDLING	REEMERGES*	REESTIEST	REFEEDS*
REDUX*	REEDLINGS	REEMERGING*	REESTING	REFEEL*
REDWARE*	REEDMACE	REEMIT*	REESTS	REFEELING*
REDWARES*	REEDMACES	REEMITS*	REESTY	REFEELS*
REDWATER	REEDMAN*	REEMITTED*	REEVE	REFEL
REDWATERS	REEDMEN*	REEMITTING*	REEVED	REFELL*
REDWING	REEDS	REEMPLOY*	REEVES	REFELLED
REDWINGS	REEDSTOP	REEMPLOYED*	REEVING	REFELLING
REDWOOD	REEDSTOPS	REEMPLOYING*	REEVOKE*	REFELS
REDWOODS	REEDUCATE*	REEMPLOYS*	REEVOKED*	REFELT*
REDYE*	REEDUCATED*	REEN	REEVOKES*	REFENCE*
REDYED*	REEDUCATES*	REENACT*	REEVOKING*	REFENCED*
REDYEING*	REEDUCATING*	REENACTED*	REEXAMINE*	REFENCES*
REDYES*	REEDY	REENACTING*	REEXAMINED*	REFENCING*
REE	REEF	REENACTS*	REEXAMINES*	REFER
REEARN*	REEFABLE*	REENDOW*	REEXAMINING*	REFERABLE

REFEREE	REFINISH*	REFLOWERS	REFOUNDED	REFUNDED
REFEREED	REFINISHED*	REFLOWING	REFOUNDER	REFUNDER
REFEREEING	REFINISHES*	REFLOWINGS	REFOUNDERS	REFUNDERS
REFEREES	REFINISHING*	REFLOWN*	REFOUNDING	REFUNDING
REFERENCE	REFIRE*	REFLOWS	REFOUNDS	REFUNDS
REFERENCED	REFIRED*	REFLUENCE	REFRACT	REFURBISH
REFERENCES	REFIRES*	REFLUENCES	REFRACTED	REFURBISHED
REFERENCING	REFIRING*	REFLUENT	REFRACTING	REFURBISHES
REFERENDA	REFIT	REFLUX	REFRACTOR	REFURBISHING
REFERENDUM*	REFITMENT	REFLUXED	REFRACTORS	REFURNISH
REFERENDUMS*	REFITMENTS	REFLUXES	REFRACTS	REFURNISHED
REFERENT	REFITS	REFLUXING	REFRAIN	REFURNISHES
REFERENTS	REFITTED	REFLY*	REFRAINED	REFURNISHING
REFERRAL	REFITTING	REFLYING*	REFRAINING	REFUSABLE
REFERRALS	REFITTINGS	REFOCUS	REFRAINS	REFUSAL
REFERRED	REFIX*	REFOCUSED	REFRAME	REFUSALS
REFERRER*	REFIXED*	REFOCUSES	REFRAMED	REFUSE
REFERRERS*	REFIXES*	REFOCUSING	REFRAMES	REFUSED
REFERRING	REFIXING*	REFOCUSSED	REFRAMING	REFUSENIK
REFERS	REFLAG	REFOCUSSES	REFREEZE	REFUSENIKS
REFFED	REFLAGGED	REFOCUSSING	REFREEZES	REFUSER
REFFING	REFLAGGING	REFOLD*	REFREEZING	REFUSERS
REFFO	REFLAGS	REFOLDED*	REFRESH	REFUSES
REFFOS	REFLATE	REFOLDING*	REFRESHED	REFUSING
REFIGHT*	REFLATED	REFOLDS*	REFRESHEN	REFUSION
REFIGHTING*	REFLATES	REFOOT	REFRESHENED	REFUSIONS
REFIGHTS*	REFLATING	REFOOTED	REFRESHENING	REFUSNIK
REFIGURE	REFLATION	REFOOTING	REFRESHENS	REFUSNIKS
REFIGURED	REFLATIONS	REFOOTS	REFRESHER	REFUTABLE
REFIGURES	REFLECT	REFOREST	REFRESHERS	REFUTABLY
REFIGURING	REFLECTED	REFORESTED	REFRESHES	REFUTAL
REFILE*	REFLECTER	REFORESTING	REFRESHING	REFUTALS
REFILED*	REFLECTERS	REFORESTS	REFRIED*	REFUTE
REFILES*	REFLECTING	REFORGE*	REFRIES*	REFUTED
REFILING*	REFLECTOR	REFORGED*	REFRINGE	REFUTER
REFILL	REFLECTORS	REFORGES*	REFRINGED	REFUTERS
REFILLED	REFLECTS	REFORGING*	REFRINGES	REFUTES
REFILLING	REFLET	REFORM	REFRINGING	REFUTING
REFILLS	REFLETS	REFORMADE	REFRONT*	REG*
REFILM*	REFLEW*	REFORMADES	REFRONTED*	REGAIN
REFILMED*	REFLEX	REFORMADO	REFRONTING*	REGAINED
REFILMING*	REFLEXED	REFORMADOES	REFRONTS*	REGAINER
REFILMS*	REFLEXES	REFORMADOS	REFROZE	REGAINERS
REFILTER*	REFLEXING	REFORMAT	REFROZEN	REGAINING
REFILTERED*	REFLEXION	REFORMATE*	REFRY*	REGAINS
REFILTERING*	REFLEXIONS	REFORMATES*	REFRYING*	REGAL
REFILTERS*	REFLEXIVE	REFORMATS	REFS	REGALE
REFINANCE*	REFLEXIVES*	REFORMATTED	REFT	REGALED
REFINANCED*	REFLEXLY	REFORMATTING	REFUEL	REGALER*
REFINANCES*	REFLIES*	REFORMED	REFUELED*	REGALERS*
REFINANCING*	REFLOAT	REFORMER	REFUELING*	REGALES
REFIND*	REFLOATED	REFORMERS	REFUELLED	REGALIA
REFINDING*	REFLOATING	REFORMING	REFUELLING	REGALIAN
REFINDS*	REFLOATS	REFORMISM	REFUELS	REGALIAS
REFINE	REFLOOD*	REFORMISMS	REFUGE	REGALING
REFINED	REFLOODED*	REFORMIST	REFUGED	REGALISM
REFINEDLY	REFLOODING*	REFORMISTS	REFUGEE	REGALISMS
REFINER	REFLOODS*	REFORMS	REFUGEES	REGALIST
REFINERIES	REFLOW	REFORTIFIED	REFUGES	REGALISTS
REFINERS	REFLOWED	REFORTIFIES	REFUGIA	REGALITIES
REFINERY	REFLOWER	REFORTIFY	REFUGING	REGALITY
REFINES	REFLOWERED	REFORTIFYING	REFUGIUM	REGALLY
REFINING	REFLOWERING	REFOUGHT*	REFULGENT	REGALS
REFININGS	REFLOWERINGS	REFOUND	REFUND	REGAR

REGARD	REGINAS	REGRAFTS*	REGUERDONED	REHEARSALS
REGARDANT	REGION	REGRANT	REGUERDONING	REHEARSE
REGARDED	REGIONAL	REGRANTED	REGUERDONS	REHEARSED
REGARDER	REGIONALS*	REGRANTING	REGULA	REHEARSER
REGARDERS	REGIONARY	REGRANTS	REGULAE	REHEARSERS
REGARDFUL	REGIONS	REGRATE	REGULAR	REHEARSES
REGARDING	REGISSEUR	REGRATED	REGULARLY	REHEARSING
REGARDS	REGISSEURS	REGRATER	REGULARS	REHEARSINGS
REGARS	REGISTER	REGRATERS	REGULATE	REHEAT
REGATHER	REGISTERED	REGRATES	REGULATED	REHEATED
REGATHERED	REGISTERING	REGRATING	REGULATES	REHEATER
REGATHERING	REGISTERS	REGRATINGS	REGULATING	REHEATERS
REGATHERS	REGISTRAR	REGRATOR	REGULATOR	REHEATING
REGATTA	REGISTRARS	REGRATORS	REGULATORS	REHEATS
REGATTAS	REGISTRIES	REGREDE	REGULI*	REHEEL
REGAUGE*	REGISTRY	REGREDED	REGULINE	REHEELED
REGAUGED*	REGIUS	REGREDES	REGULISE	REHEELING
REGAUGES*	REGIVE	REGREDING	REGULISED	REHEELS
REGAUGING*	REGIVEN	REGREEN*	REGULISES	REHEM*
REGAVE	REGIVES	REGREENED*	REGULISING	REHEMMED*
REGEAR*	REGIVING	REGREENING*	REGULIZE	REHEMMING*
REGEARED*	REGLAZE*	REGREENS*	REGULIZED	REHEMS*
REGEARING*	REGLAZED*	REGREET	REGULIZES	REHINGE*
REGEARS*	REGLAZES*	REGREETED	REGULIZING	REHINGED*
REGELATE	REGLAZING*	REGREETING	REGULO	REHINGES*
REGELATED	REGLET	REGREETS	REGULOS	REHINGING*
REGELATES	REGLETS	REGRESS	REGULUS	REHIRE*
REGELATING	REGLOSS*	REGRESSED	REGULUSES	REHIRED*
REGENCE	REGLOSSED*	REGRESSES	REGUR	REHIRES*
REGENCES	REGLOSSES*	REGRESSING	REGURS	REHIRING*
REGENCIES	REGLOSSING*	REGRESSOR*	REH	REHOBOAM
REGENCY	REGLOW*	REGRESSORS*	REHAB*	REHOBOAMS
REGENT	REGLOWED*	REGRET	REHABBED*	REHOUSE
REGENTAL*	REGLOWING*	REGRETFUL	REHABBER*	REHOUSED
REGENTS	REGLOWS*	REGRETS	REHABBERS*	REHOUSES
REGES*	REGLUE*	REGRETTED	REHABBING*	REHOUSING
REGEST	REGLUED*	REGRETTER*	REHABS*	REHOUSINGS
REGESTS	REGLUES*	REGRETTERS*	REHAMMER*	REHS
REGGAE	REGLUING*	REGRETTING	REHAMMERED*	REHUNG
REGGAES	REGMA	REGREW*	REHAMMERING*	REHYDRATE
REGGO	REGMATA	REGRIND	REHAMMERS*	REHYDRATED
REGGOS	REGNA*	REGRINDING	REHANDLE	REHYDRATES
REGICIDAL	REGNAL	REGRINDS	REHANDLED	REHYDRATING
REGICIDE	REGNANCIES*	REGROOM*	REHANDLES	REI*
REGICIDES	REGNANCY*	REGROOMED*	REHANDLING	REIF
REGIE	REGNANT	REGROOMING*	REHANDLINGS	REIFIED
REGIES	REGNUM*	REGROOMS*	REHANG	REIFIER*
REGILD*	REGO	REGROOVE*	REHANGED*	REIFIERS*
REGILDED*	REGOLITH	REGROOVED*	REHANGING	REIFIES
REGILDING*	REGOLITHS	REGROOVES*	REHANGS	REIFS
REGILDS*	REGORGE	REGROOVING*	REHARDEN*	REIFY
REGILT*	REGORGED	REGROUND	REHARDENED*	REIFYING
REGIME	REGORGES	REGROUP	REHARDENING*	REIGN
REGIMEN	REGORGING	REGROUPED	REHARDENS*	REIGNED
REGIMENS	REGOS	REGROUPING	REHASH	REIGNING
REGIMENT	REGOSOL*	REGROUPS	REHASHED	REIGNITE*
REGIMENTED	REGOSOLS*	REGROW*	REHASHES	REIGNITED*
REGIMENTING	REGRADE	REGROWING*	REHASHING	REIGNITES*
REGIMENTS	REGRADED	REGROWN*	REHEAR	REIGNITING*
REGIMES	REGRADES	REGROWS*	REHEARD	REIGNS
REGIMINAL	REGRADING	REGROWTH	REHEARING	REIK
REGINA	REGRAFT*	REGROWTHS	REHEARINGS	REIKI
REGINAE	REGRAFTED*	REGS*	REHEARS	REIKIS
REGINAL	REGRAFTING*	REGUERDON	REHEARSAL	REIKS

Words marked with an asterisk are from OTCWL

REILLUME	REINFECTING*	REINSTATING	REIVES	REKINDLED
REILLUMED	REINFECTS*	REINSURE	REIVING	REKINDLES
REILLUMES	REINFLATE*	REINSURED	REJACKET*	REKINDLING
REILLUMING	REINFLATED*	REINSURER	REJACKETED*	REKING
REIMAGE*	REINFLATES*	REINSURERS	REJACKETING*	REKNIT*
REIMAGED*	REINFLATING*	REINSURES	REJACKETS*	REKNITS*
REIMAGES*	REINFORCE	REINSURING	REJECT	REKNITTED*
REIMAGINE*	REINFORCED	REINTER	REJECTED	REKNITTING*
REIMAGINED*	REINFORCES	REINTERRED	REJECTEE*	RELABEL*
REIMAGINES*	REINFORCING	REINTERRING	REJECTEES*	RELABELED*
REIMAGING*	REINFORM	REINTERS	REJECTER	RELABELING*
REIMAGINING*	REINFORMED	REINVADE*	REJECTERS	RELABELLED*
REIMBURSE	REINFORMING	REINVADED*	REJECTING	RELABELLING*
REIMBURSED	REINFORMS	REINVADES*	REJECTION	RELABELS*
REIMBURSES	REINFUND	REINVADING*	REJECTIONS	RELACE*
REIMBURSING	REINFUNDED	REINVENT*	REJECTIVE	RELACED*
REIMMERSE*	REINFUNDING	REINVENTED*	REJECTOR	RELACES*
REIMMERSED*	REINFUNDS	REINVENTING*	REJECTORS	RELACHE
REIMMERSES*	REINFUSE	REINVENTS*	REJECTS	RELACHES
REIMMERSING*	REINFUSED	REINVEST	REJIG	RELACING*
REIMPLANT	REINFUSES	REINVESTED	REJIGGED	RELACQUER*
REIMPLANTED	REINFUSING	REINVESTING	REJIGGER	RELACQUERED*
REIMPLANTING	REINHABIT	REINVESTS	REJIGGERED	RELACQUERING*
REIMPLANTS	REINHABITED	REINVITE*	REJIGGERING	RELACQUERS*
REIMPORT	REINHABITING	REINVITED*	REJIGGERS	RELAID
REIMPORTED	REINHABITS	REINVITES*	REJIGGING	RELAPSE
REIMPORTING	REINING	REINVITING*	REJIGS	RELAPSED
REIMPORTS	REINJECT*	REINVOKE*	REJOICE	RELAPSER
REIMPOSE	REINJECTED*	REINVOKED*	REJOICED	RELAPSERS
REIMPOSED	REINJECTING*	REINVOKES*	REJOICER	RELAPSES
REIMPOSES	REINJECTS*	REINVOKING*	REJOICERS	RELAPSING
REIMPOSING	REINJURE*	REINVOLVE	REJOICES	RELATABLE*
REIN	REINJURED*	REINVOLVED	REJOICING	RELATE
REINCITE*	REINJURES*	REINVOLVES	REJOICINGS	RELATED
REINCITED*	REINJURIES*	REINVOLVING	REJOIN	RELATEDLY*
REINCITES*	REINJURING*	REIRD	REJOINDER	RELATER
REINCITING*	REINJURY*	REIRDS	REJOINDERS	RELATERS
REINCUR*	REINK*	REIS	REJOINED	RELATES
REINCURRED*	REINKED*	REISES	REJOINING	RELATING
REINCURRING*	REINKING*	REISSUE	REJOINS	RELATION
REINCURS*	REINKS*	REISSUED	REJON	RELATIONS
REINDEER	REINLESS	REISSUER*	REJONEO	RELATIVAL
REINDEERS	REINS	REISSUERS*	REJONEOS	RELATIVE
REINDEX*	REINSERT	REISSUES	REJONES	RELATIVES
REINDEXED*	REINSERTED	REISSUING	REJOURN	RELATOR
REINDEXES*	REINSERTING	REIST	REJOURNED	RELATORS
REINDEXING*	REINSERTS	REISTAFEL	REJOURNING	RELAUNCH
REINDICT*	REINSMAN	REISTAFELS	REJOURNS	RELAUNCHED
REINDICTED*	REINSMEN	REISTED	REJUDGE	RELAUNCHES
REINDICTING*	REINSPECT	REISTING	REJUDGED	RELAUNCHING
REINDICTS*	REINSPECTED	REISTS	REJUDGES	RELAX
REINDUCE*	REINSPECTING	REITBOK*	REJUDGING	RELAXANT
REINDUCED*	REINSPECTS	REITBOKS*	REJUGGLE*	RELAXANTS
REINDUCES*	REINSPIRE	REITER	REJUGGLED*	RELAXED
REINDUCING*	REINSPIRED	REITERANT	REJUGGLES*	RELAXEDLY*
REINDUCT*	REINSPIRES	REITERATE	REJUGGLING*	RELAXER*
REINDUCTED*	REINSPIRING	REITERATED	REKE	RELAXERS*
REINDUCTING*	REINSTALL	REITERATES	REKED	RELAXES
REINDUCTS*	REINSTALLED	REITERATING	REKES	RELAXIN
REINED	REINSTALLING	REITERS	REKEY*	RELAXING
REINETTE	REINSTALLS	REIVE	REKEYED*	RELAXINS
REINETTES	REINSTATE	REIVED*	REKEYING*	RELAY
REINFECT*	REINSTATED	REIVER	REKEYS*	RELAYED
REINFECTED*	REINSTATES	REIVERS	REKINDLE	RELAYING

The Chambers Dictionary is the authority for many longer words; see Introduction, page ix

RELAYS	RELIEFS	RELOADERS*	REMANDING	REMEDES
RELEARN*	RELIER	RELOADING	REMANDS	REMEDIAL
RELEARNED*	RELIERS	RELOADS	REMANENCE	REMEDIAT
RELEARNING*	RELIES	RELOAN*	REMANENCES	REMEDIATE
RELEARNS*	RELIEVE	RELOANED*	REMANENCIES	REMEDIATED*
RELEARNT*	RELIEVED	RELOANING*	REMANENCY	REMEDIATES*
RELEASE	RELIEVER	RELOANS*	REMANENT	REMEDIATING*
RELEASED	RELIEVERS	RELOCATE	REMANENTS	REMEDIED
RELEASEE	RELIEVES	RELOCATED	REMANET	REMEDIES
RELEASEES	RELIEVING	RELOCATEE*	REMANETS	REMEDING
RELEASER	RELIEVO	RELOCATEES*	REMANIE	REMEDY
RELEASERS	RELIEVOS	RELOCATES	REMANIES	REMEDYING
RELEASES	RELIGHT	RELOCATING	REMANNED	REMEET*
RELEASING	RELIGHTED	RELOCK*	REMANNING	REMEETING*
RELEASOR	RELIGHTING	RELOCKED*	REMANS	REMEETS*
RELEASORS	RELIGHTS	RELOCKING*	REMAP*	REMEID
RELEGABLE	RELIGIEUX	RELOCKS*	REMAPPED*	REMEIDED
RELEGATE	RELIGION	RELOOK*	REMAPPING*	REMEIDING
RELEGATED	RELIGIONS	RELOOKED*	REMAPS*	REMEIDS
RELEGATES	RELIGIOSE	RELOOKING*	REMARK	REMELT*
RELEGATING	RELIGIOSO	RELOOKS*	REMARKED	REMELTED*
RELEND*	RELIGIOUS	RELUCENT	REMARKER	REMELTING*
RELENDING*	RELIGIOUSES	RELUCT	REMARKERS	REMELTS*
RELENDS*	RELINE	RELUCTANT	REMARKET*	REMEMBER
RELENT	RELINED	RELUCTATE	REMARKETED*	REMEMBERED
RELENTED	RELINES	RELUCTATED	REMARKETING*	REMEMBERING
RELENTING	RELINING	RELUCTATES	REMARKETS*	REMEMBERS
RELENTINGS	RELINK*	RELUCTATING	REMARKING	REMEN
RELENTS	RELINKED*	RELUCTED	REMARKS	REMEND*
RELET	RELINKING*	RELUCTING	REMARQUE	REMENDED*
RELETS	RELINKS*	RELUCTS	REMARQUED	REMENDING*
RELETTER*	RELIQUARIES	RELUME	REMARQUES	REMENDS*
RELETTERED*	RELIQUARY	RELUMED	REMARRIED	REMENS
RELETTERING*	RELIQUE	RELUMES	REMARRIES	REMERCIED
RELETTERS*	RELIQUEFIED*	RELUMINE	REMARRY	REMERCIES
RELETTING	RELIQUEFIES*	RELUMINED	REMARRYING	REMERCY
RELEVANCE	RELIQUEFY*	RELUMINES	REMASTER	REMERCYING
RELEVANCES	RELIQUEFYING*	RELUMING	REMASTERED	REMERGE
RELEVANCIES	RELIQUES	RELUMINING	REMASTERING	REMERGED
RELEVANCY	RELIQUIAE	RELY	REMASTERS	REMERGES
RELEVANT	RELISH	RELYING	REMATCH	REMERGING
RELEVE*	RELISHED	REM	REMATCHED	REMET*
RELEVES*	RELISHES	REMADE	REMATCHES	REMEX
RELIABLE	RELISHING	REMADES	REMATCHING	REMIGATE
RELIABLES*	RELIST*	REMAIL*	REMATE*	REMIGATED
RELIABLY	RELISTED*	REMAILED*	REMATED*	REMIGATES
RELIANCE	RELISTING*	REMAILING*	REMATES*	REMIGATING
RELIANCES	RELISTS*	REMAILS*	REMATING*	REMIGES
RELIANT	RELIT	REMAIN	REMBLAI	REMIGIAL
RELIANTLY*	RELIVE	REMAINDER	REMBLAIS	REMIGRATE
RELIC	RELIVED	REMAINDERED	REMBLE	REMIGRATED
RELICENSE*	RELIVER	REMAINDERING	REMBLED	REMIGRATES
RELICENSED*	RELIVERED	REMAINDERS	REMBLES	REMIGRATING
RELICENSES*	RELIVERING	REMAINED	REMBLING	REMIND
RELICENSING*	RELIVERS	REMAINING	REMEAD	REMINDED
RELICS	RELIVES	REMAINS	REMEADED	REMINDER
RELICT	RELIVING	REMAKE	REMEADING	REMINDERS
RELICTION*	RELLISH	REMAKER*	REMEADS	REMINDFUL
RELICTIONS*	RELLISHED	REMAKERS*	REMEASURE	REMINDING
RELICTS	RELLISHES	REMAKES	REMEASURED	REMINDS
RELIDE	RELLISHING	REMAKING	REMEASURES	REMINISCE
RELIE	RELOAD	REMAN	REMEASURING	REMINISCED
RELIED	RELOADED	REMAND	REMEDE	REMINISCES
RELIEF	RELOADER*	REMANDED	REMEDED	REMINISCING

REMINT	REMOTELY	RENDED*	RENIED	RENTS
REMINTED	REMOTER	RENDER	RENIES	RENUMBER
REMINTING	REMOTES	RENDERED	RENIFORM	RENUMBERED
REMINTS	REMOTEST	RENDERER	RENIG	RENUMBERING
REMISE	REMOTION	RENDERERS	RENIGGED	RENUMBERS
REMISED	REMOTIONS	RENDERING	RENIGGING	RENVERSE
REMISES	REMOUD	RENDERINGS	RENIGS	RENVERSED
REMISING	REMOULADE	RENDERS	RENIN	RENVERSES
REMISS	REMOULADES	RENDIBLE*	RENINS	RENVERSING
REMISSION	REMOULD	RENDING	RENITENCIES	RENVERST
REMISSIONS	REMOULDED	RENDITION	RENITENCY	RENVOI
REMISSIVE	REMOULDING	RENDITIONS	RENITENT	RENVOIS
REMISSLY	REMOULDS	RENDS	RENMINBI	RENVOY
REMISSORY	REMOUNT	RENDZINA	RENMINBIS	RENVOYS
REMIT	REMOUNTED	RENDZINAS	RENNASE*	RENY
REMITMENT	REMOUNTING	RENEGADE	RENNASES*	RENYING
REMITMENTS	REMOUNTS	RENEGADED	RENNE	REOBJECT*
REMITS	REMOVABLE	RENEGADES	RENNED	REOBJECTED*
REMITTAL	REMOVABLY	RENEGADING	RENNES	REOBJECTING*
REMITTALS	REMOVAL	RENEGADO	RENNET	REOBJECTS*
REMITTED	REMOVALS	RENEGADOES*	RENNETS	REOBSERVE*
REMITTEE	REMOVE	RENEGADOS	RENNIN	REOBSERVED*
REMITTEES	REMOVED	RENEGATE	RENNING	REOBSERVES*
REMITTENT	REMOVER	RENEGATES	RENNINS	REOBSERVING*
REMITTER	REMOVERS	RENEGE	RENOGRAM*	REOBTAIN*
REMITTERS	REMOVES	RENEGED	RENOGRAMS*	REOBTAINED*
REMITTING	REMOVING	RENEGER	RENOTIFIED*	REOBTAINING*
REMITTOR	REMS	RENEGERS	RENOTIFIES*	REOBTAINS*
REMITTORS	REMUAGE	RENEGES	RENOTIFY*	REOCCUPIED
REMIX	REMUAGES	RENEGING	RENOTIFYING*	REOCCUPIES
REMIXED	REMUDA	RENEGUE	RENOUNCE	REOCCUPY
REMIXES	REMUDAS	RENEGUED	RENOUNCED	REOCCUPYING
REMIXING	REMUEUR	RENEGUER	RENOUNCER	REOCCUR*
REMIXT*	REMUEURS	RENEGUERS	RENOUNCERS	REOCCURRED*
REMNANT	REMURMUR	RENEGUES	RENOUNCES	REOCCURRING*
REMNANTS	REMURMURED	RENEGUING	RENOUNCING	REOCCURS*
REMODEL	REMURMURING	RENEST*	RENOVATE	REOFFEND
REMODELED	REMURMURS	RENESTED*	RENOVATED	REOFFENDED
REMODELING	REN	RENESTING*	RENOVATES	REOFFENDING
REMODELLED	RENAGUE	RENESTS*	RENOVATING	REOFFENDS
REMODELLING	RENAGUED	RENEW	RENOVATOR	REOFFER*
REMODELS	RENAGUES	RENEWABLE	RENOVATORS	REOFFERED*
REMODIFIED	RENAGUING	RENEWABLES	RENOWN	REOFFERING*
REMODIFIES	RENAIL*	RENEWABLY*	RENOWNED	REOFFERS*
REMODIFY	RENAILED*	RENEWAL	RENOWNER	REOIL*
REMODIFYING	RENAILING*	RENEWALS	RENOWNERS	REOILED*
REMOISTEN*	RENAILS*	RENEWED	RENOWNING	REOILING*
REMOISTENED*	RENAL	RENEWER	RENOWNS	REOILS*
REMOISTENING*	RENAME	RENEWERS	RENS	REOPEN
REMOISTENS*	RENAMED	RENEWING	RENT	REOPENED
REMOLADE*	RENAMES	RENEWINGS	RENTABLE	REOPENER
REMOLADES*	RENAMING	RENEWS	RENTAL	REOPENERS
REMOLD*	RENASCENT	RENEY	RENTALLER	REOPENING
REMOLDED*	RENATURE*	RENEYED	RENTALLERS	REOPENS
REMOLDING*	RENATURED*	RENEYING	RENTALS	REOPERATE*
REMOLDS*	RENATURES*	RENEYS	RENTE	REOPERATED*
REMONTANT	RENATURING*	RENFIERST	RENTED	REOPERATES*
REMONTANTS	RENAY	RENFORCE	RENTER	REOPERATING*
REMORA	RENAYED	RENFORCED	RENTERS	REOPPOSE*
REMORAS	RENAYING	RENFORCES	RENTES	REOPPOSED*
REMORID*	RENAYS	RENFORCING	RENTIER	REOPPOSES*
REMORSE	RENCONTRE	RENFORST	RENTIERS	REOPPOSING*
REMORSES	RENCONTRES	RENGA	RENTING	REORDAIN
REMOTE	REND	RENGAS		REORDAINED

REORDAINING	REPARKS*	REPENT	REPLASTER*	REPLUNGE*
REORDAINS	REPARTEE	REPENTANT	REPLASTERED*	REPLUNGED*
REORDER	REPARTEED	REPENTANTS	REPLASTERING*	REPLUNGES*
REORDERED	REPARTEEING	REPENTED	REPLASTERS*	REPLUNGING*
REORDERING	REPARTEES	REPENTER	REPLATE*	REPLY
REORDERS	REPASS	REPENTERS	REPLATED*	REPLYING
REORIENT	REPASSAGE	REPENTING	REPLATES*	REPO
REORIENTED	REPASSAGES	REPENTS	REPLATING*	REPOINT
REORIENTING	REPASSED	REPEOPLE	REPLAY	REPOINTED
REORIENTS	REPASSES	REPEOPLED	REPLAYED	REPOINTING
REOUTFIT*	REPASSING	REPEOPLES	REPLAYING	REPOINTS
REOUTFITS*	REPAST	REPEOPLING	REPLAYS	REPOLISH*
REOUTFITTED*	REPASTED	REPERCUSS	REPLEAD*	REPOLISHED*
REOUTFITTING*	REPASTING	REPERCUSSED	REPLEADED*	REPOLISHES*
REOVIRUS*	REPASTS	REPERCUSSES	REPLEADER*	REPOLISHING*
REOVIRUSES*	REPASTURE	REPERCUSSING	REPLEADERS*	REPOLL*
REOXIDIZE*	REPASTURES	REPERK*	REPLEADING*	REPOLLED*
REOXIDIZED*	REPATCH*	REPERKED*	REPLEADS*	REPOLLING*
REOXIDIZES*	REPATCHED*	REPERKING*	REPLED*	REPOLLS*
REOXIDIZING*	REPATCHES*	REPERKS*	REPLEDGE*	REPOMAN
REP	REPATCHING*	REPERTORIES	REPLEDGED*	REPOMEN
REPACIFIED*	REPATTERN*	REPERTORY	REPLEDGES*	REPONE
REPACIFIES*	REPATTERNED*	REPERUSAL	REPLEDGING*	REPONED
REPACIFY*	REPATTERNING*	REPERUSALS	REPLENISH	REPONES
REPACIFYING*	REPATTERNS*	REPERUSE	REPLENISHED	REPONING
REPACK	REPAVE*	REPERUSED	REPLENISHES	REPORT
REPACKAGE	REPAVED*	REPERUSES	REPLENISHING	REPORTAGE
REPACKAGED	REPAVES*	REPERUSING	REPLETE	REPORTAGES
REPACKAGES	REPAVING*	REPETEND	REPLETED	REPORTED
REPACKAGING	REPAY	REPETENDS	REPLETES	REPORTER
REPACKED	REPAYABLE	REPHRASE	REPLETING	REPORTERS
REPACKING	REPAYING	REPHRASED	REPLETION	REPORTING
REPACKS	REPAYMENT	REPHRASES	REPLETIONS	REPORTINGS
REPAID	REPAYMENTS	REPHRASING	REPLEVIED	REPORTS
REPAINT	REPAYS	REPIN*	REPLEVIES	REPOS
REPAINTED	REPEAL	REPINE	REPLEVIN	REPOSAL
REPAINTING	REPEALED	REPINED	REPLEVINED	REPOSALL
REPAINTINGS	REPEALER	REPINER	REPLEVINING	REPOSALLS
REPAINTS	REPEALERS	REPINERS	REPLEVINS	REPOSALS
REPAIR	REPEALING	REPINES	REPLEVY	REPOSE
REPAIRED	REPEALS	REPINING	REPLEVYING	REPOSED
REPAIRER	REPEAT	REPININGS	REPLICA	REPOSEDLY
REPAIRERS	REPEATED	REPINNED*	REPLICAS	REPOSEFUL
REPAIRING	REPEATER	REPINNING*	REPLICASE*	REPOSER*
REPAIRMAN	REPEATERS	REPINS*	REPLICASES*	REPOSERS*
REPAIRMEN	REPEATING	REPIQUE	REPLICATE	REPOSES
REPAIRS	REPEATINGS	REPIQUED	REPLICATED	REPOSING
REPAND	REPEATS	REPIQUES	REPLICATES	REPOSIT
REPANDLY*	REPECHAGE	REPIQUING	REPLICATING	REPOSITED
REPANEL*	REPECHAGES	REPLA	REPLICON	REPOSITING
REPANELED*	REPEG*	REPLACE	REPLICONS	REPOSITOR
REPANELING*	REPEGGED*	REPLACED	REPLIED	REPOSITORS
REPANELLED*	REPEGGING*	REPLACER	REPLIER	REPOSITS
REPANELLING*	REPEGS*	REPLACERS	REPLIERS	REPOSSESS
REPANELS*	REPEL	REPLACES	REPLIES	REPOSSESSED
REPAPER	REPELLANT	REPLACING	REPLOT*	REPOSSESSES
REPAPERED	REPELLANTS	REPLAN	REPLOTS*	REPOSSESSING
REPAPERING	REPELLED	REPLANNED	REPLOTTED*	REPOST
REPAPERS	REPELLENT	REPLANNING	REPLOTTING*	REPOSTED
REPARABLE	REPELLENTS	REPLANS	REPLUM	REPOSTING
REPARABLY	REPELLER	REPLANT	REPLUMB*	REPOSTS
REPARK*	REPELLERS	REPLANTED	REPLUMBED*	REPOSURE
REPARKED*	REPELLING	REPLANTING	REPLUMBING*	REPOSURES
REPARKING*	REPELS	REPLANTS	REPLUMBS*	REPOT

Words marked with an asterisk are from OTCWL

REPOTS	REPRISALS	REPTILE	REQUESTED	RERAN
REPOTTED	REPRISE	REPTILES	REQUESTER	REREAD
REPOTTING	REPRISED	REPTILIAN	REQUESTERS	REREADING
REPOTTINGS	REPRISES	REPTILIANS*	REQUESTING	REREADINGS*
REPOUR*	REPRISING	REPTILOID	REQUESTOR*	REREADS
REPOURED*	REPRIVE	REPUBLIC	REQUESTORS*	REREBRACE
REPOURING*	REPRIVED	REPUBLICS	REQUESTS	REREBRACES
REPOURS*	REPRIVES	REPUBLISH	REQUICKEN	RERECORD*
REPOUSSE	REPRIVING	REPUBLISHED	REQUICKENED	RERECORDED*
REPOUSSES	REPRIZE	REPUBLISHES	REQUICKENING	RERECORDING*
REPOWER*	REPRIZED	REPUBLISHING	REQUICKENS	RERECORDS*
REPOWERED*	REPRIZES	REPUDIATE	REQUIEM	REREDORSE
REPOWERING*	REPRIZING	REPUDIATED	REQUIEMS	REREDORSES
REPOWERS*	REPRO	REPUDIATES	REQUIGHT	REREDOS
REPP	REPROACH	REPUDIATING	REQUIGHTED	REREDOSES
REPPED	REPROACHED	REPUGN	REQUIGHTING	REREDOSSE
REPPING	REPROACHES	REPUGNANT	REQUIGHTS	REREDOSSES
REPPINGS	REPROACHING	REPUGNED	REQUIN*	RERELEASE*
REPPS	REPROBACIES	REPUGNING	REQUINS*	RERELEASED*
REPREEVE	REPROBACY	REPUGNS	REQUIRE	RERELEASES*
REPREEVED	REPROBATE	REPULP	REQUIRED	RERELEASING*
REPREEVES	REPROBATED	REPULPED	REQUIRER	REREMICE
REPREEVING	REPROBATES	REPULPING	REQUIRERS	REREMIND*
REPREHEND	REPROBATING	REPULPS	REQUIRES	REREMINDED*
REPREHENDED	REPROBE*	REPULSE	REQUIRING	REREMINDING*
REPREHENDING	REPROBED*	REPULSED	REQUIRINGS	REREMINDS*
REPREHENDS	REPROBES*	REPULSER*	REQUISITE	REREMOUSE
REPRESENT	REPROBING*	REPULSERS*	REQUISITES	REREPEAT*
REPRESENTED	REPROCESS	REPULSES	REQUIT	REREPEATED*
REPRESENTING	REPROCESSED	REPULSING	REQUITAL	REREPEATING*
REPRESENTS	REPROCESSES	REPULSION	REQUITALS	REREPEATS*
REPRESS	REPROCESSING	REPULSIONS	REQUITE	REREVIEW*
REPRESSED	REPRODUCE	REPULSIVE	REQUITED	REREVIEWED*
REPRESSES	REPRODUCED	REPUMP*	REQUITER	REREVIEWING*
REPRESSING	REPRODUCES	REPUMPED*	REQUITERS	REREVIEWS*
REPRESSOR	REPRODUCING	REPUMPING*	REQUITES	REREVISE
REPRESSORS	REPROGRAM	REPUMPS*	REQUITING	REREVISED
REPRICE*	REPROGRAMED*	REPUNIT	REQUITS	REREVISES
REPRICED*	REPROGRAMING*	REPUNITS	REQUITTED	REREVISING
REPRICES*	REPROGRAMMED	REPURE	REQUITTING	REREWARD
REPRICING*	REPROGRAMMING	REPURED	REQUOTE	REREWARDS
REPRIEFE	REPROGRAMS	REPURES	REQUOTED	RERIG*
REPRIEFES	REPROOF	REPURIFIED	REQUOTES	RERIGGED*
REPRIEVAL	REPROOFED	REPURIFIES	REQUOTING	RERIGGING*
REPRIEVALS	REPROOFING	REPURIFY	REQUOYLE	RERIGS*
REPRIEVE	REPROOFS	REPURIFYING	REQUOYLED	RERISE*
REPRIEVED	REPROS	REPURING	REQUOYLES	RERISEN*
REPRIEVES	REPROVAL	REPURSUE*	REQUOYLING	RERISES*
REPRIEVING	REPROVALS	REPURSUED*	RERACK*	RERISING*
REPRIMAND	REPROVE	REPURSUES*	RERACKED*	REROLL*
REPRIMANDED	REPROVED	REPURSUING*	RERACKING*	REROLLED*
REPRIMANDING	REPROVER	REPUTABLE	RERACKS*	REROLLER*
REPRIMANDS	REPROVERS	REPUTABLY	RERADIATE	REROLLERS*
REPRIME	REPROVES	REPUTE	RERADIATED	REROLLING*
REPRIMED	REPROVING	REPUTED	RERADIATES	REROLLS*
REPRIMES	REPROVINGS	REPUTEDLY	RERADIATING	REROOF*
REPRIMING	REPRYVE	REPUTES	RERAIL	REROOFED*
REPRINT	REPRYVED	REPUTING	RERAILED	REROOFING*
REPRINTED	REPRYVES	REPUTINGS	RERAILING	REROOFS*
REPRINTER*	REPRYVING	REQUERE	RERAILS	REROSE*
REPRINTERS*	REPS	REQUERED	RERAISE*	REROUTE
REPRINTING	REPTANT	REQUERES	RERAISED*	REROUTED
REPRINTS	REPTATION	REQUERING	RERAISES*	REROUTEING
REPRISAL	REPTATIONS	REQUEST	RERAISING*	REROUTES

The Chambers Dictionary is the authority for many longer words; see Introduction, page ix

REROUTING	RESCUED	RESEMBLE	RESHINE*	RESIGHTS*
RERUN	RESCUER	RESEMBLED	RESHINED*	RESIGN
RERUNNING	RESCUERS	RESEMBLER	RESHINES*	RESIGNED
RERUNS	RESCUES	RESEMBLERS	RESHINGLE*	RESIGNER
RES	RESCUING	RESEMBLES	RESHINGLED*	RESIGNERS
RESADDLE*	RESCULPT*	RESEMBLING	RESHINGLES*	RESIGNING
RESADDLED*	RESCULPTED*	RESEND*	RESHINGLING*	RESIGNS
RESADDLES*	RESCULPTING*	RESENDING*	RESHINING*	RESILE
RESADDLING*	RESCULPTS*	RESENDS*	RESHIP	RESILED
RESAID	RESEAL	RESENT	RESHIPPED	RESILES
RESAIL*	RESEALED	RESENTED	RESHIPPING	RESILIENT
RESAILED*	RESEALING	RESENTER	RESHIPS	RESILING
RESAILING*	RESEALS	RESENTERS	RESHOD*	RESILVER*
RESAILS*	RESEARCH	RESENTFUL	RESHOE*	RESILVERED*
RESALABLE*	RESEARCHED	RESENTING	RESHOEING*	RESILVERING*
RESALE	RESEARCHES	RESENTIVE	RESHOES*	RESILVERS*
RESALES	RESEARCHING	RESENTS	RESHONE*	RESIN
RESALGAR	RESEASON*	RESERPINE	RESHOOT*	RESINATA
RESALGARS	RESEASONED*	RESERPINES	RESHOOTING*	RESINATAS
RESALUTE	RESEASONING*	RESERVE	RESHOOTS*	RESINATE
RESALUTED	RESEASONS*	RESERVED	RESHOT*	RESINATED*
RESALUTES	RESEAT	RESERVER*	RESHOW*	RESINATES
RESALUTING	RESEATED	RESERVERS*	RESHOWED*	RESINATING*
RESAMPLE*	RESEATING	RESERVES	RESHOWING*	RESINED
RESAMPLED*	RESEATS	RESERVICE*	RESHOWN*	RESINER
RESAMPLES*	RESEAU	RESERVICED*	RESHOWS*	RESINERS
RESAMPLING*	RESEAUS	RESERVICES*	RESHUFFLE	RESINIFIED
RESAT	RESEAUX	RESERVICING*	RESHUFFLED	RESINIFIES
RESAW*	RESECT	RESERVING	RESHUFFLES	RESINIFY
RESAWED*	RESECTED	RESERVIST	RESHUFFLING	RESINIFYING
RESAWING*	RESECTING	RESERVISTS	RESIANCE	RESINING
RESAWN*	RESECTION	RESERVOIR	RESIANCES	RESINISE
RESAWS*	RESECTIONS	RESERVOIRED	RESIANT	RESINISED
RESAY	RESECTS	RESERVOIRING	RESIANTS	RESINISES
RESAYING	RESECURE*	RESERVOIRS	RESID*	RESINISING
RESAYS	RESECURED*	RESES	RESIDE	RESINIZE
RESCALE	RESECURES*	RESET	RESIDED	RESINIZED
RESCALED	RESECURING*	RESETS	RESIDENCE	RESINIZES
RESCALES	RESEDA	RESETTED	RESIDENCES	RESINIZING
RESCALING	RESEDAS	RESETTER	RESIDENCIES	RESINOID
RESCHOOL*	RESEE*	RESETTERS	RESIDENCY	RESINOIDS
RESCHOOLED*	RESEED*	RESETTING	RESIDENT	RESINOSES
RESCHOOLING*	RESEEDED*	RESETTLE	RESIDENTS	RESINOSIS
RESCHOOLS*	RESEEDING*	RESETTLED	RESIDER	RESINOUS
RESCIND	RESEEDS*	RESETTLES	RESIDERS	RESINS
RESCINDED	RESEEING*	RESETTLING	RESIDES	RESINY*
RESCINDER*	RESEEK*	RESEW*	RESIDING	RESIST
RESCINDERS*	RESEEKING*	RESEWED*	RESIDS*	RESISTANT
RESCINDING	RESEEKS*	RESEWING*	RESIDUA	RESISTANTS
RESCINDS	RESEEN*	RESEWN*	RESIDUAL	RESISTED
RESCORE	RESEES*	RESEWS*	RESIDUALS	RESISTENT
RESCORED	RESEIZE	RESH*	RESIDUARY	RESISTENTS
RESCORES	RESEIZED	RESHAPE	RESIDUE	RESISTER*
RESCORING	RESEIZES	RESHAPED	RESIDUES	RESISTERS*
RESCREEN*	RESEIZING	RESHAPER*	RESIDUOUS	RESISTING
RESCREENED*	RESELECT	RESHAPERS*	RESIDUUM	RESISTIVE
RESCREENING*	RESELECTED	RESHAPES	RESIDUUMS*	RESISTOR
RESCREENS*	RESELECTING	RESHAPING	RESIFT*	RESISTORS
RESCRIPT	RESELECTS	RESHAVE*	RESIFTED*	RESISTS
RESCRIPTED	RESELL	RESHAVED*	RESIFTING*	RESIT
RESCRIPTING	RESELLER*	RESHAVEN*	RESIFTS*	RESITE*
RESCRIPTS	RESELLERS*	RESHAVES*	RESIGHT*	RESITED*
RESCUABLE	RESELLING	RESHAVING*	RESIGHTED*	RESITES*
RESCUE	RESELLS	RESHES*	RESIGHTING*	RESITING*

RESUMED

RESITS	RESOLVENTS	RESPIRE	RESTAFFED	RESTORING
RESITTING	RESOLVER	RESPIRED	RESTAFFING	RESTRAIN
RESITTINGS*	RESOLVERS	RESPIRES	RESTAFFS	RESTRAINED
RESIZE*	RESOLVES	RESPIRING	RESTAGE	RESTRAINING
RESIZED*	RESOLVING	RESPITE	RESTAGED	RESTRAININGS
RESIZES*	RESONANCE	RESPITED	RESTAGES	RESTRAINS
RESIZING*	RESONANCES	RESPITES	RESTAGING	RESTRAINT
RESKETCH*	RESONANT	RESPITING	RESTAMP*	RESTRAINTS
RESKETCHED*	RESONANTS	RESPLEND	RESTAMPED*	RESTRESS*
RESKETCHES*	RESONATE	RESPLENDED	RESTAMPING*	RESTRESSED*
RESKETCHING*	RESONATED	RESPLENDING	RESTAMPS*	RESTRESSES*
RESKEW	RESONATES	RESPLENDS	RESTART	RESTRESSING*
RESKEWED	RESONATING	RESPLICE*	RESTARTED	RESTRICKEN*
RESKEWING	RESONATOR	RESPLICED*	RESTARTER	RESTRICT
RESKEWS	RESONATORS	RESPLICES*	RESTARTERS	RESTRICTED
RESKILL	RESORB	RESPLICING*	RESTARTING	RESTRICTING
RESKILLED	RESORBED	RESPLIT*	RESTARTS	RESTRICTS
RESKILLING	RESORBENT	RESPLITS*	RESTATE	RESTRIKE*
RESKILLS	RESORBING	RESPLITTING*	RESTATED	RESTRIKES*
RESKUE	RESORBS	RESPOKE	RESTATES	RESTRIKING*
RESKUED	RESORCIN	RESPOKEN	RESTATING	RESTRING
RESKUES	RESORCINS	RESPOND	RESTED	RESTRINGE
RESKUING	RESORT	RESPONDED	RESTEM	RESTRINGED
RESLATE*	RESORTED	RESPONDER	RESTEMMED	RESTRINGEING
RESLATED*	RESORTER	RESPONDERS	RESTEMMING	RESTRINGES
RESLATES*	RESORTERS	RESPONDING	RESTEMS	RESTRINGING
RESLATING*	RESORTING	RESPONDS	RESTER	RESTRINGS
RESMELT*	RESORTS	RESPONSA	RESTERS	RESTRIVE*
RESMELTED*	RESOUGHT*	RESPONSE	RESTFUL	RESTRIVEN*
RESMELTING*	RESOUND	RESPONSER	RESTFULLER	RESTRIVES*
RESMELTS*	RESOUNDED	RESPONSERS	RESTFULLEST	RESTRIVING*
RESMOOTH*	RESOUNDING	RESPONSES	RESTFULLY	RESTROOM*
RESMOOTHED*	RESOUNDS	RESPONSOR	RESTIER	RESTROOMS*
RESMOOTHING*	RESOURCE	RESPONSORS	RESTIEST	RESTROVE*
RESMOOTHS*	RESOURCED	RESPONSUM	RESTIFF	RESTRUCK*
RESNATRON	RESOURCES	RESPONSUMS	RESTIFORM	RESTRUNG
RESNATRONS	RESOURCING	RESPOT*	RESTING	RESTS
RESOAK*	RESOW*	RESPOTS*	RESTINGS	RESTUDIED*
RESOAKED*	RESOWED*	RESPOTTED*	RESTITCH*	RESTUDIES*
RESOAKING*	RESOWING*	RESPOTTING*	RESTITCHED*	RESTUDY*
RESOAKS*	RESOWN*	RESPRANG*	RESTITCHES*	RESTUDYING*
RESOD*	RESOWS*	RESPRAY	RESTITCHING*	RESTUFF*
RESODDED*	RESPACE*	RESPRAYED	RESTITUTE	RESTUFFED*
RESODDING*	RESPACED*	RESPRAYING	RESTITUTED	RESTUFFING*
RESODS*	RESPACES*	RESPRAYS	RESTITUTES	RESTUFFS*
RESOJET*	RESPACING*	RESPREAD*	RESTITUTING	RESTY
RESOJETS*	RESPADE*	RESPREADING*	RESTIVE	RESTYLE
RESOLD	RESPADED*	RESPREADS*	RESTIVELY	RESTYLED
RESOLDER*	RESPADES*	RESPRING*	RESTLESS	RESTYLES
RESOLDERED*	RESPADING*	RESPRINGING*	RESTOCK	RESTYLING
RESOLDERING*	RESPEAK	RESPRINGS*	RESTOCKED	RESUBMIT
RESOLDERS*	RESPEAKING	RESPROUT*	RESTOCKING	RESUBMITS
RESOLE	RESPEAKS	RESPROUTED*	RESTOCKS	RESUBMITTED
RESOLED	RESPECT	RESPROUTING*	RESTOKE*	RESUBMITTING
RESOLES	RESPECTED	RESPROUTS*	RESTOKED*	RESULT
RESOLING	RESPECTER	RESPRUNG*	RESTOKES*	RESULTANT
RESOLUBLE	RESPECTERS	RESSALDAR	RESTOKING*	RESULTANTS
RESOLUTE	RESPECTING	RESSALDARS	RESTORAL*	RESULTED
RESOLUTER*	RESPECTS	REST	RESTORALS*	RESULTFUL
RESOLUTES	RESPELL	RESTACK*	RESTORE	RESULTING
RESOLUTEST*	RESPELLED	RESTACKED*	RESTORED	RESULTS
RESOLVE	RESPELLING	RESTACKING*	RESTORER	RESUMABLE
RESOLVED	RESPELLS	RESTACKS*	RESTORERS	RESUME
RESOLVENT	RESPELT	RESTAFF	RESTORES	RESUMED

The Chambers Dictionary is the authority for many longer words; see Introduction, page ix

RESUMER*	RETAKER	RETEMPERS*	RETINAE	RETORTIVE
RESUMERS*	RETAKERS	RETEMS*	RETINAL	RETORTS
RESUMES	RETAKES	RETENE	RETINALS*	RETOUCH
RESUMING	RETAKING	RETENES	RETINAS	RETOUCHED
RESUMMON*	RETAKINGS	RETENTION	RETINE*	RETOUCHER
RESUMMONED*	RETALIATE	RETENTIONS	RETINENE*	RETOUCHERS
RESUMMONING*	RETALIATED	RETENTIVE	RETINENES*	RETOUCHES
RESUMMONS*	RETALIATES	RETES	RETINES*	RETOUCHING
RESUPINE	RETALIATING	RETEST*	RETINITE	RETOUR
RESUPPLIED*	RETAMA	RETESTED*	RETINITES	RETOURED
RESUPPLIES*	RETAMAS	RETESTING*	RETINITIDES*	RETOURING
RESUPPLY*	RETAPE*	RETESTS*	RETINITIS	RETOURS
RESUPPLYING*	RETAPED*	RETEXTURE	RETINITISES	RETRACE
RESURFACE	RETAPES*	RETEXTURED	RETINOID	RETRACED
RESURFACED	RETAPING*	RETEXTURES	RETINOIDS	RETRACES
RESURFACES	RETARD	RETEXTURING	RETINOL	RETRACING
RESURFACING	RETARDANT	RETHINK	RETINOLS	RETRACK*
RESURGE	RETARDANTS	RETHINKER*	RETINT*	RETRACKED*
RESURGED	RETARDATE	RETHINKERS*	RETINTED*	RETRACKING*
RESURGENT	RETARDATES	RETHINKING	RETINTING*	RETRACKS*
RESURGES	RETARDED	RETHINKS	RETINTS*	RETRACT
RESURGING	RETARDER	RETHOUGHT	RETINUE	RETRACTED
RESURRECT	RETARDERS	RETHREAD*	RETINUED*	RETRACTING
RESURRECTED	RETARDING	RETHREADED*	RETINUES	RETRACTOR
RESURRECTING	RETARDS	RETHREADING*	RETINULA	RETRACTORS
RESURRECTS	RETARGET*	RETHREADS*	RETINULAE	RETRACTS
RESURVEY	RETARGETED*	RETIA*	RETINULAR	RETRAICT
RESURVEYED	RETARGETING*	RETIAL	RETINULAS*	RETRAICTS
RESURVEYING	RETARGETS*	RETIARII	RETIRACIES	RETRAIN
RESURVEYS	RETASTE*	RETIARIUS	RETIRACY	RETRAINED
RET	RETASTED*	RETIARIUSES	RETIRAL	RETRAINING
RETABLE	RETASTES*	RETIARY	RETIRALS	RETRAINS
RETABLES	RETASTING*	RETICELLA	RETIRANT*	RETRAIT
RETACK*	RETAUGHT*	RETICELLAS	RETIRANTS*	RETRAITE
RETACKED*	RETAX*	RETICENCE	RETIRE	RETRAITES
RETACKING*	RETAXED*	RETICENCES	RETIRED	RETRAITS
RETACKLE*	RETAXES*	RETICENCIES	RETIREDLY	RETRAITT
RETACKLED*	RETAXING*	RETICENCY	RETIREE	RETRAITTS
RETACKLES*	RETCH	RETICENT	RETIREES	RETRAL
RETACKLING*	RETCHED	RETICLE	RETIRER	RETRALLY
RETACKS*	RETCHES	RETICLES	RETIRERS	RETRATE
RETAG*	RETCHING	RETICULA*	RETIRES	RETRATED
RETAGGED*	RETCHLESS	RETICULAR	RETIRING	RETRATES
RETAGGING*	RETE	RETICULE	RETITLE	RETRATING
RETAGS*	RETEACH*	RETICULES	RETITLED	RETREAD
RETAIL	RETEACHES*	RETICULUM	RETITLES	RETREADED
RETAILED	RETEACHING*	RETICULUMS	RETITLING	RETREADING
RETAILER	RETEAM*	RETIE	RETOLD	RETREADS
RETAILERS	RETEAMED*	RETIED	RETOOK	RETREAT
RETAILING	RETEAMING*	RETIES	RETOOL	RETREATED
RETAILINGS*	RETEAMS*	RETIFORM	RETOOLED	RETREATER*
RETAILOR*	RETEAR*	RETIGHTEN*	RETOOLING	RETREATERS*
RETAILORED*	RETEARING*	RETIGHTENED*	RETOOLS	RETREATING
RETAILORING*	RETEARS*	RETIGHTENING*	RETORE*	RETREATS
RETAILORS*	RETELL	RETIGHTENS*	RETORN*	RETREE
RETAILS	RETELLER	RETILE	RETORSION	RETREES
RETAIN	RETELLERS	RETILED	RETORSIONS	RETRENCH
RETAINED	RETELLING	RETILES	RETORT	RETRENCHED
RETAINER	RETELLINGS*	RETILING	RETORTED	RETRENCHES
RETAINERS	RETELLS	RETIME	RETORTER	RETRENCHING
RETAINING	RETEM*	RETIMED	RETORTERS	RETRIAL
RETAINS	RETEMPER*	RETIMES	RETORTING	RETRIALS
RETAKE	RETEMPERED*	RETIMING	RETORTION	RETRIBUTE
RETAKEN	RETEMPERING*	RETINA	RETORTIONS	RETRIBUTED

RETRIBUTES	RETUND	REVALUATE*	REVERENCE	REVICTUALED*
RETRIBUTING	RETUNDED	REVALUATED*	REVERENCED	REVICTUALING*
RETRIED	RETUNDING	REVALUATES*	REVERENCES	REVICTUALLED
RETRIES	RETUNDS	REVALUATING*	REVERENCING	REVICTUALLING
RETRIEVAL	RETUNE	REVALUE	REVEREND	REVICTUALS
RETRIEVALS	RETUNED	REVALUED	REVERENDS	REVIE
RETRIEVE	RETUNES	REVALUES	REVERENT	REVIED
RETRIEVED	RETUNING	REVALUING	REVERER	REVIES
RETRIEVER	RETURF	REVAMP	REVERERS	REVIEW
RETRIEVERS	RETURFED	REVAMPED	REVERES	REVIEWAL
RETRIEVES	RETURFING	REVAMPER*	REVERIE	REVIEWALS
RETRIEVING	RETURFS	REVAMPERS*	REVERIES	REVIEWED
RETRIEVINGS	RETURN	REVAMPING	REVERIFIED*	REVIEWER
RETRIM	RETURNED	REVAMPS	REVERIFIES*	REVIEWERS
RETRIMMED	RETURNEE	REVANCHE	REVERIFY*	REVIEWING
RETRIMMING	RETURNEES	REVANCHES	REVERIFYING*	REVIEWS
RETRIMS	RETURNER	REVEAL	REVERING	REVILE
RETRO	RETURNERS	REVEALED	REVERIST	REVILED
RETROACT	RETURNIK	REVEALER	REVERISTS	REVILER
RETROACTED	RETURNIKS	REVEALERS	REVERS	REVILERS
RETROACTING	RETURNING	REVEALING	REVERSAL	REVILES
RETROACTS	RETURNS	REVEALINGS	REVERSALS	REVILING
RETROCEDE	RETUSE	REVEALS	REVERSE	REVILINGS
RETROCEDED	RETWIST*	REVEHENT*	REVERSED	REVISABLE
RETROCEDES	RETWISTED*	REVEILLE	REVERSELY	REVISAL
RETROCEDING	RETWISTING*	REVEILLES	REVERSER	REVISALS
RETROD	RETWISTS*	REVEL	REVERSERS	REVISE
RETRODDEN	RETYING	REVELATOR	REVERSES	REVISED
RETRODICT*	RETYPE*	REVELATORS	REVERSI	REVISER
RETRODICTED*	RETYPED*	REVELED*	REVERSING	REVISERS
RETRODICTING*	RETYPES*	REVELER*	REVERSINGS	REVISES
RETRODICTS*	RETYPING*	REVELERS*	REVERSION	REVISING
RETROFIRE*	REUNIFIED	REVELING*	REVERSIONS	REVISION
RETROFIRED*	REUNIFIES	REVELLED	REVERSIS	REVISIONS
RETROFIRES*	REUNIFY	REVELLER	REVERSISES	REVISIT
RETROFIRING*	REUNIFYING	REVELLERS	REVERSO	REVISITED
RETROFIT	REUNION	REVELLING	REVERSOS	REVISITING
RETROFITS	REUNIONS	REVELLINGS	REVERT	REVISITS
RETROFITTED	REUNITE	REVELRIES	REVERTANT*	REVISOR
RETROFITTING	REUNITED	REVELRY	REVERTANTS*	REVISORS
RETROFITTINGS	REUNITER*	REVELS	REVERTED	REVISORY
RETROFLEX	REUNITERS*	REVENANT	REVERTER*	REVIVABLE
RETROJECT	REUNITES	REVENANTS	REVERTERS*	REVIVABLY
RETROJECTED	REUNITING	REVENGE	REVERTING	REVIVAL
RETROJECTING	REURGE	REVENGED	REVERTIVE	REVIVALS
RETROJECTS	REURGED	REVENGER	REVERTS	REVIVE
RETROPACK*	REURGES	REVENGERS	REVERY	REVIVED
RETROPACKS*	REURGING	REVENGES	REVEST	REVIVER
RETRORSE	REUSABLE	REVENGING	REVESTED	REVIVERS
RETROS	REUSE	REVENGINGS	REVESTING	REVIVES
RETROUSSE	REUSED	REVENGIVE	REVESTRIES	REVIVIFIED
RETROVERT	REUSES	REVENUAL*	REVESTRY	REVIVIFIES
RETROVERTED	REUSING	REVENUE	REVESTS	REVIVIFY
RETROVERTING	REUTILIZE*	REVENUED	REVET	REVIVIFYING
RETROVERTS	REUTILIZED*	REVENUER*	REVETMENT	REVIVING
RETRY	REUTILIZES*	REVENUERS*	REVETMENTS	REVIVINGS
RETRYING	REUTILIZING*	REVENUES	REVETS	REVIVOR
RETS	REUTTER	REVERABLE	REVETTED	REVIVORS
RETSINA	REUTTERED	REVERB	REVETTING	REVOCABLE
RETSINAS	REUTTERING	REVERBED	REVEUR	REVOCABLY
RETTED	REUTTERS	REVERBING	REVEURS	REVOICE*
RETTERIES	REV	REVERBS	REVEUSE	REVOICED*
RETTERY	REVALENTA	REVERE	REVEUSES	REVOICES*
RETTING	REVALENTAS	REVERED	REVICTUAL	REVOICING*

The Chambers Dictionary is the authority for many longer words; see Introduction, page ix

REVOKABLE	REWAX*	REWRITING	RHEOLOGIC	RHIPIDIUMS
REVOKE	REWAXED*	REWRITTEN	RHEOLOGIES	RHIZIC
REVOKED	REWAXES*	REWROTE	RHEOLOGY	RHIZINE
REVOKER*	REWAXING*	REWROUGHT*	RHEOMETER	RHIZINES
REVOKERS*	REWEAVE*	REWS	RHEOMETERS	RHIZOBIA
REVOKES	REWEAVED*	REWTH	RHEOPHIL*	RHIZOBIAL*
REVOKING	REWEAVES*	REWTHS	RHEOSTAT	RHIZOBIUM
REVOLT	REWEAVING*	REX	RHEOSTATS	RHIZOCARP
REVOLTED	REWED*	REXES*	RHEOTAXES	RHIZOCARPS
REVOLTER	REWEDDED*	REYNARD	RHEOTAXIS	RHIZOCAUL
REVOLTERS	REWEDDING*	REYNARDS	RHEOTOME	RHIZOCAULS
REVOLTING	REWEDS*	REZ	RHEOTOMES	RHIZOID
REVOLTS	REWEIGH	REZONE	RHEOTROPE	RHIZOIDAL
REVOLUTE	REWEIGHED	REZONED	RHEOTROPES	RHIZOIDS
REVOLVE	REWEIGHING	REZONES	RHESUS	RHIZOMA*
REVOLVED	REWEIGHS	REZONING	RHESUSES	RHIZOMATA*
REVOLVER	REWELD*	REZZES	RHETOR	RHIZOME
REVOLVERS	REWELDED*	RHABDOID	RHETORIC	RHIZOMES
REVOLVES	REWELDING*	RHABDOIDS	RHETORICS	RHIZOMIC*
REVOLVING	REWELDS*	RHABDOM	RHETORISE	RHIZOPI
REVOLVINGS	REWET*	RHABDOME*	RHETORISED	RHIZOPOD
REVOTE*	REWETS*	RHABDOMES*	RHETORISES	RHIZOPODS
REVOTED*	REWETTED*	RHABDOMS	RHETORISING	RHIZOPUS
REVOTES*	REWETTING*	RHABDUS	RHETORIZE	RHIZOPUSES
REVOTING*	REWIDEN*	RHABDUSES	RHETORIZED	RHIZOTOMIES*
REVS	REWIDENED*	RHACHIDES	RHETORIZES	RHIZOTOMY*
REVUE	REWIDENING*	RHACHIS	RHETORIZING	RHO
REVUES	REWIDENS*	RHACHISES	RHETORS	RHODAMIN*
REVUIST*	REWIN*	RHACHITIS	RHEUM	RHODAMINE
REVUISTS*	REWIND	RHACHITISES	RHEUMATIC	RHODAMINES
REVULSED*	REWINDED*	RHAGADES	RHEUMATICS	RHODAMINS*
REVULSION	REWINDER*	RHAMNOSE*	RHEUMATIZ	RHODANATE
REVULSIONS	REWINDERS*	RHAMNOSES*	RHEUMATIZES	RHODANATES
REVULSIVE	REWINDING	RHAMNUS*	RHEUMED	RHODANIC
REVVED	REWINDS	RHAMNUSES*	RHEUMIC*	RHODANISE
REVVING	REWINNING*	RHAMPHOID	RHEUMIER	RHODANISED
REVYING	REWINS*	RHAPHAE*	RHEUMIEST	RHODANISES
REW	REWIRE	RHAPHE	RHEUMS	RHODANISING
REWAKE*	REWIRED	RHAPHES	RHEUMY	RHODANIZE
REWAKED*	REWIRES	RHAPHIDE	RHEXES	RHODANIZED
REWAKEN*	REWIRING	RHAPHIDES	RHEXIS	RHODANIZES
REWAKENED*	REWOKE*	RHAPHIS	RHEXISES	RHODANIZING
REWAKENING*	REWOKEN*	RHAPONTIC	RHIES	RHODIC
REWAKENS*	REWON*	RHAPONTICS	RHIME	RHODIE
REWAKES*	REWORD	RHAPSODE	RHIMES	RHODIES
REWAKING*	REWORDED	RHAPSODES	RHINAL	RHODIUM
REWAN*	REWORDING	RHAPSODIC	RHINE	RHODIUMS
REWARD	REWORDS	RHAPSODIES	RHINES	RHODOLITE
REWARDED	REWORK	RHAPSODY	RHINITIDES*	RHODOLITES
REWARDER	REWORKED	RHATANIES	RHINITIS	RHODONITE
REWARDERS	REWORKING	RHATANY	RHINITISES	RHODONITES
REWARDFUL	REWORKS	RHEA	RHINO	RHODOPSIN
REWARDING	REWOUND	RHEAS	RHINOCERI*	RHODOPSINS
REWARDS	REWOVE*	RHEBOK*	RHINOCEROS*	RHODORA
REWAREWA	REWOVEN*	RHEBOKS*	RHINOCEROSES*	RHODORAS
REWAREWAS	REWRAP	RHEMATIC	RHINOLITH	RHODOUS
REWARM*	REWRAPPED	RHENIUM	RHINOLITHS	RHODY
REWARMED*	REWRAPPING	RHENIUMS	RHINOLOGIES	RHOEADINE
REWARMING*	REWRAPS	RHEOBASE*	RHINOLOGY	RHOEADINES
REWARMS*	REWRAPT*	RHEOBASES*	RHINOS	RHOMB
REWASH*	REWRITE	RHEOCHORD	RHIPIDATE	RHOMBI
REWASHED*	REWRITER*	RHEOCHORDS	RHIPIDION	RHOMBIC
REWASHES*	REWRITERS*	RHEOCORD	RHIPIDIONS	RHOMBOI
REWASHING*	REWRITES	RHEOCORDS	RHIPIDIUM	RHOMBOID

RHOMBOIDS	RHYTHMISING	RIBES*	RICHTS	RIDDLE
RHOMBOS	RHYTHMIST	RIBGRASS*	RICHWEED*	RIDDLED
RHOMBS	RHYTHMISTS	RIBGRASSES*	RICHWEEDS*	RIDDLER
RHOMBUS	RHYTHMIZE	RIBIBE	RICIER	RIDDLERS
RHOMBUSES	RHYTHMIZED	RIBIBES	RICIEST	RIDDLES
RHONCHAL	RHYTHMIZES	RIBIBLE	RICIN	RIDDLING
RHONCHI	RHYTHMIZING	RIBIBLES	RICING	RIDDLINGS
RHONCHIAL	RHYTHMS	RIBIER*	RICINS	RIDE
RHONCHUS	RHYTHMUS	RIBIERS*	RICINUS*	RIDEABLE
RHONE	RHYTHMUSES	RIBLESS	RICINUSES*	RIDENT
RHONES	RHYTIDOME*	RIBLET	RICK	RIDER
RHOPALIC	RHYTIDOMES*	RIBLETS	RICKED	RIDERED
RHOPALISM	RHYTINA	RIBLIKE	RICKER	RIDERLESS
RHOPALISMS	RHYTINAS	RIBOSE	RICKERS	RIDERS
RHOS	RHYTON	RIBOSES	RICKETIER	RIDERSHIP*
RHOTACISE	RHYTONS*	RIBOSOMAL	RICKETIEST	RIDERSHIPS*
RHOTACISED	RIA	RIBOSOME	RICKETILY	RIDES
RHOTACISES	RIAL	RIBOSOMES	RICKETS	RIDGE
RHOTACISING	RIALS	RIBOZYME	RICKETTIER	RIDGEBACK
RHOTACISM	RIALTO*	RIBOZYMES	RICKETTIEST	RIDGEBACKS
RHOTACISMS	RIALTOS*	RIBS	RICKETTY	RIDGED
RHOTACIZE	RIANCIES	RIBSTON	RICKETY	RIDGEL
RHOTACIZED	RIANCY	RIBSTONE	RICKEY*	RIDGELINE*
RHOTACIZES	RIANT	RIBSTONES	RICKEYS*	RIDGELINES*
RHOTACIZING	RIANTLY*	RIBSTONS	RICKING	RIDGELING*
RHOTIC	RIAS	RIBWORK	RICKLE	RIDGELINGS*
RHUBARB	RIATA	RIBWORKS	RICKLES	RIDGELS
RHUBARBS	RIATAS	RIBWORT	RICKLY	RIDGEPOLE*
RHUBARBY	RIB	RIBWORTS	RICKRACK*	RIDGEPOLES*
RHUMB	RIBALD	RICE	RICKRACKS*	RIDGER
RHUMBA	RIBALDLY*	RICEBIRD*	RICKS	RIDGERS
RHUMBAED	RIBALDRIES	RICEBIRDS*	RICKSHA	RIDGES
RHUMBAING	RIBALDRY	RICED	RICKSHAS	RIDGEWAY
RHUMBAS	RIBALDS	RICER	RICKSHAW	RIDGEWAYS
RHUMBS	RIBAND	RICERCAR	RICKSHAWS	RIDGIER
RHUS	RIBANDS	RICERCARE	RICKSTAND	RIDGIEST
RHUSES	RIBATTUTA	RICERCARES	RICKSTANDS	RIDGIL
RHY	RIBATTUTAS	RICERCARI*	RICKSTICK	RIDGILS
RHYME	RIBAUD	RICERCARS	RICKSTICKS	RIDGING
RHYMED	RIBAUDRED	RICERCATA	RICKYARD	RIDGINGS
RHYMELESS	RIBAUDRIES	RICERCATAS	RICKYARDS	RIDGLING
RHYMER	RIBAUDRY	RICERS	RICOCHET	RIDGLINGS
RHYMERS	RIBAUDS	RICES	RICOCHETED	RIDGY
RHYMES	RIBAVIRIN*	RICEY	RICOCHETING	RIDICULE
RHYMESTER	RIBAVIRINS*	RICH	RICOCHETS	RIDICULED
RHYMESTERS	RIBBAND	RICHED	RICOCHETTED	RIDICULER
RHYMING	RIBBANDS	RICHEN	RICOCHETTING	RIDICULERS
RHYMIST	RIBBED	RICHENED	RICOTTA	RIDICULES
RHYMISTS	RIBBER*	RICHENING	RICOTTAS	RIDICULING
RHYNE	RIBBERS*	RICHENS	RICRAC*	RIDING
RHYNES	RIBBIER	RICHER	RICRACS*	RIDINGS
RHYOLITE	RIBBIEST	RICHES	RICTAL	RIDLEY*
RHYOLITES	RIBBING	RICHESSE	RICTUS	RIDLEYS*
RHYOLITIC	RIBBINGS	RICHESSES	RICTUSES	RIDOTTO
RHYTA	RIBBON	RICHEST	RICY	RIDOTTOS
RHYTHM	RIBBONED	RICHING	RID	RIDS
RHYTHMAL	RIBBONING	RICHLY	RIDABLE	RIEL
RHYTHMED	RIBBONRIES	RICHNESS	RIDDANCE	RIELS
RHYTHMI	RIBBONRY	RICHNESSES	RIDDANCES	RIEM
RHYTHMIC	RIBBONS	RICHT	RIDDED	RIEMPIE
RHYTHMICS	RIBBONY	RICHTED	RIDDEN	RIEMPIES
RHYTHMISE	RIBBY	RICHTER	RIDDER	RIEMS
RHYTHMISED	RIBCAGE	RICHTEST	RIDDERS	RIESLING*
RHYTHMISES	RIBCAGES	RICHTING	RIDDING	RIESLINGS*

The Chambers Dictionary is the authority for many longer words; see Introduction, page ix

RIEVE	RIGGISH	RIGOL	RIMLESS	RINGNECKS*
RIEVER	RIGGS	RIGOLL	RIMMED	RINGS
RIEVERS	RIGHT	RIGOLLS	RIMMER*	RINGSIDE
RIEVES	RIGHTABLE	RIGOLS	RIMMERS*	RINGSIDER
RIEVING	RIGHTED	RIGOR	RIMMING	RINGSIDERS
RIF*	RIGHTEN	RIGORISM	RIMMINGS	RINGSIDES
RIFAMPIN*	RIGHTENED	RIGORISMS	RIMOSE	RINGSTAND
RIFAMPINS*	RIGHTENING	RIGORIST	RIMOSELY*	RINGSTANDS
RIFE	RIGHTENS	RIGORISTS	RIMOSITIES*	RINGSTER
RIFELY	RIGHTEOUS	RIGOROUS	RIMOSITY*	RINGSTERS
RIFENESS	RIGHTER	RIGORS	RIMOUS	RINGTAIL
RIFENESSES	RIGHTERS	RIGOUR	RIMPLE*	RINGTAILS
RIFER	RIGHTEST	RIGOURS	RIMPLED*	RINGTAW*
RIFEST	RIGHTFUL	RIGS	RIMPLES*	RINGTAWS*
RIFF	RIGHTIES*	RIGWIDDIE	RIMPLING*	RINGTOSS*
RIFFED*	RIGHTING	RIGWIDDIES	RIMROCK*	RINGTOSSES*
RIFFING*	RIGHTINGS	RIGWOODIE	RIMROCKS*	RINGWAY
RIFFLE	RIGHTISH	RIGWOODIES	RIMS	RINGWAYS
RIFFLED	RIGHTISM*	RIJSTAFEL	RIMU	RINGWISE
RIFFLER	RIGHTISMS*	RIJSTAFELS	RIMUS	RINGWORK
RIFFLERS	RIGHTIST	RIKISHA*	RIMY	RINGWORKS
RIFFLES	RIGHTISTS	RIKISHAS*	RIN	RINGWORM
RIFFLING	RIGHTLESS	RIKISHI	RIND	RINGWORMS
RIFFRAFF*	RIGHTLY	RIKSHAW*	RINDED	RINK
RIFFRAFFS*	RIGHTMOST*	RIKSHAWS*	RINDIER	RINKED
RIFFS	RIGHTNESS	RILE	RINDIEST	RINKHALS
RIFLE	RIGHTNESSES	RILED	RINDING	RINKHALSES
RIFLEBIRD*	RIGHTO	RILES	RINDLESS	RINKING
RIFLEBIRDS*	RIGHTOS	RILEY	RINDS	RINKS
RIFLED	RIGHTS	RILIER	RINDY	RINNING
RIFLEMAN	RIGHTSIZE	RILIEST	RINE	RINS
RIFLEMEN	RIGHTSIZED	RILIEVI	RINES	RINSABLE
RIFLER	RIGHTSIZES	RILIEVO	RING	RINSE
RIFLERIES*	RIGHTSIZING	RILING	RINGBARK*	RINSEABLE
RIFLERS	RIGHTWARD	RILL	RINGBARKED*	RINSED
RIFLERY*	RIGHTWARDS	RILLE	RINGBARKING*	RINSER
RIFLES	RIGHTY*	RILLED	RINGBARKS*	RINSERS
RIFLING	RIGID	RILLES	RINGBIT	RINSES
RIFLINGS	RIGIDER	RILLET	RINGBITS	RINSIBLE
RIFS*	RIGIDEST	RILLETS	RINGBOLT*	RINSING
RIFT	RIGIDIFIED	RILLETTES	RINGBOLTS*	RINSINGS
RIFTE	RIGIDIFIES	RILLING	RINGBONE	RIOJA*
RIFTED	RIGIDIFY	RILLMARK	RINGBONES	RIOJAS*
RIFTIER	RIGIDIFYING	RILLMARKS	RINGDOVE*	RIOT
RIFTIEST	RIGIDISE	RILLS	RINGDOVES*	RIOTED
RIFTING	RIGIDISED	RIM	RINGED	RIOTER
RIFTLESS	RIGIDISES	RIMA	RINGENT	RIOTERS
RIFTS	RIGIDISING	RIMAE	RINGER	RIOTING
RIFTY	RIGIDITIES	RIME	RINGERS	RIOTINGS
RIG	RIGIDITY	RIMED	RINGGIT	RIOTISE
RIGADOON	RIGIDIZE	RIMER	RINGGITS	RIOTISES
RIGADOONS	RIGIDIZED	RIMERS	RINGHALS	RIOTIZE
RIGATONI	RIGIDIZES	RIMES	RINGHALSES	RIOTIZES
RIGATONIS	RIGIDIZING	RIMESTER*	RINGING	RIOTOUS
RIGAUDON*	RIGIDLY	RIMESTERS*	RINGINGLY	RIOTOUSLY
RIGAUDONS*	RIGIDNESS	RIMFIRE*	RINGINGS	RIOTRIES
RIGG	RIGIDNESSES	RIMFIRES*	RINGLESS	RIOTRY
RIGGALD	RIGIDS	RIMIER	RINGLET	RIOTS
RIGGALDS	RIGLIN	RIMIEST	RINGLETED	RIP
RIGGED	RIGLING	RIMINESS*	RINGLETS	RIPARIAL
RIGGER	RIGLINGS	RIMINESSES*	RINGLIKE*	RIPARIAN
RIGGERS	RIGLINS	RIMING	RINGMAN	RIPARIANS
RIGGING	RIGMAROLE	RIMLAND*	RINGMEN	RIPCORD*
RIGGINGS	RIGMAROLES	RIMLANDS*	RINGNECK*	RIPCORDS*

Words marked with an asterisk are from OTCWL

RIPE	RIPTIDES	RITUAL	RIVERBEDS*	ROACHED
RIPECK	RISALDAR	RITUALISE	RIVERBOAT*	ROACHES
RIPECKS	RISALDARS	RITUALISED	RIVERBOATS*	ROACHING
RIPED	RISE	RITUALISES	RIVERED	ROAD
RIPELY	RISEN	RITUALISING	RIVERET	ROADBED*
RIPEN	RISER	RITUALISM	RIVERETS	ROADBEDS*
RIPENED	RISERS	RITUALISMS	RIVERINE	ROADBLOCK
RIPENER*	RISES	RITUALIST	RIVERLESS	ROADBLOCKED*
RIPENERS*	RISHI	RITUALISTS	RIVERLIKE	ROADBLOCKING*
RIPENESS	RISHIS	RITUALIZE	RIVERMAN	ROADBLOCKS
RIPENESSES	RISIBLE	RITUALIZED	RIVERMEN	ROADCRAFT
RIPENING	RISIBLES*	RITUALIZES	RIVERS	ROADCRAFTS
RIPENS	RISIBLY*	RITUALIZING	RIVERSIDE	ROADEO*
RIPER	RISING	RITUALLY	RIVERSIDES	ROADEOS*
RIPERS	RISINGS	RITUALS	RIVERWARD*	ROADHOUSE
RIPES	RISK	RITZ*	RIVERWAY	ROADHOUSES
RIPEST	RISKED	RITZES*	RIVERWAYS	ROADIE
RIPIENI	RISKER	RITZIER	RIVERWEED	ROADIES
RIPIENIST	RISKERS	RITZIEST	RIVERWEEDS	ROADING
RIPIENISTS	RISKFUL	RITZILY*	RIVERY	ROADINGS
RIPIENO	RISKIER	RITZINESS*	RIVES	ROADKILL*
RIPIENOS	RISKIEST	RITZINESSES*	RIVET	ROADKILLS*
RIPING	RISKILY	RITZY	RIVETED	ROADLESS
RIPOFF*	RISKINESS	RIVA	RIVETER	ROADMAN
RIPOFFS*	RISKINESSES	RIVAGE	RIVETERS	ROADMEN
RIPOST*	RISKING	RIVAGES	RIVETING	ROADS
RIPOSTE	RISKLESS*	RIVAL	RIVETINGS	ROADSHOW
RIPOSTED	RISKS	RIVALED*	RIVETS	ROADSHOWS
RIPOSTES	RISKY	RIVALESS	RIVETTED	ROADSIDE
RIPOSTING	RISOLUTO	RIVALESSES	RIVETTING	ROADSIDES
RIPOSTS*	RISOTTO	RIVALING*	RIVIERA	ROADSMAN
RIPP	RISOTTOS	RIVALISE	RIVIERAS	ROADSMEN
RIPPABLE*	RISP	RIVALISED	RIVIERE	ROADSTEAD
RIPPED	RISPED	RIVALISES	RIVIERES	ROADSTEADS
RIPPER	RISPETTI	RIVALISING	RIVING	ROADSTER
RIPPERS	RISPETTO	RIVALITIES	RIVLIN	ROADSTERS
RIPPIER	RISPING	RIVALITY	RIVLINS	ROADWAY
RIPPIERS	RISPINGS	RIVALIZE	RIVO	ROADWAYS
RIPPING	RISPS	RIVALIZED	RIVOS	ROADWORK*
RIPPINGLY	RISQUE	RIVALIZES	RIVULET	ROADWORKS
RIPPLE	RISQUES	RIVALIZING	RIVULETS	ROAM
RIPPLED	RISSOLE	RIVALLED	RIVULOSE*	ROAMED
RIPPLER	RISSOLES	RIVALLESS	RIYAL	ROAMER
RIPPLERS	RISUS	RIVALLING	RIYALS	ROAMERS
RIPPLES	RISUSES	RIVALRIES	RIZ	ROAMING
RIPPLET	RIT	RIVALROUS*	RIZA	ROAMINGS
RIPPLETS	RITARD*	RIVALRY	RIZARD	ROAMS
RIPPLIER	RITARDS*	RIVALS	RIZARDS	ROAN
RIPPLIEST	RITE	RIVALSHIP	RIZAS	ROANS
RIPPLING	RITELESS	RIVALSHIPS	RIZZAR	ROAR
RIPPLINGS	RITENUTO	RIVAS	RIZZARED	ROARED
RIPPLY	RITENUTOS	RIVE	RIZZARING	ROARER
RIPPS	RITES	RIVED	RIZZARS	ROARERS
RIPRAP	RITORNEL	RIVEL	RIZZART	ROARIE
RIPRAPPED*	RITORNELL	RIVELLED	RIZZARTS	ROARIER
RIPRAPPING*	RITORNELLS	RIVELLING	RIZZER	ROARIEST
RIPRAPS	RITORNELS	RIVELS	RIZZERED	ROARING
RIPS	RITS	RIVEN	RIZZERING	ROARINGLY
RIPSAW*	RITT	RIVER	RIZZERS	ROARINGS
RIPSAWS*	RITTED	RIVERAIN	RIZZOR	ROARS
RIPSTOP	RITTER	RIVERAINS	RIZZORED	ROARY
RIPSTOPS*	RITTERS	RIVERBANK	RIZZORING	ROAST
RIPT	RITTING	RIVERBANKS	RIZZORS	ROASTED
RIPTIDE	RITTS	RIVERBED*	ROACH	ROASTER

The Chambers Dictionary is the authority for many longer words; see Introduction, page ix

ROASTERS	ROCH	ROCQUETS	ROILED	ROLLICKY*
ROASTING	ROCHES	ROCS	ROILIER	ROLLING
ROASTINGS	ROCHET	ROD	ROILIEST	ROLLINGS
ROASTS	ROCHETS	RODDED	ROILING	ROLLMOP
ROATE	ROCK	RODDING	ROILS	ROLLMOPS
ROATED	ROCKABIES*	RODDINGS	ROILY	ROLLOCK
ROATES	ROCKABY*	RODE	ROIN	ROLLOCKS
ROATING	ROCKABYE*	RODED	ROINED	ROLLOUT
ROB	ROCKABYES*	RODENT	ROINING	ROLLOUTS
ROBALO	ROCKAWAY	RODENTS	ROINISH	ROLLOVER*
ROBALOS	ROCKAWAYS	RODEO	ROINS	ROLLOVERS*
ROBAND*	ROCKBOUND*	RODEOED*	ROIST	ROLLS
ROBANDS*	ROCKCRESS	RODEOING*	ROISTED	ROLLTOP*
ROBBED	ROCKCRESSES	RODEOS	ROISTER	ROLLWAY*
ROBBER	ROCKED	RODES	ROISTERED	ROLLWAYS*
ROBBERIES	ROCKER	RODEWAY	ROISTERER	ROM
ROBBERS	ROCKERIES	RODEWAYS	ROISTERERS	ROMA
ROBBERY	ROCKERS	RODFISHER	ROISTERING	ROMAGE
ROBBIN*	ROCKERY	RODFISHERS	ROISTERINGS	ROMAGES
ROBBING	ROCKET	RODGERSIA	ROISTERS	ROMAIKA
ROBBINS*	ROCKETED	RODGERSIAS	ROISTING	ROMAIKAS
ROBE	ROCKETEER	RODING	ROISTS	ROMAINE*
ROBED	ROCKETEERS	RODINGS	ROJI	ROMAINES*
ROBES	ROCKETER	RODLESS	ROJIS	ROMAL
ROBIN	ROCKETERS	RODLIKE	ROK	ROMALS
ROBING	ROCKETING	RODMAN	ROKE	ROMAN
ROBINGS	ROCKETRIES	RODMEN	ROKED	ROMANCE
ROBINIA	ROCKETRY	RODS	ROKELAY	ROMANCED
ROBINIAS	ROCKETS	RODSMAN	ROKELAYS	ROMANCER
ROBINS	ROCKFALL*	RODSMEN	ROKER	ROMANCERS
ROBLE	ROCKFALLS*	RODSTER	ROKERS	ROMANCES
ROBLES	ROCKFISH	RODSTERS	ROKES	ROMANCING
ROBORANT	ROCKFISHES	ROE	ROKIER	ROMANCINGS
ROBORANTS	ROCKIER	ROEBUCK	ROKIEST	ROMANISE*
ROBOT	ROCKIERS	ROEBUCKS	ROKING	ROMANISED*
ROBOTIC	ROCKIEST	ROED	ROKKAKU	ROMANISES*
ROBOTICS	ROCKILY	ROEMER	ROKS	ROMANISING*
ROBOTISE	ROCKINESS	ROEMERS	ROKY	ROMANIZE*
ROBOTISED	ROCKINESSES	ROENTGEN	ROLAG	ROMANIZED*
ROBOTISES	ROCKING	ROENTGENS	ROLAGS	ROMANIZES*
ROBOTISING	ROCKINGS	ROES	ROLAMITE*	ROMANIZING*
ROBOTISM*	ROCKLAY	ROESTONE	ROLAMITES*	ROMANO*
ROBOTISMS*	ROCKLAYS	ROESTONES	ROLE	ROMANOS*
ROBOTIZE	ROCKLESS*	ROGATION	ROLES	ROMANS
ROBOTIZED	ROCKLIKE*	ROGATIONS	ROLF*	ROMANTIC
ROBOTIZES	ROCKLING	ROGATORY	ROLFED*	ROMANTICS
ROBOTIZING	ROCKLINGS	ROGER	ROLFER	ROMAS
ROBOTRIES*	ROCKOON*	ROGERED	ROLFERS	ROMAUNT
ROBOTRY*	ROCKOONS*	ROGERING	ROLFING	ROMAUNTS
ROBOTS	ROCKROSE*	ROGERINGS	ROLFINGS	ROMELDALE*
ROBS	ROCKROSES*	ROGERS	ROLFS*	ROMELDALES*
ROBURITE	ROCKS	ROGUE	ROLL	ROMEO*
ROBURITES	ROCKSHAFT*	ROGUED	ROLLABLE	ROMEOS*
ROBUST	ROCKSHAFTS*	ROGUEING*	ROLLAWAY*	ROMNEYA
ROBUSTA	ROCKWATER	ROGUERIES	ROLLBACK*	ROMNEYAS
ROBUSTAS	ROCKWATERS	ROGUERY	ROLLBACKS*	ROMP
ROBUSTER	ROCKWEED	ROGUES	ROLLED	ROMPED
ROBUSTEST	ROCKWEEDS	ROGUESHIP	ROLLER	ROMPER
ROBUSTLY	ROCKWORK	ROGUESHIPS	ROLLERS	ROMPERS
ROC	ROCKWORKS	ROGUING	ROLLICK	ROMPING
ROCAILLE	ROCKY	ROGUISH	ROLLICKED	ROMPINGLY
ROCAILLES	ROCOCO	ROGUISHLY	ROLLICKING	ROMPISH
ROCAMBOLE	ROCOCOS	ROGUY	ROLLICKINGS	ROMPISHLY
ROCAMBOLES	ROCQUET	ROIL	ROLLICKS	ROMPS

Words marked with an asterisk are from OTCWL

ROMS*	ROOFTOP	ROOSTED	ROQUETS	ROSELLAS
RONCADOR	ROOFTOPS	ROOSTER	ROQUETTE	ROSELLE
RONCADORS	ROOFTREE	ROOSTERS	ROQUETTES	ROSELLES
RONDACHE	ROOFTREES	ROOSTING	RORAL	ROSEMARIES
RONDACHES	ROOFY	ROOSTS	RORE	ROSEMARY
RONDAVEL	ROOINEK	ROOT	RORES	ROSEOLA
RONDAVELS	ROOINEKS	ROOTAGE	RORIC	ROSEOLAR*
RONDE	ROOK	ROOTAGES	RORID	ROSEOLAS
RONDEAU	ROOKED	ROOTED	RORIE	ROSERIES
RONDEAUX	ROOKERIES	ROOTEDLY	RORIER	ROSEROOT*
RONDEL	ROOKERY	ROOTER	RORIEST	ROSEROOTS*
RONDELET*	ROOKIE	ROOTERS	RORQUAL	ROSERY
RONDELETS*	ROOKIER	ROOTHOLD	RORQUALS	ROSES
RONDELLE*	ROOKIES	ROOTHOLDS	RORT	ROSESLUG*
RONDELLES*	ROOKIEST	ROOTIER	RORTED	ROSESLUGS*
RONDELS	ROOKING	ROOTIES	RORTER	ROSET
RONDES	ROOKISH	ROOTIEST	RORTERS	ROSETED
RONDINO	ROOKS	ROOTING	RORTIER	ROSETING
RONDINOS	ROOKY	ROOTINGS	RORTIEST	ROSETS
RONDO	ROOM	ROOTLE	RORTING	ROSETTE
RONDOS	ROOMED	ROOTLED	RORTS	ROSETTED
RONDURE	ROOMER	ROOTLES	RORTY	ROSETTES
RONDURES	ROOMERS	ROOTLESS	RORY	ROSETTY
RONE	ROOMETTE	ROOTLET	ROSACE	ROSETY
RONEO	ROOMETTES	ROOTLETS	ROSACEA	ROSEWATER
RONEOED	ROOMFUL	ROOTLIKE	ROSACEAS	ROSEWATERS
RONEOING	ROOMFULS	ROOTLING	ROSACEOUS	ROSEWOOD
RONEOS	ROOMIE	ROOTS	ROSACES	ROSEWOODS
RONES	ROOMIER	ROOTSIER	ROSAKER	ROSIED
RONG	ROOMIES	ROOTSIEST	ROSAKERS	ROSIER
RONGGENG	ROOMIEST	ROOTSTOCK	ROSALIA	ROSIERE
RONGGENGS	ROOMILY	ROOTSTOCKS	ROSALIAS	ROSIERES
RONION*	ROOMINESS	ROOTSY	ROSARIA*	ROSIERS
RONIONS*	ROOMINESSES	ROOTY	ROSARIAN	ROSIES
RONNE	ROOMING	ROPABLE	ROSARIANS	ROSIEST
RONNEL*	ROOMMATE*	ROPE	ROSARIES	ROSILY
RONNELS*	ROOMMATES*	ROPEABLE	ROSARIUM	ROSIN
RONNING	ROOMS	ROPED	ROSARIUMS	ROSINATE
RONT	ROOMSOME	ROPELIKE*	ROSARY	ROSINATES
RONTE	ROOMY	ROPER	ROSCID	ROSINED
RONTES	ROON	ROPERIES	ROSCOE*	ROSINESS
RONTGEN	ROONS	ROPERS	ROSCOES*	ROSINESSES
RONTGENS	ROOP	ROPERY	ROSE	ROSING
RONTS	ROOPED	ROPES	ROSEAL	ROSINING
RONYON	ROOPIER	ROPEWALK*	ROSEATE	ROSINOL*
RONYONS	ROOPIEST	ROPEWALKS*	ROSEATELY*	ROSINOLS*
ROO	ROOPING	ROPEWAY	ROSEBAY	ROSINOUS*
ROOD	ROOPIT	ROPEWAYS	ROSEBAYS	ROSINS
ROODS	ROOPS	ROPEWORK	ROSEBOWL	ROSINWEED*
ROOF	ROOPY	ROPEWORKS	ROSEBOWLS	ROSINWEEDS*
ROOFED	ROORBACH*	ROPEY	ROSEBUD	ROSINY
ROOFER	ROORBACHS*	ROPIER	ROSEBUDS	ROSIT
ROOFERS	ROORBACK*	ROPIEST	ROSEBUSH	ROSITED
ROOFIER	ROORBACKS*	ROPILY	ROSEBUSHES	ROSITING
ROOFIEST	ROOS	ROPINESS	ROSED	ROSITS
ROOFING	ROOSA	ROPINESSES	ROSEFINCH	ROSMARINE
ROOFINGS	ROOSAS	ROPING	ROSEFINCHES	ROSMARINES
ROOFLESS	ROOSE	ROPINGS	ROSEFISH	ROSOGLIO
ROOFLIKE	ROOSED	ROPY	ROSEFISHES	ROSOGLIOS
ROOFLINE*	ROOSER*	ROQUE	ROSEHIP	ROSOLIO
ROOFLINES*	ROOSERS*	ROQUES	ROSEHIPS	ROSOLIOS
ROOFS	ROOSES	ROQUET	ROSELESS	ROSSER
ROOFSCAPE	ROOSING	ROQUETED	ROSELIKE	ROSSERS
ROOFSCAPES	ROOST	ROQUETING	ROSELLA	ROST

The Chambers Dictionary is the authority for many longer words; see Introduction, page ix

ROSTED
ROSTELLA*
ROSTELLAR
ROSTELLUM
ROSTELLUMS
ROSTER
ROSTERED
ROSTERING
ROSTERINGS
ROSTERS
ROSTING
ROSTRA
ROSTRAL
ROSTRALLY*
ROSTRATE
ROSTRATED
ROSTRUM
ROSTRUMS
ROSTS
ROSULA
ROSULAS
ROSULATE
ROSY
ROSYING
ROT
ROTA
ROTAL
ROTAMETER*
ROTAMETERS*
ROTAPLANE
ROTAPLANES
ROTARIES
ROTARY
ROTAS
ROTATABLE
ROTATE
ROTATED
ROTATES
ROTATING
ROTATION
ROTATIONS
ROTATIVE
ROTATOR
ROTATORES*
ROTATORS
ROTATORY
ROTAVATE
ROTAVATED
ROTAVATES
ROTAVATING
ROTAVATOR
ROTAVATORS
ROTAVIRUS
ROTAVIRUSES
ROTCH
ROTCHE
ROTCHES
ROTCHIE
ROTCHIES
ROTE
ROTED
ROTENONE
ROTENONES
ROTES

ROTGRASS
ROTGRASSES
ROTGUT
ROTGUTS
ROTHER
ROTHERS
ROTI
ROTIFER
ROTIFERAL
ROTIFERS
ROTIFORM*
ROTING
ROTIS
ROTL
ROTLS
ROTO*
ROTOGRAPH
ROTOGRAPHED
ROTOGRAPHING
ROTOGRAPHS
ROTOLO
ROTOLOS
ROTOR
ROTORS
ROTOS*
ROTOTILL*
ROTOTILLED*
ROTOTILLING*
ROTOTILLS*
ROTOVATE
ROTOVATED
ROTOVATES
ROTOVATING
ROTOVATOR
ROTOVATORS
ROTS
ROTTAN
ROTTANS
ROTTE*
ROTTED
ROTTEN
ROTTENER
ROTTENEST
ROTTENLY
ROTTENS
ROTTER
ROTTERS
ROTTES*
ROTTING
ROTULA
ROTULAS
ROTUND
ROTUNDA
ROTUNDAS
ROTUNDATE
ROTUNDED
ROTUNDER
ROTUNDEST
ROTUNDING
ROTUNDITIES
ROTUNDITY
ROTUNDLY
ROTUNDS
ROTURIER

ROTURIERS
ROUBLE
ROUBLES
ROUCHE*
ROUCHES*
ROUCOU
ROUCOUS
ROUE
ROUEN*
ROUENS*
ROUES
ROUGE
ROUGED
ROUGES
ROUGH
ROUGHAGE
ROUGHAGES
ROUGHCAST
ROUGHCASTED
ROUGHCASTING
ROUGHCASTS
ROUGHDRIED*
ROUGHDRIES*
ROUGHDRY*
ROUGHDRYING*
ROUGHED
ROUGHEN
ROUGHENED
ROUGHENING
ROUGHENS
ROUGHER
ROUGHERS
ROUGHEST
ROUGHHEW*
ROUGHHEWED*
ROUGHHEWING*
ROUGHHEWN*
ROUGHHEWS*
ROUGHIE
ROUGHIES
ROUGHING
ROUGHISH
ROUGHLEG*
ROUGHLEGS*
ROUGHLY
ROUGHNECK
ROUGHNECKED
ROUGHNECKING
ROUGHNECKS
ROUGHNESS
ROUGHNESSES
ROUGHS
ROUGHSHOD
ROUGHT
ROUGHY
ROUGING
ROUILLE
ROUILLES
ROUL
ROULADE
ROULADES
ROULE

ROULEAUX
ROULES
ROULETTE
ROULETTED*
ROULETTES
ROULETTING*
ROULS
ROUM
ROUMING
ROUMINGS
ROUMS
ROUNCE
ROUNCES
ROUNCEVAL
ROUNCEVALS
ROUNCIES
ROUNCY
ROUND
ROUNDARCH
ROUNDED
ROUNDEL
ROUNDELAY
ROUNDELAYS
ROUNDELS
ROUNDER
ROUNDERS
ROUNDEST
ROUNDHAND
ROUNDHANDS
ROUNDING
ROUNDINGS
ROUNDISH
ROUNDLE
ROUNDLES
ROUNDLET
ROUNDLETS
ROUNDLY
ROUNDNESS
ROUNDNESSES
ROUNDS
ROUNDSMAN
ROUNDSMEN
ROUNDUP*
ROUNDUPS*
ROUNDURE
ROUNDURES
ROUNDWOOD*
ROUNDWOODS*
ROUNDWORM
ROUNDWORMS
ROUP
ROUPED
ROUPET*
ROUPIER
ROUPIEST
ROUPILY*
ROUPING
ROUPIT
ROUPS
ROUPY
ROUSANT
ROUSE
ROUSED
ROUSEMENT

ROUSEMENTS
ROUSER
ROUSERS
ROUSES
ROUSING
ROUSINGLY
ROUSSEAU*
ROUSSEAUS*
ROUSSETTE
ROUSSETTES
ROUST
ROUSTED
ROUSTER
ROUSTERS
ROUSTING
ROUSTS
ROUT
ROUTE
ROUTED
ROUTEING
ROUTEMAN
ROUTEMEN
ROUTER
ROUTERS
ROUTES
ROUTEWAY*
ROUTEWAYS*
ROUTH
ROUTHIE
ROUTHIER
ROUTHIEST
ROUTHS
ROUTINE
ROUTINEER
ROUTINEERS
ROUTINELY
ROUTINES
ROUTING
ROUTINGS
ROUTINISE
ROUTINISED
ROUTINISES
ROUTINISING
ROUTINISM
ROUTINISMS
ROUTINIST
ROUTINISTS
ROUTINIZE
ROUTINIZED
ROUTINIZES
ROUTINIZING
ROUTOUS
ROUTOUSLY
ROUTS
ROUX
ROVE
ROVED
ROVEN*
ROVER
ROVERS
ROVES
ROVING
ROVINGLY
ROVINGS

Words marked with an asterisk are from OTCWL

ROW	ROYALIZING	RUBBERS	RUBLES	RUDDINESSES
ROWABLE	ROYALLER	RUBBERY	RUBOFF*	RUDDING
ROWAN	ROYALLEST	RUBBET	RUBOFFS*	RUDDLE
ROWANS	ROYALLY	RUBBING	RUBOUT	RUDDLED
ROWBOAT	ROYALS	RUBBINGS	RUBOUTS	RUDDLEMAN
ROWBOATS	ROYALTIES	RUBBISH	RUBRIC	RUDDLEMEN
ROWDEDOW	ROYALTY	RUBBISHED	RUBRICAL	RUDDLES
ROWDEDOWS	ROYNE	RUBBISHES	RUBRICATE	RUDDLING
ROWDIER	ROYNED	RUBBISHLY	RUBRICATED	RUDDOCK
ROWDIES	ROYNES	RUBBISHY	RUBRICATES	RUDDOCKS
ROWDIEST	ROYNING	RUBBIT	RUBRICATING	RUDDS
ROWDILY	ROYNISH	RUBBLE	RUBRICIAN	RUDDY
ROWDINESS	ROYST	RUBBLED*	RUBRICIANS	RUDDYING
ROWDINESSES	ROYSTED	RUBBLES	RUBRICS	RUDE
ROWDY	ROYSTER	RUBBLIER	RUBS	RUDELY
ROWDYDOW	ROYSTERED	RUBBLIEST	RUBSTONE	RUDENESS
ROWDYDOWS	ROYSTERER	RUBBLING*	RUBSTONES	RUDENESSES
ROWDYISH	ROYSTERERS	RUBBLY	RUBUS*	RUDER
ROWDYISM	ROYSTERING	RUBDOWN	RUBY	RUDERAL
ROWDYISMS	ROYSTERS	RUBDOWNS	RUBYING	RUDERALS
ROWED	ROYSTING	RUBE	RUBYLIKE*	RUDERIES
ROWEL	ROYSTS	RUBEFIED	RUC	RUDERY
ROWELED*	ROZELLE	RUBEFIES	RUCHE	RUDES
ROWELING*	ROZELLES	RUBEFY	RUCHED	RUDESBIES
ROWELLED	ROZET	RUBEFYING	RUCHES	RUDESBY
ROWELLING	ROZETED	RUBELLA	RUCHING	RUDEST
ROWELS	ROZETING	RUBELLAN	RUCHINGS	RUDIE
ROWEN	ROZETS	RUBELLANS	RUCK	RUDIES
ROWENS	ROZIT	RUBELLAS	RUCKED	RUDIMENT
ROWER	ROZITED	RUBELLITE	RUCKING	RUDIMENTS
ROWERS	ROZITING	RUBELLITES	RUCKLE	RUDISH
ROWING	ROZITS	RUBEOLA	RUCKLED	RUDS
ROWINGS	ROZZER	RUBEOLAR*	RUCKLES	RUE
ROWLOCK	ROZZERS	RUBEOLAS	RUCKLING	RUED
ROWLOCKS	RUANA	RUBES	RUCKS	RUEFUL
ROWME	RUANAS	RUBESCENT	RUCKSACK	RUEFULLY
ROWMES	RUB	RUBICELLE	RUCKSACKS	RUEING
ROWND	RUBABOO*	RUBICELLES	RUCKSEAT	RUEINGS
ROWNDED	RUBABOOS*	RUBICON	RUCKSEATS	RUELLE
ROWNDELL	RUBACE*	RUBICONED	RUCKUS	RUELLES
ROWNDELLS	RUBACES*	RUBICONING	RUCKUSES	RUELLIA
ROWNDING	RUBAI	RUBICONS	RUCOLA	RUELLIAS
ROWNDS	RUBAIYAT	RUBICUND	RUCOLAS	RUER*
ROWS	RUBASSE*	RUBIDIC*	RUCS	RUERS*
ROWT	RUBASSES*	RUBIDIUM	RUCTATION	RUES
ROWTED	RUBATI	RUBIDIUMS	RUCTATIONS	RUFESCENT
ROWTH	RUBATO	RUBIED	RUCTION	RUFF
ROWTHS	RUBATOS	RUBIER	RUCTIONS	RUFFE
ROWTING	RUBBABOO*	RUBIES	RUCTIOUS*	RUFFED
ROWTS	RUBBABOOS*	RUBIEST	RUD	RUFFES
ROYAL	RUBBED	RUBIFIED	RUDAS	RUFFIAN
ROYALET	RUBBER	RUBIFIES	RUDASES	RUFFIANED
ROYALETS	RUBBERED	RUBIFY	RUDBECKIA	RUFFIANING
ROYALISE	RUBBERIER	RUBIFYING	RUDBECKIAS	RUFFIANLY
ROYALISED	RUBBERIEST	RUBIGO*	RUDD	RUFFIANS
ROYALISES	RUBBERING	RUBIGOS*	RUDDED	RUFFIN
ROYALISING	RUBBERISE	RUBIN	RUDDER	RUFFING
ROYALISM	RUBBERISED	RUBINE	RUDDERS	RUFFINS
ROYALISMS	RUBBERISES	RUBINEOUS	RUDDIED	RUFFLE
ROYALIST	RUBBERISING	RUBINES	RUDDIER	RUFFLED
ROYALISTS	RUBBERIZE	RUBINS	RUDDIES	RUFFLER
ROYALIZE	RUBBERIZED	RUBIOUS	RUDDIEST	RUFFLERS
ROYALIZED	RUBBERIZES	RUBLE	RUDDILY	RUFFLES
ROYALIZES	RUBBERIZING		RUDDINESS	RUFFLIER*

RUFFLIEST*	RUINOUS	RUMKINS	RUNCIBLE	RUNTS
RUFFLIKE*	RUINOUSLY	RUMLY	RUNCINATE	RUNTY
RUFFLING	RUINS	RUMMAGE	RUND	RUNWAY
RUFFLINGS	RUKH	RUMMAGED	RUNDALE	RUNWAYS
RUFFLY*	RUKHS	RUMMAGER	RUNDALES	RUPEE
RUFFS	RULABLE	RUMMAGERS	RUNDLE	RUPEES
RUFIYAA	RULE	RUMMAGES	RUNDLED	RUPIA
RUFIYAAS	RULED	RUMMAGING	RUNDLES	RUPIAH
RUFOUS	RULELESS	RUMMER	RUNDLET	RUPIAHS
RUG	RULER	RUMMERS	RUNDLETS	RUPIAS
RUGA*	RULERED	RUMMEST	RUNDOWN	RUPTURE
RUGAE*	RULERING	RUMMIER	RUNDOWNS	RUPTURED
RUGAL*	RULERS	RUMMIES	RUNDS	RUPTURES
RUGATE	RULERSHIP	RUMMIEST	RUNE	RUPTURING
RUGBIES	RULERSHIPS	RUMMILY	RUNECRAFT	RURAL
RUGBY	RULES	RUMMINESS	RUNECRAFTS	RURALISE
RUGELACH	RULESSE	RUMMINESSES	RUNED	RURALISED
RUGGED	RULIER	RUMMISH	RUNELIKE*	RURALISES
RUGGEDER	RULIEST	RUMMY	RUNES	RURALISING
RUGGEDEST	RULING	RUMNESS	RUNFLAT	RURALISM
RUGGEDISE	RULINGS	RUMNESSES	RUNG	RURALISMS
RUGGEDISED	RULLION	RUMOR	RUNGLESS*	RURALIST
RUGGEDISES	RULLIONS	RUMORED	RUNGS	RURALISTS
RUGGEDISING	RULLOCK	RUMORING	RUNIC	RURALITE*
RUGGEDIZE	RULLOCKS	RUMOROUS	RUNKLE	RURALITES*
RUGGEDIZED	RULY	RUMORS	RUNKLED	RURALITIES
RUGGEDIZES	RUMAKI*	RUMOUR	RUNKLES	RURALITY
RUGGEDIZING	RUMAKIS*	RUMOURED	RUNKLING	RURALIZE
RUGGEDLY	RUMAL	RUMOURER	RUNLESS*	RURALIZED
RUGGELACH	RUMALS	RUMOURERS	RUNLET	RURALIZES
RUGGER	RUMBA	RUMOURING	RUNLETS	RURALIZING
RUGGERS	RUMBAED	RUMOURS	RUNNABLE	RURALLY
RUGGIER	RUMBAING	RUMP	RUNNEL	RURALNESS
RUGGIEST	RUMBAS	RUMPED	RUNNELS	RURALNESSES
RUGGING	RUMBELOW	RUMPIES	RUNNER	RURALS
RUGGINGS	RUMBELOWS	RUMPING	RUNNERS	RURBAN*
RUGGY	RUMBLE	RUMPLE	RUNNET	RURP
RUGLIKE*	RUMBLED	RUMPLED	RUNNETS	RURPS
RUGOLA*	RUMBLER	RUMPLES	RUNNIER	RURU
RUGOLAS*	RUMBLERS	RUMPLESS	RUNNIEST	RURUS
RUGOSA*	RUMBLES	RUMPLIER*	RUNNING	RUSA
RUGOSAS*	RUMBLIER	RUMPLIEST*	RUNNINGLY	RUSALKA
RUGOSE	RUMBLIEST	RUMPLING	RUNNINGS	RUSALKAS
RUGOSELY	RUMBLING	RUMPLY*	RUNNION	RUSAS
RUGOSITIES	RUMBLINGS	RUMPS	RUNNIONS	RUSCUS
RUGOSITY	RUMBLY	RUMPUS	RUNNY	RUSCUSES
RUGOUS	RUMBO	RUMPUSES	RUNOFF*	RUSE
RUGS	RUMBOS	RUMPY	RUNOFFS*	RUSES
RUGULOSE	RUME	RUMRUNNER*	RUNOUT*	RUSH
RUIN	RUMEN	RUMRUNNERS*	RUNOUTS*	RUSHED
RUINABLE	RUMENS*	RUMS	RUNOVER*	RUSHEE
RUINATE	RUMES	RUN	RUNOVERS*	RUSHEES
RUINATED	RUMINA	RUNABOUT	RUNRIG	RUSHEN
RUINATES	RUMINAL*	RUNABOUTS	RUNRIGS	RUSHER
RUINATING	RUMINANT	RUNAGATE	RUNROUND*	RUSHERS
RUINATION	RUMINANTS	RUNAGATES	RUNROUNDS*	RUSHES
RUINATIONS	RUMINATE	RUNAROUND	RUNS	RUSHIER
RUINED	RUMINATED	RUNAROUNDS	RUNT	RUSHIEST
RUINER	RUMINATES	RUNAWAY	RUNTED	RUSHINESS
RUINERS	RUMINATING	RUNAWAYS	RUNTIER	RUSHINESSES
RUING	RUMINATOR	RUNBACK	RUNTIEST	RUSHING
RUINGS	RUMINATORS	RUNBACKS	RUNTINESS*	RUSHINGS*
RUINING	RUMKIN	RUNCH	RUNTINESSES*	RUSHLIGHT
RUININGS		RUNCHES	RUNTISH	RUSHLIGHTS

RUSHLIKE
RUSHY
RUSINE
RUSK
RUSKS
RUSMA
RUSMAS
RUSSEL
RUSSELS
RUSSET
RUSSETED
RUSSETING
RUSSETINGS
RUSSETS
RUSSETY
RUSSIA
RUSSIAS
RUSSIFIED*
RUSSIFIES*
RUSSIFY*
RUSSIFYING*
RUST
RUSTABLE*
RUSTED
RUSTIC
RUSTICAL
RUSTICALS
RUSTICATE

RUSTICATED
RUSTICATES
RUSTICATING
RUSTICIAL
RUSTICISE
RUSTICISED
RUSTICISES
RUSTICISING
RUSTICISM
RUSTICISMS
RUSTICITIES
RUSTICITY
RUSTICIZE
RUSTICIZED
RUSTICIZES
RUSTICIZING
RUSTICLY*
RUSTICS
RUSTIER
RUSTIEST
RUSTILY
RUSTINESS
RUSTINESSES
RUSTING
RUSTINGS
RUSTLE
RUSTLED
RUSTLER

RUSTLERS
RUSTLES
RUSTLESS
RUSTLING
RUSTLINGS
RUSTPROOF*
RUSTRE
RUSTRED
RUSTRES
RUSTS
RUSTY
RUT
RUTABAGA
RUTABAGAS
RUTACEOUS
RUTH
RUTHENIC
RUTHENIUM
RUTHENIUMS
RUTHFUL
RUTHFULLY
RUTHLESS
RUTHS
RUTILANT
RUTILATED
RUTILE
RUTILES
RUTIN

RUTINS
RUTS
RUTTED
RUTTER
RUTTERS
RUTTIER
RUTTIEST
RUTTILY*
RUTTING
RUTTINGS
RUTTISH
RUTTISHLY*
RUTTY
RYA
RYAL
RYALS
RYAS
RYBAT
RYBATS
RYBAUDRYE
RYBAUDRYES
RYBAULD
RYBAULDS
RYE
RYEBREAD
RYEBREADS
RYEFLOUR
RYEFLOURS

RYEGRASS*
RYEGRASSES*
RYEPECK
RYEPECKS
RYES
RYFE
RYKE
RYKED
RYKES
RYKING
RYMME
RYMMED
RYMMES
RYMMING
RYND
RYNDS
RYOKAN
RYOKANS
RYOT
RYOTS
RYOTWARI
RYOTWARIS
RYPE
RYPECK
RYPECKS
RYPER

S

SAB
SABADILLA
SABADILLAS
SABATON
SABATONS
SABAYON*
SABAYONS*
SABBAT
SABBATH*
SABBATHS*
SABBATIC
SABBATICS
SABBATINE
SABBATISE
SABBATISED
SABBATISES
SABBATISING
SABBATISM
SABBATISMS
SABBATIZE
SABBATIZED
SABBATIZES
SABBATIZING
SABBATS
SABBED*
SABBING*
SABE*
SABED*
SABEING*
SABELLA
SABELLAS
SABER
SABERED
SABERING
SABERS
SABES*
SABIN
SABINE*
SABINES*
SABINS
SABIR*
SABIRS*
SABKHA
SABKHAH
SABKHAHS
SABKHAS
SABKHAT
SABKHATS
SABLE
SABLED
SABLEFISH*
SABLEFISHES*
SABLES
SABLING
SABOT

SABOTAGE
SABOTAGED
SABOTAGES
SABOTAGING
SABOTEUR
SABOTEURS
SABOTIER
SABOTIERS
SABOTS
SABRA
SABRAS
SABRE
SABRED
SABRES
SABREUR
SABREURS
SABRING
SABS
SABULINE
SABULOSE
SABULOUS
SABURRA
SABURRAL
SABURRAS
SAC
SACATON
SACATONS
SACBUT*
SACBUTS*
SACCADE
SACCADES
SACCADIC
SACCATE
SACCHARIC
SACCHARIN
SACCHARINS
SACCHARUM
SACCHARUMS
SACCIFORM
SACCOI
SACCOS
SACCOSES
SACCULAR
SACCULATE
SACCULE
SACCULES
SACCULI
SACCULUS
SACELLA
SACELLUM
SACHEM
SACHEMDOM
SACHEMDOMS
SACHEMIC
SACHEMS

SACHET
SACHETED*
SACHETS
SACK
SACKAGE
SACKAGES
SACKBUT
SACKBUTS
SACKCLOTH
SACKCLOTHS
SACKED
SACKER
SACKERS
SACKFUL
SACKFULS
SACKING
SACKINGS
SACKLESS
SACKLIKE*
SACKS
SACKSFUL*
SACLESS
SACLIKE
SACQUE
SACQUES
SACRA
SACRAL
SACRALGIA
SACRALGIAS
SACRALISE
SACRALISED
SACRALISES
SACRALISING
SACRALIZE
SACRALIZED
SACRALIZES
SACRALIZING
SACRALS*
SACRAMENT
SACRAMENTED
SACRAMENTING
SACRAMENTS
SACRARIA
SACRARIUM
SACRED
SACREDLY
SACRIFICE
SACRIFICED
SACRIFICES
SACRIFICING
SACRIFIDE
SACRIFIED
SACRIFIES
SACRIFY
SACRIFYING

SACRILEGE
SACRILEGES
SACRING
SACRINGS
SACRIST
SACRISTAN
SACRISTANS
SACRISTIES
SACRISTS
SACRISTY
SACRUM
SACRUMS*
SACS
SAD
SADDEN
SADDENED
SADDENING
SADDENS
SADDER
SADDEST
SADDHU
SADDHUS
SADDISH
SADDLE
SADDLEBAG
SADDLEBAGS
SADDLEBOW
SADDLEBOWS
SADDLED
SADDLER
SADDLERIES
SADDLERS
SADDLERY
SADDLES
SADDLING
SADDO
SADDOS
SADE
SADES
SADHE
SADHES
SADHU
SADHUS
SADI*
SADIRON
SADIRONS
SADIS*
SADISM
SADISMS
SADIST
SADISTIC
SADISTS
SADLY
SADNESS
SADNESSES

SADZA
SADZAS
SAE
SAECULUM
SAECULUMS
SAETER
SAETERS
SAFARI
SAFARIED
SAFARIING
SAFARIS
SAFARIST
SAFARISTS
SAFE
SAFED
SAFEGUARD
SAFEGUARDED
SAFEGUARDING
SAFEGUARDS
SAFELIGHT*
SAFELIGHTS*
SAFELY
SAFENESS
SAFENESSES
SAFER
SAFES
SAFEST
SAFETIED*
SAFETIES
SAFETY
SAFETYING*
SAFETYMAN
SAFETYMEN
SAFFIAN
SAFFIANS
SAFFLOWER
SAFFLOWERS
SAFFRON
SAFFRONED
SAFFRONS
SAFFRONY
SAFING
SAFRANIN
SAFRANINE
SAFRANINES
SAFRANINS
SAFROL*
SAFROLE
SAFROLES
SAFROLS*
SAFRONAL
SAFRONALS
SAG
SAGA
SAGACIOUS

SAGACITIES	SAGUARO	SAIMINS*	SAKIYEH	SALESROOMS
SAGACITY	SAGUAROS	SAIMIRI	SAKIYEHS	SALET
SAGAMAN	SAGUIN	SAIMIRIS	SAKKOI	SALETS
SAGAMEN	SAGUINS	SAIMS	SAKKOS	SALEWD
SAGAMORE	SAGUM	SAIN	SAKKOSES	SALEYARD
SAGAMORES	SAGY	SAINE	SAKSAUL	SALEYARDS
SAGANASH*	SAHIB	SAINED	SAKSAULS	SALFERN
SAGANASHES*	SAHIBA	SAINFOIN	SAL	SALFERNS
SAGAPENUM	SAHIBAH	SAINFOINS	SALAAM	SALIAUNCE
SAGAPENUMS	SAHIBAHS	SAINING	SALAAMED	SALIAUNCES
SAGAS	SAHIBAS	SAINS	SALAAMING	SALIC
SAGATHIES	SAHIBS	SAINT	SALAAMS	SALICES
SAGATHY	SAHIWAL*	SAINTDOM	SALABLE	SALICET
SAGBUT*	SAHIWALS*	SAINTDOMS	SALABLY	SALICETA
SAGBUTS*	SAHUARO*	SAINTED	SALACIOUS	SALICETS
SAGE	SAHUAROS*	SAINTESS	SALACITIES	SALICETUM
SAGEBRUSH	SAI	SAINTESSES	SALACITY	SALICETUMS
SAGEBRUSHES	SAIBLING	SAINTFOIN	SALAD	SALICIN
SAGELY	SAIBLINGS	SAINTFOINS	SALADANG*	SALICINE
SAGENE	SAIC	SAINTHOOD	SALADANGS*	SALICINES
SAGENES	SAICE	SAINTHOODS	SALADE	SALICINS
SAGENESS	SAICES	SAINTING	SALADES	SALICYLIC
SAGENESSES	SAICK	SAINTISH	SALADING	SALIENCE
SAGENITE	SAICKS	SAINTISM	SALADINGS	SALIENCES
SAGENITES	SAICS	SAINTISMS	SALADS	SALIENCIES
SAGENITIC	SAID	SAINTLIER	SALAL	SALIENCY
SAGER	SAIDEST	SAINTLIEST	SALALS	SALIENT
SAGES	SAIDS	SAINTLIKE	SALAMI	SALIENTLY
SAGEST	SAIDST	SAINTLING	SALAMIS	SALIENTS
SAGGAR	SAIGA	SAINTLINGS	SALAMON	SALIFIED
SAGGARD	SAIGAS	SAINTLY	SALAMONS	SALIFIES
SAGGARDS	SAIKEI	SAINTS	SALANGANE	SALIFY
SAGGARED*	SAIKEIS	SAINTSHIP	SALANGANES	SALIFYING
SAGGARING*	SAIKLESS	SAINTSHIPS	SALARIAT	SALIGOT
SAGGARS	SAIL	SAIQUE	SALARIATS	SALIGOTS
SAGGED	SAILABLE	SAIQUES	SALARIED	SALIMETER
SAGGER	SAILBOARD	SAIR	SALARIES	SALIMETERS
SAGGERED*	SAILBOARDS	SAIRED	SALARY	SALINA
SAGGERING*	SAILBOAT*	SAIRER	SALARYING	SALINAS
SAGGERS	SAILBOATS*	SAIREST	SALARYMAN	SALINE
SAGGIER	SAILCLOTH	SAIRING	SALARYMEN	SALINES
SAGGIEST	SAILCLOTHS	SAIRS	SALBAND	SALINITIES
SAGGING	SAILED	SAIS	SALBANDS	SALINITY
SAGGINGS	SAILER	SAIST	SALCHOW	SALINIZE*
SAGGY	SAILERS	SAITH	SALCHOWS	SALINIZED*
SAGIER	SAILFISH	SAITHE	SALE	SALINIZES*
SAGIEST	SAILFISHES	SAITHES	SALEABLE	SALINIZING*
SAGINATE	SAILING	SAITHS	SALEABLY	SALIVA
SAGINATED	SAILINGS	SAIYID*	SALEP	SALIVAL
SAGINATES	SAILLESS	SAIYIDS*	SALEPS	SALIVARY
SAGINATING	SAILOR	SAJOU	SALERATUS	SALIVAS
SAGITTA	SAILORING	SAJOUS	SALERATUSES	SALIVATE
SAGITTAL	SAILORINGS	SAKE	SALERING	SALIVATED
SAGITTARIES	SAILORLY	SAKER	SALERINGS	SALIVATES
SAGITTARY	SAILORS	SAKERET	SALEROOM	SALIVATING
SAGITTAS	SAILPLANE	SAKERETS	SALEROOMS	SALIVATOR*
SAGITTATE	SAILPLANED	SAKERS	SALES	SALIVATORS*
SAGO	SAILPLANES	SAKES	SALESGIRL*	SALIX
SAGOIN	SAILPLANING	SAKI	SALESGIRLS*	SALL*
SAGOINS	SAILROOM	SAKIA	SALESLADIES*	SALLAD
SAGOS	SAILROOMS	SAKIAS	SALESLADY*	SALLADS
SAGOUIN	SAILS	SAKIEH	SALESMAN	SALLAL
SAGOUINS	SAIM	SAKIEHS	SALESMEN	SALLALS
SAGS	SAIMIN*	SAKIS	SALESROOM	SALLE

SALLEE	SALSAS	SALTPETRE	SAMAANS	SAMLOR
SALLEES	SALSE	SALTPETRES	SAMADHI	SAMLORS
SALLES	SALSES	SALTS	SAMADHIS	SAMNITIS
SALLET	SALSIFIES	SALTUS	SAMAN	SAMNITISES
SALLETS	SALSIFY	SALTUSES	SAMANS	SAMOSA
SALLIED	SALSILLA*	SALTWATER	SAMARA	SAMOSAS
SALLIER*	SALSILLAS*	SALTWORK*	SAMARAS	SAMOVAR
SALLIERS*	SALT	SALTWORKS	SAMARITAN*	SAMOVARS
SALLIES	SALTANDO	SALTWORT	SAMARITANS*	SAMP
SALLOW	SALTANT	SALTWORTS	SAMARIUM	SAMPAN
SALLOWED	SALTANTS	SALTY	SAMARIUMS	SAMPANS
SALLOWER	SALTATE	SALUBRITIES	SAMAS	SAMPHIRE
SALLOWEST	SALTATED	SALUBRITY	SAMBA	SAMPHIRES
SALLOWING	SALTATES	SALUE	SAMBAED	SAMPI
SALLOWISH	SALTATING	SALUED	SAMBAING	SAMPIRE
SALLOWLY*	SALTATION	SALUES	SAMBAL	SAMPIRES
SALLOWS	SALTATIONS	SALUING	SAMBALS	SAMPIS
SALLOWY	SALTATO	SALUKI	SAMBAR	SAMPLE
SALLY	SALTATORY	SALUKIS	SAMBARS	SAMPLED
SALLYING	SALTBOX	SALUTARY	SAMBAS	SAMPLER
SALLYPORT	SALTBOXES	SALUTE	SAMBHAR*	SAMPLERIES
SALLYPORTS	SALTBUSH	SALUTED	SAMBHARS*	SAMPLERS
SALMI	SALTBUSHES	SALUTER	SAMBHUR*	SAMPLERY
SALMIS	SALTCAT	SALUTERS	SAMBHURS*	SAMPLES
SALMON	SALTCATS	SALUTES	SAMBO	SAMPLING
SALMONET	SALTCHUCK	SALUTING	SAMBOS	SAMPLINGS
SALMONETS	SALTCHUCKS	SALVABLE	SAMBUCA	SAMPS
SALMONID	SALTED	SALVABLY*	SAMBUCAS	SAMSARA
SALMONIDS	SALTER	SALVAGE	SAMBUKE*	SAMSARAS
SALMONOID	SALTERN	SALVAGED	SAMBUKES*	SAMSHOO
SALMONOIDS	SALTERNS	SALVAGEE*	SAMBUR	SAMSHOOS
SALMONS	SALTERS	SALVAGEES*	SAMBURS	SAMSHU
SALOL*	SALTEST	SALVAGER*	SAME	SAMSHUS
SALOLS*	SALTFISH	SALVAGERS*	SAMECH*	SAMURAI
SALOMETER*	SALTFISHES	SALVAGES	SAMECHS*	SAMURAIS*
SALOMETERS*	SALTIE*	SALVAGING	SAMEK*	SAN
SALON	SALTIER	SALVARSAN	SAMEKH	SANATIVE
SALONS	SALTIERS	SALVARSANS	SAMEKHS	SANATORIA
SALOON	SALTIES*	SALVATION	SAMEKS*	SANATORIUM*
SALOONS	SALTIEST	SALVATIONS	SAMEL	SANATORIUMS*
SALOOP	SALTILY	SALVATORIES	SAMELY	SANATORY
SALOOPS	SALTINE*	SALVATORY	SAMEN	SANBENITO
SALOP	SALTINES*	SALVE	SAMENESS	SANBENITOS
SALOPIAN	SALTINESS	SALVED	SAMENESSES	SANCAI
SALOPS	SALTINESSES	SALVER	SAMES	SANCAIS
SALP	SALTING	SALVERS	SAMEY	SANCHO
SALPA	SALTINGS	SALVES	SAMFOO	SANCHOS
SALPAE	SALTIRE	SALVETE	SAMFOOS	SANCTA
SALPAS	SALTIRES	SALVETES	SAMFU	SANCTIFIED
SALPIAN	SALTISH	SALVIA	SAMFUS	SANCTIFIES
SALPIANS	SALTISHLY	SALVIAS	SAMIEL	SANCTIFY
SALPICON	SALTLESS	SALVIFIC	SAMIELS	SANCTIFYING
SALPICONS	SALTLIKE*	SALVING	SAMIER	SANCTIFYINGS
SALPID*	SALTLY	SALVINGS	SAMIEST	SANCTION
SALPIDS*	SALTNESS	SALVO	SAMISEN	SANCTIONED
SALPIFORM	SALTNESSES	SALVOED*	SAMISENS	SANCTIONING
SALPINGES	SALTO	SALVOES	SAMITE	SANCTIONS
SALPINX	SALTOED	SALVOING*	SAMITES	SANCTITIES
SALPINXES	SALTOING	SALVOR	SAMITI	SANCTITY
SALPS	SALTOS	SALVORS	SAMITIS	SANCTUARIES
SALS	SALTPAN*	SALVOS	SAMIZDAT	SANCTUARY
SALSA	SALTPANS*	SAM	SAMIZDATS	SANCTUM
SALSAED	SALTPETER	SAMA	SAMLET	SANCTUMS
SALSAING	SALTPETERS	SAMAAN	SAMLETS	SAND

Words marked with an asterisk are from OTCWL

SANDAL	SANDMAN	SANGRIAS	SANSAS	SAPIENCY*
SANDALED*	SANDMEN	SANGS	SANSEI	SAPIENS*
SANDALING*	SANDPAPER	SANGUIFIED	SANSEIS	SAPIENT
SANDALLED	SANDPAPERED	SANGUIFIES	SANSERIF	SAPIENTLY
SANDALLING*	SANDPAPERING	SANGUIFY	SANSERIFS	SAPLESS
SANDALS	SANDPAPERS	SANGUIFYING	SANT	SAPLING
SANDARAC	SANDPEEP*	SANGUINE	SANTAL	SAPLINGS
SANDARACH	SANDPEEPS*	SANGUINED	SANTALIC*	SAPODILLA
SANDARACHS	SANDPILE*	SANGUINES	SANTALIN	SAPODILLAS
SANDARACS	SANDPILES*	SANGUINING	SANTALINS	SAPOGENIN
SANDBAG	SANDPIPER	SANICLE	SANTALOL*	SAPOGENINS
SANDBAGGED	SANDPIPERS	SANICLES	SANTALOLS*	SAPONARIA
SANDBAGGING	SANDPIT	SANIDINE	SANTALS	SAPONARIAS
SANDBAGS	SANDPITS	SANIDINES	SANTIMI*	SAPONIFIED
SANDBANK	SANDPUMP	SANIES	SANTIMS*	SAPONIFIES
SANDBANKS	SANDPUMPS	SANIFIED	SANTIR	SAPONIFY
SANDBAR*	SANDS	SANIFIES	SANTIRS	SAPONIFYING
SANDBARS*	SANDSHOE	SANIFY	SANTO*	SAPONIN
SANDBLAST	SANDSHOES	SANIFYING	SANTOL*	SAPONINE*
SANDBLASTED	SANDSOAP*	SANING*	SANTOLINA	SAPONINES*
SANDBLASTING	SANDSOAPS*	SANIOUS	SANTOLINAS	SAPONINS
SANDBLASTINGS	SANDSPOUT	SANITARIA	SANTOLS*	SAPONITE
SANDBLASTS	SANDSPOUTS	SANITARIES*	SANTON	SAPONITES
SANDBOX	SANDSPUR*	SANITARIUM*	SANTONICA	SAPOR
SANDBOXES	SANDSPURS*	SANITARIUMS*	SANTONICAS	SAPORIFIC
SANDBOY	SANDSTONE	SANITARY	SANTONIN	SAPOROUS
SANDBOYS	SANDSTONES	SANITATE	SANTONINS	SAPORS
SANDBUR*	SANDSTORM	SANITATED	SANTONS	SAPOTA
SANDBURR*	SANDSTORMS	SANITATES	SANTOS*	SAPOTAS
SANDBURRS*	SANDWICH	SANITATING	SANTOUR	SAPOTE*
SANDBURS*	SANDWICHED	SANITIES	SANTOURS	SAPOTES*
SANDDAB*	SANDWICHES	SANITISE	SANTS	SAPOUR*
SANDDABS*	SANDWICHING	SANITISED	SANTUR	SAPOURS*
SANDED	SANDWORM	SANITISES	SANTURS	SAPPAN
SANDER	SANDWORMS	SANITISING	SAOUARI	SAPPANS
SANDERS	SANDWORT	SANITIZE	SAOUARIS	SAPPED
SANDERSES	SANDWORTS	SANITIZED	SAP	SAPPER
SANDFISH*	SANDY	SANITIZES	SAPAJOU	SAPPERS
SANDFISHES*	SANE	SANITIZING	SAPAJOUS	SAPPHIC
SANDFLIES	SANED*	SANITORIA*	SAPAN	SAPPHICS
SANDFLY	SANELY	SANITORIUM*	SAPANS	SAPPHIRE
SANDGLASS	SANENESS	SANITORIUMS*	SAPANWOOD	SAPPHIRED
SANDGLASSES	SANENESSES	SANITY	SAPANWOODS	SAPPHIRES
SANDHEAP	SANER	SANJAK	SAPEGO	SAPPHISM
SANDHEAPS	SANES*	SANJAKS	SAPEGOES	SAPPHISMS
SANDHI	SANEST	SANK	SAPELE	SAPPHIST
SANDHILL	SANG	SANKO	SAPELES	SAPPHISTS
SANDHILLS	SANGA*	SANKOS	SAPFUL	SAPPIER
SANDHIS	SANGAR	SANNIE	SAPHEAD	SAPPIEST
SANDHOG*	SANGAREE	SANNIES	SAPHEADED	SAPPILY*
SANDHOGS*	SANGAREES	SANNOP*	SAPHEADS	SAPPINESS
SANDIER	SANGARS	SANNOPS*	SAPHENA	SAPPINESSES
SANDIEST	SANGAS*	SANNUP	SAPHENAE*	SAPPING
SANDINESS	SANGER*	SANNUPS	SAPHENAS	SAPPLE
SANDINESSES	SANGERS*	SANNYASI	SAPHENOUS	SAPPLED
SANDING	SANGFROID	SANNYASIN	SAPID	SAPPLES
SANDINGS	SANGFROIDS	SANNYASINS	SAPIDITIES	SAPPLING
SANDIVER	SANGH*	SANNYASIS	SAPIDITY	SAPPY
SANDIVERS	SANGHS*	SANPAN	SAPIDLESS	SAPRAEMIA
SANDLIKE*	SANGLIER	SANPANS	SAPIDNESS	SAPRAEMIAS
SANDLING	SANGLIERS	SANS	SAPIDNESSES	SAPRAEMIC
SANDLINGS	SANGOMA	SANSA	SAPIENCE	SAPREMIA*
SANDLOT*	SANGOMAS	SANSAR*	SAPIENCES	SAPREMIAS*
SANDLOTS*	SANGRIA	SANSARS*	SAPIENCIES*	SAPREMIC*

The Chambers Dictionary is the authority for many longer words; see Introduction, page ix

SAPROBE	SARDELLES	SARSARS*	SATANGS*	SATIRIST
SAPROBES	SARDELS	SARSDEN	SATANIC	SATIRISTS
SAPROBIC*	SARDINE	SARSDENS	SATANICAL	SATIRIZE
SAPROLITE	SARDINES	SARSEN	SATANISM	SATIRIZED
SAPROLITES	SARDIUS	SARSENET	SATANISMS	SATIRIZES
SAPROPEL	SARDIUSES	SARSENETS	SATANIST*	SATIRIZING
SAPROPELS	SARDONIAN	SARSENS	SATANISTS*	SATIS
SAPROZOIC	SARDONIC	SARSNET	SATANITIES	SATISFICE
SAPS	SARDONYX	SARSNETS	SATANITY	SATISFICED
SAPSAGO	SARDONYXES	SARTOR	SATARA	SATISFICES
SAPSAGOS	SARDS	SARTORIAL	SATARAS	SATISFICING
SAPSUCKER	SARED	SARTORIAN	SATAY	SATISFICINGS
SAPSUCKERS	SAREE	SARTORII	SATAYS	SATISFIED
SAPUCAIA	SAREES	SARTORIUS	SATCHEL	SATISFIER
SAPUCAIAS	SARGASSO	SARTORIUSES	SATCHELS	SATISFIERS
SAPWOOD	SARGASSOS	SARTORS	SATE	SATISFIES
SAPWOODS	SARGASSUM	SARUS	SATED	SATISFY
SAR	SARGASSUMS	SARUSES	SATEDNESS	SATISFYING
SARABAND	SARGE	SASARARA	SATEDNESSES	SATIVE
SARABANDE	SARGES	SASARARAS	SATEEN	SATORI
SARABANDES	SARGO	SASH	SATEENS	SATORIS
SARABANDS	SARGOS	SASHAY	SATELESS	SATRAP
SARAFAN	SARGOSES	SASHAYED	SATELLES	SATRAPAL
SARAFANS	SARGUS	SASHAYING	SATELLITE	SATRAPIES
SARAN*	SARGUSES	SASHAYS	SATELLITED	SATRAPS
SARANGI	SARI	SASHED	SATELLITES	SATRAPY
SARANGIS	SARIN	SASHES	SATELLITING	SATSUMA
SARANS*	SARING	SASHIMI	SATEM*	SATSUMAS
SARAPE	SARINS	SASHIMIS	SATES	SATURABLE
SARAPES	SARIS	SASHING	SATI	SATURANT
SARBACANE	SARK	SASIN	SATIABLE	SATURANTS
SARBACANES	SARKIER	SASINE	SATIABLY*	SATURATE
SARCASM	SARKIEST	SASINES	SATIATE	SATURATED
SARCASMS	SARKING	SASINS	SATIATED	SATURATES
SARCASTIC	SARKINGS	SASKATOON	SATIATES	SATURATING
SARCENET	SARKS	SASKATOONS	SATIATING	SATURATOR
SARCENETS	SARKY	SASQUATCH	SATIATION	SATURATORS
SARCOCARP	SARMENT	SASQUATCHES	SATIATIONS	SATURNIC
SARCOCARPS	SARMENTA	SASS	SATIETIES	SATURNIID
SARCODE	SARMENTS	SASSABIES	SATIETY	SATURNIIDS
SARCODES	SARMENTUM	SASSABY	SATIN	SATURNINE
SARCODIC	SARNEY	SASSAFRAS	SATINED	SATURNISM
SARCOID	SARNEYS	SASSAFRASES	SATINET	SATURNISMS
SARCOIDS	SARNIE	SASSARARA	SATINETS	SATURNIST
SARCOLOGIES	SARNIES	SASSARARAS	SATINETTA	SATURNISTS
SARCOLOGY	SAROD	SASSE	SATINETTAS	SATYR
SARCOMA	SARODE*	SASSED	SATINETTE	SATYRA
SARCOMAS	SARODES*	SASSES	SATINETTES	SATYRAL
SARCOMATA	SARODIST*	SASSIER	SATING	SATYRALS
SARCOMERE	SARODISTS*	SASSIES*	SATINING	SATYRAS
SARCOMERES	SARODS	SASSIEST	SATINPOD*	SATYRESS
SARCONET	SARONG	SASSILY*	SATINPODS*	SATYRESSES
SARCONETS	SARONGS	SASSING	SATINS	SATYRIC
SARCOPTIC	SARONIC	SASSOLIN	SATINWOOD	SATYRICAL
SARCOSOME*	SAROS	SASSOLINS	SATINWOODS	SATYRID
SARCOSOMES*	SAROSES	SASSOLITE	SATINY	SATYRIDS
SARCOUS	SARPANCH	SASSOLITES	SATIRE	SATYRISK
SARD	SARPANCHES	SASSWOOD*	SATIRES	SATYRISKS
SARDANA	SARRASIN	SASSWOODS*	SATIRIC	SATYRS
SARDANAS	SARRASINS	SASSY	SATIRICAL	SAU*
SARDAR*	SARRAZIN	SASTRUGA	SATIRISE	SAUBA
SARDARS*	SARRAZINS	SASTRUGI	SATIRISED	SAUBAS
SARDEL	SARS	SAT	SATIRISES	SAUCE
SARDELLE	SARSAR*	SATANG	SATIRISING	SAUCEBOAT*

SAUCEBOATS*	SAUTE	SAVIOUR	SAWFISH	SAYYIDS
SAUCEBOX	SAUTED	SAVIOURS	SAWFISHES	SAZ
SAUCEBOXES	SAUTEED	SAVOR	SAWFLIES*	SAZERAC
SAUCED	SAUTEEING	SAVORED	SAWFLY*	SAZERACS
SAUCEPAN	SAUTEES	SAVORER*	SAWHORSE	SAZES
SAUCEPANS	SAUTEING	SAVORERS*	SAWHORSES	SAZHEN
SAUCER	SAUTERNE*	SAVORIER*	SAWING	SAZHENS
SAUCERFUL	SAUTERNES*	SAVORIES	SAWINGS	SAZZES
SAUCERFULS	SAUTES	SAVORIEST*	SAWLIKE*	SBIRRI
SAUCERS	SAUTING	SAVORILY*	SAWLOG*	SBIRRO
SAUCES	SAUTOIR	SAVORING	SAWLOGS*	SCAB
SAUCH	SAUTOIRE*	SAVORLESS*	SAWMILL	SCABBARD
SAUCHS	SAUTOIRES*	SAVOROUS	SAWMILLS	SCABBARDED
SAUCIER	SAUTOIRS	SAVORS	SAWN	SCABBARDING
SAUCIEST	SAUTS	SAVORY	SAWNEY	SCABBARDS
SAUCILY	SAVABLE	SAVOUR	SAWNEYS	SCABBED
SAUCINESS	SAVAGE	SAVOURED	SAWPIT	SCABBIER
SAUCINESSES	SAVAGED	SAVOURER*	SAWPITS	SCABBIEST
SAUCING	SAVAGEDOM	SAVOURERS*	SAWS	SCABBILY*
SAUCISSE	SAVAGEDOMS	SAVOURIER*	SAWSHARK	SCABBING
SAUCISSES	SAVAGELY	SAVOURIES	SAWSHARKS	SCABBLE
SAUCISSON	SAVAGER	SAVOURIEST*	SAWTEETH	SCABBLED
SAUCISSONS	SAVAGERIES	SAVOURILY	SAWTIMBER*	SCABBLES
SAUCY	SAVAGERY	SAVOURING	SAWTIMBERS*	SCABBLING
SAUFGARD	SAVAGES	SAVOURLY	SAWTOOTH	SCABBY
SAUFGARDS	SAVAGEST	SAVOURS	SAWYER	SCABIES
SAUGER	SAVAGING	SAVOURY	SAWYERS	SCABIETIC*
SAUGERS	SAVAGISM	SAVOY	SAX	SCABIOSA*
SAUGH	SAVAGISMS	SAVOYARD	SAXATILE	SCABIOSAS*
SAUGHS	SAVANNA	SAVOYARDS	SAXAUL	SCABIOUS
SAUGHY*	SAVANNAH	SAVOYS	SAXAULS	SCABIOUSES
SAUL	SAVANNAHS	SAVVEY	SAXES	SCABLAND*
SAULGE	SAVANNAS	SAVVEYED	SAXHORN	SCABLANDS
SAULGES	SAVANT	SAVVEYING	SAXHORNS	SCABLIKE*
SAULIE	SAVANTS	SAVVEYS	SAXIFRAGE	SCABRID
SAULIES	SAVARIN	SAVVIED	SAXIFRAGES	SCABROUS
SAULS	SAVARINS	SAVVIER	SAXITOXIN	SCABS
SAULT	SAVATE	SAVVIES	SAXITOXINS	SCAD
SAULTS	SAVATES	SAVVIEST	SAXONIES	SCADS
SAUNA	SAVE	SAVVY	SAXONITE	SCAFF
SAUNAS	SAVEABLE*	SAVVYING	SAXONITES	SCAFFIE
SAUNT	SAVED	SAW	SAXONY	SCAFFIES
SAUNTED	SAVEGARD	SAWAH	SAXOPHONE	SCAFFOLD
SAUNTER	SAVEGARDED	SAWAHS	SAXOPHONES	SCAFFOLDED
SAUNTERED	SAVEGARDING	SAWBILL	SAXTUBA*	SCAFFOLDING
SAUNTERER	SAVEGARDS	SAWBILLS	SAXTUBAS*	SCAFFOLDINGS
SAUNTERERS	SAVELOY	SAWBLADE	SAY	SCAFFOLDS
SAUNTERING	SAVELOYS	SAWBLADES	SAYABLE	SCAFFS
SAUNTERINGS	SAVER	SAWBONES	SAYED	SCAG
SAUNTERS	SAVERS	SAWBONESES*	SAYER	SCAGLIA
SAUNTING	SAVES	SAWBUCK	SAYERS	SCAGLIAS
SAUNTS	SAVEY	SAWBUCKS	SAYEST	SCAGLIOLA
SAUREL	SAVEYED	SAWDER	SAYID	SCAGLIOLAS
SAURELS	SAVEYING	SAWDERED	SAYIDS	SCAGS
SAURIAN	SAVEYS	SAWDERING	SAYING	SCAIL
SAURIANS	SAVIN	SAWDERS	SAYINGS	SCAILED
SAURIES	SAVINE	SAWDUST	SAYNE	SCAILING
SAUROID	SAVINES	SAWDUSTED	SAYON	SCAILS
SAUROPOD	SAVING	SAWDUSTING	SAYONARA	SCAITH
SAUROPODS	SAVINGLY	SAWDUSTS	SAYONARAS	SCAITHED
SAURY	SAVINGS	SAWDUSTY	SAYONS	SCAITHING
SAUSAGE	SAVINS	SAWED	SAYS	SCAITHS
SAUSAGES	SAVIOR*	SAWER	SAYST	SCALA
SAUT	SAVIORS*	SAWERS	SAYYID	SCALABLE

The Chambers Dictionary is the authority for many longer words; see Introduction, page ix

SCALABLY*
SCALADE
SCALADES
SCALADO
SCALADOS
SCALAE
SCALAGE*
SCALAGES*
SCALAR
SCALARE*
SCALARES*
SCALARS
SCALAWAG
SCALAWAGS
SCALD
SCALDED
SCALDER
SCALDERS
SCALDFISH
SCALDFISHES
SCALDHEAD
SCALDHEADS
SCALDIC
SCALDING
SCALDINGS
SCALDINI
SCALDINO
SCALDS
SCALDSHIP
SCALDSHIPS
SCALE
SCALED
SCALELESS
SCALELIKE
SCALENE
SCALENI
SCALENUS
SCALEPAN*
SCALEPANS*
SCALER
SCALERS
SCALES
SCALEUP*
SCALEUPS*
SCALEWORK
SCALEWORKS
SCALIER
SCALIEST
SCALINESS
SCALINESSES
SCALING
SCALINGS
SCALL
SCALLAWAG
SCALLAWAGS
SCALLED
SCALLIES
SCALLION
SCALLIONS
SCALLOP
SCALLOPED
SCALLOPER*
SCALLOPERS*
SCALLOPING

SCALLOPS
SCALLS
SCALLY
SCALLYWAG
SCALLYWAGS
SCALOGRAM*
SCALOGRAMS*
SCALP
SCALPED
SCALPEL
SCALPELS
SCALPER
SCALPERS
SCALPING
SCALPINGS
SCALPINS
SCALPLESS
SCALPRUM
SCALPRUMS
SCALPS
SCALY
SCAM
SCAMBLE
SCAMBLED
SCAMBLER
SCAMBLERS
SCAMBLES
SCAMBLING
SCAMBLINGS
SCAMEL
SCAMELS
SCAMMED
SCAMMING
SCAMMONIES
SCAMMONY
SCAMP
SCAMPED
SCAMPER
SCAMPERED
SCAMPERING
SCAMPERS
SCAMPI
SCAMPIES*
SCAMPING
SCAMPINGS
SCAMPIS
SCAMPISH
SCAMPS
SCAMS
SCAN
SCAND
SCANDAL
SCANDALED*
SCANDALING*
SCANDALLED
SCANDALLING
SCANDALS
SCANDENT
SCANDIA*
SCANDIAS*
SCANDIC*
SCANDIUM
SCANDIUMS
SCANNABLE*

SCANNED
SCANNER
SCANNERS
SCANNING
SCANNINGS
SCANS
SCANSION
SCANSIONS
SCANT
SCANTED
SCANTER
SCANTEST
SCANTIER
SCANTIES
SCANTIEST
SCANTILY
SCANTING
SCANTITIES
SCANTITY
SCANTLE
SCANTLED
SCANTLES
SCANTLING
SCANTLINGS
SCANTLY
SCANTNESS
SCANTNESSES
SCANTS
SCANTY
SCAPA
SCAPAED
SCAPAING
SCAPAS
SCAPE
SCAPED
SCAPEGOAT
SCAPEGOATED
SCAPEGOATING
SCAPEGOATINGS
SCAPEGOATS
SCAPELESS
SCAPEMENT
SCAPEMENTS
SCAPES
SCAPHOID
SCAPHOIDS
SCAPHOPOD
SCAPHOPODS
SCAPI
SCAPING
SCAPOLITE
SCAPOLITES
SCAPOSE*
SCAPPLE
SCAPPLED
SCAPPLES
SCAPPLING
SCAPULA
SCAPULAE
SCAPULAR
SCAPULARIES
SCAPULARS
SCAPULARY
SCAPULAS

SCAPUS
SCAR
SCARAB
SCARABAEI
SCARABEE
SCARABEES
SCARABOID
SCARABOIDS
SCARABS
SCARCE
SCARCELY
SCARCER
SCARCEST
SCARCITIES
SCARCITY
SCARE
SCARECROW
SCARECROWS
SCARED
SCAREDER
SCAREDEST
SCAREHEAD*
SCAREHEADS*
SCARER
SCARERS
SCARES
SCAREY
SCARF
SCARFED
SCARFING
SCARFINGS
SCARFISH
SCARFISHES
SCARFPIN*
SCARFPINS*
SCARFS
SCARFSKIN
SCARFSKINS
SCARFWISE
SCARIER
SCARIEST
SCARIFIED
SCARIFIER
SCARIFIERS
SCARIFIES
SCARIFY
SCARIFYING
SCARILY*
SCARING
SCARIOSE*
SCARIOUS
SCARLESS
SCARLET
SCARLETED
SCARLETING
SCARLETS
SCARMOGE
SCARMOGES
SCARP
SCARPA
SCARPAED
SCARPAING
SCARPAS
SCARPED

SCARPER
SCARPERED
SCARPERING
SCARPERS
SCARPETTI
SCARPETTO
SCARPH
SCARPHED
SCARPHING
SCARPHS
SCARPINES
SCARPING
SCARPINGS
SCARPS
SCARRE
SCARRED
SCARRES
SCARRIER
SCARRIEST
SCARRING
SCARRINGS
SCARRY
SCARS
SCART
SCARTED
SCARTH
SCARTHS
SCARTING
SCARTS
SCARVES
SCARY
SCAT
SCATBACK*
SCATBACKS*
SCATCH
SCATCHES
SCATH
SCATHE
SCATHED
SCATHEFUL
SCATHES
SCATHING
SCATHS
SCATOLE
SCATOLES
SCATOLOGIES
SCATOLOGY
SCATS
SCATT
SCATTED
SCATTER
SCATTERED
SCATTERER
SCATTERERS
SCATTERING
SCATTERINGS
SCATTERS
SCATTERY
SCATTIER
SCATTIEST
SCATTING
SCATTINGS
SCATTS
SCATTY

SCAUD
SCAUDED
SCAUDING
SCAUDS
SCAUP
SCAUPED
SCAUPER
SCAUPERS
SCAUPING
SCAUPS
SCAUR
SCAURED
SCAURIES
SCAURING
SCAURS
SCAURY
SCAVAGE
SCAVAGER
SCAVAGERS
SCAVAGES
SCAVENGE
SCAVENGED
SCAVENGER
SCAVENGERED
SCAVENGERING
SCAVENGERINGS
SCAVENGERS
SCAVENGES
SCAVENGING
SCAVENGINGS
SCAW
SCAWS
SCAWTITE
SCAWTITES
SCAZON
SCAZONS
SCAZONTES
SCAZONTIC
SCAZONTICS
SCEAT
SCEATT
SCEATTAS
SCEDULE
SCEDULED
SCEDULES
SCEDULING
SCELERAT
SCELERATE
SCELERATES
SCELERATS
SCENA
SCENARIES
SCENARIO
SCENARIOS
SCENARISE
SCENARISED
SCENARISES
SCENARISING
SCENARIST
SCENARISTS
SCENARIZE
SCENARIZED
SCENARIZES
SCENARIZING

SCENARY
SCENAS*
SCEND
SCENDED
SCENDING
SCENDS
SCENE
SCENED
SCENEMAN
SCENEMEN
SCENERIES
SCENERY
SCENES
SCENIC
SCENICAL
SCENING
SCENT
SCENTED
SCENTFUL
SCENTING
SCENTINGS
SCENTLESS
SCENTS
SCEPSIS
SCEPSISES
SCEPTER
SCEPTERED
SCEPTERING*
SCEPTERS
SCEPTIC
SCEPTICAL
SCEPTICS
SCEPTRAL
SCEPTRE
SCEPTRED
SCEPTRES
SCEPTRING*
SCEPTRY
SCERNE
SCERNED
SCERNES
SCERNING
SCHANSE
SCHANSES
SCHANTZE
SCHANTZES
SCHANZE
SCHANZES
SCHAPPE
SCHAPPED
SCHAPPEING
SCHAPPES
SCHAPSKA
SCHAPSKAS
SCHAV*
SCHAVS*
SCHECHITA
SCHECHITAS
SCHEDULE
SCHEDULED
SCHEDULER
SCHEDULERS
SCHEDULES
SCHEDULING

SCHEELITE
SCHEELITES
SCHELLUM
SCHELLUMS
SCHELM
SCHELMS
SCHEMA
SCHEMAS*
SCHEMATA
SCHEMATIC
SCHEMATICS*
SCHEME
SCHEMED
SCHEMER
SCHEMERS
SCHEMES
SCHEMING
SCHEMINGS
SCHERZI
SCHERZO
SCHERZOS
SCHIAVONE
SCHIAVONES
SCHIEDAM
SCHIEDAMS
SCHILLER
SCHILLERS
SCHILLING
SCHILLINGS
SCHIMMEL
SCHIMMELS
SCHISM
SCHISMA
SCHISMAS
SCHISMS
SCHIST
SCHISTOSE
SCHISTOUS
SCHISTS
SCHIZIER*
SCHIZIEST*
SCHIZO
SCHIZOID
SCHIZOIDS
SCHIZONT
SCHIZONTS
SCHIZOPOD
SCHIZOPODS
SCHIZOS
SCHIZY*
SCHIZZIER*
SCHIZZIEST*
SCHIZZY*
SCHLAGER
SCHLAGERS
SCHLEMIEL
SCHLEMIELS
SCHLEMIHL
SCHLEMIHLS
SCHLEP
SCHLEPP
SCHLEPPED
SCHLEPPER
SCHLEPPERS

SCHLEPPIER
SCHLEPPIEST
SCHLEPPING
SCHLEPPS
SCHLEPPY
SCHLEPS
SCHLICH
SCHLICHS
SCHLIERE*
SCHLIEREN
SCHLIERIC*
SCHLOCK
SCHLOCKER
SCHLOCKERS
SCHLOCKIER
SCHLOCKIEST
SCHLOCKS
SCHLOCKY
SCHLOSS
SCHLOSSES
SCHLUMP*
SCHLUMPED*
SCHLUMPING*
SCHLUMPS*
SCHMALTZ
SCHMALTZES
SCHMALTZIER
SCHMALTZIEST
SCHMALTZY
SCHMALZ*
SCHMALZES*
SCHMALZIER*
SCHMALZIEST*
SCHMALZY*
SCHMEAR*
SCHMEARS*
SCHMECK
SCHMECKS
SCHMEER*
SCHMEERED*
SCHMEERING*
SCHMEERS*
SCHMELZ
SCHMELZE*
SCHMELZES
SCHMO
SCHMOCK
SCHMOCKS
SCHMOE
SCHMOES
SCHMOOS*
SCHMOOSE*
SCHMOOSED*
SCHMOOSES*
SCHMOOSING*
SCHMOOZ
SCHMOOZE
SCHMOOZED
SCHMOOZES
SCHMOOZING
SCHMOS*
SCHMUCK
SCHMUCKS
SCHMUTTER

SCHMUTTERS
SCHNAPPER
SCHNAPPERS
SCHNAPPS
SCHNAPS
SCHNAPSES
SCHNAUZER
SCHNAUZERS
SCHNECKE
SCHNECKEN
SCHNELL
SCHNITZEL
SCHNITZELS
SCHNOOK
SCHNOOKS
SCHNORKEL
SCHNORKELED*
SCHNORKELING*
SCHNORKELS
SCHNORR
SCHNORRED
SCHNORRER
SCHNORRERS
SCHNORRING
SCHNORRS
SCHNOZ*
SCHNOZZ*
SCHNOZZES*
SCHNOZZLE
SCHNOZZLES
SCHOLAR
SCHOLARCH
SCHOLARCHS
SCHOLARLIER
SCHOLARLIEST
SCHOLARLY
SCHOLARS
SCHOLIA
SCHOLIAST
SCHOLIASTS
SCHOLION
SCHOLIUM
SCHOLIUMS*
SCHOOL
SCHOOLBAG
SCHOOLBAGS
SCHOOLBOY
SCHOOLBOYS
SCHOOLDAY
SCHOOLDAYS
SCHOOLE
SCHOOLED
SCHOOLERIES
SCHOOLERY
SCHOOLES
SCHOOLING
SCHOOLINGS
SCHOOLKID*
SCHOOLKIDS*
SCHOOLMAN
SCHOOLMEN
SCHOOLS
SCHOONER

SCHOONERS	SCILLA	SCLAVE	SCOLDS	SCOPAE
SCHORL	SCILLAS	SCLAVES	SCOLECES	SCOPAS
SCHORLS	SCIMETAR*	SCLERA	SCOLECID	SCOPATE
SCHOUT	SCIMETARS*	SCLERAE*	SCOLECIDS	SCOPE
SCHOUTS	SCIMITAR	SCLERAL	SCOLECITE	SCOPED
SCHRIK*	SCIMITARS	SCLERAS	SCOLECITES	SCOPELID
SCHRIKS*	SCIMITER*	SCLERE	SCOLECOID	SCOPELIDS
SCHROD*	SCIMITERS*	SCLEREID	SCOLEX	SCOPELOID
SCHRODS*	SCINCOID	SCLEREIDE	SCOLIA	SCOPELOIDS
SCHTICK	SCINCOIDS	SCLEREIDES	SCOLICES	SCOPES
SCHTICKS	SCINTILLA	SCLEREIDS	SCOLIOMA	SCOPING
SCHTIK	SCINTILLAE*	SCLEREMA	SCOLIOMAS	SCOPS*
SCHTIKS	SCINTILLAS	SCLEREMAS	SCOLION	SCOPULA
SCHTOOK	SCIOLISM	SCLERES	SCOLIOSES	SCOPULAE*
SCHTOOKS	SCIOLISMS	SCLERITE	SCOLIOSIS	SCOPULAS
SCHTOOM	SCIOLIST	SCLERITES	SCOLIOTIC	SCOPULATE
SCHTUCK	SCIOLISTS	SCLERITIS	SCOLLOP	SCORBUTIC
SCHTUCKS	SCIOLOUS	SCLERITISES	SCOLLOPED	SCORCH
SCHUIT	SCIOLTO	SCLEROID	SCOLLOPING	SCORCHED
SCHUITS	SCION	SCLEROMA	SCOLLOPS	SCORCHER
SCHUL*	SCIONS	SCLEROMAS	SCOLYTID	SCORCHERS
SCHULN*	SCIOSOPHIES	SCLEROMATA	SCOLYTIDS	SCORCHES
SCHUSS	SCIOSOPHY	SCLEROSAL	SCOLYTOID	SCORCHING
SCHUSSED	SCIROC	SCLEROSE	SCOLYTOIDS	SCORCHINGS
SCHUSSER*	SCIROCCO	SCLEROSED	SCOMBRID	SCORDATO
SCHUSSERS*	SCIROCCOS	SCLEROSES	SCOMBRIDS	SCORE
SCHUSSES	SCIROCS	SCLEROSING	SCOMBROID	SCORECARD
SCHUSSING	SCIRRHI*	SCLEROSIS	SCOMBROIDS	SCORECARDS
SCHUYT	SCIRRHOID	SCLEROTAL	SCOMFISH	SCORED
SCHUYTS	SCIRRHOUS	SCLEROTALS	SCOMFISHED	SCORELESS*
SCHWA	SCIRRHUS	SCLEROTIA	SCOMFISHES	SCORELINE
SCHWAS	SCIRRHUSES	SCLEROTIC	SCOMFISHING	SCORELINES
SCIAENID	SCISSEL	SCLEROTICS	SCONCE	SCOREPAD*
SCIAENIDS	SCISSELS	SCLEROTIN	SCONCED	SCOREPADS*
SCIAENOID	SCISSIL	SCLEROTINS	SCONCES	SCORER
SCIAENOIDS	SCISSILE	SCLEROTIUM*	SCONCHEON	SCORERS
SCIAMACHIES	SCISSILS	SCLEROUS	SCONCHEONS	SCORES
SCIAMACHY	SCISSION	SCLIFF	SCONCING	SCORIA
SCIARID	SCISSIONS	SCLIFFS	SCONE	SCORIAC
SCIARIDS	SCISSOR	SCLIM	SCONES	SCORIAE
SCIATIC	SCISSORED	SCLIMMED	SCONTION	SCORIFIED
SCIATICA	SCISSORER	SCLIMMING	SCONTIONS	SCORIFIER
SCIATICAL	SCISSORERS	SCLIMS	SCOOG	SCORIFIERS
SCIATICAS	SCISSORING	SCOFF	SCOOGED	SCORIFIES
SCIATICS*	SCISSORS	SCOFFED	SCOOGING	SCORIFY
SCIENCE	SCISSURE	SCOFFER	SCOOGS	SCORIFYING
SCIENCED	SCISSURES	SCOFFERS	SCOOP	SCORING
SCIENCES	SCIURID*	SCOFFING	SCOOPED	SCORINGS
SCIENT	SCIURIDS*	SCOFFINGS	SCOOPER	SCORIOUS
SCIENTER	SCIURINE	SCOFFLAW	SCOOPERS	SCORN
SCIENTIAL	SCIURINES	SCOFFLAWS	SCOOPFUL	SCORNED
SCIENTISE	SCIUROID	SCOFFS	SCOOPFULS	SCORNER
SCIENTISED	SCLAFF	SCOG	SCOOPING	SCORNERS
SCIENTISES	SCLAFFED	SCOGGED	SCOOPINGS	SCORNFUL
SCIENTISING	SCLAFFER*	SCOGGING	SCOOPS	SCORNING
SCIENTISM	SCLAFFERS*	SCOGS	SCOOPSFUL*	SCORNINGS
SCIENTISMS	SCLAFFING	SCOINSON	SCOOT	SCORNS
SCIENTIST	SCLAFFS	SCOINSONS	SCOOTED	SCORODITE
SCIENTISTS	SCLATE	SCOLD	SCOOTER	SCORODITES
SCIENTIZE	SCLATED	SCOLDED	SCOOTERS	SCORPER
SCIENTIZED	SCLATES	SCOLDER	SCOOTING	SCORPERS
SCIENTIZES	SCLATING	SCOLDERS	SCOOTS	SCORPIOID
SCIENTIZING	SCLAUNDER	SCOLDING	SCOP	SCORPIOIDS
SCILICET	SCLAUNDERS	SCOLDINGS	SCOPA	SCORPION

Words marked with an asterisk are from OTCWL

SCORPIONS	SCOUTED	SCRAGGLIER	SCRAPPILY	SCREAM
SCORRENDO	SCOUTER	SCRAGGLIEST	SCRAPPING	SCREAMED
SCORSE	SCOUTERS	SCRAGGLY	SCRAPPLE	SCREAMER
SCORSED	SCOUTH	SCRAGGY	SCRAPPLES	SCREAMERS
SCORSER	SCOUTHER	SCRAGS	SCRAPPY	SCREAMING
SCORSERS	SCOUTHERED	SCRAICH	SCRAPS	SCREAMS
SCORSES	SCOUTHERING	SCRAICHED	SCRAPYARD	SCREE
SCORSING	SCOUTHERINGS	SCRAICHING	SCRAPYARDS	SCREECH
SCOT	SCOUTHERS	SCRAICHS	SCRAT	SCREECHED
SCOTCH	SCOUTHERY	SCRAIGH	SCRATCH	SCREECHER
SCOTCHED	SCOUTHS	SCRAIGHED	SCRATCHED	SCREECHERS
SCOTCHES	SCOUTING	SCRAIGHING	SCRATCHER	SCREECHES
SCOTCHING	SCOUTINGS	SCRAIGHS	SCRATCHERS	SCREECHIER
SCOTER	SCOUTS	SCRAM	SCRATCHES	SCREECHIEST
SCOTERS	SCOW	SCRAMB	SCRATCHIER	SCREECHING
SCOTIA	SCOWDER	SCRAMBED	SCRATCHIEST	SCREECHY
SCOTIAS	SCOWDERED	SCRAMBING	SCRATCHING	SCREED
SCOTOMA	SCOWDERING	SCRAMBLE	SCRATCHINGS	SCREEDED
SCOTOMAS	SCOWDERINGS	SCRAMBLED	SCRATCHY	SCREEDER
SCOTOMATA	SCOWDERS	SCRAMBLER	SCRATS	SCREEDERS
SCOTOMIA	SCOWED*	SCRAMBLERS	SCRATTED	SCREEDING
SCOTOMIAS	SCOWING*	SCRAMBLES	SCRATTING	SCREEDINGS
SCOTOMIES	SCOWL	SCRAMBLING	SCRATTLE	SCREEDS
SCOTOMY	SCOWLED	SCRAMBLINGS	SCRATTLED	SCREEN
SCOTOPIA	SCOWLER*	SCRAMBS	SCRATTLES	SCREENED
SCOTOPIAS	SCOWLERS*	SCRAMJET	SCRATTLING	SCREENER
SCOTOPIC	SCOWLING	SCRAMJETS	SCRAUCH	SCREENERS
SCOTS	SCOWLS	SCRAMMED	SCRAUCHED	SCREENING
SCOTTIE*	SCOWP	SCRAMMING	SCRAUCHING	SCREENINGS
SCOTTIES*	SCOWPED	SCRAMS	SCRAUCHS	SCREENS
SCOUG	SCOWPING	SCRAN	SCRAUGH	SCREES
SCOUGED	SCOWPS	SCRANCH	SCRAUGHED	SCREEVE
SCOUGING	SCOWRER	SCRANCHED	SCRAUGHING	SCREEVED
SCOUGS	SCOWRERS	SCRANCHES	SCRAUGHS	SCREEVER
SCOUNDREL	SCOWRIE	SCRANCHING	SCRAW	SCREEVERS
SCOUNDRELS	SCOWRIES	SCRANNEL	SCRAWL	SCREEVES
SCOUP	SCOWS	SCRANNELS*	SCRAWLED	SCREEVING
SCOUPED	SCOWTH	SCRANNIER	SCRAWLER	SCREEVINGS
SCOUPING	SCOWTHER	SCRANNIEST	SCRAWLERS	SCREICH
SCOUPS	SCOWTHERED	SCRANNY	SCRAWLIER	SCREICHED
SCOUR	SCOWTHERING	SCRANS	SCRAWLIEST	SCREICHING
SCOURED	SCOWTHERS	SCRAP	SCRAWLING	SCREICHS
SCOURER	SCOWTHS	SCRAPBOOK	SCRAWLINGS	SCREIGH
SCOURERS	SCRAB	SCRAPBOOKS	SCRAWLS	SCREIGHED
SCOURGE	SCRABBED	SCRAPE	SCRAWLY	SCREIGHING
SCOURGED	SCRABBING	SCRAPED	SCRAWM	SCREIGHS
SCOURGER	SCRABBLE	SCRAPEGUT	SCRAWMED	SCREW
SCOURGERS	SCRABBLED	SCRAPEGUTS	SCRAWMING	SCREWBALL
SCOURGES	SCRABBLER	SCRAPER	SCRAWMS	SCREWBALLS
SCOURGING	SCRABBLERS	SCRAPERS	SCRAWNIER	SCREWBEAN*
SCOURIE	SCRABBLES	SCRAPES	SCRAWNIEST	SCREWBEANS*
SCOURIES	SCRABBLIER*	SCRAPHEAP	SCRAWNY	SCREWED
SCOURING	SCRABBLIEST*	SCRAPHEAPS	SCRAWS	SCREWER
SCOURINGS	SCRABBLING	SCRAPIE	SCRAY	SCREWERS
SCOURS	SCRABBLY*	SCRAPIES	SCRAYE	SCREWIER
SCOURSE	SCRABS	SCRAPING	SCRAYES	SCREWIEST
SCOURSED	SCRAE	SCRAPINGS	SCRAYS	SCREWING
SCOURSES	SCRAES	SCRAPPAGE*	SCREAK	SCREWINGS
SCOURSING	SCRAG	SCRAPPAGES*	SCREAKED	SCREWLIKE*
SCOUSE	SCRAGGED	SCRAPPED	SCREAKIER	SCREWS
SCOUSER	SCRAGGIER	SCRAPPER*	SCREAKIEST	SCREWTOP
SCOUSERS	SCRAGGIEST	SCRAPPERS*	SCREAKING	SCREWTOPS
SCOUSES	SCRAGGILY	SCRAPPIER	SCREAKS	SCREWUP*
SCOUT	SCRAGGING	SCRAPPIEST	SCREAKY	SCREWUPS*

The Chambers Dictionary is the authority for many longer words; see Introduction, page ix

SCREWWORM*
SCREWWORMS*
SCREWY
SCRIBABLE
SCRIBAL
SCRIBBLE
SCRIBBLED
SCRIBBLER
SCRIBBLERS
SCRIBBLES
SCRIBBLIER
SCRIBBLIEST
SCRIBBLING
SCRIBBLINGS
SCRIBBLY
SCRIBE
SCRIBED
SCRIBER
SCRIBERS
SCRIBES
SCRIBING
SCRIBINGS
SCRIBISM
SCRIBISMS
SCRIECH
SCRIECHED
SCRIECHING
SCRIECHS
SCRIED
SCRIENE
SCRIENES
SCRIES
SCRIEVE
SCRIEVED
SCRIEVES
SCRIEVING
SCRIGGLE
SCRIGGLED
SCRIGGLES
SCRIGGLIER
SCRIGGLIEST
SCRIGGLING
SCRIGGLY
SCRIKE
SCRIKED
SCRIKES
SCRIKING
SCRIM
SCRIMMAGE
SCRIMMAGED
SCRIMMAGES
SCRIMMAGING
SCRIMP
SCRIMPED
SCRIMPER*
SCRIMPERS*
SCRIMPIER
SCRIMPIEST
SCRIMPILY
SCRIMPING
SCRIMPIT*
SCRIMPLY
SCRIMPS
SCRIMPY

SCRIMS
SCRIMSHAW
SCRIMSHAWED
SCRIMSHAWING
SCRIMSHAWS
SCRIMURE
SCRIMURES
SCRINE
SCRINES
SCRIP
SCRIPPAGE
SCRIPPAGES
SCRIPS
SCRIPT
SCRIPTED
SCRIPTER*
SCRIPTERS*
SCRIPTING
SCRIPTORY
SCRIPTS
SCRIPTURE
SCRIPTURES
SCRITCH
SCRITCHED
SCRITCHES
SCRITCHING
SCRIVE
SCRIVED
SCRIVENER
SCRIVENERS
SCRIVES
SCRIVING
SCROBE
SCROBES
SCROD
SCRODDLED
SCRODS
SCROFULA
SCROFULAS
SCROG
SCROGGIE
SCROGGIER
SCROGGIEST
SCROGGY
SCROGS
SCROLL
SCROLLED
SCROLLING
SCROLLS
SCROOCH*
SCROOCHED*
SCROOCHES*
SCROOCHING*
SCROOGE
SCROOGED
SCROOGES
SCROOGING
SCROOP
SCROOPED
SCROOPING
SCROOPS
SCROOTCH*
SCROOTCHED*
SCROOTCHES*

SCROOTCHING*
SCROTA
SCROTAL
SCROTUM
SCROTUMS
SCROUGE
SCROUGED
SCROUGER
SCROUGERS
SCROUGES
SCROUGING
SCROUNGE
SCROUNGED
SCROUNGER
SCROUNGERS
SCROUNGES
SCROUNGIER*
SCROUNGIEST*
SCROUNGING
SCROUNGINGS
SCROUNGY*
SCROW
SCROWDGE
SCROWDGED
SCROWDGES
SCROWDGING
SCROWL
SCROWLE
SCROWLED
SCROWLES
SCROWLING
SCROWLS
SCROWS
SCROYLE
SCROYLES
SCRUB
SCRUBBED
SCRUBBER
SCRUBBERS
SCRUBBIER
SCRUBBIEST
SCRUBBING
SCRUBBINGS
SCRUBBY
SCRUBLAND
SCRUBLANDS
SCRUBS
SCRUFF
SCRUFFIER
SCRUFFIEST
SCRUFFILY*
SCRUFFS
SCRUFFY
SCRUM
SCRUMDOWN
SCRUMDOWNS
SCRUMMAGE
SCRUMMAGED
SCRUMMAGES
SCRUMMAGING
SCRUMMED
SCRUMMIER
SCRUMMIEST
SCRUMMING

SCRUMMY
SCRUMP
SCRUMPED
SCRUMPIES
SCRUMPING
SCRUMPOX
SCRUMPOXES
SCRUMPS
SCRUMPY
SCRUMS
SCRUNCH
SCRUNCHED
SCRUNCHES
SCRUNCHIER
SCRUNCHIES
SCRUNCHIEST
SCRUNCHING
SCRUNCHY
SCRUNT
SCRUNTIER
SCRUNTIEST
SCRUNTS
SCRUNTY
SCRUPLE
SCRUPLED
SCRUPLER
SCRUPLERS
SCRUPLES
SCRUPLING
SCRUTABLE
SCRUTATOR
SCRUTATORS
SCRUTINIES
SCRUTINY
SCRUTO
SCRUTOIRE
SCRUTOIRES
SCRUTOS
SCRUZE
SCRUZED
SCRUZES
SCRUZING
SCRY
SCRYDE
SCRYER
SCRYERS
SCRYING
SCRYINGS
SCRYNE
SCRYNES
SCUBA
SCUBAS
SCUCHIN
SCUCHINS
SCUCHION
SCUCHIONS
SCUD
SCUDDALER
SCUDDALERS
SCUDDED
SCUDDER
SCUDDERS
SCUDDING
SCUDDLE

SCUDDLED
SCUDDLES
SCUDDLING
SCUDI
SCUDLER
SCUDLERS
SCUDO
SCUDS
SCUFF
SCUFFED
SCUFFING
SCUFFLE
SCUFFLED
SCUFFLER
SCUFFLERS
SCUFFLES
SCUFFLING
SCUFFS
SCUFT
SCUFTS
SCUG
SCUGGED
SCUGGING
SCUGS
SCUL
SCULK
SCULKED
SCULKER*
SCULKERS*
SCULKING
SCULKS
SCULL
SCULLE
SCULLED
SCULLER
SCULLERIES
SCULLERS
SCULLERY
SCULLES
SCULLING
SCULLINGS
SCULLION
SCULLIONS
SCULLS
SCULP
SCULPED
SCULPIN
SCULPING
SCULPINS
SCULPS
SCULPSIT
SCULPT
SCULPTED
SCULPTING
SCULPTOR
SCULPTORS
SCULPTS
SCULPTURE
SCULPTURED
SCULPTURES
SCULPTURING
SCULPTURINGS
SCULS
SCUM

SCUMBAG	SCURRY	SCYTHE	SEAFOLK	SEAMINESS
SCUMBAGS	SCURRYING	SCYTHED	SEAFOLKS	SEAMINESSES
SCUMBER	SCURS	SCYTHEMAN	SEAFOOD	SEAMING
SCUMBERED	SCURVIER	SCYTHEMEN	SEAFOODS	SEAMLESS
SCUMBERING	SCURVIES	SCYTHER	SEAFOWL	SEAMLIKE*
SCUMBERS	SCURVIEST	SCYTHERS	SEAFOWLS	SEAMOUNT
SCUMBLE	SCURVILY	SCYTHES	SEAFRONT	SEAMOUNTS
SCUMBLED	SCURVY	SCYTHING	SEAFRONTS	SEAMS
SCUMBLES	SCUSE	SDAINE	SEAGIRT*	SEAMSET
SCUMBLING	SCUSED	SDAINED	SEAGOING*	SEAMSETS
SCUMBLINGS	SCUSES	SDAINES	SEAGULL	SEAMSTER
SCUMFISH	SCUSING	SDAINING	SEAGULLS	SEAMSTERS
SCUMFISHED	SCUT	SDAYN	SEAHAWK	SEAMY
SCUMFISHES	SCUTA	SDAYNED	SEAHAWKS	SEAN
SCUMFISHING	SCUTAGE	SDAYNING	SEAHOG	SEANCE
SCUMLIKE*	SCUTAGES	SDAYNS	SEAHOGS	SEANCES
SCUMMED	SCUTAL	SDEIGN	SEAHORSE	SEANED
SCUMMER	SCUTATE	SDEIGNE	SEAHORSES	SEANING
SCUMMERS	SCUTCH	SDEIGNED	SEAHOUND	SEANNACHIES
SCUMMIER	SCUTCHED	SDEIGNES	SEAHOUNDS	SEANNACHY
SCUMMIEST	SCUTCHEON	SDEIGNING	SEAKALE	SEANS
SCUMMING	SCUTCHEONS	SDEIGNS	SEAKALES	SEAPIECE*
SCUMMINGS	SCUTCHER	SDEIN	SEAL	SEAPIECES*
SCUMMY	SCUTCHERS	SDEINED	SEALABLE*	SEAPLANE
SCUMS	SCUTCHES	SDEINING	SEALANT	SEAPLANES
SCUNCHEON	SCUTCHING	SDEINS	SEALANTS	SEAPORT
SCUNCHEONS	SCUTCHINGS	SEA	SEALCH	SEAPORTS
SCUNGE	SCUTE	SEABAG*	SEALCHS	SEAQUAKE
SCUNGED	SCUTELLA	SEABAGS*	SEALED	SEAQUAKES
SCUNGES	SCUTELLAR	SEABANK	SEALER	SEAQUARIA
SCUNGIER	SCUTELLUM	SEABANKS	SEALERIES	SEAR
SCUNGIEST	SCUTES	SEABEACH*	SEALERS	SEARAT
SCUNGILLI*	SCUTIFORM	SEABEACHES*	SEALERY	SEARATS
SCUNGILLIS*	SCUTIGER	SEABED	SEALGH	SEARCE
SCUNGING	SCUTIGERS	SEABEDS	SEALGHS	SEARCED
SCUNGY	SCUTS	SEABIRD	SEALINE	SEARCES
SCUNNER	SCUTTER	SEABIRDS	SEALINES	SEARCH
SCUNNERED	SCUTTERED	SEABLITE	SEALING	SEARCHED
SCUNNERING	SCUTTERING	SEABLITES	SEALINGS	SEARCHER
SCUNNERS	SCUTTERS	SEABOARD	SEALLIKE*	SEARCHERS
SCUP	SCUTTLE	SEABOARDS	SEALPOINT	SEARCHES
SCUPPAUG	SCUTTLED	SEABOOT*	SEALPOINTS	SEARCHING
SCUPPAUGS	SCUTTLER	SEABOOTS*	SEALS	SEARCING
SCUPPER	SCUTTLERS	SEABORNE	SEALSKIN	SEARE
SCUPPERED	SCUTTLES	SEABOTTLE	SEALSKINS	SEARED
SCUPPERING	SCUTTLING	SEABOTTLES	SEALWAX	SEARER
SCUPPERS	SCUTUM	SEACOAST	SEALWAXES	SEAREST
SCUPS	SCUZZ	SEACOASTS	SEALYHAM	SEARING
SCUR	SCUZZBALL	SEACOCK	SEALYHAMS	SEARINGLY*
SCURF	SCUZZBALLS	SEACOCKS	SEAM	SEARINGS
SCURFIER	SCUZZES	SEACRAFT	SEAMAID	SEARNESS
SCURFIEST	SCUZZIER	SEACRAFTS	SEAMAIDS	SEARNESSES
SCURFS	SCUZZIEST	SEACUNNIES	SEAMAN	SEAROBIN*
SCURFY	SCUZZY	SEACUNNY	SEAMANLY	SEAROBINS*
SCURRED	SCYBALA	SEADOG*	SEAMARK	SEARS
SCURRIED	SCYBALOUS	SEADOGS*	SEAMARKS	SEAS
SCURRIER	SCYBALUM	SEADROME	SEAME	SEASCAPE
SCURRIERS	SCYE	SEADROMES	SEAMED	SEASCAPES
SCURRIES	SCYES	SEAFARER	SEAMEN	SEASCOUT*
SCURRIL	SCYPHATE*	SEAFARERS	SEAMER	SEASCOUTS*
SCURRILE	SCYPHI	SEAFARING	SEAMERS	SEASE
SCURRING	SCYPHUS	SEAFARINGS	SEAMES	SEASED
SCURRIOUR	SCYTALE	SEAFLOOR*	SEAMIER	SEASES
SCURRIOURS	SCYTALES	SEAFLOORS*	SEAMIEST	SEASHELL

The Chambers Dictionary is the authority for many longer words; see Introduction, page ix

SEASHELLS	SEAZING	SECONDER	SECTORIZES	SEDIMENTING
SEASHORE	SEBACEOUS	SECONDERS	SECTORIZING	SEDIMENTS
SEASHORES	SEBACIC	SECONDES	SECTORS	SEDITION
SEASICK	SEBASIC*	SECONDI	SECTS	SEDITIONS
SEASICKER	SEBATE	SECONDING	SECULAR	SEDITIOUS
SEASICKEST	SEBATES	SECONDLY	SECULARLY	SEDUCE
SEASIDE	SEBESTEN	SECONDO	SECULARS	SEDUCED
SEASIDES	SEBESTENS	SECONDS	SECULUM	SEDUCER
SEASING	SEBIFIC	SECPAR*	SECULUMS	SEDUCERS
SEASON	SEBORRHEA*	SECPARS*	SECUND	SEDUCES
SEASONAL	SEBORRHEAS*	SECRECIES	SECUNDINE	SEDUCING
SEASONED	SEBUM	SECRECY	SECUNDINES	SEDUCINGS
SEASONER	SEBUMS	SECRET	SECUNDLY*	SEDUCIVE*
SEASONERS	SEBUNDIES	SECRETA	SECUNDUM	SEDUCTION
SEASONING	SEBUNDY	SECRETAGE	SECURABLE	SEDUCTIONS
SEASONINGS	SEC	SECRETAGES	SECURANCE	SEDUCTIVE
SEASONS	SECALOSE*	SECRETARIES	SECURANCES	SEDUCTOR
SEASPEAK	SECALOSES*	SECRETARY	SECURE	SEDUCTORS
SEASPEAKS	SECANT	SECRETE	SECURED	SEDULITIES
SEASTRAND*	SECANTLY	SECRETED	SECURELY	SEDULITY
SEASTRANDS*	SECANTS	SECRETER*	SECURER	SEDULOUS
SEASURE	SECATEUR*	SECRETES	SECURERS	SEDUM
SEASURES	SECATEURS	SECRETEST*	SECURES	SEDUMS
SEAT	SECCO	SECRETIN	SECUREST	SEE
SEATED	SECCOS	SECRETING	SECURING	SEEABLE
SEATER	SECEDE	SECRETINS	SECURITAN	SEECATCH
SEATERS	SECEDED	SECRETION	SECURITANS	SEECATCHIE
SEATING	SECEDER	SECRETIONS	SECURITIES	SEED
SEATINGS	SECEDERS	SECRETIVE	SECURITY	SEEDBED
SEATLESS	SECEDES	SECRETLY	SED	SEEDBEDS
SEATMATE*	SECEDING	SECRETOR*	SEDAN	SEEDBOX
SEATMATES*	SECERN	SECRETORS*	SEDANS	SEEDBOXES
SEATRAIN*	SECERNED	SECRETORY	SEDARIM*	SEEDCAKE
SEATRAINS*	SECERNENT	SECRETS	SEDATE	SEEDCAKES
SEATS	SECERNENTS	SECS	SEDATED	SEEDCASE
SEATWORK*	SECERNING	SECT	SEDATELY	SEEDCASES
SEATWORKS*	SECERNS	SECTARIAL	SEDATER	SEEDEATER*
SEAWALL*	SECESH	SECTARIAN	SEDATES	SEEDEATERS*
SEAWALLS*	SECESHER	SECTARIANS	SEDATEST	SEEDED
SEAWAN*	SECESHERS	SECTARIES	SEDATING	SEEDER
SEAWANS*	SECESHES	SECTARY	SEDATION	SEEDERS
SEAWANT*	SECESSION	SECTATOR	SEDATIONS	SEEDIER
SEAWANTS*	SECESSIONS	SECTATORS	SEDATIVE	SEEDIEST
SEAWARD	SECKEL	SECTILE	SEDATIVES	SEEDILY
SEAWARDLY	SECKELS	SECTILITIES	SEDENT	SEEDINESS
SEAWARDS	SECKLE	SECTILITY	SEDENTARY	SEEDINESSES
SEAWARE	SECKLES	SECTION	SEDER*	SEEDING
SEAWARES	SECLUDE	SECTIONAL	SEDERS*	SEEDINGS
SEAWATER	SECLUDED	SECTIONALS*	SEDERUNT	SEEDLESS
SEAWATERS	SECLUDES	SECTIONED	SEDERUNTS	SEEDLIKE
SEAWAY	SECLUDING	SECTIONING	SEDES	SEEDLING
SEAWAYS	SECLUSION	SECTIONS	SEDGE	SEEDLINGS
SEAWEED	SECLUSIONS	SECTOR	SEDGED	SEEDLIP
SEAWEEDS	SECLUSIVE	SECTORAL	SEDGELAND	SEEDLIPS
SEAWIFE	SECO	SECTORED	SEDGELANDS	SEEDMAN*
SEAWIVES	SECODONT	SECTORIAL	SEDGES	SEEDMEN*
SEAWOMAN	SECODONTS	SECTORIALS	SEDGIER	SEEDNESS
SEAWOMEN	SECOND	SECTORING	SEDGIEST	SEEDNESSES
SEAWORM	SECONDARIES	SECTORISE	SEDGY	SEEDPOD*
SEAWORMS	SECONDARY	SECTORISED	SEDILE	SEEDPODS*
SEAWORTHY	SECONDE	SECTORISES	SEDILIA	SEEDS
SEAZE	SECONDED	SECTORISING	SEDILIUM*	SEEDSMAN
SEAZED	SECONDEE	SECTORIZE	SEDIMENT	SEEDSMEN
SEAZES	SECONDEES	SECTORIZED	SEDIMENTED	SEEDTIME*

Words marked with an asterisk are from OTCWL

SEEDTIMES*
SEEDY
SEEING
SEEINGS
SEEK
SEEKER
SEEKERS
SEEKING
SEEKS
SEEL
SEELD
SEELED
SEELIER
SEELIEST
SEELING
SEELINGS
SEELS
SEELY
SEEM
SEEMED
SEEMER
SEEMERS
SEEMING
SEEMINGLY
SEEMINGS
SEEMLESS
SEEMLIER
SEEMLIEST
SEEMLIHED
SEEMLIHEDS
SEEMLY
SEEMLYHED
SEEMLYHEDS
SEEMS
SEEN
SEEP
SEEPAGE
SEEPAGES
SEEPED
SEEPIER
SEEPIEST
SEEPING
SEEPS
SEEPY
SEER
SEERESS
SEERESSES
SEERS
SEES
SEESAW
SEESAWED
SEESAWING
SEESAWS
SEETHE
SEETHED
SEETHER
SEETHERS
SEETHES
SEETHING
SEETHINGS
SEEWING
SEG
SEGAR
SEGARS

SEGETAL*
SEGGAR
SEGGARS
SEGHOL
SEGHOLATE
SEGHOLATES
SEGHOLS
SEGMENT
SEGMENTAL
SEGMENTED
SEGMENTING
SEGMENTS
SEGNI*
SEGNO
SEGNOS
SEGO
SEGOL
SEGOLATE
SEGOLATES
SEGOLS
SEGOS
SEGREANT
SEGREGANT*
SEGREGANTS*
SEGREGATE
SEGREGATED
SEGREGATES
SEGREGATING
SEGS
SEGUE
SEGUED
SEGUEING
SEGUES
SEI
SEICENTO
SEICENTOS
SEICHE
SEICHES
SEIDEL*
SEIDELS*
SEIF
SEIFS
SEIGNEUR
SEIGNEURIES*
SEIGNEURS
SEIGNEURY*
SEIGNIOR
SEIGNIORIES
SEIGNIORS
SEIGNIORY
SEIGNORAL
SEIGNORIES
SEIGNORY
SEIK
SEIKER
SEIKEST
SEIL
SEILED
SEILING
SEILS
SEINE
SEINED
SEINER
SEINERS

SEINES
SEINING
SEININGS
SEIR
SEIRS
SEIS
SEISABLE*
SEISE
SEISED
SEISER*
SEISERS*
SEISES
SEISIN
SEISING
SEISINGS*
SEISINS
SEISM
SEISMAL
SEISMIC
SEISMICAL
SEISMISM
SEISMISMS
SEISMS
SEISOR*
SEISORS*
SEISURE*
SEISURES*
SEITEN
SEITENS
SEITIES
SEITY
SEIZABLE
SEIZE
SEIZED
SEIZER
SEIZERS
SEIZES
SEIZIN
SEIZING
SEIZINGS
SEIZINS
SEIZOR*
SEIZORS*
SEIZURE
SEIZURES
SEJANT
SEJEANT
SEKOS
SEKOSES
SEKT
SEKTS
SEL
SELACHIAN
SELACHIANS
SELADANG
SELADANGS
SELAH
SELAHS
SELAMLIK*
SELAMLIKS*
SELCOUTH
SELD
SELDOM
SELDOMLY*

SELDSEEN
SELDSHOWN
SELE
SELECT
SELECTED
SELECTEE
SELECTEES
SELECTING
SELECTION
SELECTIONS
SELECTIVE
SELECTLY*
SELECTMAN*
SELECTMEN*
SELECTOR
SELECTORS
SELECTS
SELENATE
SELENATES
SELENIAN
SELENIC
SELENIDE
SELENIDES
SELENIOUS
SELENITE
SELENITES
SELENITIC
SELENIUM
SELENIUMS
SELENOUS
SELES
SELF
SELFDOM*
SELFDOMS*
SELFED
SELFHEAL
SELFHEALS
SELFHOOD
SELFHOODS
SELFING
SELFINGS
SELFISH
SELFISHLY
SELFISM
SELFISMS
SELFIST
SELFISTS
SELFLESS
SELFNESS
SELFNESSES
SELFS
SELFSAME*
SELFWARD*
SELICTAR
SELICTARS
SELKIE
SELKIES
SELL
SELLA
SELLABLE
SELLAE
SELLAS
SELLE
SELLER

SELLERS
SELLES
SELLING
SELLOTAPE
SELLOTAPED
SELLOTAPES
SELLOTAPING
SELLOUT*
SELLOUTS*
SELLS
SELS
SELSYN*
SELSYNS*
SELTZER
SELTZERS
SELVA
SELVAGE
SELVAGED
SELVAGEE
SELVAGEES
SELVAGES
SELVAGING
SELVAS
SELVEDGE
SELVEDGED
SELVEDGES
SELVEDGING
SELVES
SEMANTEME
SEMANTEMES
SEMANTIC
SEMANTICS
SEMANTIDE
SEMANTIDES
SEMANTRA
SEMANTRON
SEMAPHORE
SEMAPHORED
SEMAPHORES
SEMAPHORING
SEMATIC
SEMBLABLE
SEMBLABLES
SEMBLABLY
SEMBLANCE
SEMBLANCES
SEMBLANT
SEMBLANTS
SEMBLE
SEMBLED
SEMBLES
SEMBLING
SEME
SEMEE
SEMEED
SEMEIA
SEMEION
SEMEIOTIC
SEMEIOTICS
SEMEME
SEMEMES
SEMEMIC*
SEMEN
SEMENS

SEMES*	SEMINARIES	SENA	SENOPIA*	SENTENCE
SEMESTER	SEMINARS	SENARIES	SENOPIAS*	SENTENCED
SEMESTERS	SEMINARY	SENARII	SENOR*	SENTENCER
SEMESTRAL	SEMINATE	SENARIUS	SENORA*	SENTENCERS
SEMI	SEMINATED	SENARY	SENORAS*	SENTENCES
SEMIANGLE	SEMINATES	SENAS	SENORES*	SENTENCING
SEMIANGLES	SEMINATING	SENATE	SENORITA*	SENTENTIA*
SEMIARID*	SEMINOMAD*	SENATES	SENORITAS*	SENTENTIAE*
SEMIBALD*	SEMINOMADS*	SENATOR	SENORS*	SENTI*
SEMIBOLD	SEMINUDE*	SENATORS	SENRYU*	SENTIENCE
SEMIBOLDS	SEMIOLOGIES	SEND	SENS	SENTIENCES
SEMIBREVE	SEMIOLOGY	SENDABLE*	SENSA	SENTIENCIES
SEMIBREVES	SEMIOSES*	SENDAL	SENSATE	SENTIENCY
SEMIBULL	SEMIOSIS*	SENDALS	SENSATED*	SENTIENT
SEMIBULLS	SEMIOTIC	SENDED	SENSATELY*	SENTIENTS
SEMICOLON	SEMIOTICS	SENDER	SENSATES*	SENTIMENT
SEMICOLONS	SEMIPED	SENDERS	SENSATING*	SENTIMENTS
SEMICOMA	SEMIPEDS	SENDING	SENSATION	SENTIMO*
SEMICOMAS	SEMIPLUME	SENDINGS	SENSATIONS	SENTIMOS*
SEMIDEAF*	SEMIPLUMES	SENDOFF*	SENSE	SENTINEL
SEMIDEIFIED*	SEMIPRO*	SENDOFFS*	SENSED	SENTINELED*
SEMIDEIFIES*	SEMIPROS*	SENDS	SENSEFUL	SENTINELING*
SEMIDEIFY*	SEMIRAW*	SENDUP*	SENSELESS	SENTINELLED
SEMIDEIFYING*	SEMIRIGID*	SENDUPS*	SENSES	SENTINELLING
SEMIDOME*	SEMIRURAL*	SENE*	SENSIBLE	SENTINELS
SEMIDOMED*	SEMIS	SENECA*	SENSIBLER	SENTING
SEMIDOMES*	SEMISES	SENECAS*	SENSIBLES	SENTRIES
SEMIDRY*	SEMISOFT*	SENECIO	SENSIBLEST	SENTRY
SEMIDWARF*	SEMISOLID	SENECIOS	SENSIBLY	SENTS
SEMIDWARFS*	SEMISOLIDS	SENEGA	SENSILE	SENVIES
SEMIDWARVES*	SEMISWEET*	SENEGAS	SENSILLA	SENVY
SEMIE	SEMITAR	SENESCENT	SENSILLAE*	SENZA
SEMIERECT*	SEMITARS	SENESCHAL	SENSILLUM	SEPAD
SEMIES	SEMITAUR	SENESCHALS	SENSING	SEPADDED
SEMIFINAL	SEMITAURS	SENGI*	SENSINGS	SEPADDING
SEMIFINALS	SEMITIST*	SENGREEN	SENSISM	SEPADS
SEMIFIT*	SEMITISTS*	SENGREENS	SENSISMS	SEPAL
SEMIFLUID	SEMITONAL*	SENHOR*	SENSIST	SEPALED*
SEMIFLUIDS	SEMITONE	SENHORA*	SENSISTS	SEPALINE
SEMIGALA*	SEMITONES	SENHORAS*	SENSITISE	SEPALLED*
SEMIGLOSS*	SEMITONIC	SENHORES*	SENSITISED	SEPALODIES
SEMIGROUP*	SEMIVOWEL	SENHORITA*	SENSITISES	SEPALODY
SEMIGROUPS*	SEMIVOWELS	SENHORITAS*	SENSITISING	SEPALOID
SEMIHARD*	SEMIWILD*	SENHORS*	SENSITIVE	SEPALOUS
SEMIHIGH*	SEMIWORKS*	SENILE	SENSITIVES	SEPALS
SEMIHOBO*	SEMMIT	SENILELY	SENSITIZE	SEPARABLE
SEMIHOBOES*	SEMMITS	SENILES*	SENSITIZED	SEPARABLY
SEMIHOBOS*	SEMOLINA	SENILITIES	SENSITIZES	SEPARATA
SEMILOG*	SEMOLINAS	SENILITY	SENSITIZING	SEPARATE
SEMILUNAR	SEMPER	SENIOR	SENSOR	SEPARATED
SEMILUNE	SEMPLE	SENIORITIES	SENSORIA	SEPARATES
SEMILUNES	SEMPLER	SENIORITY	SENSORIAL	SEPARATING
SEMIMAT*	SEMPLEST	SENIORS	SENSORILY	SEPARATOR
SEMIMATT*	SEMPLICE	SENITI*	SENSORIUM	SEPARATORS
SEMIMATTE*	SEMPRE	SENNA	SENSORIUMS	SEPARATUM
SEMIMETAL*	SEMPSTER	SENNACHIE	SENSORS	SEPARATUMS
SEMIMETALS*	SEMPSTERS	SENNACHIES	SENSORY	SEPHEN
SEMIMICRO*	SEMSEM	SENNAS	SENSUAL	SEPHENS
SEMIMOIST*	SEMSEMS	SENNET	SENSUALLY	SEPIA
SEMIMUTE*	SEMUNCIA	SENNETS	SENSUM	SEPIAS
SEMINA*	SEMUNCIAE	SENNIGHT	SENSUOUS	SEPIC*
SEMINAL	SEMUNCIAL	SENNIGHTS	SENT	SEPIMENT
SEMINALLY	SEMUNCIAS	SENNIT	SENTE*	SEPIMENTS
SEMINAR	SEN	SENNITS	SENTED	SEPIOLITE

SEPIOLITES	SEPULCHRING	SERAPHS	SERIALIZE	SERMONING
SEPIOST	SEPULTURE	SERASKIER	SERIALIZED	SERMONINGS
SEPIOSTS	SEPULTURED	SERASKIERS	SERIALIZES	SERMONISE
SEPIUM	SEPULTURES	SERDAB	SERIALIZING	SERMONISED
SEPIUMS	SEPULTURING	SERDABS	SERIALLY	SERMONISES
SEPMAG	SEQUACITIES	SERE	SERIALS	SERMONISING
SEPOY	SEQUACITY	SERED	SERIATE	SERMONIZE
SEPOYS	SEQUEL	SEREIN	SERIATED	SERMONIZED
SEPPUKU	SEQUELA	SEREINS	SERIATELY	SERMONIZES
SEPPUKUS	SEQUELAE	SERENADE	SERIATES	SERMONIZING
SEPS	SEQUELS	SERENADED	SERIATIM	SERMONS
SEPSES	SEQUENCE	SERENADER	SERIATING	SEROLOGIC*
SEPSIS	SEQUENCED	SERENADERS	SERIATION	SEROLOGIES
SEPT	SEQUENCER	SERENADES	SERIATIONS	SEROLOGY
SEPTA	SEQUENCERS	SERENADING	SERIC	SERON
SEPTAL	SEQUENCES	SERENATA	SERICEOUS	SERONS
SEPTARIA	SEQUENCIES*	SERENATAS	SERICIN	SEROON
SEPTARIAN	SEQUENCING	SERENATE	SERICINS	SEROONS
SEPTARIUM	SEQUENCINGS	SERENATES	SERICITE	SEROPUS
SEPTATE	SEQUENCY*	SERENE	SERICITES	SEROPUSES
SEPTATION	SEQUENT	SERENED	SERICITIC	SEROSA
SEPTATIONS	SEQUENTS	SERENELY	SERICON	SEROSAE
SEPTEMFID	SEQUESTER	SERENER	SERICONS	SEROSAL*
SEPTEMVIR	SEQUESTERED	SERENES	SERIEMA	SEROSAS
SEPTEMVIRI	SEQUESTERING	SERENEST	SERIEMAS	SEROSITIES
SEPTEMVIRS	SEQUESTERS	SERENING	SERIES	SEROSITY
SEPTENARIES	SEQUESTRA	SERENITIES	SERIF	SEROTINAL
SEPTENARY	SEQUESTRUM*	SERENITY	SERIFED*	SEROTINE
SEPTENNIA	SEQUESTRUMS*	SERER	SERIFFED*	SEROTINES
SEPTET	SEQUIN	SERES	SERIFS	SEROTONIN
SEPTETS	SEQUINED	SEREST	SERIGRAPH	SEROTONINS
SEPTETTE	SEQUINNED	SERF	SERIGRAPHS	SEROTYPE
SEPTETTES	SEQUINS	SERFAGE	SERIN	SEROTYPED
SEPTIC	SEQUITUR*	SERFAGES	SERINE	SEROTYPES
SEPTICAL*	SEQUITURS*	SERFDOM	SERINES	SEROTYPING
SEPTICITIES	SEQUOIA	SERFDOMS	SERINETTE	SEROTYPINGS
SEPTICITY	SEQUOIAS	SERFHOOD	SERINETTES	SEROUS
SEPTICS*	SER*	SERFHOODS	SERING	SEROW
SEPTIFORM	SERA	SERFISH	SERINGA	SEROWS
SEPTIMAL	SERAC	SERFLIKE	SERINGAS	SERPENT
SEPTIME	SERACS	SERFS	SERINS	SERPENTRIES
SEPTIMES	SERAFILE	SERFSHIP	SERIOUS	SERPENTRY
SEPTIMOLE	SERAFILES	SERFSHIPS	SERIOUSLY	SERPENTS
SEPTIMOLES	SERAFIN	SERGE	SERIPH	SERPIGINES
SEPTLEVA	SERAFINS	SERGEANCIES	SERIPHS	SERPIGO
SEPTLEVAS	SERAGLIO	SERGEANCY	SERJEANCIES	SERPIGOES
SEPTS	SERAGLIOS	SERGEANT	SERJEANCY	SERPULA
SEPTUM	SERAI	SERGEANTIES*	SERJEANT	SERPULAE
SEPTUMS*	SERAIL	SERGEANTS	SERJEANTIES	SERPULITE
SEPTUOR	SERAILS	SERGEANTY*	SERJEANTS	SERPULITES
SEPTUORS	SERAIS	SERGES	SERJEANTY	SERR
SEPTUPLE	SERAL	SERGING*	SERK	SERRA
SEPTUPLED	SERANG	SERGINGS*	SERKALI	SERRAE
SEPTUPLES	SERANGS	SERIAL	SERKALIS	SERRAN
SEPTUPLET	SERAPE	SERIALISE	SERKS	SERRANID
SEPTUPLETS	SERAPES	SERIALISED	SERMON	SERRANIDS
SEPTUPLING	SERAPH	SERIALISES	SERMONED	SERRANO*
SEPULCHER	SERAPHIC	SERIALISING	SERMONEER	SERRANOID
SEPULCHERED	SERAPHIM	SERIALISM	SERMONEERS	SERRANOIDS
SEPULCHERING	SERAPHIMS	SERIALISMS	SERMONER	SERRANOS*
SEPULCHERS	SERAPHIN	SERIALIST	SERMONERS	SERRANS
SEPULCHRE	SERAPHINE	SERIALISTS	SERMONET	SERRAS
SEPULCHRED	SERAPHINES	SERIALITIES	SERMONETS	SERRATE
SEPULCHRES	SERAPHINS	SERIALITY	SERMONIC	SERRATED

The Chambers Dictionary is the authority for many longer words; see Introduction, page ix

SERRATES	SERVILISMS	SETOSE	SEVERS	SEXTAN
SERRATI	SERVILITIES	SETOUS*	SEVERY	SEXTANS
SERRATING	SERVILITY	SETOUT*	SEVICHE*	SEXTANSES
SERRATION	SERVING	SETOUTS*	SEVICHES*	SEXTANT
SERRATIONS	SERVINGS	SETS	SEVRUGA	SEXTANTAL
SERRATURE	SERVITOR	SETSCREW	SEVRUGAS	SEXTANTS
SERRATURES	SERVITORS	SETSCREWS	SEW	SEXTARII*
SERRATUS	SERVITUDE	SETT	SEWABLE*	SEXTARIUS*
SERRATUSES	SERVITUDES	SETTEE	SEWAGE	SEXTET
SERRE	SERVO	SETTEES	SEWAGES	SEXTETS
SERRED	SERVOS*	SETTER	SEWAN*	SEXTETT
SERREFILE	SESAME	SETTERED	SEWANS*	SEXTETTE
SERREFILES	SESAMES	SETTERING	SEWAR*	SEXTETTES
SERRES	SESAMOID	SETTERS	SEWARS*	SEXTETTS
SERRICORN	SESAMOIDS	SETTING	SEWED	SEXTILE
SERRIED	SESE	SETTINGS	SEWEL	SEXTILES
SERRIEDLY*	SESELI	SETTLE	SEWELLEL	SEXTO*
SERRIES	SESELIS	SETTLED	SEWELLELS	SEXTOLET
SERRING	SESEY	SETTLER	SEWELS	SEXTOLETS
SERRS	SESS	SETTLERS	SEWEN	SEXTON
SERRULATE	SESSA	SETTLES	SEWENS	SEXTONESS
SERRY	SESSES	SETTLING	SEWER	SEXTONESSES
SERRYING	SESSILE	SETTLINGS	SEWERAGE	SEXTONS
SERS*	SESSION	SETTLOR	SEWERAGES	SEXTOS*
SERUEWE	SESSIONAL	SETTLORS	SEWERED	SEXTS
SERUEWED	SESSIONS	SETTS	SEWERING	SEXTUOR
SERUEWES	SESSPOOL	SETUALE	SEWERINGS	SEXTUORS
SERUEWING	SESSPOOLS	SETUALES	SEWERS	SEXTUPLE
SERUM	SESTERCE	SETULE	SEWIN	SEXTUPLED
SERUMAL*	SESTERCES	SETULES	SEWING	SEXTUPLES
SERUMS	SESTERTIA	SETULOSE	SEWINGS	SEXTUPLET
SERVABLE*	SESTERTIUM*	SETULOUS	SEWINS	SEXTUPLETS
SERVAL	SESTET	SETUP*	SEWN	SEXTUPLING
SERVALS	SESTETS	SETUPS*	SEWS	SEXTUPLY*
SERVANT	SESTETT	SETWALL	SEX	SEXUAL
SERVANTED	SESTETTE	SETWALLS	SEXED	SEXUALISE
SERVANTING	SESTETTES	SEVEN	SEXENNIAL	SEXUALISED
SERVANTRIES	SESTETTO	SEVENFOLD	SEXER	SEXUALISES
SERVANTRY	SESTETTOS	SEVENS	SEXERS	SEXUALISING
SERVANTS	SESTETTS	SEVENTEEN	SEXES	SEXUALISM
SERVE	SESTINA	SEVENTEENS	SEXFID	SEXUALISMS
SERVED	SESTINAS	SEVENTH	SEXFOIL	SEXUALIST
SERVER	SESTINE	SEVENTHLY	SEXFOILS	SEXUALISTS
SERVERIES	SESTINES	SEVENTHS	SEXIER	SEXUALITIES
SERVERS	SESTON	SEVENTIES	SEXIEST	SEXUALITY
SERVERY	SESTONS	SEVENTY	SEXILY*	SEXUALIZE
SERVES	SET	SEVER	SEXINESS	SEXUALIZED
SERVEWE	SETA	SEVERABLE	SEXINESSES	SEXUALIZES
SERVEWED	SETACEOUS	SEVERAL	SEXING	SEXUALIZING
SERVEWES	SETAE	SEVERALLY	SEXISM	SEXUALLY
SERVEWING	SETAL*	SEVERALS	SEXISMS	SEXVALENT
SERVICE	SETBACK	SEVERALTIES	SEXIST	SEXY
SERVICED	SETBACKS	SEVERALTY	SEXISTS	SEY
SERVICER*	SETENANT*	SEVERANCE	SEXLESS	SEYEN
SERVICERS*	SETENANTS*	SEVERANCES	SEXLESSLY*	SEYENS
SERVICES	SETIFORM	SEVERE	SEXOLOGIES	SEYS
SERVICING	SETLINE	SEVERED	SEXOLOGY	SEYSURE
SERVIENT	SETLINES	SEVERELY	SEXPERT	SEYSURES
SERVIETTE	SETNESS	SEVERER	SEXPERTS	SEZ
SERVIETTES	SETNESSES	SEVEREST	SEXPOT	SFERICS
SERVILE	SETOFF*	SEVERIES	SEXPOTS	SFORZANDI
SERVILELY	SETOFFS*	SEVERING	SEXT	SFORZANDO
SERVILES	SETON	SEVERITIES	SEXTAIN*	SFORZANDOS
SERVILISM	SETONS	SEVERITY	SEXTAINS*	SFORZATI

Words marked with an asterisk are from OTCWL

SFORZATO	SHADOWIER	SHAKILY	SHAMBLED	SHANDS
SFORZATOS	SHADOWIEST	SHAKINESS	SHAMBLES	SHANDY
SFUMATO	SHADOWILY*	SHAKINESSES	SHAMBLIER	SHANGHAI
SFUMATOS	SHADOWING	SHAKING	SHAMBLIEST	SHANGHAIED
SGRAFFITI	SHADOWINGS	SHAKINGS	SHAMBLING	SHANGHAIING
SGRAFFITO	SHADOWS	SHAKO	SHAMBLINGS	SHANGHAIS
SH	SHADOWY	SHAKOES	SHAMBLY	SHANK
SHA*	SHADRACH*	SHAKOS	SHAMBOLIC	SHANKBONE
SHABBIER	SHADRACHS*	SHAKT	SHAME	SHANKBONES
SHABBIEST	SHADS	SHAKUDO	SHAMEABLE	SHANKED
SHABBILY	SHADUF	SHAKUDOS	SHAMED	SHANKING
SHABBLE	SHADUFS	SHAKY	SHAMEFAST	SHANKS
SHABBLES	SHADY	SHALE	SHAMEFUL	SHANNIES
SHABBY	SHAFT	SHALED	SHAMELESS	SHANNY
SHABRACK	SHAFTED	SHALES	SHAMER	SHANS
SHABRACKS	SHAFTER	SHALEY*	SHAMERS	SHANTEY
SHACK	SHAFTERS	SHALIER	SHAMES	SHANTEYS
SHACKLE	SHAFTING	SHALIEST	SHAMIANA	SHANTI*
SHACKLED	SHAFTINGS	SHALING	SHAMIANAH	SHANTIES
SHACKLER*	SHAFTLESS	SHALL	SHAMIANAHS	SHANTIH*
SHACKLERS*	SHAFTS	SHALLI	SHAMIANAS	SHANTIHS*
SHACKLES	SHAG	SHALLIS	SHAMING	SHANTIS*
SHACKLING	SHAGBARK*	SHALLON	SHAMISEN	SHANTUNG
SHACKO	SHAGBARKS*	SHALLONS	SHAMISENS	SHANTUNGS
SHACKOES	SHAGGED	SHALLOON	SHAMMAS*	SHANTY
SHACKOS	SHAGGIER	SHALLOONS	SHAMMASH	SHANTYMAN
SHACKS	SHAGGIEST	SHALLOP	SHAMMASHIM	SHANTYMEN
SHAD	SHAGGILY	SHALLOPS	SHAMMASIM*	SHAPABLE
SHADBERRIES	SHAGGING	SHALLOT	SHAMMED	SHAPE
SHADBERRY	SHAGGY	SHALLOTS	SHAMMER	SHAPEABLE
SHADBLOW	SHAGPILE	SHALLOW	SHAMMERS	SHAPED
SHADBLOWS	SHAGREEN	SHALLOWED	SHAMMES	SHAPELESS
SHADBUSH	SHAGREENS	SHALLOWER	SHAMMIED*	SHAPELIER
SHADBUSHES	SHAGROON	SHALLOWEST	SHAMMIES	SHAPELIEST
SHADCHAN*	SHAGROONS	SHALLOWING	SHAMMING	SHAPELY
SHADCHANIM*	SHAGS	SHALLOWINGS	SHAMMOS*	SHAPEN
SHADCHANS*	SHAH	SHALLOWLY	SHAMMOSIM	SHAPER
SHADDOCK	SHAHDOM*	SHALLOWS	SHAMMY	SHAPERS
SHADDOCKS	SHAHDOMS*	SHALM	SHAMMYING*	SHAPES
SHADE	SHAHS	SHALMS	SHAMOIS*	SHAPEUP*
SHADED	SHAIKH	SHALOM	SHAMOS*	SHAPEUPS*
SHADELESS	SHAIKHS	SHALOMS*	SHAMOSIM*	SHAPING
SHADER*	SHAIRD*	SHALOT	SHAMOY	SHAPINGS
SHADERS*	SHAIRDS*	SHALOTS	SHAMOYED	SHAPS
SHADES	SHAIRN	SHALT	SHAMOYING	SHARABLE*
SHADFLIES*	SHAIRNS	SHALWAR	SHAMOYS	SHARD
SHADFLY*	SHAITAN	SHALWARS	SHAMPOO	SHARDED
SHADIER	SHAITANS	SHALY	SHAMPOOED	SHARDS
SHADIEST	SHAKABLE	SHAM	SHAMPOOER	SHARE
SHADILY	SHAKE	SHAMA	SHAMPOOERS	SHAREABLE*
SHADINESS	SHAKEABLE	SHAMABLE	SHAMPOOING	SHARECROP
SHADINESSES	SHAKED	SHAMAN	SHAMPOOS	SHARECROPPED
SHADING	SHAKEDOWN	SHAMANIC	SHAMROCK	SHARECROPPING
SHADINGS	SHAKEDOWNS	SHAMANISM	SHAMROCKS	SHARECROPS
SHADOOF	SHAKEN	SHAMANISMS	SHAMS	SHARED
SHADOOFS	SHAKEOUT*	SHAMANIST	SHAMUS	SHAREMAN
SHADOW	SHAKEOUTS*	SHAMANISTS	SHAMUSES	SHAREMEN
SHADOWBOX*	SHAKER	SHAMANS	SHAN	SHARER
SHADOWBOXED*	SHAKERS	SHAMAS	SHANACHIE	SHARERS
SHADOWBOXES*	SHAKES	SHAMATEUR	SHANACHIES	SHARES
SHADOWBOXING*	SHAKEUP*	SHAMATEURS	SHAND	SHARESMAN
SHADOWED	SHAKEUPS*	SHAMBA	SHANDIES	SHARESMEN
SHADOWER	SHAKIER	SHAMBAS	SHANDRIES	SHAREWARE
SHADOWERS	SHAKIEST	SHAMBLE	SHANDRY	SHAREWARES

The Chambers Dictionary is the authority for many longer words; see Introduction, page ix

SHARIA	SHATTERY	SHEAL	SHEELS	SHEIK
SHARIAS	SHAUCHLE	SHEALED	SHEEN	SHEIKDOM
SHARIAT	SHAUCHLED	SHEALING	SHEENED	SHEIKDOMS
SHARIATS	SHAUCHLES	SHEALINGS	SHEENEY*	SHEIKH
SHARIF	SHAUCHLIER	SHEALS	SHEENEYS*	SHEIKHA
SHARIFIAN*	SHAUCHLIEST	SHEAR	SHEENFUL*	SHEIKHAS
SHARIFS	SHAUCHLING	SHEARED	SHEENIE*	SHEIKHDOM
SHARING	SHAUCHLY	SHEARER	SHEENIER	SHEIKHDOMS
SHARINGS	SHAUGH*	SHEARERS	SHEENIES	SHEIKHS
SHARK	SHAUGHS*	SHEARING	SHEENIEST	SHEIKS
SHARKED	SHAUL*	SHEARINGS	SHEENING	SHEILA
SHARKER	SHAULED*	SHEARLEG	SHEENS	SHEILAS
SHARKERS	SHAULING*	SHEARLEGS	SHEENY	SHEILING
SHARKING	SHAULS*	SHEARLING	SHEEP	SHEILINGS
SHARKINGS	SHAVABLE*	SHEARLINGS	SHEEPCOT*	SHEITAN*
SHARKLIKE*	SHAVE	SHEARMAN	SHEEPCOTE	SHEITANS*
SHARKS	SHAVED	SHEARMEN	SHEEPCOTES	SHEKEL
SHARKSKIN	SHAVELING	SHEARS	SHEEPCOTS*	SHEKELS
SHARKSKINS	SHAVELINGS	SHEAS	SHEEPDOG	SHELDDUCK
SHARN	SHAVEN	SHEATFISH	SHEEPDOGS	SHELDDUCKS
SHARNIER	SHAVER	SHEATFISHES	SHEEPFOLD	SHELDRAKE
SHARNIEST	SHAVERS	SHEATH	SHEEPFOLDS	SHELDRAKES
SHARNS	SHAVES	SHEATHE	SHEEPIER	SHELDUCK
SHARNY	SHAVETAIL*	SHEATHED	SHEEPIEST	SHELDUCKS
SHARP	SHAVETAILS*	SHEATHER*	SHEEPISH	SHELF
SHARPED	SHAVIE	SHEATHERS*	SHEEPMAN*	SHELFED
SHARPEN	SHAVIES	SHEATHES	SHEEPMEN*	SHELFFUL*
SHARPENED	SHAVING	SHEATHIER	SHEEPO	SHELFFULS*
SHARPENER	SHAVINGS	SHEATHIEST	SHEEPOS	SHELFIER
SHARPENERS	SHAW	SHEATHING	SHEEPSKIN	SHELFIEST
SHARPENING	SHAWED*	SHEATHINGS	SHEEPSKINS	SHELFING
SHARPENS	SHAWING*	SHEATHS	SHEEPWALK	SHELFLIKE
SHARPER	SHAWL	SHEATHY	SHEEPWALKS	SHELFROOM
SHARPERS	SHAWLED	SHEAVE	SHEEPY	SHELFROOMS
SHARPEST	SHAWLEY	SHEAVED	SHEER	SHELFS
SHARPIE	SHAWLEYS	SHEAVES	SHEERED	SHELFY
SHARPIES	SHAWLIE	SHEAVING	SHEERER	SHELL
SHARPING	SHAWLIES	SHEBANG	SHEEREST	SHELLAC
SHARPINGS	SHAWLING	SHEBANGS	SHEERING	SHELLACK*
SHARPISH	SHAWLINGS	SHEBEAN*	SHEERLEG	SHELLACKED
SHARPLY	SHAWLLESS	SHEBEANS*	SHEERLEGS	SHELLACKING
SHARPNESS	SHAWLS	SHEBEEN	SHEERLY	SHELLACKINGS
SHARPNESSES	SHAWM	SHEBEENED	SHEERNESS*	SHELLACKS*
SHARPS	SHAWMS	SHEBEENER	SHEERNESSES*	SHELLACS
SHARPY*	SHAWN*	SHEBEENERS	SHEERS	SHELLBACK
SHASH	SHAWS	SHEBEENING	SHEET	SHELLBACKS
SHASHED	SHAY	SHEBEENINGS	SHEETED	SHELLBARK
SHASHES	SHAYA	SHEBEENS	SHEETER*	SHELLBARKS
SHASHING	SHAYAS	SHECHITA	SHEETERS*	SHELLDUCK
SHASHLICK	SHAYS	SHECHITAH	SHEETFED*	SHELLDUCKS
SHASHLICKS	SHCHI	SHECHITAHS	SHEETIER	SHELLED
SHASHLIK	SHCHIS	SHECHITAS	SHEETIEST	SHELLER
SHASHLIKS	SHE	SHED	SHEETING	SHELLERS
SHASLIK*	SHEA	SHEDABLE*	SHEETINGS	SHELLFIRE
SHASLIKS*	SHEADING	SHEDDED*	SHEETLIKE*	SHELLFIRES
SHASTER	SHEADINGS	SHEDDER	SHEETS	SHELLFISH
SHASTERS	SHEAF	SHEDDERS	SHEETY	SHELLFISHES
SHASTRA	SHEAFED	SHEDDING	SHEEVE*	SHELLFUL
SHASTRAS	SHEAFIER	SHEDDINGS	SHEEVES*	SHELLFULS
SHAT	SHEAFIEST	SHEDLIKE*	SHEGETZ*	SHELLIER
SHATTER	SHEAFING	SHEDS	SHEHITA	SHELLIEST
SHATTERED	SHEAFLIKE*	SHEEL	SHEHITAH	SHELLING
SHATTERING	SHEAFS	SHEELED	SHEHITAHS	SHELLINGS
SHATTERS	SHEAFY	SHEELING	SHEHITAS	SHELLS

SHELLWORK
SHELLWORKS
SHELLY
SHELTA*
SHELTAS*
SHELTER
SHELTERED
SHELTERER
SHELTERERS
SHELTERING
SHELTERINGS
SHELTERS
SHELTERY
SHELTIE
SHELTIES
SHELTY
SHELVE
SHELVED
SHELVER*
SHELVERS*
SHELVES
SHELVIER
SHELVIEST
SHELVING
SHELVINGS
SHELVY
SHEMOZZLE
SHEMOZZLED
SHEMOZZLES
SHEMOZZLING
SHEND
SHENDING
SHENDS
SHENT
SHEOL
SHEOLS
SHEPHERD
SHEPHERDED
SHEPHERDING
SHEPHERDS
SHEQALIM*
SHEQEL*
SHERBERT*
SHERBERTS*
SHERBET
SHERBETS
SHERD
SHERDS
SHERE
SHEREEF
SHEREEFS
SHERIA
SHERIAS
SHERIAT
SHERIATS
SHERIF
SHERIFF
SHERIFFS
SHERIFIAN
SHERIFS
SHERLOCK
SHERLOCKS
SHEROOT*
SHEROOTS*

SHERPA
SHERPAS
SHERRIES
SHERRIS
SHERRISES
SHERRY
SHERWANI
SHERWANIS
SHES
SHET
SHETLAND
SHETLANDS*
SHETS
SHETTING
SHEUCH
SHEUCHED
SHEUCHING
SHEUCHS
SHEUGH
SHEUGHED
SHEUGHING
SHEUGHS
SHEVA
SHEVAS
SHEW
SHEWBREAD
SHEWBREADS
SHEWED
SHEWEL
SHEWELS
SHEWER*
SHEWERS*
SHEWING
SHEWN
SHEWS
SHH*
SHIATSU
SHIATSUS
SHIATZU
SHIATZUS
SHIBAH
SHIBAHS
SHIBUICHI
SHIBUICHIS
SHICKER
SHICKERED
SHICKERS
SHICKSA
SHICKSAS
SHIDDER
SHIDDERS
SHIED
SHIEL
SHIELD
SHIELDED
SHIELDER
SHIELDERS
SHIELDING
SHIELDINGS
SHIELDS
SHIELDUCK
SHIELDUCKS
SHIELED
SHIELING

SHIELINGS
SHIELS
SHIER
SHIERS
SHIES
SHIEST
SHIFT
SHIFTABLE*
SHIFTED
SHIFTER
SHIFTERS
SHIFTIER
SHIFTIEST
SHIFTILY
SHIFTING
SHIFTINGS
SHIFTLESS
SHIFTS
SHIFTY
SHIGELLA
SHIGELLAE*
SHIGELLAS
SHIITAKE
SHIITAKES*
SHIKAR
SHIKAREE
SHIKAREES
SHIKARI
SHIKARIS
SHIKARRED*
SHIKARRING*
SHIKARS
SHIKKER*
SHIKKERS*
SHIKSA
SHIKSAS
SHIKSE
SHIKSES
SHILINGI*
SHILL
SHILLABER
SHILLABERS
SHILLALA*
SHILLALAH
SHILLALAHS
SHILLALAS*
SHILLED
SHILLING
SHILLINGS
SHILLS
SHILPIT
SHILY
SHIM
SHIMAAL
SHIMAALS
SHIMMED
SHIMMER
SHIMMERED
SHIMMERING
SHIMMERINGS
SHIMMERS
SHIMMERY
SHIMMEY
SHIMMEYS

SHIMMIED
SHIMMIES
SHIMMING
SHIMMY
SHIMMYING
SHIMOZZLE
SHIMOZZLES
SHIMS
SHIN
SHINBONE
SHINBONES
SHINDIES
SHINDIG
SHINDIGS
SHINDY
SHINDYS*
SHINE
SHINED
SHINELESS
SHINER
SHINERS
SHINES
SHINESS
SHINESSES
SHINGLE
SHINGLED
SHINGLER
SHINGLERS
SHINGLES
SHINGLIER
SHINGLIEST
SHINGLING
SHINGLINGS
SHINGLY
SHINIER
SHINIES
SHINIEST
SHINILY*
SHININESS
SHININESSES
SHINING
SHININGLY
SHINLEAF*
SHINLEAFS*
SHINLEAVES*
SHINNE
SHINNED
SHINNERIES*
SHINNERY*
SHINNES
SHINNEY*
SHINNEYED*
SHINNEYING*
SHINNEYS*
SHINNIED
SHINNIES
SHINNING
SHINNY
SHINNYING
SHINS
SHINTIES
SHINTY
SHINY
SHIP

SHIPBOARD
SHIPBOARDS
SHIPBORNE*
SHIPFUL
SHIPFULS
SHIPLAP
SHIPLAPPED
SHIPLAPPING
SHIPLAPS
SHIPLESS
SHIPLOAD
SHIPLOADS
SHIPMAN
SHIPMATE
SHIPMATES
SHIPMEN
SHIPMENT
SHIPMENTS
SHIPOWNER*
SHIPOWNERS*
SHIPPABLE*
SHIPPED
SHIPPEN
SHIPPENS
SHIPPER
SHIPPERS
SHIPPING
SHIPPINGS
SHIPPO
SHIPPON
SHIPPONS
SHIPPOS
SHIPPOUND
SHIPPOUNDS
SHIPS
SHIPSHAPE
SHIPSIDE*
SHIPSIDES*
SHIPWAY
SHIPWAYS
SHIPWORM
SHIPWORMS
SHIPWRECK
SHIPWRECKED
SHIPWRECKING
SHIPWRECKS
SHIPYARD
SHIPYARDS
SHIR
SHIRALEE
SHIRALEES
SHIRE
SHIREMAN
SHIREMEN
SHIRES
SHIRK
SHIRKED
SHIRKER
SHIRKERS
SHIRKING
SHIRKS
SHIRR
SHIRRA
SHIRRALEE

The Chambers Dictionary is the authority for many longer words; see Introduction, page ix

SHIRRALEES	SHIVES	SHOALS	SHOGI	SHOPFRONTS
SHIRRAS	SHIVOO	SHOALWISE	SHOGIS	SHOPFUL
SHIRRED	SHIVOOS	SHOALY	SHOGS	SHOPFULS
SHIRRING	SHIVS	SHOAT	SHOGUN	SHOPGIRL*
SHIRRINGS	SHIVVED	SHOATS	SHOGUNAL	SHOPGIRLS*
SHIRRS	SHIVVING	SHOCHET	SHOGUNATE	SHOPHAR
SHIRS	SHKOTZIM*	SHOCHETIM	SHOGUNATES	SHOPHARS
SHIRT	SHLEMIEHL*	SHOCK	SHOGUNS	SHOPHROTH
SHIRTBAND	SHLEMIEHLS*	SHOCKABLE	SHOJI	SHOPLIFT*
SHIRTBANDS	SHLEMIEL	SHOCKED	SHOJIS	SHOPLIFTED*
SHIRTED	SHLEMIELS	SHOCKER	SHOLA	SHOPLIFTING*
SHIRTIER	SHLEP	SHOCKERS	SHOLAS	SHOPLIFTS*
SHIRTIEST	SHLEPP*	SHOCKING	SHOLOM	SHOPMAN
SHIRTILY	SHLEPPED	SHOCKS	SHOLOMS*	SHOPMEN
SHIRTING	SHLEPPER	SHOD	SHONE	SHOPPE*
SHIRTINGS	SHLEPPERS	SHODDEN*	SHONEEN	SHOPPED
SHIRTLESS	SHLEPPING	SHODDIER	SHONEENS	SHOPPER
SHIRTS	SHLEPPS*	SHODDIES	SHONKIER	SHOPPERS
SHIRTTAIL*	SHLEPS	SHODDIEST	SHONKIEST	SHOPPES*
SHIRTTAILS*	SHLIMAZEL	SHODDILY	SHONKY	SHOPPIER
SHIRTY	SHLIMAZELS	SHODDY	SHOO	SHOPPIEST
SHIST*	SHLOCK	SHODER	SHOOED	SHOPPING
SHISTS*	SHLOCKS	SHODERS	SHOOFLIES	SHOPPINGS
SHIT	SHLUMP*	SHOE	SHOOFLY	SHOPPY
SHITAKE*	SHLUMPED*	SHOEBILL	SHOOGIE	SHOPS
SHITAKES*	SHLUMPING*	SHOEBILLS	SHOOGIED	SHOPTALK*
SHITE	SHLUMPS*	SHOEBLACK	SHOOGIEING	SHOPTALKS*
SHITED	SHLUMPY*	SHOEBLACKS	SHOOGIES	SHOPWORN
SHITES	SHMALTZ	SHOED	SHOOGLE	SHORAN
SHITHEAD	SHMALTZES	SHOEHORN	SHOOGLED	SHORANS
SHITHEADS	SHMALTZIER	SHOEHORNED	SHOOGLES	SHORE
SHITHOLE	SHMALTZIEST	SHOEHORNING	SHOOGLIER	SHOREBIRD
SHITHOLES	SHMALTZY	SHOEHORNS	SHOOGLIEST	SHOREBIRDS
SHITING	SHMEAR*	SHOEING	SHOOGLING	SHORED
SHITS	SHMEARS*	SHOEINGS	SHOOGLY	SHORELESS
SHITTAH	SHMEK	SHOELACE	SHOOING	SHORELINE
SHITTAHS	SHMEKS	SHOELACES	SHOOK	SHORELINES
SHITTED	SHMO	SHOELESS	SHOOKS	SHOREMAN
SHITTIER	SHMOCK	SHOEMAKER	SHOOL	SHOREMEN
SHITTIEST	SHMOCKS	SHOEMAKERS	SHOOLE	SHORER
SHITTIM	SHMOES	SHOEPAC*	SHOOLED	SHORERS
SHITTIMS	SHMOOSE	SHOEPACK*	SHOOLES	SHORES
SHITTING	SHMOOSED	SHOEPACKS*	SHOOLING	SHORESIDE*
SHITTY	SHMOOSES	SHOEPACS*	SHOOLS	SHORESMAN
SHIV	SHMOOSING	SHOER	SHOON	SHORESMEN
SHIVA*	SHMOOZE	SHOERS	SHOOS	SHOREWARD
SHIVAH	SHMOOZED	SHOES	SHOOT	SHOREWARDS
SHIVAHS	SHMOOZES	SHOESHINE	SHOOTABLE	SHOREWEED
SHIVAREE	SHMOOZING	SHOESHINES	SHOOTER	SHOREWEEDS
SHIVAREED*	SHMUCK	SHOETREE	SHOOTERS	SHORING
SHIVAREEING*	SHMUCKS	SHOETREES	SHOOTING	SHORINGS
SHIVAREES	SHNAPS*	SHOFAR	SHOOTINGS	SHORL*
SHIVAS*	SHNOOK*	SHOFARS	SHOOTIST	SHORLS*
SHIVE	SHNOOKS*	SHOFROTH	SHOOTISTS	SHORN
SHIVER	SHOAL	SHOG	SHOOTOUT*	SHORT
SHIVERED	SHOALED	SHOGGED	SHOOTOUTS*	SHORTAGE
SHIVERER	SHOALER	SHOGGING	SHOOTS	SHORTAGES
SHIVERERS	SHOALEST	SHOGGLE	SHOP	SHORTARM
SHIVERIER	SHOALIER	SHOGGLED	SHOPBOARD	SHORTCAKE
SHIVERIEST	SHOALIEST	SHOGGLES	SHOPBOARDS	SHORTCAKES
SHIVERING	SHOALING	SHOGGLIER	SHOPBOY*	SHORTCUT*
SHIVERINGS	SHOALINGS	SHOGGLIEST	SHOPBOYS*	SHORTCUTS*
SHIVERS	SHOALNESS	SHOGGLING	SHOPE	SHORTCUTTING*
SHIVERY	SHOALNESSES	SHOGGLY	SHOPFRONT	SHORTED

SHORTEN	SHOUGHS	SHOWERERS*	SHREWD	SHRINING
SHORTENED	SHOULD	SHOWERFUL	SHREWDER	SHRINK
SHORTENER	SHOULDER	SHOWERIER	SHREWDEST	SHRINKAGE
SHORTENERS	SHOULDERED	SHOWERIEST	SHREWDIE	SHRINKAGES
SHORTENING	SHOULDERING	SHOWERING	SHREWDIES	SHRINKER
SHORTENINGS	SHOULDERINGS	SHOWERINGS	SHREWDLY	SHRINKERS
SHORTENS	SHOULDERS	SHOWERS	SHREWED	SHRINKING
SHORTER	SHOULDEST	SHOWERY	SHREWING	SHRINKS
SHORTEST	SHOULDST	SHOWGHE	SHREWISH	SHRIS*
SHORTFALL	SHOUT	SHOWGHES	SHREWLIKE*	SHRITCH
SHORTFALLS	SHOUTED	SHOWGIRL	SHREWMICE	SHRITCHED
SHORTGOWN	SHOUTER	SHOWGIRLS	SHREWS	SHRITCHES
SHORTGOWNS	SHOUTERS	SHOWIER	SHRI*	SHRITCHING
SHORTHAIR*	SHOUTHER	SHOWIEST	SHRIECH	SHRIVE
SHORTHAIRS*	SHOUTHERED	SHOWILY	SHRIECHED	SHRIVED
SHORTHAND	SHOUTHERING	SHOWINESS	SHRIECHES	SHRIVEL
SHORTHANDS	SHOUTHERS	SHOWINESSES	SHRIECHING	SHRIVELED
SHORTHOLD	SHOUTING	SHOWING	SHRIEK	SHRIVELING
SHORTHORN	SHOUTINGS	SHOWINGS	SHRIEKED	SHRIVELLED
SHORTHORNS	SHOUTLINE	SHOWMAN	SHRIEKER	SHRIVELLING
SHORTIA*	SHOUTLINES	SHOWMANLY	SHRIEKERS	SHRIVELS
SHORTIAS*	SHOUTS	SHOWMEN	SHRIEKIER*	SHRIVEN
SHORTIE	SHOVE	SHOWN	SHRIEKIEST*	SHRIVER
SHORTIES	SHOVED	SHOWOFF*	SHRIEKING	SHRIVERS
SHORTING	SHOVEL	SHOWOFFS*	SHRIEKINGS	SHRIVES
SHORTISH	SHOVELED*	SHOWPIECE	SHRIEKS	SHRIVING
SHORTLIST*	SHOVELER	SHOWPIECES	SHRIEKY*	SHRIVINGS
SHORTLISTS*	SHOVELERS	SHOWPLACE	SHRIEVAL	SHROFF
SHORTLY	SHOVELFUL	SHOWPLACES	SHRIEVE	SHROFFAGE
SHORTNESS	SHOVELFULS	SHOWRING*	SHRIEVED	SHROFFAGES
SHORTNESSES	SHOVELING*	SHOWRINGS*	SHRIEVES	SHROFFED
SHORTS	SHOVELLED	SHOWROOM	SHRIEVING	SHROFFING
SHORTSTOP	SHOVELLER	SHOWROOMS	SHRIFT	SHROFFS
SHORTSTOPS	SHOVELLERS	SHOWS	SHRIFTS	SHROUD
SHORTWAVE*	SHOVELLING	SHOWY	SHRIGHT	SHROUDED
SHORTWAVES*	SHOVELS	SHOWYARD	SHRIGHTS	SHROUDIER
SHORTY	SHOVELSFUL*	SHOWYARDS	SHRIKE	SHROUDIEST
SHOT	SHOVER	SHOYU	SHRIKED	SHROUDING
SHOTE	SHOVERS	SHOYUS	SHRIKES	SHROUDINGS
SHOTES	SHOVES	SHRADDHA	SHRIKING	SHROUDS
SHOTFIRER	SHOVING	SHRADDHAS	SHRILL	SHROUDY
SHOTFIRERS	SHOW	SHRANK	SHRILLED	SHROVE
SHOTGUN	SHOWABLE*	SHRAPNEL	SHRILLER	SHROVED
SHOTGUNNED*	SHOWBIZ	SHRAPNELS	SHRILLEST	SHROVES
SHOTGUNNING*	SHOWBIZZES	SHRED	SHRILLIER	SHROVING
SHOTGUNS	SHOWBIZZY	SHREDDED	SHRILLIEST	SHROW
SHOTHOLE	SHOWBOAT	SHREDDER	SHRILLING	SHROWD
SHOTHOLES	SHOWBOATED	SHREDDERS	SHRILLINGS	SHROWED
SHOTMAKER	SHOWBOATING	SHREDDIER	SHRILLS	SHROWING
SHOTMAKERS	SHOWBOATS	SHREDDIEST	SHRILLY	SHROWS
SHOTPROOF	SHOWBOX	SHREDDING	SHRIMP	SHRUB
SHOTPUT	SHOWBOXES	SHREDDINGS	SHRIMPED	SHRUBBED
SHOTPUTS	SHOWBREAD	SHREDDY	SHRIMPER	SHRUBBERIES
SHOTS	SHOWBREADS	SHREDLESS	SHRIMPERS	SHRUBBERY
SHOTT	SHOWCASE	SHREDS	SHRIMPIER	SHRUBBIER
SHOTTE	SHOWCASED	SHREEK	SHRIMPIEST	SHRUBBIEST
SHOTTED	SHOWCASES	SHREEKED	SHRIMPING	SHRUBBING
SHOTTEN	SHOWCASING	SHREEKING	SHRIMPINGS	SHRUBBY
SHOTTES	SHOWDOWN	SHREEKS	SHRIMPS	SHRUBLESS
SHOTTING	SHOWDOWNS	SHREIK	SHRIMPY	SHRUBLIKE
SHOTTLE	SHOWED	SHREIKED	SHRINAL	SHRUBS
SHOTTLES	SHOWER	SHREIKING	SHRINE	SHRUG
SHOTTS	SHOWERED	SHREIKS	SHRINED	SHRUGGED
SHOUGH	SHOWERER*	SHREW	SHRINES	SHRUGGING

SHRUGS	SHUNNERS	SHYSTERS	SICILIANA	SIDDURIM
SHRUNK	SHUNNING	SI	SICILIANE	SIDDURS*
SHRUNKEN	SHUNPIKE*	SIAL	SICILIANO	SIDE
SHTCHI	SHUNPIKED*	SIALIC	SICILIANOS	SIDEARM
SHTCHIS	SHUNPIKER*	SIALID*	SICK	SIDEARMS
SHTETEL	SHUNPIKERS*	SIALIDAN*	SICKBAY*	SIDEBAND
SHTETELACH	SHUNPIKES*	SIALIDANS*	SICKBAYS*	SIDEBANDS
SHTETELS	SHUNPIKING*	SIALIDS*	SICKBED	SIDEBAR
SHTETL	SHUNS	SIALOGRAM	SICKBEDS	SIDEBARS
SHTETLACH	SHUNT	SIALOGRAMS	SICKED	SIDEBOARD
SHTETLS	SHUNTED	SIALOID	SICKEE*	SIDEBOARDS
SHTICK	SHUNTER	SIALOLITH	SICKEES*	SIDEBONES
SHTICKS	SHUNTERS	SIALOLITHS	SICKEN	SIDEBURNS
SHTIK*	SHUNTING	SIALON	SICKENED	SIDECAR
SHTIKS*	SHUNTINGS	SIALONS	SICKENER	SIDECARS
SHTOOK	SHUNTS	SIALS	SICKENERS	SIDED
SHTOOKS	SHURA	SIAMANG	SICKENING	SIDEDNESS*
SHTOOM	SHURAS	SIAMANGS	SICKENINGS	SIDEDNESSES*
SHTUCK	SHUSH	SIAMESE	SICKENS	SIDEDRESS*
SHTUCKS	SHUSHED	SIAMESED	SICKER	SIDEDRESSES*
SHTUM	SHUSHES	SIAMESES	SICKERLY	SIDEHILL*
SHTUMM	SHUSHING	SIAMESING	SICKEST	SIDEHILLS*
SHTUP	SHUT	SIAMEZE	SICKIE	SIDEKICK
SHTUPPED	SHUTDOWN	SIAMEZED	SICKIES	SIDEKICKS
SHTUPPING	SHUTDOWNS	SIAMEZES	SICKING	SIDELIGHT
SHTUPS	SHUTE	SIAMEZING	SICKISH	SIDELIGHTS
SHUBUNKIN	SHUTED*	SIB	SICKISHLY	SIDELINE
SHUBUNKINS	SHUTES	SIBB	SICKLE	SIDELINED
SHUCK	SHUTEYE*	SIBBS	SICKLED	SIDELINER*
SHUCKED	SHUTEYES*	SIBILANCE	SICKLEMAN	SIDELINERS*
SHUCKER	SHUTING*	SIBILANCES	SICKLEMEN	SIDELINES
SHUCKERS	SHUTOFF*	SIBILANCIES	SICKLEMIA	SIDELING
SHUCKING	SHUTOFFS*	SIBILANCY	SICKLEMIAS	SIDELINING
SHUCKINGS	SHUTOUT*	SIBILANT	SICKLES	SIDELOCK
SHUCKS	SHUTOUTS*	SIBILANTS	SICKLIED	SIDELOCKS
SHUDDER	SHUTS	SIBILATE	SICKLIER	SIDELONG
SHUDDERED	SHUTTER	SIBILATED	SICKLIES	SIDEMAN
SHUDDERING	SHUTTERED	SIBILATES	SICKLIEST	SIDEMEN
SHUDDERINGS	SHUTTERING	SIBILATING	SICKLILY	SIDENOTE
SHUDDERS	SHUTTERINGS	SIBILATOR	SICKLING*	SIDENOTES
SHUDDERY	SHUTTERS	SIBILATORS	SICKLY	SIDEPATH
SHUFFLE	SHUTTING	SIBILOUS	SICKLYING	SIDEPATHS
SHUFFLED	SHUTTLE	SIBLING	SICKNESS	SIDEPIECE*
SHUFFLER	SHUTTLED	SIBLINGS	SICKNESSES	SIDEPIECES*
SHUFFLERS	SHUTTLES	SIBS	SICKNURSE	SIDER
SHUFFLES	SHUTTLING	SIBSHIP	SICKNURSES	SIDERAL
SHUFFLING	SHWA	SIBSHIPS	SICKO	SIDERATE
SHUFFLINGS	SHWANPAN*	SIBYL	SICKOS	SIDERATED
SHUFTI	SHWANPANS*	SIBYLIC	SICKOUT*	SIDERATES
SHUFTIES	SHWAS	SIBYLLIC	SICKOUTS*	SIDERATING
SHUFTIS	SHY	SIBYLLINE	SICKROOM	SIDEREAL
SHUFTY	SHYER	SIBYLS	SICKROOMS	SIDERITE
SHUL	SHYERS	SIC	SICKS	SIDERITES
SHULE	SHYEST	SICCAN	SICLIKE	SIDERITIC
SHULED	SHYING	SICCAR	SICS	SIDEROAD
SHULES	SHYISH	SICCATIVE	SIDA	SIDEROADS
SHULING	SHYLOCK*	SICCATIVES	SIDALCEA	SIDEROSES
SHULN	SHYLOCKED*	SICCED	SIDALCEAS	SIDEROSIS
SHULS	SHYLOCKING*	SICCING	SIDAS	SIDERS
SHUN	SHYLOCKS*	SICCITIES	SIDDHA	SIDES
SHUNLESS	SHYLY	SICCITY	SIDDHAS	SIDESHOOT
SHUNNABLE	SHYNESS	SICE	SIDDHI	SIDESHOOTS
SHUNNED	SHYNESSES	SICES	SIDDHIS	SIDESHOW
SHUNNER	SHYSTER	SICH	SIDDUR	SIDESHOWS

Words marked with an asterisk are from OTCWL

SIDESLIP	SIEUR*	SIGILLATE	SIGNETING	SILDS
SIDESLIPPED	SIEURS*	SIGILS	SIGNETS	SILE
SIDESLIPPING	SIEVE	SIGISBEI	SIGNEUR	SILED
SIDESLIPS	SIEVED	SIGISBEO	SIGNEURIE	SILEN
SIDESMAN	SIEVERT	SIGLA	SIGNEURIES	SILENCE
SIDESMEN	SIEVERTS	SIGLOI*	SIGNIEUR	SILENCED
SIDESPIN*	SIEVES	SIGLOS*	SIGNIEURS	SILENCER
SIDESPINS*	SIEVING	SIGMA	SIGNIFICS	SILENCERS
SIDESTEP	SIFAKA	SIGMAS	SIGNIFIED	SILENCES
SIDESTEPPED	SIFAKAS	SIGMATE	SIGNIFIEDS*	SILENCING
SIDESTEPPING	SIFFLE	SIGMATED	SIGNIFIER	SILENE
SIDESTEPS	SIFFLED	SIGMATES	SIGNIFIERS	SILENES
SIDESWIPE	SIFFLES	SIGMATIC	SIGNIFIES	SILENI
SIDESWIPED	SIFFLEUR	SIGMATING	SIGNIFY	SILENS
SIDESWIPES	SIFFLEURS	SIGMATION	SIGNIFYING	SILENT
SIDESWIPING	SIFFLEUSE	SIGMATIONS	SIGNING	SILENTER
SIDETRACK	SIFFLEUSES	SIGMATISM	SIGNINGS	SILENTEST
SIDETRACKED	SIFFLING	SIGMATISMS	SIGNIOR	SILENTLY
SIDETRACKING	SIFT	SIGMATRON	SIGNIORI*	SILENTS
SIDETRACKS	SIFTED	SIGMATRONS	SIGNIORIES*	SILENUS
SIDEWALK	SIFTER	SIGMOID	SIGNIORS	SILER
SIDEWALKS	SIFTERS	SIGMOIDAL	SIGNIORY*	SILERS
SIDEWALL	SIFTING	SIGMOIDS*	SIGNLESS	SILES
SIDEWALLS	SIFTINGLY	SIGN	SIGNOR	SILESIA
SIDEWARD	SIFTINGS	SIGNAGE	SIGNORA	SILESIAS
SIDEWARDS	SIFTS	SIGNAGES	SIGNORAS*	SILEX
SIDEWAY*	SIGANID*	SIGNAL	SIGNORE	SILEXES
SIDEWAYS	SIGANIDS*	SIGNALED	SIGNORES	SILICA
SIDEWISE	SIGH	SIGNALER	SIGNORI	SILICAS
SIDHA	SIGHED	SIGNALERS	SIGNORIA	SILICATE
SIDHAS	SIGHER	SIGNALING	SIGNORIAL	SILICATED
SIDING	SIGHERS	SIGNALINGS	SIGNORIAS	SILICATES
SIDINGS	SIGHFUL	SIGNALISE	SIGNORIES	SILICATING
SIDLE	SIGHING	SIGNALISED	SIGNORINA	SILICEOUS
SIDLED	SIGHINGLY	SIGNALISES	SIGNORINAS*	SILICIC
SIDLER*	SIGHLESS*	SIGNALISING	SIGNORINE	SILICIDE
SIDLERS*	SIGHLIKE*	SIGNALIZE	SIGNORINI	SILICIDES
SIDLES	SIGHS	SIGNALIZED	SIGNORINO	SILICIFIED
SIDLING	SIGHT	SIGNALIZES	SIGNORS	SILICIFIES
SIEGE	SIGHTABLE	SIGNALIZING	SIGNORY	SILICIFY
SIEGED	SIGHTED	SIGNALLED	SIGNPOST	SILICIFYING
SIEGER	SIGHTER	SIGNALLER	SIGNPOSTED	SILICIOUS
SIEGERS	SIGHTERS	SIGNALLERS	SIGNPOSTING	SILICIUM
SIEGES	SIGHTING	SIGNALLING	SIGNPOSTS	SILICIUMS
SIEGING	SIGHTINGS	SIGNALLINGS	SIGNS	SILICLE
SIELD	SIGHTLESS	SIGNALLY	SIJO	SILICLES
SIEMENS	SIGHTLIER	SIGNALMAN	SIJOS	SILICON
SIEN	SIGHTLIEST	SIGNALMEN	SIKA	SILICONE
SIENITE*	SIGHTLINE	SIGNALS	SIKAS	SILICONES
SIENITES*	SIGHTLINES	SIGNARIES	SIKE	SILICONS
SIENNA	SIGHTLY	SIGNARY	SIKER*	SILICOSES
SIENNAS	SIGHTS	SIGNATORIES	SIKES	SILICOSIS
SIENS	SIGHTSAW	SIGNATORY	SIKORSKIES	SILICOTIC
SIENT	SIGHTSEE	SIGNATURE	SIKORSKY	SILICOTICS
SIENTS	SIGHTSEEING	SIGNATURES	SILAGE	SILICULA
SIEROZEM*	SIGHTSEEINGS	SIGNBOARD	SILAGED	SILICULAE*
SIEROZEMS*	SIGHTSEEN	SIGNBOARDS	SILAGEING	SILICULAS
SIERRA	SIGHTSEER	SIGNED	SILAGES	SILICULE
SIERRAN	SIGHTSEERS	SIGNEE*	SILAGING	SILICULES
SIERRAS	SIGHTSEES	SIGNEES*	SILANE	SILING
SIESTA	SIGHTSMAN	SIGNER	SILANES	SILIQUA
SIESTAS	SIGHTSMEN	SIGNERS	SILASTIC	SILIQUAE*
SIETH	SIGIL	SIGNET	SILASTICS	SILIQUAS
SIETHS	SIGILLARY	SIGNETED	SILD	SILIQUE

SILIQUES	SILTS	SIMILISING	SIMPLEXES*	SINE
SILIQUOSE	SILTSTONE	SIMILIZE	SIMPLICES	SINECURE
SILK	SILTSTONES	SIMILIZED	SIMPLICIA*	SINECURES
SILKALINE*	SILTY	SIMILIZES	SIMPLIFIED	SINED
SILKALINES*	SILURID	SIMILIZING	SIMPLIFIES	SINES
SILKED	SILURIDS	SIMILOR	SIMPLIFY	SINEW
SILKEN	SILURIST	SIMILORS	SIMPLIFYING	SINEWED
SILKENED	SILURISTS	SIMIOID*	SIMPLING	SINEWIER
SILKENING	SILUROID	SIMIOUS	SIMPLINGS	SINEWIEST
SILKENS	SILUROIDS*	SIMIS	SIMPLISM	SINEWING
SILKIE	SILVA	SIMITAR	SIMPLISMS	SINEWLESS
SILKIER	SILVAE	SIMITARS	SIMPLIST	SINEWS
SILKIES	SILVAN	SIMKIN	SIMPLISTE	SINEWY
SILKIEST	SILVANS	SIMKINS	SIMPLISTS	SINFONIA
SILKILY	SILVAS	SIMLIN*	SIMPLY	SINFONIAS
SILKINESS	SILVATIC	SIMLINS*	SIMPS	SINFONIE*
SILKINESSES	SILVER	SIMMER	SIMS	SINFUL
SILKING	SILVERED	SIMMERED	SIMUL	SINFULLY
SILKLIKE*	SILVERER*	SIMMERING	SIMULACRA	SING
SILKOLINE*	SILVERERS*	SIMMERS	SIMULACRE	SINGABLE
SILKOLINES*	SILVERIER	SIMNEL	SIMULACRES	SINGALONG
SILKS	SILVERIEST	SIMNELS	SIMULACRUM*	SINGALONGS
SILKTAIL	SILVERING	SIMOLEON*	SIMULACRUMS*	SINGE
SILKTAILS	SILVERINGS	SIMOLEONS*	SIMULANT	SINGED
SILKWEED	SILVERISE	SIMONIAC	SIMULANTS	SINGEING
SILKWEEDS	SILVERISED	SIMONIACS	SIMULAR	SINGER
SILKWORM	SILVERISES	SIMONIES	SIMULARS	SINGERS
SILKWORMS	SILVERISING	SIMONIOUS	SIMULATE	SINGES
SILKY	SILVERIZE	SIMONIST	SIMULATED	SINGING
SILL	SILVERIZED	SIMONISTS	SIMULATES	SINGINGLY
SILLABUB	SILVERIZES	SIMONIZE*	SIMULATING	SINGINGS
SILLABUBS	SILVERIZING	SIMONIZED*	SIMULATOR	SINGLE
SILLADAR	SILVERLY	SIMONIZES*	SIMULATORS	SINGLED
SILLADARS	SILVERN	SIMONIZING*	SIMULCAST	SINGLES
SILLER	SILVERS	SIMONY	SIMULCASTED	SINGLET
SILLERS	SILVERY	SIMOOM	SIMULCASTING	SINGLETON
SILLIBUB*	SILVEX*	SIMOOMS	SIMULCASTS	SINGLETONS
SILLIBUBS*	SILVEXES*	SIMOON	SIMULIUM	SINGLETS
SILLIER	SILVICAL*	SIMOONS	SIMULIUMS	SINGLING
SILLIES	SILVICS*	SIMORG	SIMULS	SINGLINGS
SILLIEST	SIM	SIMORGS	SIMURG	SINGLY
SILLILY	SIMA	SIMP	SIMURGH	SINGS
SILLINESS	SIMAR	SIMPAI	SIMURGHS	SINGSONG
SILLINESSES	SIMAROUBA	SIMPAIS	SIMURGS	SINGSONGED
SILLOCK	SIMAROUBAS	SIMPATICO	SIN	SINGSONGING
SILLOCKS	SIMARRE	SIMPER	SINAPISM	SINGSONGS
SILLS	SIMARRES	SIMPERED	SINAPISMS	SINGSONGY*
SILLY	SIMARS	SIMPERER	SINCE	SINGSPIEL
SILO	SIMARUBA	SIMPERERS	SINCERE	SINGSPIELS
SILOED	SIMARUBAS	SIMPERING	SINCERELY	SINGULAR
SILOING	SIMAS	SIMPERS	SINCERER	SINGULARS
SILOS	SIMAZINE	SIMPKIN	SINCEREST	SINGULT
SILOXANE*	SIMAZINES	SIMPKINS	SINCERITIES	SINGULTS
SILOXANES*	SIMI	SIMPLE	SINCERITY	SINGULTUS
SILPHIA	SIMIAL	SIMPLED	SINCIPITA	SINGULTUSES
SILPHIUM	SIMIAN	SIMPLER	SINCIPUT	SINH*
SILPHIUMS	SIMIANS	SIMPLERS	SINCIPUTS	SINHS*
SILT	SIMILAR	SIMPLES	SIND	SINICAL
SILTATION	SIMILARLY	SIMPLESSE	SINDED	SINICISE
SILTATIONS	SIMILE	SIMPLESSES	SINDING	SINICISED
SILTED	SIMILES	SIMPLEST	SINDINGS	SINICISES
SILTIER	SIMILISE	SIMPLETON	SINDON	SINICISING
SILTIEST	SIMILISED	SIMPLETONS	SINDONS	SINICIZE
SILTING	SIMILISES	SIMPLEX	SINDS	SINICIZED

SINICIZES
SINICIZING
SINING
SINISTER
SINISTRAL
SINISTRALS
SINK
SINKABLE*
SINKAGE
SINKAGES
SINKER
SINKERS
SINKHOLE
SINKHOLES
SINKIER
SINKIEST
SINKING
SINKINGS
SINKS
SINKY
SINLESS
SINLESSLY
SINNED
SINNER
SINNERED
SINNERING
SINNERS
SINNET
SINNETS
SINNING
SINNINGIA
SINNINGIAS
SINOLOGIES*
SINOLOGUE*
SINOLOGUES*
SINOLOGY*
SINOPIA
SINOPIAS
SINOPIE*
SINOPIS
SINOPISES
SINOPITE
SINOPITES
SINS
SINSYNE
SINTER
SINTERED
SINTERING
SINTERS
SINTERY
SINUATE
SINUATED
SINUATELY
SINUATES*
SINUATING*
SINUATION
SINUATIONS
SINUITIS
SINUITISES
SINUOSE
SINUOSITIES
SINUOSITY
SINUOUS
SINUOUSLY

SINUS
SINUSES
SINUSITIS
SINUSITISES
SINUSOID
SINUSOIDS
SIP
SIPE
SIPED
SIPES
SIPHON
SIPHONAGE
SIPHONAGES
SIPHONAL
SIPHONATE
SIPHONED
SIPHONET
SIPHONETS
SIPHONIC
SIPHONING
SIPHONS
SIPHUNCLE
SIPHUNCLES
SIPING
SIPPED
SIPPER
SIPPERS
SIPPET
SIPPETS
SIPPING
SIPPLE
SIPPLED
SIPPLES
SIPPLING
SIPS
SIR
SIRCAR
SIRCARS
SIRDAR
SIRDARS
SIRE
SIRED
SIREE*
SIREES*
SIREN
SIRENIAN
SIRENIANS
SIRENIC
SIRENISE
SIRENISED
SIRENISES
SIRENISING
SIRENIZE
SIRENIZED
SIRENIZES
SIRENIZING
SIRENS
SIRES
SIRGANG
SIRGANGS
SIRI
SIRIASES
SIRIASIS
SIRIH

SIRIHS
SIRING
SIRIS
SIRKAR
SIRKARS
SIRLOIN
SIRLOINS
SIRNAME
SIRNAMED
SIRNAMES
SIRNAMING
SIROC
SIROCCO
SIROCCOS
SIROCS
SIRRA*
SIRRAH
SIRRAHS
SIRRAS*
SIRRED
SIRREE
SIRREES
SIRRING
SIRS
SIRUP
SIRUPED
SIRUPING
SIRUPS
SIRUPY*
SIRVENTE
SIRVENTES
SIS
SISAL
SISALS
SISERARIES
SISERARY
SISES
SISKIN
SISKINS
SISS
SISSERARIES
SISSERARY
SISSES
SISSIER
SISSIES
SISSIEST
SISSIFIED
SISSOO
SISSOOS
SISSY
SISSYISH*
SIST
SISTED
SISTER
SISTERED
SISTERING
SISTERLY
SISTERS
SISTING
SISTRA
SISTROID*
SISTRUM
SISTRUMS*
SISTS

SIT
SITAR
SITARIST*
SITARISTS*
SITARS
SITATUNGA
SITATUNGAS
SITCOM
SITCOMS
SITE
SITED
SITES
SITFAST
SITFASTS
SITH
SITHE
SITHED
SITHEN
SITHENCE
SITHENS
SITHES
SITHING
SITING
SITIOLOGIES
SITIOLOGY
SITOLOGIES
SITOLOGY
SITREP
SITREPS
SITS
SITTAR
SITTARS
SITTEN*
SITTER
SITTERS
SITTINE
SITTING
SITTINGS
SITUATE
SITUATED
SITUATES
SITUATING
SITUATION
SITUATIONS
SITULA
SITULAE
SITUP*
SITUPS*
SITUS
SITUSES*
SITUTUNGA
SITUTUNGAS
SITZKRIEG
SITZKRIEGS
SITZMARK*
SITZMARKS*
SIVER
SIVERS
SIWASH
SIWASHES
SIX
SIXAIN
SIXAINE
SIXAINES

SIXAINS
SIXER
SIXERS
SIXES
SIXFOLD
SIXMO*
SIXMOS*
SIXPENCE
SIXPENCES
SIXPENNIES
SIXPENNY
SIXSCORE
SIXSCORES
SIXTE
SIXTEEN
SIXTEENER
SIXTEENERS
SIXTEENMO
SIXTEENMOS
SIXTEENS
SIXTEENTH
SIXTEENTHS
SIXTES
SIXTH
SIXTHLY
SIXTHS
SIXTIES
SIXTIETH
SIXTIETHS
SIXTY
SIXTYISH*
SIZABLE
SIZABLY*
SIZAR
SIZARS
SIZARSHIP
SIZARSHIPS
SIZE
SIZEABLE
SIZEABLY*
SIZED
SIZEISM
SIZEISMS
SIZEIST
SIZEISTS
SIZEL
SIZELS
SIZER
SIZERS
SIZES
SIZIER
SIZIEST
SIZINESS
SIZINESSES
SIZING
SIZINGS
SIZISM
SIZISMS
SIZIST
SIZISTS
SIZY
SIZZLE
SIZZLED
SIZZLER

SIZZLERS	SKEARS	SKELLY	SKI	SKILL
SIZZLES	SKEARY	SKELLYING	SKIABLE	SKILLED
SIZZLING	SKEDADDLE	SKELM	SKIAGRAM	SKILLESS
SIZZLINGS	SKEDADDLED	SKELMS	SKIAGRAMS	SKILLET
SJAMBOK	SKEDADDLES	SKELP	SKIAGRAPH	SKILLETS
SJAMBOKED*	SKEDADDLING	SKELPED	SKIAGRAPHS	SKILLFUL
SJAMBOKING*	SKEE*	SKELPING	SKIAMACHIES	SKILLIER
SJAMBOKKED	SKEECHAN	SKELPINGS	SKIAMACHY	SKILLIES
SJAMBOKKING	SKEECHANS	SKELPIT*	SKIASCOPIES	SKILLIEST
SJAMBOKS	SKEED*	SKELPS	SKIASCOPY	SKILLING
SKA	SKEEING*	SKELTER	SKIATRON	SKILLINGS
SKAG	SKEELIER	SKELTERED	SKIATRONS	SKILLION
SKAGS	SKEELIEST	SKELTERING	SKIBOB	SKILLIONS
SKAIL	SKEELY	SKELTERS	SKIBOBBED	SKILLS
SKAILED	SKEEN*	SKELUM	SKIBOBBER*	SKILLY
SKAILING	SKEENS*	SKELUMS	SKIBOBBERS*	SKIM
SKAILS	SKEER	SKENE	SKIBOBBING	SKIMMED
SKAITH	SKEERED	SKENES	SKIBOBBINGS	SKIMMER
SKAITHED	SKEERIER	SKEO	SKIBOBS	SKIMMERS
SKAITHING	SKEERIEST	SKEOS	SKID	SKIMMIA
SKAITHS	SKEERING	SKEP	SKIDDED	SKIMMIAS
SKALD	SKEERS	SKEPFUL	SKIDDER	SKIMMING
SKALDIC	SKEERY	SKEPFULS	SKIDDERS	SKIMMINGS
SKALDS	SKEES*	SKEPPED	SKIDDIER*	SKIMO*
SKALDSHIP	SKEESICKS	SKEPPING	SKIDDIEST*	SKIMOBILE*
SKALDSHIPS	SKEET	SKEPS	SKIDDING	SKIMOBILES*
SKANK	SKEETER	SKEPSIS	SKIDDOO*	SKIMOS*
SKANKED	SKEETERS	SKEPSISES	SKIDDOOED*	SKIMP
SKANKING	SKEETS	SKEPTIC	SKIDDOOING*	SKIMPED
SKANKINGS	SKEG	SKEPTICAL	SKIDDOOS*	SKIMPIER
SKANKS	SKEGG	SKEPTICS	SKIDDY*	SKIMPIEST
SKART	SKEGGER	SKER	SKIDOO	SKIMPILY
SKARTH	SKEGGERS	SKERRED	SKIDOOED*	SKIMPING
SKARTHS	SKEGGS	SKERRICK	SKIDOOING*	SKIMPS
SKARTS	SKEGS	SKERRICKS	SKIDOOS	SKIMPY
SKAS	SKEIGH	SKERRIES	SKIDPAN	SKIMS
SKAT	SKEIGHER	SKERRING	SKIDPANS	SKIN
SKATE	SKEIGHEST	SKERRY	SKIDPROOF	SKINCARE
SKATED	SKEIN	SKERS	SKIDS	SKINCARES
SKATEPARK	SKEINED*	SKETCH	SKIDWAY*	SKINFLICK
SKATEPARKS	SKEINING*	SKETCHED	SKIDWAYS*	SKINFLICKS
SKATER	SKEINS	SKETCHER	SKIED	SKINFLINT
SKATERS	SKELDER	SKETCHERS	SKIER	SKINFLINTS
SKATES	SKELDERED	SKETCHES	SKIERS	SKINFOOD
SKATING	SKELDERING	SKETCHIER	SKIES	SKINFOODS
SKATINGS	SKELDERS	SKETCHIEST	SKIEY	SKINFUL
SKATOL*	SKELETAL	SKETCHILY	SKIEYER	SKINFULS
SKATOLE	SKELETON	SKETCHING	SKIEYEST	SKINHEAD
SKATOLES	SKELETONS	SKETCHY	SKIFF	SKINHEADS
SKATOLS*	SKELF	SKEW	SKIFFED	SKINK
SKATS	SKELFS	SKEWBACK	SKIFFING	SKINKED
SKATT	SKELL	SKEWBACKS	SKIFFLE	SKINKER
SKATTS	SKELLIE	SKEWBALD	SKIFFLED*	SKINKERS
SKAW	SKELLIED	SKEWBALDS	SKIFFLES	SKINKING
SKAWS	SKELLIER	SKEWED	SKIFFLING*	SKINKS
SKEAN	SKELLIES	SKEWER	SKIFFS	SKINLESS
SKEANE*	SKELLIEST	SKEWERED	SKIING	SKINLIKE*
SKEANES*	SKELLOCH	SKEWERING	SKIINGS	SKINNED
SKEANS	SKELLOCHED	SKEWERS	SKIJORER*	SKINNER
SKEAR	SKELLOCHING	SKEWEST	SKIJORERS*	SKINNERS
SKEARED	SKELLOCHS	SKEWING	SKIJORING	SKINNIER
SKEARIER	SKELLS	SKEWNESS	SKIJORINGS	SKINNIEST
SKEARIEST	SKELLUM	SKEWNESSES	SKILFUL	SKINNING
SKEARING	SKELLUMS	SKEWS	SKILFULLY	SKINNY

Words marked with an asterisk are from OTCWL

SKINS	SKITTERING	SKRANS	SKUMMERS	SKYPHOI*
SKINT	SKITTERS	SKREEGH*	SKUNK	SKYPHOS*
SKINTER	SKITTERY*	SKREEGHED*	SKUNKBIRD	SKYR
SKINTEST	SKITTISH	SKREEGHING*	SKUNKBIRDS	SKYRE
SKINTIGHT*	SKITTLE	SKREEGHS*	SKUNKED	SKYRED
SKIO	SKITTLED	SKREEN	SKUNKING	SKYRES
SKIORING*	SKITTLES	SKREENS	SKUNKS	SKYRING
SKIORINGS*	SKITTLING	SKREIGH	SKURRIED	SKYROCKET
SKIOS	SKIVE	SKREIGHED	SKURRIES	SKYROCKETED
SKIP	SKIVED	SKREIGHING	SKURRY	SKYROCKETING
SKIPJACK	SKIVER	SKREIGHS	SKURRYING	SKYROCKETS
SKIPJACKS	SKIVERED	SKRIECH	SKUTTLE	SKYRS
SKIPLANE*	SKIVERING	SKRIECHED	SKUTTLED	SKYSAIL
SKIPLANES*	SKIVERS	SKRIECHING	SKUTTLES	SKYSAILS
SKIPPABLE*	SKIVES	SKRIECHS	SKUTTLING	SKYSCAPE
SKIPPED	SKIVIE	SKRIED	SKY	SKYSCAPES
SKIPPER	SKIVIER	SKRIEGH	SKYBORN	SKYTE
SKIPPERED	SKIVIEST	SKRIEGHED	SKYBORNE*	SKYTED
SKIPPERING	SKIVING	SKRIEGHING	SKYBOX*	SKYTES
SKIPPERINGS	SKIVINGS	SKRIEGHS	SKYBOXES*	SKYTING
SKIPPERS	SKIVVIED	SKRIES	SKYCAP*	SKYWALK*
SKIPPET	SKIVVIES	SKRIK	SKYCAPS*	SKYWALKS*
SKIPPETS	SKIVVY	SKRIKS	SKYCLAD	SKYWARD
SKIPPIER	SKIVVYING	SKRIMMAGE	SKYDIVE*	SKYWARDS
SKIPPIEST	SKIVY	SKRIMMAGED	SKYDIVED*	SKYWAY
SKIPPING	SKIWEAR*	SKRIMMAGES	SKYDIVER	SKYWAYS
SKIPPINGS	SKLATE	SKRIMMAGING	SKYDIVERS	SKYWRITE*
SKIPPY	SKLATED	SKRIMP	SKYDIVES*	SKYWRITER*
SKIPS	SKLATES	SKRIMPED	SKYDIVING*	SKYWRITERS*
SKIRL	SKLATING	SKRIMPING	SKYDIVINGS*	SKYWRITES*
SKIRLED	SKLENT	SKRIMPS	SKYDOVE*	SKYWRITING*
SKIRLING	SKLENTED	SKRUMP	SKYED*	SKYWRITTEN*
SKIRLINGS	SKLENTING	SKRUMPED	SKYER	SKYWROTE*
SKIRLS	SKLENTS	SKRUMPING	SKYERS	SLAB
SKIRMISH	SKLIFF	SKRUMPS	SKYEY	SLABBED
SKIRMISHED	SKLIFFS	SKRY	SKYHOOK	SLABBER
SKIRMISHES	SKLIM	SKRYER	SKYHOOKS	SLABBERED
SKIRMISHING	SKLIMMED	SKRYERS	SKYIER	SLABBERER
SKIRMISHINGS	SKLIMMING	SKRYING	SKYIEST	SLABBERERS
SKIRR	SKLIMS	SKUA	SKYING	SLABBERING
SKIRRED	SKOAL	SKUAS	SKYISH	SLABBERS
SKIRRET	SKOALED*	SKUDLER	SKYJACK	SLABBERY
SKIRRETS	SKOALING*	SKUDLERS	SKYJACKED	SLABBIER
SKIRRING	SKOALS*	SKUG	SKYJACKER	SLABBIEST
SKIRRS	SKOFF	SKUGGED	SKYJACKERS	SLABBING
SKIRT	SKOFFED	SKUGGING	SKYJACKING	SLABBY
SKIRTED	SKOFFING	SKUGS	SKYJACKINGS	SLABLIKE*
SKIRTER	SKOFFS	SKULK	SKYJACKS	SLABS
SKIRTERS	SKOKIAAN	SKULKED	SKYLAB	SLABSTONE
SKIRTING	SKOKIAANS	SKULKER	SKYLABS	SLABSTONES
SKIRTINGS	SKOL	SKULKERS	SKYLARK	SLACK
SKIRTLESS	SKOLIA	SKULKING	SKYLARKED	SLACKED
SKIRTS	SKOLION	SKULKINGS	SKYLARKER	SLACKEN
SKIS	SKOLLIE	SKULKS	SKYLARKERS	SLACKENED
SKIT	SKOLLIES	SKULL	SKYLARKING	SLACKENING
SKITE	SKOLLY	SKULLCAP	SKYLARKINGS	SLACKENINGS
SKITED	SKOOKUM*	SKULLCAPS	SKYLARKS	SLACKENS
SKITES	SKOOSH	SKULLED*	SKYLIGHT	SLACKER
SKITING	SKOOSHED	SKULLS	SKYLIGHTS	SLACKERS
SKITS	SKOOSHES	SKULPIN	SKYLINE	SLACKEST
SKITTER	SKOOSHING	SKULPINS	SKYLINES	SLACKING
SKITTERED	SKOSH*	SKUMMER	SKYLIT*	SLACKLY
SKITTERIER*	SKOSHES*	SKUMMERED	SKYMAN	SLACKNESS
SKITTERIEST*	SKRAN	SKUMMERING	SKYMEN	SLACKNESSES

The Chambers Dictionary is the authority for many longer words; see Introduction, page ix

SLACKS	SLANGINGS	SLATTER	SLEDGES	SLEEVED
SLADANG	SLANGISH	SLATTERED	SLEDGING	SLEEVEEN
SLADANGS	SLANGS	SLATTERING	SLEDGINGS	SLEEVEENS
SLADE	SLANGUAGE*	SLATTERN	SLEDS	SLEEVELET*
SLADES	SLANGUAGES*	SLATTERNS	SLEE	SLEEVELETS*
SLAE	SLANGULAR	SLATTERS	SLEECH	SLEEVER
SLAES	SLANGY	SLATTERY	SLEECHES	SLEEVERS
SLAG	SLANK*	SLATTING	SLEECHIER	SLEEVES
SLAGGED	SLANT	SLATTINGS*	SLEECHIEST	SLEEVING
SLAGGIER	SLANTED	SLATY	SLEECHY	SLEEVINGS
SLAGGIEST	SLANTING	SLAUGHTER	SLEEK	SLEEZIER
SLAGGING	SLANTLY	SLAUGHTERED	SLEEKED	SLEEZIEST
SLAGGY	SLANTS	SLAUGHTERING	SLEEKEN	SLEEZY
SLAGS	SLANTWAYS	SLAUGHTERS	SLEEKENED	SLEIDED
SLAID	SLANTWISE	SLAVE	SLEEKENING	SLEIGH
SLAIN	SLANTY*	SLAVED	SLEEKENS	SLEIGHED
SLAINTE	SLAP	SLAVER	SLEEKER	SLEIGHER
SLAIRG	SLAPDASH*	SLAVERED	SLEEKERS	SLEIGHERS
SLAIRGED	SLAPDASHES*	SLAVERER	SLEEKEST	SLEIGHING
SLAIRGING	SLAPHAPPIER*	SLAVERERS	SLEEKIER	SLEIGHINGS
SLAIRGS	SLAPHAPPIEST*	SLAVERIES	SLEEKIEST	SLEIGHS
SLAISTER	SLAPHAPPY*	SLAVERING	SLEEKING	SLEIGHT
SLAISTERED	SLAPHEAD	SLAVERS	SLEEKINGS	SLEIGHTS
SLAISTERIES	SLAPHEADS	SLAVERY	SLEEKIT	SLENDER
SLAISTERING	SLAPJACK	SLAVES	SLEEKLY	SLENDERER
SLAISTERS	SLAPJACKS	SLAVEY	SLEEKNESS	SLENDEREST
SLAISTERY	SLAPPED	SLAVEYS	SLEEKNESSES	SLENDERLY
SLAKABLE*	SLAPPER	SLAVING	SLEEKS	SLENTER
SLAKE	SLAPPERS	SLAVISH	SLEEKY	SLENTERS
SLAKED	SLAPPING	SLAVISHLY	SLEEP	SLEPT
SLAKELESS	SLAPS	SLAVOCRAT	SLEEPER	SLEUTH
SLAKER*	SLAPSHOT	SLAVOCRATS	SLEEPERS	SLEUTHED
SLAKERS*	SLAPSHOTS	SLAW	SLEEPERY	SLEUTHING
SLAKES	SLAPSTICK	SLAWS	SLEEPIER	SLEUTHS
SLAKING	SLAPSTICKS	SLAY	SLEEPIEST	SLEW
SLALOM	SLASH	SLAYED	SLEEPILY	SLEWED
SLALOMED	SLASHED	SLAYER	SLEEPING	SLEWING
SLALOMING	SLASHER	SLAYERS	SLEEPINGS	SLEWS
SLALOMS	SLASHERS	SLAYING	SLEEPLESS	SLEY
SLAM	SLASHES	SLAYS	SLEEPLIKE*	SLEYS
SLAMMAKIN	SLASHING	SLEAVE	SLEEPOUT	SLICE
SLAMMAKINS	SLASHINGS	SLEAVED	SLEEPOUTS	SLICEABLE*
SLAMMED	SLAT	SLEAVES	SLEEPOVER	SLICED
SLAMMER	SLATCH	SLEAVING	SLEEPOVERS	SLICER
SLAMMERS	SLATCHES	SLEAZE	SLEEPRY	SLICERS
SLAMMING	SLATE	SLEAZEBAG	SLEEPS	SLICES
SLAMMINGS	SLATED	SLEAZEBAGS	SLEEPSUIT	SLICING
SLAMS	SLATELIKE*	SLEAZES	SLEEPSUITS	SLICINGS
SLANDER	SLATER	SLEAZIER	SLEEPWALK*	SLICK
SLANDERED	SLATERS	SLEAZIEST	SLEEPWALKED*	SLICKED
SLANDERER	SLATES	SLEAZILY	SLEEPWALKING*	SLICKEN
SLANDERERS	SLATEY*	SLEAZO*	SLEEPWALKS*	SLICKENED
SLANDERING	SLATHER	SLEAZY	SLEEPWEAR*	SLICKENING
SLANDERS	SLATHERED	SLED	SLEEPY	SLICKENS
SLANE	SLATHERING	SLEDDED	SLEER	SLICKER
SLANES	SLATHERS	SLEDDER*	SLEEST	SLICKERED
SLANG	SLATIER	SLEDDERS*	SLEET	SLICKERS
SLANGED	SLATIEST	SLEDDING	SLEETED	SLICKEST
SLANGER	SLATINESS	SLEDDINGS	SLEETIER	SLICKING
SLANGERS	SLATINESSES	SLEDED	SLEETIEST	SLICKINGS
SLANGIER	SLATING	SLEDGE	SLEETING	SLICKLY
SLANGIEST	SLATINGS	SLEDGED	SLEETS	SLICKNESS
SLANGILY	SLATS	SLEDGER	SLEETY	SLICKNESSES
SLANGING	SLATTED	SLEDGERS	SLEEVE	SLICKROCK*

SLICKROCKS*
SLICKS
SLID
SLIDABLE*
SLIDDEN
SLIDDER
SLIDDERED
SLIDDERING
SLIDDERS
SLIDDERY
SLIDE
SLIDED
SLIDER
SLIDERS
SLIDES
SLIDEWAY*
SLIDEWAYS*
SLIDING
SLIDINGLY
SLIDINGS
SLIER
SLIEST
SLIGHT
SLIGHTED
SLIGHTER
SLIGHTEST
SLIGHTING
SLIGHTISH
SLIGHTLY
SLIGHTS
SLILY
SLIM
SLIME
SLIMEBALL
SLIMEBALLS
SLIMED
SLIMES
SLIMIER
SLIMIEST
SLIMILY
SLIMINESS
SLIMINESSES
SLIMING
SLIMLINE
SLIMLY
SLIMMED
SLIMMER
SLIMMERS
SLIMMEST
SLIMMING
SLIMMINGS
SLIMMISH
SLIMNESS
SLIMNESSES
SLIMPSIER*
SLIMPSIEST*
SLIMPSY*
SLIMS
SLIMSIER
SLIMSIEST
SLIMSY
SLIMY
SLING
SLINGBACK

SLINGBACKS
SLINGER
SLINGERS
SLINGING
SLINGS
SLINGSHOT
SLINGSHOTS
SLINK
SLINKED*
SLINKER
SLINKERS
SLINKIER
SLINKIEST
SLINKILY*
SLINKING
SLINKS
SLINKSKIN
SLINKSKINS
SLINKWEED
SLINKWEEDS
SLINKY
SLINTER
SLINTERS
SLIP
SLIPCASE
SLIPCASED*
SLIPCASES
SLIPCOVER*
SLIPCOVERS*
SLIPE
SLIPED*
SLIPES
SLIPFORM
SLIPFORMED*
SLIPFORMING*
SLIPFORMS*
SLIPING*
SLIPKNOT
SLIPKNOTS
SLIPLESS*
SLIPOUT*
SLIPOUTS*
SLIPOVER*
SLIPOVERS*
SLIPPAGE
SLIPPAGES
SLIPPED
SLIPPER
SLIPPERED
SLIPPERIER
SLIPPERIEST
SLIPPERING
SLIPPERS
SLIPPERY
SLIPPIER
SLIPPIEST
SLIPPING
SLIPPY
SLIPRAIL
SLIPRAILS
SLIPS
SLIPSHOD
SLIPSLOP
SLIPSLOPS

SLIPSOLE*
SLIPSOLES*
SLIPT
SLIPUP*
SLIPUPS*
SLIPWARE
SLIPWARES
SLIPWAY
SLIPWAYS
SLISH
SLISHES
SLIT
SLITHER
SLITHERED
SLITHERIER
SLITHERIEST
SLITHERING
SLITHERS
SLITHERY
SLITLESS*
SLITS
SLITTED*
SLITTER
SLITTERS
SLITTING
SLIVE
SLIVED
SLIVEN
SLIVER
SLIVERED
SLIVERER*
SLIVERERS*
SLIVERING
SLIVERS
SLIVES
SLIVING
SLIVOVIC
SLIVOVICA
SLIVOVICAS
SLIVOVICES
SLIVOVITZ
SLIVOVITZES
SLIVOWITZ
SLIVOWITZES
SLOAN
SLOANS
SLOB
SLOBBER
SLOBBERED
SLOBBERER*
SLOBBERERS*
SLOBBERIER
SLOBBERIEST
SLOBBERING
SLOBBERS
SLOBBERY
SLOBBIER
SLOBBIEST
SLOBBISH
SLOBBY
SLOBLAND
SLOBLANDS
SLOBS
SLOCKEN

SLOCKENED
SLOCKENING
SLOCKENS
SLOE
SLOEBUSH
SLOEBUSHES
SLOES
SLOETHORN
SLOETHORNS
SLOETREE
SLOETREES
SLOG
SLOGAN
SLOGANEER
SLOGANEERED
SLOGANEERING
SLOGANEERINGS
SLOGANEERS
SLOGANISE
SLOGANISED
SLOGANISES
SLOGANISING
SLOGANISINGS
SLOGANIZE
SLOGANIZED
SLOGANIZES
SLOGANIZING
SLOGANIZINGS
SLOGANS
SLOGGED
SLOGGER
SLOGGERS
SLOGGING
SLOGS
SLOID
SLOIDS
SLOJD*
SLOJDS*
SLOKEN
SLOKENED
SLOKENING
SLOKENS
SLOOM
SLOOMED
SLOOMIER
SLOOMIEST
SLOOMING
SLOOMS
SLOOMY
SLOOP
SLOOPS
SLOOSH
SLOOSHED
SLOOSHES
SLOOSHING
SLOOT
SLOOTS
SLOP
SLOPE
SLOPED
SLOPER*
SLOPERS*
SLOPES
SLOPEWISE

SLOPIER
SLOPIEST
SLOPING
SLOPINGLY
SLOPPED
SLOPPIER
SLOPPIEST
SLOPPILY
SLOPPING
SLOPPY
SLOPS
SLOPWORK
SLOPWORKS
SLOPY
SLOSH
SLOSHED
SLOSHES
SLOSHIER
SLOSHIEST
SLOSHING
SLOSHINGS
SLOSHY
SLOT
SLOTBACK*
SLOTBACKS*
SLOTH
SLOTHED
SLOTHFUL
SLOTHING
SLOTHS
SLOTS
SLOTTED
SLOTTER
SLOTTERS
SLOTTING
SLOUCH
SLOUCHED
SLOUCHER
SLOUCHERS
SLOUCHES
SLOUCHIER
SLOUCHIEST
SLOUCHILY*
SLOUCHING
SLOUCHY
SLOUGH
SLOUGHED
SLOUGHIER
SLOUGHIEST
SLOUGHING
SLOUGHS
SLOUGHY
SLOVE
SLOVEN
SLOVENLIER
SLOVENLIEST
SLOVENLY
SLOVENRIES
SLOVENRY
SLOVENS
SLOW
SLOWBACK
SLOWBACKS
SLOWCOACH

SLOWCOACHES
SLOWDOWN*
SLOWDOWNS*
SLOWED
SLOWER
SLOWEST
SLOWING
SLOWINGS
SLOWISH
SLOWLY
SLOWNESS
SLOWNESSES
SLOWPOKE
SLOWPOKES
SLOWS
SLOWWORM
SLOWWORMS
SLOYD
SLOYDS
SLUB
SLUBB
SLUBBED
SLUBBER
SLUBBERED
SLUBBERING
SLUBBERINGS
SLUBBERS
SLUBBIER
SLUBBIEST
SLUBBING
SLUBBINGS
SLUBBS
SLUBBY
SLUBS
SLUDGE
SLUDGES
SLUDGIER
SLUDGIEST
SLUDGY
SLUE
SLUED
SLUEING
SLUES
SLUFF*
SLUFFED*
SLUFFING*
SLUFFS*
SLUG
SLUGABED*
SLUGABEDS*
SLUGFEST
SLUGFESTS
SLUGGABED
SLUGGABEDS
SLUGGARD
SLUGGARDS
SLUGGED
SLUGGER
SLUGGERS
SLUGGING
SLUGGISH
SLUGHORN
SLUGHORNE
SLUGHORNES

SLUGHORNS
SLUGS
SLUICE
SLUICED
SLUICES
SLUICEWAY*
SLUICEWAYS*
SLUICIER
SLUICIEST
SLUICING
SLUICY
SLUING
SLUIT
SLUITS
SLUM
SLUMBER
SLUMBERED
SLUMBERER
SLUMBERERS
SLUMBERING
SLUMBERINGS
SLUMBERS
SLUMBERY
SLUMBROUS
SLUMBRY
SLUMGUM*
SLUMGUMS*
SLUMISM*
SLUMISMS*
SLUMLORD
SLUMLORDS
SLUMMED
SLUMMER
SLUMMERS
SLUMMIER
SLUMMIEST
SLUMMING
SLUMMINGS
SLUMMOCK
SLUMMOCKED
SLUMMOCKING
SLUMMOCKS
SLUMMY
SLUMP
SLUMPED
SLUMPIER
SLUMPIEST
SLUMPING
SLUMPS
SLUMPY
SLUMS
SLUNG
SLUNGSHOT*
SLUNGSHOTS*
SLUNK
SLUR
SLURB
SLURBAN*
SLURBS
SLURP
SLURPED
SLURPER
SLURPERS
SLURPING

SLURPS
SLURRED
SLURRIED*
SLURRIES
SLURRING
SLURRY
SLURRYING*
SLURS
SLUSE
SLUSES
SLUSH
SLUSHED
SLUSHES
SLUSHIER
SLUSHIEST
SLUSHILY*
SLUSHING
SLUSHY
SLUT
SLUTS
SLUTTERIES
SLUTTERY
SLUTTIER*
SLUTTIEST*
SLUTTISH
SLUTTY*
SLY
SLYBOOTS
SLYER
SLYEST
SLYISH
SLYLY
SLYNESS
SLYNESSES
SLYPE
SLYPES
SMA
SMACK
SMACKED
SMACKER
SMACKERS
SMACKING
SMACKINGS
SMACKS
SMAIK
SMAIKS
SMALL
SMALLAGE
SMALLAGES
SMALLED
SMALLER
SMALLEST
SMALLING
SMALLISH
SMALLNESS
SMALLNESSES
SMALLPOX
SMALLPOXES
SMALLS
SMALLSAT
SMALLSATS
SMALM
SMALMED
SMALMILY

SMALMING
SMALMS
SMALMY
SMALT
SMALTI
SMALTINE*
SMALTINES*
SMALTITE
SMALTITES
SMALTO
SMALTOS
SMALTS
SMARAGD
SMARAGDE*
SMARAGDES*
SMARAGDS
SMARM
SMARMED
SMARMIER
SMARMIEST
SMARMILY
SMARMING
SMARMS
SMARMY
SMART
SMARTARSE
SMARTARSES
SMARTASS
SMARTASSES
SMARTED
SMARTEN
SMARTENED
SMARTENING
SMARTENS
SMARTER
SMARTEST
SMARTIE
SMARTIES
SMARTING
SMARTISH
SMARTLY
SMARTNESS
SMARTNESSES
SMARTS
SMARTWEED
SMARTWEEDS
SMARTY
SMASH
SMASHED
SMASHER
SMASHEROO
SMASHEROOS
SMASHERS
SMASHES
SMASHING
SMASHINGS
SMASHUP*
SMASHUPS*
SMATCH
SMATCHED
SMATCHES
SMATCHING
SMATTER
SMATTERED

SMATTERER
SMATTERERS
SMATTERING
SMATTERINGS
SMATTERS
SMAZE*
SMAZES*
SMEAR
SMEARCASE*
SMEARCASES*
SMEARED
SMEARER*
SMEARERS*
SMEARIER
SMEARIEST
SMEARILY
SMEARING
SMEARS
SMEARY
SMEATH
SMEATHS
SMECTIC
SMECTITE
SMECTITES
SMECTITIC*
SMEDDUM
SMEDDUMS
SMEE
SMEECH
SMEECHED
SMEECHES
SMEECHING
SMEEK
SMEEKED
SMEEKING
SMEEKS
SMEES
SMEETH
SMEETHS
SMEGMA
SMEGMAS
SMELL
SMELLED
SMELLER
SMELLERS
SMELLIER
SMELLIEST
SMELLING
SMELLINGS
SMELLS
SMELLY
SMELT
SMELTED
SMELTER
SMELTERIES
SMELTERS
SMELTERY
SMELTING
SMELTINGS
SMELTS
SMERK*
SMERKED*
SMERKING*
SMERKS*

Words marked with an asterisk are from OTCWL

SMEUSE	SMIRRIEST	SMOKIEST	SMOUCHED	SMUTCHING
SMEUSES	SMIRRING	SMOKILY	SMOUCHES	SMUTCHY*
SMEW	SMIRRS	SMOKINESS	SMOUCHING	SMUTS
SMEWS	SMIRRY	SMOKINESSES	SMOULDER	SMUTTED
SMICKER	SMIRS	SMOKING	SMOULDERED	SMUTTIER
SMICKERED	SMIT	SMOKINGS	SMOULDERING	SMUTTIEST
SMICKERING	SMITE	SMOKO	SMOULDERINGS	SMUTTILY
SMICKERINGS	SMITER	SMOKOS	SMOULDERS	SMUTTING
SMICKERS	SMITERS	SMOKY	SMOULDRY	SMUTTY
SMICKET	SMITES	SMOLDER	SMOUSE	SMYTRIE
SMICKETS	SMITH	SMOLDERED	SMOUSED	SMYTRIES
SMICKLY	SMITHED	SMOLDERING	SMOUSER	SNAB
SMIDDIED	SMITHERIES	SMOLDERS	SMOUSERS	SNABBLE
SMIDDIES	SMITHERS	SMOLT	SMOUSES	SNABBLED
SMIDDY	SMITHERY	SMOLTS	SMOUSING	SNABBLES
SMIDDYING	SMITHIED	SMOOCH	SMOUT	SNABBLING
SMIDGE*	SMITHIES	SMOOCHED	SMOUTED	SNABS
SMIDGEN	SMITHING	SMOOCHES	SMOUTING	SNACK
SMIDGENS	SMITHS	SMOOCHING	SMOUTS	SNACKED
SMIDGEON	SMITHY	SMOOCHY*	SMOWT	SNACKING
SMIDGEONS	SMITHYING	SMOOR	SMOWTS	SNACKS
SMIDGES*	SMITING	SMOORED	SMOYLE	SNAFFLE
SMIDGIN	SMITS	SMOORING	SMOYLED	SNAFFLED
SMIDGINS	SMITTED	SMOORS	SMOYLES	SNAFFLES
SMIERCASE*	SMITTEN	SMOOT	SMOYLING	SNAFFLING
SMIERCASES*	SMITTING	SMOOTED	SMUDGE	SNAFU
SMIGHT	SMITTLE	SMOOTH	SMUDGED	SNAFUED*
SMIGHTING	SMOCK	SMOOTHED	SMUDGER	SNAFUING*
SMIGHTS	SMOCKED	SMOOTHEN	SMUDGERS	SNAFUS
SMILAX	SMOCKING	SMOOTHENED	SMUDGES	SNAG
SMILAXES	SMOCKINGS	SMOOTHENING	SMUDGIER	SNAGGED
SMILE	SMOCKS	SMOOTHENS	SMUDGIEST	SNAGGIER
SMILED	SMOG	SMOOTHER	SMUDGILY	SNAGGIEST
SMILEFUL	SMOGGIER	SMOOTHERS	SMUDGING	SNAGGING
SMILELESS	SMOGGIEST	SMOOTHES*	SMUDGY	SNAGGY
SMILER	SMOGGY	SMOOTHEST	SMUG	SNAGLIKE*
SMILERS	SMOGLESS*	SMOOTHIE	SMUGGED	SNAGS
SMILES	SMOGS	SMOOTHIES	SMUGGER	SNAIL
SMILET	SMOILE	SMOOTHING	SMUGGEST	SNAILED
SMILETS	SMOILED	SMOOTHINGS	SMUGGING	SNAILERIES
SMILEY	SMOILES	SMOOTHISH	SMUGGLE	SNAILERY
SMILEYS	SMOILING	SMOOTHLY	SMUGGLED	SNAILIER
SMILING	SMOKABLE	SMOOTHS	SMUGGLER	SNAILIEST
SMILINGLY	SMOKE	SMOOTHY*	SMUGGLERS	SNAILING
SMILINGS	SMOKEABLE*	SMOOTING	SMUGGLES	SNAILLIKE*
SMILODON	SMOKEBUSH	SMOOTS	SMUGGLING	SNAILS
SMILODONS	SMOKEBUSHES	SMORBROD	SMUGGLINGS	SNAILY
SMIR	SMOKED	SMORBRODS	SMUGLY	SNAKE
SMIRCH	SMOKEHOOD	SMORE	SMUGNESS	SNAKEBIRD
SMIRCHED	SMOKEHOODS	SMORED	SMUGNESSES	SNAKEBIRDS
SMIRCHES	SMOKEJACK*	SMORES	SMUGS	SNAKEBIT*
SMIRCHING	SMOKEJACKS*	SMORING	SMUR	SNAKEBITE
SMIRK	SMOKELESS	SMORZANDO	SMURRED	SNAKEBITES
SMIRKED	SMOKELIKE*	SMORZATO	SMURRIER	SNAKED
SMIRKER*	SMOKEPOT*	SMOTE	SMURRIEST	SNAKELIKE
SMIRKERS*	SMOKEPOTS*	SMOTHER	SMURRING	SNAKEROOT
SMIRKIER	SMOKER	SMOTHERED	SMURRY	SNAKEROOTS
SMIRKIEST	SMOKERS	SMOTHERER	SMURS	SNAKES
SMIRKING	SMOKES	SMOTHERERS	SMUT	SNAKESKIN
SMIRKS	SMOKETREE	SMOTHERING	SMUTCH	SNAKESKINS
SMIRKY	SMOKETREES	SMOTHERINGS	SMUTCHED	SNAKEWEED
SMIRR	SMOKEY*	SMOTHERS	SMUTCHES	SNAKEWEEDS
SMIRRED	SMOKIER	SMOTHERY	SMUTCHIER*	SNAKEWISE
SMIRRIER	SMOKIES	SMOUCH	SMUTCHIEST*	SNAKEWOOD

The Chambers Dictionary is the authority for many longer words; see Introduction, page ix

SNAKEWOODS	SNASH	SNEDS	SNIDEST	SNIPPET
SNAKEY*	SNASHED	SNEE	SNIES	SNIPPETIER
SNAKIER	SNASHES	SNEED	SNIFF	SNIPPETIEST
SNAKIEST	SNASHING	SNEEING	SNIFFED	SNIPPETS
SNAKILY	SNASTE	SNEER	SNIFFER	SNIPPETY
SNAKINESS	SNASTES	SNEERED	SNIFFERS	SNIPPIER
SNAKINESSES	SNATCH	SNEERER	SNIFFIER	SNIPPIEST
SNAKING	SNATCHED	SNEERERS	SNIFFIEST	SNIPPILY*
SNAKISH	SNATCHER	SNEERFUL*	SNIFFILY	SNIPPING
SNAKY	SNATCHERS	SNEERIER	SNIFFING	SNIPPINGS
SNAP	SNATCHES	SNEERIEST	SNIFFINGS	SNIPPY
SNAPBACK*	SNATCHIER	SNEERING	SNIFFISH*	SNIPS
SNAPBACKS*	SNATCHIEST	SNEERINGS	SNIFFLE	SNIPY
SNAPHANCE	SNATCHILY	SNEERS	SNIFFLED	SNIRT
SNAPHANCES	SNATCHING	SNEERY	SNIFFLER	SNIRTLE
SNAPLESS*	SNATCHY	SNEES	SNIFFLERS	SNIRTLED
SNAPPED	SNATH	SNEESH	SNIFFLES	SNIRTLES
SNAPPER	SNATHE	SNEESHAN	SNIFFLING	SNIRTLING
SNAPPERED	SNATHES	SNEESHANS	SNIFFS	SNIRTS
SNAPPERING	SNATHS	SNEESHES	SNIFFY	SNIT*
SNAPPERS	SNAW*	SNEESHIN	SNIFT	SNITCH
SNAPPIER	SNAWED*	SNEESHING	SNIFTED	SNITCHED
SNAPPIEST	SNAWING*	SNEESHINGS	SNIFTER	SNITCHER
SNAPPILY	SNAWS*	SNEESHINS	SNIFTERED	SNITCHERS
SNAPPING	SNAZZIER	SNEEZE	SNIFTERING	SNITCHES
SNAPPINGS	SNAZZIEST	SNEEZED	SNIFTERS	SNITCHING
SNAPPISH	SNAZZY	SNEEZER	SNIFTIER	SNITS*
SNAPPY	SNEAD	SNEEZERS	SNIFTIEST	SNIVEL
SNAPS	SNEADS	SNEEZES	SNIFTING	SNIVELED*
SNAPSHOT	SNEAK	SNEEZIER	SNIFTS	SNIVELER*
SNAPSHOTS	SNEAKED	SNEEZIEST	SNIFTY	SNIVELERS*
SNAPSHOTTED*	SNEAKER	SNEEZING	SNIG	SNIVELING*
SNAPSHOTTING*	SNEAKERED*	SNEEZINGS	SNIGGED	SNIVELLED
SNAPWEED*	SNEAKERS	SNEEZY	SNIGGER	SNIVELLER
SNAPWEEDS*	SNEAKEUP	SNELL	SNIGGERED	SNIVELLERS
SNAR	SNEAKEUPS	SNELLED	SNIGGERER	SNIVELLING
SNARE	SNEAKIER	SNELLER	SNIGGERERS	SNIVELLY
SNARED	SNEAKIEST	SNELLEST	SNIGGERING	SNIVELS
SNARER	SNEAKILY	SNELLING	SNIGGERINGS	SNOB
SNARERS	SNEAKING	SNELLS	SNIGGERS	SNOBBERIES
SNARES	SNEAKISH	SNELLY	SNIGGING	SNOBBERY
SNARIER	SNEAKS	SNIB	SNIGGLE	SNOBBIER
SNARIEST	SNEAKSBIES	SNIBBED	SNIGGLED	SNOBBIEST
SNARING	SNEAKSBY	SNIBBING	SNIGGLER	SNOBBILY*
SNARINGS	SNEAKY	SNIBS	SNIGGLERS	SNOBBISH
SNARK	SNEAP	SNICK	SNIGGLES	SNOBBISM
SNARKIER*	SNEAPED	SNICKED	SNIGGLING	SNOBBISMS
SNARKIEST*	SNEAPING	SNICKER	SNIGGLINGS	SNOBBY
SNARKS	SNEAPS	SNICKERED	SNIGS	SNOBLING
SNARKY*	SNEATH	SNICKERER*	SNIP	SNOBLINGS
SNARL	SNEATHS	SNICKERERS*	SNIPE	SNOBS
SNARLED	SNEB	SNICKERING	SNIPED	SNOD
SNARLER	SNEBBE	SNICKERS	SNIPEFISH	SNODDED
SNARLERS	SNEBBED	SNICKERY*	SNIPEFISHES	SNODDER
SNARLIER	SNEBBES	SNICKET	SNIPER	SNODDEST
SNARLIEST	SNEBBING	SNICKETS	SNIPERS	SNODDING
SNARLING	SNEBS	SNICKING	SNIPES	SNODDIT
SNARLINGS	SNECK	SNICKS	SNIPIER	SNODS
SNARLS	SNECKED	SNIDE	SNIPIEST	SNOEK
SNARLY	SNECKING	SNIDELY	SNIPING	SNOEKS
SNARRED	SNECKS	SNIDENESS	SNIPINGS	SNOG
SNARRING	SNED	SNIDENESSES	SNIPPED	SNOGGED
SNARS	SNEDDED	SNIDER	SNIPPER	SNOGGING
SNARY	SNEDDING	SNIDES	SNIPPERS	SNOGS

SNOKE	SNORKELING*	SNOWDRIFT	SNOWSUITS*	SNUSHING
SNOKED	SNORKELS	SNOWDRIFTS	SNOWY	SNUZZLE
SNOKES	SNORT	SNOWDROP	SNUB	SNUZZLED
SNOKING	SNORTED	SNOWDROPS	SNUBBE	SNUZZLES
SNOOD	SNORTER	SNOWED	SNUBBED	SNUZZLING
SNOODED	SNORTERS	SNOWFALL	SNUBBER	SNY
SNOODING	SNORTIER	SNOWFALLS	SNUBBERS	SNYE
SNOODS	SNORTIEST	SNOWFIELD	SNUBBES	SNYES
SNOOK	SNORTING	SNOWFIELDS	SNUBBIER	SO
SNOOKED	SNORTINGS	SNOWFLAKE	SNUBBIEST	SOAK
SNOOKER	SNORTS	SNOWFLAKES	SNUBBING	SOAKAGE
SNOOKERED	SNORTY	SNOWFLECK	SNUBBINGS	SOAKAGES
SNOOKERING	SNOT	SNOWFLECKS	SNUBBISH	SOAKAWAY
SNOOKERS	SNOTS	SNOWFLICK	SNUBBY	SOAKAWAYS
SNOOKING	SNOTTED	SNOWFLICKS	SNUBNESS*	SOAKED
SNOOKS	SNOTTER	SNOWIER	SNUBNESSES*	SOAKEN
SNOOL	SNOTTERED	SNOWIEST	SNUBS	SOAKER
SNOOLED	SNOTTERIES	SNOWILY	SNUCK	SOAKERS
SNOOLING	SNOTTERING	SNOWINESS	SNUDGE	SOAKING
SNOOLS	SNOTTERS	SNOWINESSES	SNUDGED	SOAKINGLY
SNOOP	SNOTTERY	SNOWING	SNUDGES	SOAKINGS
SNOOPED	SNOTTIE	SNOWISH	SNUDGING	SOAKS
SNOOPER	SNOTTIER	SNOWK	SNUFF	SOAP
SNOOPERS	SNOTTIES	SNOWKED	SNUFFBOX	SOAPBARK
SNOOPIER	SNOTTIEST	SNOWKING	SNUFFBOXES	SOAPBARKS
SNOOPIEST	SNOTTILY	SNOWKS	SNUFFED	SOAPBERRIES
SNOOPILY*	SNOTTING	SNOWLAND*	SNUFFER	SOAPBERRY
SNOOPING	SNOTTY	SNOWLANDS*	SNUFFERS	SOAPBOX
SNOOPS	SNOUT	SNOWLESS	SNUFFIER	SOAPBOXES
SNOOPY	SNOUTED	SNOWLIKE	SNUFFIEST	SOAPED
SNOOT	SNOUTIER	SNOWLINE	SNUFFILY*	SOAPER
SNOOTED	SNOUTIEST	SNOWLINES	SNUFFING	SOAPERS
SNOOTFUL	SNOUTING	SNOWMAKER*	SNUFFINGS	SOAPIE
SNOOTFULS	SNOUTISH*	SNOWMAKERS*	SNUFFLE	SOAPIER
SNOOTIER	SNOUTS	SNOWMAN	SNUFFLED	SOAPIES
SNOOTIEST	SNOUTY	SNOWMELT*	SNUFFLER	SOAPIEST
SNOOTILY	SNOW	SNOWMELTS*	SNUFFLERS	SOAPILY
SNOOTING	SNOWBALL	SNOWMEN	SNUFFLES	SOAPINESS
SNOOTS	SNOWBALLED	SNOWMOLD*	SNUFFLIER	SOAPINESSES
SNOOTY	SNOWBALLING	SNOWMOLDS*	SNUFFLIEST	SOAPING
SNOOZE	SNOWBALLS	SNOWPACK*	SNUFFLING	SOAPLAND
SNOOZED	SNOWBANK*	SNOWPACKS*	SNUFFLINGS	SOAPLANDS
SNOOZER	SNOWBANKS*	SNOWPLOW*	SNUFFLY	SOAPLESS
SNOOZERS	SNOWBELL*	SNOWPLOWED*	SNUFFS	SOAPLIKE*
SNOOZES	SNOWBELLS*	SNOWPLOWING*	SNUFFY	SOAPROOT
SNOOZIER	SNOWBELT*	SNOWPLOWS*	SNUG	SOAPROOTS
SNOOZIEST	SNOWBELTS*	SNOWS	SNUGGED	SOAPS
SNOOZING	SNOWBERRIES	SNOWSCAPE	SNUGGER	SOAPSTONE
SNOOZLE	SNOWBERRY	SNOWSCAPES	SNUGGERIES	SOAPSTONES
SNOOZLED	SNOWBIRD	SNOWSHED*	SNUGGERY	SOAPSUDS
SNOOZLES	SNOWBIRDS	SNOWSHEDS*	SNUGGEST	SOAPWORT
SNOOZLING	SNOWBLINK	SNOWSHOE	SNUGGIES*	SOAPWORTS
SNOOZY	SNOWBLINKS	SNOWSHOED	SNUGGING	SOAPY
SNORE	SNOWBOARD	SNOWSHOEING	SNUGGLE	SOAR
SNORED	SNOWBOARDS	SNOWSHOER*	SNUGGLED	SOARAWAY
SNORER	SNOWBOOT	SNOWSHOERS*	SNUGGLES	SOARE
SNORERS	SNOWBOOTS	SNOWSHOES	SNUGGLING	SOARED
SNORES	SNOWBOUND	SNOWSLIDE*	SNUGLY	SOARER
SNORING	SNOWBRUSH*	SNOWSLIDES*	SNUGNESS	SOARERS
SNORINGS	SNOWBRUSHES*	SNOWSLIP	SNUGNESSES	SOARES
SNORKEL	SNOWBUSH	SNOWSLIPS	SNUGS	SOARING
SNORKELED*	SNOWBUSHES	SNOWSTORM	SNUSH	SOARINGLY
SNORKELER	SNOWCAP	SNOWSTORMS	SNUSHED	SOARINGS
SNORKELERS	SNOWCAPS	SNOWSUIT*	SNUSHES	SOARS

The Chambers Dictionary is the authority for many longer words; see Introduction, page ix

SOAVE*	SOCIALIZES	SODDIER	SOFTLY	SOKEMEN
SOAVES*	SOCIALIZING	SODDIES*	SOFTNESS	SOKEN
SOB	SOCIALLY	SODDIEST	SOFTNESSES	SOKENS
SOBBED	SOCIALS	SODDING	SOFTPASTE	SOKES
SOBBER*	SOCIATE	SODDY	SOFTS	SOKOL*
SOBBERS*	SOCIATES	SODGER	SOFTSHELL*	SOKOLS*
SOBBING	SOCIATION	SODGERS	SOFTSHELLS*	SOL
SOBBINGLY	SOCIATIONS	SODIC	SOFTWARE	SOLA
SOBBINGS	SOCIATIVE	SODIUM	SOFTWARES	SOLACE
SOBEIT	SOCIETAL	SODIUMS	SOFTWOOD	SOLACED
SOBER	SOCIETIES	SODOM*	SOFTWOODS	SOLACER*
SOBERED	SOCIETY	SODOMIES	SOFTY	SOLACERS*
SOBERER	SOCIOGRAM	SODOMISE	SOG	SOLACES
SOBEREST	SOCIOGRAMS	SODOMISED	SOGER	SOLACING
SOBERING	SOCIOLECT	SODOMISES	SOGERS	SOLACIOUS
SOBERISE	SOCIOLECTS	SODOMISING	SOGGED	SOLAH
SOBERISED	SOCIOLOGIES	SODOMIST*	SOGGIER	SOLAHS
SOBERISES	SOCIOLOGY	SODOMISTS*	SOGGIEST	SOLAN
SOBERISING	SOCIOPATH	SODOMITE	SOGGILY	SOLAND*
SOBERIZE	SOCIOPATHS	SODOMITES	SOGGINESS	SOLANDER
SOBERIZED	SOCK	SODOMITIC	SOGGINESSES	SOLANDERS
SOBERIZES	SOCKED	SODOMIZE	SOGGING	SOLANDS*
SOBERIZING	SOCKET	SODOMIZED	SOGGINGS	SOLANIN*
SOBERLY	SOCKETED	SODOMIZES	SOGGY	SOLANINE
SOBERNESS	SOCKETING	SODOMIZING	SOGS	SOLANINES
SOBERNESSES	SOCKETS	SODOMS*	SOH	SOLANINS*
SOBERS	SOCKETTE	SODOMY	SOHO	SOLANO
SOBFUL*	SOCKETTES	SODS	SOHS	SOLANOS
SOBOLE	SOCKEYE	SOEVER	SOIGNE	SOLANS
SOBOLES	SOCKEYES	SOFA	SOIGNEE	SOLANUM
SOBRIETIES	SOCKING	SOFAR	SOIL	SOLANUMS
SOBRIETY	SOCKLESS*	SOFARS	SOILAGE	SOLAR
SOBRIQUET	SOCKMAN*	SOFAS	SOILAGES	SOLARIA
SOBRIQUETS	SOCKMEN*	SOFFIONI	SOILBORNE*	SOLARISE
SOBS	SOCKO	SOFFIT	SOILED	SOLARISED
SOC	SOCKS	SOFFITS	SOILIER	SOLARISES
SOCA	SOCLE	SOFT	SOILIEST	SOLARISING
SOCAGE	SOCLES	SOFTA	SOILINESS	SOLARISM
SOCAGER	SOCMAN	SOFTAS	SOILINESSES	SOLARISMS
SOCAGERS	SOCMEN	SOFTBACK	SOILING	SOLARIST
SOCAGES	SOCS	SOFTBACKS	SOILINGS	SOLARISTS
SOCAS	SOD	SOFTBALL	SOILLESS	SOLARIUM
SOCCAGE	SODA	SOFTBALLS	SOILS	SOLARIUMS
SOCCAGES	SODAIC	SOFTBOUND*	SOILURE	SOLARIZE
SOCCER	SODAIN	SOFTCOVER	SOILURES	SOLARIZED
SOCCERS	SODAINE	SOFTCOVERS	SOILY	SOLARIZES
SOCIABLE	SODALESS*	SOFTED	SOIREE	SOLARIZING
SOCIABLES	SODALIST*	SOFTEN	SOIREES	SOLARS
SOCIABLY	SODALISTS*	SOFTENED	SOJA	SOLAS
SOCIAL	SODALITE	SOFTENER	SOJAS	SOLATE*
SOCIALISE	SODALITES	SOFTENERS	SOJOURN	SOLATED*
SOCIALISED	SODALITIES	SOFTENING	SOJOURNED	SOLATES*
SOCIALISES	SODALITY	SOFTENINGS	SOJOURNER	SOLATIA
SOCIALISING	SODAMIDE	SOFTENS	SOJOURNERS	SOLATING*
SOCIALISM	SODAMIDES	SOFTER	SOJOURNING	SOLATION
SOCIALISMS	SODAS	SOFTEST	SOJOURNINGS	SOLATIONS
SOCIALIST	SODBUSTER	SOFTHEAD	SOJOURNS	SOLATIUM
SOCIALISTS	SODBUSTERS	SOFTHEADS	SOKAH	SOLD
SOCIALITE	SODDED	SOFTIE	SOKAHS	SOLDADO
SOCIALITES	SODDEN	SOFTIES	SOKAIYA	SOLDADOS
SOCIALITIES	SODDENED	SOFTING	SOKE	SOLDAN
SOCIALITY	SODDENING	SOFTISH	SOKEMAN	SOLDANS
SOCIALIZE	SODDENLY*	SOFTLING	SOKEMANRIES	SOLDE
SOCIALIZED	SODDENS	SOFTLINGS	SOKEMANRY	SOLDER

SOLDERED	SOLEPLATE	SOLING	SOLVATING	SOMEWAY
SOLDERER	SOLEPLATES	SOLION	SOLVATION	SOMEWAYS
SOLDERERS	SOLER	SOLIONS	SOLVATIONS	SOMEWHAT
SOLDERING	SOLERA	SOLIPED	SOLVE	SOMEWHATS
SOLDERINGS	SOLERAS	SOLIPEDS	SOLVED	SOMEWHEN
SOLDERS	SOLERET*	SOLIPSISM	SOLVENCIES	SOMEWHERE
SOLDES	SOLERETS*	SOLIPSISMS	SOLVENCY	SOMEWHERES*
SOLDI	SOLERS	SOLIPSIST	SOLVENT	SOMEWHILE
SOLDIER	SOLES	SOLIPSISTS	SOLVENTLY*	SOMEWHILES
SOLDIERED	SOLEUS	SOLIQUID*	SOLVENTS	SOMEWHY
SOLDIERIES	SOLEUSES	SOLIQUIDS*	SOLVER	SOMEWISE
SOLDIERING	SOLFATARA	SOLITAIRE	SOLVERS	SOMITAL
SOLDIERINGS	SOLFATARAS	SOLITAIRES	SOLVES	SOMITE
SOLDIERLY	SOLFEGE	SOLITARIES	SOLVING	SOMITES
SOLDIERS	SOLFEGES	SOLITARY	SOMA	SOMITIC
SOLDIERY	SOLFEGGI	SOLITO	SOMAN	SOMMELIER
SOLDO	SOLFEGGIO	SOLITON	SOMANS	SOMMELIERS
SOLDS	SOLFEGGIOS	SOLITONS	SOMAS	SOMNIAL
SOLE	SOLFERINO	SOLITUDE	SOMASCOPE	SOMNIATE
SOLECISE	SOLFERINOS	SOLITUDES	SOMASCOPES	SOMNIATED
SOLECISED	SOLGEL	SOLIVE	SOMATA	SOMNIATES
SOLECISES	SOLI	SOLIVES	SOMATIC	SOMNIATING
SOLECISING	SOLICIT	SOLLAR	SOMATISM	SOMNIFIC
SOLECISM	SOLICITED	SOLLARS	SOMATISMS	SOMNOLENT
SOLECISMS	SOLICITIES	SOLLER	SOMATIST	SON
SOLECIST	SOLICITING	SOLLERET	SOMATISTS	SONANCE
SOLECISTS	SOLICITINGS	SOLLERETS	SOMBER	SONANCES
SOLECIZE	SOLICITOR	SOLLERS	SOMBERED	SONANCIES
SOLECIZED	SOLICITORS	SOLO	SOMBERER	SONANCY
SOLECIZES	SOLICITS	SOLOED	SOMBEREST	SONANT
SOLECIZING	SOLICITY	SOLOING	SOMBERING	SONANTAL*
SOLED	SOLID	SOLOIST	SOMBERLY*	SONANTIC*
SOLEI*	SOLIDAGO	SOLOISTS	SOMBERS	SONANTS
SOLEIN	SOLIDAGOS	SOLON*	SOMBRE	SONAR
SOLELESS*	SOLIDARE	SOLONCHAK	SOMBRED	SONARMAN*
SOLELY	SOLIDARES	SOLONCHAKS	SOMBRELY*	SONARMEN*
SOLEMN	SOLIDARY	SOLONETS	SOMBRER	SONARS
SOLEMNER	SOLIDATE	SOLONETSES	SOMBRERO	SONATA
SOLEMNESS	SOLIDATED	SOLONETZ	SOMBREROS	SONATAS
SOLEMNESSES	SOLIDATES	SOLONETZES	SOMBRES	SONATINA
SOLEMNEST	SOLIDATING	SOLONS*	SOMBREST	SONATINAS
SOLEMNIFIED	SOLIDER	SOLOS	SOMBRING	SONATINE*
SOLEMNIFIES	SOLIDEST	SOLPUGID	SOMBROUS	SONCE
SOLEMNIFY	SOLIDI	SOLPUGIDS	SOME	SONCES
SOLEMNIFYING	SOLIDIFIED	SOLS	SOMEBODIES	SONDAGE
SOLEMNISE	SOLIDIFIES	SOLSTICE	SOMEBODY	SONDAGES
SOLEMNISED	SOLIDIFY	SOLSTICES	SOMEDAY	SONDE
SOLEMNISES	SOLIDIFYING	SOLUBLE	SOMEDEAL	SONDELI
SOLEMNISING	SOLIDISH	SOLUBLES*	SOMEDELE	SONDELIS
SOLEMNITIES	SOLIDISM	SOLUBLY*	SOMEGATE	SONDER*
SOLEMNITY	SOLIDISMS	SOLUM	SOMEHOW	SONDERS*
SOLEMNIZE	SOLIDIST	SOLUMS	SOMEONE	SONDES
SOLEMNIZED	SOLIDISTS	SOLUS	SOMEONES	SONE
SOLEMNIZES	SOLIDITIES	SOLUTE	SOMEPLACE	SONERI
SOLEMNIZING	SOLIDITY	SOLUTES	SOMERSET	SONERIS
SOLEMNLY	SOLIDLY	SOLUTION	SOMERSETED*	SONES
SOLENESS	SOLIDNESS	SOLUTIONED	SOMERSETING*	SONG
SOLENESSES	SOLIDNESSES	SOLUTIONING	SOMERSETS	SONGBIRD
SOLENETTE	SOLIDS	SOLUTIONS	SOMERSETTED	SONGBIRDS
SOLENETTES	SOLIDUM	SOLUTIVE	SOMERSETTING	SONGBOOK
SOLENODON	SOLIDUMS	SOLVABLE	SOMETHING	SONGBOOKS
SOLENODONS	SOLIDUS	SOLVATE	SOMETHINGS	SONGCRAFT
SOLENOID	SOLILOQUIES	SOLVATED	SOMETIME	SONGCRAFTS
SOLENOIDS	SOLILOQUY	SOLVATES	SOMETIMES	SONGFEST

The Chambers Dictionary is the authority for many longer words; see Introduction, page ix

SONGFESTS	SONSIER	SOOTHSAY	SORAGES	SOREHEADS
SONGFUL	SONSIEST	SOOTHSAYING	SORAL	SOREHON
SONGFULLY	SONSY	SOOTHSAYINGS	SORAS	SOREHONS
SONGLESS	SONTAG	SOOTHSAYS	SORB	SOREL
SONGLIKE	SONTAGS	SOOTIER	SORBABLE*	SORELL
SONGMAN	SONTIES	SOOTIEST	SORBARIA	SORELLS
SONGMEN	SOOCHONG*	SOOTILY	SORBARIAS	SORELS
SONGS	SOOCHONGS*	SOOTINESS	SORBATE	SORELY
SONGSMITH	SOOEY*	SOOTINESSES	SORBATES	SORENESS
SONGSMITHS	SOOGEE	SOOTING	SORBED	SORENESSES
SONGSTER	SOOGEED	SOOTLESS	SORBENT	SORER
SONGSTERS	SOOGEEING	SOOTS	SORBENTS	SORES
SONHOOD*	SOOGEES	SOOTY	SORBET	SOREST
SONHOODS*	SOOGIE	SOP	SORBETS	SOREX
SONIC	SOOGIED	SOPAPILLA*	SORBIC*	SOREXES
SONICALLY*	SOOGIEING	SOPAPILLAS*	SORBING	SORGHO
SONICATE*	SOOGIES	SOPH	SORBITE	SORGHOS
SONICATED*	SOOJEY	SOPHERIC	SORBITES	SORGHUM
SONICATES*	SOOJEYS	SOPHERIM	SORBITIC	SORGHUMS
SONICATING*	SOOK	SOPHIES*	SORBITISE	SORGO
SONICS	SOOKS	SOPHISM	SORBITISED	SORGOS
SONLESS	SOOLE	SOPHISMS	SORBITISES	SORI
SONLIKE*	SOOLED	SOPHIST	SORBITISING	SORICINE
SONLY*	SOOLES	SOPHISTER	SORBITIZE	SORICOID
SONNE	SOOLING	SOPHISTERS	SORBITIZED	SORING
SONNES	SOOM	SOPHISTIC	SORBITIZES	SORINGS*
SONNET	SOOMED	SOPHISTRIES	SORBITIZING	SORITES
SONNETARY	SOOMING	SOPHISTRY	SORBITOL	SORITIC
SONNETED	SOOMS	SOPHISTS	SORBITOLS	SORITICAL
SONNETEER	SOON	SOPHOMORE	SORBOSE*	SORN
SONNETEERS	SOONER	SOPHOMORES	SORBOSES*	SORNED
SONNETING	SOONERS*	SOPHS	SORBS	SORNER
SONNETISE	SOONEST	SOPHY*	SORBUS	SORNERS
SONNETISED	SOOP	SOPITE	SORBUSES	SORNING
SONNETISES	SOOPED	SOPITED	SORCERER	SORNINGS
SONNETISING	SOOPING	SOPITES	SORCERERS	SORNS
SONNETIZE	SOOPINGS	SOPITING	SORCERESS	SOROBAN
SONNETIZED	SOOPS	SOPOR	SORCERESSES	SOROBANS
SONNETIZES	SOOPSTAKE	SOPORIFIC	SORCERIES	SOROCHE
SONNETIZING	SOOT	SOPORIFICS	SORCEROUS	SOROCHES
SONNETS	SOOTE	SOPOROSE	SORCERY	SORORAL
SONNETTED*	SOOTED	SOPOROUS	SORD	SORORATE
SONNETTING*	SOOTERKIN	SOPORS	SORDA	SORORATES
SONNIES	SOOTERKINS	SOPPED	SORDID	SORORIAL
SONNY	SOOTES	SOPPIER	SORDIDER	SORORISE
SONOBUOY	SOOTFLAKE	SOPPIEST	SORDIDEST	SORORISED
SONOBUOYS	SOOTFLAKES	SOPPILY	SORDIDLY	SORORISES
SONOGRAM	SOOTH	SOPPINESS	SORDINE*	SORORISING
SONOGRAMS	SOOTHE	SOPPINESSES	SORDINES*	SORORITIES
SONOGRAPH	SOOTHED	SOPPING	SORDINI	SORORITY
SONOGRAPHS	SOOTHER	SOPPINGS	SORDINO	SORORIZE
SONORANT	SOOTHERED	SOPPY	SORDO	SORORIZED
SONORANTS	SOOTHERING	SOPRA	SORDOR*	SORORIZES
SONORITIES	SOOTHERS	SOPRANI	SORDORS*	SORORIZING
SONORITY	SOOTHES	SOPRANINI	SORDS	SOROSES
SONOROUS	SOOTHEST	SOPRANINO	SORE	SOROSIS
SONOVOX*	SOOTHFAST	SOPRANINOS	SORED	SOROSISES
SONOVOXES*	SOOTHFUL	SOPRANIST	SOREDIA	SORPTION
SONS	SOOTHING	SOPRANISTS	SOREDIAL	SORPTIONS
SONSE	SOOTHINGS	SOPRANO	SOREDIATE	SORPTIVE*
SONSES	SOOTHLICH	SOPRANOS	SOREDIUM	SORRA
SONSHIP	SOOTHLY	SOPS	SOREE	SORRAS
SONSHIPS	SOOTHS	SORA	SOREES	SORREL
SONSIE	SOOTHSAID	SORAGE	SOREHEAD	SORRELS

SORRIER	SOU	SOUNDLY	SOUT	SOVIETIZE
SORRIEST	SOUARI	SOUNDMAN	SOUTACHE	SOVIETIZED
SORRILY	SOUARIS	SOUNDMEN	SOUTACHES	SOVIETIZES
SORRINESS	SOUBISE	SOUNDNESS	SOUTANE	SOVIETIZING
SORRINESSES	SOUBISES	SOUNDNESSES	SOUTANES	SOVIETS
SORROW	SOUBRETTE	SOUNDS	SOUTAR	SOVKHOZ*
SORROWED	SOUBRETTES	SOUP	SOUTARS	SOVKHOZES*
SORROWER	SOUCAR*	SOUPCON	SOUTENEUR	SOVKHOZY*
SORROWERS	SOUCARS*	SOUPCONS	SOUTENEURS	SOVRAN
SORROWFUL	SOUCE	SOUPED*	SOUTER	SOVRANLY
SORROWING	SOUCED	SOUPER	SOUTERLY	SOVRANS
SORROWINGS	SOUCES	SOUPERS	SOUTERS	SOVRANTIES
SORROWS	SOUCHONG	SOUPIER	SOUTH	SOVRANTY
SORRY	SOUCHONGS	SOUPIEST	SOUTHEAST*	SOVS
SORRYISH	SOUCING	SOUPING*	SOUTHEASTS*	SOW
SORT	SOUCT	SOUPLE	SOUTHED	SOWABLE*
SORTABLE	SOUDAN*	SOUPLED	SOUTHER	SOWANS
SORTABLY*	SOUDANS*	SOUPLES	SOUTHERED	SOWAR
SORTANCE	SOUFFLE	SOUPLING	SOUTHERING	SOWARREE
SORTANCES	SOUFFLED*	SOUPS	SOUTHERLIES*	SOWARREES
SORTATION	SOUFFLEED*	SOUPSPOON	SOUTHERLY	SOWARRIES
SORTATIONS	SOUFFLES	SOUPSPOONS	SOUTHERN	SOWARRY
SORTED	SOUGH	SOUPY	SOUTHERNS	SOWARS
SORTER	SOUGHED	SOUR	SOUTHERS	SOWBACK
SORTERS	SOUGHING	SOURBALL*	SOUTHING	SOWBACKS
SORTES	SOUGHS	SOURBALLS*	SOUTHINGS	SOWBELLIES*
SORTIE	SOUGHT	SOURCE	SOUTHLAND	SOWBELLY*
SORTIED	SOUK	SOURCED	SOUTHLANDS	SOWBREAD
SORTIEING	SOUKOUS	SOURCES	SOUTHMOST	SOWBREADS
SORTIES	SOUKOUSES	SOURCING	SOUTHPAW	SOWCAR*
SORTILEGE	SOUKS	SOURCINGS	SOUTHPAWS	SOWCARS*
SORTILEGES	SOUL	SOURDINE	SOUTHRON	SOWCE
SORTILEGIES	SOULDAN	SOURDINES	SOUTHRONS	SOWCED
SORTILEGY	SOULDANS	SOURDOUGH	SOUTHS	SOWCES
SORTING	SOULDIER	SOURDOUGHS	SOUTHSAID	SOWCING
SORTINGS	SOULDIERED	SOURED	SOUTHSAY	SOWED
SORTITION	SOULDIERING	SOURER	SOUTHSAYING	SOWENS
SORTITIONS	SOULDIERS	SOUREST	SOUTHSAYS	SOWER
SORTMENT	SOULED	SOURING	SOUTHWARD	SOWERS
SORTMENTS	SOULFUL	SOURINGS	SOUTHWARDS	SOWF
SORTS	SOULFULLY	SOURISH	SOUTHWEST*	SOWFED
SORUS	SOULLESS	SOURISHLY	SOUTHWESTS*	SOWFF
SOS	SOULLIKE*	SOURLY	SOUTS	SOWFFED
SOSS	SOULS	SOURNESS	SOUVENIR	SOWFFING
SOSSED	SOUM	SOURNESSES	SOUVENIRED	SOWFFS
SOSSES	SOUMED	SOUROCK	SOUVENIRING	SOWFING
SOSSING	SOUMING	SOUROCKS	SOUVENIRS	SOWFS
SOSSINGS	SOUMINGS	SOURPUSS	SOUVLAKI	SOWING
SOSTENUTO	SOUMS	SOURPUSSES	SOUVLAKIA	SOWINGS
SOSTENUTOS*	SOUND	SOURS	SOUVLAKIAS*	SOWL
SOT	SOUNDABLE*	SOURSE	SOUVLAKIS*	SOWLE
SOTERIAL	SOUNDBITE	SOURSES	SOV	SOWLED
SOTH*	SOUNDBITES	SOURSOP	SOVENANCE	SOWLES
SOTHS*	SOUNDBOX*	SOURSOPS	SOVENANCES	SOWLING
SOTOL*	SOUNDBOXES*	SOURWOOD*	SOVEREIGN	SOWLS
SOTOLS*	SOUNDCARD	SOURWOODS*	SOVEREIGNS	SOWM
SOTS	SOUNDCARDS	SOUS	SOVIET	SOWMED
SOTTED	SOUNDED	SOUSE	SOVIETIC	SOWMING
SOTTING	SOUNDER	SOUSED	SOVIETISE	SOWMS
SOTTINGS	SOUNDERS	SOUSES	SOVIETISED	SOWN
SOTTISH	SOUNDEST	SOUSING	SOVIETISES	SOWND
SOTTISHLY	SOUNDING	SOUSINGS	SOVIETISING	SOWNDED
SOTTISIER	SOUNDINGS	SOUSLIK	SOVIETISM	SOWNDING
SOTTISIERS	SOUNDLESS	SOUSLIKS	SOVIETISMS	SOWNDS

The Chambers Dictionary is the authority for many longer words; see Introduction, page ix

SOWNE	SPACEWARD*	SPAGERICS	SPANAEMIA	SPARAXISES
SOWNES	SPACEY	SPAGERIST	SPANAEMIAS	SPARD
SOWP	SPACIAL	SPAGERISTS	SPANAEMIC	SPARE
SOWPS	SPACIER	SPAGHETTI	SPANCEL	SPAREABLE*
SOWS	SPACIEST	SPAGHETTIS	SPANCELED*	SPARED
SOWSE	SPACING	SPAGIRIC	SPANCELING*	SPARELESS
SOWSED	SPACINGS	SPAGIRICS	SPANCELLED	SPARELY
SOWSES	SPACIOUS	SPAGIRIST	SPANCELLING	SPARENESS
SOWSING	SPACKLE*	SPAGIRISTS	SPANCELS	SPARENESSES
SOWSSE	SPACKLED*	SPAGS	SPANDEX	SPARER
SOWSSED	SPACKLES*	SPAGYRIC	SPANDEXES	SPARERIB*
SOWSSES	SPACKLING*	SPAGYRICS	SPANDREL	SPARERIBS*
SOWSSING	SPACY	SPAGYRIST	SPANDRELS	SPARERS
SOWTER	SPADASSIN	SPAGYRISTS	SPANDRIL	SPARES
SOWTERS	SPADASSINS	SPAHEE	SPANDRILS	SPAREST
SOWTH	SPADE	SPAHEES	SPANE	SPARGE
SOWTHED	SPADED	SPAHI	SPANED	SPARGED
SOWTHING	SPADEFISH	SPAHIS	SPANES	SPARGER
SOWTHS	SPADEFISHES	SPAIL*	SPANG	SPARGERS
SOX	SPADEFUL	SPAILS*	SPANGED	SPARGES
SOY	SPADEFULS	SPAIN	SPANGHEW	SPARGING
SOYA	SPADELIKE	SPAINED	SPANGHEWED	SPARID
SOYAS	SPADEMAN	SPAING	SPANGHEWING	SPARIDS
SOYBEAN*	SPADEMEN	SPAINGS	SPANGHEWS	SPARING
SOYBEANS*	SPADER	SPAINING	SPANGING	SPARINGLY
SOYLE	SPADERS	SPAINS	SPANGLE	SPARK
SOYLES	SPADES	SPAIRGE	SPANGLED	SPARKE
SOYMILK*	SPADESMAN	SPAIRGED	SPANGLER	SPARKED
SOYMILKS*	SPADESMEN	SPAIRGES	SPANGLERS	SPARKER*
SOYS	SPADEWORK	SPAIRGING	SPANGLES	SPARKERS*
SOYUZ*	SPADEWORKS	SPAIT*	SPANGLET	SPARKES
SOYUZES*	SPADGER	SPAITS*	SPANGLETS	SPARKIE
SOZIN*	SPADGERS	SPAKE	SPANGLIER	SPARKIER
SOZINE*	SPADICES	SPALD	SPANGLIEST	SPARKIES
SOZINES*	SPADILLE	SPALDS	SPANGLING	SPARKIEST
SOZINS*	SPADILLES	SPALE	SPANGLINGS	SPARKILY*
SOZZLE	SPADILLIO	SPALES	SPANGLY	SPARKING
SOZZLED	SPADILLIOS	SPALL	SPANGS	SPARKISH
SOZZLES	SPADILLO	SPALLABLE*	SPANIEL	SPARKLE
SOZZLIER	SPADILLOS	SPALLE	SPANIELLED	SPARKLED
SOZZLIEST	SPADING	SPALLED	SPANIELLING	SPARKLER
SOZZLING	SPADIX	SPALLER*	SPANIELS	SPARKLERS
SOZZLY	SPADIXES*	SPALLERS*	SPANING	SPARKLES
SPA	SPADO	SPALLES	SPANK	SPARKLESS
SPACE	SPADOES	SPALLING	SPANKED	SPARKLET
SPACEBAND*	SPADONES	SPALLINGS	SPANKER	SPARKLETS
SPACEBANDS*	SPADOS	SPALLS	SPANKERS	SPARKLIER
SPACED	SPADROON	SPALPEEN	SPANKING	SPARKLIES
SPACELESS	SPADROONS	SPALPEENS	SPANKINGS	SPARKLIEST
SPACEMAN	SPAE	SPALT	SPANKS	SPARKLING
SPACEMEN	SPAED	SPALTED	SPANLESS	SPARKLINGS
SPACEPORT*	SPAEING	SPALTING	SPANNED	SPARKLY
SPACEPORTS*	SPAEINGS*	SPALTS	SPANNER	SPARKPLUG*
SPACER	SPAEMAN	SPAM	SPANNERS	SPARKPLUGGED*
SPACERS	SPAEMEN	SPAMMED	SPANNING	SPARKPLUGGING*
SPACES	SPAER	SPAMMER	SPANS	SPARKPLUGS*
SPACESHIP	SPAERS	SPAMMERS	SPANSULE	SPARKS
SPACESHIPS	SPAES	SPAMMIER	SPANSULES	SPARKY
SPACESUIT	SPAETZLE*	SPAMMIEST	SPANWORM*	SPARLIKE*
SPACESUITS	SPAETZLES*	SPAMMING	SPANWORMS*	SPARLING
SPACEWALK*	SPAEWIFE	SPAMMINGS	SPAR	SPARLINGS
SPACEWALKED*	SPAEWIVES	SPAMMY	SPARABLE	SPAROID
SPACEWALKING*	SPAG	SPAMS	SPARABLES	SPAROIDS
SPACEWALKS*	SPAGERIC	SPAN	SPARAXIS	SPARRE

SPARRED	SPATTERS	SPEANS	SPECKLES	SPEEDWAY
SPARRER	SPATTING	SPEAR	SPECKLESS	SPEEDWAYS
SPARRERS	SPATULA	SPEARED	SPECKLING	SPEEDWELL
SPARRES	SPATULAR	SPEARER*	SPECKS	SPEEDWELLS
SPARRIER	SPATULAS	SPEARERS*	SPECKY	SPEEDY
SPARRIEST	SPATULATE	SPEARFISH	SPECS	SPEEL
SPARRING	SPATULE	SPEARFISHED*	SPECTACLE	SPEELED
SPARRINGS	SPATULES	SPEARFISHES	SPECTACLES	SPEELER
SPARROW	SPATZLE*	SPEARFISHING*	SPECTATE	SPEELERS
SPARROWS	SPAUL	SPEARGUN*	SPECTATED	SPEELING
SPARRY	SPAULD	SPEARGUNS*	SPECTATES	SPEELS
SPARS	SPAULDS	SPEARHEAD	SPECTATING	SPEER
SPARSE	SPAULS	SPEARHEADED	SPECTATOR	SPEERED
SPARSEDLY	SPAVIE	SPEARHEADING	SPECTATORS	SPEERING
SPARSELY	SPAVIES	SPEARHEADS	SPECTER	SPEERINGS
SPARSER	SPAVIET*	SPEARIER	SPECTERS	SPEERS
SPARSEST	SPAVIN	SPEARIEST	SPECTRA	SPEIL*
SPARSITIES	SPAVINED	SPEARING	SPECTRAL	SPEILED*
SPARSITY	SPAVINS	SPEARMAN	SPECTRE	SPEILING*
SPART	SPAW	SPEARMEN	SPECTRES	SPEILS*
SPARTAN	SPAWL	SPEARMINT	SPECTRUM	SPEIR
SPARTANS	SPAWLED	SPEARMINTS	SPECTRUMS*	SPEIRED
SPARTEINE	SPAWLING	SPEARS	SPECULA	SPEIRING
SPARTEINES	SPAWLS	SPEARWORT	SPECULAR	SPEIRINGS
SPARTERIE	SPAWN	SPEARWORTS	SPECULATE	SPEIRS
SPARTERIES	SPAWNED	SPEARY	SPECULATED	SPEISE*
SPARTH	SPAWNER	SPEAT	SPECULATES	SPEISES*
SPARTHE	SPAWNERS	SPEATS	SPECULATING	SPEISS
SPARTHES	SPAWNIER	SPEC	SPECULUM	SPEISSES
SPARTHS	SPAWNIEST	SPECCED*	SPECULUMS*	SPEK
SPARTS	SPAWNING	SPECCIES	SPED	SPEKBOOM
SPAS	SPAWNINGS	SPECCING*	SPEECH	SPEKBOOMS
SPASM	SPAWNS	SPECCY	SPEECHED	SPEKS
SPASMATIC	SPAWNY	SPECIAL	SPEECHES	SPELAEAN
SPASMED	SPAWS	SPECIALER*	SPEECHFUL	SPELD
SPASMIC	SPAY	SPECIALEST*	SPEECHIFIED	SPELDED
SPASMING	SPAYAD	SPECIALLY	SPEECHIFIES	SPELDER
SPASMODIC	SPAYADS	SPECIALS	SPEECHIFY	SPELDERED
SPASMS	SPAYD	SPECIALTIES	SPEECHIFYING	SPELDERING
SPASTIC	SPAYDS	SPECIALTY	SPEECHING	SPELDERS
SPASTICS	SPAYED	SPECIATE	SPEED	SPELDIN
SPAT	SPAYING	SPECIATED	SPEEDBALL	SPELDING
SPATE	SPAYS	SPECIATES	SPEEDBALLED*	SPELDINGS
SPATES	SPAZ*	SPECIATING	SPEEDBALLING*	SPELDINS
SPATFALL	SPAZZ	SPECIE	SPEEDBALLS	SPELDRIN
SPATFALLS	SPAZZED	SPECIES	SPEEDBOAT	SPELDRING
SPATHAL*	SPAZZES	SPECIFIC	SPEEDBOATS	SPELDRINGS
SPATHE	SPAZZING	SPECIFICS	SPEEDED	SPELDRINS
SPATHED	SPEAK	SPECIFIED	SPEEDER	SPELDS
SPATHES	SPEAKABLE	SPECIFIER*	SPEEDERS	SPELEAN
SPATHIC	SPEAKEASIES	SPECIFIERS*	SPEEDFUL	SPELK
SPATHOSE	SPEAKEASY	SPECIFIES	SPEEDIER	SPELKS
SPATIAL	SPEAKER	SPECIFY	SPEEDIEST	SPELL
SPATIALLY	SPEAKERS	SPECIFYING	SPEEDILY	SPELLABLE
SPATLESE	SPEAKING	SPECIMEN	SPEEDING	SPELLBIND
SPATLESEN	SPEAKINGS	SPECIMENS	SPEEDINGS	SPELLBINDING
SPATLESES	SPEAKOUT	SPECIOUS	SPEEDLESS	SPELLBINDS
SPATS	SPEAKOUTS	SPECK	SPEEDO	SPELLBOUND
SPATTED	SPEAKS	SPECKED	SPEEDOS	SPELLDOWN
SPATTEE	SPEAL	SPECKIER	SPEEDS	SPELLDOWNS
SPATTEES	SPEALS	SPECKIEST	SPEEDSTER	SPELLED
SPATTER	SPEAN	SPECKING	SPEEDSTERS	SPELLER
SPATTERED	SPEANED	SPECKLE	SPEEDUP*	SPELLERS
SPATTERING	SPEANING	SPECKLED	SPEEDUPS*	SPELLFUL

SPELLICAN
SPELLICANS
SPELLING
SPELLINGS
SPELLS
SPELT
SPELTER
SPELTERS
SPELTS
SPELTZ*
SPELTZES*
SPELUNK*
SPELUNKED*
SPELUNKER
SPELUNKERS
SPELUNKING*
SPELUNKS*
SPENCE
SPENCER
SPENCERS
SPENCES
SPEND
SPENDABLE
SPENDALL
SPENDALLS
SPENDER
SPENDERS
SPENDING
SPENDINGS
SPENDS
SPENSE*
SPENSES*
SPENT
SPEOS
SPEOSES
SPERLING
SPERLINGS
SPERM
SPERMARIA
SPERMARIES
SPERMARY
SPERMATIA
SPERMATIC
SPERMATICS
SPERMATID
SPERMATIDS
SPERMATIUM*
SPERMIC
SPERMINE*
SPERMINES*
SPERMOUS
SPERMS
SPERRE
SPERRED
SPERRES
SPERRING
SPERSE
SPERSED
SPERSES
SPERSING
SPERST
SPERTHE
SPERTHES
SPET

SPETCH
SPETCHES
SPETS
SPETSNAZ
SPETSNAZES
SPETTING
SPETZNAZ
SPETZNAZES
SPEW
SPEWED
SPEWER
SPEWERS
SPEWIER
SPEWIEST
SPEWINESS
SPEWINESSES
SPEWING
SPEWS
SPEWY
SPHACELUS
SPHACELUSES
SPHAER
SPHAERE
SPHAERES
SPHAERITE
SPHAERITES
SPHAERS
SPHAGNOUS
SPHAGNUM
SPHAGNUMS
SPHEAR
SPHEARE
SPHEARES
SPHEARS
SPHENDONE
SPHENDONES
SPHENE
SPHENES
SPHENIC
SPHENODON
SPHENODONS
SPHENOID
SPHENOIDS
SPHERAL
SPHERE
SPHERED
SPHERES
SPHERIC
SPHERICAL
SPHERICS
SPHERIER
SPHERIEST
SPHERING
SPHEROID
SPHEROIDS
SPHERULAR
SPHERULE
SPHERULES
SPHERY
SPHINCTER
SPHINCTERS
SPHINGES
SPHINGID
SPHINGIDS

SPHINX
SPHINXES
SPHYGMIC
SPHYGMOID
SPHYGMUS
SPHYGMUSES
SPIAL
SPIALS
SPIC
SPICA
SPICAE
SPICAS
SPICATE
SPICATED
SPICCATO
SPICCATOS
SPICE
SPICEBUSH
SPICEBUSHES
SPICED
SPICELESS*
SPICER
SPICERIES
SPICERS
SPICERY
SPICES
SPICEY*
SPICIER
SPICIEST
SPICILEGE
SPICILEGES
SPICILY
SPICINESS
SPICINESSES
SPICING
SPICK
SPICKER
SPICKEST
SPICKNEL
SPICKNELS
SPICKS
SPICS
SPICULA
SPICULAE
SPICULAR
SPICULATE
SPICULE
SPICULES
SPICULUM
SPICY
SPIDE
SPIDER
SPIDERIER
SPIDERIEST
SPIDERISH*
SPIDERMAN
SPIDERMEN
SPIDERS
SPIDERWEB*
SPIDERWEBS*
SPIDERY
SPIE
SPIED
SPIEGEL*

SPIEGELS*
SPIEL
SPIELED
SPIELER
SPIELERS
SPIELING
SPIELS
SPIER*
SPIERED*
SPIERING*
SPIERS*
SPIES
SPIFF
SPIFFED*
SPIFFIER
SPIFFIEST
SPIFFILY*
SPIFFING
SPIFFS*
SPIFFY
SPIGHT
SPIGHTED
SPIGHTING
SPIGHTS
SPIGNEL
SPIGNELS
SPIGOT
SPIGOTS
SPIK
SPIKE
SPIKED
SPIKEFISH
SPIKEFISHES
SPIKELET
SPIKELETS
SPIKELIKE*
SPIKENARD
SPIKENARDS
SPIKER*
SPIKERIES
SPIKERS*
SPIKERY
SPIKES
SPIKEY*
SPIKIER
SPIKIEST
SPIKILY
SPIKINESS
SPIKINESSES
SPIKING
SPIKS
SPIKY
SPILE
SPILED
SPILES
SPILIKIN
SPILIKINS
SPILING
SPILINGS
SPILITE
SPILITES
SPILITIC
SPILL
SPILLABLE*

SPILLAGE
SPILLAGES
SPILLED
SPILLER
SPILLERS
SPILLIKIN
SPILLIKINS
SPILLING
SPILLINGS
SPILLOVER
SPILLOVERS
SPILLS
SPILLWAY
SPILLWAYS
SPILOSITE
SPILOSITES
SPILT
SPILTH
SPILTHS
SPIN
SPINA
SPINACENE
SPINACENES
SPINACH
SPINACHES
SPINACHY*
SPINAE
SPINAGE
SPINAGES
SPINAL
SPINALLY*
SPINALS*
SPINAR
SPINARS
SPINAS
SPINATE
SPINDLE
SPINDLED
SPINDLER*
SPINDLERS*
SPINDLES
SPINDLIER
SPINDLIEST
SPINDLING
SPINDLINGS
SPINDLY
SPINDRIFT
SPINDRIFTS
SPINE
SPINED
SPINEL
SPINELESS
SPINELIKE*
SPINELLE*
SPINELLES*
SPINELS
SPINES
SPINET
SPINETS
SPINETTE
SPINETTES
SPINIER
SPINIEST
SPINIFEX

SPINIFEXES	SPIRALLED	SPIRY	SPLAYFEET*	SPLODGE
SPINIFORM	SPIRALLING	SPIT	SPLAYFOOT*	SPLODGED
SPININESS	SPIRALLY	SPITAL	SPLAYING	SPLODGES
SPININESSES	SPIRALS	SPITALS	SPLAYS	SPLODGIER
SPINK	SPIRANT	SPITBALL*	SPLEEN	SPLODGIEST
SPINKS	SPIRANTS	SPITBALLS*	SPLEENFUL	SPLODGILY
SPINLESS*	SPIRASTER	SPITCHER	SPLEENIER*	SPLODGING
SPINNAKER	SPIRASTERS	SPITE	SPLEENIEST*	SPLODGY
SPINNAKERS	SPIRATED	SPITED	SPLEENISH	SPLORE
SPINNER	SPIRATION	SPITEFUL	SPLEENS	SPLORES
SPINNERET	SPIRATIONS	SPITEFULLER	SPLEENY	SPLOSH
SPINNERETS	SPIRE	SPITEFULLEST	SPLENDENT	SPLOSHED
SPINNERIES	SPIREA	SPITES	SPLENDID	SPLOSHES
SPINNERS	SPIREAS	SPITFIRE	SPLENDIDER	SPLOSHING
SPINNERY	SPIRED	SPITFIRES	SPLENDIDEST	SPLOTCH
SPINNET	SPIRELESS	SPITING	SPLENDOR	SPLOTCHED
SPINNETS	SPIREM*	SPITS	SPLENDORS	SPLOTCHES
SPINNEY	SPIREME	SPITTED	SPLENDOUR	SPLOTCHIER
SPINNEYS	SPIREMES	SPITTEN	SPLENDOURS	SPLOTCHIEST
SPINNIES	SPIREMS*	SPITTER	SPLENETIC	SPLOTCHING
SPINNING	SPIRES	SPITTERS	SPLENETICS	SPLOTCHY
SPINNINGS	SPIREWISE	SPITTING	SPLENIA	SPLURGE
SPINNY	SPIRIC	SPITTINGS	SPLENIAL	SPLURGED
SPINODE	SPIRICS	SPITTLE	SPLENIC	SPLURGER*
SPINODES	SPIRIER	SPITTLES	SPLENII	SPLURGERS*
SPINOFF*	SPIRIEST	SPITTOON	SPLENITIS	SPLURGES
SPINOFFS*	SPIRILLA	SPITTOONS	SPLENITISES	SPLURGIER
SPINOR*	SPIRILLAR	SPITZ	SPLENIUM	SPLURGIEST
SPINORS*	SPIRILLUM	SPITZES	SPLENIUMS	SPLURGING
SPINOSE	SPIRING	SPIV	SPLENIUS	SPLURGY
SPINOSITIES	SPIRIT	SPIVS	SPLENIUSES	SPLUTTER
SPINOSITY	SPIRITED	SPIVVERIES	SPLENT	SPLUTTERED
SPINOUS	SPIRITFUL	SPIVVERY	SPLENTS	SPLUTTERING
SPINOUT	SPIRITING	SPIVVIER	SPLEUCHAN	SPLUTTERINGS
SPINOUTS	SPIRITINGS	SPIVVIEST	SPLEUCHANS	SPLUTTERS
SPINS	SPIRITISM	SPIVVY	SPLICE	SPLUTTERY
SPINSTER	SPIRITISMS	SPLAKE*	SPLICED	SPODE
SPINSTERS	SPIRITIST	SPLAKES*	SPLICER	SPODES
SPINTEXT	SPIRITISTS	SPLASH	SPLICERS	SPODIUM
SPINTEXTS	SPIRITOSO	SPLASHED	SPLICES	SPODIUMS
SPINTO	SPIRITOUS	SPLASHER	SPLICING	SPODOGRAM
SPINTOS*	SPIRITS	SPLASHERS	SPLIFF	SPODOGRAMS
SPINULA*	SPIRITUAL	SPLASHES	SPLIFFS	SPODUMENE
SPINULAE*	SPIRITUALS	SPLASHIER	SPLINE	SPODUMENES
SPINULATE	SPIRITUEL	SPLASHIEST	SPLINED	SPOFFISH
SPINULE	SPIRITUS	SPLASHILY	SPLINES	SPOFFY
SPINULES	SPIRITUSES	SPLASHING	SPLINING	SPOIL
SPINULOSE	SPIRITY	SPLASHINGS	SPLINT	SPOILABLE*
SPINULOUS	SPIRLING	SPLASHY	SPLINTED	SPOILAGE
SPINY	SPIRLINGS	SPLAT	SPLINTER	SPOILAGES
SPIRACLE	SPIROGRAM	SPLATCH	SPLINTERED	SPOILED
SPIRACLES	SPIROGRAMS	SPLATCHED	SPLINTERIER	SPOILER
SPIRACULA	SPIROGYRA	SPLATCHES	SPLINTERIEST	SPOILERS
SPIRAEA	SPIROGYRAS	SPLATCHING	SPLINTERING	SPOILFIVE
SPIRAEAS	SPIROID	SPLATS	SPLINTERS	SPOILFIVES
SPIRAL	SPIRT	SPLATTED	SPLINTERY	SPOILFUL
SPIRALED*	SPIRTED	SPLATTER	SPLINTING	SPOILING
SPIRALING*	SPIRTING	SPLATTERED	SPLINTS	SPOILS
SPIRALISM	SPIRTLE	SPLATTERING	SPLIT	SPOILSMAN
SPIRALISMS	SPIRTLES	SPLATTERS	SPLITS	SPOILSMEN
SPIRALIST	SPIRTS	SPLATTING	SPLITTED	SPOILT
SPIRALISTS	SPIRULA*	SPLATTINGS	SPLITTER	SPOKE
SPIRALITIES	SPIRULAE*	SPLAY	SPLITTERS	SPOKED
SPIRALITY	SPIRULAS*	SPLAYED	SPLITTING	SPOKEN

The Chambers Dictionary is the authority for many longer words; see Introduction, page ix

SPOKES	SPOOKIER	SPOROCARP	SPOTTINGS	SPRAUNCY
SPOKESMAN	SPOOKIEST	SPOROCARPS	SPOTTY	SPRAWL
SPOKESMEN	SPOOKILY	SPOROCYST	SPOUSAGE	SPRAWLED
SPOKEWISE	SPOOKING	SPOROCYSTS	SPOUSAGES	SPRAWLER
SPOKING*	SPOOKISH	SPOROGENIES	SPOUSAL	SPRAWLERS
SPOLIATE	SPOOKS	SPOROGENY	SPOUSALS	SPRAWLIER
SPOLIATED	SPOOKY	SPOROGONIES*	SPOUSE	SPRAWLIEST
SPOLIATES	SPOOL	SPOROGONY*	SPOUSED	SPRAWLING
SPOLIATING	SPOOLED	SPOROID*	SPOUSES	SPRAWLS
SPOLIATOR	SPOOLER	SPOROPHYL	SPOUSING	SPRAWLY
SPOLIATORS	SPOOLERS	SPOROPHYLS	SPOUT	SPRAY
SPONDAIC	SPOOLING	SPOROZOA*	SPOUTED	SPRAYED
SPONDAICS*	SPOOLINGS*	SPOROZOAN	SPOUTER	SPRAYER
SPONDEE	SPOOLS	SPOROZOANS	SPOUTERS	SPRAYERS
SPONDEES	SPOOM	SPOROZOON*	SPOUTIER	SPRAYEY
SPONDULIX	SPOOMED	SPORRAN	SPOUTIEST	SPRAYIER
SPONDYL	SPOOMING	SPORRANS	SPOUTING	SPRAYIEST
SPONDYLS	SPOOMS	SPORT	SPOUTINGS	SPRAYING
SPONGE	SPOON	SPORTABLE	SPOUTLESS	SPRAYS
SPONGEBAG	SPOONBAIT	SPORTANCE	SPOUTS	SPREAD
SPONGEBAGS	SPOONBAITS	SPORTANCES	SPOUTY	SPREADER
SPONGED	SPOONBILL	SPORTED	SPRACK	SPREADERS
SPONGEOUS	SPOONBILLS	SPORTER	SPRACKLE	SPREADING
SPONGER	SPOONED	SPORTERS	SPRACKLED	SPREADINGS
SPONGERS	SPOONEY	SPORTFUL	SPRACKLES	SPREADS
SPONGES	SPOONEYS	SPORTIER	SPRACKLING	SPREAGH
SPONGIER	SPOONFED	SPORTIEST	SPRAD	SPREAGHS
SPONGIEST	SPOONFUL	SPORTIF*	SPRADDLE*	SPREATHE
SPONGILY	SPOONFULS	SPORTILY	SPRADDLED*	SPREATHED
SPONGIN	SPOONHOOK	SPORTING	SPRADDLES*	SPREATHES
SPONGING	SPOONHOOKS	SPORTIVE	SPRADDLING*	SPREATHING
SPONGINS	SPOONIER	SPORTLESS	SPRAG	SPREAZE
SPONGIOSE	SPOONIES	SPORTS	SPRAGGED	SPREAZED
SPONGIOUS	SPOONIEST	SPORTSMAN	SPRAGGING	SPREAZES
SPONGOID	SPOONILY	SPORTSMEN	SPRAGS	SPREAZING
SPONGY	SPOONING	SPORTY	SPRAICKLE	SPRECHERIES
SPONSAL	SPOONS	SPORULAR	SPRAICKLED	SPRECHERY
SPONSALIA	SPOONSFUL*	SPORULATE	SPRAICKLES	SPRECKLED
SPONSIBLE	SPOONWAYS	SPORULATED	SPRAICKLING	SPRED
SPONSING	SPOONWISE	SPORULATES	SPRAID	SPREDD
SPONSINGS	SPOONY	SPORULATING	SPRAIN	SPREDDE
SPONSION	SPOOR	SPORULE	SPRAINED	SPREDDEN
SPONSIONS	SPOORED	SPORULES	SPRAINING	SPREDDES
SPONSON	SPOORER	SPOSH	SPRAINS	SPREDDING
SPONSONS	SPOORERS	SPOSHES	SPRAINT	SPREDDS
SPONSOR	SPOORING	SPOSHIER	SPRAINTS	SPREDS
SPONSORED	SPOORS	SPOSHIEST	SPRANG	SPREE
SPONSORING	SPOOT	SPOSHY	SPRANGLE	SPREED
SPONSORS	SPOOTS	SPOT	SPRANGLED	SPREEING
SPONTOON	SPORADIC	SPOTLESS	SPRANGLES	SPREES
SPONTOONS	SPORAL*	SPOTLIGHT	SPRANGLING	SPREETHE
SPOOF	SPORANGIA	SPOTLIGHTED	SPRANGS*	SPREETHED
SPOOFED	SPORANGIUM*	SPOTLIGHTING	SPRAT	SPREETHES
SPOOFER	SPORE	SPOTLIGHTS	SPRATS	SPREETHING
SPOOFERIES	SPORED*	SPOTLIT	SPRATTLE	SPREEZE
SPOOFERS	SPORES	SPOTS	SPRATTLED	SPREEZED
SPOOFERY	SPORICIDE*	SPOTTABLE*	SPRATTLES	SPREEZES
SPOOFING	SPORICIDES*	SPOTTED	SPRATTLING	SPREEZING
SPOOFS	SPORIDESM	SPOTTER	SPRAUCHLE	SPRENT
SPOOFY*	SPORIDESMS	SPOTTERS	SPRAUCHLED	SPREW
SPOOK	SPORIDIA	SPOTTIER	SPRAUCHLES	SPREWS
SPOOKED	SPORIDIAL	SPOTTIEST	SPRAUCHLING	SPRIER*
SPOOKERIES	SPORIDIUM	SPOTTILY	SPRAUNCIER	SPRIEST*
SPOOKERY	SPORING*	SPOTTING	SPRAUNCIEST	SPRIG

SPRIGGED	SPRITZED	SPUEING	SPURLING	SQUABBED
SPRIGGER*	SPRITZER	SPUES	SPURLINGS	SQUABBER
SPRIGGERS*	SPRITZERS	SPUILZIE	SPURN	SQUABBEST
SPRIGGIER	SPRITZES	SPUILZIED	SPURNE	SQUABBIER
SPRIGGIEST	SPRITZIG	SPUILZIEING	SPURNED	SQUABBIEST
SPRIGGING	SPRITZIGS	SPUILZIES	SPURNER	SQUABBING
SPRIGGY	SPRITZING	SPUING	SPURNERS	SQUABBISH
SPRIGHT	SPROCKET	SPULE	SPURNES	SQUABBLE
SPRIGHTED	SPROCKETS	SPULEBANE	SPURNING	SQUABBLED
SPRIGHTING	SPROD	SPULEBANES	SPURNINGS	SQUABBLER
SPRIGHTLIER	SPRODS	SPULEBONE	SPURNS	SQUABBLERS
SPRIGHTLIEST	SPROG	SPULEBONES	SPURRED	SQUABBLES
SPRIGHTLY	SPROGS	SPULES	SPURRER	SQUABBLING
SPRIGHTS	SPRONG	SPULYE	SPURRERS	SQUABBY
SPRIGS	SPROUT	SPULYED	SPURREY	SQUABS
SPRING	SPROUTED	SPULYEING	SPURREYS	SQUACCO
SPRINGAL	SPROUTING	SPULYES	SPURRIER	SQUACCOS
SPRINGALD	SPROUTINGS	SPULYIE	SPURRIERS	SQUAD
SPRINGALDS	SPROUTS	SPULYIED	SPURRIES	SQUADDED*
SPRINGALS	SPRUCE	SPULYIEING	SPURRIEST	SQUADDIE
SPRINGBOK	SPRUCED	SPULYIES	SPURRING	SQUADDIES
SPRINGBOKS	SPRUCELY	SPULZIE	SPURRINGS	SQUADDING*
SPRINGE	SPRUCER	SPULZIED	SPURRY	SQUADDY
SPRINGED	SPRUCES	SPULZIEING	SPURS	SQUADRON
SPRINGEING*	SPRUCEST	SPULZIES	SPURT	SQUADRONE
SPRINGER	SPRUCIER*	SPUMANTE	SPURTED	SQUADRONED
SPRINGERS	SPRUCIEST*	SPUMANTES	SPURTING	SQUADRONES
SPRINGES	SPRUCING	SPUME	SPURTLE	SQUADRONING
SPRINGIER	SPRUCY*	SPUMED	SPURTLES	SQUADRONS
SPRINGIEST	SPRUE	SPUMES	SPURTS	SQUADS
SPRINGILY	SPRUES	SPUMIER	SPURWAY	SQUAIL
SPRINGING	SPRUG	SPUMIEST	SPURWAYS	SQUAILED
SPRINGINGS	SPRUGS	SPUMING	SPUTA	SQUAILER
SPRINGLE	SPRUIK	SPUMONE*	SPUTNIK	SQUAILERS
SPRINGLES	SPRUIKED	SPUMONES*	SPUTNIKS	SQUAILING
SPRINGLET	SPRUIKER	SPUMONI*	SPUTTER	SQUAILINGS
SPRINGLETS	SPRUIKERS	SPUMONIS*	SPUTTERED	SQUAILS
SPRINGS	SPRUIKING	SPUMOUS	SPUTTERER	SQUALENE
SPRINGY	SPRUIKS	SPUMY	SPUTTERERS	SQUALENES
SPRINKLE	SPRUIT	SPUN	SPUTTERING	SQUALID
SPRINKLED	SPRUITS	SPUNGE	SPUTTERINGS	SQUALIDER
SPRINKLER	SPRUNG	SPUNGES	SPUTTERS	SQUALIDEST
SPRINKLERS	SPRUSH	SPUNK	SPUTTERY	SQUALIDLY
SPRINKLES	SPRUSHED	SPUNKED	SPUTUM	SQUALL
SPRINKLING	SPRUSHES	SPUNKIE	SPY	SQUALLED
SPRINKLINGS	SPRUSHING	SPUNKIER	SPYAL	SQUALLER
SPRINT	SPRY	SPUNKIES	SPYALS	SQUALLERS
SPRINTED	SPRYER	SPUNKIEST	SPYGLASS	SQUALLIER
SPRINTER	SPRYEST	SPUNKILY*	SPYGLASSES	SQUALLIEST
SPRINTERS	SPRYLY	SPUNKING	SPYHOLE	SQUALLING
SPRINTING	SPRYNESS	SPUNKS	SPYHOLES	SQUALLINGS
SPRINTINGS	SPRYNESSES	SPUNKY	SPYING	SQUALLS
SPRINTS	SPUD	SPUNYARN	SPYINGS	SQUALLY
SPRIT	SPUDDED	SPUNYARNS	SPYMASTER	SQUALOID
SPRITE	SPUDDER*	SPUR	SPYMASTERS	SQUALOR
SPRITEFUL	SPUDDERS*	SPURGALL*	SPYPLANE	SQUALORS
SPRITELIER	SPUDDIER	SPURGALLED*	SPYPLANES	SQUAMA
SPRITELIEST	SPUDDIEST	SPURGALLING*	SPYRE	SQUAMAE
SPRITELY	SPUDDING	SPURGALLS*	SPYRES	SQUAMATE
SPRITES	SPUDDINGS	SPURGE	SQUAB	SQUAME
SPRITS	SPUDDY	SPURGES	SQUABASH	SQUAMELLA
SPRITSAIL	SPUDS	SPURIAE	SQUABASHED	SQUAMELLAS
SPRITSAILS	SPUE	SPURIOUS	SQUABASHES	SQUAMES
SPRITZ	SPUED	SPURLESS	SQUABASHING	SQUAMOSAL

The Chambers Dictionary is the authority for many longer words; see Introduction, page ix

SQUAMOSALS	SQUAWKIEST	SQUIBBING	SQUINY	SQUOOSHES*
SQUAMOSE	SQUAWKING	SQUIBBINGS	SQUINYING	SQUOOSHIER*
SQUAMOUS	SQUAWKINGS	SQUIBS	SQUIRAGE	SQUOOSHIEST*
SQUAMULA	SQUAWKS	SQUID	SQUIRAGES	SQUOOSHING*
SQUAMULAS	SQUAWKY	SQUIDDED	SQUIRALTIES	SQUOOSHY*
SQUAMULE	SQUAWMAN	SQUIDDING	SQUIRALTY	SQUUSH*
SQUAMULES	SQUAWMEN	SQUIDGE	SQUIRARCH	SQUUSHED*
SQUANDER	SQUAWROOT*	SQUIDGED	SQUIRARCHS	SQUUSHES*
SQUANDERED	SQUAWROOTS*	SQUIDGES	SQUIRE	SQUUSHING*
SQUANDERING	SQUAWS	SQUIDGIER	SQUIREAGE	SRADDHA
SQUANDERINGS	SQUEAK	SQUIDGIEST	SQUIREAGES	SRADDHAS
SQUANDERS	SQUEAKED	SQUIDGING	SQUIRED	SRADHA*
SQUARE	SQUEAKER	SQUIDGY	SQUIREDOM	SRADHAS*
SQUARED	SQUEAKERIES	SQUIDS	SQUIREDOMS	SRI*
SQUARELY	SQUEAKERS	SQUIER	SQUIREEN	SRIS*
SQUARER	SQUEAKERY	SQUIERS	SQUIREENS	ST
SQUARERS	SQUEAKIER	SQUIFF	SQUIRELY	STAB
SQUARES	SQUEAKIEST	SQUIFFED*	SQUIRES	STABBED
SQUAREST	SQUEAKILY	SQUIFFER	SQUIRESS	STABBER
SQUARIAL	SQUEAKING	SQUIFFERS	SQUIRESSES	STABBERS
SQUARIALS	SQUEAKINGS	SQUIFFIER	SQUIRING	STABBING
SQUARING	SQUEAKS	SQUIFFIEST	SQUIRISH*	STABBINGS
SQUARINGS	SQUEAKY	SQUIFFY	SQUIRM	STABILATE
SQUARISH	SQUEAL	SQUIGGLE	SQUIRMED	STABILATES
SQUARROSE	SQUEALED	SQUIGGLED	SQUIRMER*	STABILE
SQUARSON	SQUEALER	SQUIGGLES	SQUIRMERS*	STABILES
SQUARSONS	SQUEALERS	SQUIGGLIER	SQUIRMIER	STABILISE
SQUASH	SQUEALING	SQUIGGLIEST	SQUIRMIEST	STABILISED
SQUASHED	SQUEALINGS	SQUIGGLING	SQUIRMING	STABILISES
SQUASHER	SQUEALS	SQUIGGLY	SQUIRMS	STABILISING
SQUASHERS	SQUEAMISH	SQUILGEE	SQUIRMY	STABILITIES
SQUASHES	SQUEEGEE	SQUILGEED	SQUIRR	STABILITY
SQUASHIER	SQUEEGEED	SQUILGEEING	SQUIRRED	STABILIZE
SQUASHIEST	SQUEEGEEING	SQUILGEES	SQUIRREL	STABILIZED
SQUASHILY	SQUEEGEES	SQUILL	SQUIRRELED*	STABILIZES
SQUASHING	SQUEEZE	SQUILLA	SQUIRRELING*	STABILIZING
SQUASHY	SQUEEZED	SQUILLAE*	SQUIRRELLED	STABLE
SQUAT	SQUEEZER	SQUILLAS	SQUIRRELLING	STABLEBOY
SQUATLY*	SQUEEZERS	SQUILLS	SQUIRRELS	STABLEBOYS
SQUATNESS	SQUEEZES	SQUINANCIES	SQUIRRELY	STABLED
SQUATNESSES	SQUEEZIER	SQUINANCY	SQUIRRING	STABLEMAN
SQUATS	SQUEEZIEST	SQUINCH	SQUIRRS	STABLEMEN
SQUATTED	SQUEEZING	SQUINCHED*	SQUIRT	STABLER
SQUATTER	SQUEEZINGS	SQUINCHES	SQUIRTED	STABLERS
SQUATTERED	SQUEEZY	SQUINCHING*	SQUIRTER	STABLES
SQUATTERING	SQUEG	SQUINIED	SQUIRTERS	STABLEST
SQUATTERS	SQUEGGED	SQUINIES	SQUIRTING	STABLING
SQUATTEST	SQUEGGER	SQUINNIED	SQUIRTINGS	STABLINGS
SQUATTIER	SQUEGGERS	SQUINNIER*	SQUIRTS	STABLISH
SQUATTIEST	SQUEGGING	SQUINNIES	SQUISH	STABLISHED
SQUATTING	SQUEGGINGS	SQUINNIEST*	SQUISHED	STABLISHES
SQUATTLE	SQUEGS	SQUINNY	SQUISHES	STABLISHING
SQUATTLED	SQUELCH	SQUINNYING	SQUISHIER	STABLY
SQUATTLES	SQUELCHED	SQUINT	SQUISHIEST	STABS
SQUATTLING	SQUELCHER	SQUINTED	SQUISHING	STACCATI*
SQUATTY	SQUELCHERS	SQUINTER	SQUISHY	STACCATO
SQUAW	SQUELCHES	SQUINTERS	SQUIT	STACCATOS
SQUAWFISH*	SQUELCHIER	SQUINTEST	SQUITCH	STACHYS
SQUAWFISHES*	SQUELCHIEST	SQUINTIER*	SQUITCHES	STACHYSES
SQUAWK	SQUELCHING	SQUINTIEST*	SQUITS	STACK
SQUAWKED	SQUELCHINGS	SQUINTING	SQUIZ	STACKABLE*
SQUAWKER	SQUELCHY	SQUINTINGS	SQUIZZES	STACKED
SQUAWKERS	SQUIB	SQUINTS	SQUOOSH*	STACKER
SQUAWKIER	SQUIBBED	SQUINTY*	SQUOOSHED*	STACKERS

STACKET	STAGGIER*	STAITHES	STAMINODY	STANDGALE
STACKETS	STAGGIES*	STAITHS	STAMINOID	STANDGALES
STACKING	STAGGIEST*	STAKE	STAMMEL	STANDING
STACKINGS	STAGGING	STAKED	STAMMELS	STANDINGS
STACKROOM	STAGHOUND	STAKEOUT*	STAMMER	STANDISH
STACKROOMS	STAGHOUNDS	STAKEOUTS*	STAMMERED	STANDISHES
STACKS	STAGIER	STAKES	STAMMERER	STANDOFF
STACKUP*	STAGIEST	STAKING	STAMMERERS	STANDOFFS*
STACKUPS*	STAGILY	STALACTIC	STAMMERING	STANDOUT
STACKYARD	STAGINESS	STALAG	STAMMERINGS	STANDOUTS
STACKYARDS	STAGINESSES	STALAGS	STAMMERS	STANDPAT*
STACTE	STAGING	STALE	STAMNOI	STANDPIPE
STACTES	STAGINGS	STALED	STAMNOS	STANDPIPES
STADDA	STAGNANCIES	STALELY	STAMP	STANDS
STADDAS	STAGNANCY	STALEMATE	STAMPED	STANDUP*
STADDLE	STAGNANT	STALEMATED	STAMPEDE	STANE
STADDLES	STAGNATE	STALEMATES	STAMPEDED	STANED
STADE	STAGNATED	STALEMATING	STAMPEDER*	STANES
STADES	STAGNATES	STALENESS	STAMPEDERS*	STANG
STADIA	STAGNATING	STALENESSES	STAMPEDES	STANGED
STADIAL	STAGS	STALER	STAMPEDING	STANGING
STADIALS	STAGY	STALES	STAMPEDO	STANGS
STADIAS	STAID	STALEST	STAMPEDOED	STANHOPE
STADIUM	STAIDER	STALING	STAMPEDOING	STANHOPES
STADIUMS	STAIDEST	STALK	STAMPEDOS	STANIEL
STAFF	STAIDLY	STALKED	STAMPER	STANIELS
STAFFAGE	STAIDNESS	STALKER	STAMPERS	STANINE*
STAFFAGES	STAIDNESSES	STALKERS	STAMPING	STANINES*
STAFFED	STAIG	STALKIER	STAMPINGS	STANING
STAFFER	STAIGS	STALKIEST	STAMPLESS*	STANK
STAFFERS	STAIN	STALKILY*	STAMPS	STANKS
STAFFING	STAINABLE*	STALKING	STANCE	STANNARIES
STAFFROOM	STAINED	STALKINGS	STANCES	STANNARY
STAFFROOMS	STAINER	STALKLESS	STANCH	STANNATE
STAFFS	STAINERS	STALKO	STANCHED	STANNATES
STAG	STAINING	STALKOES	STANCHEL	STANNATOR
STAGE	STAININGS	STALKS	STANCHELLED	STANNATORS
STAGEABLE*	STAINLESS	STALKY	STANCHELLING	STANNEL
STAGED	STAINLESSES*	STALL	STANCHELS	STANNELS
STAGEFUL*	STAINS	STALLAGE	STANCHER	STANNIC
STAGEFULS*	STAIR	STALLAGES	STANCHERED	STANNITE
STAGEHAND*	STAIRCASE	STALLED	STANCHERING	STANNITES
STAGEHANDS*	STAIRCASED	STALLING	STANCHERS	STANNOUS
STAGELIKE*	STAIRCASES	STALLINGS	STANCHES	STANNUM*
STAGER	STAIRCASING	STALLION	STANCHEST	STANNUMS*
STAGERIES	STAIRCASINGS	STALLIONS	STANCHING	STANYEL
STAGERS	STAIRED	STALLMAN	STANCHINGS	STANYELS
STAGERY	STAIRFOOT	STALLMEN	STANCHION	STANZA
STAGES	STAIRFOOTS	STALLS	STANCHIONED	STANZAED*
STAGEY	STAIRHEAD	STALWART	STANCHIONING	STANZAIC
STAGGARD	STAIRHEADS	STALWARTS	STANCHIONS	STANZAS
STAGGARDS	STAIRLIFT	STALWORTH	STANCHLY	STANZE
STAGGART*	STAIRLIFTS	STALWORTHS	STANCK	STANZES
STAGGARTS*	STAIRS	STAMEN	STAND	STANZO
STAGGED	STAIRWAY	STAMENED	STANDARD	STANZOES
STAGGER	STAIRWAYS	STAMENS	STANDARDS	STANZOS
STAGGERED	STAIRWELL	STAMINA	STANDAWAY*	STAP
STAGGERER	STAIRWELLS	STAMINAL	STANDBY*	STAPEDES
STAGGERERS	STAIRWISE	STAMINAS	STANDBYS*	STAPEDIAL
STAGGERING	STAIRWORK	STAMINATE	STANDEE	STAPEDII
STAGGERINGS	STAIRWORKS	STAMINEAL	STANDEES	STAPEDIUS
STAGGERS	STAITH	STAMINODE	STANDEN	STAPEDIUSES
STAGGERY*	STAITHE	STAMINODES	STANDER	STAPELIA
STAGGIE*		STAMINODIES	STANDERS	STAPELIAS

The Chambers Dictionary is the authority for many longer words; see Introduction, page ix

STAPES
STAPH
STAPHS
STAPLE
STAPLED
STAPLER
STAPLERS
STAPLES
STAPLING
STAPPED
STAPPING
STAPPLE
STAPPLES
STAPS
STAR
STARAGEN
STARAGENS
STARBOARD
STARBOARDED
STARBOARDING
STARBOARDS
STARCH
STARCHED
STARCHER
STARCHERS
STARCHES
STARCHIER
STARCHIEST
STARCHILY
STARCHING
STARCHY
STARDOM
STARDOMS
STARDRIFT
STARDRIFTS
STARDUST
STARDUSTS
STARE
STARED
STARER
STARERS
STARES
STARETS
STARETSES
STARETZ
STARETZES
STARFISH
STARFISHES
STARFRUIT*
STARFRUITS*
STARGAZE*
STARGAZED*
STARGAZER
STARGAZERS
STARGAZES*
STARGAZING*
STARING
STARINGLY
STARINGS
STARK
STARKED
STARKEN
STARKENED
STARKENING

STARKENS
STARKER
STARKERS
STARKEST
STARKING
STARKLY
STARKNESS
STARKNESSES
STARKS
STARLESS
STARLET
STARLETS
STARLIGHT
STARLIGHTS
STARLIKE
STARLING
STARLINGS
STARLIT
STARN
STARNED
STARNIE
STARNIES
STARNING
STARNOSE*
STARNOSES*
STARNS
STAROSTA
STAROSTAS
STAROSTIES
STAROSTY
STARR
STARRED
STARRIER
STARRIEST
STARRILY
STARRING
STARRINGS
STARRS
STARRY
STARS
STARSHINE
STARSHINES
STARSHIP*
STARSHIPS*
STARSPOT
STARSPOTS
STARSTONE
STARSTONES
START
STARTED
STARTER
STARTERS
STARTFUL
STARTING
STARTINGS
STARTISH
STARTLE
STARTLED
STARTLER
STARTLERS
STARTLES
STARTLING
STARTLINGS
STARTLISH

STARTLY
STARTS
STARTSY*
STARTUP*
STARTUPS*
STARVE
STARVED
STARVER*
STARVERS*
STARVES
STARVING
STARVINGS
STARWORT
STARWORTS
STASES
STASH
STASHED
STASHES
STASHIE
STASHIES
STASHING
STASIDION
STASIDIONS
STASIMA
STASIMON
STASIS
STAT*
STATABLE
STATAL
STATANT
STATE
STATEABLE*
STATED
STATEDLY
STATEHOOD
STATEHOODS
STATELESS
STATELIER
STATELIEST
STATELILY
STATELY
STATEMENT
STATEMENTED
STATEMENTING
STATEMENTINGS
STATEMENTS
STATER
STATEROOM
STATEROOMS
STATERS
STATES
STATESIDE
STATESMAN
STATESMEN
STATEWIDE
STATIC
STATICAL
STATICE
STATICES
STATICKY*
STATICS
STATIM
STATING
STATION

STATIONAL
STATIONED
STATIONER
STATIONERS
STATIONING
STATIONS
STATISM
STATISMS
STATIST
STATISTIC
STATISTICS
STATISTS
STATIVE
STATIVES*
STATOCYST
STATOCYSTS
STATOLITH
STATOLITHS
STATOR
STATORS
STATUA
STATUARIES
STATUARY
STATUAS
STATUE
STATUED
STATUES
STATUETTE
STATUETTES
STATURE
STATURED
STATURES
STATUS
STATUSES
STATUSY*
STATUTE
STATUTES
STATUTORY
STAUMREL*
STAUMRELS*
STAUNCH
STAUNCHED
STAUNCHER
STAUNCHERS
STAUNCHES
STAUNCHEST
STAUNCHING
STAUNCHINGS
STAUNCHLY
STAVE
STAVED
STAVES
STAVING
STAW
STAWED
STAWING
STAWS
STAY
STAYAWAY
STAYAWAYS
STAYED
STAYER
STAYERS

STAYING
STAYLESS
STAYMAKER
STAYMAKERS
STAYNE
STAYNED
STAYNES
STAYNING
STAYRE
STAYRES
STAYS
STAYSAIL
STAYSAILS
STEAD
STEADED
STEADFAST
STEADICAM
STEADICAMS
STEADIED
STEADIER
STEADIERS*
STEADIES
STEADIEST
STEADILY
STEADING
STEADINGS
STEADS
STEADY
STEADYING
STEAK
STEAKS
STEAL
STEALABLE*
STEALAGE*
STEALAGES*
STEALE
STEALED
STEALER
STEALERS
STEALES
STEALING
STEALINGS
STEALS
STEALT
STEALTH
STEALTHED
STEALTHIER
STEALTHIEST
STEALTHING
STEALTHINGS
STEALTHS
STEALTHY
STEAM
STEAMBOAT
STEAMBOATS
STEAMED
STEAMER
STEAMERED*
STEAMERING*
STEAMERS
STEAMIE
STEAMIER
STEAMIES
STEAMIEST

STEAMILY	STEEDIED	STEEPLED	STELLAR	STENCIL
STEAMING	STEEDIES	STEEPLES	STELLAS*	STENCILED
STEAMINGS	STEEDING	STEEPLY	STELLATE	STENCILER*
STEAMROLL*	STEEDS	STEEPNESS	STELLATED	STENCILERS*
STEAMROLLED*	STEEDY	STEEPNESSES	STELLED	STENCILING
STEAMROLLING*	STEEDYING	STEEPS	STELLERID	STENCILLED
STEAMROLLS*	STEEK	STEEPUP	STELLERIDS	STENCILLING
STEAMS	STEEKED*	STEEPY	STELLIFIED	STENCILLINGS
STEAMSHIP	STEEKING	STEER	STELLIFIES	STENCILS
STEAMSHIPS	STEEKIT	STEERABLE	STELLIFY	STEND
STEAMY	STEEKS	STEERAGE	STELLIFYING	STENDED
STEAN	STEEL	STEERAGES	STELLIFYINGS	STENDING
STEANE	STEELBOW	STEERED	STELLING	STENDS
STEANED	STEELBOWS	STEERER	STELLION	STENGAH
STEANES	STEELD	STEERERS	STELLIONS	STENGAHS
STEANING	STEELED	STEERIES	STELLS	STENLOCK
STEANINGS	STEELHEAD*	STEERING	STELLULAR	STENLOCKS
STEANS	STEELHEADS*	STEERINGS	STEM	STENNED
STEAPSIN	STEELIE*	STEERLING	STEMBOK	STENNING
STEAPSINS	STEELIER	STEERLINGS	STEMBOKS	STENO*
STEAR	STEELIES*	STEERS	STEMBUCK	STENOKIES*
STEARAGE	STEELIEST	STEERSMAN	STEMBUCKS	STENOKY*
STEARAGES	STEELING	STEERSMEN	STEME	STENOPAIC
STEARATE	STEELINGS	STEERY	STEMED	STENOS*
STEARATES	STEELMAN	STEEVE	STEMES	STENOSED
STEARD	STEELMEN	STEEVED	STEMING	STENOSES
STEARE	STEELS	STEEVELY	STEMLESS	STENOSIS
STEARED	STEELWARE	STEEVER	STEMLET	STENOTIC
STEARES	STEELWARES	STEEVES	STEMLETS	STENOTYPE*
STEARIC	STEELWORK	STEEVEST	STEMLIKE*	STENOTYPED*
STEARIN	STEELWORKS	STEEVING	STEMMA	STENOTYPES*
STEARINE	STEELY	STEEVINGS	STEMMAS*	STENOTYPIES
STEARINES	STEELYARD	STEGNOSES	STEMMATA	STENOTYPING*
STEARING	STEELYARDS	STEGNOSIS	STEMMATIC*	STENOTYPY
STEARINS	STEEM	STEGNOTIC	STEMME	STENS
STEARS	STEEMED	STEGODON	STEMMED	STENT
STEARSMAN	STEEMING	STEGODONS	STEMMER	STENTED
STEARSMEN	STEEMS	STEGODONT	STEMMERIES*	STENTING
STEATITE	STEEN	STEGODONTS	STEMMERS	STENTOR
STEATITES	STEENBOK	STEGOSAUR	STEMMERY*	STENTORS
STEATITIC	STEENBOKS	STEGOSAURS	STEMMES	STENTOUR
STEATOMA	STEENBRAS	STEIL	STEMMIER*	STENTOURS
STEATOMAS	STEENBRASES	STEILS	STEMMIEST*	STENTS
STEATOSES	STEENED	STEIN	STEMMING	STEP
STEATOSIS	STEENING	STEINBOCK	STEMMINGS	STEPBAIRN
STED	STEENINGS	STEINBOCKS	STEMMY*	STEPBAIRNS
STEDD	STEENKIRK	STEINBOK*	STEMPEL	STEPCHILD
STEDDE	STEENKIRKS	STEINBOKS*	STEMPELS	STEPCHILDREN
STEDDED	STEENS	STEINED	STEMPLE	STEPDAME
STEDDES	STEEP	STEINING	STEMPLES	STEPDAMES
STEDDIED	STEEPED	STEININGS	STEMS	STEPHANE
STEDDIES	STEEPEN	STEINKIRK	STEMSON	STEPHANES
STEDDING	STEEPENED	STEINKIRKS	STEMSONS	STEPLIKE*
STEDDS	STEEPENING	STEINS	STEMWARE*	STEPNEY
STEDDY	STEEPENS	STELA	STEMWARES*	STEPNEYS
STEDDYING	STEEPER	STELAE	STEN	STEPPE
STEDE	STEEPERS	STELAI*	STENCH	STEPPED
STEDED	STEEPEST	STELAR	STENCHED	STEPPER
STEDES	STEEPEUP	STELE	STENCHES	STEPPERS
STEDFAST	STEEPIER	STELENE	STENCHFUL*	STEPPES
STEDING	STEEPIEST	STELES	STENCHIER	STEPPING
STEDS	STEEPING	STELIC*	STENCHIEST	STEPS
STEED	STEEPISH	STELL	STENCHING	STEPSON
STEEDED	STEEPLE	STELLA*	STENCHY	STEPSONS

The Chambers Dictionary is the authority for many longer words; see Introduction, page ix

STEPT	STERNSONS	STIBIAL	STICKWORK	STILET
STEPWISE	STERNUM	STIBINE	STICKWORKS	STILETS
STERADIAN	STERNUMS	STIBINES	STICKY	STILETTO
STERADIANS	STERNWARD	STIBIUM	STICKYING	STILETTOED
STERCORAL	STERNWARDS	STIBIUMS	STICTION	STILETTOES*
STERCULIA	STERNWAY	STIBNITE	STICTIONS	STILETTOING
STERCULIAS	STERNWAYS	STIBNITES	STIDDIE	STILETTOS
STERE	STEROID	STICCADO	STIDDIED	STILING
STEREO	STEROIDAL*	STICCADOES	STIDDIEING	STILL
STEREOED*	STEROIDS	STICCADOS	STIDDIES	STILLAGE
STEREOING*	STEROL	STICCATO	STIDDYING	STILLAGES
STEREOME	STEROLS	STICCATOES	STIE	STILLBORN
STEREOMES	STERTOR*	STICCATOS	STIED	STILLBORNS*
STEREOS	STERTORS*	STICH	STIES	STILLED
STERES	STERVE	STICHARIA	STIEVE	STILLER
STERIC	STERVED	STICHERA	STIEVELY	STILLERS
STERICAL*	STERVES	STICHERON	STIEVER	STILLEST
STERIGMA	STERVING	STICHIC	STIEVEST	STILLIER
STERIGMAS*	STET	STICHIDIA	STIFF	STILLIEST
STERIGMATA	STETS	STICHOI	STIFFED	STILLING
STERILANT	STETTED	STICHOS	STIFFEN	STILLINGS
STERILANTS	STETTING	STICHS	STIFFENED	STILLION
STERILE	STEVEDORE	STICK	STIFFENER	STILLIONS
STERILELY*	STEVEDORED	STICKBALL*	STIFFENERS	STILLMAN*
STERILISE	STEVEDORES	STICKBALLS*	STIFFENING	STILLMEN*
STERILISED	STEVEDORING	STICKED	STIFFENINGS	STILLNESS
STERILISES	STEVEN	STICKER	STIFFENS	STILLNESSES
STERILISING	STEVENS	STICKERED	STIFFER	STILLROOM
STERILITIES	STEW	STICKERING	STIFFEST	STILLROOMS
STERILITY	STEWARD	STICKERS	STIFFIE	STILLS
STERILIZE	STEWARDED*	STICKFUL	STIFFIES	STILLY
STERILIZED	STEWARDING*	STICKFULS	STIFFING	STILT
STERILIZES	STEWARDRIES	STICKIED	STIFFISH	STILTBIRD
STERILIZING	STEWARDRY	STICKIER	STIFFLY	STILTBIRDS
STERLET	STEWARDS	STICKIES	STIFFNESS	STILTED
STERLETS	STEWARTRIES	STICKIEST	STIFFNESSES	STILTEDLY
STERLING	STEWARTRY	STICKILY	STIFFS	STILTER
STERLINGS	STEWBUM*	STICKING	STIFFWARE	STILTERS
STERN	STEWBUMS*	STICKINGS	STIFFWARES	STILTIER
STERNA	STEWED	STICKIT	STIFFY	STILTIEST
STERNAGE	STEWER	STICKJAW	STIFLE	STILTING
STERNAGES	STEWERS	STICKJAWS	STIFLED	STILTINGS
STERNAL	STEWIER	STICKLE	STIFLER	STILTISH
STERNEBRA	STEWIEST	STICKLED	STIFLERS	STILTS
STERNEBRAE	STEWING	STICKLER	STIFLES	STILTY
STERNED	STEWINGS	STICKLERS	STIFLING	STIME
STERNER	STEWPAN	STICKLES	STIFLINGS	STIMED
STERNEST	STEWPANS	STICKLIKE*	STIGMA	STIMES
STERNFAST	STEWPOND	STICKLING	STIGMAL*	STIMIE
STERNFASTS	STEWPONDS	STICKMAN*	STIGMAS	STIMIED
STERNING	STEWPOT	STICKMEN*	STIGMATA	STIMIES
STERNITE	STEWPOTS	STICKOUT*	STIGMATIC	STIMING
STERNITES	STEWS	STICKOUTS*	STIGMATICS	STIMULANT
STERNITIC	STEWY	STICKPIN*	STIGME	STIMULANTS
STERNLY	STEY	STICKPINS*	STIGMES	STIMULATE
STERNMOST	STEYER	STICKS	STILB	STIMULATED
STERNNESS	STEYEST	STICKSEED*	STILBENE	STIMULATES
STERNNESSES	STHENIA*	STICKSEEDS*	STILBENES	STIMULATING
STERNPORT	STHENIAS*	STICKUM*	STILBITE	STIMULI
STERNPORTS	STHENIC	STICKUMS*	STILBITES	STIMULUS
STERNPOST	STIBBLE	STICKUP*	STILBS	STIMY
STERNPOSTS	STIBBLER	STICKUPS*	STILE	STIMYING
STERNS	STIBBLERS	STICKWEED*	STILED	STING
STERNSON	STIBBLES	STICKWEEDS*	STILES	STINGAREE

Words marked with an asterisk are from OTCWL

STINGAREES	STIPITES	STIVIER	STOCKTAKINGS	STOLONIC*
STINGBULL	STIPPLE	STIVIEST	STOCKTOOK	STOLONS
STINGBULLS	STIPPLED	STIVING	STOCKWORK	STOLPORT*
STINGED	STIPPLER	STIVY	STOCKWORKS	STOLPORTS*
STINGER	STIPPLERS	STOA	STOCKY	STOMA
STINGERS	STIPPLES	STOAE	STOCKYARD	STOMACH
STINGFISH	STIPPLING	STOAI	STOCKYARDS	STOMACHAL
STINGFISHES	STIPPLINGS	STOAS	STODGE	STOMACHED
STINGIER	STIPULAR	STOAT	STODGED	STOMACHER
STINGIEST	STIPULARY	STOATS	STODGER	STOMACHERS
STINGILY	STIPULATE	STOB	STODGERS	STOMACHIC
STINGING	STIPULATED	STOBBED*	STODGES	STOMACHICS
STINGINGS	STIPULATES	STOBBING*	STODGIER	STOMACHING
STINGLESS	STIPULATING	STOBS	STODGIEST	STOMACHS
STINGO	STIPULE	STOCCADO	STODGILY	STOMACHY
STINGOS	STIPULED	STOCCADOS	STODGING	STOMAL
STINGRAY*	STIPULES	STOCCATA	STODGY	STOMAS*
STINGRAYS*	STIR	STOCCATAS	STOEP	STOMATA
STINGS	STIRABOUT	STOCIOUS	STOEPS	STOMATAL
STINGY	STIRABOUTS	STOCK	STOGEY	STOMATE*
STINK	STIRE	STOCKADE	STOGEYS	STOMATES*
STINKARD	STIRED	STOCKADED	STOGIE	STOMATIC
STINKARDS	STIRES	STOCKADES	STOGIES	STOMODAEA
STINKBUG*	STIRING	STOCKADING	STOGY	STOMODAEUM*
STINKBUGS*	STIRK	STOCKCAR*	STOIC	STOMODAEUMS*
STINKER	STIRKS	STOCKCARS*	STOICAL	STOMODEA
STINKERS	STIRLESS	STOCKED	STOICALLY	STOMODEAL*
STINKHORN	STIRP	STOCKER	STOICISM	STOMODEUM
STINKHORNS	STIRPES	STOCKERS	STOICISMS	STOMODEUMS
STINKIER*	STIRPS	STOCKFISH	STOICS	STOMP
STINKIEST*	STIRRA	STOCKFISHES	STOIT	STOMPED
STINKING	STIRRAH	STOCKHORN	STOITED	STOMPER
STINKINGS	STIRRAHS	STOCKHORNS	STOITER	STOMPERS
STINKO	STIRRAS	STOCKIER	STOITERED	STOMPING
STINKPOT*	STIRRE	STOCKIEST	STOITERING	STOMPS
STINKPOTS*	STIRRED	STOCKILY	STOITERS	STONABLE*
STINKS	STIRRER	STOCKINET	STOITING	STOND
STINKWEED*	STIRRERS	STOCKINETS	STOITS	STONDS
STINKWEEDS*	STIRRES	STOCKING	STOKE	STONE
STINKWOOD	STIRRING	STOCKINGS	STOKED	STONEBOAT
STINKWOODS	STIRRINGS	STOCKISH*	STOKEHOLD	STONEBOATS
STINKY*	STIRRUP	STOCKIST	STOKEHOLDS	STONECAST
STINT	STIRRUPS	STOCKISTS	STOKEHOLE	STONECASTS
STINTED	STIRS	STOCKLESS	STOKEHOLES	STONECHAT
STINTEDLY	STISHIE	STOCKLIST	STOKER	STONECHATS
STINTER	STISHIES	STOCKLISTS	STOKERS	STONECROP
STINTERS	STITCH	STOCKLOCK	STOKES	STONECROPS
STINTIER	STITCHED	STOCKLOCKS	STOKESIA*	STONED
STINTIEST	STITCHER	STOCKMAN	STOKESIAS*	STONEFISH
STINTING	STITCHERIES	STOCKMEN	STOKING	STONEFISHES
STINTINGS	STITCHERS	STOCKPILE	STOLE	STONEFLIES
STINTLESS	STITCHERY	STOCKPILED	STOLED	STONEFLY
STINTS	STITCHES	STOCKPILES	STOLEN	STONEHAND
STINTY	STITCHING	STOCKPILING	STOLES	STONEHANDS
STIPA	STITCHINGS	STOCKPILINGS	STOLID	STONELESS
STIPAS	STITHIED	STOCKPOT	STOLIDER	STONEN
STIPE	STITHIES	STOCKPOTS	STOLIDEST	STONER
STIPED*	STITHY	STOCKROOM	STOLIDITIES	STONERAG
STIPEL	STITHYING	STOCKROOMS	STOLIDITY	STONERAGS
STIPELS	STIVE	STOCKS	STOLIDLY	STONERAW
STIPEND	STIVED	STOCKTAKE	STOLLEN	STONERAWS
STIPENDS	STIVER	STOCKTAKEN	STOLLENS	STONERN
STIPES	STIVERS	STOCKTAKES	STOLN	STONERS
STIPITATE	STIVES	STOCKTAKING	STOLON	STONES

The Chambers Dictionary is the authority for many longer words; see Introduction, page ix

STONESHOT	STOOPBALL*	STOREROOMS	STOURE*	STRABISM
STONESHOTS	STOOPBALLS*	STORERS	STOURES*	STRABISMS
STONEWALL	STOOPE	STORES	STOURIE*	STRAD
STONEWALLED	STOOPED	STORESHIP*	STOURIER	STRADDLE
STONEWALLING	STOOPER	STORESHIPS*	STOURIEST	STRADDLED
STONEWALLINGS	STOOPERS	STOREWIDE*	STOURS	STRADDLER*
STONEWALLS	STOOPES	STOREY	STOURY	STRADDLERS*
STONEWARE	STOOPING	STOREYED	STOUSH	STRADDLES
STONEWARES	STOOPS	STOREYS	STOUSHED	STRADDLING
STONEWORK	STOOR	STORGE	STOUSHES	STRADIOT
STONEWORKS	STOORS	STORGES	STOUSHING	STRADIOTS
STONEWORT	STOOSHIE	STORIATED	STOUT	STRADS
STONEWORTS	STOOSHIES	STORIED	STOUTEN	STRAE
STONEY*	STOP	STORIES	STOUTENED	STRAES
STONG	STOPBANK	STORIETTE	STOUTENING	STRAFE
STONIED	STOPBANKS	STORIETTES	STOUTENS	STRAFED
STONIER	STOPCOCK	STORING	STOUTER	STRAFER*
STONIES	STOPCOCKS	STORK	STOUTEST	STRAFERS*
STONIEST	STOPE	STORKS	STOUTH	STRAFES
STONILY	STOPED	STORM	STOUTHRIE	STRAFF
STONINESS	STOPER*	STORMBIRD	STOUTHRIES	STRAFFED
STONINESSES	STOPERS*	STORMBIRDS	STOUTHS	STRAFFING
STONING	STOPES	STORMED	STOUTISH	STRAFFS
STONINGS	STOPGAP	STORMFUL	STOUTLY	STRAFING
STONISH*	STOPGAPS	STORMIER	STOUTNESS	STRAG
STONISHED*	STOPING	STORMIEST	STOUTNESSES	STRAGGLE
STONISHES*	STOPINGS	STORMILY	STOUTS	STRAGGLED
STONISHING*	STOPLESS	STORMING	STOVAINE	STRAGGLER
STONK	STOPLIGHT	STORMINGS	STOVAINES	STRAGGLERS
STONKER	STOPLIGHTS	STORMLESS	STOVE	STRAGGLES
STONKERED	STOPOFF	STORMS	STOVED	STRAGGLIER
STONKERING	STOPOFFS	STORMY	STOVEPIPE	STRAGGLIEST
STONKERS	STOPOVER	STORNELLI	STOVEPIPES	STRAGGLING
STONKING	STOPOVERS	STORNELLO	STOVER	STRAGGLINGS
STONKS	STOPPABLE*	STORY	STOVERS	STRAGGLY
STONN	STOPPAGE	STORYBOOK	STOVES	STRAGS
STONNE	STOPPAGES	STORYBOOKS	STOVIES	STRAICHT
STONNED	STOPPED	STORYETTE	STOVING	STRAICHTER
STONNES	STOPPER	STORYETTES	STOVINGS	STRAICHTEST
STONNING	STOPPERED	STORYING	STOW	STRAIGHT
STONNS	STOPPERING	STORYINGS	STOWABLE*	STRAIGHTED*
STONY	STOPPERS	STORYLINE	STOWAGE	STRAIGHTER
STONYING	STOPPING	STORYLINES	STOWAGES	STRAIGHTEST
STOOD	STOPPINGS	STOSS	STOWAWAY	STRAIGHTING*
STOODEN	STOPPLE	STOSSES	STOWAWAYS	STRAIGHTS
STOOGE	STOPPLED	STOT	STOWDOWN	STRAIK
STOOGED	STOPPLES	STOTINKA	STOWDOWNS	STRAIKED
STOOGES	STOPPLING	STOTINKI	STOWED	STRAIKING
STOOGING	STOPS	STOTIOUS	STOWER	STRAIKS
STOOK	STOPT*	STOTS	STOWERS	STRAIN
STOOKED	STOPWATCH	STOTTED	STOWING	STRAINED
STOOKER	STOPWATCHES	STOTTER	STOWINGS	STRAINER
STOOKERS	STORABLE	STOTTERS	STOWLINS	STRAINERS
STOOKING	STORABLES*	STOTTING	STOWN	STRAINING
STOOKS	STORAGE	STOUN	STOWND	STRAININGS
STOOL	STORAGES	STOUND	STOWNDED	STRAINS
STOOLBALL	STORAX	STOUNDED	STOWNDING	STRAINT
STOOLBALLS	STORAXES	STOUNDING	STOWNDS	STRAINTS
STOOLED	STORE	STOUNDS	STOWNLINS	STRAIT
STOOLIE	STORED	STOUNING	STOWP*	STRAITED
STOOLIES	STOREMAN	STOUNS	STOWPS*	STRAITEN
STOOLING	STOREMEN	STOUP	STOWRE	STRAITENED
STOOLS	STORER	STOUPS	STOWRES	STRAITENING
STOOP	STOREROOM	STOUR	STOWS	STRAITENS

Words marked with an asterisk are from OTCWL

STRAITER	STRAPPING	STRAWY	STREIGNING	STRIATURE
STRAITEST	STRAPPINGS	STRAY	STRELITZ	STRIATURES
STRAITING	STRAPPY	STRAYED	STRELITZES	STRICH
STRAITLY	STRAPS	STRAYER	STRELITZI	STRICHES
STRAITS	STRAPWORT	STRAYERS	STRENE	STRICK*
STRAKE	STRAPWORTS	STRAYING	STRENES	STRICKEN
STRAKED*	STRASS	STRAYINGS	STRENGTH	STRICKLE
STRAKES	STRASSES	STRAYLING	STRENGTHS	STRICKLED
STRAMACON	STRATA	STRAYLINGS	STRENUITIES	STRICKLES
STRAMACONS	STRATAGEM	STRAYS	STRENUITY	STRICKLING
STRAMASH	STRATAGEMS	STREAK	STRENUOUS	STRICKS*
STRAMASHED	STRATAL*	STREAKED	STREP	STRICT
STRAMASHES	STRATAS*	STREAKER	STREPENT	STRICTER
STRAMASHING	STRATEGIC	STREAKERS	STREPS	STRICTEST
STRAMAZON	STRATEGICS	STREAKIER	STRESS	STRICTISH
STRAMAZONS	STRATEGIES	STREAKIEST	STRESSED	STRICTLY
STRAMMEL	STRATEGY	STREAKILY	STRESSES	STRICTURE
STRAMMELS	STRATH	STREAKING	STRESSFUL	STRICTURES
STRAMONIES*	STRATHS	STREAKINGS	STRESSING	STRIDDEN
STRAMONY*	STRATI	STREAKS	STRESSOR	STRIDDLE
STRAMP	STRATIFIED	STREAKY	STRESSORS	STRIDDLED
STRAMPED	STRATIFIES	STREAM	STRETCH	STRIDDLES
STRAMPING	STRATIFY	STREAMBED*	STRETCHED	STRIDDLING
STRAMPS	STRATIFYING	STREAMBEDS*	STRETCHER	STRIDE
STRAND	STRATONIC	STREAMED	STRETCHERED	STRIDENCE
STRANDED	STRATOSE	STREAMER	STRETCHERING	STRIDENCES
STRANDER*	STRATOUS	STREAMERS	STRETCHERS	STRIDENCIES
STRANDERS*	STRATUM	STREAMIER	STRETCHES	STRIDENCY
STRANDING	STRATUMS*	STREAMIEST	STRETCHIER	STRIDENT
STRANDS	STRATUS	STREAMING	STRETCHIEST	STRIDER*
STRANG*	STRAUCHT	STREAMINGS	STRETCHING	STRIDERS*
STRANGE	STRAUCHTED	STREAMLET	STRETCHY	STRIDES
STRANGELY	STRAUCHTER	STREAMLETS	STRETTA	STRIDING
STRANGER	STRAUCHTEST	STREAMS	STRETTAS*	STRIDLING
STRANGERED	STRAUCHTING	STREAMY	STRETTE	STRIDOR
STRANGERING	STRAUCHTS	STREEK	STRETTI	STRIDORS
STRANGERS	STRAUGHT	STREEKED	STRETTO	STRIFE
STRANGEST	STRAUGHTED	STREEKER*	STRETTOS*	STRIFEFUL
STRANGLE	STRAUGHTER	STREEKERS*	STREUSEL*	STRIFES
STRANGLED	STRAUGHTEST	STREEKING	STREUSELS*	STRIFT
STRANGLER	STRAUGHTING	STREEKS	STREW	STRIFTS
STRANGLERS	STRAUGHTS	STREEL	STREWAGE	STRIG
STRANGLES	STRAUNGE	STREELED	STREWAGES	STRIGA
STRANGLING	STRAVAGE*	STREELING	STREWED	STRIGAE
STRANGURIES	STRAVAGED*	STREELS	STREWER	STRIGATE
STRANGURY	STRAVAGES*	STREET	STREWERS	STRIGGED
STRAP	STRAVAGING*	STREETAGE	STREWING	STRIGGING
STRAPHANG*	STRAVAIG	STREETAGES	STREWINGS	STRIGIL
STRAPHANGING*	STRAVAIGED	STREETBOY	STREWMENT	STRIGILS
STRAPHANGS*	STRAVAIGING	STREETBOYS	STREWMENTS	STRIGINE
STRAPHUNG*	STRAVAIGS	STREETCAR	STREWN	STRIGOSE
STRAPLESS	STRAW	STREETCARS	STREWS	STRIGS
STRAPLESSES*	STRAWED	STREETED	STREWTH	STRIKE
STRAPLINE	STRAWEN	STREETFUL	STRIA	STRIKEOUT
STRAPLINES	STRAWHAT*	STREETFULS	STRIAE	STRIKEOUTS
STRAPPADO	STRAWIER	STREETIER	STRIATA	STRIKER
STRAPPADOED	STRAWIEST	STREETIEST	STRIATE	STRIKERS
STRAPPADOING	STRAWING	STREETS	STRIATED	STRIKES
STRAPPADOS	STRAWLESS	STREETY	STRIATES	STRIKING
STRAPPED	STRAWLIKE	STREIGHT	STRIATING	STRIKINGS
STRAPPER	STRAWN	STREIGHTS	STRIATION	STRING
STRAPPERS	STRAWS	STREIGNE	STRIATIONS	STRINGED
STRAPPIER	STRAWWORM	STREIGNED	STRIATUM	STRINGENT
STRAPPIEST	STRAWWORMS	STREIGNES	STRIATUMS	STRINGER

The Chambers Dictionary is the authority for many longer words; see Introduction, page ix

STRINGERS	STRODE	STROPPERS*	STRUMOSE	STUDENTRIES
STRINGIER	STRODLE	STROPPIER	STRUMOUS	STUDENTRY
STRINGIEST	STRODLED	STROPPIEST	STRUMPET	STUDENTS
STRINGILY	STRODLES	STROPPING	STRUMPETED	STUDFARM
STRINGING	STRODLING	STROPPY	STRUMPETING	STUDFARMS
STRINGINGS	STROKE	STROPS	STRUMPETS	STUDFISH*
STRINGS	STROKED	STROSSERS	STRUMS	STUDFISHES*
STRINGY	STROKEN	STROUD	STRUNG	STUDHORSE*
STRINKLE	STROKER	STROUDING	STRUNT	STUDHORSES*
STRINKLED	STROKERS	STROUDINGS	STRUNTED	STUDIED
STRINKLES	STROKES	STROUDS	STRUNTING	STUDIEDLY
STRINKLING	STROKING	STROUP	STRUNTS	STUDIER
STRINKLINGS	STROKINGS	STROUPACH	STRUT	STUDIERS
STRIP	STROLL	STROUPACHS	STRUTS	STUDIES
STRIPE	STROLLED	STROUPAN	STRUTTED	STUDIO
STRIPED	STROLLER	STROUPANS	STRUTTER	STUDIOS
STRIPER*	STROLLERS	STROUPS	STRUTTERS	STUDIOUS
STRIPERS*	STROLLING	STROUT	STRUTTING	STUDLIER*
STRIPES	STROLLINGS	STROUTED	STRUTTINGS	STUDLIEST*
STRIPEY	STROLLS	STROUTING	STRYCHNIA	STUDLY*
STRIPIER	STROMA	STROUTS	STRYCHNIAS	STUDS
STRIPIEST	STROMAL*	STROVE	STRYCHNIC	STUDWORK
STRIPING	STROMATA	STROW	STUB	STUDWORKS
STRIPINGS	STROMATIC	STROWED	STUBBED	STUDY
STRIPLING	STROMB	STROWER	STUBBIER	STUDYING
STRIPLINGS	STROMBS	STROWERS	STUBBIES	STUFF
STRIPPED	STROMBUS	STROWING	STUBBIEST	STUFFED
STRIPPER	STROMBUSES	STROWINGS	STUBBILY*	STUFFER
STRIPPERS	STROND	STROWN	STUBBING	STUFFERS
STRIPPING	STRONDS	STROWS	STUBBLE	STUFFIER
STRIPPINGS	STRONG	STROY	STUBBLED	STUFFIEST
STRIPS	STRONGARM	STROYED	STUBBLES	STUFFILY
STRIPT*	STRONGARMED	STROYER*	STUBBLIER	STUFFING
STRIPY	STRONGARMING	STROYERS*	STUBBLIEST	STUFFINGS
STRIVE	STRONGARMS	STROYING	STUBBLY	STUFFLESS*
STRIVED	STRONGBOX	STROYS	STUBBORN	STUFFS
STRIVEN	STRONGBOXES	STRUCK	STUBBORNED	STUFFY
STRIVER	STRONGER	STRUCKEN*	STUBBORNER	STUGGIER
STRIVERS	STRONGEST	STRUCTURE	STUBBORNEST	STUGGIEST
STRIVES	STRONGISH	STRUCTURED	STUBBORNING	STUGGY
STRIVING	STRONGLY	STRUCTURES	STUBBORNS	STUIVER*
STRIVINGS	STRONGMAN	STRUCTURING	STUBBY	STUIVERS*
STROAM	STRONGMEN	STRUDEL	STUBS	STULL
STROAMED	STRONGYL	STRUDELS	STUCCO	STULLS
STROAMING	STRONGYLE	STRUGGLE	STUCCOED	STULM
STROAMS	STRONGYLES	STRUGGLED	STUCCOER	STULMS
STROBE	STRONGYLS	STRUGGLER	STUCCOERS	STULTIFIED
STROBED	STRONTIA	STRUGGLERS	STUCCOES*	STULTIFIES
STROBES	STRONTIAN	STRUGGLES	STUCCOING	STULTIFY
STROBIC	STRONTIANS	STRUGGLING	STUCCOS	STULTIFYING
STROBIL*	STRONTIAS	STRUGGLINGS	STUCK	STUM
STROBILA	STRONTIC*	STRUM	STUCKS	STUMBLE
STROBILAE	STRONTIUM	STRUMA	STUD	STUMBLED
STROBILE	STRONTIUMS	STRUMAE	STUDBOOK	STUMBLER
STROBILES	STROOK	STRUMAS*	STUDBOOKS	STUMBLERS
STROBILI	STROOKE	STRUMATIC	STUDDED	STUMBLES
STROBILS*	STROOKEN	STRUMITIS	STUDDEN	STUMBLIER
STROBILUS	STROOKES	STRUMITISES	STUDDIE*	STUMBLIEST
STROBING	STROP	STRUMMED	STUDDIES*	STUMBLING
STROBINGS	STROPHE	STRUMMEL	STUDDING	STUMBLY
STRODDLE	STROPHES	STRUMMELS	STUDDINGS	STUMER
STRODDLED	STROPHIC	STRUMMER*	STUDDLE	STUMERS
STRODDLES	STROPPED	STRUMMERS*	STUDDLES	STUMM
STRODDLING	STROPPER*	STRUMMING	STUDENT	STUMMED

Words marked with an asterisk are from OTCWL

STUMMEL	STURDIES	STYLIZED	SUBABBOT	SUBBRANCHES
STUMMELS	STURDIEST	STYLIZER*	SUBABBOTS	SUBBREED
STUMMING	STURDILY	STYLIZERS*	SUBACID	SUBBREEDS
STUMP	STURDY	STYLIZES	SUBACIDLY	SUBBUREAU
STUMPAGE	STURE	STYLIZING	SUBACRID	SUBBUREAUS
STUMPAGES	STURGEON	STYLO	SUBACT	SUBBUREAUX
STUMPED	STURGEONS	STYLOBATE	SUBACTED	SUBBY
STUMPER	STURMER	STYLOBATES	SUBACTING	SUBCANTOR
STUMPERS	STURMERS	STYLOID	SUBACTION	SUBCANTORS
STUMPIER	STURNINE	STYLOIDS	SUBACTIONS	SUBCASTE
STUMPIES	STURNOID	STYLOLITE	SUBACTS	SUBCASTES
STUMPIEST	STURNUS	STYLOLITES	SUBACUTE	SUBCAUDAL
STUMPILY	STURNUSES	STYLOS	SUBADAR	SUBCAUSE*
STUMPING	STURT	STYLUS	SUBADARS	SUBCAUSES*
STUMPS	STURTED	STYLUSES	SUBADULT	SUBCAVITIES
STUMPY	STURTING	STYME	SUBADULTS	SUBCAVITY
STUMS	STURTS	STYMED	SUBAERIAL	SUBCELL*
STUN	STUSHIE	STYMES	SUBAGENCIES	SUBCELLAR
STUNG	STUSHIES	STYMIE	SUBAGENCY	SUBCELLARS
STUNK	STUTTER	STYMIED	SUBAGENT	SUBCELLS*
STUNKARD	STUTTERED	STYMIEING	SUBAGENTS	SUBCENTER*
STUNNED	STUTTERER	STYMIES	SUBAH	SUBCENTERS*
STUNNER	STUTTERERS	STYMING	SUBAHDAR	SUBCHASER*
STUNNERS	STUTTERING	STYMY*	SUBAHDARIES	SUBCHASERS*
STUNNING	STUTTERINGS	STYMYING*	SUBAHDARS	SUBCHIEF
STUNNINGS	STUTTERS	STYPSIS	SUBAHDARY	SUBCHIEFS
STUNS	STY	STYPSISES	SUBAHS	SUBCHORD
STUNSAIL	STYE	STYPTIC	SUBAHSHIP	SUBCHORDS
STUNSAILS	STYED	STYPTICAL	SUBAHSHIPS	SUBCLAIM
STUNT	STYES	STYPTICS	SUBALAR*	SUBCLAIMS
STUNTED	STYGIAN*	STYRAX	SUBALPINE	SUBCLAN*
STUNTING	STYING	STYRAXES	SUBALTERN	SUBCLANS*
STUNTMAN	STYLAR	STYRE	SUBALTERNS	SUBCLASS
STUNTMEN	STYLATE	STYRED	SUBAPICAL	SUBCLASSED*
STUNTS	STYLE	STYRENE	SUBAQUA	SUBCLASSES
STUPA	STYLEBOOK	STYRENES	SUBARCTIC	SUBCLASSING*
STUPAS	STYLEBOOKS	STYRES	SUBARCTICS*	SUBCLAUSE
STUPE	STYLED	STYRING	SUBAREA	SUBCLAUSES
STUPED	STYLELESS	STYROFOAM	SUBAREAS	SUBCLERK*
STUPEFIED	STYLER*	STYROFOAMS	SUBARID	SUBCLERKS*
STUPEFIER	STYLERS*	STYTE	SUBAS*	SUBCLIMAX
STUPEFIERS	STYLES	STYTED	SUBASTRAL	SUBCLIMAXES
STUPEFIES	STYLET	STYTES	SUBATOM	SUBCODE*
STUPEFY	STYLETS	STYTING	SUBATOMIC	SUBCODES*
STUPEFYING	STYLI	SUABILITIES	SUBATOMICS	SUBCOLONIES*
STUPENT	STYLIFORM	SUABILITY	SUBATOMS	SUBCOLONY*
STUPES	STYLING	SUABLE	SUBAUDIO	SUBCOOL
STUPID	STYLINGS*	SUABLY	SUBAURAL	SUBCOOLED*
STUPIDER	STYLISE	SUASIBLE	SUBAXIAL*	SUBCOOLING*
STUPIDEST	STYLISED	SUASION	SUBBASAL	SUBCOOLS*
STUPIDITIES	STYLISER*	SUASIONS	SUBBASE	SUBCORTEX
STUPIDITY	STYLISERS*	SUASIVE	SUBBASES	SUBCORTEXES
STUPIDLY	STYLISES	SUASIVELY	SUBBASIN*	SUBCORTICES
STUPIDS	STYLISH	SUASORY	SUBBASINS*	SUBCOSTA
STUPING	STYLISHLY	SUAVE	SUBBASS*	SUBCOSTAE
STUPOR	STYLISING	SUAVELY	SUBBASSES*	SUBCOSTAL
STUPOROUS	STYLIST	SUAVENESS*	SUBBED	SUBCOSTALS
STUPORS	STYLISTIC	SUAVENESSES*	SUBBIE	SUBCOUNTIES*
STUPRATE	STYLISTICS	SUAVER	SUBBIES	SUBCOUNTY*
STUPRATED	STYLISTS	SUAVEST	SUBBING	SUBCRUST
STUPRATES	STYLITE	SUAVITIES	SUBBINGS	SUBCRUSTS
STUPRATING	STYLITES	SUAVITY	SUBBLOCK*	SUBCULT*
STURDIED	STYLITIC*	SUB	SUBBLOCKS*	SUBCULTS*
STURDIER	STYLIZE	SUBA*	SUBBRANCH	SUBCUTES*

The Chambers Dictionary is the authority for many longer words; see Introduction, page ix

SUBCUTIS*	SUBERINS	SUBINCISING	SUBLIMISE	SUBNICHES*
SUBCUTISES*	SUBERISE	SUBINDEX*	SUBLIMISED	SUBNIVEAL
SUBDEACON	SUBERISED	SUBINDEXES*	SUBLIMISES	SUBNIVEAN
SUBDEACONS	SUBERISES	SUBINDICES*	SUBLIMISING	SUBNODAL*
SUBDEAN	SUBERISING	SUBITEM*	SUBLIMITIES	SUBNORMAL
SUBDEANS	SUBERIZE	SUBITEMS*	SUBLIMITY	SUBNORMALS
SUBDEB*	SUBERIZED	SUBITISE	SUBLIMIZE	SUBOCTAVE
SUBDEBS*	SUBERIZES	SUBITISED	SUBLIMIZED	SUBOCTAVES
SUBDEPOT*	SUBERIZING	SUBITISES	SUBLIMIZES	SUBOCULAR
SUBDEPOTS*	SUBEROSE	SUBITISING	SUBLIMIZING	SUBOFFICE
SUBDERMAL	SUBEROUS	SUBITIZE	SUBLINE*	SUBOFFICES
SUBDEW	SUBERS	SUBITIZED	SUBLINEAR	SUBOPTIC*
SUBDEWED	SUBFAMILIES	SUBITIZES	SUBLINES*	SUBORAL*
SUBDEWING	SUBFAMILY	SUBITIZING	SUBLOT*	SUBORDER
SUBDEWS	SUBFEU	SUBITO	SUBLOTS*	SUBORDERS
SUBDIVIDE	SUBFEUED	SUBJACENT	SUBLUNAR	SUBORN
SUBDIVIDED	SUBFEUING	SUBJECT	SUBLUNARY	SUBORNED
SUBDIVIDES	SUBFEUS	SUBJECTED	SUBLUNATE	SUBORNER
SUBDIVIDING	SUBFIELD	SUBJECTING	SUBMAN	SUBORNERS
SUBDOLOUS	SUBFIELDS	SUBJECTS	SUBMARINE	SUBORNING
SUBDORSAL	SUBFILE*	SUBJOIN	SUBMARINED	SUBORNS
SUBDUABLE	SUBFILES*	SUBJOINED	SUBMARINES	SUBOVAL*
SUBDUAL	SUBFIX*	SUBJOINING	SUBMARINING	SUBOVATE
SUBDUALS	SUBFIXES*	SUBJOINS	SUBMARKET*	SUBOXIDE
SUBDUCE	SUBFLOOR	SUBJUGATE	SUBMARKETS*	SUBOXIDES
SUBDUCED	SUBFLOORS	SUBJUGATED	SUBMATRICES	SUBPANEL*
SUBDUCES	SUBFLUID*	SUBJUGATES	SUBMATRIX	SUBPANELS*
SUBDUCING	SUBFOSSIL*	SUBJUGATING	SUBMATRIXES	SUBPAR*
SUBDUCT	SUBFOSSILS*	SUBLATE	SUBMEN	SUBPART*
SUBDUCTED	SUBFRAME	SUBLATED	SUBMENTA	SUBPARTS*
SUBDUCTING	SUBFRAMES	SUBLATES	SUBMENTAL	SUBPENA*
SUBDUCTS	SUBFUSC	SUBLATING	SUBMENTUM	SUBPENAED*
SUBDUE	SUBFUSCS	SUBLATION	SUBMENU*	SUBPENAING*
SUBDUED	SUBFUSK	SUBLATIONS	SUBMENUS*	SUBPENAS*
SUBDUEDLY	SUBFUSKS	SUBLEASE	SUBMERGE	SUBPERIOD*
SUBDUER	SUBGENERA	SUBLEASED	SUBMERGED	SUBPERIODS*
SUBDUERS	SUBGENRE	SUBLEASES	SUBMERGES	SUBPHASE*
SUBDUES	SUBGENRES	SUBLEASING	SUBMERGING	SUBPHASES*
SUBDUING	SUBGENUS	SUBLESSEE	SUBMERSE	SUBPHYLA
SUBDUPLE	SUBGENUSES	SUBLESSEES	SUBMERSED	SUBPHYLUM
SUBDURAL	SUBGOAL	SUBLESSOR	SUBMERSES	SUBPLOT
SUBECHO*	SUBGOALS	SUBLESSORS	SUBMERSING	SUBPLOTS
SUBECHOES*	SUBGRADE	SUBLET	SUBMICRON	SUBPOENA
SUBEDAR	SUBGRADES	SUBLETHAL	SUBMICRONS	SUBPOENAED
SUBEDARS	SUBGRAPH*	SUBLETS	SUBMISS	SUBPOENAING
SUBEDIT	SUBGRAPHS*	SUBLETTER	SUBMISSLY	SUBPOENAS
SUBEDITED	SUBGROUP	SUBLETTERS	SUBMIT	SUBPOLAR
SUBEDITING	SUBGROUPS	SUBLETTING	SUBMITS	SUBPOTENT
SUBEDITOR	SUBGUM	SUBLETTINGS	SUBMITTAL*	SUBPRIOR
SUBEDITORS	SUBGUMS	SUBLEVEL*	SUBMITTALS*	SUBPRIORS
SUBEDITS	SUBHEAD	SUBLEVELS*	SUBMITTED	SUBPUBIC*
SUBENTIRE	SUBHEADS	SUBLIMATE	SUBMITTER	SUBRACE*
SUBENTRIES*	SUBHEDRAL	SUBLIMATED	SUBMITTERS	SUBRACES*
SUBENTRY*	SUBHUMAN	SUBLIMATES	SUBMITTING	SUBREGION
SUBEPOCH*	SUBHUMANS*	SUBLIMATING	SUBMITTINGS	SUBREGIONS
SUBEPOCHS*	SUBHUMID	SUBLIME	SUBMUCOSA	SUBRENT*
SUBEQUAL	SUBIDEA*	SUBLIMED	SUBMUCOSAE	SUBRENTS*
SUBER	SUBIDEAS*	SUBLIMELY	SUBMUCOSAS*	SUBRING
SUBERATE	SUBIMAGINES	SUBLIMER	SUBMUCOUS	SUBRINGS
SUBERATES	SUBIMAGO	SUBLIMERS*	SUBNASAL*	SUBROGATE
SUBERECT	SUBIMAGOS	SUBLIMES	SUBNET*	SUBROGATED
SUBEREOUS	SUBINCISE	SUBLIMEST	SUBNETS*	SUBROGATES
SUBERIC	SUBINCISED	SUBLIMING	SUBNEURAL	SUBROGATING
SUBERIN	SUBINCISES	SUBLIMINGS	SUBNICHE*	SUBRULE*

Words marked with an asterisk are from OTCWL

SUBRULES*	SUBSITE*	SUBTENSE	SUBTROPICS	SUCCAH
SUBS	SUBSITES*	SUBTENSES	SUBTRUDE	SUCCAHS
SUBSACRAL	SUBSIZAR	SUBTENURE	SUBTRUDED	SUCCEDENT*
SUBSALE*	SUBSIZARS	SUBTENURES	SUBTRUDES	SUCCEED
SUBSALES*	SUBSKILL*	SUBTEST*	SUBTRUDING	SUCCEEDED
SUBSAMPLE	SUBSKILLS*	SUBTESTS*	SUBTUNIC*	SUCCEEDER
SUBSAMPLED	SUBSOCIAL*	SUBTEXT	SUBTUNICS*	SUCCEEDERS
SUBSAMPLES	SUBSOIL	SUBTEXTS	SUBTYPE	SUCCEEDING
SUBSAMPLING	SUBSOILED	SUBTHEME*	SUBTYPES	SUCCEEDS
SUBSCALE*	SUBSOILER	SUBTHEMES*	SUBUCULA	SUCCENTOR
SUBSCALES*	SUBSOILERS	SUBTIDAL	SUBUCULAS	SUCCENTORS
SUBSCHEMA	SUBSOILING	SUBTIL	SUBULATE	SUCCES
SUBSCHEMATA	SUBSOILINGS	SUBTILE	SUBUNIT	SUCCESS
SUBSCRIBE	SUBSOILS	SUBTILELY*	SUBUNITS	SUCCESSES
SUBSCRIBED	SUBSOLAR	SUBTILER	SUBURB	SUCCESSOR
SUBSCRIBES	SUBSONG	SUBTILEST	SUBURBAN	SUCCESSORS
SUBSCRIBING	SUBSONGS	SUBTILIN*	SUBURBANS	SUCCI
SUBSCRIBINGS	SUBSONIC	SUBTILINS*	SUBURBED*	SUCCINATE
SUBSCRIPT	SUBSPACE*	SUBTILISE	SUBURBIA	SUCCINATES
SUBSCRIPTS	SUBSPACES*	SUBTILISED	SUBURBIAS	SUCCINCT
SUBSEA	SUBSTAGE	SUBTILISES	SUBURBS	SUCCINCTER
SUBSECIVE	SUBSTAGES	SUBTILISING	SUBURSINE	SUCCINCTEST
SUBSECT*	SUBSTANCE	SUBTILIZE	SUBVASSAL	SUCCINIC
SUBSECTOR*	SUBSTANCES	SUBTILIZED	SUBVASSALS	SUCCINITE
SUBSECTORS*	SUBSTATE	SUBTILIZES	SUBVENE*	SUCCINITES
SUBSECTS*	SUBSTATES	SUBTILIZING	SUBVENED*	SUCCINYL
SUBSELLIA	SUBSTRACT	SUBTILTIES*	SUBVENES*	SUCCINYLS
SUBSENSE*	SUBSTRACTED	SUBTILTY*	SUBVENING*	SUCCISE
SUBSENSES*	SUBSTRACTING	SUBTITLE	SUBVERSAL	SUCCOR
SUBSERE	SUBSTRACTS	SUBTITLED	SUBVERSALS	SUCCORED
SUBSERES	SUBSTRATA	SUBTITLES	SUBVERSE	SUCCORER*
SUBSERIES	SUBSTRATE	SUBTITLING	SUBVERSED	SUCCORERS*
SUBSERVE	SUBSTRATES	SUBTLE	SUBVERSES	SUCCORIES
SUBSERVED	SUBSTRATUM*	SUBTLER	SUBVERSING	SUCCORING
SUBSERVES	SUBSTRUCT	SUBTLEST	SUBVERST	SUCCORS
SUBSERVING	SUBSTRUCTED	SUBTLETIES	SUBVERT	SUCCORY
SUBSET	SUBSTRUCTING	SUBTLETY	SUBVERTED	SUCCOS
SUBSETS	SUBSTRUCTS	SUBTLY	SUBVERTER	SUCCOSE
SUBSHAFT*	SUBSTYLAR	SUBTONE*	SUBVERTERS	SUCCOT
SUBSHAFTS*	SUBSTYLE	SUBTONES*	SUBVERTING	SUCCOTASH
SUBSHELL*	SUBSTYLES	SUBTONIC	SUBVERTS	SUCCOTASHES
SUBSHELLS*	SUBSULTUS	SUBTONICS	SUBVICAR*	SUCCOTH
SUBSHRUB	SUBSULTUSES	SUBTOPIA	SUBVICARS*	SUCCOUR
SUBSHRUBS	SUBSUME	SUBTOPIAN	SUBVIRAL	SUCCOURED
SUBSIDE	SUBSUMED	SUBTOPIAS	SUBVISUAL*	SUCCOURER
SUBSIDED	SUBSUMES	SUBTOPIC*	SUBVOCAL	SUCCOURERS
SUBSIDER*	SUBSUMING	SUBTOPICS*	SUBWARDEN	SUCCOURING
SUBSIDERS*	SUBSYSTEM	SUBTORRID	SUBWARDENS	SUCCOURS
SUBSIDES	SUBSYSTEMS	SUBTOTAL	SUBWAY	SUCCOUS
SUBSIDIES	SUBTACK	SUBTOTALED*	SUBWAYED*	SUCCUBA
SUBSIDING	SUBTACKS	SUBTOTALING*	SUBWAYING*	SUCCUBAE
SUBSIDISE	SUBTASK*	SUBTOTALLED	SUBWAYS	SUCCUBAS
SUBSIDISED	SUBTASKS*	SUBTOTALLING	SUBWOOFER	SUCCUBI
SUBSIDISES	SUBTAXA*	SUBTOTALS	SUBWOOFERS	SUCCUBINE
SUBSIDISING	SUBTAXON*	SUBTRACT	SUBWORLD*	SUCCUBOUS
SUBSIDIZE	SUBTAXONS*	SUBTRACTED	SUBWORLDS*	SUCCUBUS
SUBSIDIZED	SUBTEEN	SUBTRACTING	SUBWRITER*	SUCCUBUSES
SUBSIDIZES	SUBTEENS	SUBTRACTS	SUBWRITERS*	SUCCULENT
SUBSIDIZING	SUBTENANT	SUBTREND*	SUBZERO	SUCCULENTS
SUBSIDY	SUBTENANTS	SUBTRENDS*	SUBZONAL	SUCCUMB
SUBSIST	SUBTEND	SUBTRIBE	SUBZONE	SUCCUMBED
SUBSISTED	SUBTENDED	SUBTRIBES	SUBZONES	SUCCUMBING
SUBSISTING	SUBTENDING	SUBTRIST	SUCCADE	SUCCUMBS
SUBSISTS	SUBTENDS	SUBTROPIC	SUCCADES	SUCCURSAL

The Chambers Dictionary is the authority for many longer words; see Introduction, page ix

SUCCURSALS	SUDATES	SUFFETE	SUGH*	SULCATE
SUCCUS	SUDATING	SUFFETES	SUGHED*	SULCATED
SUCCUSS	SUDATION	SUFFICE	SUGHING*	SULCATION
SUCCUSSED	SUDATIONS	SUFFICED	SUGHS*	SULCATIONS
SUCCUSSES	SUDATORIA	SUFFICER	SUI	SULCI
SUCCUSSING	SUDATORIES	SUFFICERS	SUICIDAL	SULCUS
SUCH	SUDATORIUM*	SUFFICES	SUICIDE	SULDAN*
SUCHLIKE	SUDATORIUMS*	SUFFICING	SUICIDED*	SULDANS*
SUCHNESS	SUDATORY	SUFFIX	SUICIDES	SULFA
SUCHNESSES	SUDD	SUFFIXAL	SUICIDING*	SULFAS
SUCHWISE	SUDDEN	SUFFIXED	SUID	SULFATASE
SUCK	SUDDENLY	SUFFIXES	SUIDIAN	SULFATASES
SUCKED	SUDDENS*	SUFFIXING	SUIDIANS	SULFATE
SUCKEN	SUDDENTIES	SUFFIXION	SUIDS	SULFATED
SUCKENER	SUDDENTY	SUFFIXIONS	SUILLINE	SULFATES
SUCKENERS	SUDDER	SUFFLATE	SUING	SULFATIC
SUCKENS	SUDDERS	SUFFLATED	SUINGS	SULFATING
SUCKER	SUDDS	SUFFLATES	SUINT	SULFATION
SUCKERED	SUDOR	SUFFLATING	SUINTS	SULFATIONS
SUCKERING	SUDORAL	SUFFOCATE	SUIT	SULFID*
SUCKERS	SUDORIFIC	SUFFOCATED	SUITABLE	SULFIDE
SUCKET	SUDORIFICS	SUFFOCATES	SUITABLY	SULFIDES
SUCKETS	SUDOROUS	SUFFOCATING	SUITCASE	SULFIDS*
SUCKFISH*	SUDORS	SUFFOCATINGS	SUITCASES	SULFINYL
SUCKFISHES*	SUDS	SUFFRAGAN	SUITE	SULFINYLS
SUCKING	SUDSED	SUFFRAGANS	SUITED	SULFITE
SUCKINGS	SUDSER	SUFFRAGE	SUITER*	SULFITES
SUCKLE	SUDSERS	SUFFRAGES	SUITERS*	SULFITIC*
SUCKLED	SUDSES	SUFFUSE	SUITES	SULFO*
SUCKLER	SUDSIER	SUFFUSED	SUITING	SULFONATE
SUCKLERS	SUDSIEST	SUFFUSES	SUITINGS	SULFONATED
SUCKLES	SUDSING	SUFFUSING	SUITLIKE*	SULFONATES
SUCKLESS*	SUDSLESS*	SUFFUSION	SUITOR	SULFONATING
SUCKLING	SUDSY	SUFFUSIONS	SUITORED	SULFONE
SUCKLINGS	SUE	SUFFUSIVE	SUITORING	SULFONES
SUCKS	SUEABLE	SUGAR	SUITORS	SULFONIC*
SUCRASE	SUED	SUGARALLIES	SUITRESS	SULFONIUM
SUCRASES	SUEDE	SUGARALLY	SUITRESSES	SULFONIUMS
SUCRE	SUEDED	SUGARCANE	SUITS	SULFONYL*
SUCRES	SUEDES	SUGARCANES	SUIVANTE	SULFONYLS*
SUCRIER	SUEDETTE	SUGARCOAT*	SUIVANTES	SULFOXIDE*
SUCRIERS	SUEDETTES	SUGARCOATED*	SUIVEZ	SULFOXIDES*
SUCROSE	SUEDING	SUGARCOATING*	SUJEE	SULFUR
SUCROSES	SUER	SUGARCOATS*	SUJEES	SULFURATE
SUCTION	SUERS	SUGARED	SUK	SULFURATED
SUCTIONAL*	SUES	SUGARIER	SUKH	SULFURATES
SUCTIONED*	SUET	SUGARIEST	SUKHS	SULFURATING
SUCTIONING*	SUETIER	SUGARING	SUKIYAKI	SULFURED
SUCTIONS	SUETIEST	SUGARINGS	SUKIYAKIS	SULFURET*
SUCTORIAL	SUETS	SUGARLESS	SUKKAH	SULFURETED*
SUCTORIAN	SUETTIER	SUGARLOAF	SUKKAHS	SULFURETING*
SUCTORIANS	SUETTIEST	SUGARLOAVES	SUKKOS	SULFURETS*
SUCURUJU	SUETTY	SUGARPLUM	SUKKOT	SULFURETTED*
SUCURUJUS	SUETY	SUGARPLUMS	SUKKOTH	SULFURETTING*
SUD	SUFFARI*	SUGARS	SUKS	SULFURIC
SUDAMEN	SUFFARIS*	SUGARY	SULCAL	SULFURING
SUDAMINA	SUFFECT	SUGGEST	SULCALISE	SULFURIZE*
SUDAMINAL	SUFFER	SUGGESTED	SULCALISED	SULFURIZED*
SUDARIA	SUFFERED	SUGGESTER	SULCALISES	SULFURIZES*
SUDARIES	SUFFERER	SUGGESTERS	SULCALISING	SULFURIZING*
SUDARIUM	SUFFERERS	SUGGESTING	SULCALIZE	SULFUROUS*
SUDARY	SUFFERING	SUGGESTS	SULCALIZED	SULFURS
SUDATE	SUFFERINGS	SUGGING	SULCALIZES	SULFURY*
SUDATED	SUFFERS	SUGGINGS	SULCALIZING	SULFURYL*

Words marked with an asterisk are from OTCWL

SULFURYLS*
SULK
SULKED
SULKER*
SULKERS*
SULKIER
SULKIES
SULKIEST
SULKILY
SULKINESS
SULKINESSES
SULKING
SULKS
SULKY
SULLAGE
SULLAGES
SULLEN
SULLENER
SULLENEST
SULLENLY
SULLIED
SULLIES
SULLY
SULLYING
SULPHA
SULPHAS
SULPHATE
SULPHATED
SULPHATES
SULPHATIC
SULPHATING
SULPHID*
SULPHIDE
SULPHIDES
SULPHIDS*
SULPHINYL
SULPHINYLS
SULPHITE
SULPHITES
SULPHONE
SULPHONES
SULPHUR
SULPHURED
SULPHURET
SULPHURETED
SULPHURETING
SULPHURETS
SULPHURETTED
SULPHURETTING
SULPHURIC
SULPHURING
SULPHURS
SULPHURY
SULTAN
SULTANA
SULTANAS
SULTANATE
SULTANATES
SULTANESS
SULTANESSES
SULTANIC
SULTANS
SULTRIER
SULTRIEST

SULTRILY
SULTRY
SULU
SULUS
SUM
SUMAC
SUMACH
SUMACHS
SUMACS
SUMATRA
SUMATRAS
SUMLESS
SUMMA
SUMMABLE*
SUMMAE
SUMMAND
SUMMANDS
SUMMAR
SUMMARIES
SUMMARILY
SUMMARISE
SUMMARISED
SUMMARISES
SUMMARISING
SUMMARIST
SUMMARISTS
SUMMARIZE
SUMMARIZED
SUMMARIZES
SUMMARIZING
SUMMARY
SUMMAS*
SUMMAT
SUMMATE
SUMMATED
SUMMATES
SUMMATING
SUMMATION
SUMMATIONS
SUMMATIVE
SUMMATS
SUMMED
SUMMER
SUMMERED
SUMMERIER
SUMMERIEST
SUMMERING
SUMMERINGS
SUMMERLY
SUMMERS
SUMMERSET
SUMMERSETS
SUMMERSETTED
SUMMERSETTING
SUMMERY
SUMMING
SUMMINGS
SUMMIST
SUMMISTS
SUMMIT
SUMMITAL
SUMMITED*
SUMMITEER
SUMMITEERS

SUMMITING*
SUMMITRIES
SUMMITRY
SUMMITS
SUMMON
SUMMONED
SUMMONER
SUMMONERS
SUMMONING
SUMMONS
SUMMONSED
SUMMONSES
SUMMONSING
SUMO
SUMOS
SUMOTORI
SUMOTORIS
SUMP
SUMPH
SUMPHISH
SUMPHS
SUMPIT
SUMPITAN
SUMPITANS
SUMPITS
SUMPS
SUMPSIMUS
SUMPSIMUSES
SUMPTER
SUMPTERS
SUMPTUARY
SUMPTUOUS
SUMPWEED*
SUMPWEEDS*
SUMS
SUN
SUNBACK*
SUNBAKE
SUNBAKED
SUNBAKES
SUNBAKING
SUNBATH
SUNBATHE
SUNBATHED
SUNBATHER
SUNBATHERS
SUNBATHES
SUNBATHING
SUNBATHINGS
SUNBATHS
SUNBEAM
SUNBEAMED
SUNBEAMS
SUNBEAMY
SUNBEAT
SUNBEATEN
SUNBED
SUNBEDS
SUNBELT
SUNBELTS
SUNBERRIES
SUNBERRY
SUNBIRD
SUNBIRDS

SUNBLIND
SUNBLINDS
SUNBLOCK
SUNBLOCKS
SUNBONNET*
SUNBONNETS*
SUNBOW
SUNBOWS
SUNBRIGHT
SUNBURN
SUNBURNED
SUNBURNING
SUNBURNS
SUNBURNT
SUNBURST
SUNBURSTS
SUNCHOKE*
SUNCHOKES*
SUNDAE
SUNDAES
SUNDARI
SUNDARIS
SUNDECK
SUNDECKS
SUNDER
SUNDERED
SUNDERER
SUNDERERS
SUNDERING
SUNDERINGS
SUNDERS
SUNDEW
SUNDEWS
SUNDIAL
SUNDIALS
SUNDOG
SUNDOGS
SUNDOWN
SUNDOWNER
SUNDOWNERS
SUNDOWNS
SUNDRA
SUNDRAS
SUNDRESS
SUNDRESSES
SUNDRI
SUNDRIES
SUNDRIS
SUNDROPS
SUNDRY
SUNFAST
SUNFISH
SUNFISHES
SUNFLOWER
SUNFLOWERS
SUNG
SUNGAR
SUNGARS
SUNGLASS
SUNGLASSES
SUNGLOW
SUNGLOWS
SUNHAT
SUNHATS

SUNK
SUNKEN
SUNKET
SUNKETS
SUNKIE
SUNKIES
SUNKS
SUNLAMP
SUNLAMPS
SUNLAND*
SUNLANDS*
SUNLESS
SUNLIGHT
SUNLIGHTS
SUNLIKE
SUNLIT
SUNN
SUNNA*
SUNNAH*
SUNNAHS*
SUNNAS*
SUNNED
SUNNIER
SUNNIEST
SUNNILY
SUNNINESS
SUNNINESSES
SUNNING
SUNNS
SUNNY
SUNPORCH*
SUNPORCHES*
SUNPROOF
SUNRAY
SUNRAYS
SUNRISE
SUNRISES
SUNRISING
SUNRISINGS
SUNROOF
SUNROOFS
SUNROOM*
SUNROOMS*
SUNS
SUNSCALD*
SUNSCALDS*
SUNSCREEN
SUNSCREENS
SUNSEEKER*
SUNSEEKERS*
SUNSET
SUNSETS
SUNSHADE
SUNSHADES
SUNSHINE
SUNSHINES
SUNSHINY
SUNSPOT
SUNSPOTS
SUNSTONE
SUNSTONES
SUNSTROKE
SUNSTROKES
SUNSTRUCK

The Chambers Dictionary is the authority for many longer words; see Introduction, page ix

SUNSUIT
SUNSUITS
SUNTAN
SUNTANNED
SUNTANS
SUNTRAP
SUNTRAPS
SUNUP
SUNUPS
SUNWARD
SUNWARDS
SUNWISE
SUP
SUPAWN
SUPAWNS
SUPE
SUPER
SUPERABLE
SUPERABLY
SUPERADD
SUPERADDED
SUPERADDING
SUPERADDS
SUPERATE
SUPERATED
SUPERATES
SUPERATING
SUPERB
SUPERBAD*
SUPERBANK*
SUPERBANKS*
SUPERBER
SUPERBEST
SUPERBITIES
SUPERBITY
SUPERBLY
SUPERBOLD
SUPERBOMB*
SUPERBOMBS*
SUPERBRAT
SUPERBRATS
SUPERBUG
SUPERBUGS
SUPERCAR*
SUPERCARS*
SUPERCEDE*
SUPERCEDED*
SUPERCEDES*
SUPERCEDING*
SUPERCHIC*
SUPERCITIES*
SUPERCITY*
SUPERCLUB*
SUPERCLUBS*
SUPERCOIL
SUPERCOILED*
SUPERCOILING*
SUPERCOILS
SUPERCOLD
SUPERCOOL
SUPERCOOLED
SUPERCOOLING
SUPERCOOLS
SUPERCOP*

SUPERCOPS*
SUPERCUTE*
SUPERED*
SUPEREGO
SUPEREGOS
SUPERETTE
SUPERETTES
SUPERFAN*
SUPERFANS*
SUPERFARM*
SUPERFARMS*
SUPERFAST
SUPERFINE
SUPERFIRM*
SUPERFIRMS*
SUPERFIT
SUPERFIX*
SUPERFIXES*
SUPERFLUX
SUPERFLUXES
SUPERFUND*
SUPERFUNDS*
SUPERFUSE
SUPERFUSED
SUPERFUSES
SUPERFUSING
SUPERGENE
SUPERGENES
SUPERGLUE
SUPERGLUED
SUPERGLUES
SUPERGLUING
SUPERGOOD*
SUPERGUN
SUPERGUNS
SUPERHEAT
SUPERHEATED
SUPERHEATING
SUPERHEATS
SUPERHERO
SUPERHEROES
SUPERHIT*
SUPERHITS*
SUPERHIVE
SUPERHIVES
SUPERHOT*
SUPERHYPE*
SUPERHYPED*
SUPERHYPES*
SUPERHYPING*
SUPERING*
SUPERIOR
SUPERIORS
SUPERJET
SUPERJETS
SUPERJOCK*
SUPERJOCKS*
SUPERLAIN*
SUPERLAY*
SUPERLIE*
SUPERLIES*
SUPERLOO
SUPERLOOS
SUPERLYING*

SUPERMALE*
SUPERMALES*
SUPERMAN
SUPERMART
SUPERMARTS
SUPERMEN
SUPERMIND*
SUPERMINDS*
SUPERMINI
SUPERMINIS
SUPERMOM*
SUPERMOMS*
SUPERNAL
SUPERNOVA
SUPERNOVAE
SUPERNOVAS
SUPERPIMP*
SUPERPIMPS*
SUPERPLUS
SUPERPLUSES
SUPERPORT*
SUPERPORTS*
SUPERPOSE
SUPERPOSED
SUPERPOSES
SUPERPOSING
SUPERPRO*
SUPERPROS*
SUPERRACE*
SUPERRACES*
SUPERREAL*
SUPERRICH
SUPERROAD*
SUPERROADS*
SUPERS
SUPERSAFE
SUPERSALE*
SUPERSALES*
SUPERSALT
SUPERSALTS
SUPERSEDE
SUPERSEDED
SUPERSEDES
SUPERSEDING
SUPERSELL
SUPERSELLS
SUPERSEX*
SUPERSEXES*
SUPERSHOW*
SUPERSHOWS*
SUPERSIZE*
SUPERSOFT
SUPERSPIES
SUPERSPY
SUPERSTAR
SUPERSTARS
SUPERSTUD*
SUPERSTUDS*
SUPERTAX
SUPERTAXES
SUPERTHIN
SUPERVENE
SUPERVENED
SUPERVENES

SUPERVENING
SUPERVISE
SUPERVISED
SUPERVISES
SUPERVISING
SUPERWAIF
SUPERWAIFS
SUPERWAVE*
SUPERWAVES*
SUPERWIDE*
SUPERWIFE*
SUPERWIVES*
SUPES
SUPINATE
SUPINATED
SUPINATES
SUPINATING
SUPINATOR
SUPINATORS
SUPINE
SUPINELY
SUPINES
SUPPAWN
SUPPAWNS
SUPPEAGO
SUPPEAGOES
SUPPED
SUPPER
SUPPERED
SUPPERING
SUPPERS
SUPPING
SUPPLANT
SUPPLANTED
SUPPLANTING
SUPPLANTS
SUPPLE
SUPPLED
SUPPLELY
SUPPLER
SUPPLES
SUPPLEST
SUPPLIAL
SUPPLIALS
SUPPLIANT
SUPPLIANTS
SUPPLICAT
SUPPLICATS
SUPPLIED
SUPPLIER
SUPPLIERS
SUPPLIES
SUPPLING
SUPPLY
SUPPLYING
SUPPORT
SUPPORTED
SUPPORTER
SUPPORTERS
SUPPORTING
SUPPORTINGS
SUPPORTS
SUPPOSAL
SUPPOSALS

SUPPOSE
SUPPOSED
SUPPOSER
SUPPOSERS
SUPPOSES
SUPPOSING
SUPPOSINGS
SUPPRESS
SUPPRESSED
SUPPRESSES
SUPPRESSING
SUPPURATE
SUPPURATED
SUPPURATES
SUPPURATING
SUPRA*
SUPREMACIES
SUPREMACY
SUPREME
SUPREMELY
SUPREMER
SUPREMES
SUPREMEST
SUPREMITIES
SUPREMITY
SUPREMO
SUPREMOS
SUPS
SUQ
SUQS
SUR
SURA
SURAH
SURAHS
SURAL
SURAMIN
SURAMINS
SURANCE
SURANCES
SURAS
SURAT
SURATS
SURBAHAR
SURBAHARS
SURBASE
SURBASED
SURBASES
SURBATE
SURBATED
SURBATES
SURBATING
SURBED
SURBEDDED
SURBEDDING
SURBEDS
SURBET
SURCEASE
SURCEASED
SURCEASES
SURCEASING
SURCHARGE
SURCHARGED
SURCHARGES
SURCHARGING

SURCINGLE	SURFMAN	SURPASSES	SURTAXES	SUSPENDING
SURCINGLED	SURFMEN	SURPASSING	SURTAXING	SUSPENDS
SURCINGLES	SURFPERCH	SURPLICE	SURTITLE	SUSPENS
SURCINGLING	SURFPERCHES	SURPLICED	SURTITLES	SUSPENSE
SURCOAT	SURFS	SURPLICES	SURTOUT	SUSPENSER
SURCOATS	SURFY	SURPLUS	SURTOUTS	SUSPENSERS
SURCULI	SURGE	SURPLUSES	SURUCUCU	SUSPENSES
SURCULOSE	SURGED	SURPRINT*	SURUCUCUS	SUSPENSOR
SURCULUS	SURGEFUL	SURPRINTED*	SURVEIL*	SUSPENSORS
SURCULUSES	SURGELESS	SURPRINTING*	SURVEILLE	SUSPICION
SURD	SURGENT	SURPRINTS*	SURVEILLED	SUSPICIONED
SURDITIES	SURGEON	SURPRISAL	SURVEILLES	SUSPICIONING
SURDITY	SURGEONCIES	SURPRISALS	SURVEILLING	SUSPICIONS
SURDS	SURGEONCY	SURPRISE	SURVEILS*	SUSPIRE
SURE	SURGEONS	SURPRISED	SURVEW	SUSPIRED
SURED	SURGERIES	SURPRISER	SURVEWE	SUSPIRES
SUREFIRE*	SURGERS*	SURPRISERS	SURVEWED	SUSPIRING
SURELY	SURGERY	SURPRISES	SURVEWES	SUSS
SURENESS	SURGES	SURPRISING	SURVEWING	SUSSARARA
SURENESSES	SURGICAL	SURPRISINGS	SURVEWS	SUSSARARAS
SURER	SURGIER	SURPRIZE*	SURVEY	SUSSED
SURES	SURGIEST	SURPRIZED*	SURVEYAL	SUSSES
SUREST	SURGING	SURPRIZES*	SURVEYALS	SUSSING
SURETIED	SURGINGS	SURPRIZING*	SURVEYED	SUSTAIN
SURETIES	SURGY	SURQUEDIES	SURVEYING	SUSTAINED
SURETY	SURICATE	SURQUEDRIES	SURVEYINGS	SUSTAINER
SURETYING	SURICATES	SURQUEDRY	SURVEYOR	SUSTAINERS
SURF	SURIMI*	SURQUEDY	SURVEYORS	SUSTAINING
SURFABLE*	SURING	SURRA	SURVEYS	SUSTAININGS
SURFACE	SURLIER	SURRAS	SURVIEW	SUSTAINS
SURFACED	SURLIEST	SURREAL	SURVIEWED	SUSTINENT
SURFACER	SURLILY	SURREALLY*	SURVIEWING	SUSURRANT
SURFACERS	SURLINESS	SURREBUT	SURVIEWS	SUSURRATE
SURFACES	SURLINESSES	SURREBUTS	SURVIVAL	SUSURRATED
SURFACING	SURLOIN	SURREBUTTED	SURVIVALS	SUSURRATES
SURFACINGS	SURLOINS	SURREBUTTING	SURVIVE	SUSURRATING
SURFBIRD	SURLY	SURREINED	SURVIVED	SUSURROUS*
SURFBIRDS	SURMASTER	SURREJOIN	SURVIVER*	SUSURRUS
SURFBOARD	SURMASTERS	SURREJOINED	SURVIVERS*	SUSURRUSES
SURFBOARDED*	SURMISAL	SURREJOINING	SURVIVES	SUTILE
SURFBOARDING*	SURMISALS	SURREJOINS	SURVIVING	SUTLER
SURFBOARDS	SURMISE	SURRENDER	SURVIVOR	SUTLERIES
SURFBOAT*	SURMISED	SURRENDERED	SURVIVORS	SUTLERS
SURFBOATS*	SURMISER	SURRENDERING	SUS	SUTLERY
SURFED	SURMISERS	SURRENDERS	SUSCEPTOR	SUTOR
SURFEIT	SURMISES	SURRENDRIES	SUSCEPTORS	SUTORIAL
SURFEITED	SURMISING	SURRENDRY	SUSCITATE	SUTORIAN
SURFEITER	SURMISINGS	SURREY	SUSCITATED	SUTORS
SURFEITERS	SURMOUNT	SURREYS	SUSCITATES	SUTRA
SURFEITING	SURMOUNTED	SURROGACIES	SUSCITATING	SUTRAS
SURFEITINGS	SURMOUNTING	SURROGACY	SUSES	SUTTA*
SURFEITS	SURMOUNTINGS	SURROGATE	SUSHI	SUTTAS*
SURFER	SURMOUNTS	SURROGATED*	SUSHIS	SUTTEE
SURFERS	SURMULLET	SURROGATES	SUSLIK	SUTTEEISM
SURFFISH	SURMULLETS	SURROGATING*	SUSLIKS	SUTTEEISMS
SURFFISHES	SURNAME	SURROUND	SUSPECT	SUTTEES
SURFICIAL	SURNAMED	SURROUNDED	SUSPECTED	SUTTLE
SURFIE	SURNAMER*	SURROUNDING	SUSPECTING	SUTTLED
SURFIER	SURNAMERS*	SURROUNDINGS	SUSPECTS	SUTTLES
SURFIES	SURNAMES	SURROUNDS	SUSPENCE	SUTTLETIE
SURFIEST	SURNAMING	SURROYAL	SUSPEND	SUTTLETIES
SURFING	SURPASS	SURROYALS	SUSPENDED	SUTTLING
SURFINGS	SURPASSED	SURTAX	SUSPENDER	SUTTLY
SURFLIKE*		SURTAXED	SUSPENDERS	SUTURAL

SUTURALLY	SWAIL*	SWANNERY	SWASHERS	SWEARINGS
SUTURE	SWAILS*	SWANNIER	SWASHES	SWEARS
SUTURED	SWAIN	SWANNIEST	SWASHIER	SWEARWORD*
SUTURES	SWAINING	SWANNING	SWASHIEST	SWEARWORDS*
SUTURING	SWAININGS	SWANNINGS	SWASHING	SWEAT
SUVERSED	SWAINISH	SWANNY	SWASHINGS	SWEATBAND*
SUZERAIN	SWAINS	SWANPAN*	SWASHWORK	SWEATBANDS*
SUZERAINS	SWALE	SWANPANS*	SWASHWORKS	SWEATBOX*
SVARAJ*	SWALED	SWANS	SWASHY	SWEATBOXES*
SVARAJES*	SWALES	SWANSDOWN	SWASTICA*	SWEATED
SVASTIKA	SWALIER	SWANSDOWNS	SWASTICAS*	SWEATER
SVASTIKAS	SWALIEST	SWANSKIN	SWASTIKA	SWEATERS
SVEDBERG*	SWALING	SWANSKINS	SWASTIKAS	SWEATIER
SVEDBERGS*	SWALINGS	SWAP	SWAT	SWEATIEST
SVELTE	SWALLET	SWAPPED	SWATCH	SWEATILY*
SVELTELY*	SWALLETS	SWAPPER	SWATCHES	SWEATING
SVELTER	SWALLOW	SWAPPERS	SWATH	SWEATINGS
SVELTEST	SWALLOWED	SWAPPING	SWATHE	SWEATS
SWAB	SWALLOWER	SWAPPINGS	SWATHED	SWEATSHOP*
SWABBED	SWALLOWERS	SWAPS	SWATHER*	SWEATSHOPS*
SWABBER	SWALLOWING	SWAPT	SWATHERS*	SWEATSUIT
SWABBERS	SWALLOWS	SWAPTION	SWATHES	SWEATSUITS
SWABBIE*	SWALY	SWAPTIONS	SWATHIER	SWEATY
SWABBIES	SWAM	SWARAJ	SWATHIEST	SWEDE
SWABBING	SWAMI	SWARAJES	SWATHING	SWEDES
SWABBY	SWAMIES*	SWARAJISM	SWATHS	SWEE
SWABS	SWAMIS	SWARAJISMS	SWATHY	SWEED
SWACK	SWAMP	SWARAJIST	SWATS	SWEEING
SWACKED*	SWAMPED	SWARAJISTS	SWATTED	SWEEL
SWAD	SWAMPER	SWARD	SWATTER	SWEELED
SWADDIES	SWAMPERS	SWARDED	SWATTERED	SWEELING
SWADDLE	SWAMPIER	SWARDIER	SWATTERING	SWEELS
SWADDLED	SWAMPIEST	SWARDIEST	SWATTERS	SWEENEY
SWADDLER	SWAMPING	SWARDING	SWATTING	SWEENEYS
SWADDLERS	SWAMPISH*	SWARDS	SWATTINGS	SWEENIES
SWADDLES	SWAMPLAND	SWARDY	SWAY	SWEENY
SWADDLING	SWAMPLANDS	SWARE	SWAYABLE*	SWEEP
SWADDY	SWAMPS	SWARF	SWAYBACK	SWEEPBACK
SWADS	SWAMPY	SWARFED	SWAYBACKS	SWEEPBACKS
SWAG	SWAMY*	SWARFING	SWAYED	SWEEPER
SWAGE	SWAN	SWARFS	SWAYER	SWEEPERS
SWAGED	SWANG	SWARM	SWAYERS	SWEEPIER
SWAGER*	SWANHERD	SWARMED	SWAYFUL*	SWEEPIEST
SWAGERS*	SWANHERDS	SWARMER	SWAYING	SWEEPING
SWAGES	SWANK	SWARMERS	SWAYINGS	SWEEPINGS
SWAGGED	SWANKED	SWARMING	SWAYL	SWEEPS
SWAGGER	SWANKER	SWARMINGS	SWAYLED	SWEEPY
SWAGGERED	SWANKERS	SWARMS	SWAYLING	SWEER
SWAGGERER	SWANKEST	SWART	SWAYLINGS	SWEERED
SWAGGERERS	SWANKEY	SWARTH	SWAYLS	SWEERT
SWAGGERING	SWANKEYS	SWARTHIER	SWAYS	SWEES
SWAGGERINGS	SWANKIE	SWARTHIEST	SWAZZLE	SWEET
SWAGGERS	SWANKIER	SWARTHS	SWAZZLES	SWEETCORN
SWAGGIE	SWANKIES	SWARTHY	SWEAL	SWEETCORNS
SWAGGIES	SWANKIEST	SWARTNESS	SWEALED	SWEETED
SWAGGING	SWANKILY*	SWARTNESSES	SWEALING	SWEETEN
SWAGING	SWANKING	SWARTY	SWEALINGS	SWEETENED
SWAGMAN	SWANKPOT	SWARVE	SWEALS	SWEETENER
SWAGMEN	SWANKPOTS	SWARVED	SWEAR	SWEETENERS
SWAGS	SWANKS	SWARVES	SWEARD	SWEETENING
SWAGSHOP	SWANKY	SWARVING	SWEARDS	SWEETENINGS
SWAGSHOPS	SWANLIKE	SWASH	SWEARER	SWEETENS
SWAGSMAN	SWANNED	SWASHED	SWEARERS	SWEETER
SWAGSMEN	SWANNERIES	SWASHER	SWEARING	SWEETEST

SWEETFISH	SWERVED	SWINDLERS	SWIPPLES	SWIZZLE
SWEETFISHES	SWERVER	SWINDLES	SWIRE	SWIZZLED
SWEETIE	SWERVERS	SWINDLING	SWIRES	SWIZZLER*
SWEETIES	SWERVES	SWINDLINGS	SWIRL	SWIZZLERS*
SWEETING	SWERVING	SWINE	SWIRLED	SWIZZLES
SWEETINGS	SWERVINGS	SWINEHERD	SWIRLIER	SWIZZLING
SWEETISH	SWEVEN	SWINEHERDS	SWIRLIEST	SWOB
SWEETLY	SWEVENS	SWINEHOOD	SWIRLING	SWOBBED
SWEETMEAL	SWEY	SWINEHOODS	SWIRLS	SWOBBER
SWEETMEAT	SWEYED	SWINEPOX*	SWIRLY	SWOBBERS
SWEETMEATS	SWEYING	SWINEPOXES*	SWISH	SWOBBING
SWEETNESS	SWEYS	SWINERIES	SWISHED	SWOBS
SWEETNESSES	SWIDDEN	SWINERY	SWISHER	SWOLLEN
SWEETPEA	SWIDDENS	SWING	SWISHERS	SWOLN
SWEETPEAS	SWIES	SWINGBEAT	SWISHES	SWONE
SWEETS	SWIFT	SWINGBEATS	SWISHEST	SWONES
SWEETSHOP*	SWIFTED	SWINGBOAT	SWISHIER	SWOON
SWEETSHOPS*	SWIFTER	SWINGBOATS	SWISHIEST	SWOONED
SWEETSOP	SWIFTERS	SWINGBY*	SWISHING	SWOONER*
SWEETSOPS	SWIFTEST	SWINGBYS*	SWISHINGS	SWOONERS*
SWEETWOOD	SWIFTING	SWINGE	SWISHY	SWOONING
SWEETWOODS	SWIFTLET	SWINGED	SWISS*	SWOONINGS
SWEETY	SWIFTLETS	SWINGEING	SWISSES*	SWOONS
SWEIR	SWIFTLY	SWINGER	SWISSING	SWOOP
SWEIRNESS	SWIFTNESS	SWINGERS	SWISSINGS	SWOOPED
SWEIRNESSES	SWIFTNESSES	SWINGES	SWITCH	SWOOPER*
SWEIRT	SWIFTS	SWINGIER	SWITCHED	SWOOPERS*
SWELCHIE	SWIG	SWINGIEST	SWITCHEL	SWOOPING
SWELCHIES	SWIGGED	SWINGING	SWITCHELS	SWOOPS
SWELL	SWIGGER	SWINGINGEST*	SWITCHER*	SWOOSH
SWELLDOM	SWIGGERS	SWINGINGS	SWITCHERS*	SWOOSHED
SWELLDOMS	SWIGGING	SWINGISM	SWITCHES	SWOOSHES
SWELLED	SWIGS	SWINGISMS	SWITCHIER	SWOOSHING
SWELLER	SWILL	SWINGLE	SWITCHIEST	SWOP
SWELLERS	SWILLED	SWINGLED	SWITCHING	SWOPPED
SWELLEST	SWILLER	SWINGLES	SWITCHINGS	SWOPPER
SWELLFISH*	SWILLERS	SWINGLING	SWITCHMAN	SWOPPERS
SWELLFISHES*	SWILLING	SWINGLINGS	SWITCHMEN	SWOPPING
SWELLHEAD*	SWILLINGS	SWINGMAN*	SWITCHY	SWOPPINGS
SWELLHEADS*	SWILLS	SWINGMEN*	SWITH	SWOPS
SWELLING	SWIM	SWINGS	SWITHE*	SWOPT
SWELLINGS	SWIMMABLE	SWINGTREE	SWITHER	SWORD
SWELLISH	SWIMMER	SWINGTREES	SWITHERED	SWORDED
SWELLS	SWIMMERET	SWINGY	SWITHERING	SWORDER
SWELT	SWIMMERETS	SWINISH	SWITHERS	SWORDERS
SWELTED	SWIMMERS	SWINISHLY	SWITHLY*	SWORDFISH
SWELTER	SWIMMIER	SWINK	SWITS	SWORDFISHES
SWELTERED	SWIMMIEST	SWINKED	SWITSES	SWORDING
SWELTERING	SWIMMILY*	SWINKING	SWIVE	SWORDLESS
SWELTERINGS	SWIMMING	SWINKS	SWIVED	SWORDLIKE
SWELTERS	SWIMMINGS	SWINNEY*	SWIVEL	SWORDMAN
SWELTING	SWIMMY	SWINNEYS*	SWIVELED*	SWORDMEN
SWELTRIER	SWIMS	SWIPE	SWIVELING*	SWORDPLAY
SWELTRIEST	SWIMSUIT	SWIPED	SWIVELLED	SWORDPLAYS
SWELTRY	SWIMSUITS	SWIPER	SWIVELLING	SWORDS
SWELTS	SWIMWEAR	SWIPERS	SWIVELS	SWORDSMAN
SWEPT	SWIMWEARS	SWIPES	SWIVES	SWORDSMEN
SWEPTBACK	SWINDGE	SWIPEY	SWIVET	SWORDTAIL*
SWEPTWING	SWINDGED	SWIPIER	SWIVETS	SWORDTAILS*
SWERF	SWINDGES	SWIPIEST	SWIVING	SWORE
SWERFED	SWINDGING	SWIPING	SWIZ	SWORN
SWERFING	SWINDLE	SWIPLE*	SWIZZED	SWOT
SWERFS	SWINDLED	SWIPLES*	SWIZZES	SWOTS
SWERVE	SWINDLER	SWIPPLE	SWIZZING	SWOTTED

The Chambers Dictionary is the authority for many longer words; see Introduction, page ix

SWOTTER	SYKER	SYLVANITE	SYMPATHY	SYNAPTIC
SWOTTERS	SYKES	SYLVANITES	SYMPATRIC	SYNARCHIES
SWOTTING	SYLI*	SYLVANS	SYMPATRIES*	SYNARCHY
SWOTTINGS	SYLIS*	SYLVAS	SYMPATRY*	SYNASTRIES
SWOUN	SYLLABARIES	SYLVATIC	SYMPETALIES*	SYNASTRY
SWOUND	SYLLABARY	SYLVIA	SYMPETALY*	SYNAXARIA
SWOUNDED	SYLLABI	SYLVIAS	SYMPHILE	SYNAXES
SWOUNDING	SYLLABIC	SYLVIINE	SYMPHILES	SYNAXIS
SWOUNDS	SYLLABICS	SYLVIN*	SYMPHILIES	SYNC
SWOUNE	SYLLABIFIED	SYLVINE	SYMPHILY	SYNCARP
SWOUNED	SYLLABIFIES	SYLVINES	SYMPHONIC	SYNCARPIES
SWOUNES	SYLLABIFY	SYLVINITE	SYMPHONIES	SYNCARPS
SWOUNING	SYLLABIFYING	SYLVINITES	SYMPHONY	SYNCARPY
SWOUNS	SYLLABISE	SYLVINS*	SYMPHYSES	SYNCED
SWOWND	SYLLABISED	SYLVITE	SYMPHYSIS	SYNCH
SWOWNDS	SYLLABISES	SYLVITES	SYMPHYTIC	SYNCHED
SWOWNE	SYLLABISING	SYMAR	SYMPLAST	SYNCHING
SWOWNES	SYLLABISM	SYMARS	SYMPLASTS	SYNCHRO
SWOZZLE	SYLLABISMS	SYMBION	SYMPLOCE	SYNCHRONIES
SWOZZLES	SYLLABIZE	SYMBIONS	SYMPLOCES	SYNCHRONY
SWUM	SYLLABIZED	SYMBIONT	SYMPODIA	SYNCHROS
SWUNG	SYLLABIZES	SYMBIONTS	SYMPODIAL	SYNCHS
SWY	SYLLABIZING	SYMBIOSES	SYMPODIUM	SYNCHYSES
SYBARITE	SYLLABLE	SYMBIOSIS	SYMPOSIA	SYNCHYSIS
SYBARITES	SYLLABLED	SYMBIOT*	SYMPOSIAC	SYNCING
SYBARITIC	SYLLABLES	SYMBIOTE*	SYMPOSIAL	SYNCLINAL
SYBBE	SYLLABLING	SYMBIOTES*	SYMPOSIUM	SYNCLINALS
SYBBES	SYLLABUB	SYMBIOTIC	SYMPOSIUMS*	SYNCLINE
SYBIL	SYLLABUBS	SYMBIOTS*	SYMPTOM	SYNCLINES
SYBILS	SYLLABUS	SYMBOL	SYMPTOMS	SYNCOM*
SYBO	SYLLABUSES	SYMBOLE	SYMPTOSES	SYNCOMS*
SYBOE	SYLLEPSES	SYMBOLED*	SYMPTOSIS	SYNCOPAL
SYBOES	SYLLEPSIS	SYMBOLES	SYMPTOTIC	SYNCOPATE
SYBOTIC	SYLLEPTIC	SYMBOLIC	SYN*	SYNCOPATED
SYBOTISM	SYLLOGISE	SYMBOLICS	SYNAGOG*	SYNCOPATES
SYBOTISMS	SYLLOGISED	SYMBOLING*	SYNAGOGAL	SYNCOPATING
SYBOW	SYLLOGISES	SYMBOLISE	SYNAGOGS*	SYNCOPE
SYBOWS	SYLLOGISING	SYMBOLISED	SYNAGOGUE	SYNCOPES
SYCAMINE	SYLLOGISM	SYMBOLISES	SYNAGOGUES	SYNCOPIC
SYCAMINES	SYLLOGISMS	SYMBOLISING	SYNALEPHA*	SYNCOPTIC
SYCAMORE	SYLLOGIST*	SYMBOLISM	SYNALEPHAS*	SYNCRETIC
SYCAMORES	SYLLOGISTS*	SYMBOLISMS	SYNANDRIA	SYNCS
SYCE	SYLLOGIZE	SYMBOLIST	SYNANGIA	SYNCYTIA
SYCEE	SYLLOGIZED	SYMBOLISTS	SYNANGIUM	SYNCYTIAL
SYCEES	SYLLOGIZES	SYMBOLIZE	SYNANON*	SYNCYTIUM
SYCES	SYLLOGIZING	SYMBOLIZED	SYNANONS*	SYND
SYCOMORE	SYLPH	SYMBOLIZES	SYNANTHIC	SYNDACTYL
SYCOMORES	SYLPHIC*	SYMBOLIZING	SYNANTHIES	SYNDED
SYCONIA	SYLPHID	SYMBOLLED	SYNANTHY	SYNDESES
SYCONIUM	SYLPHIDE	SYMBOLLING	SYNAPHEA	SYNDESIS
SYCOPHANT	SYLPHIDES	SYMBOLOGIES	SYNAPHEAS	SYNDESISES*
SYCOPHANTS	SYLPHIDS	SYMBOLOGY	SYNAPHEIA	SYNDET
SYCOSES	SYLPHIER	SYMBOLS	SYNAPHEIAS	SYNDETIC
SYCOSIS	SYLPHIEST	SYMITAR	SYNAPSE	SYNDETS
SYE	SYLPHINE	SYMITARE	SYNAPSED*	SYNDIC
SYED	SYLPHISH	SYMITARES	SYNAPSES	SYNDICAL
SYEING	SYLPHLIKE*	SYMITARS	SYNAPSID*	SYNDICATE
SYEN	SYLPHS	SYMMETRAL	SYNAPSIDS*	SYNDICATED
SYENITE	SYLPHY	SYMMETRIC	SYNAPSING*	SYNDICATES
SYENITES	SYLVA	SYMMETRIES	SYNAPSIS	SYNDICATING
SYENITIC	SYLVAE	SYMMETRY	SYNAPTASE	SYNDICS
SYENS	SYLVAN	SYMPATHIES	SYNAPTASES	SYNDING
SYES	SYLVANER	SYMPATHIN	SYNAPTE	SYNDINGS
SYKE	SYLVANERS	SYMPATHINS	SYNAPTES	SYNDROME

SYNDROMES
SYNDROMIC
SYNDS
SYNE
SYNECHIA
SYNECHIAS
SYNECTIC
SYNECTICS
SYNED
SYNEDRIA
SYNEDRIAL
SYNEDRION
SYNEDRIUM
SYNERESES
SYNERESIS
SYNERGIA*
SYNERGIAS*
SYNERGIC
SYNERGID
SYNERGIDS
SYNERGIES
SYNERGISE
SYNERGISED
SYNERGISES
SYNERGISING
SYNERGISM
SYNERGISMS
SYNERGIST
SYNERGISTS
SYNERGIZE
SYNERGIZED
SYNERGIZES
SYNERGIZING
SYNERGY
SYNES
SYNESES
SYNESIS
SYNESISES*
SYNFUEL
SYNFUELS
SYNGAMIC
SYNGAMIES
SYNGAMOUS
SYNGAMY
SYNGAS
SYNGASES

SYNGASSES*
SYNGENEIC
SYNGRAPH
SYNGRAPHS
SYNING
SYNIZESES
SYNIZESIS
SYNKARYON
SYNKARYONS
SYNOD
SYNODAL
SYNODALS
SYNODIC
SYNODICAL
SYNODS
SYNODSMAN
SYNODSMEN
SYNOECETE
SYNOECETES
SYNOECISE
SYNOECISED
SYNOECISES
SYNOECISING
SYNOECISM
SYNOECISMS
SYNOECIZE
SYNOECIZED
SYNOECIZES
SYNOECIZING
SYNOEKETE
SYNOEKETES
SYNOICOUS
SYNONYM
SYNONYME*
SYNONYMES*
SYNONYMIC
SYNONYMIES
SYNONYMS
SYNONYMY
SYNOPSES
SYNOPSIS
SYNOPSISE
SYNOPSISED
SYNOPSISES
SYNOPSISING
SYNOPSIZE

SYNOPSIZED
SYNOPSIZES
SYNOPSIZING
SYNOPTIC
SYNOPTIST
SYNOPTISTS
SYNOVIA
SYNOVIAL
SYNOVIAS
SYNOVITIC
SYNOVITIS
SYNOVITISES
SYNROC
SYNROCS
SYNTACTIC
SYNTAGM
SYNTAGMA
SYNTAGMAS*
SYNTAGMATA
SYNTAGMS
SYNTAN
SYNTANS
SYNTAX
SYNTAXES
SYNTECTIC
SYNTEXIS
SYNTEXISES
SYNTH
SYNTHESES
SYNTHESIS
SYNTHETIC
SYNTHETICS
SYNTHON
SYNTHONS
SYNTHRONI
SYNTHS
SYNTONIC
SYNTONIES
SYNTONIN
SYNTONINS
SYNTONISE
SYNTONISED
SYNTONISES
SYNTONISING
SYNTONIZE
SYNTONIZED

SYNTONIZES
SYNTONIZING
SYNTONOUS
SYNTONY
SYNURA*
SYNURAE*
SYPE
SYPED
SYPES
SYPH*
SYPHER
SYPHERED
SYPHERING
SYPHERS
SYPHILIS
SYPHILISE
SYPHILISED
SYPHILISES
SYPHILISING
SYPHILIZE
SYPHILIZED
SYPHILIZES
SYPHILIZING
SYPHILOID
SYPHILOMA
SYPHILOMAS
SYPHON
SYPHONED
SYPHONING
SYPHONS
SYPHS*
SYPING
SYRAH
SYRAHS
SYREN
SYRENS
SYRINGA
SYRINGAS
SYRINGE
SYRINGEAL
SYRINGED
SYRINGES
SYRINGING
SYRINX
SYRINXES
SYRLYE

SYRPHIAN*
SYRPHIANS*
SYRPHID
SYRPHIDS
SYRTES
SYRTIS
SYRUP
SYRUPED
SYRUPIER
SYRUPIEST
SYRUPING
SYRUPS
SYRUPY
SYSOP
SYSOPS
SYSSITIA
SYSSITIAS
SYSTALTIC
SYSTEM
SYSTEMED
SYSTEMIC
SYSTEMICS*
SYSTEMISE
SYSTEMISED
SYSTEMISES
SYSTEMISING
SYSTEMIZE
SYSTEMIZED
SYSTEMIZES
SYSTEMIZING
SYSTEMS
SYSTOLE
SYSTOLES
SYSTOLIC
SYSTYLE
SYSTYLES
SYTHE
SYTHES
SYVER
SYVERS
SYZYGAL*
SYZYGIAL
SYZYGIES
SYZYGY

T

TA	TABLEAU	TABOURED	TACHOGRAM	TACNODE*
TAB	TABLEAUS*	TABOURER*	TACHOGRAMS	TACNODES*
TABANID	TABLEAUX	TABOURERS*	TACHOS	TACO
TABANIDS	TABLED	TABOURET	TACHS*	TACONITE
TABARD	TABLEFUL	TABOURETS	TACHYLITE	TACONITES
TABARDED*	TABLEFULS	TABOURIN	TACHYLITES	TACOS
TABARDS	TABLELAND	TABOURING	TACHYLYTE	TACT
TABARET	TABLELANDS	TABOURINS	TACHYLYTES	TACTFUL
TABARETS	TABLEMATE*	TABOURS	TACHYON	TACTFULLY
TABASHEER	TABLEMATES*	TABRERE	TACHYONS	TACTIC
TABASHEERS	TABLES	TABRERES	TACHYPNEA	TACTICAL
TABASHIR	TABLESFUL*	TABRET	TACHYPNEAS	TACTICIAN
TABASHIRS	TABLET	TABRETS	TACIT	TACTICIANS
TABBED	TABLETED	TABS	TACITLY	TACTICITIES
TABBIED	TABLETING	TABU	TACITNESS	TACTICITY
TABBIES	TABLETOP	TABUED	TACITNESSES	TACTICS
TABBINET	TABLETOPS	TABUING	TACITURN	TACTILE
TABBINETS	TABLETS	TABULA	TACK	TACTILELY*
TABBING	TABLETTED*	TABULAE	TACKBOARD*	TACTILIST
TABBIS*	TABLETTING*	TABULAR	TACKBOARDS*	TACTILISTS
TABBISES*	TABLEWARE	TABULARLY	TACKED	TACTILITIES
TABBOULEH	TABLEWARES	TABULATE	TACKER	TACTILITY
TABBOULEHS	TABLEWISE	TABULATED	TACKERS	TACTION
TABBY	TABLIER	TABULATES	TACKET	TACTIONS
TABBYHOOD	TABLIERS	TABULATING	TACKETS	TACTISM
TABBYHOODS	TABLING	TABULATOR	TACKETY	TACTISMS
TABBYING	TABLINGS	TABULATORS	TACKEY*	TACTLESS
TABEFIED	TABLOID	TABULI*	TACKIER	TACTS
TABEFIES	TABLOIDS	TABULIS*	TACKIES	TACTUAL
TABEFY	TABLOIDY	TABUN	TACKIEST	TACTUALLY
TABEFYING	TABOGGAN	TABUNS	TACKIFIED*	TAD
TABELLION	TABOGGANED	TABUS	TACKIFIER*	TADDIE
TABELLIONS	TABOGGANING	TACAHOUT	TACKIFIERS*	TADDIES
TABER*	TABOGGANS	TACAHOUTS	TACKIFIES*	TADPOLE
TABERD	TABOO	TACAMAHAC	TACKIFY*	TADPOLES
TABERDAR	TABOOED	TACAMAHACS	TACKIFYING*	TADS
TABERDARS	TABOOING	TACAN	TACKILY	TADVANCE
TABERDS	TABOOLEY*	TACANS	TACKINESS	TAE
TABERED*	TABOOLEYS*	TACE	TACKINESSES	TAED
TABERING*	TABOOS	TACES	TACKING	TAEDIUM
TABERS*	TABOR	TACET	TACKINGS	TAEDIUMS
TABES	TABORED	TACH	TACKLE	TAEING
TABESCENT	TABORER	TACHE	TACKLED	TAEL
TABETIC	TABORERS	TACHES	TACKLER	TAELS
TABETICS	TABORET	TACHINID	TACKLERS	TAENIA
TABI	TABORETS	TACHINIDS	TACKLES	TAENIAE
TABID	TABORIN	TACHISM	TACKLESS*	TAENIAS
TABINET	TABORINE*	TACHISME	TACKLING	TAENIASES
TABINETS	TABORINES*	TACHISMES	TACKLINGS	TAENIASIS
TABIS	TABORING	TACHISMS	TACKS	TAENIATE
TABLA	TABORINS	TACHIST	TACKSMAN	TAENIOID
TABLAS	TABORS	TACHISTE	TACKSMEN	TAES
TABLATURE	TABOULI*	TACHISTES	TACKY	TAFFAREL*
TABLATURES	TABOULIS*	TACHISTS	TACMAHACK	TAFFARELS*
TABLE	TABOUR	TACHO	TACMAHACKS	TAFFEREL

Words marked with an asterisk are from OTCWL

TAFFERELS	TAIGLE	TAILSLIDE*	TAKEOVER	TALENTED
TAFFETA	TAIGLED	TAILSLIDES*	TAKEOVERS	TALENTS
TAFFETAS	TAIGLES	TAILSPIN	TAKER	TALER
TAFFETASES	TAIGLING	TAILSPINS	TAKERS	TALERS
TAFFETIES	TAIL	TAILSTOCK	TAKES	TALES
TAFFETY	TAILARD	TAILSTOCKS	TAKEUP*	TALESMAN
TAFFIA	TAILARDS	TAILWATER*	TAKEUPS*	TALESMEN
TAFFIAS	TAILBACK	TAILWATERS*	TAKHI	TALEYSIM*
TAFFIES	TAILBACKS	TAILWHEEL	TAKHIS	TALI
TAFFRAIL	TAILBOARD	TAILWHEELS	TAKI	TALIGRADE
TAFFRAILS	TAILBOARDS	TAILWIND*	TAKIER	TALION
TAFFY	TAILBONE*	TAILWINDS*	TAKIEST	TALIONIC
TAFIA	TAILBONES*	TAILYE	TAKIN	TALIONS
TAFIAS	TAILCOAT*	TAILYES	TAKING	TALIPAT
TAG	TAILCOATS*	TAILZIE	TAKINGLY	TALIPATS
TAGALONG*	TAILED	TAILZIES	TAKINGS	TALIPED
TAGALONGS*	TAILENDER*	TAIN*	TAKINS	TALIPEDS
TAGBOARD*	TAILENDERS*	TAINS*	TAKIS	TALIPES
TAGBOARDS*	TAILER*	TAINT	TAKS	TALIPOT
TAGETES	TAILERON	TAINTED	TAKY	TALIPOTS
TAGGED	TAILERONS	TAINTING	TALA	TALISMAN
TAGGEE	TAILERS*	TAINTLESS	TALAK	TALISMANS
TAGGEES	TAILFAN*	TAINTS	TALAKS	TALK
TAGGER	TAILFANS*	TAINTURE	TALANT	TALKABLE
TAGGERS	TAILGATE	TAINTURES	TALANTS	TALKATHON
TAGGIER	TAILGATED	TAIPAN	TALAPOIN	TALKATHONS
TAGGIEST	TAILGATER	TAIPANS	TALAPOINS	TALKATIVE
TAGGING	TAILGATERS	TAIRA	TALAQ	TALKBACK
TAGGINGS	TAILGATES	TAIRAS	TALAQS	TALKBACKS
TAGGY	TAILGATING	TAIS	TALAR	TALKED
TAGHAIRM	TAILING	TAISCH	TALARIA	TALKER
TAGHAIRMS	TAILINGS	TAISCHES	TALARS	TALKERS
TAGLIKE*	TAILLAMP*	TAISH	TALAS	TALKFEST
TAGLIONI	TAILLAMPS*	TAISHES	TALAUNT	TALKFESTS
TAGLIONIS	TAILLE	TAIT	TALAUNTS	TALKIE
TAGMA	TAILLES	TAITS	TALAYOT	TALKIER
TAGMATA	TAILLESS	TAIVER	TALAYOTS	TALKIES
TAGMEME	TAILLEUR	TAIVERED	TALBOT	TALKIEST
TAGMEMES	TAILLEURS	TAIVERING	TALBOTS	TALKINESS*
TAGMEMIC	TAILLIE	TAIVERS	TALBOTYPE	TALKINESSES*
TAGMEMICS	TAILLIES	TAIVERT	TALBOTYPES	TALKING
TAGRAG	TAILLIGHT*	TAJ	TALC	TALKINGS
TAGRAGS	TAILLIGHTS*	TAJES	TALCED	TALKS
TAGS	TAILLIKE*	TAJINE	TALCIER	TALKY
TAGUAN	TAILOR	TAJINES	TALCIEST	TALL
TAGUANS	TAILORED	TAK	TALCING	TALLAGE
TAHA	TAILORESS	TAKA	TALCKED	TALLAGED
TAHAS	TAILORESSES	TAKABLE	TALCKIER	TALLAGES
TAHINA	TAILORING	TAKAHE	TALCKIEST	TALLAGING
TAHINAS	TAILORINGS	TAKAHES	TALCKING	TALLAISIM*
TAHINI	TAILORS	TAKAMAKA	TALCKY	TALLAT
TAHINIS	TAILPIECE	TAKAMAKAS	TALCOSE	TALLATS
TAHR	TAILPIECES	TAKAS	TALCOUS	TALLBOY
TAHRS	TAILPIPE	TAKE	TALCS	TALLBOYS
TAHSIL	TAILPIPED	TAKEABLE	TALCUM	TALLENT
TAHSILDAR	TAILPIPES	TAKEAWAY	TALCUMS	TALLENTS
TAHSILDARS	TAILPIPING	TAKEAWAYS	TALCY	TALLER
TAHSILS	TAILPLANE	TAKEDOWN*	TALE	TALLEST
TAI	TAILPLANES	TAKEDOWNS*	TALEA	TALLET
TAIAHA	TAILRACE	TAKEN	TALEAE	TALLETS
TAIAHAS	TAILRACES	TAKEOFF*	TALEFUL	TALLIABLE
TAIGA	TAILS	TAKEOFFS*	TALEGALLA	TALLIATE
TAIGAS	TAILSKID	TAKEOUT	TALEGALLAS	TALLIATED
TAIGLACH*	TAILSKIDS	TAKEOUTS	TALENT	TALLIATES

The Chambers Dictionary is the authority for many longer words; see Introduction, page ix

TALLIATING	TAMAL	TAMENESSES	TANBARK	TANISTS
TALLIED	TAMALE	TAMER	TANBARKS	TANIWHA
TALLIER	TAMALES	TAMERS	TANDEM	TANIWHAS
TALLIERS	TAMALS	TAMES	TANDEMS	TANK
TALLIES	TAMANDU	TAMEST	TANDOOR	TANKA
TALLIS*	TAMANDUA	TAMIN	TANDOORI	TANKAGE
TALLISH	TAMANDUAS	TAMINE	TANDOORIS	TANKAGES
TALLISIM*	TAMANDUS	TAMINES	TANDOORS	TANKARD
TALLIT*	TAMANOIR	TAMING	TANE	TANKARDS
TALLITH	TAMANOIRS	TAMINGS	TANG	TANKAS
TALLITHES*	TAMANU	TAMINS	TANGA	TANKED
TALLITHIM	TAMANUS	TAMIS	TANGAS	TANKER
TALLITHS	TAMARA	TAMISE	TANGED	TANKERS
TALLITIM*	TAMARACK	TAMISES	TANGELO	TANKFUL
TALLITOTH*	TAMARACKS	TAMMAR	TANGELOS	TANKFULS
TALLNESS	TAMARAO	TAMMARS	TANGENCE*	TANKIA
TALLNESSES	TAMARAOS	TAMMIE*	TANGENCES*	TANKIAS
TALLOL*	TAMARAS	TAMMIES	TANGENCIES	TANKIES
TALLOLS*	TAMARAU	TAMMY	TANGENCY	TANKING
TALLOT	TAMARAUS	TAMOXIFEN	TANGENT	TANKINGS
TALLOTS	TAMARI	TAMOXIFENS	TANGENTS	TANKLIKE*
TALLOW	TAMARILLO	TAMP	TANGERINE	TANKS
TALLOWED	TAMARILLOS	TAMPALA*	TANGERINES	TANKSHIP*
TALLOWING	TAMARIN	TAMPALAS*	TANGHIN	TANKSHIPS*
TALLOWISH	TAMARIND	TAMPAN*	TANGHININ	TANKY
TALLOWS	TAMARINDS	TAMPANS*	TANGHININS	TANLING
TALLOWY	TAMARINS	TAMPED	TANGHINS	TANLINGS
TALLY	TAMARIS	TAMPER	TANGI	TANNA
TALLYHO*	TAMARISK	TAMPERED	TANGIBLE	TANNABLE
TALLYHOED*	TAMARISKS	TAMPERER	TANGIBLES	TANNAGE
TALLYHOING*	TAMASHA	TAMPERERS	TANGIBLY	TANNAGES
TALLYHOS*	TAMASHAS	TAMPERING	TANGIE	TANNAH
TALLYING	TAMBAC	TAMPERINGS	TANGIER	TANNAHS
TALLYMAN	TAMBACS	TAMPERS	TANGIES	TANNAS
TALLYMEN	TAMBAK*	TAMPING	TANGIEST	TANNATE
TALLYSHOP	TAMBAKS*	TAMPINGS	TANGING	TANNATES
TALLYSHOPS	TAMBALA*	TAMPION	TANGIS	TANNED
TALMA	TAMBALAS*	TAMPIONS	TANGLE	TANNER
TALMAS	TAMBER	TAMPON	TANGLED	TANNERIES
TALMUD	TAMBERS	TAMPONADE	TANGLER	TANNERS
TALMUDIC*	TAMBOUR	TAMPONADES	TANGLERS	TANNERY
TALMUDISM*	TAMBOURA	TAMPONAGE	TANGLES	TANNEST
TALMUDISMS*	TAMBOURAS	TAMPONAGES	TANGLIER	TANNIC
TALMUDS	TAMBOURED	TAMPONED	TANGLIEST	TANNIN
TALON	TAMBOURER*	TAMPONING	TANGLING	TANNING
TALONED	TAMBOURERS*	TAMPONS	TANGLINGS	TANNINGS
TALONS	TAMBOURIN	TAMPS	TANGLY	TANNINS
TALOOKA	TAMBOURING	TAMS	TANGO	TANNISH*
TALOOKAS	TAMBOURINS	TAMWORTH	TANGOED	TANNOY
TALPA	TAMBOURS	TAMWORTHS	TANGOING	TANNOYED
TALPAE	TAMBUR*	TAN	TANGOIST	TANNOYING
TALPAS	TAMBURA	TANA	TANGOISTS	TANNOYS
TALUK	TAMBURAS	TANADAR	TANGOS	TANREC
TALUKA	TAMBURIN	TANADARS	TANGRAM	TANRECS
TALUKAS	TAMBURINS	TANAGER	TANGRAMS	TANS
TALUKDAR	TAMBURS*	TANAGERS	TANGS	TANSIES
TALUKDARS	TAME	TANAGRA	TANGUN	TANSY
TALUKS	TAMEABLE	TANAGRAS	TANGUNS	TANTALATE
TALUS	TAMED	TANAGRINE	TANGY	TANTALATES
TALUSES	TAMEIN*	TANAISTE	TANH	TANTALIC
TALWEG	TAMEINS*	TANAISTES	TANHS	TANTALISE
TALWEGS	TAMELESS	TANALISED	TANIST	TANTALISED
TAM	TAMELY	TANALIZED	TANISTRIES	TANTALISES
TAMABLE	TAMENESS	TANAS	TANISTRY	TANTALISING

TANTALISINGS
TANTALISM
TANTALISMS
TANTALITE
TANTALITES
TANTALIZE
TANTALIZED
TANTALIZES
TANTALIZING
TANTALIZINGS
TANTALOUS
TANTALUM
TANTALUMS
TANTALUS
TANTALUSES
TANTARA
TANTARARA
TANTARARAS
TANTARAS
TANTI
TANTIVIES
TANTIVY
TANTO
TANTONIES
TANTONY
TANTRA
TANTRAS
TANTRIC
TANTRUM
TANTRUMS
TANUKI*
TANUKIS*
TANYARD
TANYARDS
TANZANITE*
TANZANITES*
TAO*
TAOISEACH
TAOISEACHS
TAOS*
TAP
TAPA
TAPACOLO
TAPACOLOS
TAPACULO
TAPACULOS
TAPADERA
TAPADERAS
TAPADERO
TAPADEROS
TAPALO*
TAPALOS*
TAPAS
TAPE
TAPEABLE
TAPED
TAPELESS
TAPELIKE
TAPELINE
TAPELINES
TAPEN
TAPENADE
TAPENADES
TAPER

TAPERED
TAPERER
TAPERERS
TAPERING
TAPERINGS
TAPERNESS
TAPERNESSES
TAPERS
TAPERWISE
TAPES
TAPESTRIED
TAPESTRIES
TAPESTRY
TAPESTRYING
TAPET
TAPETA
TAPETAL
TAPETI
TAPETIS
TAPETS
TAPETUM
TAPEWORM
TAPEWORMS
TAPHOLE*
TAPHOLES*
TAPHONOMIES
TAPHONOMY
TAPHOUSE*
TAPHOUSES*
TAPING
TAPIOCA
TAPIOCAS
TAPIR
TAPIROID
TAPIRS
TAPIS
TAPISES
TAPIST
TAPISTS
TAPLASH
TAPLASHES
TAPPA
TAPPABLE
TAPPAS
TAPPED
TAPPER
TAPPERS
TAPPET
TAPPETS
TAPPICE
TAPPICED
TAPPICES
TAPPICING
TAPPING
TAPPINGS
TAPPIT
TAPROOM
TAPROOMS
TAPROOT
TAPROOTS
TAPS
TAPSMAN
TAPSMEN
TAPSTER

TAPSTERS
TAPSTRY
TAPU
TAPUED
TAPUING
TAPUS
TAQUERIA
TAQUERIAS
TAR
TARA
TARAKIHI
TARAKIHIS
TARAMA*
TARAMAS*
TARAND
TARANDS
TARANTARA
TARANTARAED
TARANTARAING
TARANTARAS
TARANTAS
TARANTASES
TARANTASS
TARANTASSES
TARANTISM
TARANTISMS
TARANTULA
TARANTULAE*
TARANTULAS
TARAS
TARAXACUM
TARAXACUMS
TARBOGGIN
TARBOGGINED
TARBOGGINING
TARBOGGINS
TARBOOSH
TARBOOSHES
TARBOUSH
TARBOUSHES
TARBOY
TARBOYS
TARBUSH
TARBUSHES
TARCEL
TARCELS
TARDIED
TARDIER
TARDIES
TARDIEST
TARDILY
TARDINESS
TARDINESSES
TARDIVE
TARDO*
TARDY
TARDYING
TARDYON*
TARDYONS*
TARE
TARED
TARES
TARGE
TARGED

TARGES
TARGET
TARGETED
TARGETEER
TARGETEERS
TARGETING
TARGETS
TARGING
TARIFF
TARIFFED
TARIFFING
TARIFFS
TARING
TARINGS
TARLATAN
TARLATANS
TARLETAN*
TARLETANS*
TARMAC
TARMACKED
TARMACKING
TARMACS
TARN
TARNAL
TARNALLY
TARNATION
TARNATIONS*
TARNISH
TARNISHED
TARNISHER
TARNISHERS
TARNISHES
TARNISHING
TARNS
TARO
TAROC
TAROCS
TAROK
TAROKS
TAROS
TAROT
TAROTS
TARP
TARPAN
TARPANS
TARPAPER*
TARPAPERS*
TARPAULIN
TARPAULINS
TARPON
TARPONS
TARPS
TARRAGON
TARRAGONS
TARRAS
TARRASES
TARRE
TARRED
TARRES
TARRIANCE
TARRIANCES
TARRIED
TARRIER
TARRIERS

TARRIES
TARRIEST
TARRINESS
TARRINESSES
TARRING
TARRINGS
TARROCK
TARROCKS
TARROW
TARROWED
TARROWING
TARROWS
TARRY
TARRYING
TARS
TARSAL
TARSALGIA
TARSALGIAS
TARSALS
TARSEL
TARSELS
TARSI
TARSIA
TARSIAS
TARSIER
TARSIERS
TARSIOID
TARSIPED
TARSIPEDS
TARSUS
TART
TARTAN
TARTANA
TARTANAS
TARTANE
TARTANED
TARTANES
TARTANRIES
TARTANRY
TARTANS
TARTAR
TARTARE
TARTARES
TARTARIC
TARTARISE
TARTARISED
TARTARISES
TARTARISING
TARTARIZE
TARTARIZED
TARTARIZES
TARTARIZING
TARTARLY
TARTARS
TARTED*
TARTER
TARTEST
TARTIER
TARTIEST
TARTINE
TARTINES
TARTINESS
TARTINESSES
TARTING*

The Chambers Dictionary is the authority for many longer words; see Introduction, page ix

TARTISH	TASTED	TATTOOERS	TAVA	TAXAMETERS
TARTLET	TASTEFUL	TATTOOING	TAVAH	TAXATION
TARTLETS	TASTELESS	TATTOOIST	TAVAHS	TAXATIONS
TARTLY	TASTER	TATTOOISTS	TAVAS	TAXATIVE
TARTNESS	TASTERS	TATTOOS	TAVER	TAXED
TARTNESSES	TASTES	TATTOW	TAVERED	TAXEME*
TARTRATE	TASTEVIN	TATTOWED	TAVERING	TAXEMES*
TARTRATES	TASTEVINS	TATTOWING	TAVERN	TAXEMIC*
TARTS	TASTIER	TATTOWS	TAVERNA	TAXER
TARTUFE*	TASTIEST	TATTS	TAVERNAS	TAXERS
TARTUFES*	TASTILY	TATTY	TAVERNER	TAXES
TARTUFFE*	TASTINESS	TATU	TAVERNERS	TAXI
TARTUFFES*	TASTINESSES	TATUED	TAVERNS	TAXIARCH
TARTY	TASTING	TATUING	TAVERS	TAXIARCHS
TARWEED	TASTINGS	TATUS	TAVERT	TAXICAB
TARWEEDS	TASTY	TAU	TAVS*	TAXICABS
TARWHINE	TAT	TAUBE	TAW	TAXIDERMIES
TARWHINES	TATAMI	TAUBES	TAWA	TAXIDERMY
TARZAN*	TATAMIS	TAUGHT	TAWAS	TAXIED
TARZANS*	TATAR*	TAULD	TAWDRIER	TAXIES
TAS*	TATARS*	TAUNT	TAWDRIES	TAXIING
TASAR	TATE	TAUNTED	TAWDRIEST	TAXIMAN
TASARS	TATER	TAUNTER	TAWDRILY	TAXIMEN
TASER	TATERS	TAUNTERS	TAWDRY	TAXIMETER
TASERED	TATES	TAUNTING	TAWED	TAXIMETERS
TASERING	TATH	TAUNTINGS	TAWER	TAXING
TASERS	TATHED	TAUNTS	TAWERIES	TAXINGLY*
TASH	TATHING	TAUPE	TAWERS	TAXINGS
TASHED	TATHS	TAUPES	TAWERY	TAXIS
TASHES	TATIE	TAUPIE	TAWIE	TAXITE*
TASHING	TATIES	TAUPIES	TAWIER	TAXITES*
TASIMETER	TATLER	TAUREAN	TAWIEST	TAXITIC*
TASIMETERS	TATLERS	TAURIC	TAWING	TAXIWAY
TASK	TATOU	TAURIFORM	TAWINGS	TAXIWAYS
TASKED	TATOUAY	TAURINE	TAWNEY	TAXLESS
TASKER	TATOUAYS	TAURINES	TAWNEYS	TAXMAN
TASKERS	TATOUS	TAUS	TAWNIER	TAXMEN
TASKING	TATS	TAUT	TAWNIES	TAXOL
TASKINGS	TATT	TAUTAUG*	TAWNIEST	TAXOLS
TASKS	TATTED	TAUTAUGS*	TAWNILY*	TAXON
TASKWORK*	TATTER	TAUTED	TAWNINESS	TAXONOMER
TASKWORKS*	TATTERED	TAUTEN	TAWNINESSES	TAXONOMERS
TASLET	TATTERING	TAUTENED	TAWNY	TAXONOMIC
TASLETS	TATTERS	TAUTENING	TAWPIE	TAXONOMIES
TASS	TATTERY	TAUTENS	TAWPIES	TAXONOMY
TASSE	TATTIE	TAUTER	TAWS	TAXONS*
TASSEL	TATTIER	TAUTEST	TAWSE	TAXOR
TASSELED	TATTIES	TAUTING	TAWSED*	TAXORS
TASSELING	TATTIEST	TAUTIT	TAWSES	TAXPAID*
TASSELL	TATTILY	TAUTLY	TAWSING*	TAXPAYER*
TASSELLED	TATTINESS	TAUTNESS	TAWT	TAXPAYERS*
TASSELLING	TATTINESSES	TAUTNESSES	TAWTED	TAXPAYING*
TASSELLINGS	TATTING	TAUTOG	TAWTIE	TAXUS*
TASSELLS	TATTINGS	TAUTOGS	TAWTIER	TAXWISE*
TASSELLY	TATTLE	TAUTOLOGIES	TAWTIEST	TAXYING
TASSELS	TATTLED	TAUTOLOGY	TAWTING	TAY
TASSES	TATTLER	TAUTOMER	TAWTS	TAYASSUID
TASSET	TATTLERS	TAUTOMERS	TAX	TAYASSUIDS
TASSETS	TATTLES	TAUTONYM	TAXA	TAYBERRIES
TASSIE	TATTLING	TAUTONYMIES*	TAXABLE	TAYBERRY
TASSIES	TATTLINGS	TAUTONYMS	TAXABLES*	TAYRA
TASSWAGE	TATTOO	TAUTONYMY*	TAXABLY	TAYRAS
TASTABLE	TATTOOED	TAUTS	TAXACEOUS	TAYS
TASTE	TATTOOER	TAV*	TAXAMETER	TAZZA

TAZZAS	TEAMERS	TEASHOP*	TECTRIX	TEENTSIEST
TAZZE	TEAMING	TEASHOPS*	TECTUM	TEENTSY
TCHICK	TEAMINGS	TEASING	TED	TEENTY
TCHICKED	TEAMMATE*	TEASINGLY	TEDDED	TEENY
TCHICKING	TEAMMATES*	TEASINGS	TEDDER	TEENYBOP*
TCHICKS	TEAMS	TEASPOON	TEDDERS	TEEPEE
TCHOTCHKE*	TEAMSTER	TEASPOONS	TEDDIE	TEEPEES
TCHOTCHKES*	TEAMSTERS	TEAT	TEDDIES	TEER
TE	TEAMWISE	TEATED	TEDDING	TEERED
TEA	TEAMWORK	TEATIME	TEDDY	TEERING
TEABERRIES	TEAMWORKS	TEATIMES	TEDESCA	TEERS
TEABERRY	TEAPOT	TEATS	TEDESCHE	TEES
TEABOARD	TEAPOTS	TEAWARE*	TEDESCHI	TEETER
TEABOARDS	TEAPOY	TEAWARES*	TEDESCO	TEETERED
TEABOWL*	TEAPOYS	TEAZE	TEDIER	TEETERING
TEABOWLS*	TEAR	TEAZED	TEDIEST	TEETERS
TEABOX*	TEARABLE	TEAZEL	TEDIOSITIES	TEETH
TEABOXES*	TEARAWAY	TEAZELED	TEDIOSITY	TEETHE
TEACAKE*	TEARAWAYS	TEAZELING	TEDIOUS	TEETHED
TEACAKES*	TEARDOWN*	TEAZELLED	TEDIOUSLY	TEETHER*
TEACART*	TEARDOWNS*	TEAZELLING	TEDISOME	TEETHERS*
TEACARTS*	TEARDROP*	TEAZELS	TEDIUM	TEETHES
TEACH	TEARDROPS*	TEAZES	TEDIUMS	TEETHING
TEACHABLE	TEARED*	TEAZING	TEDS	TEETHINGS
TEACHABLY*	TEARER	TEAZLE	TEDY	TEETOTAL
TEACHER	TEARERS	TEAZLED	TEE	TEETOTALED*
TEACHERLY	TEARFUL	TEAZLES	TEED	TEETOTALING*
TEACHERS	TEARFULLY	TEAZLING	TEEING	TEETOTALLED*
TEACHES	TEARGAS*	TEBBAD	TEEL	TEETOTALLING*
TEACHIE	TEARGASES*	TEBBADS	TEELS	TEETOTALS
TEACHING	TEARGASSED*	TECH	TEEM	TEETOTUM
TEACHINGS	TEARGASSES*	TECHED*	TEEMED	TEETOTUMS
TEACHLESS	TEARGASSING*	TECHIE	TEEMER	TEF
TEACUP	TEARIER	TECHIER	TEEMERS	TEFF
TEACUPFUL	TEARIEST	TECHIES	TEEMFUL	TEFFS
TEACUPFULS	TEARILY*	TECHIEST	TEEMING	TEFILLAH
TEACUPS	TEARING	TECHILY	TEEMINGLY*	TEFILLIN
TEACUPSFUL*	TEARLESS	TECHINESS	TEEMLESS	TEFS
TEAD	TEAROOM*	TECHINESSES	TEEMS	TEG
TEADE	TEAROOMS*	TECHNIC	TEEN	TEGG
TEADES	TEARS	TECHNICAL	TEENAGE	TEGGS
TEADS	TEARSHEET	TECHNICALS*	TEENAGED	TEGMEN
TEAED	TEARSHEETS	TECHNICS	TEENAGER	TEGMENTA
TEAGLE	TEARSTAIN*	TECHNIQUE	TEENAGERS	TEGMENTAL
TEAGLED	TEARSTAINS*	TECHNIQUES	TEEND	TEGMENTUM
TEAGLES	TEARY	TECHNO	TEENDED	TEGMINA
TEAGLING	TEAS	TECHNOPOP	TEENDING	TEGMINAL*
TEAHOUSE*	TEASE	TECHNOPOPS	TEENDS	TEGS
TEAHOUSES*	TEASED	TECHNOS	TEENE	TEGU
TEAING	TEASEL	TECHS	TEENED	TEGUA*
TEAK	TEASELED	TECHY	TEENER*	TEGUAS*
TEAKETTLE*	TEASELER	TECKEL	TEENERS*	TEGUEXIN
TEAKETTLES*	TEASELERS	TECKELS	TEENES	TEGUEXINS
TEAKS	TEASELING	TECTA	TEENFUL*	TEGULA
TEAKWOOD*	TEASELINGS	TECTAL*	TEENIER	TEGULAE
TEAKWOODS*	TEASELLED	TECTIFORM	TEENIEST	TEGULAR
TEAL	TEASELLER	TECTITE*	TEENING	TEGULARLY
TEALIKE*	TEASELLERS	TECTITES*	TEENS	TEGULATED
TEALS	TEASELLING	TECTONIC	TEENSIER	TEGUMEN*
TEAM	TEASELLINGS	TECTONICS	TEENSIEST	TEGUMENT
TEAMAKER*	TEASELS	TECTONISM*	TEENSY	TEGUMENTS
TEAMAKERS*	TEASER	TECTONISMS*	TEENTIER	TEGUMINA*
TEAMED	TEASERS	TECTORIAL	TEENTIEST	TEGUS
TEAMER	TEASES	TECTRICES	TEENTSIER	TEHR

The Chambers Dictionary is the authority for many longer words; see Introduction, page ix

TEHRS	TELEMETERED	TELETEXTS	TELLURIDES	TEMPERATE
TEIGLACH*	TELEMETERING	TELETHON	TELLURION	TEMPERATED
TEIID*	TELEMETERS	TELETHONS	TELLURIONS	TEMPERATES
TEIIDS*	TELEMETRIES	TELETRON	TELLURISE	TEMPERATING
TEIL	TELEMETRY	TELETRONS	TELLURISED	TEMPERED
TEILS	TELEOLOGIES	TELEVIEW	TELLURISES	TEMPERER
TEIND	TELEOLOGY	TELEVIEWED	TELLURISING	TEMPERERS
TEINDED	TELEONOMIES	TELEVIEWING	TELLURITE	TEMPERING
TEINDING	TELEONOMY	TELEVIEWS	TELLURITES	TEMPERINGS
TEINDS	TELEOSAUR	TELEVISE	TELLURIUM	TEMPERS
TEKNONYMIES	TELEOSAURS	TELEVISED	TELLURIUMS	TEMPEST
TEKNONYMY	TELEOST	TELEVISER	TELLURIZE	TEMPESTED
TEKTITE	TELEOSTS	TELEVISERS	TELLURIZED	TEMPESTING
TEKTITES	TELEPATH	TELEVISES	TELLURIZES	TEMPESTS
TEKTITIC*	TELEPATHED	TELEVISING	TELLURIZING	TEMPI
TEL	TELEPATHIES	TELEVISOR	TELLUROUS	TEMPING
TELA	TELEPATHING	TELEVISORS	TELLUS	TEMPLAR
TELAE	TELEPATHS	TELEX	TELLUSES	TEMPLARS
TELAMON	TELEPATHY	TELEXED	TELLY	TEMPLATE
TELAMONES	TELEPHEME	TELEXES	TELLYS*	TEMPLATES
TELARY	TELEPHEMES	TELEXING	TELNET	TEMPLE
TELD	TELEPHONE	TELFER	TELNETS	TEMPLED
TELE*	TELEPHONED	TELFERAGE	TELOI*	TEMPLES
TELECAST	TELEPHONES	TELFERAGES	TELOME*	TEMPLET
TELECASTED	TELEPHONEY	TELFERED	TELOMERE	TEMPLETS
TELECASTING	TELEPHONING	TELFERIC	TELOMERES	TEMPO
TELECASTS	TELEPHONY	TELFERING	TELOMES*	TEMPORAL
TELECHIR	TELEPHOTO	TELFERS	TELOMIC*	TEMPORALS
TELECHIRS	TELEPHOTOS*	TELFORD*	TELOPHASE	TEMPORARIES
TELECINE	TELEPLAY	TELFORDS*	TELOPHASES	TEMPORARY
TELECINES	TELEPLAYS	TELIA	TELOS	TEMPORE
TELECOM	TELEPOINT	TELIAL	TELOSES	TEMPORISE
TELECOMS	TELEPOINTS	TELIC	TELOTAXES*	TEMPORISED
TELEDU	TELEPORT	TELICALLY*	TELOTAXIS*	TEMPORISES
TELEDUS	TELEPORTED	TELIUM	TELPHER	TEMPORISING
TELEFAX	TELEPORTING	TELL	TELPHERED	TEMPORISINGS
TELEFAXED	TELEPORTS	TELLABLE	TELPHERIC	TEMPORIZE
TELEFAXES	TELERAN*	TELLAR	TELPHERING	TEMPORIZED
TELEFAXING	TELERANS*	TELLARED	TELPHERS	TEMPORIZES
TELEFILM	TELERGIC	TELLARING	TELS	TEMPORIZING
TELEFILMS	TELERGIES	TELLARS	TELSON	TEMPORIZINGS
TELEGA	TELERGY	TELLEN	TELSONIC*	TEMPOS
TELEGAS	TELES*	TELLENS	TELSONS	TEMPS
TELEGENIC	TELESALE	TELLER	TELT	TEMPT
TELEGONIC	TELESALES	TELLERED	TEMAZEPAM	TEMPTABLE
TELEGONIES	TELESCOPE	TELLERING	TEMAZEPAMS	TEMPTED
TELEGONY	TELESCOPED	TELLERS	TEMBLOR	TEMPTER
TELEGRAM	TELESCOPES	TELLIES	TEMBLORES	TEMPTERS
TELEGRAMMED*	TELESCOPIES	TELLIN	TEMBLORS	TEMPTING
TELEGRAMMING*	TELESCOPING	TELLING	TEME	TEMPTINGS
TELEGRAMS	TELESCOPY	TELLINGLY	TEMED	TEMPTRESS
TELEGRAPH	TELESEME	TELLINGS	TEMENE	TEMPTRESSES
TELEGRAPHED	TELESEMES	TELLINOID	TEMENOS	TEMPTS
TELEGRAPHING	TELESES	TELLINS	TEMERITIES	TEMPURA
TELEGRAPHS	TELESIS	TELLS	TEMERITY	TEMPURAS
TELEMAN*	TELESM	TELLTALE	TEMEROUS	TEMS
TELEMARK	TELESMS	TELLTALES	TEMES	TEMSE
TELEMARKED	TELESTIC	TELLURAL	TEMP	TEMSED
TELEMARKING	TELESTICH	TELLURATE	TEMPED	TEMSES
TELEMARKS	TELESTICHS	TELLURATES	TEMPEH	TEMSING
TELEMATIC	TELESTICS*	TELLURIAN	TEMPEHS	TEMULENCE
TELEMATICS	TELETEX	TELLURIANS	TEMPER	TEMULENCES
TELEMEN*	TELETEXES	TELLURIC	TEMPERA	TEMULENCIES
TELEMETER	TELETEXT	TELLURIDE	TEMPERAS	TEMULENCY

TEMULENT
TEN
TENABLE
TENABLY*
TENACE
TENACES
TENACIOUS
TENACITIES
TENACITY
TENACULA
TENACULUM
TENACULUMS*
TENAIL
TENAILLE
TENAILLES
TENAILLON
TENAILLONS
TENAILS
TENANCIES
TENANCY
TENANT
TENANTED
TENANTING
TENANTRIES
TENANTRY
TENANTS
TENCH
TENCHES
TEND
TENDANCE
TENDANCES
TENDED
TENDENCE
TENDENCES
TENDENCIES
TENDENCY
TENDENZ
TENDENZEN
TENDER
TENDERED
TENDERER
TENDERERS
TENDEREST
TENDERING
TENDERINGS
TENDERISE
TENDERISED
TENDERISES
TENDERISING
TENDERIZE
TENDERIZED
TENDERIZES
TENDERIZING
TENDERLY
TENDERS
TENDING
TENDINOUS
TENDON
TENDONS
TENDRE
TENDRES
TENDRESSE*
TENDRESSES*
TENDRIL

TENDRILED*
TENDRILS
TENDRON
TENDRONS
TENDS
TENE
TENEBRAE
TENEBRIO
TENEBRIOS
TENEBRISM
TENEBRISMS
TENEBRIST
TENEBRISTS
TENEBRITIES
TENEBRITY
TENEBROSE
TENEBROUS
TENEMENT
TENEMENTS
TENENDUM
TENENDUMS
TENES
TENESMIC*
TENESMUS
TENESMUSES
TENET
TENETS
TENFOLD
TENFOLDS*
TENIA
TENIAE
TENIAS
TENIASES*
TENIASIS*
TENIOID
TENNE
TENNER
TENNERS
TENNES
TENNIES
TENNIS
TENNISES
TENNIST*
TENNISTS*
TENNO
TENNOS
TENNY
TENON
TENONED
TENONER
TENONERS
TENONING
TENONS
TENOR
TENORIST
TENORISTS
TENORITE
TENORITES
TENOROON
TENOROONS
TENORS
TENOTOMIES
TENOTOMY
TENOUR

TENOURS
TENPENCE
TENPENCES
TENPENNY
TENPIN*
TENPINS
TENREC
TENRECS
TENS
TENSE
TENSED
TENSELESS
TENSELY
TENSENESS
TENSENESSES
TENSER
TENSES
TENSEST
TENSIBLE
TENSIBLY*
TENSILE
TENSILITIES
TENSILITY
TENSING
TENSION
TENSIONAL
TENSIONED
TENSIONER*
TENSIONERS*
TENSIONING
TENSIONS
TENSITIES
TENSITY
TENSIVE
TENSON
TENSONS
TENSOR
TENSORS
TENT
TENTACLE
TENTACLED
TENTACLES
TENTACULA
TENTAGE
TENTAGES
TENTATION
TENTATIONS
TENTATIVE
TENTATIVES
TENTED
TENTER
TENTERED
TENTERING
TENTERS
TENTFUL
TENTFULS
TENTH
TENTHLY
TENTHS
TENTIE
TENTIER
TENTIEST
TENTIGO
TENTIGOS

TENTING
TENTINGS
TENTLESS
TENTLIKE*
TENTORIA
TENTORIAL
TENTORIUM
TENTORIUMS
TENTS
TENTWISE
TENTY
TENUE
TENUES
TENUIOUS
TENUIS
TENUITIES
TENUITY
TENUOUS
TENUOUSLY
TENURABLE
TENURE
TENURED
TENURES
TENURIAL
TENUTI*
TENUTO
TENUTOS
TENZON
TENZONS
TEOCALLI
TEOCALLIS
TEOPAN*
TEOPANS*
TEOSINTE
TEOSINTES
TEPA*
TEPAL
TEPALS
TEPAS*
TEPEE
TEPEES
TEPEFIED
TEPEFIES
TEPEFY
TEPEFYING
TEPHIGRAM
TEPHIGRAMS
TEPHILLAH
TEPHILLIN
TEPHRA
TEPHRAS
TEPHRITE
TEPHRITES
TEPHRITIC
TEPHROITE
TEPHROITES
TEPID
TEPIDARIA
TEPIDER
TEPIDEST
TEPIDITIES
TEPIDITY
TEPIDLY
TEPIDNESS

TEPIDNESSES
TEPOY*
TEPOYS*
TEQUILA
TEQUILAS
TEQUILLA
TEQUILLAS
TERAFLOP
TERAI
TERAIS
TERAKIHI
TERAKIHIS
TERAOHM*
TERAOHMS*
TERAPH
TERAPHIM
TERAPHIMS
TERAS
TERATA
TERATISM
TERATISMS
TERATOGEN
TERATOGENS
TERATOID
TERATOMA
TERATOMAS*
TERATOMATA
TERAWATT*
TERAWATTS*
TERBIA*
TERBIAS*
TERBIC
TERBIUM
TERBIUMS
TERCE
TERCEL
TERCELET
TERCELETS
TERCELS
TERCES
TERCET
TERCETS
TERCIO
TERCIOS
TEREBENE
TEREBENES
TEREBIC*
TEREBINTH
TEREBINTHS
TEREBRA
TEREBRAE
TEREBRANT
TEREBRANTS
TEREBRAS
TEREBRATE
TEREBRATED
TEREBRATES
TEREBRATING
TEREDINES
TEREDO
TEREDOS
TEREFA
TEREFAH
TEREK

TEREKS	TERPENES	TERRITORY	TESTAMUR	TETANICS
TERES	TERPENIC*	TERRITS	TESTAMURS	TETANIES
TERETE	TERPENOID	TERROR	TESTATE	TETANISE
TERETES	TERPENOIDS	TERRORFUL	TESTATES*	TETANISED
TERF	TERPINEOL	TERRORISE	TESTATION	TETANISES
TERFE	TERPINEOLS	TERRORISED	TESTATIONS	TETANISING
TERFES	TERPINOL*	TERRORISES	TESTATOR	TETANIZE
TERFS	TERPINOLS*	TERRORISING	TESTATORS	TETANIZED
TERGA	TERRA	TERRORISM	TESTATRICES	TETANIZES
TERGAL	TERRACE	TERRORISMS	TESTATRIX	TETANIZING
TERGITE	TERRACED	TERRORIST	TESTATRIXES	TETANOID
TERGITES	TERRACES	TERRORISTS	TESTATUM	TETANUS
TERGUM	TERRACING	TERRORIZE	TESTATUMS	TETANUSES
TERIYAKI	TERRACINGS	TERRORIZED	TESTCROSS*	TETANY
TERIYAKIS	TERRAE	TERRORIZES	TESTCROSSED*	TETCHED*
TERM	TERRAFORM	TERRORIZING	TESTCROSSES*	TETCHIER
TERMAGANT	TERRAFORMED	TERRORS	TESTCROSSING*	TETCHIEST
TERMAGANTS	TERRAFORMING	TERRY	TESTE	TETCHILY
TERMED	TERRAFORMINGS	TERSE	TESTED	TETCHY
TERMER	TERRAFORMS	TERSELY	TESTEE	TETE
TERMERS	TERRAIN	TERSENESS	TESTEES	TETES
TERMINAL	TERRAINS	TERSENESSES	TESTER	TETH*
TERMINALS	TERRAMARA	TERSER	TESTERN	TETHER
TERMINATE	TERRAMARE	TERSEST	TESTERNED	TETHERED
TERMINATED	TERRAMARES	TERSION	TESTERNING	TETHERING
TERMINATES	TERRANE	TERSIONS	TESTERNS	TETHERS
TERMINATING	TERRANES	TERTIA	TESTERS	TETHS*
TERMINER	TERRAPIN	TERTIAL	TESTES	TETOTUM*
TERMINERS	TERRAPINS	TERTIALS	TESTICLE	TETOTUMS*
TERMING	TERRARIA	TERTIAN	TESTICLES	TETRA
TERMINI	TERRARIUM	TERTIANS	TESTIER	TETRACID
TERMINISM	TERRARIUMS	TERTIARIES	TESTIEST	TETRACIDS*
TERMINISMS	TERRAS	TERTIARY	TESTIFIED	TETRACT
TERMINIST	TERRASES	TERTIAS	TESTIFIER	TETRACTS
TERMINISTS	TERRAZZO	TERTIUS	TESTIFIERS	TETRAD
TERMINUS	TERRAZZOS	TERTIUSES	TESTIFIES	TETRADIC
TERMINUSES	TERREEN	TERTS	TESTIFY	TETRADITE
TERMITARIES	TERREENS	TERVALENT	TESTIFYING	TETRADITES
TERMITARY	TERRELLA	TERZETTA	TESTILY	TETRADS
TERMITE	TERRELLAS	TERZETTAS	TESTIMONIED	TETRAGON
TERMITES	TERRENE	TERZETTI	TESTIMONIES	TETRAGONS
TERMITIC*	TERRENELY	TERZETTO	TESTIMONY	TETRAGRAM
TERMLESS	TERRENES	TERZETTOS	TESTIMONYING	TETRAGRAMS
TERMLIES	TERRET	TES	TESTINESS	TETRALOGIES
TERMLY	TERRETS	TESLA	TESTINESSES	TETRALOGY
TERMOR	TERRIBLE	TESLAS	TESTING	TETRAMER*
TERMORS	TERRIBLES	TESSELLA	TESTINGS	TETRAMERS*
TERMS	TERRIBLY	TESSELLAE	TESTIS	TETRAPLA
TERMTIME*	TERRICOLE	TESSELLAR	TESTON	TETRAPLAS
TERMTIMES*	TERRICOLES	TESSERA	TESTONS	TETRAPOD
TERN	TERRIER	TESSERACT	TESTOON	TETRAPODIES
TERNAL	TERRIERS	TESSERACTS	TESTOONS	TETRAPODS
TERNARIES	TERRIES	TESSERAE	TESTRIL	TETRAPODY
TERNARY	TERRIFIC	TESSERAL	TESTRILL	TETRARCH
TERNATE	TERRIFIED	TESSITURA	TESTRILLS	TETRARCHIES
TERNATELY	TERRIFIER	TESSITURAS	TESTRILS	TETRARCHS
TERNE	TERRIFIERS	TEST	TESTS	TETRARCHY
TERNED	TERRIFIES	TESTA	TESTUDINES	TETRAS
TERNES	TERRIFY	TESTABLE	TESTUDO	TETRAXON
TERNING	TERRIFYING	TESTACIES	TESTUDOS	TETRAXONS
TERNION	TERRINE	TESTACY	TESTY	TETRODE
TERNIONS	TERRINES	TESTAE	TET*	TETRODES
TERNS	TERRIT	TESTAMENT	TETANAL	TETRONAL
TERPENE	TERRITORIES	TESTAMENTS	TETANIC	TETRONALS

Words marked with an asterisk are from OTCWL

TETROXID*	TEXTURISES	THANKFULLER*	THECAE	THENAL*	
TETROXIDE	TEXTURISING	THANKFULLEST*	THECAL	THENAR	
TETROXIDES	TEXTURIZE	THANKING	THECATE	THENARS	
TETROXIDS*	TEXTURIZED	THANKINGS	THECODONT	THENCE	
TETRYL	TEXTURIZES	THANKLESS	THECODONTS	THENS	
TETRYLS	TEXTURIZING	THANKS	THEE	THEOCRACIES	
TETS*	THACK	THANKYOU	THEED	THEOCRACY	
TETTER	THACKED*	THANKYOUS	THEEING	THEOCRASIES	
TETTERED	THACKING*	THANNA	THEEK	THEOCRASY	
TETTERING	THACKS	THANNAH	THEEKED	THEOCRAT	
TETTEROUS	THAE	THANNAHS	THEEKING	THEOCRATS	
TETTERS	THAGI	THANNAS	THEEKS	THEODICIES	
TETTIX	THAGIS	THANS	THEELIN*	THEODICY	
TETTIXES	THAIM	THAR	THEELINS*	THEOGONIC	
TEUCH	THAIRM	THARM*	THEELOL*	THEOGONIES	
TEUCHAT	THAIRMS	THARMS*	THEELOLS*	THEOGONY	
TEUCHATS	THALAMI	THARS	THEES	THEOLOG*	
TEUCHER	THALAMIC	THAT	THEFT	THEOLOGER	
TEUCHEST	THALAMUS	THATAWAY	THEFTBOOT	THEOLOGERS	
TEUCHTER	THALASSIC	THATCH	THEFTBOOTS	THEOLOGIC	
TEUCHTERS	THALER	THATCHED	THEFTS	THEOLOGIES	
TEUGH	THALERS	THATCHER	THEFTUOUS	THEOLOGS*	
TEUGHER	THALIAN	THATCHERS	THEGITHER	THEOLOGUE	
TEUGHEST	THALLI	THATCHES	THEGN	THEOLOGUES	
TEUGHLY*	THALLIC	THATCHIER*	THEGNLY*	THEOLOGY	
TEUTONIZE*	THALLINE	THATCHIEST*	THEGNS	THEOMACHIES	
TEUTONIZED*	THALLIUM	THATCHING	THEIC	THEOMACHY	
TEUTONIZES*	THALLIUMS	THATCHINGS	THEICS	THEOMANCIES	
TEUTONIZING*	THALLOID	THATCHT	THEIN*	THEOMANCY	
TEW	THALLOUS	THATCHY*	THEINE	THEOMANIA	
TEWART	THALLUS	THATNESS	THEINES	THEOMANIAS	
TEWARTS	THALLUSES	THATNESSES	THEINS*	THEONOMIES	
TEWED	THALWEG	THAUMATIN	THEIR	THEONOMY	
TEWEL	THALWEGS	THAUMATINS	THEIRS	THEOPATHIES	
TEWELS	THAN	THAW	THEISM	THEOPATHY	
TEWHIT	THANA	THAWED	THEISMS	THEOPHAGIES	
TEWHITS	THANADAR	THAWER	THEIST	THEOPHAGY	
TEWING	THANADARS	THAWERS	THEISTIC	THEOPHANIES	
TEWIT	THANAGE	THAWIER	THEISTS	THEOPHANY	
TEWITS	THANAGES	THAWIEST	THELEMENT	THEORBIST	
TEWS	THANAH	THAWING	THELEMENTS	THEORBISTS	
TEXAS	THANAHS	THAWINGS	THELF	THEORBO	
TEXASES	THANAS	THAWLESS	THELITIS*	THEORBOS	
TEXT	THANATISM	THAWS	THELITISES*	THEOREM	
TEXTBOOK	THANATISMS	THAWY	THELVES	THEOREMS	
TEXTBOOKS	THANATIST	THE	THELYTOKIES	THEORETIC	
TEXTILE	THANATISTS	THEACEOUS	THELYTOKY	THEORETICS	
TEXTILES	THANATOID	THEANDRIC	THEM	THEORIC	
TEXTLESS	THANATOS*	THEARCHIC	THEMA	THEORICS	
TEXTORIAL	THANATOSES*	THEARCHIES	THEMATA	THEORIES	
TEXTPHONE	THANE	THEARCHY	THEMATIC	THEORIQUE	
TEXTPHONES	THANEDOM	THEATER	THEMATICS*	THEORIQUES	
TEXTS	THANEDOMS	THEATERS	THEME	THEORISE	
TEXTUAL	THANEHOOD	THEATRAL	THEMED	THEORISED	
TEXTUALLY	THANEHOODS	THEATRE	THEMELESS	THEORISER	
TEXTUARIES	THANES	THEATRES	THEMES	THEORISERS	
TEXTUARY	THANESHIP	THEATRIC	THEMING	THEORISES	
TEXTURAL	THANESHIPS	THEATRICS	THEMSELF	THEORISING	
TEXTURE	THANK	THEAVE	THEMSELVES	THEORIST	
TEXTURED	THANKED	THEAVES	THEN	THEORISTS	
TEXTURES	THANKEE	THEBAINE	THENABOUT	THEORIZE	
TEXTURING	THANKER	THEBAINES	THENABOUTS	THEORIZED	
TEXTURISE	THANKERS	THEBE*	THENAGE*	THEORIZER	
TEXTURISED	THANKFUL	THECA	THENAGES*	THEORIZERS	

The Chambers Dictionary is the authority for many longer words; see Introduction, page ix

THEORIZES	THERMITES	THIBETS	THIN	THIRD
THEORIZING	THERMOS*	THIBLE	THINCLAD*	THIRDED
THEORY	THERMOSES*	THIBLES	THINCLADS*	THIRDHAND*
THEOSOPH	THERMOSET*	THICK	THINDOWN*	THIRDING
THEOSOPHIES	THERMOSETS*	THICKED	THINDOWNS*	THIRDINGS
THEOSOPHS	THERMOTIC	THICKEN	THINE	THIRDLY
THEOSOPHY	THERMOTICS	THICKENED	THING	THIRDS
THEOTOKOI	THERMS	THICKENER	THINGAMIES	THIRDSMAN
THEOTOKOS	THEROID	THICKENERS	THINGAMY	THIRDSMEN
THEOW	THEROLOGIES	THICKENING	THINGHOOD	THIRL
THEOWS	THEROLOGY	THICKENINGS	THINGHOODS	THIRLAGE
THERALITE	THEROPOD	THICKENS	THINGIER	THIRLAGES
THERALITES	THEROPODS	THICKER	THINGIES	THIRLED
THERAPIES	THESAURAL*	THICKEST	THINGIEST	THIRLING
THERAPIST	THESAURI	THICKET	THINGNESS	THIRLS
THERAPISTS	THESAURUS	THICKETED	THINGNESSES	THIRST
THERAPSID	THESAURUSES	THICKETS	THINGS	THIRSTED
THERAPSIDS	THESE	THICKETY	THINGUMMIES	THIRSTER
THERAPY	THESES	THICKHEAD	THINGUMMY	THIRSTERS
THERBLIG	THESIS	THICKHEADS	THINGY	THIRSTFUL
THERBLIGS	THESPIAN	THICKING	THINK	THIRSTIER
THERE	THESPIANS	THICKISH	THINKABLE	THIRSTIEST
THEREAT	THETA	THICKLY	THINKABLY*	THIRSTILY
THEREAWAY	THETAS	THICKNESS	THINKER	THIRSTING
THEREBY	THETCH	THICKNESSES	THINKERS	THIRSTS
THEREFOR	THETCHED	THICKO	THINKING	THIRSTY
THEREFORE	THETCHES	THICKOES	THINKINGS	THIRTEEN
THEREFROM	THETCHING	THICKOS	THINKS	THIRTEENS
THEREIN	THETE	THICKS	THINLY	THIRTIES
THEREINTO	THETES	THICKSET	THINNED	THIRTIETH
THEREMIN*	THETHER	THICKSETS	THINNER	THIRTIETHS
THEREMINS*	THETIC	THICKSKIN	THINNERS	THIRTY
THERENESS	THETICAL	THICKSKINS	THINNESS	THIRTYISH
THERENESSES	THEURGIC	THICKY	THINNESSES	THIS
THEREOF	THEURGIES	THIEF	THINNEST	THISNESS
THEREON	THEURGIST	THIEVE	THINNING	THISNESSES
THEREOUT	THEURGISTS	THIEVED	THINNINGS	THISTLE
THERES	THEURGY	THIEVERIES	THINNISH	THISTLES
THERETO	THEW	THIEVERY	THINS	THISTLIER
THEREUNTO	THEWED	THIEVES	THIO*	THISTLIEST
THEREUPON	THEWES	THIEVING	THIOL	THISTLY
THEREWITH	THEWIER	THIEVINGS	THIOLIC*	THITHER
THERIAC	THEWIEST	THIEVISH	THIOLS	THITHERTO*
THERIACA	THEWLESS	THIG	THIONATE*	THIVEL
THERIACAL	THEWS	THIGGER	THIONATES*	THIVELS
THERIACAS	THEWY	THIGGERS	THIONIC*	THLIPSES
THERIACS	THEY	THIGGING	THIONIN*	THLIPSIS
THERIAN	THIAMIN	THIGGINGS	THIONINE*	THO
THERIANS	THIAMINE	THIGGIT	THIONINES*	THOFT
THERM	THIAMINES	THIGH	THIONINS*	THOFTS
THERMAE	THIAMINS	THIGHBONE	THIONYL*	THOLE
THERMAL	THIASUS	THIGHBONES	THIONYLS*	THOLED
THERMALLY	THIASUSES	THIGHED*	THIOPHEN	THOLEIITE*
THERMALS	THIAZIDE	THIGHS	THIOPHENE	THOLEIITES*
THERME*	THIAZIDES	THIGS	THIOPHENES	THOLEPIN*
THERMEL*	THIAZIN*	THILK	THIOPHENS	THOLEPINS*
THERMELS*	THIAZINE	THILL	THIOPHIL	THOLES
THERMES*	THIAZINES	THILLER	THIOTEPA*	THOLI
THERMIC	THIAZINS*	THILLERS	THIOTEPAS*	THOLING
THERMICAL	THIAZOL*	THILLS	THIOUREA	THOLOBATE
THERMIDOR	THIAZOLE*	THIMBLE	THIOUREAS	THOLOBATES
THERMION	THIAZOLES*	THIMBLED	THIR	THOLOI
THERMIONS	THIAZOLS*	THIMBLES	THIRAM	THOLOS
THERMITE	THIBET	THIMBLING	THIRAMS	THOLUS

Words marked with an asterisk are from OTCWL

THON	THOWLS	THREATS	THRIMSA	THROPPLING
THONDER	THRAE	THREAVE	THRIMSAS	THROSTLE
THONG	THRALDOM	THREAVES	THRIP*	THROSTLES
THONGED	THRALDOMS	THREE	THRIPS	THROTTLE
THONGS	THRALL	THREEFOLD	THRIPSES	THROTTLED
THORACAL	THRALLDOM	THREENESS	THRISSEL	THROTTLER
THORACES	THRALLDOMS	THREENESSES	THRISSELS	THROTTLERS
THORACIC	THRALLED	THREEP	THRIST	THROTTLES
THORAX	THRALLING	THREEPED*	THRISTED	THROTTLING
THORAXES	THRALLS	THREEPING	THRISTING	THROTTLINGS
THORIA	THRANG	THREEPIT	THRISTLE	THROUGH
THORIAS	THRANGED	THREEPS	THRISTLES	THROUGHLY
THORIC*	THRANGING	THREES	THRISTS	THROVE
THORITE	THRANGS	THREESOME	THRISTY	THROW
THORITES	THRAPPLE	THREESOMES	THRIVE	THROWAWAY
THORIUM	THRAPPLED	THRENE	THRIVED	THROWAWAYS
THORIUMS	THRAPPLES	THRENES	THRIVEN	THROWBACK
THORN	THRAPPLING	THRENETIC	THRIVER	THROWBACKS
THORNBACK	THRASH	THRENODE	THRIVERS	THROWE
THORNBACKS	THRASHED	THRENODES	THRIVES	THROWER
THORNBILL	THRASHER	THRENODIC	THRIVING	THROWERS
THORNBILLS	THRASHERS	THRENODIES	THRIVINGS	THROWES
THORNBUSH	THRASHES	THRENODY	THRO	THROWING
THORNBUSHES	THRASHING	THRENOS	THROAT	THROWINGS
THORNED	THRASHINGS	THRENOSES	THROATED	THROWN
THORNIER	THRASONIC	THREONINE	THROATIER	THROWS
THORNIEST	THRAVE	THREONINES	THROATIEST	THROWSTER
THORNILY*	THRAVES	THRESH	THROATILY	THROWSTERS
THORNING	THRAW	THRESHED	THROATING*	THRU
THORNLESS	THRAWARD	THRESHEL	THROATS	THRUM
THORNLIKE*	THRAWART	THRESHELS	THROATY	THRUMMED
THORNS	THRAWED*	THRESHER	THROB	THRUMMER
THORNSET	THRAWING	THRESHERS	THROBBED	THRUMMERS
THORNTREE	THRAWN	THRESHES	THROBBER*	THRUMMIER
THORNTREES	THRAWNLY*	THRESHING	THROBBERS*	THRUMMIEST
THORNY	THRAWS	THRESHINGS	THROBBING	THRUMMING
THORO*	THREAD	THRESHOLD	THROBBINGS	THRUMMINGS
THORON	THREADED	THRESHOLDS	THROBLESS	THRUMMY
THORONS	THREADEN	THRETTIES	THROBS	THRUMS
THOROUGH	THREADER	THRETTY	THROE	THRUPUT*
THOROUGHER	THREADERS	THREW	THROED	THRUPUTS*
THOROUGHEST	THREADFIN	THRICE	THROEING	THRUSH
THOROUGHS	THREADFINS	THRID	THROES	THRUSHES
THORP	THREADIER	THRIDACE	THROMBI	THRUST
THORPE	THREADIEST	THRIDACES	THROMBIN	THRUSTED
THORPES	THREADING	THRIDDED	THROMBINS	THRUSTER
THORPS	THREADS	THRIDDING	THROMBOSE	THRUSTERS
THOSE	THREADY	THRIDS	THROMBOSED	THRUSTFUL*
THOTHER	THREAP	THRIFT	THROMBOSES	THRUSTING
THOU	THREAPED*	THRIFTIER	THROMBOSING	THRUSTINGS
THOUED*	THREAPER*	THRIFTIEST	THROMBUS	THRUSTOR*
THOUGH	THREAPERS*	THRIFTILY	THRONE	THRUSTORS*
THOUGHT	THREAPING	THRIFTS	THRONED	THRUSTS
THOUGHTED	THREAPIT	THRIFTY	THRONES	THRUTCH
THOUGHTEN	THREAPS	THRILL	THRONG	THRUTCHED
THOUGHTS	THREAT	THRILLANT	THRONGED	THRUTCHES
THOUING	THREATED	THRILLED	THRONGFUL	THRUTCHING
THOUS	THREATEN	THRILLER	THRONGING	THRUWAY
THOUSAND	THREATENED	THRILLERS	THRONGINGS	THRUWAYS
THOUSANDS	THREATENING	THRILLIER	THRONGS	THRYMSA
THOWEL	THREATENINGS	THRILLIEST	THRONING	THRYMSAS
THOWELS	THREATENS	THRILLING	THROPPLE	THUD
THOWL	THREATFUL	THRILLS	THROPPLED	THUDDED
THOWLESS	THREATING	THRILLY	THROPPLES	THUDDING

The Chambers Dictionary is the authority for many longer words; see Introduction, page ix

THUDS	THUNKING*	THYMUSES*	TICKLIER	TIDEWATERS
THUG	THUNKS*	THYMY	TICKLIEST	TIDEWAVE
THUGGEE	THURIBLE	THYRATRON	TICKLING	TIDEWAVES
THUGGEES	THURIBLES	THYRATRONS	TICKLINGS	TIDEWAY
THUGGERIES	THURIFER	THYREOID	TICKLISH	TIDEWAYS
THUGGERY	THURIFERS	THYREOIDS	TICKLY	TIDIED
THUGGISH*	THURIFIED	THYRISTOR	TICKS	TIDIER
THUGGISM	THURIFIES	THYRISTORS	TICKSEED*	TIDIERS*
THUGGISMS	THURIFY	THYROID	TICKSEEDS*	TIDIES
THUGGO	THURIFYING	THYROIDAL*	TICKTACK*	TIDIEST
THUGGOS	THURL*	THYROIDS	TICKTACKED*	TIDILY
THUGS	THURLS*	THYROXIN	TICKTACKING*	TIDINESS
THUJA	THUS	THYROXINE	TICKTACKS*	TIDINESSES
THUJAS	THUSES	THYROXINES	TICKTOCK*	TIDING
THULIA	THUSLY*	THYROXINS	TICKTOCKED*	TIDINGS
THULIAS	THUSNESS	THYRSE	TICKTOCKING*	TIDIVATE
THULITE	THUSNESSES	THYRSES	TICKTOCKS*	TIDIVATED
THULITES	THUSWISE	THYRSI	TICKY	TIDIVATES
THULIUM	THUYA	THYRSOID	TICS	TIDIVATING
THULIUMS	THUYAS	THYRSUS	TICTAC*	TIDS
THUMB	THWACK	THYSELF	TICTACKED*	TIDY
THUMBED	THWACKED	TI	TICTACKING*	TIDYING
THUMBHOLE*	THWACKER	TIAR	TICTACS*	TIDYTIPS*
THUMBHOLES*	THWACKERS	TIARA	TICTOC*	TIE
THUMBIER	THWACKING	TIARAED	TICTOCKED*	TIEBACK
THUMBIEST	THWACKINGS	TIARAS	TICTOCKING*	TIEBACKS
THUMBING	THWACKS	TIARS	TICTOCS*	TIECLASP*
THUMBKIN*	THWAITE	TIBIA	TID	TIECLASPS*
THUMBKINS	THWAITES	TIBIAE	TIDAL	TIED
THUMBLESS	THWART	TIBIAL	TIDALLY*	TIEING*
THUMBLIKE	THWARTED	TIBIAS	TIDBIT	TIELESS
THUMBLING	THWARTER	TIC	TIDBITS	TIEPIN
THUMBLINGS	THWARTERS	TICAL	TIDDIER	TIEPINS
THUMBNAIL	THWARTING	TICALS	TIDDIES	TIER
THUMBNAILS	THWARTINGS	TICCA	TIDDIEST	TIERCE
THUMBNUT	THWARTLY	TICE	TIDDLE	TIERCED
THUMBNUTS	THWARTS	TICED	TIDDLED	TIERCEL
THUMBPOT	THY	TICES	TIDDLER	TIERCELET
THUMBPOTS	THYINE	TICH	TIDDLERS	TIERCELETS
THUMBS	THYLACINE	TICHES	TIDDLES	TIERCELS
THUMBTACK	THYLACINES	TICHIER	TIDDLEY	TIERCERON
THUMBTACKED*	THYLAKOID*	TICHIEST	TIDDLEYS	TIERCERONS
THUMBTACKING*	THYLAKOIDS*	TICHY	TIDDLIER	TIERCES
THUMBTACKS	THYLOSE	TICING	TIDDLIES	TIERCET
THUMBY	THYLOSES	TICK	TIDDLIEST	TIERCETS
THUMP	THYLOSIS	TICKED	TIDDLING	TIERED
THUMPED	THYME	TICKEN	TIDDLY	TIERING
THUMPER	THYMES	TICKENS	TIDDY	TIEROD
THUMPERS	THYMEY*	TICKER	TIDE	TIERODS
THUMPING	THYMI	TICKERS	TIDED	TIERS
THUMPS	THYMIC	TICKET	TIDELAND	TIES
THUNDER	THYMIDINE	TICKETED	TIDELANDS	TIETAC
THUNDERED	THYMIDINES	TICKETING	TIDELESS	TIETACK
THUNDERER	THYMIER	TICKETS	TIDELIKE*	TIETACKS
THUNDERERS	THYMIEST	TICKEY	TIDEMARK	TIETACS
THUNDERIER	THYMINE	TICKEYS	TIDEMARKS	TIFF
THUNDERIEST	THYMINES	TICKIES	TIDEMILL	TIFFANIES
THUNDERING	THYMOCYTE	TICKING	TIDEMILLS	TIFFANY
THUNDERINGS	THYMOCYTES	TICKINGS	TIDERIP*	TIFFED
THUNDERS	THYMOL	TICKLE	TIDERIPS*	TIFFIN
THUNDERY	THYMOLS	TICKLED	TIDES	TIFFINED*
THUNDROUS	THYMOSIN*	TICKLER	TIDESMAN	TIFFING
THUNK*	THYMOSINS*	TICKLERS	TIDESMEN	TIFFINGS
THUNKED*	THYMUS	TICKLES	TIDEWATER	TIFFINING*

Words marked with an asterisk are from OTCWL

TIFFINS	TILAPIA	TIMBERMAN*	TIMOTHIES	TINGLIEST
TIFFS	TILAPIAS	TIMBERMEN*	TIMOTHY	TINGLING
TIFOSI	TILBURIES	TIMBERS	TIMOUS	TINGLINGS
TIFOSO	TILBURY	TIMBO	TIMOUSLY	TINGLISH
TIFT	TILDE	TIMBOS	TIMPANA*	TINGLY
TIFTED	TILDES	TIMBRAL*	TIMPANI	TINGS
TIFTING	TILE	TIMBRE	TIMPANIST	TINGUAITE
TIFTS	TILED	TIMBREL	TIMPANISTS	TINGUAITES
TIG	TILEFISH	TIMBRELS	TIMPANO	TINHORN
TIGE	TILEFISHES	TIMBRES	TIMPANUM*	TINHORNS
TIGER	TILELIKE*	TIME	TIMPANUMS*	TINIER
TIGEREYE*	TILER	TIMECARD	TIMPS	TINIES
TIGEREYES*	TILERIES	TIMECARDS	TIN	TINIEST
TIGERISH	TILERS	TIMED	TINAJA	TINILY
TIGERISM	TILERY	TIMEFRAME	TINAJAS	TININESS
TIGERISMS	TILES	TIMEFRAMES	TINAMOU	TININESSES
TIGERLIKE*	TILING	TIMELESS	TINAMOUS	TINING
TIGERLY	TILINGS	TIMELIER	TINCAL	TINK
TIGERS	TILL	TIMELIEST	TINCALS	TINKED
TIGERY	TILLABLE	TIMELINE	TINCHEL	TINKER
TIGES	TILLAGE	TIMELINES	TINCHELS	TINKERED
TIGGED	TILLAGES	TIMELY	TINCT	TINKERER
TIGGING	TILLED	TIMENOGUY	TINCTED	TINKERERS
TIGHT	TILLER	TIMENOGUYS	TINCTING	TINKERING
TIGHTEN	TILLERED	TIMEOUS	TINCTS	TINKERINGS
TIGHTENED	TILLERING	TIMEOUSLY	TINCTURE	TINKERS
TIGHTENER	TILLERMAN*	TIMEOUT*	TINCTURED	TINKING
TIGHTENERS	TILLERMEN*	TIMEOUTS*	TINCTURES	TINKLE
TIGHTENING	TILLERS	TIMEPIECE	TINCTURING	TINKLED
TIGHTENS	TILLIER	TIMEPIECES	TIND	TINKLER
TIGHTER	TILLIEST	TIMER	TINDAL	TINKLERS
TIGHTEST	TILLING	TIMERS	TINDALS	TINKLES
TIGHTISH	TILLINGS	TIMES	TINDED	TINKLIER
TIGHTLY	TILLITE	TIMESCALE	TINDER	TINKLIEST
TIGHTNESS	TILLITES	TIMESCALES	TINDERBOX	TINKLING
TIGHTNESSES	TILLS	TIMETABLE	TINDERBOXES	TINKLINGS
TIGHTROPE	TILLY	TIMETABLED	TINDERS	TINKLY
TIGHTROPES	TILS	TIMETABLES	TINDERY	TINKS
TIGHTS	TILT	TIMETABLING	TINDING	TINLIKE*
TIGHTWAD	TILTABLE	TIMEWORK*	TINDS	TINMAN
TIGHTWADS	TILTED	TIMEWORKS*	TINE	TINMEN
TIGHTWIRE*	TILTER	TIMEWORN*	TINEA	TINNED
TIGHTWIRES*	TILTERS	TIMID	TINEAL	TINNER
TIGLON	TILTH	TIMIDER	TINEAS	TINNERS
TIGLONS	TILTHS	TIMIDEST	TINED	TINNIE
TIGON	TILTING	TIMIDITIES	TINEID	TINNIER
TIGONS	TILTINGS	TIMIDITY	TINEIDS	TINNIES
TIGRESS	TILTMETER*	TIMIDLY	TINES	TINNIEST
TIGRESSES	TILTMETERS*	TIMIDNESS	TINFOIL	TINNILY*
TIGRINE	TILTS	TIMIDNESSES	TINFOILS	TINNINESS*
TIGRISH	TILTYARD*	TIMING	TINFUL	TINNINESSES*
TIGRISHLY	TILTYARDS*	TIMINGS	TINFULS	TINNING
TIGROID	TIMARAU	TIMIST	TING	TINNINGS
TIGS	TIMARAUS	TIMISTS	TINGE	TINNITUS
TIKA	TIMARIOT	TIMOCRACIES	TINGED	TINNITUSES
TIKAS	TIMARIOTS	TIMOCRACY	TINGEING	TINNY
TIKE	TIMBAL	TIMOLOL*	TINGES	TINPLATE
TIKES	TIMBALE	TIMOLOLS*	TINGING	TINPLATED
TIKI	TIMBALES	TIMON	TINGLE	TINPLATES
TIKIS	TIMBALS	TIMONEER	TINGLED	TINPLATING
TIKKA	TIMBER	TIMONEERS	TINGLER	TINPOT
TIL	TIMBERED	TIMONS	TINGLERS	TINPOTS
TILAK*	TIMBERING	TIMOROUS	TINGLES	TINS
TILAKS*	TIMBERINGS	TIMORSOME	TINGLIER	TINSEL

The Chambers Dictionary is the authority for many longer words; see Introduction, page ix

TINSELED	TIPPYTOE*	TIRRIVEES	TITILLATED	TITTUPED
TINSELING	TIPPYTOED*	TIRRIVIE	TITILLATES	TITTUPING
TINSELLED	TIPPYTOEING*	TIRRIVIES	TITILLATING	TITTUPPED
TINSELLING	TIPPYTOES*	TIRRS	TITIS	TITTUPPING
TINSELLY	TIPS	TIS	TITIVATE	TITTUPPY*
TINSELRIES	TIPSIER	TISANE	TITIVATED	TITTUPS
TINSELRY	TIPSIEST	TISANES	TITIVATES	TITTUPY
TINSELS	TIPSIFIED	TISICK	TITIVATING	TITTY
TINSEY	TIPSIFIES	TISICKS	TITLARK	TITUBANCIES
TINSEYS	TIPSIFY	TISSUAL*	TITLARKS	TITUBANCY
TINSMITH	TIPSIFYING	TISSUE	TITLE	TITUBANT
TINSMITHS	TIPSILY	TISSUED	TITLED	TITUBATE
TINSNIPS	TIPSINESS	TISSUES	TITLELESS	TITUBATED
TINSTONE	TIPSINESSES	TISSUEY*	TITLER	TITUBATES
TINSTONES	TIPSTAFF	TISSUING	TITLERS	TITUBATING
TINT	TIPSTAFFS	TISSULAR*	TITLES	TITULAR
TINTACK	TIPSTAVES	TISWAS	TITLING	TITULARIES
TINTACKS	TIPSTER	TISWASES	TITLINGS	TITULARLY
TINTED	TIPSTERS	TIT	TITLIST*	TITULARS
TINTER	TIPSTOCK*	TITAN	TITLISTS*	TITULARY
TINTERS	TIPSTOCKS*	TITANATE	TITMAN*	TITULE
TINTIER	TIPSY	TITANATES	TITMEN*	TITULED
TINTIEST	TIPT	TITANESS	TITMICE	TITULES
TINTINESS	TIPTOE	TITANESSES	TITMOSE	TITULING
TINTINESSES	TIPTOED	TITANIA*	TITMOUSE	TITUP
TINTING	TIPTOEING	TITANIAS*	TITOKI	TITUPED
TINTINGS	TIPTOES	TITANIC	TITOKIS	TITUPING
TINTLESS	TIPTOP	TITANIS	TITRABLE*	TITUPPED
TINTS	TIPTOPS	TITANISES	TITRANT*	TITUPPING
TINTY	TIPULA	TITANISM	TITRANTS*	TITUPS
TINTYPE	TIPULAS	TITANISMS	TITRATE	TITUPY
TINTYPES	TIRADE	TITANITE	TITRATED	TIVY*
TINWARE	TIRADES	TITANITES	TITRATES	TIZWAS
TINWARES	TIRAMISU	TITANIUM	TITRATING	TIZWASES
TINWORK*	TIRAMISUS	TITANIUMS	TITRATION	TIZZ
TINWORKS*	TIRASSE	TITANOUS	TITRATIONS	TIZZES
TINY	TIRASSES	TITANS	TITRATOR*	TIZZIES
TIP	TIRE	TITBIT	TITRATORS*	TIZZY
TIPCART*	TIRED	TITBITS	TITRE	TJANTING
TIPCARTS*	TIREDER	TITCH	TITRES	TJANTINGS
TIPCAT	TIREDEST	TITCHES	TITS	TMESES
TIPCATS	TIREDLY	TITCHIER	TITTED	TMESIS
TIPI	TIREDNESS	TITCHIEST	TITTER	TO
TIPIS	TIREDNESSES	TITCHY	TITTERED	TOAD
TIPLESS*	TIRELESS	TITE	TITTERER	TOADEATER*
TIPOFF*	TIRELING	TITELY	TITTERERS	TOADEATERS*
TIPOFFS*	TIRELINGS	TITER	TITTERING	TOADFISH
TIPPABLE	TIRES	TITERS	TITTERINGS	TOADFISHES
TIPPED	TIRESOME	TITFER	TITTERS	TOADFLAX
TIPPER	TIRING	TITFERS	TITTIE*	TOADFLAXES
TIPPERS	TIRINGS	TITHABLE	TITTIES	TOADGRASS
TIPPET	TIRL	TITHE	TITTING	TOADGRASSES
TIPPETS	TIRLED	TITHED	TITTISH	TOADIED
TIPPIER	TIRLING	TITHER	TITTIVATE	TOADIES
TIPPIEST	TIRLS	TITHERS	TITTIVATED	TOADISH*
TIPPING	TIRO	TITHES	TITTIVATES	TOADLESS*
TIPPINGS	TIROES	TITHING	TITTIVATING	TOADLIKE*
TIPPLE	TIROS	TITHINGS	TITTLE	TOADRUSH
TIPPLED	TIRR	TITHONIA*	TITTLEBAT	TOADRUSHES
TIPPLER	TIRRED	TITHONIAS*	TITTLEBATS	TOADS
TIPPLERS	TIRRING	TITI	TITTLED	TOADSTONE
TIPPLES	TIRRIT	TITIAN	TITTLES	TOADSTONES
TIPPLING	TIRRITS	TITIANS	TITTLING	TOADSTOOL
TIPPY	TIRRIVEE	TITILLATE	TITTUP	TOADSTOOLS

Words marked with an asterisk are from OTCWL

TOADY	TODDLE	TOGE	TOKAYS	TOLLDISH
TOADYING	TODDLED	TOGED	TOKE	TOLLDISHES
TOADYISH	TODDLER	TOGES	TOKED	TOLLED
TOADYISM	TODDLERS	TOGETHER	TOKEN	TOLLER
TOADYISMS	TODDLES	TOGGED	TOKENED	TOLLERS
TOAST	TODDLING	TOGGERIES	TOKENING	TOLLGATE*
TOASTED	TODDY	TOGGERY	TOKENISM	TOLLGATES*
TOASTER	TODIES	TOGGING	TOKENISMS	TOLLHOUSE
TOASTERS	TODS	TOGGLE	TOKENS	TOLLHOUSES
TOASTIE	TODY	TOGGLED	TOKER*	TOLLING
TOASTIER*	TOE	TOGGLER*	TOKERS*	TOLLINGS
TOASTIES	TOEA	TOGGLERS*	TOKES	TOLLMAN
TOASTIEST*	TOEAS	TOGGLES	TOKING	TOLLMEN
TOASTING	TOECAP	TOGGLING	TOKO	TOLLS
TOASTINGS	TOECAPS	TOGS	TOKOLOGIES	TOLLWAY*
TOASTS	TOECLIP	TOGUE	TOKOLOGY	TOLLWAYS*
TOASTY	TOECLIPS	TOGUES	TOKOLOSHE	TOLSEL
TOAZE	TOED	TOHEROA	TOKOLOSHES	TOLSELS
TOAZED	TOEHOLD	TOHEROAS	TOKOMAK*	TOLSEY
TOAZES	TOEHOLDS	TOHO	TOKOMAKS*	TOLSEYS
TOAZING	TOEIER	TOHOS	TOKONOMA*	TOLT
TOBACCO	TOEIEST	TOHUNGA	TOKONOMAS*	TOLTER
TOBACCOES	TOEING	TOHUNGAS	TOKOS	TOLTERED
TOBACCOS	TOELESS	TOIL	TOLA	TOLTERING
TOBIES	TOELIKE*	TOILE	TOLAN*	TOLTERS
TOBOGGAN	TOENAIL	TOILED	TOLANE*	TOLTS
TOBOGGANED	TOENAILED	TOILER	TOLANES*	TOLU
TOBOGGANING	TOENAILING	TOILERS	TOLANS*	TOLUATE
TOBOGGANINGS	TOENAILS	TOILES	TOLAS	TOLUATES
TOBOGGANS	TOEPIECE*	TOILET	TOLBOOTH	TOLUENE
TOBOGGIN	TOEPIECES*	TOILETED	TOLBOOTHS	TOLUENES
TOBOGGINED	TOEPLATE*	TOILETING	TOLD	TOLUIC
TOBOGGINING	TOEPLATES*	TOILETRIES	TOLE	TOLUID*
TOBOGGINS	TOERAG	TOILETRY	TOLED	TOLUIDE*
TOBY	TOERAGGER	TOILETS	TOLEDO*	TOLUIDES*
TOC	TOERAGGERS	TOILETTE	TOLEDOS*	TOLUIDIN*
TOCCATA	TOERAGS	TOILETTES	TOLERABLE	TOLUIDINE
TOCCATAS	TOES	TOILFUL	TOLERABLY	TOLUIDINES
TOCCATE*	TOESHOE*	TOILFULLY*	TOLERANCE	TOLUIDINS*
TOCCATINA	TOESHOES*	TOILINET	TOLERANCES	TOLUIDS*
TOCCATINAS	TOETOE	TOILINETS	TOLERANT	TOLUOL
TOCHER	TOETOES	TOILING	TOLERATE	TOLUOLE*
TOCHERED	TOEY	TOILINGS	TOLERATED	TOLUOLES*
TOCHERING	TOFF	TOILLESS	TOLERATES	TOLUOLS
TOCHERS	TOFFEE	TOILS	TOLERATING	TOLUS
TOCK	TOFFEES	TOILSOME	TOLERATOR	TOLUYL*
TOCKED	TOFFIER	TOILWORN*	TOLERATORS	TOLUYLS*
TOCKING	TOFFIES	TOISE	TOLES	TOLYL*
TOCKS	TOFFIEST	TOISEACH	TOLEWARE	TOLYLS*
TOCO	TOFFISH	TOISEACHS	TOLEWARES	TOLZEY
TOCOLOGIES	TOFFS	TOISECH	TOLIDIN*	TOLZEYS
TOCOLOGY	TOFFY	TOISECHS	TOLIDINE*	TOM
TOCOS	TOFORE	TOISES	TOLIDINES*	TOMAHAWK
TOCS	TOFT	TOISON	TOLIDINS*	TOMAHAWKED
TOCSIN	TOFTS	TOISONS	TOLING	TOMAHAWKING
TOCSINS	TOFU	TOIT*	TOLINGS	TOMAHAWKS
TOD	TOFUS	TOITED*	TOLL	TOMALLEY
TODAY	TOG	TOITING*	TOLLABLE	TOMALLEYS
TODAYS	TOGA	TOITOI	TOLLAGE	TOMAN
TODDE	TOGAE*	TOITOIS	TOLLAGES	TOMANS
TODDED	TOGAED	TOITS*	TOLLBAR*	TOMATILLO
TODDES	TOGAS	TOKAMAK	TOLLBARS*	TOMATILLOES
TODDIES	TOGATE	TOKAMAKS	TOLLBOOTH	TOMATILLOS
TODDING	TOGATED	TOKAY	TOLLBOOTHS	TOMATO

TOMATOES	TOMPONING	TONIGHT	TOOLBARS	TOOTLER*
TOMATOEY	TOMPONS	TONIGHTS	TOOLBOX	TOOTLERS*
TOMB	TOMS	TONING	TOOLBOXES	TOOTLES
TOMBAC	TOMTIT	TONINGS	TOOLED	TOOTLING
TOMBACK*	TOMTITS	TONISH	TOOLER	TOOTS
TOMBACKS*	TON	TONISHLY	TOOLERS	TOOTSED
TOMBACS	TONAL	TONITE	TOOLHEAD*	TOOTSES
TOMBAK	TONALITE	TONITES	TOOLHEADS*	TOOTSIE
TOMBAKS	TONALITES	TONK	TOOLHOUSE	TOOTSIES
TOMBAL*	TONALITIES	TONKED	TOOLHOUSES	TOOTSING
TOMBED	TONALITY	TONKER	TOOLING	TOOTSY
TOMBIC	TONALLY	TONKERS	TOOLINGS	TOP
TOMBING	TONANT	TONKING	TOOLKIT	TOPARCH
TOMBLESS	TONDI	TONKS	TOOLKITS	TOPARCHIES
TOMBLIKE*	TONDINI	TONLET	TOOLLESS*	TOPARCHS
TOMBOC	TONDINO	TONLETS	TOOLMAKER	TOPARCHY
TOMBOCS	TONDINOS	TONNAG	TOOLMAKERS	TOPAZ
TOMBOLA	TONDO	TONNAGE	TOOLMAN	TOPAZES
TOMBOLAS	TONDOS	TONNAGES	TOOLMEN	TOPAZINE
TOMBOLO	TONE	TONNAGS	TOOLROOM	TOPCOAT
TOMBOLOS	TONEARM*	TONNE	TOOLROOMS	TOPCOATS
TOMBOY	TONEARMS*	TONNEAU	TOOLS	TOPCROSS*
TOMBOYISH	TONED	TONNEAUS	TOOLSHED*	TOPCROSSES*
TOMBOYS	TONELESS	TONNEAUX	TOOLSHEDS*	TOPE
TOMBS	TONEME	TONNELL	TOOM	TOPECTOMIES
TOMBSTONE	TONEMES	TONNELLS	TOOMED	TOPECTOMY
TOMBSTONES	TONEMIC	TONNER*	TOOMER	TOPED
TOMCAT	TONEPAD	TONNERS*	TOOMEST	TOPEE
TOMCATS	TONEPADS	TONNES	TOOMING	TOPEES
TOMCATTED*	TONER	TONNISH	TOOMS	TOPEK
TOMCATTING*	TONERS	TONNISHLY	TOON	TOPEKS
TOMCOD*	TONES	TONOMETER	TOONS	TOPER
TOMCODS*	TONETIC	TONOMETERS	TOORIE	TOPERS
TOME	TONETICS*	TONOMETRIES	TOORIES	TOPES
TOMENTA	TONETTE*	TONOMETRY	TOOT	TOPFLIGHT*
TOMENTOSE	TONETTES*	TONOPLAST*	TOOTED	TOPFUL*
TOMENTOUS	TONEY	TONOPLASTS*	TOOTER	TOPFULL
TOMENTUM	TONG	TONS	TOOTERS	TOPH*
TOMES	TONGA	TONSIL	TOOTH	TOPHE*
TOMFOOL	TONGAS	TONSILAR*	TOOTHACHE	TOPHES*
TOMFOOLED	TONGED	TONSILLAR	TOOTHACHES	TOPHI
TOMFOOLING	TONGER*	TONSILS	TOOTHCOMB	TOPHS*
TOMFOOLS	TONGERS*	TONSOR	TOOTHCOMBS	TOPHUS
TOMIA	TONGING	TONSORIAL	TOOTHED	TOPI
TOMIAL	TONGMAN*	TONSORS	TOOTHFUL	TOPIARIAN
TOMIUM	TONGMEN*	TONSURE	TOOTHFULS	TOPIARIES
TOMMED*	TONGS	TONSURED	TOOTHIER	TOPIARIST
TOMMIED	TONGSTER	TONSURES	TOOTHIEST	TOPIARISTS
TOMMIES	TONGSTERS	TONSURING	TOOTHILY	TOPIARY
TOMMING*	TONGUE	TONTINE	TOOTHING	TOPIC
TOMMY	TONGUED	TONTINER	TOOTHLESS	TOPICAL
TOMMYING	TONGUELET	TONTINERS	TOOTHLIKE	TOPICALLY
TOMMYROT*	TONGUELETS	TONTINES	TOOTHPICK	TOPICS
TOMMYROTS*	TONGUES	TONUS	TOOTHPICKS	TOPING
TOMOGRAM	TONGUING	TONUSES	TOOTHS	TOPIS
TOMOGRAMS	TONGUINGS	TONY	TOOTHSOME	TOPKICK*
TOMOGRAPH	TONIC	TOO	TOOTHWASH	TOPKICKS*
TOMOGRAPHS	TONICALLY*	TOOART	TOOTHWASHES	TOPKNOT
TOMORROW	TONICITIES	TOOARTS	TOOTHWORT	TOPKNOTS
TOMORROWS	TONICITY	TOOK	TOOTHWORTS	TOPLESS
TOMPION	TONICS	TOOL	TOOTHY	TOPLINE
TOMPIONS	TONIER	TOOLBAG	TOOTING	TOPLINED
TOMPON	TONIES	TOOLBAGS	TOOTLE	TOPLINER
TOMPONED	TONIEST	TOOLBAR	TOOTLED	TOPLINERS

Words marked with an asterisk are from OTCWL

TOPLINES	TOPWORKING*	TORMENTILS	TORREFYING	TORULAE
TOPLINING	TOPWORKS*	TORMENTING	TORRENT	TORULAS*
TOPLOFTIER*	TOQUE	TORMENTINGS	TORRENTS	TORULI
TOPLOFTIEST*	TOQUES	TORMENTOR	TORRET	TORULIN
TOPLOFTY	TOQUET*	TORMENTORS	TORRETS	TORULINS
TOPMAKER	TOQUETS*	TORMENTS	TORRID	TORULOSE
TOPMAKERS	TOQUILLA	TORMENTUM	TORRIDER	TORULOSES
TOPMAKING	TOQUILLAS	TORMENTUMS	TORRIDEST	TORULOSIS
TOPMAKINGS	TOR	TORMINA	TORRIDITIES	TORULUS
TOPMAN	TORA*	TORMINAL	TORRIDITY	TORUS
TOPMAST	TORAH*	TORMINOUS	TORRIDLY	TORY*
TOPMASTS	TORAHS*	TORN	TORRIFIED*	TOSA
TOPMEN	TORAN	TORNADE	TORRIFIES*	TOSAS
TOPMINNOW	TORANA	TORNADES	TORRIFY*	TOSE
TOPMINNOWS	TORANAS	TORNADIC	TORRIFYING*	TOSED
TOPMOST	TORANS	TORNADO	TORRS	TOSES
TOPNOTCH*	TORAS*	TORNADOES	TORS	TOSH
TOPOI	TORBANITE	TORNADOS	TORSADE	TOSHACH
TOPOLOGIC	TORBANITES	TORNILLO*	TORSADES	TOSHACHS
TOPOLOGIES	TORC	TORNILLOS*	TORSE	TOSHED
TOPOLOGY	TORCH	TORO*	TORSEL	TOSHER
TOPONYM	TORCHED	TOROID	TORSELS	TOSHERS
TOPONYMAL	TORCHER	TOROIDAL	TORSES	TOSHES
TOPONYMIC	TORCHERE	TOROIDS	TORSI	TOSHIER
TOPONYMICS	TORCHERES	TOROS*	TORSION	TOSHIEST
TOPONYMIES	TORCHERS	TOROSE	TORSIONAL	TOSHING
TOPONYMS	TORCHES	TOROSITIES*	TORSIONS	TOSHY
TOPONYMY	TORCHIER	TOROSITY*	TORSIVE	TOSING
TOPOS	TORCHIERE	TOROT*	TORSK	TOSS
TOPOTYPE	TORCHIERES	TOROTH*	TORSKS	TOSSED
TOPOTYPES	TORCHIERS	TOROUS	TORSO	TOSSEN
TOPPED	TORCHIEST*	TORPEDO	TORSOS	TOSSER
TOPPER	TORCHING	TORPEDOED	TORT	TOSSERS
TOPPERS	TORCHINGS	TORPEDOER	TORTE	TOSSES
TOPPING	TORCHON	TORPEDOERS	TORTEN	TOSSIER
TOPPINGLY	TORCHONS	TORPEDOES	TORTES	TOSSIEST
TOPPINGS	TORCHWOOD	TORPEDOING	TORTILE	TOSSILY
TOPPLE	TORCHWOODS	TORPEDOS	TORTILITIES	TOSSING
TOPPLED	TORCHY*	TORPEFIED	TORTILITY	TOSSINGS
TOPPLES	TORCS	TORPEFIES	TORTILLA	TOSSPOT
TOPPLING	TORCULAR	TORPEFY	TORTILLAS	TOSSPOTS
TOPS	TORCULARS	TORPEFYING	TORTIOUS	TOSSUP*
TOPSAIL	TORDION	TORPID	TORTIVE	TOSSUPS*
TOPSAILS	TORDIONS	TORPIDITIES	TORTOISE	TOSSY
TOPSIDE	TORE	TORPIDITY	TORTOISES	TOST
TOPSIDER*	TOREADOR	TORPIDLY	TORTONI	TOSTADA
TOPSIDERS*	TOREADORS	TORPIDS	TORTONIS	TOSTADAS
TOPSIDES	TORERO	TORPITUDE	TORTRICES	TOSTADO*
TOPSMAN	TOREROS	TORPITUDES	TORTRICID	TOSTADOS*
TOPSMEN	TORES	TORPOR	TORTRICIDS	TOT
TOPSOIL	TOREUTIC	TORPORS	TORTRIX	TOTABLE*
TOPSOILED*	TOREUTICS	TORQUATE	TORTRIXES*	TOTAL
TOPSOILING*	TORGOCH	TORQUATED	TORTS	TOTALED*
TOPSOILS	TORGOCHS	TORQUE	TORTUOUS	TOTALING*
TOPSPIN	TORI	TORQUED	TORTURE	TOTALISE
TOPSPINS	TORIC	TORQUER*	TORTURED	TOTALISED
TOPSTITCH*	TORIES*	TORQUERS*	TORTURER	TOTALISER
TOPSTITCHED*	TORII	TORQUES	TORTURERS	TOTALISERS
TOPSTITCHES*	TORMENT	TORQUESES*	TORTURES	TOTALISES
TOPSTITCHING*	TORMENTA	TORQUING*	TORTURING	TOTALISING
TOPSTONE*	TORMENTED	TORR	TORTURINGS	TOTALISM*
TOPSTONES*	TORMENTER	TORREFIED	TORTUROUS	TOTALISMS*
TOPWORK*	TORMENTERS	TORREFIES	TORUFFLED	TOTALIST*
TOPWORKED*	TORMENTIL	TORREFY	TORULA	TOTALISTS*

The Chambers Dictionary is the authority for many longer words; see Introduction, page ix

TOTALITIES
TOTALITY
TOTALIZE
TOTALIZED
TOTALIZER
TOTALIZERS
TOTALIZES
TOTALIZING
TOTALLED
TOTALLING
TOTALLY
TOTALS
TOTANUS
TOTANUSES
TOTAQUINE
TOTAQUINES
TOTARA
TOTARAS
TOTE
TOTED
TOTEM
TOTEMIC
TOTEMISM
TOTEMISMS
TOTEMIST
TOTEMISTS
TOTEMITE*
TOTEMITES*
TOTEMS
TOTER*
TOTERS*
TOTES
TOTHER
TOTIENT
TOTIENTS
TOTING
TOTITIVE
TOTITIVES
TOTS
TOTTED
TOTTER
TOTTERED
TOTTERER
TOTTERERS
TOTTERING
TOTTERINGS
TOTTERS
TOTTERY
TOTTIE
TOTTIER
TOTTIES
TOTTIEST
TOTTING
TOTTINGS
TOTTY
TOUCAN
TOUCANET
TOUCANETS
TOUCANS
TOUCH
TOUCHABLE
TOUCHBACK
TOUCHBACKS
TOUCHDOWN

TOUCHDOWNS
TOUCHE
TOUCHED
TOUCHER
TOUCHERS
TOUCHES
TOUCHHOLE*
TOUCHHOLES*
TOUCHIER
TOUCHIEST
TOUCHILY
TOUCHING
TOUCHINGS
TOUCHLESS
TOUCHLINE
TOUCHLINES
TOUCHMARK
TOUCHMARKS
TOUCHTONE
TOUCHUP*
TOUCHUPS*
TOUCHWOOD
TOUCHWOODS
TOUCHY
TOUGH
TOUGHED*
TOUGHEN
TOUGHENED
TOUGHENER
TOUGHENERS
TOUGHENING
TOUGHENINGS
TOUGHENS
TOUGHER
TOUGHEST
TOUGHIE
TOUGHIES
TOUGHING*
TOUGHISH
TOUGHLY
TOUGHNESS
TOUGHNESSES
TOUGHS
TOUGHY*
TOUK
TOUKED
TOUKING
TOUKS
TOUN
TOUNS
TOUPEE
TOUPEES
TOUPET
TOUPETS
TOUR
TOURACO
TOURACOS
TOURED
TOURER
TOURERS
TOURIE
TOURIES
TOURING
TOURINGS

TOURISM
TOURISMS
TOURIST
TOURISTIC
TOURISTS
TOURISTY
TOURNEDOS
TOURNEY
TOURNEYED
TOURNEYER
TOURNEYERS
TOURNEYING
TOURNEYS
TOURNURE
TOURNURES
TOURS
TOUSE
TOUSED
TOUSER
TOUSERS
TOUSES
TOUSIER
TOUSIEST
TOUSING
TOUSINGS
TOUSLE
TOUSLED
TOUSLES
TOUSLING
TOUSTIE
TOUSTIER
TOUSTIEST
TOUSY
TOUT
TOUTED
TOUTER
TOUTERS
TOUTIE
TOUTIER
TOUTIEST
TOUTING
TOUTS
TOUZE
TOUZED
TOUZES
TOUZIER
TOUZIEST
TOUZING
TOUZLE
TOUZLED
TOUZLES
TOUZLING
TOUZY
TOVARICH
TOVARICHES
TOVARISCH
TOVARISCHES
TOVARISH
TOVARISHES
TOW
TOWABLE
TOWAGE
TOWAGES
TOWARD

TOWARDLY
TOWARDS
TOWAWAY*
TOWAWAYS*
TOWBAR
TOWBARS
TOWBOAT
TOWBOATS
TOWED
TOWEL
TOWELED
TOWELETTE*
TOWELETTES*
TOWELHEAD
TOWELHEADS
TOWELING
TOWELINGS*
TOWELLED
TOWELLING
TOWELLINGS
TOWELS
TOWER
TOWERED
TOWERIER
TOWERIEST
TOWERING
TOWERLESS
TOWERLIKE*
TOWERS
TOWERY
TOWHEAD*
TOWHEADED*
TOWHEADS*
TOWHEE
TOWHEES
TOWIE*
TOWIER
TOWIES*
TOWIEST
TOWING
TOWINGS
TOWLINE
TOWLINES
TOWMON
TOWMOND
TOWMONDS
TOWMONS
TOWMONT
TOWMONTS
TOWN
TOWNEE
TOWNEES
TOWNFOLK*
TOWNHOME*
TOWNHOMES*
TOWNHOUSE
TOWNHOUSES
TOWNIE
TOWNIER
TOWNIES
TOWNIEST
TOWNISH
TOWNLAND
TOWNLANDS

TOWNLESS
TOWNLET*
TOWNLETS*
TOWNLIER
TOWNLIEST
TOWNLING
TOWNLINGS
TOWNLY
TOWNS
TOWNSCAPE
TOWNSCAPED
TOWNSCAPES
TOWNSCAPING
TOWNSCAPINGS
TOWNSFOLK
TOWNSFOLKS
TOWNSHIP
TOWNSHIPS
TOWNSKIP
TOWNSKIPS
TOWNSMAN
TOWNSMEN
TOWNWEAR*
TOWNY
TOWPATH
TOWPATHS
TOWROPE
TOWROPES
TOWS
TOWSE
TOWSED
TOWSER
TOWSERS
TOWSES
TOWSIER
TOWSIEST
TOWSING
TOWSY
TOWT
TOWTED
TOWTING
TOWTS
TOWY
TOWZE
TOWZED
TOWZES
TOWZIER
TOWZIEST
TOWZING
TOWZY
TOXAEMIA
TOXAEMIAS
TOXAEMIC
TOXAPHENE
TOXAPHENES
TOXEMIA
TOXEMIAS
TOXEMIC
TOXIC
TOXICAL
TOXICALLY
TOXICANT
TOXICANTS
TOXICITIES

TOXICITY	TRACHEARIES	TRACTRIX	TRAIKED	TRAMELS*
TOXICOSES*	TRACHEARY	TRACTS	TRAIKING	TRAMLESS*
TOXICOSIS*	TRACHEAS*	TRACTUS	TRAIKIT	TRAMLINE
TOXICS*	TRACHEATE	TRACTUSES	TRAIKS	TRAMLINED
TOXIGENIC*	TRACHEID	TRAD	TRAIL	TRAMLINES
TOXIN	TRACHEIDE	TRADABLE	TRAILABLE	TRAMMED
TOXINE*	TRACHEIDES	TRADE	TRAILED	TRAMMEL
TOXINES*	TRACHEIDS	TRADEABLE	TRAILER	TRAMMELED*
TOXINS	TRACHEOLE*	TRADED	TRAILERED	TRAMMELING*
TOXOCARA	TRACHEOLES*	TRADEFUL	TRAILERING	TRAMMELLED
TOXOCARAS	TRACHINUS	TRADELESS	TRAILERS	TRAMMELLING
TOXOID	TRACHINUSES	TRADEMARK	TRAILHEAD*	TRAMMELS
TOXOIDS	TRACHITIS	TRADEMARKED*	TRAILHEADS*	TRAMMING
TOXOPHILIES	TRACHITISES	TRADEMARKING*	TRAILING	TRAMP
TOXOPHILY	TRACHLE*	TRADEMARKS	TRAILLESS*	TRAMPED
TOY	TRACHLED*	TRADENAME	TRAILS	TRAMPER
TOYED	TRACHLES*	TRADENAMES	TRAILSIDE*	TRAMPERS
TOYER	TRACHLING*	TRADEOFF*	TRAIN	TRAMPET
TOYERS	TRACHOMA	TRADEOFFS*	TRAINABLE	TRAMPETS
TOYING	TRACHOMAS	TRADER	TRAINBAND	TRAMPETTE
TOYINGS	TRACHYTE	TRADERS	TRAINBANDS	TRAMPETTES
TOYISH	TRACHYTES	TRADES	TRAINED	TRAMPING
TOYISHLY	TRACHYTIC	TRADESMAN	TRAINEE	TRAMPINGS
TOYLESOME	TRACING	TRADESMEN	TRAINEES	TRAMPISH
TOYLESS	TRACINGS	TRADING	TRAINER	TRAMPLE
TOYLIKE	TRACK	TRADINGS	TRAINERS	TRAMPLED
TOYLSOM	TRACKABLE	TRADITION	TRAINFUL*	TRAMPLER
TOYMAN	TRACKAGE	TRADITIONS	TRAINFULS*	TRAMPLERS
TOYMEN	TRACKAGES	TRADITIVE	TRAINING	TRAMPLES
TOYO*	TRACKBALL	TRADITOR	TRAININGS	TRAMPLING
TOYON*	TRACKBALLS	TRADITORES	TRAINLESS	TRAMPLINGS
TOYONS*	TRACKED	TRADITORS	TRAINLOAD*	TRAMPOLIN
TOYOS*	TRACKER	TRADS	TRAINLOADS*	TRAMPOLINED
TOYS	TRACKERS	TRADUCE	TRAINMAN*	TRAMPOLINING
TOYSHOP	TRACKING	TRADUCED	TRAINMEN*	TRAMPOLINS
TOYSHOPS	TRACKINGS	TRADUCER	TRAINS	TRAMPS
TOYSOME	TRACKLESS	TRADUCERS	TRAINWAY*	TRAMROAD
TOYWOMAN	TRACKMAN	TRADUCES	TRAINWAYS*	TRAMROADS
TOYWOMEN	TRACKMEN	TRADUCING	TRAIPSE	TRAMS
TOZE	TRACKROAD	TRADUCINGS	TRAIPSED	TRAMWAY
TOZED	TRACKROADS	TRAFFIC	TRAIPSES	TRAMWAYS
TOZES	TRACKS	TRAFFICKED	TRAIPSING	TRANCE
TOZIE	TRACKSIDE*	TRAFFICKING	TRAIPSINGS	TRANCED
TOZIES	TRACKSIDES*	TRAFFICKINGS	TRAIT	TRANCEDLY
TOZING	TRACKSUIT*	TRAFFICS	TRAITOR	TRANCES
TRABEATE	TRACKSUITS*	TRAGEDIAN	TRAITORLY	TRANCHE
TRABEATED	TRACKWAY	TRAGEDIANS	TRAITORS	TRANCHES
TRABECULA	TRACKWAYS	TRAGEDIES	TRAITRESS	TRANCHET
TRABECULAE	TRACT	TRAGEDY	TRAITRESSES	TRANCHETS
TRABECULAS*	TRACTABLE	TRAGELAPH	TRAITS	TRANCING
TRACE	TRACTABLY	TRAGELAPHS	TRAJECT	TRANECT
TRACEABLE	TRACTATE	TRAGI	TRAJECTED	TRANECTS
TRACEABLY	TRACTATES	TRAGIC	TRAJECTING	TRANGAM
TRACED	TRACTATOR	TRAGICAL	TRAJECTS	TRANGAMS
TRACELESS	TRACTATORS	TRAGICS*	TRAM	TRANGLE
TRACER	TRACTED	TRAGOPAN	TRAMCAR	TRANGLES
TRACERIED	TRACTILE	TRAGOPANS	TRAMCARS	TRANK*
TRACERIES	TRACTING	TRAGULE	TRAMEL*	TRANKS*
TRACERS	TRACTION	TRAGULES	TRAMELED*	TRANKUM
TRACERY	TRACTIONS	TRAGULINE	TRAMELING*	TRANKUMS
TRACES	TRACTIVE	TRAGUS	TRAMELL*	TRANNIE
TRACHEA	TRACTOR	TRAHISON	TRAMELLED*	TRANNIES
TRACHEAE	TRACTORS	TRAHISONS	TRAMELLING*	TRANNY
TRACHEAL	TRACTRICES	TRAIK	TRAMELLS*	TRANQ*

TRANQS*	TRANSIENT	TRANSVESTS	TRASHCAN	TRAVESTIES
TRANQUIL	TRANSIENTS	TRANT	TRASHCANS	TRAVESTY
TRANQUILER*	TRANSIRE	TRANTED	TRASHED	TRAVESTYING
TRANQUILEST*	TRANSIRES	TRANTER	TRASHERIES	TRAVIS
TRANQUILLER	TRANSIT	TRANTERS	TRASHERY	TRAVISES
TRANQUILLEST	TRANSITED	TRANTING	TRASHES	TRAVOIS
TRANS*	TRANSITING	TRANTS	TRASHIER	TRAVOISE*
TRANSACT	TRANSITS	TRAP	TRASHIEST	TRAVOISES*
TRANSACTED	TRANSLATE	TRAPAN	TRASHILY	TRAWL
TRANSACTING	TRANSLATED	TRAPANNED	TRASHING	TRAWLED
TRANSACTS	TRANSLATES	TRAPANNING	TRASHMAN	TRAWLER
TRANSAXLE	TRANSLATING	TRAPANS	TRASHMEN	TRAWLERS
TRANSAXLES	TRANSMEW	TRAPBALL*	TRASHTRIE	TRAWLEY*
TRANSCEND	TRANSMEWED	TRAPBALLS*	TRASHTRIES	TRAWLEYS*
TRANSCENDED	TRANSMEWING	TRAPDOOR	TRASHY	TRAWLING
TRANSCENDING	TRANSMEWS	TRAPDOORS	TRASS	TRAWLINGS
TRANSCENDS	TRANSMIT	TRAPE	TRASSES	TRAWLNET*
TRANSDUCE*	TRANSMITS	TRAPED	TRAT	TRAWLNETS*
TRANSDUCED*	TRANSMITTED	TRAPES	TRATS	TRAWLS
TRANSDUCES*	TRANSMITTING	TRAPESED	TRATT	TRAY
TRANSDUCING*	TRANSMOVE	TRAPESES	TRATTORIA	TRAYBIT
TRANSE	TRANSMOVED	TRAPESING	TRATTORIAS	TRAYBITS
TRANSECT	TRANSMOVES	TRAPESINGS	TRATTORIE	TRAYFUL
TRANSECTED	TRANSMOVING	TRAPEZE	TRATTS	TRAYFULS
TRANSECTING	TRANSMUTE	TRAPEZED	TRAUCHLE	TRAYNE
TRANSECTS	TRANSMUTED	TRAPEZES	TRAUCHLED	TRAYNED
TRANSENNA	TRANSMUTES	TRAPEZIA	TRAUCHLES	TRAYNES
TRANSENNAS	TRANSMUTING	TRAPEZIAL	TRAUCHLING	TRAYNING
TRANSEPT	TRANSOM	TRAPEZII	TRAUMA	TRAYS
TRANSEPTS	TRANSOMS	TRAPEZING	TRAUMAS	TREACHER
TRANSES	TRANSONIC	TRAPEZIST*	TRAUMATA	TREACHERIES
TRANSEUNT	TRANSONICS	TRAPEZISTS*	TRAUMATIC	TREACHERS
TRANSFARD	TRANSPIRE	TRAPEZIUM	TRAVAIL	TREACHERY
TRANSFECT	TRANSPIRED	TRAPEZIUMS	TRAVAILED	TREACHOUR
TRANSFECTED	TRANSPIRES	TRAPEZIUS	TRAVAILING	TREACHOURS
TRANSFECTING	TRANSPIRING	TRAPEZIUSES	TRAVAILS	TREACLE
TRANSFECTS	TRANSPORT	TRAPEZOID	TRAVE	TREACLED
TRANSFER	TRANSPORTED	TRAPEZOIDS	TRAVEL	TREACLES
TRANSFERRED	TRANSPORTING	TRAPING	TRAVELED	TREACLIER
TRANSFERRING	TRANSPORTINGS	TRAPLIKE	TRAVELER	TREACLIEST
TRANSFERS	TRANSPORTS	TRAPLINE*	TRAVELERS	TREACLING
TRANSFIX	TRANSPOSE	TRAPLINES*	TRAVELING	TREACLY
TRANSFIXED	TRANSPOSED	TRAPNEST*	TRAVELINGS	TREAD
TRANSFIXES	TRANSPOSES	TRAPNESTED*	TRAVELLED	TREADED*
TRANSFIXING	TRANSPOSING	TRAPNESTING*	TRAVELLER	TREADER
TRANSFIXT*	TRANSPOSINGS	TRAPNESTS*	TRAVELLERS	TREADERS
TRANSFORM	TRANSSHIP	TRAPPEAN	TRAVELLING	TREADING
TRANSFORMED	TRANSSHIPPED	TRAPPED	TRAVELLINGS	TREADINGS
TRANSFORMING	TRANSSHIPPING	TRAPPER	TRAVELOG	TREADLE
TRANSFORMINGS	TRANSSHIPPINGS	TRAPPERS	TRAVELOGS	TREADLED
TRANSFORMS	TRANSSHIPS	TRAPPIER	TRAVELS	TREADLER
TRANSFUSE	TRANSUDE	TRAPPIEST	TRAVERSAL	TREADLERS
TRANSFUSED	TRANSUDED	TRAPPING	TRAVERSALS	TREADLES
TRANSFUSES	TRANSUDES	TRAPPINGS	TRAVERSE	TREADLESS*
TRANSFUSING	TRANSUDING	TRAPPOSE*	TRAVERSED	TREADLING
TRANSHIP	TRANSUME	TRAPPOUS*	TRAVERSER	TREADLINGS
TRANSHIPPED	TRANSUMED	TRAPPY	TRAVERSERS	TREADMILL
TRANSHIPPING	TRANSUMES	TRAPROCK	TRAVERSES	TREADMILLS
TRANSHIPPINGS	TRANSUMING	TRAPROCKS	TRAVERSING	TREADS
TRANSHIPS	TRANSUMPT	TRAPS	TRAVERSINGS	TREAGUE
TRANSHUME	TRANSUMPTS	TRAPT*	TRAVERTIN	TREAGUES
TRANSHUMED	TRANSVEST	TRAPUNTO	TRAVERTINS	TREASON
TRANSHUMES	TRANSVESTED	TRAPUNTOS	TRAVES	TREASONS
TRANSHUMING	TRANSVESTING	TRASH	TRAVESTIED	TREASURE

TREASURED
TREASURER
TREASURERS
TREASURES
TREASURIES
TREASURING
TREASURY
TREAT
TREATABLE
TREATED
TREATER
TREATERS
TREATIES
TREATING
TREATINGS
TREATISE
TREATISES
TREATMENT
TREATMENTS
TREATS
TREATY
TREBLE
TREBLED
TREBLES
TREBLING
TREBLY
TREBUCHET
TREBUCHETS
TREBUCKET*
TREBUCKETS*
TRECENTO
TRECENTOS
TRECK
TRECKED
TRECKING
TRECKS
TREDDLE
TREDDLED
TREDDLES
TREDDLING
TREDILLE
TREDILLES
TREDRILLE
TREDRILLES
TREE
TREED
TREEING
TREELAWN*
TREELAWNS*
TREELESS
TREELIKE*
TREEN
TREENAIL
TREENAILS
TREENS
TREENWARE
TREENWARES
TREES
TREESHIP
TREESHIPS
TREETOP
TREETOPS
TREF
TREFA

TREFAH*
TREFOIL
TREFOILED
TREFOILS
TREGETOUR
TREGETOURS
TREHALA
TREHALAS
TREHALOSE*
TREHALOSES*
TREIF
TREILLAGE
TREILLAGES
TREILLE
TREILLES
TREK
TREKKED
TREKKER
TREKKERS
TREKKING
TREKS
TRELLIS
TRELLISED
TRELLISES
TRELLISING
TREMA
TREMAS
TREMATIC
TREMATODE
TREMATODES
TREMATOID
TREMATOIDS
TREMBLANT
TREMBLE
TREMBLED
TREMBLER
TREMBLERS
TREMBLES
TREMBLIER
TREMBLIEST
TREMBLING
TREMBLINGS
TREMBLY
TREMIE
TREMIES
TREMOLANT
TREMOLANTS
TREMOLITE
TREMOLITES
TREMOLO
TREMOLOS
TREMOR
TREMORED
TREMORING
TREMORS
TREMULANT
TREMULANTS
TREMULATE
TREMULATED
TREMULATES
TREMULATING
TREMULOUS
TRENAIL
TRENAILS

TRENCH
TRENCHAND
TRENCHANT
TRENCHARD
TRENCHARDS
TRENCHED
TRENCHER
TRENCHERS
TRENCHES
TRENCHING
TREND
TRENDED
TRENDIER
TRENDIES
TRENDIEST
TRENDILY
TRENDING
TRENDS
TRENDY
TRENDYISM
TRENDYISMS
TRENISE
TRENISES
TRENTAL
TRENTALS
TREPAN
TREPANG
TREPANGS
TREPANNED
TREPANNER
TREPANNERS
TREPANNING
TREPANNINGS
TREPANS
TREPHINE
TREPHINED
TREPHINER
TREPHINERS
TREPHINES
TREPHINING
TREPHININGS
TREPID
TREPIDANT
TREPONEMA
TREPONEMAS
TREPONEMATA
TREPONEME
TREPONEMES
TRES
TRESPASS
TRESPASSED
TRESPASSES
TRESPASSING
TRESS
TRESSED
TRESSEL
TRESSELS
TRESSES
TRESSIER
TRESSIEST
TRESSING
TRESSOUR*
TRESSOURS*
TRESSURE

TRESSURED
TRESSURES
TRESSY
TREST
TRESTLE
TRESTLES
TRESTS
TRET
TRETINOIN*
TRETINOINS*
TRETS
TREVALLIES
TREVALLY
TREVET*
TREVETS*
TREVIS
TREVISES
TREVISS
TREVISSES
TREW
TREWS
TREWSMAN
TREWSMEN
TREY
TREYBIT
TREYBITS
TREYS
TREZ
TREZES
TRIABLE
TRIAC*
TRIACID
TRIACIDS*
TRIACS*
TRIACT
TRIACTINE
TRIAD
TRIADIC
TRIADICS*
TRIADISM*
TRIADISMS*
TRIADIST
TRIADISTS
TRIADS
TRIAGE
TRIAGED*
TRIAGES
TRIAGING*
TRIAL
TRIALISM
TRIALISMS
TRIALIST
TRIALISTS
TRIALITIES
TRIALITY
TRIALLED
TRIALLING
TRIALLIST
TRIALLISTS
TRIALOGUE
TRIALOGUES
TRIALS
TRIANGLE
TRIANGLED

TRIANGLES
TRIAPSAL
TRIARCH
TRIARCHIES
TRIARCHS
TRIARCHY
TRIATHLON
TRIATHLONS
TRIATIC
TRIATICS
TRIATOMIC
TRIAXIAL
TRIAXIALS
TRIAXON
TRIAXONS
TRIAZIN*
TRIAZINE*
TRIAZINES*
TRIAZINS*
TRIAZOLE*
TRIAZOLES*
TRIBADE
TRIBADES
TRIBADIC
TRIBADIES
TRIBADISM
TRIBADISMS
TRIBADY
TRIBAL
TRIBALISM
TRIBALISMS
TRIBALIST
TRIBALISTS
TRIBALLY
TRIBASIC
TRIBBLE
TRIBBLES
TRIBE
TRIBELESS
TRIBES
TRIBESMAN
TRIBESMEN
TRIBLET
TRIBLETS
TRIBOLOGIES
TRIBOLOGY
TRIBRACH
TRIBRACHS
TRIBULATE*
TRIBULATED*
TRIBULATES*
TRIBULATING*
TRIBUNAL
TRIBUNALS
TRIBUNATE
TRIBUNATES
TRIBUNE
TRIBUNES
TRIBUTARIES
TRIBUTARY
TRIBUTE
TRIBUTER
TRIBUTERS
TRIBUTES

The Chambers Dictionary is the authority for many longer words; see Introduction, page ix

TRICAR	TRICOLORS	TRIFFEST	TRIHYBRIDS	TRIMOTOR*
TRICARS	TRICOLOUR	TRIFFIC	TRIHYDRIC	TRIMOTORS*
TRICE	TRICOLOURS	TRIFFID	TRIJET*	TRIMS
TRICED	TRICORN	TRIFFIDS	TRIJETS*	TRIMTAB
TRICEPS	TRICORNE	TRIFFIDY	TRIKE	TRIMTABS
TRICEPSES	TRICORNES	TRIFID	TRIKES	TRIN
TRICERION	TRICORNS	TRIFLE	TRILBIES	TRINAL
TRICERIONS	TRICOT	TRIFLED	TRILBY	TRINARY
TRICES	TRICOTINE*	TRIFLER	TRILBYS	TRINDLE
TRICHINA	TRICOTINES*	TRIFLERS	TRILD	TRINDLED
TRICHINAE	TRICOTS	TRIFLES	TRILEMMA	TRINDLES
TRICHINAL*	TRICROTIC	TRIFLING	TRILEMMAS	TRINDLING
TRICHINAS	TRICTRAC*	TRIFLINGS*	TRILINEAR	TRINE
TRICHITE	TRICTRACS*	TRIFOCAL	TRILITH	TRINED
TRICHITES	TRICUSPID	TRIFOCALS	TRILITHIC	TRINES
TRICHITIC	TRICUSPIDS*	TRIFOLD*	TRILITHON	TRINGLE
TRICHOID	TRICYCLE	TRIFOLIES	TRILITHONS	TRINGLES
TRICHOME	TRICYCLED	TRIFOLIUM	TRILITHS	TRINING
TRICHOMES	TRICYCLER	TRIFOLIUMS	TRILL	TRINITIES
TRICHORD	TRICYCLERS	TRIFOLY	TRILLED	TRINITRIN
TRICHORDS	TRICYCLES	TRIFORIA	TRILLER*	TRINITRINS
TRICHOSES	TRICYCLIC	TRIFORIUM	TRILLERS*	TRINITY
TRICHOSIS	TRICYCLICS*	TRIFORM	TRILLING	TRINKET
TRICHROIC	TRICYCLING	TRIFORMED	TRILLINGS	TRINKETED
TRICHROME	TRICYCLINGS	TRIG	TRILLION	TRINKETER
TRICING	TRIDACNA	TRIGAMIES	TRILLIONS	TRINKETERS
TRICK	TRIDACNAS	TRIGAMIST	TRILLIUM	TRINKETING
TRICKED	TRIDACTYL	TRIGAMISTS	TRILLIUMS	TRINKETINGS
TRICKER	TRIDARN	TRIGAMOUS	TRILLO	TRINKETRIES
TRICKERIES	TRIDARNS	TRIGAMY	TRILLOES	TRINKETRY
TRICKERS	TRIDE	TRIGGED	TRILLS	TRINKETS
TRICKERY	TRIDENT	TRIGGER	TRILOBAL*	TRINKUM
TRICKIE*	TRIDENTAL	TRIGGERED	TRILOBATE	TRINKUMS
TRICKIER	TRIDENTED	TRIGGERING	TRILOBE	TRINODAL*
TRICKIEST	TRIDENTS	TRIGGERS	TRILOBED	TRINOMIAL
TRICKILY	TRIDUAN	TRIGGEST	TRILOBES	TRINOMIALS
TRICKING	TRIDUUM	TRIGGING	TRILOBITE	TRINS
TRICKINGS	TRIDUUMS	TRIGLOT	TRILOBITES	TRIO
TRICKISH	TRIDYMITE	TRIGLOTS	TRILOGIES	TRIODE
TRICKLE	TRIDYMITES	TRIGLY	TRILOGY	TRIODES
TRICKLED	TRIE	TRIGLYPH	TRIM	TRIOL*
TRICKLES	TRIECIOUS	TRIGLYPHS	TRIMARAN	TRIOLET
TRICKLESS	TRIED	TRIGNESS	TRIMARANS	TRIOLETS
TRICKLET	TRIENE*	TRIGNESSES	TRIMER	TRIOLS*
TRICKLETS	TRIENES*	TRIGO*	TRIMERIC	TRIONES
TRICKLIER	TRIENNIA*	TRIGON	TRIMEROUS	TRIONYM
TRICKLIEST	TRIENNIAL	TRIGONAL	TRIMERS	TRIONYMAL
TRICKLING	TRIENNIALS*	TRIGONIC	TRIMESTER	TRIONYMS
TRICKLINGS	TRIENNIUM*	TRIGONOUS	TRIMESTERS	TRIOR
TRICKLY	TRIENNIUMS*	TRIGONS	TRIMETER	TRIORS
TRICKS	TRIENS*	TRIGOS*	TRIMETERS	TRIOS
TRICKSIER	TRIENTES*	TRIGRAM	TRIMETHYL	TRIOSE*
TRICKSIEST	TRIER	TRIGRAMS	TRIMETRIC	TRIOSES*
TRICKSOME	TRIERARCH	TRIGRAPH	TRIMLY	TRIOXID*
TRICKSTER	TRIERARCHS	TRIGRAPHS	TRIMMED	TRIOXIDE
TRICKSTERS	TRIERS	TRIGS	TRIMMER	TRIOXIDES
TRICKSY	TRIES	TRIGYNIAN	TRIMMERS	TRIOXIDS*
TRICKY	TRIETERIC	TRIGYNOUS	TRIMMEST	TRIP
TRICLAD*	TRIETHYL	TRIHEDRA*	TRIMMING	TRIPACK*
TRICLADS*	TRIFACIAL	TRIHEDRAL	TRIMMINGS	TRIPACKS*
TRICLINIA	TRIFECTA	TRIHEDRALS	TRIMNESS	TRIPART*
TRICLINIC	TRIFECTAS	TRIHEDRON	TRIMNESSES	TRIPE
TRICLINIUM*	TRIFF	TRIHEDRONS	TRIMORPH*	TRIPEDAL
TRICOLOR	TRIFFER	TRIHYBRID	TRIMORPHS*	TRIPERIES

Words marked with an asterisk are from OTCWL

TRIPERY	TRIPTOTE	TRITER	TRIVIUMS	TROG
TRIPES	TRIPTOTES	TRITES	TRIWEEKLIES*	TROGGED
TRIPEY	TRIPTYCAS*	TRITEST	TRIWEEKLY*	TROGGING
TRIPHASE*	TRIPTYCH	TRITHEISM	TRIZONAL	TROGGS
TRIPHONE	TRIPTYCHS	TRITHEISMS	TRIZONE	TROGON
TRIPHONES	TRIPTYQUE	TRITHEIST	TRIZONES	TROGONS
TRIPIER	TRIPTYQUES	TRITHEISTS	TROAD	TROGS
TRIPIEST	TRIPUDIA	TRITHING*	TROADE	TROIKA
TRIPITAKA	TRIPUDIUM	TRITHINGS*	TROADES	TROIKAS
TRIPITAKAS	TRIPUDIUMS	TRITIATE	TROADS	TROILISM
TRIPLANE	TRIPWIRE	TRITIATED	TROAK*	TROILISMS
TRIPLANES	TRIPWIRES	TRITIATES	TROAKED*	TROILIST
TRIPLE	TRIPY	TRITIATING	TROAKING*	TROILISTS
TRIPLED	TRIQUETRA	TRITICAL	TROAKS*	TROILITE
TRIPLES	TRIQUETRAS	TRITICALE	TROAT	TROILITES
TRIPLET	TRIRADIAL	TRITICALES	TROATED	TROILUS*
TRIPLETS	TRIREME	TRITICISM	TROATING	TROILUSES*
TRIPLEX	TRIREMES	TRITICISMS	TROATS	TROIS*
TRIPLEXES	TRISAGION	TRITICUM*	TROCAR	TROKE
TRIPLIED	TRISAGIONS	TRITICUMS*	TROCARS	TROKED
TRIPLIES	TRISCELE*	TRITIDE	TROCHAIC	TROKES
TRIPLING	TRISCELES*	TRITIDES	TROCHAICS	TROKING
TRIPLINGS	TRISECT	TRITIUM	TROCHAL	TROLAND*
TRIPLITE*	TRISECTED	TRITIUMS	TROCHAR*	TROLANDS*
TRIPLITES*	TRISECTING	TRITOMA*	TROCHARS*	TROLL
TRIPLOID	TRISECTOR	TRITOMAS*	TROCHE	TROLLED
TRIPLOIDIES	TRISECTORS	TRITON	TROCHEE	TROLLER
TRIPLOIDS*	TRISECTS	TRITONE	TROCHEES	TROLLERS
TRIPLOIDY	TRISEME	TRITONES	TROCHES	TROLLEY
TRIPLY	TRISEMES	TRITONIA	TROCHI	TROLLEYED
TRIPLYING	TRISEMIC	TRITONIAS	TROCHIL*	TROLLEYING
TRIPOD	TRISHAW	TRITONS	TROCHILI*	TROLLEYS
TRIPODAL	TRISHAWS	TRITURATE	TROCHILIC	TROLLIED*
TRIPODIC*	TRISKELE	TRITURATED	TROCHILS*	TROLLIES
TRIPODIES	TRISKELES	TRITURATES	TROCHILUS	TROLLING
TRIPODS	TRISKELIA	TRITURATING	TROCHILUSES	TROLLINGS
TRIPODY	TRISMIC*	TRIUMPH	TROCHISK	TROLLIUS
TRIPOLI	TRISMUS	TRIUMPHAL	TROCHISKS	TROLLIUSES
TRIPOLIS	TRISMUSES	TRIUMPHALS	TROCHITE	TROLLOP
TRIPOS	TRISOME	TRIUMPHED	TROCHITES	TROLLOPED
TRIPOSES	TRISOMES	TRIUMPHER	TROCHLEA	TROLLOPEE
TRIPPANT	TRISOMIC	TRIUMPHERS	TROCHLEAE*	TROLLOPEES
TRIPPED	TRISOMICS*	TRIUMPHING	TROCHLEAR	TROLLOPING
TRIPPER	TRISOMIES	TRIUMPHINGS	TROCHLEARS*	TROLLOPS
TRIPPERS	TRISOMY	TRIUMPHS	TROCHLEAS	TROLLOPY
TRIPPERY	TRIST	TRIUMVIR	TROCHOID	TROLLS
TRIPPET	TRISTATE*	TRIUMVIRI	TROCHOIDS	TROLLY
TRIPPETS	TRISTE	TRIUMVIRIES	TROCHUS	TROLLYING*
TRIPPIER	TRISTESSE	TRIUMVIRS	TROCHUSES	TROMBONE
TRIPPIEST	TRISTESSES	TRIUMVIRY	TROCK	TROMBONES
TRIPPING	TRISTEZA*	TRIUNE	TROCKED	TROMINO
TRIPPINGS	TRISTEZAS*	TRIUNES	TROCKEN	TROMINOES
TRIPPLE	TRISTFUL	TRIUNITIES	TROCKING	TROMINOS
TRIPPLED	TRISTICH	TRIUNITY	TROCKS	TROMMEL
TRIPPLER	TRISTICHS	TRIVALENT	TROD	TROMMELS
TRIPPLERS	TRISUL	TRIVALVE	TRODDEN	TROMP
TRIPPLES	TRISULA	TRIVALVED	TRODE	TROMPE
TRIPPLING	TRISULAS	TRIVALVES	TRODES	TROMPED
TRIPPY	TRISULS	TRIVET	TRODS	TROMPES
TRIPS	TRITE	TRIVETS	TROELIE	TROMPING
TRIPSES	TRITELY	TRIVIA	TROELIES	TROMPS
TRIPSIS	TRITENESS	TRIVIAL	TROELY	TRON
TRIPTANE	TRITENESSES	TRIVIALLY	TROFFER*	TRONA
TRIPTANES		TRIVIUM	TROFFERS*	TRONAS

The Chambers Dictionary is the authority for many longer words; see Introduction, page ix

TRONC	TROTTING	TROVE*	TRUCKLOADS*	TRUMPINGS
TRONCS	TROTTINGS	TROVER	TRUCKMAN	TRUMPS
TRONE	TROTTOIR	TROVERS	TRUCKMEN	TRUNCAL
TRONES	TROTTOIRS	TROVES*	TRUCKS	TRUNCATE
TRONS	TROTYL	TROW	TRUCULENT	TRUNCATED
TROOLIE	TROTYLS	TROWED	TRUDGE	TRUNCATES
TROOLIES	TROUBLE	TROWEL	TRUDGED	TRUNCATING
TROOP	TROUBLED	TROWELED*	TRUDGEN	TRUNCHEON
TROOPED	TROUBLER	TROWELER*	TRUDGENS	TRUNCHEONED
TROOPER	TROUBLERS	TROWELERS*	TRUDGEON	TRUNCHEONING
TROOPERS	TROUBLES	TROWELING*	TRUDGEONS	TRUNCHEONS
TROOPIAL	TROUBLING	TROWELLED	TRUDGER	TRUNDLE
TROOPIALS	TROUBLINGS	TROWELLER	TRUDGERS	TRUNDLED
TROOPING	TROUBLOUS	TROWELLERS	TRUDGES	TRUNDLER
TROOPS	TROUGH	TROWELLING	TRUDGING	TRUNDLERS
TROOPSHIP*	TROUGHS	TROWELS	TRUDGINGS	TRUNDLES
TROOPSHIPS*	TROULE	TROWING	TRUE	TRUNDLING
TROOZ*	TROULED	TROWS	TRUEBLUE*	TRUNK
TROP*	TROULES	TROWSERS	TRUEBLUES*	TRUNKED
TROPARIA	TROULING	TROWTH*	TRUEBORN*	TRUNKFISH
TROPARION	TROUNCE	TROWTHS*	TRUEBRED*	TRUNKFISHES
TROPE	TROUNCED	TROY	TRUED	TRUNKFUL
TROPED	TROUNCER	TROYS	TRUEING	TRUNKFULS
TROPES	TROUNCERS	TRUANCIES	TRUELOVE*	TRUNKING
TROPHESIES	TROUNCES	TRUANCY	TRUELOVES*	TRUNKINGS
TROPHESY	TROUNCING	TRUANT	TRUEMAN	TRUNKS
TROPHI	TROUNCINGS	TRUANTED	TRUEMEN	TRUNNEL*
TROPHIC	TROUPE	TRUANTING	TRUENESS	TRUNNELS*
TROPHIED	TROUPED	TRUANTRIES	TRUENESSES	TRUNNION
TROPHIES	TROUPER	TRUANTRY	TRUEPENNIES	TRUNNIONS
TROPHY	TROUPERS	TRUANTS	TRUEPENNY	TRUQUAGE
TROPHYING	TROUPES	TRUCAGE	TRUER	TRUQUEUR
TROPIC	TROUPIAL	TRUCAGES	TRUES	TRUQUEURS
TROPICAL	TROUPIALS	TRUCE	TRUEST	TRUSS
TROPICS	TROUPING	TRUCED*	TRUFFE*	TRUSSED
TROPIN*	TROUSE	TRUCELESS	TRUFFES*	TRUSSER
TROPINE*	TROUSER	TRUCES	TRUFFLE	TRUSSERS
TROPINES*	TROUSERED	TRUCHMAN	TRUFFLED	TRUSSES
TROPING	TROUSERING	TRUCHMANS	TRUFFLES	TRUSSING
TROPINS*	TROUSERINGS	TRUCHMEN	TRUFFLING	TRUSSINGS
TROPISM	TROUSERS	TRUCIAL	TRUFFLINGS	TRUST
TROPISMS	TROUSES	TRUCING*	TRUG	TRUSTABLE*
TROPIST	TROUSSEAU	TRUCK	TRUGS	TRUSTED
TROPISTIC	TROUSSEAUS	TRUCKAGE	TRUING	TRUSTEE
TROPISTS	TROUSSEAUX	TRUCKAGES	TRUISM	TRUSTEED*
TROPOLOGIES	TROUT	TRUCKED	TRUISMS	TRUSTEEING*
TROPOLOGY	TROUTER	TRUCKER	TRUISTIC	TRUSTEES
TROPONIN*	TROUTERS	TRUCKERS	TRULL	TRUSTER
TROPONINS*	TROUTFUL	TRUCKFUL*	TRULLS	TRUSTERS
TROPPO	TROUTIER	TRUCKFULS*	TRULY	TRUSTFUL
TROSSERS	TROUTIEST	TRUCKIE	TRUMEAU	TRUSTIER
TROT	TROUTING	TRUCKIES	TRUMEAUX	TRUSTIES
TROTH	TROUTINGS	TRUCKING	TRUMP	TRUSTIEST
TROTHED	TROUTLESS	TRUCKINGS	TRUMPED	TRUSTILY
TROTHFUL	TROUTLET	TRUCKLE	TRUMPERIES	TRUSTING
TROTHING	TROUTLETS	TRUCKLED	TRUMPERY	TRUSTLESS
TROTHLESS	TROUTLING	TRUCKLER	TRUMPET	TRUSTOR*
TROTHS	TROUTLINGS	TRUCKLERS	TRUMPETED	TRUSTORS*
TROTLINE	TROUTS	TRUCKLES	TRUMPETER	TRUSTS
TROTLINES	TROUTY	TRUCKLINE*	TRUMPETERS	TRUSTY
TROTS	TROUVERE	TRUCKLINES*	TRUMPETING	TRUTH
TROTTED	TROUVERES	TRUCKLING	TRUMPETINGS	TRUTHFUL
TROTTER	TROUVEUR	TRUCKLINGS	TRUMPETS	TRUTHIER
TROTTERS	TROUVEURS	TRUCKLOAD*	TRUMPING	

TRUTHIEST	TSETSE	TUBECTOMIES	TUCKERBAG	TUILYIEING
TRUTHLESS	TSETSES	TUBECTOMY	TUCKERBAGS	TUILYIES
TRUTHLIKE	TSIGANE	TUBED	TUCKERBOX	TUILZIE
TRUTHS	TSIGANES	TUBEFUL	TUCKERBOXES	TUILZIED
TRUTHY	TSIMMES*	TUBEFULS	TUCKERED	TUILZIEING
TRY	TSK*	TUBELESS	TUCKERING	TUILZIES
TRYE	TSKED*	TUBELIKE	TUCKERS	TUINA
TRYER	TSKING*	TUBENOSE	TUCKET	TUINAS
TRYERS	TSKS*	TUBENOSES	TUCKETS	TUIS
TRYING	TSKTSK*	TUBER	TUCKING	TUISM
TRYINGLY	TSKTSKED*	TUBERCLE	TUCKS	TUISMS
TRYINGS	TSKTSKING*	TUBERCLED	TUCKSHOP*	TUITION
TRYMA*	TSKTSKS*	TUBERCLES	TUCKSHOPS*	TUITIONAL
TRYMATA*	TSOORIS*	TUBERCULA	TUCOTUCO	TUITIONS
TRYOUT*	TSORES*	TUBERCULE	TUCOTUCOS	TULADI*
TRYOUTS*	TSORIS*	TUBERCULES	TUCUTUCO	TULADIS*
TRYP	TSORRISS*	TUBEROID*	TUCUTUCOS	TULAREMIA
TRYPS	TSOTSI	TUBEROSE	TUFA	TULAREMIAS
TRYPSIN	TSOTSIS	TUBEROSES	TUFACEOUS	TULAREMIC
TRYPSINS	TSOURIS	TUBEROUS	TUFAS	TULBAN
TRYPTIC	TSOURISES	TUBERS	TUFF	TULBANS
TRYSAIL	TSUBA	TUBES	TUFFE	TULCHAN
TRYSAILS	TSUBAS	TUBEWORK*	TUFFES	TULCHANS
TRYST	TSUNAMI	TUBEWORKS*	TUFFET	TULE
TRYSTE*	TSUNAMIC*	TUBFAST	TUFFETS	TULES
TRYSTED	TSUNAMIS	TUBFASTS	TUFFS	TULIP
TRYSTER	TSURIS	TUBFISH	TUFOLI*	TULIPANT
TRYSTERS	TSURISES	TUBFISHES	TUFT	TULIPANTS
TRYSTES*	TSUTSUMU	TUBFUL	TUFTED	TULIPS
TRYSTING	TSUTSUMUS	TUBFULS	TUFTER	TULIPWOOD
TRYSTS	TUAN	TUBICOLAR	TUFTERS	TULIPWOODS
TRYWORKS*	TUANS	TUBICOLE	TUFTIER	TULLE
TSADDIK	TUART	TUBICOLES	TUFTIEST	TULLES
TSADDIKIM	TUARTS	TUBIFEX	TUFTILY*	TULLIBEE*
TSADDIKS	TUATARA	TUBIFEXES	TUFTING	TULLIBEES*
TSADDIQ	TUATARAS	TUBIFICID*	TUFTINGS	TULWAR
TSADDIQIM	TUATERA*	TUBIFICIDS*	TUFTS	TULWARS
TSADDIQS	TUATERAS*	TUBIFORM	TUFTY	TUM
TSADE*	TUATH	TUBING	TUG	TUMBLE
TSADES*	TUATHS	TUBINGS	TUGBOAT	TUMBLEBUG*
TSADI*	TUB	TUBIST*	TUGBOATS	TUMBLEBUGS*
TSADIS*	TUBA	TUBISTS*	TUGGED	TUMBLED
TSAMBA	TUBAE	TUBLIKE*	TUGGER	TUMBLER
TSAMBAS	TUBAGE	TUBS	TUGGERS	TUMBLERS
TSAR	TUBAGES	TUBULAR	TUGGING	TUMBLES
TSARDOM	TUBAIST*	TUBULATE	TUGGINGLY	TUMBLING
TSARDOMS	TUBAISTS*	TUBULATED	TUGGINGS	TUMBLINGS
TSAREVICH	TUBAL	TUBULATES	TUGHRA	TUMBREL
TSAREVICHES	TUBAR	TUBULATING	TUGHRAS	TUMBRELS
TSAREVNA	TUBAS	TUBULE	TUGHRIK	TUMBRIL
TSAREVNAS	TUBATE	TUBULES	TUGHRIKS	TUMBRILS
TSARINA	TUBBABLE*	TUBULIN	TUGLESS*	TUMEFIED
TSARINAS	TUBBED	TUBULINS	TUGRA	TUMEFIES
TSARISM	TUBBER	TUBULOSE*	TUGRAS	TUMEFY
TSARISMS	TUBBERS	TUBULOUS	TUGRIK	TUMEFYING
TSARIST	TUBBIER	TUBULURE*	TUGRIKS	TUMESCE
TSARISTS	TUBBIEST	TUBULURES*	TUGS	TUMESCED
TSARITSA	TUBBINESS	TUCHUN	TUI	TUMESCENT
TSARITSAS	TUBBINESSES	TUCHUNS	TUILLE	TUMESCES
TSARITZA*	TUBBING	TUCK	TUILLES	TUMESCING
TSARITZAS*	TUBBINGS	TUCKAHOE	TUILLETTE	TUMID
TSARS	TUBBISH	TUCKAHOES	TUILLETTES	TUMIDITIES
TSESSEBE	TUBBY	TUCKED	TUILYIE	TUMIDITY
TSESSEBES	TUBE	TUCKER	TUILYIED	TUMIDLY

The Chambers Dictionary is the authority for many longer words; see Introduction, page ix

TUMIDNESS	TUNES	TUQUES	TURFIER	TURNCOAT
TUMIDNESSES	TUNESMITH	TURACIN	TURFIEST	TURNCOATS
TUMMIES	TUNESMITHS	TURACINS	TURFINESS	TURNCOCK
TUMMLER*	TUNEUP*	TURACO	TURFINESSES	TURNCOCKS
TUMMLERS*	TUNEUPS*	TURACOS	TURFING	TURNDOWN*
TUMMY	TUNG*	TURACOU*	TURFINGS	TURNDOWNS*
TUMOR	TUNGS*	TURACOUS*	TURFITE	TURNDUN
TUMORAL*	TUNGSTATE	TURBAN	TURFITES	TURNDUNS
TUMORLIKE*	TUNGSTATES	TURBAND	TURFLESS*	TURNED
TUMOROUS	TUNGSTEN	TURBANDS	TURFLIKE*	TURNER
TUMORS	TUNGSTENS	TURBANED	TURFMAN	TURNERIES
TUMOUR	TUNGSTIC*	TURBANNED*	TURFMEN	TURNERS
TUMOURS	TUNIC	TURBANS	TURFS	TURNERY
TUMP	TUNICA*	TURBANT	TURFSKI*	TURNHALL*
TUMPED	TUNICAE*	TURBANTS	TURFSKIS*	TURNHALLS*
TUMPHIES	TUNICATE	TURBARIES	TURFY	TURNING
TUMPHY	TUNICATED	TURBARY	TURGENCIES*	TURNINGS
TUMPIER	TUNICATES	TURBETH*	TURGENCY*	TURNIP
TUMPIEST	TUNICIN	TURBETHS*	TURGENT	TURNIPED
TUMPING	TUNICINS	TURBID	TURGENTLY	TURNIPING
TUMPLINE*	TUNICKED	TURBIDITE	TURGID	TURNIPS
TUMPLINES*	TUNICLE	TURBIDITES	TURGIDER	TURNKEY
TUMPS	TUNICLES	TURBIDITIES	TURGIDEST	TURNKEYS
TUMPY	TUNICS	TURBIDITY	TURGIDITIES	TURNOFF
TUMS	TUNIER	TURBIDLY	TURGIDITY	TURNOFFS
TUMSHIE	TUNIEST	TURBINAL	TURGIDLY	TURNOUT
TUMSHIES	TUNING	TURBINALS	TURGITE*	TURNOUTS
TUMULAR	TUNINGS	TURBINATE	TURGITES*	TURNOVER
TUMULARY	TUNNAGE	TURBINATES	TURGOR	TURNOVERS
TUMULI	TUNNAGES	TURBINE	TURGORS	TURNPIKE
TUMULOSE*	TUNNED	TURBINED	TURION	TURNPIKES
TUMULOUS*	TUNNEL	TURBINES	TURIONS	TURNROUND
TUMULT	TUNNELED	TURBIT	TURISTA*	TURNROUNDS
TUMULTED	TUNNELER	TURBITH	TURISTAS*	TURNS
TUMULTING	TUNNELERS	TURBITHS	TURK*	TURNSKIN
TUMULTS	TUNNELING	TURBITS	TURKEY	TURNSKINS
TUMULUS	TUNNELLED	TURBO	TURKEYS	TURNSOLE
TUMULUSES*	TUNNELLER	TURBOCAR	TURKIES	TURNSOLES
TUN	TUNNELLERS	TURBOCARS	TURKIESES	TURNSPIT
TUNA	TUNNELLING	TURBOFAN	TURKIS	TURNSPITS
TUNABLE	TUNNELLINGS	TURBOFANS	TURKISES	TURNSTILE
TUNABLY	TUNNELS	TURBOJET	TURKISES	TURNSTILES
TUNAS	TUNNIES	TURBOJETS	TURKOISES*	TURNSTONE
TUNBELLIES	TUNNING	TURBOND	TURKS*	TURNSTONES
TUNBELLY	TUNNINGS	TURBONDS	TURLOUGH	TURNTABLE
TUND	TUNNY	TURBOPROP	TURLOUGHS	TURNTABLES
TUNDED	TUNS	TURBOPROPS	TURM	TURNUP*
TUNDING	TUNY	TURBOS	TURME	TURNUPS*
TUNDISH*	TUP	TURBOT	TURMERIC	TUROPHILE*
TUNDISHES*	TUPEK	TURBOTS	TURMERICS	TUROPHILES*
TUNDRA	TUPEKS	TURBULENT	TURMES	TURPETH
TUNDRAS	TUPELO	TURCOPOLE	TURMOIL	TURPETHS
TUNDS	TUPELOS	TURCOPOLES	TURMOILED	TURPITUDE
TUNDUN	TUPIK	TURD	TURMOILING	TURPITUDES
TUNDUNS	TUPIKS	TURDINE	TURMOILS	TURPS
TUNE	TUPPED	TURDION	TURMS	TURQUOIS*
TUNEABLE	TUPPENCE	TURDIONS	TURN	TURQUOISE
TUNEABLY*	TUPPENCES	TURDOID	TURNABLE*	TURQUOISES
TUNED	TUPPENNIES	TURDS	TURNABOUT	TURRET
TUNEFUL	TUPPENNY	TUREEN	TURNABOUTS	TURRETED
TUNEFULLY	TUPPING	TUREENS	TURNAGAIN	TURRETS
TUNELESS	TUPS	TURF	TURNAGAINS	TURRIBANT
TUNER	TUPTOWING	TURFED	TURNBACK	TURRIBANTS
TUNERS	TUQUE	TURFEN	TURNBACKS	TURRICAL*

TURTLE	TUT	TUTTY	TWANKY*	TWELFTH
TURTLED	TUTANIA	TUTU	TWAS	TWELFTHLY
TURTLER	TUTANIAS	TUTUS	TWASOME	TWELFTHS
TURTLERS	TUTEE	TUTWORK	TWASOMES	TWELVE
TURTLES	TUTEES	TUTWORKER	TWAT	TWELVEMO
TURTLING	TUTELAGE	TUTWORKERS	TWATS	TWELVEMOS
TURTLINGS	TUTELAGES	TUTWORKS	TWATTLE	TWELVES
TURVES	TUTELAR	TUX	TWATTLED	TWENTIES
TUSCHE	TUTELARIES	TUXEDO	TWATTLER	TWENTIETH
TUSCHES	TUTELARS	TUXEDOED*	TWATTLERS	TWENTIETHS
TUSH	TUTELARY	TUXEDOES	TWATTLES	TWENTY
TUSHED	TUTENAG	TUXEDOS	TWATTLING	TWENTYISH
TUSHERIES	TUTENAGS	TUXES	TWATTLINGS	TWERP
TUSHERY	TUTIORISM	TUYER*	TWAY	TWERPS
TUSHES	TUTIORISMS	TUYERE	TWAYBLADE*	TWIBIL*
TUSHIE	TUTIORIST	TUYERES	TWAYBLADES*	TWIBILL
TUSHIES	TUTIORISTS	TUYERS*	TWAYS	TWIBILLS
TUSHING	TUTMAN	TUZZ	TWEAK	TWIBILS*
TUSHKAR	TUTMEN	TUZZES	TWEAKED	TWICE
TUSHKARS	TUTOR	TWA	TWEAKIER*	TWICER
TUSHKER	TUTORAGE	TWADDLE	TWEAKIEST*	TWICERS
TUSHKERS	TUTORAGES	TWADDLED	TWEAKING	TWICHILD
TUSHY	TUTORED	TWADDLER	TWEAKINGS	TWICHILDREN
TUSK	TUTORESS	TWADDLERS	TWEAKS	TWIDDLE
TUSKAR	TUTORESSES	TWADDLES	TWEAKY*	TWIDDLED
TUSKARS	TUTORIAL	TWADDLIER	TWEE	TWIDDLER
TUSKED	TUTORIALS	TWADDLIEST	TWEED	TWIDDLERS
TUSKER	TUTORING	TWADDLING	TWEEDIER	TWIDDLES
TUSKERS	TUTORINGS	TWADDLINGS	TWEEDIEST	TWIDDLIER
TUSKIER	TUTORISE	TWADDLY	TWEEDLE	TWIDDLIEST
TUSKIEST	TUTORISED	TWAE	TWEEDLED	TWIDDLING
TUSKING	TUTORISES	TWAES	TWEEDLER	TWIDDLINGS
TUSKINGS	TUTORISING	TWAFALD	TWEEDLERS	TWIDDLY
TUSKLESS	TUTORISM	TWAIN	TWEEDLES	TWIER
TUSKLIKE*	TUTORISMS	TWAINS	TWEEDLING	TWIERS
TUSKS	TUTORIZE	TWAITE	TWEEDS	TWIFOLD
TUSKY	TUTORIZED	TWAITES	TWEEDY	TWIFORKED
TUSSAH	TUTORIZES	TWAL	TWEEL	TWIFORMED
TUSSAHS	TUTORIZING	TWALHOURS	TWEELED	TWIG
TUSSAL	TUTORS	TWALPENNIES	TWEELING	TWIGGED
TUSSAR*	TUTORSHIP	TWALPENNY	TWEELS	TWIGGEN
TUSSARS*	TUTORSHIPS	TWALS	TWEELY	TWIGGER
TUSSEH	TUTOYED*	TWANG	TWEEN*	TWIGGERS
TUSSEHS	TUTOYER*	TWANGED	TWEENESS	TWIGGIER
TUSSER	TUTOYERED*	TWANGER*	TWEENESSES	TWIGGIEST
TUSSERS	TUTOYERING*	TWANGERS*	TWEENIES	TWIGGING
TUSSIS	TUTOYERS*	TWANGIER	TWEENY	TWIGGY
TUSSISES	TUTRESS	TWANGIEST	TWEER	TWIGHT
TUSSIVE	TUTRESSES	TWANGING	TWEERED	TWIGHTED
TUSSLE	TUTRICES	TWANGINGS	TWEERING	TWIGHTING
TUSSLED	TUTRIX	TWANGLE	TWEERS	TWIGHTS
TUSSLES	TUTRIXES	TWANGLED	TWEEST	TWIGLESS*
TUSSLING	TUTS	TWANGLER*	TWEET	TWIGLIKE*
TUSSOCK	TUTSAN	TWANGLERS*	TWEETED	TWIGLOO
TUSSOCKS	TUTSANS	TWANGLES	TWEETER	TWIGLOOS
TUSSOCKY	TUTSED	TWANGLING	TWEETERS	TWIGS
TUSSOR*	TUTSES	TWANGLINGS	TWEETING	TWIGSOME
TUSSORE	TUTSING	TWANGS	TWEETS	TWILIGHT
TUSSORES	TUTTED	TWANGY	TWEEZE	TWILIGHTED
TUSSORS*	TUTTI	TWANK	TWEEZED	TWILIGHTING
TUSSUCK*	TUTTIES	TWANKAY	TWEEZER*	TWILIGHTS
TUSSUCKS*	TUTTING	TWANKAYS	TWEEZERS	TWILIT
TUSSUR*	TUTTINGS	TWANKIES*	TWEEZES	TWILL
TUSSURS*	TUTTIS	TWANKS	TWEEZING	TWILLED

TWILLIES
TWILLING
TWILLINGS*
TWILLS
TWILLY
TWILT
TWILTED
TWILTING
TWILTS
TWIN
TWINBERRIES*
TWINBERRY*
TWINBORN*
TWINE
TWINED
TWINER
TWINERS
TWINES
TWINGE
TWINGED
TWINGEING*
TWINGES
TWINGING
TWINIER
TWINIEST
TWINIGHT*
TWINING
TWININGLY
TWININGS
TWINJET*
TWINJETS*
TWINK
TWINKED
TWINKING
TWINKLE
TWINKLED
TWINKLER
TWINKLERS
TWINKLES
TWINKLING
TWINKLINGS
TWINKLY*
TWINKS
TWINLING
TWINLINGS
TWINNED
TWINNING
TWINNINGS
TWINS
TWINSET
TWINSETS
TWINSHIP
TWINSHIPS
TWINTER
TWINTERS
TWINY
TWIRE
TWIRED
TWIRES
TWIRING
TWIRL
TWIRLED
TWIRLER
TWIRLERS

TWIRLIER
TWIRLIEST
TWIRLING
TWIRLS
TWIRLY
TWIRP
TWIRPS
TWISCAR
TWISCARS
TWIST
TWISTABLE
TWISTED
TWISTER
TWISTERS
TWISTIER
TWISTIEST
TWISTING
TWISTINGS
TWISTOR
TWISTORS
TWISTS
TWISTY
TWIT
TWITCH
TWITCHED
TWITCHER
TWITCHERS
TWITCHES
TWITCHIER
TWITCHIEST
TWITCHILY*
TWITCHING
TWITCHINGS
TWITCHY
TWITE
TWITES
TWITS
TWITTED
TWITTEN
TWITTENS
TWITTER
TWITTERED
TWITTERER
TWITTERERS
TWITTERING
TWITTERINGS
TWITTERS
TWITTERY
TWITTING
TWITTINGS
TWIXT*
TWIZZLE
TWIZZLED
TWIZZLES
TWIZZLING
TWO
TWOCCER
TWOCCERS
TWOCCING
TWOCCINGS
TWOER
TWOERS
TWOFER*
TWOFERS*

TWOFOLD
TWOFOLDS*
TWONESS
TWONESSES
TWOPENCE
TWOPENCES
TWOPENNIES
TWOPENNY
TWOS
TWOSEATER
TWOSEATERS
TWOSOME
TWOSOMES
TWOSTROKE
TWP
TWYER
TWYERE
TWYERES
TWYERS
TWYFOLD
TWYFORKED
TWYFORMED
TYCHISM
TYCHISMS
TYCOON
TYCOONATE
TYCOONATES
TYCOONERIES
TYCOONERY
TYCOONS
TYDE
TYE
TYED
TYEE*
TYEES*
TYEING
TYER*
TYERS*
TYES
TYG
TYGS
TYING
TYKE
TYKES
TYKISH
TYLECTOMIES
TYLECTOMY
TYLER
TYLERS
TYLOPOD
TYLOPODS
TYLOSES
TYLOSIN*
TYLOSINS*
TYLOSIS
TYLOTE
TYLOTES
TYMBAL
TYMBALS
TYMP
TYMPAN
TYMPANA
TYMPANAL
TYMPANI

TYMPANIC
TYMPANICS
TYMPANIES
TYMPANIST
TYMPANISTS
TYMPANO
TYMPANS
TYMPANUM
TYMPANUMS*
TYMPANY
TYMPS
TYND
TYNDE
TYNE
TYNED
TYNES
TYNING
TYPABLE*
TYPAL
TYPE
TYPEABLE*
TYPEBAR*
TYPEBARS*
TYPECASE*
TYPECASES*
TYPECAST
TYPECASTING
TYPECASTS
TYPED
TYPEFACE*
TYPEFACES*
TYPES
TYPESET
TYPESETS*
TYPESETTING*
TYPESTYLE*
TYPESTYLES*
TYPEWRITE
TYPEWRITES
TYPEWRITING
TYPEWRITINGS
TYPEWRITTEN
TYPEWROTE
TYPEY*
TYPHLITIC
TYPHLITIS
TYPHLITISES
TYPHOID
TYPHOIDAL
TYPHOIDS
TYPHON
TYPHONIAN
TYPHONIC
TYPHONS
TYPHOON
TYPHOONS
TYPHOSE*
TYPHOUS
TYPHUS
TYPHUSES
TYPIC
TYPICAL
TYPICALLY
TYPIER*

TYPIEST*
TYPIFIED
TYPIFIER
TYPIFIERS
TYPIFIES
TYPIFY
TYPIFYING
TYPING
TYPINGS
TYPIST
TYPISTS
TYPO
TYPOGRAPH*
TYPOGRAPHED*
TYPOGRAPHING*
TYPOGRAPHS*
TYPOLOGIES
TYPOLOGY
TYPOMANIA
TYPOMANIAS
TYPOS
TYPP*
TYPPS*
TYPTO
TYPTOED
TYPTOING
TYPTOS
TYPY*
TYRAMINE
TYRAMINES
TYRAN
TYRANED
TYRANING
TYRANNE
TYRANNED
TYRANNES
TYRANNESS
TYRANNESSES
TYRANNIC
TYRANNIES
TYRANNING
TYRANNIS
TYRANNISE
TYRANNISED
TYRANNISES
TYRANNISING
TYRANNIZE
TYRANNIZED
TYRANNIZES
TYRANNIZING
TYRANNOUS
TYRANNY
TYRANS
TYRANT
TYRANTED
TYRANTING
TYRANTS
TYRE
TYRED
TYRELESS
TYRES
TYRING*
TYRO
TYROCIDIN*

Words marked with an asterisk are from OTCWL

TYROCIDINS*   TYTHE   TZAR   TZARISTS*   TZIGANE*
TYROES   TYTHED   TZARDOM*   TZARITZA*   TZIGANES*
TYRONES   TYTHES   TZARDOMS*   TZARITZAS*   TZIGANIES
TYRONIC*   TYTHING   TZAREVNA*   TZARS   TZIGANY
TYROS   TZADDIK   TZAREVNAS*   TZATZIKI   TZIMMES
TYROSINE   TZADDIKIM   TZARINA*   TZATZIKIS   TZITZIS*
TYROSINES   TZADDIKS   TZARINAS*   TZETSE   TZITZIT*
TYSTIE   TZADDIQ   TZARISM*   TZETSES   TZITZITH*
TYSTIES   TZADDIQIM   TZARISMS*   TZETZE*   TZURIS*
TYTE   TZADDIQS   TZARIST*   TZETZES*

U

UAKARI
UAKARIS
UBEROUS
UBERTIES
UBERTY
UBIETIES
UBIETY
UBIQUE
UBIQUITIES
UBIQUITY
UCKERS
UDAL
UDALLER
UDALLERS
UDALS
UDDER
UDDERED
UDDERFUL
UDDERLESS
UDDERS
UDO
UDOMETER
UDOMETERS
UDOMETRIC
UDOMETRIES*
UDOMETRY*
UDOS
UDS
UEY
UEYS
UFO
UFOLOGIES
UFOLOGIST
UFOLOGISTS
UFOLOGY
UFOS
UG
UGGED
UGGING
UGH
UGHS
UGLIED
UGLIER
UGLIES
UGLIEST
UGLIFIED
UGLIFIER*
UGLIFIERS*
UGLIFIES
UGLIFY
UGLIFYING
UGLILY
UGLINESS
UGLINESSES
UGLY

UGLYING
UGS
UGSOME
UH*
UHLAN
UHLANS
UHURU
UHURUS
UINTAHITE
UINTAHITES
UINTAITE
UINTAITES
UITLANDER
UITLANDERS
UJAMAA
UJAMAAS
UKASE
UKASES
UKE
UKELELE
UKELELES
UKES
UKULELE
UKULELES
ULAMA*
ULAMAS*
ULAN*
ULANS*
ULCER
ULCERATE
ULCERATED
ULCERATES
ULCERATING
ULCERED
ULCERING
ULCEROUS
ULCERS
ULE
ULEMA
ULEMAS
ULES
ULEX
ULEXES
ULEXITE*
ULEXITES*
ULICHON
ULICHONS
ULICON
ULICONS
ULIGINOSE
ULIGINOUS
ULIKON
ULIKONS
ULITIS
ULITISES

ULLAGE
ULLAGED
ULLAGES
ULLAGING
ULLING
ULLINGS
ULMACEOUS
ULMIN
ULMINS
ULNA
ULNAD*
ULNAE
ULNAR
ULNARE
ULNARIA
ULNAS*
ULOSES
ULOSIS
ULOTRICHIES
ULOTRICHY
ULPAN*
ULPANIM*
ULSTER
ULSTERED
ULSTERS
ULTERIOR
ULTIMA
ULTIMACIES
ULTIMACY
ULTIMAS
ULTIMATA
ULTIMATE
ULTIMATED*
ULTIMATES
ULTIMATING*
ULTIMATUM
ULTIMATUMS*
ULTIMO
ULTION
ULTIONS
ULTRA
ULTRACHIC*
ULTRACOLD*
ULTRACOOL*
ULTRADRY*
ULTRAFAST*
ULTRAFINE*
ULTRAHEAT*
ULTRAHEATED*
ULTRAHEATING*
ULTRAHEATS*
ULTRAHIGH*
ULTRAHIP*
ULTRAHOT*
ULTRAISM

ULTRAISMS
ULTRAIST
ULTRAISTS
ULTRALEFT*
ULTRALOW*
ULTRAPURE*
ULTRARARE*
ULTRARED
ULTRAREDS*
ULTRARICH*
ULTRAS
ULTRASAFE*
ULTRASLOW*
ULTRASOFT*
ULTRATHIN*
ULTRAWIDE*
ULU*
ULULANT
ULULATE
ULULATED
ULULATES
ULULATING
ULULATION
ULULATIONS
ULUS*
ULVA
ULVAS
ULYIE
ULYIES
ULZIE
ULZIES
UM
UMANGITE*
UMANGITES*
UMBEL
UMBELED*
UMBELLAR
UMBELLATE
UMBELLED*
UMBELLET*
UMBELLETS*
UMBELLULE
UMBELLULES
UMBELS
UMBER
UMBERED
UMBERING
UMBERS
UMBERY
UMBILICAL
UMBILICALS*
UMBILICI
UMBILICUS
UMBILICUSES
UMBLES

UMBO
UMBONAL
UMBONATE
UMBONES
UMBONIC*
UMBOS
UMBRA
UMBRACULA
UMBRAE
UMBRAGE
UMBRAGED
UMBRAGES
UMBRAGING
UMBRAL
UMBRAS
UMBRATED
UMBRATIC
UMBRATILE
UMBRE
UMBREL
UMBRELLA
UMBRELLAED*
UMBRELLAING*
UMBRELLAS
UMBRELLO
UMBRELLOES
UMBRELLOS
UMBRELS
UMBRERE
UMBRERES
UMBRES
UMBRETTE
UMBRETTES
UMBRIERE
UMBRIERES
UMBRIL
UMBRILS
UMBROSE
UMBROUS
UMIAC*
UMIACK*
UMIACKS*
UMIACS*
UMIAK
UMIAKS
UMIAQ*
UMIAQS*
UMLAUT
UMLAUTED
UMLAUTING
UMLAUTS
UMM*
UMP*
UMPED*
UMPH

Words marked with an asterisk are from OTCWL

UMPING*	UNANCHORED	UNBANDAGING*	UNBELT	UNBLOODY
UMPIRAGE	UNANCHORING	UNBANDED	UNBELTED	UNBLOTTED
UMPIRAGES	UNANCHORS	UNBANKED	UNBELTING	UNBLOWED
UMPIRE	UNANELED	UNBANNED*	UNBELTS	UNBLOWN
UMPIRED	UNANIMITIES	UNBANNING*	UNBEMUSED*	UNBLUNTED
UMPIRES	UNANIMITY	UNBANS*	UNBEND	UNBODIED
UMPIRING	UNANIMOUS	UNBAPTISE	UNBENDED	UNBODING
UMPS*	UNANXIOUS	UNBAPTISED	UNBENDING	UNBOLT
UMPTEEN	UNAPPAREL	UNBAPTISES	UNBENDINGS	UNBOLTED
UMPTEENTH	UNAPPARELLED	UNBAPTISING	UNBENDS	UNBOLTING
UMPTIETH	UNAPPARELLING	UNBAPTIZE	UNBENIGN	UNBOLTS
UMPTY	UNAPPARELS	UNBAPTIZED	UNBENT	UNBONE
UMQUHILE	UNAPPLIED	UNBAPTIZES	UNBEREFT	UNBONED
UMTEENTH*	UNAPT	UNBAPTIZING	UNBERUFEN	UNBONES
UMWHILE	UNAPTLY	UNBAR	UNBESEEM	UNBONING
UN	UNAPTNESS	UNBARBED	UNBESEEMED	UNBONNET
UNABASHED	UNAPTNESSES	UNBARE	UNBESEEMING	UNBONNETED
UNABATED	UNARGUED	UNBARED	UNBESEEMS	UNBONNETING
UNABLE	UNARISEN	UNBARES	UNBESPEAK	UNBONNETS
UNABRADED*	UNARM	UNBARING	UNBESPEAKING	UNBOOKED
UNABUSED*	UNARMED	UNBARK	UNBESPEAKS	UNBOOKISH
UNACCUSED	UNARMING	UNBARKED	UNBESPOKE	UNBOOT
UNACHING	UNARMORED*	UNBARKING	UNBESPOKEN	UNBOOTED
UNACTABLE	UNARMS	UNBARKS	UNBIAS	UNBOOTING
UNACTED	UNARTFUL	UNBARRED	UNBIASED	UNBOOTS
UNACTIVE	UNARY*	UNBARRING	UNBIASES	UNBORE
UNADAPTED	UNASHAMED	UNBARS	UNBIASING	UNBORN
UNADMIRED	UNASKED	UNBASED*	UNBIASSED	UNBORNE
UNADOPTED	UNASSAYED	UNBASHFUL	UNBIASSES	UNBOSOM
UNADORED	UNASSUMED	UNBATED	UNBIASSING	UNBOSOMED
UNADORNED	UNASSURED	UNBATHED	UNBID	UNBOSOMER
UNADULT*	UNATONED	UNBE	UNBIDDEN	UNBOSOMERS
UNADVISED	UNATTIRED	UNBEAR	UNBILLED*	UNBOSOMING
UNAFRAID	UNATTUNED*	UNBEARDED	UNBIND	UNBOSOMS
UNAGED*	UNAU	UNBEARED*	UNBINDING	UNBOUGHT
UNAGEING*	UNAUDITED*	UNBEARING	UNBINDINGS	UNBOUNCY*
UNAGILE*	UNAUS	UNBEARS	UNBINDS	UNBOUND
UNAGING*	UNAVENGED	UNBEATEN	UNBISHOP	UNBOUNDED
UNAI*	UNAVERAGE*	UNBED	UNBISHOPED	UNBOWED
UNAIDABLE	UNAVOIDED	UNBEDDED	UNBISHOPING	UNBOX
UNAIDED	UNAVOWED	UNBEDDING	UNBISHOPS	UNBOXED
UNAIMED	UNAWAKED*	UNBEDS	UNBITT	UNBOXES
UNAIRED	UNAWARDED*	UNBEEN	UNBITTED	UNBOXING
UNAIS*	UNAWARE	UNBEGET	UNBITTEN*	UNBRACE
UNAKIN*	UNAWARELY*	UNBEGETS	UNBITTER*	UNBRACED
UNAKING	UNAWARES	UNBEGETTING	UNBITTING	UNBRACES
UNAKITE*	UNAWED	UNBEGGED	UNBITTS	UNBRACING
UNAKITES*	UNAWESOME*	UNBEGOT	UNBLAMED	UNBRAID*
UNALIGNED	UNBACKED	UNBEGOTTEN	UNBLENDED	UNBRAIDED
UNALIKE	UNBAFFLED	UNBEGUILE	UNBLENT	UNBRAIDING*
UNALIST	UNBAG	UNBEGUILED	UNBLESS	UNBRAIDS*
UNALISTS	UNBAGGED	UNBEGUILES	UNBLESSED	UNBRAKE*
UNALIVE	UNBAGGING	UNBEGUILING	UNBLESSES	UNBRAKED*
UNALLAYED	UNBAGS	UNBEGUN	UNBLESSING	UNBRAKES*
UNALLIED	UNBAITED	UNBEING	UNBLEST	UNBRAKING*
UNALLOYED	UNBAKED	UNBEINGS	UNBLIND	UNBRANDED*
UNALTERED	UNBALANCE	UNBEKNOWN	UNBLINDED	UNBRASTE
UNAMAZED	UNBALANCED	UNBELIEF	UNBLINDING	UNBRED
UNAMENDED	UNBALANCES	UNBELIEFS	UNBLINDS	UNBREECH
UNAMERCED	UNBALANCING	UNBELIEVE	UNBLOCK	UNBREECHED
UNAMIABLE	UNBAN*	UNBELIEVED	UNBLOCKED	UNBREECHES
UNAMUSED	UNBANDAGE*	UNBELIEVES	UNBLOCKING	UNBREECHING
UNAMUSING	UNBANDAGED*	UNBELIEVING	UNBLOCKS	UNBRIDGED
UNANCHOR	UNBANDAGES*	UNBELOVED	UNBLOODED	UNBRIDLE

UNBRIDLED	UNCANDOURS	UNCHECKS	UNCLED	UNCOERCED*
UNBRIDLES	UNCANNIER	UNCHEERED	UNCLENCH	UNCOFFIN*
UNBRIDLING	UNCANNIEST	UNCHEWED	UNCLENCHED	UNCOFFINED*
UNBRIEFED*	UNCANNILY	UNCHIC*	UNCLENCHES	UNCOFFINING*
UNBRIGHT*	UNCANNY	UNCHICLY*	UNCLENCHING	UNCOFFINS*
UNBRIZZED	UNCANONIC	UNCHILD	UNCLES	UNCOIL
UNBROKE	UNCAP	UNCHILDED	UNCLESHIP	UNCOILED
UNBROKEN	UNCAPABLE	UNCHILDING	UNCLESHIPS	UNCOILING
UNBRUISED	UNCAPE	UNCHILDS	UNCLEW	UNCOILS
UNBRUSED	UNCAPED	UNCHOKE*	UNCLEWED	UNCOINED
UNBRUSHED	UNCAPES	UNCHOKED*	UNCLEWING	UNCOLORED*
UNBUCKLE	UNCAPING	UNCHOKES*	UNCLEWS	UNCOLT
UNBUCKLED	UNCAPPED	UNCHOKING*	UNCLICHED*	UNCOLTED
UNBUCKLES	UNCAPPING	UNCHOSEN	UNCLINCH*	UNCOLTING
UNBUCKLING	UNCAPS	UNCHRISOM	UNCLINCHED*	UNCOLTS
UNBUDDED	UNCAREFUL	UNCHURCH	UNCLINCHES*	UNCOMBED
UNBUDGING*	UNCARING	UNCHURCHED	UNCLINCHING*	UNCOMBINE
UNBUILD	UNCART	UNCHURCHES	UNCLING	UNCOMBINED
UNBUILDING	UNCARTED	UNCHURCHING	UNCLIP*	UNCOMBINES
UNBUILDS	UNCARTING	UNCI	UNCLIPPED	UNCOMBINING
UNBUILT	UNCARTS	UNCIA*	UNCLIPPING*	UNCOMELY
UNBULKY*	UNCASE	UNCIAE*	UNCLIPS*	UNCOMIC*
UNBUNDLE	UNCASED	UNCIAL	UNCLIPT	UNCOMMON
UNBUNDLED	UNCASES	UNCIALLY*	UNCLOAK	UNCOMMONER
UNBUNDLER	UNCASHED	UNCIALS	UNCLOAKED	UNCOMMONEST
UNBUNDLERS	UNCASING	UNCIFORM	UNCLOAKING	UNCONCERN
UNBUNDLES	UNCASKED*	UNCIFORMS*	UNCLOAKS	UNCONCERNS
UNBUNDLING	UNCATCHY*	UNCINAL*	UNCLOG	UNCONFINE
UNBUNDLINGS	UNCATE	UNCINATE	UNCLOGGED	UNCONFINED
UNBURDEN	UNCAUGHT	UNCINATED	UNCLOGGING	UNCONFINES
UNBURDENED	UNCAUSED	UNCINI	UNCLOGS	UNCONFINING
UNBURDENING	UNCE	UNCINUS	UNCLOSE	UNCONFORM
UNBURDENS	UNCEASING	UNCIPHER	UNCLOSED	UNCONFUSE*
UNBURIED	UNCERTAIN	UNCIPHERED	UNCLOSES	UNCONFUSED*
UNBURIES	UNCES	UNCIPHERING	UNCLOSING	UNCONFUSES*
UNBURNED	UNCESSANT	UNCIPHERS	UNCLOTHE	UNCONFUSING*
UNBURNT	UNCHAIN	UNCITED	UNCLOTHED	UNCONGEAL
UNBURROW	UNCHAINED	UNCIVIL	UNCLOTHES	UNCONGEALED
UNBURROWED	UNCHAINING	UNCIVILLY	UNCLOTHING	UNCONGEALING
UNBURROWING	UNCHAINS	UNCLAD	UNCLOUD	UNCONGEALS
UNBURROWS	UNCHANCIER	UNCLAIMED	UNCLOUDED	UNCOOKED
UNBURTHEN	UNCHANCIEST	UNCLAMP*	UNCLOUDING	UNCOOL
UNBURTHENED	UNCHANCY	UNCLAMPED*	UNCLOUDS	UNCOOLED*
UNBURTHENING	UNCHANGED	UNCLAMPING*	UNCLOUDY	UNCOPE
UNBURTHENS	UNCHARGE	UNCLAMPS*	UNCLOVEN	UNCOPED
UNBURY	UNCHARGED	UNCLARITIES*	UNCLOYED*	UNCOPES
UNBURYING	UNCHARGES	UNCLARITY*	UNCLOYING*	UNCOPING
UNBUSTED*	UNCHARGING	UNCLASP	UNCLUTCH	UNCORD
UNBUSY	UNCHARITIES	UNCLASPED	UNCLUTCHED	UNCORDED
UNBUTTON	UNCHARITY	UNCLASPING	UNCLUTCHES	UNCORDIAL
UNBUTTONED	UNCHARM	UNCLASPS	UNCLUTCHING	UNCORDING
UNBUTTONING	UNCHARMED	UNCLASSED	UNCLUTTER*	UNCORDS
UNBUTTONS	UNCHARMING	UNCLASSY	UNCLUTTERED*	UNCORK
UNCAGE	UNCHARNEL	UNCLE	UNCLUTTERING*	UNCORKED
UNCAGED	UNCHARNELLED	UNCLEAN	UNCLUTTERS*	UNCORKING
UNCAGES	UNCHARNELLING	UNCLEANED	UNCO	UNCORKS
UNCAGING	UNCHARNELS	UNCLEANER	UNCOATED	UNCORRUPT
UNCAKE*	UNCHARTED	UNCLEANEST	UNCOATING*	UNCOS
UNCAKED*	UNCHARY	UNCLEANLY	UNCOATINGS*	UNCOSTLY
UNCAKES*	UNCHASTE	UNCLEAR	UNCOCK	UNCOUNTED
UNCAKING*	UNCHECK	UNCLEARED	UNCOCKED	UNCOUPLE
UNCALLED	UNCHECKED	UNCLEARER	UNCOCKING	UNCOUPLED
UNCANDID	UNCHECKING	UNCLEAREST	UNCOCKS	UNCOUPLER*
UNCANDOUR		UNCLEARLY	UNCODED*	UNCOUPLERS*

UNCOUPLES	UNCURSED	UNDELIGHTS	UNDERCOOKS	UNDERGIRT
UNCOUPLING	UNCURSES	UNDELUDED	UNDERCOOL	UNDERGO
UNCOURTLY	UNCURSING	UNDENIED*	UNDERCOOLED	UNDERGOD*
UNCOUTH	UNCURTAIN	UNDER	UNDERCOOLING	UNDERGODS*
UNCOUTHER	UNCURTAINED	UNDERACT	UNDERCOOLS	UNDERGOES
UNCOUTHEST	UNCURTAINING	UNDERACTED	UNDERCUT	UNDERGOING
UNCOUTHLY	UNCURTAINS	UNDERACTING	UNDERCUTS	UNDERGONE
UNCOVER	UNCURVED	UNDERACTS	UNDERCUTTING	UNDERGOWN
UNCOVERED	UNCUS	UNDERAGE*	UNDERDECK	UNDERGOWNS
UNCOVERING	UNCUT	UNDERAGES*	UNDERDECKS	UNDERGRAD
UNCOVERS	UNCUTE*	UNDERARM	UNDERDID	UNDERGRADS
UNCOWL	UNCYNICAL*	UNDERARMS*	UNDERDO	UNDERHAND
UNCOWLED	UNDAM	UNDERATE*	UNDERDOER	UNDERHANDS
UNCOWLING	UNDAMAGED	UNDERBEAR	UNDERDOERS	UNDERHUNG
UNCOWLS	UNDAMMED	UNDERBEARING	UNDERDOES	UNDERJAW*
UNCOY*	UNDAMMING	UNDERBEARINGS	UNDERDOG	UNDERJAWS*
UNCOYNED	UNDAMNED	UNDERBEARS	UNDERDOGS	UNDERKEEP
UNCRACKED*	UNDAMPED	UNDERBID	UNDERDOING	UNDERKEEPING
UNCRATE	UNDAMS	UNDERBIDDING	UNDERDONE	UNDERKEEPS
UNCRATED	UNDARING*	UNDERBIDS	UNDERDRAW	UNDERKEPT
UNCRATES	UNDASHED	UNDERBIT	UNDERDRAWING	UNDERKING
UNCRATING	UNDATE	UNDERBITE	UNDERDRAWINGS	UNDERKINGS
UNCRAZY*	UNDATED	UNDERBITES	UNDERDRAWN	UNDERLAID
UNCREATE	UNDAUNTED	UNDERBITING	UNDERDRAWS	UNDERLAIN
UNCREATED	UNDAWNING	UNDERBITTEN	UNDERDREW	UNDERLAP
UNCREATES	UNDAZZLE	UNDERBODIES*	UNDEREAT*	UNDERLAPPED
UNCREATING	UNDAZZLED	UNDERBODY*	UNDEREATEN*	UNDERLAPPING
UNCROPPED	UNDAZZLES	UNDERBORE	UNDEREATING*	UNDERLAPS
UNCROSS	UNDAZZLING	UNDERBORNE	UNDEREATS*	UNDERLAY
UNCROSSED	UNDE	UNDERBOSS*	UNDERFED	UNDERLAYING
UNCROSSES	UNDEAD	UNDERBOSSES*	UNDERFEED	UNDERLAYS
UNCROSSING	UNDEAF	UNDERBOUGHT	UNDERFEEDING	UNDERLET
UNCROWDED	UNDEAFED	UNDERBRED	UNDERFEEDS	UNDERLETS
UNCROWN	UNDEAFING	UNDERBRIM*	UNDERFELT	UNDERLETTING
UNCROWNED	UNDEAFS	UNDERBRIMS*	UNDERFELTS	UNDERLETTINGS
UNCROWNING	UNDEALT	UNDERBUD*	UNDERFIRE	UNDERLIE
UNCROWNS	UNDEAR	UNDERBUDDED*	UNDERFIRED	UNDERLIES
UNCRUDDED	UNDEBASED	UNDERBUDDING*	UNDERFIRES	UNDERLINE
UNCRUMPLE	UNDECAYED	UNDERBUDS*	UNDERFIRING	UNDERLINED
UNCRUMPLED	UNDECEIVE	UNDERBUSH	UNDERFISH	UNDERLINES
UNCRUMPLES	UNDECEIVED	UNDERBUSHED	UNDERFISHED	UNDERLING
UNCRUMPLING	UNDECEIVES	UNDERBUSHES	UNDERFISHES	UNDERLINGS
UNCTION	UNDECEIVING	UNDERBUSHING	UNDERFISHING	UNDERLINING
UNCTIONS	UNDECENT	UNDERBUY	UNDERFLOW	UNDERLIP
UNCTUOUS	UNDECIDED	UNDERBUYING	UNDERFLOWS	UNDERLIPS
UNCUFF*	UNDECIDEDS*	UNDERBUYS	UNDERFONG	UNDERLIT*
UNCUFFED*	UNDECIMAL	UNDERCARD	UNDERFONGED	UNDERLYING
UNCUFFING*	UNDECK	UNDERCARDS	UNDERFONGING	UNDERMAN
UNCUFFS*	UNDECKED	UNDERCART	UNDERFONGS	UNDERMANNED
UNCULLED	UNDECKING	UNDERCARTS	UNDERFOOT	UNDERMANNING
UNCURABLE	UNDECKS	UNDERCAST	UNDERFOOTED	UNDERMANS
UNCURB*	UNDEE	UNDERCASTS	UNDERFOOTING	UNDERMEN
UNCURBED	UNDEEDED	UNDERCLAD	UNDERFOOTS	UNDERMINE
UNCURBING*	UNDEFACED	UNDERCLAY	UNDERFUND	UNDERMINED
UNCURBS*	UNDEFIDE	UNDERCLAYS	UNDERFUNDED	UNDERMINES
UNCURDLED	UNDEFIED	UNDERCLUB	UNDERFUNDING	UNDERMINING
UNCURED	UNDEFILED	UNDERCLUBBED	UNDERFUNDINGS	UNDERMININGS
UNCURIOUS	UNDEFINED	UNDERCLUBBING	UNDERFUNDS	UNDERMOST
UNCURL	UNDEIFIED	UNDERCLUBS	UNDERFUR	UNDERN
UNCURLED	UNDEIFIES	UNDERCOAT	UNDERFURS	UNDERNOTE
UNCURLING	UNDEIFY	UNDERCOATS	UNDERGIRD	UNDERNOTED
UNCURLS	UNDEIFYING	UNDERCOOK	UNDERGIRDED	UNDERNOTES
UNCURRENT	UNDELAYED	UNDERCOOKED	UNDERGIRDING	UNDERNOTING
UNCURSE	UNDELIGHT	UNDERCOOKING	UNDERGIRDS	UNDERNS

The Chambers Dictionary is the authority for many longer words; see Introduction, page ix

UNDERPAID	UNDERSIGNED	UNDIES	UNDUE	UNERASED*
UNDERPART	UNDERSIGNING	UNDIGHT	UNDUG	UNEROTIC*
UNDERPARTS	UNDERSIGNS	UNDIGHTING	UNDULANCIES	UNERRING
UNDERPASS	UNDERSIZE*	UNDIGHTS	UNDULANCY	UNESPIED
UNDERPASSES	UNDERSKIES	UNDIGNIFIED	UNDULANT	UNESSAYED
UNDERPAY	UNDERSKY	UNDIGNIFIES	UNDULAR*	UNESSENCE
UNDERPAYING	UNDERSOIL	UNDIGNIFY	UNDULATE	UNESSENCED
UNDERPAYS	UNDERSOILS	UNDIGNIFYING	UNDULATED	UNESSENCES
UNDERPEEP	UNDERSOLD	UNDILUTED	UNDULATES	UNESSENCING
UNDERPEEPED	UNDERSONG	UNDIMMED	UNDULATING	UNETH
UNDERPEEPING	UNDERSONGS	UNDINE	UNDULLED	UNETHICAL
UNDERPEEPS	UNDERSPIN*	UNDINES	UNDULOSE	UNEVADED*
UNDERPIN	UNDERSPINS*	UNDINISM	UNDULOUS	UNEVEN
UNDERPINNED	UNDERTAKE	UNDINISMS	UNDULY	UNEVENER
UNDERPINNING	UNDERTAKEN	UNDINTED	UNDUTEOUS	UNEVENEST
UNDERPINNINGS	UNDERTAKES	UNDIPPED	UNDUTIFUL	UNEVENLY
UNDERPINS	UNDERTAKING	UNDIVIDED	UNDY*	UNEXALTED
UNDERPLAY	UNDERTAKINGS	UNDIVINE	UNDYED	UNEXCITED
UNDERPLAYED	UNDERTANE	UNDO	UNDYING	UNEXCUSED*
UNDERPLAYING	UNDERTAX*	UNDOABLE*	UNDYINGLY	UNEXOTIC*
UNDERPLAYS	UNDERTAXED*	UNDOCILE*	UNDYNAMIC*	UNEXPERT*
UNDERPLOT	UNDERTAXES*	UNDOCK	UNEAGER*	UNEXPIRED
UNDERPLOTS	UNDERTAXING*	UNDOCKED	UNEARED	UNEXPOSED
UNDERPROP	UNDERTIME	UNDOCKING	UNEARNED	UNEXTINCT
UNDERPROPPED	UNDERTIMES	UNDOCKS	UNEARTH	UNEXTREME
UNDERPROPPING	UNDERTINT	UNDOER	UNEARTHED	UNEYED
UNDERPROPS	UNDERTINTS	UNDOERS	UNEARTHING	UNFABLED
UNDERRAN	UNDERTONE	UNDOES	UNEARTHLIER	UNFACT
UNDERRATE	UNDERTONES	UNDOING	UNEARTHLIEST	UNFACTS
UNDERRATED	UNDERTOOK	UNDOINGS	UNEARTHLY	UNFADABLE
UNDERRATES	UNDERTOW	UNDONE	UNEARTHS	UNFADED
UNDERRATING	UNDERTOWS	UNDOOMED	UNEASE	UNFADING
UNDERRUN	UNDERUSE	UNDOTTED*	UNEASES	UNFAILING
UNDERRUNNING	UNDERUSED	UNDOUBLE	UNEASIER	UNFAIR
UNDERRUNNINGS	UNDERUSES	UNDOUBLED	UNEASIEST	UNFAIRED
UNDERRUNS	UNDERUSING	UNDOUBLES	UNEASILY	UNFAIRER
UNDERSAID	UNDERVEST	UNDOUBLING	UNEASY	UNFAIREST
UNDERSAY	UNDERVESTS	UNDOUBTED	UNEATABLE	UNFAIRING
UNDERSAYE	UNDERWAY	UNDRAINED	UNEATEN	UNFAIRLY
UNDERSAYES	UNDERWEAR	UNDRAPE*	UNEATH	UNFAIRS
UNDERSAYING	UNDERWEARS	UNDRAPED	UNEATHES	UNFAITH
UNDERSAYS	UNDERWENT	UNDRAPES*	UNEDGE	UNFAITHS
UNDERSEA	UNDERWING	UNDRAPING*	UNEDGED	UNFAKED*
UNDERSEAL	UNDERWINGS	UNDRAW	UNEDGES	UNFALLEN
UNDERSEALED	UNDERWIT	UNDRAWING	UNEDGING	UNFAMED
UNDERSEALING	UNDERWITS	UNDRAWN	UNEDIBLE*	UNFAMOUS*
UNDERSEALINGS	UNDERWOOD	UNDRAWS	UNEDITED	UNFANCY*
UNDERSEALS	UNDERWOODS	UNDREADED	UNEFFACED	UNFANNED
UNDERSEAS*	UNDERWOOL*	UNDREAMED	UNELATED	UNFASTEN
UNDERSELF	UNDERWOOLS*	UNDREAMT	UNELECTED	UNFASTENED
UNDERSELL	UNDERWORK	UNDRESS	UNEMPTIED	UNFASTENING
UNDERSELLING	UNDERWORKED	UNDRESSED	UNENDED*	UNFASTENS
UNDERSELLS	UNDERWORKING	UNDRESSES	UNENDING	UNFAULTY
UNDERSELVES	UNDERWORKS	UNDRESSING	UNENDOWED	UNFAZED
UNDERSET	UNDERWROUGHT	UNDRESSINGS	UNENGAGED	UNFEARED
UNDERSETS	UNDESERT	UNDREST*	UNENTERED	UNFEARFUL
UNDERSETTING	UNDESERTS	UNDREW	UNENVIED	UNFEARING
UNDERSHOOT*	UNDESERVE	UNDRIED	UNENVIOUS	UNFED
UNDERSHOOTING*	UNDESERVED	UNDRILLED	UNENVYING	UNFEED
UNDERSHOOTS*	UNDESERVES	UNDRIVEN	UNEQUABLE	UNFEELING
UNDERSHOT	UNDESERVING	UNDROSSY	UNEQUAL	UNFEIGNED
UNDERSIDE	UNDESIRED	UNDROWNED	UNEQUALED*	UNFELLED
UNDERSIDES	UNDEVOUT	UNDRUNK	UNEQUALLY	UNFELT
UNDERSIGN	UNDID	UNDUBBED	UNEQUALS	UNFENCE*

Words marked with an asterisk are from OTCWL

UNFENCED	UNFOOLS	UNGAINFUL	UNGOWNED	UNHANDY
UNFENCES*	UNFOOTED	UNGAINLIER	UNGOWNING	UNHANG
UNFENCING*	UNFORBID	UNGAINLIEST	UNGOWNS	UNHANGED
UNFERTILE*	UNFORCED	UNGAINLY	UNGRACED	UNHANGING
UNFETTER	UNFORGED	UNGALLANT	UNGRADED	UNHANGS
UNFETTERED	UNFORGOT	UNGALLED	UNGRASSED	UNHAPPIED
UNFETTERING	UNFORKED*	UNGARBLED	UNGRAVELY	UNHAPPIER
UNFETTERS	UNFORM	UNGAUGED	UNGRAZED	UNHAPPIES
UNFEUDAL	UNFORMAL	UNGEAR	UNGREEDY*	UNHAPPIEST
UNFEUED	UNFORMED	UNGEARED	UNGROOMED	UNHAPPILY
UNFIGURED	UNFORMING	UNGEARING	UNGROUND	UNHAPPY
UNFILDE	UNFORMS	UNGEARS	UNGROUPED*	UNHAPPYING
UNFILED	UNFORTUNE	UNGENIAL	UNGROWN	UNHARBOUR
UNFILIAL	UNFORTUNES	UNGENTEEL	UNGRUDGED	UNHARBOURED
UNFILLED	UNFOUGHT	UNGENTLE	UNGUAL	UNHARBOURING
UNFILMED	UNFOUND	UNGENTLY	UNGUARD	UNHARBOURS
UNFINE	UNFOUNDED	UNGENUINE	UNGUARDED	UNHARDY
UNFIRED	UNFRAMED	UNGERMANE	UNGUARDING	UNHARMED
UNFIRM	UNFRANKED	UNGET	UNGUARDS	UNHARMFUL
UNFISHED	UNFRAUGHT	UNGETS	UNGUENT	UNHARMING
UNFIT	UNFRAUGHTED	UNGETTING	UNGUENTA*	UNHARNESS
UNFITLY	UNFRAUGHTING	UNGHOSTLY	UNGUENTS	UNHARNESSED
UNFITNESS	UNFRAUGHTS	UNGIFTED	UNGUENTUM*	UNHARNESSES
UNFITNESSES	UNFREE	UNGILD	UNGUES	UNHARNESSING
UNFITS	UNFREED	UNGILDED	UNGUESSED	UNHASP
UNFITTED	UNFREEDOM*	UNGILDING	UNGUIDED	UNHASPED
UNFITTER	UNFREEDOMS*	UNGILDS	UNGUIFORM	UNHASPING
UNFITTEST	UNFREEING*	UNGILT	UNGUILTY	UNHASPS
UNFITTING	UNFREEMAN	UNGIRD	UNGUIS	UNHASTING
UNFIX	UNFREEMEN	UNGIRDED	UNGULA	UNHASTY
UNFIXED	UNFREES*	UNGIRDING	UNGULAE	UNHAT
UNFIXES	UNFREEZE	UNGIRDS	UNGULAR*	UNHATCHED
UNFIXING	UNFREEZES	UNGIRT	UNGULATE	UNHATS
UNFIXITIES	UNFREEZING	UNGIRTH	UNGULATES	UNHATTED
UNFIXITY	UNFRETTED	UNGIRTHED	UNGULED	UNHATTING
UNFIXT*	UNFRIEND	UNGIRTHING	UNGUM	UNHATTINGS
UNFLASHY*	UNFRIENDS	UNGIRTHS	UNGUMMED	UNHAUNTED
UNFLAWED	UNFROCK	UNGIVING	UNGUMMING	UNHEAD
UNFLEDGED	UNFROCKED	UNGLAD	UNGUMS	UNHEADED
UNFLESH	UNFROCKING	UNGLAZED	UNGYVE	UNHEADING
UNFLESHED	UNFROCKS	UNGLOSSED	UNGYVED	UNHEADS
UNFLESHES	UNFROZE	UNGLOVE	UNGYVES	UNHEAL
UNFLESHING	UNFROZEN	UNGLOVED	UNGYVING	UNHEALED
UNFLESHLY	UNFUELLED	UNGLOVES	UNHABLE	UNHEALING
UNFLEXED*	UNFUMED	UNGLOVING	UNHACKED	UNHEALS
UNFLOORED	UNFUNDED	UNGLUE	UNHAILED	UNHEALTH
UNFLUSH	UNFUNNY	UNGLUED	UNHAIR	UNHEALTHIER
UNFLUSHED	UNFURL	UNGLUES	UNHAIRED	UNHEALTHIEST
UNFLUSHES	UNFURLED	UNGLUING	UNHAIRING	UNHEALTHS
UNFLUSHING	UNFURLING	UNGOD	UNHAIRS	UNHEALTHY
UNFLYABLE*	UNFURLS	UNGODDED	UNHALLOW	UNHEARD
UNFOCUSED	UNFURNISH	UNGODDING	UNHALLOWED	UNHEARSE
UNFOILED*	UNFURNISHED	UNGODLIER	UNHALLOWING	UNHEARSED
UNFOLD	UNFURNISHES	UNGODLIEST	UNHALLOWS	UNHEARSES
UNFOLDED	UNFURNISHING	UNGODLIKE	UNHALSED	UNHEARSING
UNFOLDER	UNFURRED	UNGODLILY	UNHALVED*	UNHEART
UNFOLDERS	UNFUSED*	UNGODLY	UNHAND	UNHEARTED
UNFOLDING	UNFUSSILY*	UNGODS	UNHANDED	UNHEARTING
UNFOLDINGS	UNFUSSY*	UNGORD	UNHANDIER*	UNHEARTS
UNFOLDS	UNGAG	UNGORED	UNHANDIEST*	UNHEATED
UNFOND*	UNGAGGED	UNGORGED	UNHANDILY	UNHEDGED
UNFOOL	UNGAGGING	UNGOT	UNHANDING	UNHEEDED
UNFOOLED	UNGAGS	UNGOTTEN	UNHANDLED	UNHEEDFUL
UNFOOLING	UNGAIN	UNGOWN	UNHANDS	UNHEEDILY

UNHEEDING	UNHOUSING	UNIONISED	UNITIZE	UNKINKING*
UNHEEDY	UNHUMAN	UNIONISES	UNITIZED	UNKINKS*
UNHELE	UNHUMBLED	UNIONISING	UNITIZER*	UNKISS
UNHELED	UNHUNG	UNIONISM	UNITIZERS*	UNKISSED
UNHELES	UNHUNTED	UNIONISMS	UNITIZES	UNKISSES
UNHELING	UNHURRIED	UNIONIST	UNITIZING	UNKISSING
UNHELM	UNHURT	UNIONISTS	UNITRUST*	UNKNELLED
UNHELMED	UNHURTFUL	UNIONIZE	UNITRUSTS*	UNKNIGHT
UNHELMING	UNHUSK	UNIONIZED	UNITS	UNKNIGHTED
UNHELMS	UNHUSKED	UNIONIZES	UNITY	UNKNIGHTING
UNHELPED	UNHUSKING	UNIONIZING	UNIVALENT	UNKNIGHTS
UNHELPFUL	UNHUSKS	UNIONS	UNIVALENTS	UNKNIT
UNHEPPEN	UNI	UNIPAROUS	UNIVALVE	UNKNITS
UNHEROIC	UNIALGAL*	UNIPED	UNIVALVES	UNKNITTED
UNHERST	UNIAXIAL	UNIPEDS	UNIVERSAL	UNKNITTING
UNHEWN	UNICITIES	UNIPLANAR	UNIVERSALS	UNKNOT
UNHIDDEN	UNICITY	UNIPOD	UNIVERSE	UNKNOTS
UNHINGE	UNICOLOR	UNIPODS	UNIVERSES	UNKNOTTED
UNHINGED	UNICOLOUR	UNIPOLAR	UNIVOCAL	UNKNOTTING
UNHINGES	UNICORN	UNIQUE	UNIVOCALS	UNKNOWING
UNHINGING	UNICORNS	UNIQUELY	UNJADED	UNKNOWINGS*
UNHIP	UNICYCLE	UNIQUER	UNJEALOUS	UNKNOWN
UNHIRED	UNICYCLES	UNIQUES	UNJOINED*	UNKNOWNS
UNHITCH	UNIDEAED*	UNIQUEST	UNJOINT	UNKOSHER*
UNHITCHED	UNIDEAL	UNIRAMOUS	UNJOINTED	UNLABELED*
UNHITCHES	UNIFACE*	UNIRONED	UNJOINTING	UNLACE
UNHITCHING	UNIFACES*	UNIS	UNJOINTS	UNLACED
UNHIVE	UNIFIABLE	UNISERIAL	UNJOYFUL	UNLACES
UNHIVED	UNIFIC	UNISEX	UNJOYOUS	UNLACING
UNHIVES	UNIFIED	UNISEXES*	UNJUDGED*	UNLADE
UNHIVING	UNIFIER	UNISEXUAL	UNJUST	UNLADED
UNHOARD	UNIFIERS	UNISON	UNJUSTER	UNLADEN
UNHOARDED	UNIFIES	UNISONAL	UNJUSTEST	UNLADES
UNHOARDING	UNIFILAR	UNISONANT	UNJUSTLY	UNLADING
UNHOARDS	UNIFORM	UNISONOUS	UNKED	UNLADINGS
UNHOLIER	UNIFORMED	UNISONS	UNKEMPT	UNLAID
UNHOLIEST	UNIFORMER*	UNISSUED*	UNKEND*	UNLASH
UNHOLILY	UNIFORMEST*	UNIT	UNKENNED	UNLASHED
UNHOLPEN	UNIFORMING	UNITAGE*	UNKENNEL	UNLASHES
UNHOLY	UNIFORMLY	UNITAGES*	UNKENNELED*	UNLASHING
UNHOMELY	UNIFORMS	UNITAL	UNKENNELING*	UNLAST
UNHONEST	UNIFY	UNITARD	UNKENNELLED	UNLASTE
UNHONORED*	UNIFYING	UNITARDS	UNKENNELLING	UNLATCH
UNHOOD	UNIFYINGS	UNITARIAN	UNKENNELS	UNLATCHED
UNHOODED	UNILINEAL*	UNITARIANS	UNKENT	UNLATCHES
UNHOODING	UNILINEAR*	UNITARILY*	UNKEPT	UNLATCHING
UNHOODS	UNILLUMED	UNITARY	UNKET	UNLAW
UNHOOK	UNILOBAR	UNITE	UNKID	UNLAWED
UNHOOKED	UNILOBED	UNITED	UNKIND	UNLAWFUL
UNHOOKING	UNIMBUED	UNITEDLY	UNKINDER	UNLAWING
UNHOOKS	UNIMPEDED	UNITER	UNKINDEST	UNLAWS
UNHOOP	UNIMPOSED	UNITERS	UNKINDLED	UNLAY
UNHOOPED	UNINCITED	UNITES	UNKINDLIER	UNLAYING
UNHOOPING	UNINDEXED	UNITIES	UNKINDLIEST	UNLAYS
UNHOOPS	UNINJURED	UNITING	UNKINDLY	UNLEAD
UNHOPED	UNINSTALL	UNITINGS	UNKING	UNLEADED
UNHOPEFUL	UNINSTALLED	UNITION	UNKINGED	UNLEADING
UNHORSE	UNINSTALLING	UNITIONS	UNKINGING	UNLEADS
UNHORSED	UNINSTALLS	UNITISE	UNKINGLIER	UNLEAL
UNHORSES	UNINSURED	UNITISED	UNKINGLIEST	UNLEARN
UNHORSING	UNINURED	UNITISES	UNKINGLY	UNLEARNED
UNHOUSE	UNINVITED	UNITISING	UNKINGS	UNLEARNING
UNHOUSED	UNION	UNITIVE	UNKINK*	UNLEARNS
UNHOUSES	UNIONISE	UNITIVELY	UNKINKED*	UNLEARNT

UNLEASED	UNLOCATED	UNMANTLING	UNMIXEDLY	UNNETHES
UNLEASH	UNLOCK	UNMANURED	UNMIXES*	UNNETTED
UNLEASHED	UNLOCKED	UNMAPPED*	UNMIXING*	UNNOBLE
UNLEASHES	UNLOCKING	UNMARD	UNMIXT*	UNNOBLED
UNLEASHING	UNLOCKS	UNMARKED	UNMOANED	UNNOBLES
UNLED	UNLOGICAL	UNMARRED	UNMODISH	UNNOBLING
UNLESS	UNLOOKED	UNMARRIED	UNMOLD*	UNNOISY*
UNLET	UNLOOSE	UNMARRIEDS*	UNMOLDED*	UNNOTED
UNLETHAL*	UNLOOSED	UNMARRIES	UNMOLDING*	UNNOTICED
UNLETTED*	UNLOOSEN	UNMARRY	UNMOLDS*	UNOBEYED
UNLEVEL*	UNLOOSENED	UNMARRYING	UNMOLTEN*	UNOBVIOUS
UNLEVELED*	UNLOOSENING	UNMASK	UNMONEYED	UNOFFERED
UNLEVELING*	UNLOOSENS	UNMASKED	UNMONIED	UNOFTEN
UNLEVELLED*	UNLOOSES	UNMASKER	UNMOOR	UNOILED
UNLEVELLING*	UNLOOSING	UNMASKERS	UNMOORED	UNOPEN*
UNLEVELS*	UNLOPPED	UNMASKING	UNMOORING	UNOPENED
UNLEVIED*	UNLORD	UNMASKINGS	UNMOORS	UNOPPOSED
UNLICH	UNLORDED	UNMASKS	UNMORAL	UNORDER
UNLICKED	UNLORDING	UNMATCHED	UNMOTIVED	UNORDERED
UNLID	UNLORDLY	UNMATED	UNMOULD	UNORDERING
UNLIDDED	UNLORDS	UNMATTED*	UNMOULDED	UNORDERLY
UNLIDDING	UNLOSABLE	UNMATURED	UNMOULDING	UNORDERS
UNLIDS	UNLOST	UNMEANING	UNMOULDS	UNORNATE*
UNLIGHTED	UNLOVABLE	UNMEANT	UNMOUNT	UNOWED
UNLIKABLE	UNLOVE	UNMEEK	UNMOUNTED	UNOWNED
UNLIKE	UNLOVED	UNMEET	UNMOUNTING	UNPACED
UNLIKELIER	UNLOVELIER	UNMEETLY	UNMOUNTS	UNPACK
UNLIKELIEST	UNLOVELIEST	UNMELLOW*	UNMOURNED	UNPACKED
UNLIKELY	UNLOVELY	UNMELTED	UNMOVABLE	UNPACKER
UNLIKES	UNLOVES	UNMENDED*	UNMOVABLY	UNPACKERS
UNLIMBER	UNLOVING	UNMERITED	UNMOVED	UNPACKING
UNLIMBERED	UNLUCKIER	UNMERRY*	UNMOVEDLY	UNPACKINGS
UNLIMBERING	UNLUCKIEST	UNMESH*	UNMOVING	UNPACKS
UNLIMBERS	UNLUCKILY	UNMESHED*	UNMOWN	UNPAGED
UNLIME	UNLUCKY	UNMESHES*	UNMUFFLE	UNPAID
UNLIMED	UNLYRICAL*	UNMESHING*	UNMUFFLED	UNPAINED
UNLIMES	UNMACHO*	UNMET	UNMUFFLES	UNPAINFUL
UNLIMING	UNMADE	UNMETED	UNMUFFLING	UNPAINT
UNLIMITED	UNMAILED	UNMEW	UNMUSICAL	UNPAINTED
UNLINE	UNMAIMED	UNMEWED	UNMUZZLE	UNPAINTING
UNLINEAL	UNMAKABLE	UNMEWING	UNMUZZLED	UNPAINTS
UNLINED	UNMAKE	UNMEWS	UNMUZZLES	UNPAIRED
UNLINES	UNMAKER*	UNMILKED	UNMUZZLING	UNPALSIED
UNLINING	UNMAKERS*	UNMILLED	UNMUZZLINGS	UNPANEL
UNLINK	UNMAKES	UNMINDED	UNNAIL	UNPANELLED
UNLINKED	UNMAKING	UNMINDFUL	UNNAILED	UNPANELLING
UNLINKING	UNMAKINGS	UNMINED*	UNNAILING	UNPANELS
UNLINKS	UNMAN	UNMINGLE*	UNNAILS	UNPANGED
UNLISTED	UNMANACLE	UNMINGLED	UNNAMABLE	UNPANNEL
UNLIT	UNMANACLED	UNMINGLES*	UNNAMED	UNPANNELLED
UNLIVABLE	UNMANACLES	UNMINGLING*	UNNANELD	UNPANNELLING
UNLIVE	UNMANACLING	UNMIRY	UNNATIVE	UNPANNELS
UNLIVED	UNMANAGED	UNMISSED	UNNATURAL	UNPAPER
UNLIVELY	UNMANFUL*	UNMITER*	UNNEATH	UNPAPERED
UNLIVES	UNMANLIER	UNMITERED*	UNNEEDED	UNPAPERING
UNLIVING	UNMANLIEST	UNMITERING*	UNNEEDFUL	UNPAPERS
UNLOAD	UNMANLIKE	UNMITERS*	UNNERVE	UNPARED
UNLOADED	UNMANLY	UNMITRE*	UNNERVED	UNPARTED*
UNLOADER	UNMANNED	UNMITRED*	UNNERVES	UNPARTIAL
UNLOADERS	UNMANNING	UNMITRES*	UNNERVING	UNPATHED
UNLOADING	UNMANS	UNMITRING*	UNNEST	UNPAVED
UNLOADINGS	UNMANTLE	UNMIX*	UNNESTED	UNPAY
UNLOADS	UNMANTLED	UNMIXABLE*	UNNESTING	UNPAYABLE
UNLOBED*	UNMANTLES	UNMIXED	UNNESTS	UNPAYING

The Chambers Dictionary is the authority for many longer words; see Introduction, page ix

UNPAYS	UNPLANNED	UNPREPARE	UNQUIETED	UNREEL
UNPEELED	UNPLANTED	UNPREPARED	UNQUIETER*	UNREELED
UNPEERED	UNPLAYED	UNPREPARES	UNQUIETEST*	UNREELER*
UNPEG	UNPLEASED	UNPREPARING	UNQUIETING	UNREELERS*
UNPEGGED	UNPLEATED	UNPRESSED	UNQUIETLY	UNREELING
UNPEGGING	UNPLEDGED	UNPRETTY	UNQUIETS	UNREELS
UNPEGS	UNPLIABLE	UNPRICED	UNQUOTE	UNREEVE
UNPEN	UNPLIABLY	UNPRIEST	UNQUOTED	UNREEVED
UNPENNED	UNPLIANT	UNPRIESTED	UNQUOTES	UNREEVES
UNPENNIED	UNPLOWED*	UNPRIESTING	UNQUOTING	UNREEVING
UNPENNING	UNPLUCKED	UNPRIESTS	UNRACED	UNREFINED
UNPENS	UNPLUG	UNPRIMED	UNRACKED	UNREFUTED
UNPENT	UNPLUGGED	UNPRINTED	UNRAISED	UNREIN
UNPEOPLE	UNPLUGGING	UNPRISON	UNRAKE	UNREINED
UNPEOPLED	UNPLUGS	UNPRISONED	UNRAKED	UNREINING
UNPEOPLES	UNPLUMB	UNPRISONING	UNRAKES	UNREINS
UNPEOPLING	UNPLUMBED	UNPRISONS	UNRAKING	UNRELATED
UNPERCH	UNPLUMBING	UNPRIZED	UNRANKED*	UNRELAXED
UNPERCHED	UNPLUMBS	UNPROBED*	UNRATED	UNREMOVED
UNPERCHES	UNPLUME	UNPROP	UNRAVEL	UNRENEWED
UNPERCHING	UNPLUMED	UNPROPER	UNRAVELED*	UNRENT
UNPERFECT	UNPLUMES	UNPROPPED	UNRAVELING*	UNRENTED*
UNPERPLEX	UNPLUMING	UNPROPPING	UNRAVELLED	UNREPAID
UNPERPLEXED	UNPOETIC	UNPROPS	UNRAVELLING	UNREPAIR
UNPERPLEXES	UNPOINTED	UNPROVED	UNRAVELLINGS	UNREPAIRS
UNPERPLEXING	UNPOISED	UNPROVEN	UNRAVELS	UNRESERVE
UNPERSON	UNPOISON	UNPROVIDE	UNRAZED*	UNRESERVES
UNPERSONED	UNPOISONED	UNPROVIDED	UNRAZORED	UNREST
UNPERSONING	UNPOISONING	UNPROVIDES	UNREACHED	UNRESTED*
UNPERSONS	UNPOISONS	UNPROVIDING	UNREAD	UNRESTFUL
UNPERVERT	UNPOLICED	UNPROVOKE	UNREADIER	UNRESTING
UNPERVERTED	UNPOLISH	UNPROVOKED	UNREADIEST	UNRESTS
UNPERVERTING	UNPOLISHED	UNPROVOKES	UNREADILY	UNREVISED
UNPERVERTS	UNPOLISHES	UNPROVOKING	UNREADY	UNREVOKED
UNPICK	UNPOLISHING	UNPRUNED	UNREAL	UNRHYMED
UNPICKED	UNPOLITE	UNPUCKER*	UNREALISE	UNRIBBED
UNPICKING	UNPOLITIC	UNPUCKERED*	UNREALISED	UNRID
UNPICKS	UNPOLLED	UNPUCKERING*	UNREALISES	UNRIDABLE
UNPIERCED	UNPOPE	UNPUCKERS*	UNREALISING	UNRIDDEN
UNPILE*	UNPOPED	UNPULLED	UNREALISM	UNRIDDLE
UNPILED*	UNPOPES	UNPURE*	UNREALISMS	UNRIDDLED
UNPILES*	UNPOPING	UNPURGED	UNREALITIES	UNRIDDLER
UNPILING*	UNPOPULAR	UNPURSE	UNREALITY	UNRIDDLERS
UNPILOTED	UNPOSED	UNPURSED	UNREALIZE	UNRIDDLES
UNPIN	UNPOSTED	UNPURSES	UNREALIZED	UNRIDDLING
UNPINKED	UNPOTABLE	UNPURSING	UNREALIZES	UNRIFLED
UNPINKT	UNPOTTED*	UNPURSUED	UNREALIZING	UNRIG
UNPINNED	UNPRAISE	UNPUZZLE*	UNREALLY	UNRIGGED
UNPINNING	UNPRAISED	UNPUZZLED*	UNREAPED	UNRIGGING
UNPINS	UNPRAISES	UNPUZZLES*	UNREASON	UNRIGHT
UNPITIED	UNPRAISING	UNPUZZLING*	UNREASONED*	UNRIGHTS
UNPITIFUL	UNPRAY	UNQUALIFIED	UNREASONING*	UNRIGS
UNPITYING	UNPRAYED	UNQUALIFIES	UNREASONS	UNRIMED
UNPLACE	UNPRAYING	UNQUALIFY	UNREAVE	UNRINGED
UNPLACED	UNPRAYS	UNQUALIFYING	UNREAVED	UNRINSED*
UNPLACES	UNPREACH	UNQUEEN	UNREAVES	UNRIP
UNPLACING	UNPREACHED	UNQUEENED	UNREAVING	UNRIPE
UNPLAGUED	UNPREACHES	UNQUEENING	UNREBATED	UNRIPELY*
UNPLAINED	UNPREACHING	UNQUEENLIER	UNREBUKED	UNRIPENED
UNPLAIT	UNPRECISE	UNQUEENLIEST	UNRECKED	UNRIPER
UNPLAITED	UNPREDICT	UNQUEENLY	UNRED	UNRIPEST
UNPLAITING	UNPREDICTED	UNQUEENS	UNREDREST	UNRIPPED
UNPLAITS	UNPREDICTING	UNQUELLED	UNREDUCED	UNRIPPING
UNPLANKED	UNPREDICTS	UNQUIET	UNREDY	UNRIPPINGS

UNRIPS	UNSADDLED	UNSEASONS	UNSHACKLES	UNSHRIVEN
UNRISEN	UNSADDLES	UNSEAT	UNSHACKLING	UNSHROUD
UNRIVALED*	UNSADDLING	UNSEATED	UNSHADED	UNSHROUDED
UNRIVEN	UNSAFE	UNSEATING	UNSHADOW	UNSHROUDING
UNRIVET	UNSAFELY	UNSEATS	UNSHADOWED	UNSHROUDS
UNRIVETED	UNSAFER	UNSECRET	UNSHADOWING	UNSHRUBD
UNRIVETING	UNSAFEST	UNSECULAR	UNSHADOWS	UNSHRUNK*
UNRIVETS	UNSAFETIES	UNSECURED	UNSHAKED	UNSHUNNED
UNROBE	UNSAFETY	UNSEDUCED	UNSHAKEN	UNSHUT
UNROBED	UNSAID	UNSEEABLE	UNSHALE	UNSHUTS
UNROBES	UNSAILED	UNSEEDED	UNSHALED	UNSHUTTER
UNROBING	UNSAINED	UNSEEING	UNSHALES	UNSHUTTERED
UNROLL	UNSAINT	UNSEEL	UNSHALING	UNSHUTTERING
UNROLLED	UNSAINTED	UNSEELED	UNSHAMED	UNSHUTTERS
UNROLLING	UNSAINTING	UNSEELING	UNSHAPE	UNSHUTTING
UNROLLS	UNSAINTLIER	UNSEELS	UNSHAPED	UNSICKER
UNROOF	UNSAINTLIEST	UNSEEMING	UNSHAPELIER	UNSICKLED
UNROOFED	UNSAINTLY	UNSEEMINGS	UNSHAPELIEST	UNSIFTED
UNROOFING	UNSAINTS	UNSEEMLIER	UNSHAPELY	UNSIGHING
UNROOFS	UNSALABLE	UNSEEMLIEST	UNSHAPEN	UNSIGHT
UNROOST	UNSALTED	UNSEEMLY	UNSHAPES	UNSIGHTED
UNROOSTED	UNSALUTED	UNSEEN	UNSHAPING	UNSIGHTING*
UNROOSTING	UNSAPPED	UNSEENS	UNSHARED	UNSIGHTLIER
UNROOSTS	UNSASHED	UNSEIZED	UNSHARP*	UNSIGHTLIEST
UNROOT	UNSATABLE	UNSELDOM	UNSHAVED	UNSIGHTLY
UNROOTED	UNSATED	UNSELF	UNSHAVEN	UNSIGHTS*
UNROOTING	UNSATIATE	UNSELFED	UNSHEATHE	UNSIGNED
UNROOTS	UNSATING	UNSELFING	UNSHEATHED	UNSILENT*
UNROPE	UNSAVED	UNSELFISH	UNSHEATHES	UNSINEW
UNROPED	UNSAVORY*	UNSELFS	UNSHEATHING	UNSINEWED
UNROPES	UNSAVOURY	UNSELL*	UNSHED	UNSINEWING
UNROPING	UNSAWED*	UNSELLING*	UNSHELL	UNSINEWS
UNROSINED	UNSAWN*	UNSELLS*	UNSHELLED	UNSINFUL*
UNROTTED	UNSAY	UNSELVES	UNSHELLING	UNSISTING
UNROTTEN	UNSAYABLE	UNSENSE	UNSHELLS	UNSIZABLE
UNROUGED	UNSAYING	UNSENSED	UNSHENT	UNSIZED
UNROUGH	UNSAYS	UNSENSES	UNSHEWN	UNSKILFUL
UNROUND	UNSCALE	UNSENSING	UNSHIFT*	UNSKILLED
UNROUNDED	UNSCALED	UNSENT	UNSHIFTED*	UNSKIMMED
UNROUNDING	UNSCALES	UNSERIOUS	UNSHIFTING*	UNSKINNED
UNROUNDS	UNSCALING	UNSERVED*	UNSHIFTS*	UNSLAIN
UNROUSED	UNSCANNED	UNSET	UNSHIP	UNSLAKED
UNROVE	UNSCARRED	UNSETS	UNSHIPPED	UNSLICED
UNROVEN*	UNSCARY	UNSETTING	UNSHIPPING	UNSLING
UNROYAL	UNSCATHED	UNSETTLE	UNSHIPS	UNSLINGING
UNROYALLY	UNSCENTED	UNSETTLED	UNSHOCKED	UNSLINGS
UNRUBBED	UNSCOURED	UNSETTLES	UNSHOD	UNSLUICE
UNRUDE	UNSCREW	UNSETTLING	UNSHOE	UNSLUICED
UNRUFFE	UNSCREWED	UNSETTLINGS	UNSHOED	UNSLUICES
UNRUFFLE	UNSCREWING	UNSEVERED	UNSHOEING	UNSLUICING
UNRUFFLED	UNSCREWS	UNSEW	UNSHOES	UNSLUNG
UNRUFFLES	UNSCYTHED	UNSEWED	UNSHOOT	UNSMART
UNRUFFLING	UNSEAL	UNSEWING	UNSHOOTED	UNSMILING
UNRULE	UNSEALED	UNSEWN	UNSHOOTING	UNSMITTEN
UNRULED	UNSEALING	UNSEWS	UNSHOOTS	UNSMOKED*
UNRULES	UNSEALS	UNSEX	UNSHORN	UNSMOOTH
UNRULIER	UNSEAM	UNSEXED	UNSHOT	UNSMOOTHED
UNRULIEST	UNSEAMED	UNSEXES	UNSHOUT	UNSMOOTHING
UNRULY	UNSEAMING	UNSEXING	UNSHOUTED	UNSMOOTHS
UNRUMPLED	UNSEAMS	UNSEXIST	UNSHOUTING	UNSMOTE
UNRUSHED*	UNSEARED*	UNSEXUAL	UNSHOUTS	UNSNAP
UNRUSTED*	UNSEASON	UNSEXY*	UNSHOWN	UNSNAPPED
UNS	UNSEASONED	UNSHACKLE	UNSHOWY*	UNSNAPPING
UNSADDLE	UNSEASONING	UNSHACKLED	UNSHRIVED	UNSNAPS

The Chambers Dictionary is the authority for many longer words; see Introduction, page ix

UNSNARL	UNSPENT	UNSTITCHES	UNSURER	UNTENABLE
UNSNARLED	UNSPHERE	UNSTITCHING	UNSUREST	UNTENANT
UNSNARLING	UNSPHERED	UNSTOCK	UNSUSPECT	UNTENANTED
UNSNARLS	UNSPHERES	UNSTOCKED	UNSWADDLE	UNTENANTING
UNSNECK	UNSPHERING	UNSTOCKING	UNSWADDLED	UNTENANTS
UNSNECKED	UNSPIDE	UNSTOCKS	UNSWADDLES	UNTENDED
UNSNECKING	UNSPIED	UNSTONED*	UNSWADDLING	UNTENDER
UNSNECKS	UNSPILLED	UNSTOP	UNSWATHE	UNTENTED
UNSNUFFED	UNSPILT	UNSTOPPED	UNSWATHED	UNTENTING
UNSOAKED*	UNSPLIT*	UNSTOPPER	UNSWATHES	UNTENTS
UNSOAPED	UNSPOILED	UNSTOPPERED	UNSWATHING	UNTENTY
UNSOBER*	UNSPOILT	UNSTOPPERING	UNSWAYED	UNTENURED*
UNSOCIAL	UNSPOKE	UNSTOPPERS	UNSWEAR	UNTESTED
UNSOCKET	UNSPOKEN	UNSTOPPING	UNSWEARING	UNTETHER
UNSOCKETED	UNSPOTTED	UNSTOPS	UNSWEARINGS	UNTETHERED
UNSOCKETING	UNSPRAYED*	UNSTOW	UNSWEARS	UNTETHERING
UNSOCKETS	UNSPRUNG	UNSTOWED	UNSWEET	UNTETHERS
UNSOD	UNSPUN	UNSTOWING	UNSWEPT	UNTHANKED
UNSODDEN	UNSQUARED	UNSTOWS	UNSWORE	UNTHATCH
UNSOFT	UNSTABLE	UNSTRAP	UNSWORN	UNTHATCHED
UNSOILED	UNSTABLER	UNSTRAPPED	UNTACK	UNTHATCHES
UNSOLACED	UNSTABLEST	UNSTRAPPING	UNTACKED	UNTHATCHING
UNSOLD	UNSTABLY*	UNSTRAPS	UNTACKING	UNTHAW
UNSOLDER	UNSTACK	UNSTRESS*	UNTACKLE	UNTHAWED
UNSOLDERED	UNSTACKED	UNSTRESSES*	UNTACKLED	UNTHAWING
UNSOLDERING	UNSTACKING	UNSTRING	UNTACKLES	UNTHAWS
UNSOLDERS	UNSTACKS	UNSTRINGED	UNTACKLING	UNTHINK
UNSOLEMN	UNSTAID	UNSTRINGING	UNTACKS	UNTHINKING
UNSOLID	UNSTAINED	UNSTRINGS	UNTACTFUL*	UNTHINKS
UNSOLIDLY	UNSTAMPED	UNSTRIP	UNTAGGED*	UNTHOUGHT
UNSOLVED	UNSTARCH	UNSTRIPED	UNTAILED	UNTHREAD
UNSONCY*	UNSTARCHED	UNSTRIPPED	UNTAINTED	UNTHREADED
UNSONSIE*	UNSTARCHES	UNSTRIPPING	UNTAKEN	UNTHREADING
UNSONSY	UNSTARCHING	UNSTRIPS	UNTAMABLE	UNTHREADS
UNSOOTE	UNSTATE	UNSTRUCK	UNTAMABLY	UNTHRIFT
UNSORTED	UNSTATED	UNSTRUNG	UNTAME	UNTHRIFTS
UNSOUGHT	UNSTATES	UNSTUCK	UNTAMED	UNTHRIFTY
UNSOUL	UNSTATING	UNSTUDIED	UNTAMES	UNTHRONE
UNSOULED	UNSTAYED	UNSTUFFED	UNTAMING	UNTHRONED
UNSOULING	UNSTAYING	UNSTUFFY	UNTANGLE	UNTHRONES
UNSOULS	UNSTEADIED	UNSTUFT	UNTANGLED	UNTHRONING
UNSOUND	UNSTEADIER	UNSTUNG*	UNTANGLES	UNTIDIED
UNSOUNDED	UNSTEADIES	UNSTYLISH*	UNTANGLING	UNTIDIER
UNSOUNDER	UNSTEADIEST	UNSUBDUED	UNTANNED	UNTIDIES
UNSOUNDEST	UNSTEADY	UNSUBJECT	UNTAPPED	UNTIDIEST
UNSOUNDLY	UNSTEADYING	UNSUBTLE	UNTARRED	UNTIDILY
UNSOURCED	UNSTEEL	UNSUBTLY*	UNTASTED	UNTIDY
UNSOURED	UNSTEELED	UNSUCCESS	UNTAUGHT	UNTIDYING
UNSOWED*	UNSTEELING	UNSUCCESSES	UNTAX	UNTIE
UNSOWN	UNSTEELS	UNSUCKED	UNTAXED	UNTIED
UNSPAR	UNSTEP	UNSUIT	UNTAXES	UNTIES
UNSPARED	UNSTEPPED	UNSUITED	UNTAXING	UNTIL
UNSPARING	UNSTEPPING	UNSUITING	UNTEACH	UNTILE
UNSPARRED	UNSTEPS	UNSUITS	UNTEACHES	UNTILED
UNSPARRING	UNSTERILE	UNSULLIED	UNTEACHING	UNTILES
UNSPARS	UNSTICK	UNSUMMED	UNTEAM	UNTILING
UNSPEAK	UNSTICKING	UNSUNG	UNTEAMED	UNTILLED
UNSPEAKING	UNSTICKS	UNSUNK*	UNTEAMING	UNTILTED*
UNSPEAKS	UNSTIFLED	UNSUNNED	UNTEAMS	UNTIMELIER
UNSPED	UNSTILLED	UNSUNNY	UNTEMPER	UNTIMELIEST
UNSPELL	UNSTINTED	UNSUPPLE	UNTEMPERED	UNTIMELY
UNSPELLED	UNSTIRRED	UNSURE	UNTEMPERING	UNTIMEOUS
UNSPELLING	UNSTITCH	UNSURED	UNTEMPERS	UNTIN
UNSPELLS	UNSTITCHED	UNSURELY*	UNTEMPTED	

Words marked with an asterisk are from OTCWL

UNTINGED	UNTUMBLED	UNVIEWED	UNWEBBED	UNWITTED
UNTINNED	UNTUNABLE	UNVIRTUE	UNWED	UNWITTILY
UNTINNING	UNTUNABLY	UNVIRTUES	UNWEDDED	UNWITTING
UNTINS	UNTUNE	UNVISITED	UNWEEDED	UNWITTY
UNTIPPED*	UNTUNED	UNVISOR	UNWEENED	UNWIVE
UNTIRABLE	UNTUNEFUL	UNVISORED	UNWEETING	UNWIVED
UNTIRED	UNTUNES	UNVISORING	UNWEIGHED	UNWIVES
UNTIRING	UNTUNING	UNVISORS	UNWEIGHT*	UNWIVING
UNTITLED	UNTURBID	UNVITAL	UNWEIGHTED*	UNWOMAN
UNTO	UNTURF	UNVIZARD	UNWEIGHTING*	UNWOMANED
UNTOILING	UNTURFED	UNVIZARDED	UNWEIGHTS*	UNWOMANING
UNTOLD	UNTURFING	UNVIZARDING	UNWELCOME	UNWOMANLIER
UNTOMB	UNTURFS	UNVIZARDS	UNWELDED*	UNWOMANLIEST
UNTOMBED	UNTURN	UNVOCAL	UNWELDY	UNWOMANLY
UNTOMBING	UNTURNED	UNVOICE	UNWELL	UNWOMANS
UNTOMBS	UNTURNING	UNVOICED	UNWEPT	UNWON
UNTONED	UNTURNS	UNVOICES	UNWET	UNWONT
UNTORN	UNTUTORED	UNVOICING	UNWETTED	UNWONTED
UNTOUCHED	UNTWINE	UNVOICINGS	UNWHIPPED	UNWOODED
UNTOWARD	UNTWINED	UNVULGAR	UNWHIPT	UNWOOED
UNTRACE	UNTWINES	UNWAGED	UNWHITE*	UNWORDED
UNTRACED	UNTWINING	UNWAKED	UNWIELDIER	UNWORK
UNTRACES	UNTWIST	UNWAKENED	UNWIELDIEST	UNWORKED
UNTRACING	UNTWISTED	UNWALLED	UNWIELDY	UNWORKING
UNTRACKED	UNTWISTING	UNWANING*	UNWIFELIER	UNWORKS
UNTRADED	UNTWISTINGS	UNWANTED	UNWIFELIEST	UNWORLDLIER
UNTRAINED	UNTWISTS	UNWARDED	UNWIFELY	UNWORLDLIEST
UNTREAD	UNTYING	UNWARE	UNWIGGED	UNWORLDLY
UNTREADING	UNTYINGS	UNWARELY	UNWILFUL	UNWORMED
UNTREADS	UNTYPABLE	UNWARES	UNWILL	UNWORN
UNTREATED	UNTYPICAL	UNWARIE	UNWILLED	UNWORRIED
UNTRENDY*	UNUNITED*	UNWARIER	UNWILLING	UNWORTH
UNTRESSED	UNURGED	UNWARIEST	UNWILLS	UNWORTHIER
UNTRIDE	UNUSABLE	UNWARILY	UNWIND	UNWORTHIES*
UNTRIED	UNUSABLY	UNWARLIKE	UNWINDER*	UNWORTHIEST
UNTRIM	UNUSED	UNWARMED	UNWINDERS*	UNWORTHS
UNTRIMMED	UNUSEFUL	UNWARNED	UNWINDING	UNWORTHY
UNTRIMMING	UNUSHERED	UNWARPED	UNWINDINGS	UNWOUND
UNTRIMS	UNUSUAL	UNWARY	UNWINDS	UNWOUNDED
UNTROD	UNUSUALLY	UNWASHED	UNWINGED	UNWOVE
UNTRODDEN	UNUTTERED	UNWASHEDS*	UNWINKING	UNWOVEN
UNTRUE	UNVAIL	UNWASHEN	UNWIPED	UNWRAP
UNTRUER	UNVAILE	UNWASTED	UNWIRE	UNWRAPPED
UNTRUEST	UNVAILED	UNWASTING	UNWIRED	UNWRAPPING
UNTRUISM	UNVAILES	UNWATCHED	UNWIRES	UNWRAPS
UNTRUISMS	UNVAILING	UNWATER	UNWIRING	UNWREAKED
UNTRULY	UNVAILS	UNWATERED	UNWISDOM	UNWREATHE
UNTRUSS	UNVALUED	UNWATERING	UNWISDOMS	UNWREATHED
UNTRUSSED	UNVARIED	UNWATERS	UNWISE	UNWREATHES
UNTRUSSER	UNVARYING	UNWATERY	UNWISELY	UNWREATHING
UNTRUSSERS	UNVEIL	UNWAXED*	UNWISER	UNWRINKLE
UNTRUSSES	UNVEILED	UNWAYED	UNWISEST	UNWRINKLED
UNTRUSSING	UNVEILER	UNWEAL	UNWISH	UNWRINKLES
UNTRUSSINGS	UNVEILERS	UNWEALS	UNWISHED	UNWRINKLING
UNTRUST	UNVEILING	UNWEANED	UNWISHES	UNWRITE
UNTRUSTS	UNVEILINGS	UNWEAPON	UNWISHFUL	UNWRITES
UNTRUSTY	UNVEILS	UNWEAPONED	UNWISHING	UNWRITING
UNTRUTH	UNVEINED*	UNWEAPONING	UNWIST	UNWRITTEN
UNTRUTHS	UNVENTED	UNWEAPONS	UNWIT	UNWROTE
UNTUCK	UNVERSED	UNWEARIED	UNWITCH	UNWROUGHT
UNTUCKED	UNVETTED	UNWEARY	UNWITCHED	UNWRUNG
UNTUCKING	UNVEXED	UNWEAVE	UNWITCHES	UNYEANED
UNTUCKS	UNVEXT*	UNWEAVES	UNWITCHING	UNYOKE
UNTUFTED*	UNVIABLE	UNWEAVING	UNWITS	UNYOKED

UNYOKES	UPBUILDS	UPDOVE*	UPGOING	UPHOORDED
UNYOKING	UPBUILT	UPDRAFT*	UPGOINGS	UPHOORDING
UNYOUNG*	UPBURNING	UPDRAFTS*	UPGONE	UPHOORDS
UNZEALOUS	UPBURST	UPDRAG	UPGRADE	UPHOVE*
UNZIP	UPBURSTING	UPDRAGGED	UPGRADED	UPHROE
UNZIPPED	UPBURSTS	UPDRAGGING	UPGRADER	UPHROES
UNZIPPING	UPBY	UPDRAGS	UPGRADERS	UPHUDDEN
UNZIPS	UPBYE	UPDRAW	UPGRADES	UPHUNG
UNZONED	UPCAST	UPDRAWING	UPGRADING	UPHURL
UP	UPCASTING	UPDRAWN	UPGREW	UPHURLED
UPADAISY	UPCASTS	UPDRAWS	UPGROW	UPHURLING
UPAITHRIC	UPCATCH	UPDREW	UPGROWING	UPHURLS
UPAS	UPCATCHES	UPDRIED*	UPGROWINGS	UPJET
UPASES	UPCATCHING	UPDRIES*	UPGROWN	UPJETS
UPBEAR	UPCAUGHT	UPDRY*	UPGROWS	UPJETTED
UPBEARER*	UPCHEARD	UPDRYING*	UPGROWTH	UPJETTING
UPBEARERS*	UPCHEER	UPEND	UPGROWTHS	UPKEEP
UPBEARING	UPCHEERED	UPENDED	UPGUSH	UPKEEPS
UPBEARS	UPCHEERING	UPENDING	UPGUSHED	UPKNIT
UPBEAT	UPCHEERS	UPENDS	UPGUSHES	UPKNITS
UPBEATS*	UPCHUCK	UPFIELD*	UPGUSHING	UPKNITTED
UPBIND	UPCHUCKED	UPFILL	UPHAND	UPKNITTING
UPBINDING	UPCHUCKING	UPFILLED	UPHANG	UPLAID
UPBINDS	UPCHUCKS	UPFILLING	UPHANGING	UPLAND
UPBLEW	UPCLIMB	UPFILLINGS	UPHANGS	UPLANDER
UPBLOW	UPCLIMBED	UPFILLS	UPHAUD	UPLANDERS
UPBLOWING	UPCLIMBING	UPFLING*	UPHAUDING	UPLANDISH
UPBLOWN	UPCLIMBS	UPFLINGING*	UPHAUDS	UPLANDS
UPBLOWS	UPCLOSE	UPFLINGS*	UPHEAP	UPLAY
UPBOIL	UPCLOSED	UPFLOW	UPHEAPED	UPLAYING
UPBOILED	UPCLOSES	UPFLOWED	UPHEAPING	UPLAYS
UPBOILING	UPCLOSING	UPFLOWING	UPHEAPINGS	UPLEAD
UPBOILS	UPCOAST	UPFLOWS	UPHEAPS	UPLEADING
UPBORE	UPCOIL	UPFLUNG	UPHEAVAL	UPLEADS
UPBORNE	UPCOILED	UPFOLD*	UPHEAVALS	UPLEAN
UPBOUND	UPCOILING	UPFOLDED*	UPHEAVE	UPLEANED
UPBOUNDEN	UPCOILS	UPFOLDING*	UPHEAVED	UPLEANING
UPBOW*	UPCOME	UPFOLDS*	UPHEAVER*	UPLEANS
UPBOWS*	UPCOMES	UPFOLLOW	UPHEAVERS*	UPLEANT
UPBRAID	UPCOMING	UPFOLLOWED	UPHEAVES	UPLEAP
UPBRAIDED	UPCURL	UPFOLLOWING	UPHEAVING	UPLEAPED
UPBRAIDER	UPCURLED	UPFOLLOWS	UPHELD	UPLEAPING
UPBRAIDERS	UPCURLING	UPFRONT	UPHILD	UPLEAPS
UPBRAIDING	UPCURLS	UPFURL	UPHILL	UPLEAPT
UPBRAIDINGS	UPCURVE*	UPFURLED	UPHILLS	UPLED
UPBRAIDS	UPCURVED	UPFURLING	UPHOARD	UPLIFT
UPBRAST	UPCURVES*	UPFURLS	UPHOARDED	UPLIFTED
UPBRAY	UPCURVING*	UPGANG	UPHOARDING	UPLIFTER
UPBRAYED	UPDART*	UPGANGS	UPHOARDS	UPLIFTERS
UPBRAYING	UPDARTED*	UPGATHER	UPHOIST	UPLIFTING
UPBRAYS	UPDARTING*	UPGATHERED	UPHOISTED	UPLIFTINGS
UPBREAK	UPDARTS*	UPGATHERING	UPHOISTING	UPLIFTS
UPBREAKING	UPDATE	UPGATHERS	UPHOISTS	UPLIGHT*
UPBREAKS	UPDATED	UPGAZE	UPHOLD	UPLIGHTED
UPBRING	UPDATER*	UPGAZED	UPHOLDER	UPLIGHTER
UPBRINGING	UPDATERS*	UPGAZES	UPHOLDERS	UPLIGHTERS
UPBRINGINGS	UPDATES	UPGAZING	UPHOLDING	UPLIGHTING*
UPBRINGS	UPDATING	UPGIRD*	UPHOLDINGS	UPLIGHTS*
UPBROKE	UPDIVE*	UPGIRDED*	UPHOLDS	UPLINK
UPBROKEN	UPDIVED*	UPGIRDING*	UPHOLSTER	UPLINKING
UPBROUGHT	UPDIVES*	UPGIRDS*	UPHOLSTERED	UPLINKINGS
UPBUILD	UPDIVING*	UPGIRT*	UPHOLSTERING	UPLINKS
UPBUILDING	UPDO*	UPGO	UPHOLSTERS	UPLIT*
UPBUILDINGS	UPDOS*	UPGOES	UPHOORD	UPLOAD

UPLOADED	UPREACHING*	UPSENDS	UPSTATERS*	UPTHUNDER
UPLOADING	UPREAR	UPSENT	UPSTATES*	UPTHUNDERED
UPLOADS	UPREARED	UPSET	UPSTAY	UPTHUNDERING
UPLOCK	UPREARING	UPSETS	UPSTAYED	UPTHUNDERS
UPLOCKED	UPREARS	UPSETTER	UPSTAYING	UPTICK*
UPLOCKING	UPREST	UPSETTERS	UPSTAYS	UPTICKS*
UPLOCKS	UPRESTS	UPSETTING	UPSTEP*	UPTIE
UPLOOK	UPRIGHT	UPSETTINGS	UPSTEPPED*	UPTIED
UPLOOKED	UPRIGHTED	UPSEY	UPSTEPPING*	UPTIES
UPLOOKING	UPRIGHTING	UPSEYS	UPSTEPS*	UPTIGHT
UPLOOKS	UPRIGHTLY	UPSHIFT*	UPSTIR*	UPTIGHTER
UPLYING	UPRIGHTS	UPSHIFTED*	UPSTIRRED*	UPTIGHTEST
UPMAKE	UPRISAL	UPSHIFTING*	UPSTIRRING*	UPTILT
UPMAKER	UPRISALS	UPSHIFTS*	UPSTIRS*	UPTILTED
UPMAKERS	UPRISE	UPSHOOT	UPSTOOD	UPTILTING
UPMAKES	UPRISEN	UPSHOOTING	UPSTREAM	UPTILTS
UPMAKING	UPRISER*	UPSHOOTS	UPSTREAMED	UPTIME*
UPMAKINGS	UPRISERS*	UPSHOT	UPSTREAMING	UPTIMES*
UPMANSHIP	UPRISES	UPSHOTS	UPSTREAMS	UPTOOK
UPMANSHIPS	UPRISING	UPSIDE	UPSTROKE	UPTORE
UPMARKET*	UPRISINGS	UPSIDES	UPSTROKES	UPTORN
UPMOST	UPRIST	UPSIES	UPSURGE	UPTOSS*
UPO*	UPRISTS	UPSILON	UPSURGED	UPTOSSED*
UPON	UPRIVER	UPSILONS	UPSURGES	UPTOSSES*
UPPED	UPRIVERS*	UPSITTING	UPSURGING	UPTOSSING*
UPPER	UPROAR	UPSITTINGS	UPSWARM	UPTOWN
UPPERCASE*	UPROARED	UPSOAR*	UPSWARMED	UPTOWNER
UPPERCASED*	UPROARING	UPSOARED*	UPSWARMING	UPTOWNERS
UPPERCASES*	UPROARS	UPSOARING*	UPSWARMS	UPTOWNS
UPPERCASING*	UPROLL	UPSOARS*	UPSWAY	UPTRAIN
UPPERCUT	UPROLLED	UPSPAKE	UPSWAYED	UPTRAINED
UPPERCUTS	UPROLLING	UPSPEAK	UPSWAYING	UPTRAINING
UPPERCUTTING*	UPROLLS	UPSPEAKING	UPSWAYS	UPTRAINS
UPPERMOST	UPROOT	UPSPEAKS	UPSWEEP	UPTREND
UPPERPART*	UPROOTAL	UPSPEAR	UPSWEEPING*	UPTRENDS
UPPERPARTS*	UPROOTALS	UPSPEARED	UPSWEEPS	UPTRILLED
UPPERS	UPROOTED	UPSPEARING	UPSWELL	UPTURN
UPPILE*	UPROOTER	UPSPEARS	UPSWELLED	UPTURNED
UPPILED	UPROOTERS	UPSPOKE	UPSWELLING	UPTURNING
UPPILES*	UPROOTING	UPSPOKEN	UPSWELLS	UPTURNINGS
UPPILING*	UPROOTINGS	UPSPRANG	UPSWEPT	UPTURNS
UPPING	UPROOTS	UPSPRING	UPSWING	UPTYING
UPPINGS	UPROSE	UPSPRINGING	UPSWINGING*	UPVALUE
UPPISH	UPROUSE	UPSPRINGS	UPSWINGS	UPVALUED
UPPISHLY	UPROUSED	UPSPRUNG	UPSWOLLEN	UPVALUES
UPPITY	UPROUSES	UPSTAGE	UPSWUNG*	UPVALUING
UPPROP*	UPROUSING	UPSTAGED	UPSY	UPWAFT
UPPROPPED*	UPRUN	UPSTAGES	UPTAK	UPWAFTED
UPPROPPING*	UPRUNNING	UPSTAGING	UPTAKE	UPWAFTING
UPPROPS*	UPRUNS	UPSTAIR	UPTAKEN	UPWAFTS
UPRAISE	UPRUSH	UPSTAIRS	UPTAKES	UPWARD
UPRAISED	UPRUSHED	UPSTAND	UPTAKING	UPWARDLY
UPRAISER*	UPRUSHES	UPSTANDING	UPTAKS	UPWARDS
UPRAISERS*	UPRUSHING	UPSTANDS	UPTEAR	UPWELL
UPRAISES	UPRYST	UPSTARE	UPTEARING	UPWELLED
UPRAISING	UPS	UPSTARED	UPTEARS	UPWELLING
UPRAN	UPSCALE	UPSTARES	UPTHREW	UPWELLINGS
UPRATE	UPSCALED*	UPSTARING	UPTHROW	UPWELLS
UPRATED	UPSCALES*	UPSTART	UPTHROWING	UPWENT
UPRATES	UPSCALING*	UPSTARTED	UPTHROWN	UPWHIRL
UPRATING	UPSEE	UPSTARTING	UPTHROWS	UPWHIRLED
UPREACH*	UPSEES	UPSTARTS	UPTHRUST	UPWHIRLING
UPREACHED*	UPSEND	UPSTATE	UPTHRUSTING	UPWHIRLS
UPREACHES*	UPSENDING	UPSTATER*	UPTHRUSTS	UPWIND

UPWINDING	URATE	URENAS	URINOUS	URSIFORM*
UPWINDS	URATES	URENT	URITE	URSINE
UPWOUND	URATIC*	UREOTELIC*	URITES	URSON
UPWRAP	URB*	URES	URMAN	URSONS
UPWRAPS	URBAN	URESES	URMANS	URTEXT
UPWROUGHT	URBANE	URESIS	URN	URTEXTS
UR	URBANELY	URETER	URNAL	URTICA
URACHI	URBANER	URETERAL	URNED	URTICANT
URACHUS	URBANEST	URETERIC	URNFIELD	URTICANTS*
URACHUSES	URBANISE	URETERS	URNFIELDS	URTICARIA
URACIL	URBANISED	URETHAN	URNFUL	URTICARIAS
URACILS	URBANISES	URETHANE	URNFULS	URTICAS
URAEI	URBANISING	URETHANES	URNING	URTICATE
URAEMIA	URBANISM*	URETHANS	URNINGS	URTICATED
URAEMIAS	URBANISMS*	URETHRA	URNLIKE*	URTICATES
URAEMIC	URBANIST*	URETHRAE	URNS	URTICATING
URAEUS	URBANISTS*	URETHRAL	UROCHORD	URUBU
URAEUSES	URBANITE	URETHRAS	UROCHORDS	URUBUS
URALI	URBANITES	URETIC	UROCHROME	URUS
URALIS	URBANITIES	URGE	UROCHROMES	URUSES
URALITE	URBANITY	URGED	URODELAN	URUSHIOL*
URALITES	URBANIZE	URGENCE	URODELANS	URUSHIOLS*
URALITIC	URBANIZED	URGENCES	URODELE	URVA
URALITISE	URBANIZES	URGENCIES	URODELES	URVAS
URALITISED	URBANIZING	URGENCY	URODELOUS	US
URALITISES	URBIA*	URGENT	UROGENOUS	USABILITIES
URALITISING	URBIAS*	URGENTLY	UROGRAPHIES	USABILITY
URALITIZE	URBS*	URGER	UROGRAPHY	USABLE
URALITIZED	URCEOLATE	URGERS	UROKINASE	USABLY
URALITIZES	URCEOLI	URGES	UROKINASES	USAGE
URALITIZING	URCEOLUS	URGING	UROLAGNIA	USAGER
URANIA*	URCEOLUSES	URGINGLY*	UROLAGNIAS	USAGERS
URANIAN	URCHIN	URGINGS	UROLITH	USAGES
URANIAS*	URCHINS	URIAL	UROLITHIC	USANCE
URANIC	URD	URIALS	UROLITHS	USANCES
URANIDE	URDE	URIC	UROLOGIC	USAUNCE*
URANIDES	URDEE	URICASE	UROLOGIES	USAUNCES*
URANIN	URDS	URICASES	UROLOGIST	USE
URANINITE	URDY	URIDINE	UROLOGISTS	USEABLE*
URANINITES	URE	URIDINES	UROLOGY	USEABLY*
URANINS	UREA	URINAL	UROMERE	USED
URANISCI	UREAL	URINALS	UROMERES	USEFUL
URANISCUS	UREAS	URINANT	UROPOD	USEFULLY
URANISM	UREASE*	URINARIES	UROPODAL*	USELESS
URANISMS	UREASES*	URINARY	UROPODS	USELESSLY
URANITE	UREDIA	URINATE	UROPYGIA	USER
URANITES	UREDIAL*	URINATED	UROPYGIAL	USERS
URANITIC	UREDINE	URINATES	UROPYGIUM	USES
URANIUM	UREDINES	URINATING	UROPYGIUMS	USHER
URANIUMS	UREDINIA	URINATION	UROSCOPIC	USHERED
URANOLOGIES	UREDINIAL	URINATIONS	UROSCOPIES	USHERESS
URANOLOGY	UREDINIUM	URINATIVE	UROSCOPY	USHERESSES
URANOUS	UREDINOUS	URINATOR	UROSES	USHERETTE
URANYL	UREDIUM	URINATORS	UROSIS	USHERETTES
URANYLIC	UREDO	URINE	UROSOME	USHERING
URANYLS	UREDOS*	URINED	UROSOMES	USHERINGS
URAO	UREDOSORI	URINEMIA*	UROSTEGE	USHERS
URAOS	UREIC	URINEMIAS*	UROSTEGES	USHERSHIP
URARE*	UREIDE	URINEMIC*	UROSTOMIES	USHERSHIPS
URARES*	UREIDES	URINES	UROSTOMY	USHING
URARI	UREMIA	URINING	UROSTYLE	USNEA
URARIS	UREMIAS	URINOLOGIES	UROSTYLES	USNEAS
URASE*	UREMIC	URINOLOGY	URSA*	USQUABAE*
URASES*	URENA	URINOSE	URSAE*	USQUABAES*

Words marked with an asterisk are from OTCWL

USQUE*
USQUEBAE*
USQUEBAES*
USQUES*
USTION
USTIONS
USTULATE*
USUAL
USUALLY
USUALNESS
USUALNESSES
USUALS
USUCAPION
USUCAPIONS
USUCAPT
USUCAPTED
USUCAPTING
USUCAPTS
USUFRUCT
USUFRUCTED
USUFRUCTING
USUFRUCTS
USURE
USURED
USURER
USURERS
USURES
USURESS
USURESSES

USURIES
USURING
USURIOUS
USUROUS
USURP
USURPED
USURPEDLY
USURPER
USURPERS
USURPING
USURPINGS
USURPS
USURY
USWARD
USWARDS
UT
UTA*
UTAS
UTASES
UTE
UTENSIL
UTENSILS
UTERI
UTERINE
UTERITIS
UTERITISES
UTEROTOMIES
UTEROTOMY
UTERUS

UTERUSES*
UTES
UTILE
UTILIDOR*
UTILIDORS*
UTILISE
UTILISED
UTILISER
UTILISERS
UTILISES
UTILISING
UTILITIES
UTILITY
UTILIZE
UTILIZED
UTILIZER
UTILIZERS
UTILIZES
UTILIZING
UTIS
UTISES
UTMOST
UTMOSTS
UTOPIA
UTOPIAN
UTOPIANS
UTOPIAS
UTOPIAST
UTOPIASTS

UTOPISM
UTOPISMS
UTOPIST
UTOPISTIC*
UTOPISTS
UTRICLE
UTRICLES
UTRICULAR
UTRICULI
UTRICULUS
UTS
UTTER
UTTERABLE
UTTERANCE
UTTERANCES
UTTERED
UTTERER
UTTERERS
UTTEREST
UTTERING
UTTERINGS
UTTERLESS
UTTERLY
UTTERMOST
UTTERMOSTS
UTTERNESS
UTTERNESSES
UTTERS
UTU

UTUS
UVA
UVAE
UVAROVITE
UVAROVITES
UVAS
UVEA
UVEAL
UVEAS
UVEITIC
UVEITIS
UVEITISES
UVEOUS
UVULA
UVULAE
UVULAR
UVULARLY
UVULARS*
UVULAS
UVULITIS
UVULITISES
UXORIAL
UXORIALLY
UXORICIDE
UXORICIDES
UXORIOUS

The Chambers Dictionary is the authority for many longer words; see Introduction, page ix

V

VAC
VACANCE
VACANCES
VACANCIES
VACANCY
VACANT
VACANTLY
VACATE
VACATED
VACATES
VACATING
VACATION
VACATIONED
VACATIONING
VACATIONS
VACATUR
VACATURS
VACCINA*
VACCINAL
VACCINAS*
VACCINATE
VACCINATED
VACCINATES
VACCINATING
VACCINE
VACCINEE*
VACCINEES*
VACCINES
VACCINIA
VACCINIAL
VACCINIAS
VACCINIUM
VACCINIUMS
VACHERIN
VACHERINS
VACILLANT
VACILLATE
VACILLATED
VACILLATES
VACILLATING
VACKED
VACKING
VACS
VACUA
VACUATE
VACUATED
VACUATES
VACUATING
VACUATION
VACUATIONS
VACUIST
VACUISTS
VACUITIES
VACUITY
VACUOLAR

VACUOLATE
VACUOLE
VACUOLES
VACUOUS
VACUOUSLY
VACUUM
VACUUMED
VACUUMING
VACUUMS
VADE
VADED
VADES
VADING
VADOSE
VAE
VAES
VAGABOND
VAGABONDED
VAGABONDING
VAGABONDS
VAGAL
VAGALLY*
VAGARIES
VAGARIOUS
VAGARISH
VAGARY
VAGI
VAGILE
VAGILITIES
VAGILITY
VAGINA
VAGINAE
VAGINAL
VAGINALLY
VAGINANT
VAGINAS
VAGINATE
VAGINATED
VAGINITIS
VAGINITISES
VAGINULA
VAGINULAE
VAGINULE
VAGINULES
VAGITUS
VAGITUSES
VAGOTOMIES*
VAGOTOMY*
VAGOTONIA*
VAGOTONIAS*
VAGOTONIC*
VAGRANCIES
VAGRANCY
VAGRANT
VAGRANTLY*

VAGRANTS
VAGROM
VAGUE
VAGUED
VAGUELY
VAGUENESS
VAGUENESSES
VAGUER
VAGUES
VAGUEST
VAGUING
VAGUS
VAHINE
VAHINES
VAIL
VAILED
VAILING
VAILS
VAIN
VAINER
VAINESSE
VAINESSES
VAINEST
VAINGLORIED
VAINGLORIES
VAINGLORY
VAINGLORYING
VAINLY
VAINNESS
VAINNESSES
VAIR
VAIRE
VAIRIER
VAIRIEST
VAIRS
VAIRY
VAIVODE
VAIVODES
VAKASS
VAKASSES
VAKEEL
VAKEELS
VAKIL
VAKILS
VALANCE
VALANCED
VALANCES
VALANCING*
VALE
VALENCE
VALENCES
VALENCIA*
VALENCIAS*
VALENCIES
VALENCY

VALENTINE
VALENTINES
VALERATE*
VALERATES*
VALERIAN
VALERIANS
VALERIC*
VALES
VALET
VALETA
VALETAS
VALETE
VALETED
VALETES
VALETING
VALETINGS
VALETS
VALGOID*
VALGOUS
VALGUS
VALGUSES
VALI
VALIANCE
VALIANCES
VALIANCIES
VALIANCY
VALIANT
VALIANTLY
VALIANTS
VALID
VALIDATE
VALIDATED
VALIDATES
VALIDATING
VALIDER
VALIDEST
VALIDITIES
VALIDITY
VALIDLY
VALIDNESS
VALIDNESSES
VALINE
VALINES
VALIS
VALISE
VALISES
VALKYR*
VALKYRIE*
VALKYRIES*
VALKYRS*
VALLAR
VALLARY
VALLATE*
VALLECULA
VALLECULAE

VALLEY
VALLEYS
VALLONIA
VALLONIAS
VALLUM
VALLUMS
VALONEA
VALONEAS
VALONIA
VALONIAS
VALOR
VALORISE
VALORISED
VALORISES
VALORISING
VALORIZE
VALORIZED
VALORIZES
VALORIZING
VALOROUS
VALORS
VALOUR
VALOURS
VALSE
VALSED
VALSES
VALSING
VALUABLE
VALUABLES
VALUABLY
VALUATE
VALUATED
VALUATES
VALUATING
VALUATION
VALUATIONS
VALUATOR
VALUATORS
VALUE
VALUED
VALUELESS
VALUER
VALUERS
VALUES
VALUING
VALUTA
VALUTAS
VALVAL
VALVAR
VALVASSOR
VALVASSORS
VALVATE
VALVE
VALVED
VALVELESS

VALVELET	VANDALIZE	VAPIDEST	VARES	VARIX
VALVELETS	VANDALIZED	VAPIDITIES	VAREUSE	VARLET
VALVES	VANDALIZES	VAPIDITY	VAREUSES	VARLETESS
VALVING	VANDALIZING	VAPIDLY	VARGUENO	VARLETESSES
VALVULA	VANDALS	VAPIDNESS	VARGUENOS	VARLETRIES
VALVULAE	VANDAS*	VAPIDNESSES	VARIA*	VARLETRY
VALVULAR	VANDYKE	VAPOR	VARIABLE	VARLETS
VALVULE	VANDYKED	VAPORABLE	VARIABLES	VARLETTO
VALVULES	VANDYKES	VAPORED	VARIABLY	VARLETTOS
VAMBRACE	VANDYKING	VAPORER*	VARIANCE	VARMENT
VAMBRACED	VANE	VAPORERS*	VARIANCES	VARMENTS
VAMBRACES	VANED	VAPORETTI	VARIANT	VARMINT
VAMOOSE	VANELESS	VAPORETTO	VARIANTS	VARMINTS
VAMOOSED	VANES	VAPORETTOS	VARIATE	VARNA
VAMOOSES	VANESSA	VAPORIFIC	VARIATED	VARNAS
VAMOOSING	VANESSAS	VAPORING	VARIATES	VARNISH
VAMOSE	VANG	VAPORINGS*	VARIATING	VARNISHED
VAMOSED	VANGS	VAPORISE	VARIATION	VARNISHER
VAMOSES	VANGUARD	VAPORISED	VARIATIONS	VARNISHERS
VAMOSING	VANGUARDS	VAPORISER	VARIATIVE	VARNISHES
VAMP	VANILLA	VAPORISERS	VARICELLA	VARNISHING
VAMPED	VANILLAS	VAPORISES	VARICELLAS	VARNISHINGS
VAMPER	VANILLIC*	VAPORISH*	VARICES	VARNISHY*
VAMPERS	VANILLIN	VAPORISING	VARICOSE	VAROOM*
VAMPING	VANILLINS	VAPORIZE	VARICOSED*	VAROOMED*
VAMPINGS	VANISH	VAPORIZED	VARIED	VAROOMING*
VAMPIRE	VANISHED	VAPORIZER	VARIEDLY	VAROOMS*
VAMPIRED	VANISHER	VAPORIZERS	VARIEGATE	VARROA
VAMPIRES	VANISHERS	VAPORIZES	VARIEGATED	VARROAS
VAMPIRIC	VANISHES	VAPORIZING	VARIEGATES	VARS*
VAMPIRING	VANISHING	VAPOROUS	VARIEGATING	VARSAL
VAMPIRISE	VANISHINGS	VAPORS	VARIER	VARSITIES
VAMPIRISED	VANITAS	VAPORWARE	VARIERS	VARSITY
VAMPIRISES	VANITASES	VAPORWARES	VARIES	VARTABED
VAMPIRISH*	VANITIED*	VAPORY*	VARIETAL	VARTABEDS
VAMPIRISING	VANITIES	VAPOUR	VARIETALS	VARUS
VAMPIRISM	VANITORIES	VAPOURED	VARIETIES	VARUSES
VAMPIRISMS	VANITORY	VAPOURER	VARIETY	VARVE
VAMPIRIZE	VANITY	VAPOURERS	VARIFOCAL	VARVED
VAMPIRIZED	VANMAN*	VAPOURING	VARIFOCALS	VARVEL
VAMPIRIZES	VANMEN*	VAPOURINGS	VARIFORM	VARVELLED
VAMPIRIZING	VANNED	VAPOURISH	VARIOLA	VARVELS
VAMPISH	VANNER	VAPOURS	VARIOLAR	VARVES
VAMPLATE	VANNERS	VAPOURY	VARIOLAS	VARY
VAMPLATES	VANNING	VAPULATE	VARIOLATE	VARYING
VAMPS	VANNINGS	VAPULATED	VARIOLATED	VARYINGLY*
VAN	VANPOOL*	VAPULATES	VARIOLATES	VARYINGS
VANADATE	VANPOOLS*	VAPULATING	VARIOLATING	VAS
VANADATES	VANQUISH	VAQUERO	VARIOLE	VASA
VANADIC	VANQUISHED	VAQUEROS	VARIOLES	VASAL
VANADIUM	VANQUISHES	VAR*	VARIOLITE	VASCULA
VANADIUMS	VANQUISHING	VARA	VARIOLITES	VASCULAR
VANADOUS	VANS	VARACTOR	VARIOLOID	VASCULUM
VANASPATI*	VANT	VARACTORS	VARIOLOIDS	VASCULUMS
VANASPATIS*	VANTAGE	VARAN	VARIOLOUS	VASE
VANDA*	VANTAGED	VARANS	VARIORUM	VASECTOMIES
VANDAL	VANTAGES	VARAS	VARIORUMS	VASECTOMY
VANDALIC*	VANTAGING	VARDIES	VARIOUS	VASELIKE*
VANDALISE	VANTBRACE	VARDY	VARIOUSLY	VASES
VANDALISED	VANTBRACES	VARE	VARISCITE	VASIFORM
VANDALISES	VANTS	VAREC	VARISCITES	VASOMOTOR
VANDALISING	VANWARD	VARECH	VARISIZED*	VASOSPASM*
VANDALISM	VAPID	VARECHS	VARISTOR	VASOSPASMS*
VANDALISMS	VAPIDER	VARECS	VARISTORS	VASOTOCIN*

The Chambers Dictionary is the authority for many longer words; see Introduction, page ix

VASOTOCINS*	VAULTS	VECTORING	VEGGED	VELARISE
VASOTOMIES*	VAULTY	VECTORINGS	VEGGES	VELARISED
VASOTOMY*	VAUNCE	VECTORISE	VEGGIE	VELARISES
VASOVAGAL*	VAUNCED	VECTORISED	VEGGIES	VELARISING
VASSAIL	VAUNCES	VECTORISES	VEGGING	VELARIUM
VASSAILS	VAUNCING	VECTORISING	VEGIE	VELARIZE
VASSAL	VAUNT	VECTORIZE	VEGIES	VELARIZED
VASSALAGE	VAUNTAGE	VECTORIZED	VEHEMENCE	VELARIZES
VASSALAGES	VAUNTAGES	VECTORIZES	VEHEMENCES	VELARIZING
VASSALESS	VAUNTED	VECTORIZING	VEHEMENCIES	VELARS
VASSALESSES	VAUNTER	VECTORS	VEHEMENCY	VELATE
VASSALLED	VAUNTERIES	VEDALIA	VEHEMENT	VELATED
VASSALLING	VAUNTERS	VEDALIAS	VEHICLE	VELATURA
VASSALRIES	VAUNTERY	VEDETTE	VEHICLES	VELATURAS
VASSALRY	VAUNTFUL	VEDETTES	VEHICULAR	VELD
VASSALS	VAUNTIE*	VEDUTA	VEHM	VELDS
VAST	VAUNTIER	VEDUTE	VEHME	VELDSKOEN
VASTER	VAUNTIEST	VEDUTISTA	VEHMIC	VELDSKOENS
VASTEST	VAUNTING	VEDUTISTI	VEHMIQUE	VELDT
VASTIDITIES	VAUNTINGS	VEE	VEIL	VELDTS
VASTIDITY	VAUNTS	VEEJAY*	VEILED	VELE
VASTIER	VAUNTY	VEEJAYS*	VEILEDLY*	VELES
VASTIEST	VAURIEN	VEENA	VEILER*	VELETA
VASTITIES	VAURIENS	VEENAS	VEILERS*	VELETAS
VASTITUDE	VAUS	VEEP	VEILIER	VELIGER
VASTITUDES	VAUT	VEEPEE*	VEILIEST	VELIGERS
VASTITY	VAUTE	VEEPEES*	VEILING	VELITES*
VASTLY	VAUTED	VEEPS	VEILINGS	VELL
VASTNESS	VAUTES	VEER	VEILLESS	VELLEITIES
VASTNESSES	VAUTING	VEERED	VEILLEUSE	VELLEITY
VASTS	VAUTS	VEERIES	VEILLEUSES	VELLENAGE
VASTY	VAV*	VEERING	VEILLIKE*	VELLENAGES
VAT	VAVASOR*	VEERINGLY	VEILS	VELLET
VATABLE	VAVASORIES	VEERINGS	VEILY	VELLETS
VATFUL	VAVASORS*	VEERS	VEIN	VELLICATE
VATFULS	VAVASORY	VEERY	VEINAL*	VELLICATED
VATIC	VAVASOUR	VEES	VEINED	VELLICATES
VATICAL*	VAVASOURS	VEG	VEINER*	VELLICATING
VATICIDE	VAVASSOR*	VEGA	VEINERS*	VELLON
VATICIDES	VAVASSORS*	VEGAN	VEINIER	VELLONS
VATICINAL	VAVS*	VEGANIC	VEINIEST	VELLS
VATMAN	VAW*	VEGANISM	VEINING	VELLUM
VATMEN	VAWARD	VEGANISMS	VEININGS	VELLUMS
VATS	VAWARDS	VEGANS	VEINLESS*	VELOCE
VATTED	VAWNTIE*	VEGAS	VEINLET	VELOCITIES
VATTER	VAWS*	VEGELATE	VEINLETS	VELOCITY
VATTERS	VAWTE	VEGELATES	VEINLIKE*	VELODROME
VATTING	VAWTED	VEGES	VEINOUS	VELODROMES
VATU	VAWTES	VEGETABLE	VEINS	VELOUR
VATUS	VAWTING	VEGETABLES	VEINSTONE	VELOURS
VAU	VEAL	VEGETABLY	VEINSTONES	VELOUTE
VAUDOO	VEALE	VEGETAL	VEINSTUFF	VELOUTES
VAUDOOS	VEALED*	VEGETALS	VEINSTUFFS	VELOUTINE
VAUDOUX	VEALER	VEGETANT	VEINULE*	VELOUTINES
VAULT	VEALERS	VEGETATE	VEINULES*	VELSKOEN
VAULTAGE	VEALES	VEGETATED	VEINULET*	VELSKOENS
VAULTAGES	VEALIER	VEGETATES	VEINULETS*	VELUM
VAULTED	VEALIEST	VEGETATING	VEINY	VELURE
VAULTER	VEALING*	VEGETATINGS	VELA	VELURED
VAULTERS	VEALS	VEGETE	VELAMEN	VELURES
VAULTIER*	VEALY	VEGETIST*	VELAMINA	VELURING
VAULTIEST*	VECTOR	VEGETISTS*	VELAR	VELVERET
VAULTING	VECTORED	VEGETIVE	VELARIA	VELVERETS
VAULTINGS	VECTORIAL	VEGETIVES	VELARIC	VELVET

VELVETED	VENENATES*	VENOMING	VENULAR*	VERBIFIES
VELVETEEN	VENENATING*	VENOMOUS	VENULE	VERBIFY
VELVETEENS	VENENOSE*	VENOMS	VENULES	VERBIFYING
VELVETIER	VENERABLE	VENOSE	VENULOSE*	VERBILE*
VELVETIEST	VENERABLY	VENOSITIES	VENULOUS*	VERBILES*
VELVETING	VENERATE	VENOSITY	VENUS	VERBLESS
VELVETINGS	VENERATED	VENOUS	VENUSES	VERBOSE
VELVETS	VENERATES	VENOUSLY*	VENVILLE	VERBOSELY
VELVETY	VENERATING	VENT	VENVILLES	VERBOSER
VENA	VENERATOR	VENTAGE	VERA*	VERBOSEST
VENAE	VENERATORS	VENTAGES	VERACIOUS	VERBOSITIES
VENAL	VENEREAL	VENTAIL	VERACITIES	VERBOSITY
VENALITIES	VENEREAN	VENTAILE	VERACITY	VERBOTEN
VENALITY	VENEREANS	VENTAILES	VERANDA	VERBS
VENALLY	VENEREOUS	VENTAILS	VERANDAED*	VERDANCIES
VENATIC	VENERER	VENTANA	VERANDAH	VERDANCY
VENATICAL	VENERERS	VENTANAS	VERANDAHS	VERDANT
VENATION	VENERIES	VENTAYLE	VERANDAS	VERDANTLY
VENATIONS	VENERY	VENTAYLES	VERAPAMIL*	VERDELHO
VENATOR	VENETIAN*	VENTED	VERAPAMILS*	VERDELHOS
VENATORS	VENETIANS*	VENTER	VERATRIA*	VERDERER
VEND	VENEWE	VENTERS	VERATRIAS*	VERDERERS
VENDABLE*	VENEWES	VENTIDUCT	VERATRIN	VERDEROR
VENDACE	VENEY	VENTIDUCTS	VERATRINE	VERDERORS
VENDACES	VENEYS	VENTIFACT	VERATRINES	VERDET
VENDAGE	VENGE	VENTIFACTS	VERATRINS	VERDETS
VENDAGES	VENGEABLE	VENTIGE	VERATRUM	VERDICT
VENDANGE	VENGEABLY	VENTIGES	VERATRUMS	VERDICTS
VENDANGES	VENGEANCE	VENTIL	VERB	VERDIGRIS
VENDED	VENGEANCES	VENTILATE	VERBAL	VERDIGRISED
VENDEE	VENGED	VENTILATED	VERBALISE	VERDIGRISES
VENDEES	VENGEFUL	VENTILATES	VERBALISED	VERDIGRISING
VENDER	VENGEMENT	VENTILATING	VERBALISES	VERDIN
VENDERS	VENGEMENTS	VENTILS	VERBALISING	VERDINS
VENDETTA	VENGER	VENTING	VERBALISM	VERDIT
VENDETTAS	VENGERS	VENTINGS	VERBALISMS	VERDITE
VENDEUSE	VENGES	VENTLESS*	VERBALIST	VERDITER
VENDEUSES	VENGING	VENTOSE	VERBALISTS	VERDITERS
VENDIBLE	VENIAL	VENTOSITIES	VERBALITIES	VERDITES
VENDIBLES	VENIALITIES	VENTOSITY	VERBALITY	VERDITS
VENDIBLY	VENIALITY	VENTRAL	VERBALIZE	VERDOY
VENDING	VENIALLY	VENTRALLY	VERBALIZED	VERDURE
VENDIS	VENIDIUM	VENTRALS	VERBALIZES	VERDURED
VENDISES	VENIDIUMS	VENTRE	VERBALIZING	VERDURES
VENDISS	VENIN	VENTRED	VERBALLED	VERDUROUS
VENDISSES	VENINE*	VENTRES	VERBALLING	VERECUND
VENDITION	VENINES*	VENTRICLE	VERBALLY	VERGE
VENDITIONS	VENINS	VENTRICLES	VERBALS	VERGED
VENDOR	VENIRE	VENTRING	VERBARIAN	VERGENCE
VENDORS	VENIREMAN	VENTRINGS	VERBARIANS	VERGENCES
VENDS	VENIREMEN	VENTROUS	VERBATIM	VERGENCIES
VENDUE	VENIRES	VENTS	VERBENA	VERGENCY
VENDUES	VENISON	VENTURE	VERBENAS	VERGER
VENEER	VENISONS	VENTURED	VERBERATE	VERGERS
VENEERED	VENITE	VENTURER	VERBERATED	VERGES
VENEERER	VENITES	VENTURERS	VERBERATES	VERGING
VENEERERS	VENNEL	VENTURES	VERBERATING	VERGLAS
VENEERING	VENNELS	VENTURI	VERBIAGE	VERGLASES
VENEERINGS	VENOGRAM*	VENTURING	VERBIAGES	VERIDIC*
VENEERS	VENOGRAMS*	VENTURINGS	VERBICIDE	VERIDICAL
VENEFIC	VENOM	VENTURIS	VERBICIDES	VERIER
VENEFICAL	VENOMED	VENTUROUS	VERBID	VERIEST
VENENATE*	VENOMER*	VENUE	VERBIDS	VERIFIED
VENENATED*	VENOMERS*	VENUES	VERBIFIED	VERIFIER

VERIFIERS	VERMINS	VERSERS	VERVELLED	VESTITURE
VERIFIES	VERMINY	VERSES	VERVELS	VESTITURES
VERIFY	VERMIS	VERSET	VERVEN	VESTLESS*
VERIFYING	VERMOULU*	VERSETS	VERVENS	VESTLIKE*
VERILY	VERMOUTH	VERSICLE	VERVES	VESTMENT
VERISM	VERMOUTHS	VERSICLES	VERVET	VESTMENTS
VERISMO	VERMUTH*	VERSIFIED	VERVETS	VESTRAL
VERISMOS	VERMUTHS*	VERSIFIER	VERY	VESTRIES
VERISMS	VERNACLE*	VERSIFIERS	VESICA	VESTRY
VERIST	VERNACLES*	VERSIFIES	VESICAE	VESTRYMAN
VERISTIC	VERNAL	VERSIFORM	VESICAL	VESTRYMEN
VERISTS	VERNALISE	VERSIFY	VESICANT	VESTS
VERITABLE	VERNALISED	VERSIFYING	VESICANTS	VESTURAL
VERITABLY	VERNALISES	VERSIN	VESICATE	VESTURE
VERITAS*	VERNALISING	VERSINE	VESICATED	VESTURED
VERITATES*	VERNALITIES	VERSINES	VESICATES	VESTURER
VERITE*	VERNALITY	VERSING	VESICATING	VESTURERS
VERITES*	VERNALIZE	VERSINGS	VESICLE	VESTURES
VERITIES	VERNALIZED	VERSINS	VESICLES	VESTURING
VERITY	VERNALIZES	VERSION	VESICULA	VESUVIAN
VERJUICE	VERNALIZING	VERSIONAL	VESICULAE	VESUVIANS
VERJUICED	VERNALLY	VERSIONER	VESICULAR	VET
VERJUICES	VERNANT	VERSIONERS	VESPA	VETCH
VERKRAMP	VERNATION	VERSIONS	VESPAS	VETCHES
VERLIG	VERNATIONS	VERSO	VESPER	VETCHIER
VERLIGTE	VERNICLE	VERSOS	VESPERAL	VETCHIEST
VERLIGTES	VERNICLES	VERST	VESPERALS*	VETCHLING
VERMAL	VERNIER	VERSTE*	VESPERS	VETCHLINGS
VERMEIL	VERNIERS	VERSTES*	VESPIARIES	VETCHY
VERMEILED	VERNIX*	VERSTS	VESPIARY	VETERAN
VERMEILING	VERNIXES*	VERSUS	VESPID*	VETERANS
VERMEILLE	VERONAL	VERSUTE	VESPIDS*	VETIVER
VERMEILLED	VERONALS	VERT	VESPINE	VETIVERS
VERMEILLES	VERONICA	VERTEBRA	VESPOID	VETIVERT*
VERMEILLING	VERONICAS	VERTEBRAE	VESSAIL	VETIVERTS*
VERMEILS	VERONIQUE	VERTEBRAL	VESSAILS	VETKOEK
VERMELL	VERQUERE	VERTEBRAS*	VESSEL	VETKOEKS
VERMELLS	VERQUERES	VERTED	VESSELED*	VETO
VERMES	VERQUIRE	VERTEX	VESSELS	VETOED
VERMIAN	VERQUIRES	VERTEXES	VEST	VETOER*
VERMICIDE	VERREL	VERTICAL	VESTA	VETOERS*
VERMICIDES	VERRELS	VERTICALS	VESTAL	VETOES
VERMICULE	VERREY	VERTICES	VESTALLY*	VETOING
VERMICULES	VERRUCA	VERTICIL	VESTALS	VETS
VERMIFORM	VERRUCAE	VERTICILS	VESTAS	VETTED
VERMIFUGE	VERRUCAS	VERTICITIES	VESTED	VETTING
VERMIFUGES	VERRUCOSE	VERTICITY	VESTEE*	VETTURA
VERMIL	VERRUCOUS	VERTIGINES	VESTEES*	VETTURAS
VERMILIES	VERRUGA	VERTIGO	VESTIARIES	VETTURINI
VERMILION	VERRUGAS	VERTIGOES	VESTIARY	VETTURINO
VERMILIONED	VERRY	VERTIGOS	VESTIBULA	VEX
VERMILIONING	VERS	VERTING	VESTIBULE	VEXATION
VERMILIONS	VERSAL	VERTIPORT	VESTIBULED	VEXATIONS
VERMILLED	VERSALS	VERTIPORTS	VESTIBULES	VEXATIOUS
VERMILLING	VERSANT	VERTS	VESTIBULING	VEXATORY
VERMILS	VERSANTS	VERTU	VESTIGE	VEXED
VERMILY	VERSATILE	VERTUE	VESTIGES	VEXEDLY
VERMIN	VERSE	VERTUES	VESTIGIA	VEXEDNESS
VERMINATE	VERSED	VERTUOUS	VESTIGIAL	VEXEDNESSES
VERMINATED	VERSELET	VERTUS	VESTIGIUM	VEXER
VERMINATES	VERSELETS	VERVAIN	VESTIMENT	VEXERS
VERMINATING	VERSEMAN*	VERVAINS	VESTIMENTS	VEXES
VERMINED	VERSEMEN*	VERVE	VESTING	VEXIL*
VERMINOUS	VERSER	VERVEL	VESTINGS	VEXILLA

Words marked with an asterisk are from OTCWL

VEXILLAR*	VIBRATIONS	VICIOSITIES	VIDEOS	VIGILS
VEXILLARIES	VIBRATIVE	VICIOSITY	VIDEOTAPE	VIGNERON
VEXILLARY	VIBRATO	VICIOUS	VIDEOTAPED	VIGNERONS
VEXILLUM	VIBRATOR	VICIOUSLY	VIDEOTAPES	VIGNETTE
VEXILS*	VIBRATORS	VICOMTE	VIDEOTAPING	VIGNETTED
VEXING	VIBRATORY	VICOMTES	VIDEOTEX	VIGNETTER
VEXINGLY	VIBRATOS	VICTIM	VIDEOTEXES	VIGNETTERS
VEXINGS	VIBRIO	VICTIMISE	VIDEOTEXT	VIGNETTES
VEXT	VIBRIOID*	VICTIMISED	VIDEOTEXTS	VIGNETTING
VEZIR	VIBRION*	VICTIMISES	VIDETTE	VIGOR
VEZIRS	VIBRIONIC*	VICTIMISING	VIDETTES	VIGORISH
VIA	VIBRIONS*	VICTIMIZE	VIDICON*	VIGORISHES
VIABILITIES	VIBRIOS	VICTIMIZED	VIDICONS*	VIGORO
VIABILITY	VIBRIOSES	VICTIMIZES	VIDIMUS	VIGOROS
VIABLE	VIBRIOSIS	VICTIMIZING	VIDIMUSES	VIGOROSO*
VIABLY*	VIBRISSA	VICTIMS	VIDS	VIGOROUS
VIADUCT	VIBRISSAE	VICTOR	VIDUAGE	VIGORS
VIADUCTS	VIBRONIC	VICTORESS	VIDUAGES	VIGOUR
VIAE	VIBS	VICTORESSES	VIDUAL	VIGOURS
VIAL	VIBURNUM	VICTORIA	VIDUITIES	VIGS*
VIALED*	VIBURNUMS	VICTORIAS	VIDUITY	VIHARA
VIALFUL	VICAR	VICTORIES	VIDUOUS	VIHARAS
VIALFULS	VICARAGE	VICTORINE	VIE	VIHUELA
VIALING*	VICARAGES	VICTORINES	VIED	VIHUELAS
VIALLED	VICARATE	VICTORS	VIELLE	VIKING
VIALLING*	VICARATES	VICTORY	VIELLES	VIKINGISM
VIALS	VICARESS	VICTRESS	VIER	VIKINGISMS
VIAMETER	VICARESSES	VICTRESSES	VIERS	VIKINGS
VIAMETERS	VICARIAL	VICTRIX	VIES	VILAYET
VIAND	VICARIANT*	VICTRIXES	VIEW	VILAYETS
VIANDS	VICARIANTS*	VICTROLLA	VIEWABLE	VILD
VIAS	VICARIATE	VICTROLLAS	VIEWDATA	VILDE
VIATIC*	VICARIATES	VICTUAL	VIEWDATAS	VILDLY
VIATICA	VICARIES	VICTUALED*	VIEWED	VILDNESS
VIATICAL*	VICARIOUS	VICTUALER*	VIEWER	VILDNESSES
VIATICALS	VICARLY*	VICTUALERS*	VIEWERS	VILE
VIATICUM	VICARS	VICTUALING*	VIEWIER	VILELY
VIATICUMS	VICARSHIP	VICTUALLED	VIEWIEST	VILENESS
VIATOR	VICARSHIPS	VICTUALLING	VIEWINESS	VILENESSES
VIATORES	VICARY	VICTUALS	VIEWINESSES	VILER
VIATORIAL	VICE	VICUGNA*	VIEWING	VILEST
VIATORS	VICED	VICUGNAS*	VIEWINGS	VILIACO
VIBE	VICELESS	VICUNA	VIEWLESS	VILIACOES
VIBES	VICENARY	VICUNAS	VIEWLY	VILIACOS
VIBEX	VICENNIAL	VID	VIEWPHONE	VILIAGO
VIBICES	VICEREGAL*	VIDAME	VIEWPHONES	VILIAGOES
VIBIST	VICEREINE	VIDAMES	VIEWPOINT	VILIAGOS
VIBISTS	VICEREINES	VIDE	VIEWPOINTS	VILIFIED
VIBRACULA	VICEROY	VIDELICET	VIEWS	VILIFIER
VIBRAHARP	VICEROYS	VIDENDA	VIEWY	VILIFIERS
VIBRAHARPS	VICES	VIDENDUM	VIFDA	VILIFIES
VIBRANCE*	VICESIMAL	VIDEO	VIFDAS	VILIFY
VIBRANCES*	VICHIES	VIDEODISC	VIG*	VILIFYING
VIBRANCIES	VICHY	VIDEODISCS	VIGA*	VILIPEND
VIBRANCY	VICIATE	VIDEODISK*	VIGAS*	VILIPENDED
VIBRANT	VICIATED	VIDEODISKS*	VIGESIMAL	VILIPENDING
VIBRANTLY	VICIATES	VIDEOED	VIGIA	VILIPENDS
VIBRANTS*	VICIATING	VIDEOFIT	VIGIAS	VILL
VIBRATE	VICINAGE	VIDEOFITS	VIGIL	VILLA
VIBRATED	VICINAGES	VIDEOGRAM	VIGILANCE	VILLADOM
VIBRATES	VICINAL	VIDEOGRAMS	VIGILANCES	VILLADOMS
VIBRATILE	VICING	VIDEOING	VIGILANT	VILLAE*
VIBRATING	VICINITIES	VIDEOLAND*	VIGILANTE	VILLAGE
VIBRATION	VICINITY	VIDEOLANDS*	VIGILANTES	VILLAGER

VILLAGERIES	VINDICATE	VIOLABLE	VIREMIAS*	VIROLOGY
VILLAGERS	VINDICATED	VIOLABLY	VIREMIC*	VIROSE
VILLAGERY	VINDICATES	VIOLAS	VIRENT	VIROSES
VILLAGES	VINDICATING	VIOLATE	VIREO	VIROSIS
VILLAGIO	VINE	VIOLATED	VIREOS	VIROUS
VILLAGIOES	VINEAL*	VIOLATER	VIRES	VIRTU
VILLAGIOS	VINED	VIOLATERS	VIRESCENT	VIRTUAL
VILLAGREE	VINEGAR	VIOLATES	VIRETOT	VIRTUALLY
VILLAGREES	VINEGARED	VIOLATING	VIRETOTS	VIRTUE
VILLAIN	VINEGARING	VIOLATION	VIRGA	VIRTUES
VILLAINIES	VINEGARS	VIOLATIONS	VIRGAS	VIRTUOSA
VILLAINS	VINEGARY	VIOLATIVE	VIRGATE	VIRTUOSAS*
VILLAINY	VINER	VIOLATOR	VIRGATES	VIRTUOSE
VILLAN	VINERIES	VIOLATORS	VIRGE	VIRTUOSI
VILLANAGE	VINERS	VIOLD	VIRGER	VIRTUOSIC
VILLANAGES	VINERY	VIOLENCE	VIRGERS	VIRTUOSO
VILLANIES	VINES	VIOLENCES	VIRGES	VIRTUOSOS
VILLANOUS	VINEW	VIOLENT	VIRGIN	VIRTUOUS
VILLANS	VINEWED	VIOLENTED	VIRGINAL	VIRTUS
VILLANY	VINEWING	VIOLENTING	VIRGINALLED	VIRUCIDAL
VILLAR	VINEWS	VIOLENTLY	VIRGINALLING	VIRUCIDE
VILLAS	VINEYARD	VIOLENTS	VIRGINALS	VIRUCIDES
VILLATIC	VINEYARDS	VIOLER	VIRGINED	VIRULENCE
VILLEIN	VINIC*	VIOLERS	VIRGINING	VIRULENCES
VILLEINS	VINIER	VIOLET	VIRGINITIES	VIRULENCIES
VILLENAGE	VINIEST	VIOLETS	VIRGINITY	VIRULENCY
VILLENAGES	VINIFERA*	VIOLIN	VIRGINIUM	VIRULENT
VILLI	VINIFERAS*	VIOLINIST	VIRGINIUMS	VIRUS
VILLIAGO	VINIFIED*	VIOLINISTS	VIRGINLY	VIRUSES
VILLIAGOES	VINIFIES*	VIOLINS	VIRGINS	VIS
VILLIAGOS	VINIFY*	VIOLIST	VIRGULATE	VISA
VILLIFORM	VINIFYING*	VIOLISTS	VIRGULE	VISAED
VILLOSE	VINING	VIOLONE	VIRGULES	VISAGE
VILLOSITIES	VINO	VIOLONES	VIRICIDAL	VISAGED
VILLOSITY	VINOLENT	VIOLS	VIRICIDE	VISAGES
VILLOUS	VINOLOGIES	VIOMYCIN*	VIRICIDES	VISAGIST
VILLS	VINOLOGY	VIOMYCINS*	VIRID	VISAGISTE
VILLUS	VINOS	VIPER	VIRIDIAN	VISAGISTES
VIM	VINOSITIES	VIPERINE	VIRIDIANS	VISAGISTS
VIMANA	VINOSITY	VIPERISH	VIRIDITE	VISAING
VIMANAS	VINOUS	VIPEROUS	VIRIDITES	VISARD*
VIMEN*	VINOUSLY*	VIPERS	VIRIDITIES	VISARDS*
VIMINA*	VINS	VIRAEMIA	VIRIDITY	VISAS
VIMINAL*	VINT	VIRAEMIAS	VIRILE	VISCACHA
VIMINEOUS	VINTAGE	VIRAEMIC	VIRILELY*	VISCACHAS
VIMS	VINTAGED	VIRAGO	VIRILISED	VISCERA
VIN	VINTAGER	VIRAGOES	VIRILISM	VISCERAL
VINA	VINTAGERS	VIRAGOISH	VIRILISMS	VISCERATE
VINACEOUS	VINTAGES	VIRAGOS	VIRILITIES	VISCERATED
VINAL	VINTAGING	VIRAL	VIRILITY	VISCERATES
VINALS*	VINTAGINGS	VIRALLY*	VIRILIZED	VISCERATING
VINAS	VINTED	VIRANDA	VIRING	VISCID
VINASSE	VINTING	VIRANDAS	VIRINO	VISCIDITIES
VINASSES	VINTNER	VIRANDO	VIRINOS	VISCIDITY
VINCA	VINTNERS	VIRANDOS	VIRION	VISCIDLY*
VINCAS	VINTRIES	VIRE	VIRIONS	VISCIN
VINCIBLE	VINTRY	VIRED	VIRL	VISCINS
VINCIBLY*	VINTS	VIRELAI*	VIRLS	VISCOID*
VINCULA	VINY	VIRELAIS*	VIROGENE	VISCOSE
VINCULUM	VINYL	VIRELAY	VIROGENES	VISCOSES
VINCULUMS*	VINYLIC*	VIRELAYS	VIROID	VISCOSITIES
VINDALOO	VINYLS	VIREMENT	VIROIDS	VISCOSITY
VINDALOOS	VIOL	VIREMENTS	VIROLOGIC*	VISCOUNT
VINDEMIAL	VIOLA	VIREMIA*	VIROLOGIES	VISCOUNTIES

VISCOUNTS	VISONS	VITELLI	VIVA	VIZAMENTS
VISCOUNTY	VISOR	VITELLIN	VIVACE	VIZARD
VISCOUS	VISORED	VITELLINE	VIVACES*	VIZARDED
VISCOUSLY*	VISORING	VITELLINES	VIVACIOUS	VIZARDING
VISCUM	VISORLESS*	VITELLINS	VIVACITIES	VIZARDS
VISCUMS	VISORS	VITELLUS	VIVACITY	VIZCACHA
VISCUS	VISTA	VITELLUSES*	VIVAED	VIZCACHAS
VISE	VISTAED	VITESSE*	VIVAING	VIZIED
VISED	VISTAING	VITESSES*	VIVAMENTE	VIZIER
VISEED	VISTAL	VITEX	VIVANDIER	VIZIERATE
VISEING	VISTALESS	VITEXES	VIVANDIERS	VIZIERATES
VISELIKE*	VISTAS	VITIABLE	VIVARIA	VIZIERIAL
VISES	VISTO	VITIATE	VIVARIES	VIZIERS
VISIBLE	VISTOS	VITIATED	VIVARIUM	VIZIES
VISIBLES	VISUAL	VITIATES	VIVARIUMS	VIZIR
VISIBLY	VISUALISE	VITIATING	VIVARY	VIZIRATE
VISIE	VISUALISED	VITIATION	VIVAS	VIZIRATES
VISIED	VISUALISES	VITIATIONS	VIVAT	VIZIRIAL
VISIEING	VISUALISING	VITIATOR	VIVATS	VIZIRS
VISIER	VISUALIST	VITIATORS	VIVDA	VIZIRSHIP
VISIERS	VISUALISTS	VITICETA	VIVDAS	VIZIRSHIPS
VISIES	VISUALITIES	VITICETUM	VIVE	VIZOR
VISILE	VISUALITY	VITICETUMS	VIVELY	VIZORED
VISILES	VISUALIZE	VITICIDE	VIVENCIES	VIZORING
VISING	VISUALIZED	VITICIDES	VIVENCY	VIZORS
VISION	VISUALIZES	VITILIGO	VIVER	VIZSLA
VISIONAL	VISUALIZING	VITILIGOS	VIVERRA	VIZSLAS
VISIONARIES	VISUALLY	VITIOSITIES	VIVERRAS	VIZY
VISIONARY	VISUALS	VITIOSITY	VIVERRID*	VIZYING
VISIONED	VITA	VITRAGE	VIVERRIDS*	VIZZIE
VISIONER	VITAE	VITRAGES	VIVERRINE	VIZZIED
VISIONERS	VITAL	VITRAIL	VIVERS	VIZZIEING
VISIONING	VITALISE	VITRAIN	VIVES	VIZZIES
VISIONINGS	VITALISED	VITRAINS	VIVIANITE	VLEI
VISIONIST	VITALISER	VITRAUX	VIVIANITES	VLEIS
VISIONISTS	VITALISERS	VITREOUS	VIVID	VLIES
VISIONS	VITALISES	VITREOUSES*	VIVIDER	VLY
VISIT	VITALISING	VITREUM	VIVIDEST	VOAR
VISITABLE	VITALISM	VITREUMS	VIVIDITIES	VOARS
VISITANT	VITALISMS	VITRIC	VIVIDITY	VOCAB
VISITANTS	VITALIST	VITRICS	VIVIDLY	VOCABLE
VISITATOR	VITALISTS	VITRIFIED	VIVIDNESS	VOCABLES
VISITATORS	VITALITIES	VITRIFIES	VIVIDNESSES	VOCABLY*
VISITE	VITALITY	VITRIFORM	VIVIFIC	VOCABS
VISITED	VITALIZE	VITRIFY	VIVIFIED	VOCABULAR
VISITEE	VITALIZED	VITRIFYING	VIVIFIER	VOCAL
VISITEES	VITALIZER	VITRINE	VIVIFIERS	VOCALESE
VISITER	VITALIZERS	VITRINES	VIVIFIES	VOCALESES
VISITERS	VITALIZES	VITRIOL	VIVIFY	VOCALIC
VISITES	VITALIZING	VITRIOLED*	VIVIFYING	VOCALICS*
VISITING	VITALLY	VITRIOLIC	VIVIPARA*	VOCALION
VISITINGS	VITALS	VITRIOLING*	VIVIPARIES	VOCALIONS
VISITOR	VITAMER*	VITRIOLLED*	VIVIPARY	VOCALISE
VISITORS	VITAMERS*	VITRIOLLING*	VIVISECT	VOCALISED
VISITRESS	VITAMIN	VITRIOLS	VIVISECTED	VOCALISER
VISITRESSES	VITAMINE	VITTA	VIVISECTING	VOCALISERS
VISITS	VITAMINES	VITTAE	VIVISECTS	VOCALISES
VISIVE	VITAMINS	VITTATE	VIVO	VOCALISING
VISNE	VITAS	VITTLE	VIVRES	VOCALISM
VISNES	VITASCOPE	VITTLED*	VIXEN	VOCALISMS
VISNOMIE	VITASCOPES	VITTLES	VIXENISH	VOCALIST
VISNOMIES	VITATIVE	VITTLING*	VIXENLY	VOCALISTS
VISNOMY	VITE	VITULAR	VIXENS	VOCALITIES
VISON	VITELLARY	VITULINE	VIZAMENT	VOCALITY

The Chambers Dictionary is the authority for many longer words; see Introduction, page ix

VOCALIZE	VOIDNESS	VOLITIVE	VOLUNTEERED	VORLAGES*
VOCALIZED	VOIDNESSES	VOLITIVES	VOLUNTEERING	VORPAL
VOCALIZER	VOIDS	VOLK	VOLUNTEERS	VORRED
VOCALIZERS	VOILA	VOLKS	VOLUSPA	VORRING
VOCALIZES	VOILE	VOLKSLIED*	VOLUSPAS	VORS
VOCALIZING	VOILES	VOLKSLIEDER*	VOLUTE	VORTEX
VOCALLY	VOISINAGE	VOLKSRAAD	VOLUTED	VORTEXES
VOCALNESS	VOISINAGES	VOLKSRAADS	VOLUTES	VORTICAL
VOCALNESSES	VOITURE	VOLLEY	VOLUTIN	VORTICES
VOCALS	VOITURES	VOLLEYED	VOLUTINS	VORTICISM
VOCATION	VOITURIER	VOLLEYER	VOLUTION	VORTICISMS
VOCATIONS	VOITURIERS	VOLLEYERS	VOLUTIONS	VORTICIST
VOCATIVE	VOIVODE	VOLLEYING	VOLUTOID	VORTICISTS
VOCATIVES	VOIVODES	VOLLEYS	VOLVA	VORTICITIES
VOCES	VOL	VOLOST	VOLVAS	VORTICITY
VOCODER	VOLA	VOLOSTS	VOLVATE	VORTICOSE
VOCODERS	VOLABLE	VOLPINO	VOLVE	VOTABLE*
VOCULAR	VOLAE	VOLPINOS	VOLVED	VOTARESS
VOCULE	VOLAGE	VOLPLANE	VOLVES	VOTARESSES
VOCULES	VOLAGEOUS	VOLPLANED	VOLVING	VOTARIES
VODKA	VOLANT	VOLPLANES	VOLVOX	VOTARIST
VODKAS	VOLANTE	VOLPLANING	VOLVOXES	VOTARISTS
VODOUN*	VOLANTES	VOLS	VOLVULI	VOTARY
VODOUNS*	VOLAR	VOLT	VOLVULUS	VOTE
VODUN*	VOLARIES	VOLTA	VOLVULUSES	VOTEABLE*
VODUNS*	VOLARY	VOLTAGE	VOMER	VOTED
VOE	VOLATIC	VOLTAGES	VOMERINE	VOTEEN
VOES	VOLATILE	VOLTAIC	VOMERS	VOTEENS
VOGIE	VOLATILES	VOLTAISM	VOMICA	VOTELESS
VOGIER	VOLCANIAN	VOLTAISMS	VOMICAE	VOTER
VOGIEST	VOLCANIC	VOLTE	VOMICAS	VOTERS
VOGUE	VOLCANICS*	VOLTES	VOMIT	VOTES
VOGUED	VOLCANISE	VOLTI*	VOMITED	VOTING
VOGUEING	VOLCANISED	VOLTIGEUR	VOMITER*	VOTIVE
VOGUEINGS	VOLCANISES	VOLTIGEURS	VOMITERS*	VOTIVELY*
VOGUER	VOLCANISING	VOLTINISM	VOMITING	VOTRESS
VOGUERS	VOLCANISM	VOLTINISMS	VOMITINGS	VOTRESSES
VOGUES	VOLCANISMS	VOLTMETER	VOMITIVE	VOUCH
VOGUEY	VOLCANIST	VOLTMETERS	VOMITIVES	VOUCHED
VOGUIER	VOLCANISTS	VOLTS	VOMITO	VOUCHEE
VOGUIEST	VOLCANIZE	VOLUBIL	VOMITORIA	VOUCHEES
VOGUING	VOLCANIZED	VOLUBLE	VOMITORIES	VOUCHER
VOGUINGS	VOLCANIZES	VOLUBLY	VOMITORY	VOUCHERED*
VOGUISH	VOLCANIZING	VOLUCRINE	VOMITOS	VOUCHERING*
VOICE	VOLCANO	VOLUME	VOMITOUS*	VOUCHERS
VOICED	VOLCANOES	VOLUMED	VOMITS	VOUCHES
VOICEFUL	VOLCANOS*	VOLUMES	VOMITUS	VOUCHING
VOICELESS	VOLE	VOLUMETER	VOMITUSES	VOUCHSAFE
VOICER	VOLED	VOLUMETERS	VOODOO	VOUCHSAFED
VOICERS	VOLENS	VOLUMINAL	VOODOOED	VOUCHSAFES
VOICES	VOLERIES	VOLUMING	VOODOOING	VOUCHSAFING
VOICING	VOLERY	VOLUMISE	VOODOOISM	VOUCHSAFINGS
VOICINGS	VOLES	VOLUMISED	VOODOOISMS	VOUDOU
VOID	VOLET	VOLUMISES	VOODOOIST	VOUDOUED
VOIDABLE	VOLETS	VOLUMISING	VOODOOISTS	VOUDOUING
VOIDANCE	VOLING	VOLUMIST	VOODOOS	VOUDOUS
VOIDANCES	VOLITANT	VOLUMISTS	VOR	VOUGE
VOIDED	VOLITATE	VOLUMIZE	VORACIOUS	VOUGES
VOIDEE	VOLITATED	VOLUMIZED	VORACITIES	VOULGE
VOIDEES	VOLITATES	VOLUMIZES	VORACITY	VOULGES
VOIDER	VOLITATING	VOLUMIZING	VORAGO	VOULU
VOIDERS	VOLITIENT	VOLUNTARIES	VORAGOES	VOUSSOIR
VOIDING	VOLITION	VOLUNTARY	VORANT	VOUSSOIRED
VOIDINGS	VOLITIONS	VOLUNTEER	VORLAGE*	VOUSSOIRING

Words marked with an asterisk are from OTCWL

VOUSSOIRS
VOUTSAFE
VOUTSAFED
VOUTSAFES
VOUTSAFING
VOUVRAY*
VOUVRAYS*
VOW
VOWED
VOWEL
VOWELISE
VOWELISED
VOWELISES
VOWELISING
VOWELIZE
VOWELIZED
VOWELIZES
VOWELIZING
VOWELLED
VOWELLESS
VOWELLING
VOWELLY
VOWELS
VOWER
VOWERS
VOWESS
VOWESSES
VOWING
VOWLESS*
VOWS
VOX
VOXEL

VOXELS
VOYAGE
VOYAGED
VOYAGER
VOYAGERS
VOYAGES
VOYAGEUR
VOYAGEURS
VOYAGING
VOYEUR
VOYEURISM
VOYEURISMS
VOYEURS
VOZHD
VOZHDS
VRAIC
VRAICKER
VRAICKERS
VRAICKING
VRAICKINGS
VRAICS
VRIL
VRILS
VROOM
VROOMED
VROOMING
VROOMS
VROUW
VROUWS
VROW
VROWS
VUG

VUGG*
VUGGIER
VUGGIEST
VUGGS*
VUGGY
VUGH*
VUGHS*
VUGS
VULCAN
VULCANIAN
VULCANIC
VULCANISE
VULCANISED
VULCANISES
VULCANISING
VULCANISM
VULCANISMS
VULCANIST
VULCANISTS
VULCANITE
VULCANITES
VULCANIZE
VULCANIZED
VULCANIZES
VULCANIZING
VULCANS
VULGAR
VULGARER
VULGAREST
VULGARIAN
VULGARIANS
VULGARISE

VULGARISED
VULGARISES
VULGARISING
VULGARISM
VULGARISMS
VULGARITIES
VULGARITY
VULGARIZE
VULGARIZED
VULGARIZES
VULGARIZING
VULGARLY
VULGARS
VULGATE
VULGATES
VULGO
VULGUS
VULGUSES
VULN
VULNED
VULNERARIES
VULNERARY
VULNERATE
VULNERATED
VULNERATES
VULNERATING
VULNING
VULNS
VULPICIDE
VULPICIDES
VULPINE
VULPINISM

VULPINISMS
VULPINITE
VULPINITES
VULSELLA
VULSELLAE
VULSELLUM
VULTURE
VULTURES
VULTURINE
VULTURISH
VULTURISM
VULTURISMS
VULTURN
VULTURNS
VULTUROUS
VULVA
VULVAE
VULVAL
VULVAR
VULVAS
VULVATE
VULVIFORM
VULVITIS
VULVITISES
VUM
VUMMED
VUMMING
VUMS
VYING
VYINGLY

W

WAB*	WADED	WAFFLIEST	WAGON	WAINSCOTTED
WABAIN	WADER	WAFFLING	WAGONAGE	WAINSCOTTING
WABAINS	WADERS	WAFFLINGS	WAGONAGES	WAINSCOTTINGS
WABBIT	WADES	WAFFLY	WAGONED	WAIR*
WABBLE	WADI	WAFFS	WAGONER	WAIRED*
WABBLED	WADIES	WAFT	WAGONERS	WAIRING*
WABBLER	WADING	WAFTAGE	WAGONETTE	WAIRS*
WABBLERS	WADINGS	WAFTAGES	WAGONETTES	WAIST
WABBLES	WADIS	WAFTED	WAGONFUL	WAISTBAND
WABBLIER*	WADMAAL	WAFTER	WAGONFULS	WAISTBANDS
WABBLIEST*	WADMAALS	WAFTERS	WAGONING	WAISTBELT
WABBLING	WADMAL	WAFTING	WAGONLOAD	WAISTBELTS
WABBLY*	WADMALS	WAFTINGS	WAGONLOADS	WAISTBOAT
WABOOM	WADMEL*	WAFTS	WAGONS	WAISTBOATS
WABOOMS	WADMELS*	WAFTURE	WAGS	WAISTCOAT
WABS*	WADMOL	WAFTURES	WAGSOME*	WAISTCOATS
WABSTER	WADMOLL	WAG	WAGTAIL	WAISTED
WABSTERS	WADMOLLS	WAGE	WAGTAILS	WAISTER
WACK	WADMOLS	WAGED	WAHCONDA*	WAISTERS
WACKE	WADS	WAGELESS	WAHCONDAS*	WAISTING*
WACKER	WADSET	WAGENBOOM	WAHINE	WAISTINGS*
WACKERS	WADSETS	WAGENBOOMS	WAHINES	WAISTLINE
WACKES	WADSETT	WAGER	WAHOO	WAISTLINES
WACKIER	WADSETTED	WAGERED	WAHOOS	WAISTS
WACKIEST	WADSETTER	WAGERER	WAID	WAIT
WACKILY*	WADSETTERS	WAGERERS	WAIDE	WAITE
WACKINESS	WADSETTING	WAGERING	WAIF	WAITED
WACKINESSES	WADSETTS	WAGERS	WAIFED	WAITER
WACKO	WADT	WAGES	WAIFING	WAITERAGE
WACKOS*	WADTS	WAGGED	WAIFLIKE*	WAITERAGES
WACKS	WADY	WAGGER*	WAIFS	WAITERING
WACKY	WAE	WAGGERIES	WAIFT	WAITERINGS
WAD	WAEFUL	WAGGERS*	WAIFTS	WAITERS
WADABLE*	WAENESS	WAGGERY	WAIL	WAITES
WADD	WAENESSES	WAGGING	WAILED	WAITING
WADDED	WAES	WAGGISH	WAILER	WAITINGLY
WADDER*	WAESOME	WAGGISHLY	WAILERS	WAITINGS
WADDERS*	WAESUCK*	WAGGLE	WAILFUL	WAITRESS
WADDIE	WAESUCKS	WAGGLED	WAILFULLY*	WAITRESSED*
WADDIED	WAFER	WAGGLES	WAILING	WAITRESSES
WADDIES	WAFERED	WAGGLIER	WAILINGLY	WAITRESSING*
WADDING	WAFERING	WAGGLIEST	WAILINGS	WAITS
WADDINGS	WAFERS	WAGGLING	WAILS	WAIVE
WADDLE	WAFERY	WAGGLY	WAILSOME*	WAIVED
WADDLED	WAFF	WAGGON	WAIN	WAIVER
WADDLER	WAFFED	WAGGONED	WAINAGE	WAIVERS
WADDLERS	WAFFIE*	WAGGONER	WAINAGES	WAIVES
WADDLES	WAFFIES*	WAGGONERS	WAINED	WAIVING
WADDLING	WAFFING	WAGGONING	WAINING	WAIVODE
WADDLY*	WAFFLE	WAGGONS	WAINS	WAIVODES
WADDS	WAFFLED	WAGHALTER	WAINSCOT	WAIWODE
WADDY	WAFFLER	WAGHALTERS	WAINSCOTED	WAIWODES
WADDYING	WAFFLERS	WAGING	WAINSCOTING	WAKA
WADE	WAFFLES	WAGMOIRE	WAINSCOTINGS	WAKANDA*
WADEABLE*	WAFFLIER	WAGMOIRES	WAINSCOTS	WAKANDAS*

Words marked with an asterisk are from OTCWL

WAKANE
WAKANES
WAKAS
WAKE
WAKED
WAKEFUL
WAKEFULLY
WAKELESS
WAKEMAN
WAKEMEN
WAKEN
WAKENED
WAKENER
WAKENERS
WAKENING
WAKENINGS
WAKENS
WAKER
WAKERIFE
WAKERS
WAKES
WAKF
WAKFS
WAKIKI
WAKIKIS
WAKING
WAKINGS
WALD
WALDFLUTE
WALDFLUTES
WALDGRAVE
WALDGRAVES
WALDHORN
WALDHORNS
WALDRAPP
WALDRAPPS
WALDS
WALE
WALED
WALER
WALERS
WALES
WALI
WALIER
WALIES
WALIEST
WALING
WALIS
WALISE
WALISES
WALK
WALKABLE
WALKABOUT
WALKABOUTS
WALKATHON
WALKATHONS
WALKAWAY*
WALKAWAYS*
WALKED
WALKER
WALKERS
WALKING
WALKINGS
WALKMILL

WALKMILLS
WALKOUT*
WALKOUTS*
WALKOVER*
WALKOVERS*
WALKS
WALKUP*
WALKUPS*
WALKWAY
WALKWAYS
WALKYRIE*
WALKYRIES*
WALL
WALLA
WALLABA
WALLABAS
WALLABIES
WALLABY
WALLAH
WALLAHS
WALLAROO
WALLAROOS
WALLAS
WALLBOARD
WALLBOARDS
WALLCHART
WALLCHARTS
WALLED
WALLER
WALLERS
WALLET
WALLETS
WALLEYE*
WALLEYED*
WALLEYES*
WALLFISH
WALLFISHES
WALLIE
WALLIER
WALLIES
WALLIEST
WALLING
WALLINGS
WALLOP
WALLOPED
WALLOPER
WALLOPERS
WALLOPING
WALLOPINGS
WALLOPS
WALLOW
WALLOWED
WALLOWER
WALLOWERS
WALLOWING
WALLOWINGS
WALLOWS
WALLPAPER
WALLPAPERED*
WALLPAPERING*
WALLPAPERS
WALLS
WALLSEND
WALLSENDS

WALLWORT
WALLWORTS
WALLY
WALLYDRAG
WALLYDRAGS
WALNUT
WALNUTS
WALRUS
WALRUSES
WALTIER
WALTIEST
WALTY
WALTZ
WALTZED
WALTZER
WALTZERS
WALTZES
WALTZING
WALTZINGS
WALY
WAMBENGER
WAMBENGERS
WAMBLE
WAMBLED
WAMBLES
WAMBLIER
WAMBLIEST
WAMBLING
WAMBLINGS
WAMBLY
WAME
WAMED
WAMEFOU*
WAMEFOUS*
WAMEFUL
WAMEFULS
WAMES
WAMMUS
WAMMUSES
WAMPEE
WAMPEES
WAMPISH
WAMPISHED
WAMPISHES
WAMPISHING
WAMPUM
WAMPUMS
WAMPUS
WAMPUSES
WAMUS
WAMUSES
WAN
WANCHANCY
WAND
WANDER
WANDERED
WANDERER
WANDERERS
WANDERING
WANDERINGS
WANDEROO
WANDEROOS
WANDERS
WANDLE

WANDOO
WANDOOS
WANDS
WANE
WANED
WANES
WANEY
WANG
WANGAN
WANGANS
WANGLE
WANGLED
WANGLER
WANGLERS
WANGLES
WANGLING
WANGLINGS
WANGS
WANGUN
WANGUNS
WANHOPE
WANHOPES
WANIER
WANIEST
WANIGAN
WANIGANS
WANING
WANINGS
WANION*
WANIONS*
WANK
WANKED
WANKER
WANKERS
WANKIER
WANKIEST
WANKING
WANKLE
WANKS
WANKY
WANLE
WANLY
WANNA
WANNABE
WANNABEE
WANNABEES
WANNABES
WANNED
WANNEL
WANNER
WANNESS
WANNESSES
WANNEST
WANNIGAN*
WANNIGANS*
WANNING
WANNISH
WANS
WANT
WANTAGE
WANTAGES
WANTED
WANTER
WANTERS

WANTHILL
WANTHILLS
WANTIES
WANTING
WANTINGS
WANTON
WANTONED
WANTONER
WANTONERS*
WANTONEST
WANTONING
WANTONISE
WANTONISED
WANTONISES
WANTONISING
WANTONIZE
WANTONIZED
WANTONIZES
WANTONIZING
WANTONLY
WANTONS
WANTS
WANTY
WANWORDY
WANWORTH
WANWORTHS
WANY
WANZE
WANZED
WANZES
WANZING
WAP
WAPENSHAW
WAPENSHAWS
WAPENTAKE
WAPENTAKES
WAPINSHAW
WAPINSHAWS
WAPITI
WAPITIS
WAPPED
WAPPEND
WAPPER
WAPPERED
WAPPERING
WAPPERS
WAPPING
WAPS
WAQF
WAQFS
WAR
WARATAH
WARATAHS
WARBIER
WARBIEST
WARBLE
WARBLED
WARBLER
WARBLERS
WARBLES
WARBLING
WARBLINGS
WARBONNET*
WARBONNETS*

WARBY	WARIEST	WARPERS	WARSLER*	WASHERY
WARCRAFT*	WARILY	WARPING	WARSLERS*	WASHES
WARCRAFTS*	WARIMENT	WARPINGS	WARSLES	WASHHOUSE
WARD	WARIMENTS	WARPLANE	WARSLING	WASHHOUSES
WARDCORN	WARINESS	WARPLANES	WARST	WASHIER
WARDCORNS	WARINESSES	WARPOWER*	WARSTLE*	WASHIEST
WARDED	WARING	WARPOWERS*	WARSTLED*	WASHINESS
WARDEN	WARISON	WARPS	WARSTLER*	WASHINESSES
WARDENED	WARISONS	WARPWISE*	WARSTLERS*	WASHING
WARDENING	WARK	WARRAGAL	WARSTLES*	WASHINGS
WARDENRIES	WARKED*	WARRAGALS	WARSTLING*	WASHLAND
WARDENRY	WARKING*	WARRAGLE	WART	WASHLANDS
WARDENS	WARKS	WARRAGLES	WARTED	WASHOUT
WARDER	WARLESS*	WARRAGUL	WARTHOG	WASHOUTS
WARDERED	WARLIKE	WARRAGULS	WARTHOGS	WASHPOT
WARDERING	WARLING	WARRAN	WARTIER	WASHPOTS
WARDERS	WARLINGS	WARRAND	WARTIEST	WASHRAG
WARDING	WARLOCK	WARRANDED	WARTIME	WASHRAGS
WARDINGS	WARLOCKRIES	WARRANDING	WARTIMES	WASHROOM
WARDMOTE	WARLOCKRY	WARRANDS	WARTLESS	WASHROOMS
WARDMOTES	WARLOCKS	WARRANED	WARTLIKE	WASHSTAND
WARDOG	WARLORD	WARRANING	WARTS	WASHSTANDS
WARDOGS	WARLORDS	WARRANS	WARTWEED	WASHTUB
WARDRESS	WARM	WARRANT	WARTWEEDS	WASHTUBS
WARDRESSES	WARMAKER*	WARRANTED	WARTWORT	WASHUP*
WARDROBE	WARMAKERS*	WARRANTEE	WARTWORTS	WASHUPS*
WARDROBER	WARMAN	WARRANTEES	WARTY	WASHWIPE
WARDROBERS	WARMBLOOD	WARRANTER	WARWOLF	WASHWIPES
WARDROBES	WARMBLOODS	WARRANTERS	WARWOLVES	WASHWOMAN*
WARDROOM	WARMED	WARRANTIES	WARWORK*	WASHWOMEN*
WARDROOMS	WARMEN	WARRANTING	WARWORKS*	WASHY
WARDROP	WARMER	WARRANTINGS	WARWORN*	WASM
WARDROPS	WARMERS	WARRANTOR	WARY	WASMS
WARDS	WARMEST	WARRANTORS	WAS	WASP
WARDSHIP	WARMING	WARRANTS	WASABI*	WASPIE
WARDSHIPS	WARMINGS	WARRANTY	WASABIS*	WASPIER
WARE	WARMISH	WARRAY	WASE	WASPIES
WARED	WARMLY	WARRAYED	WASEGOOSE	WASPIEST
WAREHOUSE	WARMNESS	WARRAYING	WASEGOOSES	WASPILY*
WAREHOUSED	WARMNESSES	WARRAYS	WASES	WASPISH
WAREHOUSES	WARMONGER	WARRE	WASH	WASPISHLY
WAREHOUSING	WARMONGERS	WARRED	WASHABLE	WASPLIKE*
WAREHOUSINGS	WARMOUTH*	WARREN	WASHABLES*	WASPNEST
WARELESS	WARMOUTHS*	WARRENER	WASHBALL	WASPNESTS
WAREROOM*	WARMS	WARRENERS	WASHBALLS	WASPS
WAREROOMS*	WARMTH	WARRENS	WASHBASIN	WASPY
WARES	WARMTHS	WARREY	WASHBASINS	WASSAIL
WARFARE	WARMUP*	WARREYED	WASHBOARD	WASSAILED
WARFARED	WARMUPS*	WARREYING	WASHBOARDS	WASSAILER
WARFARER	WARN	WARREYS	WASHBOWL	WASSAILERS
WARFARERS	WARNED	WARRIGAL	WASHBOWLS	WASSAILING
WARFARES	WARNER	WARRIGALS	WASHCLOTH	WASSAILINGS
WARFARIN	WARNERS	WARRING	WASHCLOTHS	WASSAILRIES
WARFARING	WARNING	WARRIOR	WASHDAY	WASSAILRY
WARFARINGS	WARNINGLY	WARRIORS	WASHDAYS	WASSAILS
WARFARINS	WARNINGS	WARRISON	WASHED	WASSERMAN
WARHABLE	WARNS	WARRISONS	WASHEN	WASSERMEN
WARHEAD	WARP	WARS	WASHER	WAST
WARHEADS	WARPAGE*	WARSAW*	WASHERED	WASTABLE
WARHORSE	WARPAGES*	WARSAWS*	WASHERIES	WASTAGE
WARHORSES	WARPATH	WARSHIP	WASHERING	WASTAGES
WARIBASHI	WARPATHS	WARSHIPS	WASHERMAN	WASTE
WARIBASHIS	WARPED	WARSLE	WASHERMEN	WASTED
WARIER	WARPER	WARSLED	WASHERS	WASTEFUL

Words marked with an asterisk are from OTCWL

WASTEL	WATCHMAN	WATERWORKS	WAURING	WAXCLOTH
WASTELAND	WATCHMEN	WATERWORN*	WAURS	WAXCLOTHS
WASTELANDS	WATCHOUT*	WATERY	WAURST	WAXED
WASTELOT	WATCHOUTS*	WATERZOOI*	WAVE	WAXEN
WASTELOTS	WATCHWORD	WATERZOOIS*	WAVEBAND	WAXER
WASTELS	WATCHWORDS	WATS	WAVEBANDS	WAXERS
WASTENESS	WATE	WATT	WAVED	WAXES
WASTENESSES	WATER	WATTAGE	WAVEFORM	WAXIER
WASTER	WATERAGE	WATTAGES	WAVEFORMS	WAXIEST
WASTERED	WATERAGES	WATTAPE*	WAVEFRONT	WAXILY
WASTERFUL	WATERBED*	WATTAPES*	WAVEFRONTS	WAXINESS
WASTERIE*	WATERBEDS*	WATTER	WAVEGUIDE	WAXINESSES
WASTERIES	WATERBIRD*	WATTEST	WAVEGUIDES	WAXING
WASTERIFE	WATERBIRDS*	WATTHOUR*	WAVELESS	WAXINGS
WASTERIFES	WATERBUCK*	WATTHOURS*	WAVELET	WAXLIKE*
WASTERING	WATERBUCKS*	WATTLE	WAVELETS	WAXPLANT*
WASTERS	WATERDOG*	WATTLED	WAVELIKE	WAXPLANTS*
WASTERY	WATERDOGS*	WATTLES	WAVELLITE	WAXWEED*
WASTES	WATERED	WATTLESS*	WAVELLITES	WAXWEEDS*
WASTEWAY*	WATERER	WATTLING	WAVEMETER	WAXWING
WASTEWAYS*	WATERERS	WATTLINGS	WAVEMETERS	WAXWINGS
WASTFULL	WATERFALL	WATTMETER	WAVEOFF*	WAXWORK
WASTING	WATERFALLS	WATTMETERS	WAVEOFFS*	WAXWORKER
WASTINGS	WATERFOWL	WATTS	WAVER	WAXWORKERS
WASTNESS	WATERFOWLS	WAUCHT	WAVERED	WAXWORKS
WASTNESSES	WATERHEN	WAUCHTED	WAVERER	WAXWORM*
WASTREL	WATERHENS	WAUCHTING	WAVERERS	WAXWORMS*
WASTRELS	WATERIER	WAUCHTS	WAVERIER	WAXY
WASTRIE*	WATERIEST	WAUFF	WAVERIEST	WAY
WASTRIES	WATERILY*	WAUFFED	WAVERING	WAYBILL
WASTRIFE	WATERING	WAUFFING	WAVERINGS	WAYBILLS
WASTRIFES	WATERINGS	WAUFFS	WAVEROUS	WAYBOARD
WASTRY	WATERISH	WAUGH	WAVERS	WAYBOARDS
WASTS	WATERLEAF*	WAUGHED	WAVERY	WAYBREAD
WAT	WATERLEAFS*	WAUGHING	WAVES	WAYBREADS
WATAP	WATERLESS	WAUGHS	WAVESHAPE	WAYED
WATAPE*	WATERLILIES	WAUGHT	WAVESHAPES	WAYFARE
WATAPES*	WATERLILY	WAUGHTED	WAVESON	WAYFARED
WATAPS	WATERLINE	WAUGHTING	WAVESONS	WAYFARER
WATCH	WATERLINES	WAUGHTS	WAVEY	WAYFARERS
WATCHABLE	WATERLOG	WAUK	WAVEYS	WAYFARES
WATCHABLES*	WATERLOGGED	WAUKED	WAVIER	WAYFARING
WATCHBAND*	WATERLOGGING	WAUKER	WAVIES	WAYFARINGS
WATCHBANDS*	WATERLOGS	WAUKERS	WAVIEST	WAYGOING*
WATCHBOX	WATERLOO*	WAUKING	WAVILY	WAYGOINGS*
WATCHBOXES	WATERLOOS*	WAUKMILL	WAVINESS	WAYGONE
WATCHCASE	WATERMAN .	WAUKMILLS	WAVINESSES	WAYGOOSE
WATCHCASES	WATERMARK	WAUKRIFE	WAVING	WAYGOOSES
WATCHCRIES*	WATERMARKED	WAUKS	WAVINGS	WAYING
WATCHCRY*	WATERMARKING	WAUL	WAVY	WAYLAID
WATCHDOG	WATERMARKS	WAULED	WAW	WAYLAY
WATCHDOGGED*	WATERMEN	WAULING	WAWE	WAYLAYER
WATCHDOGGING*	WATERPOX	WAULINGS	WAWES	WAYLAYERS
WATCHDOGS	WATERPOXES	WAULK	WAWL	WAYLAYING
WATCHED	WATERS	WAULKED	WAWLED	WAYLAYS
WATCHER	WATERSHED	WAULKER	WAWLING	WAYLEAVE
WATCHERS	WATERSHEDS	WAULKERS	WAWLINGS	WAYLEAVES
WATCHES	WATERSIDE	WAULKING	WAWLS	WAYLESS
WATCHET	WATERSIDES	WAULKMILL	WAWS	WAYMARK
WATCHETS	WATERWAY	WAULKMILLS	WAX	WAYMARKED
WATCHEYE*	WATERWAYS	WAULKS	WAXBERRIES	WAYMARKING
WATCHEYES*	WATERWEED	WAULS	WAXBERRY	WAYMARKS
WATCHFUL	WATERWEEDS	WAUR	WAXBILL	WAYMENT
WATCHING	WATERWORK	WAURED	WAXBILLS	WAYMENTED

WAYMENTING	WEAPON	WEB	WEEDERY	WEES
WAYMENTS	WEAPONED	WEBBED	WEEDICIDE	WEEST
WAYPOST	WEAPONING*	WEBBIER	WEEDICIDES	WEET
WAYPOSTS	WEAPONRIES	WEBBIEST	WEEDIER	WEETE
WAYS	WEAPONRY	WEBBING	WEEDIEST	WEETED
WAYSIDE	WEAPONS	WEBBINGS	WEEDILY*	WEETEN
WAYSIDES	WEAR	WEBBY	WEEDINESS	WEETER
WAYWARD	WEARABLE	WEBER	WEEDINESSES	WEETEST
WAYWARDLY	WEARABLES*	WEBERS	WEEDING	WEETING
WAYWISER	WEARED	WEBFED*	WEEDINGS	WEETINGLY
WAYWISERS	WEARER	WEBFEET	WEEDLESS	WEETLESS
WAYWODE	WEARERS	WEBFOOT	WEEDLIKE*	WEETS
WAYWODES	WEARIED	WEBFOOTED	WEEDS	WEEVER
WAYWORN	WEARIER	WEBLESS*	WEEDY	WEEVERS
WAYZGOOSE	WEARIES	WEBLIKE*	WEEING	WEEVIL
WAYZGOOSES	WEARIEST	WEBS	WEEK	WEEVILED
WAZIR	WEARIFUL	WEBSITE	WEEKDAY	WEEVILLED
WAZIRS	WEARILESS	WEBSITES	WEEKDAYS	WEEVILLY
WE	WEARILY	WEBSTER	WEEKE	WEEVILS
WEAK	WEARINESS	WEBSTERS	WEEKEND	WEEVILY
WEAKEN	WEARINESSES	WEBWHEEL	WEEKENDED	WEEWEE*
WEAKENED	WEARING	WEBWHEELS	WEEKENDER	WEEWEED*
WEAKENER	WEARINGLY	WEBWORK*	WEEKENDERS	WEEWEEING*
WEAKENERS	WEARINGS	WEBWORKS*	WEEKENDING	WEEWEES*
WEAKENING	WEARISH	WEBWORM	WEEKENDINGS	WEFT
WEAKENS	WEARISOME	WEBWORMS	WEEKENDS	WEFTAGE
WEAKER	WEARS	WECHT	WEEKES	WEFTAGES
WEAKEST	WEARY	WECHTS	WEEKLIES	WEFTE
WEAKFISH	WEARYING	WED	WEEKLONG*	WEFTED
WEAKFISHES	WEASAND	WEDDED	WEEKLY	WEFTES
WEAKISH*	WEASANDS	WEDDER	WEEKNIGHT	WEFTING
WEAKLIER	WEASEL	WEDDERED	WEEKNIGHTS	WEFTS
WEAKLIEST	WEASELED	WEDDERING	WEEKS	WEFTWISE*
WEAKLING	WEASELER	WEDDERS	WEEL	WEID
WEAKLINGS	WEASELERS	WEDDING	WEELS	WEIDS
WEAKLY	WEASELING	WEDDINGS	WEEM	WEIGELA
WEAKNESS	WEASELLED	WEDEL*	WEEMS	WEIGELAS
WEAKNESSES	WEASELLER	WEDELED*	WEEN	WEIGELIA*
WEAKSIDE*	WEASELLERS	WEDELING*	WEENED	WEIGELIAS*
WEAKSIDES*	WEASELLING	WEDELN	WEENIE*	WEIGH
WEAL	WEASELLY	WEDELNED	WEENIER	WEIGHABLE
WEALD	WEASELS	WEDELNS	WEENIES	WEIGHAGE
WEALDS	WEASELY*	WEDELS*	WEENIEST	WEIGHAGES
WEALS	WEASON*	WEDGE	WEENING	WEIGHED
WEALSMAN	WEASONS*	WEDGED	WEENS	WEIGHER
WEALSMEN	WEATHER	WEDGES	WEENSIER*	WEIGHERS
WEALTH	WEATHERED	WEDGEWISE	WEENSIEST*	WEIGHING
WEALTHIER	WEATHERING	WEDGIE	WEENSY*	WEIGHINGS
WEALTHIEST	WEATHERINGS	WEDGIER	WEENY	WEIGHMAN
WEALTHILY	WEATHERLY	WEDGIES	WEEP	WEIGHMEN*
WEALTHS	WEATHERS	WEDGIEST	WEEPER	WEIGHS
WEALTHY	WEAVE	WEDGING	WEEPERS	WEIGHT
WEAMB	WEAVED	WEDGINGS	WEEPHOLE	WEIGHTED
WEAMBS	WEAVER	WEDGY	WEEPHOLES	WEIGHTER*
WEAN	WEAVERS	WEDLOCK	WEEPIE	WEIGHTERS*
WEANED	WEAVES	WEDLOCKS	WEEPIER	WEIGHTIER
WEANEL	WEAVING	WEDS	WEEPIES	WEIGHTIEST
WEANELS	WEAVINGS	WEE	WEEPIEST	WEIGHTILY
WEANER	WEAZAND	WEED	WEEPING	WEIGHTING
WEANERS	WEAZANDS	WEEDED	WEEPINGLY	WEIGHTINGS
WEANING	WEAZEN	WEEDER	WEEPINGS	WEIGHTS
WEANLING	WEAZENED	WEEDERIES	WEEPS	WEIGHTY
WEANLINGS	WEAZENING	WEEDERS	WEEPY	WEIL
WEANS	WEAZENS		WEER	WEILS

WEINER*	WELFARIST	WENCHERS	WET	WHALED
WEINERS*	WELFARISTS	WENCHES	WETA	WHALELIKE*
WEIR	WELK	WENCHING	WETAS	WHALEMAN
WEIRD	WELKE	WEND	WETBACK	WHALEMEN
WEIRDED	WELKED	WENDED	WETBACKS	WHALER
WEIRDER	WELKES	WENDIGO	WETHER	WHALERIES
WEIRDEST	WELKIN	WENDIGOS	WETHERS	WHALERS
WEIRDIE	WELKING	WENDING	WETLAND	WHALERY
WEIRDIES	WELKINS	WENDS	WETLANDS	WHALES
WEIRDING	WELKS	WENNIER	WETLY	WHALING
WEIRDLY	WELKT	WENNIEST	WETNESS	WHALINGS
WEIRDNESS	WELL	WENNISH	WETNESSES	WHALLY
WEIRDNESSES	WELLADAY	WENNY	WETPROOF*	WHAM
WEIRDO	WELLADAYS*	WENS	WETS	WHAMMED
WEIRDOES*	WELLANEAR	WENT	WETTABLE*	WHAMMIES
WEIRDOS	WELLAWAY	WENTS	WETTED	WHAMMING
WEIRDS	WELLAWAYS*	WEPT	WETTER	WHAMMO
WEIRDY*	WELLBEING	WERE	WETTERS*	WHAMMOS
WEIRED	WELLBEINGS	WEREGILD	WETTEST	WHAMMY
WEIRING	WELLBORN*	WEREGILDS	WETTING	WHAMO*
WEIRS	WELLCURB*	WEREWOLF	WETTINGS*	WHAMPLE
WEISE	WELLCURBS*	WEREWOLVES	WETTISH	WHAMPLES
WEISED	WELLDOER*	WERGELD*	WETWARE	WHAMS
WEISES	WELLDOERS*	WERGELDS*	WETWARES	WHANG
WEISING	WELLED	WERGELT*	WEX	WHANGAM
WEIZE	WELLHEAD	WERGELTS*	WEXE	WHANGAMS
WEIZED	WELLHEADS	WERGILD	WEXED	WHANGED
WEIZES	WELLHOLE*	WERGILDS	WEXES	WHANGEE
WEIZING	WELLHOLES*	WERNERITE	WEXING	WHANGEES
WEKA	WELLHOUSE	WERNERITES	WEY	WHANGING
WEKAS	WELLHOUSES	WERSH	WEYARD	WHANGS
WELAWAY	WELLIE	WERSHER	WEYS	WHAP
WELCH	WELLIES	WERSHEST	WEYWARD	WHAPPED
WELCHED	WELLING	WERT	WEZAND	WHAPPER*
WELCHER	WELLINGS	WERWOLF	WEZANDS	WHAPPERS*
WELCHERS	WELLNESS	WERWOLVES	WHA	WHAPPING
WELCHES	WELLNESSES	WESAND	WHACK	WHAPS
WELCHING	WELLS	WESANDS	WHACKED	WHARE
WELCOME	WELLSITE*	WESKIT*	WHACKER	WHARES
WELCOMED	WELLSITES*	WESKITS*	WHACKERS	WHARF
WELCOMELY*	WELLY	WESSAND*	WHACKIER	WHARFAGE
WELCOMER	WELSH	WESSANDS*	WHACKIEST	WHARFAGES
WELCOMERS	WELSHED	WEST	WHACKING	WHARFED
WELCOMES	WELSHER	WESTBOUND	WHACKINGS	WHARFING
WELCOMING	WELSHERS	WESTED	WHACKO	WHARFINGS
WELD	WELSHES	WESTER	WHACKOES	WHARFS
WELDABLE	WELSHING	WESTERED	WHACKOS	WHARVE
WELDED	WELT	WESTERING	WHACKS	WHARVES
WELDER	WELTED	WESTERINGS	WHACKY	WHAT
WELDERS	WELTER	WESTERLIES	WHAISLE	WHATEN
WELDING	WELTERED	WESTERLY	WHAISLED	WHATEVER
WELDINGS	WELTERING	WESTERN	WHAISLES	WHATNA
WELDLESS	WELTERS	WESTERNER	WHAISLING	WHATNESS
WELDMENT	WELTING	WESTERNERS	WHAIZLE	WHATNESSES
WELDMENTS	WELTINGS*	WESTERNS	WHAIZLED	WHATNOT
WELDMESH	WELTS	WESTERS	WHAIZLES	WHATNOTS
WELDMESHES	WEM	WESTING	WHAIZLING	WHATS
WELDOR	WEMB	WESTINGS	WHALE	WHATSIS
WELDORS	WEMBS	WESTLIN	WHALEBACK	WHATSISES
WELDS	WEMS	WESTLINS	WHALEBACKS	WHATSIT
WELFARE	WEN	WESTMOST	WHALEBOAT	WHATSITS
WELFARES	WENCH	WESTS	WHALEBOATS	WHATSO
WELFARISM	WENCHED	WESTWARD	WHALEBONE	WHATTEN
WELFARISMS	WENCHER	WESTWARDS	WHALEBONES	WHAUP

The Chambers Dictionary is the authority for many longer words; see Introduction, page ix

WHAUPS	WHEEPLES	WHERENESS	WHIDDERS	WHIMPLED
WHAUR	WHEEPLING	WHERENESSES	WHIDDING	WHIMPLES
WHAURS	WHEEPS*	WHEREOF	WHIDS	WHIMPLING
WHEAL	WHEESH	WHEREON	WHIFF	WHIMS
WHEALS	WHEESHED	WHEREOUT	WHIFFED	WHIMSEY
WHEAR	WHEESHES	WHERES	WHIFFER	WHIMSEYS
WHEARE	WHEESHING	WHERESO	WHIFFERS	WHIMSICAL
WHEAT	WHEESHT	WHERETO	WHIFFET	WHIMSIED*
WHEATEAR	WHEESHTED	WHEREUNTO	WHIFFETS	WHIMSIER
WHEATEARS	WHEESHTING	WHEREUPON	WHIFFIER	WHIMSIES
WHEATEN	WHEESHTS	WHEREVER	WHIFFIEST	WHIMSIEST
WHEATENS*	WHEEZE	WHEREWITH	WHIFFING	WHIMSILY
WHEATIER	WHEEZED	WHEREWITHS	WHIFFINGS	WHIMSY
WHEATIEST	WHEEZER*	WHERRET	WHIFFLE	WHIN
WHEATMEAL	WHEEZERS*	WHERRETED	WHIFFLED	WHINBERRIES
WHEATMEALS	WHEEZES	WHERRETING	WHIFFLER	WHINBERRY
WHEATS	WHEEZIER	WHERRETS	WHIFFLERIES	WHINCHAT
WHEATWORM	WHEEZIEST	WHERRIED*	WHIFFLERS	WHINCHATS
WHEATWORMS	WHEEZILY	WHERRIES	WHIFFLERY	WHINE
WHEATY	WHEEZING	WHERRY	WHIFFLES	WHINED
WHEE	WHEEZINGS	WHERRYING*	WHIFFLING	WHINER
WHEECH	WHEEZLE	WHERRYMAN	WHIFFLINGS	WHINERS
WHEECHED	WHEEZLED	WHERRYMEN	WHIFFS	WHINES
WHEECHING	WHEEZLES	WHERVE*	WHIFFY	WHINEY*
WHEECHS	WHEEZLING	WHERVES*	WHIFT	WHINGE
WHEEDLE	WHEEZY	WHET	WHIFTS	WHINGED
WHEEDLED	WHEFT	WHETHER	WHIG	WHINGEING
WHEEDLER	WHEFTS	WHETS	WHIGGED	WHINGEINGS
WHEEDLERS	WHELK	WHETSTONE	WHIGGING	WHINGER
WHEEDLES	WHELKED	WHETSTONES	WHIGS	WHINGERS
WHEEDLING	WHELKIER	WHETTED	WHILE	WHINGES
WHEEDLINGS	WHELKIEST	WHETTER	WHILED	WHINGING*
WHEEL	WHELKS	WHETTERS	WHILERE	WHINIARD
WHEELBASE	WHELKY	WHETTING	WHILES	WHINIARDS
WHEELBASES	WHELM	WHEUGH	WHILING	WHINIER
WHEELED	WHELMED	WHEUGHED	WHILK	WHINIEST
WHEELER	WHELMING	WHEUGHING	WHILLIED	WHININESS
WHEELERS	WHELMS	WHEUGHS	WHILLIES	WHININESSES
WHEELIE	WHELP	WHEW	WHILLY	WHINING
WHEELIER	WHELPED	WHEWED	WHILLYING	WHININGLY
WHEELIES	WHELPING	WHEWING	WHILLYWHA	WHININGS
WHEELIEST	WHELPS	WHEWS	WHILLYWHAED	WHINNIED
WHEELING	WHEMMLE	WHEY	WHILLYWHAING	WHINNIER
WHEELINGS	WHEMMLED	WHEYEY	WHILLYWHAS	WHINNIES
WHEELLESS*	WHEMMLES	WHEYFACE*	WHILOM	WHINNIEST
WHEELMAN	WHEMMLING	WHEYFACES*	WHILST	WHINNY
WHEELMEN	WHEN	WHEYIER	WHIM	WHINNYING
WHEELS	WHENAS	WHEYIEST	WHIMBERRIES	WHINS
WHEELSMAN*	WHENCE	WHEYISH	WHIMBERRY	WHINSTONE
WHEELSMEN*	WHENCES	WHEYLIKE*	WHIMBREL	WHINSTONES
WHEELWORK	WHENCEVER	WHEYS	WHIMBRELS	WHINY
WHEELWORKS	WHENEVER	WHICH	WHIMMED	WHINYARD
WHEELY	WHENS	WHICHEVER	WHIMMER	WHINYARDS
WHEEN	WHERE	WHICKER	WHIMMIEST	WHIP
WHEENGE	WHEREAS	WHICKERED	WHIMMING	WHIPBIRD
WHEENGED	WHEREASES*	WHICKERING	WHIMMY	WHIPBIRDS
WHEENGES	WHEREAT	WHICKERS	WHIMPER	WHIPCAT
WHEENGING	WHEREBY	WHID	WHIMPERED	WHIPCATS
WHEENS	WHEREFOR	WHIDAH	WHIMPERER	WHIPCORD
WHEEP*	WHEREFORE	WHIDAHS	WHIMPERERS	WHIPCORDS
WHEEPED*	WHEREFORES	WHIDDED	WHIMPERING	WHIPCORDY
WHEEPING*	WHEREFROM	WHIDDER	WHIMPERINGS	WHIPJACK
WHEEPLE	WHEREIN	WHIDDERED	WHIMPERS	WHIPJACKS
WHEEPLED	WHEREINTO	WHIDDERING	WHIMPLE	WHIPLASH

WHIPLASHED
WHIPLASHES
WHIPLASHING
WHIPLIKE
WHIPPED
WHIPPER
WHIPPERS
WHIPPET
WHIPPETS
WHIPPIER
WHIPPIEST
WHIPPING
WHIPPINGS
WHIPPY
WHIPRAY*
WHIPRAYS*
WHIPS
WHIPSAW
WHIPSAWED
WHIPSAWING
WHIPSAWN*
WHIPSAWS
WHIPSTAFF
WHIPSTAFFS
WHIPSTALL
WHIPSTALLED
WHIPSTALLING
WHIPSTALLS
WHIPSTER
WHIPSTERS
WHIPSTOCK
WHIPSTOCKS
WHIPT
WHIPTAIL
WHIPTAILS*
WHIPWORM
WHIPWORMS
WHIR
WHIRL
WHIRLBAT
WHIRLBATS
WHIRLED
WHIRLER
WHIRLERS
WHIRLIER
WHIRLIES*
WHIRLIEST
WHIRLIGIG
WHIRLIGIGS
WHIRLING
WHIRLINGS
WHIRLPOOL
WHIRLPOOLS
WHIRLS
WHIRLWIND
WHIRLWINDS
WHIRLY
WHIRR
WHIRRED
WHIRRET
WHIRRETED
WHIRRETING
WHIRRETS
WHIRRIED

WHIRRIES
WHIRRING
WHIRRINGS
WHIRRS
WHIRRY
WHIRRYING
WHIRS
WHIRTLE
WHIRTLES
WHISH
WHISHED
WHISHES
WHISHING
WHISHT
WHISHTED
WHISHTING
WHISHTS
WHISK
WHISKED
WHISKER
WHISKERED
WHISKERS
WHISKERY
WHISKET
WHISKETS
WHISKEY
WHISKEYS
WHISKIES
WHISKING
WHISKS
WHISKY
WHISPER
WHISPERED
WHISPERER
WHISPERERS
WHISPERING
WHISPERINGS
WHISPERS
WHISPERY
WHISS
WHISSED
WHISSES
WHISSING
WHIST
WHISTED
WHISTING
WHISTLE
WHISTLED
WHISTLER
WHISTLERS
WHISTLES
WHISTLING
WHISTLINGS
WHISTS
WHIT
WHITE
WHITEBAIT
WHITEBAITS
WHITEBASS
WHITEBASSES
WHITEBEAM
WHITEBEAMS
WHITECAP
WHITECAPS

WHITECOAT
WHITECOATS
WHITED
WHITEFACE*
WHITEFACES*
WHITEFISH*
WHITEFISHES*
WHITEFLIES
WHITEFLY
WHITEHEAD
WHITEHEADS
WHITELY
WHITEN
WHITENED
WHITENER
WHITENERS
WHITENESS
WHITENESSES
WHITENING
WHITENINGS
WHITENS
WHITEOUT*
WHITEOUTS*
WHITEPOT
WHITEPOTS
WHITER
WHITES
WHITEST
WHITETAIL*
WHITETAILS*
WHITEWALL
WHITEWALLS
WHITEWARE
WHITEWARES
WHITEWASH
WHITEWASHED
WHITEWASHES
WHITEWASHING
WHITEWING
WHITEWINGS
WHITEWOOD
WHITEWOODS
WHITEY
WHITEYS
WHITHER
WHITHERED
WHITHERING
WHITHERS
WHITIER
WHITIES
WHITIEST
WHITING
WHITINGS
WHITISH
WHITLING
WHITLINGS
WHITLOW
WHITLOWS
WHITRACK*
WHITRACKS*
WHITRET
WHITRETS
WHITS
WHITSTER

WHITSTERS
WHITTAW
WHITTAWER
WHITTAWERS
WHITTAWS
WHITTER
WHITTERED
WHITTERING
WHITTERS
WHITTLE
WHITTLED
WHITTLER
WHITTLERS
WHITTLES
WHITTLING
WHITTLINGS
WHITTRET
WHITTRETS
WHITY
WHIZ
WHIZBANG
WHIZBANGS
WHIZZ
WHIZZBANG*
WHIZZBANGS*
WHIZZED
WHIZZER
WHIZZERS
WHIZZES
WHIZZING
WHIZZINGS
WHO
WHOA
WHODUNIT*
WHODUNITS*
WHODUNNIT
WHODUNNITS
WHOEVER
WHOLE
WHOLEFOOD
WHOLEFOODS
WHOLEMEAL
WHOLEMEALS
WHOLENESS
WHOLENESSES
WHOLES
WHOLESALE
WHOLESALED*
WHOLESALES
WHOLESALING*
WHOLESOME
WHOLESOMER
WHOLESOMEST
WHOLISM
WHOLISMS
WHOLIST
WHOLISTS
WHOLISTIC
WHOLLY
WHOM
WHOMBLE
WHOMBLED
WHOMBLES
WHOMBLING

WHOMEVER
WHOMMLE
WHOMMLED
WHOMMLES
WHOMMLING
WHOMP*
WHOMPED*
WHOMPING*
WHOMPS*
WHOMSO*
WHOOBUB
WHOOBUBS
WHOOF*
WHOOFED*
WHOOFING*
WHOOFS*
WHOOP
WHOOPED
WHOOPEE
WHOOPEES
WHOOPER
WHOOPERS
WHOOPING
WHOOPINGS
WHOOPLA*
WHOOPLAS*
WHOOPS
WHOOPSIE
WHOOPSIES
WHOOSH
WHOOSHED
WHOOSHES
WHOOSHING
WHOOSIS*
WHOOSISES*
WHOOT
WHOOTED
WHOOTING
WHOOTS
WHOP
WHOPPED
WHOPPER
WHOPPERS
WHOPPING
WHOPPINGS
WHOPS
WHORE
WHORED
WHOREDOM
WHOREDOMS
WHORES
WHORESON
WHORESONS
WHORING
WHORISH
WHORISHLY
WHORL
WHORLBAT
WHORLBATS
WHORLED
WHORLS
WHORT
WHORTLE*
WHORTLES*

The Chambers Dictionary is the authority for many longer words; see Introduction, page ix

WHORTS	WIDDLING	WIFEHOOD	WILDERED	WILLINGEST*
WHOSE	WIDDY	WIFEHOODS	WILDERING	WILLINGLY
WHOSEVER	WIDE	WIFELESS	WILDERS	WILLIWAU*
WHOSIS*	WIDEAWAKE	WIFELIER	WILDEST	WILLIWAUS*
WHOSISES*	WIDEAWAKES	WIFELIEST	WILDFIRE	WILLIWAW
WHOSO	WIDEBAND*	WIFELIKE	WILDFIRES	WILLIWAWS
WHOSOEVER	WIDEBODY	WIFELY	WILDFOWL	WILLOW
WHOT	WIDELY	WIFES*	WILDFOWLS	WILLOWED
WHOW	WIDEN	WIFIE	WILDGRAVE	WILLOWER*
WHUMMLE	WIDENED	WIFIES	WILDGRAVES	WILLOWERS*
WHUMMLED	WIDENER	WIFING*	WILDING	WILLOWIER
WHUMMLES	WIDENERS	WIFTIER*	WILDINGS	WILLOWIEST
WHUMMLING	WIDENESS	WIFTIEST*	WILDISH	WILLOWING
WHUMP*	WIDENESSES	WIFTY*	WILDLAND	WILLOWISH
WHUMPED*	WIDENING	WIG	WILDLANDS	WILLOWS
WHUMPING*	WIDENS	WIGAN	WILDLIFE	WILLOWY
WHUMPS*	WIDEOUT*	WIGANS	WILDLIFES	WILLPOWER
WHUNSTANE	WIDEOUTS*	WIGEON	WILDLING*	WILLPOWERS
WHUNSTANES	WIDER	WIGEONS	WILDLINGS*	WILLS
WHY	WIDES	WIGGED	WILDLY	WILLY
WHYDAH	WIDEST	WIGGERIES	WILDNESS	WILLYARD
WHYDAHS	WIDGEON	WIGGERY	WILDNESSES	WILLYART
WHYEVER	WIDGEONS	WIGGIER*	WILDS	WILLYING
WHYS*	WIDGET	WIGGIEST*	WILDWOOD	WILLYWAW*
WICCA	WIDGETS	WIGGING	WILDWOODS	WILLYWAWS*
WICCAN	WIDGIE	WIGGINGS	WILE	WILT
WICCANS	WIDGIES	WIGGLE	WILED	WILTED
WICCAS	WIDISH	WIGGLED	WILEFUL	WILTING
WICE	WIDOW	WIGGLER	WILES	WILTJA
WICH	WIDOWED	WIGGLERS	WILFUL	WILTJAS
WICHES	WIDOWER	WIGGLES	WILFULLY	WILTS
WICK	WIDOWERS	WIGGLIER	WILGA	WILY
WICKAPE*	WIDOWHOOD	WIGGLIEST	WILGAS	WIMBLE
WICKAPES*	WIDOWHOODS	WIGGLING	WILI	WIMBLED
WICKED	WIDOWING	WIGGLY	WILIER	WIMBLES
WICKEDER	WIDOWMAN	WIGGY*	WILIEST	WIMBLING
WICKEDEST	WIDOWMEN	WIGHT	WILILY	WIMBREL
WICKEDLY	WIDOWS	WIGHTED	WILINESS	WIMBRELS
WICKEDS	WIDTH	WIGHTING	WILINESSES	WIMP
WICKEN	WIDTHS	WIGHTLY	WILING	WIMPIER
WICKENS	WIDTHWAY*	WIGHTS	WILIS	WIMPIEST
WICKER	WIDTHWAYS	WIGLESS	WILJA	WIMPINESS*
WICKERED	WIDTHWISE	WIGLET*	WILJAS	WIMPINESSES*
WICKERS	WIEL	WIGLETS*	WILL	WIMPISH
WICKET	WIELD	WIGLIKE	WILLABLE	WIMPISHLY
WICKETS	WIELDABLE	WIGMAKER*	WILLED	WIMPLE
WICKIES	WIELDED	WIGMAKERS*	WILLEMITE	WIMPLED
WICKING	WIELDER	WIGS	WILLEMITES	WIMPLES
WICKINGS*	WIELDERS	WIGWAG	WILLER	WIMPLING
WICKIUP	WIELDIER	WIGWAGGED	WILLERS	WIMPS
WICKIUPS	WIELDIEST	WIGWAGGING	WILLEST	WIMPY
WICKS	WIELDING	WIGWAGS	WILLET	WIN
WICKY	WIELDLESS	WIGWAM	WILLETS	WINCE
WICKYUP*	WIELDS	WIGWAMS	WILLEY	WINCED
WICKYUPS*	WIELDY	WIKIUP*	WILLEYED	WINCER
WICOPIES*	WIELS	WIKIUPS*	WILLEYING	WINCERS
WICOPY*	WIENER*	WILCO*	WILLEYS	WINCES
WIDDER*	WIENERS*	WILD	WILLFUL	WINCEY
WIDDERS*	WIENIE	WILDCAT	WILLFULLY*	WINCEYS
WIDDIE*	WIENIES	WILDCATS	WILLIE	WINCH
WIDDIES	WIFE	WILDCATTED	WILLIED	WINCHED
WIDDLE	WIFED*	WILDCATTING	WILLIES	WINCHER*
WIDDLED	WIFEDOM*	WILDED	WILLING	WINCHERS*
WIDDLES	WIFEDOMS*	WILDER	WILLINGER*	WINCHES

WINCHING	WINDLING*	WINES	WINNER	WIPINGS
WINCHMAN	WINDLINGS*	WINESHOP*	WINNERS	WIPPEN
WINCHMEN	WINDMILL	WINESHOPS*	WINNING	WIPPENS
WINCING	WINDMILLED	WINESKIN	WINNINGLY	WIRABLE*
WINCINGS	WINDMILLING	WINESKINS	WINNINGS	WIRE
WINCOPIPE	WINDMILLS	WINESOP*	WINNLE	WIRED
WINCOPIPES	WINDOCK	WINESOPS*	WINNLES	WIREDRAW
WIND	WINDOCKS	WINEY	WINNOCK	WIREDRAWING
WINDABLE*	WINDORE	WING	WINNOCKS	WIREDRAWINGS
WINDAC	WINDORES	WINGBACK*	WINNOW	WIREDRAWN
WINDACS	WINDOW	WINGBACKS*	WINNOWED	WIREDRAWS
WINDAGE	WINDOWED	WINGBEAT	WINNOWER	WIREDREW
WINDAGES	WINDOWING	WINGBEATS	WINNOWERS	WIREHAIR*
WINDAS	WINDOWINGS	WINGBOW*	WINNOWING	WIREHAIRS*
WINDASES	WINDOWS	WINGBOWS*	WINNOWINGS	WIRELESS
WINDBAG	WINDPIPE	WINGDING	WINNOWS	WIRELESSED
WINDBAGS	WINDPIPES	WINGDINGS	WINNS	WIRELESSES
WINDBLAST*	WINDPROOF	WINGE	WINO	WIRELESSING
WINDBLASTS*	WINDRING	WINGED	WINOES*	WIRELIKE*
WINDBLOW	WINDROSE	WINGEDLY	WINOS	WIREMAN
WINDBLOWN	WINDROSES	WINGEING	WINS	WIREMEN
WINDBLOWS	WINDROW	WINGER	WINSEY	WIREPHOTO
WINDBORNE	WINDROWED	WINGERS	WINSEYS	WIREPHOTOS
WINDBOUND	WINDROWING	WINGES	WINSOME	WIRER
WINDBREAK	WINDROWS	WINGIER	WINSOMELY	WIRERS
WINDBREAKS	WINDS	WINGIEST	WINSOMER	WIRES
WINDBURN	WINDSAIL	WINGING	WINSOMEST	WIRETAP
WINDBURNED*	WINDSAILS	WINGLESS	WINTER	WIRETAPPED
WINDBURNING*	WINDSES	WINGLET	WINTERED	WIRETAPPING
WINDBURNS	WINDSHAKE	WINGLETS	WINTERER*	WIRETAPS
WINDBURNT*	WINDSHAKES	WINGLIKE*	WINTERERS*	WIREWAY
WINDCHILL*	WINDSHIP	WINGMAN*	WINTERIER	WIREWAYS
WINDCHILLS*	WINDSHIPS	WINGMEN*	WINTERIEST	WIREWORK
WINDED	WINDSOCK	WINGOVER*	WINTERING	WIREWORKS
WINDER	WINDSOCKS	WINGOVERS*	WINTERISE	WIREWORM
WINDERS	WINDSTORM	WINGS	WINTERISED	WIREWORMS
WINDFALL	WINDSTORMS	WINGSPAN	WINTERISES	WIREWOVE
WINDFALLS	WINDSURF	WINGSPANS	WINTERISING	WIRIER
WINDFLAW*	WINDSURFED	WINGTIP*	WINTERIZE	WIRIEST
WINDFLAWS*	WINDSURFING	WINGTIPS*	WINTERIZED	WIRILY
WINDGALL	WINDSURFINGS	WINGY	WINTERIZES	WIRINESS
WINDGALLS	WINDSURFS	WINIER	WINTERIZING	WIRINESSES
WINDGUN	WINDSWEPT	WINIEST	WINTERLY	WIRING
WINDGUNS	WINDTHROW	WINING	WINTERS	WIRINGS
WINDHOVER	WINDTHROWS	WINISH*	WINTERY	WIRRA*
WINDHOVERS	WINDTIGHT	WINK	WINTLE	WIRRICOW
WINDIER	WINDUP*	WINKED	WINTLED	WIRRICOWS
WINDIEST	WINDUPS*	WINKER	WINTLES	WIRY
WINDIGO	WINDWARD	WINKERS	WINTLING	WIS
WINDIGOS	WINDWARDS	WINKING	WINTRIER	WISARD
WINDILY	WINDWAY*	WINKINGLY	WINTRIEST	WISARDS
WINDINESS	WINDWAYS*	WINKINGS	WINTRILY*	WISDOM
WINDINESSES	WINDY	WINKLE	WINTRY	WISDOMS
WINDING	WINE	WINKLED	WINY	WISE
WINDINGLY	WINEBERRIES	WINKLER	WINZE	WISEACRE
WINDINGS	WINEBERRY	WINKLERS	WINZES	WISEACRES
WINDLASS	WINED	WINKLES	WIPE	WISEASS*
WINDLASSED	WINEGLASS	WINKLING	WIPED	WISEASSES*
WINDLASSES	WINEGLASSES	WINKS	WIPEOUT	WISECRACK
WINDLASSING	WINELESS*	WINLESS*	WIPEOUTS	WISECRACKED
WINDLE	WINEPRESS	WINN	WIPER	WISECRACKING
WINDLED*	WINEPRESSES	WINNA	WIPERS	WISECRACKS
WINDLES	WINERIES	WINNABLE	WIPES	WISED
WINDLESS	WINERY	WINNED*	WIPING	WISELIER*

The Chambers Dictionary is the authority for many longer words; see Introduction, page ix

WISELIEST*	WITCHEN	WITHWIND	WIZENING	WOLFERS
WISELING	WITCHENS	WITHWINDS	WIZENS	WOLFFISH*
WISELINGS	WITCHERIES	WITHY	WIZES*	WOLFFISHES*
WISELY	WITCHERY	WITHYWIND	WIZIER	WOLFHOUND
WISENESS	WITCHES	WITHYWINDS	WIZIERS	WOLFHOUNDS
WISENESSES	WITCHETTIES	WITING	WIZZEN*	WOLFING
WISENT	WITCHETTY	WITLESS	WIZZENS*	WOLFINGS
WISENTS	WITCHIER	WITLESSLY	WO	WOLFISH
WISER	WITCHIEST	WITLING	WOAD	WOLFISHLY
WISES	WITCHING	WITLINGS	WOADED	WOLFKIN
WISEST	WITCHINGS	WITLOOF	WOADS	WOLFKINS
WISEWOMAN*	WITCHKNOT	WITLOOFS	WOADWAX*	WOLFLIKE*
WISEWOMEN*	WITCHKNOTS	WITNESS	WOADWAXES*	WOLFLING
WISH	WITCHLIKE	WITNESSED	WOALD*	WOLFLINGS
WISHA*	WITCHMEAL	WITNESSER	WOALDS*	WOLFRAM
WISHBONE	WITCHMEALS	WITNESSERS	WOBBEGONG	WOLFRAMS
WISHBONES	WITCHWEED*	WITNESSES	WOBBEGONGS	WOLFS
WISHED	WITCHWEEDS*	WITNESSING	WOBBLE	WOLFSBANE
WISHER	WITCHY	WITNEY*	WOBBLED	WOLFSBANES
WISHERS	WITE	WITNEYS*	WOBBLER	WOLFSKIN
WISHES	WITED	WITS	WOBBLERS	WOLFSKINS
WISHFUL	WITELESS	WITTED	WOBBLES	WOLLIES
WISHFULLY	WITES	WITTER	WOBBLIER	WOLLY
WISHING	WITGAT	WITTERED	WOBBLIES	WOLVE
WISHINGS	WITGATS	WITTERING	WOBBLIEST	WOLVED
WISHLESS*	WITH	WITTERS	WOBBLING	WOLVER
WISING	WITHAL	WITTICISM	WOBBLINGS	WOLVERENE
WISKET	WITHDRAW	WITTICISMS	WOBBLY	WOLVERENES
WISKETS	WITHDRAWING	WITTIER	WOBEGONE	WOLVERINE
WISP	WITHDRAWN	WITTIEST	WOCK	WOLVERINES
WISPED	WITHDRAWS	WITTILY	WOCKS	WOLVERS
WISPIER	WITHDREW	WITTINESS	WODGE	WOLVES
WISPIEST	WITHE	WITTINESSES	WODGES	WOLVING
WISPILY*	WITHED	WITTING	WOE	WOLVINGS
WISPINESS*	WITHER	WITTINGLY	WOEBEGONE	WOLVISH
WISPINESSES*	WITHERED	WITTINGS	WOEFUL	WOLVISHLY
WISPING	WITHERER*	WITTOL	WOEFULLER	WOMAN
WISPISH*	WITHERERS*	WITTOLLY	WOEFULLEST	WOMANED
WISPLIKE*	WITHERING	WITTOLS	WOEFULLY	WOMANHOOD
WISPS	WITHERINGS	WITTY	WOENESS*	WOMANHOODS
WISPY	WITHERITE	WITWALL	WOENESSES*	WOMANING
WISS*	WITHERITES	WITWALLS	WOES	WOMANISE
WISSED	WITHERS	WITWANTON	WOESOME	WOMANISED
WISSES	WITHES	WITWANTONED	WOFUL	WOMANISER
WISSING	WITHHAULT	WITWANTONING	WOFULLY	WOMANISERS
WIST	WITHHELD	WITWANTONS	WOFULNESS	WOMANISES
WISTARIA	WITHHOLD	WIVE	WOFULNESSES	WOMANISH
WISTARIAS	WITHHOLDEN	WIVED	WOG	WOMANISING
WISTED	WITHHOLDING	WIVEHOOD	WOGGLE	WOMANIZE
WISTERIA	WITHHOLDS	WIVEHOODS	WOGGLES	WOMANIZED
WISTERIAS	WITHIER	WIVER*	WOGS	WOMANIZER
WISTFUL	WITHIES	WIVERN	WOIWODE	WOMANIZERS
WISTFULLY	WITHIEST	WIVERNS	WOIWODES	WOMANIZES
WISTING	WITHIN	WIVERS*	WOK	WOMANIZING
WISTITI	WITHING	WIVES	WOKE	WOMANKIND
WISTITIS	WITHINS*	WIVING	WOKEN	WOMANKINDS
WISTLY	WITHOUT	WIZ*	WOKS	WOMANLESS
WISTS	WITHOUTEN	WIZARD	WOLD	WOMANLIER
WIT	WITHOUTS*	WIZARDLY	WOLDS	WOMANLIEST
WITAN	WITHS	WIZARDRIES	WOLF	WOMANLIKE
WITBLITS	WITHSTAND	WIZARDRY	WOLFBERRIES	WOMANLY
WITBLITSES	WITHSTANDING	WIZARDS	WOLFBERRY	WOMANS
WITCH	WITHSTANDS	WIZEN	WOLFED	WOMB
WITCHED	WITHSTOOD	WIZENED	WOLFER	WOMBAT

WOMBATS
WOMBED
WOMBIER*
WOMBIEST*
WOMBING
WOMBLIKE
WOMBS
WOMBY
WOMEN
WOMENFOLK
WOMENFOLKS
WOMENKIND
WOMENKINDS
WOMERA
WOMERAS
WOMMERA*
WOMMERAS*
WON
WONDER
WONDERED
WONDERER
WONDERERS
WONDERFUL
WONDERING
WONDERINGS
WONDEROUS
WONDERS
WONDRED
WONDROUS
WONGA
WONGAS
WONGI
WONGIED
WONGIING
WONGIS
WONING
WONINGS
WONK
WONKIER
WONKIEST
WONKS
WONKY
WONNED
WONNER*
WONNERS*
WONNING
WONNINGS
WONS
WONT
WONTED
WONTEDLY*
WONTING
WONTLESS
WONTON*
WONTONS*
WONTS
WOO
WOOBUT
WOOBUTS
WOOD
WOODBIN*
WOODBIND
WOODBINDS
WOODBINE

WOODBINES
WOODBINS*
WOODBLOCK
WOODBLOCKS
WOODBOX*
WOODBOXES*
WOODCHAT
WOODCHATS
WOODCHIP
WOODCHIPS
WOODCHUCK
WOODCHUCKS
WOODCOCK
WOODCOCKS
WOODCRAFT
WOODCRAFTS
WOODCUT
WOODCUTS
WOODED
WOODEN
WOODENER
WOODENEST
WOODENLY
WOODENTOP
WOODENTOPS
WOODHEN*
WOODHENS*
WOODHOLE
WOODHOLES
WOODHORSE
WOODHORSES
WOODHOUSE
WOODHOUSES
WOODIE
WOODIER
WOODIES
WOODIEST
WOODINESS
WOODINESSES
WOODING
WOODLAND
WOODLANDS
WOODLARK
WOODLARKS
WOODLESS
WOODLICE
WOODLORE*
WOODLORES*
WOODLOT*
WOODLOTS*
WOODLOUSE
WOODMAN
WOODMEAL
WOODMEALS
WOODMEN
WOODMICE
WOODMOUSE
WOODNESS
WOODNESSES
WOODNOTE
WOODNOTES
WOODPILE
WOODPILES
WOODREEVE

WOODREEVES
WOODROOF
WOODROOFS
WOODRUFF
WOODRUFFS
WOODRUSH
WOODRUSHES
WOODS
WOODSCREW
WOODSCREWS
WOODSHED
WOODSHEDDED
WOODSHEDDING
WOODSHEDDINGS
WOODSHEDS
WOODSHOCK
WOODSHOCKS
WOODSIA
WOODSIAS
WOODSIER
WOODSIEST
WOODSKIN
WOODSKINS
WOODSMAN
WOODSMEN
WOODSPITE
WOODSPITES
WOODSTONE
WOODSTONES
WOODSTOVE*
WOODSTOVES*
WOODSY
WOODWALE
WOODWALES
WOODWARD
WOODWARDS
WOODWAX
WOODWAXEN
WOODWAXENS
WOODWAXES
WOODWIND
WOODWINDS
WOODWORK
WOODWORKS
WOODWORM
WOODWORMS
WOODWOSE
WOODWOSES
WOODY
WOODYARD
WOODYARDS
WOOED
WOOER
WOOERS
WOOF
WOOFED
WOOFER
WOOFERS
WOOFIER
WOOFIEST
WOOFING
WOOFS
WOOFTER
WOOFTERS

WOOFY
WOOING
WOOINGLY
WOOINGS
WOOL
WOOLD
WOOLDED
WOOLDER
WOOLDERS
WOOLDING
WOOLDINGS
WOOLDS
WOOLED*
WOOLEN
WOOLENS
WOOLER*
WOOLERS*
WOOLFAT
WOOLFATS
WOOLFELL
WOOLFELLS
WOOLHAT*
WOOLHATS*
WOOLIE*
WOOLIER*
WOOLIES*
WOOLIEST*
WOOLLED
WOOLLEN
WOOLLENS
WOOLLIER
WOOLLIES
WOOLLIEST
WOOLLIKE*
WOOLLILY*
WOOLLY
WOOLMAN
WOOLMEN
WOOLPACK
WOOLPACKS
WOOLS
WOOLSACK
WOOLSACKS
WOOLSEY
WOOLSEYS
WOOLSHED
WOOLSHEDS
WOOLSKIN*
WOOLSKINS*
WOOLWARD
WOOLWORK
WOOLWORKS
WOOLY*
WOOMERA
WOOMERANG
WOOMERANGS
WOOMERAS
WOON
WOONED
WOONING
WOONS
WOOPIE
WOOPIES
WOOPS*

WOOPSED*
WOOPSES*
WOOPSING*
WOORALI
WOORALIS
WOORARA
WOORARAS
WOORARI*
WOORARIS*
WOOS
WOOSEL
WOOSELL
WOOSELLS
WOOSELS
WOOSH
WOOSHED
WOOSHES
WOOSHING
WOOT
WOOTZ
WOOTZES
WOOZIER
WOOZIEST
WOOZILY
WOOZINESS
WOOZINESSES
WOOZY
WOP
WOPPED
WOPPING
WOPS
WORCESTER
WORCESTERS
WORD
WORDAGE
WORDAGES
WORDBOOK
WORDBOOKS
WORDBOUND
WORDBREAK
WORDBREAKS
WORDED
WORDGAME
WORDGAMES
WORDIER
WORDIEST
WORDILY
WORDINESS
WORDINESSES
WORDING
WORDINGS
WORDISH
WORDLESS
WORDLORE
WORDLORES
WORDPLAY
WORDPLAYS
WORDS
WORDSMITH
WORDSMITHS
WORDY
WORE
WORK
WORKABLE

The Chambers Dictionary is the authority for many longer words; see Introduction, page ix

WORKADAY	WORKTOPS	WORRITED	WOTTING	WRAPPINGS
WORKADAYS	WORKUP*	WORRITING	WOUBIT	WRAPROUND
WORKBAG	WORKUPS*	WORRITS	WOUBITS	WRAPROUNDS
WORKBAGS	WORKWEAR	WORRY	WOULD	WRAPS
WORKBENCH	WORKWEARS	WORRYCOW	WOULDEST*	WRAPT
WORKBENCHES	WORKWEEK	WORRYCOWS	WOULDS	WRASSE
WORKBOAT	WORKWEEKS	WORRYGUTS	WOULDST	WRASSES
WORKBOATS	WORKWOMAN	WORRYING	WOUND	WRASSLE*
WORKBOOK	WORKWOMEN	WORRYINGS	WOUNDABLE	WRASSLED*
WORKBOOKS	WORLD	WORRYWART	WOUNDED	WRASSLES*
WORKBOX	WORLDED	WORRYWARTS	WOUNDER	WRASSLING*
WORKBOXES	WORLDLIER	WORSE	WOUNDERS	WRAST
WORKDAY	WORLDLIEST	WORSED	WOUNDILY	WRASTED
WORKDAYS	WORLDLING	WORSEN	WOUNDING	WRASTING
WORKED	WORLDLINGS	WORSENED	WOUNDINGS	WRASTLE*
WORKER	WORLDLY	WORSENESS	WOUNDLESS	WRASTLED*
WORKERIST	WORLDS	WORSENESSES	WOUNDS	WRASTLES*
WORKERISTS	WORLDVIEW*	WORSENING	WOUNDWORT	WRASTLING*
WORKERS	WORLDVIEWS*	WORSENS	WOUNDWORTS	WRASTS
WORKFARE	WORLDWIDE	WORSER	WOUNDY	WRATE
WORKFARES	WORM	WORSES	WOURALI	WRATH
WORKFOLK	WORMCAST	WORSET*	WOURALIS	WRATHED
WORKFOLKS	WORMCASTS	WORSETS*	WOVE	WRATHFUL
WORKFORCE	WORMED	WORSHIP	WOVEN	WRATHIER
WORKFORCES	WORMER	WORSHIPED*	WOVENS*	WRATHIEST
WORKFUL	WORMERIES	WORSHIPER*	WOW	WRATHILY
WORKGIRL	WORMERS	WORSHIPERS*	WOWED	WRATHING
WORKGIRLS	WORMERY	WORSHIPING*	WOWEE	WRATHLESS
WORKGROUP	WORMHOLE	WORSHIPPED	WOWF	WRATHS
WORKGROUPS	WORMHOLED	WORSHIPPING	WOWFER	WRATHY
WORKHORSE	WORMHOLES	WORSHIPS	WOWFEST	WRAWL
WORKHORSES	WORMIER	WORSING	WOWING	WRAWLED
WORKHOUSE	WORMIEST	WORST	WOWS	WRAWLING
WORKHOUSES	WORMIL*	WORSTED	WOWSER	WRAWLS
WORKING	WORMILS*	WORSTEDS	WOWSERS	WRAXLE
WORKINGS	WORMING	WORSTING	WOX	WRAXLED
WORKLESS	WORMISH*	WORSTS	WOXEN	WRAXLES
WORKLOAD	WORMLIKE*	WORT	WRACK	WRAXLING
WORKLOADS	WORMROOT*	WORTH	WRACKED	WRAXLINGS
WORKMAN	WORMROOTS*	WORTHED	WRACKFUL	WREAK
WORKMANLY	WORMS	WORTHFUL	WRACKING	WREAKED
WORKMATE	WORMSEED	WORTHIED	WRACKS	WREAKER
WORKMATES	WORMSEEDS	WORTHIER	WRAITH	WREAKERS
WORKMEN	WORMWOOD	WORTHIES	WRAITHS	WREAKFUL
WORKOUT*	WORMWOODS	WORTHIEST	WRANG*	WREAKING
WORKOUTS*	WORMY	WORTHILY	WRANGLE	WREAKLESS
WORKPIECE	WORN	WORTHING	WRANGLED	WREAKS
WORKPIECES	WORNNESS*	WORTHLESS	WRANGLER	WREATH
WORKPLACE	WORNNESSES*	WORTHS	WRANGLERS	WREATHE
WORKPLACES	WORRAL	WORTHY	WRANGLES	WREATHED
WORKROOM	WORRALS	WORTHYING	WRANGLING	WREATHEN
WORKROOMS	WORREL	WORTLE	WRANGLINGS	WREATHER
WORKS	WORRELS	WORTLES	WRANGS*	WREATHERS
WORKSHEET	WORRICOW	WORTS	WRAP	WREATHES
WORKSHEETS	WORRICOWS	WOS	WRAPOVER	WREATHIER
WORKSHOP	WORRIED	WOSBIRD	WRAPOVERS	WREATHIEST
WORKSHOPPED	WORRIEDLY	WOSBIRDS	WRAPPAGE	WREATHING
WORKSHOPPING	WORRIER	WOST	WRAPPAGES	WREATHS
WORKSHOPS	WORRIERS	WOT	WRAPPED	WREATHY
WORKSHY	WORRIES	WOTCHER	WRAPPER	WRECK
WORKSOME	WORRIMENT	WOTS	WRAPPERED	WRECKAGE
WORKTABLE	WORRIMENTS	WOTTED	WRAPPERING	WRECKAGES
WORKTABLES	WORRISOME	WOTTEST	WRAPPERS	WRECKED
WORKTOP	WORRIT	WOTTETH	WRAPPING	WRECKER

Words marked with an asterisk are from OTCWL

WRECKERS
WRECKFISH
WRECKFISHES
WRECKFUL
WRECKING
WRECKINGS
WRECKS
WREN
WRENCH
WRENCHED
WRENCHES
WRENCHING
WRENCHINGS
WRENS
WREST
WRESTED
WRESTER
WRESTERS
WRESTING
WRESTLE
WRESTLED
WRESTLER
WRESTLERS
WRESTLES
WRESTLING
WRESTLINGS
WRESTS
WRETCH
WRETCHED
WRETCHEDER
WRETCHEDEST
WRETCHES
WRETHE
WRETHED
WRETHES
WRETHING
WRICK
WRICKED
WRICKING
WRICKS
WRIED
WRIER

WRIES
WRIEST
WRIGGLE
WRIGGLED
WRIGGLER
WRIGGLERS
WRIGGLES
WRIGGLIER
WRIGGLIEST
WRIGGLING
WRIGGLINGS
WRIGGLY
WRIGHT
WRIGHTS
WRING
WRINGED
WRINGER
WRINGERS
WRINGING
WRINGINGS
WRINGS
WRINKLE
WRINKLED
WRINKLES
WRINKLIER
WRINKLIES
WRINKLIEST
WRINKLING
WRINKLY
WRIST
WRISTBAND
WRISTBANDS
WRISTIER
WRISTIEST
WRISTLET
WRISTLETS
WRISTLOCK*
WRISTLOCKS*
WRISTS
WRISTY
WRIT
WRITABLE

WRITATIVE
WRITE
WRITER
WRITERESS
WRITERESSES
WRITERLY
WRITERS
WRITES
WRITHE
WRITHED
WRITHEN
WRITHER*
WRITHERS*
WRITHES
WRITHING
WRITHINGS
WRITHLED
WRITING
WRITINGS
WRITS
WRITTEN
WRIZLED
WROATH
WROATHS
WROKE
WROKEN
WRONG
WRONGDOER
WRONGDOERS
WRONGED
WRONGER
WRONGERS
WRONGEST
WRONGFUL
WRONGING
WRONGLY
WRONGNESS
WRONGNESSES
WRONGOUS
WRONGS
WROOT
WROOTED

WROOTING
WROOTS
WROTE
WROTH
WROTHFUL*
WROUGHT
WRUNG
WRY
WRYBILL
WRYBILLS
WRYER
WRYEST
WRYING
WRYLY
WRYNECK
WRYNECKS
WRYNESS
WRYNESSES
WRYTHEN
WUD
WUDDED
WUDDING
WUDS
WULFENITE
WULFENITES
WULL
WULLED
WULLING
WULLS
WUNNER
WUNNERS
WURLEY
WURLEYS
WURLIES
WURST
WURSTS
WURTZITE
WURTZITES
WURZEL*
WURZELS*
WUS
WUSES

WUSHU
WUSHUS
WUSS
WUSSES
WUSSIER*
WUSSIES*
WUSSIEST*
WUSSY*
WUTHER
WUTHERED
WUTHERING
WUTHERS
WUZZLE
WUZZLED
WUZZLES
WUZZLING
WYANDOTTE
WYANDOTTES
WYCH
WYCHES
WYE
WYES
WYLE*
WYLED*
WYLES*
WYLIECOAT
WYLIECOATS
WYLING*
WYN
WYND
WYNDS
WYNN
WYNNS
WYNS
WYSIWYG
WYTE
WYTED
WYTES
WYTING
WYVERN
WYVERNS

X

XANTHAM
XANTHAMS
XANTHAN
XANTHANS
XANTHATE
XANTHATES
XANTHEIN
XANTHEINS
XANTHENE
XANTHENES
XANTHIC
XANTHIN
XANTHINE
XANTHINES
XANTHINS
XANTHOMA
XANTHOMAS
XANTHOMATA
XANTHONE*
XANTHONES*
XANTHOUS
XANTHOXYL
XANTHOXYLS
XEBEC
XEBECS
XENIA
XENIAL
XENIAS
XENIC*
XENIUM
XENOCRYST
XENOCRYSTS
XENOGAMIES

XENOGAMY
XENOGENIES*
XENOGENY*
XENOGRAFT
XENOGRAFTS
XENOLITH
XENOLITHS
XENOMANIA
XENOMANIAS
XENOMENIA
XENOMENIAS
XENON
XENONS
XENOPHILE
XENOPHILES
XENOPHOBE
XENOPHOBES
XENOPHOBIES
XENOPHOBY
XENOPHYA
XENOTIME
XENOTIMES
XENURINE
XERAFIN
XERAFINS
XERANSES
XERANSIS
XERANTIC
XERAPHIM
XERAPHIMS
XERARCH
XERASIA
XERASIAS

XERIC
XEROCHASIES
XEROCHASY
XERODERMA
XERODERMAS
XEROMA
XEROMAS
XEROMATA
XEROMORPH
XEROMORPHS
XEROPHAGIES
XEROPHAGY
XEROPHILE*
XEROPHILIES
XEROPHILY
XEROPHYTE
XEROPHYTES
XEROSERE*
XEROSERES*
XEROSES
XEROSIS
XEROSTOMA
XEROSTOMAS
XEROSTOMATA
XEROTES
XEROTIC
XEROX*
XEROXED*
XEROXES*
XEROXING*
XERUS*
XERUSES*
XI

XIPHOID
XIPHOIDAL
XIPHOIDS*
XIPHOPAGI
XIS
XOANA
XOANON
XU
XYLAN*
XYLANS*
XYLEM
XYLEMS
XYLENE
XYLENES
XYLENOL
XYLENOLS
XYLIC
XYLIDIN*
XYLIDINE*
XYLIDINES*
XYLIDINS*
XYLITOL
XYLITOLS
XYLOCARP
XYLOCARPS
XYLOGEN
XYLOGENS
XYLOGRAPH
XYLOGRAPHS
XYLOID
XYLOIDIN
XYLOIDINE
XYLOIDINES

XYLOIDINS
XYLOL
XYLOLOGIES
XYLOLOGY
XYLOLS
XYLOMA
XYLOMAS
XYLOMATA
XYLOMETER
XYLOMETERS
XYLONIC
XYLONITE
XYLONITES
XYLOPHAGE
XYLOPHAGES
XYLOPHONE
XYLOPHONES
XYLORIMBA
XYLORIMBAS
XYLOSE
XYLOSES
XYLOTOMIES*
XYLOTOMY*
XYLYL
XYLYLS
XYST
XYSTER
XYSTERS
XYSTI
XYSTOI
XYSTOS
XYSTS
XYSTUS

Y

YA*
YABBER
YABBERED
YABBERING
YABBERS
YABBIE
YABBIES
YABBY
YACCA
YACCAS
YACHT
YACHTED
YACHTER
YACHTERS
YACHTIE
YACHTIES
YACHTING
YACHTINGS
YACHTMAN*
YACHTMEN*
YACHTS
YACHTSMAN
YACHTSMEN
YACK
YACKED
YACKER
YACKERS
YACKING
YACKS
YAFF
YAFFED
YAFFING
YAFFLE
YAFFLES
YAFFS
YAGER
YAGERS
YAGGER
YAGGERS
YAGI*
YAGIS*
YAH
YAHOO
YAHOOISM*
YAHOOISMS*
YAHOOS
YAHRZEIT*
YAHRZEITS*
YAHS
YAIRD*
YAIRDS*
YAK
YAKHDAN
YAKHDANS
YAKIMONO

YAKIMONOS
YAKITORI
YAKITORIS
YAKKA
YAKKAS
YAKKED
YAKKER
YAKKERS
YAKKING
YAKOW
YAKOWS
YAKS
YAKUZA
YALD
YALE
YALES
YAM
YAMALKA*
YAMALKAS*
YAMEN
YAMENS
YAMMER
YAMMERED
YAMMERER*
YAMMERERS*
YAMMERING
YAMMERINGS
YAMMERS
YAMS
YAMULKA
YAMULKAS
YAMUN*
YAMUNS*
YANG
YANGS
YANK
YANKED
YANKER
YANKERS
YANKIE
YANKIES
YANKING
YANKS
YANQUI
YANQUIS
YANTRA*
YANTRAS*
YAOURT
YAOURTS
YAP
YAPOCK
YAPOCKS
YAPOK
YAPOKS
YAPON

YAPONS
YAPP
YAPPED
YAPPER
YAPPERS
YAPPIE
YAPPIER
YAPPIES
YAPPIEST
YAPPING
YAPPS
YAPPY
YAPS
YAPSTER
YAPSTERS
YAQONA
YAQONAS
YAR*
YARD
YARDAGE
YARDAGES
YARDANG
YARDANGS
YARDARM*
YARDARMS*
YARDBIRD
YARDBIRDS
YARDED
YARDING
YARDLAND
YARDLANDS
YARDMAN
YARDMEN
YARDS
YARDSTICK
YARDSTICKS
YARDWAND
YARDWANDS
YARDWORK*
YARDWORKS*
YARE
YARELY
YARER
YAREST
YARFA
YARFAS
YARMELKE*
YARMELKES*
YARMULKA
YARMULKAS
YARMULKE
YARMULKES
YARN
YARNED
YARNER*

YARNERS*
YARNING
YARNS
YARPHA
YARPHAS
YARR
YARRAMAN
YARRAMANS
YARROW
YARROWS
YARRS
YARTA
YARTAS
YARTO
YARTOS
YASHMAC*
YASHMACS*
YASHMAK
YASHMAKS
YASMAK*
YASMAKS*
YATAGAN
YATAGANS
YATAGHAN
YATAGHANS
YATE
YATES
YATTER
YATTERED
YATTERING
YATTERINGS
YATTERS
YAUD
YAUDS
YAULD
YAUP
YAUPED*
YAUPER*
YAUPERS*
YAUPING*
YAUPON
YAUPONS
YAUPS*
YAUTIA*
YAUTIAS*
YAW
YAWED
YAWEY
YAWING
YAWL
YAWLED
YAWLING
YAWLS
YAWMETER*
YAWMETERS*

YAWN
YAWNED
YAWNER*
YAWNERS*
YAWNIER
YAWNIEST
YAWNING
YAWNINGLY
YAWNINGS
YAWNS
YAWNY
YAWP
YAWPED
YAWPER
YAWPERS
YAWPING
YAWPINGS*
YAWPS
YAWS
YAWY
YAY*
YAYS*
YBET
YBLENT
YBORE
YBOUND
YBOUNDEN
YBRENT
YCLAD
YCLED
YCLEEPE
YCLEEPED
YCLEEPES
YCLEEPING
YCLEPED
YCLEPT
YCOND
YDRAD
YDRED
YE
YEA
YEAD
YEADING
YEADS
YEAH
YEALDON
YEALDONS
YEALING*
YEALINGS*
YEALM
YEALMED
YEALMING
YEALMS
YEAN
YEANED

YEANING	YELLED	YES	YIELDINGS	YOBBOS
YEANLING	YELLER*	YESES	YIELDS	YOBS
YEANLINGS	YELLERS*	YESHIVA	YIKE	YOCK
YEANS	YELLING	YESHIVAH	YIKES	YOCKED
YEAR	YELLINGS	YESHIVAHS	YIKKER	YOCKING
YEARBOOK	YELLOCH	YESHIVAS	YIKKERED	YOCKS
YEARBOOKS	YELLOCHED	YESHIVOT	YIKKERING	YOD
YEARD	YELLOCHING	YESHIVOTH	YIKKERS	YODE
YEARDED	YELLOCHS	YESK	YILL	YODEL
YEARDING	YELLOW	YESKED	YILLS	YODELED*
YEARDS	YELLOWED	YESKING	YIN	YODELER*
YEAREND*	YELLOWER	YESKS	YINCE	YODELERS*
YEARENDS*	YELLOWEST	YESSED*	YINS	YODELING*
YEARLIES	YELLOWFIN*	YESSES	YIP	YODELLED
YEARLING	YELLOWFINS*	YESSING*	YIPE*	YODELLER
YEARLINGS	YELLOWIER	YEST	YIPES*	YODELLERS
YEARLONG	YELLOWIEST	YESTER	YIPPED	YODELLING
YEARLY	YELLOWING	YESTERDAY	YIPPEE	YODELS
YEARN	YELLOWISH	YESTERDAYS	YIPPER	YODH*
YEARNED	YELLOWLY*	YESTEREVE	YIPPERS	YODHS*
YEARNER	YELLOWS	YESTEREVES	YIPPIE*	YODLE
YEARNERS	YELLOWY	YESTERN	YIPPIES	YODLED
YEARNING	YELLS	YESTREEN	YIPPING	YODLER
YEARNINGS	YELM	YESTREENS*	YIPPY	YODLERS
YEARNS	YELMED	YESTS	YIPS	YODLES
YEARS	YELMING	YESTY	YIRD	YODLING
YEAS	YELMS	YET	YIRDED	YODS*
YEASAYER*	YELP	YETI	YIRDING	YOGA
YEASAYERS*	YELPED	YETIS	YIRDS	YOGAS
YEAST	YELPER	YETT	YIRK	YOGEE*
YEASTED	YELPERS	YETTS	YIRKED	YOGEES*
YEASTIER	YELPING	YEUK	YIRKING	YOGH
YEASTIEST	YELPINGS	YEUKED	YIRKS	YOGHOURT
YEASTILY*	YELPS	YEUKING	YIRR*	YOGHOURTS
YEASTING	YELT	YEUKS	YIRRED*	YOGHS
YEASTLIKE	YELTS	YEUKY*	YIRRING*	YOGHURT
YEASTS	YEN	YEVE	YIRRS*	YOGHURTS
YEASTY	YENNED	YEVEN	YIRTH*	YOGI
YECCH*	YENNING	YEVES	YIRTHS*	YOGIC
YECCHS*	YENS	YEVING	YITE	YOGIN
YECH	YENTA	YEW	YITES	YOGINI
YECHS*	YENTAS	YEWEN	YLEM	YOGINIS
YECHY*	YENTE*	YEWS	YLEMS	YOGINS
YEDE	YENTES*	YEX	YLIKE	YOGIS
YEDES	YEOMAN	YEXED	YLKE	YOGISM
YEDING	YEOMANLY	YEXES	YLKES	YOGISMS
YEED	YEOMANRIES	YEXING	YMOLT	YOGURT
YEEDING	YEOMANRY	YFERE	YMOLTEN	YOGURTS
YEEDS	YEOMEN	YGLAUNST	YMPE	YOHIMBINE
YEELIN*	YEP	YGO	YMPES	YOHIMBINES
YEELINS*	YEPS	YGOE	YMPING	YOICK
YEGG	YERBA	YIBBLES	YMPT	YOICKED
YEGGMAN	YERBAS	YICKER	YNAMBU	YOICKING
YEGGMEN	YERD	YICKERED	YNAMBUS	YOICKS
YEGGS	YERDED	YICKERING	YO	YOICKSED
YEH*	YERDING	YICKERS	YOB	YOICKSES
YELD	YERDS	YID*	YOBBERIES	YOICKSING
YELDRING	YERK	YIDS*	YOBBERY	YOJAN
YELDRINGS	YERKED	YIELD	YOBBISH	YOJANA
YELDROCK	YERKING	YIELDABLE	YOBBISHLY	YOJANAS
YELDROCKS	YERKS	YIELDED	YOBBISM	YOJANS
YELK	YERSINIA	YIELDER	YOBBISMS	YOK
YELKS	YERSINIAE	YIELDERS	YOBBO	YOKE
YELL	YERSINIAS	YIELDING	YOBBOES	YOKED

Words marked with an asterisk are from OTCWL

YOKEL
YOKELESS*
YOKELISH
YOKELS
YOKEMATE*
YOKEMATES*
YOKES
YOKING
YOKINGS
YOKKED
YOKKING
YOKOZUNA
YOKOZUNAS
YOKS
YOKUL
YOLD
YOLDRING
YOLDRINGS
YOLK
YOLKED
YOLKIER
YOLKIEST
YOLKS
YOLKY
YOM*
YOMIM*
YOMP
YOMPED
YOMPING
YOMPS
YON
YOND
YONDER
YONDERLY
YONDERS
YONGTHLY
YONI
YONIC*
YONIS
YONKER
YONKERS
YONKS
YONT
YOOF
YOOFS
YOOP
YOOPS
YOPPER

YOPPERS
YORE
YORES
YORK
YORKED
YORKER
YORKERS
YORKIE
YORKIES
YORKING
YORKS
YOS
YOU
YOUK
YOUKED
YOUKING
YOUKS
YOUNG
YOUNGER
YOUNGERS*
YOUNGEST
YOUNGISH
YOUNGLING
YOUNGLINGS
YOUNGLY
YOUNGNESS
YOUNGNESSES
YOUNGS
YOUNGSTER
YOUNGSTERS
YOUNGTH
YOUNGTHLY
YOUNGTHS
YOUNKER
YOUNKERS
YOUPON*
YOUPONS*
YOUR
YOURN
YOURS
YOURSELF
YOURSELVES
YOURT
YOURTS
YOUSE*
YOUTH
YOUTHEN*
YOUTHENED*

YOUTHENING*
YOUTHENS*
YOUTHFUL
YOUTHHEAD
YOUTHHEADS
YOUTHHOOD
YOUTHHOODS
YOUTHIER
YOUTHIEST
YOUTHLY
YOUTHS
YOUTHSOME
YOUTHY
YOW
YOWE
YOWED*
YOWES
YOWIE
YOWIES
YOWING*
YOWL
YOWLED
YOWLER*
YOWLERS*
YOWLEY
YOWLEYS
YOWLING
YOWLINGS
YOWLS
YOWS
YPERITE*
YPERITES*
YPIGHT
YPLAST
YPLIGHT
YPSILOID
YPSILON
YPSILONS
YRAPT
YRAVISHED
YRENT
YRIVD
YRNEH
YRNEHS
YSAME
YSHEND
YSHENDING
YSHENDS

YSHENT
YSLAKED
YTOST
YTTERBIA
YTTERBIAS
YTTERBIC*
YTTERBIUM
YTTERBIUMS
YTTRIA
YTTRIAS
YTTRIC
YTTRIOUS
YTTRIUM
YTTRIUMS
YU
YUAN
YUANS*
YUCA
YUCAS
YUCCA
YUCCAS
YUCCH*
YUCH*
YUCK
YUCKED
YUCKER
YUCKERS
YUCKIER
YUCKIEST
YUCKING
YUCKS
YUCKY
YUFT
YUFTS
YUG
YUGA
YUGAS
YUGS
YUK
YUKATA
YUKATAS
YUKE
YUKED
YUKES
YUKIER
YUKIEST
YUKING
YUKKED*

YUKKIER
YUKKIEST
YUKKING*
YUKKY
YUKO
YUKOS
YUKS
YUKY
YULAN
YULANS
YULE
YULES
YULETIDE
YULETIDES
YUM*
YUMMIER
YUMMIES*
YUMMIEST
YUMMY
YUMP
YUMPED
YUMPIE
YUMPIES
YUMPING
YUMPS
YUNX
YUNXES
YUP
YUPON
YUPONS
YUPPIE
YUPPIEDOM
YUPPIEDOMS
YUPPIES
YUPPIFIED
YUPPIFIES
YUPPIFY
YUPPIFYING
YUPPY
YUPS
YURT
YURTA*
YURTS
YUS
YWIS
YWROKE

Z

ZABAIONE
ZABAIONES
ZABAJONE*
ZABAJONES*
ZABETA
ZABETAS
ZABRA
ZABRAS
ZABTIEH
ZABTIEHS
ZACATON*
ZACATONS*
ZACK
ZACKS
ZADDICK*
ZADDIK
ZADDIKIM
ZADDIKS
ZAFFAR*
ZAFFARS*
ZAFFER
ZAFFERS
ZAFFIR*
ZAFFIRS*
ZAFFRE
ZAFFRES
ZAFTIG*
ZAG
ZAGGED
ZAGGING
ZAGS
ZAIBATSU*
ZAIKAI*
ZAIKAIS*
ZAIRE
ZAIRES*
ZAITECH
ZAITECHS
ZAKAT
ZAKATS
ZAKUSKA
ZAKUSKI
ZAMAN
ZAMANG
ZAMANGS
ZAMANS
ZAMARRA
ZAMARRAS
ZAMARRO
ZAMARROS
ZAMBO
ZAMBOMBA
ZAMBOMBAS
ZAMBOORAK
ZAMBOORAKS

ZAMBOS
ZAMBUCK
ZAMBUCKS
ZAMBUK
ZAMBUKS
ZAMIA
ZAMIAS
ZAMINDAR
ZAMINDARI
ZAMINDARIES
ZAMINDARIS
ZAMINDARS
ZAMINDARY
ZAMOUSE
ZAMOUSES
ZAMPOGNA
ZAMPOGNAS
ZAMPONE
ZAMPONI
ZANANA*
ZANANAS*
ZANDER
ZANDERS
ZANELLA
ZANELLAS
ZANIED
ZANIER
ZANIES
ZANIEST
ZANILY*
ZANINESS
ZANINESSES
ZANJA
ZANJAS
ZANJERO
ZANJEROS
ZANTE
ZANTES
ZANTHOXYL
ZANTHOXYLS
ZANY
ZANYING
ZANYISH*
ZANYISM
ZANYISMS
ZANZA*
ZANZAS*
ZANZE
ZANZES
ZAP
ZAPATA
ZAPATEADO
ZAPATEADOS
ZAPATEO*
ZAPATEOS*

ZAPOTILLA
ZAPOTILLAS
ZAPPED
ZAPPER
ZAPPERS
ZAPPIER
ZAPPIEST
ZAPPING
ZAPPY
ZAPS
ZAPTIAH
ZAPTIAHS
ZAPTIEH
ZAPTIEHS
ZARAPE
ZARAPES
ZARATITE
ZARATITES
ZAREBA
ZAREBAS
ZAREEBA
ZAREEBAS
ZARF
ZARFS
ZARIBA
ZARIBAS
ZARNEC
ZARNECS
ZARNICH
ZARNICHS
ZARZUELA
ZARZUELAS
ZASTRUGA
ZASTRUGI
ZATI
ZATIS
ZAX
ZAXES
ZAYIN*
ZAYINS*
ZAZEN*
ZAZENS*
ZEA
ZEAL
ZEALANT
ZEALANTS
ZEALFUL
ZEALLESS
ZEALOT
ZEALOTISM
ZEALOTISMS
ZEALOTRIES
ZEALOTRY
ZEALOTS
ZEALOUS

ZEALOUSLY
ZEALS
ZEAS
ZEATIN*
ZEATINS*
ZEBEC
ZEBECK
ZEBECKS
ZEBECS
ZEBRA
ZEBRAIC*
ZEBRAS
ZEBRASS
ZEBRASSES
ZEBRAWOOD*
ZEBRAWOODS*
ZEBRINA
ZEBRINAS
ZEBRINE
ZEBRINNIES
ZEBRINNY
ZEBROID
ZEBRULA
ZEBRULAS
ZEBRULE
ZEBRULES
ZEBU
ZEBUB
ZEBUBS
ZEBUS
ZECCHIN*
ZECCHINE
ZECCHINES
ZECCHINI
ZECCHINO
ZECCHINOS
ZECCHINS*
ZECHIN*
ZECHINS*
ZED
ZEDOARIES
ZEDOARY
ZEDS
ZEE
ZEES
ZEIN
ZEINS
ZEITGEBER*
ZEITGEBERS*
ZEITGEIST
ZEITGEISTS
ZEK
ZEKS
ZEL
ZELANT

ZELANTS
ZELATOR
ZELATORS
ZELATRICE
ZELATRICES
ZELATRIX
ZELATRIXES
ZELKOVA*
ZELKOVAS*
ZELOSO
ZELOTYPIA
ZELOTYPIAS
ZELS
ZEMINDAR
ZEMINDARI
ZEMINDARIES
ZEMINDARIS
ZEMINDARS
ZEMINDARY
ZEMSTVA
ZEMSTVO
ZEMSTVOS
ZENAIDA*
ZENAIDAS*
ZENANA
ZENANAS
ZENDIK
ZENDIKS
ZENITH
ZENITHAL
ZENITHS
ZEOLITE
ZEOLITES
ZEOLITIC
ZEPHYR
ZEPHYRS
ZEPPELIN
ZEPPELINS
ZERDA
ZERDAS
ZEREBA
ZEREBAS
ZERIBA
ZERIBAS
ZERK*
ZERKS*
ZERO
ZEROED
ZEROES*
ZEROING
ZEROS
ZEROTH
ZERUMBET
ZERUMBETS
ZEST

Words marked with an asterisk are from OTCWL

ZESTED	ZILLAH	ZINGERS	ZIZANIAS	ZOMBIFIES
ZESTER	ZILLAHS	ZINGIBER	ZIZEL	ZOMBIFY
ZESTERS	ZILLION	ZINGIBERS	ZIZELS	ZOMBIFYING
ZESTFUL	ZILLIONS	ZINGIER	ZIZIT*	ZOMBIISM
ZESTFULLY	ZILLIONTH	ZINGIEST	ZIZITH*	ZOMBIISMS
ZESTIER	ZILLIONTHS	ZINGING	ZIZYPHUS	ZOMBIS
ZESTIEST	ZILLS*	ZINGS	ZIZYPHUSES	ZOMBORUK
ZESTING	ZIMB	ZINGY	ZIZZ	ZOMBORUKS
ZESTLESS*	ZIMBI	ZINKE	ZIZZED	ZONA
ZESTS	ZIMBIS	ZINKED	ZIZZES	ZONAE
ZESTY	ZIMBS	ZINKENITE	ZIZZING	ZONAL
ZETA	ZIMMER	ZINKENITES	ZIZZLE*	ZONALLY*
ZETAS	ZIMMERS	ZINKES	ZIZZLED*	ZONARY
ZETETIC	ZIMOCCA	ZINKIER	ZIZZLES*	ZONATE
ZETETICS	ZIMOCCAS	ZINKIEST	ZIZZLING*	ZONATED
ZEUGMA	ZIN*	ZINKIFIED	ZLOTE*	ZONATION
ZEUGMAS	ZINC	ZINKIFIES	ZLOTIES*	ZONATIONS
ZEUGMATIC	ZINCATE*	ZINKIFY	ZLOTY	ZONDA
ZEUXITE	ZINCATES*	ZINKIFYING	ZLOTYCH*	ZONDAS
ZEUXITES	ZINCED	ZINKING	ZLOTYS	ZONE
ZEX	ZINCIC*	ZINKY	ZO	ZONED
ZEXES	ZINCIER	ZINNIA	ZOA	ZONELESS
ZEZE	ZINCIEST	ZINNIAS	ZOARIA	ZONER*
ZEZES	ZINCIFIED	ZINS*	ZOARIAL*	ZONERS*
ZHO	ZINCIFIES	ZIP	ZOARIUM	ZONES
ZHOMO	ZINCIFY	ZIPLESS*	ZOBO	ZONETIME*
ZHOMOS	ZINCIFYING	ZIPLOCK	ZOBOS	ZONETIMES*
ZHOS	ZINCING	ZIPPED	ZOBU	ZONING
ZIBELINE	ZINCITE	ZIPPER	ZOBUS	ZONINGS
ZIBELINES	ZINCITES	ZIPPERED	ZOCCO	ZONK
ZIBELLINE	ZINCKED	ZIPPERING*	ZOCCOLO	ZONKED
ZIBELLINES	ZINCKIER	ZIPPERS	ZOCCOLOS	ZONKING
ZIBET	ZINCKIEST	ZIPPIER	ZOCCOS	ZONKS
ZIBETH*	ZINCKIFIED	ZIPPIEST	ZODIAC	ZONOID
ZIBETHS*	ZINCKIFIES	ZIPPING	ZODIACAL	ZONULA
ZIBETS	ZINCKIFY	ZIPPO	ZODIACS	ZONULAE
ZIFF	ZINCKIFYING	ZIPPOS	ZOEA	ZONULAR
ZIFFIUS	ZINCKING	ZIPPY	ZOEAE	ZONULAS
ZIFFIUSES	ZINCKY	ZIPS	ZOEAL	ZONULE
ZIFFS	ZINCO	ZIPTOP	ZOEAS	ZONULES
ZIG	ZINCODE	ZIRAM*	ZOECHROME	ZONULET
ZIGAN	ZINCODES	ZIRAMS*	ZOECHROMES	ZONULETS
ZIGANKA	ZINCOID	ZIRCALOY	ZOECIA*	ZONURE
ZIGANKAS	ZINCOS	ZIRCALOYS	ZOECIUM*	ZONURES
ZIGANS	ZINCOUS	ZIRCON	ZOEFORM	ZOO
ZIGGED	ZINCS	ZIRCONIA	ZOETIC	ZOOBIOTIC
ZIGGING	ZINCY	ZIRCONIAS	ZOETROPE	ZOOBLAST
ZIGGURAT	ZINE	ZIRCONIC	ZOETROPES	ZOOBLASTS
ZIGGURATS	ZINEB	ZIRCONIUM	ZOETROPIC	ZOOCHORE
ZIGS	ZINEBS	ZIRCONIUMS	ZOFTIG*	ZOOCHORES
ZIGZAG	ZINES	ZIRCONS	ZOIATRIA	ZOOCHORIES
ZIGZAGGED	ZINFANDEL	ZIT	ZOIATRIAS	ZOOCHORY
ZIGZAGGING	ZINFANDELS	ZITE	ZOIATRICS	ZOOCYTIA
ZIGZAGGY	ZING	ZITHER	ZOIC	ZOOCYTIUM
ZIGZAGS	ZINGANI*	ZITHERIST*	ZOISITE	ZOOEA
ZIKKURAT	ZINGANO*	ZITHERISTS*	ZOISITES	ZOOEAE
ZIKKURATS	ZINGARA*	ZITHERN	ZOISM	ZOOEAL
ZIKURAT*	ZINGARE*	ZITHERNS	ZOISMS	ZOOEAS
ZIKURATS*	ZINGARI*	ZITHERS	ZOIST	ZOOECIA
ZILA	ZINGARO*	ZITI	ZOISTS	ZOOECIUM
ZILAS	ZINGED	ZITIS*	ZOMBI	ZOOGAMETE
ZILCH	ZINGEL	ZITS	ZOMBIE	ZOOGAMETES
ZILCHES	ZINGELS	ZIZ	ZOMBIES	ZOOGAMIES
ZILL*	ZINGER	ZIZANIA	ZOMBIFIED	ZOOGAMOUS

The Chambers Dictionary is the authority for many longer words; see Introduction, page ix

ZOOGAMY
ZOOGENIC
ZOOGENIES
ZOOGENOUS
ZOOGENY
ZOOGLEA*
ZOOGLEAE*
ZOOGLEAL*
ZOOGLEAS*
ZOOGLOEA
ZOOGLOEAE
ZOOGLOEAS
ZOOGLOEIC
ZOOGONIES
ZOOGONOUS
ZOOGONY
ZOOGRAFT
ZOOGRAFTS
ZOOGRAPHIES
ZOOGRAPHY
ZOOID
ZOOIDAL
ZOOIDS
ZOOKEEPER*
ZOOKEEPERS*
ZOOKS
ZOOLATER
ZOOLATERS
ZOOLATRIA
ZOOLATRIAS
ZOOLATRIES
ZOOLATRY
ZOOLITE
ZOOLITES
ZOOLITH
ZOOLITHIC
ZOOLITHS
ZOOLITIC
ZOOLOGIC*
ZOOLOGIES
ZOOLOGIST
ZOOLOGISTS
ZOOLOGY
ZOOM
ZOOMANCIES
ZOOMANCY
ZOOMANIA*
ZOOMANIAS*
ZOOMANTIC
ZOOMED
ZOOMETRIC
ZOOMETRIES
ZOOMETRY
ZOOMING
ZOOMORPH
ZOOMORPHIES

ZOOMORPHS
ZOOMORPHY
ZOOMS
ZOON
ZOONAL
ZOONIC
ZOONITE
ZOONITES
ZOONITIC
ZOONOMIA
ZOONOMIAS
ZOONOMIC
ZOONOMIES
ZOONOMIST
ZOONOMISTS
ZOONOMY
ZOONOSES
ZOONOSIS
ZOONOTIC
ZOONS
ZOOPATHIES
ZOOPATHY
ZOOPERAL
ZOOPERIES
ZOOPERIST
ZOOPERISTS
ZOOPERY
ZOOPHAGAN
ZOOPHAGANS
ZOOPHAGIES
ZOOPHAGY
ZOOPHILE
ZOOPHILES
ZOOPHILIA
ZOOPHILIAS
ZOOPHILIC*
ZOOPHILIES
ZOOPHILY
ZOOPHOBE*
ZOOPHOBES*
ZOOPHOBIA
ZOOPHOBIAS
ZOOPHORI
ZOOPHORIC
ZOOPHORUS
ZOOPHYTE
ZOOPHYTES
ZOOPHYTIC
ZOOPLASTIES
ZOOPLASTY
ZOOS
ZOOSCOPIC
ZOOSCOPIES
ZOOSCOPY
ZOOSPERM
ZOOSPERMS

ZOOSPORE
ZOOSPORES
ZOOSPORIC
ZOOSTEROL*
ZOOSTEROLS*
ZOOTAXIES
ZOOTAXY
ZOOTECHNIES
ZOOTECHNY
ZOOTHECIA
ZOOTHEISM
ZOOTHEISMS
ZOOTHOME
ZOOTHOMES
ZOOTIER*
ZOOTIEST*
ZOOTOMIC
ZOOTOMIES
ZOOTOMIST
ZOOTOMISTS
ZOOTOMY
ZOOTOXIN
ZOOTOXINS
ZOOTROPE
ZOOTROPES
ZOOTROPHIES
ZOOTROPHY
ZOOTY*
ZOOTYPE
ZOOTYPES
ZOOTYPIC
ZOOZOO
ZOOZOOS
ZOPILOTE
ZOPILOTES
ZOPPA
ZOPPO
ZORGITE
ZORGITES
ZORI
ZORIL
ZORILLA*
ZORILLAS*
ZORILLE
ZORILLES
ZORILLO
ZORILLOS
ZORILS
ZORINO
ZORINOS
ZORIS
ZORRO
ZORROS
ZOS
ZOSTER
ZOSTERS

ZOUAVE*
ZOUAVES*
ZOUK
ZOUKS
ZOUNDS
ZOWIE
ZOYSIA*
ZOYSIAS*
ZUCCHETTO
ZUCCHETTOS
ZUCCHINI
ZUCCHINIS
ZUCHETTA
ZUCHETTAS
ZUCHETTO
ZUCHETTOS
ZUFFOLI
ZUFFOLO
ZUFOLI
ZUFOLO
ZUGZWANG
ZUGZWANGS
ZULU
ZULUS
ZUMBOORUK
ZUMBOORUKS
ZUPA
ZUPAN
ZUPANS
ZUPAS
ZURF
ZURFS
ZUZ
ZUZIM
ZWIEBACK*
ZWIEBACKS*
ZYDECO
ZYDECOS
ZYGA
ZYGAENID
ZYGAENINE
ZYGAENOID
ZYGAL
ZYGANTRA
ZYGANTRUM
ZYGANTRUMS
ZYGOCACTI
ZYGODONT
ZYGOID*
ZYGOMA
ZYGOMAS
ZYGOMATA
ZYGOMATIC
ZYGON
ZYGOPHYTE
ZYGOPHYTES

ZYGOSE
ZYGOSES
ZYGOSIS
ZYGOSITIES*
ZYGOSITY*
ZYGOSPERM
ZYGOSPERMS
ZYGOSPORE
ZYGOSPORES
ZYGOTE
ZYGOTENE*
ZYGOTENES*
ZYGOTES
ZYGOTIC
ZYLONITE
ZYLONITES
ZYMASE
ZYMASES
ZYME
ZYMES
ZYMIC
ZYMITE
ZYMITES
ZYMOGEN
ZYMOGENE*
ZYMOGENES*
ZYMOGENIC
ZYMOGENS
ZYMOGRAM*
ZYMOGRAMS*
ZYMOID
ZYMOLOGIC
ZYMOLOGIES
ZYMOLOGY
ZYMOLYSES
ZYMOLYSIS
ZYMOLYTIC
ZYMOME
ZYMOMES
ZYMOMETER
ZYMOMETERS
ZYMOSAN*
ZYMOSANS*
ZYMOSES
ZYMOSIS
ZYMOTIC
ZYMOTICS
ZYMURGIES
ZYMURGY
ZYTHUM
ZYTHUMS
ZYZZYVA*
ZYZZYVAS*

Words marked with an asterisk are from OTCWL